Lecture Notes in Computer Science 4193

Commenced Publication in 1973
Founding and Former Series Editors:
Gerhard Goos, Juris Hartmanis, and Jan van Leeuwen

Thomas Philip Runarsson Hans-Georg Beyer
Edmund Burke Juan J. Merelo-Guervós
L. Darrell Whitley Xin Yao (Eds.)

Parallel Problem Solving from Nature - PPSN IX

9th International Conference
Reykjavik, Iceland, September 9-13, 2006
Procedings

Springer

Volume Editors

Thomas Philip Runarsson
University of Iceland, Reykjavik, Iceland
E-mail: tpr@hi.is

Hans-Georg Beyer
Vorarlberg University of Applied Sciences, Dornbirn, Austria
E-mail: hans-georg.beyer@fhv.at

Edmund Burke
University of Nottingham, UK
E-mail: ekb@cs.nott.ac.uk

Juan J. Merelo-Guervós
ETS Ingeniera Informatica, Granada, Spain
E-mail: jmerelo@geneura.ugr.es

L. Darrell Whitley
Colorado State University, Fort Collins, Colorado, USA
E-mail: whitley@cs.colostate.edu

Xin Yao
University of Birmingham, CERCIA, Birmingham, UK
E-mail: x.yao@cs.bham.ac.uk

Library of Congress Control Number: 2006931845

CR Subject Classification (1998): F.1-2, C.1.2, D.1-3, I.2.8, I.2.6, I.2.11, J.3

LNCS Sublibrary: SL 1 – Theoretical Computer Science and General Issues

ISSN 0302-9743
ISBN-10 3-540-38990-3 Springer Berlin Heidelberg New York
ISBN-13 978-3-540-38990-3 Springer Berlin Heidelberg New York

Springer is a part of Springer Science+Business Media

springer.com

Typesetting: Camera-ready by author, data conversion by Scientific Publishing Services, Chennai, India
Printed on acid-free paper SPIN: 11844297 06/3142 5 4 3 2 1 0

Preface

We are very pleased to present this LNCS volume, the proceedings of the 9th International Conference on Parallel Problem Solving from Nature (PPSN IX). PPSN is one of the most respected and highly regarded conference series in evolutionary computation and natural computing / computation. This biennial event was first held in Dortmund in 1990, and then in Brussels (1992), Jerusalem (1994), Berlin (1996), Amsterdam (1998), Paris (2000), Granada (2002), and Birmingham (2004). PPSN continues to be the conference of choice by researchers all over the world, who value its high quality.

We received 255 paper submissions this year. After an extensive peer review process involving more than 1000 reviews, the programme committee selected the top 106 papers for inclusion in this volume and, of course, for presentation at the conference. This represents an acceptance rate of 42%.

The papers included in this volume cover a wide range of topics, from evolutionary computation to swarm intelligence and from bio-inspired computing to real-world applications. They represent some of the latest and best research in evolutionary and natural computation. Following the PPSN tradition, all papers at PPSN IX were presented as posters. There were 7 sessions: each session consisting of around 15 papers. For each session, we covered as wide a range of topics as possible so that participants with different interests could find some relevant papers in every session.

The conference featured three distinguished keynote speakers: Herschel Rabitz, Nadia Busi, and Edward Tsang. Their backgrounds in chemistry, theoretical computer science, and financial engineering, respectively, reflect the interdisciplinary nature of PPSN IX. Herschel Rabitz's talk was on "Controlling Quantum Phenomena: The Dream Is Alive", Nadia Busi's was on "Computing with Calculi and Systems Inspired by Biological Membranes", and Edward Tsang's was on "Wind-tunnel Testing for Strategy and Market Design". Both Edward Tsang and Nadia Busi gave introductory tutorials related to their talks. Furthermore, Nadia Busi is the co-author of some notes on (Mem)Brane Computation included in this volume. We are very grateful to them for contributing valuable time from their busy schedules.

PPSN IX included 10 tutorials and 4 workshops. We were extremely fortunate to have such an impressive list of internationally leading scientists from across natural computing as tutorial speakers. They provided an excellent start to the five-day event. The workshops offered an ideal opportunity for participants to explore specific topics in natural computing in an informal setting. They were sowing the seeds for the future growth of natural computing.

To encourage and reward high-quality research in the international community, PPSN IX presented a Best Paper Award. All accepted papers were eligible to enter the competition. A separate Best Student Paper Award was also given at the conference.

The success of a conference depends on its authors, reviewers and organizers. PPSN IX was no exception. We are grateful to all the authors for their paper submissions and to all the reviewers for their outstanding work in refereeing the papers within a very tight schedule. We relied heavily upon a team of volunteers to keep the PPSN IX wheel turning. We are very grateful for their efforts.

September 2006

Thomas Philip Runarsson
Hans-Georg Beyer
Edmund Burke
Juan Julián Merelo Guervós
Darrell Whitley
Xin Yao

Organization

PPSN IX was organized and hosted by the University of Iceland.

PPSN IX Conference Committee

General Chair:	Thomas Philip Runarsson, University of Iceland
Programme Co-chairs:	Hans-Georg Beyer, Vorarlberg University of Applied Sciences Edmund Burke, University of Nottingham Alastair Channon, University of Birmingham Darrell Whitley, Colorado State University
Electronic Programme Chair:	Juan J. Merelo-Guervós, University of Granada
Local Organization Co-chairs:	Magnus Thor Jonsson, University of Iceland Olafur Petur Palsson, University of Iceland Sven Sigurdsson, University of Iceland
Tutorial Chair:	Alastair Channon, University of Birmingham
Workshop Chair:	Jim Torresen, University of Oslo
Proceedings Chair:	Xin Yao, University of Birmingham
Honorary Chair:	Hans-Paul Schwefel, University of Dortmund
Publicity Co-chairs:	Simon Lucas, University of Essex Runar Unnthorsson, University of Iceland

PPSN IX Steering Committee

David Corne	Heriot-Watt University, UK
Kenneth De Jong	George Mason University, USA
Agoston E. Eiben	Free University of Amsterdam, The Netherlands
Juan J. Merelo-Guervós	University of Granada, Spain
Thomas P. Runarsson	University of Iceland, Iceland
Marc Schoenauer	INRIA, France
Xin Yao	University of Birmingham, UK

PPSN IX Tutorials

Quantum Computing
Jaikumar Radhakrishnan

An Introduction to (Mem)Brane Computing
Nadia Busi

An Introduction to Ant Colony Optimization and Swarm Intelligence
Marco Dorigo

The Covariance Matrix Adaptation (CMA) Evolution Strategy
Nikolaus Hansen

Natural Computation in Bioinformatics
David Corne

Computational Finance and Economics
Edward Tsang

Practical Guidelines for Using Evolutionary Algorithms
Darrell Whitley

Genetic Algorithm Theory
Michael Vose

Introduction to Learning Classifier Systems
Wolfgang Stolzmann

Evolvable Computational Machines
Lukas Sekanina

PPSN IX Workshops

Workshop on Empirical Methods for the Analysis of Algorithms
Luis Paquete, Marco Chiarandini, and Dario Basso

Workshop on Evolutionary Algorithms – Bridging Theory and Practice
Borenstein Yossi, Riccardo Poli, and Thomas Jansen

Workshop on Multiobjective Problem-Solving from Nature
Joshua Knowles, David Corne, and Kalyanmoy Deb

Workshop on Bio-inspired Computing in Computational Biology
Simon Barkow, Stefan Bleuler, Dimo Brockhoff, and Eckart Zitzler

PPSN IX Programme Committee

Abbass, Hussein
Aguilar-Ruiz, Jesús S.
Alander, Jarmo
Alba, Enrique
Altenberg, Lee
Araujo, Lourdes
Bäck, Thomas
Bagnall, Tony
Banzhaf, Wolfgang
Barbosa, Helio
Barry, Alwyn
Blazewicz, Jacek
Blum, Christian
Bonarini, Andrea
Booker, Lashon B.
Bosman, Peter A.N.
Branke, Juergen
Browne, Will
Buckles, Bill
Bull, Larry
Bullinaria, John A.
Cagnoni, Stefano
Cantu-Paz, Erick
Carse, Brian
Castillo-Valdivieso, P. A.
Cayzer, Steve
Chan, Keith
Cho, Sun-Bae
Coello, Carlos
Collet, Pierre
Cordon, Cordon
Corne, David
Corr, Pat
Costa, Ernesto
Cotta, Carlos
de Castro, Leandro N.
de la Iglesia, Bea
DeJong, Ken
Deb, Kalyanmoy
Dopico, Juan Rabuñal
Dorado, Julin
Dorigo, Marco
Dozier, Gerry V.
Droste, Stefan
Duro, Richard
Eiben, Agoston E.
Engelbrecht, Andries
English, Thomas M.
Esparcia, Ana
Esquivel, Susana Cecilia
Fernandez, Francisco
Filipic, Bogdan
Floreano, Dario
Fogarty, Terence
Fogel, Gary
Fogel, David
Fonlupt, Cyril
Fonseca, Carlos M.
Freisleben, Bernd
Freitas, Alex
Gallagher, Marcus
Gambardella, Luca M.
Gamez, Jose A.
Gao, Yong
Garibaldi, Jon
Garrell-Guiu, Josep M.
Gendreau, Michel
Giannakoglou, Kyriakos
González, Jesús
Gottlieb, Jens
Gustafson, Steven
Handa, Hisashi
Handl, Julia
Hao, Jin-Kao
Hart, Bill
Hart, Emma
Hartl, Richard
Harvey, Inman
Herdy, Michael
Herrera, Francisco
Herrman, Jeffrey
Hervás, Cesar
Hidalgo, Ignacio
Hogg, Tad
Hughes, Evan J.
Hurst, Jacob
Husbands, Phil
Inza, Iñaki
Isasi, Pedro
Jansen, Thomas
Jin, Yaochu
John, Bob
Julstrom, Bryant
Kabán, Ata
Kang, Lishan
Keane, Andy
Keijzer, Maarten
Keller, Robert
Kendall, Graham
Knowles, Joshua
Kok, Joost
Kovacs, Tim
Krasnogor, Natalio
Krink, Thiemo
Kwan, Raymond
Lai, Loi Lei
Lanzi, Pier Luca
Larrañaga, Pedro
Lattaud, Claude
Le Riche, Rodolphe
Leung, K.S
Liu, Yong
Lobo, Fernando
Louis, Sushil J.
Lozano, José Antonio
Lucas, Simon
Luo, Wenjian
Lutton, Evelyne
Marchiori, Elena
Martí, Rafael
Mattfeld, Dirk
McCollum, Barry
Merz, Peter
Michalewicz, Zbigniew
Middendorf, Martin
Miller, Julian
Mohan, Chilukuri
Montana, David
Moscato, Pablo

Moshaiov, Amiram
Muruzábal, Jorge
Ochoa, Alberto
Osman, Ibrahim H.
Oudeyer, Pierre-Yves
Paechter, Ben
Paredis, Jan
Parmee, Ian
Pelikan, Martin
Petrovic, Dobrila
Petrovic, Sanja
Pipe, Tony
Pomares, Héctor
Prugel-Bennett, Adam
Raidl, Guenther
Ramos, Vitorino
Rasheed, Khaled
Reeves, Colin
Reynolds, Robert
Rivas, Víctor
Rizki, Mateen
Robilliard, Denis
Rojas, Ignacio
Romero, Gustavo
Rosca, Justinian
Rothlauf, Franz
Rowe, Jonathan
Rudolph, Guenter
Ryan, Conor
Salcedo-Sanz, Sancho
Santana, Roberto
Sareni, Bruno
Sarker, Ruhul
Schaffer, David
Schmitt, Lothar M.
Schoenauer, Marc
Schwefel, Hans-Paul
Sebag, Michele
Sendhoff, Bernhard
Shapiro, Jonathan
Sharman, Ken
Smith, Alice
Smith, James
Smith, Rob
Spears, Bill
Stewart, Paul
Stonier, Russel
Stützle, Thomas
Suganthan, Ponnuthurai
Sanchez, Luciano
Talbi, ElGhazali
Tan, Kay Chen
Tateson, Richard
Tettamanzi, Andrea
Thangiah, Sam R.
Thierens, Dirk
Thompson, Jonathan
Timmis, Jonathan
Tiňo, Peter
Tomassini, Marco
Tsahalis, Demosthenes
Tsang, Edward
Tsutsui, Shigeyoshi
Tuson, Andrew
Venturini, Gilles
Vose, Michael
Voss, Stefan
Wang, Fang
Wang, Lipo
Watson, Jean-Paul
Whigham, Peter
While, Lyndon
Wu, Annie
Wyatt, Jeremy
Yang, Shengxiang
Zhang, Byoung-Tak
Zhang, Qingfu
Zitzler, Eckart

Sponsoring Institutions

Faculty of Engineering, University of Iceland

Science Institute, University of Iceland

University of Iceland

Table of Contents

Theory

New Algorithms

Applications

Multi-objective Optimization

Evolutionary Learning

Evolutionary Optimization in Spatio–temporal Fitness Landscapes

Hendrik Richter

HTWK Leipzig, Fachbereich Elektrotechnik und Informationstechnik,
Institut Mess–, Steuerungs– und Regelungstechnik,
Postfach 30 11 66, D–04125 Leipzig, Germany
richter@fbeit.htwk-leipzig.de

Abstract. Spatio–temporal fitness landscapes that are constructed from Coupled Map Lattices (CML) are introduced. These landscapes are analyzed in terms of modality and ruggedness. Based on this analysis, we study the relationship between landscape measures and the performance of an evolutionary algorithm used to solve the dynamic optimization problem.

1 Introduction

In theoretical studies of evolutionary algorithms, concepts of fitness landscapes have shown to be a useful tool [4,7,14,16]. A fitness landscape assigns fitness values to the points of the search space through which the evolution moves. This search space can be constructed by a genotype–to–fitness mapping or more generally by encoding the set of possible solutions of an optimization problem to form a representation space for which additionally a neighborhood structure needs to be defined. Typically, the topology of the search space is considered to be constant over the run–time of the evolutionary algorithm and hence such a fitness landscape is a static concept.

As dynamic optimization turned more and more into an important topic in evolutionary computation [17,2,9,6,19], it became desirable to have concepts of fitness landscapes in dynamic environments as well. Whereas recent results have shown that such an approach is useful to characterize and classify types of dynamic landscapes [5], there is a certain lack of environments that show sufficiently complex structure in both spatial topology and temporal dynamics. In this paper, such spatio–temporal fitness landscapes are introduced and it is shown how these landscapes can be constructed from spatio–temporal dynamical systems, namely from Coupled Map Lattices (CML). CML have been the subject of intensive research, which revealed a broad variety of spatio–temporal behavior, including different types of pattern formation, spatio–temporal chaos, quasi–periodicity and emergence [8,3].

In the next section, a methodology to construct spatio–temporal fitness landscapes from CML is given. In Sec. 3, these landscapes are analyzed in terms of modality and ruggedness. Further, quantifying measures such as the number of

T.P. Runarsson et al. (Eds.): PPSN IX, LNCS 4193, pp. 1–10, 2006.

optima and the correlation structure are studied. In Sec. 4, factors contributing to problem hardness in dynamic optimization like change frequency and dynamic severity are reviewed. Numerical experiments using an evolutionary algorithm to optimize in the spatio–temporal fitness landscape are reported in Sec. 5. In the final section, the findings are summarized and conclusions are drawn.

2 Constructing Spatio–temporal Fitness Landscapes

Constructing spatio–temporal fitness landscapes should begin with defining a spatio–temporal dynamical system. Therefore, we lay out a lattice grid with $I \times J$ equally sized cells, which form a $2D$–structure. For every discrete time step k, $k = 0, 1, 2, \ldots$, each cell is characterized by its height

$$h(i, j, k), \quad i = 1, 2, \ldots, I, \quad j = 1, 2, \ldots, J, \tag{1}$$

where i, j denote the spatial indices in vertical and horizontal direction, respectively, see Fig. 1. This height $h(i, j, k)$, which we will interpret as fitness according to the geometrical metaphor of a fitness landscape, is subject to changes over time, which are described by the two–dimensional CML with nearest–neighbor coupled interaction [8,3]

$$\begin{aligned} h(i, j, k+1) = (1-\epsilon) g(h(i, j, k)) + \frac{\epsilon}{4} \Big[& g\left(h(i-1, j, k)\right) \\ & + g\left(h(i+1, j, k)\right) + g\left(h(i, j-1, k)\right) + g\left(h(i, j+1, k)\right) \Big], \end{aligned} \tag{2}$$

where $g(h(i, j, k))$ is a local mapping function and ϵ is the diffusion coupling strength. In other words, as $h(i, j, k)$ denotes the height of the $h(i, j)$–th unit bar situated in the (i, j)–lattice cell at time step k, Eq. (2) describes how this height changes over time depending on its own height and the heights of the surrounding bars, see Fig. 1a. The CML is initialized by the heights $h(i, j, 0)$ being realizations of a random variable uniformly distributed on $[0, 1]$. To complete the definition of the CML (2), we employ the logistic map

$$g(h(i, j, k)) = \alpha h(i, j, k)(1 - h(i, j, k)) \tag{3}$$

as mapping function and render the period boundary conditions

$$h(I+1, j, k) = h(1, j, k), \qquad h(i, J+1, k) = h(i, 1, k). \tag{4}$$

To summarize, the CML is a spatio–temporal dynamical system with discrete space (lattice) and time (map). The system's states, which we interpret as heights, are continuous and situated on the lattice. They dynamically interact with surrounding states via the nonlinear map (3). The spatio–temporal behavior of the CML depends on two parameters, the coupling strength ϵ and the nonlinear parameter α. These parameters span a parameter space in which different regions represent different types of spatio–temporal behavior. In this paper, we focus on the parameter ϵ.

Based on this description of a spatio–temporal dynamical system, we formulate the spatio–temporal fitness landscape. Therefore, we project the lattice

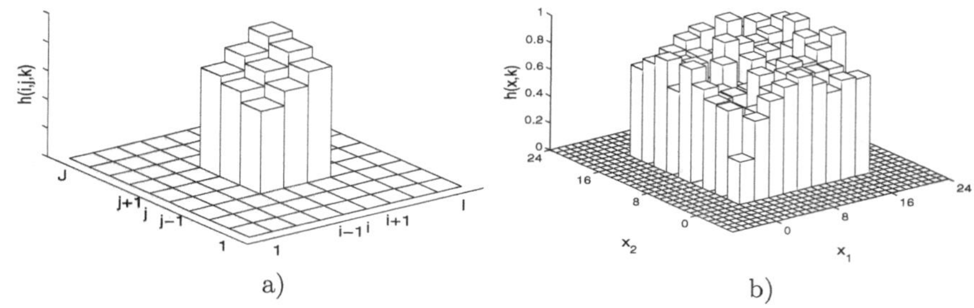

Fig. 1. Coupled map lattice: a) Generic structure. b) Spatio–temporal fitness landscape for $I = J = 9$ and $s_1 = s_2 = 0.5$.

cells on a zero plane and introduce scaling factors $s_1, s_2 \in \mathbb{R}$ for the vertical and horizontal extension. By these scaling factors, we convert the integer search space to a real value search space with step function characteristics, see Fig. 1b. The s_i can additionally be used to adjust severity of the dynamic optimization problem to be solved. Next, we define the search space variable $x = (x_1, x_2)^T$, impose a rounding condition, so that $(\lceil s_1 x_1 \rceil, \lceil s_2 x_2 \rceil)^T = (i, j)^T$ and find the spatio–temporal fitness function for the two–dimensional CML (2):

$$f(x,k) = \left\{ \begin{matrix} h(\lceil s_1 x_1 \rceil, \lceil s_2 x_2 \rceil, k) & for & \begin{matrix} 1 \leq \lceil s_1 x_1 \rceil \leq I \\ 1 \leq \lceil s_2 x_2 \rceil \leq J \end{matrix} \\ 0 & & otherwise \end{matrix} \right\}, \; k \geq 0. \tag{5}$$

The dynamic optimization problem is

$$\max_{x \in \mathbb{R}^2} f(x,k) = \max_{\substack{1 \leq \lceil s_1 x_1 \rceil \leq I \\ 1 \leq \lceil s_2 x_2 \rceil \leq J}} h(\lceil s_1 x_1 \rceil, \lceil s_2 x_2 \rceil, k), \; k \geq 0 \tag{6}$$

and solving it yields the solution trajectory

$$x_S(k) = \arg\max_{x \in \mathbb{R}^2} f(x,k) = \arg \max_{\substack{1 \leq \lceil s_1 x_1 \rceil \leq I \\ 1 \leq \lceil s_2 x_2 \rceil \leq J}} h(\lceil s_1 x_1 \rceil, \lceil s_2 x_2 \rceil, k), \; k \geq 0, \tag{7}$$

which we intend to find using an evolutionary algorithm.

The given construction of spatio–temporal fitness landscapes has the advantage that spatial topology and temporal dynamics are generated by the same system. No external driving system for inducing dynamics is required. The given formulation of a spatio–temporal fitness landscape is valid for a two–dimensional search space. An extension to n–dimensional search spaces is possible using the given framework and employing n–dimensional CML, see e.g. [13]. In addition, we only considered flat heights on the lattice cells. A generalization can be achieved by introducing morphological structures on the cell tops.

3 Properties of Spatio–temporal Fitness Landscapes

In order to evaluate the performance of an evolutionary algorithm in a spatio–temporal fitness landscape, we need a notion of how difficult a certain landscape is to optimize in. This question is addressed by concepts and quantifiers for measuring fitness landscapes. For static landscapes, this topic has been studied intensively, e.g. [18,4,16]. In the following, we adopt and modify these results to measure spatio–temporal fitness landscapes.

First, we look at the modality of the landscape by measuring the number of local maxima. Despite the continuous search space of the spatio–temporal fitness landscape (5), the local maxima need to be described within the framework of local optima in discrete search spaces. A local optimum is a solution optimal within a neighboring set of solutions, which is the same as in combinatorial optimization problems [10], p. 7. The neighborhood structure we consider here are the surrounding heights. That means the neighborhood structure $N(i,j)$ of the (i,j)–th lattice cell is

$$\begin{aligned} N(i,j) &= (i+\beta, j+\delta), \\ (\beta,\delta) &= (-1,-1) \wedge (-1,0) \wedge (-1,1) \wedge (0,-1) \wedge (0,1) \wedge (1,-1) \wedge (1,0) \wedge (1,1). \end{aligned}$$

Here, $(i,j)^T = (\lceil s_1 x_1 \rceil, \lceil s_2 x_2 \rceil)^T$. Hence, the fitness function possesses a local maximum at the time k if

$$h(i,j,k) \geq h(N(i,j),k). \tag{8}$$

Due to the countable number of lattice cells, the number of local maxima can be determined by enumeration. We denote $\#_{LM}(k)$ the number of local maxima at time k. As a spatio–temporal fitness landscape changes over time, the number of local maxima needs not to be constant. Therefore, we consider its time average:

$$\langle \#_{LM}(k) \rangle = \lim_{K \to \infty} \frac{1}{K} \sum_{k=0}^{K-1} \#_{LM}(k). \tag{9}$$

To get an approximate value of the time average number of local maxima, the $\langle \#_{LM}(k) \rangle$ is replaced by $\#_{LM} = \frac{1}{K} \sum_{k=0}^{K-1} \#_{LM}(k)$ with K sufficiently large. In Figs. 2a,c,e the average number of maxima is given for different ϵ and different lattice sizes. Here, as well as in the following experiments, we fix $\alpha = 3.999$ and consider varying ϵ. We see that the number of maxima increases steadily with increasing lattice size and that this occurs symmetrically in the vertical as well as in the horizontal direction identified by I and J. For smaller ϵ, this increase is steeper than for larger values. On the other hand, for varying ϵ there is no clear trend as to how the number of maxima scales with it, but there are also sections in the ϵ–parameter space (for instance $0.3 \leq \epsilon \leq 0.9$) for which a proportional relation can be observed. Next, we determine the ruggedness of the spatio–temporal fitness landscape modelled by the CML. A standard procedure to assert ruggedness of fitness landscapes is to analyze its correlation structure. This method works by performing a random walk on the landscape and calculating its random walk correlation function. For the spatio–temporal fitness landscape (5), this starts with generating a time series $h(\tau,k) = h(i(\tau), j(\tau), k)$, $\tau = 1,2,\ldots,T$, of the heights $h(\lceil s_1 x_1 \rceil, \lceil s_2 x_2 \rceil, k)$ with $(i,j)^T = (\lceil s_1 x_1 \rceil, \lceil s_2 x_2 \rceil)^T$. For performing the random walk, we create two times T independent realizations of an integer random variable uniformly distributed on $[-1,1]$. Starting from an initial cell, the next cell on the walk is obtained by adding the two independent realizations

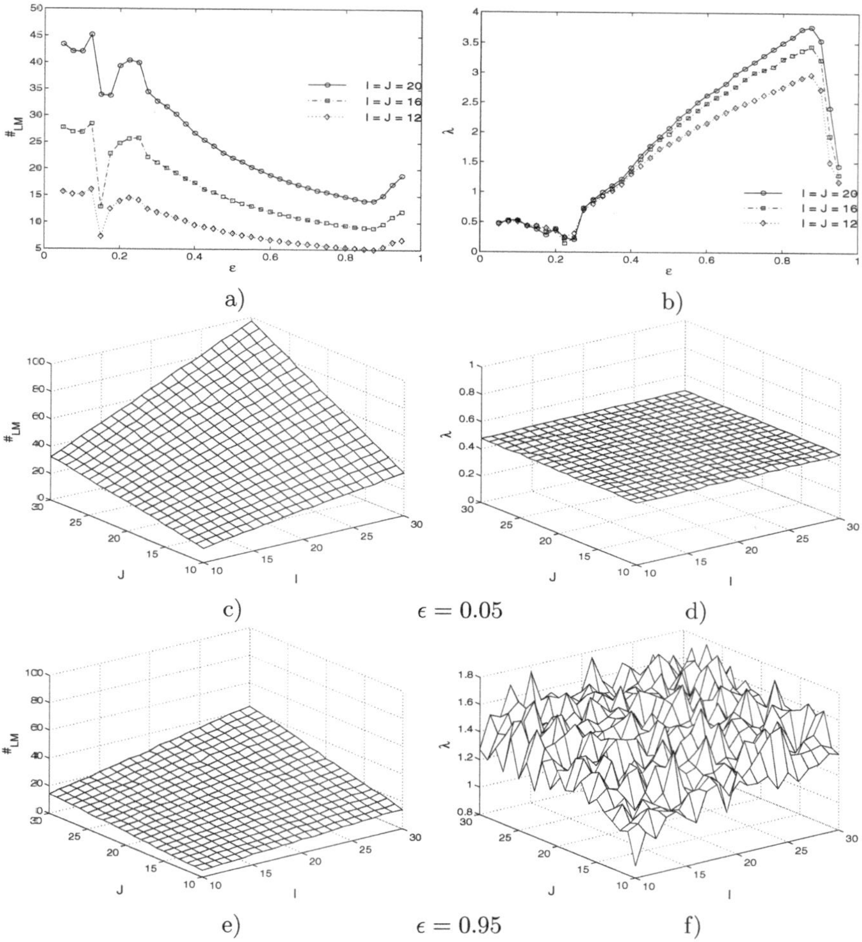

Fig. 2. Average number of local maxima $\#_{LM}$ and average correlation length λ with $\alpha = 3.999$ for $K = 1500$ and $T = 100000$

of the random variable to the current cell index (i, j). In addition, the boundary condition (4) is observed. The random walk in the two spatial dimensions as specified by $i(\tau), j(\tau)$ yields the needed time series on the spatio–temporal fitness landscape by recording the heights $h(\tau, k) = h(i(\tau), j(\tau), k)$ at time k. For this time series the spatial correlation can be calculated. The spatial correlation is widely used in determining ruggedness of static landscapes [18,4,15]. It is an estimate $r(t_L, k)$ of the autocorrelation function of the time series with time lag t_L, also called random walk correlation function:

$$r(t_L, k) = \frac{\sum_{\tau=1}^{T-t_L} \left(h(\tau, k) - \bar{h}(k)\right)\left(h(\tau + t_L, k) - \bar{h}(k)\right)}{\sum_{\tau=1}^{T} \left(h(\tau, k) - \bar{h}(k)\right)^2}, \tag{10}$$

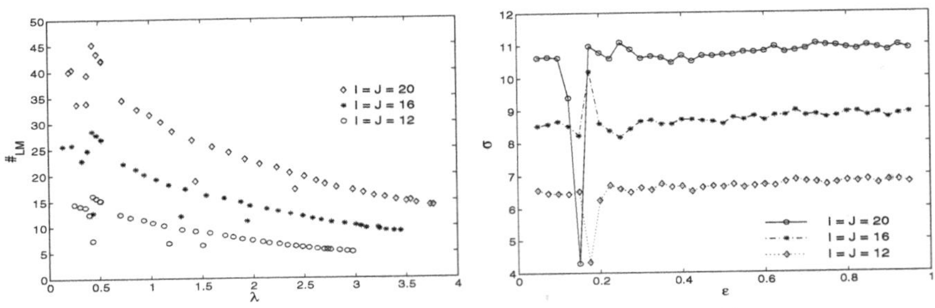

a) b)

Fig. 3. a) Correlation between number of maxima and autocorrelation. b) Severity σ for $(i,j)^T = (\lceil x_1 \rceil, \lceil x_2 \rceil)^T$.

where $\bar{h}(k) = \frac{1}{T} \sum_{\tau=1}^{T} h(\tau, k)$ and $T \gg t_L > 0$. The spatial random walk correlation function measures the correlation between different regions of the fitness landscape for a fixed k. As $r(t_L, k)$ changes over time, we consider its time average $\langle r(t_L, k) \rangle$, for which we calculate numerically an approximated value $r(t_L)$, similarly as for the average number of maxima. It has been shown that ruggedness is best reflected by the correlation length [15]

$$\lambda = -1/\ln(|r(1)|). \tag{11}$$

This quantity is given for the spatio–temporal fitness landscape, see Figs. 2b,d,f. The lower the values of λ are, the more rugged the landscape is. For varying ϵ, the correlation length scales in a similar manner as the number of maxima, compare Fig. 2a. Increasing lattice sizes lead to a small increase of λ only, see Figs. 2d,f. Also, for smaller values of ϵ, the correlation length is distributed smoother on the $I - J$-lattice size plane.

Fig. 3a shows ruggedness measured by the correlation length versus modality measured by the number of maxima. This also serves as a test on the relationship between modality and ruggedness. The results show that there is an exponential dependency between correlation length λ and the number of maxima $\#_{LM}$, which is also clearly distinct for different lattice sizes.

4 Problem Hardness in Dynamic Optimization

Optimization in spatio–temporal fitness landscapes is in essence dynamic optimization. In dynamic optimization, it is generally understood that problem hardness depends not only on the problem difficulty of the landscape but also on features of the involved dynamics [2,9]. The most prominent features are the (relative) speed of the landscape changes, which is expressed by change frequency and the (relative) strength of the landscape changes, which can be attributed by dynamic severity. Both quantities are briefly recalled. The optimization problem (6) can be solved by an evolutionary algorithm with real number representation and μ individuals $a \in \mathbb{R}^2$, which build the population $P \in \mathbb{R}^{2\times\mu}$. The dynamics

Table 1. Settings of the evolutionary algorithm and the numerical experiments

Design parameter	Symbol	Value	Setting	Symbol	Value
Population size	μ	50	Number of considered runs	R	150
Initial population width	ω^2	5	Generations in a run	T	1500
Base–mutation rate	bm	0.1	Eq. (3)	α	3.999
Hyper–mutation rate	hm	30	Severity scaling	$s = s_1 = s_2$	1

of such an evolutionary algorithm can be described by the generation transition function $\psi : \mathbb{R}^{2\times\mu} \to \mathbb{R}^{2\times\mu}$, see e.g. [1], pp. 64–65. The generation transition function includes the genetic operators selection, recombination and mutation. It generates the movement of the population within the fitness landscape by transforming a population at generation $t \in \mathbb{N}_0$ into a population at generation $t+1$,

$$P(t+1) = \psi\left(P(t)\right), \qquad t \geq 0. \tag{12}$$

Here, t represents a discrete time variable, as k does for the spatio–temporal fitness function (5). In dynamic optimization, both time scales can be related to each other by the environmental change period $\gamma \in \mathbb{N}$ (cf. [11]). Between the frequency of the changes in the population and that of the dynamic fitness landscape, we find

$$t = \gamma k. \tag{13}$$

A second prominent factor in problem hardness of dynamic optimization is dynamic severity [17,12], which measures the (relative) magnitude of the changes in the landscape by comparing k to $k+1$. In terms of the spatio–temporal fitness landscape considered here, severity means to evaluate the distance between the largest height before and after a change. Hence, severity can be calculated

$$\sigma(k+1) = \|x_S(k+1) - x_S(k)\|, \tag{14}$$

where $x_S(k)$ is the solution of the dynamic optimization problem (7). As this quantity may vary with time k, we focus on the time average severity $\langle\sigma(k)\rangle = \lim_{K\to\infty} \frac{1}{K} \sum_{k=0}^{K-1} \sigma(k)$. For the solution trajectory (7), we obtain $\langle\sigma(k)\rangle = \sigma \cdot \sqrt{s_1^2 + s_2^2}$, where σ is severity for $(i,j)^T = (\lceil x_1 \rceil, \lceil x_2 \rceil)^T$. The quantity σ is shown in Fig. 3b and can be regarded as almost constant for a given lattice size and a large majority of values of ϵ. Hence, severity of the optimization problem can be adjusted by s_1 and s_2.

5 Evolutionary Optimization

We now give experimental results on evolutionary optimization in spatio–temporal fitness landscapes modelled by CML. The performance of the evolutionary algorithm is examined depending on problem difficulty expressed by change frequency, severity and landscape measures as modality and ruggedness. The numerical experiments have been conducted with an evolutionary algorithm that

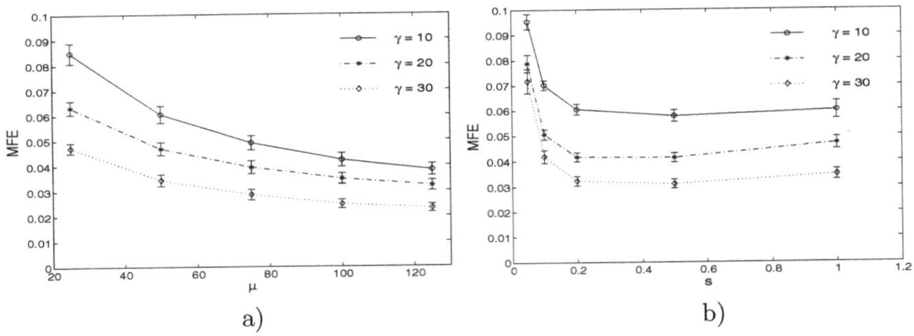

Fig. 4. Performance specified by the MFE with $\epsilon = 0.5$ and $I = J = 16$ for different γ versus: a) Population size μ for severity scaling $s = 1$. b) Severity scaling s for $\mu = 50$

uses real number representation, fixed population size, tournament selection with tournament size 2, fitness–based recombination and base– as well as hyper–mutation. The initial population is created by realizations of a random variable normally distributed on $[0, \omega^2]$. Tab. 1 summarizes the design parameters of the algorithm together with settings for the numerical experiments. The performance of the algorithm is measured by the Mean Fitness Error (MFE)

$$MFE = \frac{1}{R}\sum_{r=1}^{R}\left[\frac{1}{T}\sum_{t=1}^{T}\left(f\left(x_S, t/\gamma\right) - \max_{a \in P} f\left(a, t/\gamma\right)\right)\right], \tag{15}$$

where $f(x_s, t/\gamma)$ is the maximum fitness value at generation t, $\max_{a \in P} f(a, t/\gamma)$ is the fitness value of the best individual $a \in P$ at generation t, T is the number of generations used in the run, and R is the number of consecutive runs.

In a first experiment, we look at the design parameter population size μ and its scaling with the MFE, see Fig. 4a. Here, as well as in the following figures the MFE together with its 95% confidence interval is given. We see an exponential decrease of the MFE with increasing μ and a clear distinction between different environmental change periods γ, which is a typical result for dynamic optimization [9,11]. Next, the MFE depending on dynamic severity for $s = s_1 = s_2$ is given, see Fig. 4b. We observe a steep increase of the MFE for values of s getting smaller, which means for larger dynamic severity. Again, this is in agreement with previous findings [17,12].

In a next set of experiments, we study how the landscape measures modality and ruggedness relate to the MFE, see Fig. 5. These results stem from calculating the MFE for different values of ϵ, given in Fig. 5a. The results are the MFE for 150 runs and again the 95% confidence intervals are shown. Note that the intervals are small so that this MFE represents a good approximation of the long–term behavior. In the Figs. 5b,c the MFE is shown depending on the number of maxima $\#_{LM}$ and the correlation length λ. Within certain bounds of $\#_{LM}$ and λ, we observe that the MFE gets gradually smaller with an increasing number of maxima, while it gets larger with increasing correlation length. This trend is

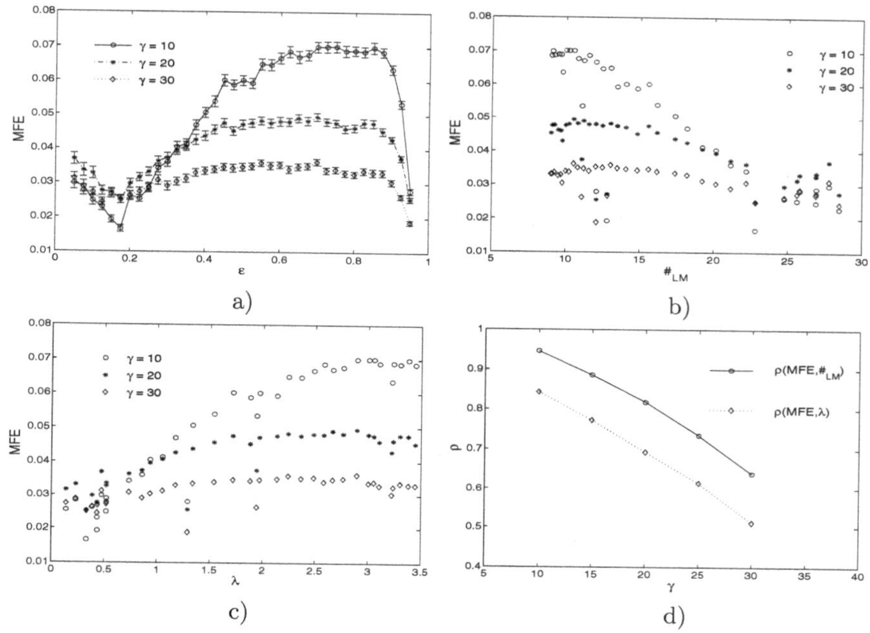

Fig. 5. The MFE as a function of: a) Diffusion coupling strength ϵ. b) Number of maxima $\#_{LM}$. c) Correlation length λ. d) Correlation between the MFE and $\#_{LM}$, λ.

particularly visible for larger environmental change periods γ. Also, within these bounds, γ is the leading factor in performance. For very large values of $\#_{LM}$ and very small values of λ, this relation vanishes. Finally, we consider the correlation between the MFE and $\#_{LM}$, denoted by $\rho(MFE, \#_{LM})$, and between the MFE and λ, denoted by $\rho(MFE, \lambda)$, respectively, depending on γ. We notice that both correlations decrease with increasing γ. This indicates that the correlation between the landscape measures and the performance gets weaker for increasing γ. For change frequency being in general the leading factor in the algorithm's performance, this can be interpreted as follows: a large number of maxima and a high ruggedness does not influence the performance strongly for the algorithm having enough time to search for the maxima. On the other hand, for small γ, these landscape measures clearly determine the performance.

6 Conclusions

In this paper, spatio–temporal fitness landscapes constructed from Coupled Map Lattices were introduced. These dynamic landscapes were analyzed in terms of modality (number of optima) and ruggedness (correlation structure). Based on these results, the relationship between landscape measures and the performance of the evolutionary algorithm used to solve the dynamic optimization problem was studied.

The results show that the landscape measures modality and ruggedness scale with the algorithm's performance and hence allow its prediction. In particular, for small change frequencies, we find a strong correlation between the performance and landscape measures, that is, modality and ruggedness. For larger change frequencies, this correlation ceases as the algorithm is more likely to find the optimum despite the problem hardness induced by the landscape.

References

1. Bäck, T.: Evolutionary Algorithms in Theory and Practice: Evolution Strategies, Evolutionary Programming, Genetic Algorithms, Oxford Univ. Press, NY (1996).
2. Branke, J.: Evolutionary Optimization in Dynamic Environments, Kluwer Academic Publishers, Dordrecht (2001).
3. Chazottes, J.R., Fernandez, B.: Dynamics of Coupled Map Lattices and of Related Spatially Extended Systems, Springer–Verlag, Berlin (2005).
4. Hordijk, W.: A Measure of Landscapes. Evolut. Comput. **4** (1996) 335–360.
5. Hordijk, W., Kauffman S.A.: Correlation Analysis of Coupled Fitness Landscapes. Complexity **10** (2005) 42–49.
6. Jin, Y., Branke, J.: Evolutionary Optimization in Uncertain Environments–A Survey. IEEE Trans. Evolut. Comput. **9** (2005) 303–317.
7. Kallel, L., Naudts, B., Reeves, C.R.: Properties of Fitness Functions and Search Landscapes. In: Kallel, L. et al. (eds.): Theoretical Aspects of Evolutionary Computing, Springer–Verlag, Berlin (2001) 177–208.
8. Kaneko, K.: The Coupled Map Lattice. In: Kaneko, K. (ed.): Theory and Application of Coupled Map Lattices, John Wiley, Chichester (1993) 1–49.
9. Morrison, R.W.: Designing Evolutionary Algorithms for Dynamic Environments, Springer–Verlag, Berlin (2004).
10. Papadimitriou, C.H., Steiglitz, K.: Combinatorial Optimization: Algorithms and Complexity, Dover, Mineola, NY (1998).
11. Richter, H.: Behavior of Evolutionary Algorithms in Chaotically Changing Fitness Landscapes. In: Yao, X. et al. (eds.): Parallel Problem Solving from Nature–PPSN VIII, Springer–Verlag, Berlin (2004) 111–120.
12. Richter, H.: A Study of Dynamic Severity in Chaotic Fitness Landscapes. In: Corne, D. (ed.): Proc. Congress on Evolutionary Computation, IEEE CEC 2005, IEEE Press, Piscataway, NJ (2005) 2824–2831.
13. Shibata, T., Kaneko, K.: Coupled Map Gas: Structure Formation and Dynamics of Interacting Mobile Elements with Internal Dynamics. Phys. **D181** (2003) 197–214.
14. Smith, T., Husbands, P., Layzell, P., O'Shea, M.: Fitness Landscapes and Evolvability. Evolut. Comput. **10** (2002) 1–34.
15. Stadler, P.F.: Landscapes and Their Correlation Functions. J. Math. Chem. **20** (1996) 1–45.
16. Stadler, P.F., Stephens, C.R.: Landscapes and Effective Fitness. Comm. Theor. Biol. **8** (2003) 389–431.
17. Weicker, K.: An Analysis of Dynamic Severity and Population Size. In: Schoenauer, M. et al. (eds.): Parallel Problem Solving from Nature–PPSN VI, Springer–Verlag, Berlin (2000) 159–168.
18. Weinberger, E.D.: Correlated and Uncorrelated Fitness Landscapes and How to Tell the Difference. Biol. Cybern. **63** (1990) 325–336.
19. Yang, S., Yao, X.: Experimental Study on Population-based Incremental Learning Algorithms for Dynamic Optimization Problems. Soft Comput. **9** (2005) 815–834.

Cumulative Step Length Adaptation on Ridge Functions

Dirk V. Arnold

Faculty of Computer Science, Dalhousie University
Halifax, Nova Scotia, Canada B3H 1W5
dirk@cs.dal.ca

Abstract. The ridge function class is a parameterised family of test functions that is often used to evaluate the capabilities and limitations of optimisation strategies. Past research with the goal of analytically determining the performance of evolution strategies on the ridge has focused either on the parabolic case or on simple one-parent strategies without step length adaptation. This paper extends that research by studying the performance of multirecombination evolution strategies with cumulative step length adaptation for a wide range of ridge topologies.

1 Introduction

It has been conjectured that ridge following is a recurring task in numerical optimisation. According to Whitley et al. [13], while the difficulties of optimising ridges "are relatively well documented in the mathematical literature on derivative free minimization algorithms [...], there is little discussion of this problem in the heuristic search literature". For evolution strategies in particular, a number of recent publications provide results that partly fill this gap.

In early work, Herdy [8] observes that mutative self-adaptation yields significantly suboptimal step lengths on the parabolic ridge, and that it fails altogether on the sharp ridge. He shows empirically that hierarchically organised strategies fare much better at generating useful step lengths. The performance of a simple hierarchically organised strategy on the parabolic ridge has recently been analysed in [2].

Oyman et al. [11, 12, 10] analytically study the performance of the $(\mu/\mu, \lambda)$-ES on the parabolic ridge. (See [5] for a comprehensive introduction to evolution strategies and the related terminology.) Recently, Arnold and Beyer [1] have extended that work by considering both the effects of noise and the performance of cumulative step length adaptation. Another extension of the initial work of Oyman et al. has been provided by Beyer [3] who considers more general ridge topologies, albeit only for one-parent strategies and without considering step length adaptation.

This paper analytically studies the performance of the $(\mu/\mu, \lambda)$-ES with cumulative step length adaptation for the ridge function class considered in [3]. It generalises the results in that reference by considering multirecombinative

T.P. Runarsson et al. (Eds.): PPSN IX, LNCS 4193, pp. 11–20, 2006.

strategies as well as cumulative step length adaptation. Moreover, it succeeds in analytically computing optimal parameter settings. This paper extends the work in [1] by considering more general ridge topologies. The results presented here thus represent a further step toward an understanding of the potential and the limitations of evolution strategies when optimising ridge functions. They are particularly interesting as they allow comparing step lengths generated using cumulative step length adaptation with optimal step lengths.

2 Algorithm and Objective Function

This section outlines the strategy considered in this paper and describes the ridge function class.

2.1 The $(\mu/\mu, \lambda)$-ES with Cumulative Step Length Adaptation

The $(\mu/\mu, \lambda)$-ES with isotropically distributed mutations is an evolution strategy used for the optimisation of functions $f : \mathbb{R}^N \to \mathbb{R}$. In every time step it computes the centroid of the population of candidate solutions as a search point $\mathbf{x} \in \mathbb{R}^N$ that mutations are applied to. Using cumulative step length adaptation as proposed by Ostermeier et al. [9], a vector $\mathbf{s} \in \mathbb{R}^N$ that is referred to as the search path is used to accumulate information about the directions of the most recently taken steps. An iteration of the strategy updates the search point along with the search path and the mutation strength of the strategy in five steps:

1. Generate λ offspring candidate solutions $\mathbf{y}^{(i)} = \mathbf{x} + \sigma\mathbf{z}^{(i)}$, $i = 1, \ldots, \lambda$, where mutation strength $\sigma > 0$ determines the step length and the $\mathbf{z}^{(i)}$ are vectors consisting of N independent, standard normally distributed components.
2. Determine the objective function values $f(\mathbf{y}^{(i)})$ of the offspring candidate solutions and compute the average
$$\mathbf{z}^{(\text{avg})} = \frac{1}{\mu}\sum_{k=1}^{\mu}\mathbf{z}^{(k;\lambda)} \tag{1}$$
of the μ best of the $\mathbf{z}^{(i)}$. The index $k;\lambda$ refers to the kth best of the λ offspring candidate solutions. Vector $\mathbf{z}^{(\text{avg})}$ is referred to as the progress vector.
3. Update the search point according to
$$\mathbf{x} \leftarrow \mathbf{x} + \sigma\mathbf{z}^{(\text{avg})}. \tag{2}$$
4. Update the search path according to
$$\mathbf{s} \leftarrow (1-c)\mathbf{s} + \sqrt{\mu c(2-c)}\mathbf{z}^{(\text{avg})} \tag{3}$$
where the cumulation parameter c is set to $1/\sqrt{N}$.
5. Update the mutation strength according to
$$\sigma \leftarrow \sigma \exp\left(\frac{\|\mathbf{s}\|^2 - N}{2DN}\right) \tag{4}$$
where damping parameter D is set to $\sqrt{N}$.

See [1] for a more thorough discussion of the algorithm and its parameters.

2.2 The Ridge Function Class

The class of objective functions considered throughout this paper is

$$f(\mathbf{x}) = x_1 - d\left(\sum_{i=2}^{N} x_i^2\right)^{\alpha/2}, \qquad \mathbf{x} = \langle x_1, \ldots, x_N \rangle \in I\!R^N \tag{5}$$

where $d > 0$ and $\alpha > 1$. The x_1-axis is referred to as the ridge axis. Notice that while in the definition used here the ridge axis is aligned with an axis of the coordinate system, that fact is irrelevant for a strategy that uses isotropically distributed mutations such as those considered in the present paper. The coordinate system could be subjected to an arbitrary rotation without affecting the strategies' performance. The parameter α is referred to as the topology parameter. Ridges with $\alpha = 2$ are referred to as parabolic ridges. The sharp ridge with $\alpha = 1$ requires extra care when using normalised variables and is not directly included in the considerations below due to space restrictions. However, it can be handled easily using the approach pursued here and indeed occurs as a limit case. Finally, as in [11, 12, 10, 3, 1], the performance of evolution strategies on ridge functions is quantified by the progress rate

$$\varphi = \mathrm{E}\left[\sigma z_1^{(\mathrm{avg})}\right] \tag{6}$$

i.e., the expected progress of the search point in the direction of the ridge axis in a single time step.

3 Performance

This section first briefly discusses the general methodology of the approach pursued in this paper. It then considers the case that the step length of strategy is static and derives optimal parameter settings. Finally, the case of adaptive step length is discussed.

3.1 Preliminaries

The performance of the $(\mu/\mu, \lambda)$-ES with cumulative step length adaptation has been studied in [1] for the parabolic ridge. The approach to the analysis for more general ridge topologies is closely analogous. Due to the symmetries of the ridge, the state of the evolution strategy can be described by a small number of variables. The algorithm described in Section 2.1 defines a stochastic mapping of those variables. After initialisation effects have faded, several state variables have a stationary limit distribution. Approximate average values of that distribution can be determined by replacing all quantities with their expected values (thus rendering the stochastic mapping deterministic) and finding a fixed point. Further simplifications are made by assuming that the search space dimensionality is high and dropping any terms from the calculations that disappear in the limit $N \to \infty$. Simulations are used to evaluate the accuracy of the approximations.

Letting $\mathbf{x}_{2\ldots N} = \langle 0, x_2, \ldots, x_N \rangle$ denote the projection of the search point onto the plane with $x_1 = 0$, throughout this paper $R = \|\mathbf{x}_{2\ldots N}\|$ denotes the distance of the search point from the ridge axis. Central to the analysis of the performance of evolution strategies on ridge functions is a decomposition of mutation and progress vectors into three mutually orthogonal components $\mathbf{z}_1$, $\mathbf{z}_A$, and $\mathbf{z}_B$. Vector $\mathbf{z}_1 = \langle z_1, 0, \ldots, 0 \rangle$ points in the direction of the ridge axis and is referred to as the axial component of $\mathbf{z}$. Letting $\mathbf{z}_{2\ldots N} = \langle 0, z_2, \ldots, z_N \rangle$, scalar quantity $z_A = -\mathbf{x}_{2\ldots N} \cdot \mathbf{z}_{2\ldots N}/R$ is the signed length of the central component $\mathbf{z}_A = -z_A \mathbf{x}_{2\ldots N}/R$ of vector $\mathbf{z}$ that points from the search point toward the ridge axis. Vector $\mathbf{z}_B$ equals $\mathbf{z}_{2\ldots N} - \mathbf{z}_A$ and is referred to as the lateral component of $\mathbf{z}$. Altogether, $\mathbf{z} = \mathbf{z}_1 + \mathbf{z}_A + \mathbf{z}_B$. See [1] for an illustration.

3.2 Static Step Length

Consider the fitness of an offspring candidate solution $\mathbf{y} = \mathbf{x} + \sigma\mathbf{z}$. Using the definitions of z_A and $\mathbf{z}_{2\ldots N}$, it follows from Eq. (5) that

$$\begin{aligned} f(\mathbf{y}) &= x_1 + \sigma z_1 - d\left(\sum_{i=2}^{N}(x_i + \sigma z_i)^2\right)^{\alpha/2} \\ &= x_1 + \sigma z_1 - d\left(R^2 - 2R\sigma z_A + \sigma^2\|\mathbf{z}_{2\ldots N}\|^2\right)^{\alpha/2}. \end{aligned} \tag{7}$$

As $\mathbf{z}$ is a mutation vector, $\|\mathbf{z}_{2\ldots N}\|^2$ is χ^2_{N-1}-distributed and has mean $N-1$ and variance $2(N-1)$. As the distribution of mutation vectors is isotropic, z_A is standard normally distributed. Let us assume that

$$R \gg \sigma\sqrt{N}. \tag{8}$$

It will be seen below that for given mutation strength σ the resulting stationary distance R of the search point from the ridge axis is such that with increasing N, $\sigma\sqrt{N}/R$ tends to zero, thus providing an a posteriori justification for Eq. (8). Under the assumption, the first term in the parentheses in Eq. (7) dominates the other two. The power term can thus be expanded into a Taylor series with terms beyond the linear one ignored, yielding

$$\begin{aligned} f(\mathbf{y}) &\overset{N\to\infty}{=} x_1 + \sigma z_1 - d\left(R^\alpha - \frac{\alpha}{2}R^{\alpha-2}\left(2R\sigma z_A - \sigma^2\|\mathbf{z}_{2\ldots N}\|^2\right)\right) \\ &= f(\mathbf{x}) + \sigma z_1 + \alpha d R^{\alpha-1}\sigma z_A - \frac{\alpha d}{2}R^{\alpha-2}\sigma^2\|\mathbf{z}_{2\ldots N}\|^2. \end{aligned} \tag{9}$$

Again using the assumption Eq. (8), for large N the variance of the term involving $\|\mathbf{z}_{2\ldots N}\|^2$ disappears relative to that involving z_A, and it is possible to treat the former as a constant. The two variable terms (those involving z_1 and z_A) are both normally distributed due to the way that mutation vectors are generated. Selection ensures that those μ candidate solutions with the largest values of $z_1 + \alpha d R^{\alpha-1} z_A$ survive. The signed lengths z_1 and z_A of the axial and central components of the mutation vectors are thus concomitants of the order statistics that result from ranking offspring candidate solutions according to their fitness. (See [6] for an introduction to concomitants of order statistics.) According to Eq. (1), the axial, central, and lateral components $\mathbf{z}_1^{(\text{avg})}$, $\mathbf{z}_A^{(\text{avg})}$, and $\mathbf{z}_B^{(\text{avg})}$ of the progress vector are the averages of the respective components of the selected mutation vectors. The following lemma that has previously been used in [1] is thus immediately applicable:

Lemma 1. *Let $X_i = Y_i + \vartheta Z_i$ for $i = 1, \dots, \lambda$, where the Y_i and the Z_i are independently standard normally distributed. Ordering the sample members by nondecreasing values of the X variates, the expected value of the arithmetic mean of those μ of the Y_i with the largest associated values of X_i is*

$$\mathrm{E}\left[\frac{1}{\mu}\sum_{k=1}^{\mu} Y_{\lambda+1-k;\lambda}\right] = \frac{c_{\mu/\mu,\lambda}}{\sqrt{1+\vartheta^2}}$$

where $Y_{j;\lambda}$ denotes the concomitant of the jth order statistic and where $c_{\mu/\mu,\lambda}$ is the $(\mu/\mu, \lambda)$-progress coefficient defined in [4].

Specifically, with $Y = z_1$, $Z = z_A$, and $\vartheta = \rho^{\alpha-1}$, where $\rho = (\alpha d)^{1/(\alpha-1)}R$ denotes the standardised distance of the search point from the ridge axis, it follows that

$$\mathrm{E}\left[z_1^{(\text{avg})}\right] \overset{N\to\infty}{=} \frac{c_{\mu/\mu,\lambda}}{\sqrt{1+\rho^{2(\alpha-1)}}}. \tag{10}$$

Similarly, with $Y = z_A$, $Z = z_1$, and $\vartheta = 1/\rho^{\alpha-1}$ it follows that

$$\mathrm{E}\left[z_A^{(\text{avg})}\right] \overset{N\to\infty}{=} \frac{c_{\mu/\mu,\lambda}\rho^{\alpha-1}}{\sqrt{1+\rho^{2(\alpha-1)}}}. \tag{11}$$

Both equations are generalisations of the corresponding results for $\alpha = 2$ obtained in [1]. Finally, as noted above, the influence of $\|\mathbf{z}_{2\dots N}\|^2$ on the relative fitness of the resulting offspring tends to zero as N increases. (The variance of the term involving $\|\mathbf{z}_{2\dots N}\|^2$ in Eq. (9) disappears compared to that involving z_A.) For $N \to \infty$, $\mathbf{z}_B^{(\text{avg})}$ is thus the average of μ uncorrelated random vectors. As seen in [4], averaging μ uncorrelated random vectors reduces the squared length of the vectors being averaged by a factor of $1/\mu$. Furthermore, the relative contribution of the central component $z_A^{(\text{avg})}$ to $\|\mathbf{z}_{2\dots N}^{(\text{avg})}\|^2$ vanishes for large N. As a result,

$$\mathrm{E}\left[\frac{\|\mathbf{z}_{2\dots N}^{(\text{avg})}\|^2}{N}\right] \overset{N\to\infty}{=} \frac{1}{\mu}. \tag{12}$$

The same result has been used in [1]. Together, Eqs. (10), (11), and (12) provide a description of the progress vector that is sufficient for obtaining a characterisation of the stationary state attained by an evolution strategy with stationary step length when tracking a ridge.

According to Eq. (2), the squared distance of the next time step's search point from the ridge axis is

$$\sum_{i=2}^{N}\left(x_i + \sigma z_i^{(\text{avg})}\right)^2 = R^2 - 2R\sigma z_A^{(\text{avg})} + \sigma^2\|\mathbf{z}_{2\ldots N}^{(\text{avg})}\|^2.$$

In order for stationarity to hold, the expected distance of the search point from the ridge axis must not change, yielding condition

$$2R\sigma\text{E}\left[z_A^{(\text{avg})}\right] = \sigma^2\text{E}\left[\|\mathbf{z}_{2\ldots N}^{(\text{avg})}\|^2\right].$$

Introducing normalised mutation strength $\sigma^* = \sigma N(\alpha d)^{1/(\alpha-1)}/(\mu c_{\mu/\mu,\lambda})$, using Eqs. (11) and (12), and squaring both sides yields after some simple transformations condition

$$4\rho^{2\alpha} = \sigma^{*2}\left(1 + \rho^{2(\alpha-1)}\right). \tag{13}$$

For given mutation strength, Eq. (13) can be used to determine the resulting average distance of the search point from the ridge axis. While for $\alpha = 2$ an analytical solution can be found (and has been presented in [1]), in general, solutions need to be obtained numerically.

From Eqs. (6) and (10) with normalisation $\varphi^* = \varphi N(\alpha d)^{1/(\alpha-1)}/(\mu c_{\mu/\mu,\lambda}^2)$, the stationary normalised progress rate on the ridge is

$$\varphi^* = \frac{\sigma^*}{\sqrt{1 + \rho^{2(\alpha-1)}}} \tag{14}$$

Figure 1 compares predictions from Eqs. (13) and (14) with measurements from runs of evolution strategies. The measurements have been made with the search point of the evolution strategy initialised to lie on the ridge axis. The simulations have been run for $40N$ time steps in order to reach the state where the distance from the ridge axis is stationary on average. Then, ρ and φ^* have been averaged over a period of 40000 time steps. It can be seen from the figure that the quality of the predictions is quite good and that it improves with increasing N. While the measurements have been made using $d = 1$, the choice of normalisations of the mutation strength and of the progress rate ensures that a different choice of d is nothing more than a uniform scaling of the search space. For any $\alpha > 1$, the accuracy of the measurements in Fig. 1 is in fact independent of the choice of d. This is not true for the case of $\alpha = 1$ which is not included in the above considerations due to the degeneracy of the normalisations used. However, for $d = 1$ it can be considered as a limit case and has been included in the figure for comparison. Finally, notice that the search space dimensionality N does not appear explicitly in Eq. (13). For $\sigma^* > 0$ and the value of ρ that solves the equation, the quotient σ^*/ρ takes on a finite value. As a consequence, it follows from reversing the normalisations of the mutation strength and the distance from the ridge axis that Eq. (8) indeed holds.

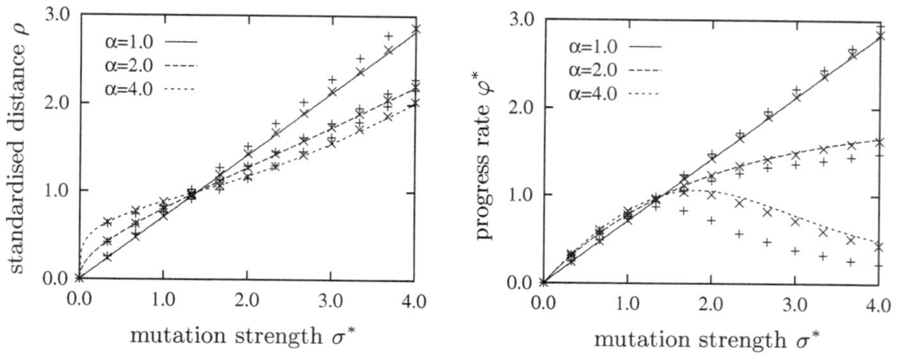

Fig. 1. Standardised distance ρ from the ridge axis and normalised progress rate φ^* plotted against normalised mutation strength σ^*. The points mark measurements made in runs of the $(3/3, 10)$-ES for $N = 40$ $(+)$ and $N = 400$ $(\times)$. The lines represent predictions obtained by numerically solving Eq. (13) for ρ and using Eq. (14) to compute φ^*.

3.3 Optimal Step Length

Interestingly, optimal settings of the mutation strength and the resulting progress rate can be determined analytically even though Eq. (13) can generally only be solved numerically. Using Eq. (13) to eliminate σ^* in Eq. (14) yields

$$\varphi^* = \frac{2\rho^\alpha}{1 + \rho^{2(\alpha-1)}}.$$

Computing the derivative

$$\frac{\mathrm{d}\varphi^*}{\mathrm{d}\rho} = \frac{2\alpha\rho^{\alpha-1}(1 + \rho^{2(\alpha-1)}) - 4(\alpha-1)\rho^{3(\alpha-1)}}{(1 + \rho^{2(\alpha-1)})^2}$$

and demanding that it be zero yields condition

$$\alpha\left(1 + \rho^{2(\alpha-1)}\right) = 2(\alpha-1)\rho^{2(\alpha-1)}$$

that must hold for maximal progress. Solving for ρ yields

$$\rho = \left(\frac{\alpha}{\alpha-2}\right)^{\frac{1}{2(\alpha-1)}} \tag{15}$$

for the optimal standardised stationary distance from the ridge axis. Using Eqs. (13) and (14), the corresponding normalised mutation strength and progress rate are

$$\sigma^* = \sqrt{\frac{2\alpha^{\frac{\alpha}{\alpha-1}}}{(\alpha-1)(\alpha-2)^{\frac{1}{\alpha-1}}}} \tag{16}$$

and

$$\varphi^* = \frac{\alpha^{\frac{\alpha}{2(\alpha-1)}}(\alpha-2)^{\frac{\alpha-2}{2(\alpha-1)}}}{\alpha-1}. \tag{17}$$

Clearly, from Eq. (15), only for $\alpha > 2$ does a nonnegative solution exist for ρ. For $\alpha \leq 2$ the optimal mutation strength is infinite, and the stationary distance of the search point from the ridge axis diverges. For $\alpha < 2$ the resulting progress rate increases indefinitely with increasing mutation strength as can be seen in Fig. 1 for the special case that $\alpha = 1$. As seen in [1], for $\alpha = 2$ a limit value of $\varphi^* = 2$ is approached as σ^* increases. For $\alpha > 2$, the optimal mutation strength is finite and results in a finite progress rate as witnessed by the curves for $\alpha = 4$ in Fig. 1. The same findings have been made by Beyer [3] for the special case of the $(1, \lambda)$-ES. However, in that reference no analytical expressions have been obtained for the optimal parameter settings. Finally, the dependence of the optimal normalised mutation strength and progress rate on the topology parameter α are illustrated by the solid lines in Fig. 2.

3.4 Adaptive Step Length

It has been seen in [1] for $\alpha = 2$ that by considering several further state variables that serve to characterise the search path, cumulative step length adaptation can be analysed using the approach described in Section 2.1. In that reference,

$$z_1^{(\text{avg})^2} + z_A^{(\text{avg})^2} = \frac{\sigma}{R} z_A^{(\text{avg})} \|\mathbf{z}_{2\ldots N}^{(\text{avg})}\|^2 \tag{18}$$

has been derived as a stationarity condition. The derivation is lengthy and cannot be reproduced here. The same argument applies in the case of more general ridge topologies, leading to the same result. The mutation strength generated by the cumulative step length adaptation mechanism can be computed from Eq. (18). Using the expected values from Eqs. (10), (11), and (12) to replace $z_1^{(\text{avg})}$, $z_A^{(\text{avg})}$, and $\|\mathbf{z}_{2\ldots N}^{(\text{avg})}\|^2$ it follows after replacing σ and R with their normalised values that

$$1 + \rho^{2(\alpha-1)} = \sigma^{*2} \rho^{2(\alpha-2)}.$$

Using Eq. (13) to eliminate the normalised mutation strength and solving the resulting equation yields $\rho = 1$ for the standardised distance from the ridge axis. Using this result in Eqs. (13) and (14) yields

$$\sigma^* = \sqrt{2} \tag{19}$$

for the normalised mutation strength generated by cumulative step length adaptation and

$$\varphi^* = 1 \tag{20}$$

for the corresponding normalised progress rate. Figure 2 compares the predictions from Eqs. (19) and (20) with measurements made in runs of evolution strategies. The experimental setup is the same as that used to generate the data points in Fig. 1, except that now the mutation strength of the strategy is subject to cumulative step length adaptation. It can be seen that although the quality of the predictions improves with increasing N, it is not as good as for static

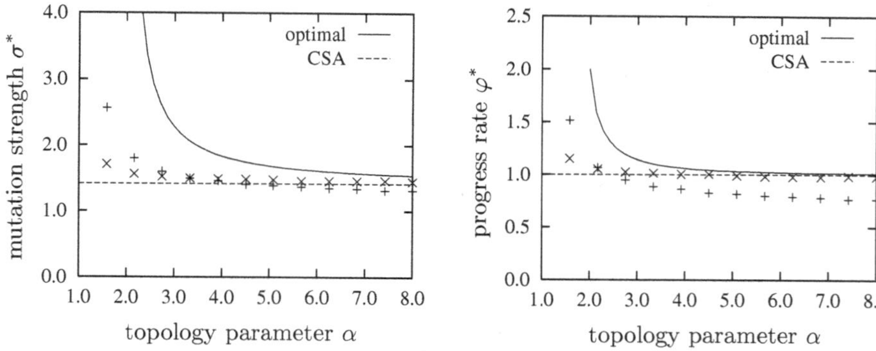

Fig. 2. Normalised mutation strength σ^* and normalised progress rate φ^* plotted against the topology parameter α. The points mark measurements made in runs of the $(3/3, 10)$-ES with cumulative step length adaptation for $N = 40$ (+) and $N = 400$ (×). The dashed lines represent predictions obtained from Eqs. (19) and (20). The solid lines reflect the optimal values described by Eqs. (16) and (17).

mutation strength. In particular, for $\alpha \gtrapprox 1$ both the mutation strength and the progress rate are severely underestimated unless the search space dimensionality is very high. A more careful analysis that helps explain those deviations remains as a task for future work and likely needs to take fluctuations of the state variables into account. Nonetheless, it is instructive to see that independent of the ridge topology, cumulative step length adaptation always generates step lengths that are shorter than optimal. For $1 < \alpha \leq 2$, it generates finite step lengths even though infinite step lengths are optimal. For the parabolic ridge where the maximal progress rate is finite, as seen in [1] cumulative step length adaptation achieves 50% of the optimal performance. For $\alpha > 2$, the gap between optimal progress rate and progress rate achieved with cumulative step length adaptation decreases with increasing values of α.

4 Conclusions

To conclude, this paper has presented an analysis of the behaviour of the $(\mu/\mu, \lambda)$-ES with cumulative step length adaptation on the ridge function class. Analytical results have been obtained for the optimal mutation strength and progress rate of the strategy, as well as for the mutation strength and progress rate generated by cumulative step length adaptation. It has been seen that the step lengths achieved using cumulative step length adaptation are consistently below the optimal values. The resulting loss in performance that has previously been seen to be a factor of two for the parabolic ridge decreases monotonically with increasing topology parameter α. How significant the failure of cumulative step length adaptation is to generate infinite step lengths for $\alpha < 2$ is debatable as arguably, it may reflect a deficiency of the ridge model rather than one of the strategy.

Future work with the goal of better understanding the behaviour of evolution strategies on ridge functions should consider alternative step length adaptation mechanisms, such as mutative self-adaptation and the use of hierarchically organised strategies. The analysis of the performance of the hierarchically organised strategy presented in [2] can be generalised beyond the parabolic ridge using the approach pursued in the present paper, and it will be interesting to see whether qualitative differences exist. Finally, strategies that use nonisotropically distributed mutations, such as the CMA-ES [7] remain to be studied.

Acknowledgements. This research was supported by the Natural Sciences and Engineering Research Council of Canada (NSERC).

References

[1] D. V. Arnold and H.-G. Beyer. Evolution strategies with cumulative step length adaptation on the noisy parabolic ridge. Technical Report CS-2006-02, Faculty of Computer Science, Dalhousie University, 2006. Available at http://www.cs.dal.ca/research/techreports/2006/CS-2006-02.shtml.

[2] D. V. Arnold and A. MacLeod. Hierarchically organised evolution strategies on the parabolic ridge. In M. Keijzer et al., editors, *Proceedings of the 2006 Genetic and Evolutionary Computation Conference*. ACM Press, New York, 2006.

[3] H.-G. Beyer. On the performance of $(1, \lambda)$-evolution strategies for the ridge function class. *IEEE Transactions on Evolutionary Computation*, 5(3):218–235, 2001.

[4] H.-G. Beyer. *The Theory of Evolution Strategies*. Springer, Heidelberg, 2001.

[5] H.-G. Beyer and H.-P. Schwefel. Evolution strategies — A comprehensive introduction. *Natural Computing*, 1(1):3–52, 2002.

[6] H. A. David and H. N. Nagaraja. Concomitants of order statistics. In N. Balakrishnan and C. R. Rao, editors, *Handbook of Statistics*, volume 16, pages 487–513. Elsevier, Amsterdam, 1998.

[7] N. Hansen and A. Ostermeier. Completely derandomized self-adaptation in evolution strategies. *Evolutionary Computation*, 9(2):159–195, 2001.

[8] M. Herdy. Reproductive isolation as strategy parameter in hierarchically organized evolution strategies. In R. Männer et al., editors, *Parallel Problem Solving from Nature — PPSN II*, pages 207–217. Elsevier, Amsterdam, 1992.

[9] A. Ostermeier, A. Gawelczyk, and N. Hansen. Step-size adaptation based on non-local use of selection information. In Y. Davidor et al., editors, *Parallel Problem Solving from Nature — PPSN III*, pages 189–198. Springer, Heidelberg, 1994.

[10] A. I. Oyman and H.-G. Beyer. Analysis of the $(\mu/\mu, \lambda)$-ES on the parabolic ridge. *Evolutionary Computation*, 8(3):267–289, 2000.

[11] A. I. Oyman, H.-G. Beyer, and H.-P. Schwefel. Where elitists start limping: Evolution strategies at ridge functions. In A. E. Eiben et al., editors, *Parallel Problem Solving from Nature — PPSN V*, pages 109–118. Springer, Heidelberg, 1998.

[12] A. I. Oyman, H.-G. Beyer, and H.-P. Schwefel. Analysis of the $(1, \lambda)$-ES on the parabolic ridge. *Evolutionary Computation*, 8(3):249–265, 2000.

[13] D. Whitley, M. Lunacek, and J. Knight. Ruffled by ridges: How evolutionary algorithms can fail. In K. Deb et al., editors, *Genetic and Evolutionary Computation — GECCO 2004*, pages 294–306. Springer, Heidelberg, 2004.

General Lower Bounds for Evolutionary Algorithms

Olivier Teytaud and Sylvain Gelly

TAO (Inria), LRI, UMR 8623(CNRS - Univ. Paris-Sud),
bat 490 Univ. Paris-Sud 91405 Orsay, France
teytaud@lri.fr

Abstract. Evolutionary optimization, among which genetic optimization, is a general framework for optimization. It is known (i) easy to use (ii) robust (iii) derivative-free (iv) unfortunately slow. Recent work [8] in particular show that the convergence rate of some widely used evolution strategies (evolutionary optimization for continuous domains) can not be faster than linear (i.e. the logarithm of the distance to the optimum can not decrease faster than linearly), and that the constant in the linear convergence (i.e. the constant C such that the distance to the optimum after n steps is upper bounded by C^n) unfortunately converges quickly to 1 as the dimension increases to ∞. We here show a very wide generalization of this result: *all comparison-based algorithms* have such a limitation. Note that our result also concerns methods like the Hooke & Jeeves algorithm, the simplex method, or any direct search method that only compares the values to previously seen values of the fitness. But it does not cover methods that use the value of the fitness (see [5] for cases in which the fitness-values are used), even if these methods do not use gradients. The former results deal with convergence with respect to the number of comparisons performed, and also include a very wide family of algorithms with respect to the number of function-evaluations. However, there is still place for faster convergence rates, for more original algorithms using the full ranking information of the population and not only selections among the population. We prove that, at least in some particular cases, using the full ranking information can improve these lower bounds, and ultimately provide superlinear convergence results.

1 Introduction

The principle of the main stream of evolutionary computation is to use only comparison between fitness values, and not the fitness values themselves. In almost all cases, the algorithm is indeed only based on comparisons between fitnesses of elements currently in a so-called "population", that has bounded size. Many algorithms, in spite of this restriction, have been proved linear (i.e. it has been proved that the logarithm of the distance to the optimum decreases linearly); see e.g. [4,1,2,10]. Some linear lower bounds also exist in various cases ([8]). In this paper, we show that :

T.P. Runarsson et al. (Eds.): PPSN IX, LNCS 4193, pp. 21–31, 2006.

- this kind of algorithms can at best be linear *w.r.t the number of comparisons*, with a constant $1-O(\frac{1}{d})$ as the dimension d increases to ∞, even with very easy fitness functions ;
- however, such algorithms can have slightly better constants *w.r.t the number of function evaluations* (theorem 4), for not too strange fitness-functions ; an interesting point is that this requires features that are not present in usual (μ,λ)-algorithms ;
- in some very particular cases, these non-standard algorithms can be superlinear if they use ranking-informations and not only selection (theorem 5).

The principle of the proof of the first point is as follows. In this informal introduction, we present it in the continuous case, but the proof is general. Consider an algorithm guided by comparisons. Then, after n_c comparisons, you have at most 2^{n_c} possible behaviors (possibly stochastic, but we may think of deterministic behaviors in this informal introduction). This is not so large in front of the entropy (here quantified by the packing number): to be precise within distance ϵ in $[0,1]^d$, you must be able of at least $\Omega(1/\epsilon^d)$ different answers, i.e. you need $d\log(1/\epsilon)$ bits of information to get a precision ϵ. This rough introduction shows already that n_c ensuring a precision ϵ must be at least such that $2^{n_c}=\Omega(1/\epsilon^d)$, i.e. ϵ decreases as $(2^{-1/d})^{n_c}$. The convergence is therefore at most linear, with a coefficient roughly $2^{-1/d}=1-O(1/d)$, hence the expected result that will be proved formally below. The reasonning also holds in the discrete case, and similar results can be derived for multi-modal optimization.

The proof of the second point, better constants *w.r.t the number of function evaluations*, is based on the information contained in rankings instead of selection. The proposed algorithm, realizing the task, is something between Nelder-Mead algorithm ([9]) and evolution strategies. The fitness is built in an ad hoc manner, but has some reasonnable properties that make the proof not too artificial. This is absolutely not the case of the proof of the last point (superlinearity w.r.t of the number of function evaluations), which uses ad hoc fitness and algorithm which are of theoretical but not practical interest. We do not know if this result also holds for more natural functions.

2 General Framework

Let D be the domain in which we look for optimal (say, minimal) values of a given real-valued function called the fitness. The packing number of a set S with respect to a metric and some $\epsilon>0$, is the maximal number of points (possibly ∞) such that (i) each point is in S (ii) any two distinct points are at distance at least ϵ. We note $|S|$ the cardinal of the set S (possibly infinite). We note $E_{y_1,y_2,\ldots,y_k}$ the expectation with respect to random variables $y_1,\ldots,y_k$. A property F being given, $\mathbf{1}_F$ denotes the function with value 1 when F holds, and 0 otherwise else. Let g_n, f, h be possibly stochastic functions. See 2 for more details on assumptions. The algorithm is as follows :

1. initialize s_1 and t_1 to some value s and t.
2. for $n=1$ to ∞, do *Epoch*(n) which is

(a) compute $(r_n, t_{n+1}) = g_n(s_n, t_n)$ with $r_n \in K_n$;
(b) $s_{n+1} = f(s_n, r_n)$.
(c) consider $x_n = h(s_n)$ as your current proposal as an approximation of the min-argument of the fitness.

The goal of this algorithm is the fast convergence of x_n to the min-argument of the fitness. No assumption is made on s_n, it can live in any domain, the only requirement is that s_{n+1} is only a function of s_n and r_n. In natural cases s_n can be a backup of all results of comparisons and of all random generations. Similarly, t_n can live in any domain, provided that t_{n+1} only depend on s_n and t_n; a natural case for us is that t_n contains all the archive of visited points with their fitness values. Also, theorems below hold for any case of K_n whenever the natural case for this paper is that r_n is the result of one or finitely many comparisons. We will now see how evolutionary algorithms fit in this framework.

Why this algorithm includes evolutionary computation. Our framework is very general, but we show here why this framework is relevant for all forms of evolutionary computation. Typically, in evolutionary computation:
- t_n is the archive of visited points with their fitness values
- r_n is the result of various comparisons (in g_n, fitness are computed and compared to other points in the population or in the archive);
- f is the method for creating generations (which might include cross-over, mutations, selection,...). Without loss of generality, we have assumed that f does not depend on n; if we want f depending on n, we just have to add the information "n" in s_n (i.e., replace s_n by (s_n, n)).

What are our hypothesis. The algorithm depends on (i) the initialization of s_1 and t_1 ; (ii) the possibly stochastic function g_n ; (iii) the possibly stochastic function f ; (iv) the possibly stochastic function h. The g_n are the only functions that use the fitness to be optimized. K_n (in which r_n has its values) is finite.

Typically, the function to be optimized is used only as a black-box. However, we will not have to assume this here in the main results. We mainly need the fact that the information provided by the fitness fits in a finite number of bits (i.e. finiteness of K_i). This is why algorithms like BFGS or even the gradient descent are not concerned by our results ; the information provided by a gradient does not fit in a finite number of bits (at least if we assume infinite precision of floating-point values). The t_n can have any structure, it may contain an archive of fitness values or not. We don't even need the fact that the computation time per epoch is bounded.

These assumptions are typically true for evolutionary algorithms. As we do not assume anything about the structure of s_n, and we do not assume anything about what is done with the fitness except that the number of bits is small, our result is much more general than only evolutionary computation.

3 Lower Bounds w.r.t of the Number of Comparisons

Entropy Lemma for Evolutionary Computation:
Consider an algorithm as in section 2. Consider a set Fit of possible fitness functions on domain D, i.e. $Fit \subset \mathbb{R}^D$, such that any $fit \in Fit$ has only one min-argument fit^*, and such that $\{fit^*; fit \in Fit\} = D$. This means that we don't know a priori where is the min-argument (Fit can be the set of sphere functions or any other very simple optimization problems).

Then, define $N(\epsilon)$ the packing number of D for 2ϵ, for some metric. Consider fit a random variable such that fit^* is uniformly distributed on the $N(\epsilon)$ elements realizing the packing number of D. Consider some fixed $\delta \in]0,1[$ and n such that the probability (on both fit and x_n) that $d(x_n, fit^*) \leq \epsilon$ (where $d(.,.)$ is the euclidean distance) verifies $P(d(x_n, fit^*) \leq \epsilon) \geq 1 - \delta$.

Then $n \geq n_{\epsilon,\delta} = \lceil \frac{\log(1-\delta)}{\log(K'_n)} + \frac{\log(N(\epsilon))}{\log(K'_n|)} \rceil$ where $K'_n = \sqrt[n]{\prod_{i=1}^n |K_i|}$.

Proof: We note S_ϵ the set of points of the domain that lie at distance $\leq \epsilon$ of the optimum fit^* for the $||.||_\infty$ norm.

Step 1: conditionning to a sequence of r_i. Consider a fixed sequence of (r_i), instead of r_i function (via g_i) of s_i and t_i. We consider a run of the algorithm, in the case in which these r_i are fixed. Then, conditionally to x_n, $E_{fit}\mathbf{1}_{\{x_n \in S_\epsilon\}} \leq \frac{1}{N(\epsilon)}$. Averaging on x_n (which can be random if the algorithm is stochastic) leads to $E_{fit}E_{x_n}\mathbf{1}_{\{x_n \in S_\epsilon\}} \leq 1/N(\epsilon)$.

Step 2: summing on all possible $(r_i)_{i\in[[1,n]]}$

$$E_{fit} \sup_{r_n} E_{x_n} \mathbf{1}_{\{x_n \in S_\epsilon\}} \leq E_{fit} \sum_{r_n} E_{x_n} \mathbf{1}_{\{x_n \in S_\epsilon\}} \leq \sum_{r_n} E_{fit} E_{x_n} \mathbf{1}_{\{x_n \in S_\epsilon\}} \leq \prod_{i=1}^{n} \frac{|K_i|}{N(\epsilon)}$$

(thanks to step 1). Note for short $K'_n = \sqrt[n]{\prod_{i=1}^n |K_i|}$. Then, $P(d(x_n, fit^*) \leq \epsilon) \geq 1 - \delta$ implies ${K'_n}^n/N(\epsilon) \geq 1 - \delta$. This implies that $n \geq \log(1-\delta)/\log(K'_n) + \log(N(\epsilon))/\log(K'_n)$. □

Note that for many algorithms, K_n is constant, and therefore K'_n is constant. An easier formulation is as follows :

Theorem 1: Entropy Theorem for Evolutionary Computation:
Consider a set Fit of possible fitness functions on domain D, i.e. $Fit \subset \mathbb{R}^D$, such that any $fit \in Fit$ has only one min-argument fit^*, and such that $\{fit^*; fit \in Fit\} = D$. This means that we don't know a priori where is the min-argument (Fit can be the set of sphere functions or any other very simple optimization problems). Consider some fixed $\delta \in]0,1[$ and n such that for any fitness in Fit, $P(d(x_n, fit^*) \leq \epsilon) \geq 1 - \delta$. Then $n \geq n_{\epsilon,\delta} = \lceil \frac{\log(1-\delta)}{log(K'_n)} + \frac{\log(N(\epsilon))}{\log(K'_n)} \rceil$ where $K'_n = \sqrt[n]{\prod_{i=1}^n K_i}$.

Proof: Assume, to get a contradiction, that n ensures $d(x_n, fit^*) \leq \epsilon$ with probability $1 - \delta$ for any fitness in Fit. Then, *a fortiori*, it ensures it with probability $1 - \delta$ on average for any distribution of fitnesses in Fit. This leads to a contradiction with the previous lemma, hence the expected result. □

This theorem provides the convergence rate with respect to the number of epochs. This is in particular interesting when (i) each epoch is parallelized ; or (ii) the cost is mainly the cost of fitness-evaluations and the number of fitness evaluations per epoch is some fixed q fitness-evaluations/epoch, what implies that the average coefficient of linear convergence per fitness evaluation r_{fe} is $r_{fe} = \sqrt[q]{r_e}$ where r_e is the coefficent of the linear convergence per epoch.

These lower bounds are absolute lowers bounds with respect to the epochs, but we might also be interested in bounds with respect to time, without neglecting the computational cost of each epoch. We can do this with a very natural assumption, very classical in evolutionary algorithms, which is that we only use comparisons on the fitness values. We can then derive a bound on the convergence rate with respect to the number of comparisons, and therefore on the convergence rate with respect to time :

Corollary 2. (entropy theorem for black-box evolutionary algorithms: complexity w.r.t. number of comparisons): *Assume the same hypothesis as in the theorem above with $K_n = 2$ corresponding to r_n equal to the result of a comparison between the fitnesses of two previously visited points. Then, with $log_2(x) = \log(x)/\log(2)$, the number of comparisons n_c required for ensuring with probability $1-\delta$ a precision ϵ is $n_c \geq \log_2(1-\delta) + \log_2(N(\epsilon))$. I.e., formally, $P(||x_{n_c} - fit^*|| < \epsilon) \geq 1-\delta \Rightarrow n_c \geq \log_2(1-\delta) + \log_2(N(\epsilon))$.*

Proof: Split the algorithm in section 2 so that each epoch contains at most one comparison. Then $|K'_n| = |K_n| = 2$ as any computation except the comparison can be put in f. Hence the expected result. □

Corollary 2': the same with respect to area. *If the domain has measure 1, and if Fit has the same property as in theorem 1, then n_c comparisons are necessary for a comparison-based algorithm in order to provide a set with measure $v < 1$ that contains fit^* with probability at least $1-\delta$, where $n_c \geq \log_2(1-\delta) + \log_2(1/v)$.* and also with notations as above, the number of epochs n verifies $n \geq \log(1-\delta)/\log(K'_n) + \log(1/v)/\log(K'_n)$.

Proof: The proof is very similar to the previous one, and is indeed simpler. Consider a fixed sequence of r_n. Consider fit a random variable on Fit such that fit^* is uniform on the domain D. Note V the set proposed by the algorithm, and that must contain fit^* with probability at least $1-\delta$.

Consider a fixed V. Then, the probability (on fit) that $fit^* \in V$ is at most v. Now, by averaging on V (conditionaly to a sequence of r_n), we have $P_V(fit^* \in V) \leq v$. If we now consider the sum of these probabilities among possible sequences of r_n, we have $P(fit^* \in V) \leq 2^{n_c}v$ and therefore $1-\delta \leq 2^{n_c}v$, which leads to $n_c \geq \log_2(1-\delta) - \log_2(v)$ where $\log_2(t) = \log(t)/\log(2)$. □

Continuous case: linear convergence w.r.t the number of comparisons. The bound above on the convergence rate depends on the packing number of the domain. This bound holds for any families of fitnesses, provided that the optimum is not known in advance (i.e. it can be anywhere in the domain). We will now apply it to the simple continuous case $D = [0,1]^d$ with the supremum norm,

$N(\epsilon) \geq (\lceil 1/\epsilon \rceil^d)$. First consider the convergence with respect to n the number of epochs in the (standard) case: $\forall i, K_i \leq K$ for some K. This implies that the guaranteed distance to the optimum, for some n and with probability at least $1-\delta$, for fixed δ, verifies $N(\epsilon) \leq K^n/(1-\delta)$ i.e. $\lceil 1/\epsilon \rceil \leq (K^n/(1-\delta))^{1/d}$, i.e. $\epsilon \geq 1/\left(1+(K^n/(1-\delta))^{1/d}\right)$. This is (at best) a linear convergence, with constant in $[1-O(1/d), 1]$. The convergence with respect to time if only comparisons are used is more strongly bounded, as shown in the corollary (without assuming anything except the fact that only comparisons of fitnesses are used) : $\epsilon \geq 1/\left(1+(2^{n_c}/(1-\delta))^{1/d}\right)$ where n_c is the number of comparisons. This is (at best) a linear convergence, with constant in $[1-O(1/d), 1]$, independent of the algorithm for a fixed K. We will see below that modifying K for example by modifying λ and μ does not significantly modify the result w.r.t the number of comparisons, but it does w.r.t the number of function-evaluations, *but only if we use full-ranking and not only selection.* Note that the bound is tight: the following problems $\{x \mapsto ||x - fit^*||_1; fit^* \in [0,1]^d\}$ is solved with constant $1-\Omega(1/d)$ by the following algorithm (close to the Hooke&Jeeves algorithm [7]), that reaches $1-\Theta(1/d)$ both w.r.t the number of fitness-evaluations and w.r.t the number of comparisons:

- initialize $x = (x_1, \ldots, x_d)$ at any point.
- in lexicographic order on $(j,i) \in \mathbb{N} \times [[0, d-1[[$:
  - try to replace the jth bit b of x_i by $1-b$;
  - if it is better, then keep the new value; otherwise else keep the old value.

4 Convergence Rate with Respect to the Number of Fitness-Evaluations: Why the $1-O(1/d)$ Is Also True for Selection-Based Algorithms

We already mentionned that our approach covers almost all existing evolutionary algorithms. We can now check the value of K, depending on the algorithm, and consider convergence rates with respect to the number of fitness-evaluations instead of the number of comparisons. The convergence rate will be $\geq 1/\sqrt[\lambda d]{K}$.

- **(μ,λ)-ES (or SA-ES):** at each step, then, we only know which are the selected points. Then, $K = \binom{\lambda}{\mu} \leq \binom{\lambda}{\lfloor \lambda/2 \rfloor} \leq (2^\lambda/\sqrt{2\pi\lambda})$ (see e.g. [3, p587] or [6] for proofs about $\binom{\lambda}{\mu}$). This leads to a convergence rate with respect to the number of FEs $> 1/\sqrt[\lambda d]{2^\lambda} \geq 1/\sqrt[d]{2}$, hence the $1-O(1/d)$ result with respect to the number of FEs ; note that the constant is *worst* if λ increases.

- Consider **more generally, any selection based algorithm**, i.e. any algorithm in which r_n encodes only a subset of μ points among λ. Then, the algorithm provides only a subset of $[[1,\lambda]]$, i.e. $K_n \leq 2^\lambda$, and $\sqrt[\lambda]{K} = O(1)$ and the convergence rate is $\geq 1-O(1/d)$ bound in distance or $\exp(-O(1))$ in area. Note that this remains true if λ depends on the epoch and even if the subset has not a fixed size defined before the fitness-evaluations. As we will show below, this $1-O(1/d)$ with respect to the number of FEs **is not true for algorithms**

using the full ranking information ; this allows the conclusion that **using *all* the ranking information can lead to better convergence rates, at least in some cases, than using *only* a *selection* information.**

- **$(\mu+\lambda)$-ES (or SA-ES):** then, we only know which are the selected points. Then, $K = (\lambda+\mu)!/(\mu!\lambda!)$. This does not allow a proof of $1-O(1/d)$ if μ increases as a function of d, but indeed, for $(\mu+\lambda)$-ES, the $1-O(1/d)$ can be proved by other means ; see e.g. [11]. Note however that for other algorithms (not $(\mu+\lambda)$-ES) with a big archive (what is somewhat similar to a big μ), we will see that the $1-O(1/d)$ does not hold.

- **Parallel $(1+\lambda)$-ES:** As the λ points are computed in parallel, we don't need to consider the $\sqrt[\lambda]{(.)}$; the convergence rate is $\geq 1/\sqrt[d]{K} = 1/\sqrt[d]{\lambda}$. Here, $K \leq \lambda$, therefore the speed up is only at most logarithmic (the number of fitness-evaluations required for a given precision decreases only as $\log(N(\epsilon))/\log(\lambda)$).

Consider the convergence rate with respect to the area as in corollary 2', with respect to epochs. For an averaged convergence rate with respect to the number of fitness-evaluations, we must consider the λth root ; the convergence rate in area is $O(\sqrt[\lambda]{\frac{2\lambda}{\sqrt{\lambda}}})$. Increasing the population size to infinity as dimension increases will therefore not improve the result in (μ,λ) schemas: this leads to $\exp(-o(1))$ instead of the $\exp(-\Theta(1))$ that can be reached by some algorithm like (1+1)-ES. Therefore, in the case of (μ,λ)-ES, either the population remains finite, and we can reach $\exp(-\Theta(1))$, or the population increases to infinity as the dimension increases and it is worse.

The case of $(\mu+\lambda)$-ES is different, as a huge μ has no cost w.r.t function evaluations (is only involves archiving). With a huge μ, as we have no restriction here on the selection method and the information stocked in memory and the computational power (we only count the number of fitness-evaluations), you can encode in an archive many specific methods, and in particular the algorithms below beating the $\exp(-O(1))$ (for area with respect to convergence rates). However, note that for standard $(\mu+\lambda)$-ES, the numerical evaluation of the bounds above, which depends on the rule for specifying μ and λ as functions of the dimension, lead to $\exp(-O(1))$ at best (for the area, with respect to the number of function evaluations).

5 Superlinearity: What About the Complexity with Respect to the Number of Fitness-Evaluations ?

K_n can run to infinity as $n \to \infty$. This implies that the computational cost of an epoch converges to infinity, but this might happen in particular if the principal cost is the evaluation of the fitness. For example in algorithms using the full archive of visited points and using the ranking of all visited points, we can compare each new point to all previously visited points. Can this improve the result in term of convergence rate with respect to the number of visited points? For the moment, we have bounds with respect to the computational time (corollary above), with respect to the number of epochs (the main theorem), but what about a bound on the convergence rate with respect to the number of fitness-evaluations, neglecting the other computational costs ? Such bounds are important as evolutionary algorithms are particularly relevant for very expensive fitnesses. Section 4 answers partially to this question for some algorithms. A positive result is a clue for designing algorithms that might be superlinear, or might have better dependencies on the dimension. We will show below that using full ranking information, it is possible to outperform the $1 - O(1/d)$ that hold, even w.r.t the number of function-evaluations for selection based algorithms.

The ultimate limit of corollary 2 w.r.t function-evaluations. Assume that we only use comparisons (but allow as many comparisons as you want per epoch). Then, let's rewrite the algorithm so that there is only one call to the fitness function per epoch. This only means that we split each epoch in the number of fitness-evaluations. Then, we see that there are at most n possible outcomes in the set of comparisons in this epoch: the rank of the newly evaluated point. This implies that $K_n \leq n$. Then, the number of epochs required to ensure a precision ϵ with probability $1 - \delta$ is $n \geq \log(1 - \delta)/\log(K'_n) + \log(N(\epsilon))/\log(K'_n)$ with $K'_n = \sqrt[n]{n!} = \Theta(n)$. In the continuous case, this is asymptotically (slightly) superlinear, but at the cost of a computation time per epoch increasing to infinity. Let's summarize these elements.

Corollary 3: convergence rate w.r.t. the number of fitness-evaluations. *Assume that K_n contains only the result of comparisons between values of the fitness at visited points. Then, the number of visited points necessary for a precision at most ϵ with probability at least $1-\delta$ is at least $n_{fe} \geq \log(1-\delta)/\log(K'_n) + \log(N(\epsilon))/\log(K'_n)$ with $K'_n = \Theta(n)$ (i.e. a superlinear convergence rate in the continuous case $[0,1]^d$).*

Whereas (as shown in corollary 2) the number of comparisons required is at least $n_c \geq \log_2(1-\delta)+\log_2(N(\epsilon))$ (i.e. a linear convergence rate in the continuous case $[0,1]^d$, with coefficient $1 - O(1/d)$).

This suggests the possible relevance of evolutionary algorithms for expensive fitnesses, for which the computational cost of each epoch out ot fitness-calls is negligible: for low-cost fitness, where the computational cost of the comparisons is not negligible, we know that we can not be superlinear, and that the constant quickly runs to 1 as the dimension increases, but we let open the possibility of superlinearity w.r.t the number of fitness evaluations, and the possibility of constants better than this $1 - O(1/d)$.

In particular, our proof above (corollary 2') forbids better than $\exp(-O(1))$ in the following terms: *if the domain has measure* 1, *then the number of comparisons required by a comparison-based algorithm for providing an area of measure $v < 1$ that contains the optimum with probability at least $1-\delta$ is as least* $n_c \geq \log_2(1-\delta) + \log_2(1/v)$. This is a bound in $\exp(-O(1))$ for the convergence rate with respect to the area, uniformly in all the possible dimensions. It is in some sense more natural, because it reflects the idea that in order to divide the area where the optimum can lie by 2, you need 1 bit of information. This bound

- holds with respect to the number of comparisons (corollary 2') ;
- holds with respect to the number of fitness-evaluations if the number of comparisons per epoch is a priori bounded independendly of the dimension or under various hypothesis including nearly all existing comparison-based algorithms ;
- but does not hold w.r.t the number of fitness-evaluations in the general case. Indeed, it is possible to avoid the $\exp(-O(1))$ if the population size increases to infinity, on some not too artificial fitness-functions. If we look to very particular cases of fitness-functions, it is also possible to be superlinear w.r.t the number of fitness-evaluations, with only comparisons. This point will be shown below.

Improved convergence rates using full ranking information. We now formalize two theorems about this precise point. The first one considers the convergence better than $\exp(-O(1))$ from the area point of view on a reasonnable fitness, thanks to the use of a bigger information than only the selected points: the algorithm uses the full ranking of the population. The second one reaches superlinearity, but for a very particular fitness and a very particular algorithm, so is only of theoretical interest.

Theorem 4: better than $\exp(-O(1))$ for the convergence rate of the area. *In spite of the various results showing bounds in* $\exp(-O(1))$ *on the constant in linear convergence rates, it is possible under the following hypotheses:*
- continuous domain with non-empty interior and dimension d;
- family of fitnesses that satisfy the hypothesis of theorem 1 (for any $fit^* \in D$*, there is at least one fitness* fit *with optimum in* fit^**) ;*
- fitnesses radially increasing ($\forall x \neq 0, t > 0, t \mapsto fit(fit^* + tx)$ *is increasing);*
- comparison-based algorithm;
to reach a $O(1/d)$ *constant from the point of view of the convergence of the area with respect to the number of function-evaluations.*

Remark: Selection is strictly less informative than ranks. Theorem 4 shows that it is possible to outperform the $\exp(-O(1))$ in area in a framework using only ranks. We have shown above that algorithms based on selections only could not outperform $\exp(-O(1))$. Therefore, at least for particular fitness-functions, full ranking is significantly more informative than selection only (i.e., can lead to $o(1)$ instead of $\exp(-O(1))$). In the same spirit, theorem 5 (superlinearity) can not be reached with selection only. The result is proved in details in `http://www.lri.fr/~teytaud/lblong.pdf`. It is based on a recursive splitting of the domain in simplices, depending on the ranking of its vertices. □

Theorem 5: superlinear convergence rates w.r.t. number of function evaluations. *There is one algorithm and one family of fitness functions such that (i) for almost all* fit^* *in the domain* D *there is a fitness* fit *with only one optimum at* fit^* *; (ii) the convergence is superlinear.*

The result is proved, thanks to very artificial fitness functions and algorithms, in `http://www.lri.fr/~teytaud/lblong.pdf`. □

6 Conclusion

We have studied algorithms that only depend on comparisons. We have shown (section 3) that ranking-based methods can not be better than linear, and that the constant runs to 1 as the dimension d runs to infinity, at least as $1-O(1/d)$. The result does not only concern comparison-based methods, it concerns all algorithms using at each epoch finitely many bits of information (what is not the case of algorithm using real numbers, at least on ideal computers). This linearity and this constant are with respect to the number of bits, e.g. the number of comparisons. In section 4, similar results are derived for the convergence with respect to the number of function evaluations. We also show that increasing λ e.g. as dimension increases does not improve the result, in a stronger sense for (λ, μ) algorithms than for $(\lambda + \mu)$-algorithms. However, these negative results, that generalize the state of the art, does not formally forbid superlinearity for comparison-based algorithms w.r.t the number of fitness-evaluations. We have then (section 5) shown that superlinearity w.r.t the number of function evaluations is possible. The contrast with the results of section 3 show that superlinear algorithms can only be superlinear w.r.t the number of function-evaluations (and not the number of comparisons), and that traditional (λ, μ)-ES or SAES or any usual algorithm can't be superlinear. Superlinear algorithms, or even linear algorithms with better constants as d increases, must use a stronger information from comparisons, typically the full ranking, and not only selection. We have exhibited such algorithms, one of them which is reasonnable (theorem 4, improving the dependency in front of the dimension by a Nelder-Mead inspired algorithm, modified for taking into account the full ranking) and one of them purely theoretical (theorem 5, superlinearity).

Acknowledgements. Talks with Anne Auger initiated this work through the idea of the class of comparison-based algorithms. Thanks also to Jens Jägersküpper, Stefan Droste, Thomas Jansen, Marc Schoenauer and various people from Dagsthul's seminar "theory of evolutionary algorithms 2006" for many interesting talks. This work was supported in part by the Pascal Network of Excellence.

References

1. A. Auger. Convergence results for (1,λ)-SA-ES using the theory of φ-irreducible markov chains. *Theoretical Computer Science*, 2005. in press.
2. A. Auger, M. Jebalia, and O. Teytaud. Xse: quasi-random mutations for evolution strategies. In *Proceedings of Evolutionary Algorithms, 12 pages*, 2005.
3. L. Devroye, L. Györfi, and G. Lugosi. *A probabilistic Theory of Pattern Recognition.* Springer, 1997.
4. S. Droste. Not all linear functions are equally difficult for the compact genetic algorithm. In *Proc. of the Genetic and Evolutionary Computation COnference (GECCO 2005)*, pages 679–686, 2005.

5. S. Droste, T. Jansen, and I. Wegener. Upper and lower bounds for randomized search heuristics in black-box optimization, 2003.
6. W. Feller. *An introduction to Probability Theory and its Applications.* Willey, 1968.
7. R. Hooke and T. A. Jeeves. Direct search solution of numerical and statistical problems. *Journal of the ACM, Vol. 8, pp. 212-229*, 1961.
8. J. Jagerskupper and C. Witt. Runtime analysis of a (mu+1)es for the sphere function. Technical report, 2005.
9. J. Nelder and R. Mead. A simplex method for function minimization. *Computer Journal 7*, pages 308–311, 1965.
10. G. Rudolph. Convergence rates of evolutionary algorithms for a class of convex objective functions. *Control and Cybernetics*, 26(3):375–390, 1997.
11. O. Teytaud, S. Gelly, and J. Mary. On the ultimate convergence rates for isotropic algorithms and the best choices among various forms of isotropy, ppsn 2006.

On the Ultimate Convergence Rates for Isotropic Algorithms and the Best Choices Among Various Forms of Isotropy

Olivier Teytaud, Sylvain Gelly, and Jérémie Mary

TAO (Inria), LRI, UMR 8623(CNRS - Univ. Paris-Sud),
bat 490 Univ. Paris-Sud 91405 Orsay, France
teytaud@lri.fr

Abstract. In this paper, we show universal lower bounds for isotropic algorithms, that hold for any algorithm such that each new point is the sum of one already visited point plus one random isotropic direction multiplied by any step size (whenever the step size is chosen by an oracle with arbitrarily high computational power). The bound is $1 - O(1/d)$ for the constant in the linear convergence (i.e. the constant C such that the distance to the optimum after n steps is upper bounded by C^n), as already seen for some families of evolution strategies in [19,12], in contrast with $1 - O(1)$ for the reverse case of a random step size and a direction chosen by an oracle with arbitrary high computational power. We then recall that isotropy does not uniquely determine the distribution of a sample on the sphere and show that the convergence rate in isotropic algorithms is improved by using stratified or antithetic isotropy instead of naive isotropy. We show at the end of the paper that beyond the mathematical proof, the result holds on experiments. We conclude that one should use antithetic-isotropy or stratified-isotropy, and never standard-isotropy.

1 Introduction: What Is the Price of Isotropy

[3] has recalled that, empirically, all evolution strategies with a relevant choice of the step size exhibit a linear convergence rate. Such a linear convergence rate has been shown in various contexts (e.g. [1]), even for strongly irregular multi-modal functions ([2]). Linearity is not so bad, but unfortunately [19,12] showed that the constant in the linear convergence, for $(1+\lambda)$-ES and $1, \lambda$-ES in continuous domains, converges to 1 as $1 - O(1/d)$ as the dimension d increases ; this has been generalized in [17] to *all* comparison-based methods. On the other hand, mathematical programming methods, using the derivatives ([4,7,9,16]), but also using only the fitness-values, reach a constant 0 in all dimensions and work in practice in huge dimension problems (see e.g. [18]).

So, we know that (i) comparison-based methods suffer from the $1-O(1/d)$ (ii) fitness-value-based methods do not. Where is the limit ? We here investigate the limit case for isotropic algorithms in two directions : (1) can isotropic algorithms avoid the $1-O(1/d)$ by using additional information such as a perfect line search

T.P. Runarsson et al. (Eds.): PPSN IX, LNCS 4193, pp. 32–41, 2006.

with computational cost zero (2) can we do better than random independent sampling for isotropic algorithms ? The answer for (1) will be essentially no : naive isotropy leads to $1 - O(1/d)$. A more optimistic answer appears for (2) : yes, some nice samplings lead to better results than naive independent uniform samplings, namely : stratified isotropy, and antithetic isotropy.

The paper is organized as follows. Section 2 shows that a random step size forbids superlinear convergence, but allows a linear convergence with rate $\exp(-\Omega(1))$. Section 3 shows that a random independent direction forbids superlinear convergence and forbids a better constant than $1 - O(1/d)$, whatever may be the family of fitness functions and the algorithm, whatever may be its step-size rule or selection procedure provided that it uses isotropic random mutations. Section 4 then shows that isotropy does not necessarily imply naive independent identically distributed sampling, and that the convergence rate of $(1 + \lambda) - ES$ on the sphere function is improved when using stratified sampling or antithetic sampling.

For the sake of clarity, without loss of generality we assume that the origin is the only optimum of the fitness (so the norm of a point is the distance to an optimum).

2 If the Step-Size Is Random

Consider an unconstrained optimization problem in $\mathbb{R}^d$. Consider any algorithm of the following form, based on at least one initial point for which the fitness has been computed (we assume that 0 has not been visited yet). Let's describe the nth epoch of the algorithm :

- Consider X_n one of the previously visited points (points for which the fitness has been computed) ; you can choose it by any algorithm you want using any information you want ;
- Choose the direction $v \in \mathbb{R}^d$ with unit norm by any algorithm you want, using any information you want.
- Then, choose the step size σ in $[0, \infty[$; for the sake of simplicity of notations, we require that $\sigma \geq 0$, but if you prefer $\sigma \in \mathbb{R}$, you simply replace v by $-v$ with probability 1/2 ;
- Evaluate the fitness at $X'_n = X_n + \sigma v$.

We assume that at each epoch σ has a non-increasing density on $[0, \infty[$. This constraint is verified by e.g. gaussian distributions (gaussian random variables have values in $]-\infty, \infty[$, but "gaussian steps + random isotropic direction" is equivalent to "absolute value of a gaussian step + random isotropic direction" and the absolute value of a gaussian step has decreasing density on $[0, \infty[$). Provided that the constraint is verified for each epoch, whatever may be the algorithm for choosing the distribution, the results below will hold. The distribution can be bounded and we do not require it to be gaussian or any other particular form of distribution. This formalism includes many algorithms ; SA-ES for example are also included. What we only require is that each point is chosen by a random jump from a previously visited point (any previously tested point) with a distribution that might be restricted to a deterministic direction (possibly the exact direction to an optimum!), with density decreasing with the distance.

In all the paper, $[a]^+ = \max(a, 0)$. Then,

Theorem 1 (step-size does matter for super-linearity).

$$E\left([-\ln([||X'_n||/||X_n||]^+)\right) \leq \int_{t>0} \min(1, \frac{2\exp(-t)}{1-\exp(-t)}) < \infty. \quad (1)$$

Moreover the variance is finite, and therefore this also implies that

$$\limsup \sqrt[n]{1/||X_n||} \leq \int_{t\geq 0} \min(1, \frac{2\exp(-t)}{1-\exp(-t)})dt. \quad (2)$$

Proof: The main tools of the proof are $E[X]^+ = \int_{t\geq 0} P(X \geq t)dt$ and the lemma $P(||X'_n||/||X_n|| \leq c) \leq \min(1, 2c/(1-c))$; the detailed proof is in `http://www.lri.fr/~teytaud/lbedalong.pdf`. □

3 If the Direction Is Random

This section generalizes [12] to any algorithm in which each newly visited point is equal to an old one plus a vector whose direction is uniform in the sphere (whenever the distance depends on the direction, i.e. is not chosen independently of the direction, even if it is optimal, and whenever the algorithm computes the gradient, the Hessian or anything else).

Consider an unconstrained optimization problem in $\mathbb{R}^d$. Consider any algorithm of the following form, based on at least one initial point for which the fitness has been computed :

- Consider X_n one of the previously visited points (points for which the fitness has been computed) ; you can choose this point, among previously visited points, by any algorithm you want using any information you want, even knowing the position of the optimum ;
- Choose the direction $v \in \mathbb{R}^d$ randomly in the unit sphere ;
- Choose the step size $\sigma > 0$ by any algorithm you want, using any information you want ; it can be stochastic as well ; it can depend on v, e.g. it can minimize the distance between $X_n + \sigma v$ and the optimum ;
- Evaluate the fitness at $X'_n = X_n + \sigma v$.

As the previously stated theorem, this result applies to a wide range of evolution strategies. We only require that each new visited point is chosen by a random jump from a previously visited point.

Then, the following holds :

Theorem 2 (direction does matter for convergence rates).
Assume $d > 1$. Then,
$E[-\ln(||X'_n||/||X_n||)]$ is finite and decreases as $O(1/d)$.

Proof: The main element of the proofs are

- the equality $E[x]+ = \int_{t\geq 0} P(x \geq t)$ for $x = -\ln(||X'_n||/||X_n||)$ which reduces the problem of the evaluation of the expectation to the evaluation of probabilities ;
- the result according to which the probability of an angle lower than α between two random independent vectors uniformly drawn on the sphere is $\frac{1}{2} - \frac{1}{2}F_\beta(cos^2(\alpha); \frac{1}{2}, (d-1)/2)$ for $\alpha < \pi/2$ and $d > 1$. This result is a theorem in [8].
- equalities of the form $\Gamma(d/2)/\Gamma((d-1)/2) = \sqrt{(d-1)/2} \times (1+o(1))$ ([10,13]) simplifying the equation above ;
- tedious evaluation of integrals.

The detailed proof of theorem 2, using these elements, can be found in `http://www.lri.fr/~teytaud/lbedalong.pdf`. □

4 Isotropic $(1+\lambda)$-ES and a Comparison Among Isotropic Samplings

We have shown that with independent isotropic mutations, even with perfect step size chosen a posteriori, we have a linear convergence rate with constant $1-O(1/d)$. We can study more carefully $(1+\lambda)$-ES with perfect step size on the sphere, in order to show the superiority of unusual isotropy. $(1+\lambda)$-ES are λ-fully-parallel ; they are probably a good choice for complex functions on which more deterministic or more structured approaches would fail, and if you have a set of λ processors for parallelizing the fitness-evaluations. Therefore, it is worth studying it. We show here that you must choose $(1+\lambda)$-ES with *stratified* isotropic or *antithetic* isotropic sampling instead of $(1+\lambda)$ *standard* isotropic sampling. We show that, at least on the sphere, it is better in all cases. The proofs below show that the convergence rate is better, but also that the distribution of the progress rate itself ($\frac{||X_{n+1}||}{||X_n||}$) is shifted in the good direction. At least for the sphere with step size equal to the distance to the optimum, we show that *all probabilities of a given progress-rate are improved.* Formally: for any c, $P(\frac{||X_{n+1}||}{||X_n||} < c)$ is greater or equal to its value in the naive case, with only equality in non-standard cases. We have postulated isotropy : this means that the probability of having one point in each given infinitesimal spherical cap is the same in any direction. This is uniformity on the unit sphere. But isotropy does not mean that all the offspring must be independent and identically distributed. We can consider independence and identical distribution (this is the naive usual case), but we can also consider independent non-identically distributed individuals (this is stratification, a.k.a. jittering, and this does not forbid overall uniformity as we will see below) and we can consider non-independently distributed individuals (this is antithetic sampling, and it is also compatible with uniformity).

Some preliminary elements will be necessary for both cases. $(1+\lambda)$-ES has a population reduced at one individual X_n at epoch n and it generates λ directions randomly on the sphere. Then, for each direction, a step-size determines a point, and the best of these λ points is selected as the new population. Let v a vector toward the optimum (so in the good direction). Let's note γ_i the angle between the ith point and v. We assume that the step size is the distance to the optimum. If $\gamma_i \geq \frac{\pi}{3}$ then the new point will not be better than X_n. Hence, we can consider $\theta_i = \min(\gamma_i, \frac{\pi}{3})$. Let $\theta = min_i \theta_i$. θ is a random variable. As we assume that the step size is the distance to the optimum, the norm of X_{n+1} is exactly $2 * |\sin(\theta/2)| ||X_n||$. In the sequel, we note for short $ssin(x) = 2\sin(x/2)||X_n||$; the norm of X_{n+1} is exactly $|ssin(\theta)|$. Then $log(||X_{n+1}||) = \log(|ssin(\min_{i\in[[1,\lambda]]}|\theta_i|)|)$. Therefore, we will have to study this quantity in sections below. For sake of clarity we assume that $||X_n|| = 1$ (without loss of generality).

4.1 Stratification Works

Let's consider a stratified sampling instead of a standard random independent sampling of the unit sphere for the choice of directions. We will consider the following simple sampling schema : (1) split the unit sphere in λ regions of same area ; (2) instead of drawing λ points independently uniformly in the sphere, draw 1 point in each of the λ regions. Such a stratification is also called *jittered* sampling (see e.g. [5]). In some cases, we define stratifications according to an auxiliary variable : let $v(.)$ a function (any function, there's no hypothesis on it) from the sphere to $[[0, \lambda - 1]]$. The ith generated point ($i \in [[0, \lambda - 1]]$) is uniformly independently distributed in $v^{-1}(i)$. We note $\pi_k(x)$ the kth coordinate of x : $x = (\pi_0(x), \pi_1(x), \pi_2(x), \ldots, \pi_{d-1}(x))$.

Let's see some examples of stratification :

1. for $\lambda = d$, we can split the unit sphere according to $v(x) = \arg\max_{i\in[[0,d-1]]}|\pi_i(x)|$. We will see below that for a good anticorrelation, this is probably not a very good choice.
2. for $\lambda = 2d$, we can split the unit sphere according to $v(x) = \arg\max_{i\in[[0,2d-1]]}(-1)^i \pi_{\lfloor \frac{i}{2} \rfloor}(x)$.
3. for $\lambda = 2^d$, we can split the unit sphere according to the auxiliary variable $v(x) = (sign(\pi_0(x)), sign(\pi_1(x)), sign(\pi_2(x)), \ldots, sign(\pi_{d-1}(x)))$.
4. for $\lambda = d + 1$, we can also split the unit sphere according to the faces of a regular simplex centered on 0.
5. for $\lambda = 2$, we can split the unit sphere with respect to any hyperplane including 0.
6. for $\lambda = d!$, we can split the unit sphere with respect to the ranking of the d coordinates.
7. for $\lambda = 2^d d!$, we can split the unit sphere with respect to the ranking of the absolute values of the d coordinates and the sign of each coordinate.

However, any stratification in λ parts $S_1, \ldots, S_\lambda$ of equal measure works (and indeed, various other stratifications also do the job). We here consider stratification randomly rotated at each generation (uniformly among rotations) and with each stratum measurable and having non-empty interior.

Theorem 3 (stratification works). *For the sphere function $x \mapsto ||x||^2$ with step size the distance to the optimum, the expected convergence rate*

$\exp(E(-\log(||X_{n+1}||/||X_n||)))$ *for* $(1+\lambda)$*-ES increases when using stratification.*

Proof: Consider the probability of $|ssin(\theta)| > c$ for some $c > 0$. $P_{naive} = P(|ssin(\theta)| > c) = P(|ssin(\theta_i)| > c)^\lambda$ if naive sampling. Consider the same probability in the case of stratification. $P_{strat} = P(|ssin(\theta)| > c) = \Pi_{i\in[[1,\lambda]]}P(|ssin(\theta_i)| > c)$. where θ_i is drawn in the ith stratum.

Let's introduce some notations. Note P_i the probability that $|ssin(v)| > c$ and that $v \in S_i$, where v is a random unit vector uniformly distributed on the sphere. Note $P(S_i)$ the probability that $v \in S_i$. Then $\Pi_i\frac{P_i}{\sum_j P_j} \leq (1/\lambda)^\lambda$ (by concavity of the logarithm). The equality is only reached if all the P_i are equal.

This implies that $\Pi_i\frac{P_i}{\sum_j P_j} \leq \Pi_i P(S_i)$, what leads to $\Pi_{i\in[[1,\lambda]]}\frac{P_i}{P(S_i)} \leq (\sum_i P_i)^\lambda$. This is exactly $P_{strat} \leq P_{naive}$. This is true for any value of c. Using $E\max(X,0) = \int_{t\geq 0}P(X>t)$ for any real-valued random variable X, this implies with $X = -\log|ssin(\theta)|$ that $E - \log(|ssin(\theta)|)$ can be worse than naive when using stratification. Indeed, it is strictly better (larger) as soon as the P_i are not all equal for at least one value of c. This is in particular the case for c small, which leads to $P_i < 1$ only for one value of i. □

Remark. We have assumed above that the step size was the distance to the optimum. Indeed, the result is very similar with other step-size-rules, provided that the probability of reaching $||X_{n+1}|| < c$ is not the same for all strata for at least an open set of values of c.

We present in figure 1 experiments on three stratifications (1 to 3 in the list above).

4.2 Antithetic Variables Work

The principle of antithetic variables is as follows (in the case of k antithetic variables): (1) instead of generating λ individuals, generate only λ/k individuals $x_0, \ldots, x_{\lambda/k-1}$ (assuming that k divides λ); (2) define $x_{i+a\lambda/k}$, for $a \in [[1,2,\ldots,k-1]]$, as $x_{i+a\lambda/k} = f_a(x_i)$ where the f_i's are (possibly random) functions. A more restricted but sufficient framework is as follows : choose a fixed set S of λ/k individuals, and choose as set of points $rot_1(S)$, $rot_2(S)$,..., $rot_k(S)$ (of overall size λ) where the r_i are independent uniform rotations in $\mathbb{R}^d$. The limit case $k=1$ (which is indeed the best one) is defining one set S of λ individuals, and using $rot(S)$ with rot a random rotation.

We first consider here a set S of 3 points on the sphere, which are $(1,0,0,\ldots,0)$, $(\cos(2\pi/3),\sin(2\pi/3),\ldots,0)$, $(\cos(4\pi/3),\sin(4\pi/3),0,\ldots,0)$ (the optimal and natural spherical code for $n=3$). The angle between two of these points is $2\pi/3$.

Theorem 4 (antithetism works). *For the sphere function* $x \mapsto ||x||^2$ *with step size equal to the distance to the optimum, the expected convergence rate* $\exp(E(-\log(||X_{n+1}||/||X_n||)))$ *for* $(1+\lambda)$*-ES increases when using antithetic sampling with the spherical code of* 3 *points.*

Proof: As previously, without loss of generality we can assume $||X_n|| = 1$. We consider $\exp(E(-\log(||X_{n+1}||)))$. As above, we show that for any c,

$$P(||X_1|| > c \text{ with antithetic variables}) \leq P(||X_{n+1}|| > c) \tag{3}$$

Using $E\max(x, 0) = \int_{t\geq 0} P(x \geq t)$, this is sufficient for the expected result. The inequality on expectations is strict as soon as it is strict in a neighborhood of some c. The probability $P(||X_{n+1}|| > c)$, in both cases, antithetic variables or not, is by independence the power $\frac{\lambda}{3}$ of the result for $\lambda = 3$. Therefore, it is sufficient to show the result for $\lambda = 3$. Yet another reduction holds on c: $c > 1$ always leads to a probability 0 as the step-size will be 0 if the direction does not permit improvement. Therefore, we can restrict our attention to $c < 1$.

So, we have to prove equation 3 in the case $c < 1$, $\lambda = 3$. In the antithetic case the candidates for X_{n+1} are $X_n + y_i$ where $y_0 = rot(x_0), y_1 = rot(x_1), y_2 = rot(x_2)$. In the naive case these candidates y_0, y_1, y_2 are randomly drawn in the sphere. We note $\gamma = \min(|angle(-y_i, X_n)|)$ (the y_i realizing this minimum verifies $X_{n+1} = X_n + y_i$ if $||X_n + y_i|| < ||X_n||$). Let θ the angle such that $\gamma \leq \theta \Rightarrow ||X_{n+1}|| < c$

In the antithetic case the the spherical caps s_i located at $-y_i$, and of angle θ are disjoint because $c < 1$ so $\theta < \frac{\pi}{3}$. But in the naive one they can overlap with non zero probability. As $P(||X_{n+1}|| < c) = P(X_n \in \cup_i s_i)$, this shows equation 3, which concludes the proof. □

The proof can be extended to show that $k = 1$ leads to a better convergence rate than $k > 1$, at least if we consider the optimal set S of λ points. But we unfortunately not succeeded in showing the same results for explicit larger numbers of antithetic variables in this framework. We only conjecture that randomly drawing rotations of explicit good spherical codes ([6]) on the sphere leads to similar results. However, we proved the following

Theorem 5 (arbitrarily large good antithetic variables exist). For any $\lambda \geq 2$, there exists a finite subset s of the unit sphere in $\mathbb{R}^d$ with cardinal λ such that the convergence rate of $(1 + \lambda)$-ES is faster with a sampling by random permutation of s than with uniform independent identically distributed sampling, with step size equal to the distance to the optimum.

Proof: We consider the sphere problem with optimum in zero and X_n of norm 1.

Let s a sample of λ random points (uniform, independent) on the unit sphere. Let $f(s) = E_{rot}(\ln ||X_{n+1}||)$ (as above rot is a random linear transformation with $rot \times rot' = 1$). If s is reduced to a single element we reach a maximum for f (as the probability of $\ln(X_{n+1}) < c$ is lower than for any set with at least two points).

$f(s)$ is therefore a continuous function, with some values larger than $E_s f(s)$. Therefore, the variance of $f(s)$ is non-zero. Therefore, thanks to this non-zero variance, there exists s' such that $f(s') < E_s f(s)$.

$E_s f(s)$ is the progress rate when using naive sampling and $f(s')$ is the progress rate when using an antithetic sampling by rotation of s'. So, this precisely means that there exists good values of s leading to an antithetic sampling that works better than the naive approach. □

We have stated the result for $(1+\lambda)$-ES with λ antithetic variables, but the same holds for λ/k antithetic variables with the same proof. This does not explicitly provided a set s', but it provides a way of optimizing it by numerical optimization of $E\ln(X_{n+1})$ that can be optimized once for all for any fixed value of λ. Despite the lack of theoretical proof, we of course conjecture that standard spherical codes are a good solution. This will be verified in experiments (figure 1, plots 4,5,6). However, we see that it works in simulations for moderate numbers of antithetic variables placed according to standard spherical codes. But for $k = 2^d$ antithetic variables at the vertices of an hypercube, it does not work when dimension increases, i.e. hypercube sampling is not a good sampling. Note that the spherical codes $\lambda = 2d$ (generalized octahedron, also termed biorthogonal spherical code) and $\lambda = d+1$ (simplex), which are nice and optimal for various points of view, seem to scale with dimension. Their benefit in terms of the reduction of the number of function evaluations behaves well when d increases. Of course, more experimental works remain to be done.

5 Conclusion

We have shown that (i) superlinear methods require a fine decision about the stepsize, with at most a very little randomization; (ii) if we accept linear convergence rates and keep the randomization of the step size, we however need, in order to break the curse of dimensionality (i.e. keeping a convergence rate far from 1), a fine decision about the direction, with at most a very little randomization. This shows the price of isotropy, which is only a choice when less randomized techniques can not work. In a second part, we have shown that isotropy can be improved; the naive isotropic method can be very easily replaced by a non i.i.d sampling, thanks to stratification (jittering) or antithetic variables. Moreover, it really works on experiments.

The main limit of this work is its restriction to isotropic methods. A second limit is that we have considered the second order of sampling *inside* each epoch, but not *between* successive epochs. In particular, Gauss-Seidel or generalized versions of Gauss-Seidel ([14,15]) are not concerned; we have not considered correlations between directions chosen at successive epochs; for example, it would be natural, at epoch $n+1$, to have directions orthogonal to, or very different from, the chosen direction at epoch n. This is beyond the simple framework here, in particular because of the optimal step size, and will be the subject of a further work.

The restriction to 3 antithetic variables in theorem 4 simplifies the theorem; this hypothesis should be relaxed in a future work. Theorem 5 shows that good point sets exist for any number of antithetic variables, theorem 4 explicitly exhibits 3 antithetic variables that work and that are equal to the optimal spherical code for $n = 3$, but figure 1 (figs. 4,5,6) suggests that more generally octahedron-sampling or simplex-sampling (which are very good spherical codes, see e.g. [6]) are very efficient, and in particular that the improvement remains strong when dimension increases. Are spherical codes ([6]) the best choice, as intuition suggests, and are there significant improvements for a number $n = \lambda/k$ of antithetic variables large in front of d ? This is directly related to the speed-up of parallelization.

Acknowledgements. This work was supported in part by the Pascal Network of Excellence. We thank A. Auger and J. Jägersküpper for fruitful discussions.

References

1. A. Auger. Convergence results for (1,λ)-SA-ES using the theory of φ-irreducible markov chains. *Theoretical Computer Science*, 2005. in press.
2. A. Auger, M. Jebalia, and O. Teytaud. Xse: quasi-random mutations for evolution strategies. In *Proceedings of Evolutionary Algorithms, 12 pages*, 2005.
3. H.-G. Beyer. *The Theory of Evolutions Strategies.* Springer, Heidelberg, 2001.
4. C. G. Broyden. The convergence of a class of double-rank minimization algorithms 2, the new algorithm. j. of the inst. for math. and applications, 6:222-231, 1970.
5. B. Chazelle. *The discrepancy method: randomness and complexity.* Cambridge University Press, New York, NY, USA, 2000.
6. J. H. Conway and N. J. Sloane. *Sphere packings, lattices and groups.* 1998.
7. R. Fletcher. A new approach to variable-metric algorithms. computer journal, 13:317-322, 1970.
8. G. Frahm and M. Junker. Generalized elliptical distributions: Models and estimation. Technical Report 0037, 2003.
9. D. Goldfarb. A family of variable-metric algorithms derived by variational means. mathematics of computation, 24:23-26, 1970.
10. U. Haagerup. The best constants in the khintchine inequality. *Studia Math.*, 70:231–283, 1982.
11. N. Hansen and A. Ostermeier. Completely derandomized self-adaptation in evolution strategies. *Evolutionary Computation*, 11(1), 2003.
12. J. Jagerskupper. In between progress rate and stochastic convergence. *Dagstuhl's seminar*, 2006.
13. Literka. A remarkable monotonic property of the gamma function. Technical report, 2005.
14. R. Salomon. Resampling and its avoidance in genetic algorithms. In V. W. Porto, N. Saravanan, D. Waagen, and A. E. Eiben, editors, *Evolutionary Programming VII*, pages 335–344, Berlin, 1998. Springer.
15. R. Salomon. The deterministic genetic algorithm: Implementation details and some results, 1999.
16. D. F. Shanno. Conditioning of quasi-newton methods for function minimization. mathematics of computation, 24:647-656, 1970.
17. O. Teytaud and S. Gelly. General lower bounds for evolutionary algorithms, ppsn 2006.
18. Z. Wang, K. Droegemeier, L. White, and I. M. Navon. Application of a new adjoint newton algorithm to the 3-d arps storm scale model using simulated data. *Monthly Weather Review, 125, No. 10, 2460-2478*, 1997.
19. C. Witt and J. Jägersküpper. Rigorous runtime analysis of a (mu+1) es for the sphere function. In *Proceedings of the 2005 Conference on Genetic and Evolutionary Computation*, pages 849–856, 2005.

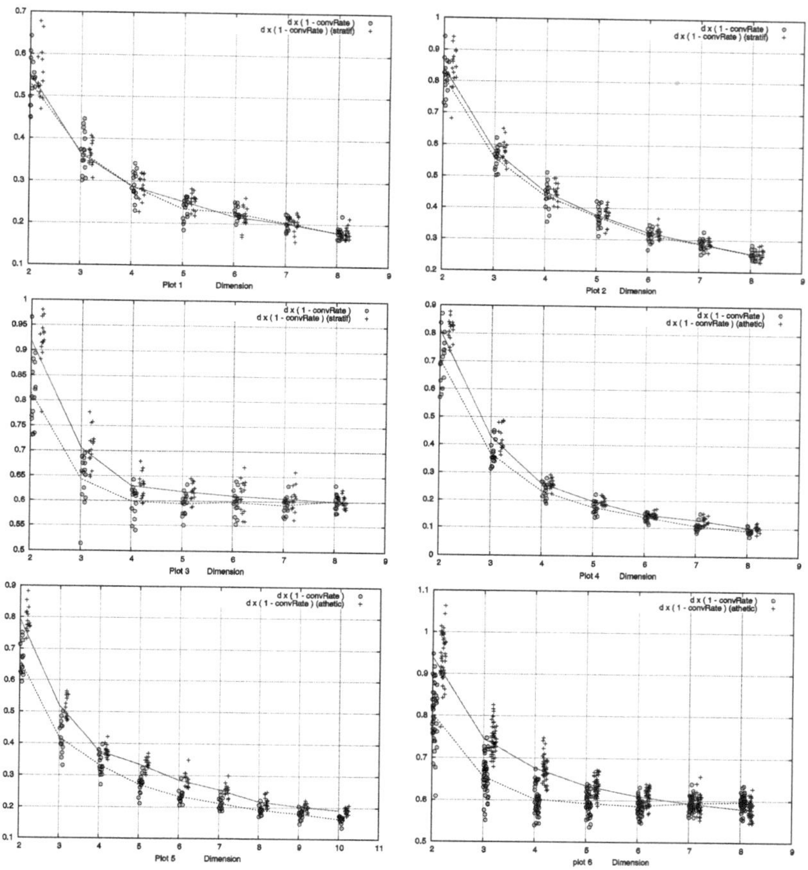

Fig. 1. *Antithetic variables look better.* Plots 1,2,3: with ρ the average progress rate $\sqrt[n\lambda]{||X_n||/||X_0||}$ on the sphere, we plot $d(1-\rho)$ in two cases (i) independent uniform sampling (ii) stratified sampling. Each point corresponds to one run. $n = 100$ for each run. The step size is equal to the optimal one. The three plots respectively deal with $\lambda = d$, $\lambda = 2d$ and $\lambda = 2^d$. The improvement in terms of number of fitness-evaluations is the ratio between the log(.) of the convergence rates. For dimension 2, the difference in terms of number of function-evaluations is close to 20 % but quickly decreases. Plots 4,5,6: with ρ the average progress rate $\sqrt[n\lambda]{||X_n||/||X_0||}$ on the sphere, we plot $d(1-\rho)$ in two cases (i) independent uniform sampling (ii) antithetic sampling with $\lambda = 3$ (plot 4) or $\lambda = d$ with an antithetic sampling by random rotation of a regular simplex (plot 5) or $\lambda = 2^d$ with an antithetic sampling by random rotation of $\{-1,1\}^d$ (plot 6). n and the step size are as for previous plots. For dimension 2 to 6, the difference in terms of number of function-evaluations for a given precision are between 12 % and 18 % for $\lambda = 2^d$ and remain close to 20 % for the octahedron $\lambda = 2d$ for any value of d. We also experiments the direct inclusion of quasi-random numbers in the Covariance-Matrix-Adaptation algorithm ([11]); the resulting algorithm, termed DCMA, in which the only difference with CMA is that the random-generator is replaced by a quasi-random generator, is more stable and faster than the classical CMA; results are presented in http://www.lri.fr/~ teytaud/resultsDCMA.pdf.

Mixed-Integer NK Landscapes

Rui Li[1], Michael T.M. Emmerich[1], Jeroen Eggermont[2], Ernst G.P. Bovenkamp[2], Thomas Bäck[1], and Jouke Dijkstra[2], and Johan H.C. Reiber[2]

[1] Natural Computing Group, Leiden University, P.O. Box 9500, 2300 CA Leiden, The Netherlands
{ruili, emmerich, baeck}@liacs.nl
[2] Division of Image Processing, Department of Radiology C2S, Leiden University Medical Center, P.O. Box 9600, 2300 RC Leiden, The Netherlands
{J.Eggermont, E.G.P.Bovenkamp, J.Dijkstra, J.H.C.Reiber}@lumc.nl

Abstract. NK landscapes (NKL) are stochastically generated pseudo-boolean functions with N bits (genes) and K interactions between genes. By means of the parameter K ruggedness as well as the epistasis can be controlled. NKL are particularly useful to understand the dynamics of evolutionary search. We extend NKL from the traditional binary case to a mixed variable case with continuous, nominal discrete, and integer variables. The resulting test function generator is a suitable test model for mixed-integer evolutionary algorithms (MI-EA) - i. e. instantiations of evolution algorithms that can deal with the aforementioned variable types. We provide a comprehensive introduction to mixed-integer NKL and characteristics of the model (global/local optima, computation, etc.). Finally, a first study of the performance of mixed-integer evolution strategies on this problem family is provided, the results of which underpin its applicability for optimization algorithm design.

1 Introduction

NK landscapes (NKL, also referred to as NK *fitness* landscapes), introduced by Stuart Kauffman [6], were devised to explore the way that epistasis controls the 'ruggedness' of an adaptive landscape. Frequently, NKL are used as test problem generators for Genetic Algorithms. NKL have two advantages. First, the ruggedness and the degree of interaction between variables of NKL can be easily controlled by two tunable parameters: the number of genes N and the number of epistatic links of each gene to other genes K. Second, for given values of N and K, a large number of NK landscapes can be created at random. A disadvantage is that the optimum of a NKL instance can generally not be computed, except through complete enumeration.

As NKL have not yet been generalized for continuous, nominal discrete, and mixed-integer decision spaces, they cannot be employed as test functions for a large number of practically important problem domains. To overcome this shortcoming, we introduce an extension of the NKL model, *mixed-integer NKL*

T.P. Runarsson et al. (Eds.): PPSN IX, LNCS 4193, pp. 42–51, 2006.

(MI-NKL), that capture these problem domains. They extend traditional NKL from the binary case to a more general situation, by taking different parameter types (continuous, integer, and nominal discrete) and interactions between them into account (cf. Figure 1).

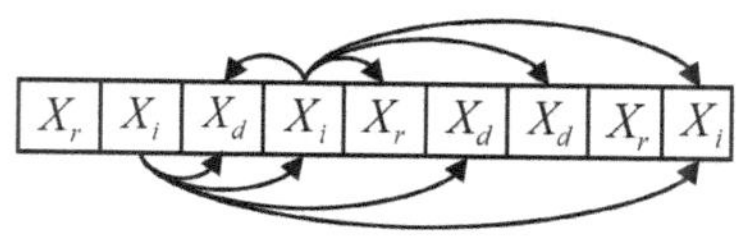

Fig. 1. Example Genes and their interaction

This paper is organized as follows. First, in Section 2, we will give a review of Kauffman's NKL and its variants. In Section 3, we extend NKL to the mixed-integer case , provide theorems on the existence and position of local and global optima, and discuss the implementation of the model. Some initial experimental results are given in Section 4 using a mixed-integer Evolution Strategy. Conclusions and topics for future research are discussed in Section 5.

2 NK Landscapes

Kauffman's NK Landscapes model defines a family of pseudo-boolean fitness functions $F : \{0,1\}^N \to \mathbb{R}^+$ that are generated by a stochastic algorithm. It has two basic components: A structure for gene interaction (using an *epistasis matrix* E), and a way this structure is used to generate a fitness function for all the possible genotypes [1]. The gene interaction structure is created as follows: The genotype's fitness is the average of N fitness components F_i, $i = 1, \ldots, N$. Each gene's fitness component F_i is determined by its own allele x_i, and also by K alleles at K $(0 \leq K \leq N-1)$ epistatic genes distinct from i. The fitness function reads:

$$F(\mathbf{x}) = \frac{1}{N} \sum_{i=1}^{N} F_i(x_i; x_{i_1}, \ldots, x_{i_k}), \ \mathbf{x} \in \{0,1\}^N \tag{1}$$

where $\{i_1, \ldots, i_k\} \subset \{1, \ldots, N\} - \{i\}$. There are two ways for choosing K other genes: '*adjacent neighborhoods*', where the K genes nearest to position i on the vector are chosen; and '*random neighborhoods*', where these positions are chosen randomly on the vector. In this paper we focus on the latter case, '*random neighborhoods*'. However, a translation to the first case is straightforward.

The computation of $F_i : \{0,1\}^K \to [0,1)$, $i = 1, \ldots, N$ is based on a *fitness matrix* F. For any i and for each of the 2^{K+1} bit combinations a random number is drawn independently from a uniform distribution over $[0,1)$. Accordingly, for the generation of one (binary) NK landscape the setup algorithm has to generate $2^{K+1}N$ independent random numbers. The setup algorithm also creates an epistasis matrix E which for each gene i contains references to its K epistatic genes. Table 1 illustrates the *fitness matrix* and *epistasis matrix* of a NKL. A more detailed description of its implementation can be found in [4].

Table 1. Epistasis matrix E (left) and fitness matrix F (right)

$E_1[1]$	$E_1[2]$	$\cdots$	$\cdots$	$\cdots$	$E_1[K]$
$E_2[1]$	$E_2[2]$	$\cdots$	$\cdots$	$\cdots$	$E_1[K]$
$\cdots$	$\cdots$	$\cdots$	$E_i[j]$	$\cdots$	$\cdots$
$E_N[1]$	$E_N[2]$	$\cdots$	$\cdots$	$\cdots$	$E_N[K]$

$F_1[0]$	$F_1[1]$	$\cdots$	$\cdots$	$\cdots$	$F_1[2^{K+1}-1]$
$F_2[0]$	$F_2[1]$	$\cdots$	$\cdots$	$\cdots$	$F_2[2^{K+1}-1]$
$\cdots$	$\cdots$	$\cdots$	$F_i[j]$	$\cdots$	$\cdots$
$F_N[0]$	$F_N[1]$	$\cdots$	$\cdots$	$\cdots$	$F_N[2^{K+1}-1]$

After having generated the epistasis and fitness matrices, for any input vector $\mathbf{x} \in \{0,1\}^N$ we can compute the fitness in $\mathcal{O}(KN)$ computational complexity via:

$$F(\mathbf{x}) = \frac{1}{N}\sum_{i=1}^{N} F_i[2^0 x_i + 2^1 x_{E_i[1]} + \cdots + 2^K x_{E_i[K]}] \qquad (2)$$

Note, that the generation of F has an exponential computational complexity and space complexity in K, while being linear in N. The computational complexity for computing function values is linear in K and N for this implementation.

2.1 Properties of NK Landscapes

Kauffman's model makes two principal assumptions: first, that the fitness of a genotype is the sum of the contributions from each gene, and second, that the effects of polygeny and pleiotropy make these interactions effectively random. Besides Kaufmann, some other researchers, e. g. Weinberger et al. [10,9], did an extensive study on NKL. Some well-known properties are:

1. $K = 0$ (no epistasis): The problem is separable and there exists a unique global optimum. Assuming a Hamming neighborhood-structure, the problem gets unimodal.
2. $1 \leq K < N-1$: For $K = 1$, a global optimum can still be found in polynomial time [10]. For $K \geq 2$, global optimization is NP-complete for the random assignment of neighbors and constant K. However, the problem can always be solved in a computational complexity of 2^N function evaluations and hence can practically be solved for problems of moderate dimension (N around 30). For adjacent neighbors, the problem can be solved in time $O(2^K N)$ (cf. Weinberger [10]).
3. $K = N-1$: This corresponds to the maximum number of interactions between genes. Practically speaking, to each bitstring of $F : \{0,1\}^N \to [0,1)$ we assign a sum of N values, each of which is drawn independently from a uniform distribution in $[0,1)$. If we choose the Hamming neighborhood on $\{0,1\}^N$ the following results apply:
   - The probability that a random bit string is a local optimum is $\frac{1}{N+1}$
   - The expected number of local optima is $\frac{2^N}{N+1}$

3 Generalized NK Landscapes

As mentioned in the previous section, Kauffman's NKL model is a stochastic method for generating fitness functions on binary strings. In order to use it as a test model for mixed-integer evolution strategies, we extend it to a more general case such that the fitness value can be computed for different parameter types. Here we consider continuous variables in $\mathbb{R}$, integer variables in $[z_{min}, z_{max}] \subset \mathbb{Z}$, and nominal discrete values from a finite set of L values. In contrast to the ordinal domain (continuous and integer variables), for the nominal domain no natural order is given. Mixed-integer optimization problems arise frequently in practise, e.g. when optimizing optical filter designs [2] and the parameters of algorithms [8].

The idea about how to extend NKL to the mixed-integer situation will be described in three steps. First we propose a model for continuous variables, then for those with integer variables and nominal discrete variables. Finally, we will discuss the case of NKL that consists of all these different variable types at the same time and allow for interaction among variables of different types. This defines the full mixed-integer NKL model.

3.1 Continuous NK Landscapes

In order to define continuous landscapes, we choose an extension of binary NKL to an N-dimensional hypercube $[0,1]^N$. Therefore, all continuous variables are normalized between $[0,1]$. In the following we describe the construction of the objective function $F : [0,1]^N \to [0,1)$:

Whenever the continuous variable takes values at the corners of the hypercube, the value of the corresponding binary NKL is returned. For values located in the interior of the hypercube or its delimiting hyperplanes, we employ a *multi-linear interpolation technique* that achieves a continuous interpolation between the function values at the corner. Note that a higher order approach is also possible but we chose a multi-linear approach for simplicity and ease of programming. Moreover, the theory of multi-linear models as used in the design and analysis of experiments, introduces intuitive notions for the effect of single variables and interaction between multiple variables of potentially different types [3]. For each of the N fitness components $F_i : [0,1]^{K+1} \to [0,1)$, we create a multi-linear function

$$F_i(\mathbf{x}) = \sum_{j=0}^{2^{K+1}-1} a_j^i x_i^{[1 \texttt{ AND } j]} \prod_{k=1}^{K} x_{i_k}^{[2^k \texttt{ AND } j]/2^k}, \tag{3}$$

where `AND` is the bitwise *and* operator and x_{i_k} is the k-th epistatic gene of x_i. For instance, in the case $K = 2$ the formula for $F_i(\mathbf{x})$ becomes[1]:
$a_{000}^i + a_{001}^i x_i + a_{010}^i x_{i_1} + a_{100}^i x_{i_2} + a_{011}^i x_i x_{i_1} + a_{101}^i x_i x_{i_2} + a_{110}^i x_{i_1} x_{i_2} + a_{111}^i x_i x_{i_1} x_{i_2}$.

[1] Note, that we use binary instead of decimal numbers for the index to make the construction more clear.

Once uniformly distributed random values have been attached to the corners of the K-dimensional hypercube (cf. Figure 2), we can identify the coefficients $a_0^i, \ldots, a_{2^{K+1}-1}^i$ by solving a linear equation system (LES). However, even for moderate K the computational complexity for applying general LES solvers would be prohibitive high. An advantage of the multi-linear form (as compared to other interpolation schemes like radial basis functions or splines) is, that it allows for an efficient computation of the coefficients by exploiting the diagonal structure of the equation system. Accordingly, a_j^i can be obtained by means of the following formula:

$$a_0^i = F_i[0], a_j^i = F_i[j] - \sum_{\ell=0}^{j-1} \left[a_\ell^i \mathrm{I}(\ell = (\ell \texttt{ AND } j))\right], j = 1, \ldots, 2^{K+1} - 1 \quad (4)$$

In order to compute the values, we have to start with $j = 0$ and increase the value of j. Hence, the number of additions we need for computing all coefficients is proportional to $(2^{K+1} - 1)(2^{K+1})/2 = 2^{2(K+1)-1} - 2^K$.

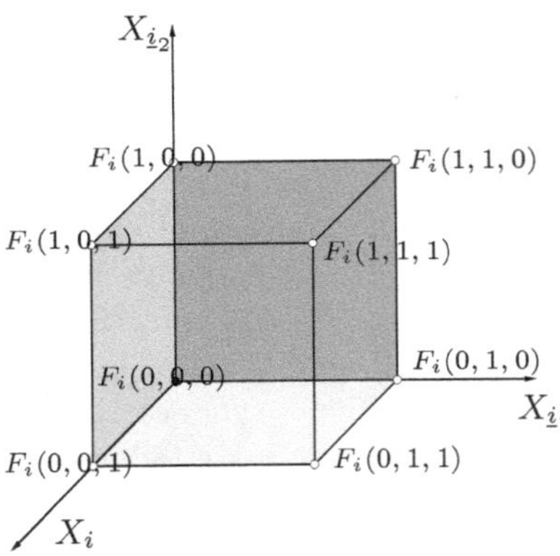

$$\begin{aligned}
a_{000}^i &= F_i(0,0,0) \\
a_{001}^i &= F_i(0,0,1) - a_{000}^i \\
a_{010}^i &= F_i(0,1,0) - a_{000}^i \\
a_{011}^i &= F_i(0,1,1) - a_{000}^i - a_{001}^i - a_{010}^i \\
a_{100}^i &= F_i(1,0,0) - a_{000}^i \\
&\vdots \\
a_{111}^i &= F_i(1,1,1) - a_{000}^i - a_{001}^i - a_{010}^i - a_{011}^i \\
&\quad - a_{100}^i - a_{101}^i - a_{110}^i
\end{aligned}$$

Fig. 2. Example HyperCube with $K = 2$ and the computation of a_j^i

Once we have the a_j^i values, we can use Equation 1 to compute the model. Of course the domain of the $\mathbf{x}$ values has to be replaced by $[0, 1]^N$ in that equation. For the computation of the global optimal value of the continuous NK landscapes the following lemma is useful:

Lemma 1. At least one global optimum of the function F will always be located in one of the corners of the N dimensional hypercube, such that the computation of the optimal function value upper bounds the computational complexity for the binary model.

Proof: The idea of the proof is that there is an algorithm that for any given input $\mathbf{x}^* \in [0, 1]^N$ determines a corner of the hypercube, the function value of which is not higher than the function value at F, given that F has a multilinear form. Basically, the proposed algorithm can be described as a path oriented algorithm that searches parallel to the coordinate axis: First we fix all variables except one, say x_1, in F. It is now crucial to see that the remaining form $F(x_1, x_2^*, \dots, x_N^*)$ is a linear function of x_1. Now, because the form is linear, it is obvious to see that either $(1, x_2^*, \dots, x_N^*)^T$ or $(0, x_2^*, \dots x_N^*)^T$ has a function value that is better or equal than the function value at $(x_1^*, \dots, x_N^*)^T$. We fix x_1 to a value for which this is the case, i. e. we move either to $(1, x_2^*, \dots, x_N^*)^T$ or to $(0, x_2^*, \dots x_N^*)^T$ without increasing the function value. For the new position $\mathbf{x}^{1*}$ we again fix all variables except one. This time x_2 is the free variable. Again we can move the value of x_2 either to zero or to one, such that the function value does not increase. Now, the new vector $\mathbf{x}^{12*}$ will either be $(x_1^{1*}, 0, x_3^*, \dots, x_N^*)^T$ or $(x_1^{1*}, 1, x_3^*, \dots, x_N^*)^T$. After continuing this process for all remaining variables x_3 to x_N we finally obtain a vector $\mathbf{x}^{12\cdots N*}$, all values of which are either zero or one, and the function value is not worse than that of $\mathbf{x}^*$. □

From Lemma 1 it follows:

Theorem 1. The problem of finding the global optimal value for a continuous NKL is NP-complete for $K \geq 2$.

Proof: Finding the optimum in the corner is equivalent to the NP-complete binary case. By applying Lemma 1, we can reduce the continuous case to the binary case. On the other hand, whenever we find the global optimal solution for the continuous case, in polynomial time we can construct a just as good solution where all optima are located at the corners in linear time. Thus, there exists a polynomial reduction of the binary case to the continuous case. □

3.2 Integer NK Landscapes

Based on our design, NKL on integer variables can be considered to be a special case of continuous NKL. The integer variables can be normalized as follows: Let $z_{min} \in \mathbb{Z}$ denote the lower bound for an integer variable, and $z_{max} \in \mathbb{Z}$ denote its upper bound. Then, for any $z \in [z_{min}, z_{max}] \subset \mathbb{Z}$ we can compute the value of $x = (z - z_{min})/(z_{max} - z_{min})$ in order to get the corresponding continuous parameter in $[0, 1]$, which can then be used in the continuous version of F to compute the NKL. Note that the properties discussed in Lemma 1 and Theorem 1 also hold for integer NKL.

3.3 Nominal NK Landscapes

To introduce nominal discrete variables in an appropriate manner a more radical change to the NKL model is needed. In this case it is not feasible to use interpolation, as this would imply some inherent neighborhood defined on a single variable's domain $x_i \in \{d_1^i, \dots, d_L^i\}$, $i = 1, \dots, N$, which, by definition, is not given for the nominal discrete case. We will now propose an extension of NKL that takes into account the special characteristics of nominal discrete variables.

Let the domain of each nominal discrete variable x_i, $i = 1, \dots, N$ be defined as a finite set of maximal size $L \geq 2$. Then for the definition of a function on a tuple of $K + 1$ such values we would need a table with L^{K+1} entries. Again, we can assign all fitness values randomly by independently drawing values from a uniform distribution. The size of the sample is upper-bounded by L^{K+1}. For $L = 2$ this corresponds to the binary case. After defining N fitness components F_i, we can then sum up the values of these components for the NKL model (eq. 1). The optimum can be found by enumerating all input values, the computational complexity of which is now L^N. The implementation of the function table and the evaluation procedures are similar to that of the binary case. Note, that for a constant value of L and K the space needed for storing the function values is given by NL^{K+1}, so is the computational complexity for generating the matrix. The time for the function evaluations is proportional to $N(K+1)$.

Equipping the discrete search space with a Hamming neighborhood, in case $K = 0$ the problem remains unimodal. For $K > 0$, we remark, that for the general problem with $L > 2$, the detection of the optimum is more difficult than in the binary case. Hence, the binary case can be reduced to the case $L > 2$, but not vice versa. For the case of full interaction (K=N-1) we show:

Lemma 2. For the nominal discrete NKL with $K = N - 1$, $L \equiv$ *constant*, and Hamming neighborhood defined on the discrete search space, the probability that an arbitrary solution $\mathbf{x}$ gets a local optimum is $\frac{1}{N(L-1)+1}$. Moreover the expected number of local optima is $\frac{L^N}{N(L-1)+1}$.

Proof: Given the preliminaries, $N(L-1)$ is the number of Hamming neighbors for any solution $\mathbf{x} \in \{1, \ldots, L\}^N$. Since we assign a different fitness value from the interval $[0, 1)$ independently to each neighbor, the probability, that the central solution, i.e. $\mathbf{x}$ itself becomes the best solution, is $1/(N(L-1)+1)$. Since, L^N is the number of search points in $\{1, \ldots, L\}^N$ we can compute the expected number of local optima as $\frac{L^N}{N(L-1)+1}$. □

3.4 Mixed Integer NK Landscapes

It is straightforward to combine these three types of variables into a single NKL with epistatic links between variables of different types (cf. Figure 1). For mixed variables of the integer and continuous types there is no problem, since integers, after normalization, are treated like continuous variables in the formula of F. If there are D nominal discrete variables that interact with a continuous variable, then the values of these discrete variables determine the values at the edges of the $K - D$ dimensional hypercube that is used for the interpolation according to the remaining continuous and integer variables. Note that for different nominal discrete values the values at the corners of the $K - D$ dimensional hypercube will change in almost every case.

Instead of describing the mixed variable case in a formal manner we give an illustrating example (cf. figure 3). This example shows one individual with three parameters (one continuous, one integer and one discrete), and each gene interacts with both other genes. For each gene, a hypercube is created. We assume there are three levels for the discrete gene X_d ($L = 3$), so the hypercube is reduced to three parallel planes, and the value of the discrete gene decides which plane is chosen. More concretely, assuming the individual has the following values: $X_d = 0, X_i = 0.4, X_r = 0.8$, the value of the discrete parameter X_d determines which square is chosen ($X_d = 0$). The value for each corner is based on the fitness matrix in Table 2 (bold displayed). As mentioned in the previous chapter, we calculate the fitness value of this individual as follows:

$$F_r(\mathbf{a}, \mathbf{x}) = a_0 + a_1 X_r + a_2 X_i + a_3 X_i X_r$$
$$a_0 = F_r(0,0) = 0.8, \quad a_1 = F_r(0,1) - a_0 = -0.1$$
$$a_2 = F_r(1,0) - a_0 = -0.1, \quad a_3 = F_r(1,1) - a_0 - a_1 - a_2 = -0.1$$
$$F_r(0.4, 0.8) = 0.648$$

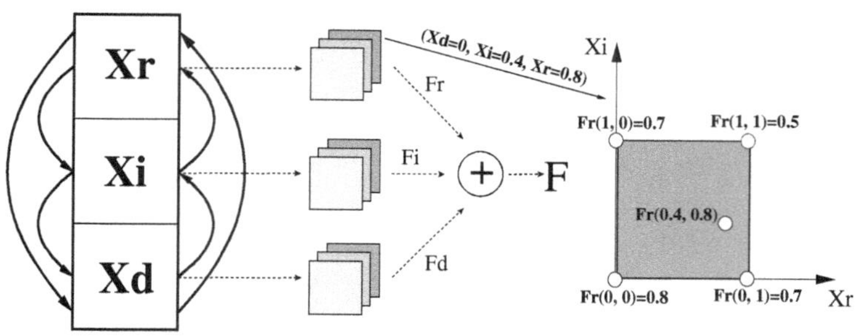

Fig. 3. Example for the computation of a MI-NK landscape

Table 2. Example epistasis matrix (left)and fitness matrix (right)

$E_r[1] = X_i$	$E_r[2] = X_d$
$E_i[1] = X_r$	$E_i[2] = X_d$
$E_d[1] = X_r$	$E_d[2] = X_i$

	0.8	***0.7***	***0.7***	***0.5***		0.3	0.7	0.2	0.9		0.5	0.6	0.3	0.5
F_r	0.5	0.8	0.4	0.7	F_i	0.2	0.3	0.7	0.9	F_d	0.9	0.8	0.2	0.7
	0.2	0.1	0.8	0.4		0.2	0.5	0.4	0.6		0.8	0.7	0.3	0.3

4 Experimental Results

In order to test our mixed-integer NKL problem generator we have tested it using a (μ,κ,λ) mixed-integer evolution strategy (MI-ES) as described in [5]. Here mutation distributions with maximal entropy are employed for the mutation of continuous variables (Gaussian distribution), integer variables (geometric distribution), and nominal discrete variables (uniform distribution). While for the first two types a step-size parameter can be learned, in the latter case a mutation probability is learned. We use a population size μ of 4, offspring size λ of 28 and $\kappa = 1$ (comma-strategie). The stepsize/mutation-probability of each variable was set to 0.1 and the standard MI-ES mutation and crossover operators are used. The maximum number of fitness evaluations is set to 3000.

To see the effect of different values of K we generated 50 problem instantiations for $N = 15$ and for each value $K \leq 14$ (750 MI-NKL problems in total) so that it is still feasable to find the global optimum by evaluating all bitstrings of length 15. Each generated problem consists of 5 continuous, 5 integer and 5 nominal discrete variables. The continuous variables are in the range [-10,10], the integer-valued variables are in the range [0,19] and we used $\{0, 1\}$ for the nominal discrete variables (Booleans). As described previously the continuous and integer-valued variables are normalized to fit in the interval $[0, 1]$ before evaluation. To compare (and average) the results of the different experiments we define the following error-measure:

$$\textbf{error} = \textbf{best found fitness - best possible fitness}$$

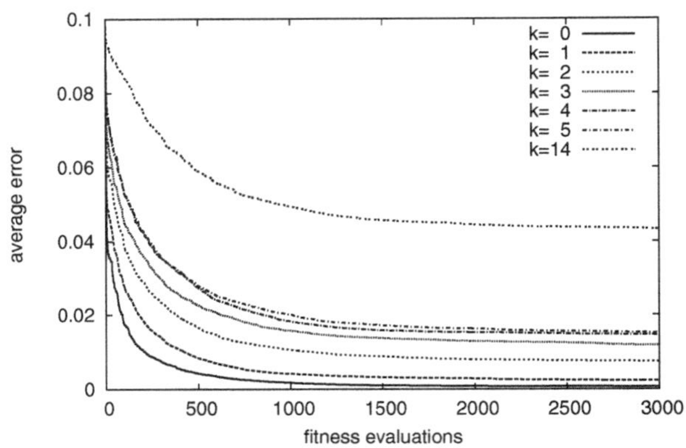

Fig. 4. The error averaged over 50 mixed-integer NK landscape problems with $N = 15$. Each problem contained 5 continuous, 5 integer-valued and 5 Boolean-valued variables.

The results are displayed in Figure 4. The x-axis shows the number of evaluations while the y-axis shows the average *error* (over 50 experiments). As can be seen an increase in K results in an increase in *error* which indicates the problem difficulty increases with K. The fact that even for $K = 0$ the MI-ES algorithm has problems achieving an average *error* of 0 is because in order to find the global optima all variables, including the continuous ones, have to be exactly either 0 or 1 (after normalization). This is hard for the continuous part of MI-ES individuals because of the mutation operator used. In the mutation, we used a reflection at the boundary method for keeping the variables within the $[0, 1]$ intervals [5]. This does not favor solutions that are directly at the boundary, as this is done by other interval treatment methods, like for example logistic transformation [2]. However, the latter mutation operator adds a bias to the search and makes it more easy to locate solutions at the boundary than in the interior, which is why we did not use it here.

5 Conclusion and Outlook

The NK landscape model has been extended to the mixed-integer problem domain. It turns out that a multi-linear interpolation approach for the continuous and integer variables provides a straightforward generalization of this model, that can also be easily implemented. Using Equation 3, function values can be computed in linear time. However, the detection of the global optimum turns out to be a NP-complete problem for $K > 2$ and can be reduced to the problem of detecting the global optimum for the binary case.

An alleged drawback of the interpolation approach is that its optima are always located in the corners of the search space. There are some ways of how this problem could be addressed. One way would be to transform the input variables by means of a periodic function and mapping them back to $[0, 1]$, e.g. to substitute x_i by $s(x_i) = \frac{1}{2} + \frac{1}{2}\cos(\pi x_i + \pi)$ and restrict x_i to the interval $[-0.5, 1.5]$ for $i = 1, \ldots, N$. It is easy to show that the optima for this transformed function are at the same position as for the original model.

For the nominal discrete variables the binary NK landscape was extended to a L-ary representation. For this the amount of random numbers increases exponentially with L. Also, for $N = K - 1$ it has been shown that the number of local optima increases exponentially with L.

One of our intentions for developing MI-NKL was to further improve the MI-ES approach. The experiments demonstrate the applicability of the MI-NKL problem generator and that the difficulty for finding the global-optimum grows with K. Future work will focus on exploring more of the characteristics of the MI-NKL, including its specializations: continuous, integer and discrete NKL.

Acknowledgements. This research is supported by the Netherlands Organisation for Scientific Research (NWO).

References

1. L. Altenberg: NK-Fitness Landscapes, In "the Handbook of Evolutionary Computation", ed. Th. Bäck, D.B. Fogel, and Z. Michalewicz, Oxford Univ. Press, 1997.
2. Th. Bäck and M. Schütz: Evolution Strategies for Mixed-Integer Optimization of Optical Multilayer Systems. Evolutionary Programming, 33 - 51, 1995.
3. G. Box, W. Hunter, and J. Hunter: Statistics for Experiments. Wiley, 1978.
4. A.E. Eiben and J.E. Smith: Introduction to Evolutionary Comp., Springer, 2003.
5. M. Emmerich, M. Groetzner, B. Groß, and M. Schütz. Mixed-integer evolution strategy for chemical plant optimization with simulators. In I. C. Parmee, editor, Proc. of ACDM'00, pages 55-67, Springer, London, 2000.
6. S.A. Kauffman: The origins of order: Self-organization and selection in evolution. Oxford University Press, NY, 1993.
7. S.A. Kauffman. and S. Levin: Towards a general theory of adaptive walks on rugged landscapes. Journey of Theoretical Biology 128: 11—45, 1987.
8. R. Li, M.T.M. Emmerich, E.G.P. Bovenkamp, J. Eggermont, Th. Bäck, J. Dijkstra and J.H.C. Reiber. Mixed-Integer Evolution Strategies and Their Application to Intravascular Ultrasound Image Analysis. In F. Rothlauf et al. eds: Applications of Evolutionary Computing, pp. 415-426, LNCS 3907, 2006, Springer.
9. R.E. Smith and J.E. Smith: An examination of tunable, random search landscapes. In "Foundations of Genetic Algorithms 5", ed. W. Banzhaf and C. Reeves, Morgan Kaufmann, San Francisco, 1999.
10. E.D. Weinberger: NP completeness of Kauffman's N-K model, a tuneable rugged fitness landscape. Working Papers 96-02-003, Santa Fe Institute, Santa Fe, NM, First circulated in 1991.

How Comma Selection Helps with the Escape from Local Optima*

Jens Jägersküpper and Tobias Storch

Dortmund University, Informatik 2, 44221 Dortmund, Germany
{JJ, Storch}@Ls2.cs.uni-dortmund.de

Abstract. We investigate (1,λ) ESs using isotropic mutations for optimization in $\mathbb{R}^n$ by means of a theoretical runtime analysis. In particular, a constant offspring-population size λ will be of interest.

We start off by considering an adaptation-less (1,2) ES minimizing a linear function. Subsequently, a piecewise linear function with a jump/cliff is considered, where a (1+λ) ES gets trapped, i. e., (at least) an exponential (in n) number of steps are necessary to escape the local-optimum region. The (1,2) ES, however, manages to overcome the cliff in an almost unnoticeable number of steps.

Finally, we outline (because of the page limit) how the reasoning and the calculations can be extended to the scenario where a (1,λ) ES using Gaussian mutations minimizes Cliff, a bimodal, spherically symmetric function already considered in the literature, which is merely Sphere with a jump in the function value at a certain distance from the minimum. For λ a constant large enough, the (1,λ) ES manages to conquer the global-optimum region – in contrast to (1+λ) ESs which get trapped.

1 Introduction

Since Schwefel has introduced the comma selection in the late 1960s (cf. Schwefel (1995)), every now and then there have been long debates about whether to favor elitist or comma selection. Unlike for the discrete search space $\{0,1\}^n$ where according to Jansen et al. (2005, p. 415) "the difference between an elitist (1+λ) EA and a non-elitist (1,λ) EA is less important", for optimization in the contiuous domain $\mathbb{R}^n$ this difference can be crucial. It seems common knowledge that comma selection should be auxiliary when a multi-modal function is to be optimized or when noise makes the function to appear multi-modal to the evolution strategy (ES) (cf. Arnold (2002)). On the other hand, it seems clear that on a smooth unimodal function elitist selection will always outperform comma selection – provided that an adequate mutation adaptation is used.

The insights about the optimzation of multimodal functions, however, base on intuition and a huge number of experimental investigations of the performance of a large variety of ESs – rather than on theoretical investigations. One reason for

* Supported by the German Research Foundation (DFG) through the collaborative research center "Computational Intelligence" (SFB 531) resp. grant We 1066/11.

T.P. Runarsson et al. (Eds.): PPSN IX, LNCS 4193, pp. 52–61, 2006.

this may be that the common progress-rate approach is unapplicable for these kinds of scenarios since it (implicitly) demands the progress to become stationary (possibly using some kind of normalization, for instance w. r. t. the distance from the optimum and/or the search space dimension). Jägersküpper (2005) at least proves that elitist selection is no good choice when the fitness landscape shows "cliffs" or "gaps"; the more challenging question whether comma selection would do better is not tackled.

The present paper tackles this question. Namely, we follow this approach and contribute to the debates by investigations that base on probabilistic runtime analysis known from the classical field of the analysis of randomized algorithms in theoretical computer science.

2 The Simplest Scenario

We consider the linear function $\text{SUM}_n\colon \mathbb{R}^n \to \mathbb{R}$ defined by

$$\text{SUM}_n(\boldsymbol{x}) := \sum_{i=1}^{n} x_i$$

which is also called ONEMAX when $\boldsymbol{x} \in \{0,1\}^n$. For a given function-value $a \in \mathbb{R}$ let $H_{\text{SUM}=a}$ denote the hyper-plane $\{\boldsymbol{x} \mid \text{SUM}(\boldsymbol{x}) = a\} \subset \mathbb{R}^n$. Obviously, $H_{\text{SUM}=a}$ and $H_{\text{SUM}=b}$ are parallel, and it is easy to see that the distance between the two hyper-planes equals $|a-b|/\sqrt{n}$. Furthermore, for a search point $\boldsymbol{c} \in \mathbb{R}^n$ let $H_{\boldsymbol{c}}$ abbreviate $H_{\text{SUM}=\text{SUM}(\boldsymbol{c})}$, i. e. $H_{\boldsymbol{c}} = \{\boldsymbol{x} \mid \text{SUM}(\boldsymbol{x}) = \text{SUM}(\boldsymbol{c})\}$. Thus, for instance, a mutation of the current search point $\boldsymbol{c}$ corresponds to a SUM-gain of 1 (we consider minimization!) iff the mutant $\boldsymbol{c}' = \boldsymbol{c}+\boldsymbol{m}$ lies in $H_{\text{SUM}=\text{SUM}(\boldsymbol{c})-1}$, implying that $\text{dist}(\boldsymbol{c}', H_{\boldsymbol{c}}) = 1/\sqrt{n}$, where "dist" denotes to the Euclidean distance – as we minimize in Euclidean n-space. Furthermore, we focus on the function (class) $\text{LINCLIFF}_n^{\Delta}\colon \mathbb{R}^n \to \mathbb{R}$ with $\Delta\colon \mathbb{N} \to \mathbb{R}_{>0}$ defined by

$$\text{LINCLIFF}_n^{\Delta} := \begin{cases} \text{SUM}_n(\boldsymbol{x}) & \text{for } \text{SUM}_n(\boldsymbol{x}) \geq 0, \\ \text{SUM}_n(\boldsymbol{x}) + \sqrt{n}\cdot\Delta(n) & \text{for } \text{SUM}_n(\boldsymbol{x}) < 0. \end{cases}$$

As we minimize, all points $\boldsymbol{x}$ with $\text{SUM}(\boldsymbol{x}) = 0$ are local optima with function value 0 (there is no global optimum); namely, the hyper-plane $H_{\text{SUM}=0}$ contains all local optima. For $\boldsymbol{x}$ with negative SUM-value a "penalty" of $\sqrt{n}\cdot\Delta$ is added, where Δ might depend on n. Thus, there are two different hyper-planes with LINCLIFF-value 0: one is $H_{\text{SUM}=0}$, which contains all local optima, and the other one is $H_{\text{SUM}=-\sqrt{n}\Delta}$. Recall that the distance between these two hyper-planes equals Δ.

When talking about "the gain" of a mutation or a step, we mean the *spatial gain* of a mutation/step (unless we explicitely state "SUM-gain", of course). The change in the SUM-value is merely used as an indicator whether the mutant of $\boldsymbol{c}$ lies in the one half-space w. r. t. the hyper-plane $H_{\boldsymbol{c}}$ or in the other.

As we focus on isotropically distributed mutation vectors, the larger the length of $\boldsymbol{m}$, the larger the expected distance between the mutant $\boldsymbol{c}'$ and $H_{\boldsymbol{c}}$ (and the larger the expected SUM-gain). To focus on the core of the reasoning, for the present we consider unit isotropic mutations, i. e. isotropic mutations the lengths of which are not random but concentrated at 1 (so that the mutation vector $\boldsymbol{m}$ is uniformly distributed upon the unit hyper-sphere). Later we show how to extend the calculations to (scaled) Gaussian mutations, the length of which follows a (scaled) χ-distribution. So, the random spatial gain

$$G := \begin{cases} \text{dist}(\boldsymbol{c}', H_{\boldsymbol{c}}) & \text{if } \text{SUM}(\boldsymbol{c}') < \text{SUM}(\boldsymbol{c}) \\ -\text{dist}(\boldsymbol{c}', H_{\boldsymbol{c}}) & \text{if } \text{SUM}(\boldsymbol{c}') \geq \text{SUM}(\boldsymbol{c}) \end{cases}$$

corresponds to the "signed distance" of the mutant from the hyper-plane containing its parent. Jägersküpper (2003) shows that the density of G at $g \in [-1, 1]$ equals $(1-g^2)^{(n-3)/2}/\Psi$ for $n \geq 4$, where $\Psi := \int_{-1}^{1}(1-g^2)^{(n-3)/2}\,\mathrm{d}g$ lies in the interval $\sqrt{2\pi}/\sqrt{n-[1.5 \pm 0.5]}$ (normalization), giving a symmetric bell-shaped function with inflection points at $\pm 1/\sqrt{n-4}$ for $n \geq 6$.

When the (1+1) ES minimizes SUM, the expected gain of a step, which consists of a (unit isotropic) mutation *and* selection, equals the expectation of the random variable (r.v.) $G^+ := G \cdot \mathbb{1}_{\{G \geq 0\}}$ since the indicator variable "$\mathbb{1}_{\{G \geq 0\}}$" implements elitist selection (in this case). We have

$$\bar{g} := \mathsf{E}[G^+] = \int_0^1 g \cdot (1-g^2)^{(n-3)/2}\,\mathrm{d}g \Big/ \Psi = (n-1)^{-1}/\Psi \in \left[\frac{0.3989}{\sqrt{n+1}}, \frac{0.4}{\sqrt{n-1}}\right].$$

For the (1,λ) ES, however, $G_{\lambda:\lambda}$, the maximum of λ independent copies of G, equals the gain of a step. The following general property of the second-order statistic of a symmetric r.v. tells us that the expected one-step gain of the (1,2) ES (when optimizing SUM) is at least as large as the one of the (1+1) ES (cf. the appendix for a proof).

Proposition 1. *Let the r.v. X be symmetric, i. e., $\mathsf{P}\{X \geq g\} = \mathsf{P}\{X \leq -g\}$ for $g \in \mathbb{R}$. Then $\mathsf{E}[X_{2:2}] \geq \mathsf{E}[X \cdot \mathbb{1}_{\{X \geq 0\}}]$ $(= \mathsf{E}[X \mid X \geq 0]/2)$.*

Hence, also the expected total gain of i steps of the (1,2) ES is at least as large as the expected i-step gain of the (1+1) ES. There is a crucial difference, though: Unlike for the (1+1) ES, for the (1,2) ES the total gain $G_{2:2}^{[i]}$ of i steps, which is formally the sum of i independent copies of $G_{2:2}$, can be negative, i. e., the evolving search point may visit the half-space consisting of all points with a larger SUM-value than the initial search point. Note that $G_{2:2}^{[i]}$ is a generalized random walk.

We are interested in the r.v. $G_{2:2}^{\inf} := \inf_{i \geq 0} G_{2:2}^{[i]}$, the maximum loss compared to the starting point. In particular, we'd like to know $\mathsf{P}\{G_{2:2}^{\inf} \geq 0\}$, the probability that the evolving search point is never (i. e. even when running the (1,2) ES ad infinitum) worse than the initial one. (As the very first step yields a negative gain with probability 1/4, obviously $\mathsf{P}\{G_{2:2}^{\inf} \geq 0\} \leq 3/4$.)

Lemma 2. $\mathsf{P}\{G_{2:2}^{\inf} \geq 0\} = \Omega(1)$.

Proof. Recall that $\mathsf{E}[G_{2:2}] \geq \bar{g}$ $(= \mathsf{E}[G^+])$. Consider the partition of $\mathbb{R}_{\geq 0}$ given by the intervals $P_i = [\bar{g} \cdot i^3; \bar{g} \cdot (i+1)^3)$ for $i \in \mathbb{N}_0$. Note that the width of P_i equals $w_i := \bar{g} \cdot (3i^2 + 3i + 1)$. We identify the current search point with the corresponding total (spatial) gain. Then we are interested in the probability of getting from P_i to $P_{>i} := \cup_{j>i} P_j$ *without* hitting $\mathbb{R}_{<0}$. In fact, we want to prove that, when starting in P_i, the probability of hitting $\mathbb{R}_{<0}$ before hitting $P_{>i}$ is $\mathrm{e}^{-\Omega(i)}$. Since, for k a constant large enough, $\sum_{i \geq k} \mathrm{e}^{-\Omega(i)} \leq 1/2$, we would know that once the current individual has made it into P_k, then with probability at least 1/2 it would never again visit the half-space corresponding to a negative total gain. On the other hand, since $\mathsf{P}\{G_{2:2} \geq \bar{g}\} \geq \mathsf{P}\{G \geq \bar{g}\} = \Omega(1)$, with probability $\mathsf{P}\{G_{2:2} \geq \bar{g}\}^{k^3} = \Omega(1)$ each of the first k^3 steps yields a gain of at least $\bar{g}$, implying that P_k is hit without visiting $\mathbb{R}_{<0}$. All in all, we'd have shown that $\mathbb{R}_{<0}$ is never visited right from the start with probability $\Omega(1) \cdot 1/2 = \Omega(1)$.

It remains to show that the probability of hitting $\mathbb{R}_{<0}$ before $P_{>i}$ when starting in P_i is in fact bounded by $\mathrm{e}^{-\Omega(i)}$. Therefore, recall that the width of P_i equals $w_i = \bar{g} \cdot (3i^2 + \Theta(i))$. Thus, the expected number of steps necessary to get from $\bar{g} \cdot i^3$ $(= \min P_i)$ into $P_{>i}$ (possibly including a visit to $\mathbb{R}_{<0}$) is at most $w_i/\bar{g} = 3i^2 + \Theta(i)$ (by using a modification of Wald's equation). As P_i is at distance $\bar{g}\, i^3$ from $\mathbb{R}_{<0}$, one may already foresee that the probability of a visit to $\mathbb{R}_{<0}$ becomes smaller and smaller as i increases.

Formally, we want to prove that this probability is $\mathrm{e}^{-\Omega(i)}$. Therefore, consider the period starting (ending) with the first visit to P_i (resp. $P_{>i}$). Assume that in each mutation in this period $|G|$ was at most $\sqrt{i} \cdot \bar{g}$. Then in each step $G_{2:2} \geq -\sqrt{i} \cdot \bar{g}$, and thus, more than $\bar{g} \cdot i^3/(\sqrt{i} \cdot \bar{g}) = i^{2.5}$ steps would be necessary for a visit to $\mathbb{R}_{<0}$ to be at all possible. For i large enough, the expected *conditional* one-step gain (under the condition $|G| \leq \sqrt{i}\, \bar{g}$) is at least $\bar{g}/2$ (see appendix), and hence, the expected number of necessary steps (under the condition on $|G|$) is at most $2 \cdot (3i^2 + \Theta(i)) = 6i^2 + \Theta(i)$. By Hoeffding's bound, for i large enough, $9i^2$ steps do *not* suffice with a probability of $\mathrm{e}^{-\Omega(i)}$ (see appendix). As the condition on $|G|$ is *not* met also with probability $\mathrm{e}^{-\Omega(i)}$ (see appendix), the total failure probability (of *not* getting from P_i into $P_{>i}$ within $9i^2$ steps such that in each of these steps $|G| \leq \sqrt{i}\, \bar{g}$ for both mutations) is upper bounded by $\mathrm{e}^{-\Omega(i)} + 2 \cdot 9i^2 \cdot \mathrm{e}^{-\Omega(i)} = \mathrm{e}^{-\Omega(i)}$. Finally note that (under the condition on $|G|$ and for i large enough) $\mathbb{R}_{<0}$ cannot be reached in $9i^2$ steps as we have already seen. In short, with probability $1 - \mathrm{e}^{-\Omega(i)}$ the search gets from P_i (in particular from $\bar{g} \cdot i^3 = \min P_i$) into $P_{>i}$ *without* visiting $\mathbb{R}_{<0}$ in at most $9i^2$ steps. □

As "$G_{2:2}^{\inf} \geq 0$" implies that $\mathbb{R}_{<0}$ is never visited, the probability of observing $b > 0$ drop-backs to $\mathbb{R}_{<0}$ is bounded above by $(1 - \Omega(1))^b = \mathrm{e}^{-\Omega(b)}$. Thus, the search drops behind the hyper-plane containing the initial search point at most n^ε times w. o. p., where we can choose the positive constant ε arbitrarily small.

Now consider the minimization of LinCliff_n^Δ where $\Delta > 0$. Recall that there are two different hyper-planes with LinCliff-value 0: $H_{\text{SUM}=0}$, which contains all local optima, and $H_{\text{SUM}=-\sqrt{n}\Delta}$. The distance between these two hyper-planes equals Δ. Call the half-space $H_{\mathrm{SUM}\geq 0} = \{\boldsymbol{x} \mid \mathrm{SUM}(\boldsymbol{x}) \geq 0\}$ local-optimum region. Then a mutant $\boldsymbol{c}'$ of $\boldsymbol{c} \in H_{\mathrm{SUM}\geq 0}$ that hits $H_{\mathrm{SUM}<0}$ (i. e., it leaves the local-optimum region) such that $\mathrm{LINCLIFF}_n^{\Delta}(\boldsymbol{c}') \leq \mathrm{LINCLIFF}_n^{\Delta}(\boldsymbol{c})$ must necessarily yield a spatial gain of at least Δ. Then $\mathsf{P}\{G \geq \Delta\}$ equals the corresponding probability of such a successful mutation. For unit isotropic mutations, the elitist (1+λ) ES cannot overcome the cliff if $\Delta \geq 1$, of course. Jägersküpper (2005) investigates how the chances of (1+λ) ES (using isotropic mutations) to get over cliffs/gaps depends on how the size of the cliff relates to the step length/mutation strength. Note that, unlike for the spherical symmetric function $\mathrm{CLIFF}_n^{\Delta}$ considered therein, for $\mathrm{LINCLIFF}_n^{\Delta}$ there is always a good chance of getting over the cliff if only the step length is made appropriately large.

In the present paper, however, we show that a (1,2) ES manages to overcome the cliff in a "short" time *independently* of how large Δ is. The challenge is to show that drop-backs to $H_{\mathrm{SUM}\geq 0}$ become more and more unlikely with the number of escapes and, in particular, to prove an upper bound on the number of steps necessary to get that far away from the local-optimum region such that there is w. o. p. no drop-back. The next result tells us that, if the current search point is "close to the cliff" in the local-optimum region, then with a "considerable" probability the local-optimum region is left in the next step once and for all.

Lemma 3. *Let the (1,2) ES minimize* $\mathrm{LINCLIFF}_n^{\Delta}$ *using unit isotropic mutations. Assume that after t steps the current search point* $\mathbf{c}^{[t]}$ *lies in the half-space* $H_{\mathrm{SUM}\geq 0}$ *such that* $\mathsf{P}\{\boldsymbol{c}^{[t]} + \boldsymbol{m} \in H_{\mathrm{SUM}<0}\} = \Omega(1)$. *Then, independently of* Δ, $\mathsf{P}\{\boldsymbol{c}^{[t+j]} \in H_{\mathrm{SUM}<0}$ *for* $j \in \mathbb{N}\} = \Omega(1)$.

Proof. Obviously, we will follow the proof of Lemma 2. With a probability of $\mathsf{P}\{\boldsymbol{c}^{[t]} + \boldsymbol{m} \in H_{\mathrm{SUM}<0}\}^2 = \Omega(1)$ both mutants of $\boldsymbol{c}^{[t]}$ generated in the next step lie in $H_{\mathrm{SUM}<0}$ so that one of them becomes $\mathbf{c}^{[t+1]}$. Subsequently, with a probability of $(\mathsf{P}\{G \geq \bar{g}\} \cdot 1/2)^{k^3} = \Omega(1)$ for the constant k from the proof of Lemma 2, in each of the k^3 following steps both mutants yield positive gains such that one of them is at least $\bar{g}$. Then a drop-back to $H_{\mathrm{SUM}\geq 0}$ is precluded within these steps, and moreover, the distance from $H_{\mathrm{SUM}\geq 0}$ is at least $k^3\bar{g}$ after these steps. From here on (when $i \geq k$), exactly the same reasoning about getting from P_i into $P_{>i}$ without ever dropping behind $H_{\mathrm{SUM}=0}$ as in the proof of Lemma 2 applies. □

As a consequence, w. o. p. we observe at most n^{ε} drop-backs, where the constant $\varepsilon > 0$ can be chosen arbitrarily small. The question is how many steps it takes the (1,2) ES until this has happend. Therefore, we must show first that, when in $H_{\mathrm{SUM}\geq 0}$, the search gets close enough to the cliff $H_{\mathrm{SUM}=0}$ for $\mathsf{P}\{\boldsymbol{c} + \boldsymbol{m} \in H_{\mathrm{SUM}<0}\}$ to be $\Omega(1)$. Note that (as Jägersküpper (2003) shows) in fact $\mathsf{P}\{\boldsymbol{c} + \boldsymbol{m} \in H_{\mathrm{SUM}<0}\} = \Omega(1) \iff \mathrm{dist}(\boldsymbol{c}, H_{\mathrm{SUM}<0}) = O(\mathsf{E}[G^+])$. The next result tells us that, when the search approaches the cliff, as long as the distance from the cliff is at least four times the (stationary one-step) drift on SUM, the drift towards the cliff is at least a quarter of this drift.

Lemma 4. *Let the (1,2) ES minimize* $\mathrm{LINCLIFF}_n^{\Delta}$ *in* $\mathbb{R}^n$ *using unit isotropic mutations. If the search point* $\mathbf{c}$ *lies in the local-optimum region* $H_{\mathrm{SUM}\geq 0}$ *such that* $\mathrm{dist}(\boldsymbol{c}, H_{\mathrm{SUM}=0}) \geq 4\mathsf{E}[G^+]$ *then* $\mathsf{E}[G_{2:2} \cdot \mathbb{1}_{\{G_1, G_2 \leq \mathrm{dist}(\boldsymbol{c}, H_{\mathrm{SUM}=0})\}}] \geq \mathsf{E}[G^+]/4$.

Proof. Recall $\bar{g} := \mathsf{E}[G^+]$. The appendix shows $\mathsf{E}[G^+ \cdot \mathbb{1}_{\{G \le \sqrt{2/n}\}}] \ge \bar{g}/2$ as well as $4\bar{g} \ge \sqrt{2/n}$, and why this implies $\mathsf{E}[G_{2:2} \cdot \mathbb{1}_{\{G_1, G_2 \le 4\bar{g}\}}] \ge \mathsf{E}[G^+]/4$. □

As a consequence, we merely get an additional factor of 4 in upper bounds on the number of steps necessary for the distance from $H_{\text{SUM}<0}$ to drop below $4\,\bar{g}$.

Theorem 5. *Let the (1,2) ES minimize* $\text{LINCLIFF}_n^{\Delta}$ *in* $\mathbb{R}^n$ *using unit isotropic mutations. Assume that the current search point* $\boldsymbol{c}$ *lies in* $H_{\text{SUM}\ge 0}$ *such that* $\text{dist}(\boldsymbol{c}, H_{\text{SUM}=0}) = O(\mathsf{E}[G^+])$. *Then, independently of* Δ, *after* $3n^{0.4}$ *steps w. o. p.* $H_{\text{SUM}\ge 0}$ *has been left once and for all.*

Proof. Let $\delta := \text{dist}(\boldsymbol{c}, H_{\text{SUM}\ge 0})$ within this proof and notice that $\delta > 0$ implies $\boldsymbol{c} \in H_{\text{SUM}<0}$. The proof of Lemma 2 directly implies (by choosing $i = n^{0.1}$, i. e. $i^3 = n^{0.3}$) that once δ has exceeded $n^{0.3}\,\bar{g}$, the local-optimum region $H_{\text{SUM}\ge 0}$ is never visited again w. o. p., namely with probability $1 - \mathrm{e}^{-\Omega(n^{0.1})}$. Using a pigeonhole-principle-like argument, we will show that, if δ does not exceed $\bar{g}\,n^{0.3}$ within at most $3n^{0.4}$ steps, then w. o. p. there must be at least $n^{0.1}$ drop-backs (from $H_{\text{SUM}<0}$ back into $H_{\text{SUM}\ge 0}$). Consequently, there would also be $n^{0.1}$ transitions from $H_{\text{SUM}\ge 0}$ into $H_{\text{SUM}<0}$, and since for each of those there is a $\Omega(1)$ probability of never dropping back (Lemma 3), those $n^{0.1}$ drop-backs happen only with probability $\mathrm{e}^{-\Omega(n^{0.1})}$. Thus, since our assumption "δ does not exceed $\bar{g}\,n^{0.3}$ within $3n^{0.4}$ steps" implies the occurrence of an event which does *not* happen w. o. p., this assumption does *not* hold true w. o. p. In other words, w. o. p. δ *does* exceed $\bar{g}\,n^{0.3}$ in at most $3n^{0.4}$ steps, finally implying the theorem.

Consider $2n^{0.3}$ steps, namely the r.v. S defined as the sum of $2n^{0.3}$ independent copies of $G_{2:2}$. A straightforward application of Hoeffding's bound (just like the one in the appendix) shows that w. o. p. S exceeds $\mathsf{E}[S]/2 = n^{0.3}\,\mathsf{E}[G_{2:2}] \ge n^{0.3}\,\bar{g}$. Thus, right after a step in which $H_{\text{SUM}\ge 0}$ was left, w. o. p. within at most $2n^{0.3}$ steps either there is a drop-back or δ exceeds $n^{0.3}\bar{g}$. In the latter case we are done; if there is a drop-back, however, the question arises how many steps it takes until the next transition from $H_{\text{SUM}\ge 0}$ into $H_{\text{SUM}<0}$ takes place w. o. p.

Therefore note that $\boldsymbol{c}$'s distance from $H_{\text{SUM}<0}$ right after a drop-back is at most $n^{0.1}\bar{g}$ w. o. p. Thus, the number of steps until the distance from the cliff drops below $4\bar{g}$ again is upper bounded by $4 \cdot 2n^{0.1}$ w. o. p. (a rather loose bound; the factor "4" stems from the lemma preceding the theorem, the factor "2" from considering twice the number of steps that would suffice in expectation to apply Hoeffding's bound again). Recall that $\text{dist}(\boldsymbol{c}, H_{\text{SUM}<0}) = O(\bar{g})$ implies $\mathsf{P}\{\boldsymbol{c} + \boldsymbol{m} \in H_{\text{SUM}<0}\} = \Omega(1)$. Thus, w. o. p. within at most $n^{0.2}$ steps after a drop-back, $H_{\text{SUM}\ge 0}$ is left anew (again a rather loose bound since one of n^{ε} trials succeeds already w. o. p.). After this leave it takes w. o. p. at most another $2n^{0.3}$ steps until either a drop-back occurs again or $\delta > n^{0.3}\,\bar{g}$, and so on. Hence, our initial assumption "$\delta \le n^{0.3}\,\bar{g}$ for $3n^{0.4}$ steps" finally implies that w. o. p. at least $3n^{0.4}/(2n^{0.3} + n^{0.2}) \ge n^{0.1}$ drop-backs take place. This was to be shown. □

We note that the theorem remains true if we substitute "$3n^{0.4}$" by "$n^{\varepsilon}, \varepsilon \in \mathbb{R}_{>0}$". Recall that a (1+$\lambda$) ES (using unit isotropic mutations) is incapable of conquering the cliff for $\Delta := 1$, for instance. It would stay in $H_{\text{SUM}\ge 0}$ forever and keep on converging towards $H_{\text{SUM}=0}$ at a declining rate – a really noticeable difference.

3 Extension to Cliff and Gaussians (Extended Outline)

As already noted, when LinCliff_n^Δ is minimized, for a fixed Δ we can always choose a step length such that also a (1+λ) ES can overcome the cliff in a short time. On the other hand, for a fixed length of an isotropic mutation, there is always a choice for Δ disabling a (1+λ) ES from conquering the cliff. One may argue that commonly the length of an isotropic mutation is also random. For instance, the length of a Gaussian mutation $\widetilde{\boldsymbol{m}} \in \mathbb{R}^n$ (each component of which is independently standard-normal distributed) follows a χ-distribution with n degrees of freedom. Then arbitrary large lengths are possible. However, since the density of $|\widetilde{\boldsymbol{m}}| = \ell$ equals $\ell^{n-1} \cdot \mathrm{e}^{-\ell^2/2} \cdot 2^{1-n/2}/\Gamma(n/2)$ (a unimodal distribution having its mode at $\sqrt{n-1}$ and inflection points at $\sqrt{n - 1/2 \pm \sqrt{2n - 7/4}}$), the probability that the length exceeds ℓ drops exponentially for $\ell \geq \sqrt{3n}$. In short, the length of a Gaussian mutation is too concentrated, and hence, if Δ is by a factor of n^ε, $\varepsilon \in \mathbb{R}_{>0}$, larger than the expected length of a Gaussian mutation, then the probability that a mutation conquers the cliff is exponentially small. An ad hoc solution to this problem could be to choose a different distribution for the length of a mutation to make large step lengths more probable, e. g. a Cauchy distribution. If the lower-level sets (success regions) are bounded (which is *not* the case for LinCliff), however, all this is pointless: Steps with immoderate length are vain anyway (they fail to hit the lower level set with high probability).

Therefore, consider the spherically symmetric function $\text{Cliff}_n^\Delta \colon \mathbb{R}^n \to \mathbb{R}$

$$\text{Cliff}_n^\Delta(\boldsymbol{x}) := \begin{cases} |\boldsymbol{x}| + \Delta(n) & \text{if } |\boldsymbol{x}| < 1 - \Delta(n), \\ |\boldsymbol{x}| & \text{otherwise,} \end{cases}$$

where $\Delta \colon \mathbb{N} \to (0, 0.3]$, introduced by Jägersküpper and Witt (2005). All points in the hyper-sphere $\{\boldsymbol{x} \mid |\boldsymbol{x}| = 1 - \Delta\} \subset \mathbb{R}^n$ are local, non-global optima. The best chances to get over the cliff, however, are at unit distance from the optimum; cf. Jägersküpper (2005). There the ratio of the gain necessary to overcome the cliff (of Δ towards the optimum/origin $\boldsymbol{o} \in \mathbb{R}^n$) to distance from $\boldsymbol{o}$ is minimal.

Consider the well-known Sphere-function ($\text{Sphere}(\boldsymbol{x}) = |\boldsymbol{x}|^2 = \sum_{i=1}^n {x_i}^2$). For any (1$\overset{+}{,}\lambda$) ES using isotropic mutations there is a distinct normalized (here w. r. t. to the distance from the origin/optimum, *not(!)* w. r. t. to n) length of an isotropic mutation resulting in maximum *expected* one-step gain. As we are interested in the number of function evaluations – which equals λ times the number of steps –, we are particularly interested in *constant* λ, i. e. λ is *not* a function of n. Then the optimum expected one-step gain (progress rate) is $O(d/n)$ where $d := |\boldsymbol{c}|$ equals the distance from the global optimum (d.g.o.). For the (1+1) ES on Sphere, an isotropic mutation of length $\ell = \Theta(d/\sqrt{n})$ results in an expected gain of $\Theta(d/n)$. A (1,2) ES (using isotropic mutations) is incapable of realizing an expected one-step gain of $\Omega(d/n)$ for Sphere. However, a straightforward calculation (Jägersküpper, 2006) shows:

1) For the (1,λ^*) ES with λ^* a constant large enough, isotropic mutations with a length of $\Theta(d/\sqrt{n})$ result in an expected one-step gain of $\Theta(d/n)$ on Sphere.

Now we can follow the reasoning for "the simplest scenario". Namely, we'd show:

2) For the (1,λ^*) ES using isotropic mutations of fixed length $\ell := \Theta(d^{[0]}/\sqrt{n})$ there is a $\Omega(1)$ probability that the d.g.o. never exceeds $d^{[0]}$, the initial one.

3) For $d^{[0]} \in [1-\Delta; 1-\Delta+\ell/\sqrt{n}]$ there is a $\Omega(1)$ probability that the first step conquers the cliff and that the search never drops back to the local optimum region afterwards, i. e. $\mathsf{P}\{d^{[i]} < 1-\Delta \text{ for } i \in \mathbb{N}\} = \Omega(1)$.

4) We'd show that 1), 2), 3) remain true when using Gaussian mutations scaled by a mutation strength $\sigma \in \mathbb{R}_{>0}$ that is $\Theta(d^{[0]}/n)$ (we would utilize the concentration of the χ-distribution already mentioned at the beginning of this section).

5) When started at a distance, say, $d^{[0]} \in [1.2, 1.3]$ then w. o. p. after $t = O(n)$ steps $d^{[t]} \in [1-\Delta; 1-\Delta+\sigma]$ such that 3) applies. After at most $n^{0.1}$ trials of conquering the cliff within at most $3n^{0.4}$ steps, the global-optimum region $\{\boldsymbol{x} \mid |\boldsymbol{x}| < 1-\Delta\} \subset \mathbb{R}^n$ is conquered such that it is never left again w. o. p.

After another $O(n)$ steps, w. o. p. d drops below $1.2/2 = 0.6 \leq 1-\Delta-0.1$, implying the following result:

Theorem 6. *Let a (1,λ) ES minimize* CLIFF_n^{Δ} *using Gaussian mutations scaled by a fixed* σ. *Assume that after initialization* $|\boldsymbol{c}^{[0]}| \in [1.2, 1.3]$ *and* $\sigma = \Theta(|\boldsymbol{c}^{[0]}|/n)$. *Then, independently of* Δ, *for* λ *a constant large enough, the number of steps* t *until* $|\boldsymbol{c}^{[t]}| \leq 0.6$ *(i. e. the distance from the optimum is halved) is* $O(n)$ *w. o. p.*

Since λ is a constant, the (1,λ) ES gets by with $O(n)$ function evaluations to halve the d.g.o. Finally, compare this with the (1+1) ES on SPHERE: It needs w. o. p. $\Omega(n)$ function evaluations to halve the d.g.o. even if the length of isotropic mutations would be adapted perfectly in each step! Thus, indeed, the cliff does not keep the (1,λ) ES from halving the d.g.o. within the asymptotically smallest possible number of function evaluations, which is $\Theta(n)$.

Since the 1/5-rule (*non*-endogenous σ-adaptation) uses an observation phase of $\Theta(n)$ steps, and since conquering the cliff takes place in a sub-linear number of steps, we are even able to extend the theorem: When the 1/5-rule is used, the number of CLIFF-evaluations to reduce the d.g.o. to a 2^{-b}-fraction of the initial one is $O(b \cdot n)$ w. o. p. – wherever the initial starting point lies (given that $1 \leq b = \text{poly}(n)$ and $\sigma^{[0]} = \Theta(|\boldsymbol{c}^{[0]}|/n$, though). This concludes the outline.

References

Arnold, D. (2002): *Noisy Optimization with Evolution Strategies.* Springer.

Hoeffding, W. (1963): *Probability inequalities for sums of bounded random variables.* American Statistical Association Journal, 58(301):13–30.

Jägersküpper, J. (2003): *Analysis of a simple evolutionary algorithm for minimization in Euclidean spaces.* In *Proc. 30th Int'l Colloquium on Automata, Languages and Programming (ICALP)*, vol. 2719 of *LNCS*, 1068–79, Springer.

Jägersküpper, J. (2005): *On the complexity of overcoming gaps with isotropic mutations and elitist selection.* In *Proc. 2005 IEEE Congress on Evolutionary Computation (CEC)*, 206–213, IEEE Press.

Jägerskupper, J. (2006): *Probabilistic runtime analysis of* $(1\overset{+}{,}\lambda)$ *ES using isotropic mutations.* Accepted for the Genetic and Evolutionary Computation Conference (GECCO).

Jägerskupper, J., Witt, C. (2005): *Rigorous runtime analysis of a (μ+1) ES for the sphere function.* In *Proc. 2005 Genetic and Evolutionary Computation Conference (GECCO)*, 849–856, ACM Press.

Jansen, T., De Jong, K. A., Wegener, I. (2005): *On the choice of the offspring population size in evolutionary algorithms.* Evolutionary Computation, 13(4):413–440.

Schwefel, H.-P. (1995): *Evolution and Optimum Seeking.* Wiley, New York.

Appendix

Proof of Proposition 1. Note that $\mathsf{P}\{X \geq 0\} = \mathsf{P}\{X \leq 0\} \geq 1/2$ due to the symmetry. As $X_{2:2} = \max\{X_1, X_2\}$, where X_1, X_2 are independent copies of X,

$$\begin{aligned}\mathsf{E}[X_{2:2}] = \; & \mathsf{E}[X_{2:2} \cdot \mathbb{1}_{\{X_1,X_2 \geq 0\}}] + \mathsf{E}[X_{2:2} \cdot \mathbb{1}_{\{X_1 \geq 0, X_2 \leq 0\}}] \\ & + \mathsf{E}[X_{2:2} \cdot \mathbb{1}_{\{X_1,X_2 \leq 0\}}] + \mathsf{E}[X_{2:2} \cdot \mathbb{1}_{\{X_1 \leq 0, X_2 \geq 0\}}].\end{aligned}$$

The first summand can be bounded from below by

$$\begin{aligned}\mathsf{E}[X_{2:2} \cdot \mathbb{1}_{\{X_1,X_2 \geq 0\}}] & \geq \mathsf{E}[X_1 \cdot \mathbb{1}_{\{X_1,X_2 \geq 0\}}] \\ & = \mathsf{E}[X_1 \cdot \mathbb{1}_{\{X_1 \geq 0\}}] \cdot \mathsf{P}\{X_2 \geq 0\} \\ & \geq \mathsf{E}[X_1 \cdot \mathbb{1}_{\{X_1 \geq 0\}}] \cdot 1/2.\end{aligned}$$

Analogously, one obtains $\mathsf{E}[X_{2:2} \cdot \mathbb{1}_{\{X_1,X_2 \leq 0\}}] \geq \mathsf{E}[X_1 \cdot \mathbb{1}_{\{X_1 \leq 0\}}]/2$ as well as $\mathsf{E}[X_{2:2} \cdot \mathbb{1}_{\{X_i \geq 0, X_{3-i} \leq 0\}}] \geq \mathsf{E}[X_i \cdot \mathbb{1}_{\{X_i \geq 0\}}]/2$ for $i \in \{1, 2\}$. Altogether,

$$\mathsf{E}\left[X^{2:2}\right] \geq 3 \cdot \mathsf{E}[X \cdot \mathbb{1}_{\{X \geq 0\}}]/2 + \mathsf{E}[X \cdot \mathbb{1}_{\{X \leq 0\}}]/2 = \mathsf{E}[X \cdot \mathbb{1}_{\{X \geq 0\}}]$$

since $\mathsf{E}[X \cdot \mathbb{1}_{\{X \leq 0\}}] = -\mathsf{E}[X \cdot \mathbb{1}_{\{X \geq 0\}}]$ because of the symmetry. □

Moreover, if $u > 0$ such that $\mathsf{E}[X \cdot \mathbb{1}_{\{u \geq X \geq 0\}}] \geq \mathsf{E}[X \cdot \mathbb{1}_{\{X \geq 0\}}]/2$, then

$$\mathsf{E}[X_{2:2} \cdot \mathbb{1}_{\{X_1,X_2 \leq u\}}] \geq 3 \cdot \frac{\mathsf{E}[X \cdot \mathbb{1}_{\{X \geq 0\}}]}{2}/2 - \mathsf{E}[X \cdot \mathbb{1}_{\{X \geq 0\}}]/2 = \mathsf{E}[X \cdot \mathbb{1}_{\{X \geq 0\}}]/4.$$

Additional Calculations for the Proof of Lemma 2. Recall that here G corresponds to the spatial gain of a unit isotropic mutation. The r.v. "$G \cdot \mathbb{1}_{\{|G| \leq \sqrt{i} \cdot \mathsf{E}[G^+]\}}$" is also symmetric, and thus, Proposition 1 applies, that is, $\mathsf{E}[\max\{G_1, G_2\} \cdot \mathbb{1}_{\{|G_1|,|G_2| \leq u\}}] \geq \mathsf{E}[G^+ \cdot \mathbb{1}_{\{|G| \leq u\}}]$. Thus, it suffices to show that

1) $\mathsf{E}[G^+ \cdot \mathbb{1}_{\{|G| \leq \sqrt{i} \cdot \mathsf{E}[G^+]\}}] \geq \mathsf{E}[G^+]/2$ for i large enough.

Recall that the density of G at $g \in [-1,1]$ equals $(1-g^2)^{(n-3)/2} \cdot \sqrt{n} \cdot (1-\Theta(1/n))$ (for $n \geq 4$). We use $(1-t/n)^n \leq \mathrm{e}^{-t}$ for $0 \leq t \leq n$. Then for $i \in [0,n]$

$$\mathsf{E}\left[G^+ \cdot \mathbb{1}_{\{|G| \leq \sqrt{i/n}\}}\right] = \int_0^{\sqrt{i/n}} g \cdot (1-g^2)^{(n-3)/2}\,\mathrm{d}g \cdot 1/\Psi =$$

$$\left[\frac{(1-x^2)^{(n-1)/2}}{-(n-1)}\right]_0^{\sqrt{i/n}} \cdot 1/\Psi = \left(\frac{1}{n-1} - \frac{(1-(i/n))^{(n-1)/2}}{n-1}\right) \cdot 1/\Psi$$

$$= \Bigl(1 - \underbrace{(1-(i/n))^{(n-1)/2}}_{\leq \mathrm{e}^{-(i/n)(n-1)/2}}\Bigr) \cdot \underbrace{\frac{1}{n-1} \cdot 1/\Psi}_{= \mathsf{E}[G^+]}$$

and $\mathrm{e}^{-(i/n)(n-1)/2} \leq \mathrm{e}^{-i \cdot 3/8} < 1/2$ for $i \geq 2$ (yet $i \leq n \geq 4$; for $i > n$ the indicator variable becomes meaningless). Thus $\mathsf{E}[G^+ \cdot \mathbb{1}_{\{G \leq \sqrt{2/n}\}}] > \mathsf{E}[G^+]/2$ and, hence, finally $\mathsf{E}\left[G^+ \cdot \mathbb{1}_{\{G \leq 4\mathsf{E}[G^+]\}}\right] > \mathsf{E}[G^+]/2$ (since $\mathsf{E}[G^+] \geq 0.3989/\sqrt{n+1}$)

2) We want $\mathsf{P}\left\{|G| > \sqrt{i/n}\right\} = \mathrm{e}^{-\Omega(i)}$.

We assume (solely for better legibility) that $\sqrt{i}$ as well as $\sqrt{n}$ are integral.

$$\mathsf{P}\left\{|G| > \sqrt{i/n}\right\} = 2\sqrt{n} \cdot (1-\Theta(1/n)) \cdot \int_{\sqrt{i/n}}^{1} (1-g^2)^{(n-3)/2}\,\mathrm{d}g$$

$$\leq 2\sqrt{n} \sum_{k=\sqrt{i}}^{\sqrt{n}} (1-k^2/n)^{(n-3)/2} \cdot \frac{1}{\sqrt{n}} \leq 2 \sum_{k=\sqrt{i}}^{\sqrt{n}} \mathrm{e}^{-(k^2/n)(n-3)/2} < 2 \sum_{k=\sqrt{i}}^{\infty} \mathrm{e}^{-k^2/8}$$

Since $\mathrm{e}^{-(k+1)^2/8}/\mathrm{e}^{-k^2/8} = \mathrm{e}^{-(2k+1)/8} < 1/2$ for $k \geq 3$, for $i \geq 3^2$ we obtain $\mathsf{P}\{|G| > \sqrt{i/n}\} \leq 2 \cdot 2 \cdot \mathrm{e}^{-i/8} = \mathrm{e}^{-\Omega(i)}$.

3) The application of Hoeffding's bound to obtain a probability of $\mathrm{e}^{-\Omega(i)}$ that $9i^2$ steps do *not* suffice to get from P_i into $P_{>i}$ (given that in each mutation $|G| \leq \sqrt{i} \cdot \bar{g}$, where i is large enough such that the expected conditional one-step gain is at least $\bar{g}/2$).

Hoeffding (1963, Theorem 2) tells us that for the r.v. S defined as the sum $X_1 + \cdots + X_k$ of k independent r.v.s $X_j \in [a_j, b_j]$ for $j \in \{1, \ldots, k\}$ we have $\mathsf{P}\{S \leq \mathsf{E}[S] - t\} \leq \mathrm{e}^{-2 \cdot t^2 / \sum_{j=1}^{k} (b_j - a_j)^2}$ for $t \geq 0$. In our case, $k := 9i^2$ so that $\mathsf{E}[S] \geq 4.5\, i^2 \bar{g}$, and furthermore, $a_j = -\sqrt{i} \cdot \bar{g}$ and $b_j = \sqrt{i} \cdot \bar{g}$. Since the necessary gain is at most $w_i = \bar{g} \cdot (3i^2 + \Theta(i)) \leq 4\, i^2 \bar{g}$ for i large enough, we can choose $t := 0.5\, i^2 \bar{g}$. Thus, the exponent becomes $-2 \cdot (0.5\, i^2 \bar{g})^2 / \sum_{j=1}^{9i^2} (2\sqrt{i}\,\bar{g})^2 = -i/72$.

When Do Heavy-Tail Distributions Help?

Nikolaus Hansen[1], Fabian Gemperle[2], Anne Auger[1], and Petros Koumoutsakos[1,2]

[1] Computational Laboratory, ETH Zurich, CH-8092, Switzerland
[2] Institute of Computational Science, ETH Zurich, CH-8092, Switzerland

Abstract. We examine the evidence for the widespread belief that heavy tail distributions enhance the search for minima on multimodal objective functions. We analyze isotropic and anisotropic heavy-tail Cauchy distributions and investigate the probability to sample a better solution, depending on the step length and the dimensionality of the search space. The probability decreases fast with increasing step length for isotropic Cauchy distributions and moderate search space dimension. The anisotropic Cauchy distribution maintains a large probability for sampling large steps along the coordinate axes, resulting in an exceptionally good performance on the separable multimodal Rastrigin function. In contrast, on a non-separable rotated Rastrigin function or for the isotropic Cauchy distribution the performance difference to a Gaussian search distribution is negligible.

1 Introduction

The optimization of multimodal objective functions is recognized as a fundamental problem in several areas of science and engineering. Stochastic search procedures such as Simulated Annealing or Evolutionary Algorithms are well-established methods to optimize multimodal objective functions. New candidate solutions are often sampled from isotropic multivariate Gaussian distributions. The choice of Gaussian distributions has several reasons. Isotropic Gaussian distributions do not favor any direction in the search space. Gaussian distributions are amenable to mathematical analysis because they are the only stable distribution—where the sum of iid variates has the same type of distribution as its summands—with finite variance. For a given variance, the Gaussian distribution has the maximal entropy, which can be interpreted in that the distribution shape contains the least additional assumptions on the objective function to be optimized. Finally, Gaussian distributions suggest themselves for bioinspired algorithms as they are widely observed in nature as for example in the distribution of phenotypic traits.

On the other hand, it is a common belief that, when employed for the optimization of *multimodal* objective functions, the exponentially decreasing tails of Gaussians are ineffective [8]. Instead, it is argued that heavy tails, such as those of the Cauchy distribution, are more appropriate, as long jumps occasionally lead to better solutions, that eventually lie within the attraction region of a better (local) optimum. Long jumps that produce worse solutions should be disregarded in general.[1] In this context several search strategies that apply heavy tail distributions have been investigated, including Fast Simulated

[1] A search strategy is highly susceptible to divergence, if worse solutions from long jumps are accepted. The danger of divergence is way smaller, if an accepted worse solution is originated from a short step. Alternatively, worse solutions from long jumps can be exploited with local optimization, which is not considered in this paper.

T.P. Runarsson et al. (Eds.): PPSN IX, LNCS 4193, pp. 62–71, 2006.

Annealing [6] and Fast Evolution Strategies [8]. In these strategies one key difference concerns the use of isotropic [6] and anisotropic [8] heavy tail distributions. The importance of the anisotropy of the coordinate-wise iid multivariate Cauchy distribution was already recognized in [5,2]. Obuchowicz [2] observed a degradation of performance of the anisotropic distribution when rotating the search space. He proposed isotropic Gauss and Cauchy distributions with norms distributed as their one-dimensional counter parts with mixed results.

Rowe and Hidovic [4] investigated the use of a scale free distribution that allowed searching simultaneously on a given range of scales. In one-dimensional problems, the scale free distribution is uniformly distributed on the log scale in that $\Pr(x \in [a, b]) \propto \log b - \log a$, given a and b are in the supported range. We found the n-dimensional version of this scale free distribution to be highly anisotropic (similar to Fig. 3, lower right). Surprisingly, even with a (1+1)-selection scheme the scale free distribution shows exceptional performance on the multimodal Rastrigin function and this is explained with the advantage of long jumps. We summarize the common hypothesis.

Hypothesis 1. *Long jumps, attributed to sampling from heavy-tail or scale free distributions, occasionally lead to better solutions. They are therefore helpful for searching multimodal objective functions.*

On the other hand, for the *unimodal* sphere model, where $f(\boldsymbol{x}) = \sum_{i=1}^{n} x_i^2$, theoretical investigations and experiments show that compared to the Cauchy distribution the Gaussian consistently leads to faster convergence of the $(1, \lambda)$-evolution strategy, regardless of the choice of λ [5].

This paper investigates why and when heavy tails can help for global optimization. The goal is (a) to *quantify* the *possible* effect of heavy tails and (b) to separate the effects of the heavy tail and the anisotropy of the search distribution in a carefully chosen experimental set-up. The paper is structured as follows: in Sect. 2 the relation between step length and search space volume is discussed. In Sect. 3 search distributions are introduced. Their characteristics and potential impact are investigated in Sect. 4. In Sect. 5 simulations of an evolutionary algorithm are presented and Sect. 6 gives a short conclusion.

2 The Search Space Volume Phenomenon

The so-called *curse of dimensionality* casts doubt on Hypothesis 1: the search space volume increases exponentially fast with increasing dimension and large steps become more and more unsuccessful. Rechenberg [3, p.160ff] analyzes the situation for the 30-dimensional Rastrigin function. He finds only a narrow evolution window for jumps that can *initiate* successful new subpopulations. Here jumps are not expected to produce better solutions but to converge to better local optima in a local optimization. Smaller steps fall back into the originating local optimum, larger steps converge into worse optima.

The volume covered by a step of length r is given by the hypersphere surface area $S_n(r) = \frac{2\pi^{n/2}}{\Gamma(n/2)}\, r^{n-1}$, where r is the distance to the center, n is the dimension, and Γ is the Gamma function. The covered volume increases with r^{n-1} making it increasingly difficult to hit a particular area of given volume.

We investigate an idealized scenario for the probability to find *a better solution* by jumping into another region of attraction, as depicted in **Fig. 1** (left).

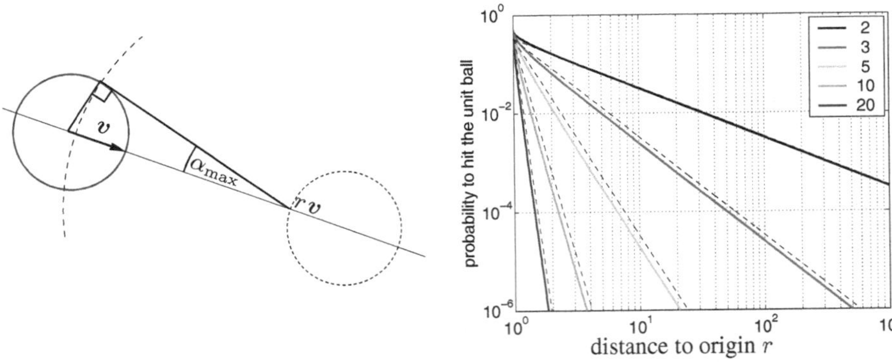

Fig. 1. Probability to hit the unit hyperball (solid) sampling from $\boldsymbol{rv}$ as mean with an optimal isotropic distribution, where $\boldsymbol{v} \in \mathbb{R}^n$ and $\|\boldsymbol{v}\| = 1$. The plots on the right show results for $n = 2, 3, 5, 10, 20$, from above to below. Dashed lines depict the approximation $\frac{1}{3\,r^{n-1}}$.

The arrow depicts a vector $\boldsymbol{v}$ with unit length. The starting point is $r\boldsymbol{v}$, located on the dotted circle on the right. Its closest local minimum is inside the dotted circle. A second volume of better solutions lies on the left, inside the unit hyperball around the coordinate system origin. We compute the probability to hit the unit hyperball by sampling around $r\boldsymbol{v}$ isotropically. We assume an optimal step-length distribution, where all steps lie on the hypersphere surface, corresponding to the dashed arc on the left. To hit the unit hyperball the angle between the sampled vector and $-\boldsymbol{v}$ has to be smaller than $\alpha_{\max} = \arcsin(1/r)$. Using the cumulative distribution function of the angle between a reference vector and a random vector uniformly distributed on the unit hypersphere [1, Theorem 9] we deduce the probability to hit the unit hyperball as

$$\frac{1}{2} - \frac{1}{2}\frac{\Gamma(n/2)}{\Gamma(1/2)\Gamma((n-1)/2)}\int_0^{1-\frac{1}{r^2}} t^{-\frac{1}{2}}(1-t)^{(n-3)/2}dt\ . \tag{1}$$

The probability is plotted as a function of r in **Fig. 1** (right) using Matlab's function `betainc`. Dashed lines depict $\frac{1}{3\,r^{n-1}}$, resembling the dependency of the hypersphere surface area on r, which turns out to be a reasonable approximation of (1). Even for moderate dimensions the probability drops fast with increasing r and becomes 10^{-4} for $r = 6, 2, 1.5$ and $n = 5, 10, 20$ respectively. For $r = 1$ the scenario resembles the sphere function and the success probability is 0.5 (for infinitesimally small step length). Our observations are summarized in an alternative hypothesis.

Hypothesis 2. *Long jumps virtually never lead to better solutions in high dimensional search spaces, because they get lost in the huge search space volume.*

3 Search Distributions

3.1 Univariate Gaussian and Cauchy Distribution

The distributions that will be used in this paper are derived from the univariate standard normal and Cauchy distribution. The univariate normal distribution with zero mean and variance σ^2 obeys the density

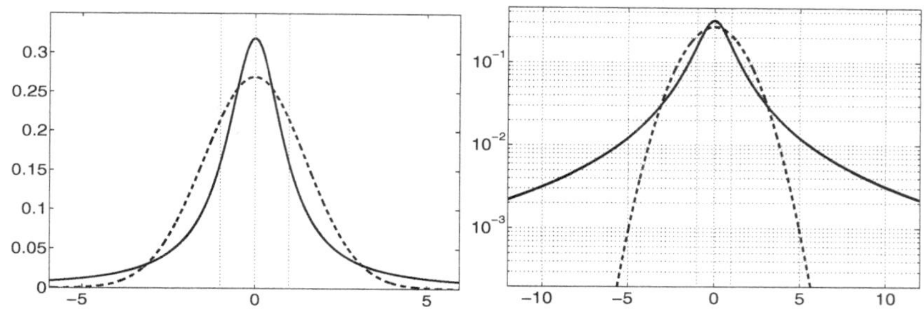

Fig. 2. Densities of the univariate normal (Gaussian) distribution (dashed) and the standard Cauchy distribution (solid) in a linear and a semi-log plot. The standard deviation of the normal distribution $\sigma = 1.4826$ is chosen such that the quartile values equal $-1, 0, 1$ (vertical dotted lines) as for the Cauchy distribution.

$$f_{\mathcal{N}(0,\sigma^2)}(x) = \frac{1}{\sigma\sqrt{2\pi}} \exp\left(-\frac{x^2}{2\sigma^2}\right) \quad . \tag{2}$$

The univariate Cauchy distribution with median zero and upper quartile τ obeys

$$f_{\mathcal{C}(0,\tau)}(x) = \frac{1}{\tau\pi}\frac{1}{x^2/\tau^2+1} = \frac{1}{\pi}\frac{\tau}{x^2+\tau^2} \quad . \tag{3}$$

A standard Cauchy distributed number, where $\tau = 1$ can be sampled by dividing two independent, standard normally distributed random numbers. Furthermore $\mathcal{C}(0,\tau) \sim \tau\mathcal{C}(0,1)$, and $\mathcal{N}(0,\sigma^2) \sim \sigma\mathcal{N}(0,1)$. **Figure 2** shows the densities of both univariate distributions.

3.2 Multivariate Distributions

We consider both isotropic and anisotropic distributions [4,7,8], and as isotropic distributions we consider a heavy-tail distribution and a distribution with exponentially fast decreasing tail.

We use $\mathcal{G}_n$ to denote an n-dimensional Gaussian (normally) distributed random vector with zero mean and identity covariance matrix. The distribution $\mathcal{G}_n$ can be sampled by sampling independent standard $(0,1)$-normally distributed random numbers from Eq. 2 for each component of a vector. Furthermore, let $\mathcal{U}_n$ denote a uniform distribution on the n-dimensional unit hypersphere, where $\Pr(\|\mathcal{U}_n\| = 1) = 1$. The distribution $\mathcal{U}_n$ can be sampled by sampling $\mathcal{G}_n$ and normalizing the resulting vector to length one, *i.e.* $\mathcal{U}_n = \mathcal{G}_n / \|\mathcal{G}_n\|$.

The following search (mutation) distributions are used.

$\mathcal{C}_n \in \mathbb{R}^n$, an (anisotropic) n-dimensional Cauchy distribution, where each coordinate is independent standard $(0,1)$-Cauchy distributed. This distribution is used, for example, in Fast Evolution Strategies [8] and Fast Evolutionary Programming [7].

$\mathcal{C}_n^{\text{iso}} \sim \|\mathcal{C}_n\| \times \mathcal{U}_n$, an *isotropic* n-dimensional distribution with the norm distributed as for $\mathcal{C}_n$.

$\mathcal{G}_n \sim \|\mathcal{G}_n\| \times \mathcal{U}_n$, the n-dimensional Gaussian (normal) distribution which is widely used in Evolutionary Algorithms such as Evolution Strategies or Evolutionary Programming. The distribution is isotropic (spherical), its norm is χ_n-distributed.

The distributions $\mathcal{C}_n$ and $\mathcal{C}_n^{\text{iso}}$ have polynomially decreasing (heavy) tails. The distributions $\mathcal{C}_n^{\text{iso}}$ and $\mathcal{G}_n$ are isotropic (spherical), and can be sampled by a product of a random number, i.e. a scalar representing the norm, and $\mathcal{U}_n$.

4 Characteristics of the Distributions

Figure 3 shows 10000 sampled points of $\mathcal{C}_2$ and $\mathcal{G}_2$ visualizing the characteristics of the distributions in 2D. For values between -3 and 3 the results of the Gaussian (first row) and the Cauchy distribution (second row) are comparable. While the Gaussian rarely realizes steps larger than five, the Cauchy distribution reveals a surprising picture. Zooming out further the distribution starts to resemble a cross parallel to the coordinate system (third row). That means, the distribution comes close to coordinate-wise sampling on the large scale.

Figure 4 presents data in the 10-dimensional case. Shown are densities of the vector norms (left) and densities along $r\boldsymbol{v} \in \mathbb{R}^{10}$, where r is a scalar and $\boldsymbol{v}$ is fixed, $\|\boldsymbol{v}\| = 1$ (right). The density for the norm of $\mathcal{C}_{10}^{\text{iso}}$ was obtained by Monte-Carlo simulations (about 10^9 samples), the respective density on the right by dividing with the hypersphere surface area $S_n(r) = \frac{2\pi^{n/2}}{\Gamma(n/2)} r^{n-1}$. The remaining densities are well-known or can be easily obtained analytically.

Comparing the lower and the upper bold graph in the right figure, again a striking difference between diagonal and coordinate axis parallel density can be recognized for $\mathcal{C}_n$. As can be derived from (3) (the multivariate density derives from a product of the univariate) the coordinate axis parallel density drops proportional to r^2, while the diagonal drops proportional to r^{2n}, for large r.

Two Gaussian densities along $r\boldsymbol{v}$ are shown. First $3.8 \times \mathcal{G}_{10}$ (dashed graph), where the median of the norm corresponds to the one of the Cauchy distributions. Second $1.25 \times \mathcal{G}_{10}$, where the density for small r compares to the one of the Cauchy distributions.

We compare the Gaussians with the isotropic Cauchy distribution (middle bold graph). In one case the density of the Gaussian drops below the Cauchy density for r larger than about 5.6. In the other case only for r between about 8 and 17 the Gaussian reveals a larger density than the isotropic Cauchy distribution $\mathcal{C}_n^{\text{iso}}$. For larger r Gaussian and Cauchy densities drop fast: for $\mathcal{C}_n^{\text{iso}}$ the slope is approximately r^{-10}. For example, the probability to hit a volume in a distance of $60 = 3 \times 20$ is about $3^{10} \approx 10^5$ times lower than to hit the same volume in distance 20, a distance where $\mathcal{C}_n^{\text{iso}}$ and $3.8 \times \mathcal{G}_n$ have comparable densities. The other way around, the volume that can be found with a comparable probability by steps being three times longer needs to be 10^5 times larger. In contrast, for the coordinate axis direction the density drops slowly and volumes far away have a considerable probability of being reached.

We can draw two conclusions from these figures. First, the anisotropy of the Cauchy distribution might have a considerable effect on the search behavior. Second, compared to the Gaussian distribution that operates on a reasonable scale of search, the heavy tails should not be of great help. Both conclusions are confirmed in our experimental results.

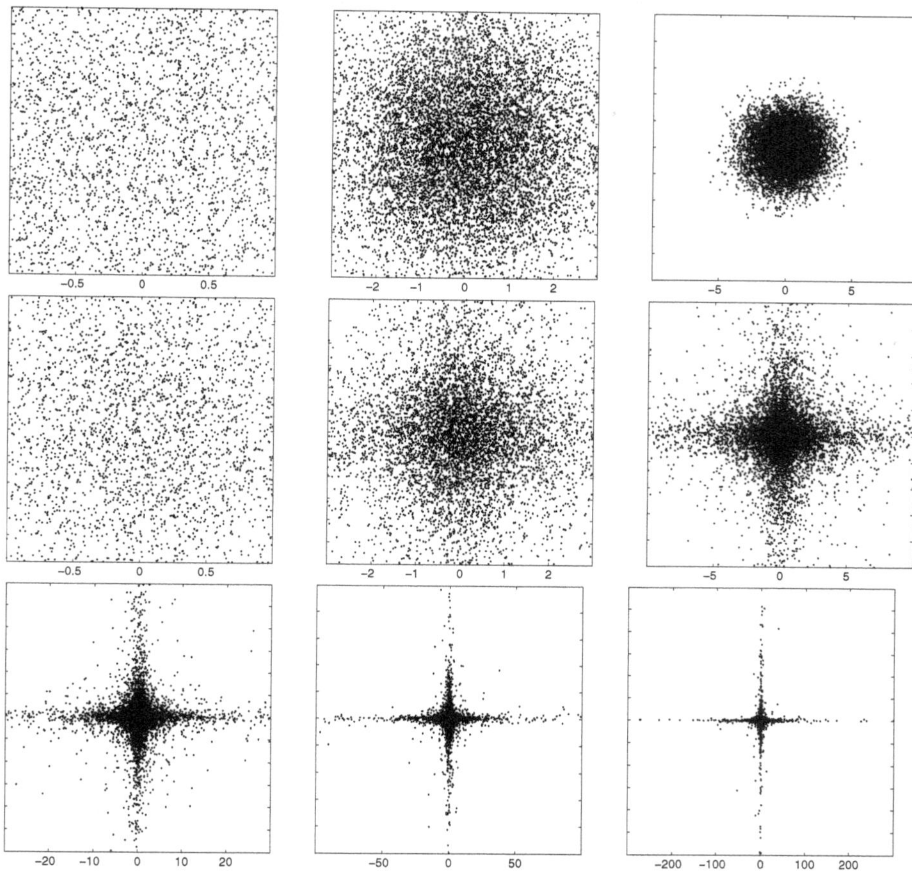

Fig. 3. Ten thousand 2D sample points from the Gaussian distribution $1.4826 \times \mathcal{G}_2$ (upper row) and the Cauchy distribution $\mathcal{C}_2$ (middle and lower row). Shown are the same sampled points on different scales ($\pm 1, \pm 3, \pm 10, \pm 30, \ldots$). The clippings contain $26, 91$, and 100% of the points for $\mathcal{G}_2$ and $25, 67, 88, 96, 98.72$, and 99.55% of the points for $\mathcal{C}_2$. For the larger scales $\mathcal{C}_n$ becomes mainly coordinate-wise sampling.

5 Simulation Results for the (1+1)-EA

5.1 The Test Functions and Evolutionary Algorithm

We use the highly multimodal Rastrigin function

$$f_{\text{Rastrigin}} : \boldsymbol{x} \mapsto 10n + \sum_{i=1}^{n} y_i^2 + 10\cos(2\pi y_i) \ ,$$

where $\boldsymbol{y} = \boldsymbol{M}\boldsymbol{x}$ and $\boldsymbol{M}$ is an orthogonal matrix ($\boldsymbol{M}^{-1} = \boldsymbol{M}^{\mathrm{T}}$). We investigate two situations. First, the axis parallel Rastrigin function $f_{\text{Rastrigin}}$, where $\boldsymbol{M} = \boldsymbol{I}$ is the identity matrix. The axis parallel Rastrigin function is separable and can therefore be

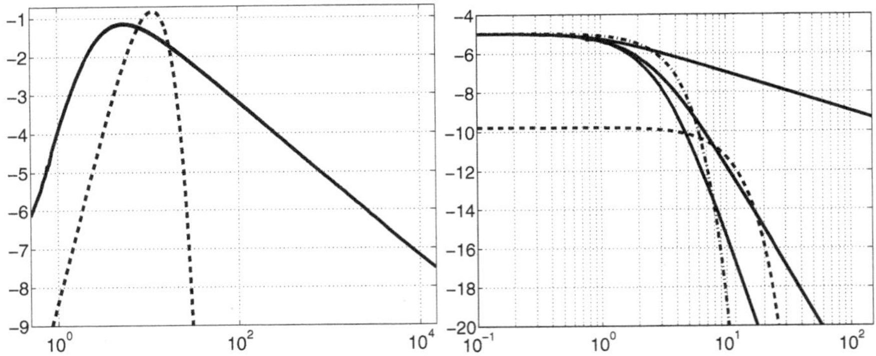

Fig. 4. Densities for $n = 10$ on the $\log_{10}$ scale. **Left**: Density of norms, $\|\mathcal{C}_{10}\|$ and $\|\mathcal{C}_{10}^{\text{iso}}\|$ (same solid graph), and $3.8 \times \|\mathcal{G}_{10}\|$ (dashed), where the factor is chosen such that the median equals to 11.7 as for $\|\mathcal{C}_{10}\|$. **Right**: densities along $r\boldsymbol{v} \in \mathbb{R}^n$ versus r, where $\|\boldsymbol{v}\| = 1$. For $\mathcal{C}_n$ (solid) in coordinate axis direction ($\boldsymbol{v} = (1, 0, \ldots, 0)^{\mathrm{T}}$, upper graph) and in diagonal direction ($\boldsymbol{v} = (1, \ldots, 1)^{\mathrm{T}}/\sqrt{10}$, lower graph), for $\mathcal{C}_n^{\text{iso}}$ (middle solid graph), for $3.8 \times \mathcal{G}_n$ (dashed), and for $1.25 \times \mathcal{G}_n$ (dashed dotted).

solved by n one-dimensional optimization procedures *parallel to the coordinate axes*. Second, we consider the rotated Rastrigin function, with a randomly chosen $\boldsymbol{M}$, where all columns of $\boldsymbol{M}$ are uniformly distributed on the unit hypersphere and orthogonal, achieved by Gram-Schmidt orthogonalization of $\mathcal{G}_n$-distributed vectors. In the relevant region for $\boldsymbol{x} \in [-5, 5]^n$, the local optima of the Rastrigin function have function values that are close to integer values, which makes the integer bin centers used for the frequency histograms below particularly meaningful.

We apply the (1+1) evolutionary algorithm (EA) as depicted in **Fig. 5 (left)** in order to address the question whether and how the heavy tails can influence the global search performance.

If not stated otherwise, we choose $\alpha = 10^{\frac{1.2}{10^4 n}}$, $\theta_{\text{final}} = 10^{-3}$, and the initial $\theta_{\text{start}} = 10^3$, leading to $50000 \times n$ iteration steps, and initial $\boldsymbol{x} = \boldsymbol{M}^{-1}(5, \ldots, 5)^{\mathrm{T}}$. The values for α result into $\alpha \approx 1.0000921, 1.0000553, 1.0000276$, for $n = 3, 5, 10$, all smaller than $1 + 10^{-4}$.

Neither (self-)adaptation nor a large population is applied so as to not interfere with the effects of the search distribution. *Adaptation* of distribution parameters, like the step-size θ, is not expected to improve the global search performance, as it usually drops step lengths much faster than the given schedule. Large populations, and eventually recombination, will usually improve the performance, but this should be true for all distributions applied. The rationale behind this set-up is to slowly move through all scales and to allow any scale, in case, to conduct the search successfully. It takes about $2500n$ iterations to reduce θ by a factor of two.

Figure 5 shows two runs *on the axis parallel* Rastrigin function, where $n = 2$ and $\alpha = 1$, one run with $\mathcal{D}_n = \mathcal{G}_n$ and $\theta = 0.25$, one run with $\mathcal{D}_n = \mathcal{C}_n$ and $\theta = 0.01$. In both cases θ is chosen much too small. While the Cauchy distribution needs about 9000 iterations, the Gaussian needs about 80000 iterations to approach the global optimum.

The Algorithm

choose $\mathcal{D}_n, \theta_{\text{start}}, \theta_{\text{final}}, \alpha$
initialize $\boldsymbol{x}$, $\theta = \theta_{\text{start}}$
while $\theta > \theta_{\text{final}}$
  $\boldsymbol{x}' = \boldsymbol{x} + \theta \times \mathcal{D}_n$
  if $f(\boldsymbol{x}') \leq f(\boldsymbol{x})$
    $\boldsymbol{x} = \boldsymbol{x}'$
  $\theta \leftarrow \theta / \alpha$

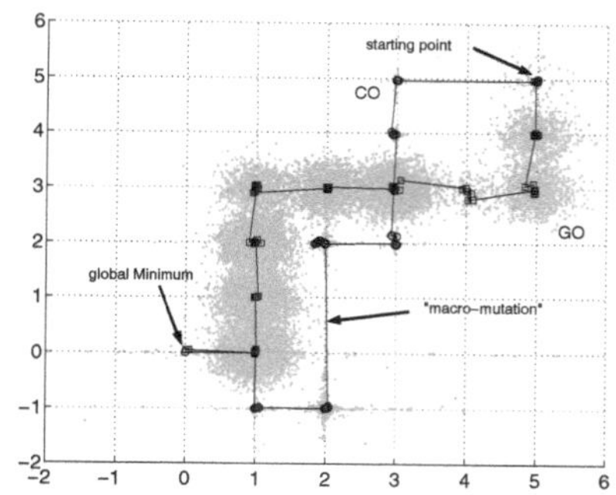

Fig. 5. The Evolutionary Algorithm (left), and paths and sampled points of two runs in 2D, where $\mathcal{D}_n = \mathcal{G}_n, \theta = 0.25$ (square marks □), and $\mathcal{D}_n = \mathcal{C}_n, \theta = 0.01$ (circle marks ∘). The marks denote realized steps, where $f(\boldsymbol{x}') \leq f(\boldsymbol{x})$. The optima lie on an axis parallel grid allowing the Cauchy distribution to reach the vicinity of the global optimum about ten times faster.

Having in mind the 2D image of the Cauchy distribution $\mathcal{C}_n$ the result and the resulting picture are not surprising.

5.2 Results

Methods. We conducted experiments on the axis parallel and the rotated Rastrigin function for dimensions $n = 3, 5, 10$, performing in each case 50 runs. We judge *performance* in terms of reached final function value and success rate to reach the global optimum with a precision of 10^{-2}. We compared success rates with the χ^2-test and the median final function values with the rank sum test.

Results. The final distribution of function values for $n = 3, 5$, and 10 is shown in **Fig. 6**.

For $n = 3$ the global optimum is found in most cases for all experimental conditions. On the axis parallel function $\mathcal{C}_n$ achieves a success probability of 100% and is slightly better than $\mathcal{C}_n^{\text{iso}}$ and $\mathcal{G}_n$. For $n = 5$ the difference becomes much more pronounced. While the success probability drops to about five percent for $\mathcal{C}_n^{\text{iso}}$ and $\mathcal{G}_n$, on the axis parallel function $\mathcal{C}_n$ has still a success probability of 100%. For $n = 10$ (Fig. 6, right) the success probability drops to zero in all cases but for $\mathcal{C}_n$ on the coordinate axis parallel function, where it is still one. The distributions in the five other cases are statistically indistinguishable and the best final function value is close to four. In all dimensions all distributions perform virtually identical on the rotated function, and only $\mathcal{C}_n$ performs significantly different from the other distributions in the coordinate axis parallel case while the performance of $\mathcal{G}_n$ and $\mathcal{C}_n^{\text{iso}}$ is invariant under rotation of the search space.

Validation of the Annealing Scheme. To investigate the influence of the choices of θ_{start} and θ_{final} we ran simulations for all combinations of values $\theta_{\text{start}} = 10^{10}, 10^9, \ldots, 10^{-5}$ and $\theta_{\text{final}} = 10^5, 10^4, \ldots, 10^{-10}$ for $n = 5$, where $\theta_{\text{start}} \geq \theta_{\text{final}}$ and the number of iterations are $50\,000 \times 5$, choosing α respectively. The best result is obtained with $\theta_{\text{start}} = 1, \theta_{\text{final}} = 0.1$ for $\mathcal{C}_5$ and $\theta_{\text{start}} = \theta_{\text{final}} = 1$ for $\mathcal{G}_5$. The respective average

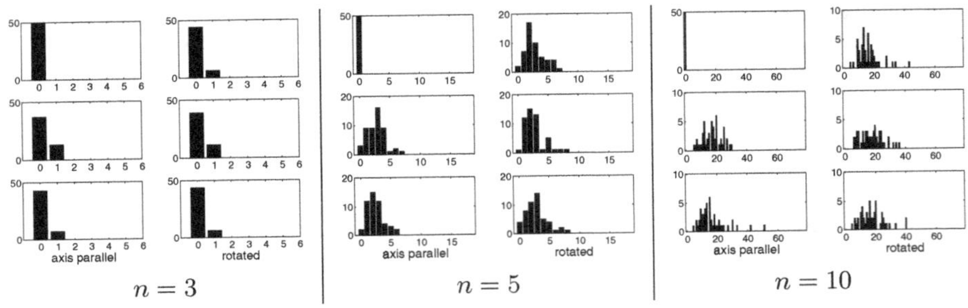

Fig. 6. Frequency of the final function value for, from above to below, $\mathcal{C}_n$, $\mathcal{C}_n^{\text{iso}}$, and $\mathcal{G}_n$. Left: $n = 3$, Middle: $n = 5$, Right: $n = 10$. For $n = 3$ on the coordinate axis parallel function $\mathcal{C}_n$ has a significantly higher success probability than $\mathcal{C}_n^{\text{iso}}$ ($p < 1.3 \times 10^{-4}$) and $\mathcal{G}_n$ ($p < 10^{-2}$). For $n = 5$ and $n = 10$ the difference regarding distribution median and success probability between $\mathcal{C}_n$ on the coordinate axis parallel function and all other cases is highly significant ($p < 10^{-15}$).

final function values are 1.7 and 1.6, compared to 2.8, and 2.4 for the set-up chosen in the last section. The results confirm that the annealing schedule is reasonably chosen and does not dominate the outcome.

6 Summary and Conclusion

We analyzed densities of isotropic and anisotropic heavy-tail Cauchy distributions with respect to their effectiveness when employed in searching for optima in multimodal objective functions. The densities are determined to a great extent by the volume of the hypersphere surface area. Consequently, for *isotropic* search distributions the density (i.e. the probability to hit a given volume) must decrease faster than r^{-n}, where r is the distance to the distribution center.[2] For Gaussian distributions the density decreases exponentially fast with r, for the investigated isotropic Cauchy distribution the dependency is r^{-2n}. Even for moderate dimensions ($n = 5$ to 10), the relevance between polynomial and exponential decrease on the search performance becomes questionable and cannot be observed in our experiments.

In contrast, the effect of anisotropy of a search distribution on the search performance can be tremendous, in particular in higher dimensions ($n \geq 10$). The Cauchy distribution, where coordinates are sampled independently, is highly anisotropic in that large steps occur most often close to the coordinate axes (see e.g. Fig. 3). Hence, it can perform exceptionally well on separable functions, like any algorithm performing coordinate-wise search. Therefore, the anisotropy of heavy-tail distributions is the most likely explanation for remarkable performance improvements on separable functions, e.g. of Fast Evolution Strategies [8] and of the so-called scale-free distribution [4]. If the coordinate system is rotated or the distribution is modified to become isotropic—keeping the distribution of the vector norm unchanged—the performance becomes indistinguishable from the Gaussian distribution in our experiments.

[2] Otherwise the density is not integrable for $r \to \infty$.

We believe that our result can be generalized beyond the specifically chosen set-up stating the following conjecture: *heavy tails are useful on multimodal objective functions (for global optimization) only if the large variations take place mainly in a low dimensional (sub-)space and the low dimensional space contains the better optima.* This is the case, for example, either if the search space by itself is low dimensional ($n \not\gg 3$), or if the search distribution is highly anisotropic with respect to the coordinate system and the objective function is separable. A challenging question arising from our conjecture is whether and how low dimensional subspaces can be found, such that the exceptional performance of the anisotropic Cauchy distribution on *separable* functions can be carried over to *non-separable* functions.

References

1. G. Frahm and M. Junker. Generalized elliptical distributions: Models and estimation. Caesar preprint, 2003. IDL 0037.
2. A. Obuchowicz. Multidimensional mutations in evolutionary algorithms based on real-valued representation. *International Journal of Systems Science*, 34(7):469–483, 2003.
3. Ingo Rechenberg. *Evolutionsstrategie '94*. Frommann-Holzboog, Stuttgart, Germany, 1994.
4. J.E. Rowe and D. Hidovic. An evolution strategy using a continuous version of the gray-code neighbourhood distribution. In K. Deb et al., editor, *Lecture Notes in Computer Science, proceedings of GECCO 2004*, volume 3102, pages 725–736. Springer-Verlag, 2004.
5. G. Rudolph. Local convergence rates of simple evolutionary algorithms with cauchy mutations. *IEEE Trans. Evolutionary Computation*, 1(4):249–258, 1997.
6. H. Szu and R. Hartley. Fast simulated annealing. *Phys. Lett. A*, 122(3,4):157–162, 1987.
7. X. Yao and Y. Liu. Evolutionary programming made faster. *IEEE Transactions on Evolutionary Computation*, 3:82–102, 1997.
8. X. Yao and Y. Liu. Fast evolution strategies. *Control and Cybernetics*, 26(3):467–496, 1997.

Self-adaptation on the Ridge Function Class: First Results for the Sharp Ridge

Hans-Georg Beyer[1,*] and Silja Meyer-Nieberg[2]

[1] Vorarlberg University of Applied Sciences, Department of Computer Science, Hochschulstr. 1, A-6850 Dornbirn, Austria
hans-georg.beyer@fhv.at
[2] Universität der Bundeswehr München, Department of Computer Science, D-85577 Neubiberg, Germany
silja.meyer-nieberg@unibw.de

Abstract. This paper presents first results of an analysis of the σ-self-adaptation mechanism on the sharp ridge for non-recombinative $(1, \lambda)$ evolution strategies (ES). To analyze the ES's evolution, we consider the so-called evolution equations which describe the one-generation change. Neglecting stochastic perturbations and considering only the mean value dynamics, we will investigate possible causes why self-adaptation can fail on the sharp ridge.

1 Introduction

The performance of evolution strategies (ES) depends on the population's distribution. During the course of an optimization run, the distribution has to be "fitted" continuously to the local characteristics of the search space in order to ensure a fast progress towards the optimum. In the case of ES, adapting the mutation strength is one of the main means. To this end, several methods have been introduced. In this paper, we will focus on self-adaptation [9,10] where the mutation strength is an integrated part of an individual's genome. Similar to the object parameters, it is subject to variation and selection processes and survives if the individual has a sufficiently good fitness.

The mechanism of self-adaptation can be examined by various means. The evolution of the ES is a stochastic process which can be described by a Markov chain. In [6], an approximate model is used to determine the system's dynamics. Other approaches analyze the Markov chain directly, e.g. [4], or study induced supermartingales, e.g. [11]. In this paper, we will follow the approach in [6] which will be described in the next section. Most of the research appears to be focused on the sphere model, i.e., on fitness functions the dependence of which can be aggregated to one variable only: the distance R to the optimizer. The ridge function class can be seen as a "natural" next step. It comprises functions of the form

$$F_{ridge}(\mathbf{y}) = y_1 - d\Big(\sum_{i=2}^{N} y_i^2\Big)^{\alpha/2} =: x - dR^{\alpha} \qquad (1)$$

* Supported by the Research Center for Process- and Product-Engineering at the Vorarlberg University of Applied Sciences.

T.P. Runarsson et al. (Eds.): PPSN IX, LNCS 4193, pp. 72–81, 2006.

with parameters d and $\alpha, \alpha > 0$. Note, we use a orthogonal representation of the general ridge function. This is not problematic as long as the ES uses isotropic mutations. As pointed out by Oyman [8], maximizations of ridge functions confront the ES with two (conflicting) goals: The distance to the ridge should be reduced while the x-component should be maximized.

Ridge functions are an interesting test case for self-adaptation. As already observed by Herdy [7], the mechanism may fail – especially on the sharp ridge, i.e, for $\alpha = 1$. It was found that in some cases self-adaptation decreases the mutation strength although the opposite behavior would be needed. It is one of the aims of this paper to investigate the reasons for this behavior. For constant mutation strengths, the behavior of ES on ridge functions was investigated before, e.g. by Oyman [8] and Beyer [5]. Recently Arnold and Beyer [2] analyzed the behavior of intermediate $(\mu/\mu_I, \lambda)$-ES on the noisy parabolic ridge applying cumulative step-size adaptation and Arnold and MacLeod [3] considered Herdy's Meta-ES [7].

We will consider the self-adaptive behavior of $(1, \lambda)$-evolution strategies. In short, a $(1, \lambda)$-ES with self-adaptation works as follows. Based on the object vector $\mathbf{y}$ of the parent, λ offspring are generated where each offspring $\mathbf{y}_l$ is obtained by adding a normally distributed random vector (*mutation vector*) with zero mean and standard deviation (*mutation strength*) ς_l. Since we are considering self-adaptation, the parental mutation strength is also subject to mutation and the descendants' mutation strengths are created by a multiplication with a random variable ζ. A common choice for ζ's distribution is the log-normal distribution with parameter (*learning parameter*) τ, i.e., ς is generated according to $\varsigma = \sigma e^{\tau \mathcal{N}(0,1)}$. The mutated mutation strength is then used to create the offspring's mutation vector. Afterwards the offspring with the best fitness value is selected as the parent of the next generation.

The paper is organized as follows. First, we introduce the so-called evolution equations which are used to model the evolution of the characteristic variables, e.g., the mutation strength. In order to continue, it is necessary to derive equations describing the variables' expected change. Afterwards, we consider the stationary state behavior on the sharp ridge trying to explain why simple self-adaptation may fail.

2 Preliminaries

Evolution strategies optimizing a ridge function can be fully characterized by three (aggregated) variables: the value on the ridge axis x, the distance to the ridge axis R, and the mutation strength ς. We will follow the approach introduced in [6] and consider the change of these variables during one generation. The change will be modeled by two components: the expected, i.e., deterministic, change of the variable and a perturbation part which covers the random fluctuations. In a first approach, the influence of the perturbation parts on the evolution will be neglected. This is a rough simplification and the results will have to be evaluated with experiments. Keeping this in mind, the evolution equations can be given by

$$x^{(g+1)} = x^{(g)} + \mathrm{E}[x^{(g+1)} - x^{(g)}] =: x^{(g)} + \varphi_x(\varsigma^{(g)}, x^{(g)}, R^{(g)}) \quad (2)$$

$$R^{(g+1)} = R^{(g)} - \mathrm{E}[R^{(g)} - R^{(g+1)}] =: R^{(g)} - \varphi_R(\varsigma^{(g)}, x^{(g)}, R^{(g)}) \quad (3)$$

$$\varsigma^{(g+1)} = \varsigma^{(g)} + \varsigma^{(g)}\mathrm{E}\Big[\frac{\varsigma^{(g+1)} - \varsigma^{(g)}}{\varsigma^{(g)}}\Big] =: \varsigma^{(g)} + \varsigma^{(g)}\psi(\varsigma^{g}, x^{(g)}, R^{(g)}). \quad (4)$$

The progress rate φ_x denotes the expected change in the direction of the ridge. The expected change of the distance to the ridge axis is given by the progress rate φ_R, also called the "radial progress" [5]. The so-called self-adaptation response (SAR) ψ is a placeholder for the expected relative change of the mutation strength. In order to continue, we need to find expressions for these functions. The progress rates were already obtained for $\tau = 0$ in [5]. Due to space restrictions, we only state the results obtained there. To simplify the notations, we will set $R = r^{(g)}$, $r := r^{(g+1)}$, $\sigma = \varsigma^{(g)}$, and $\varsigma = \varsigma^{(g+1)}$. The progress in ridge direction is given as

$$\varphi_x(\sigma, R) = \frac{\sigma c_{1,\lambda}}{\sqrt{1 + \left(d\alpha R^{\alpha-1}\right)^2 \frac{R^2+\sigma^2(N-1)/2}{R^2+\sigma^2(N-1)}}} \quad (5)$$

and depends on the distance to the ridge. The radial progress reads

$$\varphi_R(\sigma, R) = R - \sqrt{R^2 + \sigma^2(N-1)} + d\alpha R^{\alpha-1}\frac{R^2 + \sigma^2(N-1)/2}{R^2 + \sigma^2(N-1)}\varphi_x(\sigma, R). \quad (6)$$

The progress coefficient $c_{1,\lambda}$ that appears in (5) is a special case of the *higher order progress coefficients* [6, p.119]

$$d_{1,\lambda}^{(k)} := \frac{\lambda}{\sqrt{2\pi}}\int_{-\infty}^{\infty} t^k \mathrm{e}^{-\frac{t^2}{2}} \Phi(t)^{\lambda-1}\,\mathrm{d}t \quad (7)$$

with $k = 1$ and denotes the expectation of the best of λ standard normally distributed random variables. The radial component influences the progress in ridge direction. In contrast to this, there is no influence of the x-component on the evolution of R. Equations (5) and (6) were obtained under the assumption that the change $r - R$ is small compared to the parental distance to the ridge axis. In addition, both progress rates were obtained for $\tau = 0$, i.e., without considering self-adaptation. The remainder of the section is devoted to determining the self-adaptation response. The first-order self-adaptation response (SAR) denotes

$$\psi(\sigma, x^{(g)}, R) = \mathrm{E}\Big[\Big(\frac{\varsigma - \sigma}{\sigma}\Big)\Big] = \int_0^{\infty} \Big(\frac{\varsigma - \sigma}{\sigma}\Big) p_{1,\lambda}(\varsigma|\sigma, x^{(g)}, R)\,\mathrm{d}\varsigma. \quad (8)$$

The density function in (8) is the density of the mutation strength of the best offspring in λ trials. Applying the concept of induced order statistics [1], it is given by the conditional density of ς given the parental mutation strength σ. The mutation strength in turn is defined by the distribution chosen and by the probability that the mutation strength leads to the highest fitness change $Q = F_l - F(\mathbf{y}^{(g)})$ in λ trials

$$p_{1,\lambda}(\varsigma|\sigma, x^{(g)}, R) = p_\sigma(\varsigma|\sigma)\lambda\int_{-\infty}^{\infty} p(Q|\varsigma, x^{(g)}, R)P(Q|\sigma, x^{(g)}, R)^{\lambda-1}\,\mathrm{d}Q. \quad (9)$$

The probability function (cdf) $P(Q|\sigma, x^{(g)}$,R) denotes the expectation of $P(Q|s, x^{(g)}, R)$. The latter cdf and the density function (pdf) $p(Q|s, x^{(g)}, R)$ were already obtained in [5]. The probability function of Q reads

$$P(Q|s, x^{(g)}, R) = \Phi\left(\frac{Q + \alpha R^{\alpha-1}\left(\sqrt{R^2 + s^2(N-1)} - R\right)}{\sqrt{s^2 + \left(d\alpha R^{\alpha-1}\right)^2 \tilde{s}^2}}\right). \qquad (10)$$

Note, it directly depends on the parental distance to the ridge axis. The parameter $\tilde{s}$ is used to shorten the notation $\tilde{s} = s\sqrt{(R^2 + s^2(N-1)/2)/(R^2 + s^2(N-1)}$. The density function can be easily obtained by computing the derivative of (10). It was shown in [6], that the integral expression of $P(Q|\sigma, x^{(g)}, R)$ may be simplified if a log-normal distribution is considered. Provided that the learning parameter τ is sufficiently small, the cdf may be obtained by substituting s with σ in (10). We are now in a position to determine the self-adaptation response. Plugging everything into (8), the integral

$$\begin{aligned}\psi(\sigma, R) = &\int_0^\infty \left(\frac{\varsigma - \sigma}{\sigma}\right) p_\sigma(\varsigma|\sigma)\lambda \frac{1}{\sqrt{2\pi}\sqrt{\varsigma^2 + \left(d\alpha R^{\alpha-1}\right)^2 \tilde{\varsigma}^2}} \\ &\times \int_{-\infty}^\infty \Phi\left(\frac{Q + d\alpha R^{\alpha-1}\left(\sqrt{R^2 + \varsigma^2(N-1)} - R\right)}{\sqrt{\varsigma^2 + \left(d\alpha R^{\alpha-1}\right)^2 \tilde{\varsigma}^2}}\right)^{\lambda-1} \\ &\times \exp\left(-\frac{1}{2}\left(\frac{Q + d\alpha R^{\alpha-1}\left(\sqrt{R^2 + \varsigma^2(N-1)} - R\right)}{\sqrt{\varsigma^2 + \left(d\alpha R^{\alpha-1}\right)^2 \tilde{\varsigma}^2}}\right)^2\right) \mathrm{d}Q \, \mathrm{d}\varsigma \qquad (11)\end{aligned}$$

serves as the starting point for the derivation. Since there is no closed solution to (11), we will apply a similar approximation approach as in [6]. First, we will simplify the expression inside the Φ-function. Afterwards, we will expand the exponential function and the root function into their Taylor series around σ and cut them off after the first few terms. Due to space restrictions, we will only sketch the main points of the derivations. Let t stand for the expression inside the Φ-function. Rewriting it for Q gives $Q = \sqrt{\sigma^2 + \left(d\alpha R^{\alpha-1}\right)^2 \tilde{\sigma}^2} t - d\alpha R^{\alpha-1}\left(\sqrt{R^2 + \sigma^2(N-1)} - R\right)$. The integral (11) changes to the general form

$$\psi(\sigma, R) = \int_0^\infty \left(\frac{\varsigma - \sigma}{\sigma}\right) p_\sigma(\varsigma|\sigma)\lambda \int_{-\infty}^\infty \Phi\,(t)^{\lambda-1} g(\varsigma, \sigma) f(t, \varsigma, \sigma) \, \mathrm{d}t \, \mathrm{d}\varsigma$$

where g and f stand for the root and the exponential function. Both are expanded into their Taylor series' T_f and T_g around the parental mutation strength σ. We will assume $\tau \ll 1$ which allows to assume that $|\varsigma - \sigma| \ll 1$. As a result, it is possible to cut off the Taylor series after the quadratic term without introducing severe approximation errors. We will first address the integration over t. Concerning the variable t, the Taylor series T_f of f is a polynomial in t up to the fourth power

$$\begin{aligned}I_t(\varsigma, \sigma) = \lambda \int_{-\infty}^\infty \Phi(t)^{\lambda-1} \frac{\mathrm{e}^{-\frac{t^2}{2}}}{\sqrt{2\pi}} &\Big(a_0(\varsigma, \sigma) + a_1(\varsigma, \sigma)t + a_2(\varsigma, \sigma)t^2 \\ &+ a_3(\varsigma, \sigma)t^3 + a_4(\varsigma, \sigma)t^4\Big) \, \mathrm{d}t + \mathcal{O}\left((\varsigma - \sigma)^3\right). \qquad (12)\end{aligned}$$

Using the progress coefficients (7), (12) reads

$$I_t(\varsigma,\sigma) = a_0(\varsigma,\sigma) + a_1(\varsigma,\sigma)c_{1,\lambda} + a_2(\varsigma,\sigma)d^{(2)}_{1,\lambda} + a_3(\varsigma,\sigma)d^{(3)}_{1,\lambda} + a_4(\varsigma,\sigma)d^{(4)}_{1,\lambda} + \mathcal{O}\big((\varsigma-\sigma)^3\big). \tag{13}$$

The coefficients a_i depend on $\varsigma - \sigma$. Since the integration over the mutation strength remains to be done, (13) is regrouped into a polynomial in $(\varsigma - \sigma)/\sigma$

$$\begin{aligned}\psi(R,\sigma) &= \int_0^\infty \left(\frac{\varsigma-\sigma}{\sigma}\right) T_g(\varsigma,\sigma)T_f(\varsigma,\sigma)\,\mathrm{d}\varsigma \\ &= \int_0^\infty g_0 f_0 \left(\frac{\varsigma-\sigma}{\sigma}\right) + (f_0 g_1 + g_0 f_1)\sigma \left(\frac{\varsigma-\sigma}{\sigma}\right)^2 \\ &\quad + (g_1 f_1 + f_0 g_2 + g_0 f_2)\sigma^2 \left(\frac{\varsigma-\sigma}{\sigma}\right)^3 + \mathcal{O}\big((\varsigma-\sigma)^4\big)\,\mathrm{d}\varsigma \end{aligned} \tag{14}$$

where f_i and g_i denote the Taylor series's coefficients associated with $[(\varsigma - \sigma)/\sigma]^i$. In the case of the log-normal operator, the expected values of ς^k read $\overline{\varsigma^k} = \sigma^k \exp(k^2 \tau^2/2)$. The expectation of $((\varsigma - \sigma)/\sigma)^k$ can therefore be easily determined. Cutting off the resulting exponential series after τ^2, we obtain $\psi(R,\sigma) = g_0 f_0 \frac{\tau^2}{2} + (f_0 g_1 + g_0 f_1)\sigma\tau^2 + \mathcal{O}(\tau^4)$ as the first order SAR. The coefficients g_i and f_i can be obtained after a lengthy but straightforward calculation leading to

$$\begin{aligned}\psi(R,\sigma) = \tau^2 \Bigg(& d^{(2)}_{1,\lambda} - \frac{1}{2} - \frac{c_{1,\lambda} d\alpha R^{\alpha-1}(N-1)\sigma}{\sqrt{R^2 + (N-1)\sigma^2 + (d\alpha R^{\alpha-1})^2(R^2 + \frac{N-1}{2}\sigma^2)}} \\ & + (d^{(2)}_{1,\lambda} - 1)\frac{(d\alpha R^{\alpha-1})^2(N-1)\sigma^2\left(1 - 2\frac{R^2 + \frac{N-1}{2}\sigma^2}{R^2 + (N-1)\sigma^2}\right)}{2(R^2 + (N-1)\sigma^2) + 2(d\alpha R^{\alpha-1})^2(R^2 + \frac{N-1}{2}\sigma^2)}\Bigg). \end{aligned} \tag{15}$$

The first order self-adaptation response (SAR) (15) was obtained under the condition $\tau \ll 1$ which enabled several simplifications of the original equations. The basic points were the expansion of the more complicated functions into their Taylor series' around the parental mutation strength σ which due to $\tau \ll 1$ could be cut off after the first terms. Similarly to the observations made in [5], the SAR (15) depends on the distance to the ridge axis directly but *not* on the x-component.

3 Self-adaptation on the Sharp Ridge

The sharp ridge is the simplest case to be analyzed. In this case, the fitness function is given by $F(\mathbf{y}) = x - dR$. For our first analysis, we will simplify the notations by introducing normalizations similar to those used in the case of the sphere model [6]. Setting thus $\sigma^* = \sigma(N-1)/R$, the SAR changes to

$$\psi(\sigma^*, d, N) = \mathcal{O}(\tau^4) + \tau^2\Bigg(\frac{1}{2} - \frac{c_{1,\lambda} d\sigma^*}{\sqrt{1 + \frac{\sigma^{*2}}{N-1} + d^2\left(1 + \frac{\sigma^{*2}}{2(N-1)}\right)}}$$

$$+ (d^{(2)}_{1,\lambda} - 1)\left(1 + \frac{d^2 \frac{\sigma^{*2}}{N-1}\left(1 - 2\frac{1+\frac{\sigma^{*2}}{2(N-1)}}{1+\frac{\sigma^{*2}}{N-1}}\right)}{2(1 + \frac{\sigma^{*2}}{N-1}) + 2d^2(1 + \frac{\sigma^{*2}}{2(N-1)})}\right)\Bigg). \tag{16}$$

The SAR (16) has an approximately linear loss part whose non-linear components vanish with increasing search space dimensionality. In Fig. 1, Eq. (16) is compared with the results of experiments on the sharp ridge. Each data point was obtained by averaging the results of $200,000$ one-generation experiments. For the range of σ^*-values considered, (16) predicts the outcome of experiments generally well. Deviations occur for higher σ^*-values. Figure 1 also shows the influence of the d-parameter on the SAR. Larger choices of d result in an initially sharper fall of the curve and smaller zeros of the SAR. Let us now consider the limit value of (16) for $N \to \infty$ under the assumption that σ^* remains finite. We obtain after a short calculation

$$\psi_\infty(\sigma^*, d) := \lim_{N\to\infty} \psi(\sigma^*, d, N) = \mathcal{O}(\tau^4) + \tau^2\left(d^{(2)}_{1,\lambda} - \frac{1}{2} - \frac{c_{1,\lambda} d\sigma^*}{\sqrt{1+d^2}}\right) \tag{17}$$

which apart from a correction factor $d/\sqrt{1+d^2}$ closely resembles the SAR on the sphere model $\psi_{sphere}(\sigma^*) = \mathcal{O}(\tau^4) + \tau^2(d^{(2)}_{1,\lambda} - \frac{1}{2} - c_{1,\lambda}\sigma^*)$ obtained in [6] for $N \to \infty$. The zero of the SAR (17), denoted by $\sigma^*_{\psi_0}$, is easily obtained

$$\psi_\infty(\sigma^*_{\psi_0}, d) = \tau^2\left(d^{(2)}_{1,\lambda} - \frac{1}{2} - \frac{c_{1,\lambda} d\sigma^*_{\psi_0}}{\sqrt{1+d^2}}\right) = 0 \Rightarrow \sigma^*_{\psi_0} = \sqrt{1 + \frac{1}{d^2}}\,\frac{d^{(2)}_{1,\lambda} - \frac{1}{2}}{c_{1,\lambda}} \tag{18}$$

and scales with $\sqrt{1+1/d^2}$. Similarly to the SAR (15), we can determine the limit of the normalized progress rate (5) $\varphi^*_x = \varphi_x(N-1)/R$

$$\lim_{N\to\infty} \varphi^*_x(\sigma^*) = \lim_{N\to\infty} \frac{\sigma^* c_{1,\lambda}}{\sqrt{1 + d^2 \frac{1+\sigma^{*2}/(2(N-1))}{1+\sigma^{*2}/(N-1)}}} = \frac{\sigma^* c_{1,\lambda}}{\sqrt{1+d^2}} \tag{19}$$

where $\varphi^*_x = \varphi_x(N-1)/R$ and that of the normalized radial progress rate (6) $\varphi^*_R = \varphi_R(N-1)/R$

$$\lim_{N\to\infty} \varphi^*_R(\sigma^*) = \lim_{N\to\infty} (N-1)\left(1 - \sqrt{1 + \frac{\sigma^{*2}}{N-1}}\right)$$

$$+ \lim_{N\to\infty} \frac{1 + \sigma^{*2}/(2(N-1))}{1 + \sigma^{*2}/(N-1)} \frac{d c_{1,\lambda}\sigma^*}{\sqrt{1 + d^2 \frac{1+\sigma^{*2}/(2(N-1))}{1+\sigma^{*2}/(N-1)}}}$$

$$= \frac{d}{\sqrt{1+d^2}} c_{1,\lambda}\sigma^* - \frac{\sigma^{*2}}{2} \tag{20}$$

using Taylor series expansions of the roots. The radial progress rate resembles that of the sphere. It is interesting to consider a further progress measure, the quality gain, i.e., the expected one-generation change of the fitness $F(\mathbf{y}) = x - dR$ which is defined by $\overline{Q} = \mathrm{E}[F^{(g+1)} - F^{(g)}] = \mathrm{E}[x^{(g+1)} - x^{(g)}] - d\mathrm{E}[R^{(g+1)} - R^{(g)}] = \varphi_x + d\varphi_R$. Using the normalization $\overline{Q^*} = \overline{Q}(N-1)/R$, considering (19) and (20), and letting finally $N \to \infty$, we obtain

$$\overline{Q^*} = \varphi_x^* + d\varphi_R^* = \sqrt{1+d^2}c_{1,\lambda}\sigma^* - d{\sigma^*}^2/2. \tag{21}$$

Its second zero is $\sigma^*_{F_0} = 2c_{1,\lambda}\sqrt{1+d^2}/d$. It can be shown by case inspection that the zero of the SAR is smaller then the zero of the quality gain, i.e., that

$$\sigma^*_{\psi_0} < \sigma^*_{F_0} \Leftrightarrow \sqrt{1+\frac{1}{d^2}}\frac{d^{(2)}_{1,\lambda}-\frac{1}{2}}{c_{1,\lambda}} < 2\sqrt{1+\frac{1}{d^2}}c_{1,\lambda} \Leftrightarrow d^{(2)}_{1,\lambda} - \frac{1}{2} < 2c^2_{1,\lambda} \tag{22}$$

provided that $\lambda > 1$ and that $\sigma^*_{\varphi_0} < \sigma^*_{F_0} = (1+1/d^2)\sigma^*_{\varphi_0}$ holds. The consequences of these relations will be shown later on.

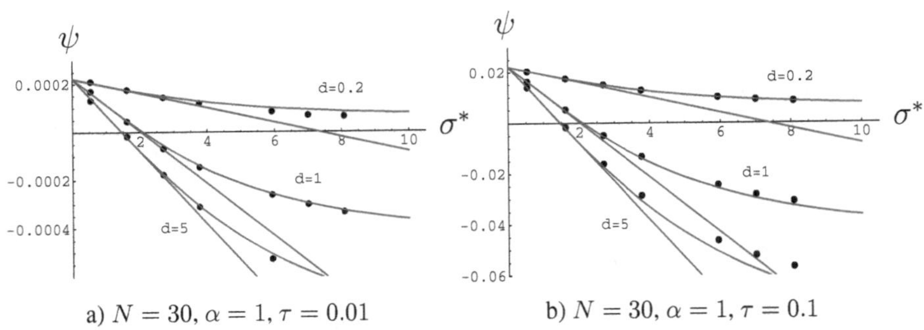

Fig. 1. The SAR (16) (blue) and its limit for $N \to \infty$ (straight lines) in comparison with the results of experiments. Each data point was sampled over 200,000 one-generation experiments.

On the sphere, the ς^*-evolution reaches a steady state for $g \to \infty$. The interesting question is whether this also occurs for the sharp ridge. Note, in the case of the non-normalized mutation strength σ, a σ-increase over time on the sharp ridge is desirable [5]. Therefore, the long-term behavior of the non-normalized σ is also of interest. Let us assume that the ES starts far away from the ridge axis so that the model appears basically as a sphere. As a result, the influence of R can be assumed to be far greater than the influence of x and the ES should initially attain a stationary normalized mutation strength. As can be seen in Fig. 2, experiments support this assumption. But what are the consequences of this stationary state? In a first analysis, we consider the SAR and the progress rates obtained for $N \to \infty$. The equation for the ς^*-evolution follows from (4). The variable ς^* is obtained by normalizing ς with $r/(N-1)$. Note, r denotes the new distance to the ridge. The new distance is given by the evolution equation (4) for r, $r = R - \varphi_R = R(1 - \varphi_R^*/(N-1))$. The ς^*-evolution is thus given by $\varsigma^* = \sigma^*(1+\psi)/(1-\varphi_R^*/(N-1)) \approx \sigma^*(1+\psi+\varphi_R^*/(N-1))$ provided that $|\varphi_R^*| \ll N-1$ holds. Stationary points, i.e., points which fulfill $\varsigma^* = \sigma^* = \sigma_{st}^*$, are then characterized by the solutions of $\psi = -\varphi_R^*/(N-1)$, i.e., by

$$\frac{d}{\sqrt{1+d^2}}c_{1,\lambda}\sigma_{st}^* - \frac{\sigma_{st}^{*\,2}}{2} = -M\tau^2\Big(d_{1,\lambda}^{(2)} - \frac{1}{2} - \frac{d}{\sqrt{1+d^2}}c_{1,\lambda}\sigma_{st}^*\Big)$$
$$\Rightarrow \sigma_{st}^* = \big(1-M\tau^2\big)\frac{d}{\sqrt{1+d^2}}c_{1,\lambda} + \sqrt{\big(1-M\tau^2\big)^2\frac{d^2c_{1,\lambda}^2}{1+d^2} - 2M\tau^2\Big(d_{1,\lambda}^{(2)} - \frac{1}{2}\Big)} \quad (23)$$

with $M = N-1$. Equation (23) is compared with the results of experiments in Fig. (3). If the search space's dimensionality is sufficiently large or τ is sufficiently small (e.g. $\tau = 1/\sqrt{N}$ as usually used in practice), the agreement with the experimental data is good. An exception appears to be a choice in the vicinity of $d = 1$ where greater deviations occur: We suspect that taking into account fluctuations is of special importance for these cases, because this scenario seems to resemble a sphere model with heavy noise. The deterministic analysis presented cannot account for these random effects.

The stationary mutation strength (23) assumes values between the zero of the radial progress rate $\sigma_{\varphi_0}^*$ and the zero of the SAR σ_{ψ}^*. The choice of the learning parameter decides whether σ_{st}^* is closer to the latter or to the former. Note, in the case of the sphere model, the zero of the SAR is generally smaller than the zero of the progress rate. Thus, the ES is able to obtain positive progress – reducing the distance to the optimizer on average. On the sharp ridge, it depends on the choice of the ridge parameter d which zero is greater as the other

$$\sigma_{\varphi_0}^* = \frac{d2c_{1,\lambda}}{\sqrt{1+d^2}} \geq \sigma_{\psi_0}^* = \frac{\sqrt{1+d^2}}{d}\frac{d_{1,\lambda}^{(2)} - \frac{1}{2}}{c_{1,\lambda}} \Rightarrow d \geq \sqrt{\frac{d_{1,\lambda}^{(2)} - \frac{1}{2}}{2c_{1,\lambda}^2 + \frac{1}{2} - d_{1,\lambda}^{(2)}}} =: d_{crit} \quad (24)$$

which holds for $2c_{1,\lambda}^2 + 1/2 - d_{1,\lambda}^{(2)} > 0$ which is generally fulfilled for $\lambda > 1$.

If $d > d_{crit}$, stationary mutation strengths given by (23) are connected with a positive radial progress and the distance R to the ridge is decreased on average. Similar to its behavior on the sphere model, the ES moves closer to the ridge axis. This has consequences for the non-normalized mutation strength σ and of course for the progress in x-direction. If R decreases and σ^* stays constant (on average) then the non-normalized mutation strength $\sigma = \sigma^* R/(N-1)$ decreases. Finally σ becomes too small to cause significant variations. The case $d > d_{crit}$ finally results in a stagnation. The ridge axis has been approached, but the ES cannot move significantly along the axis. In other words, the ES behaves as if it would optimize the sphere model.

If $d < d_{crit}$, the zero of the SAR is larger than the zero of the radial progress rate. Any stationary normalized mutation strength given by (23) causes a negative radial progress which results in an expected increase of the distance to the ridge axis. The ES does not approach the ridge axis but enlarges both components of its fitness function: the x-component of the ridge axis and the distance to the ridge R.

Both cases for d, i.e., $d > d_{crit}$ and $d < d_{crit}$ achieve a positive expected change of the normalized fitness, since the second zero of $\overline{Q^*}$, denoted by $\sigma^*_{F_0}$, is greater than the zero of the SAR $\sigma^*_{\psi_0}$ and the zero of the radial progress $\sigma^*_{\varphi_0}$. Therefore, the normalized fitness change is positive for all stationary mutation strengths (23). The fitness thus improves on average regardless of the choice of d, however, with different overall results.

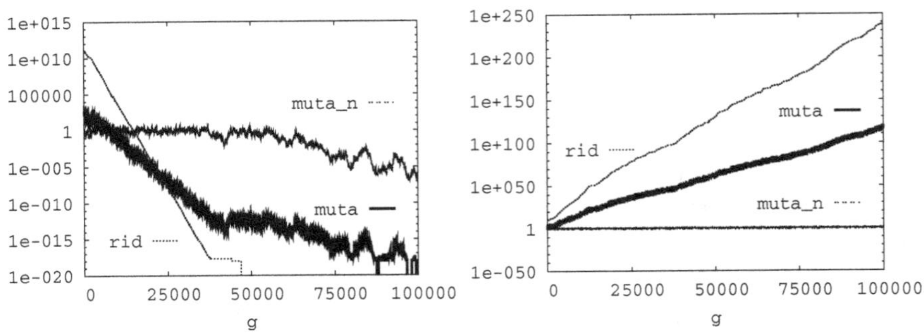

a) $\tau = 0.05$, $d = 5$ b) $\tau = 0.05$, $d = 0.2$

Fig. 2. Some typical runs of $(1, 10)$-ES on the sharp ridge for $d = 5$ and $d = 0.2$ over the first $100, 000$ generations. The search space dimensionality is $N = 1000$. Shown are the distance to the ridge (r), the mutation strength (σ, thick line) and the mutation strength (σ^*) normalized with respect to the ridge. The critical d-value is $d_{crit} = 0.936$.

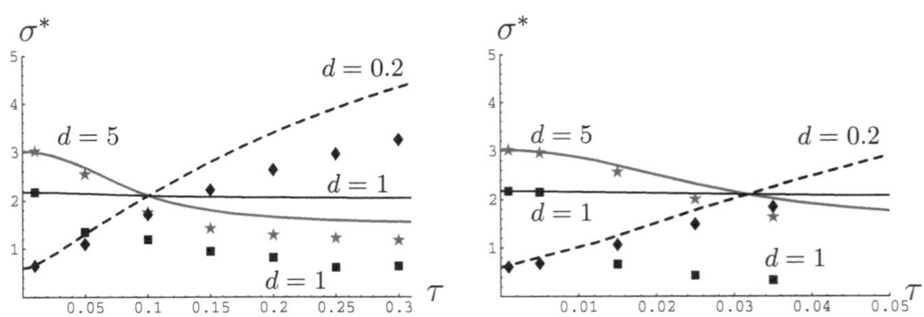

a) $N = 100$, $d = 5$ (red, stars), $d = 0.2$ (blue, dashed line, diamonds), $d = 1$ (boxes)

b) $N = 1000$, $d = 5$ (red, stars), $d = 0.2$ (blue, dashed line, diamonds), $d = 1$ (boxes)

Fig. 3. Comparison between the stationary mutation strength (23) and the stationary mutation strength obtained in experiments. The points denote the experimental results. Each data point was sampled over at least $1, 000, 000$ experiments. Due to the fast convergence of the distance to the ridge, it was necessary in some cases to restart the algorithm in order to provide an adequate data basis.

4 Conclusions

In this paper, we considered the self-adaptation behavior of $(1, \lambda)$-ES on the sharp ridge. The behavior of the ES was modeled using the evolution equation approximations. To this end, the expected one-generation changes of the state variables have to be determined: the radial and axial progress rate and the self-adaptation response. All equations obtained show an explicit dependency on the distance to the ridge axis R. In a sense, self-adaptation is deceived by this R-variable. Experiments show that the ES generally reaches a stationary normalized mutation strength. This is crucial for the long-term behavior of the algorithm. From this point on, it only depends on the choice of the ridge function parameter d whether the ES mainly decreases the distance to the ridge axis or mainly increases the speed by which it travels parallel to it. Only if d is chosen smaller than a population size dependent limit, the stationary mutation strength results in an increase of the distance to the ridge otherwise the decrease occurs. In both cases, a positive normalized fitness gain is achieved. But only if R increases, this also results in a significant gain along the ridge direction.

The analysis is far from being complete. First of all, other ridge function, e.g. the parabolic ridge, will have to be considered. Secondly, the neglected perturbation parts will have to be taken into account and the analysis must consider N-dependent progress rates and SAR.

References

1. B. C. Arnold, N. Balakrishnan, and H. N. Nagaraja. *A First Course in Order Statistics.* Wiley, New York, 1992.
2. D. V. Arnold and H.-G. Beyer. Evolution strategies with cumulative step length adaptation on the noisy parabolic ridge. Technical Report CS-2006-02 CS-2006-02, Dalhousie University, Faculty of Computer Science, January 2006.
3. D. V. Arnold and A. MacLeod. Hierarchically organised evolution strategies on the parabolic ridge. Technical Report CS-2006-03 CS-2006-03, Dalhousie University, Faculty of Computer Science, January 2006.
4. A. Auger. Convergence results for the $(1, \lambda)$-SA-ES using the theory of ϕ-irreducible Markov chains. *Theoretical Computer Science*, 334:35–69, 2005.
5. H.-G. Beyer. On the performance of $(1, \lambda)$-evolution strategies for the ridge function class. *IEEE Transactions on Evolutionary Computation*, 5(3):218–235, 2001.
6. H.-G. Beyer. *The Theory of Evolution Strategies.* Natural Computing Series. Springer, Heidelberg, 2001.
7. M. Herdy. Reproductive isolation as strategy parameter in hierarchically organized evolution strategies. In R. Männer and B. Manderick, editors, *Parallel Problem Solving from Nature, 2*, pages 207–217. Elsevier, Amsterdam, 1992.
8. A. I. Oyman. *Convergence Behavior of Evolution Strategies on Ridge Functions.* Ph.d. thesis, University of Dortmund, Department of Computer Science, 1999.
9. I. Rechenberg. *Evolutionsstrategie: Optimierung technischer Systeme nach Prinzipien der biologischen Evolution.* Frommann-Holzboog Verlag, Stuttgart, 1973.
10. H.-P. Schwefel. Adaptive Mechanismen in der biologischen Evolution und ihr Einfluß auf die Evolutionsgeschwindigkeit. Technical report, Technical University of Berlin, 1974. Abschlußbericht zum DFG-Vorhaben Re 215/2.
11. M.A. Semenov. Convergence velocity of evolutionary algorithm with self-adaptation. In *GECCO 2002*, pages 210–213, 2002.

Searching for Balance: Understanding Self-adaptation on Ridge Functions

Monte Lunacek and Darrell Whitley

Colorado State University
Fort Collins, Colorado 80523 USA

Abstract. The progress rate of a self-adaptive evolution strategy is sub-optimal on ridge functions because the global step-size, denoted σ, becomes too small. On the parabolic ridge we conjecture that σ will stabilize when *selection* is unbiased towards larger or smaller step-sizes. On the *sharp ridge*, where the bias in selection is constant, σ will continue to decrease. We show that this is of practical interest because ridges can cause even the best solutions found by self-adaptation to be of little value on ridge problems where spatially close parameters tend to have similar values.

1 Introduction

The self-adaptive evolution strategy frequently generates a step-size that is sub-optimal on *ridge* functions. This causes the progress rate to be slower than expected or even to stall [8,14,7]. We conjecture that the global step-size of a $(1, \lambda)$-ES will stabilize when the selection of σ is *unbiased* toward larger or smaller step-sizes. This occurs when the probability of selecting an individual with a smaller σ value is approximately equal to the probability of selecting an individual with a larger σ value.

We provide empirical evidence that shows when the ridge function is smooth (e.g. the parabolic ridge), self-adaptation will decrease its step-size until it is unbiased in selecting σ. On the sharp ridge, which is not continuously differentiable, the local topology in the neighborhood of the step-size does not change as σ decreases; this implies that for *any* σ value, there is a constant bias toward selecting individuals that have smaller step-sizes. Our explanation for this behavior supplements other justifications for the failure of self adaptation on the sharp ridge [14].

This is important because the *ridge* topology can greatly affects the usefulness of solutions found by self-adaptation. This is especially true when the expected global solution is smooth, a situation that arises in many real-world applications where spatially close object parameters tend to have similar values. In this paper, we discuss two such problems: 1) an atmospheric science inverse model that relates a smooth temperature profile to a set of observable measurements and 2) an artificial problem proposed by Salomon [13] that also has a smooth target profile. We show that the solutions found by self-adaptation on these problems are often unacceptable for actual use. This is because both problems have ridge topology and self-adaptation will favor the parameters of the profile that offer the greatest decrease in fitness first, and often assign incorrect values to the parameters that correspond to ridge axes (e.g. those that have less influence on the fitness function).

T.P. Runarsson et al. (Eds.): PPSN IX, LNCS 4193, pp. 82–91, 2006.

2 The Self-adaptive Evolution Strategy

The canonical *evolution strategy* is an iterative process where a population of μ parents produce λ offspring based on mutation distributions that center around the parents. This paper considers the $(1, \lambda)$ evolution strategy where the best parent is selected only from the λ offspring.

In self-adaptation, each individual in the population is described by a set of *object parameters*, which define its location in the search space, and a set of *strategy parameters*, that define its mutation distribution. In general, individuals with higher fitness, and therefore better object parameters, are more likely to survive. Unlike object parameters, strategy parameters are selected indirectly based on the assumption that the best individuals of the current generation are likely to have useful strategy parameters.

Bäck describes the typical evolution strategy for self-adapting a global step-size [2]. In the following equations, $N(0, 1)$ denotes a normally distributed random number with mean 0 and a standard deviation of 1. Before the *object parameters* are created, the step-size for each offspring is adapted.

$$\sigma^{g+1} = \sigma^g \cdot \exp(N(0, \tau^{'}))$$

The *global mutation strength* on σ is $\tau^{'} = 1/\sqrt{2n}$, where n represents the number of object parameters. The object parameters are created based on this new step-size.

$$x_i^{g+1} = x_i^g + \sigma^{g+1} \cdot N_i(0, 1)$$

Self-adaptation can be extended to adapt elliptical distributions defined by individual step-sizes, but this mutation distribution has a tendency to collapse and search only a subset of the search space [4,9,7]. *Correlated mutations* extends this idea further by estimating the covariance for each pair of object parameters, which, in theory, can describe any elliptical distribution in the search space. But Hansen *et al.* show that using correlated mutations becomes impractical when the dimensionality is higher than about ten [7] and that the performance of correlated mutations is strongly related to the initial values of the strategy parameters [6]. These shortcomings suggest that self-adapting more than one strategy parameter can be unreliable.

3 Self-adaptation and the General Ridge Function

A *ridge* in the search space occurs when there exists a different rate of change (e.g. scale) between the parameters of the objective function. The *direction* of the ridge axis is determined by the interaction of the parameter values. For a *separable* function, the ridge axis will be aligned with the coordinate axis that corresponds to the parameter with the smallest rate of decrease.

Isotropic distributions are invariant to rotations of the search space. This means that the offspring are created in an unbiased *search direction*. The implication here is that the difference in scale between the parameters of the ridge, and not the ridge orientation, is the primary characteristic that can affect performance. But being invariant with respect to rotation and being able to exploit ridge structures is not exactly the same [15].

The generalized ridge function, as defined by Beyer [3], does not have an obtainable optimal solution. Instead, this "treadmill" function is used to understand the steady-state behavior of search algorithms on the ridge. The goal is to maximize the following:

$$f(\boldsymbol{x}) = x_0 - d \cdot \left(\sum_{i=1}^{N} x_i^2 \right)^{\alpha/2}$$

where d is a *scaling* factor that determines how narrow and steep the valley will be. The α constant determines the type of ridge; the parabolic ridge corresponds to an $\alpha = 2$ and the sharp ridge forms when $\alpha = 1$. Although the *ridge axis* (denoted x_0) is aligned with a coordinate axis, this will not skew our results because, as mentioned, isotropic distributions are unbiased to the orientation of the ridge axis.

The goal is to make progress in the x_0 direction while minimizing the distance to the ridge axis in all other dimensions [12]. This creates a problem for an isotropic distribution because offspring are sampled in an unbiased way. For example, there is no adaptive mechanism that allows self-adaptation with a global step-size to search for larger values in one direction while minimizing the other parameter values.

Related Work

The theoretical and empirical behavior of evolution strategies using *constant mutation strength* and a single global step-size is well documented for the parabolic ridge function [12,10,11]. Beyer extended this work by looking at the performance properties of the $(1, \lambda)$-ES on the general class of ridge functions [3]. Recently, Arnold and Beyer have studied CSA on the noisy parabolic ridge [1].

The behavior for an evolution strategy with a *fixed mutation strength* can be summarized using two important theoretical equations (see Beyer for details [3]). First, the distance of the best individual to the ridge axis tends to fluctuate within a predictable range, R, which is called the *stationary distance* [10]. This measurement is used in the second equation, the *progress rate* (φ), that predicts the average expected change in the direction of the ridge axis given a fixed σ value. Algorithms that *creep* on the ridge will tend to have lower progress rates.

Beyer points out that the results derived using a constant mutation strength can serve as a performance benchmark for *self-adaptation* [3]. If self-adaptation is working as expected, the steady-state σ values should be close to the optimal predicted values using a constant step-size. Unfortunately, they are not.

Because an adaptive step-size is necessary in practice, it is important to understand how different adaptive strategies will perform. Oyman, Beyer, and Schwefel present conditions on the parabolic ridge where a $(1 + 10)$-ES *limps*, or *creeps* [10]. Several researchers have also noticed that non-elitist self-adaptation fails on ridge functions. Herdy showed that the self-adaptation with a single global step-size fails on the sharp ridge [8]. Salomon empirically showed that the $(1, \lambda)$-ES with a global step size failed on two instances of the *sharp ridge* [1] function [14]. Salomon found that the estimated *progress rate* is essentially negative for nearly all values $\sigma > 0$. When the population

[1] Salomon's test functions were similar to the general ridge function with $\alpha = 1$ and $\alpha = 0.5$.

size was large, which Salomon found grew exponentially with problem dimension, only a small neighborhood of acceptable σ values yield positive progress.

Given the amount of attention devoted to evolution strategies on the ridge, it is surprising that no explanation has been put forth as to why self-adaptation tends to evolve less than optimal step-sizes on the general ridge function. In the conclusion of his paper, Beyer observes that self-adaptation appears to reward the short-term goals of reducing the *stationary distance* rather than the long-term goal of making *progress* along the ridge axis [3]. In the next section, we provide evidence that supports our conjecture as to why this occurs.

4 Why Is Self-adaptation Sub-optimal?

On the ridge function there is a small "window" of improving search directions. This window gets smaller as either the dimensionality increases or the scaling factor, d, increases. This means that an unbiased isotropic distribution is more likely to sample the search space in a poor direction rather than an effective one. This creates a strong bias towards selecting smaller and smaller step-sizes.

In order to understand this bias, consider the three parabolic ridges in figure 1. The left ridge is sharp ($\alpha = 1$) whereas the other two ridges are parabolic ($\alpha = 2$). Two isotropic distributions based on σ are shown. One is slightly larger than σ and the other is slightly smaller. The base σ value in the first two graphs is 1 and decreases to $\sigma = 0.1$ for the right most graph. The "window" where the larger step size has greater fitness is less than the small step-size window in all cases. In other words, the smaller step-size has a larger region where its fitness is better than that of the larger step-size. This creates a bias towards selecting smaller σ values. Notice that on the sharp ridge, the "window" aligns perfectly with the contour lines; decreasing σ will not change the ridge bias. However, comparing the two right graphs shows that as σ decreases on the parabolic ridge, the neighborhood around the step-size becomes more linear and the bias towards smaller step-sizes is less pronounced. Given this inherent bias toward smaller step-sizes, we propose the following conjecture.

Conjecture 1. *The global step-size of a self-adaptive $(1, \lambda)$-ES will stabilize when the selection of σ is unbiased toward larger or smaller values. If the ridge bias cannot be removed, self-adaptation will continue to decrease σ by selecting smaller step-sizes.*

We found that the steady-state value of σ on the parabolic ridge occurs when the probability of selecting a small step-size is approximately equal to the probability of selecting a larger one. Self-adaptation decreases its step-size until the ridge bias diminishes. Intuitively, this makes sense. When σ is large, the *ridge bias* will drive σ towards a smaller value. If σ gets too small, the probability that a larger step-size will be selected increases. Self-adaptation tends to have a steady-state behavior that reflects this balance.

On the sharp ridge, however, the inherent bias cannot be removed. Although the sharp ridge is continuous everywhere, its gradient is discontinuous along the ridge axis. This means that as the step-size decreases, due to the inherent ridge bias, the topology in the neighborhood around σ looks identical for all values. In other words, there does not

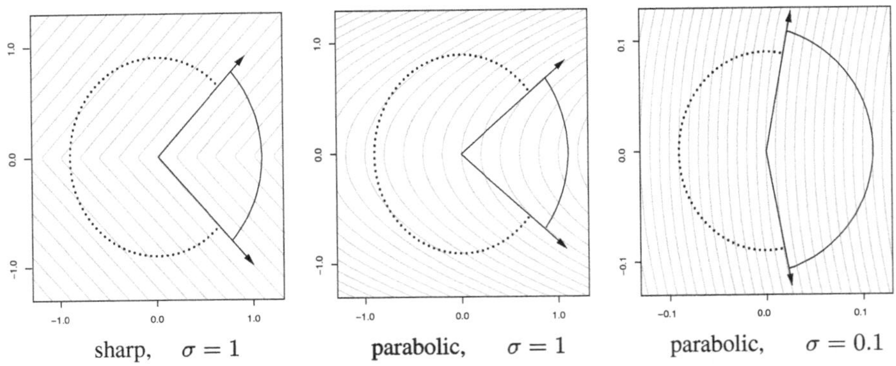

Fig. 1. Contour plots of three ridge functions. The dotted arc in each plot corresponds to the region where the smaller step-size has greater fitness. The solid arc indicates the region where the larger step-size is best.

exist a small enough step-size such that the bias toward selecting smaller σ values diminishes. This compliments Salomon's results [14]; in high dimensions, the population size needed to effectively sample the search space adequately is exponentially large. Without an adequate sample, an individual with a larger step-size will rarely search in the small window where the larger step-size is best.

In order to provide evidence for our conjecture, we would like to measure the probability that the step-size of the next generation parent is smaller than that of the current parent. If σ_g equals the step-size of generation g, then what we would like to measure is: $P(\sigma_{g+1} < \sigma_g)$. We denote this probability as ω. This will allow us to show that when σ reaches a steady-state, $\omega \approx 0.5$.

We can estimate ω by conducting a series of "single generation" experiments [2]. We do this by creating λ offspring based on a distribution defined by σ and the parent's location, $\boldsymbol{x}$. Then we evaluate the fitness of the offspring and ask the question: is the step-size of the best individual less than the value of σ? We repeat this 200 times and keep track of the number of times that a small step-size is successful. This is our estimate of ω, denoted $\hat{\omega}$.

We ran 100 trials of a $(1, 60)$-ES on both the parabolic and sharp ridge function. Each trial ran until either 1000 generations passed, which is ample to measure the stable behavior, or the step-size was below $1e - 10$, which is appropriate for measuring failure. After each generation, we estimated ω using the position and step-size of the current parent, as well as the corresponding population size, $\lambda = 60$. We tested several settings for the ridge scaling factor $d = \{1, 2, 5, 10\}$. Larger values of d create a steeper ridge function, which, given the same value for σ, increases the bias toward selecting smaller step-sizes. Figure 2 illustrates how self-adaptation behaves on a $N = 30$ dimensional ridge function where $d = 2$. The left graph shows the logarithm of σ for each generation. On the parabolic ridge, σ decreases until it reaches a steady-state value. Although this is sub-optimal, the strategy continues to make progress along the ridge axis. The step-size on the sharp ridge continues to decrease, never reaching a stable value. This

[2] An idea used by Beyer [3] for a different purpose.

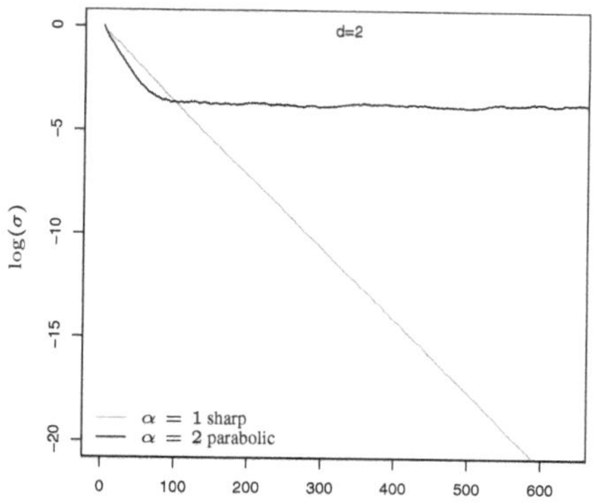

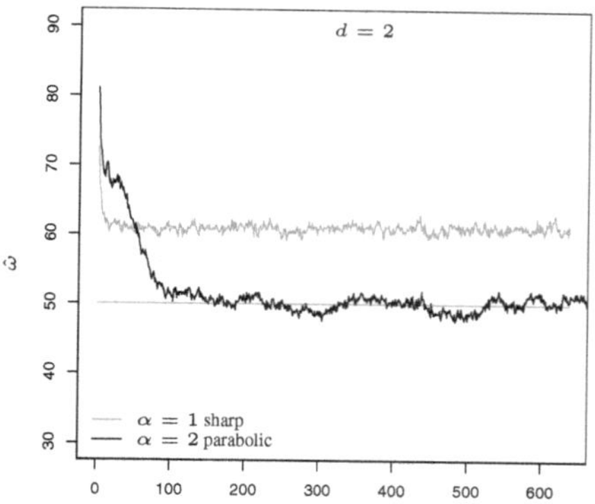

Fig. 2. The left graph shows the convergence of $\log(\sigma)$ for $\lambda = 60$ on the sharp ($\alpha = 1$) and parabolic ($\alpha = 2$) ridge. The graph on the right shows $\hat{\omega}$. The x-axis is the generation number.

is consistent with previously reported observations [8,14]. The right graph shows the average $\hat{\omega}$ for each function. The value for $\hat{\omega}$ is approximately 50% on the parabolic ridge. The step-size decreases until the topology around its expected distance from the ridge is unbiased toward selecting small or large values of σ. On the other hand, as soon as the self-adaptation finds the sharp ridge, the value for $\hat{\omega}$ is constant and greater than 50%. This is because changing the step-size does not impact the bias toward selecting smaller σ values. Therefore, the step-size will continue to decrease.

Increasing the scaling factor d increases the rate at which the last $N-1$ parameters decrease. This makes the difference between the rate of change for ridge axis (x_0) and all the other parameters more pronounced, and therefore, increases the *ridge bias*. There are two implications here. First, the steady-state σ values on the parabolic ridge will decrease as d increase. This is because it will take a smaller step-size to create an unbiased selection operator required for σ to stabilize. Second, because the bias in the sharp ridge cannot be removed, an increased ridge bias will cause the step-size to decrease at a higher rate.

Figure 3 shows how the scaling factor d can affect self-adaptation on the sharp ridge. The right box plot indicates that increasing d creates a larger bias toward selecting smaller step-sizes for the sharp ridge. The parabolic ridge still reduces it step-size until $\hat{\omega} \approx 50$, but this requires a smaller σ for larger values of d (which is not shown here). Although the $\hat{\omega}$ value for the sharp ridge with $d = 1$ appears to be close to 50, it is actually significantly different. Even this small bias will cause instability in the step-size. The right graph of figure 3 shows the convergence behavior for σ on the ridge functions with $d = 1$. The parabolic ridge balances when $\hat{\omega} \approx 50$. On the sharp ridge, a slight bias in selection ($\hat{\omega} > 50$) causes the step-size to decrease slowly. Given 1000 generations, self-adaptation makes greater progress on the unscaled ($d = 1$) sharp ridge than it does on the unscaled parabolic ridge. This is not surprising because the parabolic ridge has a much larger rate of decrease to the ridge axis than the sharp ridge, which decreases linearly.

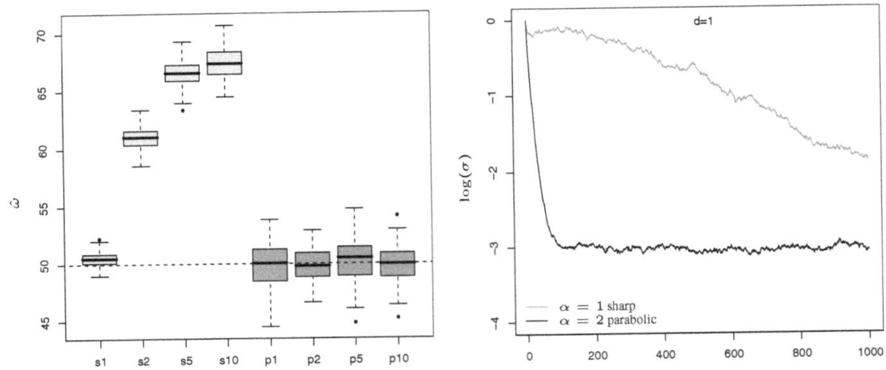

Fig. 3. The graph on the left shows $\hat{\omega}$ for all values of the ridge scaling factor *d*. Each experiment is denoted with an s or p, depending on whether the ridge is sharp or parabolic, and the *d* value. For example, $s1$ refers to the sharp ridge with $d = 1$. The right graph shows the the convergence of $\log(\sigma)$ for $\lambda = 60$ on the sharp with $d = 1$. Although $\hat{\omega}$ appears to be close to 50 for the sharp ridge with $d = 1$ (s1), it is in fact significantly higher (using a t-test with a 0.95 confidence interval).

5 Why Should We Care?

The previous section indicates that steeper more narrow ridges have a stronger inherent bias toward selecting smaller step-sizes. We also know that the *progress rate* is lower for smaller values of σ [3], which can cause an algorithm to *creep*. This means that on the general ridge function, self-adaptation will find the set of parameter values that are close to the ridge and either fail to find, or take a long time to find, the optimal value for the parameter that corresponds to the ridge axis. What is unclear here is exactly *how* the *ridge bias* can affect solution quality when more than one parameter acts like a ridge axis. We have found that self-adaptation will pay more attention to the parameters that have the largest rate of descent (e.g. large *d*) and often assign the incorrect values to the parameters that act like ridge axes. Sometimes these values are wildly different from the expected solution.

Many real-world applications that measure physical phenomena have optimal solutions such that spatially close object parameters tend to have similar values. This creates a "smooth" target profile through the parameter values of the objective function. We have recently been using search methods to find the inverse of an atmospheric science forward model that relates vertical temperature profiles to observed measurements. We actually want to solve the inverse problem: given a set of observations, what is the corresponding temperature profile? Traditional gradient-based methods can be used, which means that the function is smooth, but such methods are computationally extremely costly [5]. Unfortunately, we have found that well known, well tested evolutionary algorithms and local search methods applied to inversion problems do not always yield acceptable solutions. The primary reason for this is that there are *ridges* in fitness landscape.

Salomon demonstrated that a (1,6)-ES using self-adaptation failed to converge on an artificial test function that also contained physical continuity [13]. The test problem

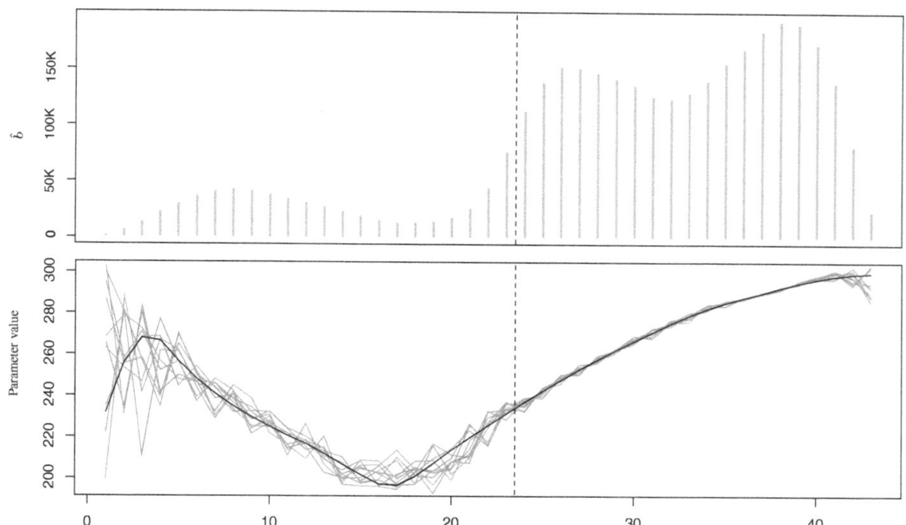

(a) The temperature inversion problem

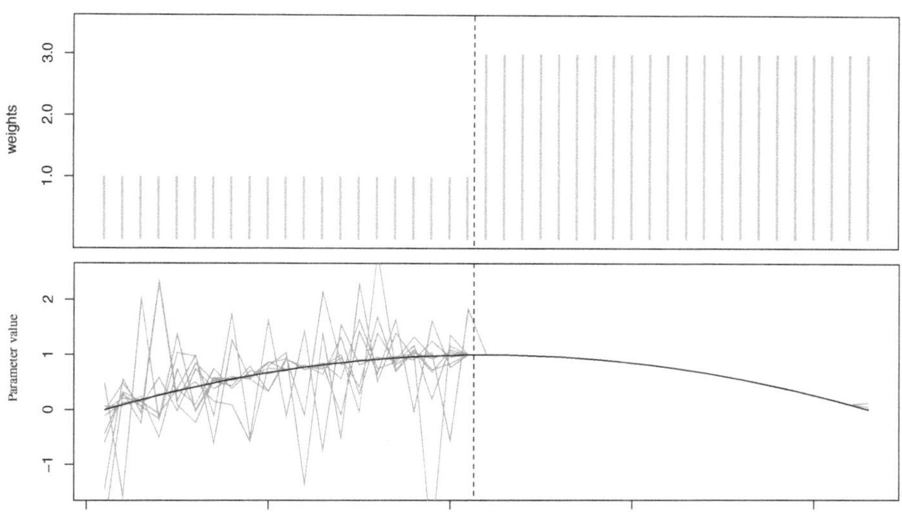

(b) Salomon's artificial test problem

Fig. 4. Self-adaptation will focus search on those parameters that offer the greatest influence on the fitness function. The top graphs are the estimated bias $\hat{b}$ (figure 4(a)) and the actual weights used on the temperature problem and Salomon's problem respectively. The vertical dashed line indicates a "transition" on the temperature problem where the parameter bias changes from small to large. The average values of $\hat{b}$ are lower for the parameters to the left of this line. We simulated this for Salomon's function by applying larger weights to the last half of the parameters.

uses a simple convex function, $f(x) = 1 - x^2$, as the *target profile*. The fitness of an individual is an approximation of the area between the current solution and the target profile (see Salomon's paper for details [13]). Since this metric is more on the order of the absolute difference between the target and current solution, and not its *square*, the test problem creates a "sharper" ridge. This is the primary cause for self-adaptation's poor performance. We found that applying different weights to the individual parameters exacerbated this problem.

We also know that the temperature problem has a strong bias toward the upper dimensions of the problem. Starting from the globally optimal solution, we varied each parameter by $\pm$ 2 units. Every move increases the objective error, which is zero when no change is applied. The average change per dimension, denoted $\hat{b}$, is a rough estimate of the expected change in the objective function associated with each object parameter near the optimal solution.

The top graph in figures 4(a) and 4(b) shows the estimated bias $\hat{b}$ for the temperature problem and the actual *weights* used to scale Salomon's problem. The bottom graph in each figure shows the *target profile* as a solid black line. The gray lines are the 10 best solutions out of 30 trials for a $(1, 100)$-ES using self-adaptation. Notice that the parameters offering the greatest opportunity to reduce the error will correspond to the largest values of the estimated bias $\hat{b}$ and artificial weights. This bias causes search algorithms to fit the "steeper" dimensions of the profile first – and to assign incorrect values to the other parameters. Unfortunately, as search continues to progress, σ becomes too small to make any dramatic changes to these solutions. From a practical point of view, the parameter values are not very useful because they "zig-zag" the actual temperature profile too much. The same is true for Salomon's problem. Even small weight values, like $w_i = 3$, create enough difference in rate of decrease to have a profound affect on how well the algorithm can fit the target profile.

6 Conclusion and Outlook

We have provided evidence to support our conjecture that self-adaptation will continue to decrease its step-size on the parabolic ridge function until it removes the bias toward selecting smaller σ values. On the sharp ridge function, this inherent bias cannot be removed, and σ will decrease on average. This explains why the performance of self-adaptation is poor on ridge functions.

From a practical point of view, ridges can cause even the best solutions found by self-adaptation to be of little value when the solution is a smooth target profile. This is because self-adaptation will favor the parameters that correspond to the largest decrease in fitness first, and leave the other parameters in potentially sub-optimal locations. This is strong evidence that isotropic distributions are not the most efficient or effective algorithms for problems that contain ridges. Strategy that directly address the ridge problem, like *Covariance Matrix Adaptation* [7], are a much better choice.

The shortcomings of *correlated mutations* and the lack of robustness that frequently occurs when adapting *individual step-sizes* leave an impression that the *only* safe way to use self-adaptation is with a single strategy parameter. And this strategy can also fail on the *sharp ridge*, a relatively harmless looking unimodal surface. To confuse the issue even more, when self-adaptation does not fail, it usually adapts step-sizes that are too small. All of these arguments seem to indicate that the self-adaptive assumption – highly fit individuals will also have useful strategy parameters – is incorrect.

On the other hand, the selected individuals *will tend to have* distributions that are more likely to explore better regions of the search space on the ridge function. A large step-size is less likely to "explore" better regions of the search space because of the inherent bias that comes with ridge functions.

This paper takes the first step towards a deeper understanding of why self-adaptation fails on the general ridge function. The results presented hold $\lambda = 60$ (for $N = 30$) constant. Future work should study how λ can affect the steady-state value of σ. Our preliminary results are counter intuitive; increasing the population size can also increase the estimated probability ($\hat{\omega}$) that a smaller step is selected.

Acknowledgments. This material is based upon work supported by the National Science Foundation under Grant No. 0117209 and Sandia National Labs.

References

1. D. V. Arnold and H.-G. Beyer. Evolution strategies with cumulative step-length adaptation on the noisy parabolic ridge. Technical report, Dalhousie University, 2006.
2. T. Bäck. *Evolutonary Algorithms in Theory and Practice.* Oxford University Press, New York, 1996.
3. H.-G. Beyer. On the Performance of $(1, \lambda)$-Evolution Strategies for the Ridge Function Class. *IEEE Transactions on Evolutionary Computation*, 5(3):218–235, 2001.
4. H.-G. Beyer and H.-P. Schwefel. Evolution strategies - a comprehensive introduction. *Natural Computing: an international journal*, 1(1):3–52, May 2002.
5. R. Englen, A. Denning, K. Gurney, and G. Stephens. Global observations of the carbon budget: I. expected satellite capabilities for emission spectroscopy in the eos and npoess eras. *Journal of Geophysical Research*, 106:20,055–20,068, 2001.
6. N. Hansen. Invariance, self-adaptation and correlated mutations in evolution strategies. In *Proceedings of Parallel Problem Solving from Nature*, pages 355–364, 2000.
7. N. Hansen and A. Ostermeier. Completely derandomized self-adaptation in evolution strategies. *Evolutionary Computation*, 9(2):159–195, 2001.
8. M. Herdy. Reproductive isolation as strategy parameter in hierarchically organized evolution strategies. In *Proceedings of Parallel Problem Solving from Nature*, pages 207–217, 1992.
9. A. Ostermeier, A. Gawelczyk, and N. Hansen. A derandomized approach to self-adaptation of evolution strategies. *Evolutionary Computation*, 2(4):369–380, 1994.
10. A. I. Oyman, H. Beyer, and H. Schwefel. Where elitists start limping evolution strategies at ridge functions. In *Parallel Problem Solving from Nature – PPSN V.*
11. A. I. Oyman and H.-G. Beyer. Analysis of the $(\mu/\mu, \lambda)$-ES on the Parabolic Ridge. *Evolutionary Computation*, 8(3):267–289, 2000.
12. A. I. Oyman, H.-G. Beyer, and H.-P. Schwefel. Analysis of the $(1, \lambda)$-ES on the Parabolic Ridge. *Evolutionary Computation*, 8(3):249–265, 2000.
13. R. Salomon. Applying evolutionary algorithms to real-world-inspired problems with physical smoothness constraints. In *Proceedings of the Congress on Evolutionary Computation.*
14. R. Salomon. The curse of high dimensional search spaces: Observing premature convergence in unimodal functions. In *Proceedings of the Congress on Evolutionary Computation*, pages 918–923. IEEE Press, 2004.
15. D. Whitley, M. Lunacek, and J. Knight. Ruffled by ridges: How evolutionary algorithms can fail. In *Proceedings of GECCO*, 2004.

Diversity Loss in General Estimation of Distribution Algorithms

Jonathan L. Shapiro

University of Manchester, Manchester, UK. M13 9PL
jls@cs.man.ac.uk

Abstract. A very general class of EDAs is defined, on which universal results on the rate of diversity loss can be derived. This EDA class, denoted SML-EDA, requires two restrictions: 1) in each generation, the new probability model is build using only data sampled from the current probability model; and 2) maximum likelihood is used to set model parameters. This class is very general; it includes simple forms of many well-known EDAs, e.g. BOA, MIMIC, FDA, UMDA, etc. To study the diversity loss in SML-EDAs, the trace of the empirical covariance matrix is the proposed statistic. Two simple results are derived. Let N be the number of data vectors evaluated in each generation. It is shown that on a flat landscape, the expected value of the statistic decreases by a factor $1-1/N$ in each generation. This result is used to show that for the Needle problem, the algorithm will with a high probability never find the optimum unless the population size grows exponentially in the number of search variables.

1 Introduction

Estimation of distribution algorithms (EDAs) are search algorithms inspired by evolutionary algorithms. Whereas evolutionary algorithms use a population of configurations to search for a solution to an optimization problem, EDAs use a probability function instead. This probability function models the population which it replaces. For this reason, EDAs are also often called "probability-model building evolutionary algorithms". A range of EDAs have been proposed and developed, both for continuous and discrete search spaces, and a number of successful applications have been reported. A recent book [1] reviews the field.

One of the appeals of EDAs is that the probability models can represent and *learn* the structure between the search variables. The earliest EDAs treated each variable independently [2,3]. Later EDAs allowed a structured relationship between the variables. This allows correlations between the variables to be maintained during search. Since the effectiveness of genetic algorithms, and most other heuristic search algorithms, is highly dependent on the move operators, the fact that EDAs can learn move operators is a very enticing feature.

Despite the appeal of EDAs and the reported successes, there are difficulties in applying them effectively. One difficulty, which is the primary issue of this paper, is that under certain circumstances certain EDAs can get into states from where they cannot find the optimum no matter how long they are run. This is because they have lost their diversity; it is analogous to fixation in a mutation-free genetic algorithm. Thus, to

T.P. Runarsson et al. (Eds.): PPSN IX, LNCS 4193, pp. 92–101, 2006.

apply EDAs effectively, the control parameters of the algorithm must be chosen to avoid this situation. However, this may be difficult to do. For independent-variable EDAs, it has been shown [4,5] that the appropriate settings of these control parameters is very different for different problems. For example, the learning rate in PBIL needs to be sufficiently small to insure that the optimum is found, and it must be exponentially small in the system size in some problems, but need only scale as low-order polynomial of the system size in others. This makes it very difficult to set this control parameter in advance. Similar results hold for UMDA, where the population size must grow as a problem-dependent function of the number variables; exponentially for some problems, polynomially in others.

It has not be known whether these results hold for EDAs with more complex variable structure. A number of different EDAs have been proposed, which are distinguished by the structure imposed on the variables and by the method used to learn the probability model. This makes theoretical analysis difficult, first because there are so many different models to analyze, and second, because the analysis of models which change their structure at each generation is difficult. Indeed, much of the theoretical work has focused on the simplest, independent-variable EDAs (e.g. [6,7,5]). An example of theoretic work on population sizing in a specific non-independent EDAs is [8].

It is worth emphasizing that although it is expected that the runtime of algorithms will depend very strongly on the problem, effective algorithms should work with fairly generic settings of the control parameters. Otherwise, one will have to dedicate substantial computational resources to searching control-parameter space, resources which could be applied to searching for the optimum using a more robust algorithm.

In this paper, two rigorous results are derived which hold for an entire class of EDAs. It is a fairly unrestricted class, including EDAs which learn structure, such as the Bayesian Optimization Algorithm (BOA) [9] in its simplest form, as well as simple EDAs such as UMDA [3] which is one of the earliest independent-variable EDAs, and many others. The first result concerns the expected diversity loss per generation when searching on a flat landscape, and the corresponding expected time to completely lose diversity (fixation). The second result is a lower bound on the minimum population size required to insure that the optimum is found when searching for a particular configuration on an otherwise flat landscape (the so-called *needle in a haystack* problem). Both results are universal for the entire class of EDAs.

2 Estimation of Distribution Algorithms

I will consider the search space to consist of L variables, all of which take values from some finite set $\mathcal{A}$, i.e. $\mathbf{x} = (x_1, x_2, \ldots, x_L) \in \mathcal{A}^L$. The goal is to find the configuration which maximize an objective function $f : \mathcal{A}^L \to \mathcal{R}$.

At the heart of the EDA is a class of probability functions from which a probability function is chosen at each generation. In general, this has two parts: the *structure* defines which variables interact with which, and the *parameters* define the form of the interaction. The structure is discrete and denoted $\mathcal{S}$; the parameters are continuous and denoted $\mathcal{P}$. To avoid confusion, the term *parameter* will always be used to refer to a parameter of the probability model; the term *control-parameter* will be used to refer to parameters of the algorithm, such as the population size.

To express this mathematically, the assumption of EDAs is that for each variable x_i, there is a set of variables, called its parents, on which it depends. Let $\pi(i)$ denote the set of parents of component i. The underlying assumption is that the joint probability of all the variables $P(\mathbf{x})$, factorizes.

$$P(\mathbf{x}) = \prod_{i=1}^{L} P(x_i|\mathbf{x}_{\pi(\mathbf{i})}). \quad (1)$$

Here, we use the shorthand $\mathbf{x}_{\pi(\mathbf{i})}$ to denote the vector consisting of just those components which are parents of i.

The set of parents for each variable is what constitutes the structure of the probability model. Once the structure has been determined, one needs to estimate values for each of the factors in equation (1). These values are what constitutes the parameters of the probability model.

The generic EDA is roughly as follows. Start with a random population of M vectors. Then implement a loop consisting of

1. Select N vectors using a selection method.
2. Learn the probability model $(\mathcal{S}, \mathcal{P})$ from the selected population.
3. Sample M vectors from the probability model.

There are many variations. Selection is often done by applying truncation selection to the sampled population. Alternatively, the selected vectors replace a fraction of the selected population from the previous generation rather than the entire population. Likewise, the probability model can be built from scratch at each generation, or or can use the model from the previous generation(s) to build the current model. Another source of variation in EDAs is in the allowed structure: UMDA treats each variable independently. MIMIC assumes a chain of interactions, so every variable except the root and the terminal variables are the parent of one node and the child of another. BOA uses a general directed acyclic graph to represent the structure. And there are many others.

2.1 SML-EDA: A Restricted Class of EDAs

In this work, we consider a restricted class of EDAs for which we will derive some simple results. We will need three assumptions.

Assumption 1. The probability distribution in each generation is built using only data which was sampled from the probability model of the previous generation.

Assumption 2. The parameters of the estimated model are chosen using maximum likelihood.

Assumption 3. The sample size M and the size of the population used to build the model N are of a constant ratio independent of the number of variables L.

Assumption 1 means that data in generation t can only affect data in generation $t+1$ through the probability model. This rules out taking data directly from previous generations to put into the current population. Thus, there can be no elitism or mixing of the population with populations from previous generations.

The results of this work apply irregardless of the mechanism used to generate the structure of the probability model. However, once the structure is chosen, Assumption 2 requires the parameters of the model are those which maximize the probability of the data given the probability model,

$$\mathcal{P}_{\text{ML}} = \text{argmax}_{\mathcal{P}} \, \text{prob}\,(\text{population}|(\mathcal{S}, \mathcal{P})). \tag{2}$$

This estimation is widely used, because it is easily computable from empirical frequencies. For example, once the structure of the model is determined, a typical model parameter will correspond to the probability that a particular component takes the particular value, given the value of its parents. If assumption 2 holds, this probability is estimated by the following ratio,

$$P(x_i|\mathbf{x}_{\pi(\mathbf{i})}) \approx \frac{N(x_i, \mathbf{x}_{\pi(\mathbf{i})})}{N(\mathbf{x}_{\pi(\mathbf{i})})}, \tag{3}$$

where $N(x, y)$ denotes the number of times in the data that x and y takes their values.

In this paper, we will explore two results which hold for all EDAs for which these two assumptions hold. For the purpose of this paper, we will refer to all such EDAs as SML-EDAs, to denote Simple, Maximum-Likelihood EDAs.

Definition 1. *The class of EDAs for which assumptions 1 and 2 hold are called SML-EDAs.*

This class includes a wide group of EDAs and can include EDAs which assume independent structure, EDAs which have non-trivial fixed structure, and EDAs which learn their structure from the data. Certainly many of the standard EDAs, such as UMDA, MIMIC, FDA, BOA, fall in this class in their simplest form.

There are two ways in which EDAs typically fail to be in the class SML-EDA. First, because they use data from several previous generations to generate the probability model. The second reason is that the parameters are not set using maximum likelihood. PBIL, for example would not be in this class because its values are estimated as a linear combination of the current values and the maximum likelihood ones. Mühlenbein and Mahnig [10] suggest setting parameters for FDA using a maximum posteriori method rather than maximum likelihood; if that is done the resulting EDA is not in this class.

Finally, in this work we are interested in asymptotic behavior for large L. Assumption 3 ensures that a single control parameter governs the population size. Under these three assumptions, the EDA works like this:

1. Initialize `sample_pop` to be a random population of size M;
2. **Repeat**
   (a) Produce `select_pop` by selecting N from `sample_pop`;
   (b) Learn the structure of the probability model $\mathcal{S}$ from `select_pop` by any means;
   (c) Learn the parameters of the probability model $\mathcal{P}$ from `select_pop` using equation (3).
   (d) Update `sample_pop` by sampling M vectors independently from the probability model defined by $(\mathcal{S}, \mathcal{P})$.
3. **Until** some stopping criterion met

3 Diversity Loss in SML-EDAs on a Flat Fitness Landscape

The first result concerns the rate of diversity loss in SML-EDAs on a flat landscape. To measure the diversity in a population of size N, we will use the *trace of empirical co-variance matrix*. Let ν_i^A be the empirical frequency at which the component i takes the value A, i.e.

$$\nu_i^A = \frac{1}{N} \sum_{\mu} \delta(x_i^{\mu} = A), \tag{4}$$

where x_i^{μ} is component i of population member μ, and δ is an indicator function; 1 if its argument is true, and 0 if its argument is false. The diversity measure we will use is,

$$v = \sum_i \frac{1}{|\mathcal{A}|} \sum_a \nu_i^a \left(1 - \nu_i^a\right), \tag{5}$$

where $|\mathcal{A}|$ is the number of values component x_i can take, which is assumed to be the same for all components.

Whenever the value of a component fixates, i.e. is the same in all members of a population, the corresponding $\sum_a \nu_i^a \left(1 - \nu_i^a\right)$ will be zero. So, complete fixation implies $v = 0$. The random population has the maximum value of v. Finally this is related to the covariance matrix which is defined as the expectation that two components both take the value A, minus the expectation that they take this value independently, summed over all values,

$$C_{ij} = \frac{1}{|\mathcal{A}|} \sum_a \left[\langle \delta(x_i = a)\delta(x_j = a)\rangle - \langle \delta(x_i = a)\rangle \langle \delta(x_j = a)\rangle\right] \tag{6}$$

where angled brackets $\langle \cdot \rangle$ denotes expectation. The quantity v_t is the trace of the empirical estimate of C at generation t.

Using this measure of diversity, it is trivial to derive the diversity loss on a flat landscape, on which all vectors have the same fitness. On a flat landscape, sampling M values followed by selection of a population of size N is equivalent to sampling a population of size N.

Theorem 1. *For EDAs in class SML-EDA on a flat landscape, the expected value of v is reduced in each generation by a factor of 1 minus the inverse population size,*

$$\langle v_t \rangle = \langle v_{t-1} \rangle \left(1 - \frac{1}{N}\right). \tag{7}$$

A detailed proof will be given elsewhere. To get from generation $t-1$ to t, there are two steps. First the probability distribution is created from the data. Second, a new population is created from the probability model. The proof is almost trivial. Starting from the value of v_{t-1}, the model is built. Since the parameters are set by maximum likelihood, the marginals are equal to the frequencies for each component. Then sampling is done. Since the landscape is flat, we can combine sampling with selecting, and replace that step with the single step of sampling N data vectors from the probability model. It is well known that empirical variance is reduced by a factor $(1 - 1/N)$ from the parent population. Thus $\langle v_t \rangle = v_{t-1}\left(1 - \frac{1}{N}\right)$. Finally, we average over the right-hand side to get the result.

This provides a prediction for the expected diversity loss which is universal for all EDA in the class SML-EDA,

$$\langle v_t \rangle = v_0 \left(1 - 1/N\right)^t , \tag{8}$$

which decays with characteristic time approximately equal to the population size for large N. Assuming a random initial population, $v_0 = L/|\mathcal{A}|(1 - 1/|\mathcal{A}|)$.

4 A Universal Bound for the Minimum Population Size in the Needle Problem

Next we consider an SML-EDA searching for a particular configuration on an otherwise flat landscape. This problem is sometimes called the *needle in the haystack* problem, or the *Needle* problem. I.e. there is one special state (the "needle") which has a high fitness value, and all other configurations have the same low fitness value.

Using the result from the previous section, it is possible to derive a lower bound for the minimum population size N needed to solve this problem. Let T_N be the time that the needle is first sampled. The shorthand $T_N = \infty$ will mean that the needle is never sampled. (Time is measured in units of iterations of the algorithm. One time-step refers to one cycle of selection, model building, and sampling.) We will assume, as above, that the search space consists of L variables, each of which takes $|\mathcal{A}|$ possible values. Asymptotics will be for large L; $|\mathcal{A}|$ is assumed to be a constant.

To derive a lower bound on the minimum population size required to ensure that the optimum is found, a bound can be derived for the probability that the needle is *never* sampled,

$$\text{prob}\left(T_N = \infty\right) \geq B(N, L). \tag{9}$$

Then, the follow holds.

Theorem 2. *In the limit that $L \to \infty$ such that $N^2 L |\mathcal{A}|^{-L} \to 0$,*

$$B(N, L) = 1 - O\left(|\mathcal{A}|^{-L/2}\right)$$

for any EDA in SML-EDA searching on the Needle problem.

This result shows that any SML-EDA will almost never find the needle if the population size is $o(\sqrt{|\mathcal{A}|^L/L})$. I.e. the population size must grow at least as fast as $\sqrt{|\mathcal{A}|^L/L}$ for the optimum to be found.

Theorem 2 will be proved in two steps. First, a time t^* is defined so that, if the algorithm has run for that length of time without finding the needle, it is highly likely that it never will find the needle. Next it is shown that if the population size grows (with L) sufficiently slowly, it is highly likely that the algorithm will run for t^* steps without finding the needle.

The first step towards proving Theorem 2 relies on the following result.

Lemma 1. *Let t^* be defined as*

$$t^* = -\frac{\frac{L}{2}\log(|\mathcal{A}|) + \log(LNv_0)}{\log(1-1/N)}. \tag{10}$$

If the needle has not been found after a time $t \geq t^*$, the probability that the needle will never be found is greater than $1-\epsilon$, where $\epsilon = |\mathcal{A}|^{-L/2}$. Mathematically, this is expressed,

$$\text{prob}\,(T_N = \infty | T_N > t^*) \geq 1 - |\mathcal{A}|^{-L/2}. \tag{11}$$

Proof. To compute $\text{prob}\,(T_N = \infty | T_N > t^*)$ first observe that at time t, the expected variance is given by equation (8) and will be very small. Because the variance is positive, the fact that the expected variance is small means that the actual variance must also be small with a high probability. The largest the actual variance can be with a probability greater than or equal to $1-\epsilon$ is $\langle v \rangle / \epsilon$, for any ϵ between 0 and 1 (see, for example, [11]). In other words,

$$\text{prob}\left[v(t) \leq \frac{\langle v(r) \rangle}{\epsilon}\right] \geq 1 - \epsilon. \tag{12}$$

The idea is to choose t^* to be large enough so that

$$v_t \leq \frac{\langle v_t \rangle}{\epsilon} \leq \frac{1}{N}\left(1 - \frac{1}{N}\right) \tag{13}$$

The reason is that if v_t is so small, there must be fixation at every component except possibly one component. (Fixation of a component i means that the variable x_i takes the same value in all vectors in the population.) Since maximum likelihood is used to build the probability model, once fixation happens at any component, that component will remain fixed for the rest of the run of the algorithm. If $L-1$ components are fixed, the needle will only be sampled if they are fixed at values found in the needle. The probability of this is no more than $|\mathcal{A}|^{-(L-1)}$. Thus, we can write

$$\text{prob}\left(T_N = \infty | T_N > t^*, v_t \leq 1/N - 1/N^2\right) > 1 - |\mathcal{A}|^{-(L-1)}. \tag{14}$$

This is the probability that the needle is never found assuming that the needle has not been found up to time greater than t^*, and given that v_t is small enough that we know that $L-1$ components are fixed.

We are not certain that v_t appropriately small, it is just probable so. However, the probability that v_t is small as we assume is ϵ. Take

$$\epsilon = |\mathcal{A}|^{-L/2}. \tag{15}$$

Then it is the leading order term and

$$\text{prob}\,(T_N = \infty | T_N > t^*) = 1 - O(\epsilon). \tag{16}$$

It only remains to compute t^*. This is done by setting equation (13) to be equality, and solving equation (8) for t. The solution is equation (10).

□

The next step in proving Theorem 2 is to consider the probability of not finding the needle during the t^* steps.

Lemma 2. *Let t^* be defined as in equation (10). The probability that the needle is not found after t^* steps obeys*

$$\mathrm{prob}\,(T_N > t^*) \geq 1 - \frac{N^2}{|\mathcal{A}|^L}\left[\frac{L}{2}\log\left(|\mathcal{A}|\right) + \log\left(LN\right)\right]. \tag{17}$$

Proof. Choose t^* as in equation 10. Since random search is optimal for this problem[1], the probability that SML-EDA does not find the needle in time t^* obeys

$$\mathrm{prob}\,(T_N > t^*) \geq \left(1 - |\mathcal{A}|^{-L}\right)^{t^* N}. \tag{18}$$

(Remembering that N vectors are considered at each time-step.)

The result is found by putting into this equation the value for t^*, and using the convexity of log and exp and other standard inequalities to simplify the expression, □

Proof of Theorem 2

Proof. The probability of never finding the needle can be decomposed into,

$$\mathrm{prob}\,(T_N = \infty) = \mathrm{prob}\,(T_N = \infty | T_N > t^*)\,\mathrm{prob}\,(T_N > t^*). \tag{19}$$

with t^* defined as previously. Lemma 1 gives a lower bound for the first factor on the right side of equation (19). Lemma 2 gives a lower bound for the second factor. Combining them gives the following,

$$\mathrm{prob}\,(T_N = \infty) \geq 1 - |\mathcal{A}|^{-(L/2)} - N^2|\mathcal{A}|^{-L}\left[\frac{L}{2}\log\left(|\mathcal{A}|\right) + \log\left(LN\right)\right] \tag{20}$$

$$+ \text{ higher order terms in } |\mathcal{A}|^{-L}. \tag{21}$$

If in the limit that $L \to \infty$, N grows sufficiently slowly that the third term vanishes, then the probability of never finding the needle will go to 1. Thus, if

$$N = o\left(\frac{|\mathcal{A}|^{L/2}}{\sqrt{L}}\right), \tag{22}$$

the leading term in equation 20 will be $1 - |\mathcal{A}|^{-L/2}$ and as $L \to \infty$ the needle will never be found. □

5 The Expected Runtime for the Needle Problem and the Limits of Universality

The content of Section 4 is basically if the algorithm runs for time t^* without finding the needle, the algorithm has likely fixated and will never find the needle. Since number

[1] Among algorithms which make no attempt to prevent visiting the same configuration multiple times.

vectors processed is tN which must be of order $|\mathcal{A}|^L$ for the needle to be found, N must be approximately the size of $|\mathcal{A}|^L/t^*$ for the needle to be found. This result is *universal*, it holds for the entire class SML-EDA.

The next task is to show that when the population size is sufficiently large, the probability of finding the optimum approaches one, and to produce an estimate of the run time when N is large enough so that the needle is typically found. It is not clear that this can be done for the entire class SML-EDA. Lemma 1 gives a universal upper bound on the search time *given the needle is found*.

Corollary 1. *If the needle is found, the time to find it is bounded above by* t^* *with probability* $1 - |\mathcal{A}|^{-L/2}$.

However, this is not very informative. If the population size is smaller than the critical value, as given in equation 22, this bound is not useful, since the needle will almost never be found. If the population grows much faster than the critical value, it is likely that this bound is not tight. For example, if the population size $N = O(|\mathcal{A}|^L)$ it is likely that the optimum will be found in the first few generations. If the population size obeys the critical scaling, $N^2 = O(|\mathcal{A}|^L/L)$, Corollary 1 suggests that the algorithm is efficient; the runtime is asymptotically the same as random search. However, the results herein are not sufficient to show that the probability of finding the optimum is needle is close to one in this case.

The reason that it is not possible to investigate the regime in which the optimum is find using the methods of this paper, is that the particular statistic, v_t gives one-sided information. When it is small, there is definitely fixation, independent of the structure of the probability model. However, when it is near its initial value, that does *not imply that there is no fixation* in models with non-trivial structure. As an example, consider a chain model with binary variables. Each variable x_i can take the values 0 or 1, and the parent of variable i is node $i-1$. Variable 1 is a root and has no parent. In other words, the assumed probability model is $P(\mathbf{x}) = P(x_1)\prod_{i=2}^{L} P(x_i|x_{i-1})$. Suppose it fixates such that $P(x_1) = 1/2$, $P(x_i = 1|x_{i-1} = 0) = 1$ and $P(x_i = 0|x_{i-1} = 1) = 1$. The only vectors which can be generated are 01010... and 101010.... This fixation would be totally invisible to the statistic v_t which would continue to equal its initial value.

One conclusion is that convergence conditions will not be universal, but will be particular to the EDA. (This paper is essentially about non-convergence conditions.) A particular statistic, sensitive to the type of probability model might be necessary. For example, the statistic used here is appropriate for SML-UMDA, for which it can be shown that if the population size N and runtime T obey $TN = O(|\mathcal{A}|^L)$ and $T/N = O(|\mathcal{A}|^{-L\delta})$ for $\delta > 0$, the algorithm behaves asymptotically like random search on the Needle problem and is therefore efficient. For other EDAs other statistics may be required to study algorithmic efficiency. Alternatively, it is possible that the decay of some general property of the covariance matrix, e.g. its rank, may be used to show convergence results for the general class SML-EDA, but that remains to be seen.

6 Conclusions

With inappropriate settings, many EDAs can reach a state from which the probability of ever finding the optimum is zero. This is due to diversity loss which cannot be restored.

If any component of the data vectors does not take one of its allowed values anywhere in the entire population, that value can never be restored. If that value is required in the optimum, the optimum will never be sampled. The flat landscape is the simplest problem in which this can be studied. We have shown that this diversity loss is the same for a whole class of EDAs. A consequence of this is that for a problem which is almost everywhere flat, such as the Needle problem, the probability of diversity loss before the optimum is sampled is also universal for the class, and we have shown that it requires an exponentially large population size to avoid this.

It is important to go beyond these results. In many other search problems, the landscape will not be flat, but there will be many directions which are essentially flat. It was shown in UMDA[5] and PBIL [4] that the rate of diversity loss relative to the rate of search in non-flat directions helped to understand how control parameters needed to be set to ensure a reasonable probability of finding the optimum. Presumably the same will be true in arbitrary EDAs. However, unlike diversity loss, I expect that search in the non-flat dimensions not to be universal, but to depend on the structure of the probability model. This remains to be investigated.

References

1. Larrañaga, P., Lozano, J.A.: Estimation of Distribution Algorithms, A New Tool for Evolutionary Computation. Kluwer Academic Publishers (2002)
2. Baluja, S.: Population-based incremental learning: A method for integrating genetic search based function optimization and competive learning. Technical Report CMU-CS-94-163, Computer Science Department, Carnegie Mellon University (1994)
3. Mühlenbein, H., Paaß, G.: From recombination of genes to the estimation of distributions i: Binary parameters. In: Proceedings of PPSN IV. (1996) 178–187
4. Shapiro, J.L.: The sensitivity of pbil to its learning rate and how detailed balance can remove it. In Jong, K.A.D., Poli, R., Rowe, J.E., eds.: Foundations of Genetic Algorithms 7. Morgan Kaufmann (2003) 115–132
5. Shapiro, J.L.: The detailed balance principle in estimation of distribution algorhithm. Evolutionary Computation **13**(1) (2005) 99–124
6. Droste, S.: Not all linear functions are equally difficult for the compact genetic algorithm. In: GECCO'05, ACM (2005) 679–686
7. Gonzalez, C., Lozano, J., Larrañaga, P.: Mathematical modelling of umcac algorithm with tournament selection: Behaviour on linear and quadratic functions. International Journal of Approximate Reasoning **31**(3) (2002) 313–340
8. Pelikan, M., Goldberg, D.E., Cantú-Paz, E.: Bayesian optimization algorithm, population sizing, and time to converge. In: Proceedings of GECCO 2000. (2000) 275–282
9. Pelikan, M.: Bayesian optimization algorithm: From single level to hierarchy. PhD thesis, University of Illinois at Urbana-Champaign, Urbana, IL (2002) Also IlliGAL Report No. 2002023.
10. Mühlenbein, H., Mahnig, T.: Evolutionary computation and beyond. In Uesaka, Y., Kanerva, P., Asoh, H., eds.: Foundations of Real-World Intelligence. CLSI Publications (2001) 123–186
11. Motwani, R., Raghavan, P.: Randomized Algorithms. Cambridge University Press (1995)

Information Perspective of Optimization

Yossi Borenstein and Riccardo Poli

University of Essex, Colchester, UK
{yboren, rpoli}@essex.ac.uk

Abstract. In this paper we relate information theory and Kolmogorov Complexity (KC) to optimization in the black box scenario. We define the set of all possible decisions an algorithm might make during a run, we associate a function with a probability distribution over this set and define accordingly its *entropy*. We show that the expected KC of the *set* (rather than the function) is a better measure of problem difficulty. We analyze the effect of the entropy on the expected KC. Finally, we show, for a restricted scenario, that any permutation closure of a single function, the finest level of granularity for which a No Free Lunch Theorem can hold [7], can be associated with a particular value of entropy. This implies bounds on the expected performance of an algorithm on members of that closure.

1 Introduction

General purpose algorithms (also known as metaheuristics, black-box algorithms or randomized search heuristics [9]) are often used when either the problem is not well defined or when there is insufficient knowledge (or resources) to construct specific algorithms [9]. In the most general case, a randomized search heuristic can be represented as a mapping from a multi-set of previously visited points to a new (not necessarily unvisited) point in the search space. Wolpert and Macready [10], Vose [8] as well as Droste, Jansen and Wegener [3,9] suggested accordingly a formal model for black-box algorithms which generalizes most, if not all, existing randomized search heuristics.

There are various theoretical approaches to analyze the expected performance of metaheuristics. Wolpert and Macready [10], using their model, proved that over all possible problems, all algorithms have the same performance. It was later shown that the same result holds even for a smaller set: the sharpened No Free Lunch Theorem (NFLT) [7] proves that a NFL result holds for any set of functions which is closed under permutation.

Rather than focusing on a set of functions, compressibility or Kolmogorov complexity is associated with a particular object. It is defined as the length of the shortest program that can generate a string and halts. When the string represents a problem, it is argued that compressible strings are associated with easy problems whereas random, incompressible strings, with difficult ones [6].

In [2], based on the information landscape framework, we derived a new way to measure the KC of a fitness function and showed the connection to the NFLTs. However, this framework was based, mainly, on a first order approximation. This paper removes this restriction. In section 2 we introduce the notion of Kolmogorov complexity – a way to measure the complexity of a fitness function f. Section 3 defines the information

T.P. Runarsson et al. (Eds.): PPSN IX, LNCS 4193, pp. 102–111, 2006.

content of f. Then, we define a way to measure its entropy, or as we put it, to quantify the amount of information a function contains. The connection between the expected difficulty of the function and its amount of information is explored in section 4. The implication of this on the sharpened NFLTs is given in section 5.

2 Kolmogorov Complexity

The Kolmogorov complexity [6] $K : \{0,1\}^* \rightarrow \mathbb{N}$ is a function from finite binary strings of arbitrary length to the natural numbers $\mathbb{N}$. It is defined on 'objects' represented by binary strings but can be extended to other types like functions.

The KC of an object, x, is defined as the length of the shortest program that prints x and halts. The program can be implemented by any universal programming language (e.g., C++, Java), in which a universal Turing Machine can be implemented. The choice of universal computer (programming language) may change the KC of x only by a fixed additive constant (which depends on the length of code required to simulate a universal computer by another). For this reason, we fix our programming language to an arbitrary language (e.g., C) and define KC w.r.t. that language. The KC of a string x is defined as: $K(x) := min_p\ l(p)$, where p is a program that prints x and halts and $l(p)$ denotes the length of program p. This definition suffices for the purpose of this paper – a more accurate definition is given in [6,5].

A simple or regular object x has a low KC. For example, a string representing a sequence consisting of n 1s (i.e., "111...1") can be represented by $K(x) = O(\log n)$ bits. The size of the program depends on the number of bits needed to encode the number n. A random object, on the other hand, with very high probability, can only be represented by $K(x) = n + O(\log n)$. That is, the shortest program to print x will be: *"print x"*. The KC of an object can only be used as a *conceptual* measure of its complexity, *it cannot be computed*. That is, it is possible to analyze the properties of a random object, or even to prove that the majority of objects are random but, given an object x, it is not possible to prove that it is random.

The notion of KC can be extended to account for functions as well. Let $f : X \rightarrow Y$ be a mapping between two finite spaces X and Y, then:

$$K(f) = min_{p_f \in \{0,1\}^*}\{l(p_f) : \forall x \in X\ p_f(x) = f(x)\}$$

where p_f is a program that given an input x returns the value $f(x)$. Any function, in the worst case, can be represented by explicitly listing the co-domain value for each domain (e.g.,*if (x="0000000000") return 1230 else...*). If the function is random, this is the *only* way to represent it. Other functions, like flat functions, can be represented in code with a constant length, e.g., *"return 0"*.

The KC of a function is sometimes used as an indicator for the expected difficulty of the function for optimization algorithms. A random function contains no regularities. For this reason, no algorithm, regardless of the search strategy, is expected to optimize it efficiently. A function with a low KC, on the other hand, contains regularities, that, in some scenarios, can be exploited by a search algorithm to find an optimal solution quickly.

Some limitation of using KC to asses problem difficulty were studied in [1]. It was concluded that KC measures how different (either better or *worse*) the expected performance (over a function) is likely to be from a random search. Moreover, some examples of difficult functions which have low KC were given. Nearly constant functions, like the needle-in-a-haystack, have minimal KC. Nevertheless, they are very difficult to optimize. This paper addresses particularly the last limitation. In this paper we make the following assumptions: Firstly, we focus, on functions which contain only a *small* number of optima. More precisely, by small, we will mean logarithmic in the size of the search space. Secondly, we assume that the algorithm has no a priori bias towards specific regions of the search space. We do not exclude deterministic decisions making – we assume, however, that the initial starting points are random. In the following section, we will define the *information content* of a function, and we will use this in section 4 to suggest a new way to calculate the KC.

3 Information Content of a Function

Let $f : X \to Y$, where X denotes a finite search space and Y is finite. Let F denote all possible fitness functions. Using Vose's notation [8], random search heuristics can be thought of as an initial collection of elements $\Psi_k \in \Psi$ chosen from some search space X together with a transition rule τ which produces from the collection Ψ_k another collection Ψ_l. The search is a sequence of iterations of τ: $\Psi_k \xrightarrow{\tau} \Psi_l \xrightarrow{\tau} \cdots$. A collection of elements is a multiset of X. We use the term *search-state* to denote a particular collection. The set of all possible such collections, the state-space, is denoted by Ψ. Without loss of generality, we assume a notion of order in Ψ. Note that we do not consider the dynamics of the algorithm and hence adjacent states do not correspond to adjacent time steps.

We restrict our attention to search algorithms for which τ depends completely on the current state, that is: $\tau : \Psi \times F \to \Psi$. Heuristics such as particle swarm optimization include other parameters such as, for example, velocity vectors. We do not consider, at this stage, such algorithms.

In reality, the transition rule $\tau(\Psi_i, f)$ if often a composition $\tau = \chi \circ \xi(\Psi_i, f)$ where $\xi(\Psi_i, f)$ denotes a *selection* operator, and χ can be thought of as the *exploration* operator. The selection phase identifies solutions with high fitness value, the exploration operator samples accordingly new solutions from X. *This section focuses solely on the selection phase of the search.*

In order to make a clear distinction between the two operators (stages) it is useful to think of an output of the selection operator, a multiset, d, which represents a possible way to choose (or select) solutions from Ψ_i. For example, in GAs, given a particular population, Ψ_i, d includes a possible mating pool. For a (1+1) evolutionary strategy, d can be either the parent or the offspring[1]. Given a state Ψ_i, we denote by S^i all possible ways of selection points. That is, S^i is a set of multisets, each multiset, $d \in S^i$, corresponds to one possible way of selecting points.

[1] The notion of a state, in that case, is not natural but, nevertheless, correct. Each state, in our notation, contains *two* solutions, then selection is applied to select one of them, and a mutation is applied in order to achieve the next state.

The dependency of the performance of a search algorithm on f is reflected by a probability distribution, P_f^i, that the selection mechanism defines for each state over S^i. The particular multiset of solutions, d, that the algorithm selects, being the only argument for the exploration operator, *defines* the next state of the search. We define the *information content* of f as the set of all such distributions.

Definition 1. *The information content of the function f is the set $\mathcal{P}_f = \{P_f^1, P_f^2, ..., P_f^n\}$ which gives for each state, Ψ_i the probability distribution P_f^i used in the selection phase.*

Usually, the algorithm does not define explicitly a probability distribution over S^i, rather, a distribution over single solutions from Ψ_i. For example, binary tournament selection defines the probability of selecting one of two possible solutions as follows:

$$\Pr_{\text{trnmnt}}\{x \mid \{x, y\}\} = \delta(f(x) > f(y)) + 0.5\delta(f(x) = f(y)) \tag{1}$$

where the function $\delta(\texttt{expr})$ returns 1 if `expr` is true, and 0 otherwise. This is used for a state (population) bigger than two points, by selecting, iteratively, uniformly at random, two points from Ψ_i and applying equation 1:

$$\Pr(x \mid \Psi_i, f) = \Pr\{x, x\} + \sum_{x \neq y} \Pr\{x, y\} \cdot \Pr_{\text{trnmnt}}\{x \mid \{x, y\}\} \tag{2}$$

Finally, P_f^i, the probability of selecting a particular multiset, d, is obtained as follows:

$$P_f^i(d \mid \Psi_i, f) = \prod_{j<|d|} \Pr(d_j \mid \Psi_i, f). \tag{3}$$

Rather than calculating the probability of selecting a particular multiset on a particular state ($P_f^i(d)$), we can measure the probability of obtaining particular sequence of decisions – this gives a full account (when, to reiterate, all the other parameters of the algorithm are fixed) for the expected performance. Let $\mathbb{D} = S^0 \times S^1 \times \cdots \times S^n$, and $D \in \mathbb{D}$ a particular decision set. Let R be a random variable taking values from $\mathbb{D}$. The probability $\mathcal{P}_f$ that the algorithm is consistent with D is:

$$\mathcal{P}_f(R = D) = \prod_{d \in D} P_f^i(d)$$

In order to understand the meaning of the distribution $\mathcal{P}_f$, it is important to explain the connection between a deterministic selection mechanism, decision set and fitness functions. For deterministic selection mechanism, f and D are synonymous: there is only one decision set which corresponds to a particular fitness function. The set of all possible fitness functions (F) corresponds therefore to a set of possible decision sets $\mathcal{D} \subset \mathbb{D}$. For stochastic selection mechanisms, a uniform P_f corresponds to choosing at each state, Ψ_i, $d \in S^i$ uniformly, at random, this can be thought of as running a deterministic search algorithm BUT choosing $f \in F$ uniformly, at random.[2] The NFLTs

[2] Assuming that the algorithm is consistent, i.e., given the same state, it always makes the same decision.

Fitness Function

X	f(x)
000	6
001	5
010	5
011	3
100	2
101	2
110	2
111	7

Information Content

X	000	001	010	011	100	101	110	111
000		1	1	1	1	1	1	0
001	0		0.5	1	1	1	1	0
010	0	0.5		1	1	1	1	0
011	0	0	0		1	1	1	0
100	0	0	0	0		0.5	0.5	0
101	0	0	0	0	0.5		0.5	0
110	0	0	0	0	0.5	0.5		0
111	1	1	1	1	1	1	1	

Possible Decision Matrix

X	000	001	010	011	100	101	110	111
000		L	L	L	L	L	L	U
001			U	L	L	L	L	U
010				L	L	L	L	U
011					L	L	L	U
100						U	L	U
101							L	U
110								U
111								

Fig. 1. Matrix representation of the information content of a function and a possible decision set

[7] imply that the expected performance, in such case, is that of a random search. The distribution $\mathcal{P}_f$ corresponds therefore to the level of randomness in the decision making of the algorithm. We define the entropy of f, in order to measure this[3]:

Definition 2. *Let Ψ denote the state-space of the algorithm. The entropy $H(f)$ of f corresponds to the entropy of P_f as defined by the algorithm.*

$$H(f) \equiv \sum_{D \in \mathbb{D}} P_f(D) \log 1/P_f(D)$$

While $K(f)$ measures how regular a function is, and thus implies how difficult it is to optimize the function, $H(f)$ measures the hardness of the search from a different perspective. It explicitly measures the randomness induced by the way an algorithm is using the function. The higher the rate of random decisions the algorithm is expected to make, the closer the performance will be to a random search.

3.1 Making It Concrete

The size of $|\Psi|$ and $|\Psi_i|$ for realistic search algorithms is usually bounded. Genetic algorithms usually use a population of fixed size, the size of a tabu-list is bounded and local-searchers often consider only two solutions at any given time. In order to have a more concrete formulation we will restrict our attention to algorithms that use a comparison of pairs of solutions in the search space.

Each state Ψ_i corresponds, therefore, to a pair of solutions (e.g., $\{x_i, x_j\}$) from which the algorithm chooses one. It follows that the number of all possible states $|\Psi| = |X|^2$, and that for each state there are $|S_i| = 2$ possible choices. In this case, if we consider various local searchers, equations 1 and 2 coincide, and therefore:

$$P_f^i(\{x\} \mid \{x, y\}) = \Pr_{\text{trnmnt}}\{x \mid \{x, y\}\} \tag{4}$$

[3] In order to have a complete understanding one has to consider the probability of obtaining a particular state during a run and calculate the expected entropy accordingly. At this stage, we assume that the uniform distribution gives a good indication to that.

Figure 1 illustrates this notion for a search space of size 8. It represents a fitness function f, the information content of the function and a possible decision set. The information content of the function is represented in the form of a matrix, in which the area above the diagonal corresponds to the search-states Ψ. Each entry in the matrix corresponds to the probability P_f^i, defined by equation 4 of choosing either of the $|S^i| = 2$ possible solutions. The decision set is defined as a possible realization of the distributions given in the information-content matrix. We used the abbreviation 'U' and 'L' to denote up and left, respectively, that is, to point the particular solutions in the matrix, which were selected.

This scenario corresponds directly to various kinds of local search algorithms. However, it can also *approximate* some population-based search algorithms, as long as they use a binary selection operator. For example, a GA with binary tournament selection, or even Memetic algorithms. *In any case, from this point on, we will consider only this restricted scenario.* Whenever Ψ is implied we assume the comparison of pairs of solutions. P_f^i is defined as in equation 4. Under this assumptions we can calculate the entropy of an algorithm.

Theorem 1. *Let* X, Ψ, f, P_f^i *defined as before. Define* $r(f) = \sum_i \delta(P_f^i = 0.5)$. *Then,* $H(f) = r(f)$.

Proof. Since for $P_i^f = 0.5$ the algorithm chooses with equal probability one of the two solutions, $P_f(D) = \prod_{d \in D} P_f^i(d)$ is uniformly distributed. Also, the number of possible decision sets is exponential with the number of entries $P_i^f = 0.5$. It follows, therefore, that $\forall_D \; P_f(D) = 1/2^{r(f)}$ which gives, $H(f) \equiv \sum_{D \in \mathbb{D}} 1/2^{r(f)} \log 2^{r(f)} = r(f)$ □

The entropy of the landscape corresponds to the number of states in which the algorithm is forced to take a random decision. The entropy will be maximal (i.e., equals $|\Psi|$) for a flat landscape (in which $\forall_i P_f^i = 0.5$). In this case, the search will be random. Note that while low entropy indicates non-random search, this does not necessarily correspond to efficient search – it simply implies that the algorithm searches according to a certain bias. The efficiency of the search depends on the matching between this bias and the problem at hand.

4 Information and Problem Hardness

In section 2 we defined the KC of f and argued that high KC implies hardness. Section 3 on the other hand, focused on the entropy of f for stochastic search algorithms. It seems that the two notions define hardness from two different perspectives: the first, $K(f)$, relates to some intrinsic property of f which measures how regular the function is. The second, $H(f)$, measures the level of randomness as reflected by the way an algorithm uses f. In this section we show that the KC of the expected *decision set* of the algorithm, integrates these two measures.

As a first step, note that given the fitness function f, we can use a fixed size program to generate the information content of f (i.e., equation 4). This, in turn, can be used to generate all the elements of the decision set which correspond to entries with a value different from 0.5. The KC of the decision vector is equivalent therefore to that of f plus the complexity which corresponds to the random decisions the algorithm makes.

The problem arises as to how to measure the part corresponding to the random decisions. It seems that it can be better described by $H(f)$ (which relates to the distribution) rather than the Kolmogorov complexity which measures the complexity of a single object. The two measurements of information, however, are closely related. The following result is taken from [6]:

Lemma 1. *Let $x = x_1x_2...$ where the individual x_i are realizations of some random variable X_i, distributed according to some distribution P. If all outcomes $X_1, X_2, ...$ are independently identically distributed (i.i.d.) with for all i, $P(X_i = 1) = p$ for some $p \in [0,1]$, the expected Kolmogorov complexity of x is:*

$$K(x_{[1:n]}) = n \cdot H(p) + o(n) \tag{5}$$

where $H(p) = -p \log p - (1-p)\log(1-p)$ is the binary entropy such that $0 \leq H(p) \leq 1$.

Lemma 1 makes the connection clear. Since the elements in the decision set which correspond to the random decision the algorithm makes are i.i.d., equation 5 gives us the expected KC for such a string. The following is a simple corollary of that.

Corollary 1. *Let X, Ψ, f, P_f^i defined as before. Let D denote the expected decision set. $K(D) > r(f)$*

Proof. The decision set D can be decomposed into two subsets: let $D^1 = \{d|P_f^i(d) \neq 0.5\}$ and $D^{0.5} = \{d|P_f^i(d) = 0.5\}$. Clearly, $K(D|f) = K(D^{0.5}) + O(1)$ (equation 4 and a simple loop can generate, given f the subset D^1). But, following lemma 1, $K(D^{0.5}) = |D^{0.5}| \cdot H(0.5) + o(|D^{0.5}|) = r(f) \cdot 1 + o(r(f))$. Which gives: $K(D) \geq K(D|f) > r(f)$ □

In order to understand the implication of this lemma, consider the expected hardness of a needle-in-a-haystack (NIAH). The NIAH describes a landscape in which all the points in the search space have the same fitness except the global optimum which has a higher one. It is known to be a very difficult problem.

For a search space of size n let f_{needle} denote the NIAH and $\mathcal{P}_f$ the corresponding information content. The average description length of f_{needle} (and therefore of $\mathcal{P}_f$ as well) is $O(\log n)$. The high compressibility of the function in contrast to its known hardness is usually given as a counterexample to the use of Kolmogorov complexity as a measure of problem difficulty [1].

This apparent contradiction can be resolved by considering the algorithm perspective of the NIAH landscape. The algorithm does not see a flat landscape. At each time step it has to make a concrete decision, namely to decide which solution to sample next. It therefore has to "interpret" the flat landscape to a landscape which contains concrete information. In other words, it selects uniformly, at random $D \in \mathbb{D}$ and selects solutions accordingly.

Following the previous lemma consider the Kolmogorov complexity of the expected decision set vs. the fitness function:

$$K(D_{needle}) \geq r(f_{needle}) = 2^{((n-1)\cdot(n-2))/2} \gg \log n$$

This illustrates the magnitude of difference between the current approach to calculate the Kolmogorov complexity of a landscapes and the one suggested in this paper. The NIAH, however, is an extreme example. Generally, moving from low entropy ($H(f) = 0$) to maximum entropy ($H(f) = |\Psi|$) we should obtain many intermediate values.

5 Information and the Sharpened NFLT

In the previous section we showed that $K(D_f) > H(f)$, where D_f is the expected decision set, given the function f. Interestingly, $H(f)$ depends on the *fitness distribution* of f alone. This allows us to make an important observation regarding the sharpened NFLT [7]. In the following we give a brief summary of the sharpened NFLT and then show how it is connected with our results.

Let $f : X \to Y$ be a function and $\sigma : X \to X$ be a permutation (i.e., σ is one-to-one and onto). The permutation σf of f is the function $\sigma f : X \to Y$ defined by $\sigma f(x) = f(\sigma^{-1}(x))$.

Define a set F of functions to be closed under permutation if for every $f \in F$, every permutation of f is also in F. Schumacher, Vose and Whitley [7] proved that the permutation closure of a single function is the finest level of granularity at which a NFL result can hold.

English [4] named each set F, a block. A distribution which is uniform within each block is called block uniform. The space of all possible problems can be divided into blocks. A block uniform distribution is necessary and sufficient for NFLT in search.

Each block (i.e., a set F) can be associated with a particular value of entropy. For each $f \in F$, $H(f)$ is:

$$H(f) = \Sigma_i \binom{|y = i|}{2} \tag{6}$$

Equation 6 counts all possible pairs of solutions which have the same fitness. It follows that the entropy depends solely on the *fitness distribution* of f. Since the permutation operator does not affect the fitness distribution of a function, all the functions which belong to F have the same fitness distribution and, therefore, the same entropy, this proves the following result:

Theorem 2. *Let F be a set of functions which is c.u.p. $\forall_{f,g \in F}\ H(f) = H(g)$. We denote the entropy of F, $H(F) = H(f \mid f \in F)$*

5.1 A *Qualitative* Plot of the Expected Hardness of a Problem

Let F be c.u.p. defined over the metric space (X, d). In this section we would like to analyze how the variance of expected performances changes for different values of $H(F)$. Let us start with $H(F) \approx |\Psi|$. It follows from corollary 1 that $\forall_{f \in F} K(D_f) > |\Psi|$, this corresponds to a random function and hence, *all the functions* in the set are expected to be very difficult to optimize. The variance, however, is expected to be very low – irrespectively of the algorithm, the expected performance on *any* function is expected to be the same, that of a random search.

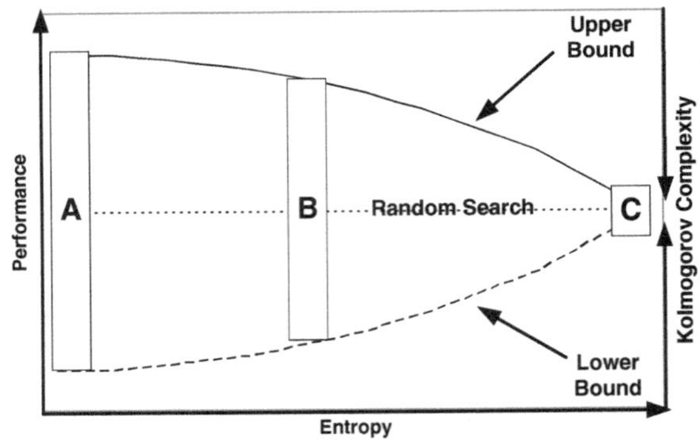

Fig. 2. The variance of expected performance as a function of the entropy. Each rectangle represents a block uniform on which a NFL result holds. The space of all possible problems is the union of all blocks. Each block is associated with a particular entropy. (A) represents a block with minimal entropy and maximum variance, (C) maximum entropy and no variance (B) is in between.

On the other hand, for $H(F) \approx 0$ we do not have any bound on the performance. We can choose, for example, a function f_1 such that $K(D_{f_1})$ is minimal. The low KC suggests that there exists an algorithm, a, which is *the best possible algorithm* to solve f. This implies that f is expected to be very easy to a, the question arises, though, as to how well the same algorithm performs on other functions from F. It is important to remember that KC gives an indication to the best performance that a realistic algorithm can have over one, specific function. It does not tell us how well the same algorithm may perform on other functions. From the sharpened NFLTs on the other hand, we know that for each problem (e.g., f_1) on which an algorithm (e.g., a) performs better than random search there exists another problem (e.g., f_2), in the same set, on which it performs as badly. It is easy to construct two functions $f_1, f_2 \in F_2$ such that one is expected to be very easy and the other very hard. For example, let:

$$f_1(x) = x$$
$$f_2(x) = \begin{cases} n+1 & \text{if } x = 0, \\ x & \text{otherwise} \end{cases}$$

We showed that for $H(F) = |\Psi|$ the variance of possible performance values is small, and, on the other hand, for $H(F) = 0$ the variance is high. More generally, moving from $H(F) = 0$ to $H(F) = |\Psi|$ the variance becomes smaller and smaller. The reason for that is derived directly from the NFLTs. An algorithm is expected to perform well on a problem (better than random search) *only if* it is aligned with the problem. The same algorithm, in that case, is misaligned with another problem and, therefore, is expected to perform badly (i.e., worse than a random search), to the same extent. The entropy $H(f)$ can be thought of as measuring how *unbiased* an algorithm is. The higher $H(f)$ the more random decisions the algorithm makes, the less bias it will be.

To summarize, corollary 1 shows that $K(D_f) > H(f)$: the entropy of a function is a lower bound to its expected KC. Theorem 2 associates each group of functions which is c.u.p with a particular entropy. Thus, each group of functions for which the NFLTs hold, are associated with a certain value of entropy which gives a bound on the expected performance of any algorithm when solving members of that group.

So, on one hand, given the entropy we have a qualitative boundary on the performance of the most efficient algorithm on the easiest landscape. On the other hand, from the sharpened NFLT we know that if the algorithm performs well on one problem there exists another problem on which it performs as badly. Combining these two aspects we can give a qualitative plot of the expected performance of the best algorithm over all possible problems w.r.t. their entropy. This is illustrated in figure 2.

6 Conclusion

This paper has provided a connection between information theory, Kolmogorov complexity and the study of optimization algorithms. The information content of a fitness function was defined, its expected effect on performance was analyzed and a novel way to compute the KC of a fitness function was introduced. This has led to new observations regarding the sharpened NFLTs: we proved that each closure can be associated with a particular entropy which implies bounds on its Kolmogorov complexity and consequently, expected difficulty. In order to make some of these connections we had to limit our attention to particular kind of algorithms (section 3.1). In future research, we plan to generalize our results.

References

1. Y. Borenstein and R. Poli. Kolmogorov complexity, optimization and hardness. CEC 2006.
2. Y. Borenstein and R. Poli. No free lunch, Kolmogorov Complexity and the information landscape. In *Proceedings of IEEE CEC 2005*, volume 3, 2005.
3. S. Droste, T. Jansen, and I. Wegener. Upper and lower bounds for randomized search heuristics in black-box optimization. *ECCC*, (048), 2003.
4. T. M. English. On the structure of sequential search: Beyond "no free lunch". In J. Gottlieb and G. R. Raidl, editors, *EvoCOP 2004*, volume 3004, pages 95–103. Springer, 2004.
5. P. Grunwald and P. Vitanyi. Shannon information and kolmogorov complexity. *IEEE Transactions on Information Theory*, 2004. In Review.
6. P. Grunwald and P. Vitanyi. Algorithmic information theory. In *Handbook on the Philosophy of Information*. Elsevier, to appear.
7. C. Schumacher, M. D. Vose, and L. D. Whitley. The no free lunch and problem description length. In L. Spector et al., editors, *GECCO-2001*, pages 565–570. Morgan Kaufmann.
8. M. D. Vose. *The Simple Genetic Algorithm: Foundations and Theory*. MIT Press, Cambridge, MA, USA, 1998.
9. I. Wegener. Towards a theory of randomized search heuristics. In B. Rovan and P. Vojtás, editors, *MFCS*, volume 2747, pages 125–141. Springer, 2003.
10. D. Wolpert and W. G. Macready. No free lunch theorems for optimization. *IEEE Trans. Evolutionary Computation*, 1(1):67–82, 1997.

A Novel Negative Selection Algorithm with an Array of Partial Matching Lengths for Each Detector

Wenjian Luo, Xin Wang, Ying Tan, and Xufa Wang

Nature Inspired Computation and Applications Laboratory,
Department of Computer Science and Technology,
University of Science and Technology of China, Hefei 230027, China
wjluo@ustc.edu.cn, sinbarwx@mail.ustc.edu.cn,
{ytan, xfwang}@ustc.edu.cn

Abstract. A novel negative selection algorithm, namely r[]-NSA, is proposed in this paper, which uses an array to store multiple partial matching lengths for each detector. Every bit of one detector is assigned a partial matching length. As for a detector, the partial matching length of one bit means that one string is asserted to be matched by the detector, if and only if the number of the maximal continuous identical bits between them from the position of the bit to the end of strings is no less than the partial matching length, and the continuous identical bits should start from the position of the bit. The detector generation algorithm and detection algorithm of r[]-NSA are given. Experimental results showed that r[]-NSA has better detector generation efficiency and detection performance than traditional negative selection algorithm.

1 Introduction

Artificial Immune System (AIS) is an emergent bio-inspired research field [1-3]. Negative Selection Algorithm (NSA) is an algorithm based on the negative selection mechanism in the course of T-Cells maturation in biological immune system [4], which has been used for anomaly detection and other applications [1-3, 5-8]. The matching rule, the detector generation algorithm and the detection algorithm are the most important components of NSA [4, 8-9].

This paper is concerned with a novel detector structure and the detector generation and detection algorithms. In this paper, a detector has an array of partial matching lengths, while not just one partial matching length as previous NSAs. Namely, every bit of one detector is assigned a partial matching length. The partial matching length of one bit means that one string is asserted to be matched by the detector, if and only if the number of the maximal continuous identical bits between them from the position of the bit to the end of strings is no less than the partial matching length, and the continuous identical bits should start from the position of the bit. For convenience, we call such kind of detectors as r[]-detector. According to such kind of detector structure, a novel negative selection algorithm, namely the r[]-NSA algorithm, is proposed with the corresponding detector generation algorithm and detection algorithm.

T.P. Runarsson et al. (Eds.): PPSN IX, LNCS 4193, pp. 112 – 121, 2006.

2 r[]-NSA

2.1 Detector Structure of r[]-NSA

The r[]-NSA is presented in binary string space in this paper. The "r-continuous-bits" matching rule is adopted here. However, in r[]-NSA, a detector no longer has only one partial matching length, but has multiple partial matching thresholds that can be saved in an array with the corresponding detector.

For convenience, r[]-detector is used to denote the detector of r[]-NSA. Fig. 1 shows the difference between r[]-detector and traditional detector.

```
l=5
Self set: 00111, 00110
Candidate detectors: 11100, 01110
Traditional detector of NSA (r=3): 11100
r[]-detector: 11100  r[5]={1, 1, 2, 1, 0}
r[]-detector: 01110  r[5]={2, 1, 0, 0, 0}
```

Fig. 1. The difference between r[]-detector and traditional detector. The detailed algorithm for generating r[]-detectors will be given in section 2.2.

In Fig. 1, the string length l is 5, the self set is {00111, 00110}. The candidate detectors are {11100, 01110}. As an example, we used r=3 for "r-continuous-bits" partial matching rule in traditional negative selection algorithm [4]. If the premature detector is {11100, 01110}, "11100" is a mature detector after negative selection, while "01110" is deleted because it matches the self string "00110". However, as for r[]-NSA, both "11100" and "01110" are valid detectors.

As for the r[]-detector "11100", r[1]=1 means that if one string is matched by the detector "11100" at the first bit, the string is an anomaly string. Similarly, r[3]=2 means that if one string is matched by the detector "11100" at both the third bit and the fourth bit, the string is an anomaly string. Especially, r[5]=0, this means that no valid matching needs to be done starting from this position. Furthermore, Fig. 2 shows the configuration of a matching length array of the 5-bit r[]-detector "11100".

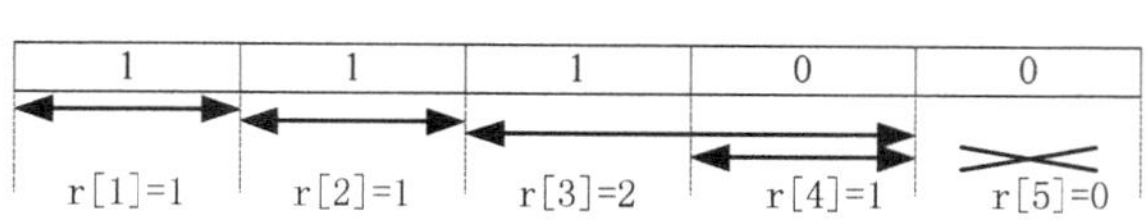

Fig. 2. The partial matching length array of the r[]-detector "11100". The string length and the self set are listed in Fig. 1.

Fig. 3 is used to further illustrate how to use the detectors. The parameters, the self set and the detector set are the same as those listed in Fig. 1.

In Fig. 3, as for the string "11101", NSA asserts that it is an anomaly one because the detector "11100" matches its first three bits. However, r[]-NSA asserts that it is

String to be detected	NSA	r[]-NSA
11101	11100	11100
00100	11100	11100
01001	---	11100 or 01110
01110	---	11100 or 01110
00110 (Self string)	---	---

Fig. 3. How the detectors are used in NSA and r[]-NSA. The bits underlined mean the matching bits between the detector and the string to be detected.

an anomaly one because the detector "11100" matches its first bit. As for the string "00100", NSA asserts that it is an anomaly because the string "00100" is matched by the detector "11100" at the last three bits, while r[]-NSA asserts that it is an anomaly because the string "00100" is matched by the detector "11100" at both the third bit and the fourth bit. For other two strings "01001" and "01110", NSA can not assert that they are anomaly ones with the detector set of {11100}. However, r[]-NSA can do it. As for the self string "00110", both NSA and r[]-NSA do not generate false alarms.

2.2 Detector Generation Algorithm

The detector generation algorithm for r[]-NSA is listed in Fig. 4. In Fig. 4, the length of a bit-string is denoted by l, and $i \in [1,l]$, r[] represents the array with elements of the partial matching lengths.

(1) Define the self set S.
(2) Generate a candidate detector d randomly.
(3) Perform the matching process between d and all self strings in S.

(3.1) For the first self string s, $r[i]$ represents the number of maximal continuous identical bits between d and s from the ith bit to the end of string, and the continuous identical bits should start from the ith bit.

(3.2) For other self strings, $r_t[i]$ represents the number of maximal continuous identical bits between d and the self bit-string from the ith bit to the end of string, and the continuous identical bits should start from the ith bit. If $r[i] < r_t[i]$, then $r[i] = r_t[i]$.

(3.3) If $r[1] = l$, go to step (2).

(3.4) For i from l to 1, if $r[i] = l - i + 1$, let $r[i] = -1$.

(3.5) For i from l to 1, $r[i] = r[i]+1$.

(4) Add (d, r[]) to the detector set. Go to step (2) if the number of detectors is not enough.

Fig. 4. The detector generation algorithm for r[]-NSA. Only the candidate string that completely matches one self string will be discarded at step (3.3). Therefore, every non-self string could be a valid detector.

To analyze the time complexity and space complexity of the detector generation algorithm of r[]-NSA, some symbols used are given as follows.

l: The string length.

N_{RO}: The number of the candidate detectors (namely the immature detectors).

N_R: The number of detectors.

N_S: The size of the self set.

According to above detector generation algorithm, every string that is not in the self set could be a detector. Therefore,

$$N_R = N_{RO}(1-\frac{N_S}{2^l}) \ . \tag{1}$$

To generate N_R detectors, the number of candidate detectors needed is

$$N_{RO} = N_R \frac{2^l}{2^l - N_S} \ . \tag{2}$$

For any candidate detector, the time complexities of both step (3.1) and step (3.2) are $O(l)$. In fact, the expected total number of bit comparisons in step (3.1) is $2l$. It is also $2l$ in step (3.2). The time complexities of both step (3.4) and step (3.5) are also $O(l)$. Therefore, the time complexity for generating N_R detectors is

$$O(N_R \frac{2^l}{2^l - N_S} \cdot N_S \cdot l) \ . \tag{3}$$

Every detector needs an array with size of l to store the partial matching lengths for each bit of the detector. The space cost for generating N_R detectors is:

$$O(N_R l) \ . \tag{4}$$

2.3 Detection Algorithm

According to above detection algorithm, the time cost of the detection algorithm is $O(N_R \cdot l)$. The detection algorithm needs a temporary array with size of l to store the

t: string to be detected; R: the detector set
(1) For any detector d in the detector set R
(1.1) For i from 1 to l
(1.1.1) If $r[i] == 0$, go to (1).
(1.1.2) Calculate $r_t[i]$. $r_t[i]$ means the number of the maximal continuous identical bits between t and d from the ith bit to the end of string, and the continuous identical bits should start from the position of the bit.
(1.1.3) If $r_t[i] \geq r[i]$, an anomaly change has been detected.

Fig. 5. The detection algorithm for r[]-NSA

number of the continuous matching bits between t and d. Therefore, the space cost of the detection algorithm is $O(l)$.

3 Experiments and Analyses

The r[]-NSA is compared with the traditional NSA in this paper. The binary string length l is 10, and then the size of global string space O is 1024. The parameter u, which denotes the proportion of the self set among the global string space O, namely $u = N_S / 2^l$, is set to {0.05, 0.15, 0.25, 0.35, 0.45, 0.55, 0.65, 0.75, 0.85, 0.95} respectively to observe the changes of the results against it.

The "r-continuous-bits" matching rule is adopted here and the partial matching length r of traditional NSA is fixed to 9.

The self set of every independent run is generated randomly, and is identical for both r[]-NSA and traditional NSA.

There are two parameters taken to make the comparisons, N_R and P_f. Where N_R is the number of mature detectors. In an independent run, it is assumed that FN is the number of non-self strings missed (i.e. undetected), and TP is the number of non-self strings detected as non-self. And then $P_f = FN / (FN + TP)$ [4].

3.1 Comparisons on N_R and P_f When N_{R0} Is Fixed

In experiments, the size of initial immature detector set is fixed to 300. The results take the average values over 20 independent runs for every value of the parameter u.

Table 1. Comparisons on N_R between r[]-NSA and traditional NSA when N_{R0} is fixed

	N_R			
	r[]-NSA		NSA	
u	Experimental	Theoretical	Experimental	Theoretical
0.05	285.70 (9.87)	285.06	258.70 (20.87)	258.31
0.15	254.75 (4.94)	254.88	183.85 (7.49)	190.94
0.25	227.15 (5.99)	225.00	128.15 (6.75)	141.55
0.35	193.30 (6.43)	195.12	81.90 (7.09)	104.94
0.45	163.50 (7.24)	164.94	51.10 (6.81)	77.57
0.55	134.00 (5.42)	135.06	26.45 (6.14)	57.51
0.65	106.55 (6.24)	104.88	14.10 (3.11)	42.51
0.75	76.15 (6.30)	75.00	4.90 (2.59)	31.52
0.85	46.50 (4.85)	45.12	1.40 (1.23)	23.36
0.95	15.55 (4.35)	14.94	0.05 (0.22)	17.27

Both the experimental values and theoretical values of N_R are given in Table 1, where the standard deviations of experimental values are in the parenthesizes. According to the experimental values in Table 1, it is obvious that the sizes of the detector sets of r[]-NSA are lager than those of traditional NSA. Therefore, the detector generation efficiency of r[]-NSA is much better than traditional NSA.

The theoretical values of r[]-NSA in Table 1 is calculated according to equation (1) in section 2. The theoretical values of traditional NSA are computed by the methods provided in reference [4]. Theoretically, with fixed N_{RO}, the number of detectors linearly decreases as N_S increases for r[]-NSA. However, with fixed N_{RO},, the number of detectors exponentially decreases as N_S increases for traditional NSA [4, 9]. It is note that the assumption, in reference [4], that the detectors are independent is not entirely valid as N_S and P_m increase [4, 9] (P_m is the probability of a match between two random strings). This is also verified by the experimental values in Table 1. When u is large, the experimental values of traditional NSA are much smaller than the theoretical values. However, as for r[]-NSA, its experimental values are always almost equal to the theoretical values.

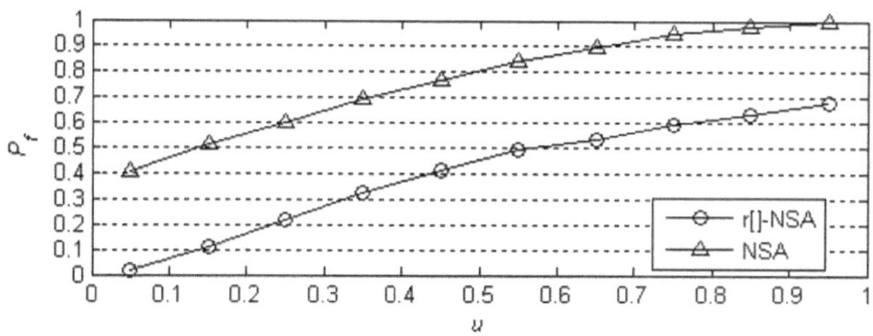

Fig. 6. Comparisons on P_f between r[]-NSA and traditional NSA

Fig. 6 shows the comparisons on P_f between two algorithms when N_{RO} is fixed (the numbers of detectors are shown in Table 1). It is shown that the values of P_f of r[]-NSA are clearly lower than those of traditional NSA when N_{RO} is fixed.

3.2 Estimate P_f After N_R Detectors Are Generated

In this subsection, some experiments are done to show how to estimate P_f after some detectors are generated. Firstly, a method for estimating P_f of r[]-NSA is given.

As for a detector d with an array r[], the probability that one string can be matched by d is denoted by P_m. Assume the array of r[] has π non-zero elements, and these π non-zero elements are denoted by $r_{x_1}, r_{x_2}, r_{x_3}, \cdots, r_{x_\pi}$. Therefore, we have

$$P_m = \sum_{1\le i\le\pi} \frac{1}{2^{r_{x_i}}} - \sum_{1\le i\ne j\le\pi} \frac{1}{2^{r_{x_i}+r_{x_j}}} + \sum_{1\le i\ne j\ne k\le\pi} \frac{1}{2^{r_{x_i}+r_{x_j}+r_{x_k}}} - \cdots + (-1)^{\pi} \frac{1}{2^{r_{x_1}+r_{x_2}+r_{x_3}+\cdots+r_{x_\pi}}} \quad (5)$$

Obviously, we assume that all these probabilities of one string being matched at $x_1, x_2, x_3, \cdots, x_\pi$ positions are independent.

When the self set is absolutely very large, one detector is prone to matching only one string, and then $P_m \approx 1/2^l$. When the self set is not very large, we have

$$P_m \approx \sum_{1 \le i \le \pi} \frac{1}{2^{r_{x_i}}} - \sum_{1 \le i \ne j \le \pi} \frac{1}{2^{r_{x_i} + r_{x_j}}} \,. \tag{6}$$

Let the size of the detector set R is N_R, and the P_{m_i} is the probability that one string can be matched by the *i*th detector. Assume that every detector is independent because every candidate detector is generated randomly. Therefore,

$$P_f \approx \prod_i (1 - P_{m_i}) \,. \tag{7}$$

P_f : the expected value.
(1) Initialize $P_{f\_temp} = 1$.
(2) Repeat
  (2.1) Generate a detector *d* according to the algorithm in Fig. 4.
  (2.2) Add *d* to the detector set R.
  (2.2) Compute P_m of *d*.
  (2.3) let $P_{f\_temp} = P_{f\_temp} \cdot (1 - P_m)$.
(3) Until $P_{f\_temp} \le P_f$.

Fig. 7. Estimate P_f of r[]-NSA after some detectors are generated

When the expected P_f of r[]-NSA is given, the pseudo-codes in Fig. 7 show how to generate enough detectors for the expected P_f [16].

(1) count=0.
(2) Generate the self set S randomly.
(3) Predefine the expected value of P_f.
(3) Generate the detector set R according to the algorithm in Fig. 7.
(4) For every string in global string space but not in the self set
  (4.1) If this string can be detected by the detector set R, then counter= counter+1.
(5) Set the real values of P_f as $count/(2^l - N_S)$.

Fig. 8. Verify the real P_f of r[]-NSA after the estimated number of detectors are generated

The experimental procedure is given Fig. 8. By generating enough detectors for the expected P_f according to the method given in Fig. 7, the pseudo-codes in Fig. 8 is also used to verify the real values of P_f.

Table 2 gave the results when the expected value of P_f is 0.1. And Table 3 gave the results when the expected value of P_f is 0.05. All results are the average values of 100 independent runs. And the standard deviations are in the parentheses.

In Table 2 and Table 3, as for r[]-NSA, "N_R" means the size of the detector set that generated according to the algorithm in Fig. 7, "P_f (real)" means the real value of P_f that is calculated according to the algorithm in Fig. 8. As for traditional NSA, "N_R (theoretical)" means the theoretical value that is computed according to the equation (2) in reference [9], while "N_R (experiment)" means the real number of the detectors that traditional NSA really can be generated. Because traditional NSA could not generate sufficient number of detectors, the values of "N_R (experiment)" are smaller than the theoretical values when u is larger.

Table 2. Comparisons between r[]-NSA and traditional NSA when P_f is fixed to 0.1

	r[]-NSA		NSA		
u	N_R	P_f (real)	N_R (theoretical)	N_R (Experiment)	P_f (real)
0.05	30.32 (4.75)	0.31881 (0.04734)	785	785 (0)	0.02282 (0.00682)
0.15	121.51 (12.41)	0.27654 (0.02677)	785	626.12 (9.33)	0.05954 (0.00720)
0.25	241.99 (21.18)	0.19909 (0.02644)	785	431.4 (11.29)	0.15630 (0.01192)
0.35	381.33 (29.51)	0.11482 (0.02125)	785	280.59 (11.46)	0.28119 (0.01583)
0.45	538.53 (26.46)	0.00950 (0.01191)	785	169.12 (12.44)	0.42892 (0.02233)
0.55	461 (0)	0 (0)	785	92.07 (9.20)	0.57456 (0.02767)
0.65	358 (0)	0 (0)	785	43.67 (7.74)	0.72277 (0.03626)
0.75	256 (0)	0 (0)	785	15.78 (4.45)	0.84383 (0.03496)
0.85	154 (0)	0 (0)	785	3.22 (1.98)	0.94247 (0.03275)
0.95	51 (0)	0 (0)	785	0.12 (0.38)	0.99294 (0.02256)

Table 3. Comparisons between r[]-NSA and traditional NSA when P_f is fixed to 0.05

	r[]-NSA		NSA		
u	N_R	P_f (real)	N_R (theoretical)	N_R (Experiment)	P_f (real)
0.05	39.88 (6.23)	0.25239 (0.04693)	1021	878.69 (3.23)	0.00762 (0.00321)
0.15	160.97 (16.45)	0.20786 (0.02758)	1021	625.84 (9.83)	0.05986 (0.00697)
0.25	314.58 (25.28)	0.13773 (0.02188)	1021	429.81 (11.93)	0.15512 (0.01305)
0.35	496.79 (34.16)	0.05165 (0.01600)	1021	279.67 (10.86)	0.28353 (0.01447)
0.45	563 (0)	0 (0)	1021	170.51 (10.86)	0.42393 (0.02442)
0.55	461 (0)	0 (0)	1021	92.71 (9.84)	0.57508 (0.02829)
0.65	358 (0)	0 (0)	1021	44.70 (7.29)	0.71704 (0.02781)
0.75	256 (0)	0 (0)	1021	16.40 (4.78)	0.84219 (0.03505)
0.85	154 (0)	0 (0)	1021	3.40 (2.15)	0.93844 (0.03435)
0.95	51 (0)	0 (0)	1021	0.13 (0.56)	0.99392 (0.02080)

As shown in Table 2 and Table 3, as for r[]-NSA, when u>0.25, the real values of P_f are almost equal or smaller than the expected values of P_f. Therefore, the algorithm in Fig. 7 can be used to estimate the number of detectors. However, when u<0.25, the real values of P_f is larger than the expected values. This is because the detectors of r[]-NSA is not entirely independent when u is smaller. Since the r[]-NSA has better performance to generate valid detectors than traditional NSA as shown in subsection 3.1, this problem can be easily avoided by adding more detectors.

As for traditional NSA, the results are not very ideal when u>0.25. The real values of P_f are much higher than the expected values.

4 Related Works and Discussions

Negative Selection Algorithm (NSA) is presented by S. Forrest and her colleagues [4, 8], and is mainly applied as a change detection algorithm in artificial immune systems. P. D'haeseleer and S. Forrest presented a greedy algorithm that attempts to reduce the size of the detector set and maximize the coverage areas of the detector set when "r-continuous-bits" matching rule is adopted, and proposed an approach to counting the number of holes [10]. Wierzcho also analyzed the negative selection algorithm with the r-contiguous bits matching rule in [14-15]. Z. Ji and D. Dasgupata proposed an augmented NSA with variable-coverage detectors for real-valued space [11-12]. In their works, other than having one unique partial matching threshold for all the detectors, every detector can have an appropriate matching threshold different from others. By this way, the coverage of different detectors can be different, and the number of holes is reduced at a certain extent. Their works mainly describes the experiments of variable-sized detectors in real-valued space. And effects of the two main control parameters, the self radius and expected coverage, are discussed and experimentally tested [11-12]. In addition, Z. Heng et al. proposed an r-adjustable NSA, and their works focused on the binary string space [13].

Anyway, in all current works, one detector has only one partial matching length. In this paper, a novel r[]-NSA is proposed, in which a detector no longer has just one matching threshold, but has multiple thresholds that can be saved in an array with the corresponding detector. By this way, the coverage of a detector can be improved, and the survivability of an immature detector is improved, i.e., the efficiency of detector generation is improved, which has been proved by the experiments.

5 Conclusions

A novel negative selection algorithm, namely r[]-NSA, is proposed in this paper. This novel algorithm can improve the efficiency of detector generation greatly. The performance of this new algorithm has been proved and verified by the experiments. The candidate detector of r[]-NSA is generated randomly in this paper. In the future, a more efficient detector generation algorithm for r[]-NSA needs to be designed to maximize the coverage of a detector set with a certain number of detectors. And the r[]-NSA for a higher dimensionality and real world problems will be studied.

Acknowledgements. This work is partly supported by the National Natural Science Foundation of China (NO. 60404004, NO. 60428202) and Nature Science Major Foundation from Anhui Education Bureau (NO. 2004kj360zd).

References

1. Dasgupta, D., Zhou, J., Gonzalez, F.: Artificial Immune System (AIS) Research in the Last Five Years. Proceedings of Congress on Evolutionary Computation, Canberra (2003) 123-130
2. Castro, L.N.d., Timmis, J.: Artificial Immune Systems: A New Computational Intelligence Approach. Springer-Verlag, London (2002)

3. Taraknaov, A.O., Skormin, V.A., Sokolova, S.P.: Immunocomputing: Principles and Applications. Springer-Verlag (2003)
4. Forrest, S., Perelson, A.S., Allen, L., Cherukuri, R.: Self-Nonself Discrimination in a Computer. Proceedings of 1994 IEEE Symposium on Research in Security and Privacy. Los Alamitos, CA (1994) 202-212
5. Aickelin, U., Greensmith, J., Twycross, J.: Immune System Approaches to Intrusion Detection - A Review. Proceedings of 3rd International Conference on Artificial Immune Systems (ICARIS-2004), LNCS 3239, Springer-Verlag, Catania, Italy (2004) 316-329
6. Kim, J., Bentley, P.: Towards an Artificial Immune System for Network Intrusion Detection: an Investigation of Clonal Selection with a Negative Selection Operator. Proceedings of IEEE Congress on Evolutionary Computation. Seoul, Korea (2001) 27-30
7. Luo, W., Wang, X., et al.: Evolutionary Negative Selection Algorithms for Anomaly Detection. Proceedings of 8th Joint Conference on Information Sciences, Vol. 1-3. Salt Lake City, Utah (2005) 440-445
8. Ayara, M., Timmis, J., Lemos, L.N.d., et al.: Negative Selection: How to Generate Detectors. Proceedings of First International Conference on Artificial Immune Systems (2002) 89-98
9. D'haeseleer, P., Forrest, S., Helman, P.: An Immunological Approach to Change Detection: Algorithms, Analysis and Implications. Proceedings of 1996 IEEE Symposium on Security and Privacy. Los Alamitos, CA (1996) 110-119
10. D'haeseleer, P.: Further Efficient Algorithms for Generating Antibody Strings. Tech. Rep. CS95-3. Dept. Comput. Sci., Univ. New Mexico (1995)
11. Zhou, J., Dasgupata, D.: Augmented Negative Selection Algorithm with Variable-Coverage Detectors. Proceedings of 2004 Congress on Evolutionary Computation, (2004) 1081-1088
12. Zhou, J., Dasgupata, D.: Real-Valued Negative Selection Algorithm with Variable-Sized Detectors. Proceedings of 2004 Genetic and Evolutionary Computation Conference, Washington (2004) 287-298
13. Zhang, H., Wu, L., Zhang, Y., Zeng, Q.: An Algorithm of r-Adjustable Negative Selection Algorithm and Its Simulation Analysis (in Chinese). Chinese Journal of Computers, Vol. 28(10) (2005) 1614-1619
14. Wierzcho, S.T.: Deriving Concise Description of Non-Self Patterns in an Artificial Immune System. In: Jain, L.C., Kacprzyk, J. (eds.): New Learning Paradigms in Soft Computing. Physica-Verlag, ISBN 3-7908-1436-9 (2002) 438-458
15. Wierzcho, S.T.: Generating Optimal Repertoire of Antibody Strings in an Artificial Immune System. In: Kopotek, M.A., Michalewicz, M., Wierzcho, S.T. (eds.): Intelligent Information Systems. Physica-Verlag/Springer Verlag, (2000) 119-133
16. Wenjian Luo, Zeming Zhang, Xufa Wang: A Heuristic Detector Generation Algorithm for Negative Selection Algorithm with Hamming Distance Partial Matching Rule. Proceedings of 5th International Conference on Artificial Immune Systems, Oeiras, Portugal, 4th-6th September (2006)

Hierarchical BOA, Cluster Exact Approximation, and Ising Spin Glasses

Martin Pelikan[1], Alexander K. Hartmann[2], and Kumara Sastry[3]

[1] Missouri Estimation of Distribution Algorithms Laboratory (MEDAL), 320 CCB; University of Missouri in St. Louis; One University Blvd.; St. Louis, MO 63121
pelikan@cs.umsl.edu

[2] Institut für Theoretische Physik; Universität Göttingen; Friedrich-Hund-Platz 1; 37077 Göttingen, Germany
hartmann@physik.uni-goettingen.de

[3] Illinois Genetic Algorithms Laboratory (IlliGAL), 117 TB; University of Illinois at Urbana-Champaign; 104 S. Mathews Ave., Urbana, IL 61801
kumara@illigal.ge.uiuc.edu

Abstract. This paper analyzes the hierarchical Bayesian optimization algorithm (hBOA) on the problem of finding ground states of Ising spin glasses with $\pm J$ couplings in two and three dimensions. The performance of hBOA is compared to that of the simple genetic algorithm (GA) and the univariate marginal distribution algorithm (UMDA). The performance of all tested algorithms is improved by incorporating a deterministic hill climber (DHC) based on single-bit flips and cluster exact approximation (CEA). The results show that hBOA significantly outperforms GA and UMDA with both types of local search and that CEA enables all tested algorithms to solve larger spin-glass instances than DHC. Using advanced hybrid methods created by combining competent genetic and evolutionary algorithms with advanced local searchers thus proves advantageous in this challenging class of problems.

1 Introduction

Ising spin glasses are prototypical models for disordered systems and have played a central role in statistical physics during the last three decades [1,2,3,4]. Examples of experimental realizations of spin glasses are metals with magnetic impurities, e.g. gold with a small fraction of iron added. Spin glasses represent also a rich class of challenging problems for optimization algorithms [5,6,7] where the task is to minimize energy of a given spin-glass instance [8,9,10,11,12,13]. States with the lowest energy are called *ground states* and thus the problem of minimizing the energy of spin-glass instances can be formulated as the problem of finding ground states of these instances. There are two main challenges that must be tackled to find ground states of spin glasses efficiently and reliably: (1) There are many local optima in the energy landscape (the number of local optima may grow exponentially with problem size). (2) The local minima are often surrounded by high-energy configurations, which make it difficult for local operators to escape the local optimum once they get trapped in it. That is

T.P. Runarsson et al. (Eds.): PPSN IX, LNCS 4193, pp. 122–131, 2006.

why even state-of-the-art Markov chain Monte Carlo (MCMC) methods require exponential time to locate ground states [14].

This paper analyzes the hierarchical Bayesian optimization algorithm (hBOA) [15,16] on a broad spectrum of instances of the problem of finding ground states of Ising spin glasses with $\pm J$ couplings and periodic boundary conditions. The performance of hBOA is compared to that of the simple genetic algorithm (GA) and the univariate marginal distribution algorithm (UMDA). We build on the prior work [12] where we combined several evolutionary algorithms with the deterministic hill climber to solve various classes of 2D and 3D spin glasses. However, here we consider also cluster exact approximation (CEA) [17], which provides an efficient method to perform large updates of spin glass configurations to decrease their energy. CEA is incorporated into hBOA and GA, and the resulting hybrids are tested on a number of spin-glass problem instances. CEA is shown to significantly improve performance of all tested algorithms, allowing a practical solution of much larger problems than DHC.

The paper is organized as follows. Section 2 describes the problem of finding ground states of Ising spin glasses. Section 3 outlines the algorithms hBOA, GA and UMDA; additionally, the section describes the deterministic hill climber and cluster exact approximation, which are incorporated into all tested algorithms to improve their performance. Section 4 presents and discusses experiments. Finally, Section 5 summarizes and concludes the paper.

2 Ising Spin Glass

A very simple model to describe a finite-dimensional Ising spin glass is typically arranged on a regular 2D or 3D grid where each node i corresponds to a spin s_i and each edge $\langle i, j \rangle$ corresponds to a coupling between two spins s_i and s_j. Each edge has a real value associated with it that defines the relationship between the two connected spins. To approximate the behavior of the large-scale system, periodic boundary conditions are often used that introduce a coupling between the first and the last element along each dimension.

For the classical Ising model, each spin s_i can be in one of two states: $s_i = +1$ or $s_i = -1$. Note that this simplification corresponds to highly anisotropic systems, which do indeed exist in some experimental situations. Nevertheless, the two-state Ising model comprises all basic effects also found in models with more degrees of freedom. A specific set of coupling constants defines a spin-glass instance. Each possible setting of all spins is called a spin configuration.

Given a set of coupling constants $J_{i,j}$, and a spin configuration $C = \{s_i\}$ ($i = 1, \ldots, n$), the energy can be computed as

$$E(C) = \sum_{\langle i,j \rangle} s_i J_{i,j} s_j \ , \tag{1}$$

where the sum runs over all couplings $\langle i, j \rangle$.

Given a set of coupling constants, the usual task in statistical physics is to integrate a known function over all possible configurations of spins, assuming the Boltzmann distribution of spin configurations; that means, the probability of each configuration C is proportional to $\exp(-E(C)/T)$ where $E(C)$ is energy of C and T is the temperature. From the physics point of view, it is also interesting to know the ground states (configurations associated with the minimum possible energy). Finding extremal energies then corresponds to sampling the Boltzmann distribution with temperature approaching 0 and thus the problem of finding ground states is simpler *a priori* than integration over a wide range of temperatures. However, most of the conventional methods based on sampling the above Boltzmann distribution, such as the flat-histogram Markov chain Monte Carlo [18], fail to find the ground states because they get often trapped in a local minimum [14].

In order to obtain a quantitative understanding of the disorder in a spin glass system introduced by the random spin-spin couplings, one generally analyzes a large set of random spin-glass instances for a given distribution of the spin-spin couplings. For each spin glass instance, the optimization algorithm is applied and the results are analyzed to obtain a measure of computational complexity. Here we consider the $\pm J$ spin glass, where each spin-spin coupling constant is set randomly to either $+1$ or -1 with equal probability.

3 Compared Algorithms

This section outlines the algorithms compared in this paper: (1) The hierarchical Bayesian optimization algorithm (hBOA), (2) the genetic algorithm (GA), and (3) the univariate marginal distribution algorithm (UMDA). hBOA and UMDA are estimation of distribution algorithms (EDAs) [19,20,21], where standard variation operators are replaced by building and sampling probabilistic models. The section also describes the deterministic hill climber (DHC) and cluster exact approximation (CEA), which are used to improve performance of compared algorithms. Candidate solutions are represented by n-bit binary strings where each bit specifies the value of one of the n spins (0 represents state -1 and 1 represents state $+1$).

3.1 Hierarchical Bayesian Optimization Algorithm (hBOA)

The hierarchical Bayesian optimization algorithm (hBOA) [15,16] evolves a population of candidate solutions. The population is initially generated at random according to a uniform distribution over all n-bit strings. Each iteration starts by selecting a population of promising solutions using any common selection method of genetic and evolutionary algorithms, such as tournament and truncation selection; we use binary tournament selection. New solutions are generated by building a Bayesian network with decision trees [22,23] for the selected solutions and sampling the built Bayesian network. To ensure useful diversity maintenance, the new candidate solutions are incorporated into the original population using restricted tournament replacement (RTR) [24]. The run is terminated when termination criteria are met.

3.2 Genetic Algorithm (GA)

The genetic algorithm (GA) [25,26] also evolves a population of candidate solutions starting with a population generated at random. Each iteration starts by selecting promising solutions from the current population. New solutions are created by applying variation operators to the population of selected solutions. Specifically, crossover is used to exchange bits and pieces between pairs of candidate solutions and mutation is used to perturb the resulting solutions. Here we use one-point crossover and bit-flip mutation. The new candidate solutions are incorporated into the original population using RTR. The run is terminated when termination criteria are met.

3.3 Univariate Marginal Distribution Algorithm (UMDA)

The univariate marginal distribution algorithm (UMDA) [19] also evolves a population of candidate solutions represented by binary strings, starting with a random population. Each iteration starts by selection. Then, the probability vector is learned that stores the proportion of 1s in each position of the selected population. Each bit of a new candidate solution is then set to 1 with the probability equal to the proportion of 1s in this position; otherwise, the bit is set to 0. Consequently, the variation operator of UMDA preserves the proportions of 1s in each position while decorrelating different string positions. The new candidate solutions are incorporated into the original population using RTR. The run is terminated when termination criteria are met.

The only difference between hBOA and the UMDA variant discussed in this paper is the type of the probabilistic model used to model promising candidate solutions and generate the new ones. The comparison between hBOA and UMDA should therefore indicate whether in this problem domain effective exploration necessitates complex probabilistic models that can efficiently encode large-order interactions between spins, as it is the case for hBOA. For analogical reasons, the comparison between hBOA and GA will indicate whether it is important to use advanced variation operators that adapt to the problem like in hBOA.

3.4 Deterministic Hill Climber

Like in previous work [12], we incorporate a deterministic hill climber (DHC) into hBOA, GA and UMDA to improve their performance. DHC takes a candidate solution represented by an n-bit binary string on input. Then, it performs one-bit changes on the solution that lead to the maximum improvement of solution quality (maximum decrease in energy). DHC is terminated when no single-bit flip improves solution quality and the solution is thus locally optimal. Here, DHC is used to improve every solution in the population before the evaluation is performed. The hybrids created by incorporating DHC into hBOA, GA and UMDA are referred to as hBOA+DHC, GA+DHC and UMDA+DHC, respectively.

3.5 Cluster Exact Approximation (CEA)

Due to the complex structure of the energy landscape of spin glasses, many local minima exist, which have energies very close to the ground-state energy.

Usually these minima differ from the true ground states by flips of large domains. Hence, as already mentioned, the minima are surrounded by high energy barriers from the viewpoint of single-spin-flip dynamics. This leads to poor performance of algorithms that apply single-bit (spin) changes as DHC. For this reason, we also consider *cluster exact approximation* (CEA) [17], which provides an efficient method that can change many spins at the same time optimally (assuming that the remaining spins remain fixed).

CEA starts by constructing a non-frustrated cluster of spins; a non-frustrated cluster contains spins that can be set to some values without breaking any interactions between them. The selected cluster is first transformed so that all interactions become ferromagnetic (negative coupling). All spins outside the cluster are fixed and treated as local magnetic fields. All cluster spins are computed leading to an optimal spin configuration with respect to the non-cluster spins, which remain fixed. The computation can be performed in polynomial time using graph-theoretical methods [27,28]: an equivalent network is constructed [29], the maximum flow is calculated [30,31] and the spins of the cluster are set to orientations leading to a minimum in energy.

The CEA update step ensures that the spins in the cluster minimize energy assuming that the remaining (non-cluster) spins remain fixed to their current values. Each CEA iteration either decreases the energy or the energy remains the same, which is the case when all cluster spins have been already set to their optimal values. In this work, we use CEA to improve all obtained candidate solutions and we repeat the CEA update step until the update fails to decrease the energy for a predefined number of iterations; specifically, the bound on the number of failures is $\sqrt{n}$ for 2D spin glasses and it is $\sqrt[3]{n}$ for 3D spin glasses.

4 Experiments

This section presents and discusses experimental results.

4.1 Tested Spin-Glass Instances

Both 2D and 3D Ising spin-glass instances with $\pm J$ couplings and periodic boundary conditions were considered. To analyze scalability, for 2D spin glasses, instances of size 6×6 (36 spins) to 50×50 (2500 spins) have been considered; 1000 random instances have been generated for each problem size. For 3D spin glasses, instances of size $4 \times 4 \times 4$ (64 spins) to $10 \times 10 \times 10$ (1000 spins) have been considered. In the experiments on 3D spin glasses without CEA, only 8 random instances have been generated for each problem size because of the increased computational resources required to solve the 3D instances; for CEA-based algorithms, 1000 random instances were used for each problem size.

4.2 Description of Experiments

All compared algorithms use binary tournament selection to select promising solutions. As a replacement strategy, RTR is used where the window size w is set to the number of bits in solution strings but it is always ensured to be at most 5% of the population size, $w = \min(n, N/20)$. GA+DHC and GA+CEA use one-point crossover with the probability of crossover $p_c = 0.6$ and bit-flip mutation with the probability of flipping each bit $p_m = 1/n$.

For each problem instance, bisection is run to determine the minimum population size to ensure convergence in 5 independent runs (out of 5 runs total). Each run is terminated either when the algorithm has found the optimum or when the algorithm has failed to find the optimum for a large number of iterations. The optimum for most 2D instances was verified with the branch-and-cut algorithm provided at the Spin-Glass Ground State Server at the University of Köln [32]. The remaining 2D instances with ground states were obtained from S. Sabhapandit and S. N. Coppersmith from the University of Wisconsin who identified the ground states using flat-histogram Markov chain Monte Carlo simulations [14]. All 3D instances with their ground states were obtained from previous simulations of one of the authors [10].

The upper bound on the number of iterations (generations) is determined by combining convergence theory [33,34] with empirical results so that the number of iterations is sufficiently large for all tests. In general, the bound on the number of iterations for GA+DHC is larger than that for hBOA+DHC and UMDA+DHC because of the slower mixing with one-point crossover [35].

The performance of hBOA+DHC, GA+DHC and UMDA+DHC is measured by the number of evaluated spin glass configurations until the optimum has been found. Since one update step of CEA is usually more computationally expensive than the entire evaluation of a spin configuration [36], the time complexity of hBOA+CEA and GA+CEA is measured by the number of iterations of CEA as opposed to the number of evaluations.

4.3 Results

Figure 1a compares the performance of hBOA+DHC, UMDA+DHC and GA+DHC on 2D $\pm J$ spin glasses with periodic boundary conditions. The results indicate that the number of evaluations for hBOA+DHC grows with a low-order polynomial of problem size, specifically, it is bounded by $O(n^{1.63})$. Furthermore, the results show that hBOA significantly outperforms GA+DHC and UMDA+DHC. The worst performance is achieved by UMDA+DHC, the time complexity of which grows faster than polynomially. Recall that for spin glasses, one-point crossover performs relatively well because one-point crossover rarely breaks important interactions between spins due to the used representation. Nonetheless, this behavior cannot be generalized to other similar slowly equilibrating problems that exhibit different energy landscapes, such as protein folding or polymer dynamics.

For 2D Ising spin glasses, a polynomial algorithm [37,38] with complexity $O(n^{3.5})$ exists that computes the number of states at each energy level, including the ground state. It was shown [39] that on 2D $\pm J$ Ising spin glasses, hBOA+DHC achieves asymptotic performance of the polynomial algorithm without any prior knowledge about spin glasses.

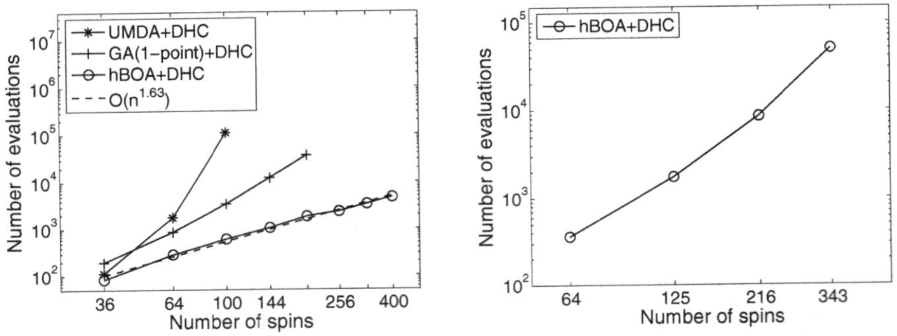

(a) 2D $\pm J$ spin glass. (b) 3D $\pm J$ spin glass.

Fig. 1. Performance of hBOA+DHC, UMDA+DHC, and GA+DHC on random 2D and 3D $\pm J$ Ising spin glasses

Figure 1b shows the performance of hBOA+DHC on 3D $\pm J$ spin glasses. Since both GA+DHC and UMDA+DHC have not been capable of solving most 3D instances even with enormous computational resources, we only include the results for hBOA+DHC. The results show that the performance of hBOA+DHC appears to grow exponentially fast. This behavior is expected because the problem of finding ground states of 3D spin glasses is NP-complete [40]. However, we see that hBOA+DHC is still capable of solving instances of several hundreds spins, which are intractable with most standard optimization algorithms, such as genetic algorithms and simulated annealing.

Figure 2a shows the performance of hBOA+CEA and GA+CEA on 2D Ising spin glasses with $\pm J$ couplings. The results indicate that hBOA+CEA significantly outperforms GA+CEA and thus hBOA retains superior performance even with CEA. The results also show that incorporating CEA leads to a somewhat faster asymptotic growth of time complexity with problem size; on the other hand, the use of CEA provides a significant decrease of running time for the tested range of problems and, consequently, much larger problem sizes can be treated currently as compared to hBOA+DHC. Nonetheless, based on these results, it can be hypothesized that hBOA+DHC will become faster than hBOA+CEA for much larger spin-glass instances. It is also important to note that the size of spin glass instances solved in this paper is orders of magnitude larger than the size of problems solved by other EDAs [41,42,43,12].

Figure 2b shows the performance of hBOA+CEA and GA+CEA on 3D Ising spin glasses with $\pm J$ couplings. The results indicate that the performance of both algorithms grows faster than polynomially even with the use of CEA as is expected from the NP-completeness of this problem. However, CEA improves the performance of GA significantly and makes the difficult 3D instances tractable even with GA. Nonetheless, hBOA+CEA still retains superior performance, yielding several times fewer evaluations than GA+CEA.

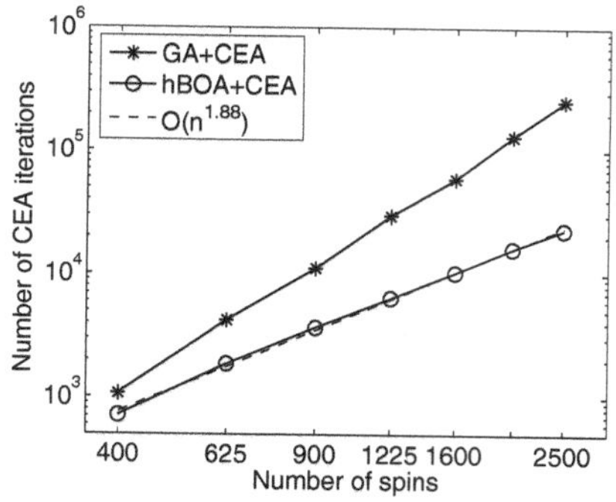

(a) 2D $\pm J$ Ising spin glass.

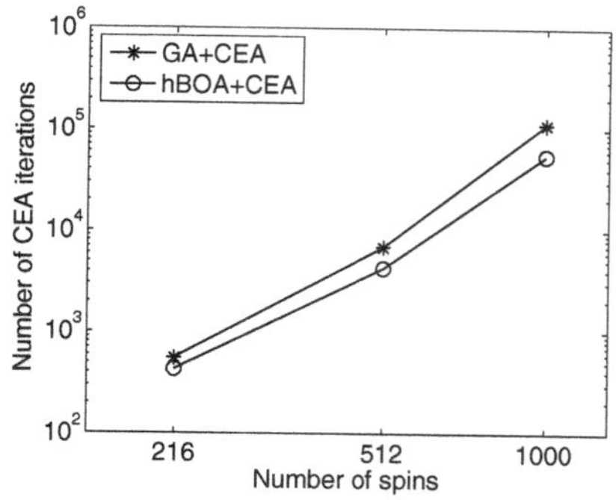

(b) 3D $\pm J$ Ising spin glass.

Fig. 2. Performance of hBOA+CEA and GA+CEA on $\pm J$ Ising spin glasses

5 Summary and Conclusions

This paper tested the hierarchical Bayesian optimization algorithm (hBOA), the simple genetic algorithm (GA) and the univariate marginal distribution algorithm (UMDA) on a large number of instances of the problem of finding ground states of Ising spin glasses with random couplings in two and three dimensions. All algorithms were hybridized by using either a simple deterministic hill climber (DHC) or the cluster exact approximation (CEA). The results showed that hBOA significantly outperforms all other compared methods in all cases and that CEA allows all algorithms to solve much larger instances than DHC. The results presented in this paper thus confirm that using hierarchical decomposition for solving difficult optimization problems with little problem-specific knowledge holds a big promise and that advanced estimation of distribution algorithms offer a robust and scalable class of optimization algorithms applicable to important classes of difficult problems.

Acknowledgments. The authors thank Fabien Alet, Martin V. Butz, David E. Goldberg, Jiri Ocenasek, Simon Trebst and Matthias Troyer. This work was supported by the National Science Foundation under CAREER grant ECS-0547013, by the Air Force Office of Scientific Research, Air Force Materiel Command, USAF, under grant FA9550-06-1-0096, by the University of Missouri in St. Louis through the High Performance Computing Collaboratory sponsored by Information Technology Services, and the Research Award and Research Board programs, and by the *VolkswagenStiftung* (Germany) within the program "Nachwuchsgruppen an Universitäten". Most experiments were done using the hBOA software developed by Martin Pelikan and David E. Goldberg at the University of Illinois at Urbana-Champaign.

References

1. Binder, K., Young, A.: Spin-glasses: Experimental facts, theoretical concepts and open questions. Rev. Mod. Phys. **58** (1986) 801
2. Mezard, M., Parisi, G., Virasoro, M.: Spin glass theory and beyond. World Scientific, Singapore (1987)
3. Fischer, K., Hertz, J.: Spin Glasses. Cambridge University Press, Cambridge (1991)
4. Young, A., ed.: Spin glasses and random fields. World Scientific, Singapore (1998)
5. Hartmann, A.K., Rieger, H.: Optimization Algorithms in Physics. Wiley-VCH, Weinheim (2001)
6. Hartmann, A.K., Rieger, H., eds.: New Optimization Algorithms in Physics. Wiley-VCH, Weinheim (2004)
7. Hartmann, A.K., Weigt, M.: Phase Transitions in Combinatorial Optimization Problems. Wiley-VCH, Weinheim (2005)
8. Mühlenbein, H., Mahnig, T.: Convergence theory and applications of the factorized distribution algorithm. Journal of Computing and Information Technology **7**(1) (1999) 19–32
9. Naudts, B., Naudts, J.: The effect of spin-flip symmetry on the performance of the simple GA. Parallel Problem Solving from Nature (1998) 67–76
10. Hartmann, A.K.: Ground-state clusters of two, three and four-dimensional +/-J Ising spin glasses. Phys. Rev. E **63** (2001) 016106
11. Van Hoyweghen, C.: Detecting spin-flip symmetry in optimization problems. In Kallel, L., et al., eds.: Theoretical Aspects of Evolutionary Computing. Springer, Berlin (2001) 423–437
12. Pelikan, M., Goldberg, D.E.: Hierarchical BOA solves Ising spin glasses and MAXSAT. Proceedings of the Genetic and Evolutionary Computation Conference (GECCO-2003) **II** (2003) 1275–1286
13. Fischer, S., Wegener, I.: The Ising model on the ring: Mutation versus recombination. Proceedings of the Genetic and Evolutionary Computation Conference (GECCO-2004) (2004) 1113–1124
14. Dayal, P., Trebst, S., Wessel, S., ürtz, D., Troyer, M., Sabhapandit, S., Coppersmith, S.: Performance limitations of flat histogram methods and optimality of Wang-Langdau sampling. Physical Review Letters **92**(9) (2004) 097201
15. Pelikan, M., Goldberg, D.E.: Escaping hierarchical traps with competent genetic algorithms. Proceedings of the Genetic and Evolutionary Computation Conference (GECCO-2001) (2001) 511–518
16. Pelikan, M.: Hierarchical Bayesian optimization algorithm: Toward a new generation of evolutionary algorithms. Springer-Verlag (2005)
17. Hartmann, A.K.: Cluster-exact approximation of spin glass ground states. Physica A **224** (1996) 480
18. Wang, F., Landau, D.P.: Efficient, multiple-range random walk algorithm to calculate the density of states. Physical Review Letters **86**(10) (2001) 2050–2053
19. Mühlenbein, H., Paaß, G.: From recombination of genes to the estimation of distributions I. Binary parameters. Parallel Problem Solving from Nature (1996) 178–187
20. Larrañaga, P., Lozano, J.A., eds.: Estimation of Distribution Algorithms: A New Tool for Evolutionary Computation. Kluwer, Boston, MA (2002)
21. Pelikan, M., Goldberg, D.E., Lobo, F.: A survey of optimization by building and using probabilistic models. Computational Optimization and Applications **21**(1) (2002) 5–20

22. Chickering, D.M., Heckerman, D., Meek, C.: A Bayesian approach to learning Bayesian networks with local structure. Technical Report MSR-TR-97-07, Microsoft Research, Redmond, WA (1997)
23. Friedman, N., Goldszmidt, M.: Learning Bayesian networks with local structure. In Jordan, M.I., ed.: Graphical models. MIT Press, Cambridge, MA (1999) 421–459
24. Harik, G.R.: Finding multimodal solutions using restricted tournament selection. Proceedings of the International Conference on Genetic Algorithms (ICGA-95) (1995) 24–31
25. Holland, J.H.: Adaptation in natural and artificial systems. University of Michigan Press, Ann Arbor, MI (1975)
26. Goldberg, D.E.: Genetic algorithms in search, optimization, and machine learning. Addison-Wesley, Reading, MA (1989)
27. Claiborne, J.: Mathematical Preliminaries for Computer Networking. Wiley, New York (1990)
28. Swamy, M., Thulasiraman, K.: Graphs, Networks and Algorithms. Wiley, New York (1991)
29. Picard, J.C., Ratliff, H.: Minimum cuts and related problems. Networks **5** (1975) 357
30. Träff, J.: A heuristic for blocking flow algorithms. Eur. J. Oper. Res. **89** (1996) 564
31. Tarjan, R.: Data Structures and Network Algorithms. Society for industrial and applied mathematics, Philadelphia (1983)
32. Spin Glass Ground State Server. `http://www.informatik.unikoeln.de/ls_juenger/research/sgs/sgs.html` (2004) University of Köln, Germany.
33. Thierens, D., Goldberg, D.E., Pereira, A.G.: Domino convergence, drift, and the temporal-salience structure of problems. Proceedings of the International Conference on Evolutionary Computation (ICEC-98) (1998) 535–540
34. Mühlenbein, H., Schlierkamp-Voosen, D.: Predictive models for the breeder genetic algorithm: I. Continuous parameter optimization. Evol. Comp. **1**(1) (1993) 25–49
35. Sastry, K., Goldberg, D.E.: Analysis of mixing in genetic algorithms: A survey. IlliGAL Report No. 2002012, University of Illinois at Urbana-Champaign, Illinois Genetic Algorithms Laboratory, Urbana, IL (2002)
36. Middleton, A., Fisher, D.S.: The three-dimensional random field Ising magnet: Interfaces, scaling, and the nature of states. Phys. Rev. B **65** (2002) 134411
37. Galluccio, A., Loebl, M.: A theory of Pfaffian orientations. I. Perfect matchings and permanents. Electr. J. of Combinatorics **6**(1) (1999) Research Paper 6.
38. Galluccio, A., Loebl, M.: A theory of Pfaffian orientations. II. T-joins, k-cuts, and duality of enumeration. Electronic Journal of Combinatorics **6**(1) (1999) Research Paper 7.
39. Pelikan, M., Ocenasek, J., Trebst, S., Troyer, M., Alet, F.: Computational complexity and simulation of rare events of Ising spin glasses. Proceedings of the Genetic and Evolutionary Computation Conference (GECCO-2004) **2** (2004) 36–47
40. Barahona, F.: On the computational complexity of Ising spin glass models. Journal of Physics A: Mathematical, Nuclear and General **15**(10) (1982) 3241–3253
41. Höns, R.: Estimation of Distribution Algorithms and Minimum Relative Entropy. PhD thesis, University of Bonn, Bonn, Germany (2006)
42. Shakya, S., McCall, J., Brown, D.: Solving the ising spin glass problem using a bivariate eda based on markov random fields. In: Proceedings of IEEE Congress on Evolutionary Computation (CEC 2006). (2006) To appear.
43. Santana, R.: Estimation of distribution algorithms with Kikuchi approximations. Evolutionary Computation **13**(1) (2005) 67–97

Towards an Adaptive Multimeme Algorithm for Parameter Optimisation Suiting the Engineers' Needs

Wilfried Jakob

Forschungszentrum Karlsruhe GmbH
Institute for Applied Computer Science
P.O. Box 3640, 76021 Karlsruhe, Germany
wilfried.jakob@iai.fzk.de

Abstract. Important factors for the easy usage of an Evolutionary Algorithm (EA) are numbers of fitness calculations as low as possible, its robustness, and the reduction of its strategy parameters as far as possible. Multimeme Algorithms (MMA) are good candidates for the first two properties. In this paper a cost-benefit-based approach shall be introduced for the adaptive control of both meme selection and the ratio between local and global search. The latter is achieved by adaptively adjusting the intensity of the search of the memes and the frequency of their usage. It will be shown in which way the proposed kind of adaptation fills the gap previous work leaves. Detailed experiments in the field of continuous parameter optimisation demonstrate the superiority of the adaptive MMA over the simple MA and the pure EA.

1 Introduction

Wide application of Evolutionary Algorithms (EA) to real-world problems presently is being prevented by two major obstacles: by the variety of strategy parameters, the appropriate adjustment of which may be crucial to success, and by the large number of evaluations required. The latter is of relevance in particular when the individual evaluation requires a high expenditure, because it is based on e.g. a simulation run. For the EA to become a standard tool of the engineer, a significant reduction of relevant strategy parameters is as necessary as a reduction of fitness calculations.

Concerning EA strategy parameters like mutation rates and crossover parameters, a lot of research effort has been taken successfully, see [1, 2] and [3] for a survey. The large number of evaluations is caused by the property of EA of being strong in discovering interesting regions of a given search space (*exploration*), but unfortunately weak in finding the precise optimum (*exploitation*) due to their lacking exploitation of local information. This is why most applications of EAs to real-world problems use some sort of hybridisation with other procedures and techniques, such as local searchers (LS) or heuristics, see [4-9, 12-15, 19-24]. These add-ons frequently introduce some sort of domain-specific knowledge in the until then generally applicable EA and change it into a domain-specific tool. This is the usually paid price for the speed-up achieved. In [6] and [7] it was shown for parameter optimisation that this drawback can be overcome by using application-independent local searchers. The resulting hybrid combines the global nature of the search and the convergence reliability of the

T.P. Runarsson et al. (Eds.): PPSN IX, LNCS 4193, pp. 132 – 141, 2006.

EA with a decrease of the evaluations required to reach a given solution by factors of up to 100 compared to the pure EA.

Hybridisation can be done in the following ways: by improving all or a fraction of the start population [8], by improving all or some offspring [5], by some sort of post-optimisation of the EA results [9], or by combinations thereof. This was investigated and compared in detail in [6] and [7], and an important result is that offspring improvement works best and that all strategy parameters and the choice of an appropriate local searcher are application-dependent. This paper will focus on offspring improvement, a kind of hybridisation which is also known as Memetic Algorithm (MA) [10]. This term was introduced by Moscato [11] and the idea is to imitate the effect of learning and social interaction during the life span of an individual by some kind of (local) improvement mechanisms (*memes*) applied to the offspring created by the common operators of an EA.

The aim of the work presented here is to find a mechanism for the adaptive control of as many strategy parameters of an MA for continuous parameter optimisation as possible. The cost-benefit-based approach proposed for adaptation controls both meme selection and the intensity of their work, and thus the balance between global and local search. The procedure can be applied to all population-based EAs, and it is desirable, but not necessary to have more than one offspring per mating.

In section 2 the approach will be compared to other adaptive MAs and it will be shown in which way it fills the gap previous work leaves. The approach will be described in detail in section 3, while the results of in-depth experiments using five test functions and two real-world problems shall be presented in section 4. The paper will be concluded by a summary and an outlook in section 5.

2 Related Work

For MAs an appropriate choice of the local search method employed has a major impact on the search performance, as shown for example by Hart [12], Krasnogor [13], Ong [14], and our own results [6, 7]. As it is usually not known a priori which LS performs best or at least well, multimeme EAs (MMA) were introduced by Krasnogor and Smith [15] and applied to two bioinformatics problems [13]. The difference to "simple MAs" (MAs with one meme and without any adaptation will be referred to as *simple MA* (SMA)) is that multimeme EAs do not employ one complex or sophisticated LS, but a set of more or less simple LSs. From this set, it is selected adaptively which one is to be used for different individuals in the course of evolution. Another big step in this direction is Krasnogor's "Self-Generating Memetic Algorithm" which is able to create its own local searchers and to co-evolve their behaviours as required to successfully solve a given problem [13]. Here, the classification of adaptation given in [16] shall be used: "*Adaptive dynamic adaptation* takes place if there is some form of feedback from the EA that is used to determine the direction and magnitude of the change to the strategy parameters." In the case of *self-adaptation*, "the parameters to be adapted are encoded onto the chromosome(s) of the individual and undergo mutation and recombination."

On addition to LS selection, the distribution of computing resources between local and global search is another important issue. It is usually controlled by the intensity of the local search and the fraction of offspring, to which the LS is applied, see e.g. [12].

Furthermore, it must be decided, whether this partitioning shall be static or change during the progress of search. Goldberg and Voessner [17] presented a first analysis on a system level, where two scenarios were investigated: the attempt to obtain a specified solution quality in a minimum time or the goal of achieving the best possible solution quality in a given time. This work was continued by Sinha, Chen, and Goldberg [18], but is still "based on a number of assumptions which may require information unavailable in practice", as the authors stated themselves.

In Table 1 a classification of the different approaches to adaptive MAs as to *how* and *what* is adaptively controlled is presented together with the researchers, who introduced and investigated them in detail (publications on single problems or aspects of MAs are omitted here). Furthermore, it is indicated whether a given quality or time frame limits the run of the particular MA and whether it was applied mainly to combinatorial or parameter optimisation. The table also shows how the work reported here complements previous research in this area. In addition to the table the work of Hart [12] and Lozano et al. [19] must be mentioned here. They experimented with different local search intensities and showed that the best number of iterations is application-dependent. From this it can be concluded that it should be adjusted adaptively.

Table 1. Classification of different adaptive MAs

<table>
<tr><th></th><th colspan="2">Adaptive Dynamic Adaptation</th><th>Self-adaptation</th></tr>
<tr><td>Meme selection</td><td>Ong & Keane [14]
quality, param. opt.</td><td rowspan="2">Jakob et al.
[7, 22]
quality, param. opt.</td><td>Krasnogor, Smith [13, 15, 23]
quality, comb. and param. opt.</td></tr>
<tr><td>Intensity of the search of the meme(s)</td><td>Zitzler et al. [20, 21]
time, comb. opt.</td><td></td></tr>
</table>

The cost-benefit-based adaptation scheme used by Ong and Keane [14] is close to that used here and it was obviously developed in parallel (cf. [7] and [22]), but it is used for meme selection only. The number of allowed evaluations per LS run is fixed to 100, which means that local search is stopped before convergence in many cases [14]. Ong and Keane investigated two kinds of selection mechanisms for a set of nine different LSs and found that their approach performed closely to the best SMA. This is a great advantage, as the decision which meme to use can now be left to the adaptation without any danger of a relevant performance lost. While Ong and Kane concentrate on the selection of an LS, the work presented here focuses more on the intensity of an LS run. Hence, both complement each other.

The approach by Zitzler et al. [20] is based on a fixed time budget. They use parameterised local searchers, where the amount of iterations and, thus, accuracy can be controlled. They start with low accuracy and increase it according to a given schedule comparable to simulated annealing. In a later and enhanced version Bambha et al. [21] replace the fixed schedules by dynamic ones which take the observed increase of solution quality produced by the LS into account. Still, their framework is based on a fixed time budget. Their detailed investigation demonstrates the superiority of adaptation of the intensity of local search over SMAs, where the number of iterations of the LS is fixed and usually set high for achieving a good accuracy [21]. We share the idea of adaptively increasing the precision of the local search in the course of evolution.

The main difference is the fixed time frame, upon which their algorithm is constructed. Especially for new problems, only rough estimates of the time required to at least get a feasible solution may be obtained. Despite the fact that there are applications where adhering to a fixed time frame is essential, we think that a more general approach which attempts to yield the best within the shortest possible time, also has its significance.

The motivation for using an external mechanism for adaptation rather than self-adaptation, as it is done by Krasnogor and Smith [13, 15, 23, 24] and others, is as follows: self-adaptation has proved its suitability when e.g. applied to control the mutation rate as it is the case with the ES. This works well, because only fitness improvements play a role, as the cost for a mutation is independent of the chosen step size. The choice of different LSs, however, implies different numbers of evaluations (costs), unless they are stopped uniformly. These costs should be taken into account. Therefore, an external control mechanism, such as the cost-benefit-based adaptation introduced, is required. Another argument is that the self-adaptation of strategy parameters of the evolutionary mechanism is somewhat different from self-adapting the control parameters of an additional algorithm like an LS. Krasnogor et al. [24] state: "The rationale is to propagate local searchers (i.e. memes) that are associated with fit individuals, as those individuals were probably improved by their respective memes." Or they were improved by recent evolution! This cannot be concluded from the fitness value alone, because the fitness sums up the fitness coming from evolution and that originated from local search. Despite the success reported by the authors of co-evolution, we think that these are arguments in favour of the investigation of the cost-benefit-based approach introduced.

3 Concept of Cost-Benefit-Based Adaptation

The adaptive mechanism is based on the fitness gain obtained by local search and the effort spent that is measured in evaluations. This mechanism is described for the case of scheduling local searchers. Initially, all LSs have the same probability of being selected. The relative fitness gain *rfg* and the required evaluations *eval* are summed up. A normalised fitness function in the range of 0 and f_{max} is used, which turns every task into a maximisation problem. The relative fitness gain is the ratio between the achieved fitness improvement and the possible one, as shown in (1), where f_{LS} is the fitness obtained by the LS and f_{evo} the fitness of the offspring as produced by the evolution. The probabilities of applying the local searchers are adjusted, if either each LS was used at minimum $usage_{min}$ times or there have been $matings_{max}$ matings in total since the last adjustment. The new relation between the local searchers *LS1, .. , LSn* is calculated as shown in (1).

The sums are reset to zero after the adjustment, such that the adaptation is faster. If the probability for one LS is worse than P_{min} for three consecutive alterations, it is ignored from then on. To avoid premature deactivation, the probability is set to P_{min} for the first time it drops below P_{min}. For the experiments P_{min} was set to 0.1.

$$rfg = \frac{f_{LS} - f_{evo}}{f_{\max} - f_{evo}} \qquad \frac{\sum rfg_{i,LS1}}{\sum eval_{i,LS1}} : \ldots : \frac{\sum rfg_{j,LSn}}{\sum eval_{j,LSn}} \tag{1}$$

This approach can be extended easily for strategy parameters to be adapted like the maximum permissible iterations of an LS. For each parameter, a set of levels is defined corresponding to appropriate values like iteration limits or termination thresholds. In contrast to the selection of LSs, however, where all LSs have a certain chance of being selected unless they prove their infeasibility, only three consecutive levels are allowed to be active here (i.e. to have a probability p greater than zero) at the same time. Initially, a likeliness of 0.5 is assigned to the lowest level, 0.3 to the next one, and 0.2 to the last one, ensuring that the search will start coarsely. If the lowest or highest active level is given a probability of more than 0.5, the next lower or higher, respectively, is added. The level at the opposite end is dropped and its likeliness is added to its neighbour. The new level is given a probability equal to 20% from the sum of the probabilities of the other two levels. This causes a move of three consecutive levels along the scale of possible ones according to their performance determined by the achieved fitness gain and the required evaluations. To ensure mobility in both directions none of the three active levels may have a probability below 0.1. An example of a movement of the active levels is shown in Fig. 1.

For EAs that create more than one offspring per mating, such as the one used here, a choice must be made between locally optimising the best (called *best-improvement*) or a fraction of up to all of these offspring (called *all-improvement*). This is controlled adaptively in the following way: the best offspring always undergoes LS improvement and for its siblings the chance of being treated by the LS is adaptively adjusted as described before, with the following peculiarities. After having processed all selected offspring, f_{LS} is estimated as the fitness of the best locally improved child and f_{evo} as that of the best offspring from pure evolution.

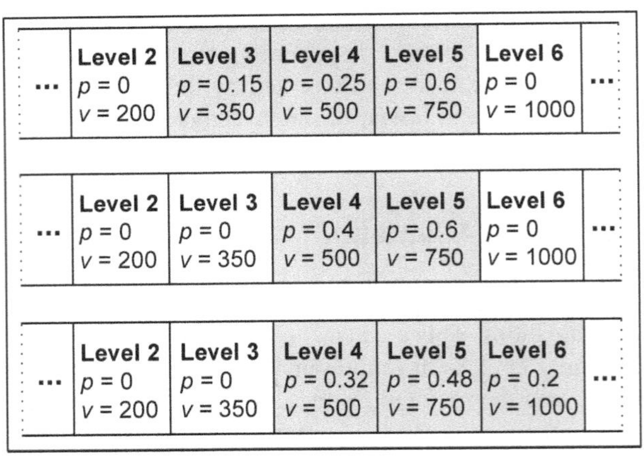

Fig. 1. Three phases of a level movement. p denotes the probability of the levels and v the associated strategy parameter value, which is just an illustrating example here. Active levels are marked by a grey background.

4 Experiments

Due to the lack of space, the basic algorithms used for the experiments shall be described briefly only and the interested reader is referred to the given literature. Suitable local search algorithms must be derivative-free and able to handle restrictions in order to preserve the general applicability of the resulting MA. The Complex and the Rosenbrock algorithm, two well-known procedures from the sixties, were chosen, since they meet these requirements and are known to be powerful local search procedures. The Rosenbrock algorithm is a modified coordinate strategy that uses a rotating coordinate system which points in the direction that appears to be most favorable. The Complex procedure is a polyhedron strategy using expansion, reflection, and contraction for improving the polyhedron. The implementation is based on Schwefel [25], who gives a detailed description of both algorithms together with experimental results. Hereinafter, the algorithms are abbreviated by R and C.

The EA used is GLEAM (General Learning Evolutionary Algorithm and Method) [26], an EA of its own that combines elements from Evolution Strategy (ES) and real-coded Genetic Algorithms with data structuring concepts from computer science. The coding is based on chromosomes consisting of problem-configurable gene types. The definition of a gene type constitutes its set of real, integer or Boolean parameters together with their ranges of values. There are different rules for constructing chromosomes from gene types covering the range of pure parameter and combinatorial optimisation including chromosomes of variable length. Based on the gene type definitions a set of standard genetic operators is defined. This provides users with a flexible mechanism for naturally mapping their problem to the chromosomes and genes, often resulting in genotypes from which phenotypic properties can be derived easily. Among others, GLEAM contains mutation operators influenced by the ES insofar, as small parameter changes are more likely than greater ones. GLEAM uses ranking-based selection, elitist offspring acceptance, and a structured population based on a neighbourhood model [27], that causes an adaptive balance between exploration and exploitation and avoids premature convergence. This is achieved by maintaining niches within the population for a longer period of time and thus, sustains diversity. Hence, GLEAM can be regarded a more powerful EA compared to simple ones, which makes it harder to gain improvement by adding local search. On the other hand, if an improvement can be achieved by adding and applying memes adaptively, then at least the same advantage if not better can be expected by using a simpler EA.

These procedures were integrated and the resulting hybrid GLEAM (HyGLEAM) covers all kinds of hybridisation mentioned in the first section. Detailed investigations of the SMA included in HyGLEAM showed that Lamarckian evolution, where the chromosomes are updated according to the LS improvement, performs better than without updates [6, 7, 22]. The danger of premature convergence, which was observed by other researchers, is avoided by the neighbourhood model used [26, 27].

Adaptive HyGLEAM controls meme selection and four strategy parameters controlling the intensity of local search (th_R, $limit_R$, and $limit_C$) and the frequency of meme application (*all_impr*) as shown in Table 2. th_R is a termination threshold value of the Rosenbrock procedure, while $limit_R$ and $limit_C$ margin the LS iterations. In case

Table 2. Adaptively controlled strategy parameters of the Multimeme Algorithm (MMA)

Strategy parameter	Values used for the experiments
th_R	10^{-1}, 10^{-2}, 10^{-3}, 10^{-4}, 10^{-5}, 10^{-6}, 10^{-7}, 10^{-8}, 10^{-9}
$limit_R$, $limit_C$	100, 200, 350, 500, 750, 1000, 1250, 1500, 1750, 2000
all-impr	0, 0.2, 0.4, 0.6, 0.8, 1.0

of all-improvement (see also section 3), the probability of the siblings of the best offspring being treated by a meme is denoted *all_impr.*

4.1 Strategy Parameters of the Adaptation Scheme

First experiments and thorough observations of the adaptation process have led to the insight that adaptation should be allowed to develop differently for dissimilar fitness levels. The experiments were carried out with three parameterisations for the fitness levels and three different adaptation speeds (see also section 3), as shown in Tables 3 and 4. Together with the choice between best- and all-improvement, this results in three new strategy parameters, and a crucial question related to the experiments is, whether they can be set to common values without any relevant loss of performance.

Tables 3 and 4. Strategy parameters of the adaptive Multimeme Algorithm (AMMA)

Fitness Levels	Fitness Ranges in % of f_{max}
fl1	40 70 100
fl2	35 65 85 100
fl3	30 55 75 90 100

Adaptation Speed	Meme Selection		Parameter Adaptation	
	$usage_{min}$	$matings_{max}$	$usage_{min}$	$matings_{max}$
fast	3	15	3	12
medium	5	20	4	15
slow	8	30	7	25

4.2 Test Cases

Appropriate test cases must be representative of real-world applications, their calculation must be comparatively fast for statistical investigations, and the exact or an acceptable solution must be known. We used five test functions taken from GENEsYs [28] and two real-world problems, see Table 5. Due to the lack of space they are described very briefly only, and the interested reader is referred to the given literature and to [6, 7, 22]. We used rotated versions of Shekel's Foxholes and the Rastrigin function in order to make them harder, see [7, 22]. The scheduling task is solved largely by assigning start times to the production batches.

Table 5. Important properties of the test cases used. *fi* are the function numbers of [28].

Test Case	Para-meter	Modality	Implicit Restrict.	Range	Target Value
Schwefel's Sphere[28, f1]	30 real	unimodal	no	$[-10^{10}, 10^{10}]$	0.01
Shekel's Foxholes [28, f5]	2 real	multimodal	no	[-500, 500]	0.998004
Gen. Rastrigin f. [28, f7]	5 real	multimodal	no	[-5.12, 5.12]	0.0001
Fletcher & Powell f. [28, f16]	5 real	multimodal	no	[-3.14, 3.14]	0.00001
Fractal f. [28, f13]	20 real	multimodal	no	[-5, 5]	-0.05
Design optimisation [29]	3 real	multimodal	no		
Scheduling + resource opt.[30]	87 int.	multimodal	yes		

4.3 Experimental Results

The comparisons were based on one hundred runs per *job* (an algorithm together with a setting of its strategy parameters). The effort was measured by the average number of evaluations needed for success, i.e. reaching the target value of Table 5 or a given solution quality in case of the real-world problems. Only jobs where all runs were successful were taken into account for comparison to ensure high convergence reliability. The different jobs were evaluated by the improvement in effort achieved compared with the best hand-tuned GLEAM job. Table 6 shows the results for the best jobs of the basic EA GLEAM, the two simple MAs SMA-R ($th_{R,}$, best/all) and SMA-C (best/all) using the Rosenbrock or the Complex procedure respectively, and two parameterisations of the adaptive Multimeme Algorithm (AMMA): best AMMA (adaptation speed, fitness levels, best/all) and recommended AMMA (see next section). The hand-tuned strategy parameters are given in brackets except for the population size μ, which was always tuned.

Table 6 shows that the effort required could be reduced massively when using the appropriate SMA or the AMMA and that the choice of a suitable LS for the SMA is application-dependent. Based on a detailed statistical analysis of the results, the following best setting of the strategy parameters of the AMMA (cf. Tables 3 and 4) can be given: all-improvement, fitness level fl1, and slow adaptation speed. On the average, the best jobs of this recommended AMMA reach 83% of the observed effort reduction of the best hand-tuned AMMA. The differences between best and recommended AMMA are not significant for the scheduling and the design optimisation task. Thus, the recommended AMMA performs only a little worse for three test cases: sphere, Fletcher's, and fractal function. The great span of population sizes from 5 to 11,200 used with the basic EA GLEAM could be reduced to a range between 5 and 90, which simplifies the estimation of the appropriate value for that last remaining strategy parameter. Fig. 2 illustrates the improvements obtained. For a correct interpretation of the outstanding results reached with one of the two SMAs for three test cases, it must be considered that they all require careful and cumbersome tuning and that it is some sort of peak-shaped optimum in the case of the scheduling task. Furthermore, both AMMA parameterisations yield better results than the best SMA in case of Shekel's foxholes, the Rastrigin, and the fractal function.

Table 6. Effort (evaluations) for best hand-tuned basic EA GLEAM, two SMAs, best AMMA and recommended AMMA and their best population sizes μ. "-" indicates no success.

Test Case	Basic EA GLEAM		SMA-R		SMA-C		Best AMMA		Rec.AMMA	
	μ	eval.	μ	eval.	μ	eval	μ	eval.	μ	eval.
Sphere	5	278,102	10	2,518		-	5	9,316	5	18,718
Fletcher	600	483,566	10	13,535	5	4,684	10	11,808	5	14,449
Sched.	1,800	5,376,334	5	69,448		-	30	235,410	20	257,951
Foxholes	350	103,192	30	10,710	20	8,831	20	6,209	20	6,209
Rastrigin	11,200	3,518,702	70	315,715	150	3,882,531	90	265,892	90	265,892
Fractal	20	195,129	5	30,626	10	1,065,986	5	20,753	5	28,644
Design	210	5,773	10	4,222	5	1,041	10	1,201	5	1,440

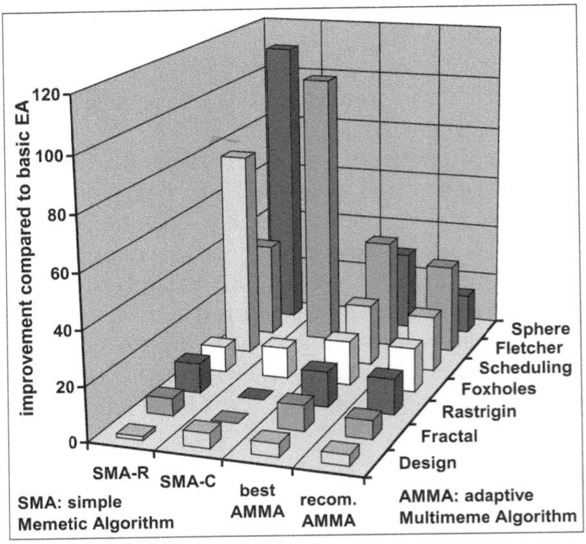

Fig. 2. Comparison of the best SMA and AMMA jobs. Empty fields indicate an insufficient success rate (below 100%), while flat fields denote the fulfilling of the optimisation task, but with greater effort than the basic EA. The given improvements are the ratio between the means of the evaluations of the basic EA and the compared algorithm.

5 Conclusions and Outlook

We introduced a cost-benefit-based adaptation for both meme selection and intensity and frequency of meme usage, which defines the balance between global and local search. It was shown how this approach fits into the gap previous work in the field left open. Finally, a common parameterisation of the adaptive Multimeme Algorithm suggested was developed, which requires only one strategy parameter to be adjusted, the population size. For this, it is recommended to start with a value of 20 or more for problems that are assumed to be very complex.

As the proposed adaptation scheme can be applied to any other EA, it is hoped to meet the engineer's needs for an easy-to-apply EA for the task on hand. As the results are based on five test functions and two real-world app-lications, they should be verified by further applications or test cases. The addition of more local searchers and improvements of the adaptation mechanism are also interesting fields of further research.

References

1. Grefenstette, J.J.: Optimization of Control Parameters for Genetic Algorithms. IEEE Transactions on Systems, Man, and Cybernetics, vol. 16 (1) (1986) 122-128
2. Srinivas, M., Patnaik, L.M.: Adaptive Probabilities of Crossover and Mutation in Genetic Algorithms. IEEE Trans. on Systems, Man, and Cybernetics, vol. 24 (4) (1994) 17-26
3. Eiben, A.E, Hinterding, R., Michalewicz, Z.: Parameter Control in Evolutionary Algorithms. IEEE Trans. on Evolutionary Computation, vol. 3 (2) (1999) 124-141
4. L. Davis, L. (ed), Handbook of Genetic Algorithms. Van Nostrand Reinhold, NY (1991)
5. Hart, W.E., Krasnogor, N., Smith, J.E. (eds.): Recent Advances in Memetic Algorithms. Studies in Fuzziness and Soft Computing, vol. 166, Springer, Berlin (2005)
6. Jakob, W.: HyGLEAM – An Approach to Generally Applicable Hybridization of Evolutionary Algorithms. In: Merelo, J.J., et al. (eds.): Conf. Proc. PPSN VII, LNCS 2439, Springer, Berlin (2002) 527–536
7. Jakob, W: A New Method for the Increased Performance of Evolutionary Algorithms by the Integration of Local Search Procedures. In German, PhD thesis, Univ. of Karlsruhe, FZKA 6965, March 2004, see also: http://www.iai.fzk.de/~jakob/HyGLEAM/main-gb.html

8. Lienig, J., Brandt, H.: An Evolutionary Algorithm for the Routing of Multi Chip Modules. In: Davidor, Y., Schwefel, H.-P., Männer, R. (eds.): Conf. Proc. PPSN III, LNCS 866, Springer, Berlin (1994) 588-597
9. Cox jr., L.A., Davis, L., Oiu, Y.: Dynamic Anticipatory Routing in Circuit Switches Telecommunications Networks. In [4] (1991) 124-143
10. Krasnogor, N., Smith, J.E.: A Tutorial for Competent Memetic Algorithms: Model, Taxonomy, and Design Isssues. IEEE Trans. on Evol. Comp., vol. 9 (5) (2005) 474-488
11. Moscato, P.: On Evolution, Search, Optimization, Genetic Algorithms and Martial Arts - Towards Memetic Algorithms. Tech. rep. 826, California Inst. Technol., Pasadena (1989)
12. Hart, W.E.: Adaptive Global Optimization with Local Search. PhD thesis, University of California, San Diego, CA, USA (1994)
13. Krasnogor, N.: Studies on the Theory and Design Space of Memetic Algorithms. PhD thesis, Faculty Comput., Math. and Eng., Univ. West of England, Bristol, U.K. (2002)
14. Ong, Y.S., Keane, A.J.: Meta-Lamarckian Learning in Memetic Algorithms. IEEE Trans. on Evolutionary Computation, vol. 8, no. 2 (2004) 99-110, citation: p.100
15. Krasnogor, N., Smith, J.E.: Emergence of Profitable Search Strategies Based on a Simple Inheritance Algorithm. In: Conf. Proc. GECCO 2001, M. Kaufmann, S. Francisco, 432-439
16. Hinterding, R., Michalewicz, Z., Eiben, A.E.: Adaptation in Evolutionary Computation: A Survey. In: Conf. Proc. IEEE Conf. on Evol. Comp. (CEC 97), IEEE press (1997) 65-69
17. Goldberg, D.E., Voessner, S.: Optimizing Global-Local Search Hybrids. In: Conf. Proc. GECCO 99, Morgan Kaufmann, San Mateo, CA (1999) 220-228
18. Shina, A., Chen, Y., Goldberg, D.E.: Designing Efficient Genetic and Evolutionary Algorithm Hybrids. In [5] (2005) 259-288
19. Lozano, M., Herrera, F., Krasnogor, N., Molina, D.: Real-Coded Memetic Algorithms with Crossover Hill-Climbing. Evolutionary Computation Journal, vol 12(2) (2004) 273-302
20. Zitzler, E., Teich, J., Bhattacharyya, S.S.: Optimizing the Efficiency of Parameterized Local Search within Global Search: A Preliminary Study. In: Conf. Proc CEC 2000, IEEE press, Piscataway, NJ (2000). 365-372
21. Bambha, N.K., Bhattacharyya, S.S., Zitzler, E., Teich, J.: Systematic Integration of Parameterized Local Search into Evolutionary Algorithms. IEEE Trans. on Evolutionary Computation, vol. 8(2) (2004) 137-155
22. Jakob, W., Blume, C., Bretthauer, G.: Towards a Generally Applicable Self-Adapting Hybridization of Evolutionary Algorithms. In: Conf. Proc. GECCO 2004, LNCS 3102, Springer, Berlin (2004) 790-791 and vol. Late Breaking Papers
23. Smith, J.E.: Co-evolving Memetic Algorithms: A learning approach to robust scalable optimisation. In: Conf. Proc. CEC 2003, IEEE press, Piscataway, N.J. (2003) 498-505
24. Krasnogor, N., Blackburne, B.P., Burke, E.K., Hirst, J.D.: Multimeme Algorithms for Protein Structure Prediction. In: Conf. Proc. PPSN VII, LNCS 2439, Springer, Berlin (2002) 769-778, citation: p.772
25. Schwefel, H.-P.: Evolution and Optimum Seeking. John Wiley & Sons, New York (1995)
26. Blume, C., Jakob, W.: GLEAM – An Evolutionary Algorithm for Planning and Control Based on Evolution Strategy. In: Cantú-Paz, E. (ed): GECCO 2002, vol. Late Breaking Papers (2002) 31-38
27. Gorges-Schleuter, M.: *Genetic Algorithms and Population Structures - A Massively Parallel Algorithm.* Dissertation, Dept. Comp. Science, University of Dortmund, 1990
28. Bäck, T.: GENEsYs 1.0 (1992) ftp://lumpi.informatik.uni-dortmund.de/pub/GA/
29. Sieber, I. Eggert, H., Guth, H., Jakob, W.: Design Simulation and Optimization of Microoptical Components. In: Bell, K.D. et al. (eds): Proceedings of Novel Optical Systems and Large-Aperture Imaging. SPIE, vol.3430 (1998) 138-149
30. Blume, C., Gerbe, M.: Deutliche Senkung der Produktionskosten durch Optimierung des Ressourceneinsatzes. atp 36, 5/94, Oldenbourg Verlag, München (in German) (1994) 25-29

Niche Radius Adaptation in the CMA-ES Niching Algorithm

Ofer M. Shir[1] and Thomas Bäck[1,2]

[1] Leiden Institute of Advanced Computer Science
Universiteit Leiden
Niels Bohrweg 1, 2333 CA Leiden
The Netherlands
[2] NuTech Solutions
Martin-Schmeisser-Weg 15
44227 Dortmund
Germany

Abstract. Following the introduction of two *niching methods* within Evolution Strategies (ES), which have been presented recently and have been successfully applied to theoretical high-dimensional test functions, as well as to a real-life high-dimensional physics problem, the purpose of this study is to address the so-called *niche radius problem*.

A new concept of *adaptive individual niche radius*, introduced here for the first time, is applied to the ES Niching with Covariance Matrix Adaptation (CMA) method. The proposed method is described in detail, and then tested on high-dimensional theoretical test functions.

It is shown to be robust and to achieve satisfying results.

1 Introduction

Evolutionary Algorithms (EAs) have the tendency to converge quickly into a single solution [1,2,3], i.e. all the individuals of the artificial population evolve to become nearly identical. Given a problem with multiple solutions, the traditional EAs will locate a single solution. This is the desired result for many complex tasks, but a problem arises when multimodal domains are considered and multiple optima are required. For instance, consider an optimization problem for a high-dimensional real-world application, which requires the location of highly-fit multiple solutions with high diversity among them - a result which a sequential multiple-restart algorithm doesn't aim for. *Niching methods*, the extension of EAs to multi-modal optimization, address this problem by maintaining the diversity of certain properties within the population - and this way they allow parallel convergence into multiple good solutions. Up to date, *niching methods* have been studied mainly within the field of Genetic Algorithms (GAs). The research in this direction has yielded various successful methods which have been shown to find multiple solutions efficiently [1], but naturally were limited to low-dimensional real-valued problems. Evolution Strategies (ES) are a *canonical EA for real-valued function optimization*, due to their straightforward encoding,

T.P. Runarsson et al. (Eds.): PPSN IX, LNCS 4193, pp. 142–151, 2006.

their specific variation operators, the self-adaptation of their mutation distribution as well as to their high performance in this domain in comparison with other methods on benchmark problems. The higher the dimensionality of the search space, the more suitable a task becomes for an ES (see, e.g. [3], pp. 149-159). Two ES niching methods have been proposed lately [4,5]. Upon their successful application to high-dimensional theoretical functions, those methods were successfully applied to a real-world high-dimensional physics problem, namely the *optimization of dynamic molecular alignment by shaped laser pulses* [6]. In that application, the niching technique was shown to be clearly qualitatively inferior with respect to multiple restart runs with a single population, for locating highly-fit unique optima which had not been obtained otherwise.

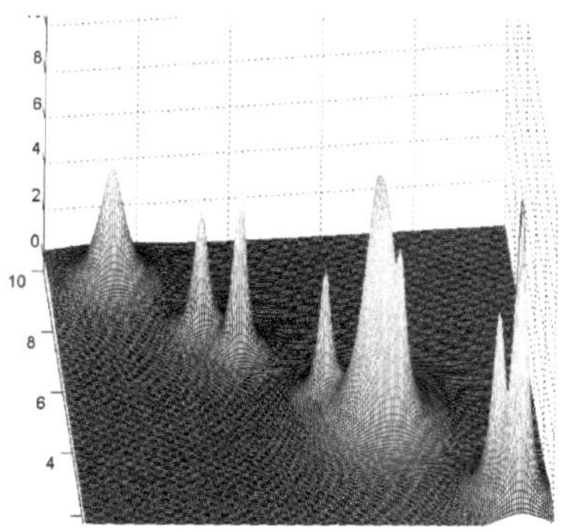

Fig. 1. $\mathcal{S}$, $n = 2$

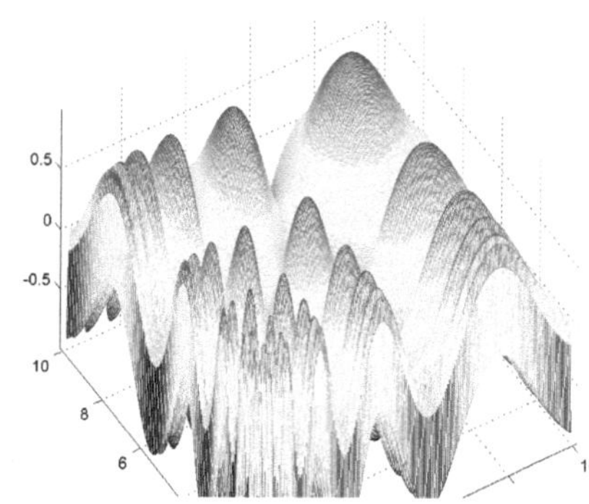

Fig. 2. $\mathcal{V}$, $n = 2$

The ES niching methods, as the majority of the GA niching methods, hold an assumption concerning the fitness landscape, stating that the peaks are far enough from one another with respect to some threshold distance, called the *niche radius*, which is estimated for the given problem and remains fixed during the course of evolution. Obviously, there are landscapes for which this assumption isn't applicable, and where those niching methods are most likely to fail (for example see Fig. 1, 2). There were several GA-oriented studies which addressed this so-called *niche radius problem*, aiming to drop this assumption, such as the cooling-based UEGO [7] or the clustering-based DNC [8]. A more theoretical study of a clustering-based niching can be found in [9]. Moreover, an iterative statistical-based approach was introduced lately [10] for learning an optimal niche radius (without relaxing the fitness landscape assumption).

Our proposed method introduces a new concept to the niche radius problem, inspired by the ES self-adaptation concept - an **adaptive individual niche radius**. The idea is that each individual carries and adapts a niche radius along with its adaptive strategy parameters. This method is an "adaptive extension" to the *CMA-ES dynamic niching algorithm* [5], as will be explained.

The remainder of the paper is organized as follows: In section 2 we introduce the background for the various components of our proposed algorithm. Section 3 introduces our proposed algorithm. In section 4 the test functions as well as the methodology for the performance study are outlined, where the numerical results are presented and analyzed in section 5. Section 6 provides summary and conclusion.

2 From Fitness Sharing to the CMA-ES Niching Method

2.1 Fitness Sharing

The *fitness sharing* approach [11] was the pioneering GA niching method. Its idea is to consider the fitness as a shared resource and by that to aim to decrease redundancy in the population. Given the similarity metric of the population, which can be genotype or phenotype based, the *sharing function* is given by:

$$sh(d_{ij}) = \begin{cases} 1 - \left(\frac{d_{ij}}{\rho}\right)^{\alpha_{sh}} & \text{if } d_{ij} < \rho \\ 0 & \text{otherwise} \end{cases} \tag{1}$$

where d_{ij} is the distance between individuals i and j, ρ (traditionally noted as σ_{sh}) is the fixed radius of every niche, and α_{sh} is a control parameter, usually set to 1. Using the *sharing function*, the *niche count* is then defined as follows:

$$m_i = \sum_{j=1}^{N} sh(d_{ij}) \tag{2}$$

Given an individual's raw fitness f_i, the *shared fitness* is then defined by:

$$f_i^{sh} = \frac{f_i}{m_i} \tag{3}$$

2.2 Dynamic Niche Sharing

The *dynamic niche sharing* method [12], which succeeded the fitness sharing method, aims to dynamically recognize the q peaks of the forming niches, and with this information to classify the individuals as either members of one of the niches, or as members of the "non-peaks domain". Explicitly, let us introduce the *dynamic niche count*:

$$m_i^{dyn} = \begin{cases} n_j & \text{if individual } i \text{ is within dynamic niche } j \\ m_i & \text{otherwise (non-peak individual)} \end{cases} \tag{4}$$

where n_j is the size of the jth dynamic niche, and m_i is the standard *niche count*, as defined in Eq. 2. The shared fitness is then defined respectively:

$$f_i^{dyn} = \frac{f_i}{m_i^{dyn}} \tag{5}$$

The identification of the dynamic niches can be done in the greedy approach, as proposed in [12] as the Dynamic Peak Identification (DPI) algorithm.

2.3 Dynamic Niching in Evolution Strategies

The ES dynamic niching algorithm [4] was introduced recently as a niching method for the Evolution Strategies framework. The inspiration for this algorithm was given by various niching algorithms from the GA field, and in particular by the *fitness sharing* [11] and its dynamic extension [12], as well as by the *crowding* concept [13]. The basic idea of the algorithm is to *dynamically identify the various fitness-peaks of every generation* that define the niches, *classify all the individuals into those niches*, and apply *a mating restriction scheme which allows competitive mating only within the niches*: in order to prevent *genetic drift*, every niche can produce the same number of offspring, following a *fixed mating resources* concept.

For more details we refer the reader to [14].

2.4 Dynamic Niching with Covariance Matrix Adaptation ES

The dynamic niching with CMA-ES algorithm [5] was the successor of *the ES dynamic niching algorithm*, where the CMA replaces the mutative step-size control. We provide here a short overview of the CMA-ES method, followed by a description of the algorithm.

The $(1, \lambda)$-CMA-ES: A Brief Overview. The *covariance matrix adaptation evolution strategy* [15], is a variant of ES that has been successful for treating correlations among object variables. This method tackles the critical element of Evolution Strategies, the adaptation of the mutation parameters. We provide here a short description of the principal elements of the $(1, \lambda)$-CMA-ES.

The fundamental property of this method is the exploitation of information obtained from previous successful mutation operations. Given an initial search point $\boldsymbol{x}^0$, λ offspring are sampled from it by applying the mutation operator. The best search point out of those λ offspring is chosen to become the parent of the next generation.

Explicitly, the action of the *mutation operator* for generating the λ samples of search points in generation $g+1$ is defined as follows:

$$\boldsymbol{x}^{g+1} \sim \mathcal{N}\left(\boldsymbol{x}_k^{(g)}, \sigma^{(g)^2}\mathbf{C}^{(g)}\right), \qquad k = 1, ..., \lambda \tag{6}$$

where $\mathcal{N}(\boldsymbol{m}, \mathbf{C})$ denotes a normally distributed random vector with mean $\boldsymbol{m}$ and covariance matrix $\mathbf{C}$. The matrix $\mathbf{C}$, the crucial element of this process, is initialized as the *unity matrix* and is learned during the course of evolution, based on cumulative information of successful mutations (the so-called *evolution path*). The global step size, $\sigma^{(g)}$, is based on information from the *principal component analysis* of $\mathbf{C}^{(g)}$ (the so-called *"conjugate" evolution path*). We omit most of the details and refer the reader to Hansen and Ostermeier [15].

Dynamic Niching with CMA. The algorithm uses the $(1, \lambda)$-CMA ES as its evolutionary core mechanism. A brief description of the algorithm follows. Given q, the estimated/expected number of peaks, $q + p$ "CMA-sets" are initialized, where a CMA-set is defined as the collection of all the dynamic variables of the CMA algorithm which uniquely define the search at a given point of time. Such dynamic variables are the current search point, the covariance matrix, the step size, as well as other auxiliary parameters. At every point in time the algorithm stores exactly $q + p$ CMA-sets, which are associated with $q + p$ search points: q for the peaks and p for the "non-peaks domain". The $(q + 1)^{th}...(q + p)^{th}$ CMA-sets are individuals which are randomly re-generated in every generation as potential candidates for niche formation. Until stopping criteria are met, the following procedure takes place. Each search point samples λ offspring, based on its evolving CMA-set. After the fitness evaluation of the new $\lambda \cdot (q + p)$ individuals, the classification into niches of the entire population is done using the DPI algorithm, and the peaks become the new search points. Their CMA-sets are inherited from their parents and updated according to the CMA method.

2.5 The Niche Radius Problem

The traditional formula for the niche radius for *phenotypic sharing* in GAs was derived by Deb and Goldberg [16]. By following the trivial analogy and considering the decision parameters as the decoded parameter space of the GA, the same formula was applied to the ES niching methods. It is important to note that this formula depends on q, the expected/desired number of peaks in the solution space:

$$\rho = \frac{r}{\sqrt[n]{q}} \tag{7}$$

where given lower and upper boundary values $x_{k,min}$, $x_{k,max}$ of each coordinate in the decision parameters space, r is defined as $r = \frac{1}{2}\sqrt{\sum_{k=1}^{n}(x_{k,max} - x_{k,min})^2}$. For the complete derivation see, e.g., [6].

Hence, by applying this niche radius approach, two assumptions are held:

1. The expected/desired number of peaks, q, is given or can be estimated.
2. **All peaks are at least in distance 2ρ from each other**, where ρ is the fixed radius of every niche.

3 The Proposed Algorithm: Niche Radius Adaptation in the CMA-ES Niching Algorithm

Our new algorithm tackles the *niche radius problem*, in particular the assumption regarding the fitness landscape: it introduces the concept of an individual niche radius which adapts during the course of evolution. The idea is to *couple* the niche radius to the global step size σ, whereas the *indirect selection* of the niche radius is applied through the demand for λ individuals per niche. This is implemented through a quasi *dynamic fitness sharing* mechanism.

The *CMA-ES Niching method* is used as outlined earlier (Sec. 2.4), with the following modifications. q is given as an input to the algorithm, but it's now merely a prediction or a demand for the number of solutions, with no effect on the nature of the search. A niche radius is initialized for each individual in the population, noted as ρ_i^0. The update step of the niche radius of individual i in generation $g+1$ is based on the parent's radius and on its step-size:

$$\rho_i^{g+1} = \left(1 - c_i^{g+1}\right) \cdot \rho_{parent}^{g} + c_i^{g+1} \cdot \sigma_{parent}^{g+1} \tag{8}$$

where c_i^g is the individual learning coefficient, which is updated according to the *delta of the step size* σ:

$$c_i^{g+1} = \frac{1}{5} \cdot \left(1 - \exp\left\{\alpha \cdot \Delta\sigma_i^{g+1}\right\}\right) \qquad \Delta\sigma_i^{g+1} = \left|\sigma_{parent}^{g+1} - \sigma_{parent}^{g}\right| \tag{9}$$

This profile is chosen in order to keep the learning coefficient close to $\frac{1}{5}$ for big changes in the global step size, but make it exponentially approach 0 as the global step size vanishes, i.e. convergence is achieved. The parameter α determines the nature of this profile, and it seems to become problem dependent for some landscapes (a discussion concerning this parameter will follow).

The DPI algorithm is run using the **individual niche radii**, for the identification of the peaks and the classification of the population.
Furthermore, introduce:

$$g(x,\lambda) = 1 + \Theta(\lambda - x) \cdot \frac{(\lambda - x)^2}{\lambda} + \Theta(x - \lambda) \cdot (\lambda - x)^2 \tag{10}$$

where $\Theta(y)$ is the *Heaviside step function*. Given a fixed λ, $g(x,\lambda)$ is a parabola with unequal branches, centered at $(x = \lambda,\ g = 1)$. An explanation will follow. Then, by applying the calculation of the *dynamic niche count* m_i^{dyn} (Eq. 4), based on the appropriate radii, we **define** the *niche fitness* of individual i by:

$$f_i^{niche} = \frac{f_i}{g\left(m_i^{dyn}, \lambda\right)} \tag{11}$$

The selection of the next parent in each niche is based on this *niche fitness*. Eq. 11 enforces the requirement for having a fixed resource of λ individuals per niche, since $g(x,\lambda)$ obtains values greater than 1 for any niche count different than λ. The anti-symmetry of $g(x,\lambda)$ is therefore meant to penalize more the niches which exceeded λ members, in comparison to those with less than λ members. This equation is a variant of the dynamic shared fitness (Eq. 5), and is used now in the context of niche radius adaptation.

A single generation of the method is summarized as Algorithm 1.

4 Test Functions and Experimental Procedure

Table 1 summarizes the unconstrained multimodal test functions [3,5,17,18], as well as their initialization intervals. Some of the functions have a symmetric or equal distribution of optima ($\mathcal{A}$, $\mathcal{L}$, $\mathcal{B}$, $\mathcal{M}$, $\mathcal{G}$), and some do not ($\mathcal{F}$, $\mathcal{V}$, $\mathcal{S}$). Some

Algorithm 1. $(1,\lambda)$-CMA-ES Dynamic Niching with Adaptive Niche Radius

for all $i = 1..q+p$ search points
  Generate λ samples based on the CMA distribution of i
  Update the niche radius ρ_i^{g+1} according to Eq.8
endfor
Evaluate Fitness of the population.
Compute the Dynamic Peak Set of the population using the DPI, based on individual radii
Compute the Dynamic Niche Count (Eq.4) of every individual
for every given peak of the dynamic-peak-set do:
  Compute the Niche Fitness (Eq. 11)
  Set indiv. with best niche fitness as a search point of the next generation
  Inherit the CMA-set and update it respectively
endfor
if N_{dps} =size of dynamic-peak-set < q
  Generate $q - N_{dps}$ new search points, reset CMA-sets
endif
Reset the $(q+1)^{th}...(q+p)^{th}$ search points

of the functions are *non-separable.* The *CMA-ES dynamic niching* algorithm (with a fixed niche radius) was tested on $\{\mathcal{A},\ \mathcal{L},\ \mathcal{F}\}$ [5], whereas it was not applied to the rest of the functions given here. Some of those additional test functions $\{\mathcal{M},\ \mathcal{B},\ \mathcal{G}\}$ are benchmark multimodal functions that will further test the robustness of the algorithm as a niching method, and the others $\{\mathcal{V},\ \mathcal{S}\}$ focus on the *niche radius problem.*

$\mathcal{M}$ is meant to test the stability of a particularly large number of niches: In the interval $[0,1]^n$ this function has 3^n maxima, equally distributed as a *hyper-grid*, with equal function values of 1. $\mathcal{V}$ is a sine function with decreasing frequency (6^n optima in the interval $[0.25,10]^n$). $\mathcal{S}$, suggested in [18], introduces a landscape with dramatically uneven spread of optima. Both $\mathcal{V}$ and $\mathcal{S}$ are not likely to be tackled by a niching method with a fixed niche radius.

The algorithm is tested on the specified functions for various dimensions. Each test case includes 100 runs. All runs are performed with a core mechanism of

Table 1. Test functions to be *minimized* and initialization domains

Name	Function	Init
Ackley	$\mathcal{A}(\boldsymbol{x}) = -c_1 \cdot \exp\left(-c_2\sqrt{\frac{1}{n}\sum_{i=1}^n x_i^2}\right) - \exp\left(\frac{1}{n}\sum_{i=1}^n \cos(c_3 x_i)\right) + c_1 + e$	$[-10,10]^n$
$\mathcal{L}$	$\mathcal{L}(\boldsymbol{x}) = -\prod_{i=1}^n \sin^k(l_1\pi x_i + l_2) \cdot \exp\left(-l_3\left(\frac{x_i - l_4}{l_5}\right)^2\right)$	$[0,1]^n$
Fletcher-Powell	$\mathcal{F}(\boldsymbol{x}) = \sum_{i=1}^n (A_i - B_i)^2$ $A_i = \sum_{j=1}^n (a_{ij} \cdot \sin(\alpha_j) + b_{ij} \cdot \cos(\alpha_j))$ $B_i = \sum_{j=1}^n (a_{ij} \cdot \sin(x_j) + b_{ij} \cdot \cos(x_j))$	$[-\pi,\pi]^n$
$\mathcal{M}$	$\mathcal{M}(\boldsymbol{x}) = -\frac{1}{n}\sum_{i=1}^n \sin^\alpha(3\pi x_i)$	$[0,1]^n$
Bohachevsky	$\mathcal{B}(\boldsymbol{x}) = \sum_{i=1}^{n-1}(x_i^2 + 2x_{i+1}^2$ $-0.3 \cdot \cos(3\pi x_i) - 0.4 \cdot \cos(4\pi x_{i+1}) + 0.7)$	$[-10,10]^n$
Grienwank	$\mathcal{G}(\boldsymbol{x}) = \frac{1}{4000}\sum_{i=1}^n x_i^2 - \prod_{i=1}^n \cos\left(\frac{x_i}{\sqrt{i}}\right) + 1$	$[-10,10]^n$
Shekel	$\mathcal{S}(\boldsymbol{x}) = -\sum_{i=1}^{10} \frac{1}{k_i(\boldsymbol{x}-\boldsymbol{a}_i)(\boldsymbol{x}-\boldsymbol{a}_i)^T + c_i}$	$[0,10]^n$
Vincent	$\mathcal{V}(\boldsymbol{x}) = -\frac{1}{n}\sum_{i=1}^n \sin(10 \cdot \log(x_i))$	$[0.25,10]^n$

a $(1, 10)$-strategy per niche and initial points are sampled uniformly within the initialization intervals. Initial step sizes, as well as initial niche radii, are set to $\frac{1}{6}$ of the intervals. The parameter q is set based on a-priori knowledge when available, or arbitrarily otherwise; p is set to 1. The default value of α is -10, but it becomes problem dependent for some cases, and has to be tuned. Each run is stopped after 10^5 generations ($(q + 1) \cdot 10^6$ evaluations).

We consider three measures as the performance criteria: the saturation M.P.R. (*maximum peak ratio*; see, e.g., [5]), the global optimum location percentage, and the number of optima found (with respect to the desired value, q).

5 Numerical Results

The results of the simulations are summarized in table 2. As reflected by those results, our method performs in a satisfying manner. A comparison shows that the performance of the new niching method is not harmed by the introduction of the niche radius adaptation mechanism with respect to the same multimodal test functions reported in [5], except for the *Ackley* function in high dimensions. The latter seems to become deceptive for the adaptation mechanism as the dimensions go up: it requires the tuning of the parameter α, but no longer obtains satisfying results for $n > 15$. This occurs since the global minimum has a far stronger basin of attraction in comparison to the local minima, and many niches are formed in this basin. However, our confidence in the method is further reassured by the results on the functions $\{\mathcal{M}, \mathcal{B}, \mathcal{G}\}$ which are quite satisfying. Concerning the landscapes with the "deceptive" distribution of optima, i.e. $\mathcal{V}$ and $\mathcal{S}$, our method performed well, and managed to tackle the niche radius problem successfully. The tuning of α is also required for $\mathcal{S}$.

A visualizations of the runs on $\mathcal{V}$ and $\mathcal{S}$ for $n = 1$ are given as Fig. 3 and Fig. 4.

Table 2. Performance Results

Function	M.P.R.	Global	Optima/q	Function	M.P.R.	Global	Optima/q
$\mathcal{A}: n=3$	1	100%	7/7	$\mathcal{M}: n=3$	1	100%	100/100
$\mathcal{A}: n=20$	0.6984	59%	22.6/41	$\mathcal{M}: n=10$	0.9981	100%	99.1/100
$\mathcal{A}: n=40$	0.3186	43%	20.8/81	$\mathcal{M}: n=40$	0.7752	100%	87.2/100
$\mathcal{L}: n=4$	0.9832	100%	4.4/5	$\mathcal{B}: n=3$	0.9726	100%	3.96/5
$\mathcal{L}: n=10$	0.7288	47%	3.4/11	$\mathcal{B}: n=10$	0.5698	82%	2.21/5
$\mathcal{F}: n=2$	1	100%	4/4	$\mathcal{B}: n=20$	0.1655	61%	1.21/5
$\mathcal{F}: n=4$	0.881	100%	3.0/4	$\mathcal{G}: n=2$	0.7288	100%	3.96/5
$\mathcal{F}: n=10$	0.783	67%	2.3/4	$\mathcal{G}: n=10$	0.398	53%	2.2/5
$\mathcal{V}: n=1$	0.8385	100%	5.05/6	$\mathcal{S}: n=1$	0.9676	100%	7.833/8
$\mathcal{V}: n=2$	0.8060	100%	17.86/36	$\mathcal{S}: n=2$	0.8060	100%	6.33/8
$\mathcal{V}: n=5$	0.9714	100%	39.16/50	$\mathcal{S}: n=5$	0.7311	91%	4.37/8
$\mathcal{V}: n=10$	0.9649	100%	36.9/50	$\mathcal{S}: n=10$	0.7288	79%	3.41/8

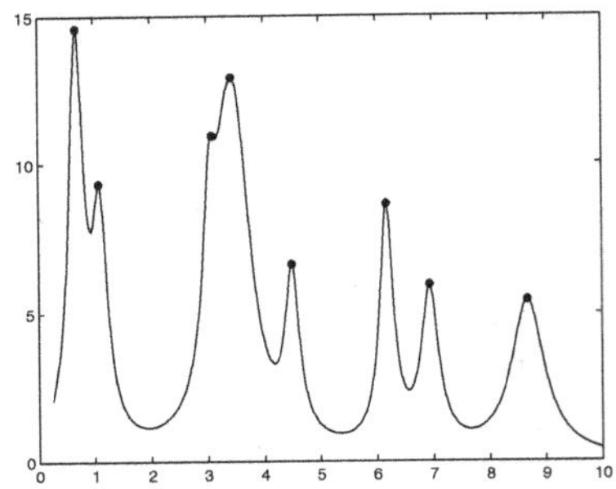

Fig. 3. $\mathcal{S}$ ($n = 1$): final population

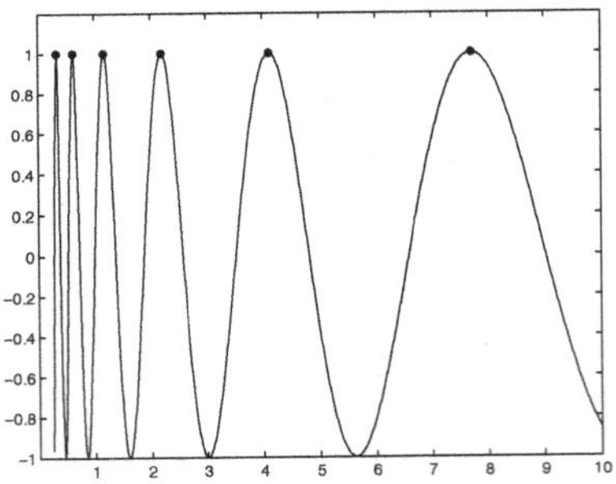

Fig. 4. $\mathcal{V}$ ($n = 1$): final population

6 Summary and Conclusion

We have proposed a new niching algorithm, with a niche-radius adaptation mechanism, for Evolution Strategies. In particular, this method relies on the CMA-ES algorithm, and couples the individual niche radius to the individual step size. The method is tested on a set of highly multimodal theoretical functions for various dimensions. It is shown to perform in a satisfying manner in the location of the desired optima of functions which were tested in the past on the predecessor of this method, using a fixed niche radius. The *Ackley* function in high dimensions seems to be deceptive for this method. More importantly, the *niche radius problem* is tackled successfully, as demonstrated on functions with unevenly spread optima. In these cases the performance was satisfying as well.

The function of the learning coefficients has to be tuned (through the parameter α) in some cases. Although this is an undesired situation, i.e., the adaptation mechanism is problem dependent, this method makes it possible to locate all desired optima on landscapes which could not be handled by the old methods of fixed niche radii, or would require the tuning of q parameters.

Acknowledgments

The authors would like to thank Michael Emmerich for the fruitful discussions.

This work is part of the research programme of the 'Stichting voor Fundamenteel Onderzoek de Materie (FOM)', which is financially supported by the 'Nederlandse organisatie voor Wetenschappelijk Onderzoek (NWO)'.

References

1. Mahfoud, S.: Niching Methods for Genetic Algorithms. PhD thesis, University of Illinois at Urbana Champaign (1995)
2. Bäck, T.: Selective pressure in evolutionary algorithms: A characterization of selection mechanisms. In Michalewicz, Z., Schaffer, J.D., Schwefel, H.P., Fogel, D.B., Kitano, H., eds.: Proc. First IEEE Conf. Evolutionary Computation (ICEC'94), Orlando FL. Volume 1., Piscataway, NJ, USA, IEEE Press (1994)

3. Bäck, T.: Evolutionary algorithms in theory and practice. Oxford University Press, New York, NY, USA (1996)
4. Shir, O.M., Bäck, T.: Niching in evolution strategies. In: Proceedings of the Genetic and Evolutionary Computation Conference, GECCO-2005, New York, NY, USA, ACM Press (2005)
5. Shir, O.M., Bäck, T.: Dynamic niching in evolution strategies with covariance matrix adaptation. In: Proceedings of the 2005 Congress on Evolutionary Computation CEC-2005, Piscataway, NJ, USA, IEEE Press (2005)
6. Shir, O.M., Siedschlag, C., Bäck, T., Vrakking, M.J.: Niching in evolution strategies and its application to laser pulse shaping. In: Lecture Notes in Computer Science. Volume 3871., Springer (2006)
7. Jelasity, M.: Uego, an abstract niching technique for global optimization. In: Parallel Problem Solving from Nature - PPSN V. Volume 1498., Amsterdam, Springer (1998)
8. Gan, J., Warwick, K.: Dynamic niche clustering: A fuzzy variable radius niching technique for multimodal optimisation in GAs. In: Proceedings of the 2001 Congress on Evolutionary Computation CEC2001, COEX, World Trade Center, 159 Samseong-dong, Gangnam-gu, Seoul, Korea, IEEE Press (2001)
9. Preuss, M., Schönemann, L., Emmerich, M.: Counteracting genetic drift and disruptive recombination in (μ, λ)-ea on multimodal fitness landscapes. In: GECCO '05: Proceedings of the 2005 conference on Genetic and evolutionary computation, New York, NY, USA, ACM Press (2005)
10. Cioppa, A.D., Stefano, C.D., Marcelli, A.: On the role of population size and niche radius in fitness sharing. IEEE Trans. Evolutionary Computation **8** (2004)
11. Goldberg, D.E., Richardson, J.: Genetic algorithms with sharing for multimodal function optimization. In: Proceedings of the Second International Conference on Genetic Algorithms on Genetic algorithms and their application, Mahwah, NJ, USA, Lawrence Erlbaum Associates, Inc. (1987)
12. Miller, B., Shaw, M.: Genetic algorithms with dynamic niche sharing for multimodal function optimization. In: Proceedings of the 1996 IEEE International Conference on Evolutionary Computation (ICEC'96), New York, NY, USA (1996)
13. Jong, K.A.D.: An analysis of the behavior of a class of genetic adaptive systems. PhD thesis (1975)
14. Shir, O.M., Bäck, T.: Niching in evolution strategies. Technical report (2005)
15. Hansen, N., Ostermeier, A.: Completely derandomized self-adaptation in evolution strategies. Evolutionary Computation **9** (2001)
16. Deb, K., Goldberg, D.E.: An investigation of niche and species formation in genetic function optimization. In: Proceedings of the third international conference on Genetic algorithms, San Francisco, CA, USA, Morgan Kaufmann Publishers Inc. (1989)
17. Hansen, N., Kern, S.: Evaluating the cma evolution strategy on multimodal test functions. In: Parallel Problem Solving from Nature - PPSN V. Volume 1498., Amsterdam, Springer (1998)
18. Törn, A., Zilinskas, A.: Global Optimization. Volume 350. Springer (1987)

A Tabu Search Evolutionary Algorithm for Solving Constraint Satisfaction Problems

B.G.W. Craenen and B. Paechter

Napier University
10 Colinton Rd, Edinburgh, EH10 5DT
{b.craenen, b.paechter}@napier.ac.uk
http://www.soc.napier.ac.uk

Abstract. The paper introduces a hybrid Tabu Search-Evolutionary Algorithm for solving the constraint satisfaction problem, called STLEA. Extensive experimental fine-tuning of parameters of the algorithm was performed to optimise the performance of the algorithm on a commonly used test-set. The performance of the STLEA was then compared to the best known evolutionary algorithm and benchmark deterministic and non-deterministic algorithms. The comparison shows that the STLEA improves on the performance of the best known evolutionary algorithm but can not achieve the efficiency of the deterministic algorithms.

1 Introduction

The last two decades saw the introduction of many evolutionary algorithms (EAs) for solving the constraint satisfaction problem (CSP). In [1], the performance of a representative sample of these EAs was compared on a large randomly generated test-set of CSP-instances. In [2] a more extensive comparison, including a large number of algorithm variants, was included, this time on a test-set generated by the latest random CSP generator. One variant algorithm, the Stepwise-Adaptation-of-Weights EA with randomly initialisated domain sets (rSAWEA) outperformed all other EAs. However, when the effectivity and the efficiency of this algorithm was compared to non-evolutionary algorithms, it was found that the effectivity of the other algorithms was approached by the rSAWEA but that the efficiency still fell short of the other algorithms.

A major reason for this lack of efficiency is that EAs tend to recheck previously checked candidate solutions during their run, wasting computational effort. This paper investigates a way of reducing this waste: the use of a tabu list.

Tabu lists are used in Tabu Search (TS) algorithms ([3]). They are used to ensure that the algorithm does not return to an already searched neighbourhood or check a candidate solution twice. Tabu lists and TS have found their way into EAs before (i.e. [4,5,6]) but to the authors' knowledge never for EAs solving the CSP. Tabu lists, in essence, store already checked candidate solutions. The algorithm can use the list to determine future search avenues or simply to forgo checking the candidate solution: making it tabu. Because the (more simple) tabu lists are used as reference memory (only insertion and lookup is allowed), they

T.P. Runarsson et al. (Eds.): PPSN IX, LNCS 4193, pp. 152–161, 2006.

can be implemented efficiently as a hash set. This ensures a constant time cost ($O(1)$) when a suitable hash function is used and the table is sufficiently large. This paper will show that combining EAs with tabu lists will provide both an effective and efficient CSP solving algorithm.

The article is organised in the following way: in section 2, the constraint satisfaction problem is defined. Section 3 defines the proposed algorithm. The experimental setup is explained in section 4. Section 5 discusses the results of the experiments. Finally, the paper is concluded in section 6.

2 Constraint Satisfaction Problems

The *Constraint Satisfaction Problem* (CSP) is a well-known satisfiability problem that is NP-complete ([7]). Informally, the CSP is defined as a set *variables* X and a set of *constraints* C between these variables. Variables are only assigned values from their respective *domains*, denoted as D. Assigning a value to a variable is called *labelling* a variable and a *label* is a variable-value pair, denoted: $\langle x, d\rangle$. The simultaneous assignment of several values to their variables is called a *compound label*. A constraint is a set of compound labels, this set used to determine when a constraint is *violated*. If a compound label is not in a constraint, it *satisfies* the constraint. A compound label that violates a constraint is called a *conflict*. A *solution* of the CSP is defined as the compound label containing all variables in such a way that no constraint is violated. The number of distinct variables in the compound labels of a constraint is called the *arity* of the constraint and these variables are said to be relevant to the constraint. The arity of a CSP is the maximum arity of its constraints. In this paper we consider only CSPs with an arity of two, called *binary CSPs*. All constraints of a binary CSP have arity two.

In this paper we will use the test-set constructed in [2]. The test-set consists of model F generated solvable CSP-instances ([8]) with 10 variables and a uniform domain size of 10 values. Complexity of the instances is determined by two commonly used complexity measures for the CSP: density (p_1) and average tightness ($\overline{p_2}$), both presented as a real number between 0.0 and 1.0 inclusive. The mushy region is the region in the density-tightness parameter space where the hard-to-solve CSP-instances can be found. The nine density-tightness combinations used are $1 : (0.1, 0.9)$, $2 : (0.2, 0.9)$, $3 : (0.3, 0.8)$, $4 : (0.4, 0.7)$, $5 : (0.5, 0.7)$, $6 : (0.6, 0.6)$, $7 : (0.7, 0.5)$, $8 : (0.8, 0.5)$, and $9 : (0.9, 0.4)$. For these density-tightness combinations 25 CSP-instances were selected from a population of 1000 generated CSP instances (for selection criteria see [2]) for a total of 225 CSP-instances. The test-set can be downloaded at: `http://www.emergentcomputing.org/csp/testset_mushy.zip`.

3 The Algorithm

The proposed EA is called the *Simple Tabu List Evolutionary Algorithm* (STLEA) and is a hybrid between a TS algorithm and an EA. In keeping with the simple definition of TS as "a meta-heuristic superimposed on another heuristic" ([3]), the STLEA only uses the tabu list. The tabu list is used to ensure that the STLEA does not check a compound label twice during a run. The basic structure of the STLEA is similar to other EAs and is shown in algorithm 1. A population P of *popsize* individuals is initialised (line 2) and the compound labels in the population are added to the tabu list (line 3). The individuals' representation and how they are initialised are described in section 3.1, the tabu list is described in section 3.3. The STLEA iterates for a number of generations (line 4 to 10) until either a solution is found or the maximum number of conflict checks allowed (*maxCC*) has been reached or exceeded (The *stop condition* in line 4). At each iteration parents are selected from P into offspring population S using biased linear ranking selection ([9]) with bias *bias* (line 5). The offspring population creates a new population using the variation operator (line 6), further described in section 3.4. The new offspring population is then evaluated by the objective function (line 7), described in section 3.2. Each new individual in the offspring population is also added to the tabu list (line 8). Finally, the survivor selection operator selects individuals from the offspring population (S) into an emptied population (P) to be used for the next generation (line 9). The survivor operator selects individuals with the best fitness value (see section 3.1) until the new population (P) is equal to *popsize*.

Algorithm 1: STLEA

```
1  funct STLEA(popsize, maxCC, bias) ≡
2    P := initialise(popsize);
3    updateTabuList(P);
4    while ¬solutionFound(P) ∨ CC < maxCC do
5        S := selectParents(P, bias);
6        S := variationOperator(S);
7        evaluate(S);
8        updateTabuList(S);
9        P := selectSurvivors(S);
10   od
```

3.1 Representation and Initialisation

An individual in the STLEA consists of three parts: a compound label over all variables of the CSP used as the candidate solution; the subset of constraints of the CSP that are violated by the compound label; and a parameter indicating which variable was altered in the previous generation (changed variable parameter). A new individual is then initialised by: uniform randomly labelling all variables in the compound label from the respective domains of each variable; adding each constraint violated by the compound label to the set of violated constraints; and leaving the changed variable parameter *unassigned*. The biggest difference to other commonly used representations is that this representation maintains: the actual set of violated constraints instead of the derivative *number* of violated constraints; and the variable changed in the previous generation. The size of the constraint set is used if a fitness value for the individual is needed. By numbering the constraints of the CSP, we can store only this number as a reference to the actual constraint.

3.2 Objective Function

The objective of STLEA is to minimise the number of violated constraints, thus finding a solution. The objective function then maintains the set of violated constraints of an individual. The number of conflict checks needed for one fitness evaluation is reduced by only considering the constraints relevant to the last changed constraint. First all constraints relevant to the last changed variable are removed from the set of violated constraints of the individual. The objective function then checks each constraint relevant to the last changed variable of the individual. If it is violated, the constraint is added to the set of violated constraints of the individual.[1]

3.3 Simple Tabu List

The STLEA maintains a simple tabu list of compound labels implemented as a hash set. The tabu list is used in only two ways: adding a compound label (insertion), and checking if a compound label is in the list (lookup). There is no need to alter or remove a compound label once it has been added to the tabu list. New compound labels are added immediately after the new individuals have been evaluated. Depending on the quality of the hash-function and given adequate size of the hash table, insertion and lookup in a hash table set constant time ($O(1)$).

3.4 Variation Operator

The variation operator takes a single individual to produce many children (offspring). The basic premise of the variation operator is simple: select a variable from the CSP and generate children for all not previously checked values in the domain of the selected variable. The variation operator uses the tabu list to check whether a child has already been checked. All not previously checked children are added to the offspring population, and the last changed variable parameter is set to the selected variable.

If all children are in the tabu list, the variation operator iterates the procedure with another variable selected. No variable will be selected twice in one operator invocation per individual. It is possible that after all variables have been selected, no unchecked child was found. At this stage, the search environment around the individual has been exhaustively searched and the search path can be terminated. At this point the variation operator inserts a new randomly initialised individual into the offspring population, in effect, starting a random new search path. This is, in essence, a gradual restart strategy. The variation operator never selects

[1] This objective function only works when only one variable is changed, although a version where more than one variable is changed can be defined analogously.

the variable selected in the previous generation, since all values for that variable have already been checked in the previous generation of the algorithm.

The variation operator selects the variable in three stages, uniform randomly from the set of variables:

1. relevant to the constraints violated by the individual's compound label (*first stage variable set*);
2. related to but excluding the variables in the first stage variable set by constraint arc (*second stage variable set*); and
3. that are not in the previous two sets (*third stage variable set*).

The first stage variable set is created by adding all relevant variables for each constraint in the violated constraints set of the individual to a multiset. A multiset is used so that variables relevant to more than one violated constraint have a higher chance of being selected. This provides a higher chance to satisfy more than one constraint by a single relabelling.

The second stage variable set is a multiset of variables, excluding the variables of the first stage variable set but including those variables that are relevant to constraints that have a relevant variable in the first stage variable set. These variables are said to be *relevant-by-arc* to a violated constraint. After all variables from the first stage variable set have been tried, it is necessary to expand the local-search neighbourhood. It may be useful to change the value of a relevant-by-arc variable to another value first to escape the local-search neighbourhood. The second stage variable set gives a higher selection chance to variables that are relevant-by-arc to more violated constraints.

The third stage variable set includes all variable not in the previously two variable sets. Since no preference can be established, all variables in the set have equal probability for selection.

4 Experimental Setup

The STLEA is run on the test-set used in [2] (see section 2). Two measures are used to assess the performance of the algorithm: the success rate (*SR*), and the average number of conflict checks to solution (*ACCS*). The *SR* will be used to describe the effectiveness of the algorithm, the *ACCS* will be used to describe the efficiency of the algorithms.

The *SR* of an algorithm is calculated by dividing the number of successful runs by the total number of runs. A successful run is a run in which the algorithm solved the CSP-instance. The *SR* is given as a real number between 0.0 and 1.0 but can also be expressed as a percentage. A *SR* of 1.0 means that all runs were successful. The *SR* is the most important performance measure to compare algorithms on, after all, an algorithm which finds more solutions should be valued over an algorithm that does not. The accuracy of the *SR* measure is influenced by the total number of runs.

The *ACCS* of an algorithm is calculated by averaging the number of conflict checks needed by an algorithm over several successful runs. A conflict check is the check made to see if a compound label is in a constraint. Unsuccessful runs of an algorithm are discarded, and if all runs of an algorithm are unsuccessful, the *ACCS* measure is undefined. The *ACCS* measure is a secondary measure for comparing an algorithm and its accuracy is affected by the number of successful runs as well as the total number of runs of an algorithm (the ratio of which is the *SR*).

A efficiency performance measure has to account for the computational effort of an algorithm. The *ACCS* measure uses the number of conflict checks as the atomic measure to quantify the computational effort. The STLEA, however, also spends computational effort on the maintenance of the tabu list. It was found that the computational effort needed to insert and lookup compound labels in the tabu list was negligible in comparison to the computational effort of performing a conflict check when the CSP-instance to solve was sufficiently complex. The computational effort needed to maintain the tabu list became relatively substantial when the average number of relevant constraints to a variable in the CSP-instance is smaller than two. This was not the case for the CSP-instances in the test-set.

The STLEA has relatively few parameters to fine-tune: the *popsize*; the *maxCC* allowed; and the bias of the biased linear ranking parent selection operator. We chose to select an equal number of parents for use by the variation operator as there were individuals in the population (*popsize*). A bias of 1.5 for the biased linear ranking selection operator was used because this gave the best performance in preliminary experiments, and is also used in other studies ([1,2]).

This leaves just the *popsize* and *maxCC* parameters to fine-tune. With EAs for solving CSPs it is common practice to use a small population size. The reasoning is that with a small population to maintain, more computational effort can be spend on increasing the fitness of the individuals, following the (small number of) search paths of which they are part. Large populations, on the other hand, need a lot of computational effort to maintain but provide for more search avenues to explore; in general keeping population diversity high. The trade-off, is investing computational effort, either in following a few search paths in depth, or in maintaining many search paths but (perhaps) following them to a lesser depth. The STLEA, however, doesn't seem to lend itself well to conventional wisdom. The combination of a tabu list and a powerful local search technique appears to address both issues at simultaneously. Since the common practice does not seem to apply to the STLEA, only experimentation with a large number of combinations for the *popsize* and *maxCC* parameters can provide guidelines.

The experimental setup for the proposed algorithm is then as follows: all 225 CSP-instance in the test-set the algorithm is run 10 times for a total of 2250 runs. The *popsize* and *maxCC* parameters are varied. The *popsize* parameter is taken from the following set: $\{10\} \cup \{50, 100, \ldots, 5000\}$. The *maxCC* is taken from the following set: $\{100000, 200000, \ldots, 5000000\}$. In total $2250 \cdot 101 \cdot 50 = 11,362,500$ runs were performed.

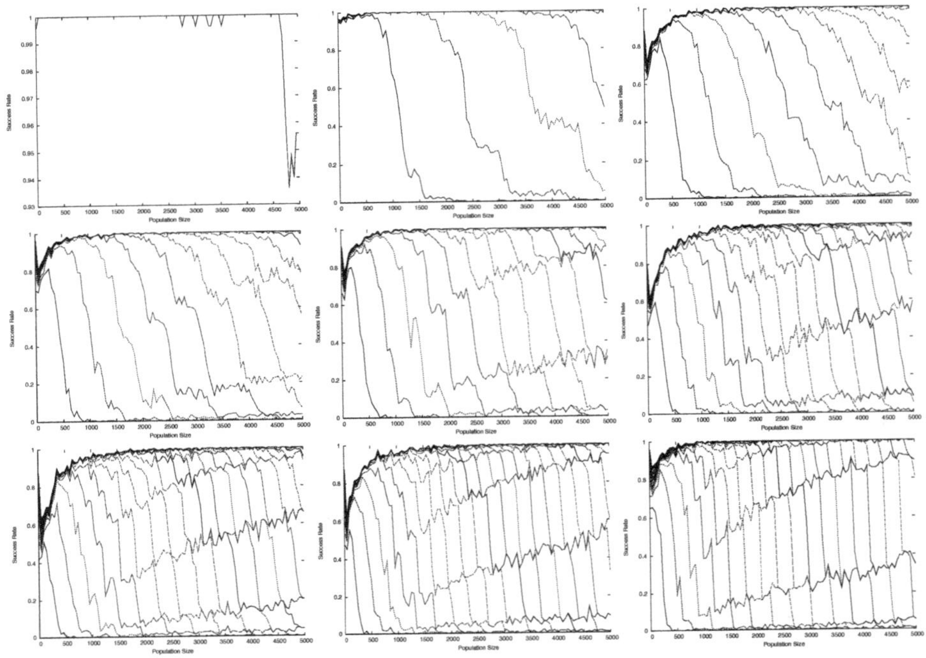

Fig. 1. The relationship between the population size (x-axis) and the success rate (y-axis) of the algorithm for different maximum number of conflict checks allowed

5 Results

The results of the experiments are summarised in figure 1. Figure 1 consists of 9 graphs, each showing the result for each density-tightness combination in the test-set. The top row shows the results for density-tightness combinations 1 to 3, the middle row the results for density-tightness combinations 4 to 6, and the bottom row the results for density-tightness combinations 7 to 9.

Figure 1 shows the influence of different values for *maxCC* on the *SR* for different values of *popsize*. The trend for the *SR* is the same for all different density-tightness combinations. The *SR* increases when larger values for *popsize* are used. The *SR* drops abruptly when *popsize* gets too large relative to *maxCC*. At the point where the algorithm achieves maximum *SR*, *maxCC* is just enough to allow the algorithm to reach this peak but not much more. If the *popsize* is increased beyond this point, the *maxCC* for maintaining a population of this size are not available and the *SR* drops abruptly. The inner most arc seen from the left-bottom corner of the graph (worst performance) invariably depicts the experiments with the least *maxCC*. Note that the difference in complexity of the density-tightness combinations in the test-set is also apparent by the *maxCC* allowed. Density-tightness combination 1 for example is known to be easier to solve than density-tightness combination 9, and the number of conflict checks

Table 1. Success rate (*SR*) and average conflict checks to solution (*ACCS*) for the best population size (*popsize*) and maximum conflict checks allowed (*maxCC*) parameters

	SR	ACCS	popsize	maxCC
1	1.0	2576	50	100000
2	1.0	67443	550	200000
3	1.0	313431	1650	500000
4	1.0	397636	1800	600000
5	1.0	319212	1150	500000
6	1.0	469876	1350	800000
7	1.0	692888	1750	1100000
8	1.0	774929	1700	1400000
9	1.0	442323	900	800000

needed to sustain the population while reaching a success rate of 1.0 is therefore lower for the first then for the latter. Note also the stepwise drop in *SR* after the optimal *SR* has been reached. Each step is caused be the inability of the algorithm to perform another generation. The slight increase in *SR* at each step is cause by the maximisation of the *popsize* for the number of generations that can still be performed.

Table 1 shows the first parameter-combination (*popsize*-*maxCC*) for which the *SR* is 1.0 for each density-tightness, with *popsize* minimised first and *maxCC* second. There is significant difference between the parameter values for different density-tightness combinations. CSP-instances for density-tightness combination 1 for example can be solved with *popsize* = 50 and *maxCC* = 100000 while density-tightness combination 7 needs *popsize* = 1750 and *maxCC* = 1100000. This reflects the difference in effort needed for solving the CSP-instances for the different density-tightness combination more then an inherent aptitude for the different density-tightness combinations of the algorithm.

Table 2 shows a comparison of the performance of the STLEA with the best algorithm from [2] and some benchmark algorithms. Table 2 clearly shows that the STLEA outperforms rSAWEA in *SR* and *ACCS* on all but density-tightness combination 9. Especially the fact that, given a large enough population and allowed number of conflict checks to work, the STLEA has a success rate of 1.0 is an improvement on rSAWEA. The STLEA also compares favourable with the HCAWR algorithm, with efficiency of the algorithm on average several magnitudes better (except density-tightness combination 9). Compared with the deterministic algorithms CBA and FCCDBA, however, the STLEA still has, on average, inferior efficiency, both algorithms outperforming it by several orders of magnitude (except for density-tightness combinations 1 and 2 for CBA). Overall, the STLEA is more effective and efficient then the best EA published so far but, although a step in the right direction, is still unable to beat deterministic algorithms on efficiency.

In [2] the notion of *memetic overkill* was introduced as well. Memetic overkill occurs when an algorithm for solving CSPs incorporates a heuristic so capable of finding solutions that the evolutionary components actually hamper performance. Especially hybrid algorithms are susceptible to suffer from memetic overkill. De-evolutionarising the STLEA through additional experiments (as explained in [2]) showed that the STLEA does not suffer from memetic overkill.

Table 2. Comparing the success rate and average conflict checks to solution of the STLEA, the Stepwise-Adaptation-of-Weights EA with randomly initialised domain sets (rSAWEA), Hillclimbing algorithm with Restart (HCAWR), Chronological Backtracking Algorithm (CBA), and Forward Checking with Conflict-Directed Backjumping Algorithm (FCCDBA)

	STLEA		rSAWEA		HCAWR		CBA		FCCDBA	
	SR	ACCS	SR	ACCS	SR	ACCS	SR	ACCS	SR	ACCS
1	1.0	2576	1.0	9665	1.0	234242	1.0	3800605	1.0	930
2	1.0	67443	0.988	350789	1.0	1267015	1.0	335166	1.0	3913
3	1.0	313431	0.956	763903	1.0	2087947	1.0	33117	1.0	2186
4	1.0	397636	0.976	652045	1.0	2260634	1.0	42559	1.0	4772
5	1.0	319212	1.0	557026	1.0	2237419	1.0	23625	1.0	3503
6	1.0	469876	1.0	715122	1.0	2741567	1.0	44615	1.0	5287
7	1.0	692888	1.0	864249	1.0	3640630	1.0	35607	1.0	4822
8	1.0	774929	1.0	1012082	1.0	2722763	1.0	28895	1.0	5121
9	1.0	442323	1.0	408016	1.0	2465975	1.0	15248	1.0	3439

6 Conclusion

In this paper we introduced a hybrid Tabu Search — Evolution Algorithm for solving the CSP, called Simple Tabu List Evolutionary Algorithm (STLEA). In [2] it was found that EAs for solving the CSP were able to approach the effectiveness of other (deterministic) algorithms but that they were still far behind in efficiency while doing so. A reason behind this lack of efficiency is the tendency of EAs to recheck previously checked compound labels during their search for a solution. The rational behind the STLEA is to reduce this rechecking by using a tabu list, effectively making previously checked compound labels tabu. The basic structure of the STLEA resembles the basic EA structure but incorporates a local-search technique into a single variation operator. A slightly altered representation allows for further efficiency improvement as well. A large number of experiments were performed for different combinations of the algorithm's parameters in order to find the best parameter settings. Using these parameters, it was found that the STLEA outperforms the best EA for solving the CSP published so far but still has inferior efficiency to deterministic algorithms.

Future research is focussed on comparing the relative behaviour of the STLEA to other algorithms when the complexity of the CSP-instances is increased (scale-up experiments) and the effects on the performance of the STLEA when other kinds of tabu lists are used.

References

1. Craenen, B., Eiben, A., van Hemert, J.: Comparing evolutionary algorithms on binary constraint satisfaction problems. IEEE Transactions on Evolutionary Computing **7**(5) (2003) 424–445
2. Craenen, B.: Solving Constraint Satisfaction Problems with Evolutionary Algorithms. Doctoral dissertation, Vrije Universiteit Amsterdam, Amsterdam, The Netherlands (2005)
3. Glover, F., Laguna, M.: Tabu search. In Reeves, C., ed.: Modern Heuristic Techniques for Combinatorial Problems. Blackwell Scientific Publishing, Oxford, England (1993) 70–141
4. Costa, D.: An evolutionary tabu search algorithm and the nhl scheduling problem. Orwp 92/11, Ecole Polytechnique Fédérale de Lausanne, Département de Mathématiques, Chaire de Recherche Opérationelle (1992)
5. Burke, E., Causmaecker, P.D., VandenBerghe: A hybrid tabu search algorithm for the nurse rostering problem. In: Proceedings of the Second Asia-Pasific Conference on Simulated Evolution and Learning. Volume 1 of Applications IV. (1998) 187–194
6. Greistorfer, P.: Hybrid genetic tabu search for a cyclic scheduling problem. In Voß, S., Martello, S., Osman, I., Roucairol, C., eds.: Meta-Heuristics: Advances and Trends in Local Search Paradigms for Optimization, Boston, MA, Kluwer Academic Publishers (1998) 213–229
7. Rossi, F., Petrie, C., Dhar, V.: On the equivalence of constrain satisfaction problems. In Aiello, L., ed.: Proceedings of the 9th European Conference on Artificial Intelligence (ECAI'90), Stockholm, Pitman (1990) 550–556
8. MacIntyre, E., Prosser, P., Smith, B., Walsh, T.: Random constraint satisfaction: theory meets practice. In Maher, M., Puget, J.F., eds.: Principles and Practice of Constraint Programming – CP98, Springer Verlag (1998) 325–339
9. Whitley, D.: The genitor algorithm and selection pressure: Why rank-based allocation of reproductive trials is best. In Schaffer, J., ed.: Proceedings of the 3rd International Conference on Genetic Algorithms, San Mateo, California, Morgan Kaufmann Publisher, Inc. (1989) 116–123

cAS: Ant Colony Optimization with Cunning Ants

Shigeyoshi Tsutsui

Hannan University, Matsubara Osaka 580-8502, Japan
tsutsui@hannan-u.ac.jp

Abstract. In this paper, we propose a variant of an ACO algorithm called the *cunning* Ant System (cAS). In cAS, each ant generates a solution by borrowing a part of a solution which was generated in previous iterations, instead of generating the solution entirely from pheromone density. Thus we named it, cunning ant. This *cunning* action reduces premature stagnation and exhibits good performance in the search. The experimental results showed cAS worked very well on the TSP and it may be one of the most promising ACO algorithms.

1 Introduction

As a bio-inspired computational paradigm, ant colony optimization (ACO) has been applied with great success to a large number of hard problems. They include the traveling salesman problem (TSP) [1,2,3], the quadratic assignment problem [4], scheduling problem [5], and vehicle routing problem [6], among others.

The first ACO algorithm was called the Ant System (AS) [1], and is applied to the TSP. Since then, many advanced ACO algorithms are proposed as extensions of AS. Typical of these are AS with elitist strategy and ranking (AS_{rank}) [6], Ant Colony System (ACS) [2], and MAX-MIN Ant System (MMAS) [3]. These advanced ACO algorithms include a strong exploitation of the best solutions found during the search. However, strong exploitation causes premature stagnation of the search. The most successful ones, such as ACS and MMAS, have explicit features to avoid this premature stagnation [7]. Thus for developing a successful variant of ACO, we need to incorporate a good balance between exploitation and exploration.

In this paper, we propose a variant of an ACO algorithm called the *cunning Ant System* (cAS). In cAS, each ant generates a solution by borrowing a part of a solution from a previous iteration, instead of generating the solution entirely from pheromone density. From this behavior, we call them *cunning ants*. This *cunning* action reduces premature stagnation and exhibits good performance in the search.

Although the basic background is different, the idea of using partial solutions to seed the ants' solution construction is inspired by our previous study on the edge histogram based sampling algorithm (EHBSA) [8] within the EDA [9] framework for permutation domains. Using partial solutions to seed solution

T.P. Runarsson et al. (Eds.): PPSN IX, LNCS 4193, pp. 162–171, 2006.

construction in ACO framework has been performed by combining an external memory implementation in [10,11]. In [12], some solution components generated according to ACO are removed, resulting in a partial candidate solution. Starting from the partial solution, a complete candidate solution is reconstructed by a greedy construction heuristic.

In the remainder of this paper, Section 2 gives a brief overview of MMAS. Then, Section 3 describes how the solutions with *c*AS are constructed, and the empirical analysis is given in Section 4. Finally, Section 5 concludes this paper.

2 A Brief Review of MMAS

Since *c*AS uses the MMAS framework in pheromone density updating, in this section we give a brief overview of MMAS.

MMAS allows the deposit of pheromone by either the *iteration-best*, or *best-so-far* ant to introduce a strong exploitation feature in the search. To counteract the stagnation caused by this, MMAS introduced an important mechanism to limit the possible range of pheromone trail density within the interval $[\tau_{min}, \tau_{max}]$. By limiting the influence of the pheromone trails we can avoid the relative differences between the pheromone trails from becoming too extreme during the run of the algorithm. MMAS also introduced schemes of pheromone trail reinitialization and/or pheromone trail smoothing (PTS) to prevent stagnation of the search. In MMAS, the values of τ_{max} and τ_{min} are defined as

$$\tau_{\max}(t) = 1/(1-\rho) \times 1/C_t^{best-so-far}, \tag{1}$$

$$\tau_{min}(t) = \frac{\tau_{max} \cdot (1 - \sqrt[n]{p_{best}})}{(n/2-1) \cdot \sqrt[n]{p_{best}}}, \tag{2}$$

where $C_t^{best-so-far}$ is the fitness of *best-so-far* solution at t and n is the problem size and p_{best} is a control parameter. With a smaller value of p_{best}, the value of τ_{min} becomes larger.

3 Cunning Ant System (*c*AS)

3.1 Cunning Ant

In traditional ACO algorithms, each ant generates a solution probabilistically or pseudo-probabilistically based on the current pheromone trail $\tau_{ij}(t)$. In this paper, we introduce an agent called *cunning ant* (*c-ant*). The *c-ant* differs from traditional ants in the manner of solution construction. It constructs a solution by borrowing a part of existing solutions. The remainder of the solution is constructed based on $\tau_{ij}(t)$ probabilistically as usual. In a sense, since this agent in part appropriates the work of others to construct a solution, we named the agent *c-ant* after the metaphor of its cunning behavior. In the remainder of this paper a solution constructed by a *c-ant* is also represented with the same notation, *c-ant*. Also, an agent which has constructed a solution borrowed by a *c-ant* is called a *donor ant* (*d-ant*) and the solution is also represented with the notation *d-ant*.

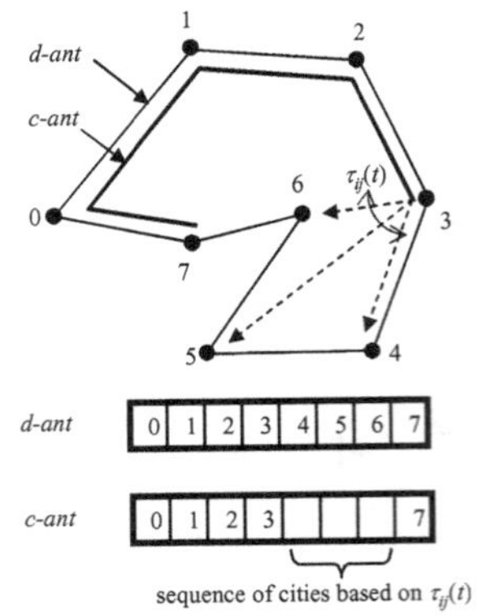

Fig. 1. *c-ant* and *d-ant* in TSP

Fig. 1 shows an example of the relationship between *c-ant* and *d-ant* in TSP. Here note again the notations *c-ant* and *d-ant* are used both for agents and solutions. In this example, the *c-ant* borrows part of the tour, 7→0→1→2→3, from the *d-ant* directly. The *c-ant* constructs the remainder of the tour for cities 4, 5, and 6 according to $\tau_{ij}(t)$ probabilistically. Using *c-ant* in this way, we can prevent premature stagnation the of search, because only a part of the cities in a tour are newly generated, and this can prevent over exploitation caused by strong positive feedback to $\tau_{ij}(t)$ (see Section 4.2).

3.2 Colony Model of *c*AS

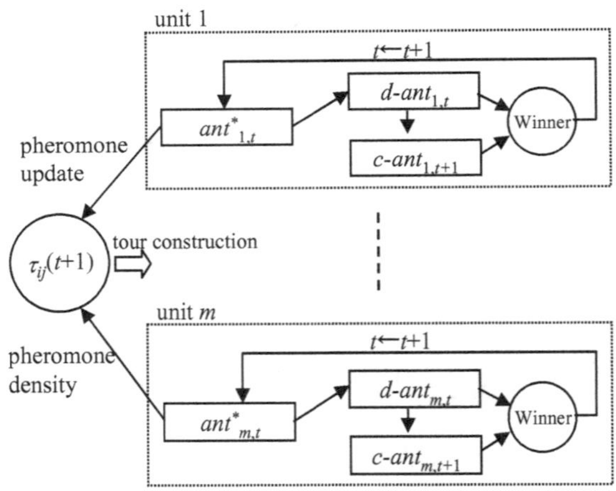

Fig. 2. Colony model of *c*AS

In *c*AS, we use a colony model as shown in Fig. 2, which is similar to the colony model proposed for real parameter optimization with ACO framework [13]. It consists of m *units*. Each unit consists of only one $ant^*_{k,t}$ (k = 1, 2, ..., m). At iteration t in unit k, a new $c\text{-}ant_{k,t+1}$ creates a solution with the existing ant in the unit (i.e., $ant^*_{k,t}$) as the $d\text{-}ant_{k,t}$. Then, the newly generated $c\text{-}ant_{k,t+1}$ and $d\text{-}ant_{k,t}$ are compared, and the better one becomes the next $ant^*_{k,t+1}$ of the unit.

Thus, in this colony model, $ant^*_{k,t}$, the best individual of unit k, is always reserved. Pheromone density is then updated with $ant^*_{k,t}$ (k=1, 2, ..., m) and $\tau_{ij}(t+1)$ is obtained as:

$$\tau_{ij}(t+1) = \rho \cdot \tau_{ij}(t) + \sum\nolimits_{k=1}^{m} \Delta^* \tau^k_{ij}(t), \tag{3}$$

$$\Delta^* \tau^k_{ij}(t) = 1/C^*_{k,t}\text{: if } (i,\, j) \in ant^*_{k,t},\ 0\text{: otherwise}, \tag{4}$$

where $C^*_{k,t}$ is the fitness of $ant^*_{t,k}$.

In *c*AS, pheromone update is performed with m $ant^*_{k,t}$ (k=1,2,..., m) by Eq. 3 within $[\tau_{min}, \tau_{max}]$ as in MMAS [3]. Here, τ_{max} for *c*AS is defined as

$$\tau_{\max}(t) = \frac{1}{1-\rho} \times \sum\nolimits_{k=1}^{m} \frac{1}{C^*_{k,t}}, \tag{5}$$

and τ_{min} is given by Eq. 2 of MMAS. Here, note that τ_{max} of Eq. 5 is obtained by modifying Eq. 1 of MMAS.

In this colony model, a *d-ant* is the best ant of each unit. By using ant^* as a *d-ant* in each unit we can expect an appropriate level of exploitation. Further, the comparison method in each sub-colony is similar to the tournament selection in genetic algorithms (GAs), being well known that tournament selection can maintain diversity of a population, though it differs from traditional tournament selection in that the comparison restricted to being performed inside of each unit. Thus, we can also expect this colony model to maintain the diversity of ant^*_k in the system.

3.3 Number of Sampling and Borrowing Nodes

A crucial question when *c-ant* creates a new solution is how to determine which part of the solution the *c-ant* will borrow from the *d-ant.* To ensure robustness across a wide spectrum of problems, it should be advantageous to introduce variation both in the portion and the number of nodes of the partial solution that is borrowed from *d-ant.* First it is reasonable to choose the starting node position of the partial solution randomly. Thereafter, the number of nodes of the partial solution must be determined. Let us represent the number of nodes that are constructed based on $\tau_{ij}(t)$, by l_s. Then, l_c, the number of nodes of partial solution, which *c-ant* borrows from *d-ant*, is $l_c = n–l_s$. Here, let us introduce a control parameter γ which can define $E(l_s)$ (the average of l_s) by $E(l_s) = n\times\gamma$.

In previous studies [8], when generating a permutation string, part of the permutation elements were copied from a *template* string. To determine the sampling portion in a string, we used the c cut-point approach. We sampled nodes for only one randomly chosen segment from c segments obtained by applying c cut points to the template. With this approach, l_s distributes in the range [0, n], and $E(l_s) = n\times 1/c$. Thus, with c cut-point method above, $E(l_s)$ is $n/2$, $n/3$, ... for c = 2, 3, and so on, and, γ corresponds to $1/c$, i.e., γ can take only the values of 0.5, 0.333, and 0.25, corresponding to c = 2, 3, 4 and so on.

In the current research, we extend this elementary method to a more flexible technique which allows for γ taking values in the rage [0.0, 1.0]. The probability density function of l_s with the c cut-point approach is [14]:

$$f_s(l) = \frac{(c-1)}{n}\left(1-\frac{l}{n}\right)^{c-2}, \; 0 < l < n, \; c \geq 2. \tag{6}$$

Here, we extend c so that it can take a continuous value ($c \geq$2). Then, we can obtain a generalized $f_s(l)$ by setting $c = 1/\gamma$ in Eq. 6 for $0.5 \geq \gamma >$0 as follows:

$$f_s(l) = \frac{1-\gamma}{n\gamma}\left(1-\frac{l}{n}\right)^{\frac{1-2\gamma}{\gamma}}. \quad (7)$$

For 0.5 $<\gamma<$1, we further extend the above logic as follows. First we consider distribution of $l' = n-l$ and $p'_s = 1-\gamma$ in Eq. 7. Then we can obtain the following equation for 0.5 $<\gamma<$ 1.

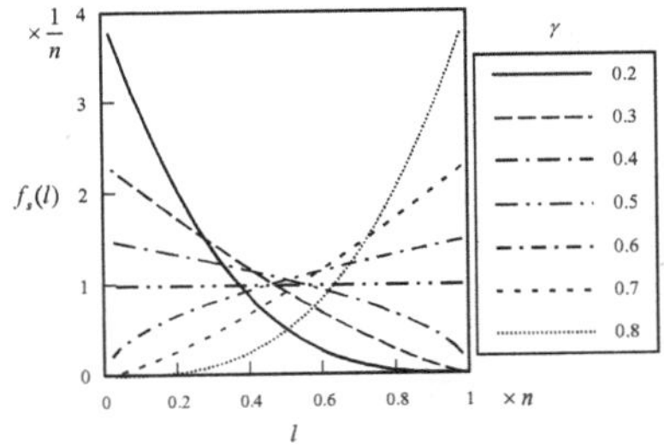

Fig. 3. Distribution of l_s for various γ

$$f_s(l) = \frac{\gamma}{n(1-\gamma)}\left(\frac{l}{n}\right)^{\frac{2\gamma-1}{1-\gamma}}. \quad (8)$$

Fig. 3 shows $f_s(l)$ for γ = 0.2, 0.3, 0.4, 0.5, 0.6, 0.7, and 0.8. We can see from this figure that for a smaller γ, shorter lengths of l_s become dominant, and for a larger γ, longer lengths of l_s become dominant.

The algorithm of cAS is summarized in Fig. 4.

1. $t \leftarrow 0$
2. Set the initial density $\tau_{ij}(t) = C$(an arbitrary large value, e.g. 10)
3. Sample two individuals randomly for each unit k, then choose the best one in the unit and set it as $ant^*_{k,0}$ (k=1,2,. . . , m)
4. Update $\tau_{ij}(t)$ according to Eq. 3 with τ_{max}, τ_{min} of Eqs. 5 and 2
5. Sample $c\text{-}ant_{k,t+1}$ for k=1,2,. . . , m according to $d\text{-}ant_{k,t}$ (: $ant^*_{k,t}$) and $\tau_{ij}(t+1)$
6. Compare $c\text{-}ant_{k,t+1}$ and $d\text{-}ant_{k,t}$, set the best one as $ant^*_{k,t+1}$ for i=1,2,. . . , m
7. $t \leftarrow t+1$
8. If the termination criteria are met, terminate the algorithm. Otherwise, go to 4

Fig. 4. Algorithm description of cAS

4 Experiments

Here we evaluate cAS on TSP. Unless explicitly indicated otherwise, the following default parameter settings are used, which are the same values as used with MMAS in [3] except for p_{best}, i.e., $\alpha = 1$, $\beta = 2$ (α and β are parameters that control the relative importance of the trail and the heuristic value [3]), $m = n$ (m is the number of units and n is the number of cities), a candidate list [3] with a size of 20. For cAS, p_{best} value of 0.005 and γ value of 0.4 were used. All test instances are taken from TSPLIB.

4.1 Performance of cAS

The performance of cAS was compared with MMAS and ACS, both of which outperform other existing ACO algorithms [7]. The comparison was performed on the same number of tour constructions for all algorithms as is described in [15] and [3]; this number was chosen as $k \times n \times 10000$, where $k = 1$ for symmetric TSPs and $k = 2$ for asymmetric TSPs (ATSPs). 25 runs were performed. Performance of each algorithm was compared using $Best_{avg}$ (average of the best tour length) and *Error* (average excess rate from optimum length) over 25 runs.

Table 1 summarizes the results. The results of MMAS+PTS and MMAS are taken from [3] and those of ACS are from [15]. We also showed the results of *non-c*AS; i.e., we use colony model shown in Fig. 2 but no cunning action is applied. This correspond to *c*AS with $\gamma = 1$. The values in bold show the best performance for each instance. From this table, we can see that *c*AS outperforms almost all instances used in the experiments except for d198. Further, we can observe that even *non-c*AS has similar performance to MMAS and thus the effectiveness of using the colony model in Fig 2 is also confirmed.

Table 1. Results of *c*AS $Best_{avg}$ is average best solution over 25 runs and *Error* indicates average excess (%) of $Best_{avg}$ from optimal in 25 runs

	TSP	opt	*c* AS						MMAS				ACS	
			c AS (=0.4)			*non-c* AS (=1)			MMAS+pts		MMAS			
			Best $_{avg}$	*std**	*Error* (%)	*Best* $_{avg}$	*std**	*Error* (%)	*Best* $_{avg}$	*Error* (%)	*Best* $_{avg}$	*Error* (%)	*Best* $_{avg}$	*Error* (%)
STSP	eil51	426	**426.2**	0.5	**0.06**	427.3	0.7	0.31	427.1	0.26	427.6	0.38	428.1	0.48
STSP	kroA100	21282	**21282.0**	0.0	**0.00**	21332.4	48.5	0.24	21291.6	0.05	21320.3	0.18	21420.0	0.65
STSP	d198	15780	**15954.1**	35.6	**1.10**	15958.5	10.9	1.13	15956.8	1.12	15972.5	1.22	16054.0	1.74
ATSP	ry48p	14422	**14465.4**	34.9	**0.30**	14509.5	46.7	0.61	14523.4	0.70	14553.2	0.91	14565.5	0.99
ATSP	ft70	38673	**38736.1**	77.1	**0.16**	39105.8	169.5	1.12	38922.7	0.65	39040.2	0.95	39099.1	1.10
ATSP	kro124p	36230	**36303.2**	120.3	**0.20**	36734.1	261.1	1.39	36573.6	0.95	36773.5	1.50	36857.0	1.73
ATSP	ftv170	2755	2827.1	8.7	2.62	2820.6	14.8	2.38	**2817.7**	**2.28**	2828.8	2.68	2826.5	2.59

* *std* : standard deviation of *Best* $_{avg}$

4.2 Parameter Values for γ

Fig. 5 shows the variations of *Error* for various γ values. Here, γ values were varied starting from 0.1 to 0.9 with step 0.1. Except for d198 and ftv170, γ values of [0.2, 0.6], which are in the smaller value range of γ, showed good performance. On ftv170, *c*AS with γ values of 0.2 showed good performance. On d198, γ values of [0.4, 0.9], which are in the larger value range of γ, showed good performance.

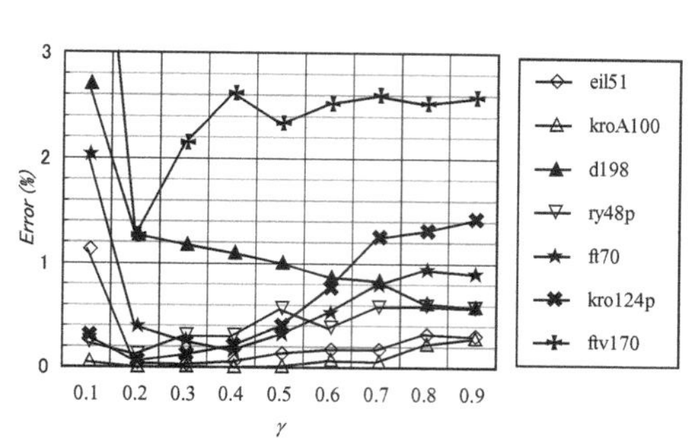

Fig. 5. Variation of *Error* for γ

Fig. 6 shows the convergence process of change of *Error* on kroA100 (100-city symmetric TSP) for γ values of 0.1, 0.3, 0.5, 0.7, and 0.9. Early stagnations of search can be observed with γ vales of 0.7 and 0.9. With γ values of 0.3 and 0.5, stagnations of search occur much later in the search. With a γ value of

0.1, no stagnation can be observed. But the convergence process is very slow. Thus we can see that using appropriate small values of γ can prevent over exploitation with strong positive feedback to $\tau_{ij}(t)$ and lead to success searches.

4.3 Parameter Values for ρ

With the ACO scheme, parameter ρ also plays an important role in controlling the search process. With a larger value of ρ, the search proceeds slowly, but it prevents the stagnation of the search. On the other hand, with a smaller value of ρ, the search proceeds rapidly, but it causes stagnation.

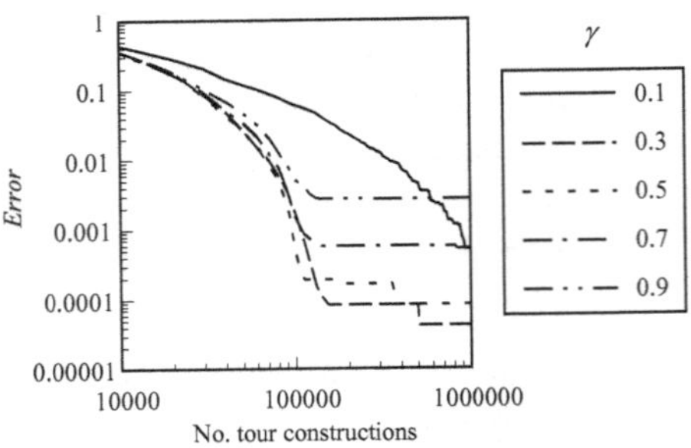

Fig. 6. Convergence process on kroA100

In cAS, as seen in Section 4.2, parameter γ has an effect similar to that of ρ. Fig. 7 shows the effects of variations of the value of ρ on the quality of solutions on kroA100 with γ values of 0.2 (left) and 0.6 (right). With $\gamma = 0.6$, though the performance is bad compared with $\gamma = 0.2$, ρ having a strong effect. On the other hand, with $\gamma = 0.2$, we can see the effect of variation of ρ is weaker compared with $\gamma = 0.6$. But still an appropriate value of ρ (ρ =0.98) leads to successful runs. Thus, we can see the synergy effect of parameters γ and ρ.

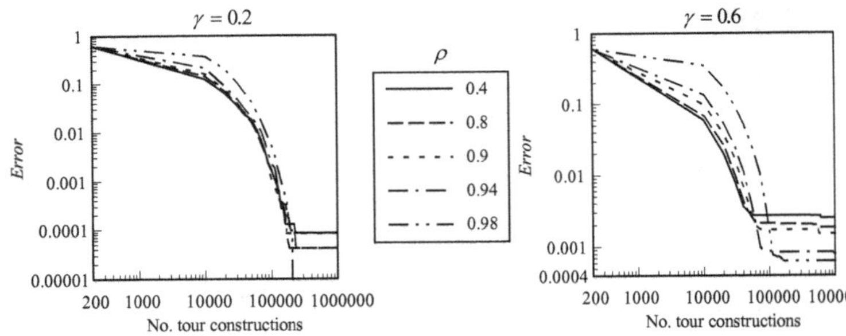

Fig. 7. Effect of ρ values on kroA100. *Error* is average over 25 runs.

4.4 Improving Performance of cAS with Local Search

Here we study cAS with a local search on symmetrical TSP. One of the best performing local searches for TSP is the well-known Lin-Kernighan algorithm (LK) [16]. The implementation of LK is complex compared with 2-OPT and 3-OPT heuristics. There are many variant implementations for LK. An important, and widely adopted scheme is the repeated use of the basic LK algorithm. The scheme is referred to as Chained Lin-Kernighan [17], or Iterated Lin-Kernighan [18]. In addition to the basic LK, Chained LK repeatedly utilizes a method for perturbing a given tour which is called *kick*. We used a Chained LK called

Table 2. Results of *c*AS with LK on symmetrical TSP. I_{avg} and T_{avg} are average iterations and time in second to find optimal in successful runs. *Error* indicates average excess (%) from optimal in 25 runs.

TSP	*c*AS								MMAS				Chained LK			T_{max}
	*c*AS (γ=0.4)				*non-c*AS (γ=1)											
	#OPT	*Error* (%)	I_{avg}	T_{avg} [min, max]	#OPT	*Error* (%)	I_{avg}	T_{avg} [min, max]	#OPT	*Error* (%)	I_{avg}	T_{avg} [min, max]	#OPT	*Error* (%)	T_{avg} [min, max]	
att532 (n=532)	25	0.00	1.8	7.8 [1.4, 27.8]	24	0.00	1.9	8.2 [1.4, 32.9]	25	0.00	2.4	10.5 [1.4, 32.6]	17	0.02	6.11 [0.3, 28.5]	40
d1291 (n=1291)	25	0.00	5.7	27.4 [6.0, 54.4]	24	0.00	7.4	35.9 [6.0, 56.9]	22	0.00	10.3	48.8 [6.1, 74.1]	6	0.12	17.0 [4.0, 61.3]	80
vm1748 (n=1748)	25	0.00	5.6	72.4 [8.4, 171.0]	24	0.00	5.6	77.5 [8.1, 169.8]	21	0.00	5.6	78.4 [8.3, 173.0]	1	0.06	72.8 [-]	200
pr2392 (n=2392)	25	0.00	10.1	104.9 [33.7, 190.0]	24	0.00	13.4	137.2 [57.3, 205.9]	12	0.00	20.4	211.3 [170.3, 233.2]	4	0.17	122.4 [40.2, 222.1]	240
fl3795 (n=3795)	25	0.00	9.8	435.1 [102.8, 1228.7]	15	0.00	13.9	615.9 [119.4, 1138.2]	17	0.00	17.6	770.7 [159.9, 1081.1]	0	0.57	-	1400
rl5934 (n=5934)	25	0.00	43.2	1336.1 [729.1, 1996.8]	1	0.00	59.6	1854.6 [-]	10	0.00	82.8	2533.6 [1499.2, 2897.0]	0	0.27	-	3300

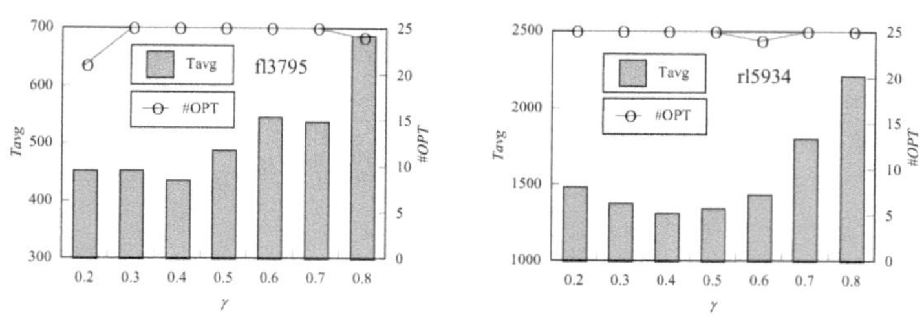

Fig. 8. Variations of *Error* for various values on fl3795 and rl5934

Concorde TSP solver (Concorde) developed by D. Applegate et.al, which is available for research purposes at [19]. *c*AS is written in JAVA and Concorde is written in C. So we combined it with *c*AS using Java Native Interface (JNI). Concorde was compiled using *MinGW* on Windows XP. For each tour generated by *c*AS, we applied it n iterations of Chained LK with *random-walk kicks*, which is reported to have the best performing *kick* [17].

The following six instances, which range in hundreds and thousands of cities, were used: att532, d1291, vm1748, pr2392, fl3795, and rl5934. The maximum execution time (T_{max}) of the *c*AS with LK for each instance is set to 40, 80, 200, 240, 1400, and 3300 seconds, respectively. The machine we used had two Opteron 275 (2.4GHz) processors, 2GB main memory, and 32-bit WindowsXP. For unit size, $m = 5$ was used for all instances. For other parameters, we used $\rho = 0.5$. γ =0.4. For τ_{min}, we used $\tau_{min} = \tau_{min}/2n$ to attain somewhat tighter bounds on the allowed pheromone trail strength according to the recommendation in [3].

To confirm the effectiveness of combining *c*AS with LK, we also tested the following three algorithms: *non-c*AS with LK (i.e., γ=1, see Section 4.1), MMAS with LK, and Chained LK alone. For MMAS, we used our implementation with Java. ρ value of 0.8 was used. For MMAS, we tuned by testing all combinations of $m = \{5, 10\}$ and pheromone update strategy = {iteration-best, best-so-far, and the schedule described in [3] for use with LK}. The results of the combination of $\{m = 5\} \times$ {pheromone update strategy = best-so-far} scored the best *#OPT* on bigger problems (i.e., pr2392, fl3795, and rl5934) and we used this combination for MMAS with LK. We ran Concorde iterating the basic LK with *random-walk kicks* until the achieving time defined by T_{max}. In the Chained LK, the initial tour affects the performance. In this experiment, we chose the *Quick-Borka* tour which has good performance on medium runs [17].

Table 2 summarizes the results. We can see all algorithms of *c*AS, *non-c*AS, and MMAS showed very small values of *Error* by combining LK and thus the advantage of combining these algorithms with LK is very clear. However, when we focus our attention on the results of *#OPT*, all algorithms except for *c*AS could not attain *#OPT* = 25 for d1291,vm1748, pr2392, fl3795, and rl5934. In contrast to this, *c*AS could attain *#OPT* = 25 for all test instances within the allowed run time T_{max} showing the smallest T_{avg} (average time in seconds to find optimal in successful runs) among algorithms tested. Here we notice again that even *non-c*AS shows very similar *#OPT* results to MMAS, as were observed without local search in Section 4.1. Thus, we can see that the effectiveness of using the combination of the proposed colony model and *c-ant* holds true for *c*AS with local search also. Fig. 8 shows the variations of *Error* for various γ values. Here, γ values were varied starting from 0.2 to 0.8 with step 0.1. We can see that cAS with γ values within range [0.3, 0.5] shows small T_{avg} with *#OPT* = 25.

5 Conclusions

In this paper, we proposed the *c*AS, a new ACO algorithm, and evaluated the performance using TSP instances available at TSPLIB. The results showed that *c*AS worked well on the test instances and has performance that may be one of the most promising ACO algorithms. We also evaluate *c*AS when it is combined with LK local search heuristics using larger sized TSP instances. The results also showed promising performance.

*c*AS introduced two important schemes. One is to use the colony model divided into units, which has a stronger exploitation feature while maintaining a certain degree of diversity among units. The other is to use a scheme, we call cunning, when constructing new solutions, which can prevent premature stagnation by reducing strong positive feedback to the trail density.

However, we need more analytical study on the relationships between these schemes and traditional schemes with ACO, including the further tuning of competitor algorithms. To apply *c*AS to other applications, such as the scheduling problem and the quadratic assignment problems, also remains for future work.

Acknowledgements. The author would like to acknowledge to the reviewers for their insightful comments on improving this paper. This research is partially supported by the Ministry of Education, Culture, Sports, Science and Technology of Japan under Grant-in-Aid for Scientific Research number 16500143.

References

1. Dorigo, M., Maniezzo, V., Colorni, A.: The ant system: Optimization by a colony of cooperating agents. IEEE Trans. on SMC-Part B **26**(1) (1996) 29–41
2. Dorigo, M., Gambardella, L.M.: Ant colony system: A cooperative learning approach to the traveling salesman problem. IEEE TEC **1**(1) (1997) 53–66
3. Stützle, T., Hoos, H.: Max-min ant system. Future Generation Computer Systems **16**(9) (2000) 889–914
4. Gambardella, L.M., Taillard, E.D., Dorigo, M.: Ant colony for the quadratic assignment problem. J. of the Operational Research Society **50** (1999) 167–176
5. Stützle, T.: An ant approach to the flowshop problem. Proc. of the 6th European Congress in Intelligent Thech. and Com. **3** (1998) 1560–1564
6. Bullnheimer, B., Hartl, R.F., Strauss, C.: An improved ant system algorithm for the vehicle routing problem. Annals of Operations Research **89** (1999) 319–328
7. Dorigo, M., Stützle, T.: Ant Colony Optimization. MIT press, Massachusetts (2004)
8. Tsutsui, S.: Probabilistic model-building genetic algorithms in permutation representation domain using edge histogram. Proc. of the 7th Int. Conf. on Parallel Problem Solving from Nature (PPSN VII) (2002) 224–233
9. Pelikan, M., Goldberg, D.E., F.Lobo: A survey of optimization by building and using probabilistic models. Computational Optimization and Applications **21**(1) (2002) 5–20
10. Acan, A.: An external memory implementation in ant colony optimization. Proc. of the Fourth International Workshop on Ant Algorithms and Swarm Intelligence (ANTS-2004 (2004) 73–84
11. Acan, A.: An external partial permutations memory for ant colony optimization. Proc. of the 5th European Conference on Evolutionary Computation in Combinatorial Optimization (2005) 1–11
12. Wiesemann, W., Stützle, T.: An experimental investigation of iterated ants for the quadratic assign-ment problem. IRIDIA Technical Report Series Technical Re-port TR/IRIDIA/2006-003 (2006)
13. Tsutsui, S.: An enhanced aggregation pheromone system for real-parameter optimization in the aco metaphor. Proc. of the Fifth International Workshop on Ant Algorithms and Swarm Intelligence (ANTS-2006) (2006)
14. Tsutsui, S., Pelikan, M., Goldberg, D.E.: Using edge histogram models to solve permutation problems with probabilistic model-building genetic algorithms. IlliGAL Report No. 2003022 (2003)
15. Gambardella, L.M., Dorigo, M.: Solving symmetric and asymmetric tsps by ant colonies. Proc. the IEEE Int. Conf. on Evo. Comp.(ICEC'96) (1996) 622–627
16. Lin, S., Kernighan, B.W.: An effective heuristic algorithm for the traveling salesman problem. Operations Research **21** (1973) 498–516
17. Applegate, D., Cook, W., Rohe, A.: Chained lin-kernighan for large traveling salesman problems. INFORMS J. on Computing **15** (2003) 82–92
18. Johnson, D.S.: Experimental analysis of heuristics for the stsp. G. Gutin and A. P. Punnen (ed.), The Traveling Salesman Problem and Variations **9** (2002) 369–443
19. http://www.tsp.gatech.edu/concorde.html. Concorde tsp solver, Ansi c code as gzipped tar file (2005)

Genetic Algorithm Based on Independent Component Analysis for Global Optimization

Gang Li, Kin Hong Lee, and Kwong Sak Leung

Department of Computer Science and Engineering
The Chinese University of Hong Kong
Shatin, N.T. Hong Kong

Abstract. We design a new Genetic Algorithm based on Independent Component Analysis for unconstrained global optimization of continuous function. We use Independent Component Analysis to linearly transform the original dimensions of the problem into new components which are independent from each other with respect to the fitness. We project the population on the independent components and obtain corresponding sub-populations. We apply genetic operators on the sub-populations to generate new sub-populations, and combine them as a new population. In other words, we use Genetic Algorithm to find the optima on the independent components, and combine the optima as the global optimum for the problem. As we actually reduce the original high-dimensional problem into sub-problems of much fewer dimensions, the solution space decreases exponentially and thus the problem becomes easier for Genetic Algorithm to solve. The experiment results verified that our algorithm produced optimal or close-to-optimal solutions better than or comparable to those produced by some of other Genetic Algorithms and it required much less fitness evaluations of individuals.

Keywords: Genetic Algorithm, Independent Component Analysis, Estimation of Distribution Algorithms, Global Optimization.

1 Introduction

Genetic Algorithm (GA) [1][2] is a branch of Evolutionary Computation inspired by Darwin's theory of natural evolution. GA can solve the unconstrained continuous global optimization problem as formulated in Definition 1. GA encodes the problem solution in a vector of variables as an individual. The objective function in Definition 1 evaluates the fitness of the individual. GA randomly generates a population of individuals to search in the solution space at first, focuses on the promising solution areas via genetic operators gradually, and finally converges to the global optimum.

Definition 1. *An unconstrained global optimization problem is solving the following continuous objective function:*

$$maximize\ f(x),\ subject\ to\ l \le x \le u$$

where $l \le x \le u$ defines the function domain, i.e. the solution space.

T.P. Runarsson et al. (Eds.): PPSN IX, LNCS 4193, pp. 172–181, 2006.

GA can fail to find the optima in some high-dimensional problems, because the size of the solution space grows exponentially with the dimension of the problem. To reduce the size of the solution space, a possible approach is dividing the original problem into several sub-problems by its dimensions. Afterwards GA is applied to the sub-problems to find their sub-optima separately. Finally the sub-optima are combined as the optimum of the original problem. Since a sub-problem has fewer dimensions than the original problem, its solution space is smaller than that of the original problem, so it is easier for GA to solve.

The difficulty of this approach is that the dimensions of the problem are usually interdependent on each other with respect to the fitness. In other words, the fitness of a sub-solution for a sub-problem depends on the sub-solutions for the other sub-problems. Suppose we have found the sub-optimum for a sub-problem, if the other sub-solutions change, the original sub-optimum might not be optimal any more. Therefore, even if we find the sub-optima for all the sub-problems, combining them does not give us the optimum for the original problem.

We propose a new Genetic Algorithm based on Independent Component Analysis (GA/ICA) to resolve this difficulty in this paper. We use Independent Component Analysis (ICA) to find a set of components which are linear transformations of the original dimensions. The components are independent from each other with respect to the fitness, so the sub-solutions on the independent components do not affect each other. Afterwards, the original problem is converted into a new problem defined on the independent components. Consequently, we can decompose the new problem into sub-problems by the independent components, and use GA to solve the sub-problems separately. There are primarily three issues to be solved to make our algorithm work,

1. ICA is a statistical method while GA is an optimization algorithm. Therefore, we need to transform the original problem into an equivalent new problem so that we can apply ICA on it.
2. When we use GA to solve the sub-problems, we need to know their fitness functions. However, we only have the fitness function for the original problem with all the dimensions together. Therefore, we need to infer the fitness in the sub-problems from the original fitness.
3. A solution could become a local optimum on a certain dimension when it cannot increase its fitness in either direction along the dimension, so a single modal problem could induce multi-modal sub-problems. Therefore, we need to take extra care when we apply GA on the sub-problems.

The rest of the paper is organized as follows. Section 2 reviews related work. Section 3 described GA/ICA in detail. Section 4 presents the experiment results on some benchmark problems. Section 5 concludes the paper.

2 Related Work

Estimation of Distribution Algorithm (EDA) [6] is a branch of GA with statistical analysis. In each generation, EDA selects good individuals from the population, and learns the distribution of these good individuals, then it generates a new population according to the distribution. In continuous domain, a Gaussian distribution is often used as the distribution model of the individuals.

Univariate Marginal Distribution Algorithm (UMDA) [5] is a kind of EDA. It assumes that the variables of the individual are independent from each other with respect to the fitness. Therefore, the joint probability density function is a product of Gaussian distributions of variables as Eq. 1, where m is the number of variables, μ_i is the mean of the ith variable, and σ_i is the corresponding standard deviation.

$$p_{\mathcal{N}}(x;\mu,\sigma) = \prod_{i=1}^{m} p_{\mathcal{N}}(x_i;\mu_i,\sigma_i) = \prod_{i=1}^{m} \frac{1}{\sqrt{2\pi}\sigma_i} e^{-\frac{1}{2}(\frac{x_i-\mu_i}{\sigma_i})^2} \tag{1}$$

Univariate Marginal Distribution Algorithm with Independent Component Analysis (UMDA/ICA) [10] incorporates ICA into UMDA to resolve the interdependence between the dimensions of the problem. In each generation, it uses ICA on the good individuals to find the independent components of the original dimensions. Then it transforms the population from the original space into the new space defined by the independent components. Afterwards, it applies UMDA to the transformed population. However, we think there are three disadvantages of UMDA/ICA. First, UMDA/ICA uses only part of the population for ICA and UMDA, so it may not find the true independent components and it loses the information contained in the rest of the population. Second, the selected individuals are treated equally in ICA and UMDA disregarding the differences between their fitness. Finally, it uses only crossover in the evolution on each independent component, which may not be very effective for difficult problems. [8] proposed a similar approach to UMDA/ICA. By applying ICA to the population, it transforms the coordinate system of the solution space so as to increase the separability of the fitness function, and then the component-wise crossover is applied.

3 Genetic Algorithm with Independent Component Analysis

UMDA is inappropriate for the problems whose variables are highly interdependent on each other with respect to the fitness. To circumvent this restriction, an approach is to linearly transform the original variables into a set of new independent variables so that we can apply UMDA on the new variables. ICA is an appropriate method for this task.

3.1 Independent Component Analysis

Independent Component Analysis (ICA) [4] is originally used as a data transformation method, especially for Blind Source Separation (BSS). Suppose we observe N m-dimensional data $x^t, t = 1,2...N$, we try to find a linear transformation $y = Wx$, where W is the demixing matrix, so as to make the variables $y_i, i = 1\cdots m$ as statistically independent from each other as possible. In BSS, we try to find the mixing model $x = As$, where s is the recovered source signals and A is the mixing matrix. It is proved that y equals s up to a multiplicative constant and permutation. The difficulty of ICA is that we know neither A nor s. In statistics, the variables $y_1, y_2, \cdots, y_m$ are mutually independent, if their joint density function can be factorized as Eq. 2, where $p_i(y_i)$ is the marginal density of y_i.

$$p(y) = p(y_1, y_2, \cdots, y_m) = \prod_{i=1}^{m} p_i(y_i) \tag{2}$$

Suppose our optimization problem is as defined in Definition 1. For ICA to find the independent components with respect to the fitness, we need to associate the fitness to the probability density. Intuitively, we should have more individuals of higher fitness than individuals of lower fitness. If the objective function $f(x)$ has a lower bound $L = inf\{f(x)|l \leq x \leq u\}$, we can define $f'(x) = f(x) - L \geq 0$ as the new fitness of the individual. Further suppose $\int_l^u f'(x)dx$ is the integral of $f'(x)$ over the domain $[l,u]$, then $g(x)$ as defined in Eq. 3 can be treated as a probability density function as it satisfies the two conditions following its definition.

$$g(x) = \frac{f'(x)}{\int_l^u f'(x)dx} = \frac{f(x) - L}{\int_l^u (f(x) - L)dx}, \; where \; g(x) \geq 0 \; \& \int_l^u g(x)dx = 1 \tag{3}$$

It is difficult to calculate $g(x)$ because we do not have the analytical form of $f(x)$ in the integral. However, we can generate a new population of individuals whose distribution roughly follows the probability density function $g(x)$. Note that $\int_l^u (f(x) - L)dx$ is the same for the $g(x)$ of all the individuals, so we have $f(x) - L \propto g(x)$. Therefore, we replicate each individual x^i for $\lfloor C \cdot (f(x^i - L)) \rfloor$ times, where C is an appropriate constant to make $C \cdot (f(x^i - L)) \geq 1$. This way, the copies of the individual is approximately proportionate to its density of $g(x)$. Then we apply ICA on this new population to find the independent components satisfying the statistical independent equation Eq. 4, where $g'(s)$ is the joint density function defined on the independent components and $g_i'(s_i)$ is the univariate marginal density function, which can be treated as the implicit fitness function defined on the ith independent component.

$$g(x) = g(As) = g'(s) = \prod_{i=1}^{m} g_i'(s_i) \tag{4}$$

GA/ICA uses ICA in a different way than UMDA/ICA does. First, it uses all the individuals in the population for ICA. Second, it uses the fitness of the individuals for the probability densities in ICA.

3.2 Algorithm

GA/ICA consists of two stages. In the first stage, GA/ICA samples a large population of individuals uniformly in the solution space. Then it uses ICA on the population to find the independent components. In the second stage, GA/ICA actually evolves the population to find the solution. It projects the population on the independent components and gets one 1-dimensional sub-population on each independent component, so it is able to evolve on the independent components separately. The basic steps of the second stage are shown in Algorithm 1 with the independent components as the inputs. At first GA/ICA randomly initializes a new population, evaluates the fitness of its individuals, and remembers the best individual in the population. Then it evolves the population for at most 1000 generations. In each generations, it runs the following steps until termination,

1. First we need to decide which genetic operator to use mostly in the current generation. Usually, crossover shrinks the solution area covered by the population, while mutation makes the population explore a large solution area. Because a single modal problem could induce a multimodal sub-problem on an independent component, we use the mutation as the primary genetic operator. When the best-so-far individual has not been improved for a relatively long time, we switches to crossover to focus on the neighborhood of the best-so-far individual. On the contrary, UMDA/ICA uses crossover only.
2. We project the population in the original space into the new space defined by the independent components according to the ICA demixing formula $y = Wx$. Then we divide the population by the independent components into m 1-dimensional sub-populations.
3. In the function *estimatePop*, we estimate the new fitness of the 1-dimensional individuals in the sub-populations. The new fitness in stead of the original fitness is used in the evolution later. We will explain this in detail in **Fitness Estimation**. However, UMDA/ICA uses the original fitness directly in UMDA.
4. On each of the independent components, we sample a new 1-dimensional sub-population out of its corresponding 1-dimensional sub-population via the genetic operator we have chosen in step 1. The details of the function *icaSample* are described in **Independent Component Sampling**. This step is totally different from UMDA.
5. After completing the evolutions on all the independent components, we combine all the new 1-dimensional sub-populations into a new m-dimensional population. Then we project the new population back into the original space using the ICA mixing formula $x = As$, and evaluate the fitness of its individuals.
6. Finally, we check how many generations the best-so-far individual has not been improved for. If the number is larger than 50, we terminate the program and return the best-so-far individual.

Fig. 1 illustrates combining the 1-dimensional sub-populations into a m-dimensional population. On the left, each row of the table is a sub-population. The individuals in the ith 1-dimensional sub-population are denoted as $\{s_i^1, s_i^2, \cdots, s_i^N\}$. On the right, each column of the table is a m-dimensional individual. The jth individual in the population is denoted as $(s_1^j s_2^j \cdots s_m^j)^T$. Now we elaborate on the functions of *estimatePop* and *icaSample*.

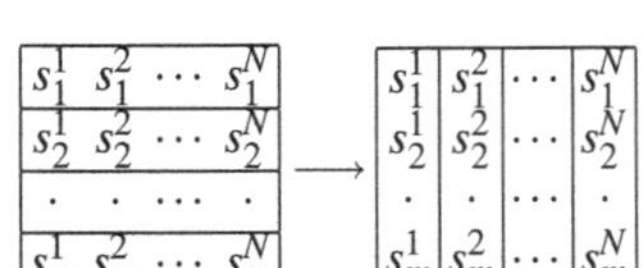

Fig. 1. Combine the 1-dimensional sub-populations into a true m-dimension population. Row vectors on the left table are the 1-dimensional sub-populations. Column vectors on the right table are the individuals in the population.

Algorithm 1. Evolution with the Independent Components

```
Input: W, A
Output: bestInd
pop ← initPop();
fitness ← evaluate(pop);
bestInd ← bestFunc(pop, fitness);
for gi ← 1 to 1000 do
    [pop, genOp ] ← checkOp(bestInd, pop, fitness, stagnancy);
    icaOldPop ← W × pop;
    for di ← 1 to dim do
        [icaPop_di, icaFit_di] ← estimatePop(icaOldPop_di, fitness, icaPop_di,
        icaFit_di);
        icaNewPop_di ← icaSample(icaPop_di, icaFit_di, genOp);
    end
    pop ← A × icaNewPop;
    fitness ← evaluate(pop);
    [stagnancy bestInd ]← checkState(pop, fitness, bestInd);
    if stagnancy > 50 then
        break;
    end
end
```

Fitness Estimation. When we perform GA on the 1-dimensional sub-population on the independent component s_i, we need to know the fitness of its 1-dimensional individuals. UMDA/ICA uses the fitness of the original individuals for evolution, i.e. $f(As)$. However, $f(As)$ does not only depends on s_i, but on the other independent components as well, so $f(As)$ is not the true measure of the goodness of the 1-dimensional individuals on s_i. The ideal measure should be $g_i'(s_i)$ in Eq. 4. The difficulty of this measure is that all that we have is $g'(s)$, while $g_i'(s_i)$ is only an implicit term. However, in ICA, theoretically, we can calculate the marginal density function $p_i(y_i)$ in Eq. 2 as in Eq. 5, where $-i$ represents the dimensions other that i.

$$p_i(y_i) = \int_{l_{-i}}^{u_{-i}} p(y_{-i}y_i)dy_{-i} \tag{5}$$

Similarly, we have the theoretical and empirical formulas for calculating $g_i'(s_i)$ as Eq. 6, where S_i is the set of individuals whose ith variables equal s_i. The problem is that we do not have many individuals which have the same s_i value, especially in high-dimensional space. Therefore, we have to take the nearby individuals into account as well, calculate the average of their fitness, and give bigger weight to the nearer individuals. This method results in a Parzen window like regression in Eq. 7, where σ is the average distance between the individuals and their nearest neighbors. In this way, GA/ICA is able to estimate the fitness of an individual in a sub-population as in the *estimatePop* function in Algorithm 1.

$$g_i'(s_i) = \int_{l_{-i}}^{u_{-i}} g'(s_{-i}s_i)ds_{-i} \; or \; g_i'(s_i) = \frac{1}{|S_i|} \sum_{s^j \in S_i} g'(s^j) \tag{6}$$

$$g'_i(s_i^j) = \frac{\sum_{k=1}^N \varphi(s_i^j, s_i^k) g'(s^k)}{\sum_{j=1}^N \varphi(s_i^j, s_i^k)}, \textit{ where } \varphi(s_i^j, s_i^k) = \frac{1}{\sqrt{2\pi}\sigma} e^{\frac{(s_i^j - s_i^k)^2}{2\sigma^2}} \tag{7}$$

Independent Component Sampling. The central part of GA/ICA is generating new 1-dimensional sub-populations on the independent components. EDA samples new individuals from the distribution model of the previous individuals. However, GA/ICA does not build such a distribution model. It generates new individuals by applying genetic operators to the previous individuals directly. The function *independentSample* in Algorithm 1 follows the basic framework of GA except the part of individual evaluation (because it cannot evaluate individuals of only one dimension). In addition, it has some advantages over GA, including adaptive genetic operators, fitness prediction and high population diversity.

At first, it calculates the average distance of the individuals to their nearest neighbors, i.e. σ, which is used as the parameter to control the scale of crossover and mutation. In the initial population, the individuals are randomly generated in the whole solution space, so σ is relatively large. As the population converges, σ drops gradually. With this method, crossover and mutation of GA/ICA adapt to the current sub-populations. Then it runs the following steps iteratively:

1. GA/ICA uses the tertiary-tournament. It randomly selects three individuals, uses the best two individuals for crossover and mutation, and replaces the worst individual with the offspring.
2. GA/ICA then generates two random numbers. One number follows the Cauchy distribution, while the other number follows the Gaussian distribution. GA/ICA uses the Gaussian random number for crossover. Cauchy distribution has bigger tails than Gaussian distribution. GA/ICA uses the Cauchy random number for mutation to make it more likely for the offspring to jump out of the local optimum [9].
3. In each generation, GA/ICA chooses crossover or mutation as the primary genetic operator in the current evolution. When it chooses crossover, *independentSample* does two crossovers of opposite directions and one mutation, so it makes the population converge. When it chooses mutation instead, *independentSample* does two mutations of opposite directions and one crossover, so it keeps the individuals search in different solution areas.
4. GA/ICA cannot evaluate the fitness of the offspring candidates directly because they are of only 1 dimension. Instead, it uses the Parzen window like regression, as described in the function *estimatePop*, on the current sub-population to predict the fitness of the candidates. Then it chooses one of them as the offspring probabilistically, with bigger probabilities given to better candidates. This technique enables it to search in more promising directions and avoid wasting evaluation time on bad candidates.
5. As discussed in Section 1, the number of local optima could increase on an independent component, so GA/ICA need to make the population diverse to search in a large solution space. Before the offspring is actually put in the new sub-population, it is adjusted to maintain the sub-population diversity. *independentSample* keeps an ordered list of offspring already generated, and finds the location where to insert

the new offspring. If the new offspring's distance to either its pre-neighbor or next-neighbor in the list is smaller than the current σ, it is adjusted to make the distance at least σ if possible, otherwise as large as possible. In this way, the offspring are pushed away from each other to maintain the sub-population diversity.

4 Experiment

In order to test the performance of GA/ICA, we used GA/ICA to find the global optima of the following 7 testing functions.

$$f_1 = \sum_{i=1}^{30} (x_i \sin(\sqrt{|x_i|}))$$

$$f_2 = -\sum_{i=1}^{30} (x_i^2 - 10\cos(2\pi x_i) + 10)$$

$$f_3 = 20\exp\left(-0.2\sqrt{\frac{1}{30}\sum_{i=1}^{30} x_i^2}\right) + \exp\left(\frac{1}{30}\sum_{i=1}^{30} \cos(2\pi x_i)\right) - 20 - e$$

$$f_4 = -\frac{1}{4000}\sum_{i=1}^{30} x_i^2 + \prod_{i=1}^{30} \cos\left(\frac{x_i}{\sqrt{i}}\right) - 1$$

$$f_5 = -\frac{\pi}{30}\left\{10\sin^2(\pi y_1) + \sum_{i=1}^{29} (y_i - 1)^2 \cdot [1 + 10\sin^2(\pi y_{i+1})] + (y_{30} - 1)^2\right\} - \sum_{i=1}^{30} u(x_i, 10, 100, 4)$$

where

$$y_i = 1 + \frac{1}{4}(x_i + 1) \text{ and } u(x_i, a, k, m) = \begin{cases} k(x_i - a)^m, & x_i > a \\ 0, & -a \le x_i \le a \\ k(-x_i - a)^m, & x_i < -a \end{cases}$$

$$f_6 = \sum_{i=1}^{100} \sin(x_i)\sin^{20}\left(\frac{i \times x_i^2}{\pi}\right)$$

$$f_7 = -\frac{1}{100}\sum_{i=1}^{100} (x_i^4 - 16x_i^2 + 5x_i)$$

All the above functions are multimodal functions with many local optima besides the global optima. The functions of f_1 to f_5 have 30 dimensions, and the functions of f_6 and f_7 have 100 dimensions. The functions' feasible solution spaces, global optimal function values and the population sizes GA/ICA used are shown in Table 1. The ICA algorithm we used was FastICA [3]. Note that ICA did not know the original dimensions of some functions are actually independent, so they sufficed to verify the capability of ICA to discover the independent components.

Other researchers have also tested their algorithms on these problems, so we can use their results directly for comparison. The algorithms that we compared ours to are:

Table 1. The Experiment Settings

Function	Function Space	Optimum	Pop Size
f_1	$[-500,500]^{30}$	12569.5	200
f_2	$[-5.12,5.12]^{30}$	0	400
f_3	$[-32,32]^{30}$	0	400
f_4	$[-600,600]^{30}$	0	400
f_5	$[-50,50]^{30}$	0	200
f_6	$[0,\pi]^{100}$	99.2784	600
f_7	$[-5,5]^{100}$	78.33236	600

Table 2. Experiment Results

Test function	Mean number of function evaluations				Mean function value (standard deviation)			
	OGA/Q	CGA	FES	GA/ICA	OGA/Q	CGA	FES	GA/ICA
f_1	302,166	458,653	900,030	34,420	12569.45	8444.76	12556.4	12569.47
f_2	224,710	335,993	500,030	56,760	0	-22.97	-0.16	-4.24×10^{-4}
f_3	112,421	336,481	150,030	44,400	-4.44×10^{-16}	-2.70	-1.2×10^{-2}	-5.0×10^{-6}
f_4	134,000	346,971	200,030	45,160	0	-1.26	-3.7×10^{-2}	-1.4×10^{-8}
f_5	134,556	346,800	150,030	26,840	-6.02×10^{-6}	-3.74×10^{-1}	-2.8×10^{-6}	-1.40×10^{-8}
f_6	302,773	338,417	NA	115,020	92.83	83.27	NA	97.61
f_7	245,930	268,286	NA	86,220	78.31	59.05	NA	78.33

1. Orthogonal Genetic Algorithm with Quantization (OGA/Q) [7]: OGA/Q uses orthogonal array to generate the initial population and the offspring in crossover.
2. Conventional Genetic Algorithm (CGA) [7]: This is the conventional Genetic Algorithm, with standard random initialization, crossover and mutation.
3. Fast Evolution Strategy (FES) [9]: FES is ES but with Cauchy mutation.

Table 2 shows the experiment results. We performed GA/ICA on each of the test functions for 10 runs. For each test function in the 10 runs, we recorded the mean number of the function evaluations, the mean function value of the best individuals and their standard deviation. As described in Section 3.2, we randomly sampled and evaluated 20,000 individuals before the evolution, and then we used FastICA to find the independent components. The 20,000 individuals were not counted in the mean number of the function evaluations, but the good ones among them were not used in the evolution either. In the future work, GA/ICA may use these 20,000 individuals in evolution, as ignoring them would be a huge waste of computation.

For all the test functions except f_5, where FES obtained slightly better solution than OGA/Q, OGA/Q and GA/ICA outperformed CGA and FES in terms of the function values of the solutions and the numbers of the function evaluations. For the functions f_1, f_5, f_6 and f_7, GA/ICA produced better solutions than OGA/Q. For the functions f_2, f_3 and f_4, the solutions of GA/IGA were slightly worse than those of OGA/Q. While for all the test functions, the numbers of the function evaluations that GA/ICA used were significantly less than those used by OGA/Q. Therefore, the results verified that GA/ICA was able to produce optimal or close-to-optimal solutions better than or comparable to those of OGA/Q while requiring much less function evaluations.

5 Conclusion

We have proposed GA/ICA as a new GA employing ICA to solve unconstrained continuous global optimization problems in this paper. It first uses ICA to identify the independent components of the solution space with respect to the fitness, then it divides the population into sub-populations and evolves on the independent components separately, finally it combines their optima as the global optimum for the original problem. As the high-dimensional problem is divided into many 1-dimensional sub-problems, the solution space is exponentially reduced, so the problem becomes easier for GA to solve. The experiment results showed that GA/ICA required much less function evaluations to produce optimal or close-to-optimal solutions which are better than or comparable to those produced by OGA/Q on the benchmark problems tested in this paper.

References

1. D. E. Goldberg. *Genetic Algorithms in Search, Optimization & Machine Learning*. Addison-Wesley, Reading, MA, 1989.
2. J. H. Holland. *Adaptation in Natural and Artificial Systems*. MIT Press, Cambridge, Mass., 2nd edition, 1992.
3. A. Hyvaerinen. Fast and robust fixed-point algorithms for independent component analysis. *IEEE-NN*, 10(3):626, May 1999.
4. A. Hyvärinen and E. Oja. Independent component analysis: Algorithms and applications. *Neural Networks*, 13(4–5):411–430, 2000.
5. P. Larranaga, R. Etxeberria, J. A. Lozano, and J. M. Pena. Optimization in continuous domains by learning and simulation of gaussian networks. In *Optimization By Building and Using Probabilistic*, pages 201–204, Las Vegas, Nevada, USA, 8 July 2000.
6. P. Larrañaga and J. A. Lozano. *Estimation of Distribution Algorithms: A New Tool for Evolutionary Computation*. Kluwer Academic Publishers, Norwell, MA, USA, 2001.
7. Y.-W. Leung and Y. Wang. An orthogonal genetic algorithm with quantization for global numerical optimization. *IEEE-EC*, 5:41–53, Feb. 2001.
8. M. Takahashi and H. Kita. A crossover operator using independent component analysis for real-coded genetic algorithms. In *Proceedings of the 2001 Congress on Evolutionary Computation CEC2001*, pages 643–649, COEX, World Trade Center, 159 Samseong-dong, Gangnam-gu, Seoul, Korea, 27-30 May 2001. IEEE Press.
9. X. Yao and Y. Liu. Fast evolution strategies. In P. J. Angeline, R. G. Reynolds, J. R. McDonnell, and R. Eberhart, editors, *Evolutionary Programming VI*, pages 151–161, Berlin, 1997. Springer. Lecture Notes in Computer Science 1213.
10. Q. Zhang, N. M. Allinson, and H. Yin. Population optimization algorithm based on ICA. In *IEEE Symposium on Combinations of Evolutionary Computation and Neural Networks*, pages 33–36, May 02 2000.

Improved Squeaky Wheel Optimisation for Driver Scheduling

Uwe Aickelin, Edmund K. Burke, and Jingpeng Li*

School of Computer Science and Information Technology
The University of Nottingham
Nottingham, NG8 1BB
United Kingdom
{uxa, ekb, jpl}@cs.nott.ac.uk

Abstract. This paper presents a technique called Improved Squeaky Wheel Optimisation (ISWO) for driver scheduling problems. It improves the original Squeaky Wheel Optimisation's (SWO) effectiveness and execution speed by incorporating two additional steps of *Selection* and *Mutation* which implement evolution within a single solution. In the ISWO, a cycle of *Analysis-Selection-Mutation-Prioritization-Construction* continues until stopping conditions are reached. The *Analysis* step first computes the fitness of a current solution to identify troublesome components. The *Selection* step then discards these troublesome components probabilistically by using the fitness measure, and the *Mutation* step follows to further discard a small number of components at random. After the above steps, an input solution becomes partial and thus the resulting partial solution needs to be repaired. The repair is carried out by using the *Prioritization* step to first produce priorities that determine an order by which the following *Construction* step then schedules the remaining components. Therefore, the optimisation in the ISWO is achieved by solution disruption, iterative improvement and an iterative constructive repair process performed. Encouraging experimental results are reported.

1 Introduction

Personnel scheduling problems have been addressed by mangers, operational researchers and computer scientists over the past forty years. During this period, there has been a wealth of literature on automated personnel scheduling including several survey papers that generalise the problem classification and the associated approaches (Burke et al., 2004; Ernst et al., 2004).

In brief, personnel scheduling is the problem of assigning staff members to shifts or duties over a scheduling period (typically a week or a month) so that certain constraints (organizational and personal) are satisfied. The scheduling process normally consists of two stages: the first stage involves determining how many staff must be employed in order to meet the service demand; the second stage involves allocating individual staff members to shifts and then assigning duties to individuals for each

* Authors are in alphabetical order. Please send all correspondence to Jingpeng Li.

T.P. Runarsson et al. (Eds.): PPSN IX, LNCS 4193, pp. 182 – 191, 2006.

shift. Throughout the process, all industrial regulations associated with the relevant workplace agreements must be complied with.

Since personnel scheduling problems are general NP-hard combinatorial problems (Garey and Johnson, 1979) which are unlikely to be solved optimally in polynomial time, various methods such as local search-based heuristics (Li and Kwan, 2005), knowledge based systems (Scott and Simpson, 1998) and hyper-heuristics (Burke, Kendall, and Soubeiga, 2003) have been studied. Over the last few years, meta-heuristics have attracted the most attention. Genetic Algorithms (GAs) form an important class of meta-heuristics (Aickelin 2002), and have been extensively applied to personnel scheduling problems (Aickelin and Dowsland 2000 & 2003; Aickelin and White, 2004; Easton and Mansour, 1999 Li and Kwan, 2003; Wren and Wren, 1995). A number of attempts have also been made using other meta-heuristics (Shen and Kwan, 2001; Aickelin and Li 2006). The methods and techniques that have been used over the years to tackle personnel scheduling problems have tended to draw on problem-specific information and particular heuristics. In this paper, we are trying to deal with the goal of developing more general personnel scheduling systems, i.e. a method which is not designed with one particular problem in mind, but is instead applicable to a range of problems and domains.

The work that is presented here is based on the observation that, in most real world problems, the solutions consist of components which are intricately woven together. Each solution component, e.g. a shift pattern assigned to a particular employee, may be a strong candidate in its own right, but it also has to fit well with other components. To deal with these components, Joslin and Clements (1999) proposed a technique called Squeaky Wheel Optimisation (SWO), and claimed it could be a general approach for various combinatorial optimisation problems. In this paper, we analyse the limitations of the original SWO and revise it by incorporating some evolutionary features into the searching process. We term the revised version the improved SWO (ISWO). Its general idea is to break a solution down into its components and assign a score to each by an evaluation function working under dynamic environments. The scores are employed in two ways: first as fitness values which determine the chances for the components to survive in the current solution, and then they are sorted to obtain an order in which a greedy algorithm reschedules deleted components.

2 A General Description of the ISWO

SWO belongs to the class of non-systematic search techniques. In SWO, a priority ordering of problem components is given to a greedy algorithm that constructs a solution. That solution is then analyzed to find trouble spots, i.e. those components that are not handled as well as they could be, relative to some lower bound. The priority of the components that are trouble spots is then increased. All components, sorted in the new priority ordering are then given to the greedy constructor, with the likely result that those components will be handled better in the next solution. This construct-analyze-prioritize cycle continues until a stopping condition is reached. Joslin and Clements (1999) applied this technique on production line scheduling problems and graph colouring problems with some satisfactory results. Burke and Newall (2004) developed an adaptive heuristic framework for examination timetabling problems which was based on SWO. A hybridisation of this method (Burke and Newall, 2002) with exam timetabling methodology based upon the Great Deluge algorithm was shown to be effective on benchmark problems (Burke et al 2004).

In essence, SWO finds good quality solutions quickly by searching in two spaces simultaneously: the traditional solution space and the new priority space. Hence it avoids many problems that other local search methods often encounter. These features allow SWO to effectively make large coherent moves to escape from unpromising regions in the search space. The construct-analyze-prioritize loop learns as it executes: problem components that are hard to handle tend to rise in the priority queue, and components that are easy to handle tend to sink.

Although SWO has achieved success in certain problems of realistic size, there exist two limitations which restrict its wider applications in domains with large problem sizes, such as many practical scheduling and rostering problems. The first limitation lies in its scalability, which is caused by SWO's construction step using greedy algorithms to construct a solution from scratch at each iteration. If the construction process could start from partial solutions which contain information of past solutions, the optimisation process would speed up significantly.

The second limitation lies in its aspect of convergence: although SWO has the ability to make large coherent moves, it is, however, poor at making small tuning moves in the solution space. Ironically, this weakness is caused by its feature of operating on dual search spaces (a "strength"). Compared to the solution of the previous iteration, a small change in the sequence of components generated by the *Prioritization* step may correspond to a large change in the corresponding solution generated by the *Construction* step. For example, moving a component forward in the sequence can significantly change its state in the actual solution, because any components occurring after it in the sequence must accommodate that component's state. However, if it was possible to restrict changes of components to the trouble-makers, e.g. by delaying part of the sequence without going through the full *Analysis* and *Prioritization* cycle, then the changes in the corresponding solutions would be relatively small.

To address the above two issues, this paper presents a new technique called ISWO, which incorporates two additional steps of *Selection* and *Mutation* into the loop. These two steps enable the ISWO to implement search by simulating an evolutionary process on a single solution. Each component in the solution has to continuously demonstrate its worthiness to stay in the solution. Hence in each iteration, a number of components will be deemed not worth keeping. The evolutionary strategy adopted may also throw out, with a low probability, some worthy components. Any deleted component is then rescheduled by using a greedy algorithm one at a time, in the order they occur in the priority sequence. Of key importance is that the admittance of a new component is analyzed by a dynamic evaluation function, which takes account of how well the prospective component will fit in with others already in the solution. The above processes are iterated together with the remainder of the classical SWO. Thus the global optimisation procedure is based on solution disruption and iterative improvement, while a constructive process is performed within.

As outlined, our proposed algorithm operates a sequence of *Analysis*, *Selection*, *Mutation*, *Prioritization* and *Construction* steps in a loop on one solution. Besides these five steps, some input parameters (e.g. stopping conditions) and a valid starting solution are initialized. In the *Analysis* step, the fitness of each component in the current solution is computed. By analyzing a solution, well-fitting and ill-fitting components can be identified. The fitness measure is then used probabilistically to select components to be discarded in the *Selection* step. Components with high fitness have a lower probability of being discarded. To get out of local optima in the solution space, it is necessary to incorporate the ability to make for uphill moves. This is achieved by the *Mutation* step which probabilistically discards even superior components of the solution.

After the above steps, a previously complete solution becomes partial due to the removal of some components, and thus the resulting partial solution needs to be repaired. Before making any repairs, the *Prioritization* step uses the results of the *Analysis* step to create priorities that in turn determine the scheduling order for the recently removed components. In this step, the previous sequence of 'trouble' components (i.e. recently removed ones) is modified: problem components with lower fitness values (i.e. more trouble-making ones) are moved towards the front of the sequence: The lower the value, the further the component is moved towards the front of the sequence. Finally, the *Construction* step repairs a broken solution by applying a greedy algorithm to reschedule the removed components, in the order that they appear in the component sequence produced by the *Prioritization*. Throughout the iteration, the best solution is retained and finally presented as the final solution.

3 ISWO for Driver Scheduling

3.1 Problem Description

Bus and rail driver scheduling is represents process of partitioning blocks of work, each of which is serviced by one vehicle, into a set of legal driver shifts. The main objectives are to minimize the total number of shifts and the total shift costs. This problem has attracted much interest since the 1960's. Wren and Rousseau (1995) gave an overview of the main approaches, many of which have been reported in a series of international workshop conferences, e.g. (Voß and Daduna, 2001).

To clarify the problem, we start by introducing some terminologies used in driver scheduling (Li and Kwan, 2003). A *Relief Opportunity* (RO) is a time and place where a driver can leave the current vehicle, for reasons such as taking a meal-break, or transferring to another vehicle. The work between two consecutive ROs on the same vehicle is called *a piece of work*. The work that a single driver carries out in a day is called *a shift*, which is composed of several *spells* of work. A *spell* contains a number of consecutive pieces of work on the same vehicle, and a *schedule* is a solution that contains a set of shifts that cover all the required work. The subsequent packaging of work for actual drivers is usually performed on a weekly basis, allowing for rest days and taking into account issues such as fairness and safety regulations.

The driver scheduling problem can be formulated as a set covering integer linear programming problem: all the legal potential shifts are first constructed by heuristics that are usually highly parameterized to reflect on the driver work rules of individual companies, and then a least cost subset covering all the work is selected to form a solution schedule. In practice, the model has been extended to cater for other practical objectives and constraints (Fores et al., 2002). A typical problem may have a solution schedule requiring over 100 shifts chosen from a potential set of about 50,000.

3.2 Implementation

This section details how to apply the ISWO to the driver scheduling problem. Based on our problem-specific knowledge, we first set up five criteria to evaluate the structure of a shift from different aspects. Since each criterion bears some degree of uncertainty, we characterize them as individual fuzzy membership functions and aggregated these membership functions together by the way of fuzzy evaluation. The resulting aggregated function is used in a general evaluation function to analyze the fitness of each solution component (i.e. shift), and then incorporated into a constructing heuristic to enable shift selection. The steps of *Analysis, Selection, Mutation, Prioritization* and *Construction* are executed in a loop to improve a given initial solution iteratively. During each iteration, an unfit portion of the working schedule is removed. Broken schedules are repaired by the constructing heuristic. Throughout the iterations, the best is retained and finally returned as the preserved solution.

3.2.1 Analysis

The first *Analysis* step is to evaluate the current arrangement for each shift in a schedule. In this step, the fitness of the individual shift in a complete schedule is computed. The purpose of computing this measure is to determine, besides the structural fitness of shifts, which shifts are in positions that lead to less overlapping work time, and which shifts contribute unnecessarily to large amounts of overlapping work time. Hence we can formulate a normalized evaluation function as

$$F(S_j) = f_1(S_j) \times f_2(S_j), \ \forall j \in J \tag{1}$$

where S_j denotes the shift contained in the current schedule J with an index number j, $0 \le f_1(S_j) \le 1$ is the structural coefficient of shift S_j, and $0 \le f_2(S_j) \le 1$ is the over-cover penalty which reflects the coverage status for shift S_j.

1) Structural coefficient

Five fuzzified criteria u_i (i= 1 ,…, 5), characterized by associated membership functions, have been abstracted for the evaluation of the shift structure (Li 2002): Total work-time u_1, the ratio u_2 of total work-time to spreadover (i.e. the paid hours for a driver from sign on to sign off), the number of pieces of work u_3, the number of spells u_4 contained in a shift, and the fractional cover u_5 which is given by a linear programming relaxation. Since the evaluations by individual criteria refer to the local features of each criterion, an overall evaluation (i.e. the calculation of the structural coefficient $f_1(S_j)$ for shift S_j) could be made by the aggregation of these five criteria as

$$f_1(S_j) = \sum_{i=1}^{5} w_i \mu_{\tilde{A}_i}, \forall j \in \{1, \ldots, n\} \tag{2}$$

where $\tilde{A}_i$ is the fuzzy subset on the i-th criterion and w_i is the weight of criterion u_i, s.t.

$$\sum_{i=1}^{5} w_i = 1, w_i \ge 0 \tag{3}$$

The design of the membership functions for these five criteria can be briefly described as follows. Since the fitness of shift S_j generally increases with the total work-time, ratio of total work-time to spreadover and number of pieces of work, respectively, the membership function $\mu_{\tilde{A}i}$ (i = 1, 2, 3) for these three factors takes the same form as

$$\mu_{\tilde{A}_i} = \begin{cases} 2\left(\dfrac{x_i - b_i}{a_i - b_i}\right)^2, & a_i \le x_i < \dfrac{a_i + b_i}{2} \\ 1 - 2\left(\dfrac{x_i - a_i}{a_i - b_i}\right)^2, & \dfrac{a_i + b_i}{2} \le x_i \le a_i \end{cases} \tag{4}$$

where x_1 is the total work-time of S_j, a_1 is the maximum total work-time, b_1 is the minimum total work-time, x_2 is the ratio of total work-time to spreadover for S_j, a_2 is the maximum ratio, b_2 is the minimum ratio, x_3 is the number of pieces of work contained in S_j, a_3 is the maximum number of pieces of work and b_3 is the minimum number of pieces of work.

With respect to the criterion u_4, in most practical problems, the number of spells in a shift is limited to be at most four. 2-spell shifts are generally more effective than others, and 3-spell shifts are more desirable than 1-spell or 4-spell shifts. Hence, the membership function $\mu_{\tilde{A}4}$ is defined as

$$\mu_{\tilde{A}_4} = \begin{cases} 0, & \text{if } x_4 = 1 \text{ or } x_4 = 4 \\ 0.5, & \text{if } x_4 = 3 \\ 1, & \text{if } x_4 = 2 \end{cases} \tag{5}$$

where x_4 is the number of spells contained in S_j.

With respect to the last criterion u_5, extensive studies have shown that the fractional cover by linear programming relaxation provides some useful information about the significance of some of the shifts identified in the relaxed solution. In general, the higher the fractional value of the variable for a shift, the higher chance that it is present in the integer solution (Kwan et al., 2001). We use the following Gaussian distribution function $\mu_{\tilde{A}5}$ to define criterion u_5. More details about this criterion can be found in (Li 2002).

$$\mu_{\tilde{A}_5} = \begin{cases} e^{\frac{\ln 0.01}{(a-b)^2}(x_5 - a)^2} & \text{, if } S_j \text{ is in the fractional cover} \\ 0 & \text{, otherwise} \end{cases} \tag{6}$$

where x_5 is the fractional value of S_j in the relaxed LP solution, a is the maximum value in fractional cover and b is the minimum value in fractional cover.

2) Over-cover penalty

The ratio of the overlapped work time to total work time in S_j, is also regarded as an important criterion, which can be formulated as over-cover penalty $0 \le f_2(S_j) \le 1$,

$$f_2(S_j) = \sum_{k=1}^{|S_j|} (\alpha_{jk} \times \beta_{jk}) \bigg/ \sum_{k=1}^{|S_j|} \beta_{jk}, \ \forall j \in J \tag{7}$$

where $|S_j|$ is the number of pieces of work in S_j, $_{jk}$ is 0 if work piece k in S_j has been covered by any other shifts S_i in J and 1 otherwise, and $_{jk}$ is the work-time for work pieces k in S_j.

3.2.2 Selection

This step is to decide whether a shift in a current schedule should be retained or discarded. The decision is made by comparing its fitness value $F(S_j)$ to $(p_s - p)$ where p_s is a variable generated randomly for each iteration satisfying $0 \leq p_s \leq 1$, and p is a constant no larger than 1. If $F(S_j)$ is larger than $(p_s - p)$, then S_i will remain in its present allocation, otherwise S_j will be removed from the current schedule. The pieces of work that S_j covers are then released unless they are also covered by other remaining shifts in the schedule. By using *Selection*, shift S_j with larger fitness $F(S_j)$ has higher probability to survive in the current schedule. Note that the purpose of subtracting p from p_s is to improve the efficiency of *Selection*. Without this operator, for example, almost all shifts in the current schedule will be removed when p_s is close to 1.

3.2.3 Mutation

The *Mutation* step follows to mutate the retained shifts S_j, i.e. randomly discarding them from the partial solution at a small rate p_m. The pieces of work that S_j covers are then released unless they are also covered by other remaining shifts in the schedule. Compared with the selection rate which is randomly generated for each iteration, the mutation rate p_m should be much smaller to ensure convergence.

3.2.4 Prioritization

The *Prioritization* step first generates a sequence of problem shifts that need to be rescheduled (i.e. the ones that have been removed by the previous steps of *Selection* and *Mutation*). Using the results of *Analysis*, the problem shifts are sorted in ascending order of their fitness values, with poor-scheduled shifts being earlier in the sequence.

The obtained sequence of problem shifts is then used indirectly to determine the order in which a new solution is constructed. Since each shift constitutes a number of pieces of work, the sequence of shifts can be transformed into a longer sequence of pieces of work, with pieces that have already been covered by earlier shifts not appearing again. Thus, the new sequence consists of all the uncovered pieces of work, in the order that they would be covered by the construction heuristic described below.

3.2.5 Construction

The *Construction* task is to assign shifts to all uncovered pieces of work to repair a broken schedule. By considering all potential shifts with respect to the pieces of work to be covered, it is possible to build a coverage list for each piece containing all shifts that are able to cover it. The greedy constructor assumes that the desirability of adding shift $S_j(j)$ into the partial schedule increases with its function value $F(S_j)$. The reconstructing heuristic is to assign shifts until every piece of work is covered. Candidate shifts are then assigned to the unassigned pieces of work sequentially. The criterion of choosing the next uncovered piece of work for assignment is to locate the first piece of work appearing in the priority sequence, obtain its corresponding coverage list, and randomly select a shift with one of the k-largest function value $F(S_j)$. For a feasible solution obtained in such a way, over-cover is often inevitable and ultimately has to be resolved by manual editing before the schedule is implemented: In practise, the intervention is simply to decide a shift that should contain the over-covered pieces of work and then remove this piece from the other shifts.

Note that the evaluation function used in the *Constructing* heuristic takes the same form as the one used in the *Analysis* step. The major difference is that the former one needs to evaluate all unused shifts from the large possible legal shift set, for the purpose of selecting some shifts to form a feasible schedule, while the latter only evaluates shifts in the current schedule.

3.3 Experimental Results

Among various heuristic and meta-heuristic approaches developed in recent years for driver scheduling, the Self-Adjusting Approach (SAA) performs generally best on a set of standard test problems (Li and Kwan, 2005). It uses the following weighted-sum objective function, which combines the two main objectives of minimizing total cost and number of shifts into a weighted-sum cost function:

$$\text{Minimize} \sum_{i=1}^{L} (c_{J_i} + 2000) \tag{8}$$

where L is the number of shifts in the schedule, c_{Ji} is the cost of the i-th shift, and 2000 is used to give priority to the first objective of minimizing the number of shifts.

For a benchmark comparison, the same objective function is used in the ISWO coded in C++ and implemented on a Pentium IV 2.1 GHz machine under Window XP. Thirteen real world instances from medium to very large size are used as the test-bed. Starting from an initial solution generated by a genetic algorithm (Li and Kwan, 2003), we set the stopping criterion equal to 1000 iterations without further improvement. Also, we apply a fixed weight distribution of membership functions, W=(0.20, 0.10, 0.10, 0.20, 0.40), in equation (3) to all thirteen data instances. In addition, we set parameter p_s in Section 3.2.2 to be 0.3, the mutation rate p_m in Section 3.2.3 to be

Table 1. Comparative results. B – Bus, T – Train, R – Tram, **M – Mean**. *S – best shift, C – best cost, CPU – mean CPU time in seconds.* SAA – Self-Adjusting Approach, SWO - Squeaky Wheel Optimisation, ISWO – Improved Squeaky Wheel Optimisation, TRACS – TRACS II by Fores et al. The last two columns show % between ISWO and TRACS II.

	SAA *S*	SAA *C*	SAA *CPU*	SWO *S*	SWO *C*	SWO *CPU*	ISWO *S*	ISWO *C*	ISWO *CPU*	*S* %	*C* %
B1	35	294	28	37	321	>999	34	292	121	0.0	1.2
B2	35	294	26	36	319	>999	35	291	61	2.9	0.5
B3	74	830	216	81	908	>999	73	828	203	-2.7	-2.7
T1	62	507	131	67	554	>999	62	507	141	0.0	0.4
T2	117	998	167	124	1097	>999	116	994	176	0.0	-0.9
T3	51	406	11	56	455	>999	50	403	19	0.0	-0.2
T4	62	572	530	67	632	>999	61	569	536	-4.7	1.2
T5	243	2249	981	262	2488	>999	242	2248	873	0.0	0.0
T6	271	2102	130	314	2410	>999	270	2082	135	-2.2	-0.0
T7	343	2662	358	399	3091	>999	342	2662	318	-2.0	0.0
T8	390	3239	986	447	3686	>999	389	3200	928	-1.5	2.0
R1	49	420	23	53	444	>999	49	420	27	0.0	0.0
R2	49	414	59	54	437	>999	49	411	74	0.0	0.6
M	**137**	**1153**	**280**	**154**	**1295**	**>999**	**136**	**1147**	**278**	**-0.8**	**0.1**

0.05, and the k value in Section 3.2.5 to be 2. For each instance, we run the program ten times by using different random seeds.

Table 1 lists the comparative results of the ISWO against the results of the ILP and the SAA, respectively. It also lists the results of the original SWO, which are far from optimal. Each data instance was run ten times by fixing the parameters and varying the pseudo random number seed at the beginning. Compared with the solutions of the ILP approach, our best solutions are 0.78% better in terms of total shift numbers, and are only 0.11% more expensive in terms of total cost. However, our results are much faster in general, especially for larger cases. Compared with the SAA which outperforms other meta-heuristics available in the literature (Li and Kwan, 2005), our ISWO performs better for all data instances using similar execution times.

4 Conclusions

This paper presents a new technique to solve personnel scheduling problems by using the original idea of SWO but by adding two steps of *Selection* and *Mutation* into its loop of *Analysis / Prioritization / Construction*. With these two additional steps, the drawbacks of the original SWO in terms of optimisation ability and execution speed are successfully dealt with. Taken as a whole, the ISWO implements evolution on a single solution and carries out search by solution disruption, iterative improvement and an iterative constructive process. The experiments have demonstrated that the ISWO performs very efficiently and competitively. In general, it outperforms the previous best-performing approaches reported in the literature.

The architecture of the ISWO is innovative, and thus there is still some room for further improvement. For example, we currently only use one fixed rule. We believe that by adding some more flexible rules into the search, solution quality could be improved further. This would be particularly interesting if we have more difficult instances to solve. In the future, we are also looking at more advanced methods of *Analysis*, *Selection* and *Mutation*.

Acknowledgements. The research described in this paper was funded by the Engineering and Physical Sciences Research Council (EPSRC), under grant GR/S70197/1.

References

U. Aickelin, "An Indirect Genetic Algorithm for Set Covering Problems," *Journal of the Operational Research Society*, 53(10), pp 1118-1126, 2002.

U. Aickelin and J. Li, "An Estimation of Distribution Algorithm for Nurse Scheduling," *Annals of Operations Research*, in print, 2006.

U. Aickelin and K. Dowsland, "Exploiting problem structure in a genetic algorithm approach to a nurse rostering problem", *Journal of Scheduling*, 3(3), pp 139-153, 2000.

U. Aickelin and K. Dowsland, "An indirect genetic algorithm for a nurse scheduling problem," *Computers and Operations Research*, vol. 31, pp. 761-778, 2003.

U. Aickelin and P. White, "Building better nurse scheduling algorithms," *Annals of Operations Research*, vol. 128, pp. 159-177, 2004.

E.K. Burke, Y. Bykov, J.P. Newall and S. Petrovic, "A Time-Predefined Local Search Approach to Exam Timetabling Problems", *IIE Transactions*, 36(6), pp 509-528, 2004.

E.K. Burke, P. Causmaecker, G. Vanden Berghe, and H. Landeghem, "The state of the art of nurse rostering," *Journal of Scheduling*, vol. 7, no. 6, pp. 441-499, 2004.

E.K. Burke, G. Kendall, and E. Soubeiga, "A tabu-search hyperheuristic for timetabling and rostering," *Journal of Heuristics*, vol. 9, no. 6, pp. 451-470, 2003.

E.K. Burke and J.P. Newall, "Solving Examination Timetabling Problems through Adaptation of Heuristic Orderings", *Annals of Operations Research* 129, pp 107-134, 2004.

E.K. Burke and J.P. Newall, "Enhancing Timetable Solutions with Local Search Methods", PATAT IV, Lecture Notes in Computer Science 2740, pages 195-206, 2003.

F.F. Easton and N. Mansour, "A distributed genetic algorithm for deterministic and stochastic labor scheduling problems," *European Journal of Operational Research*, vol. 118, pp. 505–523, 1999.

A.T. Ernst, H. Jiang et al, "Staff scheduling and rostering: a review of applications, methods and models," *European Journal of Operational Research*, vol. 153, pp. 3-27, 2004.

S. Fores, L. Proll, and A. Wren, "TRACS II: a hybrid IP/heuristic driver scheduling system for public transport," *Journal of the OR Society*, vol. 53, pp. 1093-1100, 2002.

M.R. Garey and D.S. Johnson, *Computers and Intractability: a Guide to the Theory of NP-Completeness*. Freeman, San Francisco, 1979.

R.S.K. Kwan, A.S.K. Kwan, and A. Wren, "Evolutionary driver scheduling with relief chains." *Evolutionary Computation*, vol 9, pp. 445–460, 2001.

J. Li, *Fuzzy Evolutionary Approach for Bus and Rail Driver Scheduling*. PhD Thesis, University of Leeds, UK, 2002.

J. Li and R.S.K. Kwan, "A fuzzy genetic algorithm for driver scheduling," *European Journal of Operational Research*, vol. 147, pp. 334-344, 2003.

J. Li and R.S.K. Kwan, "A self-adjusting algorithm for driver scheduling," *Journal of Heuristics*, vol. 11, pp. 351-367, 2005.

D.E. Joslin and D.P. Clements, "Squeak wheel optimisation," *Journal of Artificial Intelligence*, Morgan Kaufmann Publishers, vol. 10, pp. 353-373, 1999.

S. Scott and R.M. Simpson, "Case-bases incorporating scheduling constraint dimensions: experiences in nurse rostering," in Smyth and Cunningham (eds.), *Advances in Case-Based Reasoning*, vol. 1488, pp. 392-401, Springer LNAI, 1998.

Y. Shen and R.S.K. Kwan, "Tabu search for driver scheduling," *Computer-Aided Scheduling of Public Transport*, pp. 121-135, Springer-Verlag, 2001.

S. Voß and J.R. Daduna (Eds.), *Computer-Aided Scheduling of Public Transport, Proceedings*, Berlin, Germany, Springer-Verlag, 2001.

A. Wren and D.O. Wren, "A genetic algorithm for public transport driver scheduling," *Computers and Operations Research*, vol. 22, pp. 101-110, 1995.

A. Wren and J.M. Rousseau, "Bus driver scheduling – an overview," in Computer-*Aided Transit Scheduling*, pp. 173-187, Springer-Verlag, 1995.

A Local Genetic Algorithm for Binary-Coded Problems*

Carlos García-Martínez[1], Manuel Lozano[2], and Daniel Molina[3]

[1] Dept. of Computing and Numerical Analysis, Univ. of Córdoba, 14071, Spain
in1gamac@uco.es
[2] Dept. of Computer Science and Artificial Intelligence, Univ. of Granada, 18071, Spain
lozano@decsai.ugr.es
[3] Dept. of Software Engineering, Univ. of Cádiz, 11002, Spain
daniel.molina@uca.es

Abstract. *Local Genetic Algorithms* are search procedures designed in order to provide an effective *local search*. Several Genetic Algorithm models have recently been presented with this aim. In this paper we present a new *Binary-coded Local Genetic Algorithm* based on a *Steady-State Genetic Algorithm* with a *crowding replacement method*. We have compared a *Multi-Start Local Search* based on the Binary-Coded Local Genetic Algorithm with other instances of this metaheuristic based on Local Search Procedures presented in the literature. The results show that, for a wide range of problems, our proposal consistently outperforms the other local search approaches.

1 Introduction

Local Search Procedures (LSPs) are optimisation methods that maintain a solution, known as *current solution*, and explore the search space by steps within its *neighbourhood*. The interest on LSPs comes from the fact that they may effectively and quickly explore the basin of attraction of optimal solutions, finding an optimum with a high degree of accuracy and within a small number of iterations. In fact, these methods are a key component of metaheuristics that are *state-of-the-art* of many optimisation problems, such as *Multi-start Local Search* ([3]), *Greedy Randomised Adaptive Search Procedures*, *Iterated Local Search*, *Variable Neighbourhood Search*, and *Memetic Algorithms* ([2]).

Genetic Algorithms (GAs) ([9,14]) have been seen as search procedures that can locate high performance regions of vast and complex search spaces, but they are not well suited for fine-tuning solutions ([17]). However, the components of the GAs may be *specifically designed* and their parameters *tuned*, in order to provide an *effective local search* as well. In fact, several GA models have recently been presented with this aim ([17,18]). These algorithms are called *Local Genetic Algorithms* (LGAs).

* This research was supported by the Spanish MEC project TIN2005-08386-C05-01.

T.P. Runarsson et al. (Eds.): PPSN IX, LNCS 4193, pp. 192–201, 2006.

LGAs present some advantages over classic LSPs. Most LSPs lack the ability to follow the proper path to the optimum on complex search landscapes. This difficulty becomes much more evident when the search space contains very narrow paths of arbitrary direction, also known as ridges. That is due to LSPs attempt successive steps along orthogonal directions that do not necessarily coincide with the direction of the ridge. However, it was observed that LGAs are capable of following ridges of arbitrary direction in the search space regardless of their direction, width, or even, discontinuities ([17]). Thus, the study of LGAs becomes a promising way to allow the design of more effective metaheuristics based on LSPs ([6,13,17,18,22]).

In this paper, we propose a *Binary-coded LGA* (BLGA) based on a *Steady-State Genetic Algorithm* (SSGA) with a *crowding replacement method*. It iteratively crosses a *leader solution* with individuals of the population belonging to the nearest niches. Then, the best solution between the leader one and the offspring becomes the new leader solution, and the other one is inserted in the population by means of the *Restricted Tournament Selection* ([11]). We have compared a Multi-start Local Search based on the new LGA with other instances of this metaheuristic based on LSPs proposed in the literature. The results show that, for a wide range of problems, this LGA consistently outperforms the other local search approaches.

The paper is organised as follows. In Section 2, we present the LGAs. In Section 3, we propose the BLGA. In Section 4, we compare the performance of the BLGA with LSPs presented in the literature. Finally, in Section 5, we provide some conclusions.

2 Local Genetic Algorithms

There are two primary factors in the search carried out by a GA ([23]):

- *Selection pressure.* In order to have an effective search there must be a search criterion (the fitness function) and a selection pressure that gives individuals with higher fitness a higher chance of being selected for reproduction, mutation, and survival. Without selection pressure, the search process becomes random and promising regions of the search space would not be favoured over non-promising regions.
- *Population diversity.* It is crucial to a GA's ability in order to continue the fruitful exploration of the search space.

Selection pressure and population diversity are inversely related: increasing selection pressure results in a faster loss of population diversity, while maintaining population diversity offsets the effect of increasing selection pressure.

Traditionally, GA practitioners have carefully designed GAs in order to obtain a balanced performance between selection pressure and population diversity. The main objective is to obtain their beneficial advantages simultaneously: to allow the most promising search space regions to be reached (*reliability*) and refined (*accuracy*).

Due to the flexibility of the GA architecture, it is possible to design GA models specifically aimed to provide *effective local search*. In this way, their unique objective is to obtain *accurate* solutions. These algorithms are named *Local Genetic Algorithms*. LGAs arise as an alternative choice to classical LSPs, in order to design metaheuristics based on LSPs. In fact, some LGAs were considered for this task ([6,13,17,18,22]).

3 Binary-Coded Local GA

In this section, we present a Binary-coded LGA (BLGA) that may be used to design metaheuristics based on LSPs. It is a *Steady-state GA* ([20,23]) that inserts one single new member into the population (P) in each iteration. It uses a *crowding replacement method* (*restricted tournament selection* (RTS) ([11])) in order to force a member of the current population to perish and to make room for the new offspring. It is important to know that RTS favours the formation of niches in P (groups of chromosomes with high quality located in different and scattered regions of the search space). In addition, the BLGA maintains an external chromosome, the *leader chromosome* (C^L), which is always selected as one of the parents for the crossover operation. The following sections indicate the main components of the BLGA.

3.1 General Scheme of the Binary-Coded LGA

Let's suppose that a particular metaheuristic applies the BLGA as LSP. When the metaheuristic calls the BLGA to refine a particular solution, the BLGA will consider this solution as C^L. Then, the following steps (Figure 1) are carried out during each iteration:

1. *Mate selection.* m chromosomes, $Y^1, Y^2, ..., Y^m$, are selected from the population applying the positive assortative mating m times (Section 3.2).
2. *Crossover.* C^L is crossed over with $Y^1, Y^2, ..., Y^m$ by applying the multiparent uniform crossover operator, generating an offspring Z (Section 3.3).
3. *Update of the leader solution and replacement.* If Z is better than C^L, then C^L is inserted into the population using the restricted tournament selection (Section 3.4) and Z becomes the new C^L. Otherwise, Z is inserted in the population using the same replacement scheme.

These steps are carried out until the stop condition described in Section 3.5 is achieved.

3.2 Positive Assortative Mating

Assortative mating is the natural occurrence of mating between individuals of similar phenotype more or less often than expected by chance. Mating between individuals with similar phenotype more often is called positive assortative mating and less often is called negative assortative mating. Fernandes et al. ([5])

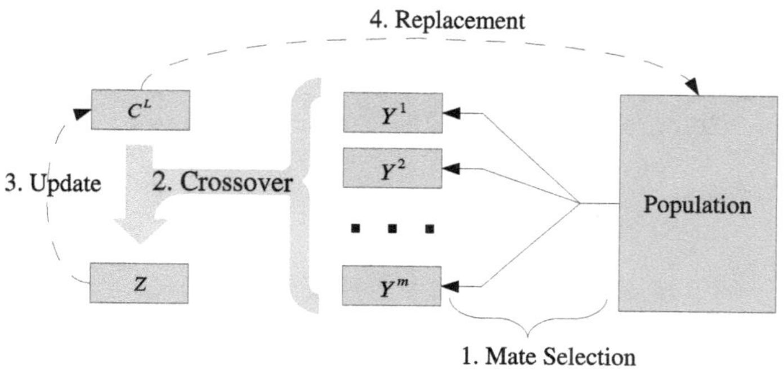

Fig. 1. Model of the BLGA

implement these ideas to design two mating selection mechanisms. A first parent is selected by the roulette wheel method and n_{ass} chromosomes are selected with the same method (in BLGA all the candidates are selected at random). Then, the similarity between each of these chromosomes and the first parent is computed (similarity between two binary-coded chromosomes is defined as the Hamming distance between them). If assortative mating is negative, then the one with less similarity is chosen. If it is positive, the genome more similar to the first parent is chosen to be the second parent. In the case of BLGA, the first parent is the leader chromosome and the method is repeated m times.

3.3 Multiparent Uniform Crossover Operator

The BLGA uses a *multiparent* version of the *Uniform crossover* (UX) ([20]) with a *short term memory* mechanism that avoids the generation of any offspring previously created. The pseudocode is shown in Figure 2, where $U(0,1)$ is a random number in $[0,1]$, $RI(1,m)$ is a random integer in $\{1,2,...,m\}$, and p_f is the probability of choosing genes from C^L (p_f is set to a high value in order to create offspring similar to C^L).

The short term memory remembers the genes of C^L that have been flipped at generating an offspring Z_k. Then, it avoids flipping those genes of C^L, in order to prevent the creation of Z_k once again. In order to do that, this mechanism maintains a mask, $M = (M_1, \ldots, M_n)$, where $M_i = 1$ indicates that the gene c_i^L can not be flipped in order to create an offspring. Initially, and when C^L is updated with a better solution, any gene can be flipped, so M_i is set to 0 for all $i \in \{1, \ldots, n\}$.

The multiparent UX with short term memory creates the offspring $Z = (z_1, \ldots, z_n)$ with:

- z_i is set to c_i^L for all $i = 1, \ldots, n$ with $M_i = 1$.
- If $M_i = 0$, then z_i is set to c_i^L with probability p_f. Otherwise, z_i is set to the ith gene of a randomly chosen parent Y^j. The mask is updated if z_i is different from c_i^L.

```
multiparent_UX(C^L, Y^1, ..., Y^m, m, p_f)
   For i = 1, ..., n
      If M_i = 1 OR U(0,1) < p_f //short term memory mechanism
         z_i ⟵ c_i^L;
      Else
         k ⟵ RI(1,m);
         z_i ⟵ Y_i^k;
         If z_i ≠ c_i^L
            M_i ⟵ 1; //update the mask
   If Z = C^L
      j ⟵ RI(1,n) such as M_j = 0;
      M_j ⟵ 1; //update the mask
      z_j ⟵ 1 − z_j;
   Return Z;
```

Fig. 2. Pseudocode of the multiparent UX with short term memory

– If Z is equal to C^L, then a gene chosen at random, i with $M_i = 0$, is flipped and the mask is updated.

The short term memory mechanism shares ideas with the one of the *Tabu Search* (TS) ([7]). Both of them help the sampling operator to efficiently explore the neighbourhood of the current solution C^L. Both of them avoid sampling previous solution more than once. The main difference is that the mechanism of the BLGA is entirely reset every time an offspring Z becomes better than C^L, whereas the elements in the one of the TS are eliminated, one by one, when their *tabu tenure* expires (usually, a fix number of algorithm iterations).

3.4 Restricted Tournament Selection

BLGA considers the *Restricted Tournament Selection* (RTS) ([11]) as *crowding method*. Its main idea is to replace the closest chromosome R to the one being inserted in the population, I, from a set of n_T randomly selected ones, if I is better than R.

The application of RTS together with the use of high population size may favour the creation of groups of chromosomes with high quality in P, which become located in different and scattered regions of the search space (*niches*).

3.5 Stop Condition

It is important to notice that, when every bit of the mask of the short term memory is set to 1 (Section 3.3), then, C^L will not be further improved, because the crossover operator will create new solutions exactly equal to C^L. Thus, this condition will be used as stop condition for the BLGA.

4 Experiments: Comparison with Other LSPs

The aim of this section is to compare the BLGA with other LSPs for binary-coded problems presented in the literature:

- the *First LSP* ([2]) that changes a random component of the current solution, which improves its fitness value,
- the *Best LSP* ([2]), which changes the bit that makes the best improvement, and,
- the *RandK LSP* ([16,19]) that examines a *k-variable* neighbourhood (it looks for solutions changing k components).

We have implemented four instances of the simplest LSP based metaheuristic, the Multi-start Local Search ([3]), each one with a different LSP. Multi-start Local Search iteratively creates a random solution and apply a LSP on it, until a stop condition is reached. At last, Multi-start Local Search returns the best solution obtained so far.

The four Multi-start Local Search instances will be called as follows:

- MS-First-LS: Multi-start with the First LSP.
- MS-Best-LS: Multi-start with the Best LSP.
- MS-RandK-LS: Multi-start with the RandK LSP.
- MS-BLGA: Multi-start with the BLGA.

We have chosen the Multistart Local Search metaheuristic in order to avoid possible synergies between the metaheuristic and the LSP. In this way, comparisons among the LSPs are fairer. All the algorithms were executed 50 times, each one performing 100,000 evaluations.

The BLGA uses 500 individuals as the population size, $p_f = 0.95$ and $m = 10$ mates for the crossover operator, $n_{ass} = 5$ for the Positive Assortative Mating, and $n_T = 15$ for the Restricted Tournament Selection. The population of the BLGA does not undergoes initialisation after the iterations of the Multistart Local Search, i.e. the initial population of the BLGA at the jth iteration of the MS-BLGA is the last population of the $(j-1)$th iteration. On the other hand, the leader chromosome is randomly generated at the beginning of the iterations of this metaheuristic.

4.1 Test Suite

Table 1 shows the test function used, their dimension, optimisation criterion (to maximise/minimise), optimum value and reference. Some comments are needed:

- Trap(4) consists on applying Trap(1) to a chromosome with 4 groups of 36 genes. Each group is evaluated with Trap(1), and the overall fitness of the chromosomes is the sum of the fitness of each group.

Table 1. Used test problems

Name	Dim	Criterion	f^*	Ref
Onemax(400)	400	min	0	
Deceptive(13)	39	min	0	[8]
Deceptive(134)	402	min	0	[8]
Trap(1)	36	max	220	[21]
Trap(4)	144	max	880	[21]
Maxcut(G11)	800	max	Not known	[15]
Maxcut(G12)	800	max	Not known	[15]
Maxcut(G17)	800	max	Not known	[15]
Maxcut(G18)	800	max	Not known	[15]
Maxcut(G43)	1000	max	Not known	[15]
M-Sat(100,1200,3)	100	max	1[1]	[4]
M-Sat(100,2400,3)	100	max	1[1]	[4]
NkLand(48,4)	48	max	1[1]	[4]
NkLand(48,12)	48	max	1[1]	[4]
BQP('gka')	50	max	3414[2]	[1,10]
BQP(50)	50	max	2098[2]	[1,10]
BQP(100)	100	max	7970[2]	[1,10]
BQP(250)	250	max	45607[2]	[1,10]
BQP(500)	500	max	116586[2]	[1,10]

- We have used 5 instances of the Max-cut problem (G11, G12, G17, G18, G43) from [12].
- We have used two set of instances of the Max-Sat problem with 100 variables (n), 3 variables by clause (l), and 1200 and 2400 clauses (m) respectively ([4]). They are denoted as M-Sat(n, m, l).
- We have used two set of instances of the NK-Landscape problem: one with $N = 48$ and $K = 4$, and another with $N = 48$ and $K = 12$ ([4]). They are denoted as NKLand(N, K).
- We have used 5 instances of the *Binary Quadratic Problem* (BQP) with different dimensions (n). They have been taken from the OR-Library. They are the first instances of the files 'bqpgka', 'bqp50', 'bqp100', 'bqp250', 'bqp500'. They are called BQP('gka'), BQP(50), BQP(100), BQP(250), and BQP(500), respectively.

4.2 Results

The results for all the algorithms are included in Table 2. It shows the average and the standard deviation of the best fitness function found over 50 executions. We have added, in parenthesis, the times the MS-BLGA is slower than the average of the other algorithms (the time consumed by the MS-BLGA divided by the average of the time consumed by the remainder, which were extremely similar). In addition, a two-sided *t-test* at 0.05 level of significance was applied in order to ascertain if the differences in the performance of MS-BLGA are significant when compared against the ones for the other algorithms. We denote the direction of any significant differences as follows:

[1] 1 is the maximum possible fitness value, however it may not exist any optimal solution with that fitness value, depending on the current problem instance.

[2] Best known values presented in [1].

Table 2. Comparison of the MS-BLGA with other Multistart LSP instances

		MS-First-LS	MS-Best-LS	MS-RandK-LS	MS-BLGA	+ ~ -
Onemax(400)	average	0	0	0	0	
	sd	0 ~	0 ~	0 ~	0 (753.12)	0 3 0
Deceptive(13)	average	8.68	3.36	14.32	8.68	
	sd	1.11 ~	1.24 −	0.94 +	1.43 (1162.51)	1 1 1
Deceptive(134)	average	177.6	128.4	201.6	185.84	
	sd	5.03 −	10.5 −	7.51 +	9.56 (742.11)	1 0 2
Trap(1)	average	213.12	219.1	201.86	218.38	
	sd	2.54 +	1.94 ~	2.41 +	2.39 (873.49)	2 1 0
Trap(4)	average	790.08	828.92	781.78	869.3	
	sd	7.17 +	8.09 +	7.88 +	6.97 (562.19)	3 0 0
Maxcut(G11)	average	437.36	349.6	441	506.64	
	sd	7.37 +	17.11 +	10.78 +	6.92 (52.47)	3 0 0
Maxcut(G12)	average	425.6	335.16	431.32	497.36	
	sd	7.23 +	15.65 +	12.17 +	6.97 (52.44)	3 0 0
Maxcut(G17)	average	2920.82	2824.66	2946.58	2975.7	
	sd	5.97 +	15.59 +	11.06 +	8.15 (51.16)	3 0 0
Maxcut(G18)	average	849.86	628.32	873.82	898.08	
	sd	11.30 +	22.15 +	18.68 +	15.98 (51.37)	3 0 0
Maxcut(G43)	average	6427.44	5735.84	6463.1	6463.18	
	sd	16.27 +	40.74 +	26.20 ~	24.86 (49.3)	2 1 0
M-Sat(100,1200,3)	average	0.9551	0.9526	0.9563	0.9566	
	sd	3.7e-3 +	3.9e-3 +	3.3e-3 ~	3.2e-3 (21.59)	2 1 0
M-Sat(100,2400,3)	average	0.9332	0.9314	0.9335	0.9338	
	sd	2.0e-3 ~	2.5e-3 +	2.2e-3 ~	1.9e-3 (11.25)	1 2 0
NkLand(48,4)	average	0.7660	0.7647	0.7694	0.7750	
	sd	1.4e-2 +	1.3e-2 +	1.4e-2 +	1.4e-2 (13.48)	3 0 0
NkLand(48,12)	average	0.7456	0.7442	0.7493	0.7468	
	sd	8.3e-3 ~	7.7e-3 ~	1.0e-2 ~	9.5e-3 (9.39)	0 3 0
BQP('gka')	average	3414	3414	3414	3414	
	sd	0 ~	0 ~	0 ~	0 (143.8)	0 3 0
BQP(50)	average	2098	2094.08	2096.72	2098	
	sd	0 ~	15.68 ~	9.05 ~	0 (146.11)	0 3 0
BQP(100)	average	7890.56	7831.7	7881.52	7927.56	
	sd	33.79 +	57.75 +	38.01 +	43.15 (96,4)	3 0 0
BQP(250)	average	45557.16	45171.38	45504.22	45510.96	
	sd	33.68 ~	295.46 +	99.28 +	128.92 (62.92)	2 1 0
BQP(500)	average	115176.88	108588.26	115335.34	115256.3	
	sd	494.89 ~	2210.02 +	527.97 ~	814.44 (50.14)	1 2 0
+/ ~ /−		10 / 8 / 1	12 / 5 / 2	11 / 8 / 0		

- A plus sign (+): the average of MS-BLGA is better than the one of the corresponding algorithm.
- A minus sign (−): the algorithm improves the average of MS-BLGA.
- An approximate sign (~): non significant differences.

We have added the last three columns and the last three rows that count the number of improvements, non-differences and reductions according to the t-test by functions and by algorithms, respectively.

The last three rows indicate that the BLGA arises as a promising algorithm to deal with binary-coded optimisation problems because it achieves many improvements and very few reductions versus the other approaches.

On the other hand, two remarks are worth being mentioned from the last three columns:

- MS-BLGA is one of the best algorithms for almost the 90% of the test functions. Concretely, MS-BLGA achieves better or equivalent results than

the ones of the other algorithms for all the functions, except on the two Deceptive ones.
- MS-BLGA returns the best results for 4 from up to 5 Max-cut problems.

It can be seen that these good results do not come for free. MS-BLGA invest runtime in order to obtain better results than the ones obtained by the other LSPs, performing the same number of fitness evaluations. However, it is interesting to notice that the differences become smaller when the dimension of the problem increases. The design of less time consuming LGAs, including parallel GAs, arises as an important idea from this study.

To sum up, we may conclude that the BLGA, working within the Multistart Local Search metaheuristic, is very competitive with classic LSPs, because it obtains better or equivalent results for almost all the test problems considered in this study.

5 Conclusions

In this paper, we have presented the BLGA, a LGA instance that incorporates specific mate selection mechanism, crossover operator, and replacement strategy to direct the local search towards promising search regions represented in the proper BLGA population.

An experimental study, including 19 binary coded test problems, has shown that when we incorporate the BLGA into a Multistart Local Search metaheuristic, this metaheuristic may improve their results with regards to the use of other LSP instances that are frequently used to implement it.

Several ideas for future developments arise from this study:

- Analyse the behaviour of the BLGA when it is used by different metaheuristics based on LSPs ([3,2]).
- Extend our investigation to different test-suites (other coding schemes) and real-world problems.
- Study adaptive mechanisms that control the parameters of the algorithm according to the current state of the search process.

References

1. J.E. Beasley. Heuristic algorithms for the unconstrained binary quadratic programming problem. Technical Report, Management School, Imperial College, UK, 1998.
2. C. Blum, A. Roli. Metaheuristics in combinatorial optimization: overview and conceptual comparison. ACM Computing Surveys (CSUR) 35:2, 2003, pp. 268-308.
3. K.D. Boese and S. Muddu. A new adaptive multi-start technique for combinatorial global optimizations. Operations Research Letters 16, 1994, pp. 101-113.
4. K. De Jong, M.A. Potter, W.M. Spears. Using problem generators to explore the effects of epistasis. Proc. of the Seventh International Conference on Genetic Algorithms, 1997, pp. 338-345.

5. C. Fernandes, A. Rosa. A study on non-random mating and varying population size in genetic algorithms using a royal road function. Proc. of the 2001 Congress on Evolutionary Computation, IEEE Press, Piscataway, New Jersey, 2001, pp. 60-66.
6. C. García-Martínez, M. Lozano, F. Herrera, D. Molina, A.M. Sánchez. Global and local real-coded genetic algorithms based on parent-centric crossover operators. European Journal of Operational Research, 2006. In press.
7. F. Glover, M. Laguna. Tabu search. Operational Research Society Journal 50:1, 1999, pp. 106-107.
8. D.E. Goldberg, B. Korb, K. Deb. Messy genetic algorithms: motivation, analysis, and first results. Complex Systems 3, 1989, pp. 493-530.
9. D.E. Goldberg. Genetic algorithms in search, optimization, and machine learning. Addison-Wesley, Reading, MA, 1989.
10. V.P. Gulati, S.K. Gupta, A.K. Mittal. Unconstrained quadratic bivalent programming problem. European Journal of Operational Research 15, 1984, pp. 121-125.
11. G. Harik. Finding multimodal solutions using restricted tournament selection. Proc. of the 6th International Conference on Genetic Algorithms, L.J. Eshelman, editor, Morgan Kaufmann, San Mateo, California, 1995, pp. 24-31.
12. C. Helmberg, F. Rendl. A spectral bundle method for semidefinite programming. Siam Journal of Optimization 10:3, 2000, pp. 673-696.
13. F. Herrera, M. Lozano. Gradual distributed real-coded genetic algorithms. IEEE Transactions on Evolutionary Computation 4:1, 2000, pp. 43-63.
14. J.H. Holland. Adaptation in natural and artificial systems. The University of Michigan Press (The MIT Press, London, 1992).
15. R.M. Karp. Reducibility among combinatorial problems. In R. Miller and J. Thatcher, editors, Complexity of Computer Computations, Plenum Press, New York, 1972, pp. 85-103.
16. K. Katayama, H. Narihisa. A variant *k-opt* local search heuristic for binary quadratic programming. Trans. IEICE (A) J84-A:3, 2001, pp. 430-435.
17. S.A. Kazarlis, S.E. Papadakis, J.B. Theocharis, V. Petridis. Microgenetic algorithms as generalized hill-climbing operators for GA optimization. IEEE Transactions on Evolutionary Computation 5:3, 2001, pp. 204-217.
18. M. Lozano, F. Herrera, N. Krasnogor, D. Molina. Real-coded memetic algorithms with crossover hill-climbing. Evolutionary Computation Journal 12:3, 2004, pp. 273-302.
19. P. Merz, K. Katayama. Memetic algorithms for the unconstrained binary quadratic programming problem. Bio Systems 79:1-3, 2004, pp. 99-118.
20. G. Sywerda. Uniform crossover in genetic algorithms. Proc. of the third international conference on Genetic algorithms, 1989, pp. 2-9.
21. D. Thierens. Population-based iterated local search: restricting neighborhood search by crossover. Proc. of the Genetic and Evolutionary Computation Conference, LNCS 3103, 2004, pp. 234-245.
22. S. Tsutsui, A. Ghosh, D. Corne, Y. Fujimoto. A real coded genetic algorithm with an explorer and an exploiter population. Proc. of the Seventh International Conference on Genetic Algorithms, T. Bäck, editor, Morgan Kaufmann Publishers, San Francisco, 1997, pp. 238-245.
23. D. Whitley. The GENITOR algorithm and selection pressure: why rank-based allocation of reproductive trials is best. Proc. of the Third International Conference on Genetic Algorithms, J. David Schaffer, editor, Morgan Kaufmann, San Mateo, 1989, pp. 116-121.

Hill Climbers and Mutational Heuristics in Hyperheuristics

Ender Özcan, Burak Bilgin, and Emin Erkan Korkmaz

Yeditepe University,
Department of Computer Engineering,
34755 Kadıköy/İstanbul, Turkey
{eozcan, bbilgin, ekorkmaz}@cse.yeditepe.edu.tr

Abstract. Hyperheuristics are single candidate solution based and simple to maintain mechanisms used in optimization. At each iteration, as a higher level of abstraction, a hyperheuristic chooses and applies one of the heuristics to a candidate solution. In this study, the performance contribution of hill climbing operators along with the mutational heuristics are analyzed in depth in four different hyperheuristic frameworks. Four different hill climbing operators and three mutational operators are used during the experiments. Various subsets of the heuristics are evaluated on fourteen well-known benchmark functions.

1 Introduction

The term hyperheuristics refers to a recent approach in search methodologies [2, 4, 5, 7, 17, 23]. The hyperheuristic concept involves a higher level of abstraction than metaheuristic methods. This term describes an iterative search approach which controls a set of heuristics. The method keeps track of the non problem-specific data such as the fitness change, the execution time and applies a heuristic at each iteration. Studies involving a number of heuristic selection and acceptance mechanism combinations are reported in the literature [2, 3, 4, 7, 17]. A comprehensive study on the performance of different heuristic selection and move acceptance strategies is reported in [3].

In this paper, the synergy of various heuristics and their contribution to the performance is evaluated on a set of benchmark functions. Furthermore, four different hyperheuristic frameworks that utilize a set of hill climbers as heuristics in addition to a set of mutational heuristics, are defined and assessed as well. The new frameworks are derived from the commonly used framework. The intention of this study is to answer the following questions: What type of heuristics is useful to be used in hyperheuristics? Do the hill climbers improve the performance if used within hyperheuristics? Can we use only hill climbers as heuristics? At which stage(s) and how can hill climbers be used to improve the performance? Is it possible to identify the problem domains where a specific framework might perform better as compared to the others?

2 Preliminaries

In general, exhaustive methods are impractical for solving real world problems, whereas meta-heuristics provide better means by intelligently seeking optimal solutions within

T.P. Runarsson et al. (Eds.): PPSN IX, LNCS 4193, pp. 202–211, 2006.

a search space. For many practical problems meta-heuristics provide state-of-the-art solutions. Their success is due to the problem-specific implementations, which utilize knowledge about the problem domain and properties. The deployment of meta-heuristics requires expert level knowledge and experience on the problem tackled. Furthermore, fine tuning might be required [4, 23]. Hyperheuristics are general search methods that can be applied to any optimization problem easily [7]. Hyperheuristics describe a set of strategies that are used to choose a heuristic from a set of low level heuristics as illustrated in Fig. 1. There are very simple strategies that can be coded easily. Yet, a meta-heuristic can be used as a heuristic underneath a hyperheuristic as well as a hyperheuristic itself within this framework.

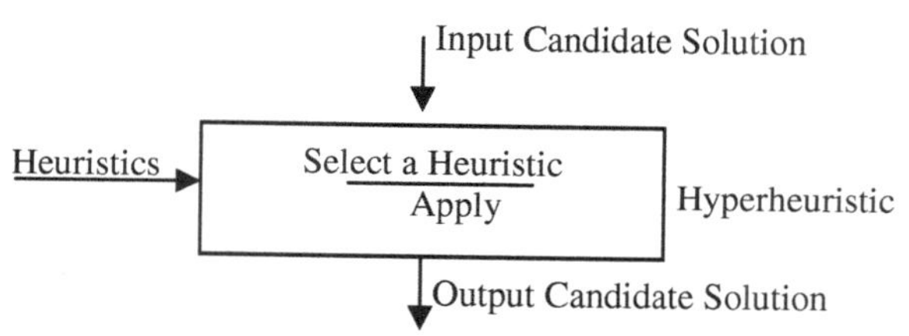

Fig. 1. Traditional hyperheuristic framework

Hyperheuristics operate on the search space of heuristics instead of candidate solutions. Non problem-specific data like heuristic execution time and changes in the fitness function can be used by hyperheuristics to select and apply a heuristic [2]. Although the methods of this type are reported in the literature before, the term hyperheuristic is first proposed by Cowling et al. [7] to name this approach. The early studies date back to Fisher and Thompson. They used a hyperheuristic based on probabilistic weighting of heuristics to solve the job-shop scheduling problem [12]. Kitano [19] used a genetic algorithm as a hyperheuristic for designing neural network topology. The hyperheuristic approach is utilized by Gratch et al. [15] to schedule earth-orbiting satellites and ground stations communications. Fang et al. [11] utilized this approach using the genetic algorithm to tackle the open-shop problem. Hart and Ross [17] tackled the dynamic job-shop problem with a similar approach. Hyperheuristics are applied to university exam timetabling problems by Terashima-Marin et al. [25].

A single iteration of a hyperheuristic method can be decomposed in two stages, heuristic selection and movement acceptance. In the previous studies, hyperheuristics might be named without discriminating between heuristic selection and acceptance criterion. Examples of heuristic selection methods are Simple, Greedy, Choice Function [7], Tabu-Search [5], and Case Based Heuristic Selection Methods [6]. Simple Hyperheuristics utilize randomized processes to select heuristics. Greedy Hyperheuristic chooses the best performing heuristic at each iteration. Choice Function Hyperheuristic keeps track of previous performance of each heuristic and makes a choice between them by evaluating their performance via a choice function. Two types of deterministic acceptance criteria are used in [5, 7]: All Moves Accepted (AM) and Only Improving Moves Accepted (OI). Non-deterministic acceptance criteria can be found in [2, 17]. Monte Carlo Hyperheuristic accepts all of the improving moves and the non-improving moves can be accepted based on a probabilistic framework [2]. Great Deluge Hyperheuristic utilizes the Great Deluge Algorithm as the acceptance criterion [17]. Monte Carlo and Great Deluge Hyperheuristics both use Simple Random as heuristic selection method in [2, 17]. An experimental study on the performance of various heuristic selection and acceptance criterion combinations yielded that the combination of Choice Function, Improving and Equal Moves Accepted (IE) strategy and bit modifying heuristics performed the best on benchmark functions [3]. Hence, during the experiments this combination is used.

2.1 Benchmark Functions

A set of benchmark functions can be used to represent a broad range of optimization problems with various fitness landscapes. For the performance evaluation of different heuristic sets within different hyperheuristic frameworks, fourteen different benchmark functions are utilized. Characteristics of each benchmark function and the sources where they are obtained are summarized in Table 1.

Table 1. Characteristics of benchmark functions: *lb* indicates lower bound, *ub* upper bound, *opt* optimum point, *dim* number of dimensions, *bits* number of bits per dimension, *Conti.* continuity, *Cont.* continuous, *Disc.* discrete, and *Multi.* multimodal

Label	*lb*	*ub*	*opt*	*dim*	*bits*	*Conti.*	*Modality*	*Source*
F1	-5.12	5.12	0	10	30	Cont.	Unimodal	[8]
F2	-2.048	2.048	0	10	30	Cont.	Unimodal	[8]
F3	-5.12	5.12	0	10	30	Cont.	Unimodal	[8]
F4	-1.28	1.28	1	10	30	Cont.	Multi.	[8]
F5	-65.536	65.536	0	2	30	Cont.	Multi.	[8]
F6	-5.12	5.12	0	10	30	Cont.	Multi.	[15]
F7	-500	500	0	10	30	Cont.	Multi.	[16]
F8	-600	600	0	10	30	Cont.	Multi.	[12]
F9	-32.768	32.768	0	10	30	Cont.	Multi.	[1]
F10	-100	100	-1	10	30	Cont.	Unimodal	[1]
F11	-65.536	65.536	0	10	30	Cont.	Unimodal	[8]
F12	-	-	0	8	8	Disc.	-	[14]
F13	-	-	0	30	3	Disc.	-	[10]
F14	-	-	0	6	4	Disc.	-	[18]

2.2 Heuristics for Benchmark Function Optimization

Heuristics are classified as *mutational heuristics* and *hill climbers* in this paper. Hill climbers generate a *better* output candidate solution as a local search component, after they are applied to an input candidate solution. Mutational heuristics do not necessarily generate a better output candidate solutiono. 4 hill climbing algorithms and 3 mutational heuristics are implemented as heuristics to be used for solving binary encoded problems.

Hill climbing algorithms are as follows: Davis' Bit Hill Climbing Algorithm (DBHC) [8], Next Descent Hill Climbing Algorithm (NDHC) Random Bit Hill

Climbing Algorithm (RBHC) and Steepest Descent Hill Climbing Algorithm (SDHC) [19]. All hill climbers make a set of modifications on a given candidate solution and each modification is accepted if there is an improvement in the generated solution. Assuming that a candidate solution is represented by a binary string, in each NDHC step a bit is inverted. The whole string is scanned bit by bit starting from the first until to the last. A DBHC differs from NDHC due to the scanning order. DBHC predetermines a random sequence to apply a hill climbing step and scans through the candidate solution according to it. During each RBHC step a bit is selected randomly and inverted for a number of iterations. SDHC checks each single bit inversion variant of the input candidate and accepts the one with the *best* improvement.

Mutational heuristics are Swap Dimension (SWPD), Dimensional Mutation (DIMM) and Hyper-mutation (HYPM). Swap Dimension heuristic randomly chooses two different dimensions in a candidate solution and swaps them. Dimensional Mutation heuristic randomly chooses a dimension and inverts all bits in this dimension with a probability of 0.5. Hyper-mutation randomly inverts each bit in the candidate solution with a probability of 0.5.

2.3 Hyperheuristic Frameworks

Recent studies presented in [21] shows that in memetic algorithms, using a single efficient hill climber instead of using a set of hill climbers where the operator selection is carried out self adaptively, might yield better solutions. As a result, different frameworks based on the general hyperheuristic approach can be defined in order to make better use of hill climbers as heuristics. In this study, four different frameworks are used; F_A, F_B, F_C and F_D, as summarized in Fig. 2.

F_A is the traditional framework and the others are the newly proposed ones. Hill climbers are used together with the mutational hill climbers. In some situations, after applying a mutational heuristic a hill climbing might be desirable. For example, if IE is used in the hyperheuristic, then most of the mutational heuristic moves will be declined. To avoid this phenomenon and to make better use of diversity provided by mutational heuristics, a hill climber can be utilized additionally. F_B represents such a framework. If the hyperheuristic chooses a mutational heuristic, then a predefined single hill climber is applied to the candidate solution. Notice that F_B still uses all heuristics together. In F_C, hill climbers are separated from the mutational heuristics. Hyperheuristic chooses only an appropriate mutational heuristic. Application of a selected heuristic to a candidate solution is followed by a hill climbing. A single hill climber is predefined by the user. F_D is a more general form of F_C. Two hyperheuristic modules are used; one for selecting an appropriate mutational heuristic and one for selecting an appropriate hill climber. F_D can be implemented in two ways. The acceptance mechanism of the hyperheuristic for hill climbers can get a feedback from the intermediate candidate solution (Fig. 2- F_D, marked solid lines) or from the initial candidate solution (Fig. 2-F_D, dashed line).

3 Experiments

The experiments are performed on Pentium IV, 2 GHz Linux machines with 256 Mb memory. Fifty runs are performed for each heuristic set and problem instance

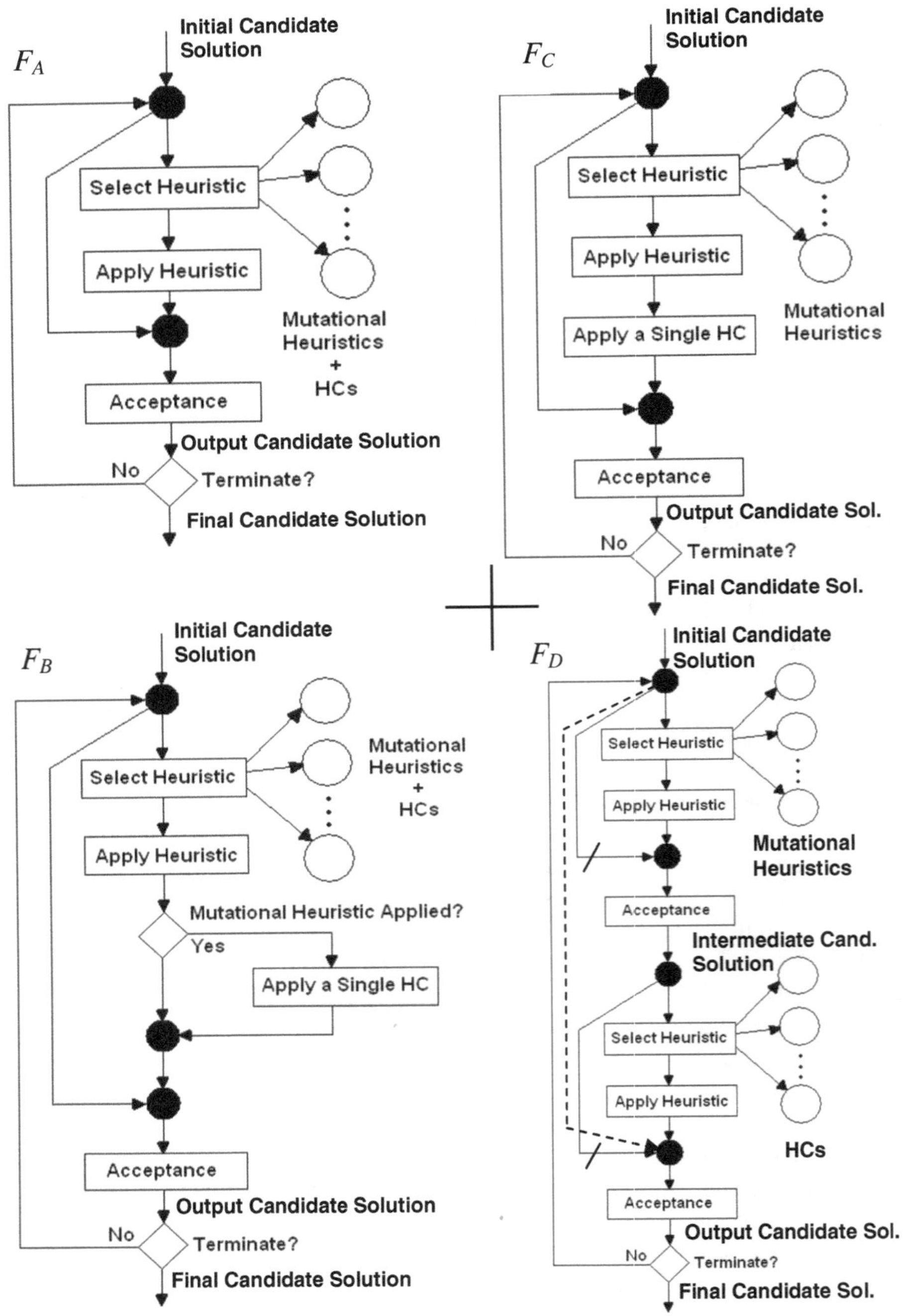

Fig. 2. Different hyperheuristic frameworks combining mutational heuristics and hill climbers

pair. For each problem instance, a set of fifty random initial candidate solutions are created. Each run in an experiment is performed starting from the same initial candidate solution. The experiments are allowed to run for 600 CPU seconds. If the global optimum of the objective function is found before the time limit is exhausted than the experiment is terminated.

3.1 Experimental Settings

The candidate solutions are encoded as bit strings. The continuous functions in benchmark set are encoded in gray code. The discrete functions have their own direct encoding. Linear combinations of deceptive function variables are created to make them multidimensional. F5 has default dimension of 2. The default number of bits per dimension parameter is set to 8, 3, and 4 for the F12, F13, and F14 respectively. The rest of them have 10 dimensions and 30 bits are used to encode a variable (Table 1).

Hyperheuristic pattern is defined as the set of heuristics and the framework utilized in a hyperheuristic algorithm. The experimental set consists of eleven different hyperheuristic patterns; H1-H11 (Table 2). The frameworks F_A and F_B are tested combining hill climbers (HCs) with each mutational heuristic to observe the contribution of each one. If just hill climbers are used without having any mutational heuristics in the system, then both frameworks F_B and F_D reduce to F_A and F_C becomes local search. Hyperheuristic patterns are tested on 14 different benchmark functions. Choice Function and IE pair is used as a hyperheuristic during the experiments, except for H11. This pair is used on hill climbers, while Simple Random and AM pair is used on mutational heuristics. The single hill climber within the frameworks F_B and F_C is chosen as *DBHC* during the experiments.

3.2 Experimental Results

The runs, where the global optimum is found before time limit is exceeded, are considered to be successful. *Success rate*, the ratio of successful runs to all runs, is used as a performance criterion. There exists at least one hyperheuristic pattern that obtains an optimal solution during the runs for each benchmark function, except F4, which represents a search space with noise.

The average number of evaluations of the hyperheuristic patterns achieving full success during all runs on each benchmark function is depicted in Fig. 3. The traditional framework F_A with hill climbers performed poorly on most of the benchmark functions. There is always a better framework than F_A for all cases, except for F1. Even for F1, the performance of F_A is not significantly better than the rest. The framework F_B with all hill climbers and *SWPD* heuristic performed well on the benchmark functions F2, F9, and F11. These functions carry epistasis between dimensions. The experiments with F_A, F_B and each mutational heuristics showed that in some cases a good choice of mutational heuristics might yield a better performance. For example, *DIMM* provided a significantly better performance compared to the rest of the mutational heuristics in F_A and F_B for F6 and F11. Furthermore, in some cases, the framework might generate a synergy between operators providing an improved performance. For example, F_B performed significantly better than F_A when all hill climbers are used and *SWPD* in F2 and F8.

Table 2. Heuristic set and the framework used in each hyperheuristic pattern; H1-H11, where + and * indicate that the corresponding heuristic is controlled by the same hyperheuristic and – points out the heuristic that is used as the single hill climber within the related framework

Sets:	H1	H2	H3	H4	H5	H6	H7	**H8**	**H9**	**H10**	**H11**
NDHC	+	+	+	+	+	+	+	+	+		+
DBHC	+	+	+	+	+/–	+/–	+/–	+/–	+	–	+
RBHC	+	+	+	+	+	+	+	+	+		+
SDHC	+	+	+	+	+	+	+	+	+		+
SWPD		+			+			+	+	+	*
DIMM			+			+		+	+	+	*
HYPM				+			+	+	+	+	*
Framework	F_A	F_A	F_A	F_A	F_B	F_B	F_B	F_B	F_A	F_C	F_D

The framework F_C with all mutational heuristics and *DBHC* hill climber performed well on F3, F6, F7, and F10 which are continuous benchmark functions either unimodal or multimodal. Furthermore, F_C yielded a significantly better performance in solving discrete deceptive problems as compared to the rest. F_D was the only framework generating full success in all the runs for F5. This framework also performed well on F8. Both functions represent continuous and highly multimodal search spaces.

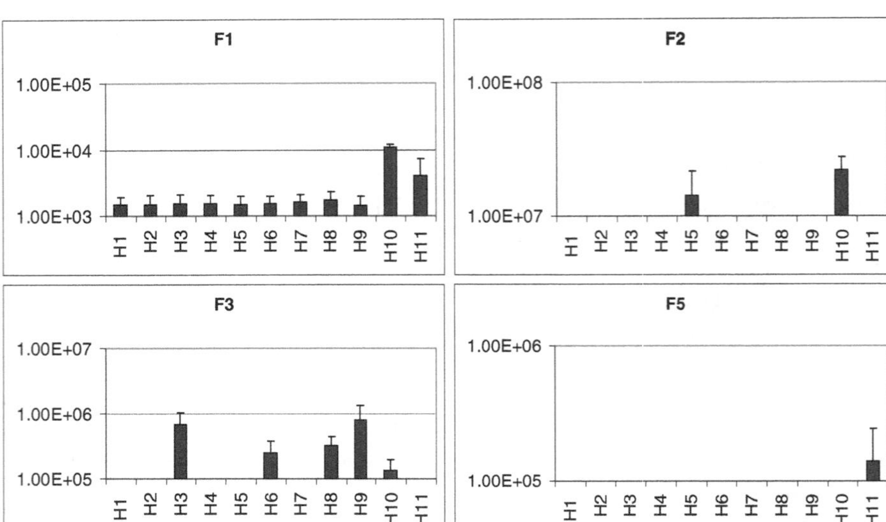

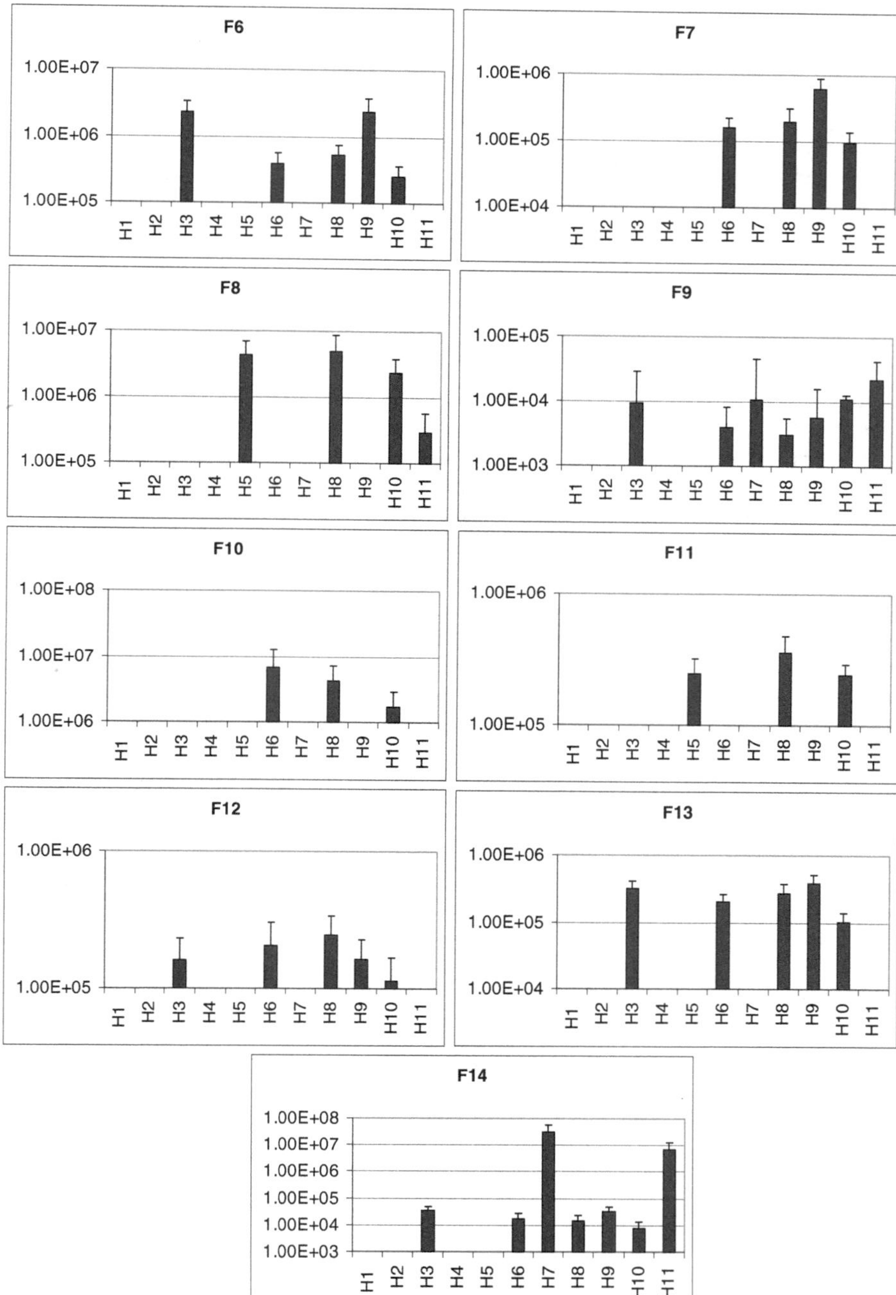

Fig. 3. Average number of fitness evaluations and their standard deviations for each hyperheuristic pattern having full success in all the runs

4 Conclusion

The traditional hyperheuristics framework is extended to embed hill climbers as heuristics in various ways. Three different new frameworks are proposed and experimented on a set of benchmark functions, together with the traditional framework. Additionally, in order to observe the effects of mutational heuristics combined with hill climbers, an extra set of experiments is arranged.

The empirical results indicate that two of the newly proposed frameworks F_B and F_C have a better average performance than the traditional one. The third framework proposed turns out to be significantly successful for solving two highly multimodal benchmark functions compared to the rest. Furthermore, a hyperheuristic framework does not perform well, if it contains only hill climbers as heuristics. Obviously, most of the problems require utilization of a mutational heuristic in order not to get stuck at local optima. It has been observed that the choice of heuristics, whether it is a hill climber or a mutational heuristic determines the performance along with the choice of the framework. Exploitation and exploration capability of a hyperheuristic algorithm is determined by the heuristics used within. Mutational heuristics and hill climbers, combined underneath a decent framework might generate a synergy, yielding a better performance.

It seems that the traditional perturbation approaches are appropriate to be used as mutational heuristics. For example, random perturbation of a locus in a candidate solution, similar to mutation in evolutionary algorithms seems to perform well. Dimensional or content swapping operators can be helpful. Even, a hypermutation like heuristic, generating a random candidate solution might become handy, especially, whenever a hill climber is invoked afterwards. In our experiments, *SWPD* was useful in the benchmark problems with interdimensional epistasis, while *DIMM* and *HYPM* were very useful in multimodal benchmark functions to escape from the local optima.

Acknowledgement. This research is funded by TUBİTAK (The Scientific and Technological Research Council of Turkey) under grant number 105E027.

References

1. Ackley, D.: An Empirical Study of Bit Vector Function Optimization. Genetic Algorithms and Simulated Annealing, (1987) 170-215
2. Ayob, M. and Kendall, G.: A Monte Carlo Hyperheuristic To Optimise Component Placement Sequencing For Multi Head Placement Machine. Proc. of the Int. Conference on Intelligent Technologies, InTech'03, Chiang Mai, Thailand, Dec 17-19 (2003) 132-141
3. Bilgin, B., Ozcan, E., Korkmaz, E.E., An Experimental Study on Hyper-heuristics and Final Exam Scheduling, Proc. of the 6th Int. Conf. on PATAT 2006, to appear (2006)
4. Burke, E. K., Kendall, G., Newall, J., Hart E., Ross, P., Schulenburg, S.: Hyperheuristics: An Emerging Direction in Modern Search Technology. In: Glover, F., Kochenberger, G. A. (eds.): Handbook of Metaheuristics. International Series in OR & Management Science, Vol. 57. Kluwer Academic Publishers, Boston Dordrecht London (2003) 457–474
5. Burke, E.K., Kendall, G., and Soubeiga, E: A Tabu-Search Hyperheuristic for Timetabling and Rostering. Journal of Heuristics Vol 9, No. 6 (2003) 451-470

6. Burke E.K., Petrovic, S. and Qu, R.: Case Based Heuristic Selection for Timetabling Problems. Journal of Scheduling, Vol.9 No2. (2006) 115-132
7. Cowling P., Kendall G., and Soubeiga E.: A Hyperheuristic Approach to Scheduling a Sales Summit. LNCS vol. 2079, PATAT 2000, selected papers (2000) 176-190
8. Davis, L.: Bit Climbing, Representational Bias, and Test Suite Design, Proceeding of the 4th International conference on Genetic Algorithms (1991) 18-23
9. De Jong, K.: An Analysis of the Behaviour of a Class of Genetic Adaptive Systems. PhD thesis, University of Michigan (1975)
10. Easom, E. E.: A Survey of Global Optimization Techniques. M. Eng. thesis, Univ. Louisville, Louisville, KY (1990)
11. Fang, H-L., Ross, P. M. and Corne, D.: A Promising Hybrid GA/Heuristic Approach for Open-Shop Scheduling Problems. Proc. of the 11th European Conf. on Artificial Intelligence (1994) 590-594
12. Fisher H. and Thompson, G. L.: Probabilistic Learning Combinations of Local Job-shop Scheduling Rules. Factory Scheduling Conf., Carnegie Institute of Tech., May 10-12 1961.
13. Goldberg, D. E.: Genetic Algorithms and Walsh Functions: Part I, A Gentle Introduction. Complex Systems (1989) 129-152
14. Goldberg, D. E.: Genetic Algorithms and Walsh Functions: Part II, Deception and Its Analysis. Complex Systems (1989) 153-171
15. Gratch, J., Chein, S. and de Jong, G.: Learning Search Control Knowledge for Deep Space Network Scheduling. Proc. of 10th Int. Conf. on Machine Learning (1993) 135-142
16. Griewangk, A.O.: Generalized Descent of Global Optimization. Journal of Optimization Theory and Applications, 34 (1981) 11-39
17. Hart, E., and Ross, P. M.: A Heuristic Combination Method for Solving Job-Shop Scheduling Problems. PPSN V, LNCS Vol. 1498, Springer Berlin (1998) 845-854
18. Kendall, G. and Mohamad M.: Channel Assignment in Cellular Communication Using a Great Deluge Hyperheuristic, Proc. of the IEEE Int. Conf. on Network (2004) 769-773
19. Kitano, H.: Designing Neural Networks Using Genetic Algorithms with Graph Generation Systems. Complex Systems 4(4) (1990) 461-476
20. Mitchell, M., and Forrest, S.: Fitness Landscapes: Royal Road Functions. Handbook of Evolutionary Computation, Baeck, T., Fogel, D., Michalewiz, Z., (eds.), Institute of Physics Publishing and Oxford University (1997) 1-25
21. Ozcan, E.: An Empirical Investigation on Memes, Self-generation and Nurse Rostering, Proc. of the 6th Int. Conf. on PATAT 2006, to appear (2006)
22. Rastrigin, L. A.: Extremal Control Systems. In Theoretical Foundations of Engineering Cybernetics Series, Moscow, Nauka, Russian (1974)
23. Ross, P.: Hyperheuristics. In: Burke, E. K., Kendall, G. (eds.): Search Methodologies: Introductory Tutorials in Optimization and Decision Support Techniques. Springer-Verlag, Berlin Heidelberg New York (2005) 529–556
24. Schwefel, H. P.: Numerical Optimization of Computer Models, John Wiley & Sons (1981), English translation of Numerische Optimierung von Computer-Modellen mittels der Evolutionsstrategie (1977)
25. Terashima-Marin, H., Ross, P. M., and Valenzuela-Rendon, M.: Evolution of Constraint Satisfaction Strategies in Examination Timetabling. Proc. of Genetic and Evolutionary Computation Conference – GECCO, (1999) 635-642
26. Whitley, D.: Fundamental Principles of Deception in Genetic Search. In G. J. E. Rawlins (eds.), Foundations of Genetic Algorithms, Morgan Kaufmann, San Matco, CA (1991)

A Multi-level Memetic/Exact Hybrid Algorithm for the Still Life Problem

José E. Gallardo, Carlos Cotta, and Antonio J. Fernández

Dept. Lenguajes y Ciencias de la Computación, ETSI Informática,
University of Málaga, Campus de Teatinos, 29071 - Málaga, Spain
{pepeg, ccottap, afdez}@lcc.uma.es

Abstract. Bucket elimination (BE) is an exact technique based on variable elimination. It has been recently used with encouraging results as a mechanism for recombining solutions in a memetic algorithm (MA) for the still life problem, a hard constraint optimization problem based on Conway's game of life. This paper studies expanded multi-level models in which this exact/metaheuristic hybrid is further hybridized with branch-and-bound techniques. A novel variable clustering based recombination operator is also explored, with the aim of reducing the inherent time complexity of BE. Multi-parent recombination issues are analyzed as well. The obtained results are of higher quality than any previous metaheuristic approach, with large instances being solved to optimality.

1 Introduction

Conway's game of life [1] consists of an infinite checkerboard in which the only player places checkers on some of its squares. Each square has eight neighbors: the eight cells that share one or two corners with it. A cell is alive if there is a checker on it, and dead otherwise. The state of the board evolves iteratively according to three rules: (i) if a cell has exactly two living neighbors then its state remains the same in the next iteration, (ii) if a cell has exactly three living neighbors then it is alive in the next iteration, and (iii) if a cell has fewer than two or more than three living neighbors, then it is dead in the next iteration. The *maximum density still life problem* (MDSLP) is a challenging constraint optimization problem based on Conway's game. The problem is to find stable configurations, called *still lifes*, consisting of finite board configurations (of size $n \times n$) with a maximum number of living cells not changing along time. This problem has many practical applications in the control of discrete systems [2,3] and is very hard to solve; though it has not been proven to be NP-hard, no polynomial-time algorithm for it is known.

The MDSLP has been tackled using different approaches. Bosch and Trick [4] used a hybrid approach mixing integer programming and constraint programming to solve the cases for $n = 14$ and $n = 15$ in about 6 and 8 days of CPU time respectively. Smith [5] considered a pure constraint programming approach to tackle the problem and proposed a formulation of the problem as a constraint satisfaction problem with 0-1 variables and non-binary constraints.

T.P. Runarsson et al. (Eds.): PPSN IX, LNCS 4193, pp. 212–221, 2006.

A dual formulation of the problem was also considered, and it was proven that this dual representation outperformed the initial one (although it could only solve instances up to $n = 10$). The best results for this problem were reported in [6], showing the usefulness of *bucket elimination* (BE). Their basic approach could solve the problem for $n = 14$ in about 10^5 seconds. Further improvements pushed the solvability boundary forward to $n = 20$ in about the same time. At any rate, it is clear that these exact approaches are inherently limited for increasing problem sizes, and their capabilities as anytime algorithms are unclear. Later, Cheng and Yap [7] tackled the problem via the use of ad-hoc constraints, but their results are far from the ones obtained previously by Larrosa *et al.*

To the best of our knowledge, the only evolutionary approach to the problem has been proposed by Gallardo *et al.* [8]. Their work showed that a MA endowed with BE could provide optimal or near-optimal solutions at an acceptable computational cost. A study of partial Lamarckism was also conducted, revealing that applying always the BE operator provides the best results. In this paper, we consider extended hybrid models in which the hybridization with exact techniques takes place at two levels: inside the MA, as an embedded operator, and outside it, in a cooperative model. We also study variants based on an alternative recombination operator, and on multi-parent recombination [9]. Experimental results reveal that the performance of the algorithm is improved significantly, showing that MAs stand as a practical alternative to exact techniques employed so far to obtain still-life patterns.

2 Bucket Elimination and the Still Life Problem

Bucket elimination [10] is a generic algorithm particularly adequate for solving *weighted constraint satisfaction problems* (WCSPs) [11]. A WCSP is defined by a set $X = \{x_1, \cdots, x_n\}$ of variables taking values from a set D of finite domains ($D_i \in D$ is the domain of x_i) and a set F of cost functions (also called soft constraints). Each $f \in F$ is defined over a subset of variables $var(f) \subseteq X$, called its *scope*. For each assignment t of all variables in the scope of a soft constraint f, $t \in f$ (i.e., t is *permitted*) if, and only if, t is allowed by the soft constraint. A complete assignment that satisfies every soft constraint represents a solution to the WCSP. The valuation of an assignment t is defined as the sum of costs of all functions whose scope is assigned by t. Permitted assignments receive finite costs expressing their degree of preference and forbidden assignments receive cost ∞. The optimization goal consists of finding the solution with the lowest valuation.

BE is based upon two operators over functions: (1) the sum of two functions f and g denoted $(f+g)$ is a new function with scope $var(f) \cup var(g)$ which returns for each tuple the sum of costs of f and g defined as $(f + g)(t) = f(t) + g(t)$; (2) the elimination of variable x_i from f, denoted $f \Downarrow i$, is a new function with scope $var(f) - \{x_i\}$ which returns for each tuple t the minimum cost extension of t to x_i, defined as $(f \cdot i)(t) = min_{a \in D_i}\{f(t \cdot (x_i, a))\}$ where $t \cdot (x_i, a)$ means the extension of t to the assignment of a to x_i. Observe that when f is a unary function, eliminating the only variable in its scope produces a constant.

BE works in two phases. In the first phase, the algorithm eliminates variables one at a time in reverse order according to an arbitrary variable ordering o. In the second phase, the optimal assignment is computed processing variables in increasing order. The elimination of variable x_i is done as follows: initially, all cost functions in F having x_i in their scope are stored in B_i (the so called *bucket of* x_i). Next, BE creates a new function g_i defined as the sum of all functions in B_i in which variable x_i has been eliminated. Then, this function is added to F, which is also updated by removing the functions in B_i. The consequence is that the new F does not contain x_i (all functions mentioning x_i were removed) but preserves the value of the optimal cost. The elimination of the last variable produces an empty scope function (i.e., a constant) which is the optimal cost of the problem. The second phase generates an optimal assignment of variables. It uses the set of buckets that were computed in the first phase: starting from an empty assignment t, variables are assigned from first to last according to o. The optimal value for x_i is the best value regarding the extension of t with respect to the sum of functions in B_i.

In order to apply the general BE template to the MDSLP, let us first introduce some notation. A board configuration for a $n \times n$ instance will be represented by a n-dimensional vector $(r_1, r_2, \ldots, r_n)$. Each vector component encodes (as a binary string) a row, so that the j-th bit of row r_i (noted r_{ij}) indicates the state of the j-th cell of the i-th row (a value of 1 represents an alive cell and a value of 0 a dead cell). Let $Zeroes(r)$ be the number of zeroes in binary string r and let $Adjacents(r)$ be the maximum number of adjacent living cells in row r. If r_i is a row and r_{i-1} and r_{i+1} are the rows above and below r, then $Stable(r_{i-1}, r, r_{i+1})$ is a predicate satisfied if, and only if, all cells in r are stable.

The formulation has n cost functions f_i ($i \in \{1..n\}$). For $i \in \{2..n-1\}$, f_i is ternary with scope $var(f_i) = \{r_{i-1}, r_i, r_{i+1}\}$ and is defined as:

$$f_i(a,b,c) = \begin{cases} \infty & : \neg Stable(a,b,c) \\ \infty & : a_1 = b_1 = c_1 = 1 \\ \infty & : a_n = b_n = c_n = 1 \\ Zeroes(b) & : \text{otherwise} \end{cases} \tag{1}$$

As to f_1 and f_n, they are binary with scopes $var(f_1) = \{r_1, r_2\}$ and $var(f_n) = \{r_{n-1}, r_n\}$, and are defined similarly to $f_i(\cdot)$, assuming a boundary of dead cells. Notice in these definitions that stability is not only required within the pattern, but also in the surrounding dead cells.

Due to the sequential structure of the corresponding constraint graph [6], the model can be readily approached with BE. Figure 1 shows the corresponding algorithm. Function BE takes two parameters: n, the size of the instance to be solved, and D, the domain for each variable (row) in the solution. If domain D is set to $\{0..2^n - 1\}$ (i.e., a set containing all possible rows) the function implements an exact method that returns the optimal solution for the problem instance (as the number of dead cells) and a vector corresponding to the rows of that solution.

```
function BE(n, D)
    for a, b ∈ D do
        g_n(a, b) := min_{c∈D}{f_{n-1}(a, b, c) + f_n(b, c)}
    end for
    for i := n − 1 downto 3 do
        for a, b ∈ D do
            g_i(a, b) := min_{c∈D}{f_{i-1}(a, b, c) + g_{i+1}(b, c)}
        end for
    end for
    (r_1, r_2) := argmin_{a,b∈D}{g_3(a, b) + f_1(a, b)}
    opt := g_3(r_1, r_2) + f_1(r_1, r_2)
    for i := 3 to n − 1 do
        r_i := argmin_{c∈D}{f_{i-1}(r_{i-2}, r_{i-1}, c) + g_{i+1}(r_{i-1}, c)}
    end for
    r_n := argmin_{c∈D}{f_{n-1}(r_{n-2}, r_{n-1}, c) + f_n(r_{n-1}, c)}
    return (opt, (r_1, r_2, ..., r_n))
end function
```

Fig. 1. Bucket Elimination for the MDSLP

3 Memetic and Hybrid Algorithms for the MDSLP

As mentioned before, the algorithmic model we consider is based on the hybridization of MAs with exact techniques at two levels: within the MA (as an embedded operator), and outside it (in a cooperative model). An overall description of the basic hybridization scheme at the first level is provided in next subsection. Subsequently, we will explore some variants based on variable clustering and multi-parent recombination, before proceeding to the second level of hybridization.

3.1 A Memetic Algorithm with BE for the MDSLP

The MA described in [8] evolves configurations represented as binary $n \times n$ matrices; infeasible solutions are dealt via a stratified penalty-based fitness function:

$$f(r) = n^2 - \sum_{i=1}^{n}\sum_{j=1}^{n} r_{ij} + K\sum_{i=0}^{n+1}\sum_{j=0}^{n+1}\left[r'_{ij}\phi_1(\eta_{ij}) + (1 - r'_{ij})\phi_0(\eta_{ij})\right] \quad (2)$$

where r' is an $(n+2) \times (n+2)$ binary matrix obtained by embedding r in a frame of dead cells, K and K' are constants, η_{ij} is the number of alive neighbors of cell (i, j), and ϕ_0, $\phi_1 : \mathbb{N} \longrightarrow \mathbb{N}$ are two functions that take the number of alive neighbors of a cell, and return how many of them should be flipped to have a stable configuration (depending on whether the central cell is alive or not). Constants K and K' are set with the primary goal of decreasing the number of cells in an unstable state; if this were not possible, the secondary goal was to decrease the level of instability of these cells.

It turns out that this fitness function is easily decomposable, a fact that is exploited within the MA by means of a local improvement strategy based on tabu search (TS). This TS strategy explores the neighborhood $\mathcal{N}(r) = \{s \mid \text{Hamming}(r, s) = 1\}$, i.e., the set of solutions obtained by flipping exactly one cell in the configuration.

The binary representation allows the use of standard recombination operators for binary strings, but these blind operators performed poorly. Hence, problem-aware operators were considered. To be precise, BE was used to implement a recombination operator that explored the dynastic potential [12] (possible children) of the solutions being recombined, providing the best solution that could be constructed without introducing implicit mutation. That is, let $x = (x_1, x_2, \cdots, x_n)$ and $y = (y_1, y_2, \cdots, y_n)$ be two board configurations for a $n \times n$ instance of the MDSLP. Then, $\text{BE}(n, \{x_1, x_2, \cdots, x_n, y_1, y_2, \cdots, y_n\})$ calculates the best feasible configuration that can be obtained by combining rows in any of the parents (x and y). Notice that the described operator can be generalized to recombine any number of board configurations like $\text{BE}(n, \cup_{x \in S}\{x_i \mid i \in \{1..n\}\})$ where S is a set comprising the solutions to be recombined. This is one of the algorithmic variants that will be explored next.

3.2 Variable Clustering and Multi-parent Recombination

The complexity of BE depends on the problem structure (as captured by its constraint graph G) and the ordering o of variable elimination. According to [13], the complexity of BE along ordering o is time $\Theta(Q \times n \times d^{w^*(o)+1})$ and space $\Theta(n \times d^{w^*(o)})$, where d is the largest domain size, Q is the cost of evaluating cost functions (usually assumed $\Theta(1)$), and $w^*(o)$ is the maximum width of nodes in the induced graph of G relative to o (check [13] for details).

A well-known technique for reducing this computational cost in the context of constraint processing is variable clustering [14]. This approach merges several variables into a metavariable preserving the problem semantics. Inspired by this technique, variables corresponding to consecutive rows in a MDSLP solution can be clustered. We will denote by C_iBE the recombination operator that performs bucket elimination on a new domain obtained by clustering every group of i consecutive rows in a metavariable. This recombination operator thus provides the best feasible configuration that can be obtained by combining groups of i rows taken from the parents. Figure 2 shows the resulting algorithm for C_2BE when n is even. The procedure starts by defining the new domain for variables obtained by grouping every two consecutive rows in the original domain. Then, bucket elimination is performed for the new domain. The number of iterations of the loop in line 5 is reduced to one half with respect to the original algorithm, and the range for loops instantiating variables is also halved, thus reducing the time complexity of the algorithm at the expense of losing information.

One of the possibilities for alleviating the loss of alternatives for combining the information is the consideration of multi-parent recombination [9]. Following the scheme depicted in Section 3.1, an arbitrary number of solutions can contribute their constituent rows for constructing a new solution. In the worst case, this results in a linear increase in the size of domains, and thus does not affect the asymptotical complexity of BE, as long as the number of parents is bounded by a constant. One of the goals of the experimentation has been to check whether there exists some optimal tradeoff between these two strategies

```
function C2BE (n, D)
    D' := { {D_{2i-1}, D_{2i}} | i ← {1..|D|/2} }
    for a, b ∈ D' do
        g_n(a, b) := min_{c∈D'} {f_{n-4}(a_1, a_2, b_1) + f_{n-3}(a_2, b_1, b_2) + f_{n-2}(b_1, b_2, c_1)+
                                 f_{n-1}(b_2, c_1, c_2) + f_n(c_1, c_2)}
    end for
    for i := 1 to (n-6)/2 do
        for a, b ∈ D' do
            g_{n-i}(a, b) := min_{c∈D'} { f_{n-2(i+2)+1}(a_1, a_2, b_1) + f_{n-2(i+2)}(a_2, b_1, b_2)+
                                          g_{n-i+1}(b, c)}
        end for
    end for
    κ := n - (n-6)/2
    (α, β) := argmin_{a,b∈D'} {g_κ(a, b) + f_1(a_1, a_2)}
    r_1 := α_1; r_2 := α_2; r_3 := β_1; r_4 := β_2
    opt := g_κ(α, β) + f_1(r_1, r_2)
    for i := 5 to n - 3 step 2 do
        κ := κ + 1
        α := argmin_{a∈D'} {f_{i-1}(r_{i-3}, r_{i-2}, r_{i-1}) + g_κ(r_{i-1}, a)}
        r_i := α_1; r_{i+1} := α_2
    end for
    α := argmin_{a∈D'} {f_{n-1}(r_{n-2}, a_1, a_2) + f_n(a_1, a_2)}
    r_{n-1} := α_1; r_n := α_2
    return (opt, (r_1, r_2, ..., r_n))
end function
```

Fig. 2. BE with clusters formed by two rows for even sizes for the MDSLP

(variable clustering and multi-parent recombination), and indeed whether any of them can contribute to the global improvement of the hybrid algorithm.

3.3 A Beam Search Hybrid Algorithm

Gallardo *et al.* [15] have shown that hybridizing a MA with a branch-and-bound-based Beam Search (BS) algorithm can provide excellent results for some combinatorial optimization problems. We show here that this is also the case for the MDSLP. We consider a hybrid algorithm that executes the BS and the MA in an interleaved way. The goal is combining synergistically these two different approaches, exploiting the capability of BS for identifying provably good regions of the search space, and the strength of the MA for exploring these.

The resulting algorithm is depicted in Figure 3. Here, $\overline{r}$ denotes the reflection value of r, and $v +\!\!+ r$ is the vector obtained by concatenating r to the end of v. Function Hybrid(n, k, l_0) constructs a branch and bound tree whose leaves are all possible $n \times n$ board configurations whose rows are symmetric (this symmetry constraint is required to keep the branching factor at a manageable level for the range of instance sizes considered). Internal nodes at level i represent partially specified (up to the ith row) board configurations. The tree is traversed using a BS algorithm that explores the tree in a breadth-first way maintaining only the best k nodes at each level of the tree. In order to rank nodes, a quality measure is defined on them, whose value is either ∞ if the partial configuration is unstable, or its number of dead cells otherwise. Parameter l_0 indicates how many levels the BS descends before starting running the MA, and can be used to control the balance between the MA and the BS. For each execution of the MA, its population is initialized using the best *popsize* nodes in the current level

```
function Hybrid (n, k, l0)
    sol := ∞
    q := { () }
    for i := 1 to n do
        q' := {}
        for c ∈ q do
            for r := 0 to 2^⌈n/2⌉ − 1 do
                q' := q' ∪ {c++(r or r̄)}
            end for
        end for
        q := select best k nodes from q'
        if (i ≥ l0) then
            initialize MA population with best nodes from q'
            run MA
            sol := min (sol, MA solution)
        end if
    end for
    return sol
end function
```

Fig. 3. Hybrid algorithm for the MDSLP

of exploration. Since these are partial solutions, they must be first converted into full solutions, e.g., by completing remaining rows randomly. After running the MA, its solution is used to update the incumbent solution. This process is repeated until the search tree is exhausted.

4 Experimental Results

A set of experiments for problem sizes from $n = 12$ up to $n = 20$ has been realized (recall that optimal solutions are known up to $n = 20$). The experiments were done in all cases using a steady-state MA ($popsize = 100$, $p_m = 1/n^2$, $p_X = 0.9$, binary tournament selection). Aiming to maintaining diversity, duplicated individuals were not allowed in the population. For the different versions of the hybrid algorithm described in Section 3.3, the setting of parameters was $k = 2000$ and $l_0 = 0.3n$, i.e, the best 2000 nodes were kept on each level of the BS algorithm, and 30% of the levels of the BS tree were initially descended before starting running the MA. All algorithms were run until an optimal solution was found or a time limit was exceeded. This time limit was set to 3 minutes —on a P4 (2.4GHz and 512MB RAM) under SuSE Linux— for problem instances of size 12 and were gradually incremented by 60 seconds for each size increment. For each algorithm and each instance size, 20 independent executions were run.

First of all, experiments have been done to explore the effects of multi-parent recombination in a MA endowed with BE for performing recombination as described in Section 3.1 (MA-BE). Figure 4 (left) shows the results obtained by MA-BE for different number of parents being recombined (arities 2, 4 and 8). For $arity = 2$, the algorithm was able to find the optimum solution for all instances except for $n = 18$ and $n = 20$ (the relative distance to the optimum is less than 1.04% in these cases). Note that results for $n = 19$ and $n = 20$ were obtained in just 10 and 11 minutes per run respectively. As a comparison, recall that the approach in [6] respectively requires over 15 hours and over 2

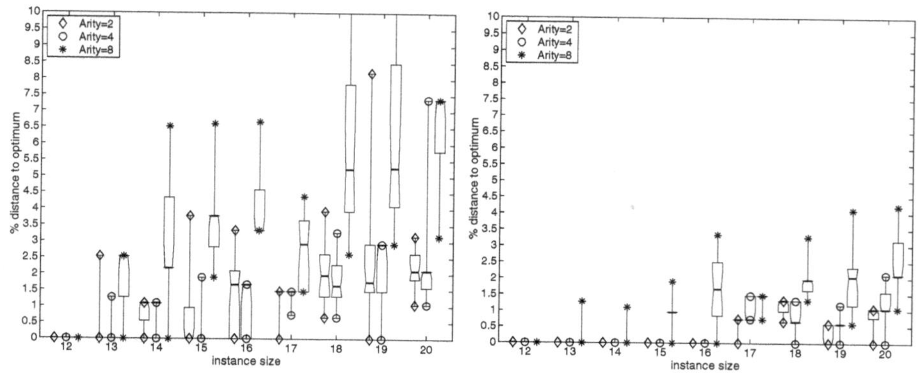

Fig. 4. Relative distances to optimum for different arities for MA-BE (left) and HYB-MA-BE (right) for sizes ranging from 12 up to 20. Each box summarizes 20 runs.

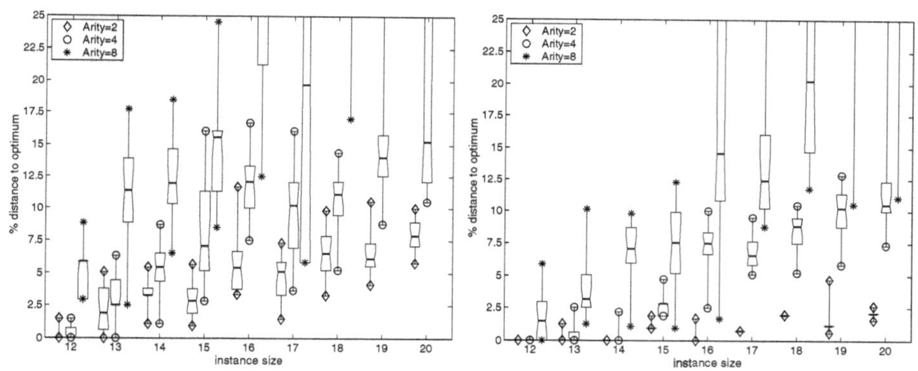

Fig. 5. Relative distances to optimum for different arities for MA-C_2BE (left) and HYB-MA-C_2BE (right) for sizes from 12 up to 20. Each box summarizes 20 runs.

days for these same instances, and that other approaches are unaffordable for $n > 15$. Executions with $arity = 4$ cannot find optimum solutions for the remaining instances, but note that the distribution always improves. Clearly, the performance of the algorithm degrades when combining more than 4 parents due to the higher computational cost.

Subsequent experiments were conducted to evaluate the C_iBE recombination operator for $i \in \{2, 3\}$. Results are shown in Figure 5 (left) and 6 (left), and reveal that the performance of the algorithm is worse, as it only finds the optimal solution for the smallest instance sizes. The computational costs saved by clustering variables does not compensate the loss of information induced, even in the presence of multi-parent recombination, and the combination of these two strategies is counter-productive.

We finally approach the two-level hybrid algorithm. Figures 4 (right), 5 (right), and 6 (right) show the results obtained using MA-BE, MA-C_2BE, and MA-C_3BE

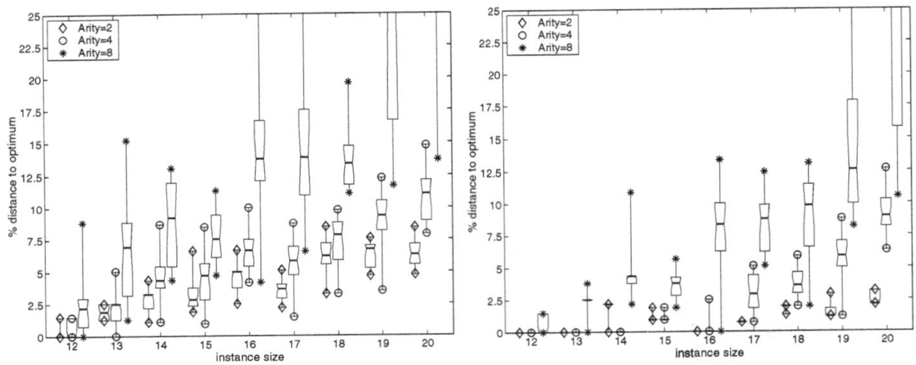

Fig. 6. Relative distances to optimum for different arities for MA-C_3BE (left) and HYB-MA-C_3BE (right) for sizes from 12 up to 20. Each box summarizes 20 runs.

in the MA part. The performance is significantly improved over the original MA. Note that HYB-MA-BE using an arity of 2 parents is able to find the optimum for all cases except for $n = 18$ (this instance is solved with $arity = 4$). All distributions for different instance sizes are improved in an significant manner. For $n < 17$ and $arity \in \{2, 4\}$, the algorithm consistently finds the optimum in all runs. For other instances and $arity = 2$, the solution provided by the algorithm is always within a 1.05 % of the optimum, except for $n = 18$, for which the relative distance to the optimum for the worst solution is 1.3%. The results of HYB-MA-C_2BE and HYB-MA-C_3BE are worse than those of HYB-MA-BE, but note however that the hybridization with the BS algorithm is beneficial also in this case, as it improves the distributions with respect to MA-C_2BE and MA-C_3BE.

5 Conclusions and Future Work

The high space complexity of BE as an exact technique [10], makes this approach impractical for large instances. In this work, we have presented several proposals for the hybridization of Bucket Elimination (BE) with MAs and BS, and showed that it represents a worthwhile model. The experimental results have been very positive, solving to optimality large instances of a hard constrained problem. We have also studied the influence that variable clustering and multi-parent recombination have on the performance of the algorithm. The results indicate that variable clustering is detrimental in this problem, but multi-parent recombination can help to improve the results obtained by previous approaches.

One interesting extension to this work is to improve the bounds used in the BS algorithm. To do so, we are currently considering the technique of mini–buckets [16]. Work is in progress in this area.

Acknowledgements. This work was partially supported by Spanish MCyT under contracts TIN2004-7943-C04-01 and TIN2005-08818-C04-01.

References

1. Gardner, M.: The fantastic combinations of John Conway's new solitaire game. Scientific American **223** (1970) 120–123
2. Gardner, M.: On cellular automata, self-reproduction, the garden of Eden and the game of "life". Scientific American **224** (1971) 112–117
3. Gardner, M.: Wheels, Life, and Other Mathematical Amusements. W.H. Freeman, New York (1983)
4. Bosch, R., Trick, M.: Constraint programming and hybrid formulations for three life designs. In: CP-AI-OR. (2002) 77–91
5. Smith, B.M.: A dual graph translation of a problem in 'life'. In Hentenryck, P.V., ed.: Principles and Practice of Constraint Programming - CP'2002. Volume 2470 of Lecture Notes in Computer Science., Ithaca, NY, USA, Springer (2002) 402–414
6. Larrosa, J., Morancho, E., Niso, D.: On the practical use of variable elimination in constraint optimization problems: 'still life' as a case study. Journal of Artificial Intelligence Research **23** (2005) 421–440
7. Cheng, K., Yap, R.: Ad-hoc global constraints for life. In van Beek, P., ed.: Principles and Practice of Constraint Programming – CP'2005. Volume 3709 of Lecture Notes in Computer Science., Sitges, Spain, Springer (2005) 182–195
8. Gallardo, J.E., Cotta, C., Fernández, A.J.: A memetic algorithm with bucket elimination for the still life problem. In Gottlieb, J., Raidl, G.R., eds.: EvoCOP. Volume 3906 of Lecture Notes in Computer Science., Springer (2006) 73–85
9. Eiben, A., Raue, P.E., Ruttkay, Z.: Genetic algorithms with multi-parent recombination. In Davidor, Y., Schwefel, H.P., Männer, R., eds.: Parallel Problem Solving From Nature III. Springer-Verlag (1994) 78–87, LNCS 866
10. Dechter, R.: Bucket elimination: A unifying framework for reasoning. Artificial Intelligence **113** (1999) 41–85
11. Bistarelli, S., Montanari, U., Rossi, F.: Semiring-based constraint satisfaction and optimization. Journal of the ACM **44** (1997) 201–236
12. Radcliffe, N.: The algebra of genetic algorithms. Annals of Mathematics and Artificial Intelligence **10** (1994) 339–384
13. Larrosa, J., Morancho, E.: Solving 'still life' with soft constraints and bucket elimination. In Rossi, F., ed.: Principles and Practice of Constraint Programming - CP 2003. Volume 2833 of Lecture Notes in Computer Science., Kinsale, Ireland, Springer (2003) 466–479
14. Dechter, R., Pearl, J.: Tree clustering for constraint networks. Artificial Intelligence (1989) 353–366
15. Gallardo, J., Cotta, C., Fernández, A.: On the hybridization of memetic algorithms with branch-and-bound techniques. IEEE Transactions on Systems, Man and Cybernetics, part B (2006) (to appear).
16. Dechter, R.: Mini-buckets: A general scheme for generating approximations in automated reasoning. In: Proceedings of the Fifteenth International Joint Conference on Artificial Intelligence, Nagoya, Japan, Morgan Kaufmann (1997) 1297–1303

Transmission Loss Reduction Based on FACTS and Bacteria Foraging Algorithm

M. Tripathy[1], S. Mishra[1], L.L. Lai[2], and Q.P. Zhang[2]

[1] Department of Electrical Engineering,
Indian Institute of Technology, Delhi, India
[2] Energy Systems Group, City University,
London EC1V 0HB, United Kingdom
sukumar@ee.iitd.ac.in, l.l.lai@city.ac.uk

Abstract. An optimal location and parameters of an UPFC along with values of OLTC taps are tuned with a view to minimize the real power losses of a mesh power network. This issue is formulated as a non-linear equality and inequality constrained optimization problem with an objective function incorporating power loss. A new evolutionary algorithm known as Bacteria Foraging is applied for solving, the optimum location and the amount of series injected voltage for the UPFC, and the best values of the taps present in the system. The same problem is also solved with Interior Point Successive Linearization technique using the LINPROG command of MATLAB. A comparison between the two suggests the superiority of the proposed algorithm.

1 Introduction

Optimal Power Flow (OPF) is a static non-linear program that intends to schedule the controls of the power system in such a manner that certain objective function like real power loss is optimized with some operating equipment and security requirement, limit constraints forced on the solution. The OPF problem has been solved from different perspectives like studying the effects of load increase/decrease on voltage stability/power flow solvability, generation rescheduling to minimize the cost of power generation, controls like taps, shunts and other modern VAR sources adjustments to minimize real power losses in the system.

The OPF is solved by varieties of methods like Successive Linear Programming(SLP)[1], Newton based non-linear programming method[2], and with varieties of recently proposed Interior Point Methods(IPM) [3]. With the advent of Flexible AC Transmission Systems (FACTS) technology a new possibility of optimizing the power flow without resorting to generation rescheduling or topology changes has arisen. UPFC the most advanced in the family of these devices can provide a lot of flexibility in OPF by injecting a controlled series and shunt compensation [4].

Proper coordination of the UPFC with the existing OLTC transformer taps already present in the system will certainly improve the steady state operating limit of any power system. Even though the OPF problem when incorporated with FACTS devices becomes non-convex and thus is prone to be trapped in local optima, but still

T.P. Runarsson et al. (Eds.): PPSN IX, LNCS 4193, pp. 222–231, 2006.

the conventional techniques of OPF solution can be satisfactorily applied. However, the disadvantage with the classical techniques lies in the fact that they are highly sensitive to starting points owing to a non-monotonic solution surface. To eliminate such problems evolutionary techniques have been applied in solving the OPF problem [5]. In [5] authors have applied Particle Swarm Optimization (PSO) to the problem of OPF. Such algorithms, based on food searching behavior of species (like birds etc.), compute both global and local best positions at each instant of time, to decide the best direction of search.

In this paper the authors have applied a new algorithm from the family of Evolutionary Computation, known as Bacteria Foraging (BF) Algorithm, to solve OPF problem of real power loss minimization, along with improved voltage profile. BF has been recently proposed [6] and further applied for harmonic estimation problem in power systems [7]. The algorithm is based on the foraging behavior of E.coli bacteria present in human intestine. The UPFC location, series injection voltage and transformer tap positions are simultaneously adjusted as control variables, so that the overall bus voltages profile is maintained flat, keeping an eye to all specified constraints. The results so obtained show its strength in solving highly non-linear *epistatic* problems like that of OPF. The main objectives of this paper are as follows:

1) By optimizing the values of OLTC transformer taps present in a multi machine power network, so that the real power loss of the system is minimized. The OPF solution is carried out with the Bacteria Foraging Algorithm (BFA) and also with Successive Linear Programming (SLP) technique integrated with Interior Point Method, so as to get a comparative idea of the performances of the two. The Interior Point Successive Linear Programming (IPSLP) is solved by using the MATLAB command LINPROG.
2) By fixing the tap positions at the optimized values, Unified Power Flow Controller (UPFC) is introduced in the system. The best location and injection voltages of the UPFC are again optimized using BFA and IPSLP to seek a comparison.

2 Bacteria Foraging Optimization

The idea is based on the fact that, natural selection tends to eliminate animals with poor foraging strategies and favor those having successful foraging strategies. After many generations, poor foraging strategies are either eliminated or reshaped into good ones. The *E. coli* bacteria that are present in our intestines also undergo a foraging strategy. Four processes basically govern the bacteria namely Chemotaxis, Swarming, Reproduction, Elimination and Dispersal [6].

a) Chemotaxis: This process is achieved through swimming and tumbling. Depending upon the rotation of the flagella in each bacterium it decides whether it should move in a predefined direction (swimming) or an altogether different direction (tumbling), in the entire lifetime of the bacterium. To represent a tumble, a unit length random direction, say $\phi(j)$, is generated; this will be used to define the direction of movement after a tumble. In particular

$$\theta^i(j+1,k,l)=\theta^i(j,k,l)+C(i)\phi(j) \tag{1}$$

Where $\theta^i(j,k,l)$ represents the ith bacterium at j[th] chemotactic k[th] reproductive and l[th] elimination and dispersal step. C(i) is the size of the step taken in the random direction specified by the tumble (run length unit).

b) Swarming: It is always desired that the bacterium which has searched optimum path of food search should try to attract other bacteria so that they reach the desired place more rapidly. Swarming makes the bacteria congregate into groups and hence move as concentric patterns of groups with high bacterial density. Mathematically, Swarming can be represented by

$$J_{cc}(\theta, P(j,k,l)) = \sum_{i=1}^{S} J_{cc}^{i}\left(\theta, \theta^i(j,k,l)\right)$$
$$= \sum_{i=1}^{S}\left[-d_{attract}\exp\left(-\omega_{attract}\sum_{m=1}^{p}(\theta_m - \theta_m^i)^2\right)\right] \tag{2}$$
$$+ \sum_{i=1}^{S}\left[h_{repelent}\exp\left(-\omega_{repelent}\sum_{m=1}^{p}(\theta_m - \theta_m^i)^2\right)\right]$$

where $J_{cc}(\theta, P(j,k,l))$ is the cost function value to be added to the actual cost function to be minimized to present a time varying cost function. 'S' is the total number of bacteria. 'p' the number of parameters to be optimized which are present in each bacterium. $d_{attract}, \omega_{attract}, h_{repelent}, \omega_{repelent}$ are different coefficients that are to be chosen judiciously.

c) Reproduction: The least healthy bacteria die and the other healthiest bacteria each split into two bacteria, which are placed in the same location. This makes the population of bacteria constant.

d) Elimination and Dispersal: It is possible that in the local environment the life of a population of bacteria changes either gradually (e.g., via consumption of nutrients) or suddenly due to some other influence. Events can occur such that all the bacteria in a region are killed or a group is dispersed into a new part of the environment. They have the effect of possibly destroying the chemotactic progress, but they also have the effect of assisting in chemotaxis, since dispersal may place bacteria near good food sources. From a broad perspective, elimination and dispersal are parts of the population-level long-distance motile behavior. It helps in reducing the behavior of *stagnation,*(i.e. being trapped in a premature solution point or local optima) often seen in such parallel search algorithms. This section is based on the work in [6]. The detailed mathematical derivations as well as theoretical aspect of this new concept are presented in [6,7].

3 Simulation System

Simulations have been carried out to solve the real power bus voltage constrained loss minimization of 10 machine New England power systems [8], connected with UPFC by using IPSLP and BFA. Both the sequential and simultaneous allocation of taps and UPFC are carried out for comparison. This is done in the following manner:

a) A total of 12 transformer taps present in the system are optimally positioned.
b) Introducing an UPFC at the most suitable location in the system and then injecting the desired voltage, through its series converter keeping the above values of taps fixed.

In this paper the 10-machine, 39-bus New England power system shown in Fig.1 is considered for study. The system data in detail, including the 12 transformers' nominal tap values are given in [8]. The system diagram is shown in Fig.1.

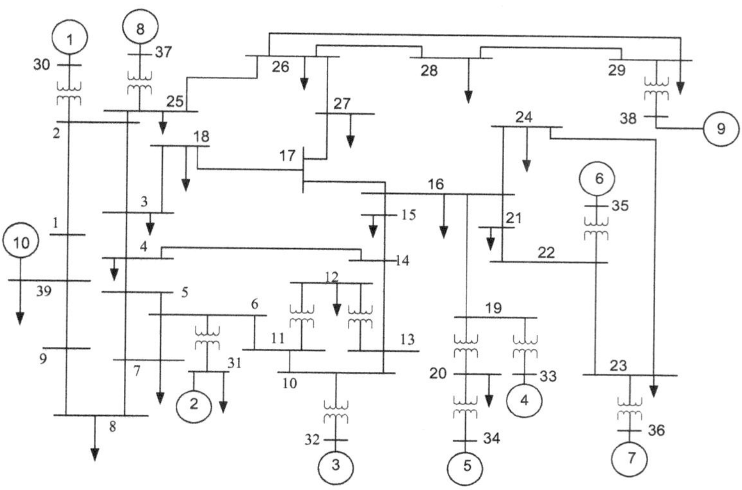

Fig. 1. New England Power System Layout

The OPF problem is a static constrained non linear optimization problem, the solution of which determines the optimal settings of control variables in a power network respecting various constraints. So the problem is to solve a set of nonlinear equations describing optimal solution of power system. It is expressed as:

$$\text{Minimize} \quad F(x,u) \tag{3}$$

$$\text{Subject to} \quad \begin{matrix} g(x,u) = 0 \\ h(x,u) \le 0 \end{matrix}$$

The objective function F, is real power loss of the mesh connected multi machine test system. $g(x,u)$ is a set of non-linear equality constraints (i.e. power flow) and $h(x,u)$ is a set of non-linear inequality constraints(i.e. bus voltages, transformer/line MVA limits, etc.). Vector x consists of dependent variables and u consists of control variables. For the above problem the control variables are the OLTC transformer taps and both the magnitude and phase angle of UPFC series injected voltage (V_{se}). The non-linear optimization problem of equation (3) is solved by both BFA and IPSLP methods.

4 Bacterial Foraging: The Algorithm

The BF algorithm suggested in [7] is modified so as to expedite the convergence. The modifications are discussed below.

1) In [7], the author has taken the average value of all the chemotactic cost functions, to decide the health of particular bacteria in that generation, before sorting is carried out for reproduction. In this paper, instead of the average value, the minimum value of all the chemotactic cost functions is retained for deciding the bacterium's health. This speeds up the convergence, because in the average scheme [7], it may not retain the fittest bacterium for the subsequent generation. On the contrary in this paper the global minimum bacteria among all chemotactic stages passes on to the subsequent stage.
2) For swarming, the distances of all the bacteria in a new chemotactic stage are evaluated from the global optimum bacterium till that point, and not the distances of each bacterium from rest others as suggested in [6,7].

The algorithm is discussed below:

Step1-Initialization

The following variables are initialized.

i. Number of bacteria (S) to be used in the search.
ii. Number of parameters (p) to be optimized.
iii. Swimming length $N_{s.}$
iv. N_c the number of iteration in a chemotactic loop. ($N_c > N_s$).
v. N_{re} the no of reproduction.
vi. N_{ed} the no of elimination and dispersal events.
vii. P_{ed} the probability of elimination and dispersal.
viii. Location of each bacterium P(p,S,1) i.e. random numbers on [0-1].
ix. The values of $d_{attract}$, $\omega_{attract}$, $h_{repelent}$ and $\omega_{repelent}$.

Step-2 Iterative algorithm for optimization

This section models the bacterial population chemotaxis, swarming, reproduction, elimination and dispersal (initially, $j=k=l=0$). For the algorithm updating θ^i automatically results in updating of 'P'.

1) Elimination-dispersal loop: $l=l+1$
2) Reproduction loop: $k=k+1$
3) Chemotaxis loop: $j=j+1$
   a) For $i=1,2,\ldots,S$, calculate cost function value for each bacterium i as follows.
      - Compute value of cost function $J(i, j, k, l)$. Let $J_{sw}(i, j, k, l) = J(i, j, k, l) + J_{cc}(\theta^i(j,k,l), P(j,k,l))$ $P(j,k,l)$ is the location of bacterium corresponding to the global minimum cost function out of all the generations and chemotactic loops till that point (i.e., add on the cell-to-cell attractant effect for swarming behavior).
      - Let $J_{last} = J_{sw}(i, j, k, l)$ to save this value since we may find a better cost via a run.
      - End of For loop

b) For i=1,2,….S take the tumbling/swimming decision

- Tumble: Generate a random vector $\Delta(i) \in \Re^p$ with each element $\Delta_m(i)$ m=1,2,..p, a random number on [0,1].
- Move: let

$$\theta^i(j+1,k,l) = \theta^i(j,k,l) + C(i)\frac{\Delta(i)}{\sqrt{\Delta^T(i)\Delta(i)}}$$

Fixed step size in the direction of tumble for bacterium i is considered.

- Compute J(i, j+1, k, l) and then let $J_{sw}(i, j+1, k, l)$= J(i, j+1, k, l)+ $J_{cc}(\theta^i(j+1,k,l), P(j+1,k,l))$
- Swim :
  - i) Let m=0; (counter for swim length)
  - ii) While m<N_s (have not climbed down too long)
    - Let m=m+1
    - If $J_{sw}(i, j+1, k, l) < J_{last}$ (if doing better), let J_{last}= $J_{sw}(i, j+1, k, l)$ and let

$$\theta^i(j+1,k,l) = \theta^i(j,k,l) + C(i)\frac{\Delta(i)}{\sqrt{\Delta^T(i)\Delta(i)}}$$

and use this $\theta^i(j+1,k,l)$ to compute the new J(i, j+1, k, l)

- Else, let m=N_s. This is the end of the while statement.

c) Go to next bacterium (i+1) if $i \neq S$ (i.e. go to b) to process the next bacterium.

4. If j < N_c, go to step 3. In this case, continue chemotaxis since the life of the bacteria is not over.

5. Reproduction
   a) For the given k and l, and for each i=1,2,..S, let $J^i_{health} = \min_{j\in\{1\cdots N_c\}} \{J_{sw}(i,j,k,l)\}$ be the health of the bacterium i. Sort bacteria in order of ascending cost J_{health} (higher cost means lower health).
   b) The S_r=S/2 bacteria with highest J_{health} values die and other S_r bacteria with the best value split (and the copies that are made are placed at the same location as their parent)
6. If k < N_{re} go to 2, in this case, we have not reached the number of specified reproduction steps, so we start the next generation in the chemotactic loop.
7. Elimination-dispersal: For i=1,2,..S, with probability P_{ed}, eliminates and disperses each bacterium (this keeps the number of bacteria in the population constant). To do this, if you eliminate a bacterium, simply disperse one to a random location on the optimization domain.

5 Simulation and Results

The objective function of the real power loss minimization problem is formulated by introducing penalty factors for voltage and transformer MVA and transmission line limit violations. These penalty factors are added to the total real power loss in the system.

$$F = pf_1 + pf_2 + pf_3 + of \text{ , where} \tag{4}$$

of = Real Power Loss

$$pf_1 = 10 * abs(sign(V_{\min} - 0.8) - 1) + 10 * abs(sign(V_{\max} - 1.2) + 1)$$

$$pf_2 = 10 * abs(sign(trans_{\max} - 15) + 1)$$

$$pf_3 = 10 * abs(sign(line_{\max} - 20) + 1)$$

pf_1, pf_2 and pf_3 are the penalty factors added with the real power loss (of), so that a constrained solution is achieved. $V_{\max}$ and $V_{\min}$ are the maximum and minimum limits of bus voltages of all buses. Similarly $trans_{\max}$ and $line_{\max}$ are respectively the maximum MVA limits of the transformers and lines in the system. The values of $trans_{\max}$ and $line_{\max}$ are chosen at double the maximum nominal values of respective quantities. The methodology adopted for optimization with both the BFA and IPSLP techniques are discussed here in brief.

A. Optimization with only OLTC taps as control variables

Bacteria Foraging (*Without Swarming*): Initially the Swarming effect is excluded from the algorithm so as to study the convergence behavior. The values of bacteria number (S) and the chemotactic loops number (N_c) are chosen in steps and the algorithm is run for number of times. For a whole cycle of elimination and dispersal loop when the cost function remains unchanged, then the algorithm is said to have converged. The speed of convergence differs with different combinations of S and N_c. It was found that S=10 and N_c=6 gives the fastest convergence. A comparison of convergence by taking the average value of each bacterium [7] in the chemotactic

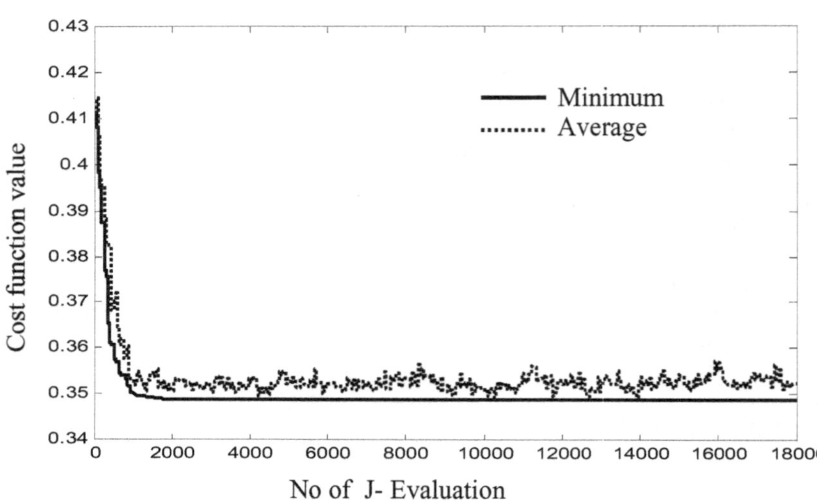

Fig. 2. Reproduction Schemes Proposed (Min) vs. [7] (Average)

stage to that of Global Minimum (as proposed) for reproduction is shown in Fig.2. It is found that with the proposed scheme the algorithm converges faster. Also for the particular problem the algorithm proposed in [7] fails to converge but tend to oscillate around the point of convergence.

Bacteria Foraging (*With Swarming*):
As established above swarming is included now considering the global minimum. To choose the parameters of swarming, the algorithm is run for different values of $d_{attract}$, $\omega_{attract}$, $h_{repelent}$ and $\omega_{repelent}$.

It was found that these values when chosen as 0.1, 0.1, 0.1,10 respectively, it gives the fastest convergence. Fig.3 shows the relative improvement of convergence when swarming effect is included as compared to without swarming. It is seen that though the loss minimization is same with both the techniques, there is a difference in the values of tap positions to which the algorithms have converged. These tap values are highlighted in Table-1. From Fig.3 it is obvious that the BFA converges faster if the swarming effect is included in it, though there is a negligible improvement seen for the particular problem.

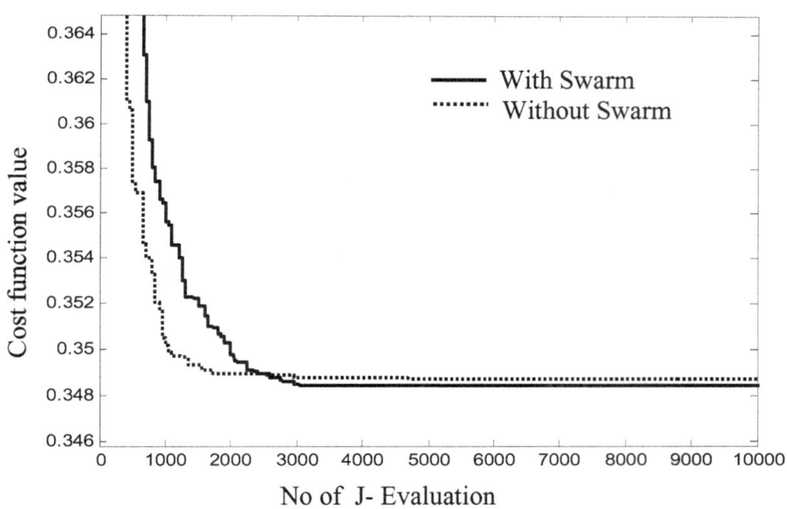

Fig. 3. Performance of Algorithms

B: Sequential optimization of UPFC location and its injection voltage:
With the optimized tap positions obtained previously, the UPFC location and its series injection voltage is then evaluated. The power injection model as discussed in section III is used for modeling the UPFC. In both BFA and IPSLP methods, 14 lines (out of total 46 lines), containing transformers or feeding generator powers to the network are excluded for connecting the UPFC. The UPFC is connected at the left hand side bus as per line notation given in [8]. For BFA, the line at which UPFC should be connected is decided randomly out of 32 lines selected in the initial stage. Hence the line number in which UPFC is to be connected becomes a control variable along with

the usual control variables of series injection voltage magnitude and its phase angle. On the other hand the UPFC location in terms of line number can't be used as a control variable for IPSLP technique as it cannot be linearized through perturbation. Therefore the UPFC is connected to all the 32 lines, considering one at a time. The best location and the UPFC injection voltage in each succession of linearization are retained.

Table 1. Results

<table>
<tr><th colspan="7">Optimization of only Taps</th><th colspan="2">Sequential Optimization of UPFC</th></tr>
<tr><th>Line Number</th><th>Nominal Taps</th><th>Loss</th><th>Optimized Discrete Taps (BFA)</th><th>Loss</th><th>Optimized Discrete Taps (IPSLP)</th><th>Loss</th><th>UPFC Optimized Parameter</th><th>Loss</th></tr>
<tr><td>2 - 30</td><td>1.025</td><td rowspan="12">0.3900 p.u.</td><td>1.05</td><td rowspan="12">0.3548 p.u.</td><td>1.05</td><td rowspan="12">0.3548 p.u.</td><td rowspan="7">BFA:
$|V_{se}| = 0.0079$ p.u.
$\angle V_{se} = 5.0998$ rad
Location:
line 14-15</td><td rowspan="7">0.2764 p.u</td></tr>
<tr><td>10 - 32</td><td>1.070</td><td>1.20</td><td>1.20</td></tr>
<tr><td>12 - 11</td><td>1.006</td><td>**1.05**</td><td>**0.80**</td></tr>
<tr><td>12 - 13</td><td>1.006</td><td>**1.05**</td><td>**0.80**</td></tr>
<tr><td>19 - 33</td><td>1.070</td><td>1.15</td><td>1.15</td></tr>
<tr><td>19 - 20</td><td>1.060</td><td>1.00</td><td>1.00</td></tr>
<tr><td>20 - 34</td><td>1.009</td><td>1.15</td><td>1.15</td></tr>
<tr><td>22 - 35</td><td>1.025</td><td>1.15</td><td>1.15</td><td rowspan="5">IPSLP:
$|V_{se}| = 0.1245$ p.u.
$\angle V_{se} = 3.6767$ rad
Location:
line 21-22</td><td rowspan="5">0.3351 p.u</td></tr>
<tr><td>23 - 36</td><td>1.000</td><td>1.10</td><td>1.10</td></tr>
<tr><td>25 - 37</td><td>1.025</td><td>1.05</td><td>1.05</td></tr>
<tr><td>29 - 38</td><td>1.025</td><td>1.10</td><td>1.10</td></tr>
<tr><td>31 - 6</td><td>1.070</td><td>0.85</td><td>0.85</td></tr>
</table>

6 Conclusions

The new evolutionary technique, Bacteria Foraging has been used for solving a highly non-linear and non-convex problem of Optimal Power Flow solution. It is found that the BFA technique succeeds in better loss minimization as compared to conventional IPSLP technique.

References

1. P.Ristanovic, "Successive linear programming based OPF solution," Optimal Power Flow: Solution techniques, requirements and challenges, IEEE Power Engineering Society, 1996.
2. D.Sun et al., "Optimal power flow by Newton approach," IEEE Transactions on Power Apparatus and Systems, Vol. PAS-103 No.10, pp.2864-2875, Oct. 1984.
3. J.L.Martinez .Ramos, A.G.Exposito and V.Quintana, "Transmission loss reduction by interior point methods: implementation issues and practical experience," IEE Proceedings on Generation, Transmission and Distribution, Vol. 152, No.1, pp.90-98, Jan.2005.

4. M.Noroozian, L.Angquist, M.Ghandhari and G.Anderson, "Use of UPFC for optimal Power flow control," IEEE Transactions on Power Delivery, Vol. 12, No.4, pp.1629-1634, Oct. 1997.
5. Ahmed A. A.Esmin, G.Torres and A.C.Z.de Souza, "A hybrid particle swarm optimization applied to loss power minimization," IEEE Transactions on Power System, Vol. 20, No. 2 pp.859-866, May.2005.
6. K.M.Passino, "Biomimicry of bacterial foraging for distributed optimization and control", IEEE Control System Magazine, pp.52-67, June 2002.
7. S.Mishra, "A hybrid least square-fuzzy bacteria foraging strategy for harmonic estimation" IEEE Transactions on Evolutionary Computation, Vol. 9, No. 1, pp.61-73, Feb. 2005.
8. M.A. Pai, Energy Function Analysis for Power System Stability. Norwell, MA: Kluwer.

Substructural Neighborhoods for Local Search in the Bayesian Optimization Algorithm

Claudio F. Lima[1], Martin Pelikan[2], Kumara Sastry[3], Martin Butz[4], David E. Goldberg[3], and Fernando G. Lobo[1]

[1] University of Algarve, Portugal
[2] University of Missouri at St. Louis, USA
[3] University of Illinois at Urbana-Champaign, USA
[4] University of Würzburg, Germany
clima@ualg.pt, pelikan@cs.umsl.edu, ksastry@uiuc.edu, mbutz@psychologie.uni-wuerzburg.de, deg@uiuc.edu, flobo@ualg.pt

Abstract. This paper studies the utility of using substructural neighborhoods for local search in the Bayesian optimization algorithm (BOA). The probabilistic model of BOA, which automatically identifies important problem substructures, is used to define the structure of the neighborhoods used in local search. Additionally, a surrogate fitness model is considered to evaluate the improvement of the local search steps. The results show that performing substructural local search in BOA significatively reduces the number of generations necessary to converge to optimal solutions and thus provides substantial speedups.

1 Introduction

Estimation of distribution algorithms (EDAs) [1,2], a new class of genetic and evolutionary algorithms (GEAs), have frequently been found to be more efficient than traditional GEAs that use fixed, problem-independent variation operators. The conceptual difference is that EDAs replace the traditional variation operators of GEAs by building and sampling a probabilistic model of promising solutions. In essence, this procedure tries to mimic the behavior of an ideal recombination operator that combines subsolutions with minimal disruption.

Although EDAs are effective at exploring the search space to find promising regions, they inherit a common drawback from traditional GEAs: slower convergence to optimal solutions when compared with appropriate local searchers that start the search within the basin of attraction of the optima. This observation has led to the combination of GEAs with local search methods known as hybrid GEAs or memetic algorithms [3,4]. In this context EDAs are no exception and many applications in real-world optimization have been accomplished with the help of some sort of local search. However, systematic methods for hybridizing and designing competent global and local-search methods that automatically identify the problem decomposition and important problem substructures are still scarce. For instance, the probabilistic models of EDAs contain useful information about the underlying problem structure that can be exploited to speedup the convergence of EDAs to optimal solutions.

T.P. Runarsson et al. (Eds.): PPSN IX, LNCS 4193, pp. 232–241, 2006.

In this paper we use substructural neighborhoods to perform local search in the Bayesian optimization algorithm (BOA) [5]. These neighborhoods are defined by the dependency groups learned by the probabilistic model of BOA. Additionally, we use a surrogate fitness model that also makes use of substructural information to evaluate the alternatives while performing hillclimbing in the subsolution search space. The results show that incorporating substructural local search in BOA leads to a significant reduction in the number of generations, providing relevant speedups in terms of number of evaluations.

The next section gives an outline of the Bayesian optimization algorithm and how fitness can be modeled under this framework. In Section 3, we introduce several substructural neighborhoods, followed by the incorporation of a substructural hillclimber in BOA. Section 5 presents and discusses empirical results. The paper ends with a summary and major conclusions.

2 Bayesian Optimization Algorithm

Estimation of distribution algorithms [1,6] replace traditional variation operators of GEAs by building a probabilistic model of promising solutions (that survive selection) and sampling the corresponding probability distribution to generate the offspring population. The Bayesian optimization algorithm [5,6] uses Bayesian networks as the probabilistic model to capture the (in)dependencies between the variables of the problem.

Like traditional GAs, BOA starts with an initial population (usually randomly generated) that is evaluated and submitted to a selection operator that gives preference to high-quality solutions. The set of selected individuals is then used as the *training dataset* to learn the probabilistic model for the present generation. After obtaining the model structure and parameters, the offspring population is generated by sampling from the distribution of modeled individuals. The new solutions are then evaluated and incorporated into the original population. Here, we use a simple replacement scheme where new solutions fully replace the original population.

2.1 Modeling (in)Dependencies Between Variables in BOA

Bayesian networks [7] are powerful graphical models that combine probability theory with graph theory to encode probabilistic relationships between variables of interest. A Bayesian network is defined by a structure and corresponding parameters. The structure is represented by a directed acyclic graph where the nodes correspond to the variables of the data to be modeled and the edges correspond to conditional dependencies. The parameters are represented by the conditional probabilities for each variable given any instance of the variables that this variable depends on. More formally, a Bayesian network encodes the following joint probability distribution,

$$p(X) = \prod_{i=1}^{\ell} p(X_i|\Pi_i), \tag{1}$$

where $X = (X_1, X_2, \ldots, X_\ell)$ is a vector of all the variables of the problem, Π_i is the set of *parents* of X_i (nodes from which there exists an edge to X_i), and $p(X_i|\Pi_i)$ is the conditional probability of X_i given its parents Π_i.

In BOA, both the structure and the parameters of the probabilistic model are searched and optimized to best fit the data (set of promising solutions). To learn the most adequate structure for the Bayesian network a greedy algorithm is usually used for a good compromise between search efficiency and model quality.

The parameters of a Bayesian network are represented by a set of conditional probability tables (CPTs) specifying the conditional probabilities for each variable given all possible instances of the parent variables Π_i. Alternatively, these conditional probabilities can be stored in the form of local structures such as decision trees or decision graphs, allowing a more efficient and flexible representation of local conditional distributions. In this work, decision trees are used to encode the parameters of the Bayesian network.

2.2 Modeling Fitness in BOA

Pelikan and Sastry [8] extended the Bayesian networks used in BOA to encode a surrogate fitness model that is used to estimate the fitness of a proportion of the population, thereby reducing the total number of function evaluations. For each possible value x_i of every variable X_i, an estimate of the marginal fitness contribution of a subsolution with $X_i = x_i$ is stored for each instance π_i of X_i's parents Π_i. Therefore, in the binary case, each row in the CPT is extended by two additional entries. The fitness of an individual can then be estimated as

$$f_{est}(X_1, X_2, \ldots, X_\ell) = \bar{f} + \sum_{i=1}^{\ell} \left(\bar{f}(X_i|\Pi_i) - \bar{f}(\Pi_i) \right), \tag{2}$$

where $\bar{f}$ is the average fitness of all solutions used to learn the surrogate, $\bar{f}(X_i|\Pi_i)$ is the average fitness of solutions with X_i and Π_i, and $\bar{f}(\Pi_i)$ is the average fitness of all solutions with Π_i.

Fitness information can also be incorporated in Bayesian networks with decision trees or graphs in a similar way. In this case, the average fitness of each instance for every variable must be stored in every leaf of the decision tree or graph. The fitness averages in each leaf are now restricted to solutions that satisfy the condition specified by the path from the root of the tree to the leaf.

3 Substructural Neighborhoods

One of the key requirements for designing an efficient mutation operator is to ensure that it searches in the correct neighborhood. This is often accomplished by exploiting and incorporating domain- or problem-specific knowledge in the design of neighborhood operators. While these neighborhood operators are designed for a particular search problem, oftentimes on an ad-hoc basis, they do not generalize their efficiency beyond a small number of applications. On the other hand, simple bitwise hillclimbers are frequently used as local search methods with more general applicability, providing inferior but still competitive results, especially when combined with population-based search procedures. Clearly, there is a tradeoff between generalization and efficiency for neighborhood operators with fixed structure. Therefore, it is important to study systematic methods for designing neighborhood operators that can solve a broad class of search problems.

The exploration of neighborhoods defined by the probabilistic models of EDAs is an approach that exploits both the underlying problem structure while not loosing the generality of application. The resulting mutation operators explore a more *global*, problem-dependent neighborhood than traditional local, purely representation-dependent search procedures.

Recently, it has been shown that a selectomutative algorithm that performs hillclimbing in the substructural space can successfully solve problems of bounded difficulty with subquadratic scalability [9]. Sastry and Goldberg [10] proposed a building-block-wise mutation algorithm based on the probabilistic model of the extended compact genetic algorithm (eCGA) [11], where linkage information is used to perform local search among competing subsolutions. Lima *et. al.* [12] extended the regular eCGA by incorporating local search in the subsolution search space and concluded that this hybrid approach is more robust than both single-operator-based approaches [11,10].

In this paper we extend the concept of exploring substructural neighborhoods to the Bayesian optimization algorithm. Given the structure of the Bayesian network, several neighborhood topologies can be considered to perform random or improvement-guided mutations. For a given variable X_i, the corresponding set of parent nodes Π_i, and set of child nodes Ω_i (nodes to where an edge arrives from node X_i), we define three different substructural neighborhoods:

Parental neighborhood considers variable X_i together with the parent variables Π_i. This neighborhood is therefore defined by $K = 1 + |\Pi_i|$ different variables, resulting in 2^K possible values in the binary realm.

Children neighborhood considers variable X_i together with the child variables Ω_i. Thus this neighborhood is defined by $K = 1 + |\Omega_i|$ variables.

Parental+Children neighborhood considers variable X_i together with both parent variables Π_i and child variables Ω_i. This neighborhood is composed by $K = 1 + |\Pi_i| + |\Omega_i|$ variables.

These three neighborhoods explore the structure captured by the Bayesian network to different extends. In this paper, we focus on the parental neighborhood to define the neighborhood topology to be used by local search.

A somewhat related approach has been recently proposed by Handa [13], where the traditional bitwise mutation operator is employed in the estimation of Bayesian networks algorithm (EBNA) [14] and consequently variables that depend on the mutated node are resampled according to the conditional probabilities for the new instance. Although this mutation operator takes into account the dependencies between variables, it is specifically designed to perturb solutions in order to maintain diversity in the population. Our approach is to interpret the structure of the Bayesian network as a set of linkage groups that are used to define neighborhoods to be explored by local search.

4 BOA with Substructural Hillclimbing

This section introduces a hillclimber that uses the parental neighborhood defined in the previous section to perform hillclimbing in the substructural space of an individual. This hillclimbing is performed for a proportion of the population in BOA to speedup convergence to good solutions, as in traditional hybrid GEAs. After the offspring population is sampled from the probabilistic model and evaluated, each individual is submitted to substructural hillclimbing with probability p_{ls}. The substructural hillclimber can be described as follows:

1. Consider the first variable X_i according with the ancestral reverse ordering of variables in the Bayesian network.
2. Choose the values (x_i, π_i) associated with the maximal substructural fitness $\bar{f}(X_i|\Pi_i)$.
3. Set variables (X_i, Π_i) of the considered individual to values (x_i, π_i) if the overall fitness of the individual is improved by doing so, otherwise leave the individual unchanged.
4. Repeat steps 2-3 for all remaining variables following the ancestral reverse order of variables.

Some details need further explanation. First, we use the reverse order of that used to sample the variables of new solutions, where each node is preceded by its parents. By doing so, higher-order dependencies within the same linkage group are *optimized* first. This procedure aims to reduce the possibility of doing incorrect decisions when considering problems whose lower-order statistics lead the search away from global optima.

Also, we consider two different versions of the substructural hillclimber in our study, that only differ in step 3. The first version uses the estimated fitness of the individual (Equation 2) to decide if the best substructure (according to $\bar{f}(X_i|\Pi_i)$) for a given neighborhood should be accepted, while the second version uses the actual fitness function to make the decision. After performing substructural hillclimbing for all variables, the resulting individual is evaluated with the fitness function before it is inserted back into the population. This avoids the propagation of error possibly introduced by using surrogate fitness. Thus, the surrogate is only used to perform local search in the substructural neighborhoods.

We also note that searching within the same substructural neighborhoods for different individuals yields results whose similarity increase with the accuracy of the linkage model. However, in practice, performing local search on different individuals helps to overcome incorrect biases from the errors in the substructural models.

5 Experiments

This section describes the test problems used, presents the results obtained for varying proportions of local search p_{ls}, and empirically analyzes the scalability of the proposed method with increasing problem size.

5.1 Test Problems and Experimental Setup

Two different problems are used to test the proposed method: OneMax and Trap functions. These problems represent two important bounds on a class of additively decomposable problems with bounded difficulty. In OneMax the fitness is simply given by the sum of ones in a binary string. This is a simple linear function with the optimum in the solution with all ones. Therefore, there is no need of linkage learning to be able to solve this problem. While the optimization of the OneMax problem is easy, the probabilistic models build by EDAs such as eCGA and BOA, however, are known to be only partially correct and include spurious linkages. Therefore, the results on this function will indicate if the effect of using partially correct linkage mapping on the accuracy of the surrogate is significant, and consequently if performing substructural local search under these conditions is still advantageous. This paper considers a OneMax function with size $\ell = 50$.

The second problem considered is a concatenated 5-bit Trap function [15]. This problem consists in concatenating a number of copies of the Trap function with size $k = 5$. The Trap function used is defined as follows

$$f_{Trap}(u) = \begin{cases} 5 & \text{if } u = 5 \\ 4 - u & \text{otherwise,} \end{cases} \tag{3}$$

where u is the number of ones in the substring of 5 bits. In this problem the accurate identification and exchange of the building-blocks is critical to achieve success, because processing substructures of lower order will lead to exponential scalability. Ten concatenated copies of the 5-bit Trap are used, which makes the total problem size also $\ell = 50$.

For each problem, we perform experiments for different proportions of local search p_{ls}. The proportions tested are $0.001, 0.005, 0.01, 0.03, 0.05, 0.1, 0.15, 0.2$. For the 10x5-bit Trap function, an additional value of 0.0005 is also considered. The minimal number of function evaluations required to obtain the optimal solution is empirically determined using a bisection method over the population size. For each experiment, 10 independent bisection runs are performed. Each bisection run searches for the minimal population size required to find the optimum in 10 out of 10 independent runs. Therefore, the results for the minimal sufficient population size are averaged over 10 bisection runs, while the results for the number of function evaluations and the number of generations spent are averaged over 100 (10×10) independent runs. For all experiments, binary tournament selection without replacement is used.

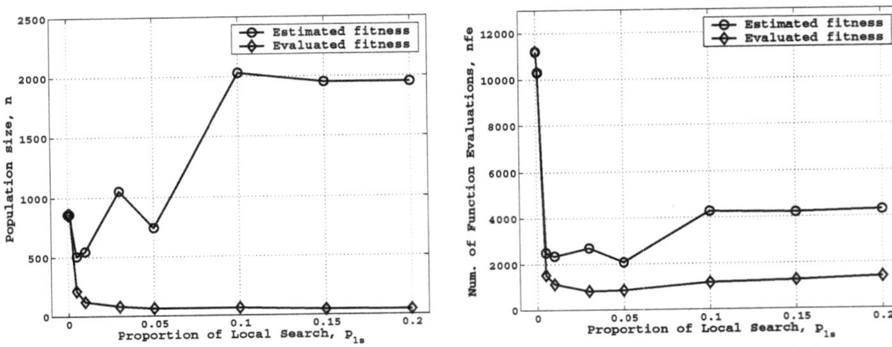

Fig. 1. Population size and number of function evaluations required to solve the 50-bit OneMax problem

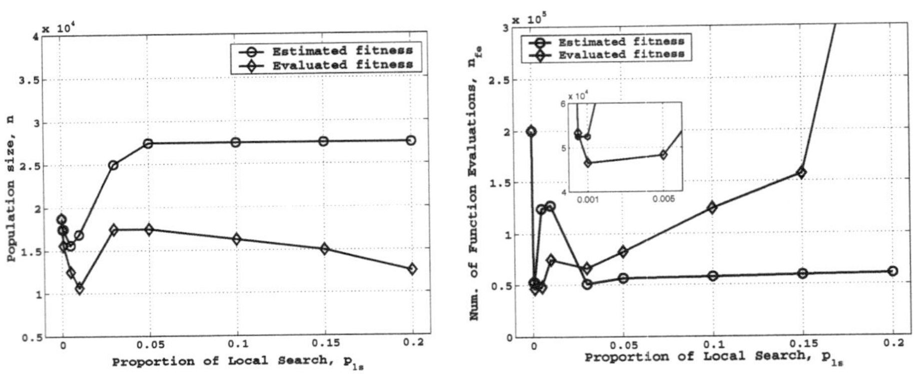

Fig. 2. Population size and number of function evaluations required to solve the 10x5-bit Trap problem

5.2 Results and Discussion

The results obtained are shown in figures 1 and 2. For both problems, the number of evaluations is significatively reduced when using local search that explores substructural neighborhoods. Also, both versions of the acceptance criteria in the substructural hillclimber reduce the cost to solve the problem. However, different dynamics can be observed for each problem.

For OneMax, using the actual fitness function when deciding if substructures should be accepted or not provides slightly better results than using estimated fitness, while the population size required is significatively smaller, in particular for higher proportions of local search. Note that the correctness of the substructural neighborhoods is not crucial when solving OneMax using local search because there is no linkage. However, the choice of the best alternative in each neighborhood is based on the substructural fitness contribution that is estimated by the surrogate whose correctness relies on the accuracy of the linkage model.

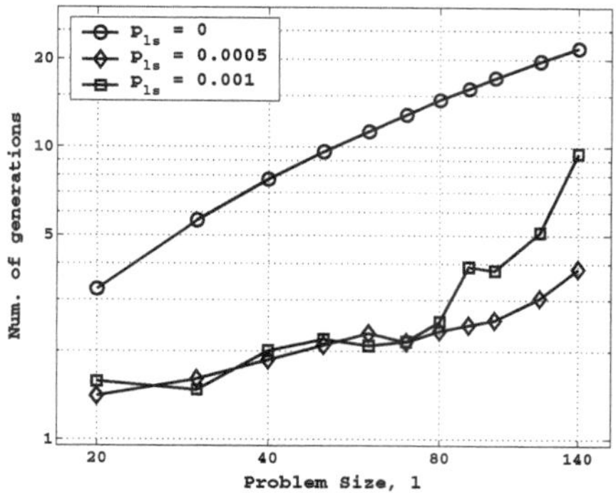

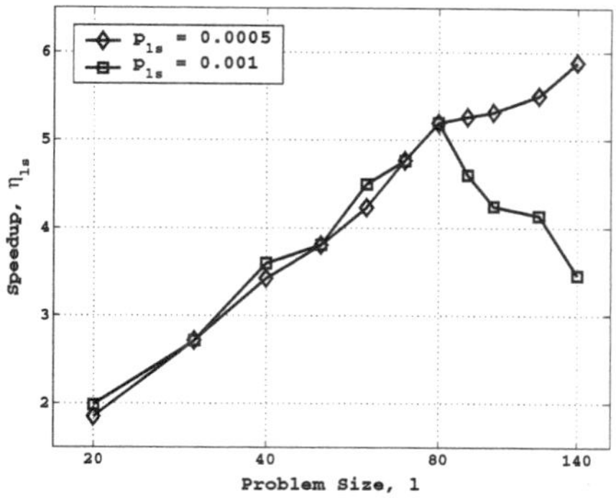

Fig. 3. Number of generations required to get the optimum and the speedup obtained by performing substructural local search on a number of concatenated 5-bit Trap functions. The speedup scales as $\mathcal{O}(\ell^{0.45})$ for $\ell \leq 80$. For $\ell > 80$ the speedup grow is more moderate for the *optimal* value of $p_{ls} = 0.0005$, while for higher proportions of local search the speedup starts to decrease due to diversity reduction in the population.

But even more important is the acceptance (or not) of the substructures. By using real fitness evaluation in this decision, only those building-blocks that really improve the fitness of the individual are accepted, which drastically reduces the need of having an accurate surrogate fitness model (and consequently a larger population size). For the hillclimber that uses only estimated fitness, the population size required grows even more for higher proportions of local search because the diversity in the population is quickly reduced, which requires the surrogate to be accurate enough to solve the problem in the first generation.

In the 10x5-bit Trap, the identification of the correct substructures is crucial to solve the problem, requiring the accuracy of the probabilistic model of BOA to be high. Therefore, both hillclimbers perform similar for small proportions of local search. Here, however, the cost of using fitness function calls at each step of the substructural hillclimber shows to be an expensive overhead for higher values of p_{ls}. Similar to OneMax, there is a transition phase in the population size required for the hillclimber that uses surrogate fitness. For $p_{ls} \geq 0.05$, the population size stagnates at a value where the model is accurate enough to solve the problem in the first generation by performing substructural local search.

Figure 3 presents the results obtained for increasing number of concatenated 5-bit Trap functions for BOA with the hillclimber that uses estimated fitness. The number of generations required to reach optima and the speedup of performing local search are shown. Note that the speedup is simply the ratio of the number of evaluations required by BOA without and with local search. Several proportions of local search were tested between 0.0001 and 0.005, but for clarity only two illustrative cases are plotted: 0.0005 and 0.001. The population size required (not plotted) scales similarly for all tested p_{ls} values.

The results show that while obtaining a significant reduction in the number of generations, substantial speedups are provided by using substructural local search in BOA. The speedup grows approximately as $\mathcal{O}(\ell^{0.45})$ for $\ell \leq 80$. For larger problem sizes the increase in speedup becomes more moderate for $p_{ls} = 0.0005$, while for higher proportions of local search the speedup decreases. This is due to the population size required for larger problems, increasing the number of individuals that undergo local search for the same value of p_{ls}, and thereby reducing diversity in the population. Note that the resulting individuals from substructural hillclimbing are very similar. On the other hand, smaller proportions of local search (not plotted) lead to a curve with similar slope to that obtained for the best proportion but with inferior speedups. As a final remark, while $p_{ls} = 0.0005$ was found to be the most adequate value the spectrum of problem sizes tested, the optimal proportion should decrease for larger problems than considered here.

The reduction of the slope in the speedup curve for larger problem sizes is also related to the structure of the model learned by BOA. Analyzing the dependency groups captured by the Bayesian network with decision trees, it can be observed that the number and size of spurious linkages increases with problem size. By spurious linkage we mean additional variables that are considered together with a correct linkage group. Although the structure of the Bayesian network captures such spurious dependencies, the conditional probabilities nearly express independency between the spurious variables and the correct linkage, therefore not affecting the capability of sampling such variables as if they were independent. In fact, this capability of decision trees to detect more complex dependencies is one of the keys in hierarchical BOA [6] to solve more complex decomposable problems such as hierarchical problems.

6 Summary and Conclusions

In this paper, we have introduced the use of substructural neighborhoods to perform local search in BOA. Three different substructural neighborhoods—based on the structure of the learned Bayesian network—were proposed. A hillclimber that effectively searches in the subsolution search space was incorporated in BOA, using a surrogate fitness model to evaluate competing substructures. The results showed that incorporating substructural local search in BOA leads to a significant reduction in the number of generations necessary to solve the problem, while providing substantial speedups in terms of number of evaluations. More importantly, the relevance of designing and hybridizing competent operators that automatically identify the problem decomposition and important problem substructures have been empirically highlighted.

Acknowledgements. This work was sponsored by the Air Force Office of Scientific Research, Air Force Materiel Command, USAF, under grant FA9550-06-1-0096, the National Science Foundation under CAREER grant ECS-0547013, ITR grant DMR-03-25939 at Material Computation Center, UIUC, and Portuguese Foundation for Science and Technology (FCT/MCES) under grant SFRH-BD-16980-2004. The work was also supported by the High Performance Computing Collaboratory sponsored by Information Technology Services, the Research Award and the Research Board at the University of Missouri in St. Louis.

The views and conclusions contained herein are those of the authors and should not be interpreted as necessarily representing the official policies or endorsements, either expressed or implied, of the Air Force Office of Scientific Research, or the U.S. Government.

References

1. Larrañaga, P., Lozano, J.A., eds.: Estimation of distribution algorithms: a new tool for Evolutionary Computation. Kluwer Academic Publishers, Boston, MA (2002)
2. Pelikan, M., Goldberg, D.E., Lobo, F.: A survey of optimization by building and using probabilistic models. Computational Optimization and Applications **21**(1) (2002) 5–20 Also IlliGAL Report No. 99018.
3. Moscato, P.: On evolution, search, optimization, genetic algorithms and martial arts: Towards memetic algorithms. Technical Report C3P 826, Caltech Concurrent Computation Program, California Institute of Technology, Pasadena, CA (1989)
4. Hart, W.E.: Adaptive global optimization with local search. PhD thesis, University of California, San Diego, San Diego, CA (1994)
5. Pelikan, M., Goldberg, D.E., Cantú-Paz, E.: BOA: The Bayesian Optimization Algorithm. In Banzhaf, W., et al., eds.: Proceedings of the Genetic and Evolutionary Computation Conference GECCO-99, San Francisco, CA, Morgan Kaufmann (1999) 525–532 Also IlliGAL Report No. 99003.
6. Pelikan, M.: Hierarchical Bayesian Optimization Algorithm: Toward a New Generation of Evolutionary Algorithms. Springer (2005)
7. Pearl, J.: Probabilistic reasoning in intelligent systems: Networks of plausible inference. Morgan Kaufmann, San Mateo, CA (1988)
8. Pelikan, M., Sastry, K.: Fitness inheritance in the Bayesian optimization algorithm. In Deb, K.e.a., ed.: Proceedings of the Genetic and Evolutionary Computation Conference (GECCO-2004), Part II, LNCS 3103, Springer (2004) 48–59
9. Sastry, K., Goldberg, D.E.: Let's get ready to rumble: Crossover versus mutation head to head. In Deb, K., et al., eds.: Proceedings of the Genetic and Evolutionary Computation Conference (GECCO-2004), Part II, LNCS 3103, Springer (2004) 126–137 Also IlliGAL Report No. 2004005.
10. Sastry, K., Goldberg, D.E.: Designing competent mutation operators via probabilistic model building of neighborhoods. In Deb, K., et al., eds.: Proceedings of the Genetic and Evolutionary Computation Conference (GECCO-2004), Part II, LNCS 3103, Springer (2004) 114–125 Also IlliGAL Report No. 2004006.
11. Harik, G.R.: Linkage learning via probabilistic modeling in the ECGA. IlliGAL Report No. 99010, Illinois Genetic Algorithms Laboratory, University of Illinois at Urbana-Champaign, Urbana, IL (1999)
12. Lima, C.F., Sastry, K., Goldberg, D.E., Lobo, F.G.: Combining competent crossover and mutation operators: A probabilistic model building approach. In Beyer, H., et al., eds.: Proceedings of the ACM SIGEVO Genetic and Evolutionary Computation Conference (GECCO-2005), ACM Press (2005)
13. Handa, H.: The effectiveness of mutation operation in the case of estimation of distribution algorithms. Journal of Biosystems (2006) (to appear).
14. Etxeberria, R., Larrañaga, P.: Global optimization using Bayesian networks. In Rodriguez, A., et al., eds.: Second Symposium on Artificial Intelligence (CIMAF-99), Habana, Cuba (1999) 332–339
15. Deb, K., Goldberg, D.E.: Analyzing deception in trap functions. Foundations of Genetic Algorithms 2 (1993) 93–108

Theory and Practice of Cellular UMDA for Discrete Optimization*

E. Alba[1], J. Madera[2], B. Dorronsoro[1], A. Ochoa[3], and M. Soto[3]

[1] Department of Computer Science, University of Málaga, Spain
{eat, bernabe}@lcc.uma.es
[2] Department of Computing, Camagüey University, Cuba
jmadera@inf.reduc.edu.cu
[3] The Institute of Cybernetics, Mathematics and Physics, La Habana, Cuba
{ochoa, mrosa}@icmf.inf.cu

Abstract. A new class of estimation of distribution algorithms (EDAs), known as cellular EDAs (cEDAs), has recently emerged. In these algorithms, the population is decentralized by partitioning it into many small collaborating subpopulations, arranged in a toroidal grid, and interacting only with its neighboring subpopulations. In this work, we study the simplest cEDA —the cellular univariate marginal distribution algorithm (cUMDA). In an attempt to explain its behaviour, we extend the well known takeover time analysis usually applied to other evolutionary algorithms to the field of EDAs. We also give in this work empirical arguments in favor of using the cUMDAs instead of its centralized equivalent.

1 Introduction

Evolutionary Algorithms (EAs) are stochastic search techniques designed as an attempt to solve adaptive and hard optimization tasks on computers [1]. In fact, it is possible to find this kind of algorithms applied for solving complex problems like constrained optimization tasks, problems with a noisy objective function, or problems having high epistasis and multimodality [2]. These algorithms work over a set (*population*) of potential solutions (*individuals*) by applying some stochastic operators, called *variation operators* (e.g., natural selection, recombination, or mutation), on them in order to search for the best solutions.

Estimation of Distribution Algorithms (EDAs) [3,4] are an alternative family to traditional EAs in which a different kind of variation operators is used. The successive generations of individuals are created by using estimations of distributions observed in the current population instead of evolving the population with the typical variation operators (like crossover and mutation) used in other EAs. Hence, the main feature distinguishing EDAs from other more classical EAs is that EDAs learn the interactions among variables (building blocks) in the problem to be solved. At the same time, it is the main drawback of EDAs due to the complexity of this learning and simulation task.

* E. Alba, and B. Dorronsoro acknowledge the support by FEDER and MEC under contract TIN2005-08818-C04-01 (the OPLINK project: http://oplink.lcc.uma.es).

T.P. Runarsson et al. (Eds.): PPSN IX, LNCS 4193, pp. 242–251, 2006.

The application of EDAs to optimization problems has been intense during the last decade [4]. The motivation is, in part, that in many of the reported results EDAs overcome other EAs such as genetic algorithms [4, 5, 6]. Due to the high computational costs of many EDAs, the current state-of-art of the field requires the development of new and more powerful strategies for implementing them.

One interesting and simple approach for dealing with that problem consists in decentralizing the population. In many cases [7], decentralizing the population provides a better sampling of the search space, and thus improves the numerical behavior of the algorithm. In this paper, we propose a decentralization of the population of EDAs by partitioning it into many small collaborating subpopulations, such that they are allowed to interact only with their neighboring subpopulations for computing the estimation of distribution. This estimation is then used for computing the next generation of the considered subpopulation. The result are the so called cellular EDAs (cEDAs) [8,9]. Note that MIDEA [10] can seem as a similar approach to the proposed one, but in MIDEA the space of solutions is clustered for obtaining the estimation of distribution for each cluster, and then all the performed estimations are mixed to obtain a unique one for computing the whole next population. However, we are using one estimation of distribution for each population in our approach.

The main contribution of this paper is a comparative study on the behavior of both cEDAs and EDAs. For this study, we face an extended benchmark of discrete problems with UMDA (a simple EDA) and 4 different cellular versions of UMDA (cUMDAs). This study extends the one previously made in [8], where a UMDA and a cUMDA were compared on one simple problem, and confirms the obtained results in that work. As a second contribution, we extend the study of the selection pressure of an algorithm to the field of EDAs in order to include a brief comparison on the theoretical behavior of the proposed algorithms. To the best of our knowledge, this is the first time that this selection pressure study is applied to an EDA, and it constitutes a good empirical approach for studying the behavior of an algorithm.

The paper is structured as follows. In the next section we present the cellular EDA approach studied in this paper. The benchmark we have used in this work is presented in Section 3, while our results, as well as an explanation of the algorithms used, are given in Section 4. Finally, we finish this paper giving our main conclusions an some future research lines.

2 Cellular Estimation of Distribution Algorithms

Cellular EAs (cEAs) are endowed of an internal spatial structure that allows fitness and genotype diversity for a larger number of iterations [11] than centralized EAs. Additionally, some works [12, 13] have established the advantages of using cEAs over other EA models for complex optimization tasks where high efficacy and a low number of steps are needed.

Cellular EDAs were introduced in [9] as a decentralized version of EDAs, and also as a generalization of the cellular models developed for other evolutionary algorithms [14, 12]. In a cEDA the population is decentralized by partitioning it into many small collaborating subpopulations (called *cells* or *member algorithms*), arranged in a toroidal grid, and interacting only with the neighboring subpopulations. One distinctive feature of this class of algorithm is that selection is decentralized at the level of the member algorithms, while in other cellular EAs selection usually occurs at the recombination level.

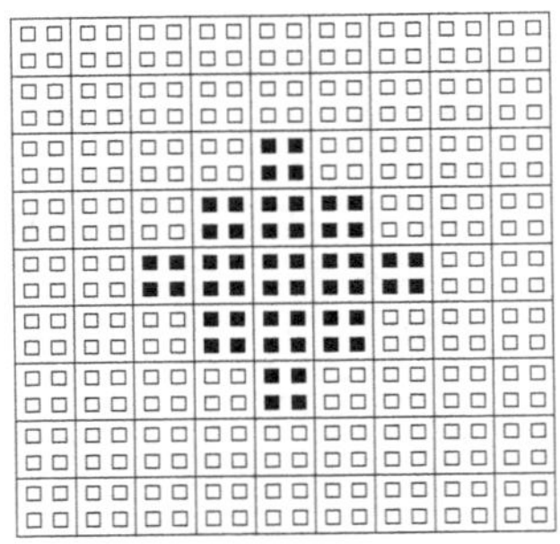

Fig. 1. A cEDA with a C13 neighborhood and the population shape $2 \times 2 - 9 \times 9$

The organization of cEDAs is based on the traditional 2D structure of overlapped neighborhoods. That structure is better understood in terms of two grids, i.e. one consisting of strings and another consisting of disjoint sets of strings (cells). Figure 1 shows a global population of 18×18 strings (small squares) partitioned in a 9×9 toroidal grid of cells (large squares) containing 4 strings each. The neighborhood used is the so called C13, which is composed by the considered subpopulation plus its 12 nearest cells (measured with the manhattan distance). We adopt the same notation used in [9] for describing the shape of the population: it consists of the shape of cells in terms of strings plus the shape of the whole population taking into account the cells (composed of one or more strings). For example, following this nomenclature, the grid of Fig. 1 is labelled as $2 \times 2 - 9 \times 9$.

In Algorithm 1 we present a pseudocode of the proposed cEDA approach. Each iteration of a cEDA consists of exactly one iteration of all the member algorithms. Each of these member algorithms is responsible for updating exactly one subpopulation, and this is made by applying a local EDA model to the population composed of its strings and those of its neighbor subpopulations (lines 5 to 7). In the implementation of cEDA carried out in this paper, the successive populations replace each other at once (line 10), so the new individuals generated by the local learning and sampling steps are placed in a temporal population (line 8). This policy for updating individuals is called *synchronous*, since all the individuals are updated at the same time in the population. An alternative to this synchronous updating is the so called *asynchronous* update method, and lies in placing the offsprings directly in the current population by following some rules [15] instead of updating all the individuals simultaneously. The asynchronous issue is not explored here because of the many implications and numerous existing asynchronous policies.

Algorithm 1. Pseudocode of a simple cEDA

```
1: Set t ← 1;
2: Generate N >> 0 points randomly;
3: while termination criteria are not met do
4:    for every cell do
5:       Select locally M ≤ SizeOf(Neighborhood) × SizeOf(cell) strings of the neigh-
         borhood according to a selection method;
6:       Estimate the distribution p^s(x, t) of these M selected strings;
7:       Generate SizeOf(cell) new points according to the distribution p^s(x, t);
8:       Insert the generated points in the same cell of an auxiliary population;
9:    end for
10:   Replace the current population with the auxiliary one;
11:   Compute and update the statistics;
12:   Set t ← t + 1;
13: end while
```

In the replacement step (line 10), the old population can be taken into account (i.e., replacing a string if the new one is better) or not (always adding the new string to the next population). The first issue (called *elitism*) is the preferred one for this study. Finally, computing basic statistics (line 11) is rarely found in the pseudocodes of other authors in the EA field. However, it can be used for monitoring the algorithm and decide changes in the adaptive search, when needed.

A critical issue in a cEDA is the computation of the probabilistic model due to the high computational cost it usually supposes. The reader is referred to [9,8] for an explanation of several alternative learning schemes for cellular EDAs. Notice that the use of UMDA as the member algorithm, implies that we do not need to learn the structure of the model (it is known), but just the univariate marginal frequencies.

3 Set of Test Functions

We present in this section the set of test functions we have selected for our study. It is composed of five problems having many different features: OneMax [16], Plateau [17], IsoPeak [18], P-PEAKS [19] and the minimum tardy task problem (MTTP) [20]. In Table 1 we present, for each of these problems, its name, its fitness function (to be maximized), the size of the studied instance, the chromosome representing the optimal solution to the problem, and the value of this optimum. In all the cases, n represents the dimension of the problem, and a binary genotype is used ($x_i \in \{0,1\}$).

The Onemax problem simply consists in maximizing the number of ones in a bit-string. In the Plateau function, the chromosome is divided into groups of three genes, and the fitness value is the number of sets containing three ones. IsoPeak is a non separable function, and it is composed of functions $Iso1$ and $Iso2$. The P-PEAKS problem consists in finding one of P randomly generated binary strings. Finally, MTTP is a task scheduling problem in which the tasks

Table 1. Benchmark of problems

Problem	Fitness function	n	Solution chromosome	Optimum
Onemax	$f_{OneMax}(\boldsymbol{x}) = \sum_{i=1}^{n} x_i$	1000	(1,1,1,1,...,1,1)	1000
Plateau	$f_{Plateau}(\boldsymbol{x}) = \sum_{i=1}^{m} g(\boldsymbol{s_i})$ where $\boldsymbol{s_i} = (x_{3i-2}, x_{3i-1}, x_{3i})$, and $m = \frac{n}{3}$; $g(x_1, x_2, x_3) = \begin{cases} 1 \text{ if } x_1 = x_2 = x_3 = 1 \\ 0 \text{ otherwise} \end{cases}$	300	(1,1,1,1,...,1,1)	100
IsoPeak	$f_{IsoPeak(\boldsymbol{x})} = Iso2\,(x_1, x_2) + \sum_{i=2}^{m} Iso1\,(x_{2i-1}, x_{2i})\,; m = \frac{n}{2}$; $Iso1(x_1, x_2) = m - mx_1 - mx_2 + (2m-1)x_1x_2$; $Iso2(x_1, x_2) = mx_1x_2$	100	(1,1,0,0,...,0,0)	2500
P-PEAKS	$f_{P-PEAKS}(\boldsymbol{x}) = \frac{1}{N} \max_{1 \leq i \leq p}(N - HammingD(\boldsymbol{x}, Peak_i))$	100	One of the peaks	1.0
MTTP	$f_{MTTP}(\boldsymbol{x}) = \sum_{i=1}^{n} x_i \cdot w_i$	100	$\boldsymbol{x} = (x_1, x_2, ..., x_n)$; $x_i = 1 \Rightarrow$ Task $\in S$; $x_i = 0 \Rightarrow$ Task $\notin S$	0.005

have a given length (the time its execution takes), a deadline before which a task must be scheduled (and its execution completed), and a weight. The objective is to maximize the weights of the scheduled tasks S from a set of tasks T, subject to that a task can not be scheduled before any previous one has finished, and every task finishes before its deadline.

4 Experimentation

We present in this section the experiments we have made in this work. In Section 4.1 we briefly explain the functioning of the UMDA algorithm, the simple EDA we have selected for our study. Later, in Section 4.2 we show and analyze the results of our tests.

4.1 Univariate Marginal Distribution Algorithm

The Univariate Marginal Distribution Algorithm (UMDA) was presented for the first time by Müehlenbein and Paaß in [3]. UMDA is one of the simplest algorithm in the EDAs family. A pseudocode of UMDA is presented in Algorithm 2. In UMDA, it is considered that variables are independent from the others, so there are no dependencies between them. The current generation evolves towards the new one by computing the frequencies of values of the variables on each position in the selected set of promising solutions (lines 4 and 5). These frequencies are then used to compute new solutions (line 6), which replace the old ones. Due to its simplicity, it is a very efficient algorithm (converges quickly), and its behavior is particularly good for linear problems.

We have used common parameterizations in our tests in order to make a meaningful comparison among the studied algorithms. The details are shown in Table 2. As can be seen, we have defined four different configurations of cUMDAs. These cUMDAs differ in the population and the neighborhood used. The

Algorithm 2. Univariate Marginal Distribution Algorithm

```
Set t ← 1;
Generate N >> 0 points randomly;
while termination criteria are not met do
    Select M ≤ N points according to a selection method;
    Compute the marginal frequencies p^s(x_i, t) of the selected set;
    Generate N new points according to the distribution p^s(x, t) = ∏_{i=1}^{n} p^s(x_i, t);
    Set t ← t + 1;
end while
```

population is always composed of 400 individuals, but in the case of the cUMDAs it can be structured in two different ways ($1 \times 1 - 20 \times 20$ and $2 \times 2 - 10 \times 10$). The neighborhoods used are C25 and C41 (see Fig. 2), and they are composed by the considered cell plus the nearest 24 (for C25) and 40 (in the case of C41) cells measured in manhattan distance. The selection method used is the truncation selection (with $\tau = 0.5$), applied into the local subpopulation pool. Finally, all the algorithms implement a mutation step in order to introduce some diversity into the population. Although it is not usual in EDAs, we apply this mutation due to the good results obtained in some preliminary experiments. The proposed mutation simply consists in flipping the genes of the newly generated individuals with a given probability.

Table 2. Parameterization used in all the compared algorithms

Parameter	Value
Population Size	400 individuals
Selection of Parents	Truncation selection, $\tau = 0.5$
Mutation	Bit-flip, $p_m = 1/n$
Replacement	Replace-if-Better
Stop Condition	Optimum reached or 400000 fitness evaluations
Member Algorithm	UMDA
Cellular Case	*Neighborhood Shape:* $C25$ and $C41$
	Population Shape: $1 \times 1 - 20 \times 20$ and $2 \times 2 - 10 \times 10$

We finally include in this section a brief study of the theoretical behavior of all the proposed algorithms in terms of their selection pressure. Selection pressure is related to the concept of *takeover time*, which is defined for EAs as the time it takes for a single best individual to colonize the whole population with copies of itself under the effects of selection only. Shorter takeover times mean a more intense selection. For calculating the takeover time in EDAs, we compute the proportion of the best individuals in the population (after truncating), and use it for generating the new one with elitism (best individuals are kept).

In Fig. 3 we plot the growth curves of UMDA and the four cUMDAs. In order to obtain meaningful results, we have enlarged the population up to 64000

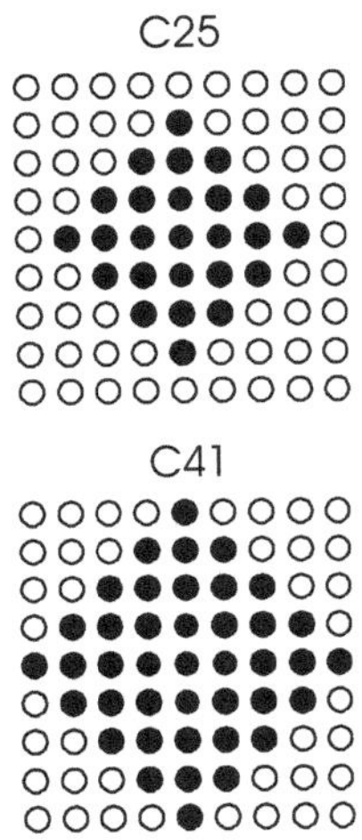

Fig. 2. Neighborhoods

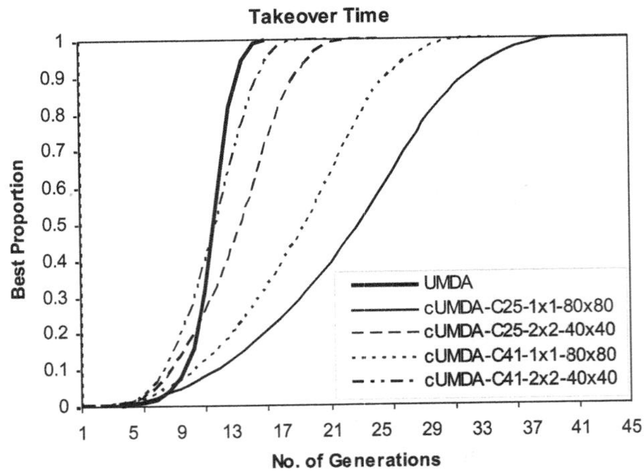

Fig. 3. Takeover curves for the studied algorithms

individuals for this study. As can be seen, the higher selection pressure (shorter takeover time) corresponds to UMDA. Regarding the cUMDAs, the two algorithms having one individual per cell are those with lower selection pressure (longer takeover time). The reason is that in the cases of the cUMDAs with four individuals per cell the exploration capabilities of the algorithm are penalized since the number of individuals in the neighborhood is multiplied by four.

4.2 Results

In this section we turn to present and analyze the results we have obtained in our experiments for the five problems previously proposed in Section 3. As we stated in the previous section, the algorithms we have studied in our comparison are the standard UMDA plus four different proposed cellular versions. All these five algorithms include a mutation operator. The studied cUMDAs are those using the C25 neighborhood and one or four strings per cell (called C25-1×1-20×20, and C25-2×2-10×10, respectively), and these same two population structures with the neighborhood C41: C41-1×1-20×20 and C41-2×2-10×10.

In order to get statistically significant results, we have made 100 runs for each test, and computed the analysis of variance (ANOVA) or Kruskal-Wallis tests for comparing our results (depending on whether the data follows a normal distribution or not). For these statistical tests, we consider in this work a significance level of 95% (p-value under 0.05). Both UMDA and cUMDA are written in C++ and executed in a Pentium 4 2.4 GHz under Linux with 512 MB of RAM.

We present in Table 3 the percentage of runs in which the algorithms found the optimal solution to the problems (success –or hit– rate). As can be seen, UMDA has difficulties for finding the optimum in the case of MTTP (74% of the runs), and was not able to get it in any run for the IsoPeak problem. Conversely,

Table 3. Success Rate

Neighborhood	OneMax	Plateau	IsoPeak	P-PEAKS	MTTP
UMDA	100%	100%	0%	100%	74%
cUMDA C25-1×1-20×20	100%	100%	100%	100%	100%
cUMDA C25-2×2-10×10	100%	100%	100%	100%	100%
cUMDA C41-1×1-20×20	100%	100%	100%	100%	100%
cUMDA C41-2×2-10×10	100%	100%	100%	100%	100%

its four cellular versions studied here did not find any difficulty for obtaining the optimal value for all the problems in every run (100% of success rate).

Table 4. Function evaluations

Neighborhood	OneMax	Plateau	IsoPeak	P-PEAKS	MTTP
UMDA	26072.00	18972.00	—	15040.00	169713.51
	±463.20	±1054.86	—	±1448.37	±106624.49
cUMDA C25-1×1-20×20	23298.11	16337.83	176878.71	**13460.97**	14976.44
	±382.76	±584.86	±36384.01	±1650.01	±1348.01
cUMDA C25-2×2-10×10	22037.60	14961.16	218190.00	34994.20	14418.12
	±346.74	±511.65	±47518.06	±13342.22	±1116.66
cUMDA C41-1×1-20×20	22500.89	15454.92	**176138.77**	16915.08	14469.85
	±361.14	±510.05	±41834.80	±3091.56	±981.36
cUMDA C41-2×2-10×10	**21851.72**	**14773.64**	253725.44	41795.32	**14235.52**
	±340.30	±469.24	±58172.59	±15362.06	±1203.63
p-value	+	+	+	+	+

In Table 4 we present the average number of evaluations and the standard deviation needed by the five studied algorithms for solving the problems. In the last row of the table we present the p-values obtained in our statistical tests when comparing all the algorithms for each problem. The '+' symbol stands for statistical confidence in the comparison of the five algorithms, i.e. the results of almost two of the compared algorithms are statistically different. As can be seen, the most efficient algorithm (lowest number of evaluations) for every problem (**bolded** values) is always one of the studied cellular versions of UMDA.

In Fig. 4 we graphically show the results of Table 4. It is easy to see that the less efficient algorithm for all the problems is UMDA, with the exception of P-PEAKS. With respect to the different cellular versions of UMDA, cUMDA C41-2×2-10×10 is the most efficient for three of the five studied problems (OneMax, Plateau, and MTTP), although it is the worst one for the two other problems. However, the differences among the studied cUMDAs are, in general, very low (no statistical confidence was found in the comparison of the cUMDAs).

Finally, in Fig. 5 we plot an example of the evolution of the best fitness value for UMDA and the 4 proposed cUMDAs when solving the Plateau problem. The value plotted in each generation is computed as the average of 100 executions. As can be seen, the two algorithms that converge earlier to the optimum are the two cUMDAs with the population 2×2-10×10, which show a similar behavior (almost

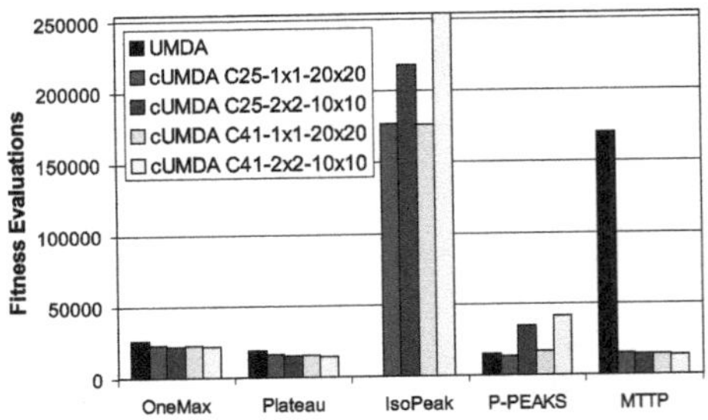

Fig. 4. Efficiency of the algorithms

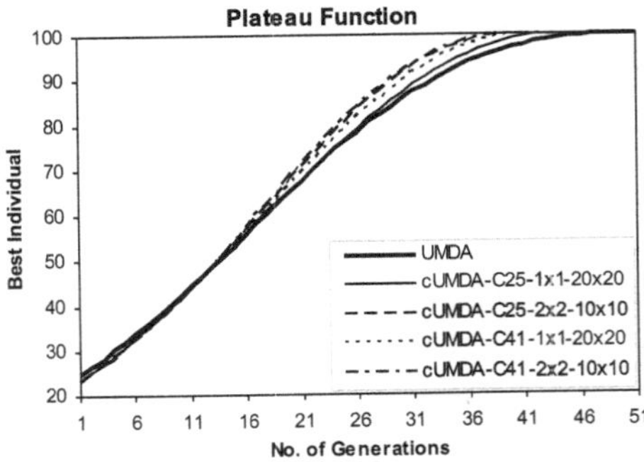

Fig. 5. Evolution of the best fitness value for Plateau

indistinguishable), as we previously obtained in the analysis of the takeover time. The slowest of the studied algorithms for this problem is UMDA, which finds more difficulties than the cUMDAs for avoiding local optima and converge to the global optimum due to its higher solution pressure.

5 Conclusions and Further Work

In this paper we have investigated an algorithm from a new class of decentralized EDAs, called cellular EDA, based on the functioning of other existing cellular EAs. Our main motivation has been to advance in the field of EDAs by studying a new kind of decentralized population, easily parallelizable, that has been demonstrated to obtain highly competitive results in other kind of EAs. Four approaches based on UMDA have been tested. The comparison between the four new cUMDAs and UMDA reports very advantageous results for the cellular models, since UMDA (centralized) is, in general, the worst algorithm both in terms of efficacy (success rate) and efficiency (number of evaluations to reach an optimum) for all the problems.

The comparison of the cellular EDA versus other kinds of algorithms is out of the scope of this paper. Our objective here is not competing with other existing algorithms, but presenting a study of a new kind of EDA and analyze its behavior versus their centralized counterpart. The algorithms investigated herein are only a first approach, and are susceptible of high improvements after a fine tuning of the parameters. The comparison between EDAs and cEDAs was carried out in terms of the selection pressure and the resolution of a diverse benchmark of discrete problems. In the two cases, the centralized EDA was outperformed by the four new cellular models (cEDAs) compared.

Thus, in this paper we have advanced in the development a new wide research field, and hence there exists a huge number of possible future lines of work. Specifically, we suggest some direct further works from this paper, like the study of the other alternatives proposed (but not studied) in [8] for the cEDAs learning schemes, the fine tuning of the parameters used, the comparison of our cEDAs to other existing algorithms in the literature, and the study on the behavior of other cellular models based on EDAs distinct than UMDA. There exist also some other future lines of work, such as the study on the effects of the synchronicity in the population updating, the algorithm parallelization, or adopting existing algorithmic improvements from other cellular EAs.

References

1. Bäck, T., Fogel, D., Michalewicz, Z., eds.: Handbook of Evolutionary Computation. Oxford University Press (1997)
2. Alba, E., Dorronsoro, B.: The exploration/exploitation tradeoff in dynamic cellular evolutionary algorithms. IEEE TEC **9**(2) (2005) 126–142
3. Mühlenbein, H., Paab, G.: From recombination of genes to the estimation of distributions I. Binary parameters. In: PPSN IV, Springer (1996) 178–187
4. Larrañaga, P., Lozano, J.A., eds.: Estimation of Distribution Algorithms. A New Tool for Evolutionary Computation. Kluwer Academic Publishers (2002)
5. Cantú-Paz, E.: Feature subset selection by estimation of distribution algorithms. In: GECCO, San Francisco, CA, Morgan Kaufmann (2002) 303–310
6. Pelikan, M., Mühlenbein, H.: The bivariate marginal distribution algorithm. Advances in Soft Computing-Engineering Design and Manufacturing (1999) 521–535
7. Alba, E., Troya, J.: Improving flexibility and efficiency by adding parallelism to genetic algorithms. Statistics and Computing **12**(2) (2002) 91–114
8. Madera, J., Alba, E., Ochoa, A.: Parallel Estimation of Distribution Algorithms. In Alba, E., ed.: Parallel Metaheuristics: A New Class of Algorithms, John Wiley & Sons (2005) 203–222
9. Ochoa, A., Soto, M., Alba, E.: Cellular estimation of distribution algorithms. In preparation (2006)
10. Bosman, P., Thierens, D.: Advancing continuous IDEAs with mixture distributions and factorization selection metrics. In: OBUPM. (2001) 208–212
11. Spiessens, P., Manderick, B.: A massively parallel genetic algorithm. In Belew, R., Booker, L., eds.: 4th ICGA, Morgan Kaufmann (1991) 279–286
12. Baluja, S.: Structure and performance of fine-grain parallelism in genetic search. In Forrest, S., ed.: 6th ICGA, Morgan Kaufmann (1993) 155–162
13. Mühlenbein, H., Schomish, M., Born, J.: The parallel genetic algorithm as a function optimizer. Parallel Computing **17** (1991) 619–632
14. Manderick, B., Spiessens, P.: Fine-grained parallel genetic algorithm. In: 3rd ICGA. (1989) 428–433
15. Giacobini, M., Alba, E., Tomassini, M.: Selection intensity in asynchronous cellular evolutionary algorithms. In: GECCO, Springer Verlag (2003) 955–966
16. Schaffer, J., Eshelman, L.: On crossover as an evolutionary viable strategy. In: 4th ICGA, Morgan Kaufmann (1991) 61–68
17. Mühlenbein, H., Schlierkamp-Voosen, D.: The science of breeding and its application to the breeder genetic algorithm (BGA). Evol. Comp. **1** (1993) 335–360
18. Mahnig, T., Mühlenbein, H.: Comparing the adaptive Boltzmann selection schedule SDS to truncation selection. In: CIMAF. (1999) 121–128
19. Jong, K.D., Potter, M., Spears, W.: Using problem generators to explore the effects of epistasis. In: 7th ICGA, Morgan Kaufman (1997) 338–345
20. Stinson, D.: An Introduction to the Design and Analysis of Algorithms. The Charles Babbage Research Center, Canada (1985 (second edition, 1987))

A Memetic Approach to Golomb Rulers

Carlos Cotta[1], Iván Dotú[2], Antonio J. Fernández[1], and Pascal Van Hentenryck[3]

[1] Dpto. de Lenguajes y Ciencias de la Computación, Universidad de Málaga, Spain
[2] Dpto. de Ingeniería Informática, Universidad Autónoma de Madrid, Spain
[3] Brown University, Box 1910, Providence, RI 02912
{ccottap, afdez}@lcc.uma.es, ivan.dotu@uam.es, pvh@cs.brown.edu

Abstract. Finding Golomb rulers is an extremely challenging optimization problem with many practical applications. This problem has been approached by a variety of search methods in recent years. We consider in this work a hybrid evolutionary algorithm that incorporates ideas from greedy randomized adaptive search procedures (GRASP), tabu-based local search methods (TS) and scatter search (SS). In particular, GRASP and TS are embedded into a SS algorithm to serve as initialization and restarting methods for the population and as improvement technique respectively. The resulting memetic algorithm significantly outperforms earlier approaches (including other hybrid EAs, as well as hybridizations of local search and constraint programming), finding optimal rulers where the mentioned techniques failed.

1 Introduction

Golomb Rulers [1,2] are a class of undirected graphs that, unlike usual rulers, measure more discrete lengths than the number of marks they carry. More formally, a n-mark Golomb ruler is an ordered sequence of n distinct nonnegative integers $\langle m_1, \ldots, m_n \rangle$ $(m_i < m_{i+1})$ such that all distances $m_j - m_i$ $(1 \leqslant i < j \leqslant n)$ are distinct. Each integer m_i corresponds to a mark on the ruler and the *length* of the ruler is the difference $m_n - m_1$. By convention, the first mark m_1 can be placed in position 0, in which case the length is given by m_n.

The particularity of Golomb Rulers that on any given ruler, all differences between pairs of marks are unique makes them really interesting in many practical applications (cf. [3,4]). It turns out that finding optimal or near-optimal Golomb rulers (a n-mark Golomb ruler is optimal if there exists no n-mark Golomb ruler of smaller length) is an extremely challenging combinatorial problem. The search for an optimal 19-marks Golomb ruler took approximately 36,200 CPU hours on a Sun Sparc workstation using a very specialized algorithm [5]. Optimal solutions for 20 up to 24 marks were obtained by massive parallelism projects, taking from several months up to several years for each of those instances [4,6,7,8]. Finding optimal Golomb rulers has thus become a standard benchmark to evaluate and compare a variety of search techniques. In particular, evolutionary algorithms (EAs), constraint programming (CP), local search (LS), and their hybridizations have all been applied to this problem (e.g., [3,9,10,11,12,13]).

T.P. Runarsson et al. (Eds.): PPSN IX, LNCS 4193, pp. 252–261, 2006.

In this paper, we present a hybrid EA designed to find optimal or near-optimal Golomb Rulers. This algorithm makes use of both an indirect approach and a direct approach in different stages of the search. More specifically, the indirect approach is used in the phases of initialization and restarting of the population and takes ideas borrowed from the GRASP-based evolutionary approach published in [9]. The direct approach is considered in the stages of recombination and local improvement; particularly, the local improvement method is based on the tabu search (TS) algorithm described in [14]. Experimental results show that this algorithm succeeds where other evolutionary algorithms did not. OGRs up to 15 marks (included) can now be found. Moreover, the algorithm produces Golomb rulers for 16 marks that are very close to the optimal value (i.e., 1.1% far), thus significantly improving the results reported in the EA literature.

2 Related Work

Two main approaches can be essentially considered for tackling the OGR problem with EAs. The first one is the *direct* approach, in which the EA conducts the search in the space $\mathcal{S}_G$ of all possible Golomb rulers. The second one is the *indirect* approach, in which an auxiliary $\mathcal{S}_{aux}$ space is used by the EA. In this latter case, a decoder [15] must be utilized in order to perform the $\mathcal{S}_{aux} \longrightarrow \mathcal{S}_G$ mapping. Examples of the former (direct) approach are the works of Soliday *et al.* [13], and Feeney [3]. As to the latter (indirect) approach, we can cite the work by Pereira *et al.* [10] (based on the notion of random-keys [16]), and Cotta and Fernández [9] (based on ideas from GRASP [17]). This latter paper is particularly interesting since generalizations of the core idea presented there have been used in this work. To be precise, the key idea was using a problem-aware procedure (inspired in GRASP) to perform the genotype-to-phenotype mapping. This method ensured the generation of feasible solutions, and was shown to outperform other previous approaches.

Another very relevant proposal has been recently presented by Dotú and Van Hentenryck [14]. They used a hybrid evolutionary algorithm (GROHEA) that incorporated a tabu-search algorithm for mutation. The basic idea was to optimize the length of the rulers indirectly by solving a sequence of feasibility problems (starting from an upper bound l and producing a sequence of rulers of length $l_1 > l_2 > \ldots > l_i > \ldots$). This algorithm performed very efficiently and was able to find OGRs for up to 14 marks. Notice that this method requires an estimated initial upper bound, something that clearly favored its efficiency. At any rate, GROHEA outperforms earlier approaches and will be used to benchmark our algorithm.

3 Scatter Search for the OGR Problem

Scatter search (SS) is a metaheuristic based on population-based search whose origin can be traced back to the 1970s in the context of combining decision rules and problem constraints [18]. Among the salient features of SS we can cite the absence of biological motivation, and the emphasis put in the use of problem-aware mechanisms, such as specialized recombination procedures, and LS techniques. In a striking example of convergent evolution, these are also distinctive features of memetic algorithms (MAs) [19]. Indeed, although SS evolved independently from MAs, SS can be regarded with hindsight as a particular case of MA (or, at least, as an alternative formulation of a common underlying paradigm). There is just one remarkable methodological difference between mainstream versions of SS and MAs: unlike other population-based approaches, SS relies more on deterministic strategies rather than on randomization. At any rate, this general methodological principle is flexible. This is particularly the case in our approach, in which we use a non-deterministic component within our algorithm. For this reason, we will use the terms MA and SS interchangeably in the context of this work. In the following we will describe each of the components of our algorithm.

3.1 Diversification Generation Method

The diversification generation method serves two purposes in the SS algorithm considered: it is used for generating the initial population from which the reference set will be initially extracted, and it is utilized for refreshing the reference set whenever a restart is needed.

The generation of new solutions is performed by using a randomized procedure that tries to generate diverse solutions. The basic method utilizes the GRASP-decoding techniques introduced in [9]. Solutions are incrementally constructed as follows: in the initial step, only mark $m_1 = 0$ is placed; subsequently, at each step i, an ordered list is built using the n first integers $l_1, \cdots, l_n$ such that placing a new mark $m_i = m_{i-1} + l_j$, $1 \leqslant j \leqslant n$, would result in a feasible Golomb ruler. A random element is drawn from this list, and used to place mark m_i. This process is iterated until all marks have been placed. Notice that the outcome is a feasible solution.

A variant of this process is used in subsequent invocations to this method for refreshing the population. This variant is related to an additional dynamic constraint that is imposed in the algorithm: in any solution, it must hold that $m_n < L$, where L is the length of the best feasible Golomb ruler found so far. To fulfill this constraint, new solutions are constructed by generating two feasible rules following the procedure described before, and submitting them to the combination method (see Sect. 3.3), which guarantees compliance with the mentioned constraint.

3.2 Local Improvement Method

The improvement method is responsible for enhancing raw solutions produced by the diversification generation method, or by the solution combination method. In this case, improvement is achieved via the use of a tabu-search algorithm. This TS algorithm works on tentative solutions that may be infeasible, i.e., there may exist some repeated distances between marks. The goal of the algorithm is precisely to turn infeasible rulers into feasible ones, respecting the dynamic constraint $m_n < L$. Whenever this is achieved, a new incumbent solution is obviously found.

To guide the search, the algorithm uses a notion of constraint violations on the distances. The violation $v_\sigma(d)$ of a distance d in a n-mark ruler σ is the number of times distance d appears between two marks in the ruler σ beyond its allowed occurrences, i.e.,

$$v_\sigma(d) = \left(\sum_{1 \leqslant i < j \leqslant n} 1(d_{ij} = d) \right) - 1 \tag{1}$$

where $d_{ij} = m_j - m_i$, and $1(\texttt{TRUE}) = 1$ and $1(\texttt{FALSE}) = 0$. The overall violation $v(\sigma)$ of a n-mark ruler σ is simply the sum of the violations of its distances d, i.e., $v(\sigma) = \sum_{d \in D} v_\sigma(d)$, where $D = \{d_{ij} \mid 1 \leqslant i < j \leqslant n\}$.

A move in the local search consists of changing the value of a single mark. Since marks are ordered, a mark m_x can only take a value in the interval $I_\sigma(x) = [m_{x-1}+1, m_{x+1}-1]$. As a consequence, the set of possible moves is $\mathcal{M}(\sigma) = \{(x,p) \mid (1 < x < n) \wedge (p \in I_\sigma(x))\}$. Observe that m_1 is fixed to 0, and m_n is not allowed to grow. To prevent cycling, a tabu list of movements is kept. The list stores triplets $\langle x, p, i \rangle$, where x is a mark, p is a possible position for mark x, and i represents the first iteration where mark x can be assigned to p again. The tabu tenure, i.e., the number of iterations (x, p) stays in the list, is dynamic and randomly generated in the interval $[4, 100]$. For a ruler σ and an iteration k, the set of legal moves is thus defined as

$$\mathcal{M}^+(\sigma, k) = \{(x,p) \in \mathcal{M}(\sigma) \mid \neg \mathit{tabu}(x,p,k)\}. \tag{2}$$

where $\mathit{tabu}(x,p,k)$ holds if the assignment $m_x \leftarrow p$ is tabu at iteration k. The tabu status can be overridden whenever an assignment reduces the smallest number of violations found so far. Thus, if σ^* is the ruler with the smallest number of violations found so far, the neighborhood also includes the moves

$$\mathcal{M}^*(\sigma, \sigma^*) = \{(x,p) \in \mathcal{M}(\sigma) \mid v(\sigma[m_x \leftarrow p]) < v(\sigma^*)\} \tag{3}$$

where $\sigma[m_x \leftarrow p]$ denotes the ruler σ where variable m_x is assigned to p. To intensify the search, the current solution is reinitialized to the initial ruler σ_0 (in the current TS run) whenever no improvement in the number of violations took place for *maxStable* iterations. The algorithm returns the best solution σ^* found. Fig. 1 shows the complete pseudocode of the TS algorithm.

3.3 Solution Combination Method

The combination of solutions is performed using a procedure that bears some resemblance with the GRASP-decoding mentioned in Sect. 3.1. There are some important differences though: firstly, the procedure is fully deterministic; secondly, the solution produced by the method is entirely composed of marks taken

TS(σ_0)
    tabu $\leftarrow \{\}$;
    $\sigma^* \leftarrow \sigma_0$; $\sigma \leftarrow \sigma_0$;
    $k \leftarrow 0$;
    $s \leftarrow 0$;
    while $k \leqslant maxIt$ & $v(\sigma) > 0$ **do**
        select $(x,p) \in \mathcal{M}^+(\sigma,k) \cup \mathcal{M}^*(\sigma,\sigma^*)$ **minimizing** $v(\sigma[m_x \leftarrow p])$;
        $\tau \leftarrow$ RANDOM([4,100]);
        tabu $\leftarrow$ *tabu* $\cup \{\langle x,p,k+\tau\rangle\}$;
        $\sigma \leftarrow \sigma[m_x \leftarrow p]$;
        if $v(\sigma) < v(\sigma^*)$ **then**
            $\sigma^* \leftarrow \sigma$;
            $s \leftarrow 0$;
        else if $s > maxStable$ **then**
            $\sigma \leftarrow \sigma_0$;
            $s \leftarrow 0$;
            tabu $\leftarrow \{\}$;
        else
            $s{+}{+}$;
        $k{+}{+}$;
    return σ^*;

Fig. 1. Pseudocode of the TS algorithm

from either of the parents; finally, the method ensures that the $m_n < L$ constraint is fulfilled.

The combination method begins by building a list $\mathcal{L}$ of all marks x present in either of the parents, such that $x < L$ [1]. Then, starting from $m_1 = 0$, a new mark x is chosen at each step i such that (i) $m_{i-1} < x$, (ii) there exist $n-i$ marks greater than x in $\mathcal{L}$, and (iii) a local quality criterion is optimized. This latter criterion is minimizing $\sum_{j=1}^{i-1} v_\sigma(x-m_j)^2 + (x - m_{i-1})$, where σ is the partial ruler. This expression involves minimizing the number of constraints violated when placing the new mark, as well as the subsequent increase in length of the ruler. The first term is squared to raise its priority in the decision-making.

3.4 Subset Generation and Reference Set Update

This subset generation method creates the groups of solutions that will undergo combination. The combination method used is in principle generalizable to an arbitrary number of parents, but we have considered the standard two-parent recombination. Hence the subset generation method has to form pairs of solutions. This is done exhaustively, producing all possible pairs. It must be noted that since the combination method utilized is deterministic, it does not make

[1] It might happen that the number of such marks is not enough to build a new ruler. In that case, a dummy solution with length ∞ (the worst possible value) is returned.

sense to combine again pairs of solutions that were already coupled before. The algorithm keeps track of this fact to avoid repeating computations.

As to the reference set update method, it must produce the reference set for the next step by using the current reference set and the newly produced offspring (or by using the initial population generated by diversification at the beginning of the run or after a restart). Several strategies are possible. Quality is an obvious criterion to determine whether a solution can gain membership to the reference set: if a new solution is better than the worst existing solution, the latter is replaced by the former. In the OGR, we consider a solution x is better than a solution y if the former violates less constraints, or violates the same number of constraints but has a lower length. It is also possible to gain membership of the reference set via diversity. To do so, a subset of *diverse* solutions (i.e., *distant* solutions to the remaining high-quality solutions in the set – an appropriate definition of a distance measure is needed for this purpose) is kept in the reference set, and updated whenever a new solution improves the diversity criterion.

If at a certain iteration of the algorithm no update of the reference set takes place, the current population is considered stagnated, and the restart method is invoked[2]. This method works as follows: let μ be the size of the reference set; the best solution in the reference set is preserved, $\lambda = \mu(\mu - 1)/2$ solutions are generated using the diversification generation method and the improvement method, and the best $\mu - 1$ out of these λ solutions are picked and inserted in the reference set.

4 Experimental Results

To evaluate our memetic approach, a set of experiments for problem sizes ranging from 10 marks up to 16 marks has been realized. In all the experiments, the maximum number of iterations for the tabu search was set to 10,000, the size of the population and reference set was 190 and 20 respectively, and the arity of the combination method was 2. The reference set is only updated on the basis of the quality criterion. One of the key points in the experimentation has been analyzing the influence of the local search strategy with respect to the population-based component. To this end, we have experimented with partial Lamarckism [20], that is, applying the local improvement method just on a fraction of the members of the population. To be precise, we have considered a probability p_{ts} for applying LS to each solution. The values $p_{ts} \in \{0.1, 0.2, 0.4, 0.6, 0.8, 1.0\}$ have been considered. All algorithms were run 20 times until an optimal solution was found, or a limit in the whole number of evaluations was exceeded. This number of evaluations was set so as to allow a fixed average number e of LS invocations ($e = 10,000$ TS runs). Thus, the number of evaluations was limited in each of the instances to e/p_{ts}. This is a fair measure since the computational cost is dominated by the number of TS invocations.

[2] Notice that the TS method used for local improvement is not deterministic. Thus, it might be possible that further applications of TS on the stagnated population resulted in an improvement. However, due to the computational cost of this process, it is advisable to simply restart.

Table 1. Relative distances to optimum for different probabilities of the MA and the algorithms GROHEA and HGRASP. Globally best results (resp. globally best median results) for each instance size are shown in boldface (resp. underlined). Results of HGRASP and GROHEA are not available for 10 marks.

		number of marks						
		10	11	12	13	14	15	16
HGRASP	Best	N/A	2.8	10.6	4.7	6.3	7.3	6.8
	Median	N/A	2.8	11.8	7.5	9.4	11.9	11.3
GROHEA	Best	N/A	**0**	**0**	**0**	3.1	4.6	5.6
	Median	N/A	0	7.1	5.6	7.1	8.6	10.2
MA1.0	Best	**0**	**0**	**0**	**0**	1.6	**0**	4.0
	Median	0	0	0	0	2.4	4.0	6.2
MA0.8	Best	**0**	**0**	**0**	**0**	0.8	1.3	2.3
	Median	0	0	0	0	1.6	3.3	5.6
MA0.6	Best	**0**	**0**	**0**	**0**	0.8	**0**	2.8
	Median	0	0	0	0	1.6	4.0	6.2
MA0.4	Best	**0**	**0**	**0**	**0**	**0**	1.3	**1.1**
	Median	0	0	0	0	1.6	4.0	5.6
MA0.2	Best	**0**	**0**	**0**	**0**	**0**	0.7	3.4
	Median	0	0	0	0	1.6	4.0	6.2
MA0.1	Best	**0**	**0**	**0**	**0**	**0**	0.7	3.4
	Median	0	0	0	0	1.6	3.3	5.6

Table 1 reports the experimental results for the different instances considered. Row MAxx corresponds to the execution of the MA with a local improvement rate of $p_{ts} = xx$. The table reports the relative distance (percentage) to the known optimum for the best and median solutions obtained. The table also shows the results obtained by the algorithms described in [9] (HGRASP) and [14] (GROHEA). Algorithm HGRASP is grounded on the evolutionary use of the GRASP-based solution generation method used in the basic diversification method of our algorithm. As to GROHEA, it provides the best results reported in the literature for this problem via a population-based approach, and therefore it is the benchmark reference for our algorithm. Specifically for this latter algorithm, as reported in [14], the maximum number of iterations for the tabu search was also $10,000$, the size of the population was 50, and the probabilities p_m and p_X were both set to 0.6. Both algorithms (GROHEA and HGRASP) were run 30 times for each ruler.

The results are particularly impressive. Firstly, observe that our memetic algorithm systematically finds optimal rulers for up to 13 marks. GROHEA is also capable of eventually finding some optimal solutions for these instance sizes, but notice that the median values are drastically improved in the MA. In fact, the median values obtained by the MA for these instances correspond exactly to their optimal solutions. Comparatively, the results are even better in larger OGR instances: our MA can find optimal ORGs even for 14 and 15 marks, and computes high-quality near-optimal solutions for 16 (i.e., 1.1% from the optimum). These

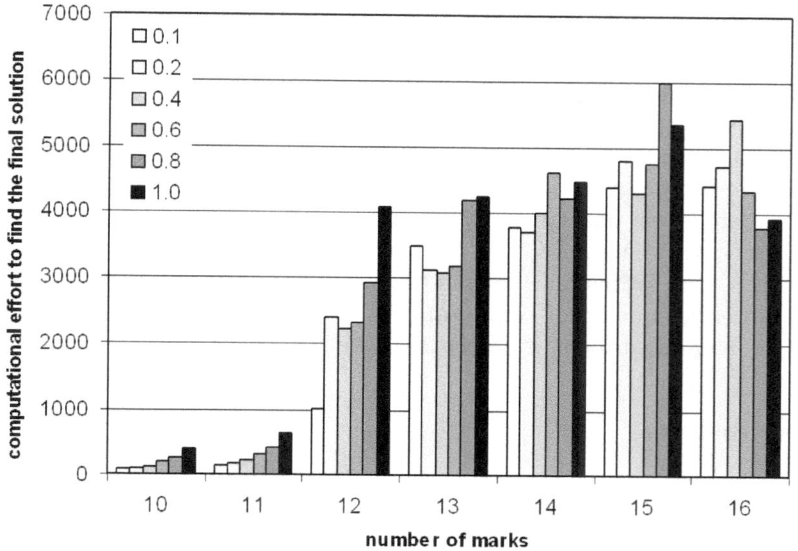

	0.1	0.2	0.4	0.6	0.8	1.0
0.1	•	− + + − − − −	+ + + − − − −	+ + + − − − −	+ + + − − − −	+ + + − − − −
0.2	− + + − − − −	•	− − − − − − −	+ + − − − − −	+ + − − − − −	+ + + − − − −
0.4	+ + + − − − −	− − − − − − −	•	+ + − − − − −	+ − − − − − +	+ + − − − − −
0.6	+ + + − − − −	+ + − − − − −	+ + − − − − −	•	+ + − − − − −	+ + + − − − −
0.8	+ + + − − − −	+ + − − − − −	+ − − − − − +	+ + − − − − −	•	+ + − − − − −
1.0	+ + + − − − −	+ + + − − − −	+ + − − − − −	+ + + − − − −	+ + − − − − −	•

Fig. 2. (Top) Computational effort (measured in number of TS invocations) to find the best solution. (Bottom) Statistical comparison of the computation effort. In each cell, the results ('+'=significant, '−'=non-significant) correspond from left to right to instance sizes from 10 up to 16.

results clearly outperform GROHEA; indeed, the latter cannot provide optimal values for instance sizes larger than 14 marks. Moreover, all MAxx significantly improve the median values obtained by GROHEA on the larger instances of the problem. These results clearly indicate the potential of hybrid EAs for finding optimal and near-optimal rulers.

We have also conducted statistical tests to ascertain whether there are significant performance differences between the different LS application rates. This has been done using a non-parametric Wilcoxon ranksum test (results are not normally distributed). Except in three head-to-head comparisons for 14 marks (p_{ts} = 1.0 vs p_{ts} = 0.8 and p_{ts} = 0.1, and p_{ts} = 0.4 vs p_{ts} = 0.1), there is no statistically significant difference (at the standard 0.05 level) in any instance size for the different values of p_{ts}. While this is consistent with the fact that the average number of TS invocations is constant, it raises the issue of whether the associated computational cost is the same or not. The answer to this question can be seen in Fig. 2. As expected, the computational cost increases with the size of the problem. Quite interestingly, the average cost decreases for 16 marks.

This behavior owes to the higher difficulty of the problem for this latter size: the algorithm quickly reaches a near-optimal value (a remarkable result), and then stagnates (longer runs would be required to improve the solutions from that point on). The table at the bottom of Fig. 2 shows the outcome of the statistical comparison between the computational cost of the MAxx for a given instance size. As it can be seen, the differences are almost always significant for the lower range of sizes, and progressively become non-significant as the size increases. For 16 marks, there is just one case of statistically significant difference of computational cost ($p_{ts} = 0.4$ vs $p_{ts} = 0.8$). Since the small values of p_{ts} imply a lower computational cost for instance sizes in the low range, and there is no significant difference in either quality or computational cost with respect to higher values of p_{ts} in the larger instances, it seems that values $p_{ts} \in \{0.1, 0.2\}$ are advisable.

5 Conclusions

We have presented a memetic approach for the optimal Golomb ruler problem. The MA combines, in different stages of the algorithm, a GRASP-like procedure (for diversification and recombination) and tabu search (for local improvement) within the general template of scatter search. The results of the MA have been particularly good, clearly outperforming other state-of-the-art evolutionary approaches for this problem. One of the aspects on which we have focused is the influence of the LS component. We have shown that lower rates of Lamarckism achieve the best tradeoff between computational cost and solution quality.

We are currently exploring alternatives for some of the operators used in our algorithm. Preliminary experiments with multi-tier reference sets –i.e., including a diversity section– do not indicate significant performance changes. A deeper analysis is nevertheless required here. In particular, it is essential that the particular distance measure used to characterize diversity correlates well with the topology of the search landscape induced by the reproductive operators. Related to this issue, we plan to test alternative recombination methods based on exhaustive techniques used in constraint programming. Defining appropriate distance measures in this context (and indeed, checking their usefulness in practice) will be the subsequent step.

Acknowledgements. This work was partially supported by Spanish MCyT under contracts TIN2004-7943-C04-01 and TIN2005-08818-C04-01.

References

1. Babcock, W.: Intermodulation interference in radio systems. Bell Systems Technical Journal (1953) 63–73
2. Bloom, G., Golomb, S.: Aplications of numbered undirected graphs. Proceedings of the IEEE **65** (1977) 562–570
3. Feeney, B.: Determining optimum and near-optimum golomb rulers using genetic algorithms. Master thesis, Computer Science, University College Cork (2003)

4. Rankin, W.: Optimal golomb rulers: An exhaustive parallel search implementation. Master thesis, Duke University Electrical Engineering Dept., Durham, NC (1993)
5. Dollas, A., Rankin, W.T., McCracken, D.: A new algorithm for Golomb ruler derivation and proof of the 19 mark ruler. IEEE Transactions on Information Theory **44** (1998) 379–382
6. Garry, M., Vanderschel, D., et al.: In search of the optimal 20, 21 & 22 mark golomb rulers. GVANT project, `http://members.aol.com/golomb20/index.html` (1999)
7. Shearer, J.B.: Golomb ruler table. Mathematics Department, IBM Research, `http://www.research.ibm.com/people/s/shearer/grtab.html` (2001)
8. Schneider, W.: Golomb rulers. MATHEWS: The Archive of Recreational Mathematics, `http://www.wschnei.de/number-theory/golomb-rulers.html` (2002)
9. Cotta, C., Fernández, A.: A hybrid GRASP - evolutionary algorithm approach to Golomb ruler search. In Yao, X., et al., eds.: Parallel Problem Solving From Nature VIII. Number 3242 in Lecture Notes in Computer Science, Birmingham, UK, Springer (2004) 481–490
10. Pereira, F., Tavares, J., Costa, E.: Golomb rulers: The advantage of evolution. In Moura-Pires, F., Abreu, S., eds.: Progress in Artificial Intelligence, 11th Portuguese Conference on Artificial Intelligence. Number 2902 in Lecture Notes in Computer Science, Berlin Heidelberg, Springer-Verlag (2003) 29–42
11. Prestwich, S.: Trading completeness for scalability: Hybrid search for cliques and rulers. In: Third International Workshop on the Integration of AI and OR Techniques in Constraint Programming for Combinatorial Optimization Problems CPAIOR 2001, Ashford, Kent, England (2001)
12. Smith, B., Stergiou, K., Walsh, T.: Modelling the golomb ruler problem (1999)
13. Soliday, S., Homaifar, A., Lebby, G.: Genetic algorithm approach to the search for golomb rulers. In Eshelman, L., ed.: 6th International Conference on Genetic Algorithms (ICGA'95), Pittsburgh, PA, USA, Morgan Kaufmann (1995) 528–535
14. Dotú, I., Hentenryck, P.V.: A simple hybrid evolutionary algorithm for finding golomb rulers. In et. al., D.C., ed.: Congress on Evolutionary Computation Conference (CEC2005). Volume 3., Edinburgh, Scotland, IEEE (2005) 2018–2023
15. Koziel, S., Michalewicz, Z.: A decoder-based evolutionary algorithm for constrained parameter optimization problems. In Bäeck, T., Eiben, A., Schoenauer, M., Schwefel, H.P., eds.: Parallel Problem Solving from Nature V. Volume 1498 of Lecture Notes in Computer Science. Springer-Verlag, Berlin Heidelberg (1998) 231–240
16. Bean, J.: Genetic algorithms and random keys for sequencing and optimization. ORSA Journal on Computing **6** (1994) 154–160
17. Resende, M., Ribeiro, C.: Greedy randomized adaptive search procedures. In Glover, F., Kochenberger, G., eds.: Handbook of Metaheuristics. Kluwer Academic Publishers, Boston MA (2003) 219–249
18. Laguna, M., Martí, R.: Scatter Search. Methodology and Implementations in C. Kluwer Academic Publishers, Boston MA (2003)
19. Moscato, P., Cotta, C.: A gentle introduction to memetic algorithms. In Glover, F., Kochenberger, G., eds.: Handbook of Metaheuristics. Kluwer Academic Publishers, Boston MA (2003) 105–144
20. Houck, C., Joines, J., Kay, M., Wilson, J.: Empirical investigation of the benefits of partial lamarckianism. Evolutionary Computation **5** (1997) 31–60

Some Notes on (Mem)Brane Computation*

Nadia Busi[1] and Miguel A. Gutiérrez-Naranjo[2]

[1] Dipartimento di Scienze dell'Informazione - Università di Bologna
Mura Anteo Zamboni 7, I-40127 Bologna, Italy
busi@cs.unibo.it

[2] Dpto. de Ciencias de la Computación e Inteligencia Artificial
Universidad de Sevilla
Avda. Reina Mercedes s/n, 41012, Sevilla, Spain
magutier@us.es

Abstract. Membrane Computing and Brane Calculi are two recent computational paradigms in the framework of Natural Computing. They are based on the study of the structure and functioning of living cells as living organisms able to process and generate information. In this paper we give a short introduction to both areas and point out some open research lines.

1 Introduction

Natural Computing studies new computational paradigms inspired from various well known natural phenomena in physics, chemistry and biology. This paper is devoted to a new field in Natural Computing: The study of the structure and functioning of cells as living organisms able to process and generate information.

The starting point is the fact that the cell is the smallest living thing, and at the same time it is a marvellous machinery, with a complex structure, an intricate inner activity self-regulated in a quite efficient way. Assuming that cells can be seen as computational devices, two different branches of Natural Computing can be found in the literature: *Membrane Computing* and *Brane Calculi*.

The notions of membrane investigated in these new paradigms of computation are abstract entities which try to mimic some features of the functioning of membranes in living cells. The basic function of biological membranes is to *define compartments* and to *relate compartments to their environment*, including neighbouring compartments. The currently accepted model of the membrane structure is the so-called *fluid-mosaic model*, proposed in 1972 by S. Singer and G. Nicholson. According to this model, a membrane is a phospholipid bilayer in which protein molecules (as well as other molecules) are totally or partially embedded.

The first paradigm of computation we present is *Membrane Computing*. It was introduced by Gh. Păun in [22] under the assumption that the processes

* The second author acknowledges the support by project TIN2005-09345-C04-01 of Ministerio de Educación y Ciencia of Spain, cofinanced by FEDER funds, and by the Project of Excellence TIC-581 of the Junta de Andalucía.

T.P. Runarsson et al. (Eds.): PPSN IX, LNCS 4193, pp. 262–271, 2006.

taking place in the compartmental structure of a living cell can be interpreted as computations. The devices of this model are called *P systems*. Roughly speaking, a P system consists of a membrane structure, in the compartments of which one places multisets of objects which evolve according to given rules in a synchronous nondeterministic maximally parallel manner.

The second one, *Brane Calculi* was introduced by L. Cardelli in [9] on the assumption that in living cells membranes are not merely containers, but they are highly dynamic entities that actively participate in the cell life. In this way, computation happens on the membrane, not inside it.

The paper is organised as follows: Section 2 is devoted to a brief presentation of Membrane Computing. In a similar way, a short introduction to Brane Calculi is presented in Section 3. The paper ends with some final remarks.

2 Membrane Computing

Membrane Computing[1] starts with the explicit goal of abstracting computing models from the *structure* and the *functioning* of a living cell. The literature of the domain is very large (already in 2003, Thompson Institute for Scientific Information, ISI, has qualified the initial paper as "fast breaking" and the domain as "emergent research front in computer science" – see `http://esi-topics.com`) and it progresses rather rapidly, so that the presentation here is quite general.

The basic idea is to consider a distributed and parallel computing device, structured like a cell, by means of a hierarchical arrangement of membranes which delimit compartments where various chemicals (we call them *objects*) evolve according to local reaction rules. The objects can be described by symbols or by strings of symbols from a given alphabet. These objects can also pass through membranes, under the control of specific rules. Because the chemicals from the compartments of a cell are swimming in an aqueous solution, the data structure we consider is that of a *multiset* – a set with multiplicities associated with its elements. Also, in close analogy with what happens in a cell, the reaction rules are applied in a parallel manner. This means that in each computational step a maximal (multi)set of nondeterministically chosen rules is applied.

The *membrane structure* of a P system is a hierarchical arrangement of membranes (understood as three dimensional vesicles), embedded in a *skin* membrane, the one which separates the system from its *environment*. A membrane without any membrane inside is called *elementary*. Each membrane defines a *region*. For an elementary membrane this is the space enclosed by it, while the region of a non-elementary membrane is the space in-between the membrane and the membranes directly included in it. Membranes are labelled. Each region contains a multiset of *objects*, and a set of (*evolution*) *rules*. The objects are represented by symbols from a given alphabet. Typically, an evolution rule from region r is of the form $ca \to cb_{in_j} d_{out} d_{here}$, and it "says" that a copy of the

[1] A layman-oriented introduction can be found in [30], a comprehensive presentation can be found in [23] and further updated bibliography in [34]. A presentation of applications can be found in [14].

object a, in the presence of a copy of the *catalyst* c (this is an object which is never modified, it only assists the evolution of other objects), is replaced by a copy of the object b and two copies of the object d. Moreover, the copy of b has to enter "immediately" the inner membrane of region r labelled by j (hence to enter region j), one copy of object d is sent out through the membrane of region r, and one copy of d remains in region r. Note that the considered evolution rule can be applied in the region r only if this region includes the membrane j.

Membrane systems are *synchronous*, in the sense that a global clock is assumed. In each time unit a transformation of a *configuration* of the system takes place by applying the rules in each region, in a *nondeterministic* and *maximally parallel manner*. This means that the objects to evolve and the rules governing this evolution are chosen in a nondeterministic way; this choice is "exhaustive" in the sense that, after the choice was made, no rule can be applied anymore in the same evolution step (there are not enough objects available anymore for any rule to be applied now – this is the maximality of application). In this way, one gets *transitions* between the configurations of the system. A maximal sequence of transitions is called a *computation*. A configuration is *halting* if no rule is applicable in any region. A computation is *halting* if it reaches a halting configuration. The *result* of a (halting) computation is the *number* of objects sent (through the skin membrane) to the environment during the computation.

Many variants/extensions of this very basic model sketched above are discussed in the literature.

2.1 Variants of the Basic Model

Here we will briefly mention a few variants of the basic model. For instance, there are a number of ways of weakening the programming power provided by in_j: to only indicate *in* (an object associated with this command has to enter any adjacently lower membrane; the choice of a membrane to enter is nondeterministic), to associate *electrical charges* both with objects and with membranes (a polarised object will enter the region of any adjacently lower membrane of the opposite polarisation; the polarisation of objects and of membranes may change during the computation).

Coming closer to the trans-membrane transfer of molecules, we can consider purely communicative systems, based on the three classes of such transfer known in the biology of membranes: *uniport*, *symport*, and *antiport*. Symport refers to the transport where two molecules pass together through a membrane in the same direction, antiport refers to the transport where two molecules pass through a membrane simultaneously, but in opposite directions, while the case when a molecule does not need a "partner" for a passage is referred to as uniport.

Another important extension is to consider a priority relation among rules. Furthermore, we can have rules for handling membranes (creating, destroying, dividing, merging, etc.), the rules can have promoters or inhibitors, their use can be regulated by a priority relation, the permeability of membranes can be controlled by the used rules and so on and so forth, either with a biological or with a mathematical motivation. In short, we abstract as much as possible/necessary, in order to obtain a mathematical model which is intended to be (i) minimalistic (as elegant as possible, containing as restricted ingredients as possible), but (ii) without losing the biological inspiration (hence remaining as "realistic" as possible), with (iii) good computability properties (as *powerful* as possible and as *efficient* as possible).

2.2 Computational Power and Efficiency

Many classes of P systems, combining various ingredients described above, are capable of simulating Turing machines, hence they are *computationally complete.* Note that in the case when we deal with P systems which compute numbers, we consider Turing machines as number recognisers; in the case of string-objects we can obtain the family of languages which are recognised by Turing machines (the recursively enumerable languages). Always, the proofs of results of this type are constructive, and this has the important consequence from the computability point of view that we can get *universal* (hence *programmable*) P systems: starting from a universal Turing machine, we get an equivalent universal P system.

The computational power is one of the important questions to be dealt with when defining a new computing model. The other fundamental question concerns the computational *efficiency.*

One of the explicit goals of various branches of natural computing is to find ways to address computationally hard problems (typically, **NP**-complete problems) in order to solve them (in a strict sense or in a probabilistic sense) in a feasible (that is, in polynomial) time. The rules of a P system are used in parallel, that is, in each membrane all objects evolve simultaneously, and, in turn, at the level of the system all membranes evolve simultaneously. This is a good degree of parallelism, which, however, is not sufficient to devise polynomial time solutions to **NP**-complete problems (unless $\mathbf{P} = \mathbf{NP}$). However, biology suggests operations with membranes which, sometimes surprisingly, make possible polynomial (often linear) solutions to **NP**-complete problems. Among these operations, the most investigated so far in membrane computing have been membrane division and membrane creation.

We do not enter here into details, but we refer, e.g., to the chapter from [14] devoted to this topic. Anyway, these results are of a clear theoretical interest (new characterisations of the standard complexity classes were given, as well as a characterisation of the relation $\mathbf{P} = \mathbf{NP}$ problem, intriguing borderlines between efficiency and non-efficiency were found – with many challenging open problems still waiting to be considered).

2.3 Applications

As mentioned above, Membrane Computing was initiated having as primary goals computability in general, and Natural Computing in particular, without aiming to faithfully model biological facts in such a way as to provide a modelling framework for the use of biologists. However, after significantly developing at the theoretical level, the domain started to be useful for biological and medical applications.

For example, the modelling of some dynamical systems, where we are not interested in halting configurations, but in the evolution of the process itself (see [34] and the corresponding chapter from [14]).

Another important application field is the study of processes related to cancer. We only mention the simulation of p53 protein pathways control (the interaction between proteins p53 and MdM2) through a P system, as carried out by Y. Suzuki and his co-workers (details can be found in [14]), and the modelling of EGFR (epidermal growth factor receptor) signalling network [31].

A very promising application is the study of approximate algorithms for hard optimisation problems (see [20]). These algorithms can be considered as high level (distributed and dynamically evolving their structure during the computation) evolutionary algorithms. The strategy has been checked for the travelling salesman problem and the results were more than encouraging.

Besides applications in biology, membrane computing has also been considered in other areas, such as computer graphics [33], cryptography [19], modelling in a uniform way parallel architectures [12], economics [25,26], etc. Some theoretical applications of (notions and ideas central to) P systems has also been considered in several papers: to artificial life [18], for simulating the photosynthesis [21], to linguistics [2], etc.

3 Brane Calculi

In recent years, the modeling and analysis of the biological matter has attracted the interest of the researchers in the area of concurrent process calculi.

Indeed, a network of biochemical cells can be seen as a computing machinery, made of processing agents which interact and cooperate to achieve a common goal. This informal description applies to concurrent system as well, hence it is natural to use techniques from the concurrency theory field to study the behaviour of biological cells.

Particularly promising is the use of process calculi, which are formalisms used to describe concurrent and mobile systems. Process calculi are equipped with a formal semantics describing their behaviour, and plenty of tools for the static and dynamic analysis of systems have been produced. These tools can therefore be used in the field of biological organisms, as well.

Starting from the seminal work of Buss and Fontana [17] on the use of a process calculus for the modeling of biological entities, the field has been fruitfully explored by other research groups, either by using existing calculi or by defining new, biologically inspired calculi (see, e.g., [29,28,13,32,15,27], just to mention a few).

Brane Calculi [9] are a family of process calculi proposed for modeling the behavior of biological membranes. In a process algebraic setting, Brane Calculi represent an evolution of BioAmbients [32], a variant of Mobile Ambients [10] based on a set of biologically inspired primitives of interaction. The main novelty of Brane calculi consists in the fact that the active entities reside on membranes, and not inside membranes.

While Membrane Computing is now a well-established research field, Brane Calculi can be considered to be a newborn, rather unexplored research field. In the following, we present a brief overview of the calculi, as well as of the main existing (and ongoing) works.

In [9] two basic instances of Brane Calculi are defined: the Phago/Exo/Pino (PEP) and the Mate/Bud/Drip (MBD) calculi.

The interaction primitives of PEP are inspired by *endocytosis* (the process of incorporating external material into a cell by engulfing it with the cell membrane) and *exocytosis* (the reverse process). A relevant feature of such primitives is *bitonality*, a property ensuring that there will never be a mixing of what is inside a membrane with what is outside, although external entities can be brought inside if safely wrapped by another membrane.

As endocytosis can engulf an arbitrary number of membranes, it turns out to be a rather uncontrollable process. Hence, it is replaced by two simpler operations: *phagocytosis*, that is engulfing of just one external membrane, and *pinocytosis*, that is engulfing zero external membranes.

The primitives of MBD are inspired by membrane fusion (mate) and fission (mito).

Because membrane fission is an uncontrollable process that can split a membrane at an arbitrary place, it is replaced by two simpler operations: *budding*, that is splitting off one internal membrane, and *dripping*, that consists in splitting off zero internal membranes.

An encoding of the MBD primitives in PEP is provided in [9].

In [6] we provided a stronger separation result between PEP and MBD.

On the one hand, we showed that PEP is a Turing powerful language, by providing a deterministic encoding of Random Access Machines (a Turing–equivalent formalism).

On the other hand, we proved that the existence of a divergent (i.e., infinite) computation is a decidable property in MBD. This means that there exist no divergence-preserving encoding of PEP in MBD.

After the introduction of the two basic brane calculi PEP and MBD, containing only membranes and membrane interaction primitives, in [9] the calculus is extended with small molecules, freely floating either in the external environment or inside a membrane, and with a molecule–membrane interaction primitive.

Biological membranes contain catalysts that can cause molecules, floating respectively inside and outside the membrane, to interact with each other without crossing the membrane. Membranes can bind molecules on either sides of their surface, and can release molecules on either sides of their surface. Usually, such an operation occurs in an atomic (all-or-nothing) way. The *bind&release* operation permits to simultaneously bind and release multiple molecules.

In [4] we extend the decidability result presented in [6] in two directions. On the one hand, we showed the decidability of divergence to the calculus with molecules, and with all the molecule–membrane and membrane–membrane interaction primitives, except the *phago* operation. On the other hand, we extended the decidability result on the full calculus without *phago* to other biologically relevant properties, such as, e.g., control state maintainability, inevitability and boundedness.

Control state maintainability can be used to check safety properties, such as, e.g., the fact that all the derivatives of a system contain at least one occurrence of a given molecule (or at least two occurrences of molecules belonging to some specified set). Inevitability can be used to check, e.g., if in all the computation a state is eventually reached that does contain no occurrences of a given molecule. Boundedness can be used to check if the number of membranes or of molecules can arbitrarily grow during the computation.

The decidability results in [4] are all constructive, i.e., they provide a computable procedure for deciding the systems properties. We plan to develop a tool for the animation and the analysis of Brane Calculus systems, also based on the results presented in this work.

We also recently started to use Brane Calculi for the modeling of biological pathways, and to apply the analysis techniques developed in [4]. A preliminary step in this direction is represented by [8], where the LDL Cholesterol Degradation Pathway [1] is modeled both in Brane Calculi and in Membrane Computing. Moreover, we also discuss an application of the analysis techniques developed in [4] to check behavioural properties of this pathway.

4 Final Remarks

In the last years, two branches of Natural Computing, *Membrane Computing* and *Brane Calculi*, have been developed, with a continuous afflux of new ideas, notions, problems, and with a series of applications, especially in modelling biological phenomena. No lab implementation was intended, and no such implementation is known to be planned for the near future[2].

Brane Calculi are somewhat dual to Membrane Computing, as they work with objects placed on membranes (corresponding to proteins attached to or embedded in the real membranes), with membranes operations controlled by these objects, and trying to stay as close to the biology as possible; also the tools and the goals are different – process algebra and systems biology, respectively.

A notable difference between Brane Calculi and P systems is concerned with the semantics of the two formalisms: whereas Brane Calculi are usually equipped with an interleaving, sequential semantics (each computational step consists of the execution of a single instruction), the usual semantics in membrane computing is based on maximal parallelism (a computational step is composed of a maximal set of independent interactions).

The fist attempt of bridging both research areas was made in [11] by the *fathers* of the disciplines L. Cardelli and Gh. Păun and as they point out Membrane Computing and Brane Calculi *have different objectives and develop in different directions. While Membrane Computing tries to abstract computing models, in*

[2] For Membrane Computing, several *simulators* have been implemented. We refer to [34] and to the corresponding chapter from [14] for details.

the Turing sense, from the structure and the functioning of the cell (...), Brane Calculi pay more attention to the fidelity to the biological reality (...).

In [11] a variant of P systems with the mate and drip operations – inspired by the corresponding primitives in Brane Calculi – is defined and proved to be Turing powerful. The *Projective Brane Calculus* [16] is a refinement of Brane Calculi, where the interaction primitives reside either on the external side or on the internal side of the membrane. In [3] a projective variant of the P systems, defined in [11], is defined and shown to be computationally complete.

In [5] the computational power of the MBD Brane Calculus equipped with two different semantics is investigated. The first semantics is the classical interleaving semantics of process calculi, whereas the second semantics is the maximal parallelism semantics used for Membrane Computing. An expressiveness gap has been found, thus confirming the intuition that the maximal parallelism semantics turns out to be a very powerful synchronization mechanism.

Recently, a bridge has been crossed the other way [7]. Instead of expressing Brane Calculi operations in terms of the Membrane Computing formalism, a problem is taken from Computer Science (the generation of the set $\{n^2 \mid n \geq 1\}$) and it is shown how it can be implemented both in Membrane Computing and in Brane Calculi.

In the last years, Membrane Computing has turned out to be a useful framework for building models with biological relevance, and the number of applications of this type is steadily increasing and becoming more and more advanced and elaborate.

This leads to considerations concerning the significance of membrane based calculi and systems (for biology, for mathematics, and for computing). The approach is clearly motivated from a mathematical point of view, not only because it is natural to (try to) model the cell computational behaviour, but also because the new computing model has a number of intrinsically interesting features. Examples of such features are: the use of multisets, the inherent parallelism, the possibility of devising computations which can solve exponential (intractable) problems in polynomial time (by making use of an exponential space created in a natural manner). At this moment, all these features are only *potentially* useful from a practical computational point of view. How should the implementation problem be approached? All these questions (and some more presented at [24]) should be explored in the future.

References

1. B. Alberts, A. Johnson, J. Lewis, M. Raff, K. Roberts and P. Walter. *Molecular Biology of The Cell.* Garland Science, 4th edition, (2002).
2. G. Bel Enguix and M.D. Jiménez-López. Linguistic Membrane Systems and Applications. In [14], 347–388.
3. D. Besozzi, N. Busi, G. Franco, R. Freund and Gh. Păun. Two Universality Results for (Mem)Brane Systems. In *Proceedings of the Fourth Brainstorming Week on Membrane Computing, Vol. I* (M.A. Gutiérrez Naranjo, Gh. Păun, A. Riscos-Núñez, F.J. Romero-Campero, eds.), Fénix Editora, (2006).

4. N. Busi. Deciding behavioural properties in Brane Calculi. *Computational Methods in System Biology 2006* (CMSB 2006), to appear.
5. N. Busi. On the Computational Power of the Mate/Bud/Drip Brane Calculus: Interleaving vs. Maximal Parallelism. Workshop on Membrane Computing 2005, LNCS 3850, (2006), 144–158.
6. N. Busi and R. Gorrieri. On the Computational Power of Brane Calculi. *Transactions on Computational Systems Biology*, LNCS, Springer, to appear. An extended abstract appeared in Proc. Computational Methods in System Biology 2005 (CMSB 2005).
7. N. Busi and M. A. Gutiérrez Naranjo. A Case Study in (Mem)Brane Computation: Generating $\{n^2 \mid n \geq 1\}$. In *Proceedings of the Fourth Brainstorming Week on Membrane Computing, Vol. I* (M.A. Gutiérrez Naranjo, Gh. Păun, A. Riscos-Núñez, F.J. Romero-Campero, eds.), Fénix Editora, (2006), 81–97.
8. N. Busi and C. Zandron. Modeling and Analysis of Biological Processes by Mem(Brane) Calculi and Systems. *Winter Simulation Conference 2006*, to appear.
9. L. Cardelli. Brane Calculi. In *Computational Methods in Systems Biology 2004* (V. Danos, V. Schachter, eds.), LNBI 3082, (2005) 257–278.
10. L.Cardelli and A.D. Gordon. Mobile Ambients. *Theoretical Computer Science*, 240(1), (2000), 177–213.
11. L. Cardelli and Gh.Păun. An Universality Result for a (Mem)Brane Calculus Based on Mate/Drip Operations. In *Cellular Computing (Complexity Aspects)* (M.A. Gutiérrez-Naranjo, Gh. Păun and M.J. Pérez-Jiménez, eds.) Fénix Editora, Sevilla, Spain, (2005). 75–94.
12. R. Ceterchi and M.J. Pérez-Jiménez. On simulating a class of parallel architectures. *International Journal of Foundations of Computer Science*, 17, 1 (2006), 91–110.
13. D. Chiargugi, M. Curti, P. Degano and R. Marangoni. VICE: A VIrtual CEll.In *Computational Methods in Systems Biology 2004* (V. Danos, V. Schachter, eds.), LNBI 3082, (2005), 207–220.
14. G. Ciobanu, Gh. Păun, M.J. Pérez–Jiménez, eds.: *Applications of Membrane Computing*. Springer, (2005).
15. V. Danos and C. Laneve. Core formal Molecular Biology. In *Programming Languages and Systems*, (P. Degano, ed.), LNCS 2618, (2003), 302–318.
16. V. Danos and S. Pradalier. Projective Brane Calculus. *Computational Methods in Systems Biology 2004* (V. Danos, V. Schachter, eds.), LNBI 3082, (2005), 134–148.
17. W.Fontana and L.W. Buss. The barrier of objects: from dynamical system to bounded organizations, Addison - Wesley, (1996), 56–116.
18. Suzuki, Y., Fujiwara, Y., Takabayashi, J. and Tanaka, H.: Artificial life applications of a class of P systems: Abstract rewriting systems on multisets. *Multiset Processing. Mathematical, Computer Science, and Molecular Computing Points of View* (C. Calude, Gh. Păun, G. Rozenberg, and A. Salomaa, eds.), LNCS 2235, (2001), 299–346.
19. S.N. Krishna and R. Rama: Breaking DES Using P Systems. *Theoretical Computer Sci.*, 299, 1-3 (2003), 495–508.
20. T.Y. Nishida. An Approximate Algorithm for NP-Complete Optimization Problems Expoiting P Systems. *Workshop on Uncertainty in Membrane Computing*, Palma de Mallorca, (2004), 185–192.
21. T.Y. Nishida. A Membrane Computing Model for Photosynthesis. In [14], 181–202.
22. Gh. Păun. Computing with membranes. *Journal of Computer and System Sciences*, 61, 1 (2000), 108–143.
23. Gh. Păun. Membrane Computing – An Introduction. Springer-Verlag, Berlin, (2002).

24. Gh. Păun. 2006 Research Topics in Membrane Computing. In *Proceedings of the Fourth Brainstorming Week on Membrane Computing, Vol. II* (C. Graciani Díaz, Gh. Păun, A. Romero-Jiménez, F. Sancho-Caparrini, eds.), Fénix Editora, (2006), 235–251.
25. Gh. Paun and R. Paun. Membrane Computing and Economics: Numerical P Systems. *Fundamenta Informaticae*, 73, 1-2, (2006), 213–227.
26. Gh. Paun and R. Paun. Membrane computing as a framework for modeling economic processes. Submitted, (2005).
27. C. Priami and P. Quaglia. Beta binders for biological interactions. *Computational Methods in Systems Biology 2004* (V. Danos, V. Schachter, eds.), LNBI 3082, Springer-Verlag, Berlin, (2005), 20–33.
28. C.Priami, A.Regev, W.Silverman and E.Shapiro. Application of a stochastic passing-name calculus to representation and simulation of molecular processes. Information Processing Letters, 80, (2001), 25-31.
29. A. Regev and E. Shapiro. Cells as computations. Nature, 419, 343, (2002).
30. Gh. Păun and M.J. Pérez-Jiménez: Recent computing models inspired from biology: DNA and membrane computing. *Theoria*, 18 (2003), 72–84.
31. M.J. Pérez–Jiménez and F.J. Romero–Campero. A Study of the Robustness of the EGFR Signalling Cascade Using Continuous Membrane Systems. In *Mechanisms, Symbols, and Models Underlying Cognition. First International Work-Conference on the Interplay between Natural and Artificial Computation*, IWINAC 2005 (J. Mira, J.R. Alvarez, eds.), LNCS 3561, Springer, Berlin, (2005), 268–278.
32. A. Regev, E. M. Panina, W. Silverman, L. Cardelli and E. Shapiro. BioAmbients: An Abstraction for Biological Compartments. *Theoretical Computer Science*, 325, 1, (2004), 141–167.
33. A. Romero-Jiménez, M.A. Gutiérrez-Naranjo and M.J. Pérez-Jiménez. Graphical Modelling of Higher Plants Using P Systems. Accepted paper at Seventh Workshop on Membrane Computing, Leiden (The Netherlands), July 2006.
34. The P Systems Website: `http://psystems. disco.unimib.it`.

Evolutionary Local Search for Designing Peer-to-Peer Overlay Topologies Based on Minimum Routing Cost Spanning Trees

Peter Merz and Steffen Wolf*

Department of Computer Science
University of Kaiserslautern, Germany
{pmerz, wolf}@informatik.uni-kl.de

Abstract. Finding overlay topologies for peer-to-peer networks on top of the Internet can be regarded as a network design problem, in which a graph with minimum communication costs is desired. An example of such a graph is a spanning tree connecting all nodes in the overlay. We present evolutionary algorithms incorporating local search for the minimum routing cost spanning tree problem in which the overall routing/communication cost is minimized. We present three types of local search for this problem as well as an evolutionary framework for finding (near)optimal solutions to the problem. Moreover, we present results from a fitness landscape analysis for the three types of local optima that reveal interesting properties of the problem data based on real measurements in the Internet. We demonstrate that our proposed algorithms find near optimum solutions reliably by comparing against a lower bound of the problem.

1 Introduction

Peer-to-peer (P2P) systems have become popular due to development of file-sharing applications like Gnutella [1,2], Kazaa or Bit-Torrent [3]. However, the P2P paradigm is useful in many other application scenarios such as Distributed Computing [4,5], Distributed Storage/Backup [6], or Distributed Database Systems [7]. An important aspect in the development of a P2P protocol is the design of the overlay topology. The topology defines which nodes are directly connected to each other. More formally, we can think of the topology as a graph, in which the nodes are networked computers and the edges are communication links between them. The goal of the design is to find a graph which is robust in respect to failures of nodes and links and/or which reduces the communication overhead and time within the network. In this paper, we concentrate on the latter by minimizing the routing and hence communication time between any pair of nodes in the network. Since the graph should be easy to maintain as well as to repair and routing algorithms should be simple, we focus on spanning trees.

* This work was partially supported by the Rhineland-Palatinate Cluster of Excellence 'Dependable Adaptive Systems and Mathematical Modelling'.

T.P. Runarsson et al. (Eds.): PPSN IX, LNCS 4193, pp. 272–281, 2006.

Since the forming of the topology is a self-organizing process, we are interested in distributed online algorithms for the network design problem. However, we concentrate in this paper on the offline case, where we search for the optimum topology given the global view on the network. The purpose of this approach is twofold. Firstly, the offline algorithms provide a basis for analyzing the performance of online algorithms. Secondly, by analyzing local search algorithms we gain valuable insight for the development of distributed algorithms for the online optimization problem.

The paper is organized as follows. In section 2, an overview is given for network optimization problems with focus on the minimum routing cost spanning tree (MRT) problem as well as local search algorithms. A new evolutionary heuristics for the MRT problem is presented in section 3. In section 4, results from various experiments with the new heuristics as well as a landscape analysis are presented based on measured Internet (PlanetLab) data. Conclusions and an outline for future research is provided in section 5.

2 Network Optimization and Local Search

A P2P overlay topology can be represented by a weighted graph $G = (V, E, d)$ where the nodes are the peers and the edges are communication links between the peers used for communicating in the P2P system. The weight $d(i, j)$ of an edge (i, j) denotes message delay on the communication link from peer i to peer j, or the average round-trip-time (RTT) between peer i to peer j. A spanning tree is a subgraph $T \subseteq G$ with $|V| - 1$ edges connecting all nodes in V. Given a spanning tree, multicast/broadcast can be implemented simply by flooding. In this preliminary work, we focus on spanning trees as topologies for P2P overlays since they require a minimum number of edges (connections) and are easily maintained. Since in a P2P system peers may join or leave at any time, the graph is changing over time. In order to study the effectiveness of the optimization methods, we concentrate on the case where the graph remains constant for the time of optimization.

2.1 Problem Definition

In order to minimize the time for multicast or unicast routing, a tree with optimum routing cost is sought. The problem of finding a spanning tree with minimum routing cost is defined as follows. Given a graph $G = (V, E, d)$, finding a spanning tree T of G such that

$$C(T) = \sum_{u,v \in V} d_T(u, v) \tag{1}$$

is minimal is called the *Minimum Routing Cost Spanning Tree (MRT) Problem*, where $d_T(u, v)$ denotes the distance/length of the path from u to v in T (message delay from u to v). The problem is a special case of the optimum communication spanning tree problem, which is known to be NP-hard [8,9], but known to admit a polynomial-time approximation scheme (PTAS) [9,10].

The MRT problem is closely related to the Shortest-Path-Tree (SPT) Problem. In fact, there is a vertex such that any SPT rooted at the vertex is a 2-approximation of the MRT. The SPT problem can be solved in polynomial time with Dijkstra's algorithm [11] or the algorithm of Bellman and Ford [12,13]. However, resulting trees may degenerate to stars if the triangle inequality is obeyed.

2.2 Related Work

Only few research has been done on the optimization of network topologies, in particular overlay topologies, focusing on combinatorial optimization techniques. In [14], two combinatorial problems are addressed, a minimum spanning tree problem, and a traveling salesman problem. In both cases, centralized heuristics/algorithms are proposed. In [15], evolutionary algorithms for self-organized networks are proposed. However, the authors do not consider the MRT objective and it is unclear how their algorithms can work in a fully decentralized distributed system. A centralized approximation algorithm for application-layer multicast trees is presented in [16]. The approach concentrates on an NP-hard optimization problem in which each node has a nonnegative processing delay the model differs also from our problem regarding the objective. The MeshTree approach [17] is a decentralized approach differentiating between backbone and delivery trees. Each node has a maximum neighbor degree. It is unclear how effective the optimization is in terms of approaching the optimum or a lower bound. Moreover, the benefits from using a minimum spanning tree (MST) as a backbone tree are not obvious. Since finding a degree-constrained MST is an NP-hard problem it can be expected to be harder for heuristic search than the degree-constrained SPT. Summarizing, to the best of our knowledge the MRT problem has not yet been addressed by (evolutionary) heuristics.

2.3 Local Search for the MRT Problem

Local search in the MRT Problem works by searching for a better solution (in terms of fitness/cost function) in the neighborhood of the current solution. The neighborhood itself consists of all trees reachable from a given tree by applying simple 'moves'. Such a move modifies the tree in a simple non-destructive way. Two types of moves considered in our algorithms are shown in Fig. 1. In the first move (a), a node (i) is connected to a new parent (q). We denote a neighborhood based on this move a 1-opt neighborhood. The second move (b) is actually a combination of two moves of type (a): two nodes, denoted i and j exchange their parents. We denote the neighborhood of this move a 2-opt neighborhood.

In order to compute the gain associated with a move, we make use of the following formula. The objective can be rewritten as

$$C(T) = \sum_{v \in V} C_v(T) \quad \text{with } C_v(T) = 2\, c(v)\, (N - c(v))\, d(v, p^v), \tag{2}$$

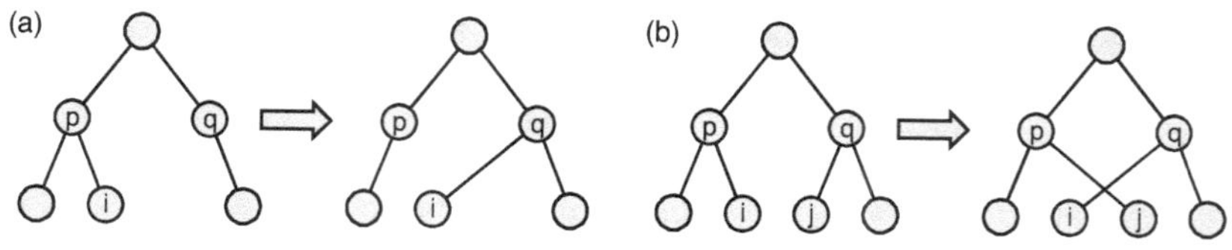

Fig. 1. Two types of tree moves

where $N = |V|$, p^v denotes the parent of node v and $c(v)$ denotes the size of the subtree rooted at v (number of children + 1). We assume here that the tree is rooted with an arbitrary root. With the formula, the cost of a tree can be computed in linear time. Also, this formula can be used to calculate the gain of a move efficiently. For both moves, only those C_v have to be recalculated that do change. These are those nodes for which the number of children or parent edges change and hence all nodes on the path P on the tree from i to parent q (or node j):

$$\Delta C(T \rightarrow T') = C(T) - C(T') = \sum_{v \in P} (C_v(T) - C_v(T')) \tag{3}$$

Hence, the number of updates is expected to be in $O(\log N)$ but in the worst case linear in N (if the tree degenerates to a single path). If we except an expected path length of $O(\log N)$, the time to search the complete neighborhood (denoted by $N_{\text{2-opt}}$) becomes $O(N^2 \log N)$. As a consequence, a local search based on these neighborhoods may not scale well with the problem size. Therefore, we propose two variants of the local search.

The first one considers only the nodes incident to the parent node p as candidates for the new parent q in move (a). Hence, the path from p to q consists of just p and q. A move of type (b) is only performed if $c(i) = c(j)$ and hence no update of C_v is needed along the path from p to q. Furthermore, not all pairs (i, j) are considered here. Instead, in each iteration of the local search, for each node i a node j is selected randomly. Therefore, the time complexity for searching the neighborhood reduces to $O(N)$ if we assume that the node degree in the tree is bounded by a constant. In the following we refer to this neighborhood as the constant update neighborhood N_{const}.

Since a local search based only on constant time/local changes may get stuck too early in local optima, we considered another neighborhood. In addition to N_{const} we also check for non-local moves of type (a) by randomly selecting j for each node i. This way, the time required for searching the neighborhood remains sub-quadratic but global moves are also considered to a certain degree. We call this neighborhood N_{fast}.

3 An Evolutionary Algorithm for the MRT Problem

Since the local search alone may not be sufficient to find optimum or near optimum solutions, we propose an evolutionary framework for improving local optimum solutions. The framework is similar to *iterated local search* [18] or *memetic algorithms* [19,20]. Unlike other memetic algorithms for combinatorial problems, it uses only mutation.

Since the general framework is independent of the considered problem, we provide a problem independent description in the following.

3.1 The General Evolutionary Framework

After creating initial solutions or an application of the mutation operator, a local search is applied to find a new local optimum. The general outline is shown in Fig. 2.

The framework is especially useful if not much is known about a problem. It accepts three parameters: the number of generations κ, the number of offspring per iteration λ, and the mutation adaptation rate α. The algorithm can be considered as a $(1+\lambda)$-EA incorporating local search. The product of generations and offspring defines the number of local searches to perform. The higher the number of offspring the higher the selection pressure. The adaptation rate defines by which factor the number of mutation steps is to be reduced if an iteration was not successful, i. e. there was no better solution. This approach is meaningful if the optimum mutation strength of problem is not known. Especially if an optimum mutation rate exists but is unknown, the adaptation allows to try different mutation rates or no mutation at all if multiple starts (init+local search) are sufficient. Since the number of mutation steps is adapted only if there was no improvement, the algorithm is capable of selecting an effective mutation rate depending on the state of convergence.

```
function EALS( κ: Integer; λ: Integer; α: Real) : Solution;
 begin
   s := Init ();
   s := LocalSearch(s);
   mutationSteps := ProblemSize(s);
   for iter := 0 to κ do begin
     sbest := s;
     for i := 0 to λ do begin
       if mutationSteps = ProblemSize(s) then stemp := Init()
         else stemp := Mutate(s, mutationSteps);
       stemp := LocalSearch(stemp);
       if stemp < sbest then sbest := stemp;
     end;
     if sbest < s then s := sbest
       else mutationSteps := round(mutationSteps * α);
   end;
   return s;
 end;
```

Fig. 2. The Evolutionary Local Search Framework

3.2 The Local Search Operator for the MRT Problem

It is not obvious which local search is best suited in the above evolutionary framework. Therefore, we decided to realize all three local search procedures described above, namely N_{const} local search, N_{fast} local search and $N_{\text{2-opt}}$ local search.

3.3 The Mutation Operator for the MRT Problem

The mutation operator is parameterized by a the number of mutation steps to apply. A single step consists of a random move as used in the local search, more precisely, type (a) described above. Hence, within the mutation operator such a move with a randomly selected node and a randomly selected new parent is applied k times with k denoting the number of mutation steps (mutationSteps in the pseudo code). As a consequence of mutation with k steps will remove k edges from the tree and insert k random edges such that the resulting graph is again a tree.

4 Results

We performed several experiments to evaluate the effectiveness of the local search variants as well as the evolutionary framework. In the experiments, we used data collected in experiments performed on the PlanetLab [21], a world-wide platform for performing Internet measurements. The PlanetLab consist of more than 400 computers distributed over more than 200 sites around the world. The measurements are simple 'ping' measurements measuring the RTT of messages using the ICMP protocol from any host to any other host in the PlanetLab. These RTTs were used in our experiments as the communication cost for the edges in the overlay graph. The higher the RTT, the higher the cost for a link/edge. In the experiments, we used the daily collected data by Jeremy Stribling reported in [21]. For each month of the year, we selected the first measurement (denoted by 01-2005, ..., 12-2005). All CPU times reported in this section refer to a Pentium IV (3 GHz, running Java). All results are averaged over at least 30 runs.

4.1 EALS Performance Evaluation

In a first set of experiments, we ran our evolutionary algorithms with varying parameters on the set of 12 instances. We varied the number of generations κ, the number of offspring λ, and the local search variant used in the EA. In all experiments we fixed the adaptation rate to $\alpha = 0.8$. The results for some of the experiments are shown in Table 1. In the displayed experiments the number of offspring was set to 1, and the number of generations to 1000. The cost of the best known solution is shown in column Best. It can be seen that with increasing neighborhood size $|N_{\text{const}}| < |N_{\text{fast}}| < |N_{\text{2-opt}}|$ both runtime and solution quality (shown as the percentage excess over the best known solution) increase. The constant update neighborhood local search performs very poor on some of the instances with a high deviation of more than 27 % from the best solution.

Table 1. Results for three Evolutionary Locals Search algorithm variants, with $(\kappa, \lambda, LS) = (1000, 1, \{\text{const}, \text{fast}, \text{2-opt}\})$, κ denoting the number of generations, λ the number of offspring per generation, and LS the local search neighborhood

		(1000,1,const)		(1000,1,fast)		(1000,1,2-opt)	
Instance	Best	Time	Excess	Time	Excess	Time	Excess
01-2005	2743556	0.9 s	3.86	1.4 s	1.33	37.2 s	0.26
02-2005	17567152	3.6 s	8.86	5.7 s	1.46	313.1 s	0.34
03-2005	19288320	3.5 s	10.02	5.6 s	1.72	286.2 s	0.52
04-2005	751404	0.5 s	1.03	0.7 s	0.50	8.5 s	0.09
05-2005	19175890	4.4 s	39.06	7.6 s	1.58	513.6 s	0.17
06-2005	20312884	4.1 s	16.27	7.1 s	1.61	409.1 s	0.29
08-2005	30540984	4.9 s	6.78	7.9 s	0.86	542.9 s	0.26
09-2005	25712960	5.3 s	30.76	8.7 s	1.58	535.4 s	0.26
11-2005	26797284	5.3 s	9.39	8.5 s	0.62	527.2 s	0.17

In order to study the influence of the number of generated offspring per generation, we performed additional experiments. The most relevant results are summarized in Table 2. The time required (Time) as well as percentage excess over the best known solution in percent (Ex) are reported. Here, we can see that increasing the number of offspring significantly increases average solution quality. Moreover, the N_{fast} local search EA appears to be close to the $N_{\text{2-opt}}$ local search EA in terms of tree cost, given approximately the same CPU time. The results clearly indicate that the 2-opt local search EA performs the best but the fast local search EA can achieve also very good results. It may scale better with the problem size if the networks become larger than investigated here. The slight modification of the fast variant compared to the const variant has a tremendous effect on the solution quality for several instances considered. The 2-opt variant with 100 generations and 100 offspring per generation finds the best solutions very frequently as indicated in the last column of the table.

4.2 Problem Instance Analysis

In the next set of experiments, we looked at the deviation of our best solutions found from two bounds, the all-pairs-shortest-path (APSP) lower bound and the best-shortest-path-tree (SPT) upper bound. The former measures the overall communication cost if we consider for each node the shortest path tree instead of a single shared tree as in the MRT. The latter is the best shortest path tree among all possible shortest path trees in terms of our cost function. This tree is a 2-approximation to the optimum solution. The results are shown in Table 3. Interestingly, it turns out that there is a relatively small gap of 10 % to 13 % between the best solutions we found and the simple APSP lower bound for all instances independent of their size. The gap to the upper bound of 4 % up to 14 % indicates that it is worth using heuristics for the MRT problem instead of using the shortest path tree approximation.

In a final set of experiments, we were interested in the properties of the local optima using the three neighborhoods. We calculated the average percentage

Table 2. Results for three Evolutionary Locals Search algorithm variants, with $(\kappa, \lambda, LS) = \{(100, 100, \text{fast}), (10, 10, \text{2-opt}), (100, 100, \text{2-opt})\}$, κ denoting the number of generations, λ the number of offspring per generation, and LS the neighborhood used in the local search

		(100,100,fast)		(10,10,2-opt)		(100,100,2-opt)		
Instance	Best	Time	Ex	Time	Ex	Time	Ex	Best
01-2005	2743556	18.2 s	0.29	9.9 s	0.13	157.6 s	0.00	52/53
02-2005	17567152	108.7 s	0.28	97.6 s	0.20	3260.0 s	0.00	34/50
03-2005	19288320	105.3 s	0.22	92.5 s	0.07	2633.5 s	0.00	42/48
04-2005	751404	5.4 s	0.05	2.0 s	0.01	26.6 s	0.00	48/48
05-2005	19175890	166.2 s	1.17	155.7 s	0.08	3244.8 s	0.00	43/48
06-2005	20312884	148.8 s	0.26	132.2 s	0.07	5558.5 s	0.00	34/48
08-2005	30540984	162.7 s	0.31	168.5 s	0.12	4067.4 s	0.00	39/47
09-2005	25712960	195.0 s	0.25	185.2 s	0.03	3840.2 s	0.00	35/48
11-2005	26797284	178.1 s	0.16	177.9 s	0.03	6407.2 s	0.00	40/48

Table 3. Overview of all considered instances. For each instance, the network size, the best solution found, the All-Pairs-Shortest-Path lower bound and an upper bound based on the Best Shortest Path Tree are shown.

Instance	Size	Best	Lower Bound (APSP)	Upper Bound (SPT)
01-2005	127	2743556	2447260 (12.1%)	3025120 (10.3%)
02-2005	321	17567152	15868464 (10.7%)	19607936 (11.6%)
03-2005	324	19288320	17164734 (12.4%)	20842606 (08.1%)
04-2005	70	751404	663016 (13.3%)	787856 (04.9%)
05-2005	374	19175890	17324082 (10.7%)	19949036 (04.0%)
06-2005	365	20312884	18262984 (11.2%)	22217312 (09.4%)
08-2005	402	30540984	27640136 (10.5%)	32209226 (05.5%)
09-2005	419	25712960	23195568 (10.9%)	27223336 (05.9%)
11-2005	407	26797284	23694130 (13.1%)	29322480 (09.4%)

Table 4. Properties of the local optima. For each local search neighborhood, the deviation from the best solution, the fitness distance correlation coefficient, and the average distance to the best solution is provided.

	LS const			LS 2-opt			LS fast		
Instance	Ex(%)	FDC	Dist	Ex(%)	FDC	Dist	Ex(%)	FDC	Dist
01-2005	68.8	0.25	91.3	5.5	0.32	52.7	13.7	0.40	80.3
02-2005	51.5	0.24	237.0	4.1	0.43	134.7	12.0	0.46	207.6
03-2005	47.0	0.22	245.6	3.6	0.37	145.5	11.3	0.40	216.2
04-2005	21.0	0.33	41.2	2.9	0.28	27.2	7.2	0.30	35.6
05-2005	86.9	0.15	282.9	3.0	0.39	143.5	32.7	0.50	245.3
06-2005	51.2	0.23	274.0	3.8	0.49	144.8	14.8	0.49	235.9
08-2005	34.1	0.31	291.5	2.8	0.48	158.3	8.0	0.52	250.9
09-2005	73.4	0.27	311.0	3.4	0.36	164.9	29.6	0.45	270.9
11-2005	43.3	0.31	293.8	3.2	0.45	156.9	10.2	0.44	255.0

excess (Ex) over the best solution found, the fitness distance correlation coefficient (FDC) of the local optima and the average distance (Dist) in the solution space to the best known solution. This distance is calculated by counting the edges of one tree not contained in the other. The results are displayed in Table 4. It can be observed that average tree quality and correlation are significantly lower for the simplest local search. The average distance to the best solution is very high. The other local search variants have a lower distance to the best solution and a significantly higher FDC. In all cases the FDC is below or equal to 0.52, indicating that recombination may not be very helpful for these landscapes, since respectful recombination is known to be effective on correlated landscapes [22,23]. Hence, the evolutionary local search algorithms based on mutation appear to be a good choice for effectively finding (near)optimum solutions to the MRT problem.

5 Conclusions

We have presented highly effective evolutionary algorithms incorporating local search for the minimum routing cost spanning tree problem arising in the design of P2P overlay topologies. The results show that the proposed algorithms are capable of approaching a lower bound on the problem effectively as well as improving upper bounds found by shortest path tree algorithms significantly. We proposed and investigated three types of local search in an evolutionary framework using a self-adapting mutation operator. The results show that either using a strong but time-consuming local search or using a scalable fast local search yields a solution quality below 0.5 % in short time.

There are several issues for future research. The influence of the adaptation rate used in our evolutionary framework has to be studied in detail. Moreover, it is important to investigate the scalability of the variants. Since there is no PlanetLab data with larger networks than those used here, we are forced to generate random instances with similar properties. Finally, we are working on distributed online algorithms for the MRT problem.

References

1. Gnutella: Gnutella Protocol v. 0.4 (2000) http://www.clip2.com/.
2. Ripeanu, M., Iamnitchi, A., Foster, I.: Mapping the Gnutella Network. IEEE Internet Computing (2002)
3. Cohen, B.: Incentives Build Robustness in BitTorrent. In: Workshop on Economics of Peer-to-Peer Systems, Berkeley, CA, USA (2003)
4. Chakravarti, A.J., Baumgartner, G., Lauria, M.: The Organic Grid: Self-Organizing Computation on a Peer-to-Peer Network. In: Proceedings of the International Conference on Autonomic Computing (ICAC '04), New York, NY (2004)
5. Merz, P., Gorunova, K.: Efficient Broadcast in P2P Grids. In: Proceedings of the IEEE/ACM International Symposium on Cluster Computing and the Grid (CCGrid 2005), Cardiff, UK (2005)

6. Kubiatowicz, J., *et al.*: OceanStore: An Architecture for Global-Scale Persistent Storage. In: Proc. of the 9th International Conference on Architectural Support for Programming Languages and Operating Systems (ASPLOS 2000). (2000) 190–201
7. Demers, A.J., Greene, D.H., Hauser, C., Irish, W., Larson, J.: Epidemic algorithms for replicated database maintenance. In: Proceedings of the Sixth Annual ACM Symposium on Principles of Distributed Computing. (1987) 1–12
8. Johnson, D.S., Lenstra, J.K., Kan, A.H.G.R.: The Complexity of the Network Design Problem. Networks **8** (1978) 279–285
9. Wu, B.Y., Lancia, G., Bafna, V., Chao, K.M., Ravi, R., Tang, C.Y.: A Polynomial-Time Approximation Scheme for Minimum Routing Cost Spanning Trees. SIAM Journal on Computing **29** (1999) 761–778
10. Wu, B.Y., Chao, K.M., Tang, C.Y.: Approximation Algorithms for Some Optimum Communication Spanning Tree Problems. Discrete Applied Mathematics **102** (2000) 245–266
11. Dijkstra, E.W.: A Note on Two Problems in Connexion with Graphs. Numerische Mathematik **1** (1959) 269–271
12. Bellman, R.E.: On a Routing Problem. Quart. of Appl. Mathem. **16** (1958) 87–90
13. Ford, Jr., L.R., Fulkerson, D.R.: Flows in Networks. Princeton Univ. Press (1962)
14. Sobeih, A., Wang, J., Yurcik, W.: Performance Evaluation and Comparison of Tree and Ring Application-Layer Multicast Overlay Networks. In: Proceedings of the 1st International Computer Engineering Conference: New Technologies for the Information Society (ICENCO), Cairo, Egypt (2004)
15. Lehmann, K.A., Kaufmann, M.: Evolutionary Algorithms for the Self-Organized Evolution of Networks. In et al., H.G.B., ed.: GECCO 2005: Proceedings of the 2005 Conference on Genetic and Evolutionary Computation. Volume 1., Washington DC, USA, ACM Press (2005) 563–570
16. Brosh, E., Shavitt, Y.: Approximation and Heuristic Algorithms for Minimum-Delay Application Layer Multicast Trees. In: The 23rd International Conference on Computer Copmunications, IEEE INFOCOM, Hong Kong (2004)
17. Tan, S.W., Waters, A., Crawford, J.: MeshTree: A Delay optimised Overlay Multicast Tree Building Protocol. Tech. R. 5-05, Univ. of Kent, Canterbury, UK (2005)
18. Lourenco, H.R., Martin, O., Stützle, T.: Iterated Local Search. In Glover, F., Kochenberger, G., eds.: Handb. of Metaheuristics. Kluwer Acad. Publ. (2003)
19. Moscato, P.: On Evolution, Search, Optimization, Genetic Algorithms and Martial Arts: Towards Memetic Algorithms. Technical Report C3P Report 826, Caltech Concurrent Computation Program, California Institue of Technology (1989)
20. Merz, P., Freisleben, B.: Memetic Algorithms for the Traveling Salesman Problem. Complex Systems **13** (2001) 297–345
21. Banerjee, S., Griffin, T., Pias, M.: The Interdomain Connectivity of PlanetLab Nodes. In Barakat, C., Pratt, I., eds.: Proceedings of the 5th International Workshop on Passive and Active Network Measurement, (PAM 2004). Volume 3015 of Lecture Notes in Computer Science., Springer (2004)
22. Merz, P., Freisleben, B.: Fitness Landscape Analysis and Memetic Algorithms for the Quadratic Assignment Problem. IEEE Transactions on Evolutionary Computation **4** (2000) 337–352
23. Merz, P.: Advanced Fitness Landscape Analysis and the Performance of Memetic Algorithms. Evolutionary Computation, Special Issue on Memetic Evolutionary Algorithms **12** (2004) 303–326

Nature-Inspired Algorithms for the Optimization of Optical Reference Signals

Sancho Salcedo-Sanz*, José Saez-Landete, and Manuel Rosa-Zurera

Department of Signal Theory and Communications, Universidad de Alcalá, 28871 Alcalá de Henares, Madrid, Spain
{sancho.salcedo, jose.saez, manuel.rosa}@uah.es

Abstract. This paper presents two nature-inspired approaches to the design of Zero Reference Codes (ZRC) for optical applications, both in one and two dimensions. Specifically we present a genetic algorithm and a simulated annealing hybridized with a restricted search operator to cope with the problem constraints. Extensive experiments have shown that nature-inspired approaches proposed can improve the results of existing techniques for this problem.

1 Introduction

The absolute measure of the position in grating measurement systems, and the detection of a reference position in mask alignment systems, are critical problems in metrology. They are very similar problems: both need a reference signal to detect an absolute position, and both can be tackled by solving an optimization problem. These systems are especially important in precision engineering, nanoscience and nanotechnology.

In grating measurement systems, a reference signal (or zero reference signal) is necessary to obtain an absolute measure. Traditionally, zero reference signals are generated by means of optical correlation of two binary transmittances, named Zero Reference Codes (ZRCs). Since 1986 gratings with adjacent zero reference codes has been developed [2]. Each ZRC consists of a group of specially coded transparent and opaque slits, see Figure 1 (a). A collimated beam propagates through both codes and the total amount of transmitted light is registered by means of a photodiode. The transmitted light depends on the relative displacement between the ZRCs and the signal registered in the photodiode is the correlation of the transmittances of the ZRCs. The characterization and design of optimum codes to obtain suitable reference signals has been studied in [3] and [4].

Chen et al. proposed a two-dimensional version of the ZRCs for precise mask alignment [6]. The system operation is similar to the one used to generate the zero reference signal in grating measurement systems, see Figure 1 (b). When

* This work has been partially supported by a CAM-UAH grant number: CAM-UAH2005/019.

T.P. Runarsson et al. (Eds.): PPSN IX, LNCS 4193, pp. 282–291, 2006.

the movement takes place on the XY plane, the signal is obtained as the two-dimensional correlation of the ZRCs. The design of two-dimensional ZRCs are considerably harder to design than its one-dimensional counterpart because the number of variables in a two-dimensional problem is $n \times n$, with n the number of variables of the one-dimensional version of the problem.

In this paper we explore the possibility of applying nature-inspired approaches to the design of ZRCs. Specifically we develop a genetic algorithm and a simulated annealing to deal with the problem of designing good ZRCs. We will show that these techniques are not limited by the number of variables, and are able to obtain good quality codes better than the codes obtained with previous approaches to the problem, even for large codes, with hundreds of variables.

The rest of the paper is structured as follows: next section describes the ZRC design problems tackled in this paper. Section 3 presents the nature-inspired algorithms we propose in this paper to solve the ZRC design problems. In Section 4 we provide several computational evidences of the good performance of our approaches in both problems. Section 5 closes de paper with some final remarks.

2 Optical Reference Signals Problems

The systems used in generation of optical reference signals are displayed in Figure 1. In Figure 1 (a) we show the generation in a grating measurement system (one-dimensional ZRC) and, in Figure 1 (b) we show a mask alignment system for optical lithography (two-dimensional ZRC). Note that in both examples, the ZRCs are parallel to each other and at least one of them is set in an XY (or X) mobile stage. A collimated beam passes through them in the perpendicular direction and the total transmitted flux is detected in a photodiode. The output signal depends on the relative displacements between ZRCs. In order to increase the maximum of this signal, the two codes are made identical so that the reference signal becomes the autocorrelation of the same ZRC. Although one and two-dimensional cases are different problems, two dimensional problem can be treated like a generalization of the one-dimensional problem.

The structure of a general ZRC can be represented by the following matrix of binary data:

$$\mathbf{c} = [c_{ij}] = \begin{bmatrix} c_{11} & \cdots & c_{1n} \\ \vdots & \ddots & \vdots \\ c_{n1} & \cdots & c_{nn} \end{bmatrix}, \quad c_{ij} \in \{0,1\}, \tag{1}$$

where n is the total number of elements of the ZRC, $c_{ij} = 1$ if a transparent pixel is located at the ij-position, and $c_{ij} = 0$ elsewhere. The number of transparent pixels is n_1. The sizes of the transparent and opaque regions in the ZRC are integer multiples of the width of a single pixel. In two-dimensional ZRC, a transparent pixel is a square aperture, whereas in one-dimensional ZRC, a transparent pixel is a rectangular slit, $\mathbf{c} = \begin{bmatrix} c_1 \, c_2 \cdots c_n \end{bmatrix}$, $c_j = \{0,1\}$, $j = 1, \ldots, n$. The one-dimensional case can be obtained from two-dimensional case substituting c_{ij} by c_i and removing the index j.

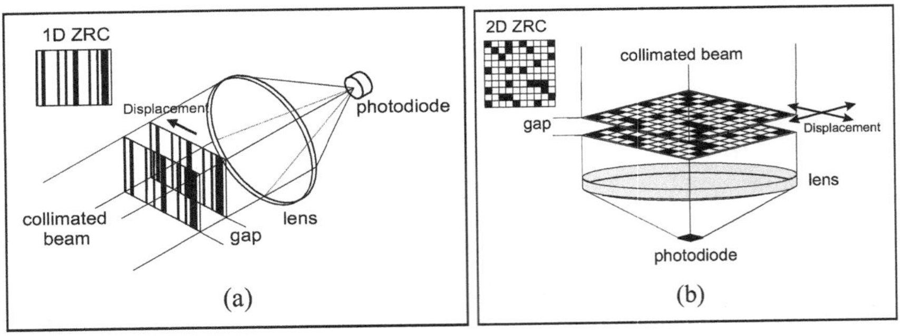

Fig. 1. Examples of systems using ZRCs; (a) Generation system of optical reference signals in grating measurement systems (one-dimensional ZRC); (b) Mask alignment system for optical lithography (two-dimensional ZRC)

We will assume that the illuminating light is a parallel ray beam and diffraction effects are negligible. This approach is valid when the gap between ZRCs is small with regard to the size of the pixels (or slits) in the code and this size is greater than wavelength of the illuminating light.

When the two ZRC have relative displacements of k and l units in the X and Y directions respectively, the signal registered in the photodiode is proportional to

$$S_{kl} = \sum_{i=1}^{n-k} \sum_{j=1}^{n-l} c_{ij} c_{i+k,\ j+l}, \tag{2}$$

where $k,\ l = -n+1, \ldots, n-1$, and the signal S_{kl} is the autocorrelation matrix of the two ZRC defined in equation (1). S_{00} is the signal obtained when the relative displacement between the ZRCs is zero. It is the central maximum and is equal to the number of transparent pixels, n_1

$$S_{00} = \sum_{i=1}^{n} \sum_{j=1}^{n} c_{ij}^2 = \sum_{i=1}^{n} \sum_{j=1}^{n} c_{ij} = n_1. \tag{3}$$

The secondary maximum of the signal is

$$\sigma = \max_{k^2+l^2 \neq 0} [S_{kl}] \tag{4}$$

where $k^2 + l^2 \neq 0$ implies that $k \neq 0$ and $l \neq 0$ at the same time.

The most important parameter that characterize a zero reference signal is the ratio between the secondary and the main maximum, $K = \sigma / S_{00}$. A good zero reference signal must be a single and well distinct peak, so the secondary maxima of the correlation signal must be low. The smaller K value, the higher the sensitivity and robustness of the zero reference signal.

In absence of diffraction, the size of the pixels of the ZRC defines the width of the central peak of the reference signal and this width is the resolution of the alignment system. The diameter of the light beam limits the number of pixels in the ZRC and in addition, the sensitivity of the photodiode determines the minimum value for the central maximum of the signal, i. e., the number of transparent pixels of the ZRC. According with these working requirements, we have n and n_1 predetermined and we must minimize the second maximum of the signal, σ. In [4] and [7] the authors calculate a theoretical lower bound for the second maximum in a one and two-dimensional problem, respectively. The lower bound in one-dimensional problem is

$$\sigma \geq \frac{\left[(2n+1) - \sqrt{(2n+1)^2 - 4n_1(n_1-1)}\right]}{2}, \qquad (5)$$

and in the two dimensional case is

$$\sigma \geq \frac{-\left(2n^2+n-1\right) + \sqrt{\left(2n^2+n-1\right)^2 + 4\left(1+\frac{1}{n}\right)n_1(n_1-1)}}{-2\left(1+\frac{1}{n}\right)}. \qquad (6)$$

Although there are some simple cases in which this bound is reached, there is no evidence that, for any values of n and n_1 at least one ZRC could be found for which the equality sign holds. The objective of the ZRC design problem is the calculation a ZRCs whose autocorrelation has the minimum second maximum. Table 1 shows a summary of the objective functions as well as the constraints for the one and two-dimensional cases.

Table 1. Main features of the set of benchmark problems considered

$\min_{c \in \text{binary}} f(\mathbf{c})$	one-dimensional	two-dimensional
Objective function	$f(\mathbf{c}) = \max\{S_1, \ldots, S_{n-1}\}$ $S_k = \sum_{j=1}^{n-k} c_j \cdot c_{j+k}$	$f(\mathbf{c}) = \max_{k^2+l^2 \neq 0} \{S_{kl}\}$ $S_{kl} = \sum_{i=1}^{n-k} \sum_{j=1}^{n-l} c_{ij} c_{i+k,\, j+l}$
Constraints	$\sum_{i=1}^{n} c_i = n_1$	$\sum_{i=1}^{n} \sum_{j=1}^{n} c_{ij} = n_1$

Traditionally, the design of the ZRCs has been based on properties of the autocorrelation function, since they establish the necessary conditions to achieve a suitable signal. The main difficulty for designing good ZRCs, is that there is not a systematic method of calculus from which arbitrary length ZRCs can be obtained. Some hints are given by Yajun in [3] and [4] in one-dimensional ZRC and [6] in two-dimensional ZRC to heuristically construct optimum ZRCs according to predefined criteria. The method consists of filling the code with ones or zeros to fulfill the necessary conditions of optimality, these conditions are only applicable to small-length ZRC, up to 30-40 elements. Recently, a new approach to the design of ZRCs based on optimization techniques has been presented [5]. The design problem is transformed into a minimization problem with binary variables, and the algorithm known as DIRECT is applied to solve it. We compare the nature-inspired algorithms presented in this paper with the results of DIRECT algorithm.

3 Nature-Inspired Algorithms Proposed

In this paper we aim to show the performance of standard implementations of a genetic algorithm and a simulated annealing for solving one and two-dimensional ZRC design problems. In both cases, there is a constraint related to the number of 1s in the encoding of the problem (number of slits (n_1), see Table 1). This section briefly describes the standard implementations of a GA and a SA, and also the restricted search operator used to include the problem constraints, and how to include it into the algorithms.

3.1 A Genetic Algorithm

GAs are robust problem's solving techniques based on natural evolution processes. They are population-based techniques which codifies a set of κ possible solutions to the problem, and evolve them through the application of the so called *genetic operators* [1]. The standard genetic operators in a GA are:

- Selection, where the individuals of a new population are selected from the old one. In the standard implementation of the Selection operator, each individual has a probability of surviving for the next generation proportional to its associated fitness value (roulette wheel).
- Crossover, where new individuals are searched starting from couples of individuals in the population. Once the couples are randomly selected, the individuals have the possibility of swapping parts of themselves with its couple, the probability of this happens is usually called *crossover probability*, P_c.
- Mutation, where new individuals are searched by randomly changing bits of current individuals with a low probability P_m (*probability of mutation*).

Outline of a GA:

```
Initialize GA population of κ individuals at random;
while(max. number of generations not reached)
        for(every individual c)
                Calculate the objective function f(c);
        endfor
        Selection;
        Crossover;
        Mutation;
end while
```

3.2 The Simulated Annealing

SA has been widely applied to solve combinatorial optimization problems [10], [11]. It is inspired by the physical process of heating a substance and then cooling it slowly, until a strong crystalline structure is obtained. This process is simulated by lowering an initial temperature by slow stages until the system reaches an equilibrium point, and no more changes occur. Each stage of the process consists in changing the configuration several times, until a thermal equilibrium is reached, and a new stage starts, with a lower temperature. The solution of the problem is the configuration obtained in the last stage. In the standard SA, the changes in the configuration are performed in the following way: A new configuration is built by a random displacement of the current one. If the new configuration is better, then it replaces the current one, and if not, it may replace the current one probabilistically. This probability of replacement is high in the beginning of the algorithm, and decreases in every stage. This procedure allows the system to move toward the best configuration. Although SA is not guaranteed to find the global optima, it is still better than others algorithms in escaping from local optima. The solution found by SA can be considered a "good enough" solution, but it is not guaranteed to be the best.

Outline of the SA heuristic:

$k \leftarrow 0$;
$T \leftarrow T_0$;
Initialize a potential solution $\mathbf{c}$ at random;
do{
Calculate $f(\mathbf{c})$;
repeat
    for $j = 0$ **to** ξ
        $\mathbf{c}_{mut} \leftarrow$ **mutate**($\mathbf{c}$);
        Calculate($f(\mathbf{c}_{mut})$);
        if(($f(\mathbf{c}_{mut}) < f(\mathbf{c}_{best})$)) OR ($random(0,1) < e^{(\frac{-a}{T})}$)) then
            $\mathbf{c} \leftarrow \mathbf{c}_{mut}$
            $\mathbf{c}_{best} \leftarrow \mathbf{c}_{mut}$
        endif
    endfor
    $T \leftarrow f_T(T_0, k)$;
    $k \leftarrow k + 1$;
until($T < T_{min}$);

where k counts the number of iterations performed; T keeps the current temperature; T_0 is the initial temperature; T_{min} is the minimum temperature to be reached; $\mathbf{c}$ stands for the current configuration, $\mathbf{c}_{mut}$ for the new configuration after the mutation operator is applied and $\mathbf{c}_{best}$ for the configuration obtained after applying the tabu search; f represents the objective function considered; ξ is the number of changes performed with a given temperature T; f_T is the cooling function; and a is a previously fixed constant. Parameter a and the initial temperature T_0 are calculated in order to have an initial acceptance probability equal to 0.8, which is the value tipically used. *In order to increase the rate of convergence* we do not allow the probability of acceptance worse solutions than the current one to be less than 0.005 until the last 50 iterations of the algorithm. The cooling function is defined as

$$f_T = \frac{T_0}{1+k}. \tag{7}$$

The minimum temperature T_{min} is calculated on the basis of the desired number of iterations as:

$$T_{min} = f_T(T_0, numIt). \tag{8}$$

3.3 The Restricted Search

The restricted search strategy consists of fixing the number of desired transparent slits in the ZRC (1s in the binary string), by means of the so-called restricted search operator. This operator works in the following way: after the application of the crossover and mutation operators in the genetic algorithm, or the mutation in the simulated annealing, the individual **c** will have p 1s that, in general, will be different from the desired number of transparent slits n_1. If $p < n_1$ the restricted search operator adds $(n_1 - p)$ 1s randomly and if $p > n_1$, the restricted search operator randomly selects $(p - n_1)$ 1s and removes them from the binary string. This operator can be described in pseudo-code, as follows:

The restricted search operator

```
Select n1 (number of transparent slits) before running the GA or SA algorithms.
for every generation of the GA or SA:
    for every individual of the GA population or state of the SA:
        check the number of 1s p.
            if(p < n1)
                Add_ones(n1 - p);
            else
                Remove_ones(p - n1)
            end(if)
    end(individual)
end(generation)
```

Note that this operator forces the genetic algorithm or the simulated annealing to search in a reduced search space. In fact, the standard genetic algorithm and simulated annealing search in a space of size 2^n, whereas introducing the restricted search operator, the size of the search space is reduced to $\binom{n}{n_1} \ll 2^n$. This operator has been used before in different applications such as feature selection [9]. Note also that the application of the restricted search in the GA or SA heuristic is straightforward: it must be applied after the crossover and mutation operators in the GA and after the mutation operator in the SA.

4 Experiments and Results

In order to test the performance of our approaches in the design of ZRCs, we have run simulations in the case one and two dimensional ZRCs of different length. Specifically we propose two simulations: the first one is the design of one dimensional ZRCs, with length $n = 256$, and a variable number of slits (n_1), from 1 to 255. The second experiment simulates the design of two dimensional ZRCs, with length 16×16, also with number of slits variable from 1 to 255. We have run the GA with parameters $P_c = 0.6$, $P_m = 0.01$ (standard values suggested in [1]), 300 generations and a population of 100 individuals. The SA parameters are $k = 300$ and $\xi = 100$. Note that both algorithms perform the same number of function evaluations.

In order to compare the results obtained, we have implemented the DIRECT algorithm in the same problems [5], with the same number of function evaluations. DIRECT is a sampling algorithm developed by Donald R. Jones et al. for finding the global minimum of a multivariate function subject to simple bounds, using no derivative information [8]. The name DIRECT comes from *DIviding RECTangles*, which describes the way the algorithm moves towards the minimum. The first step in the algorithm is to transform the search space in a unit hypercube. The function is then sampled at the center of this hypercube. The hypercube is then divided into smaller hyperrectangles whose center-points are also sampled. Normally, the Lipschitz constant of the objective function is utilized for determining the next rectangle to sample. As the Lipschitz is not known, DIRECT identifies a set of "potentially optimal" rectangles corresponding to all the combinations of Lipschitz constants and rectangles sizes in each iteration. All "potentially optimal" rectangles are further divided into smaller rectangles whose centers are sampled. For more information about DIRECT algorithm see reference [5], [7].

Figure 2 (left) shows the comparison among the algorithms implemented, together with the lower bound for the one dimensional ZRC design problem. Note that both the GA and the SA obtains very similar results, much better than the DIRECTs. In this figure is difficult to appreciate differences in the behavior of our nature-inspire approaches. To do this, we can do a zoom in the graph, between 160 and 200 slits (Figure 2 (right)). This figure shows that the GA seems to perform slightly better, though there are points where the SA obtains a better value. Anyway, there are few differences between the proposed nature-inspired approaches in this one dimension case.

Figure 3 (left) shows the results obtained in the two-dimensional ZRCs code design. Again the results obtained with DIRECT algorithm and the lower bound in Section 2 have been depicted for comparison. In this problem it is apparent that the proposed nature-inspired algorithms perform much better than the DIRECT algorithm. The performance of GA and the SA is similar, but there are small differences between them, more accused than in the one dimensional case. This can be better seen in Figure 3 (right), where it is easy to appreciate that the GA obtains solutions with second maximum of autocorrelation smaller than the SA solution.

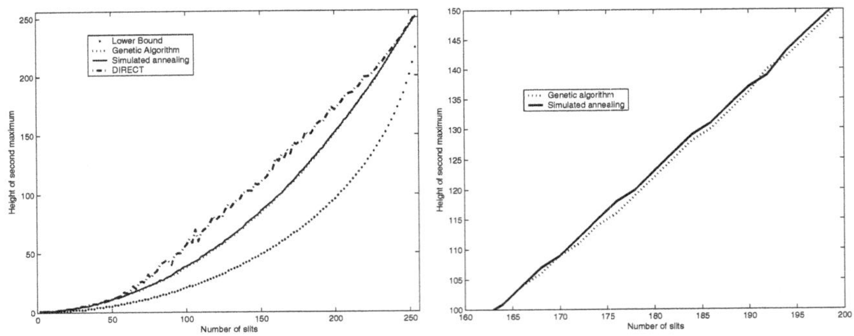

Fig. 2. Comparison of the second maximum of autocorrelation reached with the Genetic algorithm, the Simulated annealing, the DIRECT algorithm and the theoretical lower bound for the one dimensional ZRC design problem; Complete simulation on the left; Zoom $n_1 = 160$ to 200 on the right

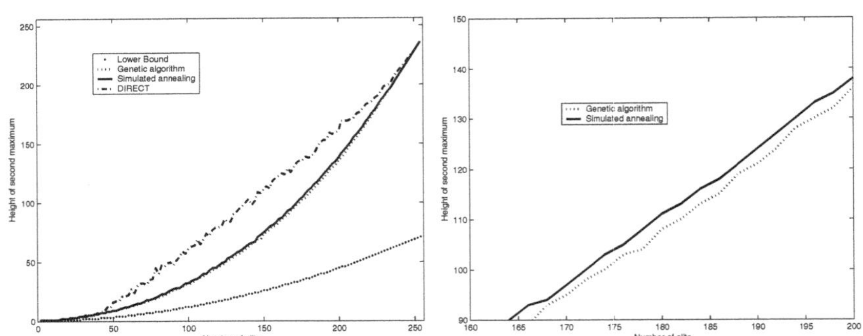

Fig. 3. Comparison of the second maximum of autocorrelation reached with the Genetic algorithm, the Simulated annealing, the DIRECT algorithm and the theoretical lower bound for the two-dimensional ZRC design problem; Complete simulation on the left; Zoom $n_1 = 160$ to 200 on the right

5 Conclusions

The design of optimum ZRCs is a very demanding task in terms of computing. In this paper we have analyzed the performance of a genetic algorithm and a simulated annealing algorithms in the design of reference signal in optics. We have shown that these meta-heuristic techniques are able to improve the results obtained previously by a DIRECT technique. The ZRCs obtained by our nature-inspired approaches are excellent reference signals for mask alignment in optical lithography and also in grating measurement systems.

Future work includes the modification of the problem's objective function, for taking into account not only the second maximum of the signal (as in the present application), but also the code structure, in such a way that the diffraction between ZRCs can be taken into account.

References

1. Goldberg, D. E., *Genetic algorithms in search, optimization and machine learning*, Reading:MA, Addison-Wesley, 1989.
2. Yang, X. and Yin, C. "A new method for the design of zero reference marks for grating measurement systems", *J. Phys. E Sci. Instrum.*, vol. 19, pp. 34-37, 1986.
3. Yajun, L., "Autocorrelation function of a bar code system", *J. Mod. Opt*, vol. 34, pp. 1571-5, 1987.
4. Yajun, L., "Optical valve using bar codes", *Optik*, vol. 79, pp. 67-74, 1988.
5. Sáez-Landete, J., Alonso, J. and Bernabeu, E., "Design of zero reference codes by means of a global optimization method", *Optics Express*, vol. 13, pp. 195-201, 2004.
6. Chen, Y., Huang, W. and Dang, X., "Design and analysis of two-dimensional zero-reference marks for alignment systems", *Review of Scientific Instruments*, vol. 74, pp. 3549-3553, 2003.
7. Séz-Landete, J., Alonso, J. and Bernabeu, E., "Design of two-dimensional zero reference codes by means of a global optimization method," *Optics Express*, vol. 13, pp. 4230-4236, 2005.
8. Jones, D. R. "DIRECT Global optimization algorithm", in Encyclopedia of Optimization (Kluwer Academic Publishers, Dordrecht, 2001).
9. S. Salcedo-Sanz, S., Camps-Vals, G., Pŕez-Cruz, F., Sepúlveda-Sanchís, J. and Bousoño-Calzón, C., "Enhancing genetic feature selection through restricted search and walsh analysis", *IEEE Trans. System, Man and Cybern. Part C*, vol. 34, no. 4, pp. 398-406, 2005.
10. Kirpatrick, S., Gerlatt, C. D., and Vecchi, M. P. (1983). "Optimization by simulated annealing," *Science*, 220, 671-680.
11. Kirpatrick, S. (1984). "Optimization by simulated annealing–Quantitative studies," *J. Stat. Phys.*, 34, 975-986.

Optimum Design of Surface Acoustic Wave Filters Based on the Taguchi's Quality Engineering with a Memetic Algorithm

Kiyoharu Tagawa[1] and Mikiyasu Matsuoka[2]

[1] Dept. of Electrical and Electronics Engineering, Kobe University,
Kobe, Hyogo 657-8501, Japan
tagawa@kobe-u.ac.jp
http://www2.kobe-u.ac.jp/~tagawa/index.html
[2] Graduate School of Science and Technology, Kobe University; ditto

Abstract. For deciding suitable structures of surface acoustic wave (SAW) filters based on the computer simulation, the equivalent circuit model of interdigital transducer (IDT), which includes several uncertain constant parameters, is usually used. In order to cope with the imperfections of the optimum design caused by the inevitable dispersion of these constant parameters, a technique based on the Taguchi's quality engineering coupled with a memetic algorithm (MA) is presented. Besides the traditional Taguchi's two-step design approach maximizing the robustness of SAW filters before realizing their specified functions, the proposed MA enables us to improve their robustness and functions simultaneously.

1 Introduction

In recent years, surface acoustic wave (SAW) filters have played an important role as a key device in various mobile and wireless communication systems, such as personal data assistants (PDAs) and cellular phones[1,2]. Especially, resonator type SAW filters are wildly used in the inter-stages of cellular phones, because they provide small, rugged and cost-competitive mechanical bandpass filters with outstanding frequency response characteristics such as high attenuations[3].

The frequency response characteristics of SAW filters are governed primarily by their geometrical structures, namely, the configurations of interdigital transducers (IDTs) and grating reflectors fabricated on piezoelectric substrates. Consequently, for realizing desirable functions of SAW filters, we need to decide their suitable structures. Even though a number of optimum design techniques coupling optimization methods with computer simulations are proposed for deciding the suitable structures of SAW filters[4,5,6,7], conventional optimum design techniques have rarely discussed the accuracy of computer simulations. The underlying models might have some error factors that deteriorate the precision of simulations. Actually, in order to estimate the performances of SAW filters based on the computer simulation, we have been constrained to use the equivalent circuit model of IDT including several uncertain constant parameters[8].

T.P. Runarsson et al. (Eds.): PPSN IX, LNCS 4193, pp. 292–301, 2006.

In this paper, we present a robust optimum design technique to tackle the imperfections of the optimum design of SAW filters caused by the inevitable dispersion of constant parameters included in the equivalent circuit model of IDT. Among robust optimum design approaches developed recently[9,10,11], the design for six sigma (DFSS)[10] may be the most popular one. However, DFSS needs to be used with the time-consuming Monte Carlo simulation for evaluating the robustness of products. Therefore, we employ the quality engineering[11], which is also called "the Taguchi method". Then, according to the Taguchi method, we define a signal-to-noise ratio (SNR) for measuring the robustness of resonator type SAW filters. Since the value of SNR is obtained with less experiments, we can save a lot of time by using the Taguchi method.

The Taguchi method recommends the two-step design approach maximizing the SNR of products before realizing their ideal functions. First of all, we obey the Taguchi's precept and enhance the robustness of SAW filters before achieving their functions by solving two kinds of optimization problems sequentially. Then we propose a concurrent design approach for improving robustness and functions simultaneously. Exactly, we formulate the robust optimum design of SAW filters as a constrained optimization problem in which the SNR of SAW filters is maximized under the constraints of their specified functions.

In order to solve the above optimization problems, we propose a memetic algorithm (MA), which are also referred as genetic local searches or hybrid genetic algorithms (GAs)[12]. A favorite trick of MAs is to improve respective solutions, or individuals, by using exclusive local searches. Therefore, we introduce a new local search, i.e., a revised version of the variable neighborhood search (VNS) offered by authors[6]. Because any restart mechanism isn't used in the MA, a distance-based mutation is also proposed to keep the diversity of population.

In the next section, we briefly describe a structure of SAW filter. We also explain the equivalent circuit model of IDT. In Section 3, we formulate two types of robust design approaches of SAW filters into optimization problems. In Section 4, we present a MA for solving the above optimization problems. In Section 5, we demonstrate the proposed design techniques on the robust optimum design of practical SAW filters. Finally, we offer some conclusions in Section 6.

2 Resonator Type SAW Filter

2.1 Structure of SAW Filter

Figure 1 shows the fundamental structure of resonator type SAW filter consisting of five components: one receiver IDT (IDT-1), two transmitter IDTs (IDT-2) and two grating reflectors realized by shorted metal strip array (SMSA). Each of IDTs is composed of some pairs of electrodes, which are called fingers, and used for SAW excitation and detection. Because resonator type SAW filters are designed to resonate SAW stably, they have symmetric structures.

The frequency response characteristics of SAW filters depend on their structures, or the configurations of components fabricated on piezoelectric substrates.

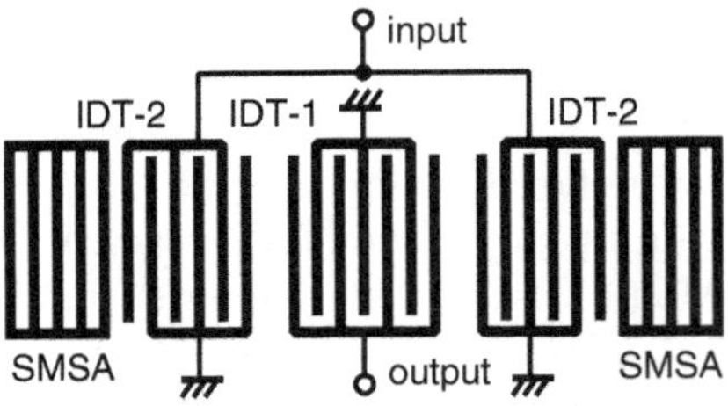

Fig. 1. Resonator type SAW filter

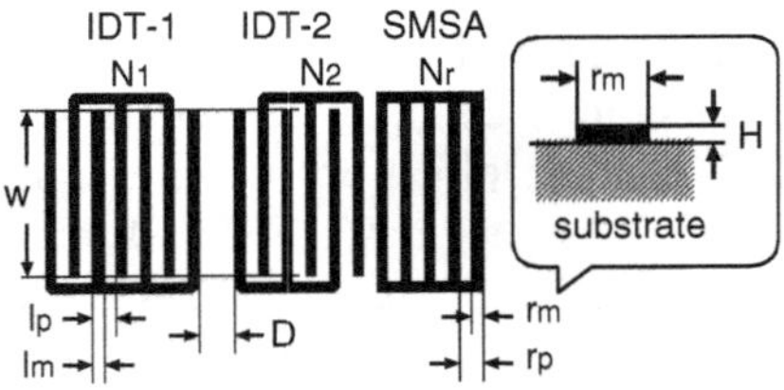

Fig. 2. Design parameters

For example, in order to decide a suitable structure of the SAW filter in Fig.1, we have to adjust nine design parameters listed in Fig.2, namely, overlap between electrodes W, number of fingers of IDT-1 N_1, ditto of IDT-2 N_2, number of strips of SMSA N_r, gap between IDT-1 and IDT-2 D, metallization ratio of IDT ξ, ditto of SMSA ξ_r, pitch ratio of SMSA ρ_r and thickness of electrode H. The metallization ratio of IDT is defined as $\xi = l_m/l_p$ with the pitch of fingers l_p and their metal width l_m. Similarly, the metallization ratio of SMSA is defined as $\xi_r = r_m/r_p$. The pitch ratio of SMSA to IDT is given by $\rho_r = r_p/l_p$.

According to the terminology of the Taguchi method[11], design parameters describing the structure of SAW filter are referred as control factors. We represent control factors by a vector of n-elements $\mathbf{x} = (x_1, \cdots, x_n)$. Some control factors, such as the number of IDTs' fingers, are positive integers. Also the lithographic resolution for shaping electrodes and strips on substrates is restricted into a finite value. Therefore, we introduce a minimum unit value e_i into each of $x_i \in \mathbf{x}$. Then we suppose that control factors $x_i \in \mathbf{x}$ take discrete values within the regions bounded by their parametric limitations as follows.

$$\underline{x}_i \leq x_i \leq \overline{x}_i, \quad i = 1, \ldots, n. \tag{1}$$

where, $(\overline{x}_i - \underline{x}_i) \mod e_i \equiv 0, \;\; e_i > 0, \;\; i = 1, \ldots, n.$

2.2 Equivalent Circuit Model of IDT

The entire circuit models of SAW filters are made up from the equivalent circuit models of their components, namely, IDTs and SMSAs[2,8]. The N-pair of IDTs illustrated in Fig.3 can be modeled by using a three-port circuit shown in Fig.4, where port-1 and port-2 are acoustic ports, and port-3 is electric port[8]. If we short the electric port-3, we can obtain the equivalent circuit model of SMSA. Circuit elements included in Fig.4, namely, transconductances A_{10}, A_{20}, admittance Y_m and impedances Z_1, Z_2, depend on the image admittance F_s and the image transfer constant γ_s derived from some parameters as follows.

$$F_s = \sqrt{pq}, \qquad \gamma_s = 2\tanh^{-1}\left(\sqrt{\frac{p}{q}}\right) \tag{2}$$

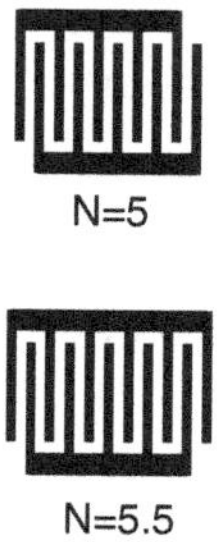

Fig. 3. N-pair of IDT

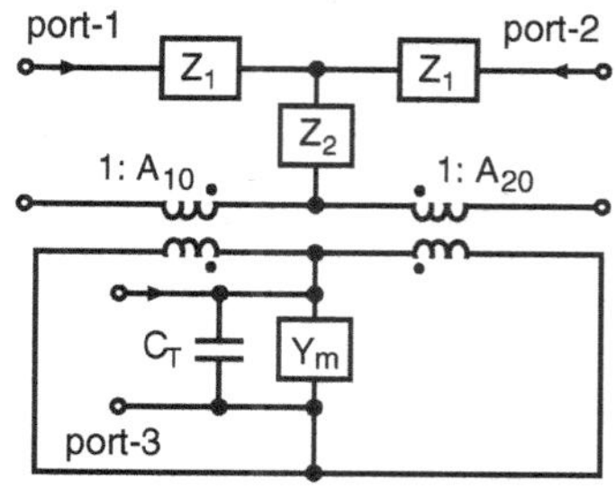

Fig. 4. Equivalent circuit model of IDT

$$\left[\begin{array}{ll} p = \dfrac{\tanh(\phi) + \tau \tanh\left(\dfrac{\psi}{2}\right) + y_s}{1 + \tanh(\phi)\left(\tau \tanh\left(\dfrac{\psi}{2}\right) + y_s\right)}, & \phi = \left(\alpha_o + j\,\dfrac{\omega}{v_o}\right)\dfrac{(l_p - l_m)}{2} \\ q = \dfrac{\tanh(\phi) + \tau \coth\left(\dfrac{\psi}{2}\right) + y_s}{1 + \tanh(\phi)\left(\tau \coth\left(\dfrac{\psi}{2}\right) + y_s\right)}, & \psi = \left(\alpha_m + j\,\dfrac{\tau_v\,\omega}{v_o}\right)\dfrac{l_m}{2} \end{array}\right.$$

where, $y_s = g_s + j\,b_s$; g_s and b_s denote bulk wave loss and phase susceptance at the edge of electrode. v_o is the velocity of SAW. ω denotes frequency[8].

The accuracy of the equivalent circuit model of IDT depends on the reliability of three constant parameters, namely, velocity ratio τ_v, discontinuous coefficient τ and phase susceptance b_s included in (2). However, because these constant parameters vary with the qualities of the materials of substrates and electrodes, we can't decide their values exactly. Therefore, in the robust design of SAW filters based on the computer simulation, we should consider the dispersion of these constant parameters. From now on, constant parameters (τ_v, τ, b_s) are referred as error factors[11] and represented by a vector $\mathbf{c} = (c_1, c_2, c_3)$.

3 Robust Optimum Design

3.1 Evaluation of Robustness

In order to evaluate the robustness of SAW filters, we define the signal-to-noise ratio (SNR) in accordance with the Taguchi method[11]. First of all, as a signal factor, we choose the following resonant frequency of single IDT[8].

$$\omega_o = \frac{\pi\, v_o}{(1 + \xi\,(\tau_v - 1))\, l_p} \tag{3}$$

We suppose that each error factor $c_j \in \mathbf{c}$ $(j = 1, \ldots, 3)$ takes three levels, namely, nominal $\acute{c}_j$, minimum $\underline{c}_j$ and maximum $\overline{c}_j$; thus we consider $3^3 = 27$

variations of error factors $\mathbf{c}^r$ $(r = 1, \ldots, 27)$. We pay our attention to the transmission coefficient s_{21}[2] between the input- and the output-ports of SAW filter. Since s_{21} depends on control factor $\mathbf{x}$, error factor $\mathbf{c}$ and frequency ω, we evaluate the values of $s_{21}(\mathbf{c}^r, \mathbf{x}, \omega_o)$ under the signal factor ω_o in (3) and a given $\mathbf{x}$ against every $\mathbf{c}^r$ $(r = 1, \ldots, 27)$. For minimizing the dispersion of these $s_{21}(\mathbf{c}^r, \mathbf{x}, \omega_o)$, we try to maximize the SNR of SAW filters defined as follows.

$$\eta(\mathbf{x}) = 10 \log \left(\frac{\mu^2(\mathbf{x})}{\sigma^2(\mathbf{x})} \right) \tag{4}$$

where, μ^2 is mean square of s_{21}, while σ^2 is deviation of $(\mu - s_{21})$.

3.2 Evaluation of Function

As a criterion for discussing the ideal functions of SAW filters, we adopt the attenuation Γ defined from the transmission coefficient s_{21} as follows[2].

$$\Gamma(\mathbf{c}, \mathbf{x}, \omega) = -20 \log(|s_{21}(\mathbf{c}, \mathbf{x}, \omega)|) \tag{5}$$

Let Ω be a set of frequencies $\omega \in \Omega$ sampled from the remarkable range of a target SAW filter. $\Gamma(\acute{\mathbf{c}}, \mathbf{x}, \omega)$ denotes the value of the attenuation evaluated at $\omega \in \Omega$ with a given design factor $\mathbf{x}$ and the nominal value of error factor $\acute{\mathbf{c}}$. By using the upper $U(\omega)$ and the lower $L(\omega)$ bounds, $\Gamma(\acute{\mathbf{c}}, \mathbf{x}, \omega)$ is specified at each $\omega \in \Omega$. Consequently, in order to realize the specified characteristics of the SAW filter, we have only to minimize the following objective function.

$$f(\mathbf{x}) = \sum_{\omega \in \Omega} \frac{\nabla U(\mathbf{x}, \omega) + \nabla L(\mathbf{x}, \omega)}{|\Omega|} \tag{6}$$

$$\left[\begin{array}{l} \nabla U(\mathbf{x}, \omega) = \max\{ \Gamma(\acute{\mathbf{c}}, \mathbf{x}, \omega) - U(\omega), 0 \} \\ \nabla L(\mathbf{x}, \omega) = \max\{ L(\omega) - \Gamma(\acute{\mathbf{c}}, \mathbf{x}, \omega), 0 \} \end{array} \right.$$

3.3 Formulation of Two-Step Design Approach

The Taguchi method recommends the two-step design approach, because it is more difficult to reduce the variability than to adjust the average response to the target value[11]. According to the two-step approach, the first design problem for maximizing the robustness of SAW filters is formulated as follows.

$$\tilde{\mathbf{x}} = \arg \max_{\mathbf{x} \in \mathcal{X}} \eta(\mathbf{x}) = \arg \min_{\mathbf{x} \in \mathcal{X}} - \eta(\mathbf{x}) \tag{7}$$

where $\mathcal{X}$ is a set of control factors $\mathbf{x} \in \mathcal{X}$ that satisfy the constraints in (1).

After solving the first design problem in (7), we evaluate the SNR for each of the best control factors $\tilde{x}_i \in \tilde{\mathbf{x}}$ $(i = 1, \ldots, n)$ by using orthogonal array with three levels, namely, $\tilde{x}_i$ and $\tilde{x}_i \pm e_i$, and decide their optimal levels x_i^o.

We choose several effective control factors $x_j \in \mathbf{x}$ for raising the SNR and fix their values in the optimal levels x_j^o. Let $\mathcal{Z} \subseteq \mathcal{X}$ be a set of control factors $\mathbf{x} \in \mathcal{X}$ that satisfy the constraint: $\mathbf{x} \in \mathcal{Z} \Rightarrow x_j^o \in \mathbf{x}$. Then the second design problem for realizing the functions of SAW filters is formulated as follows.

$$\tilde{\mathbf{x}} = \arg \min_{\mathbf{x} \in \mathcal{Z}} f(\mathbf{x}) \tag{8}$$

3.4 Formulation of Concurrent Design Approach

The Taguchi's two-step design approach assumes that we can realize the functions of SAW filters sufficiently by solving the second design problem under the constraint $\mathbf{x} \in \mathcal{Z} \subseteq \mathcal{X}$. But there is no evidence for the assumption. Therefore, in order to guarantee the specified functions of SAW filters with a ceiling ε ($\varepsilon \geq 0$), we present the concurrent design problem formulated as follows.

$$\tilde{\mathbf{x}} = \arg \min_{\mathbf{x} \in \mathcal{F}} -\eta(\mathbf{x}), \qquad \mathcal{F} = \{\, \mathbf{x} \in \mathcal{X} \mid \varepsilon \geq f(\mathbf{x}) \,\}. \tag{9}$$

Incidentally, for deciding an appropriate value of the ceiling ε in (9), we can refer to the minimum value of the objective function $f(\tilde{\mathbf{x}})$ obtained by solving the following conventional optimum design problem of SAW filters[6,7].

$$\tilde{\mathbf{x}} = \arg \min_{\mathbf{x} \in \mathcal{X}} f(\mathbf{x}) \tag{10}$$

4 Memetic Algorithm

4.1 Variable Neighborhood Search

The k-degree-neighborhood $N_k(\mathbf{x})$ ($k \leq n$) is defined as follows[6]: every solution $\mathbf{x}' \in N_k(\mathbf{x})$ differs from the solution $\mathbf{x}$ in just k elements, and the differences between respective $x_i' \in \mathbf{x}'$ and $x_i \in \mathbf{x}$ are equivalent to their units such as $e_i = |x_i' - x_i|$. Therefore, $N_k(\mathbf{x})$ contains the following number of solutions.

$$|N_k(\mathbf{x})| = 2^k\, {}_nC_k \tag{11}$$

The original VNS explores $N_k(\mathbf{x})$ ($k = 1, \ldots, \overline{k}$) and jumps from there to a new one if and only if an improvement was made[6]. Consequently, the quality of solution seems to be improved by using more and more neighborhoods. However, the computation time spent by VNS increases with their numbers.

In order to reduce the computational time arbitrarily, we introduce the limits of the total number of solutions to be examined $\overline{t}$. Supposing that we solve the unconstrained optimization problem in (10), the procedure of the restricted VNS is described as follows. Since we employ the first improvement strategy[13], the incumbent $\mathbf{x}$ is always replaced by the first objective-improving solution $\mathbf{x}'$ found in $\mathcal{L} = N_k(\mathbf{x}) \cap \mathcal{X}$. Furthermore, we choose a candidate $\mathbf{x}' \in \mathcal{L}$ randomly.

Procedure of restricted VNS

get an initial $\mathbf{x} \in \mathcal{X}$; $k := 1$; $t := 0$;
while ($k < \overline{k}$ and $t < \overline{t}$) {
  $\mathcal{L} := N_k(\mathbf{x}) \cap \mathcal{X}$; flag := 0;
  while ($\mathcal{L} \neq \emptyset$ and $t < \overline{t}$) {
    choose $\mathbf{x}' \in \mathcal{L}$; $\mathcal{L} := \mathcal{L} - \{ \mathbf{x}' \}$; $t := t + 1$;
    if ($f(\mathbf{x}') < f(\mathbf{x})$) { $\mathbf{x} := \mathbf{x}'$; flag := 1; break; }
  }
  if (flag = 1) $k := 1$; else $k := k + 1$;
}
return $\mathbf{x}$;

4.2 Genetic Operators

As we have mentioned before, we adopt a general procedure of MA[12], while we apply the above restricted VNS to every offspring generated by crossover or mutation. For keeping the diversity of population, we employ a discrete version of the blend crossover (BLX-α)[14] with $\alpha = 50$ [%]. Furthermore, we use the distance-based mutation that modifies more than $\overline{k}$ elements $x_i \in \mathbf{x}$ of a parent $\mathbf{x}$ to generate its offspring $\mathbf{x}'$ as $x'_i := x_i \pm e_i$; $(x'_i \in \mathbf{x}')$. Therefore, $\mathbf{x}'$ is never included initially within any neighborhood $N_k(\mathbf{x})$ $(k = 1, \ldots, \overline{k})$ of parent.

4.3 Constraint Handling

When we apply our MA to the constrained optimization problem in (9), we minimize the following penalty function $g_1(\mathbf{x})$ $(\mathbf{x} \in \mathcal{X})$ with the above VNS.

$$g_1(\mathbf{x}) = -\eta(\mathbf{x}) + \beta \max\{ f(\mathbf{x}) - \varepsilon, \; 0 \}, \qquad \beta > 0. \tag{12}$$

On the other hand, in accordance with the criterion $g_2(\mathbf{x})$ in (13) to be minimized, a new generation is formed by selecting the best individuals from the current population $\mathcal{P}$. As a result, the values of $g_2(\mathbf{x})$ for feasible solutions $\mathbf{x} \in \mathcal{F}$ are always smaller than those of infeasible ones $\mathbf{x} \in \overline{\mathcal{F}} = (\mathcal{X} - \mathcal{F})$[15].

$$\left[\begin{array}{ll} g_2(\mathbf{x}) = -\eta(\mathbf{x}), & \mathbf{x} \in \mathcal{F}. \\ g_2(\mathbf{x}) = -\eta(\mathbf{x}) - \min\limits_{\mathbf{x}' \in \overline{\mathcal{F}} \cap \mathcal{P}} \{ -\eta(\mathbf{x}') \} + \max\limits_{\mathbf{x}'' \in \mathcal{F} \cap \mathcal{P}} \{ -\eta(\mathbf{x}'') \}, & \mathbf{x} \notin \mathcal{F}. \end{array}\right. \tag{13}$$

5 Computational Experiments

5.1 Example of Two-Step Design Approach

We applied the two-step approach to the robust optimum design of the SAW filter shown in Fig.1. Table 1 shows the search space $\mathcal{X}$, i.e., the upper and lower bounds of $x_i \in \mathbf{x}$ $(i = 1, \ldots, 9)$ in Fig.2 and their units e_i. For each of $c_j \in \mathbf{c}$ $(j = 1, 2, 3)$, we assigned three levels: $\acute{c}_j$, $\underline{c}_j = 0.99\,\acute{c}_j$ and $\overline{c}_j = 1.01\,\acute{c}_j$. Then,

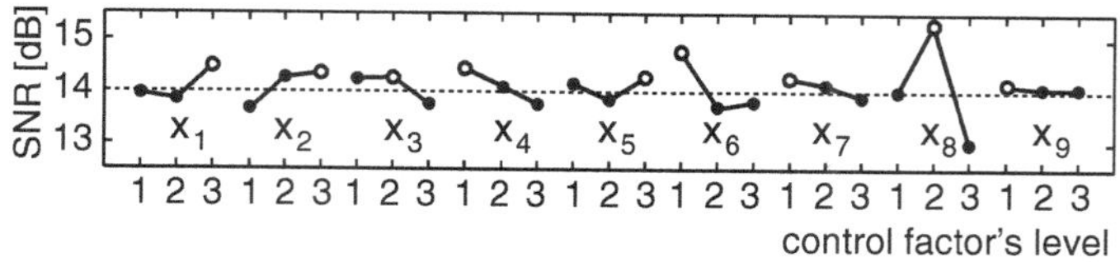

Fig. 5. Factor effect graph for SNR (optimal level: ∘)

Table 1. Search space of control factors

i	x_i	$[\underline{x}_i, \quad \overline{x}_i]$	e_i
1	W	[200, 400]	10
2	N_2	[11.0, 21.0]	0.5
3	N_1	[12.5, 32.5]	1.0
4	N_r	[50, 150]	5
5	D	[0.88, 1.28]	0.02
6	ξ	[0.30, 0.70]	0.05
7	ξ_r	[0.30, 0.70]	0.05
8	ρ_r	[0.98, 1.22]	0.02
9	H	[2900, 3100]	10

Table 2. Comparison of solutions

problem	$\eta(\tilde{\mathbf{x}})$	$f(\tilde{\mathbf{x}})$	time
(7)	16.63	4.65	2.21×10^5
(9)	9.74	0.62	3.28×10^5
(10)	6.66	0.53	3.28×10^5

- Taguchi's first design problem: (7)
- concurrent design problem: (9)
- conventional design problem: (10)

we solved the first design problem in (7) by using the MA with population size: 20, the numbers of offspring generated by crossover: 10 and mutation: 10 in each generation, terminal generation: 40, $\overline{k} = 3$ and $\overline{t} = 400$. We chose these values carefully through some preliminary experiments and the knowledge from (11). As a result, we obtained the best solution $\tilde{\mathbf{x}}$ with $\eta(\tilde{\mathbf{x}}) = 16.63$ [dB].

Figure 5 shows the factor effect for the SNR about $\tilde{x}_i \in \tilde{\mathbf{x}}$ analyzed with the orthogonal array. From Fig.5, we decided optimal levels x_i^o and fixed several $x_j \in \mathbf{x}$ as $x_j = x_j^o$. Also we specified the upper and lower bounds of $\Gamma(\acute{\mathbf{c}}, \mathbf{x}, \omega)$ in (6) at $\omega \in \Omega$ ($|\Omega| = 200$). Then we applied the above MA to the second design problem in (8), changing the number of $x_j^o \in \mathbf{x}$ fixed in $\mathcal{Z} \subseteq \mathcal{X}$.

The best solution $\tilde{\mathbf{x}}$ minimizing the objective function $f(\tilde{\mathbf{x}})$ in (8) might lose its initial value of the SNR $\eta(\tilde{\mathbf{x}})$ achieved at the first design problem in (7). Figure 6 shows the values of $f(\tilde{\mathbf{x}})$ and $\eta(\tilde{\mathbf{x}})$ obtained for the best solutions $\tilde{\mathbf{x}}$ of the second design problems in (8) under various numbers of $x_j^o \in \mathbf{x}$ selected in effective order. From the results in Fig.6, we can observe a trade-off relationship between the robustness and the function of the SAW filter.

5.2 Example of Concurrent Design Approach

(1) Small-sized SAW Filter: We applied the concurrent approach to the robust optimum design of the SAW filter shown in Fig.1. By using the above MA, we solved the optimization problem in (9) under a ceiling $\varepsilon = 1.0$.

Table 2 compares the best feasible solution of the problem in (9) with those of the problems in (7) and (10) on their robustness $\eta(\tilde{\mathbf{x}})$, functions $f(\tilde{\mathbf{x}})$ and the total numbers of solutions examined by MA. Undoubtedly, the concurrent approach was able to improve the robustness of the best solution of the conventional optimum design problem in (10) without losing its function.

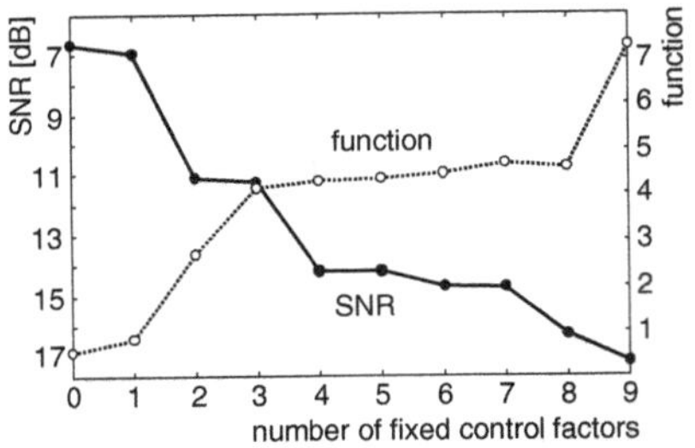

Fig. 6. Robustness and functions

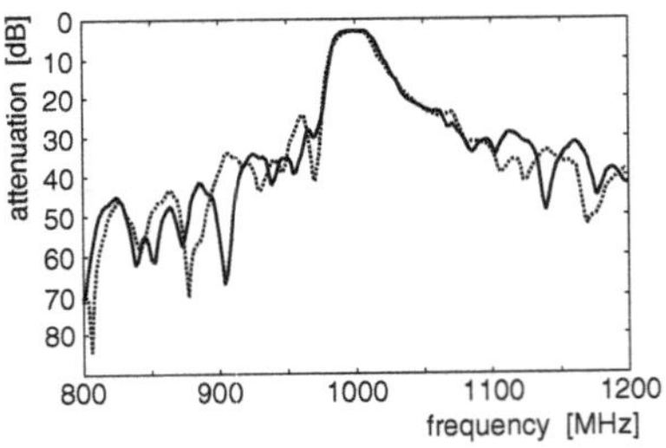

Fig. 7. Frequency response characteristics

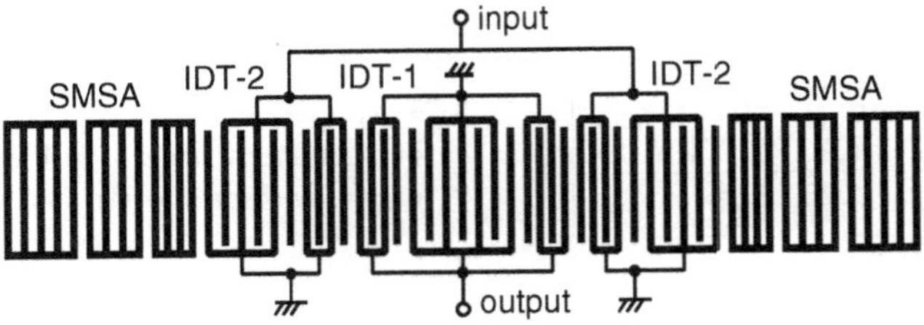

Fig. 8. Large-sized SAW filter with pitch-modulated IDTs and SMSAs

(2) Large-sized SAW Filter: Since we could verify that the concurrent approach was more efficient than the two-step approach, we applied the former approach to the robust optimum design of a large-sized SAW filter illustrated in Fig.8. The complex structure of the large-sized SAW filter including pitch-modulated IDTs and SMSAs is described with 14 control factors[16].

By using the above MA, we obtained the best solution $\tilde{\mathbf{x}}$ of the problem in (9) with $\eta(\tilde{\mathbf{x}}) = 12.51$ [dB] and $f(\tilde{\mathbf{x}}) = 0.49$. On the other hand, the best solution $\tilde{\mathbf{x}}'$ of the problem in (10) became $\eta(\tilde{\mathbf{x}}') = 5.90$ [dB] and $f(\tilde{\mathbf{x}}') = 0.31$. Figure 7 compares the attenuation $\Gamma(\acute{\mathbf{c}}, \tilde{\mathbf{x}}, \omega)$ (solid line) with $\Gamma(\acute{\mathbf{c}}, \tilde{\mathbf{x}}', \omega)$ (broken line). We can't see so much difference between $\Gamma(\acute{\mathbf{c}}, \tilde{\mathbf{x}}, \omega)$ and $\Gamma(\acute{\mathbf{c}}, \tilde{\mathbf{x}}', \omega)$.

6 Conclusions

As a practical application of evolutionary computation in industry track, we have presented a MA equipped with the restricted VNS for the robust optimum design of resonator type SAW filters. Through the computational experiments, we have disclosed that there is a trade-off relationship between the robustness and the functions of SAW filters. Therefore, for realizing an ideal function of SAW filter, the traditional Taguchi's two-step approach demands to solve the second design problems repeatedly, changing the number of fixed control factors. On the other hand, the concurrent approach can offer a proper solution, if the MA is executed twice at most. Consequently, the concurrent design approach is applicable to large-sized SAW filters, as we have demonstrated in this paper.

Future work will focus on the multi-criteria optimization of SAW filters for designing their robustness and functions comprehensively. Also evolutionary computations including MAs are suitable for the multi-criteria optimization.

References

1. C. K. Campbell: Surface Acoustic Wave Devices for Mobile and Wireless Communications, Academic Press (1998)
2. K. Hashimoto: Surface Acoustic Wave Devices in Telecommunications: Modeling and Simulation, Springer-Verlag, Berlin Heidelberg New York (2000)
3. M. Kadota, T. Yoneda, K. Fujimoto, T. Nakao and E. Takata: "Resonator filters using shear horizontal-type leaky surface acoustic wave consisting of heavy-metal electrode and quartz substrate," IEEE Trans. on Ultrasonics, Ferroelectrics, and Frequency Control, vol. 51, no. 2, pp. 202–210 (2004)
4. E. V. Bausk: "Optimization of broadband withdrawal weighted interdigital transducers for high selective SAW filters," IEEE Trans. on Ultrasonics, Ferroelectrics, and Frequency Control, vol. 46, no. 5, pp. 1276–1282 (1999)
5. V. Prabhu, B. S. Panwar and Priyanka: "Linkage learning genetic algorithm for the design of withdrawal weighted SAW filters," Proc. of IEEE Ultrasonics Symposium, pp. 357–360 (2002)
6. K. Tagawa, T. Tokunaga, H. Haneda, T. Igaki and S. Seki: "Optimal design of three-IDT type SAW filter using local search," Proc. of the 28th Annual Conference of the IEEE Industrial Electronics Society (2002)
7. K. Tagawa, T. Yamamoto, T. Igaki and S. Seki: "An Imanishian genetic algorithm for the optimum design of surface acoustic wave filter," Proc. of Congress on Evolutionary Computation pp. 2748–2755 (2003)
8. T. Kojima and T. Suzuki: "Fundamental equations of electro-acoustic conversion for an interdigital surface-acoustic-wave transducer by using force factors," Japanese Journal of Applied Physics Supplement, vol. 31, pp. 194–197 (1992)
9. D. Wiesmann, U. Hammel and T. Bäck: "Robust design of multilayer optical coatings by means of evolutionary algorithms," IEEE Trans. on Evolutionary Computation, vol. 2, no. 4, pp. 162–167 (1998)
10. M. J. Harry and R. Stewart: Six Sigma Mechanical Design Tolerancing, Motorola University Press (1988)
11. G. Taguchi, S. Chowdhury and Y. Wu: Taguchi's Quality Engineering, John Wiley & Sons, Hoboken New Jersey (2005)
12. P. Merz and B. Freisleben: "Fitness landscape analysis and memetic algorithms for the quadratic assignment problem," IEEE Trans. on Evolutionary Computation, vol. 4, no. 4, pp. 337–352 (2000)
13. E. Aarts and J. K. Lenstra: Local Search in Combinatorial Optimization, John Wiley & Sons (1997)
14. L. J. Eshelman and J. D. Schaffer: "Real-coded genetic algorithms and interval-schemata," Foundations of Genetic Alg. 2, Morgan Kaufmann, pp. 187–202 (1993)
15. K. Deb: "An efficient constraint handling method for genetic algorithms," Computer Methods in Applied Mechanics and Engineering, vol. 186, pp. 311–338 (2000)
16. O. Kawachi, S. Mitobe, M. Tajima, T. Yamaji, S. Inoue and K. Hashimoto: "A low-loss and wide-band DMS filter using pitch-modulated IDT and reflector structures," Proc. of UFFC 50th Anniversary Conference, pp. 298–301 (2004)

Genetic Algorithm for Burst Detection and Activity Tracking in Event Streams*

Lourdes Araujo[1], José A. Cuesta[2], and Juan J. Merelo[3]

[1] Departamento de Sistemas Informáticos y Programación, Universidad Complutense de Madrid, Spain
lurdes@sip.ucm.es

[2] Grupo Interdisciplinar de Sistemas Complejos (GISC), Departamento de Matemáticas, Universidad Carlos III de Madrid, Spain
cuesta@math.uc3m.es

[3] Departamento de Arquitectura y Tecnología de Computadores, Universidad de Granada, Spain
jmerelo@geneura.ugr.es

Abstract. We introduce a new model for detection and tracking of bursts of events in a discrete temporal sequence, its only requirement being that the time scale of events is long enough to make a discrete time description meaningful. A model for the occurrence of events using with Poisson distributions is proposed, which, applying Bayesian inference transforms into the well-known Potts model of Statistical Physics, with Potts variables equal to the Poisson parameters (frequencies of events). The problem then is to find the configuration that minimizes the Potts energy, what is achieved by applying an evolutionary algorithm specially designed to incorporate the heuristics of the model. We use it to analyze data streams of very different nature, such as seismic events and weblog comments that mention a particular word. Results are compared to those of a standard dynamic programming algorithm (Viterbi) which finds the exact solution to this minimization problem. We find that, whenever both methods reach a solution, they are very similar, but the evolutionary algorithm outperforms Viterbi's algorithm in running time by several orders of magnitude, yielding a good solution even in cases where Viterbi takes months to complete the search.

1 Introduction and State of the Art

Suppose you are the marketing manager of a publishing house which has recently released a book targeted at being a new best-seller, you have launched a marketing and PR campaign and want to know its impact. One thing you can do is to collect e-mails from public discussion forums on books and check for those that talk about the topic the new book deals with. Once these messages have

* Supported by MEC projects TIC2003-09481-C04 (LA and JJM) and BFM2003-0180 (JAC), CAM-UC3M project UC3M-FI-05-007 (JAC), and CAM project S-0505/ESP/000299 MOSSNOHO (JAC).

T.P. Runarsson et al. (Eds.): PPSN IX, LNCS 4193, pp. 302–311, 2006.

been selected, you end up with a temporal sequence of events. The campaign can be considered successful if after the targeted advertising campaign, references to the book show up as a burst of activity in your temporal series.

In the area of "topic detection and tracking" (TDT) [1], once the document topics have been identified, the sequence of documents for a particular topic can be regarded and analyzed as any other temporal series. There are many natural and social phenomena that produce such temporal series of events: seisms, books or CDs sales, news, e-mails and citations to a scientific paper, to name a few. In all of them, events roughly concentrate in bursts in which, loosely speaking, the frequency of their occurrence first rises, stays there for a while and then fades away. In a graphical representation of such sequences these bursts are more or less visible; however, a precise automatic detection of these bursts and of the frequency of events in them is not trivial because the sequence of events is a stochastic process and noise hides the relevant information. Even in the middle of the burst, events can apart from each other. On the contrary, even if there is no such burst, a few events may be close together. Discriminating whether these are just noise or a significant part of a burst is the real problem that we address in this paper.

Different statistical techniques[6,3,5] have been applied to analyse temporal changes in document streams. In particular, Kleinberg proposed in [6] a probabilistic automaton to model the frequency of document arrival, e-mails with a given topic in his case. High activity episodes or bursts correspond to intervals of high frequency of arrival. The most probable sequence of frequencies follows from Bayesian inference through Viterbi's dynamic programming algorithm [4,7]. A similar analysis using an evolutionary algorithm (EA) instead was recently proposed by some of us [2].

However, there is a limitation in Kleinberg model: events can happen at any time instant, which is true for a certain kind of them (for instance, the problem that motivated Kleinberg, which was e-mail classification). However, the timescale of some events is so long that this may be too much information for a proper modeling. For instance, low intensity earthquakes have a timescale of days; sales are registered with a timescale of days or even weeks, and e-mails on a given topic in a discussion forum also have a timescale of days (an accurate registering of time leads to some modeling issues as the difference between day and night, for instance). A typical sequence of such events consists of the number of occurrences per day, per week, per month or other adequate time period, which is a discrete temporal sequence that cannot be correctly modeled by Kleinberg's model. That is the main reason why we propose here a new automaton model for such a kind of sequences and apply it to several data streams of this type. The search for the most probable sequence of frequencies is made with both Viterbi's algorithm and an EA. When the complexity of the temporal sequence is high enough, the latter, which we present here, is shown to perform much better, even in cases in which Viterbi is infeasible.

The rest of the paper is organized as follows: section 2 describes the probabilistic model, section 3 introduces the EA to obtain the most probable sequence of event frequencies, and section 4 shows the performance in applications to different kinds of data. Results are summarized in section 5.

2 Potts Model for Event Streams

Suppose we have an event log along T time units (days, months, years...) that registers the number of events which occurred at all times $t = 0, 1, \ldots, T$. If events arrive at a constant average frequency, λ, independently of each other, the number of events at any given time, n, follows a Poisson distribution

$$P(n|\lambda) = e^{-\lambda}\frac{\lambda^n}{n!}, \qquad n = 0, 1, 2 \ldots \tag{1}$$

Frequencies may be different at different times, so assuming independence of events occurring at different times, the probability that we observe a certain stream of events $\{n_1, n_2, \ldots, n_T\}$ will be given by

$$P(n_1, n_2, \ldots, n_T|\lambda_1, \lambda_2, \ldots, \lambda_T) = \prod_{t=1}^{T} P(n_t|\lambda_t), \tag{2}$$

where λ_t denotes the event frequency at time t, and $P(n|\lambda)$ is given by (1).

In a typical experiment we have the stream $\{n_1, n_2, \ldots, n_T\}$ and what we want to estimate is the sequence of frequencies which these events have occurred with. Thus we apply Bayesian inference and express

$$\begin{aligned} P(\lambda_1, \ldots, \lambda_T|n_1, \ldots, n_T) &= \frac{P(n_1, \ldots, n_T|\lambda_1, \ldots, \lambda_T)P(\lambda_1, \ldots, \lambda_T)}{P(n_1, \ldots, n_T)} \\ &= \frac{\exp\left\{\sum_{t=1}^{T}(n_t \ln \lambda_t - \lambda_t)\right\} P(\lambda_1, \ldots, \lambda_T)}{P(n_1, \ldots, n_T)\prod_{t=1}^{T} n_t!}, \end{aligned} \tag{3}$$

where we have inserted (2) once 1 has been substituted into it.

Our problem is now to make a sensible choice of the *prior* $P(\lambda_1, \ldots, \lambda_T)$, given the situation we want to model. To begin with, we will assume that the sequence of frequencies is a Markov process, i.e. the frequency that the events a time t have arrived with only depends on the frequency of arrival at the previous time step. This is, of course, a simplification; if the process that models the frequencies has memory, its modeling is hopeless unless we have further information on it. On the other hand, most stochastic processes in real life are Markov processes, so this is a reasonable assumption. Therefore,

$$P(\lambda_1, \ldots, \lambda_T) = P(\lambda_1)P(\lambda_2|\lambda_1)\cdots P(\lambda_T|\lambda_{T-1}). \tag{4}$$

For practical purposes we will assume that frequencies can only take values from a discrete set Λ. Then we take $P(\lambda_1) = 1/E$, with E the number of frequencies in Λ, i.e. any frequency is considered as likely to be observed initially as any other. This reflects our lack of knowledge about the initial the state. For $P(\lambda'|\lambda)$

we make the hypothesis that if the process has frequency λ at time $t-1$, then it will tend to have the same frequency at time t; so with probability p, $\lambda' = \lambda$, and with probability $1-p$, $\lambda' \neq \lambda$ and will equiprobably take any other value of the frequency. Thus,

$$P(\lambda'|\lambda) = p\,\delta_{\lambda',\lambda} + \frac{1-p}{E-1}(1-\delta_{\lambda',\lambda}), \tag{5}$$

where $\delta_{\lambda',\lambda} = 1$ if $\lambda' = \lambda$ and 0 otherwise. A more convenient rewriting is

$$P(\lambda'|\lambda) = \frac{1-p}{E-1}(1-\delta_{\lambda',\lambda} + e^{K}\,\delta_{\lambda',\lambda}) = \frac{1-p}{E-1}\,e^{K\delta_{\lambda',\lambda}}, \tag{6}$$

where we have introduced the new parameter $K = \log[p(E-1)/(1-p)]$.

If we now introduce the prior (4), with these choices, into equation (3),

$$P(\lambda_1,\ldots,\lambda_T|n_1,\ldots,n_T) = \frac{\exp\left\{\sum_{t=1}^{T}(n_t\ln\lambda_t - \lambda_t) + \sum_{t=2}^{T} K\delta_{\lambda_t,\lambda_{t-1}}\right\}}{Z(K;n_1,\ldots,n_T)}, \tag{7}$$

where

$$Z(K;n_1,\ldots,n_T) = E\left(\frac{E-1}{1-p}\right)^{T-1} P(n_1,\ldots,n_T)\prod_{t=1}^{T} n_t! \tag{8}$$

is a normalizing factor and therefore can also be written

$$Z(K;n_1,\ldots,n_T) = \sum_{\{\lambda_t\in\Lambda\}_{t=1}^{T}} \exp\left\{\sum_{t=1}^{T}(n_t\ln\lambda_t - \lambda_t) + \sum_{t=2}^{T} K\delta_{\lambda_t,\lambda_{t-1}}\right\}. \tag{9}$$

Expressions (7) and (9) define the well-known *Potts model* of Statistical Physics [8] in a one-dimensional lattice, with λ_t the Potts variable at site t, K the coupling constant and $\varphi(\lambda_t) = n_t\ln\lambda_t - \lambda_t$, for fixed n_t, an external field acting on λ_t.

Once we have an expression for $P(\lambda_1,\ldots,\lambda_T|n_1,\ldots,n_T)$ we can obtain the desired estimation for the sequence of frequencies $\{\lambda_1,\ldots,\lambda_T\}$ as that which maximizes this probability. Since $Z(K;n_1,\ldots,n_T)$ is independent on the frequencies and the numerator of (7) is an exponential, maximizing this probability is equivalent to maximizing the argument of the exponential (i.e. minus the energy of the configuration in the Potts model), namely

$$f(\lambda_1,\ldots,\lambda_T) = \sum_{t=1}^{T}(n_t\ln\lambda_t - \lambda_t) + K\sum_{t=2}^{T}\delta_{\lambda_t,\lambda_{t-1}}, \tag{10}$$

which turns into a well-defined *fitness function* for an evolutionary algorithm. Please note that the two sums have competing effects on the frequencies: the first one gets maximized when every λ_t is as close as possible to n_t, while the second one reaches its maximum when all frequencies are equal. The "coupling" K is then a parameter that tunes the "stiffness" of the estimation, i.e. the larger

K, the more new events will be assumed to have arrived with the same frequency as the previous ones. Playing with K we can smooth out the intrinsic noise that the data unavoidably contain, and at the same time capture net differences in the frequencies.

3 Evolutionary Algorithm for Event Frequency Tracking

We propose an EA to perform the search of the sequence of event frequencies which maximizes (10). First of all, we need to estimate the model parameters. An estimate of the minimum, λ_{min}, and maximum, λ_{max}, frequencies can be $\lambda_{min} = (1/2)T^{-1}$, $\lambda_{max} = 2M$, with T the longest interval without events, and M the maximum number of events registered in a time unit. The value of E, i.e. the number of different frequencies (states of the automaton) considered is then given by $E = \lambda_{max}/\lambda_{min}$. Thus the possible frequencies are $\lambda_\alpha = \alpha\lambda_{min}$, $\alpha = 1, \cdots, E$.

The choice of p (see 5) is rather arbitrary. However, it enters the model through K (see 6), and this parameter is rather insensitive to the precise value of p provided it is in the range $\sim$ 0.3–0.7. Thus, after checking that other choices lead to the same results, we have taken $p = 0.5$.

The fitness function is directly provided by (10). In what follows we define the remaining ingredients of the EA.

3.1 Individuals and Initial Population

The most immediate representation of the individuals of our EA would be a sequence of T frequencies, one for each time unit. Accordingly, an individual would be a list of T genes g_t, where $g_t \in \{0, \cdots, E\}$ is the frequency at time t, α_t.

However, many adjacent times can be assigned the same frequency, so the sequence of transitions can be compacted. Thus, an individual is a variable length list, in which each position, or gene, represents a time interval with the same frequency. Each gene is composed of a frequency and of an identifier of the first and the last time of the interval.

g_1	g_2	·········	g_f
α_1, $[1, t_2 - 1]$	α_{t_2}, $[t_2, t_3 - 1]$	·········	α_{t_f}, $[t_f, T]$

The initial population of our algorithm is composed of individuals composed of randomly generated sequences of frequency transitions. The simplest way of creating one such sequence is to choose a few times at random and use them to split the whole period of time into intervals, every one of which is assigned a random frequency. Some preliminary experiments have shown, however, that such a naive strategy gives rise to a search space much too large for the algorithm to be efficient. Accordingly, we propose a different strategy. We again choose a random set of times for splitting, but remove those for which the number of events in the preceding interval differ in less than 50%. Afterwards, the first interval is assigned a random frequency and subsequent intervals are assigned a random higher frequency if they have more events than the preceding interval or a random lower frequency if they have less events.

3.2 Crossover Operator

We have adopted the classic one point crossover, which creates two offsprings by splitting two individuals at a crossover point and swapping their second bits. Then, the best offspring replaces the worst parent (steady state, elitist strategy).

There are some details that have to be dealt with, though. The crossover point lies in genes g and g' of both parents, respectively. Thus after swapping, unless both g and g' have the same frequency, each of these genes will become two, one on the left of the crossover point and one on the right, with different frequencies. Several strategies have been tested, but the most efficient one is to leave them as two genes if the number of events at the crossover instant and the preceding instant differ more than 50%; otherwise both the left and right genes are assigned the frequency of g or g' at random, and thus converted back in a single gene.

3.3 Mutation Operator

We have implemented three different mutation operators and each time a mutation occurs one of them is applied at random. The operators are:

1. Choose a gene at random and with equal probability increment or decrement its frequency to the next or previous one.
2. Join two consecutive genes to produce a single one with a frequency randomly taken from one of the original genes.
3. Split a gene in two and assign a different frequency to each piece: one of them is given the frequency of the original gene and the other one is incremented or decremented (depending on whether the number of events is larger or smaller than that of the other piece) a random amount. This operator is only applied if the resulting number of events at both sides of the partition differ more than 50%.

4 Experimental Results

The present model relies on two assumptions: (i) that events occur with a Poisson distribution and (ii) that frequency changes occur with a constant probability and contiguous frequencies are uncorrelated. In order to test the Bayesian reconstruction with our EA independently of these two assumptions we have first tested the model against data streams artificially created using Poisson distributions of different frequencies. The sequence `art_poisson1` presents short periods of constant frequency and small frequency jumps, and the sequence `art_poisson2` presents long periods of constant frequency and large frequency jumps. The outcome of our EA has been compared with that of Viterbi's algorithm (an exhaustive search algorithm for Markov chains) as well as with the

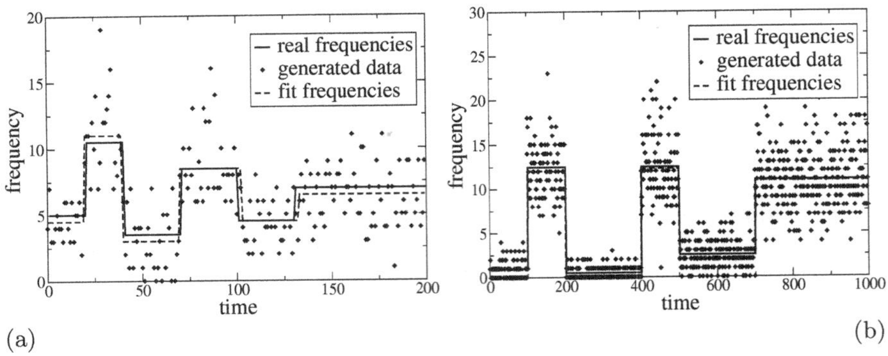

Fig. 1. Artificial sequences created to test the EA: `art_poisson1` (a), and `art_poisson2` (b). We plot the exact sequence of frequencies (full lines), the number of events generated with this sequence along 200 (a) or 1000 (b) time steps (dots), and the result from the EA as well as Viterbi's algorithm (dashed line; both results are indistinguishable in the plot).

exact sequence of frequencies. Both algorithms have been implemented in C++ and run on a Pentium IV 2.4MHz and 1Gb of memory running Linux. Results appear in Figure 1. First of all, we can observe that Viterbi's algorithm reproduces with high accuracy the sequence of frequencies, which proves the validity of the Bayesian inference applied to this model, but the EA yields results which are indistinguishable from them, which proves the validity of the EA —at least for these simple sequences.

The next step taken has consisted in tuning the parameters of the EA. For this purpose we have chosen `art_poisson2`. Figure 2 shows the final fitness attained by the EA for different population sizes (a) as well as its evolution with time for a fixed population (b). Plotted data are averages over 5 different EA runs. Figure 2(a) shows that fitness improves with the population size for any setting of the remaining parameters, although beyond 10^3 individuals and using intermediate values for crossover and mutation rates, no further improvement is obtained. Figure 2(b) shows the fast increase of fitness to its maximum, which is faster the larger the population is (although actual differences are negligible). Figure 3 shows the effect of crossover and mutation on the fitness, also for `art_poisson2`. It can be observed that the best results are obtained with a crossover rate $\sim$ 30–60% and a mutation rate $\sim$ 15–25%.

4.1 Results on Real Data

We have applied our EA to real streams of events of very different nature. The first one, shown in Figure 4, provides the daily number of earthquakes of magnitude ≥ 2 which occurred in Spain in the period 2002/01/01–2004/11/22[1]. Figure 4(a) illustrates the fit produced by the EA with 10^3 individuals, a 30%

[1] Data taken from the "Advance National Seismic System Catalog", web page www.ncedc.org/cnss/catalog-search.html.

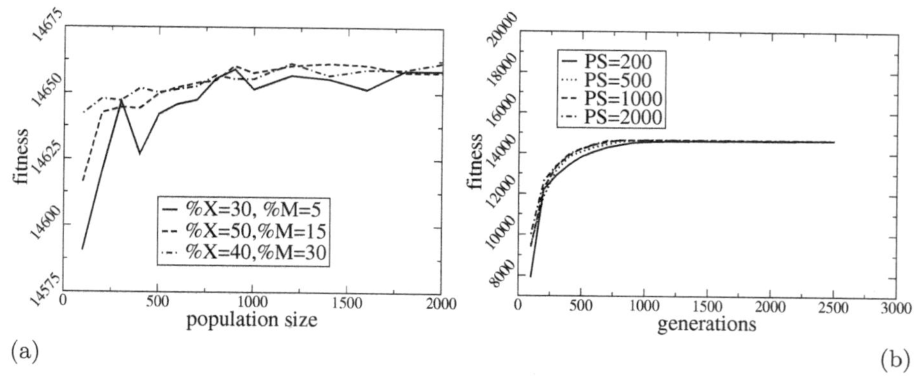

Fig. 2. (a) Final fitness attained with different population sizes for several values of crossover and mutation rates. (b) Evolution of the fitness along 10^4 generations (crossover rate = 50%, mutation rate = 15%), for different population sizes.

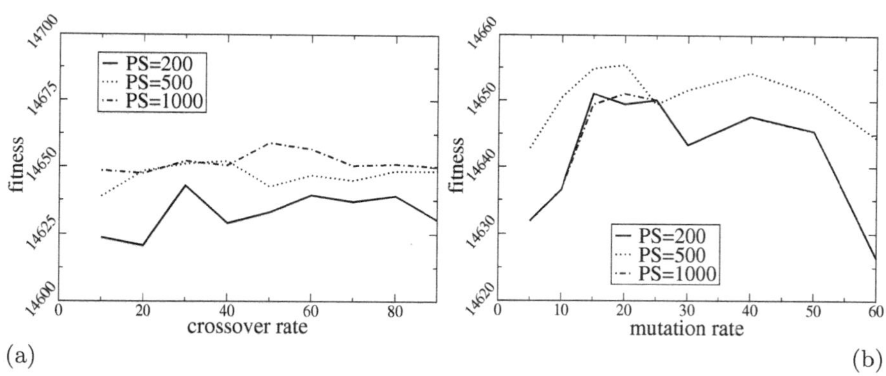

Fig. 3. Fitness reached with different values of the crossover rate (with a 15% of mutation) (a) as well as of the mutation rate (with a 50% of crossover) (b), for several population sizes. Total number of generations: 10^4.

of crossover, a 5% of mutation and run for 5×10^3 generations. Figure 4(b) is a cumulative plot of the same results. The goodness of the fit is more evident in this latter plot, so the remaining data are plotted using this representation. The second and third set of data are formed by the comments on 'blog' and 'Google', respectively, sent to all blogs hosted in Blogalia (http://blogalia.com) during the period January 2002-January 2006. A cumulative plot of these data, as well as the fits produced by the EA with 10^3 individuals, a 50% of crossover, a 15% of mutation and run for 10^4 generations, appear in Figure 5. Despite being data of a very different nature, the fit is as good as that for the earthquakes. One of the most important aspects to remark about our experiments is the comparison of the execution times needed by the EA and by the Viterbi's algorithm. As it can be seen in Table 1, Viterbi required about two orders of magnitude more time to reach the solution than the EA. In fact, in two of the cases Viterbi was stopped

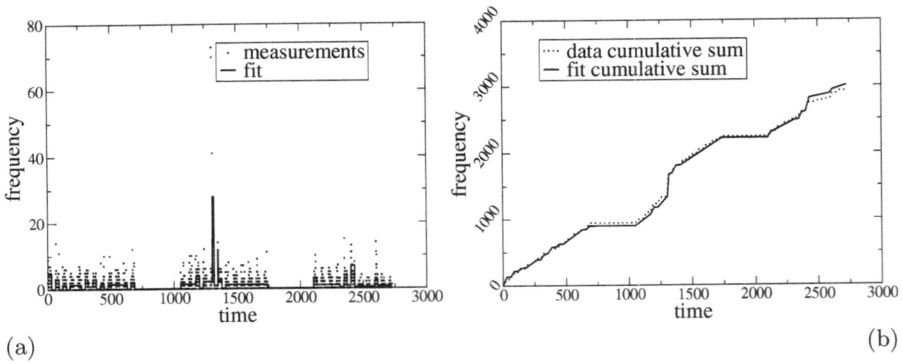

Fig. 4. Fit to the daily number of earthquakes of magnitude ≥ 2 which occurred in Spain in the period 2002/01/01–2004/11/22.

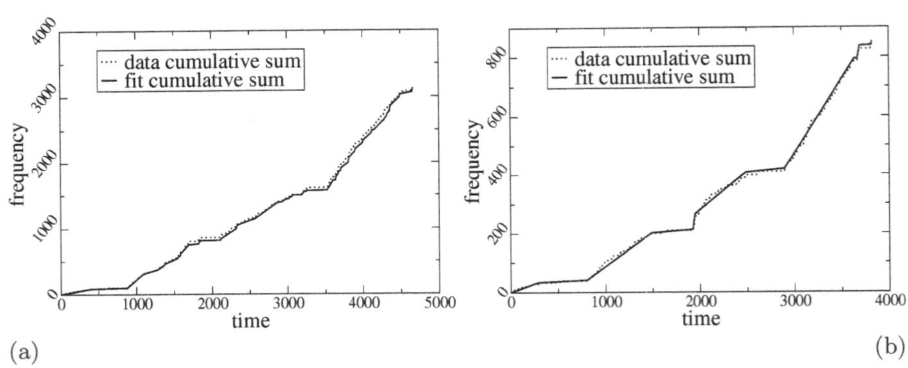

Fig. 5. Time sequence of comments on 'blog' and 'Google' during the period January 2002-January 2006

without reaching a solution, and the time to get it was estimated extrapolating from the time required to compute every time step. The main reason for such an impressive improvement in performance is the fact that the EA conducts a search very much guided by the heuristics on the particular problem under study that can be implemented in the evolution operators (in our case, for instance, the way crossover and mutation are implemented eliminates trials which assign different frequencies to segments with similar number of events). This dramatically reduces the size of the search space, so much as to render feasible problems that

Table 1. Execution times required by the EA and estimated for Viterbi

	Viterbi		EA	
earthquakes	7140862 s	(> 82 days)	27514.2 s	(7.64 hours)
coment_blogs	697412 s	(> 8 days)	25139.3 s	(7.00 hours)
coment_google	237800 s	(> 2 days)	35609.4 s	(9.89 hours)

would not be so with a standard algorithm like Viterbi's. These two elements: the accuracy of the results, and the dramatic increase in performance, justify the application of an EA to this problem.

5 Conclusions

In this paper we have proposed a model for detection and tracking of bursts in data streams coming from a wide range of problems. The model applies to those problems which are well represented by a discrete temporal series where we have a log of the number of events every time unit (day, week, month, year...). We model event occurrences by Poisson distributions and apply Bayesian inference to find the sequence of Poisson parameters that maximizes the likelihood. The problem is shown to be equivalent to minimizing the energy of the well-known Potts model of Statistical Physics. We use the negative of this energy as the fitness of a special purpose evolutionary algorithm to solve this problem, and apply it to streams of data obtained from earthquake detection and from weblog comments. The results are very similar to those obtained from Viterbi's algorithm, which is guaranteed to find the absolute maximum of such problems. However, execution times for the evolutionary algorithm are about two orders of magnitude smaller than those employed by Viterbi, thus leaving the evolutionary algorithm as the only available tool to reach a solution in a reasonable time for real collections of data.

References

1. James Allan. *Topic Detection and Tracking: Event-Based Information Organization.* Kluwer Academic Publishers, 2002.
2. Lourdes Araujo and Juan J. Merelo. Automatic detection of trends in dynamical text: An evolutionary approach, 2006.
3. Ella Bingham, Ata Kabán, and Mark Girolami. Topic identification in dynamical text by complexity pursuit. *Neural Process. Lett.*, 17(1):69–83, 2003.
4. G. D. Forney. The Viterbi algorithm. *Proceedings of The IEEE*, 61(3):268–278, 1973.
5. Mark Girolami and Ata Kaban. Simplicial mixtures of Markov chains: Distributed modelling of dynamic user profiles. In Sebastian Thrun, Lawrence Saul, and Bernhard Schölkopf, editors, *Advances in Neural Information Processing Systems 16.* MIT Press, Cambridge, MA, 2004.
6. J. Kleinberg. Bursty and hierarchical structure in streams. In *Proc. 8th ACM SIGKDD Intl. Conf. on Knowledge Discovery and Data Mining*, pages 91–101. ACM, 2002.
7. Lawrence R. Rabiner. A tutorial on hidden Markov models and selected applications in speech recognition. In *Readings in speech recognition*, pages 267–296. Morgan Kaufmann Publishers Inc., 1990.
8. F. Y. Wu. The potts model. *Review of Modern Physics*, 54:235–268, 1982.

Computationally Intelligent Online Dynamic Vehicle Routing by Explicit Load Prediction in an Evolutionary Algorithm*

Peter A.N. Bosman and Han La Poutré

Centre for Mathematics and Computer Science,
P.O. Box 94079, 1090 GB Amsterdam, The Netherlands
{Peter.Bosman, Han.La.Poutre}@cwi.nl

Abstract. In this paper we describe a computationally intelligent approach to solving the dynamic vehicle routing problem where a fleet of vehicles needs to be routed to pick up loads at customers and drop them off at a depot. Loads are introduced online during the actual planning of the routes. The approach described in this paper uses an evolutionary algorithm (EA) as the basis of dynamic optimization. For enhanced performance, not only are currently known loads taken into consideration, also possible future loads are considered. To this end, a probabilistic model is built that describes the behavior of the load announcements. This allows the routing to make informed anticipated moves to customers where loads are expected to arrive shortly. Our approach outperforms not only an EA that only considers currently available loads, it also outperforms a recently proposed enhanced EA that performs anticipated moves but doesn't employ explicit learning. Our final conclusion is that under the assumption that the load distribution over time shows sufficient regularity, this regularity can be learned and exploited explicitly to arrive at a substantial improvement in the final routing efficiency.

1 Introduction

The goal in solving dynamic optimization problems is to provide solutions during a timespan such that the result of a certain function, integrated over that timespan, is optimized [5,7]. In practice, such problems typically have to be solved online, i.e. as time actually goes by. To solve such problems, often a myopic approach is taken. The quality of a decision is then taken only to be how good it is in the current situation. This approach however is blind to the important issue of time-dependence: decisions taken now have consequences in the future. To establish a non–myopic approach, the system's future response to earlier decisions must be known. In practice however, this information is typically not available. Therefore, to be able to anticipate the system's future behavior, this information needs to be learned from experience that is gained as time goes by.

* This work is part of DEAL (Distributed Engine for Advanced Logistics) supported as project EETK01141 under the Dutch EET programme.

T.P. Runarsson et al. (Eds.): PPSN IX, LNCS 4193, pp. 312–321, 2006.

Recently, a framework has been proposed to deal with anticipating the future in the problem to be optimized [4]. The framework is based on a synergy in computational intelligence: evolutionary algorithms (EAs) and statistical/machine learning (ML/SL). EAs are known to be a good problem–solving methodology for dynamic optimization with respect to the efficiency of tracking optima as these optima shift through the search space as time goes by [5]. Often this is a virtue of properly maintaining diversity in the population. As such, EAs provide a solid basis for building a robust non–myopic approach to dynamic optimization. The ML/SL techniques are used to explicitly predict for future times the observed values of problem–specific variables and/or the quality of decisions. The EA optimizes decisions not only with respect to the current situation but also future decisions with respect to future, predicted, situations (i.e. it builds a plan/strategy). It was shown, as a proof of principle, that this approach is capable of outperforming strategies that do not use explicit future prediction.

In this paper we tailor this approach to a key dynamic optimization problem that is important to the transportation and logistics industry: the dynamic vehicle routing problem [6]. In this problem, routes have to be planned for a fleet of vehicles to pick up loads at customers. The problem is dynamic because the loads to be transported are announced while the vehicles are already on-route.

Intuitively, one can construct a more efficient routing, resulting in the delivery of more loads, if one would know beforehand when the loads will become ready for transport. It would then be possible to send a vehicle to a customer that currently has no load available, but it is known that a load will be available at that customer upon arrival of the vehicle. Alternatively stated, this information allows us to see that a current decision to send a vehicle to pick up a currently available load may in the end not be the best thing to do. This corresponds exactly to the non-myopic approach for which the earlier mentioned framework has been developed. However, this optimal information about future introduction of new loads is not readily available. The only option left is to learn it.

A few studies currently exist in which information is used about future loads [3,8,10,11,14]. Most approaches employ a waiting strategy. For each vehicle, upon its arrival at a customer, a waiting window is defined within which a new load is expected to arrive at that customer or at a nearby customer. During that waiting period, the vehicle doesn't move because it anticipates on having to move only a little in the near future to pick up a new load. In this paper, similar to [14], we opt for an approach in which the vehicles keep driving, unless they are at a centrally located depot. The rationale behind this idea is the principled notion that as long as there are loads to be transported, we don't want to have any vehicles waiting around. To move the vehicles as efficiently as possible, we propose to learn the distribution of load announcements at the customers. We use this information to predict the number of future expected loads at a certain customer. By directly integrating this expected value into the fitness of solutions, i.e. vehicle routes, the evolutionary algorithm (EA) that we use in this paper is able to make informed decisions about anticipated moves (i.e. moves to customers that currently don't have a load ready). Not only do the results show an improvement compared to building routes solely on the basis of currently available loads, our explicit–learning approach also outperforms the EA proposed in [14] that uses anticipated moves without explicit learning.

The remainder of this paper is organized as follows. In Section 2 we describe the dynamic vehicle routing problem as targeted in this paper. Subsequently, in Section 3 we describe the approach that we take to solving the problem. In addition to describing a base dynamic EA, we describe both an existing approach from the literature to using anticipation and our explicit–learning approach to using anticipation. In Section 4 we present results of running experiments with the various EAs. Finally, some conclusions are drawn in Section 5.

2 Problem Definition

The definition of the dynamic vehicle routing problem that we use in this paper is the same as the one used by Van Hemert and La Poutré [14]. Exact mathematical details are in extenso formulated in [14]. Due to space constraints we shall restrict ourselves here to an intuitive, yet concise, description of the problem at hand.

A set of customers is predefined. Each customer has a certain location defined by 2D coordinates. The distance between two locations is taken to be the Euclidean distance. The goal in solving the problem is to deliver as many loads as possible. Each load has to be picked up at a certain customer and must be delivered to the central depot. A load has a certain announcement time (i.e. the time from which it is available for pickup). Each load must be delivered to the depot within a certain delivery window, starting from the moment of announcement. Beyond this delivery window the load is no longer accepted by the depot. The size of the delivery window is fixed and is denoted Δ.

To transport the loads, a fleet of vehicles is available. All vehicles have the same capacity. All loads have the same size. Both the size of the loads and the capacity of the vehicles is integer. Initially, all vehicles are located at the depot.

At any time t^{now}, the solver must be able to return a list of actions to be performed; one separate action for each vehicle in the fleet. Actions are either to go and pick up a load at a customer, to go to a certain customer without a pickup assignment (i.e. an anticipated move) or to go back to the depot to drop off all loads that are currently being carried.

To ensure that loads are only picked up if they can be delivered on time and to furthermore ensure that loads that have actually been picked up are indeed delivered on time, constraints exist to ensure that such solutions are infeasible. The optimization approach must now only return feasible solutions.

3 Optimization Approach

3.1 The Dynamic Solver

The dynamic solver updates the optimization problem whenever a change occurs, i.e. when a new load becomes available for pick up. In addition, the dynamic solver controls the EA. It runs the EA and announces changes to the EA so that these changes may be accounted for in the solutions that the EA is working with. It also requests the currently best available solution from the EA whenever changes occur and presents that solution to the real world as the plan to be executed. In our case, the problem changes whenever a new load is announced, whenever a load is picked up or whenever loads are delivered. In addition, the currently executed solution changes whenever a vehicle arrives at a customer, regardless of whether a load is to be picked up there.

The EA is run between changes (also called events). In practice, the time that is available for running equals the time between events. Because computing fitness evaluations takes up most of the time, in our simulated experiments we ensured that the number of evaluations that the EA was allowed to perform between two subsequent events is linearly proportional to the time between events in the simulation. For each time unit of the simulation the EA may perform one generation. Since the population size will be fixed, the EA will thus perform a fixed number of evaluations in one simulation run.

The whole simulation operates by alternatively running the EA and the simulated routing problem. The routing simulator calculates when the next event will occur, e.g., a vehicle will pick up or deliver a load, or, a load is announced for pickup. Then, the EA may run up until this event occurs. This way we simulate an interrupt of the EA when it needs to adapt to changes in the real world. The best individual from the last generation before the interrupt is used to update the assignments of the vehicles in the routing simulation. Then, the routing problem is advanced up until the next event. Afterwards, the individuals of the EA are updated by removing assignments that are no longer applicable (i.e. delivered loads or loads that have passed their delivery window) and by adding assignments to pick up loads that have recently been made available.

3.2 Base EA: Routing Currently Available Loads

With the exception of the selection method, the base EA that we use is the same as the one used by Van Hemert and La Poutré [14].

Representation
The representation is a set of action lists, one separate list for each vehicle in the fleet. An action list describes all actions that the vehicle will perform in that order. In the case of the base EA, this action list contains only pickup actions. The first action in the list for a specific vehicle is the action that is currently being executed by that vehicle. Properties such as the number of loads that a vehicle already carries is stored in the simulation and is not subject to search.

New loads
Whenever the solver announces new loads to the EA, these loads are injected randomly into the action list of a single vehicle in each member of the population.

Variation
Only mutation is considered. In the mutation of an individual, two vehicles are chosen randomly. These two vehicles may actually be the same vehicle. From these two vehicles, two actions from their lists are chosen randomly. These actions

are swapped. This operator allows visits to customers to be exchanged between vehicles or to be re–ordered in the route of a single vehicle directly.

Selection
The selection scheme that we employ ensures elitism. We use truncation selection to select half of the population. The other half is discarded. Using variation, the discarded half is replaced with new individuals. Hence, elitism of the best half of the population is employed. Although this selection operator is rather strict, enough diversity is introduced as a result of mutation and the random introduction of new loads. As a result, selecting more strictly allows the EA to weed out bad solutions more efficiently.

Decoding
It is important to note that as a result of load introduction and of variation, action lists may come to represent an infeasible solution. For example the action list may cause the vehicle to be on–route too long for the loads that it is carrying to be returned to the depot within the delivery window. For this reason a decoding mechanism is used that decodes the representation into a valid solution, i.e., a solution where none of the constraints are violated. The representation itself is not altered. Assignments that violate one or more time constraints are ignored upon decoding. When a vehicle reaches its capacity or when adding more assignments will violate a time constraint, the decoder inserts a visit to the depot into the action list. Afterwards, this vehicle may be deployed to service customers again. This procedure is the same as used in [9]. The fitness of the individual will be based on the decoded solution. Although the decoding process may have a large impact on the fitness landscape, it is necessary as in a dynamic environment we must be able to produce valid solutions on demand.

Fitness
The fitness of an individual corresponds to the number of loads that is returned to the depot, i.e. the number of loads picked up when executing the current decoded action lists for all vehicles. It should be noted that this representation already provides, in part, a way to oversee future consequences of current decisions. To see this, note that the only decision required to be taken at each point in time from the problem's perspective is what to let each vehicle in the fleet do next. By having a list of actions to perform after the first next move, planning ahead is made possible, which consequently allows for more efficient routing. However, this anticipation at time t^{now} covers only the non–stochastic information about the problem that is available at time t^{now}. It might be possible to improve the benefits of anticipation further by considering some of the stochastic information about the problem at time t^{now}. This is the goal of introducing anticipated moves.

3.3 Enhanced EA: Anticipated Moves

Implicit anticipation. The first approach that we describe to introducing anticipated moves into the EA is the one originally proposed in [14]. In this approach, there is no explicit link between making an anticipated move and the expected reward to be gained from that move. Instead, the mechanism behind anticipated moves is implicit and focuses on ensuring that anticipated moves do not cause the resulting routing to violate any constraints. Ultimately, this results in slight deviations from routes that are built based upon currently available loads, otherwise the loads will not be returned to the depot in time. It is only over multiple generations and over time that in retrospect an anticipated move can be found to have been advantageous.

Variation
To guide the introduction of anticipated moves, an anticipated–move–rate α is used. Upon mutation, this parameter represents the probability of introducing an anticipated move into the route of a single vehicle. Similar to mutation in evolution strategies [2], this parameter is subject to self–mutation.

Fitness
To prevent selection of individuals with a large α that cause many constraint–violating anticipated moves to be introduced, the fitness function is extended with a penalty term. The penalty term grows linearly with the number of constraint–violating anticipated moves in a solution.

Explicit anticipation. The results reported in [14] already indicate an improvement over the base EA for certain values of the delivery window Δ. However, there is no directly apparent reason that the anticipated moves will actually result in the collection of more loads. A bigger improvement is to be expected if a proper, direct and explicit reason for making anticipated moves is introduced. To this end, we opt for an explicit means of anticipation. We still use the basic strategy of introducing anticipated moves randomly, i.e. we use the same variation technique. To bias the search toward feasible anticipated moves with a positive number of expected future loads, we alter the fitness function.

Fitness
First, assume that we have an oracle that can tell us for each customer exactly when future loads will become available at that customer. In that case the fitness of a decoded action list can be computed by not only counting the number of loads that are picked up along the route as a result of premeditated pickup actions, but also the number of loads that are available at customers upon arrival there. Care must be taken that the capacity of the vehicle is not exceeded in computing the number of additional loads. Moreover, only the loads that can still be brought back to the depot on time should be counted. Also, each load should only be counted once to avoid overrating the goodness of anticipated moves when two or more vehicles have planned a visit to the same specific customer. As we now know exactly how fruitful certain anticipated moves are, this extension allows for a much more efficient search of anticipated moves.

In practice we do not have such perfect information. Hence, the only thing left that we can do is estimate it. The closer the estimation, the closer we get to the case of optimal information. For each customer we propose to estimate the distribution of the time between two subsequent loads becoming available for transport. To estimate this distribution, we use the normal distribution. How to compute maximum–likelihood estimates for the normal distribution is well known from the literature [1,13]. The expected number of loads that will become available at a certain customer c_i between the current time t^{now} and the time of arrival of a vehicle at that specific customer t^{arrive} is just $(t^{\text{arrive}} - t^{\text{now}})/\mu^{c_i}$ where μ^{c_i} is the mean of the distribution of the time between two subsequent loads at customer c_i. Similar to the case of perfect information we have to make sure that we only count the expected loads that can still be brought back to the depot in time. Also the capacity of the vehicle and the possibility of multiple vehicles planning an anticipated trip need to be taken into account. This can be done exactly the same way as in the case of perfect information.

4 Experiments

4.1 Experimental Setup

In practice, customers are often clustered into regions as opposed to scattered around uniformly [12]. We therefore use a particular arrangement of the customers by clusters, similar to the arrangement used in [14]. First a set of points called the set of cluster centers C is created by randomly selecting points (x, y) in the 2–dimensional space such that these points are uniformly distributed in that space. Then for each cluster center $(x, y) \in C$ a set of locations $R(x, y)$ is created such that these locations are scattered around the cluster center by using a Gaussian random distribution with an average distance of τ to choose the diversion from the center. This way we get clusters with a circular shape. The set of customer nodes N is defined as $N = \{n | n \in R(x, y) \wedge (x, y) \in C\}$. The set of locations form the nodes of the graph $G = (N, E)$. This graph is a full graph and its edges E are labeled with the costs to traverse them. For each $(n_1, n_2) \in E$, this cost is equal to the Euclidean distance between n_1 and n_2.

A set of loads is randomly generated, which represents the work that needs to be routed. Every load starts at a customer node and needs to be carried to a central depot, which is located in the center of the map. Each customer generates loads where the time between two subsequent loads is normally distributed with a mean of μ^{Loads} and a standard deviation of σ^{Loads}. Typically customers are manufacturers. Therefore, the internal process of preparing loads is often quite regular. The larger the standard deviation, the less regular the process is assumed to be and the more randomly generated the loads will appear to be.

We have randomly generated 25 problem instances and have run the EA without anticipation, the EA with implicit anticipation, the EA with optimal–information anticipation and the EA with learned–information anticipation for $1 \cdot 10^5$ time units. We have varied the standard deviation of the time between subsequent loads, the delivery window and the capacity of the vehicles. An overview of all involved parameters used in our experimental setup is given in Table 1.

4.2 Results

Figure 1 shows the efficiency of the various EAs with respect to the problems in our test suite for a standard deviation of the time spread of the loads of 40. The use of truncation selection and elitism compared to the use of tournament

Table 1. Parameter settings used in our experiments

Parameter	Value
Maximum width and height of the map	200×200
Number of locations	$\|N\| = 50$
Number of clusters	$\|C\| = 5$
Spread of locations in a cluster	$\tau = 10$
Number of vehicles	$\|V\| = 10$
Capacity constraint	$q \in \{1, 5\}$
Delivery time constraint	$\Delta \in \{20, 40, \ldots, 400\}$
Average time spread of loads	$\mu^{\text{Loads}} = 400$
Standard dev. time spread of loads	$\sigma^{\text{Loads}} \in \{20, 40, \ldots, 200\}$

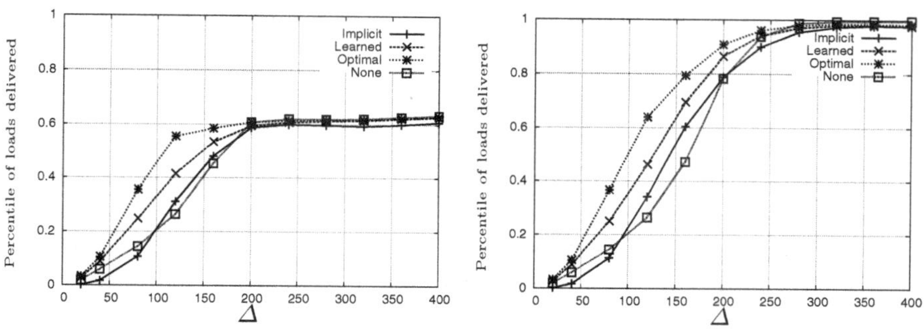

Fig. 1. Routing efficiency in percentage of loads delivered as a function of the delivery window for all tested algorithms and a standard deviation of the time spread of the loads of $\sigma^{\text{Loads}} = 40$. Vehicle capacity is 1 in the left graph and 5 in the right graph.

selection and a generational scheme that was used in the EA that employed implicitly anticipated moves [14] was observed to give better results. This causes the ratio of improvement of the implicit anticipation approach compared to using no anticipation to be smaller than was found in the earlier research.

Similar to the results by Van Hemert and La Poutré [14], there is a clear shift in problem difficulty when varying the length of the delivery time window. If this time window is very small, anticipatory routing only pays off if one is certain that there will be loads that can be picked up upon arrival at a certain customer. The number of loads that can be picked up and delivered on time is so small that uninformed anticipatory moves directly cause a drop in the number of loads that could have been delivered otherwise. Indeed, if the learned information or the perfect information is used, an improvement can be found over not using anticipatory moves, where the perfect information of course leads to the biggest improvements. For an average Δ there is much room for improvement. Indeed all anticipatory approaches are capable of obtaining better results than the non-anticipatory approach. However, the use of explicit learning and predicting the announcement of new loads is able to obtain far better results than when the implicit means of anticipation is used. If the delivery window becomes too large, there is ample time to fully use the capacity of the fleet to the maximum and hence there is no longer any difference between using anticipation and using no anticipation. The problem thus becomes easier.

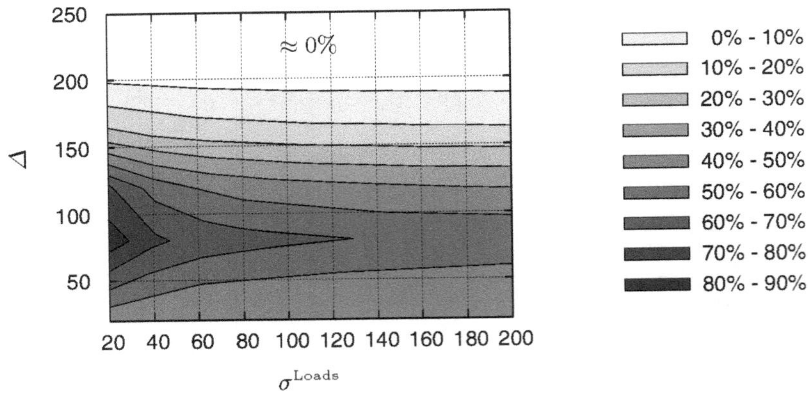

Fig. 2. Relative performance increase of our proposed anticipation–by–explicit–learning EA over the non–anticipatory EA for various values of the delivery window and the standard deviation of the time spread of the loads

Figure 2 shows a contour graph of the relative performance increase that can be obtained when using our explicit prediction approach to anticipation as compared to the EA that doesn't use anticipatory moves. This height–map shows clearly the phase–shift with respect to the delivery time window. There are clear bounds within which an improvement can be obtained. This graph also shows the influence of the randomness of the problem. The larger the standard deviation of the time between subsequent loads, the smaller the performance increase becomes. Clearly, the largest performance increase can be obtained if the variance goes down to 0, which corresponds to the case of using the optimal information. Although the best results only comprise a small area of the graph and thus correspond only to a specific type of problem settings, the range of problem settings for which an improvement can be obtained is large and rather robust with respect to an increase in randomness. Hence we can conclude that our explicit anticipatory approach provides a robust means of improving the quality of online dynamic vehicle routing that is generally speaking preferable compared to an implicit means of anticipatory routing.

5 Conclusions

In this paper we have revisited a dynamic vehicle routing model that defines a load collection problem, i.e. the pickup and delivery of loads to a central depot. Conforming to earlier work, we have argued that the use of anticipatory moves to customers where currently no load is available can improve the quality of routing. As an extension to earlier work, we have argued that such anticipatory routing can be greatly improved if decisions for making anticipatory moves are well–informed. We have used this observation in an evolutionary algorithm by following an existing framework that integrates evolutionary computation with learning techniques to predict future situations and to simultaneously base current decisions on the currently available information as well as the predicted information. Specifically, we have learned the times between subsequent loads at customers and used this information to predict when new loads will become available. This information is explicitly used to define the fitness of a planned route that possibly contains anticipatory moves. By doing so, we have found, similar to earlier work, transition points in varying problem–specific parameters between which it makes sense to employ anticipatory routing. Moreover, our explicit learning approach clearly outperformed an earlier approach that introduced anticipatory moves in an implicit manner. Hence, by analyzing carefully what it is that should be predicted, learning this information from past experience and explicitly incorporating it in anticipating the consequences of current decisions, better results can be obtained than when using no prediction or when using an implicit means of prediction.

References

1. T. W. Anderson. *An Introduction to Multivariate Statistical Analysis.* John Wiley & Sons Inc., New York, New York, 1958.
2. T. Bäck. *Evolutionary Algorithms in Theory and Practice.* Oxford University Press, Oxford, 1996.
3. R. Bent and P. van Hentenryck. Scenario–based planning for partially dynamic vehicle routing with stochastic customers. *Operations Research*, 52:977–987, 2004.
4. P. A. N. Bosman. Learning, anticipation and time–deception in evolutionary online dynamic optimization. In S. Yang and J. Branke, editors, *Proceedings of the Evolutionary Algorithms for Dynamic Optimization Problems EvoDOP Workshop at the Genetic and Evolutionary Computation Conference — GECCO–2005*, pages 39–47, New York, New York, 2005. ACM Press.
5. J. Branke. *Evolutionary Optimization in Dynamic Environments.* Kluwer, Norwell, Massachusetts, 2001.
6. G. Ghiani, F. Guerriero, G. Laporte, and R. Musmanno. Real–time vehicle routing: Solution concepts, algorithms and parallel computing strategies. *European Journal of Operational Research*, 151(1):1–11, 2004.
7. M. Grötschel, S. O. Krumke, and J. Rambau. *Online optimization of large scale systems.* Springer Verlag, Berlin, 2001.
8. S. Ichoua, M. Gendreau, and J.-Y. Potvin. Exploiting knowledge about future demands for real–time vehicle dispatching. 2006. Forthcoming in *Transportation Science.*
9. G. Laporte, F. Louveaux, and H. Mercure. The vehicle routing problem with stochastic travel times. *Transportation science*, 26:161–170, 1992.
10. S. Mitrovic-Minic, R. Krishnamurti, and G. Laporte. Double–horizon based heuristics for the dynamic pickup and delivery problem with time windows. *Transportation Science B*, 38:669–685, 2004.
11. S. Mitrovic-Minic and G. Laporte. Waiting strategies for the dynamic pickup and delivery problem with time windows. *Transportation Science B*, 38:635–655, 2004.
12. M. Solomon. The vehicle routing problem and scheduling problems with time window constraints. *Operations Research*, 35:254–265, 1987.
13. M. M. Tatsuoka. *Multivariate Analysis: Techniques for Educational and Psychological Research.* John Wiley & Sons Inc., New York, New York, 1971.
14. J. I. van Hemert and J. A. La Poutré. Dynamic routing problems with fruitful regions: Models and evolutionary computation. In X. Yao et al., editors, *Parallel Problem Solving from Nature — PPSN VIII*, pages 690–699. Springer–Verlag, 2004.

Novel Approach to Develop Rheological Structure-Property Relationships Using Genetic Programming

Elsa Jordaan, Jaap den Doelder, and Guido Smits

Dow Benelux B.V., Core R&D,
P.O. Box 48, 4530 AA Terneuzen, The Netherlands
{EMJordaan, CFDenDoelder, GFSmits}@dow.com

Abstract. Rheological structure-property models play a crucial role in the manufacturing and processing of polymers. Traditionally rheological models are developed by design of experiments that measure a rheological property as a function of the moments of molar mass distributions. These empirical models lack the capacity to apply to a wide range of distributions due the limited availability of experimental data. In recent years fundamental models were developed to satisfy a wider range of distributions, but they are in terms of variables not readily available during processing or manufacturing. Genetic programming can be used to bridge the gap between the practical, but limited, empirical models and the more general, but less practical, fundamental models. This is a novel approach of generating rheological models that are both practical and valid for a wide set of distributions.

Keywords: genetic programming, rheology, molar mass distribution.

1 Introduction

Structure-property relationships of materials, like plastics, are very important in the manufacturing and application of materials. Over the last thirty years, a multidisciplinary field of relating the performance and function of matter in an application to its micro-, nano-, and atomic-structure, has developed [1]. This field is known as materials science. At the basis of all materials science is to understand how the desired properties of a material in a certain application are related to the material's structure and vice versa. The way in which the material is processed (formed or created) is an important determinant of the structure and thus of its properties. Radical materials advances can drive the creation of new products or even new industries. Industrial applications of materials science include materials design, cost/benefit tradeoffs in the production of materials, and improving processing and analytical techniques.

One particular field of research in materials science is rheology. Rheology is the science of the flow and deformation of matter [2]. It is associated to the so-called visco-elastic materials, which have a complex dynamic behavior. All materials act as solids when deformation is fast and as liquids when deformation is slow.

T.P. Runarsson et al. (Eds.): PPSN IX, LNCS 4193, pp. 322–331, 2006.

An every day example of this is glass. When impacted by fast movement, glass will shatter. However, over time the glass in windows will "flow" to the bottom under force of gravity. The general flow and relaxation behavior of materials is therefore a combination of elastic and viscous response.

Important visco-elastic materials are polymers (plastics). Many of the commercially available polymers are produced in chemical plants, accounting for a multi-billion dollar market. The rheology of polymers is essential in various aspects. It is a characterization tool as rheology is very sensitive to molecular structure. It is also key to the complex processes that transform the material into a final product, such as a plastic bag, an insulating foam sheet, or a car bumper. During such processes, the polymer is typically molten after which a time-dependent force and motion is imposed. Rheology governs the response of the molten material to the deformation.

The modeling of materials is quite difficult for a number of reasons. One reason is the difficulty in observing everything that is needed to describe the materials completely despite the vast array of techniques that exist to characterize them. A second major reason is the inherent multi-scale nature of the composition and properties of many materials in terms of length scales (from nanometers to meters) and time scales (from nanoseconds to years). Parts of this spectrum can be covered by fundamental models but many gaps exist that need to be bridged by (semi-)empirical models.

This paper describes a novel approach to develop desired rheological models by making use of genetic programming. The layout of this paper is as follows. The next section describes the classical approaches to develop rheological models. It also discusses briefly the limitations of each approach and proposed a new strategy of modelling rheology. The third section shows how traditional power-law fitting fails to develop satisfactory models using the new strategy. Finally, in Section Four, Genetic Programming (GP) is employed as a novel approach to generate the desired models.

2 Classical Rheology Modelling

Polymer synthesis kinetics leads to systems that consist of a distribution of chains cite3. Each chain has a different number of monomers incorporated. In general, it is a huge task to characterize and describe the distribution, especially when the architecture contains side branches. Focusing on purely linear chains, the description is considerably simplified. A full description would then consist of a table of chain lengths or masses and the corresponding number, volume, or weight fraction of chains of that specific mass. Still, such a description is rather complex, because thousands of different chain lengths are typically present. Therefore, for practical reasons, most distributions are captured by a couple of indicators, such as some moments of the so-called molar mass distribution (MMD). Fig. 1 shows an example of the moments of a MMD. The lower moments are M_n, the number-average molar mass, and M_w, the weight-average molar mass. Higher moments are M_z, the z-average moment, and M_{z+1}, with $M_{z+1} \geq M_z \geq M_w \geq M_n$. The distribution and its moments are either available from knowledge of the synthesis kinetics or from measurements on a small sample of the material. An example of such an experiment is gel permeation chromatography, where the chains are led through a porous medium, which separates the chains according to length because of their different residence time in the medium.

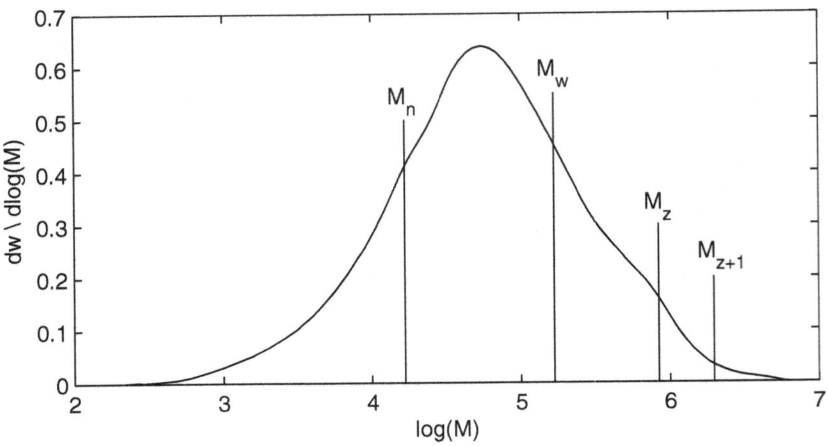

Fig. 1. Moments of a molar mass distribution

There are many different ways of determining the rheology of polymers [2]. From an experimental point of view, in shear experiments, cylindrical pieces of polymer of a couple of centimeter in diameter and a millimeter in height are put in between two metal disks. The sample is heated to the desired temperature and a prescribed deformation of the disks is executed as a function of time. The polymer will respond to the deformation in a viscoelastic manner. Forces are measured during the experiment and relevant rheological quantities are derived from the deformation-force profile. Two main rheological indicators are taken as examples in the present paper. The zero-shear viscosity η_0 is a measure of the viscous character of the polymer. The recoverable compliance J_e^0 is a measure of the elastic character of the polymer.

One of the most important challenges in rheology is to relate the molar mass distribution to the rheological properties. This is of prime importance to a polymer producer, because such knowledge enables design of materials for specific applications.

2.1 Empirical and Fundamental Modelling

Historically, per polymer type, empirical models have been derived to relate structure to rheology [2]. A number of samples is characterized both in terms of distribution moments and main rheological quantities. Statistical methods are used to derive fit equations. Since the dynamic range of inputs and outputs is large in this field, the variables are typically logarithmically transposed. The limited number of data points has led to using linear fit functions in the log-space, which results in power-law functions in the original variable space. Two examples of such relations are given here. The zero-shear viscosity is found to be well-described by only using M_w: $\eta_0 \propto (M_w)^{3.4}$. The recoverable compliance is often described by a function of a ratio of M_z and M_w: $J_e^0 \propto (M_z/M_w)^3$.

The main limitation of these models is that they are built upon a limited number of samples. It is suspected that certain cases require higher moments to accurately describe the compliance, but the limited data provide no statistical basis for it. Higher moments are also difficult to determine experimentally.

Recently, physics-based models have been derived to relate structure to rheology. Such models typically require the full distribution to calculate viscosity and compliance. The fundamental model under consideration is the double reptation model in the time-dependent diffusion (DRmTDD) form by [4]. The need to use the entire distribution as input is a limitation for the practical use of this fundamental model.

2.2 Enhanced Empirical Modelling with Fundamentals

In this section a strategy is proposed that combines the advantages of both classical approaches. A large set of theoretical distributions is generated with significant variability in all aspects of the distribution, such as bimodality and the presence of high molar mass tails. These full distributions are the inputs for the fundamental model which generates the relevant rheological quantities. The moments of each distribution are also calculated. Finally, models are built relating the rheology to the moments.

The models are allowed to contain the first four moments of the distribution, because higher moments are not obtainable from experiments. This is important, because the resulting models will ultimately also be used in connection with further experimentation. A conventional way of relating the inputs and outputs is as follows:

$$\begin{aligned}\eta_0(\cdot) &= \eta_0\left(M_w, \frac{M_w}{M_n}, \frac{M_z}{M_w}, \frac{M_{z+1}}{M_z}\right) \\ &\equiv \eta_0\left(M_w, 1, 1, \ldots\right) \eta_{rel}\left(M_w, \frac{M_w}{M_n}, \frac{M_z}{M_w}, \frac{M_{z+1}}{M_z}\right) \end{aligned} \tag{1}$$

$$\begin{aligned}J_e^0(\cdot) &= J_e^0\left(M_w, \frac{M_w}{M_n}, \frac{M_z}{M_w}, \frac{M_{z+1}}{M_z}\right) \\ &\equiv J_e^0\left(M_w, 1, 1, \ldots\right) J_{rel}\left(M_w, \frac{M_w}{M_n}, \frac{M_z}{M_w}, \frac{M_{z+1}}{M_z}\right). \end{aligned} \tag{2}$$

Note that the second (polydisperse) part of the right hand side of each equation is in general still depending on M_w. The first (monodisperse) part is easy to find by conventional modeling. The polydisperse part is less obvious.

3 Traditional Power-Law Moment Fits

The previous section introduced a new approach of modeling rheological structure-property relationships. Recall that the empirically derived models were only valid for a limited range of molecular weight distributions, whereas the input data for the fundamental models were not easily obtained. The ideal model is one that is valid for a larger range of molecular weight distributions, but using easy-to-measure input data.

For the learning input data we used three types of molecular weight distributions. Set I consisted of 13 strictly monodisperse polymers, i.e. all molecules have the same mass. Since these are monodisperse polymers their molecular weight distribution can be characterized by one moment only, e.g. M_w. Set II consisted of 75 log-normal distributions. The log-normal distribution is characterized by two moments, namely M_w and M_n. The distributions were designed on a grid of (5 M_w) x (15 M_w/M_n) values. The polydispersity of the distributions used in this set ranged from 1 to 20. Set III was constructed using 198 blends of two log-normal distributions with 5 degrees of freedom. The blends were designed using the M_w and M_n of the individual log-normal components and the weight fraction of the low mass component w_1. The distributions were designed on a grid of (1 M_{w_1}) x (3 M_{w_1}/M_{n_1}) x (2 M_{w_2}) x (3 M_{w_2}/M_{n_2}) x (11 w_1) values. The individual component polydispersity in this set ranged from 2 to 10. The three sets combined resulted in a total of 289 input data observations.

The DRmTDD-model was then used to predict the output for the theoretical molecular weight distributions. From the multiple outputs that the model provides, only the relative rheological properties η_{rel} and J_{rel} are of interest.

The designed data were used in a normal least squares fit approach. An initial analysis showed that the relative properties η_{rel} and J_{rel} could not be described using a polynomial function of a single moment ratio, e.g. M_w/M_n [5]. Rheologists typically use multiplicative power-laws of higher moments of the form:

$$y_{fit} = \left(\frac{M_w}{M_n}\right)^a \left(\frac{M_z}{M_2}\right)^b \left(\frac{M_{z+1}}{M_z}\right)^c, \qquad y = \eta_{rel}, J_{rel}. \tag{3}$$

The log-normal results of Set II also showed that the multiplicative power-law fit of Eq. 3 cannot explain the curvature in the log-log relationships [5]. Furthermore, such a description was unable to handle the variability through M_w. Incorporating more moments, e.g. M_{z+2}/M_{z+1}, did not improve the fits either. In order to obtain more accurate fits, the input variables were transformed to the following three variables:

$$x_1 = \log(M_w),\ x_2 = \log\left(M_z/M_w\right),\ \text{and } x_3 = \log\left(M_{z+1}/M_z\right).$$

The output variable y is also transformed logarithmically where $y = \log(\eta_{rel})$ or $y = \log(J_{rel})$. Note that the first polydispersity index (M_w/M_n) is not used since it showed little correlation with especially J_{rel}. Using the transformed data, a least squares fit of a first degree polynomial was fitted again:

$$\log(\eta_{rel}) = 0.1730 - 0.0467x_1 + 0.4814x_2 - 0.2030x_3 \tag{4}$$

$$\log(J_{rel}) = -0.1373 + 0.0620x_1 + 2.2034x_2 + 1.5788x_3. \quad (5)$$

The performance of these models on the learning data is given in Fig. 2. The accuracy of the models, especially that of the model in Eq. 4, was not good enough for all application purposes and therefore it was decided to try and derive better models using GP.

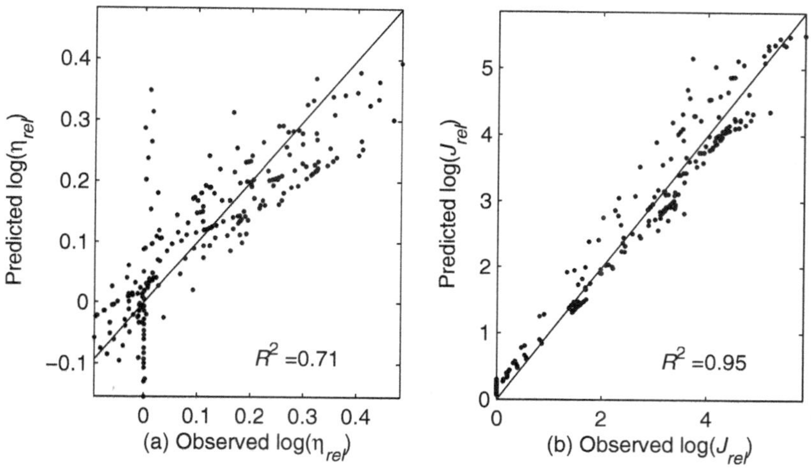

Fig. 2. Performance of the linearised models on the learning data

4 Moment Fits Using GP-Generated Models

It was shown in the previous section that following the traditional empirical fitting of power laws could not produce the desired rheological model. In this section we describe how genetic programming is used to develop the "ideal" rheology model [6].

Three GP-experiments with different settings were made using a MATLAB toolbox developed internally in The Dow Chemical Company. The experiments used the transformed input data (x_1, x_2, x_3) and the output $y = \log(\eta_{rel})$ and $y = \log(J_{rel})$ as learning data. The settings used in the different experiments are given in Table 1.

Several thousand empirical models are generated in a typical GP-experiment. Most of the models have similar performance and selecting the best model is not trivial. Often researchers simply use the R^2-statistic as criterion to select the "best" model based on the fitness measure at the end of the run.

A drawback of this fitness measure is that it does not take complexity of the function into account. The complexity is a very important factor for the robustness of a model. It is often possible to obtain a far less complex function for a slightly decreased in the performance. Less complex models typically have higher robustness and are therefore more stable in a noisy environment. Since the

Table 1. GP-experiment parameter settings

	Experiment 1	**Experiment 2**	**Experiment 3**
Number of independent runs	5	10	10
Number of cascades	10	20	10
Number of generations	30	30	25
Total number of generations	10x30=300	20x30=600	10x25=250
Population size	500	300	200

intended use of this particular model is to emulate a known fundamental model, it is important it does not violate any physical laws. For this the experience of the rheologist is needed. Therefore, it is necessary to extract a manageable number of models to inspect for complexity and compliance to physics.

One indicator of the complexity of GP-models is the number of nodes used to define the model. The measure may be misleading for it does not discern between the types of operators used in each node. For example, no distinction is made between an addition operator and an operator that is an exponential function. Clearly there is a huge difference in complexity. Another measure of complexity is the level of nonlinearity or smoothness in model. In [7] an expressional complexity measure was developed and this measure is used in further analyses.

In order to find the right trade-off between complexity and accuracy, the Pareto-front is constructed. The Pareto-front is a concept commonly used in multi-objective optimization [8]. In multi-objective (MO) optimization, apart from the solution space, which is constructed by the constraints, there is also an objective space. The objective space is a mapping of the solution space onto the objectives. The MO-problem is typically written as a single objective optimization problem by defining an *a priori* weighted sum. The solution of this new problem is one point in the objective space. Since the optimal weighted sum is seldom known *a priori*, it is often better to make the final decision from a set of weight-independent solutions. This set of solutions is given by the Pareto-front.

The task of model selection is essentially a MO-problem (i.e. accuracy vs. complexity). Therefore the fundamentals of the Pareto-front can be applied. Using the Pareto-front for the GP-models has a number of advantages [9]. Firstly, the structural risk minimization principle can be easily applied to GP-models [10]. Secondly, it effectively displays the trade-off between the measures, which enables the user to make an unbiased decision. Thirdly, as only a small fraction of the generated GP-models will end up on the Pareto-front, the number of models that need to be inspected individually is decreased tremendously.

In Fig. 3 the Pareto-front is displayed for the GP-models in terms of two objectives, namely the complexity measure and R^2. The complexity measure needs to be minimised. The second objective, R^2 is a measure of the performance of the models. Using 1-R^2 instead allows easier interpretation as both objectives are minimized. The Pareto-front models are models for which no improvement on one objective can be obtained without deteriorating another objective. The optimal model will therefore lie somewhere on the Pareto-front. If the complexity

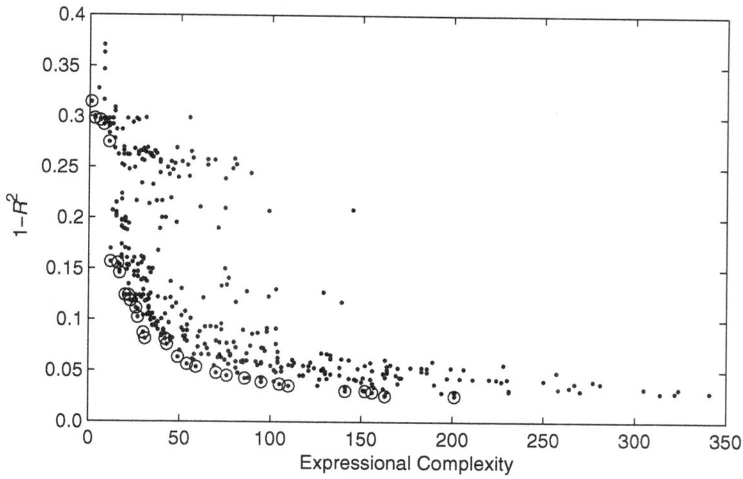

Fig. 3. Pareto-front of GP-generated rheological models

and performance have equal importance then the optimal model would lie in the lower left corner of the Pareto-front. It is clear from Fig. 3 that there are several models that can reach high R^2-values for relatively low complexity estimates. Using the Pareto-front, the following model was selected for $y = \log(\eta_{rel})$

$$y = 2.220 \cdot 10^{-2}(3 + x_2)\left((x_1 - x_3)x_2 \cos(x_1 + \exp(\exp(-x_2))) - x_3\right). \quad (6)$$

The same approach was used to develop a model for $y = \log(J_{rel})$. The selected GP-model is

$$y = 1.7768\,(x_2(1 + \exp(-x_2)) + x_3 \cos(x_1 + x_2)). \quad (7)$$

The performance of the GP-model in Eq. 6 on the learning data is given in Fig. 4(a). Although there are no physical grounds for using periodic functions, it is perfectly acceptable to use one period of the cosine to approximate a smooth function. It is only a matter of scaling. The resulting fit of the model in Eq. 6 is not very good ($R^2 = 0.89$), although it is significantly better than when using Eq. 4 ($R^2 = 0.71$). However, when the model in Eq. 6 is combined with the dominant dependence of η_0/η_{rel} on M_w an excellent overall description is obtained. For such a strong main M_w-dependence is absent, which makes the fit of J_{rel} in Eq. 7 more critical. Fig. 4(b) shows the performance of the GP-model in Eq. 7 on the learning data. Although the R^2 of the model is very high ($R^2 = 0.99$), the fit is still not perfect because on the linear scale (opposed to the logarithmic scale) the mean square error is 6.9x10^3. On the other hand, the fit is much better than when using Eq. 5 ($R^2 = 0.95$).

Fig. 5 shows the performance of the model in Eq. 7 on some validation data. The validation data consisted of three test sets. The first test set had 28 observations of a similar design as Set III but using lower values for M_w. These

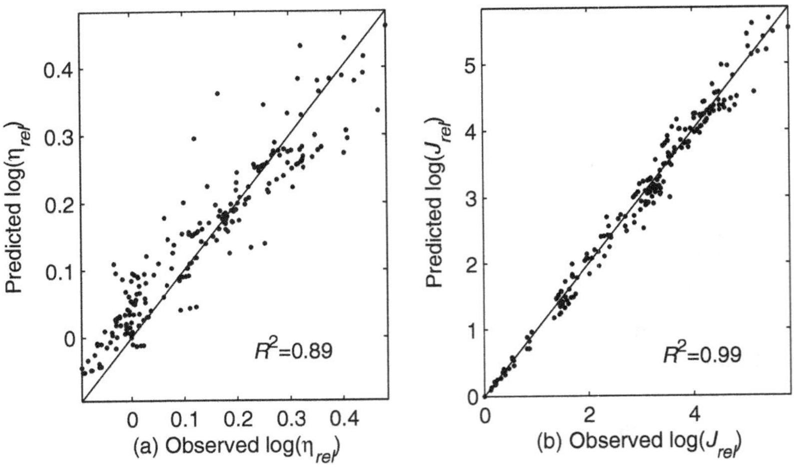

Fig. 4. Performance of GP-generated models on the learning data

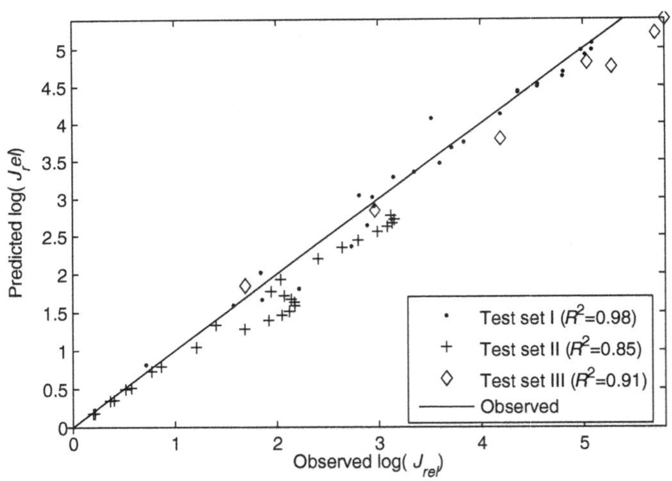

Fig. 5. Extrapolation capability of GP-generated rheological model

lower M_w-values are in the range of the Set II M_w, but differ in polydispersity. The second test set consisted of 30 unimodal log-normal distributions at the same polydispersity values as Set II, but with higher M_w-values. The third test set consisted of 7 unimodal log-normal distributions at the same M_w-values as Set II, but of higher polydispersity. The extrapolation of the model in terms of polydispersity is good ($R^2 = 0.91$). However, the extrapolation in terms of M_w leads to predicted values that are too high and the resulting performance of the model is not satisfactory ($R^2 = 0.85$). Therefore, in general the model should be used with care when extrapolating outside the known learning space.

The models have not been validated using data obtained by laboratory experiments because of time and cost constraints.

5 Conclusions

Rheological structure-property models play a crucial role in the manufacturing and processing of polymers. Classical rheology modelling approaches lack either broad application of easily obtainable input data.

In this paper we have shown a novel approach to develop complex rheological models that are not only in terms of easily obtained parameters, but also valid for a wide range of polymers. The new approach uses the fundamental model to predict a specific rheological output by using an artificial full MMD. The output combined with the calculated moments of the full MMD form a learning data set to be used by Genetic Programming. The resulting nonlinear models have a much better performance than the classical regression models. It was also shown that these models are capable of extrapolating with reasonable accuracy.

Genetic programming has given rheologists a new way of modelling complex structure-property relationships that are both practical and valid for a broad set of molar mass distribution.

References

1. Osswald, T.A. and Menges, G.: Materials science of polymers for engineers. 2nd edn, Hanser Gardner, Cincinnati OH (2003)
2. Macosko, C.W.: Rheology, principles, measurements, and applications. Wiley VCH, New York (1994)
3. Bamford, C.H., Tompa, H.: The calculation of molecular weight distributions from kinetic schemes. Trans. Faraday Soc. 50 (1954) 1097
4. Van Ruymbeke, E., Keunings, R., Stphenne, V., Hagenaars, A., Bailly, C.: Evaluation of reptation models for predicting the linear viscoelastic properties of entangled linear polymers. Marcomolecules 35 (2002) 2689–2699
5. Den Doelder, J.: Viscosity and compliance from molar mass distributions using double reptation,. Accepted for Rheology Acta (2006)
6. Koza, J.: Genetic Programming. On the Programming of Computers by Means of Natural Selection. MIT Press, Cambridge MA (1992)
7. Vladislavleva, C.: Symbolic Regression via Genetic Programming. Masters thesis. Eindhoven University of Techonology, Eindhoven (2005)
8. Deb K.: Multi-Objective Optimization Using Evolutionary Algorithms. Wiley, Chichester UK (2001)
9. Smits, G. and Kotanchek, M.: Pareto-Front Exploitation in Symbolic Regression. In: Riolo, R. and Worzel, B. (eds): Genetic Programming Theory and Practice. Kluwer, Boston (in press) (2004)
10. Vapnik, V.: Statistical Learning Theory. Wiley, New York (1998)

An Evolutionary Approach to the Inference of Phylogenetic Networks

Juan Diego Trujillo and Carlos Cotta

Dept. Lenguajes y Ciencias de la Computación, ETSI Informática,
University of Málaga, Campus de Teatinos, 29071 - Málaga - Spain
ccottap@lcc.uma.es

Abstract. Phylogenetic networks are models of the evolution of a set of organisms that generalize phylogenetic trees. By allowing the existence of reticulation events (such as recombination, hybridization, or horizontal gene transfer), the model is no longer a tree but a directed acyclic graph (DAG). We consider the problem of finding a phylogenetic network to model a set of sequences of molecular data, using evolutionary algorithms (EAs). To this end, the algorithm has to be adequately designed to handle different constraints regarding the structure of the DAG, and the location of reticulation events. The choice of fitness function is also studied, and several possibilities for this purpose are presented and compared. The experimental evaluation indicates that the EA can satisfactorily recover the underlying evolution model behind the data. A computationally light fitness function seems to provide the best performance.

1 Introduction

Phylogenies are used to represent the evolutionary history of a collection of organisms (represented by phenotypical information, or –as assumed throughout this paper– by molecular sequence data). Typically, this evolutionary history is represented as a tree, i.e., a hierarchy showing the degree of closeness among the organisms under study. As it turns out, inferring the *best* hierarchy is a formidably difficult task under several formulations [1,2]. This hardness barrier can be circumvented using heuristic approaches; indeed, evolutionary algorithms (EAs) have been used in this domain with encouraging results, e.g., [3,4,5,6,7] among others. At any rate, there is an additional important fact we should not lose sight of: trees oversimplify our view of evolution, as it has been long recognized by biologists. There are many events in natural evolution in which the genetic material is not transferred in a hierarchical way, e.g., hybrid speciation, horizontal gene transfer, etc. These phenomena, usually called reticulations, give rise to edges that connect nodes from different branches of a tree, creating a directed acyclic graph structure that is usually called a phylogenetic network [8].

No single methodology for network reconstruction is widely accepted to date [9]. For example, the detection and identification of reticulation events has been approached by Hallett *et al.* [10] (focusing on horizontal gene transfer), and by Posada *et al.* [11] (focusing on recombination events). Nakhleh *et al.* [12] have

T.P. Runarsson et al. (Eds.): PPSN IX, LNCS 4193, pp. 332–341, 2006.

proposed a method that combines pre-existing consensus trees into a network with a single reticulation event. Finally, Gusfield *et al.* [13,14] have devised several algorithms for binary input sequences, under different assumptions on where reticulation events take place, and how they work.

The methods mentioned above are in general based in deterministic approaches for finding provably good solutions, and hence the well-known limitations arising from the $P \neq NP$ conjecture apply. To the best of our knowledge, the inference problem has not been approached with metaheuristic techniques so far. However, this latter approach seems natural in this domain, given the success history of these techniques (EAs in particular) on the inference of phylogenetic trees. In this work, we propose an evolutionary approach to the phylogenetic-network inference problem, and show that it can be a useful tool in this domain.

2 Phylogenetic Networks

As mentioned in previous section, there exist some evolutionary events that do not fit in the tree-like view of evolution, e.g., hybrid speciation, recombination, and horizontal gene transfer. In general, these events require the use of rooted directed acyclic graphs (DAGs) for representing them. In the following, we will describe the notation used henceforth, as well as some crucial notions such as time coexistence, and topological distance metrics on phylogenetic networks.

2.1 Notation

Let $G(V, E)$ be a DAG. We will use the notation $E(G)$ and $V(G)$ to denote respectively the set of edges and vertices of a DAG G. A directed path P of length k from u to v in a graph G ($u, v \in V(G)$), is a sequence $P = \langle u_0, u_1, \cdots, u_k \rangle$ of nodes where $u = u_0$, $v = u_k$, and $(u_i, u_{i+1}) \in E(G)$ for $0 \leqslant i < k$. Let $\alpha(P) = u_0$, and $\omega(P) = u_k$ be the endpoints of path P. A node v is reachable from u in G if there exists a directed path from u to v; in that case, u is an ancestor of v. Unlike trees, there may be more that one directed path between two nodes in a DAG. These paths are also termed *positive time directed paths* for reasons that will be clear at a later point.

We can now define the in-degree $\delta^{\downarrow}$ of a node as the number of edges arriving to that node, and the out-degree $\delta^{\uparrow}$ as the number of edges that depart from that node. There are some degree constraints in DAGs representing phylogenetic networks. To be precise, a node $v \in V(E)$ is a *tree node* if (a) $\delta^{\downarrow}(v) = 0$ and $\delta^{\uparrow}(v) = 2$ [root (unique)], (b) $\delta^{\downarrow}(v) = 1$ and $\delta^{\uparrow}(v) = 0$ [leaf], or (c) $\delta^{\downarrow}(v) = 1$ and $\delta^{\uparrow}(v) = 2$ [internal tree node]. If a node v is not a tree node, then it must have $\delta^{\downarrow}(v) = 2$ and $\delta^{\uparrow}(v) = 1$. Such nodes are termed *network nodes*. An edge $e = (u, v) \in E(G)$ is a *tree edge* if and only if v is a tree node, and it would be a *network edge* otherwise. Notice that tree nodes describe mutations, and network nodes describe reticulation events. Fig. 1(a) shows an example of phylogenetic network. If given any edge in the network at least one of its endpoints is a tree node (and provided some constraints on the structure of reticulation events are fulfilled, see Sect. 2.2), the network is termed *reconstructible* [9].

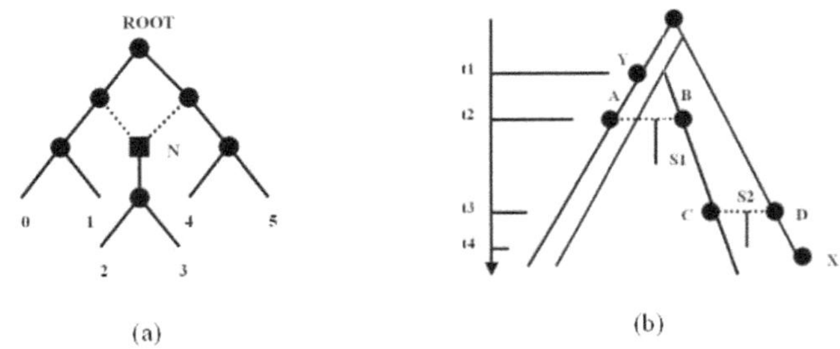

Fig. 1. (a) A phylogenetic network N on six observed species (and seven ancestral species). Tree nodes and network nodes are depicted with circles and squares respectively. Likewise, solid lines denote tree edges, and dashed lines denote the network edges. (b) X and Y cannot coexist in time.

2.2 Time Coexistence

A crucial consideration that must be taken into account in phylogenetic networks is the fact that each reticulation event defines a *simultaneity plane*: in order to have two species recombining their genomes, or having some genetic information transferred from a species to another, they must coexist in time. This way, the set of nodes $V(G)$ of a phylogenetic network G are implicitly ordered in time according to the particular reticulation events existing in G. To be precise, we can assign a specific time-stamp $t(v)$ to each node v in the network. Actually, the absolute values of these time-stamps are not relevant; what matters is their relative ordering. Thus, if there exists a time directed path between node u and node v, we would logically have $t(u) < t(v)$, i.e., u is an ancestor of v. However, if $e = (u, v)$ is a network edge, then $t(u) = t(v)$ because the reticulation events are instantaneous in the evolution time scale.

Consider Fig. 1(b). Let $t(Y) = t_1$ and $t(X) = t_4$, and let reticulation events s_1 and s_2 happen at time t_2 and t_3 respectively. Now notice that there does not exist a positive time directed path from Y to X. However, even though Y is not an ancestor of X, it is impossible to have a reticulation event between these two nodes: Y is an ancestor of A, that coexists with B; B is in turn an ancestor of C that coexist with D, an ancestor of X. Hence, $t_1 < t_2 < t_3 < t_4$. More formally, we say that two nodes $u, v \in V(G)$ cannot coexist in time if:

(a) u is an ancestor of v (or vice versa), or
(b) there is a sequence of positive time directed paths $P = \{P_1, P_2, \cdots, P_k\}$ such that $\alpha(P_1) = u$ (resp. v), $\omega(P_k) = v$ (resp. u), and for $1 \leqslant i < k$, there exists a network node whose parents are $\omega(P_i)$, and $\alpha(P_{i+1})$.

Time coexistence thus imposes constraints on where reticulation events can take place, and therefore on which DAGs actually represent a feasible phylogenetic network. These constraints will have to be observed when evolving networks within the inference algorithms.

2.3 Topological Distance Metrics on Phylogenetic Networks

Metrics for measuring the topological distance between networks are essential to interpret the results of an inference algorithm. They can be used to determine to which extent the features of a target network have been successfully recovered. For this purpose, we can resort to generalizations of well-known distance metrics for trees, such as the Robinson-Foulds (RF) distance [15].

The RF distance on trees uses the notion of *bipartition*: given an edge e in a tree T, we can partition the leaf set $\mathcal{L}$ of T into two disjoint sets $A(e)$ and $C(e)$, respectively comprising the leaves in $\mathcal{L}$ that are reachable from the root (resp. unreachable) through edge e. The notion of bipartition in trees is readily generalizable to *tripartitions* in networks. In this latter case, an edge e induces a tripartition $\langle A(e), B(e), C(e)\rangle$, where $A(e)$ comprising the leaves that are reachable from the root only through edge e, $B(e)$ comprises the leaves that are reachable from the root by a path that goes through e, and at least by another path that does not pass through e, and $C(e)$ is defined as before.

We denote by $\phi(e) = \langle A(e), B(e), C(e)\rangle$ the tripartition induced by the e. Two tripartitions $\phi(e_1)$ and $\phi(e_2)$ are equivalent ($\phi(e_1) \equiv \phi(e_2)$) if, and only if, $A(e_1) = A(e_2)$, $B(e_1) = B(e_2)$, and $C(e_1) = C(e_2)$. Now, two edges e_1, e_2 are compatible ($e_1 \equiv e_2$) if, and only if, $\phi(e_1) \equiv \phi(e_2)$. Let $\delta : \mathbb{B} \rightarrow \{0,1\}$ be defined as $\delta(\texttt{TRUE}) = 1$ and $\delta(\texttt{FALSE}) = 0$. Let $\Gamma(G_1, G_2)$ be defined as

$$\Gamma(G_1, G_2) = \frac{1}{|E(G_1)|} \sum_{e_1 \in E(G_1)} \left(1 - \sum_{e_2 \in E(G_2)} \delta(e_1 \equiv e_2)\right) \qquad (1)$$

It is then possible to define the *false negative rate* $FN(G, \tilde{G}) = \Gamma(\tilde{G}, G)$, and the *false positive rate* $FP(G, \tilde{G}) = \Gamma(G, \tilde{G})$ between an inferred network G and a target network $\tilde{G}$. Finally, the RF distance for networks can be estimated as $D_{RF}(G, \tilde{G}) = (FN(G, \tilde{G}) + FP(G, \tilde{G}))/2$. Notice that the RF distance is 0.0 for two identical networks, and 1.0 for two networks without any compatible edge.

3 EAs for Inferring Phylogenetic Networks

In order to tackle the inference of phylogenetic networks with EAs, we consider a direct approach in which the search is directly conducted on the space of all possible phylogenetic networks with given leaf set. Thus, each individual in the population of the EA represents a feasible phylogenetic network, internally encoded as an adjacency matrix. This means that (i) an initialization process producing feasible networks must be used, and (ii) the reproductive operators used must respect feasibility, i.e., they must always produce feasible offspring. The details of these operators will be described in Sect. 3.1.

Another central element in this EA is the fitness function. The RF metric defined in the previous section can be used for the off-line assessment of the results, but it cannot obviously be used during the evolution. On the contrary, the fitness function must evaluate a phylogenetic network on the basis of the

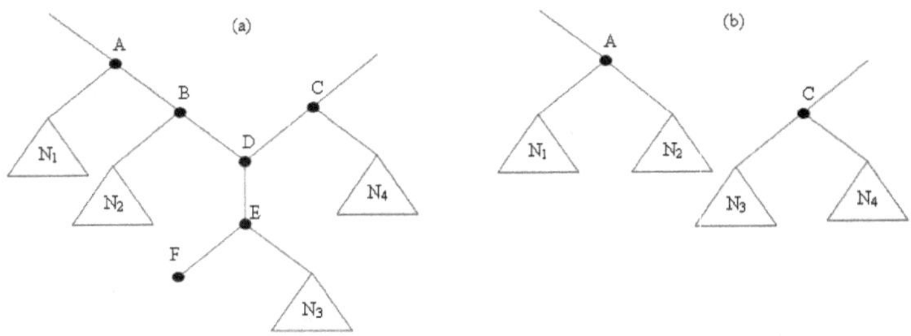

Fig. 2. After deleting node F, the subnetwork in (a) takes the shape shown in (b)

particular dataset of molecular sequences to be modelled. Several choices have been explored for this purpose. These are described in Sect. 3.2.

3.1 Evolutionary Operators

The first issue to be tackled in the EA is the generation of feasible networks for insertion in the initial population. To do so, each time a new network is required a random tree is firstly generated (this is done by firstly constructing a random permutation of the leaves; then, an initial tree is built with the first two leaves in the permutation, and the remaining leaves are subsequently inserted at random points of the partial tree until it is finally completed). Once the tree has been obtained, network nodes are inserted by randomly selecting pairs of tree nodes that can coexist in time.

After having generated a population of feasible networks, adequate reproductive operators must be used. Let us firstly consider the recombination operator. As usual, this operator takes information pieces from two individuals, and combines them to create a new feasible solution. In this case, these information pieces take the shape of subnetworks, and hence we can express the process in terms of pruning and grafting subnetworks. Let G_1 and G_2 be the networks to recombine, and let trees be represented in LISP notation. The process is as follows:

1. Select a random subnetwork N (rooted at a tree node) from G_1.
2. **for each** leaf $u \in N$ **do**
   (a) Find subnetwork U in G_2 such that $U = (h, (u), U')$ or $U = (h, U', (u))$.
   (b) Replace U by U' in G_2.
3. Select a random subnetwork V from G_2.
4. Replace V by $V' = (h', N, V)$, where h' is a new internal tree node.

This operator can be regarded as a generalization of the Prune-Delete-Graft (PDG) operator for trees [5,6]. Thus, we have termed it NetPDG. Notice that some network node might be broken during the recombination process. This could happen either in step 1 (if there were a reticulation event between a node in N and another node not in N), or in step 2b (if a grandson of a network node were removed). Fig. 2 shows an example of this latter situation.

As to the mutation operator, it is based on rearranging the topology of a portion of the network. More precisely, to mutate network G, this operator (NetSCRAMBLE) selects a random subnetwork N from G, and generates another random network, spanning the same set of leaves, and having the same number of internal network nodes (network nodes with one parent in N and other parent outside N are broken). Notice that not only the number of network nodes in the child might be lower than that of the parental solution(s) (if some such nodes are broken during recombination –as described before– or during subnetwork scrambling in mutation); it can be also higher than it if no network node is broken, and new ones are transferred during recombination. In this work, we have opted for keeping a fixed, predefined number of network nodes in solutions. Hence, whenever a new solution has a higher or lower number of network nodes, it is repaired (breaking randomly selected network nodes, or adding new ones).

3.2 The Fitness Function

As it is the case for phylogenetic trees, the accuracy with which a phylogenetic network model the evolutionary history of a certain dataset can be computed via sequence-based methods (i.e., maximum parsimony [16], or maximum likelihood [17]) and distance-based methods [18]. Among these approaches, maximum likelihood is an appealing way of assessing the quality of a proposed phylogenetic model: they consider all possible evolutionary pathways compatible with the molecular data available, and are known to be asymptotically accurate [19]. We have thus opted for a maximum likelihood approach here.

The general setting is the following: we have a collection D of n sequences, representing some molecular data from n different species. Here, these sequences are taken from the alphabet $\Sigma = \{\mathtt{A}, \mathtt{C}, \mathtt{G}, \mathtt{T}\}$, i.e., they represent DNA sequences. We assume a certain evolution model at the molecular level, indicating the likelihood that a certain character (nucleotides in this case) mutates into another one, say $\Pi = \{\pi_{ij}\}_{i,j \in \Sigma}$. Each site in the sequence is assumed to evolve independently. Likewise, we assume a certain mechanics for reticulation events, i.e., network nodes indicate recombinations, and these produce organisms whose genetic sequence is, e.g., the result of a uniform crossover of the parental sequences. When this general evolutionary framework is superimposed on a particular network N, we can calculate $P(D|N)$, that is, the likelihood that N gave rise to D. A potential drawback of this method is its computational cost. Related to this issue, we have considered several alternative formulations of the fitness function to estimate $P(D|N)$, as described below.

The first method is based on the formula used for likelihood calculation in trees. Let L^r_{k,s_k} be the likelihood of a network rooted at node k, given that that node has nucleotide s_k in site r. If node k is the parent of nodes i and j in the network, and both are tree nodes, then,

$$L^r_{k,s_k} = \left(\sum_{s_i \in \Sigma} \pi_{s_k,s_i} L^r_{i,s_i} \right) \left(\sum_{s_j \in \Sigma} \pi_{s_k,s_j} L^r_{j,s_j} \right) . \qquad (2)$$

In case node i were a network node, the first term in Eq. (2) would have to be changed accordingly. To be precise, the state of node i would depend on the state of node k, and also on the state of the other parent, say node z. This bivariate dependency precludes the fast recursive evaluation of Eq. (2). To circumvent this issue, we can take into account the fact that, due to the semantics of recombination, the state of node k propagates with 1/2 probability to node i. Thus, we approximate this first term as $1/2 \cdot L^r_{v,s_k}$, where v is the unique child of node i in the network. The same reasoning would apply to node j were it a network node. While this is a mere approximation of the exact likelihood of these network nodes, it allows a very fast recursive evaluation of the overall likelihood of the complete network. This evaluation is completed by noting that (i) the likelihood $L^r_{w,s}$ of a leaf is 1.0 if the rth site of the wth sequence is s, and 0.0 otherwise, and (ii) the complete likelihood of the network for site r is $L^r = \sum_{s_0 \in \Sigma} \pi_{s_0} L^r_{0,s_0}$, where π_s is the marginal probability of nucleotide s. Finally, since sites evolve independently, the likelihood of the network for the whole data is $L = \prod_{i=i}^m L^i$, m being the length of sequences. We term this evaluation method ABE (after approximate bayesian estimation).

Monte Carlo (MC) methods constitute an alternative to ABE providing an asymptotically exact numerical estimation of the network likelihood. This estimation is obtained by constructing N samples of the states of internal nodes in the network, and computing

$$L^r = \frac{1}{N} \sum_{i=1}^{N} \prod_{w} \pi_{s^i_{w'}, s_w} \tag{3}$$

where the inner product ranges over all leaves w of the network, w' is the parent node of a certain w, $s^i_{w'}$ is the ith sampled state in the rth site for node w', and s_w is the actual state in the rth site of the wth sequence. In order to have a correct MC integration, the probability of each sample must be proportional to its real likelihood. This can be easily accomplished by assuming a random state at the network root (following the marginal probabilities π_s), and simulating the evolution of this site along the network, using the stochastic model Π considered.

The MC method provides an asymptotically more accurate estimation of the exact likelihood, but it has a much higher computational cost than ABE. In order to alleviate this cost partially, a combined method (CMB) has been considered. The basic idea is identifying all the subtrees in the network (that is, maximal subgraphs without network nodes), using the MC method just to sample the states for the remaining nodes. Subsequently,

$$L^r = \frac{1}{N} \sum_{i=1}^{N} \prod_{v} L^r_{v,s^i_v} \prod_{w} \pi_{s^i_{w'}, s_w} \tag{4}$$

where the first product ranges over all internal nodes v being the root of a maximal subtree, s^i_v is the corresponding value in the ith sample, the second product ranges over all leaves that are not part of a maximal subtree, and w', $s^i_{w'}$, and s_w are interpreted as before. Thus, the exact likelihood value is computed for maximal subtrees, and the cost of the MC component is reduced.

4 Experimental Results

The data used in the experiments have been synthetically generated from known evolution models, in order to allow an objective measurement of the extent to which the inference algorithms were capable of recovering the underlying model. The process consists of generating a random network with the desired number of leaves (n) and network nodes (k), and then constructing nucleotide sequences by simulating the evolution of r sites throughout the network. The stochastic evolution of sequences is done assuming the Kimura 2-parameter model [20] with transition rate $\alpha = 0.05$ and transversion rate $\beta = .025$. We have considered networks with $n \in \{10, 25\}$ leaves, $k \in \{0, 1, 2\}$ network nodes, and $r \in \{100, 250\}$ sites per sequence. Both the procedure for generating the dataset, and the parameters used are similar in related woks [12,16].

A steady-state EA with standard parameters ($popsize = 100$, $p_X = .9$, $p_m = 1/\ell$, ℓ being the number of nodes, $maxevals = 1000n$, binary tournament selection) has been used in the experiments. No fine tuning of these parameters has been attempted. To allow a wider exploration of the capabilities of the EA, a different problem instance has been used in each run. This way we are evaluating the algorithm on many samples of the whole problem class, rather than just on a couple of instances. Results have been obtained for the three fitness functions described in Sect. 3.2. Twenty runs have been done for each parameter set for functions MC and CMB. Function ABE turns out to be around 50 times faster than MC (using 500 samples per evaluation), so we have conducted 1000 runs for it per parameter set. The best networks found are evaluated in terms of the RF distance with respect to the "real" network. For the network model considered, the most related approach in the literature is [12]. Unfortunately, the SPNET program used there is not available. For this reason, we have devised an combination of greedy-exhaustive heuristic for comparison purposes: we firstly construct a tree using an agglomerative technique such as complete-link (CL) or single-link (SL), and then exhaustively check all locations where to place the network nodes (one at a time), keeping the best network.

Complete results are shown in Fig. 3. As expected, the ABE function performs very well in the $k = 0$ case (i.e., tree models) since it captures the exact likelihood of each tentative solution. For $n = 10$, $k > 0$, the MC function provides better results than ABE (the MC estimation may be better than the approximation used in ABE); however, for $n = 25$, $k > 0$, the differences are negligible (not statistically significant, using a Wilcoxon ranksum test [21] since data is not normally distributed), and the best results of ABE are even better than those of MC for $k = 1$. In general, CMB performs similarly to ABE, and all three evolutionary approaches are much better (statistically significant) than CL and SL. Notice also that ABE can recover the original network in at least one run for all parameter settings except $n = 25$, $k = 2$. We have also conducted similar experiments with networks generated with an additional constraint: the parents of network nodes must be located at the same depth. The results are essentially the same as depicted in Fig. 3 for unconstrained networks.

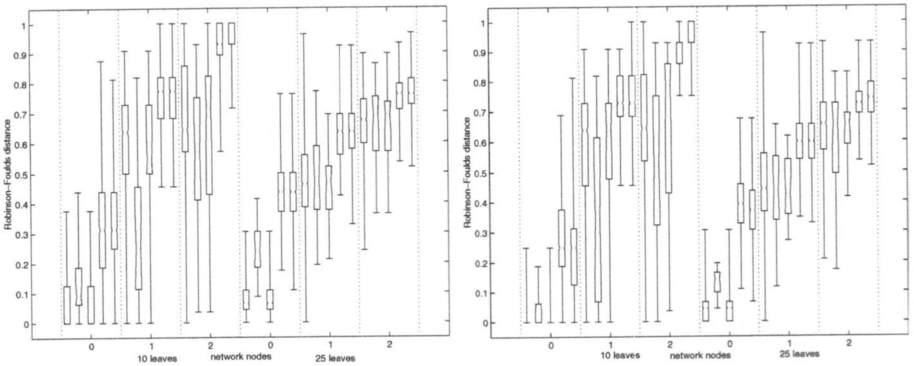

(a) (b)

Fig. 3. Results for different instance sizes (from left to right in each group of five boxes: ABE, MC, CMB, CL, and SL). The boxes comprise the second and third quartile, and the whiskers indicate the range of the data. (a) Sequences of 100 nucleotides. (b) Sequences of 250 nucleotides.

5 Conclusions

We have analyzed several evolutionary approaches for the inference of phylogenetic networks from molecular data. The results indicate that EAs can be a useful tool in this domain, since it has been shown that they can provide network models very close to the real evolutionary model hidden in the data (sometimes recovering it in full), outperforming some ad-hoc heuristics as well. We have compared three different fitness functions for guiding the evolution. The ABE function seems to provide the best tradeoff between the quality of the results, and the computational cost implied.

Future work will be directed to analyze the generalizability of this evolutionary approach to other reticulation events. For example, recombination can be analyzed on diploid organisms (the offspring would inherit a full DNA sequence from each of the parents). The approach can be also readily adapted to tackle alternative assessment models such as maximum parsimony.

Acknowledgements. Thanks are due to Jorge Muruzábal for useful comments on bayesian methods and Monte Carlo integration. The second author is partially supported by MCyT project TIN2005-08818-C04-01.

References

1. Foulds, L., Graham, R.: The Steiner problem in phylogeny is NP-complete. Advances in Applied Mathematics **3** (1982) 439–49
2. Day, W., Johnson, D., Sankoff, D.: The computational complexity of inferring rooted phylogenies by parsimony. Mathematical Biosciences **81** (1986) 33–42

3. Matsuda, H.: Protein phylogenetic inference using maximum likelihood with a genetic algorithm. In Hunter, L., Klein, T.E., eds.: 1st Pacific Symposium on Biocomputing '96, London, World Scientific (1996) 512–523
4. Lewis, P.: A genetic algorithm for maximum-likelihood phylogeny inference using nucleotide sequence data. Molecular Biology and Evolution **15** (1998) 277–283
5. Moilanen, A.: Searching for the most parsimonious trees with simulated evolution. Cladistics **15** (1999) 39–50
6. Cotta, C., Moscato, P.: Inferring phylogenetic trees using evolutionary algorithms. In Merelo, J., et al., eds.: Parallel Problem Solving From Nature VII. Volume 2439 of Lecture Notes in Computer Science. Springer-Verlag, Berlin (2002) 720–729
7. Shen, J., Heckendorn, R.: Discrete branch length representations for genetic algorithms in phylogenetic search. In Raidl, G., et al., eds.: Applications of Evolutionary Computing 2004. Volume 3005 of Lecture Notes in Computer Science., Coimbra, Portugal, Springer (2004) 94–103
8. Huson, D., Bryant, D.: Application of phylogenetic networks in evolutionary studies. Molecular Biology and Evolution **23** (2006) 254–267
9. Moret, B., Nakhleh, L., Warnow, T., Linder, C., Tholse, A., Padolina, A., Sun, J., Timme, R.: Phylogenetic networks: Modeling, reconstructibility, and accuracy. IEEE Transactions on Computational Biology and Bioinformatics **1** (2004) 13–23
10. Hallett, M., Lagergren, J., Tofigh, A.: Simultaneous identification of duplications and lateral transfers. In: 8th Annual International Conference on Computational Molecular Biology. (2004) 347–356
11. Posada, D., Crandall, K.: The effect of recombination on the accuracy of phylogeny estimation. Journal of Molecular Evolution **54** (2002) 396–402
12. Nakhleh, L., Warnow, T., Linder, C.: Reconstructing reticulate evolution in species – theory and practice. In: 8th Annual International Conference on Computational Molecular Biology. (2004) 337–346
13. Gusfield, D., Eddhu, S., Langley, C.: Optimal, efficient reconstruction of phylogenetic networks with constrained recombination. Journal of Bioinformatics and Computational Biology **2** (2004) 173–213
14. Song, Y., Wu, Y., Gusfield, D.: Efficient computation of close lower and upper bounds on the minimum number of recombinations in biological sequence evolution. Bioinformatics **21** (2005) i413–i422
15. Robinson, D., Foulds, L.: Comparison of phylogenetic trees. Mathematical Biosciences **53** (1981) 131–147
16. Nakhleh, L., Jin, G., Zhao, F., Mellor-Crummey, J.: Reconstructing phylogenetic networks using maximum parsimony. In: Computational Systems Bioinformatics Conference 2005, IEEE Press (2005) 93–102
17. Strimmer, K., Moulton, V.: Likelihood analysis of phylogenetic networks using directed graphical models. Molecular Biology and Evolution **17** (2000) 875–881
18. Makarenkov, V., Kevorkov, D., Legendre, P.: Modeling phylogenetic relationships using reticulated networks. Zoologica Scripta **33** (2005) 89–96
19. Huelsenbeck, J., Crandall, K.: Phylogeny estimation and hypothesis testing using maximum likelihood. Annual Review of Ecology and Systematics **28** (1997) 437–466
20. Kimura, M.: Estimation of evolutionary distances between homologous nucleotide sequences. Proceedings of the Natural Academy of Sciences **78** (1981) 454–458
21. Lehmann, E.: Nonparametric Statistical Methods Based on Ranks. McGraw-Hill, New York NY (1975)

An Evolutive Approach for the Delineation of Local Labour Markets

Francisco Flórez-Revuelta[1],
José Manuel Casado-Díaz[2], and Lucas Martínez-Bernabeu[1]

[1] Research Unit on Industrial Computing and Computer Networks, University of Alicante, P.O. Box 99, E-03080, Alicante, Spain
florez@dtic.ua.es, lucas.martinez@ua.es
http://www.us.es/i2rc
[2] Institute of International Economics, University of Alicante, P.O. Box 99, E-03080, Alicante, Spain
jmcasado@ua.es
http://iei.ua.es

Abstract. This paper presents a new approach to the delineation of local labour markets based on evolutionary computation. The main objective is the regionalisation of a given territory into functional regions based on commuting flows. According to the relevant literature, such regions are defined so that (a) their boundaries are rarely crossed in daily journeys to work, and (b) a high degree of intra-area movement exists. This proposal merges municipalities into functional regions by maximizing a fitness function that measures aggregate intra-region interaction under constraints of inter-region separation and minimum size. Real results are presented based on the latest database from the Census of Population in the Region of Valencia. Comparison between the results obtained through the official method which currently is most widely used (that of British Travel-to-Work Areas) and those from our approach is also presented, showing important improvements in terms of both the number of different market areas identified that meet the statistical criteria and the degree of aggregate intra-market interaction.

1 Introduction

Delineating local labour markets (LLMs) is an exercise that has become very common in the last decades across developed countries [1]. These sets of functional areas are seen as an alternative to the use of local and regional administrative areas as the relevant geography for statistical purposes and for the design, implementation and monitoring of labour market and other public policies in related fields such education and housing markets. The reason for this is that administrative areas are defined by boundaries that very frequently derive from historical reasons, and so it is not assured that they provide a meaningful insight of the territorial functional reality. Most countries have opted for defining markets through the aggregation of units which are intimately related in terms of exchange of flows. Thus accordingly to their nature

T.P. Runarsson et al. (Eds.): PPSN IX, LNCS 4193, pp. 342 – 351, 2006.

in most developed countries travel-to-work commuting flows have been used to identify LLMs instead of defining markets characterized by the homogeneity of the constituting geographical basic units in certain attributes (a review of procedures which concentrate on this last option can be found in [19]).

A LLM represents an area where the majority of the interaction between workers seeking jobs and employers recruiting labour occurs. This refers to what Goodman [2] called external perfection (the boundary of the area is rarely crossed in daily journeys to work) and is joined by high degree of intra-market movement (so that the defined market is internally active and so as unified as possible) to form the basis of the ideal LLM. More than a decade ago Eurostat [3] established a code of good practices to guide the selection of a specific procedure: (1) the ideal map of LLMs should be based on statistical criteria, thus defined in a consistent way to allow comparison for statistical and policy purposes, (2) the procedure should allow the delineation of boundaries between areas within which most people both live and work, (3) each basic spatial unit should be in one, and only one LLM, (4) contiguity should be respected, (5) a certain degree of self-containment should be reached, so that most of the LLM's workers live in that area and most of the area's employed residents should work locally, (6) the map should consist on homogeneous units whose size should overpass a minimum threshold, (7) the areas defined should not be unnecessarily complex from a topographic point of view, (8) the map of LLMs should respect where possible the standard administrative top tier boundaries, this being considered advantageous from both statistical and policy points of view and finally (9) the procedure should be flexible enough to allow evaluation and adjustment, although the possibility of varying the statistical criteria between regions must be excluded. The preference for detail (delineating as many criteria-meeting LLMs as possible) is also frequently included as one additional criterion.

Despite sharing a common basic view about the ideal features of such an area, current official methods have a very diverse nature and are mostly based in sets of rules whose sophistication substantially varies nationally and, to a certain degree, temporally. In [4] several classifications of these official procedures are presented. One of the procedures that has been more successfully applied is that of Coombes et al. [5] which has been used in the United Kingdom for the delineation of LLMs (so-called *Travel-to-Work Areas*, TTWAs) since the 80s. This procedure has also been used, with minor changes, to define LLMs in Italy [6], [7], [8], Spain [9], New Zealand [10] and Australia [11], among other countries. This is the procedure that serves as inspiration for the one proposed in the article. In our proposal the regionalisation problem is presented as the maximization of markets' internal cohesion in terms of travel-to-work subject to a number of restrictions among which stands meeting certain self-containment and minimum size (in terms of occupied population) thresholds, with the aim of identifying as many independent markets as possible, and without making use of contiguities constrictions or distance measures. Unlike most current procedures, the method proposed here meet the criteria listed above and means a significant improvement in measurable indicators such as the number of LLMs identified which meet the stated criteria compared with alternative methods.

Given the size of the problem, which can be characterized as NP-complete, an exhaustive search of the solution is not possible, this is the reason why an evolutive approach is proposed where specific operators and strategies have been designed and implemented in experimentation using the latest figures available for Spain [12].

2 Problem Description

Let $A=\{A_1,A_2,\ldots,A_n\}$ be a set of areas (territory). The objective is to obtain the set of regions $R=\{R_1,R_2,\ldots,R_m\}$ so as $\bigcup_{i=1}^{m} R_i = A$ and $R_i \cap R_j = \varnothing, \forall i,j \in [1,m], i \neq j$, that maximizes the fitness function

$$\mathrm{card}(R)\cdot \sum_{\forall i \in A} f(i) \tag{1}$$

where

$$f(i)=\frac{W^2_{\{i\},R(i)-\{i\}}}{W_{\{i\},A}\cdot W_{A,R(i)-\{i\}}}+\frac{W^2_{R(i)-\{i\},\{i\}}}{W_{R(i)-\{i\},A}\cdot W_{A,\{i\}}} \tag{2}$$

being $R(i)$ the region containing area i, and

$$W_{R_s,R_t}=\sum_{\forall i\in R_s}\sum_{\forall j\in R_t} W_{ij} \tag{3}$$

where W_{ij} is the number of commuters from area i to area j, that is the number of employed residents in area i that work in area j.

$f(\cdot)$ represents the interaction index between an area and the rest of the region to which it belongs, while the introduction of the number of regions tries to maximize the division of the territory.

Besides, each one of the regions $R_i \in R$ must fulfil two constraints of self-containment (β_1, β_2), $\beta_2 \geq \beta_1$ and minimal size (β_3, β_4), $\beta_3 \geq \beta_4$:

$$\min\left(\frac{W_{R_i,R_i}}{W_{R_i,A}};\frac{W_{R_i,R_i}}{W_{A,R_i}}\right)\geq \beta_1 \tag{4}$$

$$W_{R_i,A}\geq \beta_4 \tag{5}$$

A trade-off between both constraints has been introduced similarly to [5], but in the formulation proposed by Casado [9]. According to this trade off, the self-containment absolute requisite is relaxed for regions which are sufficiently large following a linear relationship. This trade-off establishes a new constraint:

$$\begin{gathered}\min\left(\frac{W_{R_i,R_i}}{W_{R_i,A}};\frac{W_{R_i,R_i}}{W_{A,R_i}}\right)\geq a+b\cdot W_{R_i,A}\\ a=\beta_2-b\beta_4\\ b=\frac{\beta_2-\beta_1}{\beta_4-\beta_3}\end{gathered} \tag{6}$$

We have also included a requisite to guarantee some degree of contiguity by employing only commuting data: an area can only belong to a region if some of the areas to/from it has more output/input commuting flows is also part of that region.

3 Evolutive Proposal

The structure of the evolutive algorithm for the regionalisation of the territory is:

```
Produce a random initial population of size n
Repeat
      Evaluate fitness of all individuals
      Generate new individuals by recombination
      Generate new individuals by mutation
      Evaluate fitness of all new individuals
      Order all individuals (old and new) by fitness
      Generate a new population choosing the n best indi-
      viduals
Until there were no change in the best individual for a
number of iterations
```

3.1 Individual Representation

The individuals of the population represent feasible solutions, that is, the aggregation of all the geographical basic areas composing territory A into no over-lapping local labour markets (regions). Each individual is represented by a vector of n components, each of which corresponds to an area of A, and takes the value of the identifier of the region the area belongs to.

1	2	1	3	2	1	3	2	3	4	Individual

$R_1 = \{a_1, a_3, a_6\}$ $R_2 = \{a_2, a_5, a_8\}$ $R_3 = \{a_4, a_7, a_9\}$ $R_4 = \{a_{10}\}$

3.2 Selection

Selection of the individuals to be affected by recombination and mutation operations is performed following a ranking method [13], according to which those individuals scoring higher in the fitness function have a larger probability of being selected.

3.3 Recombination Operators

Due to the large number of constraints that the individuals must fulfil, and very notably to the fact that in a regionalisation exercise it is important to guarantee the exhaustive coverage of the territory and the avoidance of overlapping between regions, the usual operator of recombination does not in many cases lead to feasible solutions. This is the reason why we have designed a wide group of specific operators which allow a more rapid evolution of the population to acceptable solutions:

- *Rec1*: a crossover point is randomly selected. Offspring is generated by taking the initial part of one of the parents and the final part of the other one. This is the usual operator employed in genetic algorithms. However, unacceptable offspring is a frequent result of this operator in this specific case, since frequently there is not a compatible correspondence between the region identifiers of both parents.

Parent #1	1	2	1	**3**	2	1	**3**	2	3	4	
Offspring	1	2	1	**3**	2	3	**4**	2	4	5	Crossover point= 4
Parent #2	1	2	3	**4**	2	3	**4**	2	4	5	

To avoid such discrepancies in the codification of the regions of both parents two new operators of recombination have been introduced:

- *Rec2*: A region identifier belonging to parent #1 is randomly chosen. The areas with identifiers lower or equal to the chosen one are inherited by the offspring. The rest of the areas are then assigned the identifiers of parent #2, except for the cases when this involves a region for which one or more of its constituting areas were already in the offspring. In such cases, the areas take the identifiers from parent #1.

Parent #1	1	2	1	3	2	1	3	2	3	4	
Offspring	1	2	1	4	2	**1**	4	2	4	5	Crossover region = 2
Parent #2	1	2	3	4	2	3	4	2	4	5	

- *Rec3*: a crossover point is randomly selected. For the areas previous to that point, the offspring takes the values of parent #1. From that crossover point, values from parent #2 are inherited, unless this involves a region with an area already set in the offspring, when the identifier of parent #1 is used.

Parent #1	1	2	1	3	2	1	3	2	3	4	
Offspring	1	2	1	3	2	**1**	**3**	2	**3**	5	Crossover point = 4
Parent #2	1	2	3	4	2	3	4	2	4	5	

Since the areas characterised by lower identifiers are also assigned to regions with lower identifiers, their probability of being taken from parent #1 is greater than that of areas with high identifiers. To cope with this we have added two recombination operators (*Rec4* and *Rec5*), as variations of Rec2 and Rec3 respectively. In them a random recoding of the regions in the representation of both parents is performed previously to the recombination.

3.4 Mutation Operators

We have designed an extensive set of mutation operators, some of them specifically intended for the delineation of local labour market areas, with the aim to accelerate the obtaining of individuals with adequate fitness:

- *Mut1*: This is the mutation operator usually employed in evolutionary computation. The only difference is that instead of muting just one gene (area), we mute a randomly selected number of genes, changing the region they belong to.

– *Mut2*: This operator is analogous to Mut1. In this case, however, instead of choosing the region assigned to the muted area on a random basis, such area is merged with its optimal region, that is, the region with a higher interaction index with it:

$$R'(i) = \underset{\forall R_j \in R - R(i)}{\arg\max} \left(\frac{W^2_{\{i\},R_j}}{W_{\{i\},A} \cdot W_{A,R_j}} + \frac{W^2_{R_j,\{i\}}}{W_{R_j,A} \cdot W_{A,\{i\}}} \right) \quad (7)$$

– *Mut3*: In this case, two randomly selected regions are merged.
– *Mut4*: A region is randomly chosen. Each of its constituting areas is then merged with its optimal region (see Mut2). So, as results of this operator, the number of regions in the offspring is one less compared to its parent.
– *Mut5*: This operator divides a region into two. The splitting process is as follows:
   1. A region R_i is randomly selected. This region must fulfil two constraints: (a) $W_{R_i,A} > 2\beta_4$ and (b) $W_{R_i,A} - W_{focus(R_i),A} > \beta_4$ where $focus(R_i) = \arg\max_{\forall a \in R_i}(W_{\{a\},A} + W_{A,\{a\}})$ (that is, the region is large enough).
   2. An area belonging to R_i is randomly chosen. It is then assigned to the new region $R_i^{'}$.
   3. Another area belonging to R_i is randomly chosen. It is then assigned to the new region $R_i^{''}$.
   4. The rest of the areas belonging to R_i are taken at random, being assigned to region $R_i^{'}$ or $R_i^{''}$ which they have a greater interaction index with.
– *Mut6*: This operator creates a new region from another one by removing from the latter a number of areas sufficiently large so as to form a valid market:
   1. Similar to Mut5.
   2. An area belonging to R_i is chosen at random, being assigned to the new region $R_i^{'}$.
   3. If region $R_i^{'}$ does not fulfil the size constraint (equation 5), it takes the area belonging to R_i with which it has a higher interaction index. This process is repeated until $R_i^{'}$ is large enough.
– *Mut7*: This operation removes from a region the areas that score lower in the interaction index when measured with regards the rest of the region. Such areas are then assigned to their optimal regions:
   1. Similar to Mut5.
   2. The area to remove is selected as:

$$s = \underset{\forall j \in R_i}{\arg\min} \left(\frac{W^2_{\{j\},R_i-\{j\}}}{W_{\{j\},A} \cdot W_{A,R_i-\{j\}}} + \frac{W^2_{R_i-\{j\},\{j\}}}{W_{R_i-\{j\},A} \cdot W_{A,\{j\}}} \right) \quad (8)$$

   3. If $W_{R_i-\{s\},A} > \beta_4$ (R_i is large enough), the area s is assigned to its optimal region, and step 2 is repeated. If that condition is not fulfilled, mutation is finished.

- *Mut8*: An exchange of areas between regions is performed. One area is randomly chosen and it is assigned to its optimal region. One area of that optimal region is then transferred to the source region.
- *Mut9*: This operator is similar to Mut2 in the sense that areas are assigned to their optimal regions. In this case, however, instead of a single area a group of them is transferred. Such a group is chosen so that the relationships among its component areas are high. The process is as follows:
  1. An area i is randomly selected.
  2. The k areas belonging to $R(i)$ with which area i has more interaction are also selected. k is chosen at random.
  3. All the selected areas are assigned to the optimal region for area i.
- *Mut10*: As, in some cases, there is a great interaction between regions, this operator tries to redistribute areas in such regions. The procedure is:
  1. A number $k \geq 2$ of regions to mute is randomly chosen.
  2. A region R_i is selected at random.
  3. The k-1 regions that have a higher degree of interaction with R_i are selected.
  4. These regions are then disintegrated into their constituting areas.
  5. k areas from this new group are selected at random. These areas act as seeds for the new regions.
  6. The rest of unassigned areas are individually taken at random and merged with their optimal region among those k new regions.

4 Experimentation

Our proposal has been implemented for the delineation of local labour markets in the Region of Valencia, Spain, using data about travel-to-work derived from the Spanish Census of Population [12]. This data allow us to build a 541x541 matrix (541 is the number of municipalities constituting the Region), where each cell represents W_{ij}.

Parameters employed in the following examples are: size population = 100, offspring size = 123 with the following individuals from the application of the different operators of recombination and mutation (5 for each recombination operator, 30 for mutations 5 and 6; and 6 for each one of the other mutation operator), iterations without changes in the best individual to stop the process = 1,000. Since one of the criteria stated in the introduction section of the paper is Detail, i.e. reaching the highest possible number of independent LLMs, division operators are over considered.

The thresholds for the self-containment and minimum size conditions (equations 4 to 6) are: $\beta_1 = 0.7$, $\beta_2 = 0.75$, $\beta_3 = 20{,}000$ and $\beta_4 = 3{,}500$; that is, the levels used in the British procedure for the delineation of Travel-to-Work Areas. This allows the comparison of our results with those from that procedure. Parameter γ of "neighbourhood" is established to 5.

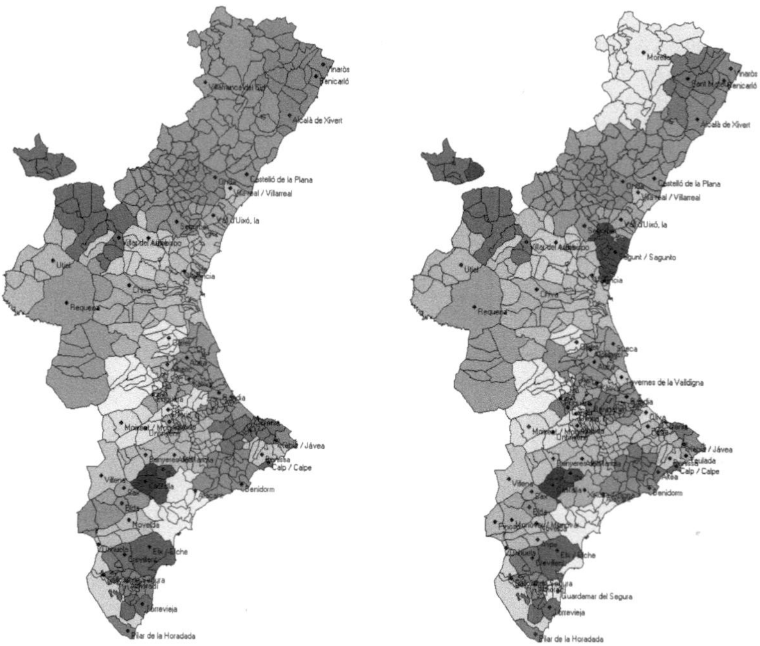

Fig. 1. Comparison between the delineation employing Coombes method (left) and our evolutionary approach (right)

Our algorithm has been executed 100 times. Results depicted in Table 1 and Figure 1 are quite straightforward. The number of independent markets identified through the evolutive procedure is approximately 35 per cent larger compared to the results reached through the use of the British official method which has become the standard in the field. In this sense, this procedure performs clearly better according to one of the good practices criteria listed in Section 1, that of Detail. In territorial terms it is clear that the evolutive procedure manages to identify independent LLMs following a nested pattern in which LLMs identified in the TTWAs' method are divided into LLMs which keep on meeting the statistical requisites which are the same (notably self-containment, criterion 5, and minimum size, criterion 6), but with little variation of the external boundaries of such markets. Also criteria 2 and 3 are fully met by our procedure. Regarding criterion (1), the procedure proposed here is clearly based on statistical properties of the areas considered, and it is not subject to subjectivism (which is the main concern in that criterion), although as in any other genetic algorithm procedure, it is affected by a lack of determinism in the results that could at least potentially be relevant in a policymaking context. Assessing the degree of accomplishment of criterion (8) is difficult here due to space constraints, although it can be stated that the procedure proposed meets this criterion in a degree that is at least equal to that of the TTWAs procedure. Finally, and concerning criterion (4), the number of discontinuities is higher in our evolutionary approach (although the absolute number remains low considering that no information on geographical distance or contiguity between basic areas has been used in the procedure). It is important to state, however, that these are raw results, and that the observed discontinuities can be solved in any case, as it was in the TTWAs case, through the application of a final calibration stage in which residual areas are assigned to LLMs they share boundaries with trough a decision rule based on an interaction measure.

Table 1. Comparative results between Coombes method and our evolutionary proposal

	Coombes method	Our proposal		
		Best individual	Mean	Standard deviation
Number of labour markets	46	62	59.76	1.07
Fitness function	129.18	191.03	182.43	3.29
Non-contiguous regions	4	7	-	-

5 Conclusions and Current Works

The degree of success in the delineation, implementation and monitoring of public policies in different contexts (Statistics, labour markets, housing markets, transportation, urban planning…) heavily depends on the adequateness of the geographical reference. Official methods for the delineation of functional areas which serve as a reference for these purposes have until now rely on procedures that very frequently were designed some decades ago and that can now be improved through the use of new procedures such evolutionary computation that allow to deal with complex datasets in a different way so as to reach better results. In this piece of work we model the regionalisation problem as one of optimisation which is then solved through a genetic algorithm based on operators and strategies that have been designed to meet the specificity of the problem. The need for exhaustively covering the territory and avoiding overlapping is one of the more characteristic features of the regionalisation problems. The experimental results show that, once the respect of statistical constraints such minimum size or minimum separation between functional regions is granted, the proposed method performs better and identifies a number of LLMs that is significantly larger than that resulting from current official methods whilst it manages to meet all the criteria that has been included in the codes of good practices like such of Eurostat, the Statistical Office of the European Commission.

The major concern in this policy making context is undoubtedly the fact that the use of our evolutionary approach does not guarantee that the results of the regionalisation exercise would remain unaltered in different trials. Despite giving place to worse results in the referred terms, traditional methods are consistent through different applications. Further research is needed on the way the convergence can be assured in a reasonable time and on the reduction of uncertainty. Different solutions are to be explored in immediate research: statistics extracted from different independent executions [14], [15], parallel evolutionary algorithms [16], application of other evolutionary proposals for clustering as the Grouping Genetic Algorithms [17] and multi-objective optimization [18].

Acknowledgements

José M. Casado-Díaz has received financial support from the Spanish Department of Education and Science (ref. BEC2003-02391) through a program partly funded by the European Regional Development Fund (ERDF). Lucas Martínez-Bernabeu acknowledges financial support from the Spanish Dept. of Education and Science, the European Social Fund (ESF) and the University of Alicante.

References

1. OECD: Redefining Territories. The Functional Regions. OECD Publications, Paris (2002)
2. Goodman, J.F.B: The Definition and Analysis of Local Labour Markets: Some Empirical Problems. British Journal of Industrial Relations, 8(2) (1970) 179-196.
3. EUROSTAT, Coombes, M.G.: Étude sur les zones d'emploi. Document E/LOC/20. Office for Official Publications of the European Communities, Luxembourg (1992)
4. Casado-Díaz, J.M., Coombes, M.G.: The Delineation of 21st Century Local Labour Market Areas (LLMAs). In Proceedings of the 8th Nectar Conference, Las Palmas C.G. (2005)
5. Coombes, M.G., Green, A.E., Openshaw, S.: An efficient algorithm to generate official statistical reporting areas: the case of the 1984 Travel-to-Work Areas revision in Britain. Journal of the Operational Research Society, 37 (1986) 943-953
6. ISTAT-IRPET: I mercati locali del lavoro in Italia, Milan, Angeli (1989)
7. ISTAT: I sistemi locali del lavoro 1991, Rome, Istat (1997)
8. ISTAT: I sistemi locali del lavoro 2001, available at http://www.istat.it (2005)
9. Casado-Díaz, J.M.: Local Labour Market Areas in Spain: A Case Study. Regional Studies, 34(9) (2000) 843-856
10. Papps, K., Newell, J.O.: Identifying Functional Labour Market Areas in New Zealand: A Reconnaissance Study Using Travel-to-Work Data. Discussion Paper n°. 443. Bonn, Institute for the Study of Labor (IZA) (2002)
11. Watts, M.: Local Labour Markets in New South Wales: Fact or Fiction?, Centre of Full Employment and Equity, WP 04-12, The University of Newcastle, Australia. (2004)
12. Censo de poblaciön (2001): Detailed results available at http://www.ine.es
13. Tomassini, M.: A Survey of Genetic Algorithms. In: Stauffer (ed.): Annual Reviews of Computational Physics, III. World Scientific, Singapore (1995) 87-118
14. Szpiro, G.G.: Tinkering with Genetic Algorithms: Forecasting and Data Mining in Finance and Economics. In: Chen, S.H. (ed.): Evolutionary Computation in Economics and Finance, tudies in Fuzziness and Soft Computing, 100. Heidelberg: Physica-Verlag (2002) 273-285
15. Fogel, D.B.: Evolutionary Computation. Towards a New Philosophy of Machine Intelligence, Third Edition. John Wiley & Sons (2006)
16. Nowostawski, M., Poli, R.: Parallel Genetic Algorithm Taxonomy. In Proceedings of the Third International Conference on Knowledge-based Intelligent Information Engineering Systems. IEEE Computer Society (1999) 88-92
17. Falkenauer, E.: Genetic Algorithms and Grouping Problems. John Wiley & Sons (1998)
18. Coello, C., Lamont, G.B. (eds.): Applications Of Multi-Objective Evolutionary Algorithms. Advances in Natural Computation, vol. 1. World Scientific Publishing Co. (2004)
19. Duque, J.C.: Design of homogeneous territorial units: A methodological proposal and Applications. Unpublished PhD dissertation, Universidad de Barcelona, Spain (2004)

Direct Manipulation of Free Form Deformation in Evolutionary Design Optimisation

Stefan Menzel, Markus Olhofer, and Bernhard Sendhoff

Honda Research Institute Europe GmbH,
Carl-Legien-Str. 30, D-63073 Offenbach/Main, Germany
{stefan.menzel, markus.olhofer, bs}@honda-ri.de

Abstract. The choice of an adequate representation plays a major role in any kind of evolutionary design optimisation. A flexible and preferably adaptive description of the shape is advantageous in many aspects as it guarantees a wide variety of geometry changes while keeping a low number of parameters. In the past free form deformation methods which are well known from the field of computer graphics have already been combined successfully with evolutionary optimisation. In the present paper general free form deformation (FFD) techniques are compared to the so-called direct manipulation (DM) of free form deformations method which promises several advantages in a design optimisation of complex systems. A general optimisation framework which allows the combination of these representations with evolutionary algorithms is described in detail. Its applicability is illustrated in a turbine blade test scenario to analyze the effects of the representations in evolutionary design optimisation.

1 Introduction

A crucial step when applying Evolutionary Algorithms to design optimisation problems is the definition of a representation of the design to be optimised by a set of parameter. Since the representation is highly problem specific various representations have been proposed for different application areas. Splines probably represent the most commonly used method for shape descriptions. A set of control points is used to define a spline curve or a spline surface which represents the cross-section or the surface of a geometry. This representation has been successfully used predominantly for the optimisation of relatively simple structures like turbine blades [1], aircraft wings or heat exchangers [2]. A major drawback of spline representations is the fact, that a large number of parameters is required to represent very complex shapes, i.e., the complexity of the representation is directly related to the complexity of the design. Additionally, if computational fluid dynamics calculations are required to determine the quality of new shapes, new grids have to be calculated. While automatic grid generation is possible for simple shapes, it is difficult or sometimes even impossible for complex designs. For these cases, the generation of the computational grid is a difficult and time consuming manual process. In particular, in the context of evolutionary algorithms, manual grid generation does not seem to be feasible.

An alternative representation that alleviates both problems (complex shapes and grid generation) is the free form deformation (FFD) method. In the FFD method

T.P. Runarsson et al. (Eds.): PPSN IX, LNCS 4193, pp. 352 – 361, 2006.

deformations of an initial design are described instead of the geometry itself. Therefore, the number of parameters is independent of the complexity of the shape. It is solely determined by the required flexibility of the deformation. FFD techniques have been introduced in the field of computer graphics and computer animation for object manipulation [3]. They have been applied to shape optimisation of aerodynamic problems by Perry et al. in [5] and together with evolutionary algorithms by Menzel et al. in [6]. It has been shown that FFD methods realize a good trade-off between shape flexibility and a low number of parameter which in turn results in a low dimensional search space for the optimisation. Furthermore, it has been demonstrated that the shape deformations defined by the FFD method can equally well be applied to deform a grid for computational fluid dynamics calculations. This way it is possible to omit the manual grid generation even for complex geometries. In many cases, design optimisation of complex shapes only becomes feasible when FFD methods are used for the representation.

An FFD system, which is described in Section 2 in more detail, is generally defined by a lattice of control points. A modification of the control point positions results in a deformation of the geometry inside the control volume. For the optimisation it is important to minimize the number of parameters. This is achieved by a proper initialisation of the control volume because the number and position of control points determines the shape flexibility.

One important aspect is to maximize the influence of the control points on the shape by placing control points close to the sensitive regions of the geometry. For the search process it is advantageous to generate a set of control points with which geometrical variations can be realized without the need for correlated changes of control points. Furthermore, the transformation should allow changes that are sufficiently local.

Therefore, this step of constructing an optimal control volume requires experience of the designer with the representation and more crucially with the problem at hand. Using an online adaptation of the grid of control points, which has been suggested in [6], can alleviate the problem of an optimal initial grid, however at the expense of an additional burden on the search process that is likely to result in additional evaluations and increased computing time.

Whereas the first problem addresses the dimensionality and flexibility of the representation, the second problem emerges purely due to the position of the control points in the design space. The position determines the structure of the search space and influences the optimisation process.

For both the dynamics of the search process and the design freedom, it would be desirable to *directly* specify shape variations instead of changing positions of control points in a grid that result in deformations of the "attached" shape as it is the case in standard FFD.

Direct Manipulation of Free Form Deformation (DMFFD) allows this. DMFFD decouples the control point grid of the FFD from the design modifications. Instead of defining the parameter of the transformation function, a set of "handles" to the design – usually surface points – are defined. The effect is a well defined influence of parameter on the shape. Furthermore, the search dimension is independent of the control volume, keeping all other attributes of the underlying free form deformation.

In this paper, we apply both methods, the standard free form deformation and the direct manipulation of Free Form Deformation, to a design optimization problem and compare the results with respect to quality, stability and convergence time. The optimization of a 2D transonic gas turbine stator blade does not represent the complex shape problem for which the FFD methods are actually most suitable. However, it indicates the strong and weak points of both representations and serves as a kind of intermediate benchmark problem.

The remainder of this paper is organized as follows. In Section 2, FFD and DMFFD are described in more detail. The combination of both representations with evolutionary computation is illustrated in the turbine blade test scenario in Section 3 and the effects of the representations are discussed. We conclude in Section 4.

2 Direct Manipulation of Free Form Deformations

2.1 Free Form Deformation (FFD)

The basic idea of the free form deformation is depicted in Fig. 1 a). The sphere represents the object which is the target of the optimisation. It is embedded in a lattice of control points (CP). Firstly, the coordinates of the object have to be mapped to the coordinates in the spline parameter space, a procedure which is called 'freezing'. If the object is a surface point cloud of the design or a mesh which originates from an aerodynamic computer simulation (as in our example in Section 3) each grid point has to be converted into spline parameter space to allow the deformations. For this calculation various methods have been proposed, e.g. Newton approximation or similar gradient based methods [4], [7]. After freezing the object can be modified by moving a control point to a new position. The new control point positions are the inputs for the spline equations and the updated geometry is calculated. Since *everything* in the control volume is deformed, a grid from computational fluid dynamics that is attached to the shape is also adapted. Hence, the deformation affects not only the shape of the design but at the same time the grid points of the computational mesh which is needed for the Computational Fluid Dynamics (CFD) evaluations of the proposed designs. The new shape and the corresponding CFD mesh are generated at the same time without the need for an automated or manual re-meshing procedure. This feature significantly reduces the computational costs and allows a high degree of automation [5], [6], [8]. Thus, by applying FFD the grid point coordinates are changed but the grid structure is kept.

As mentioned in the introduction the main disadvantage is the sensitivity of the FFD method to the initial placement of the control points. An inappropriate set-up increases the necessary size of the parameter set and therefore the dimensionality of the search space. One of the reasons is for example that the influence of a control point on an object decreases with the distance from the object. Even a small object variation requires a large modification of the control point if the initial distance between object and control point is large (this also violates the strong causality condition that is important in particular for Evolution Strategies). This in turn often modifies other areas of the design space which has to be compensated for by the movement of other control points. Hence, often correlated mutations of control points are necessary for a local change of the object geometry.

To reduce the influence of the initial positions of the control points direct manipulation is introduced as a representation for evolutionary optimisation which

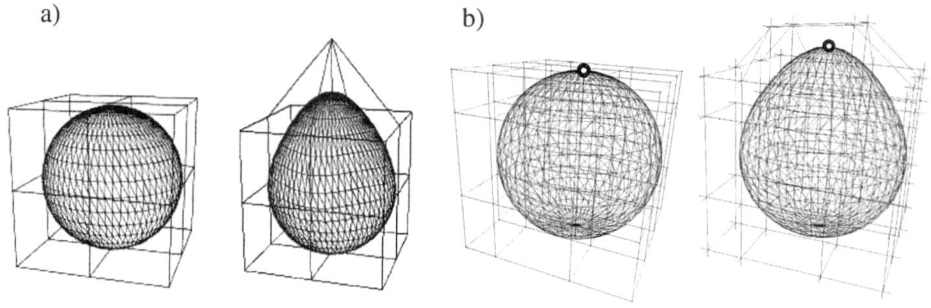

Fig. 1. a) Free Form Deformation [5]. The design is embedded within a lattice of control points. The modification of control points affects the shape as well as everything else inside the control volume. – b) Direct Manipulation of Free Form Deformations. The object point is chosen directly on the surface and the required movements of the control points to realize the target movement of the object point are calculated e.g. by the least squares method. The dotted control volume is invisible to the designer as s/he works directly on the object points; the control volume can be chosen arbitrarily.

allows to determine variations directly on the shape. Therefore local deformations of the object depend only on the so called object point.

2.2 Direct Manipulation of Free Form Deformations

Direct manipulation of free form deformations as an extension to the standard FFD has been introduced in [9]. Instead of moving control points (CP), whose influence on the shape is not always intuitive, the designer is encouraged to modify the shape directly by specifying so called object points (OP).

Although the initial setup of the control volume is similar to FFD, the control volume becomes invisible to the user and necessary correlated modifications are calculated analytically. In a first step, a lattice of control points has to be constructed and the coordinates of the object and the CFD mesh have to be frozen. But the control volume can be arbitrary, i.e., the number and positions of control points do not need to have any logical relationship to the embedded object, besides the fact that the number of control points determines the degree of freedom for the modification. In the next step, the designer specifies object points, which define handles to the represented object that can be repositioned. The shape is modified by *directly* changing the positions of these object points. The control points are determined analytically so that the shape variations (induced by the object point variations) are realized by the deformations associated with the new control point positions. In other words, the control points are calculated in such a way that the object points meet the given new positions under the constraint of minimal movement of the control points in a least square sense. Of course the object variations must be realizable by the deformations from the calculated new control point positions, i.e., if the number of control points is too small, some variations given by new object point positions might not be representable by a deformation.

In Fig. 1 b) an object point has been specified at the top of the sphere. The designer is able to move this object point upwards without any knowledge of the "underlying" control volume which can be initialized arbitrarily. The direct manipulation algorithm calculates the corresponding positions of the control points to mimic the targeted object point movement. The solution is shown in Fig. 1 b).

Direct manipulation of free form deformation has several advantages when combined with evolutionary optimization as compared to standard FFD. The construction of the control volume and the number and distribution of control points are not as important as in standard FFD. Furthermore, the number of optimisation parameters equals the number of object points.

3 FFD and Direct Manipulation of FFD in Evolutionary Design Optimisation

3.1 General Remarks on the Optimisation Set-Up

For a comparison of both representations a design optimisation test scenario has been set up. Four optimisation runs have been executed, one based on the standard free form deformation method and three using the direct manipulation technique.

All optimisations were based on an evolutionary strategy with covariance matrix adaptation (CMA-ES), an algorithm which combines fast convergence (few function evaluations) with high performance and small population sizes. This is especially significant for optimisations in which CFD calculations are required for fitness evaluation. There are mainly three features of the CMA-ES which distinguish it from standard evolutionary strategy algorithms. Firstly, the stochastic influence in the mutation step is reduced by introducing only one stochastic source which is used for modifying both, the object as well as the strategy parameters. Secondly, the so-called cumulative step-size adaptation is applied which extracts information from past generations to speed up and stabilize the adaptation of the strategy parameter. Thirdly, an adaptation of the full covariance matrix of the probability density vector takes place instead of independent variances for each single parameter. Therefore, correlated mutations can be realized which can significantly increase the convergence speed of the algorithm [1, 9, 10].

In all four optimisations the population size has been set to 32 individuals and an approximation model has been applied. In a pre-evaluation step all 32 individuals have been evaluated with a neural network and only the 16 most promising ones have been simulated with CFD to determine the individual fitness. The fitness values have also been used to train the neural network. From the 16 CFD results the best individual has been selected and considered as the parent for the next generation, so a (1,32(16))-strategy has been applied.

The details for each run can be found in Table 1. The number of parameters refers to the dimension of the search space. Their distribution on the design is depicted in Figure 3. The number of control points refers to the control point coordinates which can be modified in the FFD control volume. This is different from the total number of control point coordinates because points at the upper, lower and left border have to be constant due to CFD mesh consistency. Additionally, control points on the right edge of the control volume can be modified only in y-direction in order to fix the x-length of the design. For run 1 to run 3 the same FFD control mesh is used which is shown in Figure 3 in the upper left part for run 1.

Table 1. Type and number of parameters

Run	Type	Number of parameters	Number of control points
1	control points	10	10
2	object points	5	10
3	object points	13	10
4	object points	13	36

3.2 Turbine Blade Test Scenario

In this section, the results of a study on a turbine blade optimisation are presented, for details of the aerodynamic application and its parameters the reader is referred to [1].

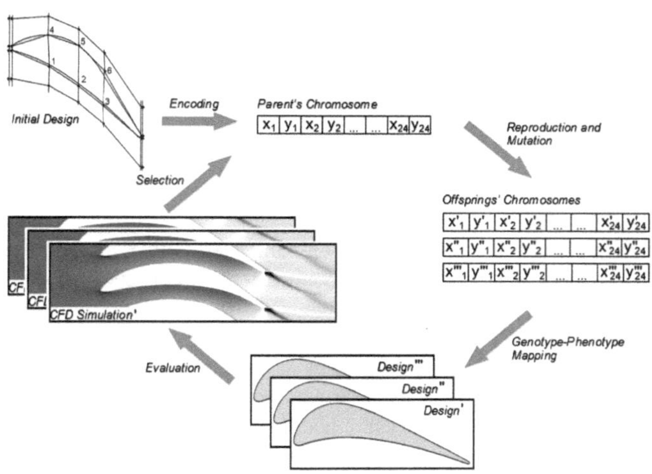

Fig. 2. The generation cycle in evolutionary design optimisation, see [6]

In Figure 2, the general workflow of the design optimisation is depicted and is now explained in more detail for run1, i.e., the standard free form deformation technique. A control volume consisting of 4x4 control points has been set up in which the turbine blade is embedded, see Figure 3. For easier visualization the CFD mesh is not plotted. However, we should keep in mind that during the deformation step the blade geometry *as well as* the CFD mesh are modified which allows the omission of the costly re-meshing process.

The control points CP_1-CP_4 can be freely moved in the x-y plane during the optimisation, while CP_5 and CP_6 are only allowed to move in vertical direction as stated above. After the encoding of these parameters (x and y coordinates of points CP_1 to CP_4 and the y-coordinate of CP_5 and CP_6) in the chromosome of the parent individual the control point positions are optimized. This includes the mutation of the control points, the deformation of the CFD grid based on the free form deformation algorithm and the execution of the CFD flow solver. As described in the previous section, the ES-CMA is used together with a neural network meta-model.

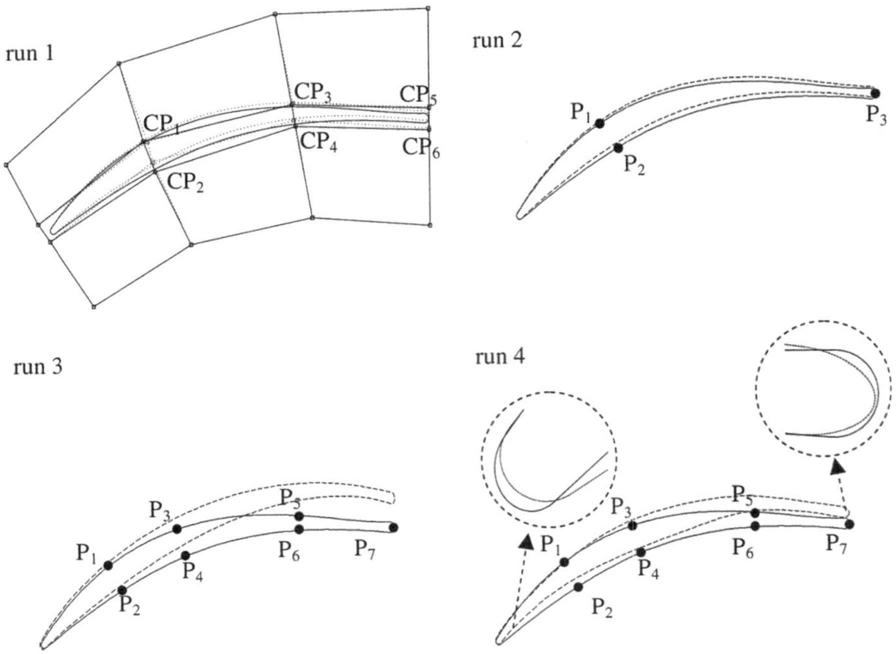

Fig. 3. Number and distribution of optimisation parameters. run1: 10 parameters (P_1-P_4: x, y; P_5, P_6: y); run2: 5 parameters (P_1, P_2: x, y; P_3: y); run3: 13 parameters (P_1-P_6: x, y; P_7: y); run4: 13 parameters (P_1-P_6: x, y; P_7: y). The closed line marks the initial designs, the dashed lines the optimized ones. The control volume is only drawn for run1. The control volumes for run2 and run3 are the same as for run1. Run4 has been modified in such a way that two rows and columns of control points have been inserted corresponding to a simple knot insertion algorithms as explained in [7]. For run4 the modifications at the leading and trailing edge are shown in a higher resolution to illustrate the occurring deformations. Initial circular or ellipsoid arcs are not kept after deformation because they turn out to be inferior to other leading and trailing edge geometries.

Run 2, 3 and 4 are identical besides that the direct manipulation of free form deformations is applied to modify the control points directly. The two major differences are the following:

1. The chromosomes contain object point positions (P_i) instead of control point positions (CP_i) as parameter sets.
2. The control points are calculated based on the encoded object points with the method for direct manipulation. Here the object points given in Figure 3 are used in the three runs. Based on the calculated control points the deformations of the design and CFD grid are updated in the same way as in run 1.

The results, i.e. the fitness progression, of this optimisation of all optimisation runs are summarized in Figure 4.

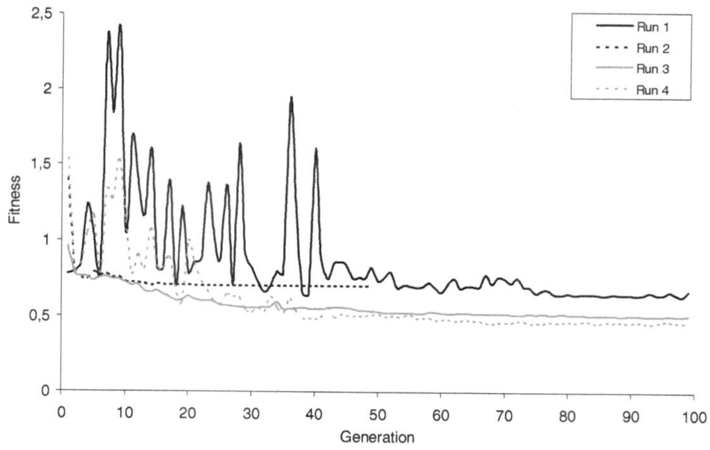

Fig. 4. The progress of the fitness of the runs 1 - 4

One major drawback of the direct manipulation method as presented in Section 2 is that the calculation of the control points is not unique in every case and constraints necessary for the deformation of the CFD grid are neglected. Especially negative volumes can emerge which can be described as loops in the design space.

This constraint is usually fulfilled by keeping the order of control points during the deformation step. However, when using direct manipulation the effect can occur that a targeted movement of an object point can only be achieved if large control point modifications are applied. These modifications can result in a change of the order of control points with the effect of producing grid cells with negative volumes. Methods for repairing and improving the structure of control points are therefore topic of our current research. To guarantee valid CFD meshes in the present optimisations the order of control points is checked after every mutation step. If the order of the control points is changed the mutation is repeated until a valid individual is generated.

3.3 Experimental Results

Figure 4 summarizes the results of the optimisations. Base run 1 that uses the standard FFD representation resulted in a converged fitness of 0.62 which means a 37% gain compared to the fitness of the initial turbine blade of 0.98.

According to Figure 3 three object points have been chosen for run 2. It resulted in a fitness of 0.7 but it needed less than half the number of generations and the optimization run is very stable. This is due to the reduced number of parameter which is only 5 (2 object points movable in x- and y-, 1 object point movable in y-direction) but it also shows that the flexibility of the design is limited by the choice of object points. This demonstrates that an optimisation using direct manipulation is limited by two factors. On the one hand a low number of object points restricts the flexibility of the design because these are the parameters which are optimized. On the other hand the number of control points limits the degree of realizable shape variations because the control points *actually* induce the targeted object point modifications through the defined deformations. If the number of control points is too low the targeted object points movements cannot be achieved.

In run 3 the number of object points (OP) has been increased to 7, i.e. 13 optimisation parameters (6 OP movable in x- and y-, 1 OP movable in y-direction) to improve the flexibility of the design. The fitness decreased to 0.5. This is an improvement compared to the optimisation run 1. This improvement is particularly interesting because the optimisation is based on the same control point grid as run 1. Even if the number of parameter for the optimisation is larger in run 3 the parameter for the deformations are identical because they are limited by the control point grid. Since the number and distribution of control points did not change between both runs the optimisation of run 1 must have converged to a local optimum. The structure of the search space seems to be changed by the direct manipulation in a way that the local maximum is circumvented in this optimisation run.

As a consequence, for this optimisation it can be seen that the usage of object points has been more successful. The fitness decreased faster and also at an earlier generation which is particularly important when dealing with time consuming evaluation functions like CFD simulations.

To analyze whether the performance could be even more increased by allowing more flexibility in the possible deformations two rows and columns of control points have been inserted into the control volume, resulting in 36 control points in run 4 while the number of object points was kept at 7. The fitness improved due to the control point insertion only slightly to 0.45. This is also a promising observation because the number of optimisation parameters is still 13 and the course of the fitness is quite similar to the one of run 3. Hence, the increase of flexibility by control point insertion did not affect the convergence behaviour.

4 Conclusions

In this paper, the standard free form deformation technique as well as direct manipulation of free form deformation have been combined with evolutionary optimisation. Both representations provide a fair trade-off between a low number of parameter and shape flexibility. To compare the performance a test scenario has been set up: a two dimensional turbine blade optimisation. The test scenario is a trade-off between a simple shape approximation benchmark problem and a truly complex shape optimization which is too computationally expensive for the comparison presented here. The expensive computational CFD simulations did not allow to perform several optimisations for averaging. By changing the representation and applying different numbers of object points the effect of the representation on the design optimisation has been studied.

In summary, we have shown that in this optimisation the usage of the new direct manipulation with free form deformation method has been advantageous.

If only 3 object points are chosen like in run 2 the convergence speed improved drastically and resulted still in a good performance index compared to the optimisation of the control points in run 1. This can be explained by the lower number of parameters in the optimisation. If the number of object points is increased like in run 3 and at the same time keeping the control points fixed, the fitness can be further improved although the possible transformations are kept constant in all three experiments. Here obviously the re-structuring of the search space by the introduction of the direct manipulation methods is beneficial.

Even an increase of control points in the control volume as it has been done in run 4 did not slow down the optimisation. This is a very promising result since the influence of the number of control points did not affect the convergence speed but the number of object points did. As a consequence one could argue to choose a high number of control points in the optimisation to achieve a high flexibility of the transformation and less constraints for the modification due to restrictions in the transformation. This definitely decreases the effect of the control point position and reduced the necessary prior knowledge about the optimisation problem while setting up the control volume.

Therefore, direct manipulation is a very promising representation because it provides the advantages of the standard free form deformation techniques while adding its own advantages as the arbitrary initialization of control volumes as well as the more direct impact of the object points on the geometry which improves the efficiency of the evolutionary algorithm.

References

[1] Sonoda, T., Yamaguchi, Y., Arima, T., Olhofer, M., Sendhoff, B., Schreiber, H-A.: Advanced High Turning Compressor Airfoils for Low Reynolds Number Condition, Part 1: Design and Optimization. Journal of Turbomachinery, 126: 350-359, 2004

[2] Foli, K., Okabe, T., Olhofer, M., Jin, Y., Sendhoff, B.: Optimization of Micro Heat Exchanger: CFD, Analytical Results and Multi-objective Evolutionary Algorithms. International Journal of Heat and Mass Transfer, vol. 49, no 5-6, pp. 1090-1099, 2006

[3] Sederberg, T. W., Parry, S. R.: Free-Form Deformation of Solid Geometric Models. Computer Graphics, 20(4):151-160, 1986

[4] Coquillart, S.: Extended Free-Form Deformation: A Sculpturing Tool for 3D Geometric Modeling. Computer Graphics, 24(4):187-196, August 1990

[5] Perry, E. C., Benzley, S. E., Landon, M., Johnson, R.: Shape Optimization of Fluid Flow Systems. Proceedings of ASME FEDSM'00. ASME Fluids Engineering Summer Conference, Boston, 2000.

[6] Menzel, S., Olhofer, M., Sendhoff, B.: Application of Free Form Deformation Techniques in Evolutionary Design Optimisation. 6th World Congress on Multidisciplinary and Structural Optimisation, Rio de Janeiro, 2005

[7] Piegl, L., Tiller, W.: The NURBS Book. Springer-Verlag Berlin Heidelberg 1995 and 1997

[8] Menzel, S., Olhofer, M., Sendhoff, B.: Evolutionary Design Optimisation of Complex Systems integrating Fluent for parallel Flow Evaluation. European Automotive CFD Conference, 2005

[9] Hsu, W. M., Hughes, J. F., Kaufman, H.: Direct Manipulations of Free-Form Deformations. Computer Graphics, 26:177-184, July 1992

[10] Jin, Y., Olhofer, M., Sendhoff, B.: Managing Approximate Models in Evolutionary Aerodynamic Design Optimization. Congress on Evolutionary Computation (CEC), vol. 2, pp. 592-599, 2001.

[11] Hansen, N., Ostermeier, A.: Completely Derandomized Self-adaptation in Evolution Strategies. Evolutionary Computation, vol. 9, no. 2, pp. 159-196, 2001

An Evolutionary Approach to Shimming Undulator Magnets for Synchrotron Radiation Sources

Olga Rudenko and Oleg Chubar

Synchrotron Soleil,
L'orme des Merisiers - Saint-Aubin - BP48
91192 Gif-sur-Yvette Cedex, France
olga.roudenko@synchrotron-soleil.fr, oleg.chubar@synchrotron-soleil.fr

Abstract. Undulator magnets shimming is a stage of the undulator production cycle that has a major influence on the quality of a synchrotron radiation. Despite the high complexity of the underlying decision making process, shimming is traditionally performed in a semi-empirical way using a high level expert knowledge. Such a labor intensive approach introduces additional cost and delay in undulator production. The present study introduces an automated decision making procedure for shimming based on an appropriate formalization of this task. Our approach consists in formulating the corresponding constrained optimization problem, which can be efficiently solved by an evolutionary algorithm using 3D magnetostatic methods and magnetic measurement for fitness calculation. Such automation allows us to reduce the time and cost of the undulator production and it leads to results of a quality level that is hardly attainable empirically considering the high complexity of the optimization problem.

Introduction

Synchrotron Radiation (SR) is nowadays routinely used for complex experiments in protein crystallography (for determination of the protein structure and drug design), in photoelectron spectroscopy (for inorganic material microanalysis) and many other sub-domains of physics, chemistry, biology and material science. Undulators are periodic multi-pole magnet structures installed at SR facilities in order to bring to the emitted radiation a number of particular features (such as high spectral brightness, tunability of the photon energy or tunability of the polarization state) needed by the SR users. Therefore, the undulator performance strongly conditions the quality of the synchrotron beam delivered for the scientific experiments.

Physically, an undulator is composed of a large number (from tens to hundreds) of magnets, each of which can be characterized by its magnetic error (the deviation of its magnetic characteristics from the ideal ones), inevitably resulting from the magnets' production technology. The impact of the individual magnets' imperfections on the performance of the whole undulator can be partly

T.P. Runarsson et al. (Eds.): PPSN IX, LNCS 4193, pp. 362–371, 2006.

compensated during the assembly stage making a series of appropriate decisions concerning the precise location of each of the available magnets in the undulator structure. The so-called *shimming* procedure plays a very important part in this scenario. It is applied after the undulator has been mounted and consists of relatively small discrete valued horizontal or/and vertical displacements of a limited number of magnets. The problem to be solved at this stage consists of choosing the locations at which the magnets will be displaced and to define the direction and the number of displacement steps for each chosen location so as to improve undulator performance. Moreover, a constraint on the maximum number of shimmed magnets is imposed by the technical complexity and loss of precision associated with the shimming process.

The paper is organized as follows. Section 1 describes the application, introducing the criteria of undulator performance and the degrees of freedom available to improve these criteria. Section 2 formulates the corresponding optimization problem in terms of Evolutionary Computation and evaluates the efficiency of different combinations of variation operators specifically tailored for this application. Section 3 shows the first practical results obtained with our approach, used for shimming of one of the undulators recently built at Soleil [10].

1 Shimming of Undulator Magnets

1.1 Undulator Performance

Undulator performance is evaluated, on one hand, by the quality of the emitted radiation (i.e. from the SR users point of view), and, on the other hand, by the amount of undesired perturbations inevitably introduced by an undulator to the electron beam, which must remain as steady as possible in the storage ring (See Fig. 1 (Left)).

The main characteristics of the magnet system are derived from transverse components of the 3D magnetic field created by the undulator, $B_x(x, y, z)$ and $B_y(x, y, z)$, where x, y and z are horizontal, vertical and longitudinal Cartesian coordinates respectively (see Fig. 1 (Right)).

The high spectral flux and brightness of undulator radiation, which are of a paramount importance for most user experiments, result from the constructive interference of electromagnetic waves emitted by an electron at different undulator periods. For maximum constructive interference to take place, the electromagnetic waves must be emitted in the same phase at all the periods, i.e. with minimal phase error from one period to another. Let us note $\Phi(z)$ the phase of electromagnetic waves. The phase error can then be defined as follows

$$Err(\Phi) \equiv \sum_{j=1}^{N_p} (\Delta\Phi_j - \overline{\Delta\Phi})^2, \tag{1}$$

where $\Phi_j = \Phi(z_0 + \lambda_u j)$ with period λ_u and arbitrary longitudinal position in the first period z_0, N_p is the number of full periods and $\Delta\Phi_j = \Phi_j - \Phi_{j-1}$.

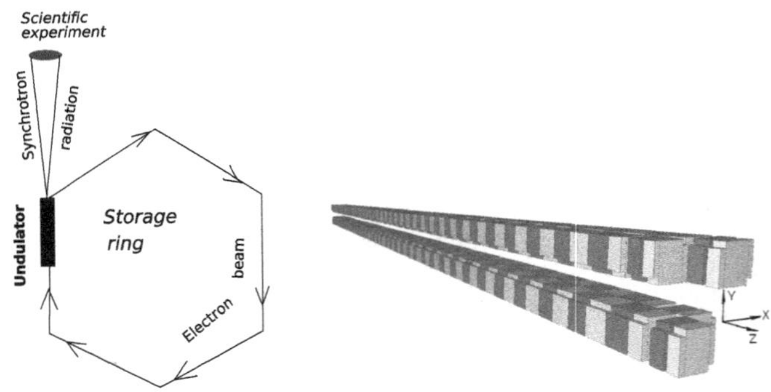

Fig. 1. Left: Scheme of a typical SR facility **Right:** Example of the undulator structure: APPLE-II type undulator (the magnets with vertical and longitudinal directions of the magnetization are shown by different tones)

Another feature conditioning the quality of the beam delivered for the user experiments is the *straightness* of the electron trajectory in the undulator. Let $x_e(z)$ and $y_e(z)$ be the transversal components of the electron trajectory. The requirement of the straightness can be formalized as minimization of the deviations of both components from their mean values:

$$Dev(x_e) \equiv \sum_{j=1}^{N_p} (x_{ej} - \overline{x}_e)^2, \qquad Dev(y_e) \equiv \sum_{j=1}^{N_p} (y_{ej} - \overline{y}_e)^2, \tag{2}$$

where $x_{ej} = x_e(z_0 + \lambda_u j)$. Note that these requirements on the electron trajectory and on the electromagnetic phase are, in fact, the requirements on the undulator magnetic field as x_e, y_e and Φ are given by the second integrals of the expressions depending on $B_x(0,0,z)$ and $B_y(0,0,z)$ [4].

In order to minimize perturbations introduced by an undulator with respect to the electron beam in the synchrotron ring, the undulator magnetic field must satisfy several more requirements. These can be formulated through the first horizontal and vertical field integrals taken in the direction of the electron trajectory before the undulator (i.e. z axis) and considered as functions of the transverse position:

$$I_x(x,y) = \int_{-\infty}^{+\infty} B_x(x,y,z)dz, \qquad I_y(x,y) = \int_{-\infty}^{+\infty} B_y(x,y,z)dz. \tag{3}$$

Minimizing the integrals (3) within a given range of the horizontal position in the median plane ($y = 0$), i.e. the sums

$$S_x(I_x) \equiv \sum_{k=0}^{N_x - 1} I_x^2(x_0 + k\delta x, 0), \qquad S_x(I_y) \equiv \sum_{k=0}^{N_x - 1} I_y^2(x_0 + k\delta x, 0), \tag{4}$$

is very important for preserving the dynamical aperture of an electron beam during many turns in the storage ring.

Finally, in order to prevent an undesired residual focusing introduced by the undulator to the electron beam, the horizontal derivatives of the field integrals on the electron beam axis ($x = y = 0$)

$$\Delta_x(I_x) \equiv |\frac{\partial I_x}{\partial x}(0,0)|, \qquad \Delta_x(I_y) \equiv |\frac{\partial I_y}{\partial x}(0,0)|, \tag{5}$$

must be minimized. Note that if $S_x(I_x)$ and $S_x(I_y)$ (Eq. (4)), could be minimized to a value approaching zero, there would be no point in minimizing $\Delta_x(I_x)$ and $\Delta_x(I_y)$. In practice, however, this is generally not the case.

1.2 Shimming for Restoring Undulator Performance

The so-called permanent magnet materials have a series of important advantages, which make them widely used in undulator production. However, because of their intrinsically stochastic domain structure, the permanent magnets unavoidably have some inhomogeneities of the remnant magnetization over their volumes and fluctuations of the volume-averaged remnant magnetization from one block to another. These effects cause the deviations of the magnetic characteristics from their reference values, that perturbs the magnetic field in the undulator enough to considerably degrade its performance.

The cumulated undesirable effect of individual magnet imperfections varies as a function of positions of the different magnets in the undulator structure. This effect can be partly reduced by an intelligent sorting of the available magnets (i.e. deciding where to put each magnet as a function of its magnetic characteristics) before and during the assembly stage. However, the efficiency in sorting is *a priori* limited because of either a lack of precise knowledge of the individual magnetic errors, or a lack of the accuracy of the mathematical model used to evaluate the undulator performance as a function of different magnet permutations.

The procedure of shimming [1] is applied when the undulator is assembled and different quantities defining its performance can be directly measured. The procedure consists of making small transverse displacements of the magnets. Doing so introduces magnetic system variations, which can considerably change (and, potentially, improve) the undulator performance defined as the minimization of the quantities (1), (2), (4) and (5).

In practice, the displacement of a magnetic block consists of dismounting and remounting it after inserting a *shim* (a piece of non-magnetic foil). The thickness of a shim can only take discrete step values within a given range. The perturbations of the magnetic characteristics resulting from the insertion of a shim of a minimal (one step) thickness are called *shim signatures*, and they can be calculated using magnetostatic calculation tools such as RADIA [2], used in this study. As the magnet displacements are much smaller then the distance between the magnets and the median plane of the undulator, the perturbation of the magnetic characteristics, resulting from the insertion of a shim of thickness n, is given by the corresponding shim signature multiplied by n. The calculation of the system state after shimming is then achieved by adding the effect of the perturbations to the initial (measured) characteristics' values.

2 Evolutionary Optimization for Magnets Shimming

2.1 Optimization Parameters and EA Representation

As follows from Section 1.2, the degrees of freedom for planning the shimming procedure are thicknesses of vertical and horizontal shims for each of the magnets composing the undulator. These thicknesses taking discrete values, an EA individual can be represented as a vector of pairs of integer numbers, each of which corresponds to the number of shim steps in horizontal and vertical directions respectively. A mapping between such vectors (genotypes) and the undulator structure (phenotype) allows us to assign to any *shimming configuration* a fitness value corresponding to the undulator performance.

The actual representation used in this work is a little more complex than the vector of pairs described above. Indeed, the magnets composing, for example, the undulator HU80 (described in more details in Section 3) are divided into two groups: magnets with vertical and longitudinal magnetization (see Fig. 1 (Right) for illustration). The displacements of the magnets with vertical magnetization tend to have stronger influence on the undulator performance, which we seek to improve by shimming. In order to make use of this expert knowledge, the vector-individual has been divided into two sub-vectors, corresponding one to the vertically and the other to the longitudinally magnetized magnets. An importance weight has then been assigned to each of the sub-vectors, allowing to bias the evolutionary search at the initialization stage as well as when applying the variation operators. (See Section 2.4 for more details.)

2.2 Optimization Criteria and EA Fitness

As we already mentioned in Section 1.2, since shimming is applied to an entirely assembled undulator, such quantities as magnetic field transverse components and their integrals can be directly measured before shimming. Having the shim signatures and taking advantage of the linearity of our system (briefly explained at the end of Section 1.2), we can calculate magnetic field and field integrals for every possible shimming configuration. This enables calculation of the function

$$F \equiv w_{\Phi} Err(\Phi) + w_{x_e} Dev(x_e) + w_{y_e} Dev(y_e) + \\ w_{I_x} S_x(I_x) + w_{I_y} S_x(I_y) + w_{\delta I_x} \Delta_x(I_x) + w_{\delta I_y} \Delta_x(I_y). \tag{6}$$

which is a weighted sum of the undulator performance criteria defined by the equations (1), (2), (4) and (5). The function F is used in this study as the fitness function, i.e. the criterion for comparing the performance of different shimming configurations.

We leave the aspect related to the multi-objective nature of the shimming optimization out of the scope of the present work, concentrating especially on designing the variation operators appropriate for our particular representation. We will however briefly discuss this potentially very interesting and important issue in Section 4.

2.3 Limited Shims Number and EA Constraint Handling

As explained in Section 1.2, to shim a magnet, one must dismount it from the undulator. The procedure of dismounting and remounting the magnets in practice is time consuming and hard to perform without loss of precision of the magnet position. Hence, a constraint on the number of shimmed magnets must be introduced. To give an idea of a real shimming procedure, for the undulator described in the Section 3, at most 30 of 332 magnets can be accepted for shimming. This constraint actually limits the efficiency of the shimming procedure.

In the Evolutionary framework, two basic types of constraint handling methods can be distinguished: the methods modifying individual evaluation so as to guide the search towards the feasible region (e.g. penalty based [7] constraint handling) and the methods which consist in sampling the feasible space and using variation operators preserving feasibility of solutions(see for example, [9]). Taking advantage of the fact that, in our case, it is easy to build feasible solutions, we designed variation operators, which preserve the feasibility of EA individuals.

2.4 Variation Operators

In addition to preserving individual feasibility, another issue has to be kept in mind when designing variation operators for our application: the importance weights assigned to the sub-vectors of the vector-individual corresponding to the vertically and horizontally magnetized magnets. The use of the sub-vectors' weights is clarified by the following initialization procedure. For each new individual, a number of non-zero positions n_s is chosen randomly in the range $(0, n_s^{max}]$, where n_s^{max} is a maximum number of shimmed magnets. To choose each of these positions, we choose first in which sub-vector it will lie (i.e. if a vertically or a longitudinally magnetized magnet will be shimmed). The roulette-wheel draws one of two sub-vectors using their importance weights as proportional probabilities. In the so chosen sub-vector, the non-zero position is drawn randomly as well as the horizontal and vertical shim thicknesses.

GA-inspired Crossover and Mutation. Given that the constraint on the number of shims was chosen to be controlled by the variation operators (i.e. feasible parents may produce only feasible offspring), an individual should be seen not only as a vector of pairs of integers but also as a set of zero (no shim) and non-zero (shim) valued elements. Such a view immediately inspires the analogy with the binary representation used by the traditional Genetic Algorithm [5]. The following crossover and mutation have, therefore, been designed by analogy with 1-point binary crossover [6] and bit-flip mutation [5].

The crossover divides all the components of the vector-individual in two groups in such a way that, in the phenotypic space, it corresponds to cutting the undulator structure in two parts at a randomly chosen longitudinal position. To not surpass the maximum number of shims after switching the parts, as in the traditional one-point crossover, all the shims are preserved in one (randomly chosen) of two parts, while the shims to be kept in the other part are randomly selected one by one until there are no shims anymore or the maximum number of shims is attained. One-point crossover has been used actually because for more division points it is less easy to control the maximum shim number in the offspring.

The one-bit-flip mutation is used with the changed "bit" drawn randomly following exactly the same procedure as for the initialization described above.

"Small" Mutation. This operator has been designed to enable the exploration in the very near neighborhood of the good solutions, which is particularly important at an advanced stage of the evolutionary search. It consists of mutating the number of shim steps for one or many locations where this number is already non-zero. A new shim value is drawn following the binomial law, whose mean is equal to the previous value. The experiments (which are not shown here for space reasons) confirm that a binomial law is more efficient than uniform sampling to refine the search at the end of the evolution.

2.5 Experimental Results

Problem Parameters. All the numerical results presented in this section and in Section 3, were obtained for the HU80 undulator [10] built out of 332 permanent magnets: 164 vertically-magnetized and 168 longitudinally-magnetized. The maximum shim sizes are 6 and 9 steps in horizontal and vertical directions respectively. All the results shown or mentioned in this section were obtained with maximum number of shims set to 15.

EA Scheme and Experimental Setup. Our evolutionary algorithm uses tournament selection with diversity preserving low selection pressure (each individual encounters only one randomly chosen opponent), which is balanced by a highly elitist replacement, merging 100 parents and 100 offspring to choose the 100 best individuals for the next generation. Variation operators are combined sequentially, i.e. they are applied to an individual one after another. The crossover is applied with probability 0.6, the "small" mutation with probability 1, and the bit-flip mutation with probability 0.7 when combined with the "small" mutation and with probability 1 when combined with the crossover only. The curves in Figure 2 represent the best fitness values, averaged over 21 runs, at each generation. The same set of 21 initial populations was used to test different operator combinations.

Let us note that bit-flip mutation (called GA-mutation in the figure legends) was introduced later than the crossover and "small" mutation. The efficiency of this operator, especially when combined with "small" mutation, is clearly shown in Figure 2 (Left). The number in brackets assigned to the "small" mutation refers to the number of the mutated components. It is natural that, in absence of the bit-flip mutation, mutating more components gives better results. But, when combining all three operators, the smallest "small" mutation (1 mutated component) appears to be the best choice (See Fig. 2 (Right)).

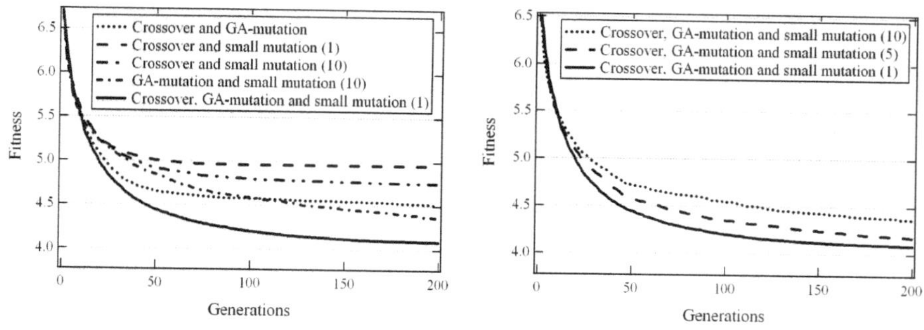

Fig. 2. Comparison of different combinations of variation operators

We are keen to mention another positive effect of the one-bit-flip mutation (which is not illustrated here for space reasons): it significantly and systematically improves the reproducibility of the quality of results from one run to another. This aspect is indeed very important when evaluating the efficiency of a stochastic optimization method.

The effect of different assignments of the importance weights to the vertically and longitudinally magnetized blocks has also been studied. For the criteria weights $w_{\Phi} = w_{I_y} = 0.15$, $w_{x_e} = w_{y_e} = 0.2$, $w_{I_x} = 0.26$, $w_{\delta I_x} = w_{\delta I_y} = 0.02$ (see Eq. (6)), used to obtain all the results shown in this paper, the difference is not spectacular but the tendency is neat: the higher the weight of a vertically magnetized blocks, the better the optimization results. However, in Section 4 we will explain why one should interpret this conclusion carefully.

3 Practical Results

The practical results of the evolutionary-based shimming of the HU80 undulator recently assembled at Soleil are very satisfactory and were highly appraised by the Soleil Machine division. Note that they were obtained when the study dedicated to adapting an EA to this application (notably, tuning variation operators) was still on-going. This means that there is a room for further improvement of the shimming efficiency for the other undulators being currently built at Soleil.

As one can readily see from Figures 3 and 4, the shimming procedure resulted in considerable reduction of the residual horizontal and vertical field integrals within about 100mm range along the x axis and, at the same time, in improvement of the "straightness" of the electron trajectory in the central part of the undulator so as to match the ideal trajectory very closely. Let us note that the variations of magnetic field integrals (Fig. 3) cannot be completely suppressed by shimming. This is related to the fact that the shim signatures do not constitute a full basis, i.e. a set of functions sufficient for an accurate approximation of any other function by their linear combination. The correction of remaining non-zero residual field integrals is generally done using a special technique applied, if necessary, after shimming.

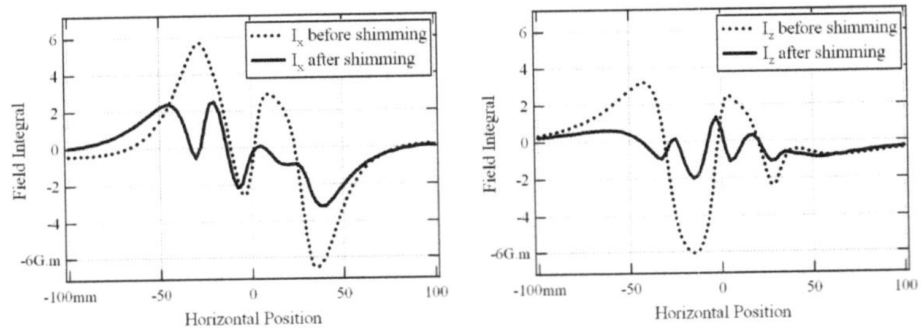

Fig. 3. Measured horizontal and vertical magnetic field integrals as functions of the horizontal position in the median plane of HU80

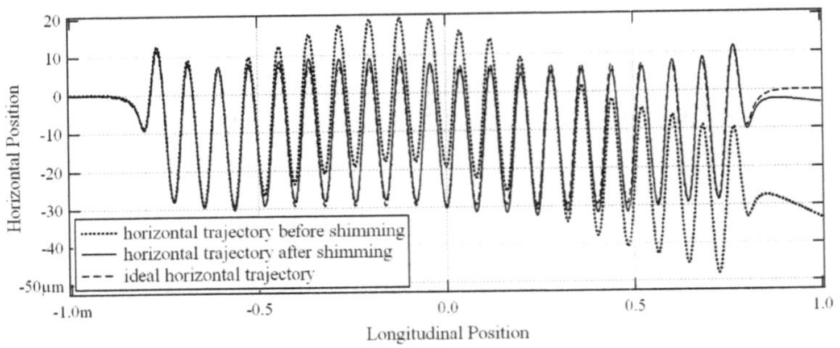

Fig. 4. Horizontal components of electron trajectories, calculated from the measured on-axis vertical magnetic field

4 Discussion and Future Work

This paper presents the first experience of applying EAs to shimming undulator magnets. The comparison of different combinations of EA variation operators specifically designed for this application is also provided.

The efficiency of the proposed approach is supported by practical experience: indeed, HU80 became the first of a whole series of undulators being assembled at Soleil that are or will be shimmed using our method. Unfortunately, as we are presenting here a recent industrial application, we do not have any reference solution, which would allow for a quantitative comparative evaluation of the obtained results. However, it is fairly unlikely for a semi-empirical approach to ensure a sufficient exploration of a search space of size $\binom{332}{15} \cdot 9 \cdot 6$ (the number of all possible shimming configurations for the values given in the beginning of the subsection 2.5) in a reasonably short period of time.

When implementing the idea of assigning a higher priority to the vertically magnetized blocks, particular attention must be paid to the weights of the different performance criteria. Indeed, while most criteria are influenced especially by displacements of vertically magnetized blocks, the phase is sensitive to displacements of both magnet types. Hence, if the phase weight is relatively small, the optimization of the weighted sum (6) may suggest to completely remove the longitudinally magnetized blocks from consideration, while, in fact, it can undesirably limit phase improvement during optimization.

We recognize here a very important multi-objective aspect of shimming. There exists a particular kind of EAs, referred to in the literature as Multi-Objective Evolutionary Algorithms (MOEAs) [3]. These methods do not need user-defined weights to be assigned to the different optimization criteria as they are designed to find multiple trade-off solutions of multi-objective optimization problem in a single run. Application of MOEAs to the problem of shimming is currently an on-going project. One particular interest of this type of methods is that having a well sampled trade-off surface, one can analyze the interactions between different objectives, which allows for a deeper understanding of the physical phenomenon at the origin of the problem.

Acknowledgments. The first author is supported under the European Commission's BIOXHIT Project (LHSG-CT-2003-503420).

References

1. J. Chavanne and P. Elleaume. Undulator and Wiggler Shimming. *Synchrotron Radiation News*, Vol. 8, Num. 1, pp. 18-22, 1995.
2. O. Chubar, P. Elleaume and J. Chavanne. A 3D Magnetostatics Computer Code for Insertion Devices. *Journal of Synchrotron Radiation*, Vol. 5, pp. 481-484, 1998
3. K. Deb. *Multi-Objective Optimization using Evolutionary Algorithms.* John Wiley, 2001.
4. P. Elleaume. Undulator Radiation. In H. Onuki and P. Elleaume eds. *Undulators, Wigglers and their Applications.* Taylor and Francis, 2003.
5. D. E. Goldberg. *Genetic algorithms in search, optimization and machine learning.* Addison Wesley, 1989.
6. J.H. Holland. Outline for a logical theory of adaptive systems. *Journal of the association of computing machinery*, Vol. 3, pp. 297-314, 1962.
7. J.A. Joines and C.R. Houck. On the Use of Non-Stationary Penalty Functions to Solve Nonlinear Constrained Optimization Problems With GAs. In Z. Michalewicz and al. eds. *ICEC94 proceedings*, IEEE Press, pp. 579-584, 1994.
8. S. Sasaki. Analyses for a planar variably-polarizing undulator. *Nuclear Instruments and Methods in Physics Research*, Vol. A347, pp. 83-86, 1994
9. M. Schoenauer and S. Xanthakis. Constrained GA Optimization. In S. Forrest ed. *ICGA93 proceedings*, Morgan Kaufmann, pp. 573-580, 1993.
10. Synchrotron Soleil: Insertion devices, http://www.synchrotron-soleil.fr/anglais/machine/accelerators/insertion-devices/index.html

New EAX Crossover for Large TSP Instances

Yuichi Nagata

Graduate School of Information Sciences,
Japan Advanced Institute of Science and Technology
nagatay@jaist.ac.jp

Abstract. We propose an evolutionary algorithm (EA) that applies to the traveling salesman problem (TSP). The EA uses edge assembly crossover (EAX), which is known to be efficient and effective for solving TSPs. Recently, a fast implementation of EAX and an effective technique for preserving population diversity were proposed. This makes it possible to compare the EA with EAX comparable to state-of-the-art TSP heuristics based on Lin-Karnighan heuristics. We further improved the performance of EAs with EAX, especially for large instances of more than 10,000 cities. Our method can find optimal solutions for instances of up to 24978 cities within a day using a single Itanium 2 1.3-GHz processor. Moreover, our EA found three new best tours for unsolved national TSP instances in a reasonable computation time.

1 Introduction

The traveling salesman problems (TSPs) are widely cited NP-hard combinatorial optimization problems because they are so intuitive and easy to state. In Johnson and McGeoch's surveys [1][2], the most efficient approximation methods for TSPs were based on Lin-Kernighan local searches (LKLS) [3]. The chained Lin-Kernighan algorithm (CLK) [4] is a more sophisticated LKLS. Helsgaun [5] proposed another type of efficient LKLS (LKH). The tour-merging method [12] has been thought be a very powerful approximation method; the best tour is searched for on a restricted graph constructed of the union of dozens of high-quality solutions obtained using CKL or LKH.

Many evolutionary algorithms (EAs) have been applied to TSPs. Much effort has been devoted to designing effective crossovers suitable for TSPs because the performances of EAs are highly dependent on the design of crossovers. The edge assembly crossover (EAX) proposed by Nagata and Kobayashi [6] is known to be an effective crossover for TSPs.

However, EAs without LKLS have been found to be less effective than state-of-the-art TSP heuristics based on LKLS. Therefore, hybrid algorithms composed of EAX and CLK have been proposed [7]. On the other hand, Nagata [11] proposed a fast implementation of EAX and an effective method of preserving population diversity. This technique significantly improved the performance of EAs using EAX and demonstrated that EAs without LKLS can perform as well as state-of-the-art TSP heuristics based on LKLS.

T.P. Runarsson et al. (Eds.): PPSN IX, LNCS 4193, pp. 372–381, 2006.

In this paper, we further improve EAX to apply EAs to large instances of more than 10,000 cities because we found that the EAX used in [11] is not appropriate for large instances. The remainder of this paper is organized as follows. In Section 2, we look at existing work related to EAX. Our improvement of EAX for large instances is described in Section 3. In Section 4, we discuss our experiments and results. Section 5 is the conclusion.

2 Previous Work

In this section, we will introduce work related to this paper. First, we will briefly describe the algorithm of EAX [6] (See Ref. [6] or [11] for details). Then, some strategies for using EAX effectively, proposed in [10] and [11], are also described.

2.1 Outline of EAX

The following and Fig. 1 is an outline of EAX.

Step 1: Denote a pair of parents as tour-A and tour-B, and define G_{AB} as a graph constructed by merging tour-A and tour-B.
Step 2: Divide the edges on G_{AB} into *AB-cycles*, where an *AB-cycle* is defined as a closed loop on G_{AB} that can be generated by alternately tracing the edges of tour-A and tour-B.
Step 3: Construct an *E-set* by selecting *AB-cycles* according to a given rule.
Step 4: Generate an intermediate solution by applying the *E-set* to tour-A, *i.e.,* by removing tour-A's edges in the *E-set* from tour-A and adding tour-B's edges in the *E-set* to it.
Step 5: Modify the intermediate solution to generate a valid tour by connecting its sub-tours. Two sub-tours are connected by deleting one edge from each sub-tour and adding two edges to connect them. Which sub-tours are connected and which edges are deleted are determined heuristically.

The following are comments that are helpful in Section 3.

- The union of all *AB-cycles* generated in step (2) is equal to G_{AB}.
- In practice, *AB-cycles* constructed of duplicated edges are neglected in step (3) because they have no effect on step (4). These *AB-cycles* are called *ineffective AB-cycles*. The other are called *effective AB-cycles*.

In step (3), the *E-set* can be constructed from any combination of *AB-cycles*. The following two methods were proposed in previous reports [6][10].

EAX-Rand: The *E-set* is constructed by randomly selecting *AB-cycles* with provability 0.5. The intermediate solution tends to equally include edges of tour-A and tour-B.
EAX-1AB: The *E-set* is constructed from a single *AB-cycle*. The intermediate solution tends to be similar to tour-A; i.e., children are generated by removing a small number of edges from tour-A and adding the same number of edges to it.

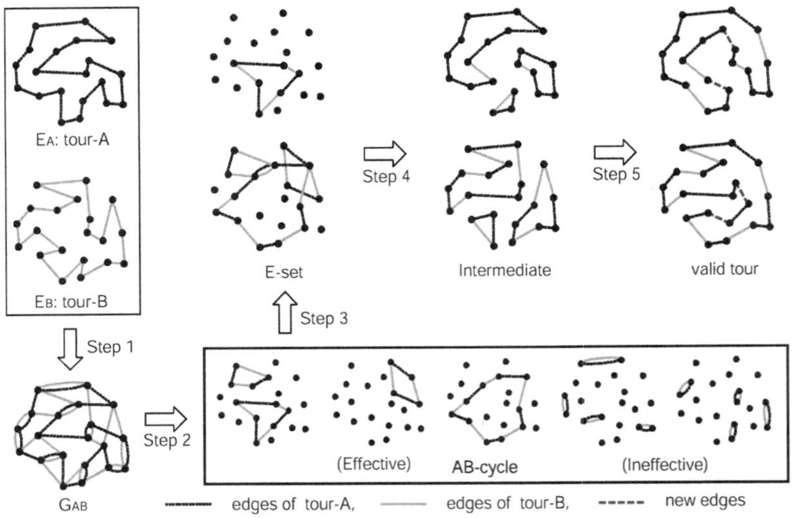

Fig. 1. Outline of EAX

2.2 Some Strategies for EAX

In previous work [10,11], these two methods were bifurcated according to the quality of the solutions in the population.

Stage I: EAX-1AB is used until no improvements in the shortest tour length in the population are observed over a period of time.
Stage II: EAX-Rand is used after stage I is finished, i.e., when EAX-1AB can no longer improve individuals in the population.

The reasons for using stage I are (i) the efficiency of the computational cost of EAX-1AB and (ii) the capability of preserving the population diversity. When EAX-1AB is used, changes of edges in the EAX algorithm are localized, and calculation is sped up. An especially efficient implementation of EAX-1AB was proposed by Nagata [11]. Moreover, EAX-1AB can prevent the population from converging wastefully by eliminating changes of edges that do not shorten the tour length [10].

Stage II is useful because EAX-Rand can produce wider varieties of children than can EAX-1AB. Stage II can actually improve individuals in the population even when EAX-1AB can no longer improve them [10,11].

3 Proposed Method

In this section, we propose a new EAX used in stage II instead of EAX-Rand.

First, we define some notation. The *size of an E-set* and the *size of an AB-cycle* are defined as the number of tour-A edges included in the *E-set* and the *AB-cycle*, respectively. $Gain_{Modi}$ is an improvements of tour length from an intermediate solution to a valid tour which is defined by $Gain_{Modi} = \sum_{e \in E_{remove}} w(e) - \sum_{e \in E_{add}} w(e)$, where E_{add} and E_{remove} are sets of edges that are added and removed, respectively, in step (5) of the EAX algorithm. $w(e)$ is a weight of an edge e.

3.1 Limitations of EAX-1AB and EAX-Rand

Let *POP* be a population that EAX-1AB can no longer improve. Such a population is usually highly refined. Therefore, each individual in *POP* is trapped in a deep local optima. To further improve individuals in *POP*, intermediate solutions should be formed so as to satisfy the following two conditions.

(C-I) Intermediate solutions should be formed by changing tour-A extensively. In other words, the size of the *E-set* should be large to overcome deep local optima.
(C-II) The number of sub-tours in an intermediate solution should be as small as possible.

The reason for C-II is a limitation of step (5) of the EAX algorithm. If an intermediate solution consists of k sub-tours, they must be connected into a valid tour by $k-1$ operations like 2-opt moves. 2-opt move is a transition from one tour to another by exchanging two edges. Indeed, step (5) of the EAX algorithm usually increases the tour length of a resulting valid tour ($Gain_{Modi} < 0$) when tour-A is highly refined because 2-opt moves are the most restricted method of connecting two sub-tours. Thus, the number of sub-tours in an intermediate solution should be restricted to increase $Gain_{Modi}$.

However, C-I and C-II usually conflict because the number of sub-tours in an intermediate solution tends to increase as the size of *E-set* increases. Considering C-I and C-II, the drawbacks of EAX-1AB and EAX-Rand can be summarized as the following three hypotheses. Typical examples of intermediate solutions for each case are illustrated in Fig. 2. We will verify these hypotheses in Section 3.3.

(i) If an *E-set* is constructed from a single small-sized *AB-cycle*, C-I is not satisfied.
(ii) If an *E-set* is constructed from a single large-sized *AB-cycle*, C-II is not satisfied.
(iii) If an *E-set* is constructed by randomly selecting multiple *AB-cycles* (EAX-Rand), C-II is not satisfied. However, this method can produce improved tours from *POP* at least in principle because a wide variety of *E-sets* can be constructed. However, the likelihood is very low.

3.2 EAX-Block

In this subsection, we propose a method of selecting *AB-cycles* for constructing an *E-set* that can produce an intermediate solution satisfying C-I and C-II. We call EAX using this method EAX-Block.

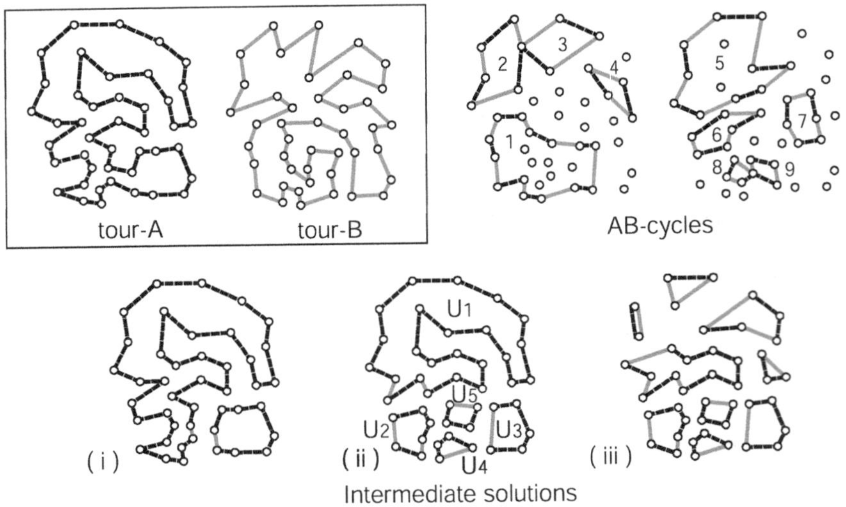

Fig. 2. Typical examples of intermediate solutions generated by *E-sets* constructed of (i) a single small-sized *AB-cycle* (*AB-cycle* 9), (ii) a single large-sized *AB-cycle* (*AB-cycle* 1), and (iii) randomly selected multiple *AB-cycles* (*AB-cycle* 1, 2, 3, 4). Tour-A, tour-B and *AB-cycles* are also illustrated (Ineffective *AB-cycles* are omitted).

EAX-Block:

1. Select a large-sized *AB-cycle*. Let it be a center *AB-cycle*. Note that the top N_{ch} largest-sized *AB-cycles* are selected as center ones when N_{ch} children are generated from a pair of parents.
2. Apply the center *AB-cycle* to tour-A and form an intermediate solution. Let U_i $(i = 1, \ldots, k)$ be the i-th sub-tour, where k is the number of sub-tours. Let U_1 be the largest sub-tour, i.e., including the largest number of edges.
3. Select *AB-cycles* that satisfy the following conditions.
   -(c1): They have connections to vertices in U_i $(i = 2, \ldots, k)$.
   -(c2): Their sizes are smaller than that of the center *AB-cycle*.
4. Construct an *E-set* from the center *AB-cycle* and the *AB-cycles* selected in step 3.

Fig. 2 and Fig. 3 illustrate an example of EAX-Block. In step (1), *AB-cycle* 1 illustrated in Fig. 2 is selected as a center *AB-cycle*. Therefore, an intermediate solution (ii) in Fig. 2 is produced in step (2). In step (3) and (4), an *E-set* is constructed of *AB-cycles* 1, 6, 7, 8 and 9 as shown in Fig. 3, where ineffective *AB-cycles* satisfying (c1) are also included in the *E-set* for the sake of simplicity of an explanation described below. A resulting intermediate solution produced by the *E-set* is illustrated in Fig. 3.

Now, properties of EAX-Block are described. For the sake of simplicity, ineffective *AB-cycles* can be selected in step (3), and condition (c2) is not considered here. First, we define the following terms.

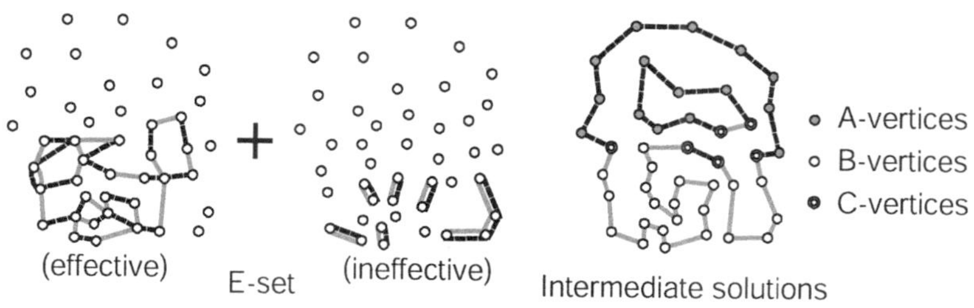

Fig. 3. Typical example of an *E-set* and an intermediate solution generated by EAX-Block. The *E-set* is constructed of *AB-cycles* 1, 6, 7, 8 and 9 illustrated in Fig. 2 and ineffective *AB-cycles* adjacent to $U_2, \ldots, U_5$.

A-vertex: A vertex that is connected to no tour-A (tour-B) edge in the *E-set*. It is connected to two tour-A edges in intermediate solutions.

B-vertex: A vertex that is connected to two tour-A (tour-B) edges in the *E-set*. It is connected to two tour-B edges in intermediate solutions.

C-vertex: A vertex that is connected to one tour-A (tour-B) edge in the *E-set*. It is connected to one tour-A edge and one tour-B edge in intermediate solutions.

All vertices in $U_2, \ldots, U_k$ are B-vertices because of condition (c1) in step (3) (Remember the comments mentioned in Section 2.1.). Vertices in U_1 that are geographically far from the other sub-tours tend to be A-vertices if the sizes of *AB-cycles* selected in step (3) are small. Other vertices are C-vertices, which are located between A-vertices and B-vertices. In Fig. 3, vertices in the intermediate solution are divided into A-, B- and C-vertices. When the number of C-vertices increase, the number of sub-tours tend to increase as shown in Fig. 2.

The advantage of EAX-Block over EAX-1AB and EAX-Rand is that intermediate solutions can be generated by assembling a block of tour-A edges and a block of tour-B edges. If the sizes of all *AB-cycles* selected in step (3) are small, the number of C-vertices tends to be small. In this case, EAX-Block has an ideal property and can satisfy the conditions (C-I) and (C-II).

3.3 Behaviors

Now, we demonstrate the behaviors of EAX-1AB, EAX-Rand, and EAX-Block.

The distribution frequency of sizes of *AB-cycles* that are obtained by applying EAX to a pair of parents is shown in Fig. 4 (a). These data are averaged over 150 pairs of parents selected from *POP* by random sampling without replacement, where *POP* was generated by stage I with EAX-1AB as described in Section 4.1. The instance usa13509 [9] was used for these experiments.

On average, 124.6 *AB-cycles* are generated from a pair of parents[1]. As shown in Fig. 4 (a), while most *AB-cycles* have sizes smaller than 10, relatively large

[1] 95% edges are removed as ineffective*AB-cycles* because individuals in *POP* are similar to each other.

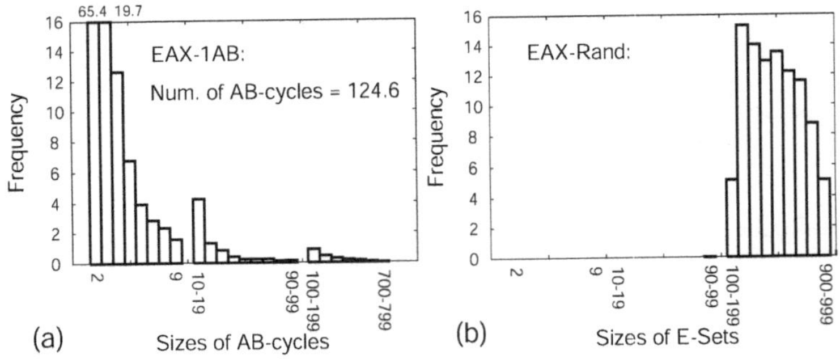

Fig. 4. (a) Distribution frequency of size of *AB-cycles*. (b) Distribution frequency of size of *E-sets*. Note that scales of x-axes are different.

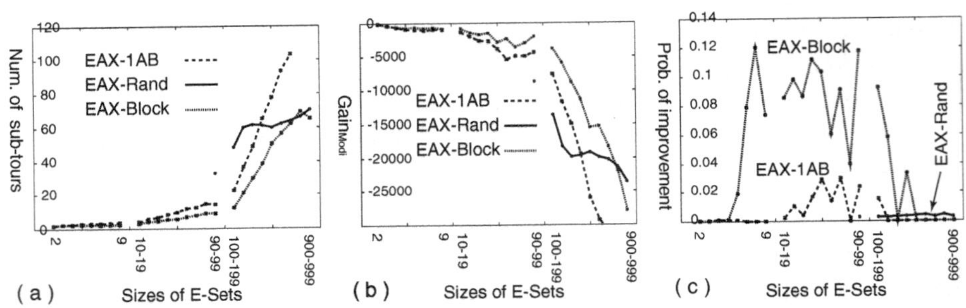

Fig. 5. Behaviors of EAX-1AB, EAX-Rand, and EAX-Block. Note that scales of x-axes are different.

AB-cycles having sizes of larger than 100 are usually contained in this example. Figure 4 (b) shows the distribution frequency of the size of *E-sets* that were obtained by applying EAX-Rand to the same population, where 100 *E-sets* are generated form a pair of parents. Obviously, the sizes of the *E-sets* generated by EAX-Rand are larger than those generated by EAX-1AB.

The behaviors of the three EAXs are shown in Fig. 5. The data are averaged over each size of an *E-set*. Figure (a) shows the number of sub-tours in intermediate solutions generated by the three types of EAXs. As shown, the number of sub-tours tends to increase as the size of the *E-set* increases. On the other hand, Fig. (b) shows that $Gain_{Modi}$ tend to decrease as the size of the *E-set* increases. We can see that the graphs in Figs. (a) and (b) are symmetric with respect to the x-axis. Thus, the number of sub-tours and $Gain_{Modi}$ have a negative correlation. Based on the condition (C-II), EAX-Block is the best method among the three types of EAXs because the number of sub-tours ($Gain_{Modi}$) of EAX-Block is the smallest (largest) among them. Consequently, EAX-Block can improve tour-A more frequently than can EAX-1AB and EAX-Rand, as shown in Fig. (c). Fig. (c) shows the probabilities of obtaining improved individuals from tour-A using *E-sets* constructed by the three types of EAXs.

4 Experiments

4.1 Experimental Setting

We compared EAX-1AB, EAX-Rand, and EAX-Block on several TSP benchmarks. Experiment setting is the same as the Nagata's works [11] where the edge entropy measure was used to maintain population diversity, and the fast implementation of EAX was used. This experiments are implemented in C++ and executed using Itanium 2 1.3-GHz single processor with 126 GB of RAM.

Stage I: EAX-1AB was applied to TSP benchmarks using selection model I [11], where the population size (N_p) was set to 300, and an initial population was generated by the 2-opt local search. The number of children generated from a pair of parents (N_{ch}) was set to 30. If the shortest tour length in the population stagnated over 150 generations, then the run was terminated. Ten trials were executed for each instance. The resulting population is denoted as POP_i $(i = 1, \ldots, 10)$ for each run.

Stage II: For $(i = 1, \ldots, 10)$, EAX-Rand or EAX-Block was applied to TSP benchmarks using POP_i as the initial population. Selection model I was used. Although N_p was necessarily 300, N_{ch} was set to 100 in this case to enhance the searches. The termination conditions were the stagnation of 100 generations for EAX-Rand or 50 for EAX-Block.

4.2 Results

In these experiments, eight large instances were chosen from TSPLIB [9] and twelve large instances from the national TSPs [13]. The results of EAX-1AB, EAX-Rand, and EAX-Block are listed in Table 1. As shown, EAX-Rand improved the qualities of the solutions obtained by EAX-1AB with a few exceptions. Although EAX-Rand can usually find optimal (best known) solutions for the instances with up to 10,000 cities, it fails larger instances. In contrast, EAX-Block can find optimal (best known) solutions for instances of up to 24978 cities. Moreover, the CPU times needed to terminate runs of EAX-Block were about 10 times faster than those of EAX-Rand.The reasons are that (i) EAX-Block can improve populations more rapidly than EAX-Rand and that (ii) EAX-Block can generate individuals faster than EAX-Rand.

In this experiment, EAX-Block found three new best solutions to the national TSPs benchmarks. This is the first improvement in several years. The new best tours (tour lengths) are pa8079 (114855), ho14473 (177092), and bm33708 (959291).

We compare EAX-Block with other state-of-the-art TSP heuristic algorithms. Our proposed approach is categorized as approximation methods for TSPs that consume relatively large time but aim at finding very near-optimal solution. So, we chose HeSEA [7] and tour-merging technique [12] that are categorized as the same class. HeSEA is a hybrid algorithm composed of EAX and CLK [4]. Tour-merging method look for a best tour on a restricted graph consisting of the union of set of tours obtained by LKH[5].

Table 1. Comparisons of performances of EAs using three types of EAX. "Opt." column indicates number of trials that reached optimal solutions in ten trials. "Err." indicates average length by which best tour exceeded optimal tour in each trial. "Gen." indicates average generation required to reach best individual in each trial. "Time" means average CPU time in seconds required for one trial. For unsolved instances, a number of trials that reach best tour known today is listed in "Opt.", and "–" is filled in "Err.". If new best tour is found, "Improve (number of these trials)" is filled in "Opt.".

	EAX-1AB (Stage I)				EAX-Block (Stage II)				EAX-Rand (Stage II)			
Instances	Opt.	Err. (%)	Gen.	Time (sec)	Opt.	Err. (%)	Gen.	Time (sec)	Opt.	Err. (%)	Gen.	Time (sec)
fnl4461	0	0.0014	848	1512	10	0.0000	3	42	10	0.0000	30	185
rl5915	10	0.0000	319	992	10	0.0000	0	36	10	0.0000	0	125
rl11849	0	0.0041	1252	7646	10	0.0000	15	298	9	0.0000	61	2533
usa13509	0	0.0126	2486	13249	6	0.0001	43	496	0	0.0019	173	7164
brd14051	0	0.0129	2729	15550	10	0.0000	31	712	0	0.0033	216	10193
d15112	0	0.0181	3076	21244	4	0.0001	107	1662	0	0.0081	165	40060
d18512	0	0.0186	3496	25392	8	0.0000	77	1526	0	0.0047	253	14037
pla33810	0	0.0182	5014	38424	0	0.0076	79	1892	0	0.0124	456	18930
pm8079	Improve (5)		800	1596	Improve (9)		1	128	Improve (9)		6	830
ei8246	0	--	1476	4556	9	--	1	439	5	--	53	4511
ar9152	0	--	1226	7038	9	--	2	135	9	--	10	217
ja9847	0	0.0057	1664	4705	3	0.0017	6	275	3	0.0028	31	1574
kz9976	0	--	1700	5967	9	--	21	532	1	--	119	5685
fi10639	0	--	1891	6955	5	--	34	808	0	--	169	9276
mo14185	0	--	2379	10481	9	--	44	1089	0	--	0	10756
ho14473	0	--	1218	3365	Improve (10)		57	359	Improve (7)		67	5445
it16862	0	0.0173	3094	14778	2	0.0007	109	892	0	0.0173	0	19778
vm22775	0	0.0089	3814	21346	1	0.0007	45	3457	0	0.0089	0	20686
sw24978	0	0.0209	4522	36946	3	0.0010	129	2500	0	0.0209	0	26542
bm33708	0	--	6339	56305	Improve (1)		168	5094	0	--	0	36087

Table 2 show the results. As compared with the results of HeSEA and Tour-merging, EAX-Block could find optimal solutions in some large instances with smaller CPU times even where other method could not find them.

5 Conclusion

We improved the edge assembly crossover (EAX) to apply EAs using EAX to large TSP instances having more than 10,000 cities. Our results demonstrated that EAX-Block is suitable for large TSP instances.

We observed that the following two conditions are needed to improve highly refined near-optimal solutions using EAX for large instances. (C-I) The *E-set* should be large enough to overcome deep local optima. (C-II) The number of sub-tours in an intermediate solution should be as small as possible. We proposed EAX-Block to satisfy these conditions. The key idea of EAX-Block is assembling blocks of tour-A edges and blocks of tour-B edges to generate intermediate solutions. We demonstrated that EAX-Block is better than EAX-1AB and EAX-Rand in terms of the above conditions.

The experimental results show that the EA with EAX-Block can find optimal solutions for large instances of up to 24978 cities in a reasonable CPU time. Moreover, three new best tours were found for unsolved national TSP instances.

Table 2. Performances of other state-of-the-art TSP heuristics. These Data are copied from the original papers (Data are not available in Blank cells). HeSEA and Tour-merging were executed twenty and one trials for each instance, respectively. CPU time of HeSEA and Tour-merging are based on Pentium IV 1.2-GHz and EV6 Compaq Alpha 500-MHz processors, respectively.

	HeSEA			Tour-merging		
Instances	Opt.	Err. (%)	Time (sec)	Opt.	Err. (%)	Time (sec)
fnl4461	16/20	0.0005	2,349			
rl5915	19/20	0.0001	2,773	1/1	0.0000	63,954
r11849				1/1	0.0000	646,483
usa13509	0/20	0.0074	34,948	0/1	0.0001	968,473
brd14051				0/1	0.0030	1,676,314
d15112				1/1	0.0000	1976,174
d18512				0/1	0.0071	3,704,852
pla33810				0/0	0.0998	43,632,379

References

1. D. S. Johnson: Local Optimization and the Traveling Salesman Problem, Automata, Languages and Programming, Lecture note in Computer Science 442, pringer, Heidelberg, pp. 446–461.
2. 8-th DIMACS Implementation Challenge: The Traveling Salesman Problem, http://www.research.att.com/ dsj/chtsp.
3. S. Lin and B. Kernighan, Effective heuristic algorithms for the traveling salesman problem, Oper. Res., vol. 21, pp. 498–516, 1973.
4. D. Applegate, R. Bixby, V. Chvatal, and W. Cook, "Finding tours in the TSP. Technical Report 99885, Forschungsinstitut fur Diskrete Mathematik, Universitat Bonn, 1999.
5. K. Helsgaun, "An effective implementation of the Lin-Kernighan traveling salesman heuristic, "Eur. J. Oper. Res., vol. 126, no.1, pp. 106–130, 2000.
6. Y. Nagata and S. Kobayashi, Edge Assembly Crossover: A High-power Genetic Algorithm for the Traveling Salesman Problem, Proc. of the 7th Int. Conference on Genetic Algorithms, pp. 450-457, 1997.
7. H. K. Tsai, J. M. Yang, Y. F. Tsai, and C. Y. Kao, An Evolutionary Algorithm for Large Traveling Salesman Problem, IEEE Transaction on SMC-part B, vol. 34, no. 4, pp. 1718- 1729, 2004.
8. K. Maekawa, N. Mori, H. Kita, and H.Nishikawa, A Genetic Solution for the Traveling Salesman Problem by Means of a Thermodynamical Selection Rule, Proc. 1996 IEEE Int. Conference on Evolutionary Computation, pp. 529-534, 1996.
9. TSPLIB95, http://www.iwr.uni-heidelberg.de/iwr/compt/soft/TSPLIB95
10. Y. Nagata, The EAX algorithm considering diversity loss, Proc. of the 8th Int. Conference on Parallel Problem Solving from Nature, pp. 332–341, 2004.
11. Y. Nagata, Fast EAX algorithm Considering Population Diversity for Traveling Salesman Problems, Proc. of the 6th Int. Conference on EvoCOP2006, pp. 171–182, 2006.
12. W. Cook and P. Seymour, Tour Merging via Branch-Decomposition, INFORMS Journal on Computing, vol. 15, no. 3, pp. 233–248, 2003.
13. National Traveling Salesman Problems.http://www.tsp.gatech.edu/world/countries.html.

Functional Brain Imaging with Multi-objective Multi-modal Evolutionary Optimization

Vojtech Krmicek[1,2] and Michèle Sebag[2]

[1] Department of Computer Science
Masaryk University, CZ-602 00 Brno
[2] IA-TAO, CNRS – INRIA – LRI
Université Paris Sud, FR-91405 Orsay
{krmicek, sebag}@lri.fr

Abstract. Functional brain imaging is a source of spatio-temporal data mining problems. A new framework hybridizing multi-objective and multi-modal optimization is proposed to formalize these data mining problems, and addressed through Evolutionary Computation (EC).

The merits of EC for spatio-temporal data mining are demonstrated as the approach facilitates the modelling of the experts' requirements, and flexibly accommodates their changing goals.

1 Introduction

Functional brain imaging aims at understanding the mechanisms of cognitive processes through non-invasive technologies such as magnetoencephalography (MEG). These technologies measure the surface activity of the brain with a good spatial and temporal resolution [8,15], generating massive amounts of data.

Finding "interesting" patterns in these data, e.g. assemblies of active neuronal cells, can be viewed as a Machine Learning or a Data Mining problem. However, contrasting with ML or DM applications [6], the appropriate search criteria are not formally defined up to now; in practice the detection of active cell assemblies is manually done.

Resuming an earlier work [17], this paper formalizes functional brain imaging as a multi-objective multi-modal optimization (MoMOO) problem, and describes the evolutionary algorithm called *4D-Miner* devised to tackle this problem. In this paper, the approach is extended to the search of discriminant patterns; additional criteria are devised and accommodated in order to find patterns specifically related to particular cognitive activities.

The paper is organized as follows. Section 2 introduces the background and notations; it describes the targeted spatio-temporal patterns (STP) and formalizes the MoMOO framework proposed. Section 3 describes the *4D-Miner* algorithm designed for finding STPs, hybridizing multi-objective [5] and multi-modal [12] heuristics, and it reports on its experimental validation. Section 4 presents the extension of *4D-Miner* to a new goal, the search for discriminant STPs. Section 5 discusses the opportunities offered by Evolutionary Data Mining, and the paper concludes with perspectives for further research.

T.P. Runarsson et al. (Eds.): PPSN IX, LNCS 4193, pp. 382–391, 2006.

2 Background and Notations

This section introduces the notations and criteria for Data Mining in functional brain imaging, assuming the reader's familiarity with multi-objective optimization [5]. Let N be the number of sensors and let T denote the number of time steps. The i-th sensor is characterized by its position M_i on the skull ($M_i = (x_i, y_i, z_i) \in \mathbb{R}^3$) and its activity $C_i(t), 1 \leq t \leq T$ along the experiment. Fig. 1 depicts a set of activity curves.

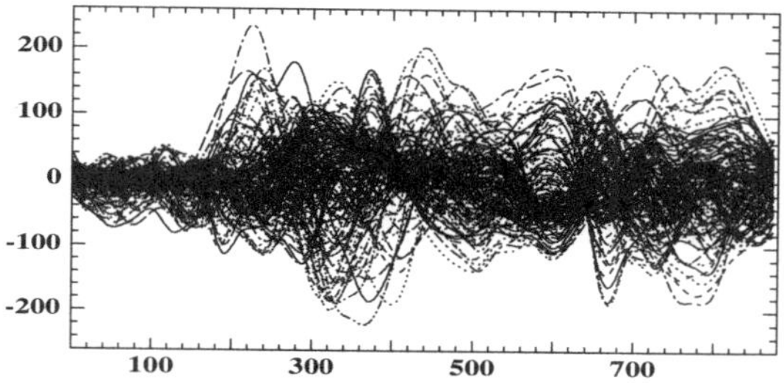

Fig. 1. Magneto-Encephalography Data (N = 151, T = 875)

A spatio-temporal pattern noted $X = (I, i, w, r)$ is characterized from its temporal interval I ($I = [t_1, t_2] \subset [1, T]$) and a spatial region $\mathcal{B}(i, w, r)$. For the sake of convenience, spatial regions are restricted to axis-parallel ellipsoids centered on some sensor; region $\mathcal{B}(i, w, r)$ is the ellipsoid centered on the i-th sensor, which includes all sensors j such that $d_w(M_i, M_j)$ is less than radius $r > 0$, with

$$d_w(M_i, M_j)^2 = w_1(x_i - x_j)^2 + w_2(y_i - y_j)^2 + w_3(z_i - z_j)^2 \qquad w_1, w_2, w_3 > 0$$

This paper focuses on the detection of assemblies of active neuronal cells, informally viewed as large spatio-temporal regions with correlated sensor activities. Formally, let $I = [t_1, t_2]$ be a time interval, and let $\bar{C}_i^I$ denote the average activity of the i-th sensor over I. The I-alignment $\sigma_I(i, j)$ of sensors i and j over I is defined as:

$$\sigma_I(i,j) = \frac{\sum_{t=t_1}^{t_2} C_i(t).C_j(t)}{\sqrt{\sum_{t=t_1}^{t_2} C_i(t)^2} \times \sqrt{\sum_{t=t_1}^{t_2} C_j(t)^2}} \times \left(1 - \frac{|\bar{C}_i^I - \bar{C}_j^I|}{|\bar{C}_i^I|}\right),$$

To every spatio-temporal pattern $X = (I, i, w, r)$, are thus associated i) its duration or length $\ell(X)$ $(= t_2 - t_1)$; ii) its area $a(X)$ (the number of sensors in $\mathcal{B}(i, w, r)$); and iii) its alignment $\sigma(X)$, defined as the average of $\sigma_I(i, j)$ for j ranging in $\mathcal{B}(i, w, r)$. An *interesting* candidate pattern is one with large length, area and alignment.

Naturally, the sensor alignment tends to decrease as a longer time interval or a larger spatial region are considered, everything else being equal; conversely, the alignment increases when the duration or the area decrease. It thus comes to characterize the STP detection problem as a multi-objective optimization problem (MOO) [5], searching for large spatio-temporal regions X with correlated sensor activities, i.e. patterns X simultaneously maximizing criteria $\ell(X)$, $a(X)$ and $\sigma(X)$. The best compromises among these criteria, referred to as Pareto front, are the solutions of the problem.

Definition 1 (Pareto-domination).
Let $c_1, \ldots, c_K$ denote K criteria to be simultaneously maximized on Ω. X is said to Pareto-dominate X' if X improves on X' with respect to all criteria, and the improvement is strict for at least one criterion. The Pareto front includes all solutions which are not Pareto-dominated.

However, the MOO setting fails to capture the true target patterns: The Pareto front defined from the above three criteria could be characterized and it does include a number of patterns; but all of these actually represent the same spatio-temporal region up to some slight variations of the time interval and the spatial region. This was found unsatisfactory as neuroscientists are actually interested in *all* active areas of the brain; X might be worth even though its alignment, duration and area are lower than that of X', provided that X and X' are situated in different regions of the brain.

The above remark leads to extend multi-objective optimization goal in the spirit of multi-modal optimization [12]. Formally, a new optimization framework is defined, referred to as *multi-modal multi-objective optimization* (MoMOO). MoMOO uses a relaxed inclusion relationship, noted p-inclusion, to relax the Pareto domination relation.

Definition 2 (p-inclusion).
Let A and B be two subsets of a measurable set Ω, and let p be a positive real number ($p \in [0, 1]$). A is p-included in B iff $|A \bigcap B| > p \times |A|$, where $|A|$ denotes the measure of set A.

Definition 3 (multi-modal Pareto domination).
Let X and Y denote two spatio-temporal patterns with respective supports $Sup(X)$ and $Sup(Y)$ ($Sup(X), Sup(Y) \subset \mathbb{R}^d$). X p-mo-Pareto dominates Y iff the support of Y is p-included in that of X, and X Pareto-dominates Y.

Finally, the interesting STPs are all spatio-temporal patterns which are not p-mo-Pareto dominated.

It must be emphasized that MoMOO differs from MOO with diversity enforcing heuristics (see e.g., [3,11]): diversity-based heuristics in MOO aim at a better sampling of the Pareto front defined from fixed objectives; MoMOO is interested in a new Pareto front, including diversity as a new objective.

3 4D-Miner

This section describes the *4D-Miner* algorithm designed for the detection of stable spatio-temporal patterns, and reports on its experimental validation.

3.1 Overview of 4D-Miner

Following [4], special care is devoted to the initialization step. In order to both favor the generation of relevant STPs and exclude the extremities of the Pareto front (patterns with insufficient alignment, or insignificant spatial or temporal amplitudes), every initial pattern $X = (i, w, I, r)$ is generated after a constrained sampling mechanism:

- Center i is uniformly drawn in $[1, N]$;
- Vector w is set to $(1, 1, 1)$ (d_w is initialized to the Euclidean distance);
- Interval $I = [t_1, t_2]$ is such that t_1 is drawn with uniform distribution in $[1, T]$; the length $t_2 - t_1$ of I_j is drawn according to a Gaussian distribution $\mathcal{N}(min_\ell, min_\ell/10)$, where min_ℓ is a user-supplied length parameter.
- Radius r is deterministically computed from a user-supplied threshold min_σ, corresponding to the minimal I-alignment desired.

$$r = min_k\{d_w(i,k)\ s.t.\ \sigma_I(i,k) > min_\sigma)\}$$

- Last, the spatial amplitude $a(X)$ of individual X is required to be more than a user-supplied threshold min_a; otherwise, the individual is non admissible and it does not undergo mutation or crossover.

The user-supplied min_ℓ, min_σ and min_a thus govern the proportion of admissible individuals in the initial population. The computational complexity of the initialization phase is $\mathcal{O}(P \times N \times min_\ell)$, where P is the population size, N is the number of measure points and min_ℓ is the average length of the intervals.

The variation operators go as follows. From parent $X = (i, w, I, r)$, mutation generates an offspring by one among the following operators: i) replacing center i with another sensor in $\mathcal{B}(i, w, r)$; ii) mutating w and r using self-adaptive Gaussian mutation; iii) incrementing or decrementing the bounds of interval I; iv) generating a brand new individual (using the initialization operator).

The crossover operator is subjected to restricted mating (only sufficiently close patterns are allowed to mate); it proceeds by i) swapping the centers or ii) the ellipsoid coordinates of the two individuals, or iii) merging the time intervals.

A steady state evolutionary scheme is considered. In each step, a single admissible parent individual is selected and it generates an offspring via mutation or crossover; the parent is selected using a Pareto archive-based selection [5], where the size of the Pareto archive is 10 times the population size. The offspring either replaces a non-admissible individual, or an individual selected after inverse Pareto archive-based selection.

3.2 Experimental Results

This subsection reports on the experiments done using *4D-Miner* on real-world datasets[1], collected from subjects observing a moving ball. Each dataset involves

[1] Due to space limitations, the reader is referred to [17] for an extensive validation of *4D-Miner*. The retrieval performances and scalability were assessed on artificial datasets, varying the number T of time steps and the number N of sensors up to 8,000 and 4,000 respectively; the corresponding computational runtime (over a 456Mo dataset) is 5 minutes on PC-Pentium IV.

151 measure points and the number of time steps (milliseconds) is 875. As can be noted from Fig. 1, the range of activities widely varies along time. The runtime on the available data is less than 20 seconds on PC Pentium 2.4 GHz.

The parameters used in the experiments are as follows. The population size is $P = 200$; the stop criterion is based on the number of fitness evaluations per run, limited to 40,000. A few preliminary runs were used to adjust the operator rates; the mutation and crossover rates are respectively set to .7 and .3. For computational efficiency, the p-inclusion is computed as: X is p-included in Y if the center i of X belongs to the spatial support of Y, and there is an overlap between their time intervals. *4D-Miner* is written in C^{++}.

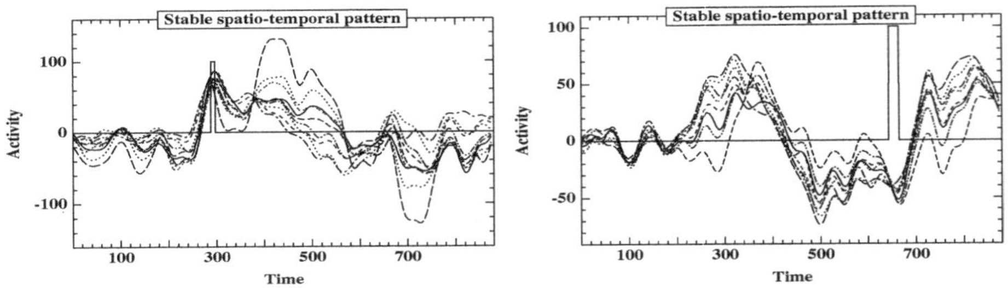

(a): $\ell(X) = 8,\ a(X) = 8,\ \sigma(X) = .29$ (b): $\ell(X) = 20,\ a(X) = 9,\ \sigma(X) = .396$

Fig. 2. Two stable spatio-temporal patterns ($N = 151,\ T = 875$)

Typical STPs found in the real datasets are shown in Fig. 2.(a) and (b), displaying all activity curves belonging to the STP plus the time-window of the pattern. Both patterns are considered relevant by the expert; note that the STP on the right is Pareto dominated by the one of the left.

All experiments confirm the importance of the user-defined thresholds (min_ℓ, min_a, min_σ), defining the minimum requirements on solution individuals. Raising the thresholds beyond certain values leads to poor final results as the optimization problem becomes over constrained; lowering the thresholds leads to a crowded Pareto archive, increasing the computational time and adversely affecting the quality of the final solutions. Indeed, the coarse tuning of the parameters can be achieved based on the desired proportion of admissible individuals in the initial population. However, the fine-tuning of the parameters could not be automatized up to now, and it still requires running *4D-Miner* a few times. For this reason, the control of the computational cost (through the population size and number of generations) is of utmost importance.

4 Extension to Discriminant STPs

After some active brain areas have been identified, the next task in the functional brain imaging agenda is to relate these areas to specific cognitive processes, using contrasted experimental settings. In this section, the *catch* versus *no-catch* experiment is considered; the subject sees a ball, which s/he must respectively catch (*catch* setting) or let go (*no-catch* setting). Cell assemblies that are found active in the *catch* setting and inactive in the *no-catch* one, are conjectured to relate to motor skills.

More generally, the mining task becomes to find STPs that behave differently in a pair of (positive, negative) settings, referred to as discriminant STPs. The notations are modified as follows. To the i-th sensor are attached its activities in the positive and negative settings, respectively noted $C_i^+(t)$ and $C_i^-(t)$; its positions are similarly noted M_i^+ and M_i^-.

The fact that the sensor position differs depending on the setting entails that the genotype of the sought patterns must be redesigned. An alternative would have been to specify the 3D coordinates of a pattern instead of centering the pattern on a sensor position. However, the spatial region of a pattern actually corresponds to a set of sensors; in other words it is a discrete entity. The use of a 3D (continuous) spatial genotype would thus require to redesign the spatial mutation operator, in order to ensure effective mutations. However, calibrating the continuous mutation operator and finding the right trade-off between ineffective and disruptive modifications of the pattern position proved to be trickier than extending the genotype.

Formally, the STP genotype noted $X(i, j, I, w, r)$ now refers to a pair of sensors i, j, which are closest to each other across both settings[2]. The STP is assessed from:

- its spatial amplitude $a^+(X)$ (resp. $a^-(X)$) defined as the size of $\mathcal{B}^+(i, w, r)$, including all sensors k such that $d_w(M_i^+, M_k^+) < r$ (resp. $\mathcal{B}^-(j, w, r)$, including all sensors k such that $d_w(M_j^-, M_k^-) < r$)).
- its spatio-temporal alignment $\sigma^+(X)$ (respectively $\sigma^-(X)$), defined as the activity alignment of the sensors in $\mathcal{B}^+(i, w, r)$ (resp. in $\mathcal{B}^-(j, w, r)$), over time interval I.

The next step regards the formalization of the goal. Although neuroscientists have a clear idea of what a discriminant STP should look like, turning this idea into a set of operational requirements is by no way easy. Several formalizations were thus considered, modelling the search criteria in terms of new objectives (e.g. maximizing the difference between σ^+ and σ^-) or in terms of constraints ($|\sigma^+(X) - \sigma^-(X)| > min_{d\sigma}$). The extension of the *4D-Miner* system to accommodate the new objectives and constraints was straightforward.

The visual inspection of the results found along the various modellings led the neuroscientists to introduce a new feature noted $d(X)$, the difference of the average activity in $\mathcal{B}^+(i, w, r)$ and $\mathcal{B}^-(j, w, r)$ over the time interval I. Finally, the search goal was modelled as an additional constraint on the STPs, expressed as $|d(X)| > min_d$ where min_d is a user-supplied threshold.

Also, it was deemed neurophysiologically unlikely that a functional difference could occur in the early brain signals; only differences occurring after the motor program was completed by the subject, i.e. 200ms after the beginning of the

[2] With $j = arg\,min\{d_w(M_i^+, M_k^-), k = 1..N\}$; $i = arg\,min\{d_w(M_k^+, M_j^-), k = 1..N\}$.

experiment, are considered to be relevant. This requirement was expressed in a straightforward way, through a new constraint on admissible STPs, and directly at the initialization level (e.g., drawing t_1 uniformly in $[200, T]$, section 3.1).

Figs. 3.(a) and 3.(b) show two discriminant patterns, that were found to be satisfactory by the neuroscientists. Indeed, this assessment of the results pertains to the field of data mining more than discriminant learning. It is worth mentioning that the little amount of data available in this study, plus the known variability of brain activity in the general case (between different persons and for a same person at different moments, see e.g. [10]), does not permit to assess discriminant patterns (e.g. by splitting the data into training and test datasets, and evaluating the patterns extracted from the training set onto the test set).

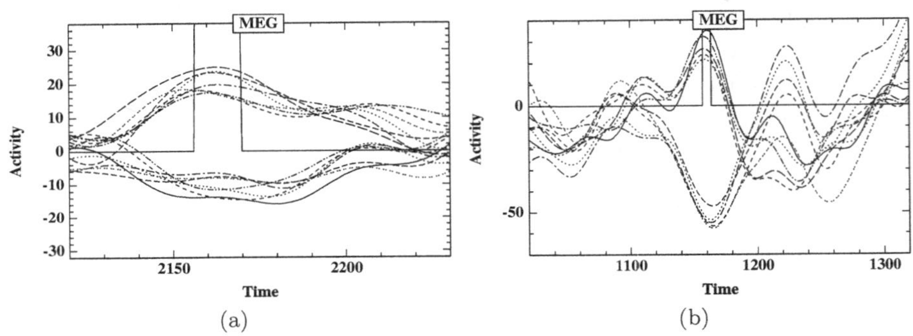

Fig. 3. Two discriminant stable spatio-temporal patterns. Sensors display a positive (resp. negative) activity in the catch (resp. nocatch) case. ($N = 151$, $T = 2500$)

Overall, the extension of *4D-Miner* to the search of discriminant STPs required i) a small modification of the genotype and ii) the modelling of two additional constraints. An additional parameter was introduced, the minimum difference min_d on the activity level, which was tuned by a few preliminary runs. Same parameters as in section 3.2 were used; the computational cost is less than 25 seconds on PC-Pentium.

5 State of the Art and Discussion

The presented approach is concerned with finding specific patterns in databases describing spatial objects along time.

Many approaches have been developed in signal processing and computer science to address such a goal, ranging from Fourier Transforms to Independent Component Analysis [7] and mixtures of models [2]. These approaches aim at particular pattern properties (e.g. independence, generativity) and/or focus on particular data characteristics (e.g. periodicity).

Functional brain imaging however does not fall within the range of such wide spectrum methods, for two reasons. Firstly, the sought spatio-temporal patterns are not periodic, and not independent. Secondly, and most importantly, it appears useless to build a general model of the spatio-temporal activity, while the "interesting" activity actually corresponds to a minuscule fragment of the total activity – the proverbial needle in the haystack.

In the field of spatio-temporal data mining (see [18,16] for comprehensive surveys), typical applications such as remote sensing, environmental studies, or medical imaging, involve complete algorithms, achieving an exhaustive search or building a global model. The stress is put on the scalability of the approach.

Spatio-temporal machine learning mostly focuses on clustering, outlier detection, denoising, and trend analysis. For instance, [2] used EM algorithms for non-parametric characterization of functional data (e.g. cyclone trajectories), with special care regarding the invariance of the models with respect to temporal translations. The main limitation of such non-parametric models, including Markov Random Fields, is their computational complexity; therefore the use of randomized algorithms is attracting an increasing for sidestepped by using randomized search for model estimates.

Many developments are targeted at efficient access primitives and/or complex data structures (see, e.g., [19]); another line of research is based on visual and interactive data mining (see, e.g., [9]), exploiting the unrivaled capacities of human eyes for spotting regularities in 2D-data.

More generally, the presented approach can be discussed with respect to the *generative* versus *discriminative* dilemma in Machine Learning. Although the learning goal is most often one of discrimination, generative models often outperform discriminative approaches, particularly when considering low-level information, e.g. signals, images or videos (see e.g. [14]). The higher efficiency of generative models is frequently explained as they enable the modelling and exploitation of domain knowledge in a powerful and convenient way, ultimately reducing the search space by several orders of magnitude.

In summary, generative ML extracts faithful models of the phenomenon at hand, taking advantage of whatever prior knowledge is available; these models can be used for discriminative purposes, though discrimination is not among the primary goals of generative ML. In opposition, discriminative ML focuses on the most discriminant hypotheses in the whole search space; it does not consider the relevance of a hypothesis with respect to the background knowledge *per se*.

To some extent, the presented approach combines generative and discriminative ML. *4D-Miner* was primarily devised with the extraction of interesting patterns in mind. The core task was to model the prior knowledge through relevance criteria, combining optimization objectives (describing the expert's preferences) and constraints (describing what is *not* interesting). The extraction of discriminant patterns from the relevant ones was relatively straightforward, based on the use of additional objectives and constraints. This suggests that extracting discriminant patterns from relevant ones is much easier than searching discriminant patterns, and thereafter sorting them out to find the relevant ones.

6 Conclusion and Perspectives

This paper has proposed a stochastic approach for mining stable spatio-temporal patterns. Indeed, a very simple alternative would be to discretize the spatio-temporal domain and compute the correlation of the signals in each cell of the discretization grid. However, it is believed that the proposed approach presents several advantages compared to the brute force, discretization-based, alternative.

Firstly, *4D-Miner* is a fast and frugal algorithm; its good performances and scalability have been successfully demonstrated on real-world problems and on large-sized artificial datasets [17]. Secondly, data mining applications specifically involve two key steps, exemplified in this paper: i) understanding the expert's goals and requirements; ii) tuning the parameters involved in the specifications. With regard to both steps, the ability of Evolutionary Computation to work under bounded resources is a very significant advantage. Evolutionary algorithms intrinsically are any-time algorithms, allowing the user to check at a low cost whether the process can deliver useful results, and more generally enabling her to control the trade-off between the computational resources needed and the quality of the results.

A main perspective for further research is to equip *4D-Miner* with learning abilities, facilitating the automatic acquisition of the constraints and modelling the expert's expectations. A first step would be to automatically adjust the thresholds involved in the constraints, based on the expert's feedback. Ultimately, the goal is to design a truly user-centered mining system, combining advanced interactive optimization [13], online learning [1] and visual data mining [9].

Acknowledgments. We heartily thank Sylvain Baillet, Cognitive Neurosciences and Brain Imaging Lab., La Piti Salptrire and CNRS, who provided the data and the interpretation of the results. The authors gratefully acknowledge the support of the Pascal Network of Excellence (IST 2002506778).

References

1. N. Cesa-Bianchi, A. Conconi, and C. Gentile. On the generalization ability of on-line learning algorithms. *IEEE Transactions on Information Theory*, 50(9):2050–2057, 2004.
2. D. Chudova, S. Gaffney, E. Mjolsness, and P. Smyth. Translation-invariant mixture models for curve clustering. In *Proc. of the Ninth Int. Conf. on Knowledge Discovery and Data Mining*, pages 79–88. ACM, 2003.
3. D. Corne, J. D. Knowles, and M. J. Oates. The Pareto envelope-based selection algorithm for multi-objective optimisation. In *Proc. of PPSN - VI*, LNCS, pages 839–848. Springer Verlag, 2000.
4. J. Daida. Challenges with verification, repeatability, and meaningful comparison in genetic programming: Gibson's magic. In *Proc. of GECCO 99*, pages 1069–1076. Morgan Kaufmann, 1999.
5. K. Deb. *Multi-Objective Optimization Using Evolutionary Algorithms.* John Wiley, 2001.

6. T. Hastie, R. Tibshirani, and J. H. Friedman. *The Elements of Statistical Learning: Data Mining, Inference, and Prediction.* Springer Series in Statistics, 2001.
7. A. Hyvarinen, J. Karhunen, and E. Oja. *Independent Component Analysis.* Wiley New York, 2001.
8. M. Hmlinen, R. Hari, R. Ilmoniemi, J. Knuutila, and O. V. Lounasmaa. Magnetoencephalography: theory, instrumentation, and applications to noninvasive studies of the working human brain. *Rev. Mod. Phys*, 65:413–497, 1993.
9. D. A. Keim, J. Schneidewind, and M. Sips. Circleview: a new approach for visualizing time-related multidimensional data sets. In *Proc. of Advanced Visual Interfaces*, pages 179–182. ACM Press, 2004.
10. T. Lal. *Machine Learning Methods for Brain-Computer Interfaces.* PhD thesis, Max Plank Institute for Biological Cybernetics, 2005.
11. M. Laumanns, L. Thiele, K. Deb, and E. Zitsler. Combining convergence and diversity in evolutionary multi-objective optimization. *Evolutionary Computation*, 10(3):263–282, 2002.
12. J.-P. Li, M. E. Balazs, G. T. Parks, and P. J. Clarkson. A species conserving genetic algorithm for multimodal function optimization. *Evolutionary Computation*, 10(3):207–234, 2002.
13. X. Llorà, K. Sastry, D. E. Goldberg, A. Gupta, and L. Lakshmi. Combating user fatigue in IGAs: partial ordering, support vector machines, and synthetic fitness. In *Proc. of GECCO 05*, pages 1363–1370. ACM, 2005.
14. I. McCowan, D. Gatica-Perez, S. Bengio, G. Lathoud, M. Barnard, and D. Zhang. Automatic analysis of multimodal group actions in meetings. *IEEE Trans. on Pattern Analysis and Machine Intelligence (PAMI)*, 27(3):305–317, 2005.
15. D. Pantazis, T. E. Nichols, S. Baillet, and R. Leahy. A comparison of random field theory and permutation methods for the statistical analysis of MEG data. *Neuroimage*, 25:355–368, 2005.
16. J. Roddick and M. Spiliopoulou. A survey of temporal knowledge discovery paradigms and methods. *IEEE Trans. on Knowledge and Data Engineering*, 14(4):750–767, 2002.
17. M. Sebag, N. Tarrisson, O. Teytaud, S. Baillet, and J. Lefevre. A multi-objective multi-modal optimization approach for mining stable spatio-temporal patterns. In *Proc. of Int. Joint Conf. on AI, IJCAI'05*, pages 859–864, 2005.
18. S. Shekhar, P. Zhang, Y. Huang, and R. R. Vatsavai. Spatial data mining. In H. Kargupta and A. Joshi, editors, *Data Mining: Next Generation Challenges and Future Directions.* AAAI/MIT Press, 2003.
19. K. Wu, S. Chen, and P. Yu. Interval query indexing for efficient stream processing. In *ACM Conf. on Information and Knowledge Management*, pages 88–97. ACM Press, 2004.

A New Neural Network Based Construction Heuristic for the Examination Timetabling Problem

P.H. Corr, B. McCollum, M.A.J. McGreevy, and P. McMullan

Queens University of Belfast, Northern Ireland
p.corr@qub.ac.uk

Abstract. This paper examines the application of neural networks as a construction heuristic for the examination timetabling problem. Building on the heuristic ordering technique, where events are ordered by decreasing scheduling difficulty, the neural network allows a novel dynamic, multi-criteria approach to be developed. The difficulty of each event to be scheduled is assessed on several characteristics, removing the dependence of an ordering based on a single heuristic. Furthermore, this technique allows the ordering to be reviewed and modified as each event is scheduled; a necessary step since the timetable and constraints are altered as events are placed. Our approach uses a Kohonen self organising neural network and is shown to have wide applicability. Results are presented for a range of examination timetabling problems using standard benchmark datasets.

1 Introduction

The examination timetabling problem is principally concerned with the scheduling of a number of events into a restricted number of time-periods, subject to a set of constraints [1]. Conflicting events which have students in common must not be scheduled into the same time-period. This essential condition is a *hard constraint*. Another such hard constraint is that seating capacity must not be exceeded in any time-period (the so called capacitated problem). A timetable satisfying all hard constraints with all events scheduled is a *feasible* solution. While there may be many feasible solutions to a given problem, the timetabler's task is to find a good quality solution, satisfying as many desirable conditions as possible. These desirable conditions, or *soft constraints*, often vary between data sets but typically involve placing events such that each student has a reasonable gap between any two exams. These conditions are rarely, if ever, completely satisfied, and often vary extensively between data sets. The degree to which the soft constraints are met - and hence the quality of the timetable - is measured by a cost function or penalty function. Therefore, the principal objective of the timetabler is to construct a timetable with an acceptably low, ideally optimum, penalty function.

Over the years various researchers have considered several methods of timetable construction. A detailed discussion of these techniques is given by Carter et al [2] and an excellent overview of recent research directions. [3].

T.P. Runarsson et al. (Eds.): PPSN IX, LNCS 4193, pp. 392 – 401, 2006.

Early approaches include techniques such as Graph Colouring and Constraint Programming (see, for example [1,2,3]). Subsequently, metaheuristic approaches have been used to help improve the solution. Simulated annealing [4], tabu search [5], evolutionary approaches [8,9] and other techniques such as great deluge [6] have all proved useful. In general metaheuristic approaches have performed well on benchmark problems though they are time consuming compared with graph colouring based approaches. Hybrid approaches involving combinations of heuristics and metaheuristics such as genetic algorithms and hill climbing techniques [7, 10, 11] have produced good results on benchmark datasets. Other successful methods taken include multi-criteria approaches [12], constraint based techniques [13], case based reasoning [14], and recently hyper-heuristics [15]. Recent papers note that, on the whole, methods used to tackle the examination problem tend to use problem specific information and heuristics.

Construction of a timetable is often accomplished in two phases. An initial timetable is built using a *construction heuristic*; this initial timetable is then enhanced using an *improvement heuristic* [2]. Heuristic ordering is one approach to the construction phase. Events are ordered in decreasing order of perceived scheduling difficulty and then placed sequentially into available positions in the timetable within the conditions imposed by the hard constraints. If necessary, events are left unscheduled at this initial stage rather than violating the constraints with a high penalty being attributed to the incomplete timetable. Heuristic ordering may take either a static or a dynamic approach to construction. In the static approach a complete ordering is established at the start of the construction phase prior to scheduling and remains constant throughout the process. Events may be ordered using a single heuristic such as; largest degree, weighted degree, or exam size, all of which contribute to scheduling difficulty. In the dynamic approach, the order in which events are placed may change as the timetable is built. For example, if events are scheduled by the number of available slots remaining in the timetable (saturated degree) the placement order will change as events are placed in the timetable.

In recent years, improvement heuristics have received much more attention from researchers than the construction phase. As outlined above, a wide range of different techniques have been applied, such as simulated annealing, tabu-search, genetic algorithms, great deluge algorithm, and hybridised methods. The research reported here focuses on the construction phase and seeks to improve the quality of the initial timetable produced prior to the application of an improvement heuristic.

The well-established heuristic ordering approach has proved very effective and offers a firm foundation for further development. However, a feature of the approach is that the order in which events are scheduled is typically determined based on a single heuristic. However, recent work by Asmuni et al [16] has shown how fuzzy techniques that incorporate characteristics from a number of established heuristic orderings can be used in establishing the initial order. Another approach explored in recent research has focused on heuristic adaptability, in which the scheduling order is adapted to suit the problem leading to an improvement in the quality of the initial timetable [17]. Heuristic adaptability also introduces a degree of generality to the system since the solution, as it develops, adapts to the environment. Each time an event is scheduled, the timetabling environment has been altered. In essence, an available position has been removed from the timetable, resource availability is reduced and a new and more difficult problem has been created. It is into this modified environment, a partially completed timetable, that the remaining events must be placed. As the timetable is generated, the scheduling order must be reviewed after every placement, and modified if necessary, to ensure that the most difficult exam is scheduled at each stage. In this paper we propose a novel, neural network based multi-criteria methodology for dynamically modifying scheduling order during the construction of an initial examination timetable.

2 The Timetabling System

In order to investigate the effectiveness of the neural network as a multi-criteria adaptive scheduling component the construction of a feasible timetable is viewed conceptually as a two stage process. Firstly, the neural network ranks all remaining exams by perceived difficulty and chooses the most difficult to be scheduled next. A placement component then places the chosen exam in the timetable. Following placement, the process repeats – the remaining exams are ranked by difficulty and the most difficult is placed in the timetable – until all exams have been placed or the chosen exam cannot be placed. The quality of the final timetable is determined by a penalty function which measures the extent to which each student's exams are spread across the available periods. Clearly, before the neural network can rank exams by difficulty it must be appropriately trained. Details of both network training and the penalty function used are given later.

2.1 The Neural Network

The system is based on a Kohonen self-organising neural network. As illustrated in figure 1, the network consists of two layers of processing elements or neurons; an input layer and a mapping layer. Neurons (prototypes) in the mapping layer are spatially arranged as a 2-D grid of five neurons by eight. The network employs an unsupervised learning algorithm in which it is not necessary to know in advance the 'correct' output for a given input. Once trained the organised network topology reflects the statistical regularities of the input data. Inputs (feature vectors) are projected onto the prototypes in the mapping layer such that the topology of the input space is preserved.

During training the Kohonen layer undergoes a self-organising process in which a two-dimensional map is produced representing the higher dimensional input space. An essential feature of the map produced is that it preserves the topology of the input space in that inputs which are 'close together' in input space are mapped to points 'close together' on the Kohonen layer. In effect, points on the Kohonen map represent prototypes, or cluster centres, for the feature vectors used during training. Thus, a feature vector input to the trained network will be represented by a single prototype on the mapping layer.

The choice of inputs and the extent to which the data used to train the network is an accurate and adequate representation of the problem are crucial to the success of the network. The purpose of the network is to determine the difficulty of each event such that the most difficult exam can be scheduled at each point during the construction phase. As such, it is important that the feature vectors that form the input to the network reflect those characteristics of the problem which contribute to scheduling difficulty. At any point during the construction of the timetable the concept of difficultly is highly dependent upon both the data set and the current state of the timetable. An examination may be perceived as 'easy' or 'difficult' based on characteristics such as, for example, the number of conflicts (degree), the number of students enrolled (exam size) or the number of available slots left (saturation degree). The input feature vector used in this work contains both static components, such as degree, weighted degree and exam size, and a dynamic component reporting the current state of the timetable.

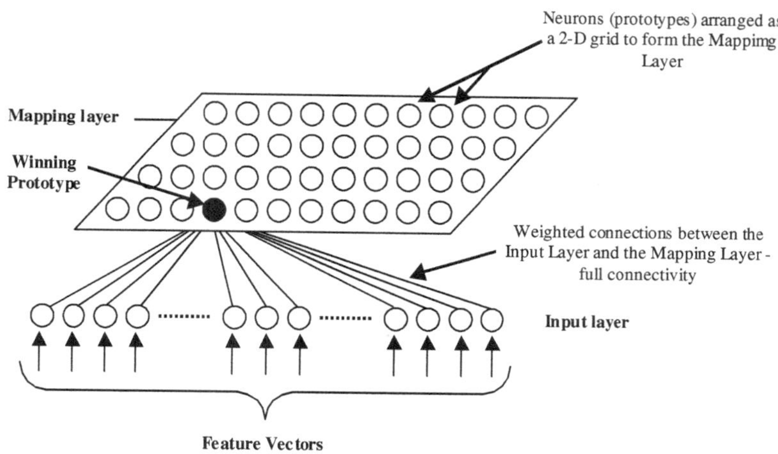

Fig. 1. Schematic of the Kohonen Network. Further information on the Kohonen network and neural networks in general may be found in Haykin [18]

2.2 The Training Process

Having defined the input feature vector it is necessary to establish a corpus of vectors which are representative of the particular timetabling problem and which may be used to train the network. In defining the training data it is essential that the corpus should capture the complexities of the scheduling problem. In this work the training data was generated by building a series of timetables using a random ordering heuristic. An event is chosen at random and an attempt made to schedule it using the placement system described above. Should placement succeed, the characteristics (of both the event and the current state of the timetable) are recorded and stored to the training corpus as a valid feature vector. Nothing is stored should placement fail. In this way a corpus of feature vectors is constructed containing examples of successful scheduling situations for the problem in hand. This approach allows each exam to be encountered in a variety of ordering positions; scheduled early, mid or late in the construction. The training corpus then contains a wide spread of possible scenarios that may arise during the course of building the timetable.

The Kohonen network is trained using a competitive learning algorithm. As input data is presented to the network the neurons on the mapping layer compete amongst each other for activation, resulting in a winning neuron. The weights associated with this winning neuron are then adjusted as dictated by the learning algorithm to align more closely with the input [18]. Through this process the neurons on the mapping layer become tuned to particular input patterns. The mapping layer is initially arranged as a two dimensional lattice of neurons as shown in figure 1. As the neurons become tuned, and patterns are identified, they arrange topologically so that their position is representative of the input characteristics.

As training progresses, a two-dimensional, topological preserving map of the input space is formed, made up of prototypes representing a range of inputs. The essence of the methodology then is to label each prototype represented in the Kohonen layer with a relative scheduling difficulty. Since the Kohonen network uses an unsupervised learning algorithm it is not necessary to know *a priori* how difficult it is to actually schedule the event represented by each of the feature vectors. However, it is a fundamental assumption in this work that feature vectors (events) that map to the same prototype on the Kohonen mapping layer, and are therefore 'close together' in input space, will have a similar scheduling difficulty.

Since all components in the feature vector are individually positively correlated with perceived difficulty it is possible to allocate a relative difficulty to each prototype based on a simple linear distance measure based on the normalised values of the prototype's weighted inputs. Prototypes with the largest value represent the most difficulty exams to schedule; prototypes with the smallest value represent the easiest exams to place. This method presupposes that all features contribute equally to scheduling difficulty. In reality, some features are more influential than others and some can exhibit non-linear relationships with scheduling difficulty. The relative importance of the features and their non-linear relationships must be accounted for by a preprocessing stage prior to input to the network.

2.3 Construction of a Timetable

Construction of a timetable can begin once the network has been trained and the prototypes labelled. Scheduling begins with an empty timetable. A feature vector is generated for each event to be placed and presented in turn to the trained network. The order of presentation is irrelevant. The network will map each input to one of the forty prototypes. Since each prototype is labelled with perceived relative difficulty, it is relatively straightforward to find all those events which are perceived to be most difficult at this stage. One of this group of events is chosen to be placed; at the moment the choice is random since each event in the group is assumed to be equally difficult. The chosen event is placed using the placement algorithm already described.

When an event is successfully placed, the resulting change in the timetable can increase the scheduling difficulty of events yet be timetabled. These changes are captured in the updated feature vectors which are again presented to the network as the first stage in choosing the next event to be scheduled. And so the process continues with the scheduling difficulty of the remaining events changing and adapting as more events are scheduled until either a feasible solution is obtained or the selected event cannot be placed.

3 Results

The proposition to use a neural network as a critical component in a multi-criteria adaptive scheduling system is entirely new. In order to accurately evaluate the contribution of the network to the overall scheduling task it is important that the experimental system is kept stable and simple. To that end, a two-phase iterative timetable construction system was developed as outlined above. Determining the order in which exams should be placed in the timetable is the responsibility of the first phase. In the second phase a placement system schedules exams in the chosen order. In all of the results reported below, timetables are produced by a construction heuristic only; improvement heuristics have not been used.

A relatively straightforward placement system is used in this work. When an exam is to be placed all remaining slots in the timetable which do not contravene a hard constraint are considered. The exam is placed in the slot which contributes least to the overall penalty. Should more than one timetable slot meet this criteria, the exam is placed randomly in one of these slots. Importantly, recursive backtracking is not used during timetable construction; once placed, an exam cannot be moved. This simplistic placement regime is necessary to ensure that the impact of the neural network component is clearly visible and, in the context of proving the neural network based approach, can be evaluated without masking by an unnecessarily complex placement algorithm.

3.1 Establishing Feasibility of the Method

The first experimental task was to verify that the neural network could act as a multi-criteria adaptive component in a scheduling system. Carter's collection of benchmark examination datasets was used for this purpose[1].

Each dataset was ordered by degree, weighted degree and exam size. These static orderings were passed to the placement system and exams scheduled in the established order. To enable a range of possible timetables, exams were placed randomly in the timetable with the only proviso being that placement did not break a hard constraint. It is practically impossible to generate a feasible timetable using such a simplistic placement mechanism. A number of runs were made for each ordering and the number of unplaced exams was recorded.

An eight-by-five Kohonen network was then constructed and trained for each dataset as described above. A number of timetables were constructed for each dataset. For each run, the number of unplaced exams was recorded. Again, the objective is not to construct a feasible timetable but to determine the contribution of the neural network.

Results of the experiment are shown in table 1.

[1] Benchmark datasets may be downloaded from ftp://ftp.mie.utoronto.ca/pub/carter/testprob

Table 1. Number of unplaced events in the construction of a timetable

Data Set	By Degree	By Size	By W.Degree	Best Result	Best Result using NN
CAR-F-92	15	17	19	15	1
CAR-S-91	22	21	15	15	5
EAR-F-83	8	13	14	8	3
HEC-S-92	3	8	6	3	0
KFU-S-93	13	12	8	8	3
LSE-F-91	7	5	7	5	0
STA-F-83	31	31	30	30	22
UTA-S-92	6	7	7	7	1
UTE-S-92	9	7	11	5	0
TRE-S-92	10	10	5	6	0
YOR-F-83	15	28	26	15	10

In all cases, use of the network component has reduced the number of unplaced events, sometimes significantly, when compared to the use of established event ordering heuristics based on a single criterion. Indeed, despite the highly restrictive placement algorithm, use of the neural network to order events for placement generated feasible timetables for four of the datasets. It was not possible to produce a feasible timetable for any of the datasets using traditional ordering heuristics.

3.2 Refining the Methodology

Having established the feasibility of the neural network based methodology the task now is to tune the method so that high quality feasible timetables can be produced for all datasets. For this it is necessary to introduce a penalty function so that the quality of the final timetable can be determined and results compared with those of other researchers.

The penalty function is motivated by the goal of spreading out each student's examination schedule. If two exams, i and j, scheduled for a particular student are t time slots apart, the weight is set to

$$w_t = 2^{5-t} \quad \text{where} \quad t \in \{1,2,3,4,5\} \tag{1}$$

The weight is multiplied by the number of students that sit for both of the scheduled exams. The average penalty per student is calculated by dividing the total penalty by total number of students T. The goal is to minimise the following formulation:

$$\frac{1}{T}\sum_{i=1}^{N-1}\sum_{j=i+1}^{N} s_{ij}\, w_{|p_j - p_i|} \tag{2}$$

where N is the number of exams, s_{ij} is the number of students enrolled in both exam i and j, p_i is the time slot where exam i is scheduled, subject to $1 \le |p_j - p_i| \ge 5$.

A number of refinements were made to the methodology. In particular, the network training regime was revised. Training data was originally generated using the method outline above in which events are chosen at random and a feature vector added to the training corpus if that event can be scheduled. This method takes no account of difficulty during training and can result in feature vectors representing intrinsically easy events (e.g. small events with low degree) scheduled early in the process being added to the training corpus. Similarly, it is inevitable that the training data will contain feature vectors representing intrinsically difficult events (e.g. large events with high degree) scheduled late in the process. Neither of these eventualities is likely to occur while the timetable is being constructed. Consequently, it can be argued that the network should not be trained with such unlikely exemplars.

New training data was generated for each of the datasets. In each case events were ordered by each of the established ordering heuristics before placement. A number of random orderings were retained in generating the training data. In addition, the placement system used was modified such that the chosen event was placed by least cost. For each dataset, a new trained network was developed and used in the construction of a timetable. The results are shown in table 2.

Table 2. Best cost achieved for each dataset using the revised training method. The ease with which timetables can be generated and an indication of time taken is also shown. The work was carried out using a standard desktop PC with AMD Athlon (tm) XP 1800+ 1.54GHz processor and 256MB RAM.

Data Set	Proportion of feasible timetables	Best Cost	Average time to produce a timetable(sec)	Best Reported Results -see[16]
CAR-F-92	0.002	6.2456	10.51	4.1
CAR-S-91	0.008	7.2129	17.28	4.65
EAR-F-83	0.0004	49.4436	2.03	29.3
HEC-S-92	0.095	13.57	0.60	9.2
KFU-S-93	0.008	19.9	3.17	13.5
LSE-F-91	0.0504	14.9938	2.25	9.6
STA-F-83	0.24275	159.2831	0.96	134.9
UTA-S-92	0.04	4.489	14.04	3.2
UTE-S-92	0.30436	31.25	1.31	24.4
TRE-S-92	0.0584	10.7791	3.01	8.3
YOR-F-83	0	1 unplaced	2.07	36.2

With the modified training regime feasible timetables were constructed for all datasets with the exception of YOR-F-83. For some datasets generating a feasible timetable is relatively straightforward, for others it is problematic. For example, 30% of attempts to generate a timetable for the UTE-S-92 dataset result in a feasible solution. With the exception of the YOR-F-83 dataset, EAR-F-83 was found to be most difficult with only 0.04% of attempts resulting in a feasible timetable.

The costs recorded for each dataset represent the value of the penalty function at the end of the construction phase only; improvement heuristics have not been used in this work. As such, our results are not directly comparable with other published results for these datasets, invariably recorded after an improvement phase. Our primary motivation in this work is to prove the effectiveness of the neural network as a multi-criteria, adaptive construction heuristic; not necessarily to obtain best results on these test datasets. With this proviso, best published results are also shown in table 2.

3.3 Application to of the Methodology to Capacitated Data

The datasets above do not contain constraints on the seating available in each period. Such uncapacitated data is useful for developing and proving the methodology but most real-world problems will have a limited set of rooms of varying capacities available. In reality, different institutions must satisfy a range of different constraints in generating an institution-wide timetable [19]. The neural network methodology has been applied to a rich dataset from the University of Nottingham – Nottingham 94. This dataset contains many constraints additional to those found in the benchmark datasets used above. Extra conditions include; specific period assignments, room assignments, timetabling events in a particular order, the requirement for some events to be placed in a room of their own and groups of events to be scheduled together in the same period/room. A neural network was trained, using the technique presented above, with all of these conditions treated as hard constraints. This presents a much more realistic, highly constrained scheduling problem than that posed by the benchmark datasets considered previously. Again, without the use of recursive backtracking or an improvement heuristic the neural network based system succeeded in constructing valid timetables but only by contravening the desirable condition that conflicting events should be scheduled at least one period apart.

It is important to note that the methodology used to order events for placement has not changed from that used with the benchmark datasets. The only component of the timetabling system which is, of necessity, tailored to the institution is the placement system; this component must be tuned such that all institution-specific hard constraints are respected when events are scheduled. This is a significant result. Taken with the results on the benchmark datasets it illustrates that the neural network methodology has general applicability across a range of data and can be used successfully in real timetabling situations. In essence, the neural network provides a generalisation technique, designed to recognise patterns in the data that may be exploited in the generation of high quality timetables. This provides a high degree of generality resulting in a methodology which is largely independent of institution or dataset.

4 Conclusions and Further Work

The work presented here has shown the feasibility of using a neural network based methodology as a generally applicable, multi-criteria, adaptive, construction heuristic for the examination timetabling problem. Work is progressing on two fronts; firstly, to refine the method to improve both the proportion of feasible timetables produced and the quality of the final schedule and secondly, to evaluate the applicability of the methodology to related scheduling problems such as course timetabling for example.

References

1. Burke, E.K., Jackson, K.S., Kingston, J.H. and Weare R.F., *Automated Timetabling: The State of the Art,* The Computer Journal, Vol 40, No 9, pp 565-571, 1997.
2. Carter. M.W., and Laporte, G. *Recent developments in practical examination timetabling.* Practice and Theory of Automated Timetabling, Lecture Notes in Computer Science Vol 1153, Springer, pp3-21, 1996.
3. Burke, E.K. and Petrovic, S. *Recent research directions in automated timetabling.* European Journal of Operational Research 140 pp 266-280, 2002.
4. Thompson, J.M. and Dowsland, K.A. *A Robust Simulated Annealing Based Examination Timetabling System.* Computers and Operations Research 25(7-8), pp 637-648, 1998.
5. White, G.M. and Xie B.S. *Examination Timetables and Tabu Search with Longer-Term Memory.* Practice and Theory of Automated Timetabling III, Lecture Notes in Computer Science Vol 2079, pp 85-103, 2001
6. Burke, E.K. and Newall, J.P. *Enhancing Timetable Solutions with Local Search Methods.* Practice and Theory of Automated Timetabling IV, Lecture Notes in Computer Science Vol 2740, pp. 195-206, 2003.
7. Burke, E.K., Newall, J.P. and Weare, R.F. *A Memetic Algorithm for University Exam Timetabling.* Practice and Theory of Automated Timetabling, LNCS, Vol 1153, Springer, pp 241-250, 1996
8. Corne, D., Fang, H.L. and Mellish, C. *Solving the Modular Exam Scheduling Problem with Genetic Algorithms.* In Proc of the 6th International Conference on Industrial and Engineering Applications of Artificial Intelligence and Expert systems, pp 370-373, 1993.
9. Ross, P., Corne, D. and Fang, H.L. *Improving Evolutionary Timetabling and Delta Evaluation and Directed Mutation.* In Y. Davidor, H. P. Schwefel, and R.Manner (eds.), Parallel Program Solving in Nature, Vol. III, pp. 565-566. Berlin: Springer. 1994
10. Burke, E.K., Newall, J.P. and Weare, R.F. *Initialisation Strategies and Diversity in Evolutionary Timetabling.* Evolutionary Computation 6(1), pp 81-103, 1998
11. Burke, E.K. and Newall, J.P. *A Multi-Stage Evolutionary Algorithm for the Timetabling Problem.* IEEE Transactions on Evolutionary Computation 3(1), pp 63-74, 1999.
12. Burke, E.K., Bykov, Y and Petrovic, S. *A Multi-Criteria Approach to Examination Timetabling*, Practice and Theory of Automated Timetabling III, LNCS Vol 2079, Springer, pp 118-131, 2001.
13. Merlot, L.T.G, Boland, N, Hughes, B. D. Stuckey, P.J, A Hybrid Algorithm for the Examination Timetabling Problem, Practice and Theory of Automated Timetabling IV, pp 207-231, Springer, 2003.
14. Burke, E.K, Petrovic, S and Qu, R. Case Based Heuristic Selection for Timetabling Problems, Journal of Scheduling, Vol 9 issue 2, 2006, pp 115-132.
15. Burke, E.K., McCollum, B., Meisels, A., Petrovic, S. and Qu, R., *A Graph-Based Hyper-Heuristic for Timetabling Problems*, accepted for publication in the European Journal of Operational Research, to appear 2006.
16. Asmuni, H., Burke, E.K., Garibaldi, J.M. and McCollum, B. *Fuzzy Multiple Heuristic Ordering for Examination Timetabling.* Practice and Theory of Automated Timetabling V, Lecture Notes in Computer Science Vol 3616, pp 334-353, 2004.
17. Burke, E.K. and Newall, J.P. *Solving Examination Timetabling Problems through the Adaption of Heuristic Orderings.* Annals of Operational Research 129, pp 107-134, 2004.
18. Haykin, S.S. and Saher S. *Neural Networks: a comprehensive foundation. - 2nd ed.. -* Englewood Cliffs, N.J. : Prentice Hall, 1998 . -ISBN 0132733501
19. Burke, E.K., Elliman, D.G., Ford, P. and Weare, R.F. *Examination Timetabling in British Universities: A survey.* Practice and Theory of Automated Timetabling, LNCS, Vol 1153 pp76-90. 1996.

Optimisation of CDMA-Based Mobile Telephone Networks: Algorithmic Studies on Real-World Networks

Paul Weal[1], David Corne[2], and Chris Murphy[3]

[1] SECaM , Harrison Building, University of Exeter, EX4 4QF, UK
P.D.Weal@ex.ac.uk
[2] MACS, Earl Mountbatten Building, Heriot-Watt University, Edinburgh EH14 8AS, UK
dwcorne@macs.hw.ac.uk
[3] Motorola Ltd, Thamesdown Drive, Swindon, Wiltshire, SN25 4XY, UK
Chris.Murphy@motorola.com

Abstract. CDMA and WCDMA mobile phone networks depend on a network of antennae, each defining a geographic 'cell' that handles the transmissions to and from users' handsets within that cell. These antennae have adjustable settings whose values have a large effect on both quality of service (and consequent subscriptions) and resource consumption. We consider the optimisation of these parameters, and describe experiments that compare a range of optimisation algorithms with the methods currently used in the field for this purpose. The aim of the current project was to achieve faster (necessary) and better (if possible) results than the existing methods used by field engineers. We find that certain evolutionary algorithm configurations achieve both of these requirements on test problems arising from real data from a high-traffic urban environment. To some extent the ideal algorithm depends on the size and load in the network being optimised, and this is the main topic of ongoing research.

1 Introduction

We report on a project aimed at improving the dynamic service delivery infrastructure of a mobile phone network provider, via exploring a small number of algorithms for optimising aspects of that infrastructure. We specifically address optimisation of infrastructural elements of a mobile telephone network based on Code Division Multiple Access (CDMA) technology. A mobile telephone communications service provider needs to maintain a network of antennae, each defining a geographic 'cell' and responsible for providing transmission services for handsets within (or near) that cell. A cell's extent must be such that subscribers may move from the coverage area of one cell to another with continuous service. That is, there should be an area of overlap between neighbouring cells. But too much overlap would lead to too much interference, resulting in excessive powers and reduced capacity to support many subscribers. Each antenna will have at least one CDMA downlink radio carrier which is used to transmit signals to mobiles in that cell. There are many parameters associated with each carrier that are significant for adjusting the geographical relationship between cells; one of these is the 'pilot power'. This is adjustable typically via a database in the central operations and maintenance centre, and relates directly to the strength of

T.P. Runarsson et al. (Eds.): PPSN IX, LNCS 4193, pp. 402 – 412, 2006.

signal received by users' mobile devices when it is choosing its serving cell. We also consider the adjustment of other parameters, which we discuss later.

A suite of tools has previously been developed for modelling and simulating the interactions between cells given defined user loads and system parameters. Two optimisation methods are in this suite, which, using the simulator to evaluate configurations, attempt to find good configurations of pilot powers for specific periods of the day. These are an iterative local/greedy search style algorithm (which we call ILS), and a simple evolutionary algorithm (IGA). Engineers in the field currently use ILS, since it works quickly (within a few hours on modest spec hardware), and gives acceptable results in that time. IGA is capable of producing better solutions, but currently the time taken is unacceptable to the field engineers.

The remainder is set out as follows. In Sect. 2 we review some relevant related material. Sect. 3 then further describes and details certain specifics of the optimisation problem we address and the test data. In Sect. 4 we describe algorithms and experiments and present the results, and we end with a brief discussion in Sect. 5.

2 Related Work

There are several optimisation issues involved in CDMA mobile telephone networks, but they fall cleanly into three categories, being mainly concerned with issues such as the realtime scheduling of signals at a single base station, the initial design and planning (e.g. antenna placement) of a new network, or the continual optimisation and management of an established network (in response to subscriber growth, for example). As an example of the first category, [1] considers the case of high data rate customers using a network that also carries a large number of voice users; based on a mathematical model, they derive principles and an associated optimal downlink (from antenna to user) signal scheduling algorithm that minimises interference between data and voice users. Another example in the first category is [2], in which an evolutionary algorithm (EA) is proposed that works separately within each cell; it regularly samples user traffic and attributes at that cell, and the EA determines optimal bit rate and power setting for each mobile user, and transmits that information back to them. In tests this yielded significant quality of service improvement.

Meanwhile, concerning initial design and planning, this is often solved by experienced engineers using simulators with Monte Carlo methods to generate good initial parameterisations. However [3] considers together the location and pilot powers of base stations (antenna), in order to maximise network capacity, based on a mathematical model that enables a mixed integer programming (MIP) formulation, solved via both MIP and adaptive simulated annealing [4]. They addressed small problems (fewer than 30 cells). [5] and [6] consider a similar problem, and address it with tabu search and evolutionary algorithms respectively, achieving (according to the model) close to optimal performance for some large networks; these both relate to initial network design, combined with initial or 'typical' power settings. In our work, the problem is to respond dynamically to existing demand in an already established network.

In practice the third category of continual 're'-optimisation of an existing network is traditionally done by teams of engineers performing *drive tests* around the network, with test mobiles and spectrum scanners for measuring received signal code power of the pilot channels. This identifies problems of poor coverage or interference, and attempts are made to fix them by intuitive tuning of system parameters in the region. There is relatively little published work to date in this category, perhaps owing to a relative perceived difficulty in the logistics of applying this optimisation. Given a revised collection of antenna adjustments for an urban network spanning (say) 100 square miles, engineers need to visit each antenna and make adjustments; this effort is hard to justify unless the predicted benefit is quite significant, which is hard to guarantee since the models used contain many approximations. However, work on such a model [7] together with its use to derive optimisation heuristics, showed, in a major city-wide setting, that the resulting optimised pilot powers led to significant gains over the use of uniform pilot settings and traditional 'ad hoc' optimisation. As well as significant improvement in pilot interference, there was also gain in forward link coverage and capacity, allowing a substantial reduction in deployment efforts spent in optimising pilot powers. Our work builds on [7] in two main ways, by using a recently developed model that considerably improves accuracy, and by exploring evolutionary and similar algorithms for the optimisation process. Meanwhile, with the advent of remotely adjustable antennae it is becoming much simpler and cheaper to adjust the antenna downtilt, azimuth and beamwidth parameters.

Finally, it should be noted that there is much, but considerably less closely related work in the general field of telecommunications. A sample covering the main application areas (optimisation of various kinds of network design, and optimisation of routing through an established network) using evolutionary computation, includes [8—17]. There are also specialised books and proceedings on this specific area [18—20].

3 The CDMA Network Optimisation Problem

In a CDMA network, there may be several hundred or more antennae in a reasonably large city. Each defines a 'cell', corresponding to the geographic region around it within which it is the preferred base station for users' handsets in that area. The overall quality of service experienced by users depends on various attributes of these antennae. Amongst these attributes is the 'pilot power', which is essentially the strength of a beacon signal provided by it for mobiles to use when choosing which cell to request a service from. Other adjustable attributes include those concerned with the directional nature of the signal, namely the antenna's *azimuth* and *downtilt*.

A healthy network will be tuned such that the areas of overlap are minimised without compromising the coverage offered. It will also keep power and hence interference to a minimum by ensuring that mobiles are served by the most optimum cell without allowing certain cells to carry disproportionately high traffic. The desire to minimise interference by keeping power under control leads to a complex optimisation problem in finding a balance between quality of service provision and cost, as power for one user is interference to another.

As indicated, 'pilot power' is one parameter available for adjustment. Another is the downtilt of the antenna; the larger this is, the less area an antenna's signal will cover. Another parameter is 'azimuth', this being the antenna's angle from magnetic north, which is often set in relation to topological restraints.

The specific deployed commercial network used in most of our tests, which we call N1, contains 207 cells, of which 59 cells have fixed pilot powers for operational reasons. The remaining 148 cells can have their pilot powers adjusted between 1.0 watts and 3.0 watts in increments of 0.1 watts. Another deployed commercial network that appears in some of the tests, which we call N2, contains 97 cells, all of which can have their powers adjusted in the same way as with N1.

The fitness function is an equally weighted sum of the following. 1: Mean traffic channel power per user; 2: Percentage of users who don't receive a sufficiently strong pilot signal; 3: Mean pilot pollution factor (number of non-dominant pilot signals received within a 5dB margin of the dominant); 4: Mean downlink traffic channel outage (users unable to get a usable signal for voice or data services); 5: Penalties associated with the Linear Power Amplifier driving the transmissions on an antenna of which more power than it can provide is demanded. This is as a result of users' excessive requirements for a usable signal; 6: Penalty for users served by a cell other than that closest in terms of propagation loss. This arises from having non-uniform pilot powers across the network and takes account of uplink optimisation, which may conflict with downlink optimisation which is the focus of this paper.

Naturally this can be treated via multiobjective algorithms [21—23], and such is the topic of ongoing related work, however, for this problem these tend to be substantially slower to optimise a network to the extent that they are of little use currently in operational network optimisation. In the present work there is a need to stay close to the current practice of engineers who would use the system, who are familiar with, and require the speed, of the existing single-objective fitness function.

4 Algorithms, Experiments and Results

Algorithms**:** The in-house CDMA network model (developed by the third author) can with suitable accuracy estimate the fitness function described above. The present work was conducted specifically to see if the speed (in particular) and quality of results provided by the incumbent methods (ILS and IGA) could be improved by using alternative algorithms, yet under the constraint that these should be relatively parameter-light and straightforward (implementable readily in this and other scenarios by non-expert practitioners). To this end we explored hillclimbing (HC), simulated annealing (SA), particle swarm optimisation (PSO) and an alternative evolutionary algorithm (SSGA). Each is briefly described below.

ILS is relatively fast, but found less effective in terms of solution quality. We can broadly describe ILS as follows. It takes a parameter *h*, which refers to the number of cells that will be involved in a *hotspot*. For each group of *h* cells, where those groups are considered in a specific order based on network data, ILS estimates the quality of all configurations of available pilot power levels for cells in the hotspot (clearly this becomes infeasible for moderate *h*); the best such configuration is retained, and ILS moves on to consider the next hotspot. This process is repeated for a given number of passes, where one pass involves considering all hotspots in the network in turn.

IGA is a classical, generational genetic algorithm incorporating elitism [24]; it uses binary encoding, single point crossover, bitflip mutation and fitness proportionate selection. Since the problem is one of minimisation, proportionate selection works with the reciprocal of the fitness.

SSGA is a steady state genetic algorithm [25], using real-number encoding, uniform crossover [26], Gaussian mutation and binary tournament selection. In some experiments we also employ swap mutation (two randomly chosen genes are swapped). In one generation of SSGA, two parents are selected, and one child is generated by uniform crossover, and then mutation is applied to that child, and it is evaluated. If the child's fitness is better or equal to that of the population's current worst, then it enters the population overwriting a worst chromosome; otherwise, the child is discarded.

PSO is a standard implementation of Particle Swarm Optimisation (PSO) [27], with parameters c_1 and c_2 both set at 1, and $V_{max} = 1$. Some preliminary investigation of alternative parameters was done, but none improved significantly on these.

HC is straightforward stochastic 'hill climbing'. Maintaining a single chromosome (initially random), called the 'current', HC iterates the following process: the current is copied and mutated, producing a mutant. If the mutant is fitter than or equally as fit as the current, then the mutant becomes the new current solution; otherwise the mutant is discarded. HC used the same mutation operators as the SSGA.

SA was a simple implementation of simulated annealing [28, 29] with a linearly reducing temperature schedule which was engineered to change the probability of accepting a worse solution from 0.3 at the beginning of the run to 0 at the end. Limited preliminary parametric investigation was done, confirming this as a valid choice.

Encodings and Operators: In the cases of HC, PSO, SA and SSGA, a 'pilots only' *chromosome* comprises L real numbers where L is the number of antennae whose pilot powers are not pre-specified, each representing the pilot power of a specific antenna, and the value is constrained in [1, 3]. Let the value of gene i be v_i; when gene i is interpreted, it indicates a setting of p for the pilot power associated with gene i, where p is the closest value to v_i in the set {1.0, 1.1, 1.2, ..., 3.0} (the available pilot power settings). In the case of IGA, the encoding is binary, where each power is encoded in an 8-bit string similarly interpreted in [1, 3]. With ILS, the encoding is immaterial (since there is no interaction with genetic operators). In the cases when we optimise each of pilots, tilts and azimuths (see Sect. 3), a chromosome is of length $3L$, each group of three genes denoting pilot power, tilt and azimuth values respectively. Each is interpreted similarly as one of the permitted vales for the corresponding parameter. The possible pilot powers are as stated above, while tilts and azimuths each have 20 possible settings.

As well as the Gaussian mutation operator described, the SSGA experiments and some of the HC and SA experiments also used a swap operator. This was tried after observing (in work otherwise not reported here) a high diversity in solutions from different runs (also observed in [7]). Ideal solutions tend to be characterised by a pattern in which low power antennae are compensated for by higher power antennae nearby, which in turn suggests that swap mutation is a reasonable tool to explore this space. When it is used, it is in combination with the Gaussian mutation operator: a number k of swaps are done (where $k = 0$ defaults to Gaussian mutation), followed by application of the Gaussian mutation. In each SA, HC and SSGA case, preliminary experiments explored values of k from 0 to 3. In the results reported here, we use only the thus-found best k for each algorithm/problem combination.

Parameters: Each of IGA, SSGA and PSO used a population size of 100. Whenever Gaussian mutation was used, it employed a mean of 0 and a standard deviation of 0.3, and was applied with a strength of $3/L$ (that is, mutation was applied to three randomly chosen genes). These values were arrived at on the basis of preliminary experiments. As was implicit before, crossover and mutation were always applied (i.e. crossover rate and mutation rate were both 1).

Experiments and Results: The fitness function is computationally highly expensive, so our experiments were oriented towards examining the number of evaluations required to achieve acceptable solutions; this is why we are interested in convergence-over-time curves in the following. In every experiment, the 'solution quality' result indicates the best solution after 100,000 fitness evaluations. First, each algorithm was compared on problem N1, optimising only the pilot powers. Fig. 1 shows early convergence plots, while Table 1 summarises a statistical analysis of the results using 10,000-sample Randomisation tests [29] based on 10 trial runs of each algorithm. (In many cases a single trial run of one algorithm consumed 24hrs elapsed time – we were unable to do further runs for the current publication). The same collection of algorithms, but omitting ILS, were compared on problem N2, also optimising only pilot powers. We omit the equivalent of Fig 1 for space reasons, which was highly similar to the convergence curves for N1; however we provide a statistical summary in Table 2. Next we investigated optimising pilots, tilts and azimuths on the larger network N1, using only the more promising algorithms in the previous tests, while keeping IGA for baseline comparison. As before, the HC and SSGA results provided are for the configuration (number of swaps) that was best in preliminary tests. Fig. 2 shows convergence behaviour, and Table 3 summarises pairwise results statistically, while we recognize that this is not sufficient on which to base claims concerning multiple algorithm comparisons.

Table 1. Summary of statistical comparison of SSGA, HC, IGA, ILS, PSO and SA on N1, pilot powers optimisation. Based on best of 10 runs of 100,000 evaluations for each algorithm.

Comparison	Conclusions
SSGA vs HC	SSGA superior, p-value < .00001; HC superior at short timescales
SSGA vs IGA	p-value = 0.116 at 100,000 evals, p-value < 0.00001 at 50,000 evals; SSGA superior at short and medium timescales but superior with only low confidence at 100,000 evals point.
IGA vs HC	IGA superior with >97% confidence, p-value = 0.023
Others	At 100,000 evals, each of HC, SSGA,IGA were superior to the various ILS versions, SA and PSO with p-value < .00001

Basic Observations: In the pilots-only/larger network case, SSGA (1-swap) and HC (0-swap) are superior to the others in terms of both finding good solutions quickly and final solution quality. Both ILS and IGA are outperformed significantly. At around the 15,000 evaluations mark (beyond which ILS never improves), both SSGA and HC outperform ILS and IGA, in time very acceptable to the field engineers. Relative performance was similar on the smaller network N2, except that the difference between HC and SSGA in early stages was less pronounced. Again, SSGA provided better overall results and both outperformed ILS and IGA over long and short timescales. Interestingly, in both 'pilots only' cases, the better version of SSGA (hence the one reported here) was that involving 1 swap before the Gaussian mutation, but the better version of HC was that with Gaussian mutation alone.

Table 2. Summary of statistical comparison of SSGA, HC, IGA, on problem N2, (abbreviated to these for space reasons); pilot powers optimisation. Based on best from 10 runs of 100,000 evaluations for each algorithm.

Comparison	Conclusion	*p*-value
SSGA vs HC	SSGA superior, >99% confidence	0.0016
SSGA vs IGA	SSGA is superior	< 0.00001
HC vs IGA	HC superior, >99% confidence	0.0014

Table 3. Summary of statistical comparisons of SSGA, HC, IGA, on problem N1; pilot powers, tilts and azimuths optimisation. Based on best of 10 runs of 100,000 evaluations.

Comparison	Conclusion	*p*-value
HC vs SSGA	Inconclusive	0.36
HC vs IGA	HC is superior	< 0.00001
SSGA vs IGA	SSGA is superior	< 0.00001

Concerning the 'pilots, tilts and azimuths' problem on N1, it is notable that in very early stages the chromosomes are much less fit than in the corresponding stages of the 'pilot powers only' runs. This arises because tilts and azimuths are randomly assigned in the initial population, rather than given a predetermined reasonable assignment in the pilots-only case. However, being able to adjust these extra parameters clearly leads to benefits, with cost falling to around 27 in these experiments rather than 30. Again, HC and SSGA both outperform the incumbent IGA. ILS results in this case were poor and are omitted for space reasons. Finally, it is notable that swap mutation was not useful in this case; both the SSGA and HC use Gaussian mutation alone.

5 Concluding Discussion

Mobile phone networks based on CDMA technology present a plethora of challenges for service provision and maintenance, and these in turn demand sophisticated computational models, up-to-date optimisation approaches and much empirical investigation to address. Also, in common with a pattern typical in the commercial world, new developments in engineering and technology yield even more opportunities and challenges. Hence, as adjustment of more attributes of base station antenna becomes more routine and easy, the challenge of optimising these parameters comes to the fore.

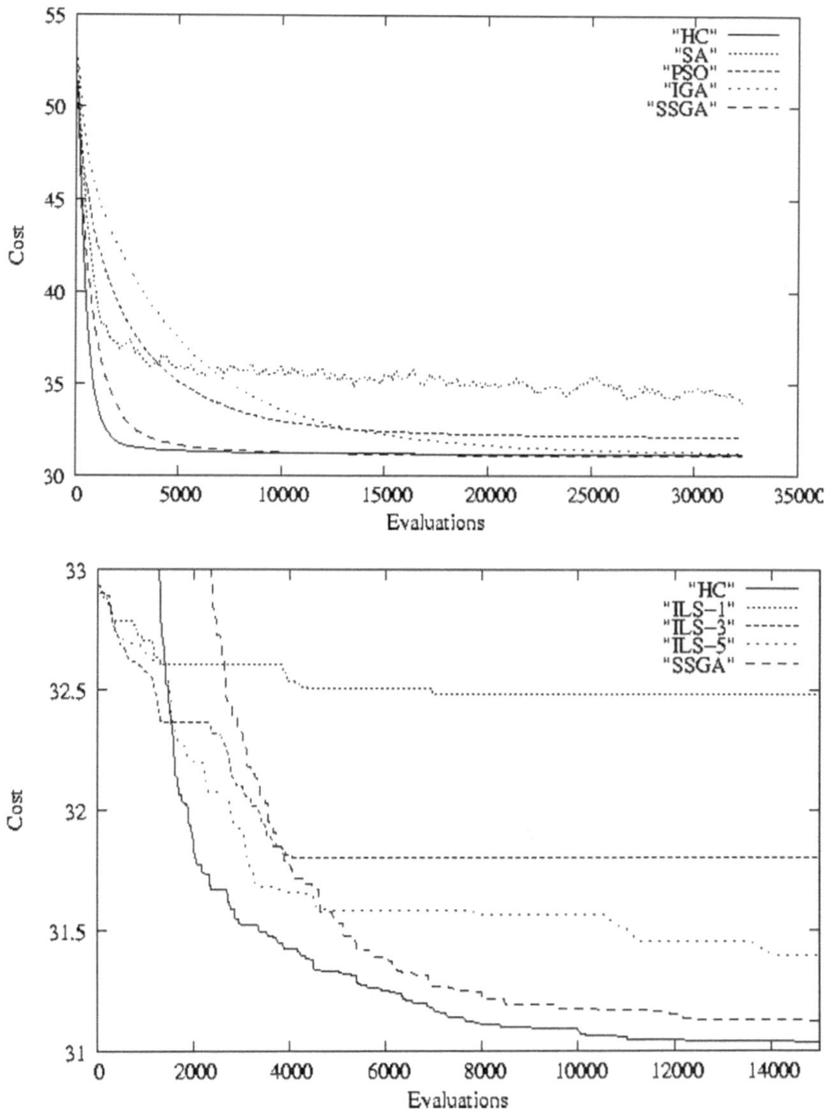

Fig. 1. Early convergence behaviour on network N1, optimising pilot powers only. Each curve is mean of ten runs; upper plot shows first 30,000 evaluations of a 100,000 evaluation run, so that we can highlight behaviour early in the run; lower plot provides the results for ILS with different levels of k, contrasted with SSGA and HC, for approx. first 15000 evaluations. None of the ILS runs improved beyond the best level in this plot.

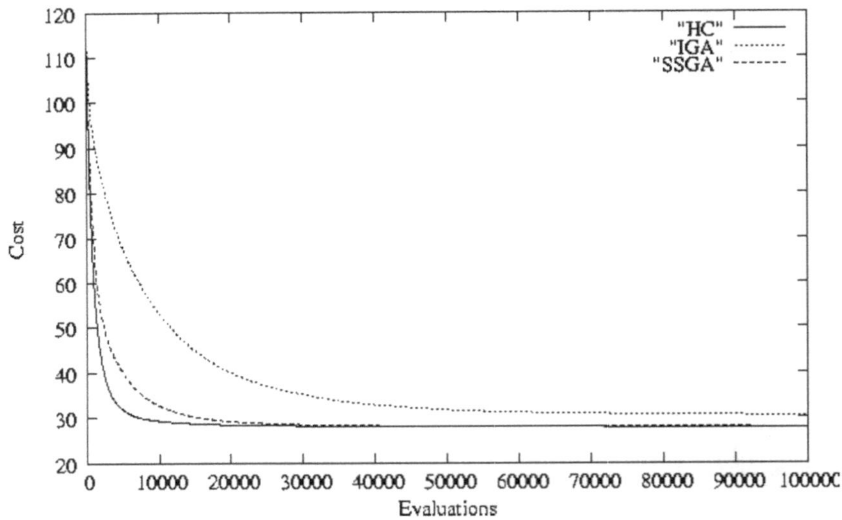

Fig. 2. Convergence behaviour of SSG, HC, and IGA on network N2 (97 adjustable antennae), optimising pilot powers, tilts and azimuths. Each curve is the mean of ten runs.

We have explored the optimisation of pilot powers in CDMA networks, and also the problem of optimising each of pilots, tilts and azimuths. Our test data came from two established networks, and we were able to find improvements to the incumbent optimisation methods, that are able to find better solutions, and more quickly. On the basis of these results, an ongoing project will deploy the updated methods in the field at a selection of regions. However, this study has been necessarily limited by the computational expense of the fitness function (a single trial run of 100,000 evaluations on network N1 typically takes 24 hrs on a modest spec workstation), and by the fact that it has been difficult so far to obtain additional network data beyond the two reported on here; meanwhile much more needs to be done to understand how suitably to choose the algorithm based on the (ideally) easily measurable details of the network under study and its user load. In our view it is more urgent, however, to find a way to significantly accelerate the speed of experiments on these problems. We are currently addressing this issue via using these CDMA optimisation problems as a case study/research vehicle for landscape state machines (LSMs) [30, 31]. The idea here is that data from previous runs are used to build an approximate landscape model, which can then be used for ultra-fast approximate performance evaluation via running algorithms on the *model*. Meanwhile the LSMs themselves may be visualised and so yield further insight into the relationships between problem and algorithm choice.

Acknowledgements

We are grateful for the careful work and suggestions of several reviewers. We acknowledge the support of EPSRC in the form of a CASE studentship for the first author (this award was obtained thanks in part to the efforts of Sameer Singh).

References

[1] Bedakar, A., Borst, S., Ramanan, K., Whiting, P. and Yeh, E. (1999), Downlink scheduling in CDMA data networks, in Proc. Global Telecomms. Conf., 1999. GLOBECOM'99, vol 5, pp. 2653—2657.

[2] Moustafa, M., Habib, I., Naghshineh, M. (2001) Wireless resource management using genetic algorithm for mobiles equilibrium, Proc.6th IEEE Symp. on Computers and Comms., pp. 586—591.

[3] Akl, R.G., Hegde, M.V., Naraghi-Pour, M. and Min, P.S. (2001) Multicell CDMA network design, IEEE Transactions on Vehicular Technology, 50(3):711—722.

[4] Chen, S. and Luk, B.L. (1999) Adaptive simulated annealing for optimization in signal processing applications, Signal Processing, 79(1): 117—128.

[5] Lee, C.Y. and Kang, H.G. (2000) Cell planning with capacity expansion in mobile communications: a tabu search approach, IEEE Transactions on Vehicular Technology, 49(5):1678—1691.

[6] Maple, C., Guo, L. and Zhang, J. (2004) Parallel Genetic Algs. for Third Generation Mobile Network Planning, Proc Int'l. Conf. on Parallel Comp. in Elec. Eng. (PARELEC'04) pp. 229—236.

[7] Love, R.T. Beshir, K.A. Schaeffer, D. and Nikides, R.S. (1999), A pilot optimization technique for CDMA cellular systems, in Proc. 50th IEEE VTS Vehicular Technology Conf., vol. 4, pp. 2238—2242.

[8] Sinclair, M. (1993) The application of a genetic algorithm to trunk network routing table optimisation, in Proc. 10th UK Teletraffic Symp.: Performance Engineering in Telecomms. Networks, 2/1—2/6.

[9] Abuali, F.N., Schoenefeld, D. and Wainwright, R.L. (1994) Designing telecommunications networks using genetic algorithms and probabilistic minimum spanning trees, in Proceedings of the 1994 ACM symposium on Applied computing, pp. 242—246.

[10] Celli, G., Costamagna, E. and Fanni, A. (1995) Genetic algorithms for telecommunication network optimization, in Proc. IEEE Int'l Conf. on Systems, Man and Cybernetics, vol 2, pp. 1227—1232.

[11] Kumar, A., Pathak, R.M. and Gupta, Y.P. (1995) Genetic-algorithm-based reliability optimization for computer network expansion, IEEE Transactions on Reliability, 44(1).

[12] Ko, K-T., Tang, K-S., Chan, C-Y., Man, K-F. and Kwong, S. (1997) Using genetic algorithms to design mesh networks, COMPUTER, 30(8):56—61.

[13] Webb, A., Turton, B.C.H. and Brown, J.M. (1998) Application of genetic algorithm to a network optimisation problem, in Proc. 6th IEE Conference on Telecommunications, pp. 62—66.

[14] Knowles, J., Oates, M. and Corne, D. (2000) Advanced Multi-Objective Evolutionary Algorithms Applied to Two Problems in Telecommunications, BT Technology Journal, 18(4).

[15] Hsinghua C., Premkumar, G. and Chao-Hsien, C. (2001), Genetic algs. for commus. network design - an empirical study of the factors that influence performance, IEEE Trans. E.C., 5(3):236—249.

[16] Weicker, N., Szabo, G., Weicker, K, Widmayer, P. (2003) Evolutionary multiobjective optimization for base station transmitter placement with frequency assignment, IEEE Trans. E.C.., 7(2):189—203

[17] Crepu, J.-C., Koukam, A., Lissajoux, T., Caminada, A. (2005) Automatic mesh generation for mobile network dimensioning using evolutionary approach, IEEE Trans Evol. Comp., 9(1):18—30.

[18] Corne, D., Smith, G.D., Oates, M. (eds.) (2000) Telecommunications Optimization: Heuristic and Adaptive Techniques, John Wiley & Sons, 416pp.

[19] Pedrycz, W. (ed.) (2000) Computational Intelligence in Telecommuns. Networks, CRC Press, 450pp.

[20] Wang, L. (ed.) (2003) Soft Computing in Communications, Springer, 2003, 408pp.

[21] Deb, K. (2001) Multiobjective Optimization using Evolutionary Algorithms, Wiley, 518pp.
[22] Corne, D., Deb, K., Fleming, P. and Knowles, J. (2003) The good of the many outweighs the good of the one: evolutionary multiobjective optimization, coNNectionS, 1(1), pp9-13, IEEE Neur. Net. Soc.
[23] Collete, Y., Siarry, P. (2004) Multiobjective optimization: principles & case studies, Springer, 293pp.
[24] Goldberg, D. (1989), Genetic algs. in search, optimization and machine learning, Addison Wesley
[25] Syswerda, G. (1991) A study of reproduction in steady state genetic algorithms, FOGA I, Morgan Kaufmann, pp. 94—101.
[26] Syswerda, G. (1989) Uniform crossover in genetic algorithms, Proc. 3rd Int'l Conf. on Genetic Algorithms, pp. 2—9, Morgan Kaufmann.
[27] Kennedy, J., and Eberhart, R. C. (1995). Particle Swarm Optimization, Proc. IEEE International Conference on Neural Networks , IEEE Service Center, 1942-1948.
[28] Kirkpatrick, S., Gelatt, C.D, Vecchi, M.P. (1983), Science, 220(4598) : 671—680.
[29] Edgington, E.S. (1995) Randomization Tests, Marcel Dekker, 424pp.
[30] Corne, D., Oates, M., Kell, D. (2003) Landscape state machines: tools for evolutionary algorithm performance analyses and landscape /algorithm mapping,. EvoCop '03, Springer LNCS, pp. 187—198.
[31] Rowe, W., Corne, D., Knowles, J. (2006) Predicting Stochastic Search Algorithm Performance using Landscape State Machines, Proc. IEEE Con. Evol. Comp. 2006, to appear.

Evolving Novel and Effective Treatment Plans in the Context of Infection Dynamics Models: Illustrated with HIV and HAART Therapy

Rebecca Haines[1] and David Corne[2]

[1] SECaM, Harrison Building, University of Exeter, Exeter EX4 4QF, UK
r.i.haines@ex.ac.uk
[2] MACS, Earl Mountbatten Building, Heriot-Watt University, Edinburgh EH14 8AS, UK
dwcorne@macs.hw.ac.uk

Abstract. Several diseases involve complex interplay between an infection and the body's defences. Concerning AIDS, for example, this corresponds to developments in the immune system's responses and the HIV virus' counter-responses. Treatment for such diseases involves, at specific times, delivery of an agent that inhibits the infection. We hypothesise that: given a credible model of the combined dynamics of infection and response, the timing and quantities involved in treatment can be valuably investigated using that model. In particular, we investigate searching for optimised treatment plans with an evolutionary algorithm (EA). Our test case is a cellular automaton (CA) model of HIV dynamics, extended to incorporate HAART therapy (a favoured HIV treatment).An EA is wrapped around this model, and searches for treatments that maximally delay onset of AIDS, given certain constraints. We find that significant improvements over default HAART strategy are readily discovered in this way.

1 Introduction

Several viral and bacterial diseases are characterised in terms of the complex interplay over time between the infection and the body's defences. E.g., with AIDS, three distinct phases have been observed, corresponding to developments in the immune system's responses to the attack, and the HIV virus' counter-responses. Any treatment strategy will involve intervention at specific times, with the delivery of an agent that is believed to somehow inhibit the course of the infection. We hypothesise that: given a credible model of the combined dynamics of the infection and the body's response, the timing and quantities involved in any treatment can be valuably investigated in terms of that model. In particular, we investigate the notion of searching for optimised treatment plans with an evolutionary algorithm (EA). Our test case is a cellular automaton (CA) model of the dynamics of HIV infection, which we extend to incorporate the modeling of treatment via HAART therapy (a currently favoured HIV treatment). A simple EA is wrapped around this extended model, and searches for treatment plans that maximise the time taken for AIDS to take hold, in the context of a constraints concerned with harmful effects of prolonged continuous therapy. We

T.P. Runarsson et al. (Eds.): PPSN IX, LNCS 4193, pp. 413 – 422, 2006.

fiind that, insofar as the models hint at reality, treatment plans that improve on default HAART strategies can be readily discovered by this method.

The paper is set out as follows. In section 2 we set out relevant introductory material on HIV/AIDS, mathematical and computational modeling thereof, HAART therapy. Section 3 then details the models and algorithms employed, aimed at providing a replicable account of the HIV and HAART CA model, and the EA that searches using this model within the fitness function. Experiments and their results are described in section 4, and a concluding discussion appears in section 5.

2 Background Material

HIV, AIDS and HAART Therapy: The Human Immunodeficiency Virus (HIV) has been subject to intense research over the last two decades. Although major progress has been achieved in understanding different aspects of the virus-host interaction, the mechanisms by which HIV causes AIDS still remain unexplained. HIV can lie dormant for years, invisible to the body's surrounding immune defenses.

The following is summarised from [1—5]. Infection begins when an HIV particle enters the body and enters a CD4+ T lymphocyte. Since these cells are key to the immune response, this is a central reason for HIV's impact. A small number of cells harbour HIV in a stable, inactive form, so that HIV can lie dormant for years, invisible to the body's immune defences. Once in the cytoplasm of a cell, HIV reverse transcriptase converts viral RNA into DNA. This stage is important to drug therapy development and modeling as seven of the antiviral drugs approved in the US for HIV treatment (AZT, ddC, etc.) function by interfering with this stage. The HIV DNA travels to the cell's nucleus and is spliced into the host's DNA. Once incorporated into the cell's genes, HIV DNA is now a 'provirus'. The cell is now co-erced into manufacturing more virus particles; viral RNA and associated proteins are packaged and released from the lymphocyte surface, taking with them a swatch of lymphocyte membrane containing viral surface proteins. These proteins will then bind to the receptors on other immune cells facilitating continued infection.

Broadly, the infection is characterized by three stages: In stage 1, lasting only a few weeks, there is an initial increase in the viral load followed by a sharp decrease. A large amount of HIV is in the peripheral blood and the immune system produces antibodies and cytotoxic lymphocytes. This stage is present in the left hand side of figure 1 which is plotted from clinical data. In stage 2, which can last 10 or more years, HIV level in peripheral blood drops very low but people remain infectious. HIV is not dormant during this stage, but is actually very active in the lymph nodes, wherein many T helper cells are infected and die and a large quantity of virus is produced. This stage is the mid-area of figure 1. Finally, in stage 3, the immune system starts to fail (see right end of figure 1). HIV becomes more prevalent and varied, leading to destruction of more T helper cells. The body fails to continually replace these. As the immune system continues to fail, mild symptoms develop. As the immune system deteriorates the symptoms worsen, resulting in the onset of AIDS.

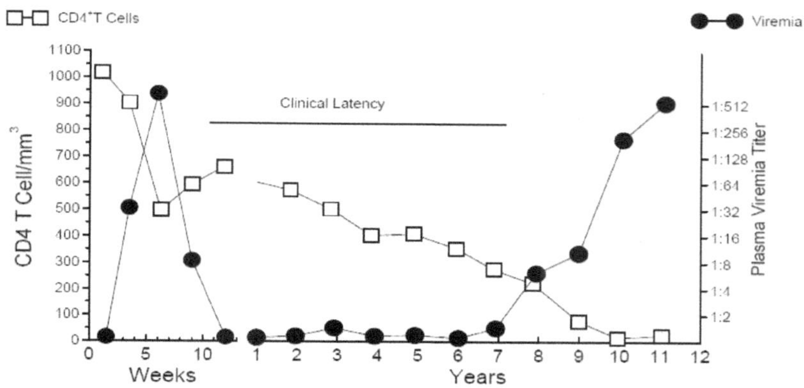

Fig. 1. The graph of patient cell and viral measurements from [22]. Notice the change in horizontal scale following the 10-weeks point. The first 10 weeks show the intial phase of infection following which the density of healthy cells (squares) recovers, but the HIV virus `incubates' for several years until an acceleration in viral count that heralds the onset of AIDS.

At present, there are fifteen drugs licensed for HIV treatment [6]. But, individual therapies each have their drawbacks, as, e.g., HIV develops specific resistance to it. Currently, theory and clinical trials indicate that maximal viral suppression is through highly active anti-retroviral therapy (HAART), which consists of triple therapy with two nucleoside analogues and a protease inhibitor [6]. We concentrate on HAART as the therapy to model since at this time it is the most effective at reducing the time for onset if AIDS. However, due to the development of drug resistance, evolution of viral strains, or poor patient compliance, it fails to effectively contain the virus long-term in the majority of patients. Recent research has investigated Structured Treatment Interrupts [19, 20] in which treatment is interrupted by periods of several weeks. This, further discussed later, forms the basis of our experiments.

Modelling HIV, AIDS and Potential Therapies: Several mathematical models of HIV infection have been proposed (e.g. [8-10]), but all fail to describe some important aspects of the infection's dynamics. Typically, models proposed so far have problems in maintaining biological plausibility while producing a qualitative match to the known dynamics of cell concentrations, the main difficulty being that characteristic dynamics occur at two quite distinct timescales (see figure 1, showing timescales over the first few weeks, and over several years, respectively). A recent example is [10], who integrate a CA approach with a graph percolation model, focusing on HIV's long-term dynamics and the distribution of incubation periods, but this does not account for the characteristic dynamics of the first few weeks of infection.

However, the recent CA model reported by Dos Santos & Coutinho [11] clearly shows the different time scales of the infection and has a broad qualitative agreement to the density of healthy and infected cells observed *in vivo*. This sets it apart as a promising candidate for further research, although [12] notes that this qualitative agreement is quite parameter sensitive. Nevertheless, Dos Santos and Coutinho's approach is clearly of interest (as is also pointed out in [12]), and unique in capturing the multi-timescale dynamics with apparently biologically plausible rules; we believe this model is sufficient as the basis of this study in terms of proving feasibility of our approach; meanwhile we are investigating improvements and alternatives [13].

There have been several attempts to model drug therapy and continued progress has led to the development of various types of therapy. *Multiple* drug therapy is considered to increase long term survival moreso than single-drug therapy. The appearance of virus resistance against HAART is apparently more delayed than with combined drug therapy [6], but long-term survival data with HAART is unknown. Mathematical models have difficulties with single treatment models and also have difficulties with unifying multiple therapies into one model [6]. This (as mentioned above) is again a difficulty in capturing the dynamics at different time scales. However, Sloot et al's system [6] echoes the nature of dos Santos and Coutinho's model and extends to model a variety of therapies; they show good qualitative agreement to clinical treatment data. We base our work on such a combined HIV/HAART model.

Optimisation and Therapy Models: Finally, generalizing away from the HIV/AIDS context, we note that other work has considered the use optimisation methods to generate therapy plans in different contexts, our sample being [14—17]. In [14] and [16], the model under study predicts the effect (on both tumours and surrounding healthy tissue) of radiotherapy beams, and optimization is done to find ideal parameters for the radiotherapy. In [15] and [17], the module under consideration is a differential-equation based treatment of accumulated toxicity over time of cancer chemotherapy, and advanced optimization methods are used to find ideal chemotherapy schedules.

3 Models and Algorithms

The CA / HAART Therapy Model: First we describe our implementation of the HIV Infection model [11]; this is how our model operates during periods when treatment is *off*; further rules below, following [6], define how the model operates when simulated therapy is in operation.

As [11], we use a 2D synchronous CA with a square lattice, and the Moore neighbourhood (a cell's neighbourhood are its N, NE, E, SE, S, SW, W and NW neighbours). Cells can be in one of four states: healthy (H), infected-1 (I1), infected-2 (I2), or dead (D). Initially, cells are mainly H, but a small random proportion p_{HIV} are infected. We use $p_{HIV} = .025$, in common with [11]. 'HAART off' operation then continues according to the following four rules; one application of these rules to every grid cell results in simulating 1 week's progress. Biological justification of these rules is in [11]; we provide brief notes on this point.

Rule 1 - If an H cell has at least one I1 neighbour, or if has at least k I2 neighbours, then it becomes I1. Otherwise, it stays healthy.

Rule 2 – An I1 cell becomes I2 after τ time steps (simulated weeks). (to operate this the CA maintains a counter associated with each I1 cell).

Rule 3 - An I2 cell becomes D.

Rule 4 – A D cell becomes: H, with probability $p_{repl}(1 - p_{Infec})$; I1, with probability $p_{repl}\, p_{Infec}$; otherwise, it remains D

Rule 1 models spread of infection by contact prior to development of immune response. As [11], we use $k = 4$. An I2 cell represents one against which an immune response has finally been developed (note that each infected cell will harbour a different HIV strain), which happens after roughly τ weeks; as [11], we use $\tau = 4$. Rule 4 simulates the replenishment of new healthy cells in the context of maintained infection. In common with [11] we use $p_{repl} = 0.99$ and $p_{Infec} = 0.00001$.

Now we turn to the integration of simulated HAART. The following rules, gleaned from [6], are designed to model the effects of HAART's anti viral-replication activity. These rules become operative in the model when therapy is switched on, replacing the corresponding rules above. Note that in the case of HAART-Rule 1, it is convenient to write and implement it as one which updates its *neighbours* on the basis of its own state, rather than updating a cell on the basis of its neighbours' states:

HAART-Rule 1: Given an I1 cell, the following is done to its neighbours at the next time step: with prob. $p_{response}(t)$ (where t is current week of infection), a randomly chosen N ($7 \geq N \geq 0$) of neighbouring H cells become I1; otherwise, all 8 become I1.

HAART-Rule 3 - An I2 cell becomes dead after 2 time steps.

Meanwhile, rules 2 and 4 remain unchanged. HAART-Rule 1 models the inhibition of viral replication, with N representing the effectiveness of the HAART drugs. Without therapy, Rule 1 provides (implicitly) that all H neighbours of an I1 cell will become infected at the next time step. On therapy, with probability $p_{response}(t)$, this falls to N. The smaller N, the more efficient the therapy. Meanwhile, the larger $p_{response}(t)$, the more effective is the therapy. This models the response function for the HAART drug therapy, and incorporates the fact that the therapy will not immediately influence all of the I1 cells, but will affect some of them at each time step [3]. We used a response function based on the work in [6] but adapted to model the use of varied treatments and in line with current knowledge about the HAART mechanism. Also, given the increasingly high quality of the HAART drug, and observations that show relatively prolonged long-term survival for the highly inhibitive drugs [3], we use $N = 0$. The model maintains the possibility for other values of N, which may become useful in prolonged treatments involving different flavours of HAART.

The change to rule 3 reflects the fact that, during HAART therapy, an I2 cell will take longer to die while viral propagation is inhibited. Finally, we note various parameters that have not yet been specified. We use a lattice size of 700×700 - as noted later, this is a minimal size at which the basic HIV infection model yields quite repeatable results. Our CA boundary conditions are *fixed* – e.g. a cell at the right hand edge of the grid has no right hand neighbours. This is unlike the [11] case, but we feel it better models the physical conditions, in which the dynamics of infection occur in the relatively restricted space of the thymus.

Structured Treatment Interruptions: Rather than prolonged, continual HAART, many believe that structured treatment interruptions (STIs - scheduled periods without treatment) may *improve* the immune system by increasing HIV's sensitivity to antiretroviral drugs. Interruptions draw viral mutant selection pressure away from drug resistance, thus breeding a more drug-susceptible virus [5].

Implementing STIs is straightforward in our model, and is done by switching between the normal ruleset while off treatment and the HAART ruleset during treatment. STI based therapy is not the same as Intermittent Therapy, which has shorter cycles of switching on and off the antiviral drugs, such as 'five days on two days off' and has in some research proved ineffective and lead quickly to drug resistance. Meanwhile, STI (with on/off periods measured in several weeks) has proven beneficial in trials. By optimising STIs we can investigate vastly more possible treatments that can be done with clinical trials.

Optimisation: We use a very simple evolutionary algorithm [18—21] (EA). With a population of 10 randomly generated solutions, it continues for v generations as follows: a parent is selected by binary tournament selection, and then subject to mutation. If the mutant is fitter than (or equally as fit as) the current worst in the population, then it replaces this worst. This represents a first-choice method, in the context of having very limited opportunity to experiment with several different algorithms owing to the very time-complex nature of the evaluation function in this case. On the basis of the results we feel both that this algorithm design suffices for now, and that alternatives will be worth investigating in future when we come to understand the landscapes involved in this and related problems.

4 Experiments and Results

A number of experiments were done to investigate optimizing STI plans using a simple evolutionary algorithm. Each candidate solution (*chromosome*) specified a schedule of treatment interruptions to start from the 300-week stage; this is the mean point at which the viral load is at a threshold that indicates HAART therapy should begin. The fitness function consisted of running the CA for 690 simulated weeks, using the chromosome to indicate when to simulate the therapy. Fitness itself is the week number at which the density of infected and healthy cells becomes equal (called the 'set point') *and* the healthy density does not recover past this point in later weeks. Such a point essentially heralds the onset of AIDS, while earlier weeks at which the 'set point' may be reached do not develop into AIDS owing to the introduction of treatment. There are various 'repeating-pattern' STI schemes that have been investigated in clinical trials, and limited simulations have found these tend to yield fitnesses between 400 and 500 in our model.

It is worth noting the time complexity of the experiments. Given an N by N CA grid, a single iteration involves N^2 cell updates, each of which involves several operations. A run of a black-box search algorithm for v evaluations would therefore have a complexity of $690vN^2$ cell updates. Ideally, to compensate for the fact that multiple runs of the CA do not have identical behaviour, it would make sense for a single evaluation to return the mean result from $s > 1$ simulations. But, initial tests and observations [11, 13] show that variation is also markedly reduced with grid size. Here we chose to raise N to a level where variation became acceptably low (N = 700), allowing us to set s=1. Each evaluation still involved $> 3\times10^8$ cell updates, and certain pragmatics and resource issues mean that we can only here report on (at most) 50-evaluation runs. The main reason for high N, rather than s>1, is that lower N can lead to simulations that do not always follow the stages of infection, quickly settling down to an `all-healthy' state. This would of course corrupt the evaluation of STI plans and the optimisation.

Structured Treatment Experiments: We report here on three experiments, differing in terms of the space of possible structured treatment interrupts (STIs) that were explored. Clinical studies show that there is a serious risk of constant HAART therapy leading to drug resistant HIV strains emerging. These then dominate the viral strand population resulting in *acceleration* of the onset of AIDS. It is thought that STI, in which constant prolonged therapy is avoided, can *harness* this to the patient's advantage. When the virus population is no longer subject to selection pressure from the drugs (i.e during a therapy-free period), the population reverts to non-resistant forms.

To broadly illustrate the issues, and modeling this for illustration via a binary string, where '1' means 8 weeks of treatment and '0' means 8 weeks without treatment, the following shows a possible 48-week treatment plan: '110000'; We will assume that treatment starts at week 300 following initial infection. In this simple plan, which is actually the standard HAART therapy plan (repeated each 48 weeks following consultation and review), there is 16 weeks' treatment followed by 32 weeks off treatment. The alternative 48-week plan '110110' potentially provides a dangerous level of treatment from the viewpoint of developing resistance, while a plan such as '000101' perhaps starts dangerously late. Of particular interest is the effect of such patterns over a much longer period, and the potential use of treatments without a repeating pattern, but structured to interact with the dynamics of the infection in such a way as to indefinitely delay the onset of AIDS.

We do not explicitly model the effect whereby resistant strains increase during treatment (and reduce in treatment-free periods), but we incorporate a bias against overly prolonged stretches of treatment by enforcing a limit on 'treatment-weeks' in each experiment. The problem we address is therefore to find optimised structured treatment interrupt (STI) plans under a maximal treatment-week constraint.

Encodings and Operators: In expt. 1, an initial exploratory test, we evolved 10-bit binary chromosomes for 20 iterations (evaluations), where a '0' stood for 8 weeks treatment, and a '1' stood for 16 weeks off treatment. These were subject to a maximum of 6 stretches of treatment. Mutation was binary flip of a randomly chosen gene.

In expt. 2, we used 20-bit binary chromosomes, where '0' stood for 16 weeks of treatment and '1' stood for 16 weeks without treatment, constrained to have precisely 6 1s. (hence searching a space of STI plans each spanning 6 years and involving precisely 96 weeks' treatment, which represents a clearly safe 'density' of HAART therapy). The 16 weeks on and 16 weeks off stretches correspond with practice in some clinical trials [23] In this case, mutation was a single swap of a randomly chosen '1' with a randomly chosen '0'. This experiment also ran for only 20 iterations.

The third experiment was designed after prolonged consideration of data from recent STI clinical trials. In short, the essential notion behind STI is that the off-treatment periods 'jump start' the immune system to take active control over the virus. However this revived defence can only last for short periods of time, hence a recent leaning in trials towards 8 weeks 'off' periods [24]. Meanwhile, this and other summaries and reviews indicate that a 16-week or longer period on treatment may be relatively safe; after 2 years on continuous HAART treatment, 10% of patients develop resistance (in which the HAART drugs no longer have any effect), and this increases to 20% after 4 years and 30% after 6 years of continuous treatment. For the third experiment, we therefore evolved chromosomes of length 20 where a '1' represented 16 weeks of treatment, and a 0 represented 8 weeks off treatment. The number of 1s was maintained at 12, using the swap operator, and contiguous periods on treatment were limited to 80 weeks (5 1s). In this case we ran for 50 iterations.

In all cases, the chromosome's treatment plan is implemented from week 301 onwards, matching clinical practice in terms of the level of viral load at that point.

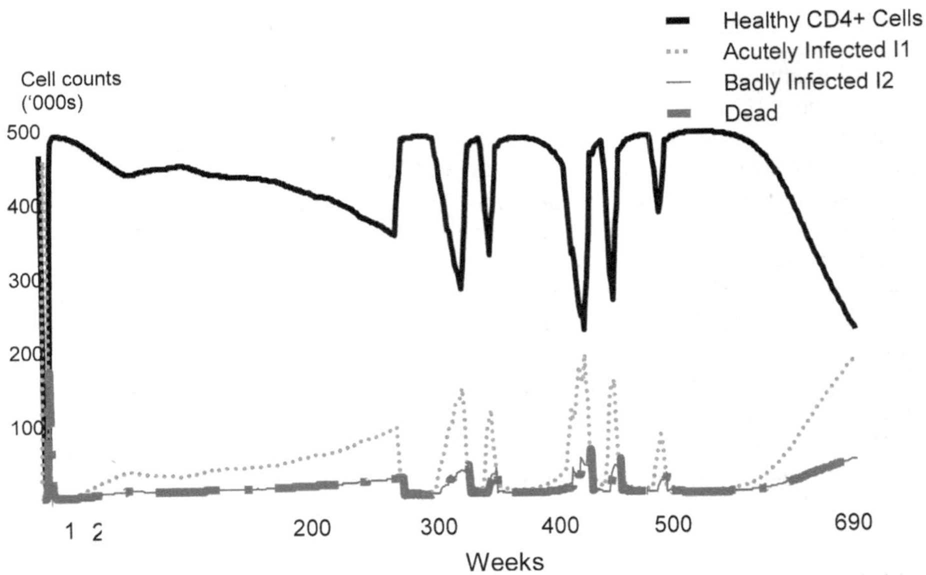

Fig. 2. Effects of an optimal STI treatment from expt. 3. Infected cell counts do not start to approach the set point until > week 690 (though came close around week 430).

Results: Expt 1 results confirmed to us that optimization was feasible in this space, as we found that a short EA run could find the optimum discovered (later) by an exhaustive search. We do not report further on this expt, and turn now to cases where exhaustive search was infeasible. In experiment 2, the best solution had a fitness of 578, and encoded the following STI plan:

000000001111000000000000111100111100000

We omit the plot for space reasons, but report dynamics in which the treatment seems to exploit the dynamics that occur when infected and healthy-cell counts are close, resulting in a series of healthy periods interspersed with near-onset periods.

Finally, in experiment 3, all solutions in the final population had fitness 690 (indicating no onset of the set point throughout the simulation). We could not therefore 'ignore' such cases as with experiment 1. Given that each of these solutions was from a random initial configuration, in a model of robust size, and involving slightly different chromosomes (treatment plans); meanwhile, the initial population in this case tended to have fitnesses around 550, owing to the enforced high density of treatment, so overall we consider this result to be robust. An example optimal solution is as follows, with the treatment shown in figure 3.

1111110001111111110001101111011

5 Concluding Discussion

In this preliminary investigation we have found support for the possibility of evolving STI plans that exploit the dynamics of infection and treatment as simulated in a model. The work reported so far has many limitations, but each has been or is being addressed in ongoing work. We have not yet evolved treatment plans that we are sure are robust (as would be evidenced, e.g., by several simulations per evaluation); although 700 by 700 grids tend to be produce repeatable results in the HIV model, the parameter sensitivity of this particular model is known [12, 13], and we do not really know the sensitivity yet of the *combined* HIV/HAART model as a function of grid size. Longer runs would also be desirable, of individual simulations, but in particular of the EA, to provide greater opportunity to find interesting and high-quality results.

Perhaps the most material limitation is the validity of the HIV/HAART model itself. The Dos Santos and Coutinho HIV infection model [11] is unique in providing a good qualitative agreement with real-data on cell counts, but has been criticised for its robustness [12, 13]. The qualitative agreement, arising from simple and apparently biologically plausible rules, is a considerable achievement, and the lack of robustness to parameters is not in itself a denial of the model's validity (real disease dynamics is not necessarily 'robust' in this sense), but this is associated with questions about the way that the biological observation has been translated into rule probabilities and other attributes, E.g., in the model, an infected cell always dies after 5 weeks, rather than different cells varying in their survival time around a mean.

However, we do not claim any great degree of validity for this model (and are developing others which seem more robust in related work [13]), but stress the promise of the overall approach, which consists of wrapping a complex disease/treatment dynamics model within an optimisation framework to yield high-quality suggested treatment plans for further consideration, and thus potentially narrowing down on novel strategies that may otherwise never have gone on to the stage of clinical trials. In ongoing work we are repeating and extending these experiments for longer runs, and including multiple simulations per run, and also plan working with encodings finer-grained stretches of treatment. On the modeling side, we are also considering the use of more robust HIV/treatment models that may arise from an approach investigated in [13]. We also plan to investigate this general approach for other diseases and associated treatments, especially where a robust model exists that reflects all the relevant dynamics with good qualitative accuracy, *and* (unlike the situation with HIV) allows us to computationally quickly simulate or calculate a treatment plan.

Acknowledgements. We thank Jonathan Owen for his preliminary research work involving the Dos Santos and Coutinho model, we thank Martin Oates for useful discussions about the model, and we thank Ron Yang for partial supervision of the first author.

References

[1] Laurie Garrett (1995) *New View of How HIV* Works, http://ww2.aegis.org/news/ newsday/ 1995/

[2] The national institute of infectious diseases fact sheet http://www.albany.edu/AIDS/ howhiv. html

[3] Kevin Robert Frost, Amfar AIDS research- http://www.amfar.org/cgi-bin/iowa/bridge. html
[4] Hethcote, H.W. (1992) Modeling HIV Transmission and AIDS in the United States, Springer-Verlag.
[5] Medic Eric S. Daar, M.D and Jay W. Marks, M.D. (2004) Human Immunodeficiency Virus (HIV Management), http://www.medicinenet.com/human_immunodeficiency_virus_hiv_aids/ article.htm
[6] Sloot, P., Chen, F., Boucher, C. (2002) Cellular Automata Model of Drug Therapy for HIV Infection, in *Proc. 5th Int'l Conf. on Cellular Automata for Research and Industry*, Springer LNCS 2493: 282—293.
[7] Kirschner, D. (1996) Using Mathematics to Understand HIV Immune Dynamics, http://www.cnd.mcgill.ca/courses_mackey/pdf%20files/kirschner.pdf
[8] Perelson, A.S. and Nelson, P.W. (1999) Mathematical analysis of HIV-1 dynamics in vivo, *SIAM Review*, **41**(1): 3—44.
[9] Wodarz, D. and Nowak, M.A. (2002) Mathematical models of HIV parthogenesis and treatment, *Bioessays*, **24**(12): 1178—1187.
[10] Kamp, C. and Bornholdt, S. (2002) From HIV infection to AIDS: a dynamically induced percolation transition?, *Proc. Royal Society B: Biological Sciences*, **269**(1504): 235—2040.
[11] dos Santos, R., Coutinho, S. (2001) Dynamics of HIV Infection: A Cellular Automata Approach, *Phys. Rev. Lett.*, **87**(16): 168102-1, 4pp.
[12] Strain, M.C. and Levine, H. (2002) Comment on "Dynamics of HIV infection: a cellular automata approach", *Phys. Rev. Lett.*, **89**(21): 219805.
[13] Corne, D., Frisco, P. (2006) Dynamics of HIV Infection studied with cellular automata and conformon-P systems, *Biosystems*, submitted.
[14] Knowles, J.D., Corne, D.W., Bishop, M. (1998) Evolutionary Training of Artificial Neural Networks for Radiotherapy Treatment of Cancers. In *Proc. 1998 International Conference on Evolutionary Computation (ICEC'98)*, pp. 398-403.
[15] Tan, K.C., Khor, E.F., Cai, J., Heng C.M., and Lee, T.H. (2002) Automating the drug scheduling of cancer chemotherapy via evolutionary computation, *Artificial Intelligence in Medicine* **25**(2):169--185.
[16] Schreibmann, E., Lahanas, M., Xing, L. and Baltas, M. (2004) Multiobjective evolutionary optimization of the number of beams, their orientations and weights for intensity-modulated radiation therapy, *Phys. Med. Biol.* **49** 747-770.
[17] Liang, Y., Leung, K.S. and Mok, T.S.K. (2006) A Novel Evolutionary Drug Scheduling Model in Cancer Chemotherapy, *IEEE Transactions on Information Technology in Bio-Medicine*, **10**(2):237-245.
[18] Fogel, L.J., A.J. Owens, and M.J. Walsh (1966) *Artificial Intelligence Through Simulated Evolution*, John Wiley, New York.
[19] Holland, J. (1975) *Adaptation in Natural and Artificial Systems*, U. of Michigan Press, Ann Arbor, MI.
[20] Schwefel, H.-P. (1981) *Numerical Optimization of Computer Models*, John Wiley, Chichester, U.K.
[21] Goldberg. D. (1989) *Genetic algorithms in search, optimization and machine learning*, Addison-Wesley.
[22] Pantaleo, G., Graziozi, G. Fauci, A.S. (1993) *New England J. Medicine*, **328**(327).
[23] Coffey, S. (2003) Structured Treatment Interruption (STI) HIV InSite's Coverage of the 10th Conf. on Retroviruses and Opportunistic Infections, *HIV InSite*, http://hivinsite.ucsf.edu/InSite?page=cf10croi-04
[24] Franco Lori*, Andrea Foli and Julianna Lisziewicz (2002) Structured treatment interruptions as a potential alternative therapeutic regimen for HIV-infected patients: a review of recent clinical data and future prospects, *Journal of Antimicrobial Chemotherapy* **50**, 155-162.

Automatic Test Pattern Generation with BOA

Tiziana Gravagnoli, Fabrizio Ferrandi, Pier Luca Lanzi, and Donatella Sciuto

Dipartimenti di Elettronica e Informazione
Politecnico di Milano, Milano, Italy
{ferrandi, lanzi, sciuto}@elet.polimi.it

Abstract. We introduce a Bayesian Optimization algorithm (BOA) for the automatic generation of test sequences (ATPG) for digital circuit. We compare our approach, named BOATPG, to the two most known evolutionary approaches to ATPG (GATTO and STRATEGATE) and the currently most promising non-evolutionary approach to ATPG (namely, SPECTRAL ATPG). We show that our simple approach can easily outperform GATTO and performs as good as a more complex evolutionary approach like STRATEGATE. We also show that when BOATPG is coupled with spectral approach for seeding the population of initial test sequences, the resulting hybrid system, SBOATPG, performs better than the plain BOATPG although the improvements over SPECTRAL ATPG are limited.

1 Introduction

Modern integrated circuits are complex devices manufactured through complicated fabrication processes. At any stage of the production process physical defects can occur which impair the resulting devices. Accordingly, circuit testing is one of the most expensive and most crucial steps of circuit production. It is performed by applying several signals to the circuit inputs and verifying whether the circuit works correctly. The area of test pattern generation deals with the problem of finding all those input signals, those *test patterns*, which allow the detection of all the possible faults in a given circuit. The tools for automatic test pattern generation (ATPG) fall into two main categories: (i) *deterministic* approaches [1] build test sequences by analyzing the structure of the circuit; (ii) *simulation based* approaches analyze the effects of the application of the test sequences to the circuit (gate and flip-flop values, and total amount of faults detected) and they modify the test sequences in order to detect more faults. Some simulation based test generators, such as GATTO [4] and STRATEGATE [8], exploit genetic algorithms to drive the search of test sequences. Other simulation based methods take a radically different viewpoint. For instance, Spectral ATPG [5] views the circuit as a black-box system, and builds test sequences as a set of waveforms (*spectra*) by filtering unwanted noise from them.

In this paper, we introduce a simulation based approach to ATPG based on Bayesian optimization algorithms (BOA) [12]. Our approach is an extension of Jiri Ocenasek's AMBOA [11] for ATPG problems in which the simulation part

T.P. Runarsson et al. (Eds.): PPSN IX, LNCS 4193, pp. 423–432, 2006.

is performed using the HOPE fault simulator [9]. We compare our approach, BOATPG, against (i) STRATEGATE [8], a state-of-the-art ATPG tool, (ii) GATTO [4], a pure evolutionary approach to ATPG, and (iii) Spectral ATPG [5], one of the most promising techniques in this area. We also introduce a hybrid approach which couples BOATPG and Spectral ATPG [5], named SBOATPG, which first applies Spectral ATPG to seed the initial population of BOATPG. Experimental results for the three approaches demonstrate the effectiveness and robustness of BOATPG compared to state-of-the-art test generators.

The paper is organized as follows. In Section 2 we briefly overview Automatic Test Pattern Generation and the evolutionary techniques that have been introduced in the literature to tackle these types of applications. In Section 3 we describe the version of BOA we applied to ATPG and compare its performance of the three state-of-the-art heuristic techniques for ATPG taken from the literature. In Section 4 we compare our version of BOA for ATPG, BOATPG, to the two major evolutionary approaches for ATPG (GATTO and STRATEGATE) and to SPECTRAL. Finally, in Section 6, we draw some conclusions and delineate future research directions.

2 Automatic Test Pattern Generation

Automatic Test Pattern Generation (ATPG) [1] is the process of generating a set of test vectors for a circuit that are capable of inducing different behaviors in good and in faulty circuits. Test vectors can be applied only to the circuit primary inputs (the input pins) and faults can be observed only on the circuit primary outputs (the output pins). The quality of a test sequence is measured by the *fault coverage*, i.e., the percentage of faults detected by the sequence over all possible faults. The application cost of a test sequence is measured by the number of test vectors that must be applied to the circuit primary inputs to obtain a given fault coverage. The computation time required to the application of the test sequence grows with the number of test vectors. Accordingly, ATPG algorithms aim at generating short test sequences (i.e., consisting of few test vectors) with a high fault coverage (i.e., capable of detecting a high percentage of faults). There are two types of ATPG algorithms: deterministic ones and simulation based ones.

Deterministic Test Generators. This class of ATPG algorithms build test sequences by analyzing the circuit structure. Deterministic test generators involve two steps [1]: *fault activation* and *fault propagation*. Fault activation of a line l with respect to a binary value v consists of the application of input signals to the primary inputs of the circuit capable of inducing on l the complement value of v. Fault propagation consists of applying the input signals to the primary inputs of the circuit capable of inducing on one or more primary output the complement of the value obtained in the fault-free circuit. The intersection of the test vector for fault activation and the test vector for fault propagation leads to the test vector for the fault on line l. Algorithms of this class include the D algorithm [15], the "9 value" algorithm [3], and HITEC [10]–the state-of-the-art deterministic test generator for sequential circuits. Deterministic test generators require long computation time to generate a test sequence, mainly due to the justification phase.

Simulation Based Test Generators do not take into account the circuit structure, instead candidate test sequences are *fault simulated*; as a result the fault simulation returns the values of the flip-flops and the primary outputs due to the application of the test sequence, along with the number of faults detected by the sequence. The candidate test sequences are then modified according to the results of the simulation. The whole process stops when some criterion is met. GATTO [4] is a simulation-based test generator which uses a genetic algorithm to produce fault-detecting sequences. In GATTO [4], an individual is a test sequence of variable length that represents a series of input vectors that must be applied to the circuit. One strong assumption in GATTO [4] (not present in other approaches) is that the circuit starts from its reset state and therefore it can be applied to circuits which include an input reset signal. To each individual, to each sequence, an *evaluation function* is associated which measures how close the sequence is to the detection of a fault based on two heuristics: (i) the weighted number of gates with different values in the good and faulty circuits, and on (ii) the weighted number of flip-flops with different values in the good and in the faulty circuits. STRATEGATE [8] is one of the state-of-the-art algorithms for ATPG. It is based on (i) finding the states of the circuit (i.e., all the flip-flop values) capable of activating target faults, and on (ii) finding the test sequences capable of driving the circuit from one state to another (they are called state-transfer sequences). STRATEGATE use genetic algorithms both to derive and manipulate dynamic state-transfer sequences and in the overall test generation process. SPECTRAL ATPG [5] views the circuit as a black-box system that has to be identified from its input-output signals. The testing of sequential systems is mapped into the problem of constructing a set of waveforms which, when applied at the primary inputs of the circuit, can excite and propagate targeted faults in the circuit. The input waveforms have specific *spectral* characteristics. To capture such spectral characteristics for a given signal, a clean representation of the signal is desired: wider spectra lead to more unpredictable/random signals. Accordingly, any embedded noise should be filtered. Static test set compaction [14,7] reduces the size of the test set by removing any unnecessary vectors while retaining the useful ones. In other words, static compaction filters unwanted noise from the derived test sequence, leaving a cleaner signal (narrower spectrum) to analyze. The spectral information obtained offers a way to predict intelligent vectors based on the vectors generated so far, see [14,7,6,5] for details.

Table 1 reports (a) the descriptions of the circuits from ISCAS89 [2] family, a typical testbed for ATPG algorithms, and (b) the performance of the three approaches (STRATEGATE [8], GATTO [4], and SPECTRAL [5]) on the ISCAS89 circuits. In Table 1a, **Name** identifies the circuit, **PI** and **PO** are the number of primary inputs and primary outputs, **FF** is the number of flip-flops, **Gates** is the number of gates in the circuit, **Depth** is the sequential depth of

Table 1. Performance of STRATEGATE, SPECTRAL ATPG, and GATTO on the circuits of the ISCAS89 family

Circuit	PI	PO	FF	Gates	Depth	Faults
s298	3	6	14	119	9	308
s344	9	11	15	160	20	342
s382	3	6	21	158	9	399
s444	3	6	21	181	11	474
s526	3	6	21	193	9	555
s641	35	24	19	379	74	446
s713	35	23	19	393	74	560
s820	18	19	5	289	10	816
s832	18	19	5	287	10	836
s1196	14	14	18	529	24	1214
s1238	14	14	18	508	22	1327
s1423	17	5	74	657	59	1515
s1488	8	19	6	653	17	1470
s1494	8	19	6	647	17	1490
s5378	35	49	179	2779	25	4601

(a)

Circuit			STRATEGATE		SPECTRAL		GATTO	
Name	Level	Faults	Cov	Vec	Cov	Vec	Cov	Vec
s298	9	308	86,04	194	-	-	88,64	189
s344	20	324	96,20	86	-	-	98,46	241
s382	9	399	91,23	1486	91,23	567	70,43	559
s386	11	384	-	-	-	-	81,51	423
s444	11	474	89,45	1945	-	-	61,18	409
s510	12	564	-	-	-	-	99,82	626
s526	9	555	81,80	2642	-	-	81,08	1618
s641	74	465	86,51	166	-	-	87,10	598
s713	74	581	81,93	176	81,93	89	82,62	820
s820	10	850	95,76	590	-	-	56,82	2012
s832	10	869	94,02	701	-	-	53,51	471
s953	16	1079	-	-	-	-	98,98	1284
s1196	24	1242	99,76	574	99,76	244	98,79	2509
s1238	22	1355	94,61	625	94,69	255	94,10	4205
s1423	59	1515	93,33	3943	93,47	927	90,50	2388
s1488	17	1486	97,17	593	97,17	384	97,11	1549
s1494	17	1506	96,48	540	96,48	388	94,29	1662
s5378	25	4603	79,06	11481	79,14	734	73,91	1586
s9234	58	6927	-	-	-	-	5,85	198
s13207	59	9815	-	-	-	-	20,15	147
s35932	29	39094	89,78	257	-	-	89,36	1121
s38417	47	31180	-	-	-	-	17,90	839

(b)

the circuit in terms of flip-flops, **Faults** is the number of faults that can be injected in the circuit. In Table 1b, column **Name** identifies the circuit and for each algorithm considered, **Cov** is the percentage of fault coverage (our performance) that the algorithm can identify using **Vec** test vectors. Note that the data in Table 1 are taken from the literature [8,4,5] thus some values are missing (those corresponding to a "-" symbol) because not available. As the table shows, GATTO performs better than STRATEGATE in some circuits (s298, s344, s641, s713), but worse in others (s382, s444, s820, s832). SPECTRAL can reach maximum fault coverages for all the circuits, with a limited number of test vectors. In several cases, SPECTRAL outperforms STRATEGATE, which is the state-of-the-art in the area of ATPG. Thus Spectral ATPG is currently considered very promising.

3 BOA for Automatic Test Pattern Generation

BOA for Automatic Test Pattern Generation, BOATPG, has been implemented as an extension of Jiri Ocenasek's AMBOA code [11] and basically works as the most typical BOA. Individuals are bitstrings of fixed length representing candidate test sequences. The population is randomly initialized. At each generation, half the population is selected and model building is performed using decision graphs [13]. The decision graphs obtained are then used to generate offsprings, which replace half of the original population. Then the Bayesian network is destroyed and the process starts again. The fitness takes into account the number of faults detected by the test sequence and two heuristic parameters, flip-flop observability and gate observability, which estimate the easiness of propagating a flip-flop or gate value to a primary output. These heuristics are the same used in GATTO [4] and they have been implemented from the code of GATTO that is publically available. Note however, that the fitness in BOATPG combines these heuristics in a different way with respect to what done in GATTO. In BOATPG, a test sequence has a high fitness if (i) it detects more faults and (ii) it propagates the effects of not yet detected faults to crucial elements (such as flip-flops) so as to improve the probability of its future detection. A detailed description of the fitness function is available in [6]. To compute fitness we integrated the HOPE [9] fault simulator into BOATPG to fault simulate test sequences; we also modified the code of HOPE to allow the computation of flip-flop observability and gate observability that our fitness function requires.

In addition, BOATPG includes a test sequence extension mechanism that we designed for ATPG application. In BOATPG, test sequences are of fixed length as needed by the Bayesian networks building. However, when the fitness of individuals does not improve for a certain number of generations, the best sequence in the population is appended to the final test set, and a new set of fixed length sequences is optimized. Thus, in BOATPG each individual represents T test vectors, i.e., $T \times P_I$ bits, where P_I is the number of primary inputs of the circuit. If the best value of the fitness function remains unchanged for S_g generations, a new population is generated by appending to the best individual generated so fare other T test vectors. When M_g generations passed without an improvement in the fitness function, the program terminates. The parameter T represents the size of the step that the system is willing to undertake for exploring longer sequences. To keep the approach simple, T is fixed from the beginning and it is set to the initial number of test sequences in the initial individuals.

4 Experiments with BOATPG

We compared BOATPG with (i) the two most popular ATPG methods based on genetic algorithms (GATTO [2] and STRATEGATE [8]) and one of the most promising non evolutionary approaches to ATPG, SPECTRAL ATPG [5]. We conducted two sets of experiments. In the first set of experiments, we applied BOATPG to typical testbeds using very small populations containing at most 100 individuals. The parameters S_g and M_g have been set to 50 and 250 generations respectively, to ensure adequate exploration of the space of solutions before extending test sequences, and to guarantee an adequate number of sequence extensions before termination. For each problem, we performed ten trials, i.e., we run BOATPG ten times with different seeds. The second set of experiments has been performed on the most hard-to-test circuits. In this case, we have used populations of 1000 individuals. The parameters S_g and M_g have been increased to 100 and 500 respectively, to increase the exploration of the solution space.

4.1 Comparison with GATTO

The fitness of BOATPG is based on the same heuristics used in GATTO [4]. this comparison can be actually viewed as a comparison between a probabilistic

Table 2. BOATPG compared to GATTO. The best fault coverage is showed in bold.

Circuit	GATTO		BOATPG			
	Cov	Vec	Cov	$\overline{\text{Cov}}$	Vec	$\overline{\text{Vec}}$
s298	**88.64**	189	**88.64**	88.64± 0.00	100	100.00± 0.00
s344	98.46	241	**98.54**	98.54±0.00	50	50.00±0.00
s382	70.43	559	**91.73**	86.19± 3.08	500	420.00±78.88
s444	61.18	409	**89.66**	74.77±10.04	300	245.00±36.89
s526	81.08	1618	**81.80**	75.59±7.42	770	623.00±61.29
s641	87.10	598	**87.37**	87.37±0.00	52	40.30±4.11
s713	**82.62**	820	**82.62**	82.62±0.00	48	40.80±6.20
s820	56.82	2012	**95.29**	91.18±3.46	400	306.00±80.58
s832	53.51	471	**93.68**	90.84±2.23	510	397.80±78.60
s1196	98.79	2509	**99.76**	99.76±0.00	480	384.00±65.86
s1238	94.10	4205	**94.69**	94.69±0.00	462	353.10±56.20
s1423	90.50	2388	**96.77**	95.25±0.85	468	385.20±53.80
s1488	97.11	1549	**97.31**	97.29±0.03	540	459.00±78.80
s1494	94.29	1662	**96.61**	96.54 ±0.08	420	331.80± 57.55
s5378	73.91	1586	**80.01**	78.61±0.64	576	340.20±100.56

model building approach and a plain genetic algorithm in the context of ATPG applications. One strong assumption made in GATTO [4] is that the target circuit has a reset signal that can be used to initialize all the flip-flop values to zero. This means that in GATTO [4] test sequences are applied starting from a known state since the circuit have been initially resetted. For this reason, in this first comparison we have applied the same initialization scheme with BOATPG.

Table 2 compares the performance of GATTO as reported in [4] and the performance of BOATPG. While in [4], the performance is simply measured as the highest covering obtained (column Cov in Table 2) and the corresponding number of test vectors (column Vec Table 2), for BOATPG we report the best evolved solution and the corresponding vector size (columns **Cov** and **Vec**) but also the average covering obtained in the ten runs (column $\overline{\text{Cov}}$) and the average test vector size (column $\overline{\text{Vec}}$).

As can be noted, BOATPG outperforms GATTO on all the circuits. The difference in the performances is more evident especially on some hard-to-test circuits, such as s382, s444, s820, s832 and s1423. In those circuits in which the fault coverages of GATTO and BOATPG are the same (such as s298 and s713), BOATPG evolves solutions which require fewer test vectors, i.e., when BOATPG does not improve the coverage produced by GATTO, it can still produce better (more compact) solutions. A comparison of the execution time between GATTO and BOATPG is infeasible. The statistics for GATTO reported in [4] were performed on a different systems and from the publicly available code of GATTO we were not able to duplicate the results in [4] mainly because the fault simulator used in [4] was not available to us. Nevertheless, we can certainly state that GATTO should be generally much faster than BOATPG due to the major model building phase required by the latter. On the other hand, in this type of application execution time might not be a relevant issue since the designers are generally willing to invest more computation time to obtain better sequences.

4.2 Comparison with STRATEGATE and SPECTRAL ATPG

As discussed in the previous section, GATTO [4] assumes that flip-flops can be initialized using a reset input signal so that the initial state of the circuit is determined. This assumption simplifies the generation of test sequences but it is generally infeasible. since most circuits do not provide such possibility. Accordingly, most ATPG methods, like STRATEGATE and SPECTRAL ATPG, do not make this assumption. To compare BOATPG against STRATEGATE and SPECTRAL ATPG, BOATPG is applied without flip-flop initialization, thus the performances for BOATPG reported in this section are different from those reported in Table 2.

Table 3 compares the performances of (i) STRATEGATE, as reported in [8], (ii) SPECTRAL ATPG, as reported in [5], and (iii) BOATPG. For each circuit and for each algorithm, Table 3 reports the best coverage reached (column `Cov`) and the corresponding number of test vectors found (column `Vec`); for BOATPG also the averages are reported (columns $\overline{\texttt{Col}}$ and $\overline{\texttt{Vec}}$). For some circuits the results of multiple BOATPG experiments are reported. All the experiments have been performed using very small populations of 100 individuals, the rows in Table 3 preceded by an asterisk to experiments with populations of 1000 individuals.

In many circuits, more precisely in 8 out of 17 circuits considered, BOATPG performs as well as STRATEGATE and/or SPECTRAL ATPG while producing generally shorter and thus better test sequences than STRATEGATE. In almost every circuit, the difference between the best and the average performance of BOATPG is small, which suggests that the approach is rather robust. Note that for the other approaches [4,8] such statistics is not available. It is worth noting that in big circuits (e.g. s5378) and hard-to-test circuits (e.g., s820 and s832) the coverage obtained by BOATPG is just a little lower than that obtained by the state-of-the-art STRATEGATE and SPECTRAL. In large problems, the test sequences obtained by SPECTRAL ATPG are much shorter than those evolved by BOATPG. This result was expected and it is basically due to the static test set compaction algorithms used with SPECTRAL ATPG [5]. However, BOATPG test sequences are more compact than the ones obtained by STRATEGATE, the state-of-the-art of evolutionary based ATPG. In s382, s444, s526 and s1423, the performance of BOATPG is lower than that of STRATEGATE and SPECTRAL. Experiments with increased population size results in little improvements. On the other hand, such low performances are probably due to a difficult initialization phase of these circuits. In fact, when the presence of a reset signal is assumed, BOATPG results for the same circuits are much higher (see Table 2). This suggests that our fitness function may be not adequate to guide the search of circuit initialization sequences, while it is effective to guide the search of fault detecting sequences. Accordingly, we coupled BOATPG with SPECTRAL that we used to seed the initial populations.

Also in this case, a comparison of the computation time required by the three methods considered here is infeasible. A rough analysis of the data in [8], in [5], and our execution of BOATPG (see [6] for details on BOATPG execution times)

Table 3. BOATPG compared to STRATEGATE and SPECTRAL

Circuit	STRATEGATE		SPECTRAL		BOATPG			
	Cov	Vec	Cov	Vec	Cov	$\overline{\text{Cov}}$	Vec	$\overline{\text{Vec}}$
s298	**86.04**	194	-	-	**86.04**	**86.04±0.00**	120	116.00± 12.65
s344	**96.20**	86	-	-	**96.20**	**96.20**±0.00	80	52.00±19.32
s382	**91.23**	1486	**91.23**	567	87.22	74.56±10.89	350	189.00±104.61
s444	**89.45**	1945	-	-	87.13	75.76±8.72	360	198.00±98.18
* s444	**89.45**	1945	-	-	80.80	80.53±0.48	400	320.00±42.16
* s526	**81.80**	2642	-	-	79.64	72.00±4.12	880	704.00±140.10
s526	**81.80**	2642	-	-	79.64	72.18±2.63	900	700.00±94.28
s641	**86.51**	166	-	-	**86.51**	86.51±0.00	54	54.00±0.00
s713	**81.93**	176	**81.93**	89	**81.93**	81.93±0.00	50	43.00±4.83
s820	**95.76**	590	-	-	95.18	93.44±1.43	544	418.20±60.08
s832	**94.02**	701	-	-	93.56	91.07±1.32	425	310.00±57.97
s1196	**99.76**	574	**99.76**	244	**99.76**	99.74±0.03	425	310.00±54.26
s1238	94.61	625	**94.69**	255	**94.69**	94.65±0.07	400	325.00±54.01
s1423	93.33	3943	**93.47**	927	92.08	91.52±0.47	550	390.00±79.23
s1488	**97.17**	593	**97.17**	384	**97.17**	97.11±0.09	400	335.00± 33.75
s1494	**96.48**	540	**96.48**	388	**96.48**	96.47±0.03	400	360.00± 31.62
s5378	79.06	11481	**79.14**	734	78.99	77.67±0.00	552.00	420.00±222.35

shows that SPECTRAL ATPG is an order of magnitude faster than STRATEGATE and BOATPG. Again, this was expected: STRATEGATE employs two genetic algorithms, BOATPG performs complex probabilistic model building, while SPECTRAL ATPG performs simple operations like matrix multiplications. Nonetheless, BOATPG execution times seem to be comparable to those of STRATEGATE, which is the state-of-the-art in the field.

5 Coupling BOA with Spectral

The results discussed in the previous section suggest that the fitness definition in BOATPG may be not adequate to guide the search of circuit initialization sequences. Accordingly, we coupled coupled SPECTRAL ATPG and BOATPG: SPECTRAL ATPG is used to generate candidate test sequences which are then used to seed the population of BOATPG. This hybrid approach, named SBOATPG, first applies SPECTRAL ATPG to extract candidate test sequences that are then used to seed BOATPG populations and to supply interesting test sequences to feed the extension mechanism. To implement these extensions, we reimplemented SPECTRAL ATPG following the description in [5]. Unfortunately, although we carefully followed the description in [5], we were not able to fully duplicate the original results but it generally performs slightly worse than what presented in [5].

Table 4 compares BOATPG, the original SPECTRAL ATPG, and SBOATPG on the subset of the ISCAS89 testbed for which the performance of SPECTRAL ATPG was available. As can be noted, SBOATPG performs better than the plain BOATPG in all the circuits in which BOATPG reaches lower fault coverages (such as s832 and s526). However, the improvement in fault detection obtained by evolutionary phase of SBOATPG is limited with respect to the fault coverages achieved by SPECTRAL alone. This suggests that the coupling

Table 4. SBOATPG compared to BOATPG. The best fault coverage is showed in bold.

Circuit	BOATPG				SPECTRAL				SBOATPG			
	Cov	$\overline{\text{Cov}}$	Vec	$\overline{\text{Cov}}$	Cov	$\overline{\text{Cov}}$	Vec	$\overline{\text{Cov}}$	Cov	$\overline{\text{Cov}}$	Vec	$\overline{\text{Cov}}$
s382	87.22	74.56	350	189.00	**89.47**	50.03	511	174.30	**89.47**	89.47	800	640.00
s382	87.22	74.56	350	189.00	89.47	31.55	607	83.37	**90.48**	89.37	1000	760.00
s444	87.13	75.76	360	198.00	84.60	18.61	265	39.20	**87.76**	87.34	800	640.00
s820	95.18	93.44	544	418.20	95.41	74.09	680	334.80	**95.65**	95.53	680	503.20
s832	93.56	91.07	425	310.00	93.91	81.74	1138	515.40	**94.02**	93.95	850	646.00
s1196	**99.76**	99.74	425	310.00	99.52	98.95	247	230.20	**99.76**	99.71	514	514.00
s1196	**99.76**	99.74	425	310.00	99.67	97.39	247	223.14	**99.76**	99.76	602	516.24

of spectral and Bayesian approaches may not provide interesting improvements while being computationally expensive. On the other hand, we note that spectral approach have high variances in both in the coverage and in the length of the test sequences (in fact the difference between the average performance and the best performance is usually large). In contrast, BOA based approaches seems more robust in that the difference between best and average performances is very small. Finally, the improvements obtained by BOATPG over the other evolutionary approaches and the additional improvements obtained by SBOATPG seem to suggest that BOA approaches may provide an interesting direction for ATPG application.

6 Conclusions

We have presented a Bayesian Optimization algorithm for ATPG, named BOATPG, and compared its performance with the two mostly known evolutionary approach to ATPG and with SPECTRAL ATPG, a very promising non evolutionary approach to ATPG. The initial results we discussed show that our simple approach can easily outperform GATTO and performs as good as a more complex evolutionary approach like STRATEGATE. When BOATPG is coupled with an effective strategy to seed the population, the performance increases, although the improvements with respect to plain SPECTRAL ATPG appear to be limited. This work, which we consider rather preliminary, opens future research directions. Among the others, the fitness function should be improved to better deal with hard-to-initialize circuits. In addition, much larger populations and other model building schemes should be tested to improve the model building phase.

References

1. M. Abramovici, M. A. Breuer, and A. D. Friedman. *Digital systems testing and testable design*. Computer Science Press, 1990.
2. F. Brglez, Bryant D., and K. Kozminski. Combinational profiles of sequential benchmark circuits. *Proc. International Symposium on Circuits Systems*, pages 1929–1934, 1989.

3. C. W. Cha, W. E. Donath, and F. Ozguner. 9-v algorithm for test pattern generation of combinational digital circuits. *IEEE Transactions on Electronic Computers*, C-27(3):193–200, March 1978.
4. Fulvio Corno, Paolo Prinetto, Maurizio Rebaudengo, and Matteo Soriza Reorda. Gatto: A genetic algorithm for automatic test pattern generation for large synchronous sequential sircuits. *IEEE Trans. on Computer-Aided Design of Integrated Circuits and Systems*, 15(8):991–1000, August 1996.
5. Ashish Giani, Shuo Sheng, Michael S. Hsiao, and Vishwani Agrawal. Efficient spectral techniques for sequential atpg. *Proc. IEEE Design Automation and Test in Europe Conf.*, pages 204–208, March 2001.
6. Tiziana Gravagnoli. Test generation based on probabilistic model building genetic algorithms and spectral analysis. Master's thesis, April 2006. Master thesis supervisor: Prof. Pier Luca Lanzi.
7. Ruifeng Guo, Irith Pomeranz, and Sudhakar M. Reddy. Procedures for static compaction of test sequences for synchronous sequential circuits based on vector restoration. *Proc. Design Automation and Test in Europe*, pages 583–587, 1998.
8. Michael S. Hsiao, Elizabeth M. Rudnick, and Janak H. Patel. Sequential circuit test generation using dynamic state traversal. *Proc. European Design and Test Conference*, pages 22–28, March 1996.
9. H. K. Lee and D. S. Ha. Hope: An efficient parallel fault simulator for synchronous sequential circuits. *Proc. 29th Design Automation Conf.*, pages 336–340, June 1992.
10. T. Niermann and J. H. Patel. Hitec: A test generator package for sequential circuits. *Proc. European Design Automation Conf.*, pages 214–218, 1991.
11. Jiri Ocenasek, Stefan Kern, Nikolaus Hansen, and Petros Koumoutsakos. A mixed bayesian optimization algorithm with variance adaptation. In Xin Yao, Edmund K. Burke, José Antonio Lozano, Jim Smith, Juan J. Merelo Guervós, John A. Bullinaria, Jonathan E. Rowe, Peter Tiño, Ata Kabán, and Hans-Paul Schwefel, editors, *PPSN*, volume 3242 of *Lecture Notes in Computer Science*, pages 352–361. Springer, 2004.
12. Martin Pelikan. *Hierarchical Bayesian Optimization Algorithm.* Springer Verlag, Berlin, 2005.
13. Martin Pelikan, David E. Goldberg, and Kumara Sastry. Bayesian optimization algorithm, decision graphs, and occam's razor. *Proceedings of the Genetic and Evolutionary Computation Conference*, pages 519–526, 2001. Also IlliGAL Report No. 2000020.
14. Irith Pomeranz and Sudhakar M. Reddy. Vector restoration based static compaction of test sequences for synchronous sequential circuits. *Proc. Int. Conf. Computer Design*, pages 360–365, 1997.
15. J. P. Roth. Diagnosis of automata failures: a calculus and a method. *IBM Journal of Research and Development*, 10(4):278–291, July 1996.

Multiobjective Genetic Programming for Natural Language Parsing and Tagging*

L. Araujo

Dpto. Sistemas Informáticos y Programación.
Universidad Complutense de Madrid. Spain
lurdes@sip.ucm.es

Abstract. Parsing and Tagging are very important tasks in Natural Language Processing. Parsing amounts to searching the correct combination of grammatical rules among those compatible with a given sentence. Tagging amounts to labeling each word in a sentence with its lexical category and, because many words belong to more than one lexical class, it turns out to be a disambiguation task. Because parsing and tagging are related tasks, its simultaneous resolution can improve the results of both of them. This work aims developing a multiobjective genetic program to perform simultaneously statistical parsing and tagging. It combines the statistical data about grammar rules and about tag sequences to guide the search of the best structure. Results show that any of the implemented multiobjective optimization models improve on the results obtained in the resolution of each problem separately.

1 Introduction

Parsing and tagging are very important tasks in Natural Language Processing. They are usually a prior step to carry on many natural language processing processes such as machine translation, information retrieval, speech recognition, etc. Parsing amounts to searching the correct combination of grammatical rules among those compatible with a given sentence. Tagging amounts to labeling each word in a sentence with its lexical category (noun, verb, etc), disambiguating those words which belong to more than one lexical class. Languages are ambiguous and many words belong to more than one lexical class. Thus, disambiguation methods are required to proceed with tagging. The research in automatic part-of-speech tagging [1] and parsing [2] has increased a lot in the past few years, probably due to the increasing availability of large annotated corpora.

Often, tagging is a prior step to parsing. Grammatical ambiguity is highly reduced if lexical ambiguity has been eliminated. In fact, Dalrymple [5] has shown that if a perfect tagger were available, we could obtain a reduction in ambiguity of about 50%.

On the other hand, a perfect disambiguation of a lexical tagging requires taking into account at least the parsing, but sometimes also discourse analysis

* Supported by project TIC2003-09481-C04.

T.P. Runarsson et al. (Eds.): PPSN IX, LNCS 4193, pp. 433–442, 2006.

and world knowledge. Thus, the simultaneous resolution of tagging and parsing can improve on the results of both of them.

This work aims at developing an evolutionary multiobjective optimization algorithm to perform simultaneously statistical parsing and tagging. It combines the statistical data about grammar rules and about sequences of lexical tags to guide the search of the best structure. The work relies on previous works which apply separately genetic programming to perform parsing [2] and an evolutionary algorithm for solving tagging [1]. Because, even separately the results provided by these evolutionary systems are comparable or even better than those obtained with algorithms of exhaustive search, it is expected than the multiobjective genetic program can improve on the results for both problems.

Parsing is essentially a Multi-Objective Optimization process: a search for the most probable combination of grammar rules as well as for the most probable combination of lexical categories for the words of the sentence. An evolutionary multiobjective algorithm for this problem can take advantage of several evolutionary multiobjective models which have appeared in the literature [6,4]. Some of the simplest ones, usually known as aggregative functions, amounts to combining the different objectives into a single function or linear fitness combination, *i.e.*, to adding all the objective functions together using different weighting coefficients for each of them, thus transforming the problem into a scalar optimization one. Some alternative approaches are based on the concept of Pareto optimum[1]. Solutions included in the Pareto optimal set are called nondominated. The approaches considered herein have been an aggregative function, and some Pareto-optimum approaches: MOGA (Multi-Objective Genetic Algorithm, in which the rank of an individual corresponds to the number of individuals in the population by which it is dominated) [8], NSGA (Non-dominated Sorting Genetic Algorithm, which considers several layers of classification of individuals) [11], and NSGA-II (which improves NSGA with elitism and a crowded comparison operator to keeps diversity without additional parameters) [7].

The rest of the paper proceeds as follows: Section 2 and 3 are respectively devoted to state the two problems considered: parsing and tagging, presenting the main elements of a genetic program to solve parsing and the objective function for tagging; Section 4 presents and discusses the experimental results, and Section 5 draws the main conclusions of this work.

2 Evolutionary Statistical Parsing

To implement our evolutionary multiobjective algorithm for parsing and tagging we have started from the genetic program for parsing, which produces the parse tree for a sentence, which in its turn determines the tagging of the sentence. The fitness function combines the probabilistic evaluation of the parse tree with

[1] A solution $\mathbf{x} \in \mathcal{X}$ is a Pareto optimum (minimum) if there is no better solution $\mathbf{y} \in \mathcal{X}$ for some objective: $\nexists y \in \mathcal{X}$ such that
$f_i(y) \leq f_i(x)(\forall i = 1, \cdots, k)$ and
$f_j(y) < f_j(x)$ for some j.

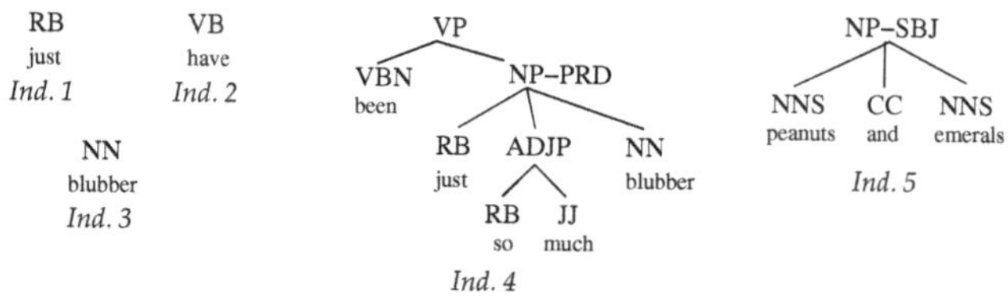

Fig. 1. Examples of individuals for the sentence *To her peanuts and emeralds would have been just so much blubber.* RB stands for adverb, VB for verb (base form), NN for noun (singular or mass), VBN for verb (past participle), NNS for noun (plural), CC for coordinating conjunction, ADJP for adjective phrase, NP-PRD for predicate noun phrase, VP for verb phrase, and NP-SBJ for subject noun phrase.

the context based evaluation of the tagging. This combination is performed in different ways for the different models considered here.

A bottom-up parser starts with the sequence of lexical classes of the words and its basic operation is to take a sequence of symbols that match the right-hand side of the grammar rules. Stochastic grammars [3,2], whose rules are assigned a probability, allow us evaluating the possible parses of a sentence, and thus solving ambiguity by selecting the most probable one. The stochastic grammar can be extracted from a linguistic corpus syntactically annotated (treebanks).

We have developed a probabilistic bottom-up parser based on genetic programming which works with a population of partial parses, *i.e.*, parses of sentence segments.

2.1 Chromosome Representation

Individuals in our system are parses of segments of the sentence, that is, they are trees obtained by applying the probabilistic context free grammar to a sequence of words of the sentence. Each individual is assigned a syntactic category: the left-hand side of the top-level rule of the parse. The probability of this rule is also registered. Every tree is composed of a number of subtrees, each of them corresponding to the required syntactic category of the right-hand side of the rule. Figure 1 shows some individuals for the sentence *To her peanuts and emeralds would have been just so much blubber*, used as a running example, which has been extracted from the Penn Treebank [9]. We can see that there are individuals composed of a single word, such as *1*, while others, such as *4*, are a parse tree obtained by applying different grammar rules. For the former, the category is the chosen lexical category of the word (a word can belong to more than one lexical class); *e.g.*, the category of *1* is *RB*. For the latter, the category is the left hand-side of the top level rule; *e.g.*, the category of *4* is *VP*.

Initial Population. The first step to parse a sentence is to find the possible lexical tags of each word. They are obtained, along with their frequencies, from

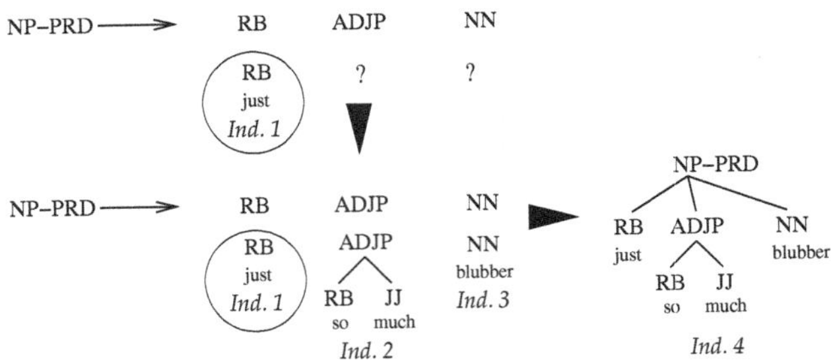

Fig. 2. Example of application of the crossover operator. Individual 1, whose syntactic category is RB, is randomly selected for crossover. The rule NP-PRD → RB ADJP NN is selected among those rules whose right-hand side begins with RB. Finally, the population is searched for individuals corresponding to the remaining syntactic categories of the rule, provided its sequence of words is appropriate to compose a segment of the sentence.

a dictionary. Because parses are built in a bottom-up manner, the initial population is composed of individuals that are leave trees formed only by a lexical category of the word. The system generates a different individual for each lexical category of the word.

2.2 Genetic Operators

Chromosomes in the population of subsequent generations which did not appear in the previous one are created by means of two genetic operators: *crossover* and *cut*. The crossover operator combines a parse with other parses present in the population to satisfy a grammar rule; cut creates a new parse by randomly selecting a subtree from an individual of the population. A classic genetic operator which has not been used in our algorithm is mutation. Because our system only works with correct parses, mutation should substitute a subtree by another subtree in the population which parses exactly the same sequence of words and has the same syntactic symbol that the substituted one. But this effect is obtained by the combination of crossover and cut.

Crossover. The crossover operator produces a new individual by combining an individual selected from the population with an arbitrary number of other ones. Notice that the crossover in this case does not necessarily acts on pairs of individuals. The individuals to be crossed are randomly selected. This selection does not consider the fitness of the individuals because some grammar rules may require, to be completed, individuals of some particular syntactic category for which there are no representatives with higher fitness.

Let us assume that the individual *1* of Figure 1 is selected. The syntactic category (label of the root) of this individual is *RB*. The next step requires selecting among the grammar rules those whose right-hand side begins with this syntactic category, *i.e.*, *RB*. Some examples from the grammar used in this work are (NP-PRD → RB ADJP NN), (ADJP → RP JJ), (ADVP → RB RB), etc. Let us assume that we choose the first of these rules. Now, the crossover operator searches in the population for individuals whose syntactic category matches the remaining categories at the right-hand side of the rule, and whose sequence of words is the continuation of the words of the previous individual (Figure 2). In the example, we look for an individual of category *ADJP* and for another of category *NN*. The sequence of words of the individual of category *ADJP* must begin with the word *so*, the one following the words of individual *1*. Accordingly, the individual *2* of Figure 2 is a possible candidate (likewise, individuals *3* is also chosen for the crossover). This process produces the individual *4* of Figure 2, whose syntactic category is the left-hand side of the rule (NP-PRD), and which is composed of the subtrees selected in the previous steps. This new individual is added to the population. With this scheme, the crossover of one individual may produce no descendant at all, or may produce more than one descendant. In the latter case all descendants are added to the population. The process of selection is in charge of reducing the population down to the specified size.

Crossover increases the mean size of the individuals every generation. Though this is advantageous because at the end we are interested in providing as solution individuals which cover the whole sentence, it may also induce some problems. If the selection process removes small individuals which can only be combined in later generations, the parses of these combinations will never be produced. This situation is prevented by introducing the *cut* operator, as well as by applying some constraints in the selection process, which reduces the size of the population by erasing individuals according to their fitness but always ensuring that each of their words is present in at least another individual. The cut operator produces a new individual out of another one by cutting off a subtree of its parse tree at random. The new individual is added to the population.

2.3 Objective Function for Parsing

The fitness function is basically a measure of the probability of the parse. It is computed as the average probability of the grammar rules used to construct the parse:

$$f_{par} = \frac{\sum_{s \in T} prob(s)}{nn(T)}$$

where T is the tree to evaluate, s each of its nodes and $nn(T)$ is the number of nodes. For the lexical category, the probability is the relative frequency of the chosen tag.

3 Objective Function for Tagging

A tagging of the considered sentence is a sequence of tags assigned to the words of the sentence. The model for tagging deals with disambiguation by assigning

This	the	therapist	may	pursue	in	later	questioning	.
DT	AT	NN	NNP	VB	RP	RP	VB	.
QL			MD	VBP	NNP	RB	NN	
					RB	JJ	JJ	
					NN	JJR		
					FW			
					IN			

Fig. 3. Tags for the words in a sentence extracted from the Penn corpus. Underlined tags are the correct ones, according to the corpus. Tags correspond to the tag set defined in the Penn corpus: DT stands for determiner/pronoun, AT for article, NN for common noun, MD for modal auxiliary, VB for uninflected verb, IN for preposition, JJR for comparative adjective, etc.

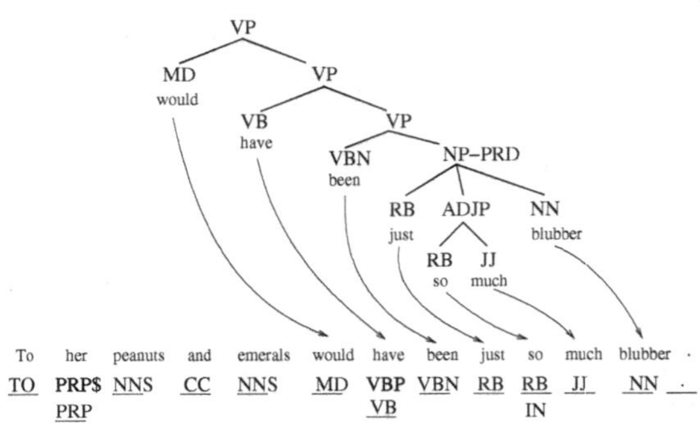

Fig. 4. Example of construction of the tagging of a sentence out the partial parse

different probabilities to a given tag depending on which are the neighbouring tags (*context*) on both sides of the word. Figure 3 shows an example of sentence extracted from the Penn corpus. The word *questioning* can be disambiguated as a common name (NN) if the preceding tag is disambiguated as an adjective (JJR). But it might happen that the preceding word were ambiguous, so there may be many dependencies which must be resolved simultaneously. The computation of the fitness (f_{tag}) of a tagging is based on the list of contexts (*training table*) extracted from a training hand-tagged corpus. This table records the different contexts of each tag, along with its number of occurrences, for every tag in the training text.

The genetic parser works with partial parses of the sentences. Thus the tagging obtained from an individual is a partial tagging of the whole sentence. We complete the tagging by choosing tags for the remaining words, randomly selected among the valid tags for the word (according to the dictionary), proportionally to their probabilities. Figure 4 shows an example. The tags selected to compose the tagging corresponding to the individual appear underlined. The tag PRP for the word *her* is randomly selected among those of the word (PRP$, possessive pronoun, and PRP, personal pronoun), while the tag VB (verb in base form) selected for *been* is given by the parse tree. The f_{tag} of an individual is a measure of the total probability of its sequence of tags, according to the data from the training table. It is computed as the sum of the fitness of its genes, $\sum_i f(g_i)$. The fitness of a gene g is defined as

$$f(g) = \log P(T|LC, RC)$$

where $P(T|LC, RC)$ is the probability that the tag of gene g is T, given that its context is formed by the sequence of tags LC to the left and the sequence RC to the right (the logarithm is taken in order to make fitness additive). This probability is estimated from the training table as

$$P(T|LC, RC) \approx \frac{occ(LC, T, RC)}{\sum_{T' \in \mathcal{T}} occ(LC, T', RC)}$$

where $occ(LC, T, RC)$ is the number of occurrences of the list of tags LC, T, RC in the training table, and $\mathcal{T}$ is the set of all possible tags of g.

4 Experimental Results

Once we have defined the two objective functions, we can apply the different evolutionary multiobjective methods as for any pair of functions. In particular, the application of an aggregative function to the fitness functions computed for parsing and tagging is straightforward. We only have to take into account that both functions should vary within a similar range of values.

Another consideration concerns NSGA, in which the computation of the sharing function for each front requires the computation of the phenotypic distance between two individuals. Because individuals in our system are partial parses, corresponding in general to different segments of the sentence, they can not be directly compared. Accordingly, a phenotypic distance is defined as the number of words which are parsed in one of the individuals but not in the other.

The system, implemented on a PC in C++ language, has been applied to sentences extracted from two linguistic corpora: the Penn Treebank [9] and the Susanne corpus [10], both databases of English sentences manually annotated with syntactic information. The probabilistic grammar for parsing has also been obtained from the corpora. Each grammar rule is assigned a probability computed as its relative frequency with respect to other rules with the same left-hand side.

In order to evaluate the quality of the obtained parses we have used the most common measures for parsing evaluation, defined assuming a bracket representation [2] of the parse tree: *precision*[3] and *recall*[4].

[2] For example, the parse tree for individual *5* of Figure 1 corresponds to the bracket expression NP-SBJ(NNS(peanuts), CC(and), NNS(emeralds)).

[3] Given by the number of brackets in the parse to evaluate matching those of the correct tree.

[4] A coverage measure given by the number of brackets in the correct tree which also appear in the parse.

Table 1. Study (tagging accuracy, precision and recall) of the sharing parameter for MOGA in Penn corpus (PS=450, IT=1500, %X=20, %C=20, TC=5) and in Susanne corpus (PS=200, IT=500, %X=20, %C=10, TC=3)

	Penn corpus			Susanne corpus		
Sharing	Acc. Tag.	Prec.	Recall	Acc. Tag.	Prec.	Recall
10%	99.61	90.50	90.08	99.61	98.04	96.56
20%	99.61	91.72	89.16	99.80	97.83	97.50
30%	99.61	92.40	90.38	99.61	99.74	98.46
40%	96.12	89.54	92.14	99.80	98.81	97.53

From the Susanne corpus, we have used a training text set of 470082 words, and a test text of 520 words (17 sentences). From the Penn Treebank, we have taken a set of training text of 16233 words, using a test text of 269 words (11 sentences).

4.1 Studying the Sharing Parameters

First of all, we have adjusted the parameters of the algorithms considered in this paper. Table 1 shows the results obtained in both corpora for MOGA with different values of the sharing parameter. This is defined as a percentage of the distance between the best and worst values of the objective parsing. We can observe that the best results on both corpora are obtained with a sharing value of 30%.

Table 2 shows the results obtained for NSGA with different values of the sharing parameter. In this case, individuals of a same niche are those of the same level which differ in a number of words below a threshold value. A sharing distance of 3 words provides the best results in this case.

In the case of the aggregative function, we have also studied the use of different weights for the contributions to the fitness of parsing and tagging. Table 3 shows the results obtained in both corpora. In this case, the best results are obtained by assigning the same weight to both objective functions.

A general observation is that the most significant results are obtained with the Penn Treebank. This is due to the large sets of lexical and syntactic tags used in the Susanne corpus, which lead to very specific grammar rules, for which the results are very similar in all cases.

Table 2. Study (tagging accuracy, precision and recall) of the sharing parameter for NSGA in Penn corpus (PS=450, IT=1500, %X=20, %C=20, TC=5) and in Susanne corpus (PS=200, IT=500, %X=20, %C=10, TC=3)

	Penn corpus			Susanne corpus		
Sharing	Acc. Tag.	Prec.	Recall	Acc. Tag.	Prec.	Recall
1	96.51	90.66	91.15	99.61	99.74	98.30
2	96.51	90.66	91.15	99.61	99.74	98.30
3	99.61	91.98	91.34	99.80	99.74	98.46
4	99.61	87.37	87.23	99.61	99.74	98.44

Table 3. Study (tagging accuracy, precision and recall) of the coefficient for the aggregative function in Penn corpus (PS=450, IT=1500, %X=20, %C=20, TC=5) and in Susanne corpus (PS=200, IT=500, %X=20, %C=10, TC=3)

	Penn corpus			Susanne corpus		
Coef.	Acc. Tag.	Prec.	Recall	Acc. Tag.	Prec.	Recall
1/2+1/2	99.61	89.90	87.93	100	98.45	97.79
1/3+2/3	99.61	87.91	89.80	99.80	98.16	97.54
2/3+1/3	100	87.92	87.10	99.61	97.97	97.05

Table 4. Comparison of the results (tagging accuracy, precision, recall and execution time in seconds) obtained performing parsing separately and with different evolutionary multiobjective optimization algorithms. *Chart p.* stands for a classic chart parser algorithm, and *Wout tag.* for parsing without tagging with a genetic programming algorithm. The parameters of the algorithms in Penn corpus are population size (PS)=450, iteration number (IT)=1500, crossover rate(%X)=20, cut rate(%C)=20) and in Susanne corpus (PS=200, IT=500, %X=20, %C=10).

	Penn corpus				Susanne corpus			
Algorithm	Acc. Tag.	Prec.	Recall	Time(s)	Acc. Tag.	Prec.	Recall	Time(s)
Chart p.	99.22	88.66	85.81	15.33	97.30	94.52	96.41	9.25
Wout tag.	96.51	87.88	90.59	20.37	99.61	83.44	81.82	10.93
AF	99.61	89.90	87.93	15.59	100	98.45	97.79	10.13
MOGA	99.61	92.40	90.38	20.93	100	99.74	98.46	14.24
NSGA	99.61	91.98	91.34	34.26	99.80	99.74	98.46	13.33
NSGA-II	100	91.56	90.85	43.91	99.61	99.23	99.23	14.31

4.2 Comparing the Models

In order to compare the evolutionary algorithm with a classic parser, we have implemented a classic *best-first chart parsing* (BFCP) algorithm. Table 4 shows the precision, recall, and tagging accuracy results obtained for each algorithm (figures represent the best result with respect precision out of ten independent runs). MOGA is run with a sharing parameter of 30%, NSGA with a sharing distance of 3 words, and the aggregative function with a linear combination of 0.5 + 0.5. We can observe that the results of any evolutionary algorithm improve on those of a classic chart parser. We can also observe that all methods provide similar results, though it is MOGA which provides the best results in precision (in particular for the Peen Treebank, for which there is larger differences for different methods). This can be due to the fact that this model allows tuning the weight of each objective function more precisely. MOGA distributes the population over the Pareto-optimal region by a niching method based on objective function values. The sharing distance for NSGA is defined as a function of the sentence words, what can be too coarse for tuning the algorithm. Concerning NSGA-II, the differences among the fitness value of each objective function for individuals in the same level (used to evaluate the crowding distance) can be little significant in some cases because individuals may parse different segments of the sentence.

Execution times are similar for the different methods, being NSGA-II the one which requires a larger time.

5 Conclusions

We have tested different evolutionary multiobjective optimization algorithms for two related problems of natural language processing: parsing and tagging. Parsing can be regarded as a multi-objective optimization process in nature, since it amounts to searching the most probable combination of grammar rules as well as the most probable combination of lexical categories for the words of the sentence. The implementation of the tested models (aggregative function, MOGA, NSGA and NSGA-II) has been adapted to our particular problems, defining specific sharing parameters and distances, according to the structure of our individuals.

A relevant result is the improvement achieved by any of the evolutionary multiobjective models with respect to the resolution of each problem separately, regardless of whether a classic exhaustive search method or an evolutionary algorithm is applied to the isolated problems. The comparison of the applied models has also revealed that MOGA performs better than the other methods.

References

1. L. Araujo. Part-of-speech tagging with evolutionary algorithms. In *Proc. of the Int. Conf. on Intelligent Text Processing and Computational Linguistics (CICLing-2002)*, pages 230–239. Springer-Verlag, 2002.
2. L. Araujo. Genetic programming for natural language parsing. In *Proc. of the European Conf. on Genetic Programming (EuroGP2004)*, pages 230–239. Springer-Verlag, 2004.
3. E. Charniak. *Statistical Language Learning.* MIT press, 1993.
4. C. A. Coello Coello, D. A. Van Veldhuizen, and G. B. Lamont. *Evolutionary Algorithms for Solving Multi-Objective Problems.* Kluwer Academic, 2002.
5. M. Dalrymple. How much can tagging help parsing? Technical report, Department of Computer Science, King's College London, 2004.
6. K. Deb and D. Kalyanmoy. *Multi-Objective Optimization Using Evolutionary Algorithms.* John Wiley & Sons, 2001.
7. K. Deb, A. Pratab, S. Agarwal, and T. Meyarivan. A fast and elitist multiobjective genetic algorithm: Nsga-ii. *IEEE transactions on Evolutionary Computations*, 6(2):182–197, 2002.
8. Carlos M. Fonseca and Peter J. Fleming. Genetic algorithms for multiobjective optimization: Formulation, discussion and generalization. In *Genetic Algorithms: Proc. of the Fifth Int. Conf.*, pages 416–423. Morgan Kaufmann, 1993.
9. Mitchell P. Marcus, Beatrice Santorini, and Mary Ann Marcinkiewicz. Building a large annotated corpus of english: The penn treebank. *Computational Linguistics*, 19(2):313–330, 1994.
10. G. Sampson. *English for the Computer.* Clarendon Press, Oxford, 1995.
11. N. Srinivas and Kalyanmoy Deb. Multiobjective optimization using nondominated sorting in genetic algorithms. *Evolutionary Computation*, 2(3):221–248, 1994.

Modelling the Population Distribution in Multi-objective Optimization by Generative Topographic Mapping

Aimin Zhou[1], Qingfu Zhang[1], Yaochu Jin[2], Bernhard Sendhoff[2], and Edward Tsang[1]

[1] Department of Computer Science, University of Essex, Colchester, CO4 3SQ, U.K.
[2] Honda Research Institute Europe, Carl-Legien-Str. 30, 63073, Offenbach, Germany

Abstract. Under mild conditions, the Pareto set of a continuous multi-objective optimization problem exhibits certain regularity. We have recently advocated taking into consideration such regularity in designing multi-objective evolutionary algorithms. Following our previous work on using Local Principal Component Analysis for capturing the regularity, this paper presents a new approach for acquiring and using the regularity of the Pareto set in evolutionary algorithms. The approach is based on the Generative Topographic Mapping and can be regarded as an Estimation of Distribution Algorithm. It builds models of the distribution of promising solutions based on regularity patterns extracted from the previous search, and samples new solutions from the models thus built. The proposed algorithm has been compared with two other state-of-the-art algorithms, NSGA-II and SPEA2 on a set of test problems.

1 Introduction

Multi-objective optimization problems (MOP) arise from many practical applications where several objectives have to be optimized. In this paper, we consider the following continuous MOP:

$$\begin{array}{ll} \text{minimize } F(x) = (f_1(x), f_2(x), \ldots, f_m(x))^T \\ \text{subject to} \qquad\qquad x \in X \end{array} \tag{1}$$

where $X \in R^n$ is the decision (variable) space, $F : X \rightarrow R^m$ consists of m continuous objective functions and R^m is called the objective space. Very often, no point in X minimizes all the objectives simultaneously. The best tradeoffs among these objectives can be defined in terms of Pareto optimality.

Let $u, v \in R^m$, u is said to *dominate* v if and only if $u_i \leq v_i$ for every $i \in \{1, 2, \ldots, m\}$ and $u_j < v_j$ for at least one index $j \in \{1, 2, \ldots, m\}$. A point $x^* \in S$ is *Pareto optimal* to (1) if there is no point x such that $F(x)$ dominates $F(x^*)$. $F(x^*)$ is then called a *Pareto optimal (objective) vector*. The set of all the Pareto optimal points is called the *Pareto set (PS)* and the set of all the Pareto optimal objective vectors is the *Pareto front (PF)*.

A number of evolutionary algorithms (EA) for dealing with multi-objective optimization problems , have been suggested over the past two decades [1,2]. These multi-objective evolutionary algorithms (MOEA) work with a population of candidate solutions and are able to produce a set of Pareto optimal vectors for approximating the PF. Most of these algorithms can be regarded as extensions of EAs for scalar optimization

T.P. Runarsson et al. (Eds.): PPSN IX, LNCS 4193, pp. 443–452, 2006.

problems. Selection, crossover and mutation are major operators in EAs. Conventional crossover and mutation operators can be used without any modification in MOEAs (although these operators may not lead to satisfactory performances in MOEAs), while the selection operators in scalar optimization EAs cannot be directly applied to MOPs. A major research issue in the area of MOEAs is the so-called fitness assignment [3], which assigns a relative fitness to each individual in a population for facilitating selection.

Estimation Distribution Algorithms (EDA) are a new class of EAs [4,5,6]. There is no traditional crossover or mutation in EDAs. Instead they explicitly extract global statistical information from the previous search and build a posterior probability distribution model of promising solutions, based on the extracted information. New trial solutions are sampled from the model thus built. Several EDAs for continuous MOPs have been proposed, among them are Mixture-based Iterated Density Estimation Evolutionary Algorithms (MIEDA) [7], EDAs based on Bayesian networks [8] and Voronoi-based Estimation of Distribution Algorithm (VEDA) [9].

Under mild conditions, the PS (or PF) of a continuous MOP is a piecewise continuous $(m-1)$ dimensional manifold where m is the number of the objectives. This property has been used in several mathematical programming methods for approximating the PF [10]. In fact, it has also been found that, for the most widely-used test problems of continuous multi-objective optimization in the evolutionary computations, their PS are $(m-1)$ dimensional linear or piecewise linear manifolds [11,12]. This regularity has been ignored in most current MOEAs.

Recently, we suggested that such regularity should be used in MOEAs for improving the algorithms' performances. We have proposed three EDAs [13,14,15] which employ Local Principal Component Analysis algorithms [16] for capturing and modeling the regularity of the Pareto set in a continuous MOP. The experimental results are very encouraging, the algorithms outperform NSGA-II [17] and SPEA2 [3] on several test problems with high interactions among the decision variables. Bueche et al [18] also attempted to use self-organizing mapping to learn the shape of the Pareto set of a MOP, although they have not explicitly discussed their method in the context of the regularity.

The Generative Topographic Mapping (GTM) [19] is a tool for extracting regularity from data. This paper continues our work on improving MOEAs by utilizing the regularity. We propose to use GTM in EDAs for extracting the regularity of the PS of (1). GTM can provide a probability model of promising solutions in terms of latent variables. Such a model is very easy for sampling new trial solutions.

The remainder of this paper is organized as follows: Section 2 gives a brief introduction to GTM. Section 3 presents the details of the model building and sampling techniques. The framework of the proposed algorithm is given in Section 4. Section 5 compares our proposed algorithm with NSGA-II and SPEA2 on a set of test problems. The final section provides concluding remarks.

2 The Generative Topographic Mapping

GTM can discover some underlying regularity of a set of unlabeled data in a high dimensional space. It considers a nonlinear transformation mapping from a latent-variable space with lower dimensionality L to the data space:

$$x = y(v, W) = W\phi(v)$$

where x is a point in the data space, v is the latent variable. W is a parameter matrix and $\phi(v)$ is a vector of prefixed basis functions.

GTM models the distribution of data x, for given value of W and v, to be a radially-symmetric Gaussian centered on $y(v, W)$ with variance β^{-1}:

$$p(x|v, W, \beta) = (\frac{\beta}{2\pi})^{-n/2}\exp\{-\frac{\beta}{2}\|W\phi(v) - x\|^2\}$$

Therefore, $x = W\phi(v)$ can be envisaged as a central L-D manifold of the data, as illustrated in Fig. 1.

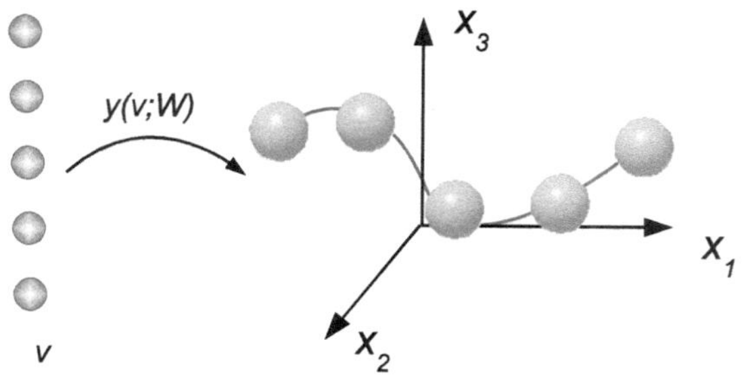

Fig. 1. Generative Topographic Mapping from 1-D latent space (left) to data space (right)

Given a number of points $x^1, x^2, \ldots, x^N$ in the data space, GTM estimates the values of W and β by maximizing the following log likelihood:

$$L(W, \beta) = \ln \prod_{i=1}^{N} \int p(x^i|v, W, \beta)p(v)dv.$$

where $p(v)$ is the distribution of v. In our experiments, we use the GTM code developed by NCRG group at Aston University[1]. The details of GTM can be found in [19].

3 Model Building Based on GTM

3.1 Basic Idea

The population in a MOEA for (1) will hopefully approximate to the PS and be uniformly distributed around the PS as the search goes on. Therefore, we can envisage the solutions in the population as independent observations of a random vector whose center is an approximation of the PS of (1). Since the PS is a piecewise continuous $(m-1)$

[1] The source codes are from http://www.ncrg.aston.ac.uk/GTM

dimensional manifold, a promising solution x can be regarded as an observation of the following n-D random vector:

$$\xi = \xi_1 + \xi_2 \qquad (2)$$

where ξ_1 is uniformly distributed along a $(m-1)$ dimensional manifold Φ. ξ_2 is a random noise vector. Φ is called the central manifold of ξ in this paper. For simplicity, we assume that ξ_1 and ξ_2 are independent of each other.

Under the above assumption, the modeling of promising solutions consists of two tasks: the modeling of the central manifold Φ and noise ξ_2.

3.2 Modeling and Sampling

Given a population, which is a data set in R^n, we apply the GTM with $(m-1)$ latent variables to it (where m is the number of objectives) and obtain the values of W and β. In GTM training procedure, we set the range of the latent variable $v = (v_1, \ldots, v_{m-1})$ as:

$$-1 \leq v_i \leq 1 \;\; i = 1, 2, \ldots, m-1.$$

Since the population often can not cover the whole PS thus the central manifold found can only approximate part of the PS. To overcome this problem and explore more ranges, in [13] , [14] and [15], the search range is extended along the center manifold when we do sampling. In this paper, this idea is implemented by extending the range of the latent variables by 20%.

Sampling a new point x from the model built by the GTM is quite straightforward. We can do it in the following way:

Step 1: Uniformly and randomly select a v from $[-1.1, 1.1]^{m-1}$. Set $x^1 = y(v, W)$.
Step 2: Sample x^2 from $N(0, \frac{1}{\beta}I)$.
Step 3: Set $x = x^1 + x^2$.

where m is the objective number, I is a $n \times n$ identity matrix and n is the variable dimension.

4 Algorithm Framework

Our proposed modeling and sampling approach can be adopted as operators for producing new solutions in most current MOEAs. In this paper, we use the following algorithm framework:

Step 0 Initialization: Randomly generate a population P of N solutions, N is the population size.
Step 1 Reproduction:
  Step 1.1 Modeling: Build a probability model based on statistical information extracted from P;
  Step 1.2 Sampling: Sample N new solutions from the model and store them in Q.

Step 2 Selection: Select N solutions from $P \cup Q$. Let these selected solutions to replace all the solutions in P.

Step 3 Stopping Condition: If the stopping condition is met, stop; otherwise, go to **Step 1**.

In our implementation, we use the selection scheme of NSGA-II in Step 2. We call our algorithm the model-based evolutionary algorithm with GTM (MEA/GTM).

5 Experimental Results

We use five test problems shown in Table 1 in our simulation studies.

Table 1. Test problems

MOP	n	Constraints	Objectives
$FON2$ [1]	30	$x \in [-2, 2]^n$	$f_1(x) = 1 - \exp(-\sum_{i=1}^{n}(x_i - \frac{1}{\sqrt{n}})^2)$ $f_2(x) = 1 - \exp(-\sum_{i=1}^{n}(x_i + \frac{1}{\sqrt{n}})^2)$
$OKA4$ [20]	2	$x \in [0, 8]^n$	$f_1(x) = 2 - \frac{1}{4}(x_1 - x_2 + 4)$ $+\frac{1}{4}\sqrt{-x_1^2 - x_2^2 - 16 + 2x_1x_2 + 8x_1 + 8x_2}$ $f_2(x) = \frac{1}{4}(x_1 - x_2 + 4)$ $+\frac{1}{4}\sqrt{-x_1^2 - x_2^2 - 16 + 2x_1x_2 + 8x_1 + 8x_2}$ $x_1 - 4\sqrt{x_1} - x_2 + 4 \leq 0$ $x_1 + 4\sqrt{x_1} - x_2 + 4 \geq 0$
$ZDT1.2$ [13]	30	$x \in [0, 1]^n$	$f_1(x) = x_1$ $f_2(x) = g(x) \times (1.0 - \sqrt{\frac{f_1(x)}{g(x)}})$ $g(x) = 1.0 + \frac{9}{n-1}\Sigma_{i=2}^{n}(x_i^2 - x_1)^2$
$ZDT2.2$ [13]	30	$x \in [0, 1]^n$	$f_1(x) = \sqrt{x_1}$ $f_2(x) = g(x) \times (1.0 - (\frac{f_1(x)}{g(x)})^2)$ $g(x) = 1.0 + \frac{9}{n-1}\Sigma_{i=2}^{n}(x_i^2 - x_1)^2$
$DTLZ2.2$	10	$x \in [0, 1]^n$	$f_1(x) = \cos(\frac{\pi}{2}x_1)\cos(\frac{\pi}{2}x_2)(1 + g(x))$ $f_2(x) = \cos(\frac{\pi}{2}x_1)\sin(\frac{\pi}{2}x_2)(1 + g(x))$ $f_3(x) = \sin(\frac{\pi}{2}x_1)(1 + g(x))$ $g(x) = \sum_{i=3}^{n}(x_i^2 - x_1)^2$

$ZDT1.2$, $ZDT2.2$ and $DTLZ2.2$[2] are a respective modified version of $ZDT1$ [1], $ZDT2$ [1] and $DTLZ2$ [21]. In their original versions, the Pareto set is parallel to a coordinate axis which makes the problems easy to tackle.

We compared the performances of MEA/GTM, NSGA-II[3] and SPEA2[4] on the test problems in Table 1. The parameter setting of these algorithms are as follows: The

[2] ZDT 1.2, ZDT 2.2 and DTLZ2.2 are provided by Hui Li.

[3] The source codes are from http://www.iitk.ac.in/kangal/codes.shtml

[4] The source codes are from http://www.tik.ee.ethz.ch/pisa

population size for all the algorithms is set to 100 for 2-objective test instances and 200 for the 3-objective test instances. To have a fair comparison, the other parameters in NSGA-II and SPEA2 are set as in the default setting in their source codes. In GTM, the number of training steps is 15, the latent points number is 1×25 for 2-objective test instances and 5×5 in case of 3 objective, the basis function number is 2 for 2-objective problems and 2×2 in case of 3-objective and other parameters take their default values in their source codes. All the algorithms stops after 200 generations. We run each algorithm for each test instances 20 times.

To measure the performances of the algorithms, we use Υ [17] metric to measure the convergence of a population to the PF, and Δ [17] metric to measure the diversity of a population.

Υ [17] metric is defined as:

$$\Upsilon(S, S^*) = \frac{1}{|S|} \sum_{x \in S} d(x, S^*), \tag{3}$$

where

$$d(x, S^*) = \min_{y \in S^*} ||F(x) - F(y)||^2.$$

S is an obtained non-dominated set by an algorithm, S^* is a set which is uniformly distributed in Pareto Front.

Δ [17][5] metric is defined as:

$$\Delta(S, S^*) = \frac{\sum_{i=1}^{m} d(e_i, S) + \sum_{x \in S} |d(x, S) - \bar{d}|}{\sum_{i=1}^{m} d(e_i, S) + |S|\bar{d}}, \tag{4}$$

where $\{e_1, \ldots, e_m\}$ are m extreme solutions in S^* and

$$d(x, S) = \min_{y \in S, y \neq x} ||F(x) - F(y)||^2,$$

$$\bar{d} = \frac{1}{|S|} \sum_{y \in S} d(y, S).$$

It should be noticed that $d(x, S)$ measures the distance between point x and its nearest neighbor which is different from the original definition.

Table 2 gives the means and standard derivations of Υ and Δ on 20 runs at different stages, generation 40, 80, 120, 160 and 200, of the algorithms for each problem. Fig.2 shows the distributions of nondominated solutions generated in 20 runs in the objective space for each algorithm for each problem.

From the values of Δ in Table 2 it is clear that MEA/GTM outperforms NSGA-II and SPEA2 in terms of the diversity of the nondominated solutions found. Fig.2 also supports this claim. For all five test problems, MEA/GTM can cover the whole Pareto Fronts, while NSGA-II can only cover the Pareto Fronts of OKA4 and DTLZ2.2 and

[5] We notice this metric is only fit in the case of small m.

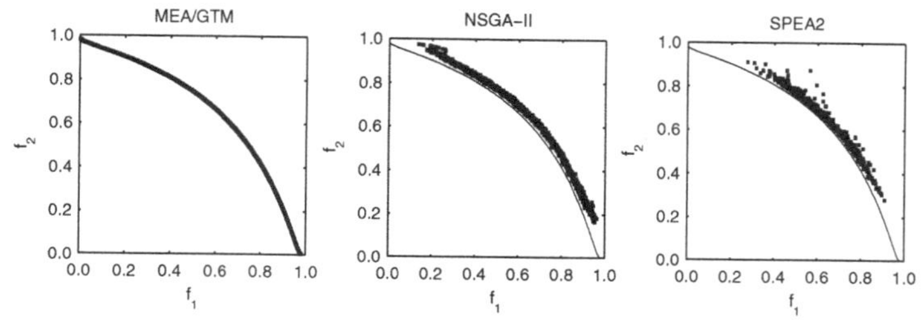

(a) FON2

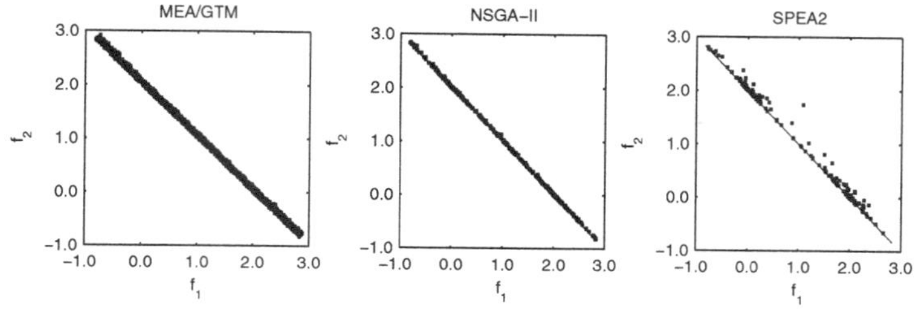

(b) OKA4

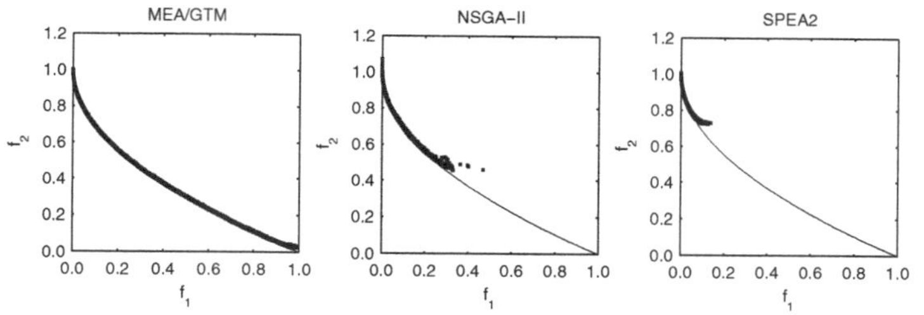

(c) ZDT1.2

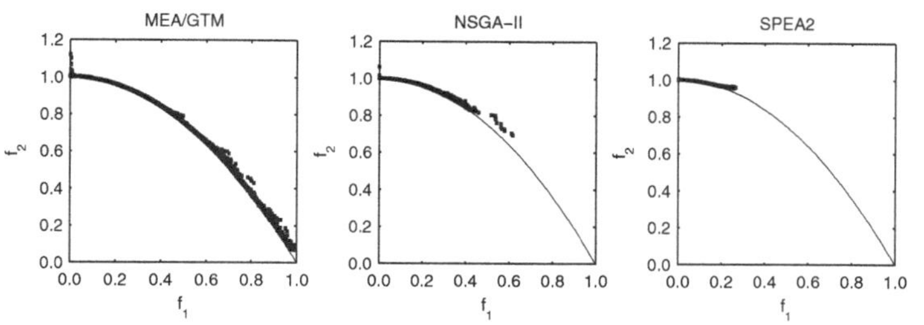

(d) ZDT2.2

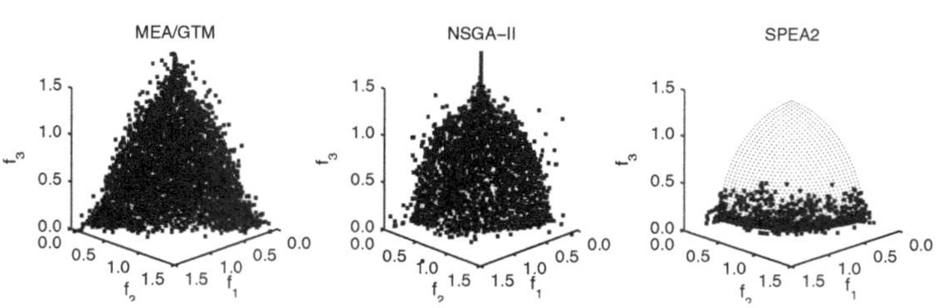

(e) DTLZ2.2

Fig. 2. Pareto fronts produced by MEA/GTM, NSGA-II and SPEA2

Table 2. Experimental results

Gen	MEA/GTM		NSGA-II		SPEA2	
	Υ	Δ	Υ	Δ	Υ	Δ
FON2						
40	0.022 ± 0.002	**0.500**± 0.071	0.215± 0.027	0.849± 0.049	**0.184**± 0.025	0.769± 0.118
80	**0.002**± 0.000	**0.160**± 0.019	0.075± 0.007	0.748± 0.037	0.061± 0.009	0.726± 0.079
120	**0.002**± 0.000	**0.154**± 0.016	0.049± 0.003	0.690± 0.038	0.037± 0.005	0.750± 0.075
160	**0.002**± 0.000	**0.151**± 0.017	0.036± 0.003	0.629± 0.051	0.029± 0.003	0.786± 0.069
200	**0.002**± 0.000	**0.156**± 0.018	0.029± 0.002	0.514± 0.040	0.023± 0.003	0.798± 0.053
OKA4						
40	0.086± 0.008	**0.483**± 0.069	**0.035**± 0.005	0.706± 0.110	0.038± 0.012	0.730± 0.263
80	0.065± 0.005	**0.485**± 0.055	**0.020**± 0.003	0.821± 0.104	0.025± 0.010	0.757± 0.286
120	0.055± 0.005	**0.468**± 0.044	**0.016**± 0.003	0.873± 0.108	0.018± 0.005	0.815± 0.274
160	0.049± 0.004	**0.449**± 0.048	**0.014**± 0.003	0.878± 0.125	0.015± 0.006	0.899± 0.322
200	0.045± 0.003	**0.399**± 0.057	**0.012**± 0.002	0.841± 0.149	0.017± 0.011	0.811± 0.318
ZDT1.2						
40	0.013± 0.002	**0.806**± 0.053	0.024± 0.005	0.890± 0.043	**0.012**± 0.003	0.915± 0.025
80	0.008± 0.001	**0.425**± 0.085	0.011± 0.002	0.814± 0.022	**0.005**± 0.000	0.928± 0.013
120	0.006± 0.001	**0.273**± 0.042	0.009± 0.001	0.792± 0.020	**0.005**± 0.001	0.917± 0.010
160	**0.004**± 0.000	**0.225**± 0.023	0.008± 0.001	0.783± 0.028	0.005± 0.000	0.921± 0.013
200	**0.004**± 0.000	**0.206**± 0.018	0.007± 0.001	0.775± 0.019	0.005± 0.001	0.915± 0.013
ZDT2.2						
40	0.047± 0.021	0.937± 0.112	0.024± 0.010	**0.933**± 0.017	**0.019**± 0.007	0.968± 0.038
80	0.013± 0.006	**0.765**± 0.168	0.009± 0.004	0.947± 0.018	**0.004**± 0.001	0.965± 0.012
120	0.009± 0.003	**0.551**± 0.242	0.006± 0.002	0.915± 0.030	**0.003**± 0.000	0.981± 0.016
160	0.007± 0.002	**0.412**± 0.213	0.005± 0.003	0.870± 0.020	**0.002**± 0.000	0.982± 0.014
200	0.006± 0.001	**0.329**± 0.207	0.005± 0.003	0.870± 0.031	**0.002**± 0.000	0.984± 0.012
DTLZ2.2						
40	0.156± 0.031	**0.491**± 0.056	0.145± 0.036	0.647± 0.074	**0.144**± 0.113	0.950± 0.260
80	**0.113**± 0.024	**0.473**± 0.075	0.218± 0.292	0.602± 0.077	0.643± 0.393	0.798± 0.215
120	**0.099**± 0.021	**0.448**± 0.068	0.462± 0.640	0.576± 0.057	0.603± 0.384	0.832± 0.222
160	**0.092**± 0.019	**0.433**± 0.067	0.829± 0.725	0.563± 0.083	0.675± 0.506	0.814± 0.227
200	**0.081**± 0.012	**0.427**± 0.066	1.121± 0.499	0.532± 0.035	0.717± 0.441	0.875± 0.240

SPEA2 can not cover any of the Pareto Fronts. The reason may be: (1) MEA/GTM can cover the whole Pareto Fronts by extension and (2) MEA/GTM uniformly samples new solutions from the model.

In terms of Υ metric, MEA/GTM performances much better than NSGA-II and SPEA2 on FON2 and DTLZ2.2. Υ values in MEA/GTM is slightly higher than in SPEA2 on ZDT1.2 and ZDT2.2, it does not imply that MEA/GTM is worse. Since NSGA-II and SPEA2, as shown in Fig.2, cannot cover the whole Pareto Front as MEA/GTM does. Only on OKA4, MEA/GTM performs worse than NSGA-II and SPEA2. From Fig.2, however, EA/GTM can also approximate the Pareto Front very well.

These algorithms have been run in a desktop computer (Pentium(R) 4 3.40GHz CPU, 1.00GB of RAM). The average run time (in seconds) are listed in Table 3. Although

Table 3. Average run time(in seconds)

Method	FON2	OKA4	ZDT1.2	ZDT2.2	DTLZ2.2
NSGA-II	0.323	0.172	0.323	0.327	1.106
SPEA2	1.611	1.662	1.669	1.565	7.207
MEA/GTM	15.206	3.634	10.727	12.354	15.972

MEA/GTM needs more time to optimize each test problem than NSGA-II and SPEA2, it is still affordable especially when the fitness evaluation is much time consuming.

6 Conclusions

Incorporating problem-specific knowledge into evolutionary algorithms is a basic strategy for enhancing their performances [22]. The Pareto set of a continuous MOP is usually a piecewise continuous $(m-1)$-D manifold. Most current MOEAs ignore this regularity. Our recent work has showed that such regularity could be beneficial for modeling the population distribution in estimation of distribution algorithms for continuous multi-objective optimization. This paper demonstrated that GTM can be used for capturing and modeling the regularity and proposed an estimation of distribution algorithms with GTM for multi-objective optimization. The preliminary experiments show that our proposed method outperforms NSGA-II and SPEA2.

Our previous work in [13], [14] and [15] and this paper are on the design of EDAs by making the use of the regularity property. In the future, we plan to study how to incorporate such regularity and other properties of MOPs into other evolutionary algorithms.

References

1. Kalyanmoy Deb. *Multi-Objective Optimization using Evolutionary Algorithms.* John Wiley & Sons, LTD, Baffins Lane, Chichester, 2001.
2. Ashish Ghosh and Satchidananda Dehuri. Evolutionary algorithms for multi-criterion optimization: A survey. *International Journal of Computing & Information Sciences*, 2(1):38–57, 2004.
3. Eckart Zitzler, Marco Laumanns, and Stefan Bleuler. A tutorial on evolutionary multiobjective optimization. In *Workshop on Multiple Objective Metaheuristics (MOMH 2002)*, volume 535 of *Lecture Notes in Economics and Mathematical Systems*, pages 3–37, Berlin, Germany, 2004. Springer-Verlag.
4. Pedro Larrañaga and Jose A Lozano, editors. *Estimation of distribution algorithms : a new tool for evolutionary computation.* Kluwer Academic Publishers, Norwell, MA, USA, 2001.
5. Qingfu Zhang. On stability of fixed points of limit models of univariate marginal distribution algorithm and factorized distribution algorithm. *IEEE Transactions on Evolutionary Computation*, 8(1):80–93, 2004.
6. Qingfu Zhang and Heinz Mühlenbein. On the convergence of a class of estimation of distribution algorithms. *IEEE Transactions on Evolutionary Computation*, 8(2):127–136, 2004.
7. Peter A N Bosman and Dirk Thierens. The naive MIDEA: A baseline multi-objective EA. In *Third International Conference on Evolutionary Multi-Criterion Optimization(EMO 2005)*, volume 3410 of *Lecture Notes in Computer Science*, pages 428–442, Guanajuato, Mexico, 2005. Springer.
8. Kumara Sastry, Martin Pelikan, and David E Goldberg. Decomposable problems, niching, and scalability of multiobjective estimation of distribution algorithms. IlliGAL Report 2005004, Illinois Genetic Algorithms Laboratory, 2005.
9. Tatsuya Okabe, Yaochu Jin, Bernhard Sendhoff, and Markus Olhofer. Voronoi-based estimation of distribution algorithm for multi-objective optimization. In *Proceedings of the Congress on Evolutionary Computation (CEC 2004)*, pages 1594–1601, Portland, Oregon, USA, June 2004. IEEE Press.

10. Oliver Schütze, Sanaz Mostaghim, Michael Dellnitz, and Jürgen Teich. Covering Pareto sets by multilevel evolutionary subdivision techniques. In *Second International Conference on Evolutionary Multi-Criterion Optimization (EMO 2003)*, volume 2632 of *Lecture Notes in Computer Science*, pages 118–132, Faro, Portugal, April 2003. Springer.
11. Yaochu Jin and Bernhard Sendhoff. Connectedness, regularity and the success of local search in evolutionary multi-objective optimization. In *Proceedings of the Congress on Evolutionary Computation (CEC 2003)*, pages 1910–1917, Canberra, Australia, December 2003. IEEE Press.
12. Tatsuya Okabe, Yaochu Jin, Markus Olhofer, and Bernhard Sendhoff. On test functions for evolutionary multi-objective optimization. In *Parallel Problem Solving from Nature (PPSN VIII)*, volume 3242 of *Lecture Notes in Computer Science*, pages 792–802, Birmingham, UK, September 2004. Springer.
13. Aimin Zhou, Qingfu Zhang, Yaochu Jin, Edward Tsang, and Tatsuya Okabe. A model-based evolutionary algorithm for bi-objective optimization. In *Proceedings of the Congress on Evolutionary Computation (CEC 2005)*, pages 2568–2575, Edinburgh, U.K, September 2005. IEEE Press.
14. Aimin Zhou, Yaochu Jin, Qingfu Zhang, Tatsuya Okabe, and Edward Tsang. Combining model-based and genetics-based offspring generation for multi-objective optimization using a convergence criterion. to be published in Proceedings of the Congress on Evolutionary Computation (CEC 2006).
15. Qingfu Zhang, Aimin Zhou, and Yaochu Jin. Modelling the regularity in estimation of distribution algorithm for continuous multi-objective evolutionary optimization with variable linkages. 2006. to be submitted.
16. Nandakishore Kambhatla and Todd K. Leen. Dimension reduction by local principal component analysis. *Neural Computation*, 9(7):1493–1516, October 1997.
17. Kalyanmoy Deb. A fast and elitist multiobjective genetic algorithm: NSGA-II. *IEEE Transactions on Evolutionary Computation*, 6(2):182–197, 2002.
18. Dirk Büche, Michele Milano, and Petros Koumoutsakos. Self-organizing maps for multi-objective optimization. In *Proceedings of Genetic and Evolutionary Computation Conference (GECCO 2002)*, pages 152–155, New York, July 2002. Morgan Kaufmann Publishers.
19. Christopher M. Bishop, Markus Svensén, and Christopher K. I. Williams. GTM:the generative topographic mapping. *Neural Computation*, 10(1):215–234, 1998.
20. Tatsuya Okabe. *Evolutionary Multi-Objective Optimization: On the Distribution of Offspring in Parameter and Fitness Space*. PhD thesis, Honda Research Institute Europe GmbH, 2004.
21. Kalyanmoy Deb, Lothar Thiele, Marco Laumanns, and Eckart Zitzler. Scalable test problems for evolutionary multi-objective optimization. Technical Report 112, Computer Engineering and Networks Laboratory (TIK),Swiss Federal Institute of Technology (ETH), 2001.
22. Yaochu Jin, editor. *Knowledge Incorporation in Evolutionary Computation*. Number 167 in Studies in Fuzziness and Soft Computing. Springer, Berlin Heidelberg, 2004.

Multiobjective Optimization of Ensembles of Multilayer Perceptrons for Pattern Classification

P.A. Castillo[1], M.G. Arenas[2], J.J. Merelo[1], V.M. Rivas[2], and G. Romero[1]

[1] Department of Architecture and Computer Technology
University of Granada (Spain)
[2] Department of Computer Science
University of Jaén (Spain)
pedro@atc.ugr.es

Abstract. Pattern classification seeks to minimize error of unknown patterns, however, in many real world applications, type I (false positive) and type II (false negative) errors have to be dealt with separately, which is a complex problem since an attempt to minimize one of them usually makes the other grow. Actually, a type of error can be more important than the other, and a trade-off that minimizes the most important error type must be reached. Despite the importance of type-II errors, most pattern classification methods take into account only the global classification error. In this paper we propose to optimize both error types in classification by means of a multiobjective algorithm in which each error type and the network size is an objective of the fitness function. A modified version of the GProp method (optimization and design of multilayer perceptrons) is used, to simultaneously optimize the network size and the type I and II errors.

Keywords: multiobjective optimization, multiobjective evolutionary algorithms, Pareto optimality, artificial neural networks optimization, gprop, pattern classification.

1 Introduction

There are two types of errors that can be made when classifying patterns. The first is the spurius detection of a non-existent effect (type I error or false positive), the second, the non-detection of an existent effect (type II error or false negative). For instance, if we conclude from a toxicity test that the tested substance is toxic when it is in fact not, then we have committed a type I error. If we conclude that a substance is not toxic when it in fact is, then we have committed a type II error [14]. This exemplifies how these errors are different in the real world, and usually have to be dealt with separately. Another example is bankruptcy prediction [5]: false positives can lead to lawsuits, while false negatives will usually lead only to loss of a customer. The most commonly used statistical measure, statistical significance, is a measure of type I error (the absence of a significative effect does not mean that the effect is inexistent). On the other hand, Neyman-Pearson's

T.P. Runarsson et al. (Eds.): PPSN IX, LNCS 4193, pp. 453–462, 2006.

test is based on the minimization of type II error after establishing a limit to the type I error [31,6].

There are many examples of incorrect conclusions due to type II error [30,25], and caution must be taken not to interpret 'no evidence of effect' as 'evidence of no effect' [28]. Despite the importance of type II error in some real problems (medical problems, judging a person to be sick or not [21], or forecasting business failure [5]), most methods compute the global classification error, without paying attention to its distinction in different types.

Most real optimization problems present several objective variables to be optimized at the same time. Solving those multiobjective problems where some objectives enter in conflict is a complex task. In these cases, instead of searching for a single solution, the method must obtain a set of solutions; later on, one solution (or several) will be used to solve the problem.

Multiobjective optimization methods range from the weighted sum of the objectives which, nowadays is usually not considered the best method available, to techniques based on the Pareto front [11,12,22,33].

This paper continues the research presented in [26,27] where a comparison between statistical methods (logistic regression) and evolutionary artificial neural networks (G-Prop) for the bankruptcy prediction was carried out. Discovering when a company is going to fail is a problem traditionally approached heuristically, which requires a wide knowledge about that company, so that it only can be carried out by means of accounting experts. The interest in pinpointing a firm's financial state of health runs from the management, who can thus count on early warning signs to aid them in taking decisions to correct foreseeable financial distress. This also applies to medical problems, such as the prediction of cancer or diabetes.

G-Prop [7,9] was designed to optimize both the architecture of the multilayer perceptron (MLP) and its classification ability.

In the present paper we propose to improve the type I and type II errors using a multiobjective evolutionary algorithm (called MG-Prop) that optimizes both errors and also the MLP architecture. Our target is to design small networks that produce small type I and II errors. Approaching this problem as a multiobjective optimization task makes unnecesary weight the different objectives, and the solutions based on Pareto optimality guarantee the diversity of the final population.

As a mixture of predictors usually improves the results, our method uses the final Pareto front to form an ensemble.

The multiobjective problem deals with three objectives: minimizing type I and II errors, and the network size. To test the ability of the proposed method, two real pattern classification problems have been used (bankruptcy prediction and breast cancer).

The remainder of this paper is structured as follows: section 2 reviews the literature on multiobjective optimization of artificial neural networks (ANN). In section 3 it is detailled the proposed method. Section 4 describes the experiments and the results obtained, followed by a brief conclusion in Section 5.

2 Neural Network Optimization Using Multi-objective Methods

Evolving neural networks [34,7,10] is an efficient way of searching the neural net problem space. However, most of these methods either calculate a weighted sum of the objectives (i.e. minimizing both the errors and the number of weights) or assign some priority to one of the objectives [7,10].

On the other hand, ANNs act as a black box that give their prediction on an input pattern. This might be a problem for the expert that uses an ANN-based method, due to the difficulty to explain the way the method calculated its output.

To face the problem of optimizing all the parameters and objectives related to the ANN, some authors propose the use of multiobjective optimization methods, such as the Pareto differential evolution (PDE), by Abbass [4]. This algorithm is an adaptation of the original differential evolution introduced by Storn and Price [32], and was also tested successfully for evolving neural networks (Memetic Pareto Artificial Neural Network [1,3]).

Recently, Abbass casted the problem of simultaneous optimization of the network architecture and the corresponding training error as a multiobjective optimization problem [3], obtaining that combining backpropagation (BP) with an multiobjective evolutionary algorithm, a considerable reduction in the computational cost can be achieved. In a latter research, Abbass [2] proposes two multiobjective formulations to the formation of neuro ensembles: the first one splits the training set into two non-overlapping stratified subsets and form an objective to minimize the training error on each subset. The second formulation adds random noise to the training set to form a second objective.

Jin et al. [17] presented a modified version of two multiobjective optimization algorithms (Dynamic Weighted Aggregation and NSGA-II) to address the neural network regularization problem from a multiobjective optimization point of view (both the structure and parameters of the neural network are optimized).

In the last years, ANN research focus on neural network ensembles [23] because they are a powerful tool to face complex problems. Using an ensemble (mixture of predictors) usually results in an improvement in the prediction accuracy [16]. Many studies [18,19,20,29] focus on the construction of ensembles using artificial neural networks.

Some authors establish the set of networks that form the ensemble by means of evolutive [19,20], coevolutive [15], and multiobjective methods, as Abbass proposes in [3] (using the Pareto front networks as the ensemble components).

Althogh most of these methods calculate only the global classification error, we think that both type I and II errors should be taken into account.

3 MG-Prop: MultiObjective Evolution of MLP

In this paper, a multiobjective method designed to optimize both type I and II errors and the network size is proposed. The objectives might confict, so if one is improved, the other could get worse.

This method is based on the multiobjective evolutionary algorithm SFGA (Single Front Genetic Algorithm), developed by De Toro et al. and uses the elitist scheme selection proposed in [13].The idea is to copy into the next population, instead of the full elite set (non-dominated individuals) a reduced set, with individuals distributed homogeneouslly among the search space.

However, this algorithm had to be adapted to our particular problem. After some experimentation, we have found that, as the evolution advances, the number of non-dominated individuals-MLP increases considerably. Moreover, some networks might commit no error at all classifying class A patterns (0%), but fail on class B patterns (100%). That infeasible individuals are non-dominated, however, they should be eliminated. The population of individuals selected to mate and generate the next generation is formed by those in the Pareto front. The designed algorithm is specified in the following pseudocode, which is an adaptation of the previously published G-Prop algorithm [7,9]:

1. Generate a population of N individuals (*Population*)
2. Evaluate the N individuals: train them using the training set and obtain their fitness (type I and type II errors) on the validation set and the network size.
3. Repeat for G generations:
   (a) Copy *Population* into P_0
   (b) Remove Pareto dominated individuals from *Population* (obtaining P_1)
   (c) Remove infeasible individuals from P_1 (obtaining P_2)
   (d) Prune P_2 using clustering to limit the number of individuals
   (e) Select S individuals from P_2 and apply genetic operators to copies of them (obtaining *Offspring*)
   (f) Evaluate the new individuals in *Offspring*
   (g) Fill the *Population* using nondominated individuals (P_2) and *Offspring*
   (h) If N is greater than the number of individuals in *Population*, then use dominated individuals in P_0 to fill *Population*
4. Remove Pareto dominated and infeasible individuals from *Population*
5. Use nondominated individuals (MLPs) as an ensemble to classify the testing set and to obtain the total, type I and type II errors.

On termination, it takes a set of not previously seen patterns, and it classifies them obtaining both error types and the network size.

The networks on the Pareto set will be potentially good, however, as a single MLP with good performance on the training set may not be the best network in terms of generalization, we will use all individual-MLP in the Pareto front as an ensemble to classify the test-patterns, as proposed in [2].

We have used three methods to obtain the ensemble classification: (a) the predicted class is obtained as majority voting; (b) for each pattern, the class is obtained taking into account the largest activation between all the outputs of all the networks; (c) computing the average outputs for all networks. Thus, an expert who has to decide if a person is ill (or a company is bankrupt) or not, has more information available about that case than if a single ANN was used.

4 Experiments and Results

Following Prechelt's advice [24], at least two real world problems should be used to test an algorithm. In any case, the best way to test the algorithm ability as well as its limitations is to use it to solve real world problems.

Thus, we have tested our method on two real world classification problems: the well known breast-cancer problem, and a bankruptcy benchmark problem (see below for details).

4.1 Breast-Cancer Problem

The dataset comes from the UCI machine learning dataset Wisconsin breast cancer database (http://www.ics.uci.edu/~mlearn/MLSummary.html), which was compiled from the University of Wisconsin Hospitals and Clinics in Madison by Dr. William H. Wolberg [21]. Each sample has 10 attributes plus the class attribute: sample code number, clump thickness, uniformity of cell size, uniformity of cell shape, marginal adhesion, single epithelial cell size, bare nuclei, bland chromatin, normal nucleoli, mitoses, class (0 for benign, 1 for malignant). The class distribution in the original set is as follows: 65.5% benign and 34.5% malignant.

4.2 Bankruptcy Problem

The dataset comes from the Infotel database (http://www.axesor.com). The sample of companies contains 450 non-financial firms taken from the Infotel database, of which half are companies that have failed and the other half present a good financial health. A further 76 firms, not included in the aforementioned group, have been used as a validation sample for the models obtained. The group of financial failures corresponds to those firms that had suspended payments or had declared legal bankruptcy, in accordance with Spanish Law, while the healthy firms were randomly selected from among 150.000 companies. The comparison was made using the same sample referring to the same time period: 1998 and 1999. The dependent variable takes a value of 1 in the case of legal failure, and of 0 in the case of a healthy firm. The independent variables are quantitative ratios taken from financial statements, along with qualitative information, and their description is included in Table 1.

4.3 Methodology

Experiments were set using 50 generations,a population size of 50 individuals, and 500 training epochs in order to avoid too long a run.

The remaining parameters (population size, selection rate, operator application rates, mutation probability, initial weights range, etc) where set using statistical methods (see [10] for details).

Mean and standard deviation, shown in tables (see section 4.4), where obtained after 30 runs in each method.

Statistical *t-Student* tests are used in order to evaluate the difference in means, as these can be used even in the case of small samples. This method calculates a value p that represents the error probability if the null hypothesis is accepted, that is, the error probability assuming that there is no difference between the

Table 1. Description of independent variables

VARIABLE	DESCRIPTION
L: Liabilities	Liabilities/Equity
DE: Debt Expiration	Long-Term Liabilities/Current Liabilities
WC: Working Capital	Working Capital/Total Assets
CashR: Cash Ratio	Cash equivalent/Current Liabilities
AT: Acid Test	(Cash equivalent+Marketable Securities+ Net receivables)/Current Liabilities
CR: Current Ratio	Current Assets/Current Liabilities
DR: Debt Ratio	Total Assets/Total Liabilites
DPA: Debt Paying Ability	Operating Cash Flow/Total Liabilities
AT: Asset Turnover	Net Sales/Average Total Assets
ST: Stock Turnover	Cost of sales/Average Inventory
RT: Receivable Turnover	Net Sales/Average Receivables
ROPA: Return on Operating Assets	Operating Income/Average Operating Assets
OIM: Operating Income Margin	Operating Income/Net Sales
ROA: Return on Assets	Net Income/Average Total Assets
ROE: Return on Equity	Net Income/Average Total Equity
DC: Debt Cost	Interest Cost/Total Liabilities
IC: Interest Cost	Interest Cost/Sales
LAG: Date	The time lag in reporting annual accounts
L: Lawsuits	(sums challenged)/(total liabilities)
I: Incidences	Relative to auctions, impounds, etc.

levels of the observations in the population. Thus, t-Student statistical tests were used to check the validity of the results obtained (average and standard deviation), and to test whether differences among them were significant.

4.4 Results Obtained

Results on Breast Cancer are shown in table 2. As can be seen the multiobjective method obtains results comparable to those obtained using G-Prop (priorizes one objective). Although MG-Prop does not outperform G-Prop, slightly better global classification error is achieved, and differences between type I and II errors minimize (homogeneity between error types grows). On the other hand, better results are obtained using the majority voting to obtain the ensemble classification.

As far as the network size is concerned, as the ensemble is composed by several MLPs, the total number of weights is higher than those obtained using G-Prop. However, network size of individual MLPs is slightly smaller than those obtained using G-Prop.

T-Student tests were used to verify the results. No significant differences were found between global classification and type I errors for G-Prop and MG-Prop. However, differences in type II error was significant to level of 99%. In any case, Cancer is a problem such as G-Prop correctly classifies most of the patterns

Table 2. Average results for the **Breast Cancer** problem. This table shows the global error rate, the type I and II errors and size of networks. Results have been obtained using G-Prop [8] and MG-Prop. Majority voting (V), average output (A) and largest activation (B) have been used to obtain the ensemble classification. The network size is expressed in terms of number of parameters of the net, that is, the number of weights of the net. In the case of MG-Prop, an ensemble is obtained, thus both the number of components of the ensemble and the average number of weights for each MLP in the ensemble is reported.

Method		Global error	Type I error	Type II error	Network size
G-Prop [8]		1.2 ± 0.1	1.1 ± 0.1	1.3 ± 0.1	173 ± 22
	(V)	1.2 ± 0.5	1.3 ± 0.9	0.7 ± 0.6	*ensemble of*
MG-Prop	(A)	1.4 ± 0.4	1.9 ± 0.8	0.5 ± 0.5	15±1 *MLPs of*
	(B)	1.6 ± 0.4	2.0 ± 0.9	0.7 ± 0.8	120 ± 44 *weights*

(small type I and II errors are committed), and that makes difficult to find differences between models.

Table 3 shows the results obtained on the Bankruptcy problem using logistic regresion, G-Prop and MG-Prop.

Table 3. Average results for the **Bankruptcy** problem using logistic regresion (logit), G-Prop [26,27] and MG-Prop

Method		Global error	Type I error	Type II error	Network size
Logit [26,27]		15.92	17.24	14.48	-
G-Prop [26,27]		17.26	11.21	23.32	1042
	(V)	12 ± 2	13 ± 2	12 ± 3	*ensemble of*
MG-Prop	(A)	13 ± 2	13 ± 3	13 ± 2	16±1 *MLPs of*
	(B)	15 ± 3	14 ± 3	16 ± 4	1120 ± 60 *weights*

Previous research [26,27] showed that the forecasting ability of multilayer perceptrons is slightly lower than that of logistic regression, in type II and total error, although better results are obtained in type I errors. In G-Prop, however, the fitness measure used to evolve perceptrons only take into account the total error, instead of using the type I and/or type II errors.

Results obtained using MG-Prop are slightly better than those obtained using previous methods [26,27]. As in the previous problem, differences in type I and II errors, as well as the global error decrease. As can be seen, better results are obtained using the majority voting to obtain the ensemble classification.

As in previous problem, G-Prop finds just an MLP, while MG-Prop finds an ensemble (several MLPs). Thus, total number of weights is much higher for MG-Prop, although for individual MLPs, sizes are comparable.

After applying t-Student tests to verify the results, differences between methods in terms of errors obtained were significant when the confidence level was 99%.

5 Conclusions and Work in Progress

In this paper we address the problem of optimizing the MLP classification ability as a multiobjective optimization problem: the type I and type II errors, and the network size are minimized. As a single MLP may not be the best network in terms of generalization, we have used the MLPs in the Pareto front as an ensemble to increase the generalization ability. The Pareto set defines the size of the ensemble and ensures that the networks in the ensemble are different and will contribute to optimize the objectives.

MG-Prop takes into account error types and obtains comparable (or even better) results to GProp method (that priorizes some objectives), carrying out the trade-off between objectives (optimizes the error types obtaining similar network sizes).

The method has been tested on two real pattern classification problems, breast cancer and bankruptcy, and has been found to be competitive to other methods in the literature. Although results are not much better than those obtained using other methods, slightly better global classification error is achieved and differences between type I and II errors minimize. In any case, the idea of optimizing the type I and II errors and the network size as a multiobjective problem is interesting and could be applied to improve other classification methods.

In the bankruptcy problem, the model has been obtained for one year before the failure. As future work, it would be interesting to obtain it for two or more years prior to the declaration of bankruptcy. On the other hand, Zhou et al. [35] analyzed the relationship between the ensemble and its component neural networks, obtaining better results ensembling some of the neural networks instead of all of them. Taking into account these results, it would be interesting to carry out the selection of components using automatic methods, such as cooperative models.

In general, majority voting seems to work better for this kind of problems.

Acknowledgements

This work has been supported by CICYT TIC2003-09481-C04-04 project.

References

1. H.A. Abbass. A memetic Pareto evolutionary approach to artificial neural networks. *In M. Stumptner, D.Corbett and M. Brooks, editors, Proceedings of the 14th Australian Joint Conference on Artificial Intelligence (AI'01), pages 1-12, Berlin*, 2001.
2. H.A. Abbass. Pareto neuro-evolution: constructive ensemble of neural networks using multi-objective optimization. *IEEE Congress on Evolutionary Computation (CEC2003), IEEE-Press, Vol. 3, pp. 2074-2080, Canberra, Australia*, 2003.
3. H.A. Abbass. Speeding up back-propagation using multiobjective evlutionary algorithms. *Neural Computation, MIT Press, Vol. 15, No 11, pp. 2705-2726*, 2003.

4. H.A. Abbass, R.A. Sarker, and C.S. Newton. PDE: A Pareto-frontier differential evolution approach for multi-objective optimization problems. *In Proc. of the IEEE Congress on Evolutionary Computation (CEC2001), vol.2,pp.971-978,Piscataway,NJ, IEEE Press*, 2001.
5. E.I. Altman. The success of business failure prediction models. an international survey. *Journal of Banking, Accounting and Finance, 8:171-198*, 1984.
6. R.J. Barton. Neyman-Pearson Hypothesis TestingSignal. *ECE 6333 - Signal Detection and Estimation. http://www2.egr.uh.edu/~rbarton/Classes/ECE6333/files.pdf/Notes/Notes_9-19-05.pdf*, 2005.
7. P. A. Castillo, J. Carpio, J. J. Merelo, V. Rivas, G. Romero, and A. Prieto. Evolving Multilayer Perceptrons. *Neural Processing Letters, vol. 12, no. 2, pp.115-127. October*, 2000.
8. P. A. Castillo, J. González, J. J. Merelo, V. Rivas, G. Romero, and A. Prieto. G-Prop-III: Global Optimization of Multilayer Perceptrons using an Evolutionary Algorithm. *In Congress on Evolutionary Computation,In Genetic and Evolutionary Computation Conference, ISBN:1-55860-611-4, Volume I, pp. 942, Orlando, USA*, 1999.
9. P. A. Castillo, J. J. Merelo, V. Rivas, G. Romero, and A. Prieto. G-Prop: Global Optimization of Multilayer Perceptrons using GAs. *Neurocomputing, Vol.35/1-4, pp.149-163*, 2000.
10. P.A. Castillo, J.J. Merelo, G. Romero, A. Prieto, and I. Rojas. Statistical Analysis of the Parameters of a Neuro-Genetic Algorithm. *in IEEE Transactions on Neural Networks, vol.13, no.6, pp.1374-1394, ISSN:1045-9227, november*, 2002.
11. C.A. Coello Coello, D.A. Van-Veldhuizen, and G.B. Lamont. Evolutionary algorithms for solving multi-objective problems. *Kluwer Academic Publishers, New York, ISBN 0-3064-6762-3*, 2002.
12. Carlos A. Coello Coello and Nareli Cruz Cortés. Solving Multiobjective Optimization Problems using an Artificial Immune System. *Genetic Programming and Evolvable Machines, Vol. 6, No. 2, pp. 163–190*, 2005.
13. F. de Toro, J. Ortega, J.Fernandez, and A.F Diaz. Parallel genetic algorithm for multiobjective optimization. *10th Euromicro Workshop on Parallel, Distributed and Network-based processing, IEEE Computer Society, pp. 384-391*, 2002.
14. J.A. Freiman, T.C. Chalmers, and H. Smith. The importance of beta, the type II error and sample size in the design and interpretation of the randomized control trial. *New England Journal of Medicine, 299:690-694*, 1978.
15. N. Garcia-Pedrajas, C. Hervas-Martinez, and D. Ortiz-Boyer. Cooperative coevolution of artificial neural network ensembles for pattern classification. *IEEE Trans. Evolutionary Computation 9(3): 271-302*, 2005.
16. H. Ishibuchi and T. Yamamoto. Evolutionary multiobjective optimization for generating an ensemble of fuzzy rule-based classifiers. *In Proc. of the Genetic and Evolutionary Computation Conference (GECCO2003), Lecture Notes in Computer Science (LNCS), pp.1077-1088, Chicago, IL*, 2003.
17. Y. Jin, T. Okabe, and B. Sendhoff. Neural network regularization and ensembling using multiobjective evolutionary algorithms. *Congress on Evolutionary Computation, CEC2004. Vol.1, pp.1-8. ISBN:0-7803-8515-2*, 2005.
18. A. Krogh and J. Vedelsby. Neural network ensembles, cross validation and active learning. *In G. Tesauro, D.S. Touretzky and T.K. Leen editors, Advances in Neural Information Processing Systems, vol.7, pp.231-238. MIT Press*, 1995.
19. Y. Liu and X. Yao. Ensemble leagning via negative correlation. *Neural Networks, 12(10):1399-1404*, 1999.

20. Y. Liu, X. Yao, and T. Higuchi. Evolutionary ensembles with negative correlation learning. *IEEE Transactions on Evolutionary Computation, 4(4):380-387*, 2000.
21. O. L. Mangasarian, R. Setiono, and W.H. Wolberg. Pattern recognition via linear programming: Theory and application to medical diagnosis. *Large-scale numerical optimization, Thomas F. Coleman and Yuying Li, editors, SIAM Publications, Philadelphia 1990, pp 22-30*, 1990.
22. J. Olvander. Robustness considerations in multi-objective optimal design. *Journal of Engineering Design, Vol. 16, No. 5, pp. 511–523*, 2005.
23. M.P. Perrone and L.N. Cooper. When networks disagree: Ensemble methods for hybrid neural networks. *Neural Networks for Speech and Image Processing, R.J.Mammone, Ed., pp.126-142*, 1993.
24. L. Prechelt. PROBEN1 — A set of benchmarks and benchmarking rules for neural network training algorithms. Technical Report 21/94, Fakultät für Informatik, Universität Karlsruhe, D-76128 Karlsruhe, Germany, September 1994.
25. C. Rolf, T.G. Cooper, C.H. Yeung, and E. Nieschlag. Antioxidant treatment of patients with asthenozoospermia or moderate oligoasthenozoospermia with high-dose vitamin C and vitamin E: a randomized, placebo-controlled, double blind study. *Hum. Reprod., 14, 1028-1033*, 1999.
26. I. Roman, J.M. de la Torre, P.A. Castillo, and J.J. Merelo. Sectorial bankruptcy prediction analysis using artificial neural networks: The spanish companies case. *25th Annual Congress European Accounting Association. Pp. 237, Copenhagen, April*, 2002.
27. I. Roman, J.M. de la Torre, M.E. Gomez, P.A. Castillo, and J.J. Merelo. Bankruptcy prediction adapted to firm characteristics. an empirical study. *26th Annual Congress European Accounting Association. Congress Book. pp. A-108. Sevilla, April*, 2003.
28. J. Savulescu, I. Chalmers, and J. Blunt. Are research ethics committees behaving unethically? some suggestions for improving performance and accountability. *Br. Med. J., 313, 1390-1393*, 1996.
29. A.J.C. Sharkey. On combining artificial neural nets. *Connection Science, 8:299-313*, 1996.
30. S.M Smith. Statistical scrotal effect. *Nature, 368, 501-502*, 1994.
31. Jonathan A.C. Sterne. Teaching hypothesis tests - time for significant change? *STATISTICS IN MEDICINE. 21:985-994 (DOI: 10.1002/sim.1129)*, 2002.
32. R. Storn and K. Price. Differential evolution: a simple and efficient adaptive scheme for global optimization over continuous spaces. *Technical Report TR-95-012, International Computer Science Institute, Berkeley*, 1995.
33. D.A. Van-Veldhuizen and G.B. Lamont. Multiobjective evolutionary algorithms: analyzing the state-of-the-art. *Evolutionary Computation 8(2): 125-147*, 2000.
34. X. Yao. Evolving artificial neural networks. *Proceedings of the IEEE, 87(9):1423-1447*, 1999.
35. Z.H. Zhou, J. Wu, and W. Tang. Ensembling neural networks: many could be better than all. *Artificial Intelligence, vol.137, no.1-2, pp.239-253*, 2002.

Multi-Objective Equivalent Random Search

Evan J. Hughes

Department of Aerospace, Power and Sensors,
Cranfield University, Shrivenham, Swindon,
Wiltshire, England. SN6 8LA
e.j.hughes@cranfield.ac.uk

Abstract. This paper introduces a new metric vector for assessing the performance of different multi-objective algorithms, relative to the range of performance expected from a random search. The metric requires an ensemble of repeated trials to be performed, reducing the chance of overly favourable results. The random search baseline for the function-under-test may be either analytic, or created from a Monte-Carlo process: thus the metric is repeatable and accurate.

The metric allows both the median and worst performance of different algorithms to be compared directly, and scales well with high-dimensional many-objective problems. The metric *quantifies* and is sensitive to the *distance* of the solutions to the Pareto set, the *distribution* of points across the set, and the *repeatability* of the trials. Both the Monte-Carlo and closed form analysis methods will provide accurate analytic confidence intervals on the observed results.

1 Introduction

This paper details a new metric, *Multi-Objective Equivalent Random Search (MOERS)*, that quantifies the performance of an algorithm on an objective function relative to the expected performance of a random search. The metric returns the size of the random search that would be required to achieve results of the same quality. The metric is calculated through a non-parametric statistical analysis of the best solutions found by the optimiser over an ensemble of trials, reducing the chances of occasional overly favourable results biasing the comparison.

The metric focusses on both the median and worst performance of the optimiser under test. Often when we run an optimiser many times, we only remember the good results. Some optimisation routines are capable of providing spectacular results with moderate frequency, but typical results are poor. Other optimisers generate satisfactory results every time, but rarely produce spectacular solutions. If optimisation is being used in a design phase where many repeated runs are possible, then the first algorithm that can produce occasional spectacular results may be preferred. However, in a situation where the optimisation is time-critical, the reliable algorithm is a better choice.

Much research has been performed on different metrics for assessing optimiser performance [7,6,5]. The true performance of a multi-objective optimiser cannot be summarised with a single number, or with only a single trial run. For a given test function and optimiser, the MOERS metric provides 10 key performance measures, 5 for the median performance and 5 for the worst-case performance. Each of the 5 is comprised

T.P. Runarsson et al. (Eds.): PPSN IX, LNCS 4193, pp. 463–472, 2006.

of 2 outer confidence intervals (indicate the distribution of points along the Pareto set), 2 inner confidence intervals (relate to the repeatability of the results) and the median behaviour over the ensemble of trials (indicates the distance to the Pareto set).

In order to remove the effects of constraints, multi-modalities, discontinuous Pareto sets etc., the optimiser results (i.e. the Pareto points) are normalised using the Cumulative probability Density Function (CDF) of the objective surface.[1] The CDF may be calculated analytically from the objective functions and constraints, or generated using a large Monte-Carlo random search (for problems without simple analytic solutions). The metric may be calculated very quickly if an analytic solution to the CDF is used.

Section 2 summarises the Equivalent Random Search metric for single objective problems, and section 3 expands the theory to encompass multi-objective problems. Section 4 demonstrates the metric on a bi-objective function where the analytic CDF has been calcuated, and also demonstrates that a true random search returns the correct metric results. Finally section 6 concludes.

2 Equivalent Random Search Metric

2.1 Introduction

The Equivalent Random Search (ERS) metric assesses the performance of an algorithm, relative to the expected performance of a random search on the same objective function [4]. The metric gives a direct indication of how many points would be needed in a random search to achieve the same solution quality. The metric can then be compared to the actual number of objective evaluations used by the optimiser in order to assess the effectiveness of the optimisation algorithm. For example, if 1000 objective calculations were used by the optimisation process, but the ERS metric reported that 10,000 points would be needed by a random search to achieve equivalent results, then the algorithm is performing well.

2.2 Objective Normalisation

To get a reliable assessment, the optimisation process is repeated M times and the best optima results, $Y_i : i = 1 \ldots M$, gathered. Each of the M results are transformed via the cumulative probability density function of the objective surface, $D(Y)$, to generate the probability of obtaining an objective value *better* than the best value observed in each of the M runs. This normalisation process allows even very rough, multi-modal and deceptive functions to be used for evaluating the optimisers.

The function $D(Y)$ can be generated for any objective functions by performing a large uniform-random sample of the objective surfaces. Further details on Monte-Carlo CDF generation are given in [4]. It is also possible (but not always trivial) to obtain an analytic solution for the CDF if the equations for the objective function are known. This allows the ERS metric to be calculated quickly, but more importantly, will allow functions that have a very low density of points at the Pareto surface to be analysed without resorting to massive Monte-Carlo searches.

[1] Each objective function provides a unique problem to the optimiser, but a set of optimisers may be compared directly if the results are generated for a common multi-objective function.

2.3 Metric Calculation

Once we have calculated the probability of a solution better than Y existing, $D(Y)$, we can compare the result directly to a random search. For the random search, if we generated a single random point, there would be a probability $D(Y)$ that the point would be better than Y, and a probability $1 - D(Y)$ that the point will be worse than Y. If we generate N independent random points, then we will not find a better solution than Y with a probability of $(1 - D(Y))^N$. Therefore the probability of finding *at least one* solution better than Y with an N point random search is given by:

$$D'(Y) = 1 - (1 - D(Y))^N \tag{1}$$

For example, if $D(Y) = 1/1000$ and we generated $N = 100$ random points, the probability of at least one of the N solutions being better than Y is $D'(Y)$ =9.5%.

Importantly, the new cumulative density function, $D'(Y)$ in equation 1, describes the probability that a random search of N points would find an optimum value better than Y. If we repeated an N-point random search M times, $D'(Y)$ would describe the distribution of the M results. Thus the median value of Y from our M searches would be an approximation of the value of Y necessary to make $D'(Y) = 0.5$. We can exploit this property of $D'(Y)$ to create a metric that uses a simple random search as its reference. As the reference can be described analytically, we can use the metric to **quantify** the performance of any optimisation algorithm on any evaluation function.

The ERS metric is calculated by performing M independent runs of our optimisation algorithm under test, and then exploiting (1) to calculate a value for N, given the observed values for Y from our optimiser. By setting $D'(Y_{median}) = 0.5$, where Y_{median} is chosen to be the median result from our M trials of the optimiser, we can calculate the value for N to give us an equivalent size of random search that we would have to perform to achieve the same median result.

Therefore we can re-arrange (1) (and taking logarithms) to give:

$$N_{median} = \frac{\log(0.5)}{\log(1 - D(Y_{median}))} \tag{2}$$

Ultimately, the calculated value for N_{median} is only an estimate and is subject to sampling error (median is calculated by ranking the M values for Y and finding the central value). If we consider that the probability of the true value of N_{median} being less than the estimate is 0.5, and the probability of the true value being greater is also 0.5, we can describe the error in the estimate using a binomial distribution of the rank locations with the two probabilities being $p = 0.5$ and $q = 1 - 0.5$. A binomial distribution can be approximated by a normal distribution when $Mp \geq 5$ and $Mq \geq 5$. Thus a minimum value of $M = 10$ trials will suffice. The variance is given by $Mpq = M/4$ and therefore the standard deviation by $\sigma = \sqrt{M}/2$. The 95% confidence limits of a normal distribution are given by $\pm 1.96\sigma$. Therefore the the upper and lower bounds to give 95% confidence intervals on the estimate of the median correspond to the values of Y from the ranked data in indexes $(M + 1)/2 \pm 1.96\sqrt{M}/2$.

We can also process other statistics such as the best and worst values of Y and associate them to the best and worst values expected from a random search. In practice, the *best* value found is subject to very wide confidence bounds unless a very large M is used (for example, to find the 99th percentile, $p = 0.01$, $q = 0.99$, $\therefore M > 500$). However although the estimate of the *worst* value of Y should also require a large number of samples, in practice it is far better behaved, and also a far more useful indicator of algorithm performance.

For the random search, the probability given by $D'(Y)^M$ is the probability that M searches will all return values better than Y. Therefore the cumulative probability distribution in (3) is the distribution of probabilities that at least one worse value than Y will be found in M trials. The distribution $D''(Y)$ is therefore the distribution of the worst optimisation results from M trials.

$$D''(Y) = 1 - D'(Y)^M \tag{3}$$

Equation 4 shows equations (3) and (1) re-arranged to obtain a median estimate and the 95% confidence limits of the worst optimisation value.

$$\begin{aligned}
N_{worst_{upper}} &= \frac{\log(1 - \sqrt[M]{0.025})}{\log(1 - D(Y_{worst}))} \\
N_{worst_{median}} &= \frac{\log(1 - \sqrt[M]{0.5})}{\log(1 - D(Y_{worst}))} \\
N_{worst_{lower}} &= \frac{\log(1 - \sqrt[M]{0.975})}{\log(1 - D(Y_{worst}))}
\end{aligned} \tag{4}$$

The metric N_{median} in (2) is the size of the random search optimisation that must be performed, that when repeated M times, will obtain a median optima Y_{median}. This metric is an indicator of typical algorithm performance (distance to the true global objective value) and a value of N_{median} larger than the actual number of function evaluations used indicates an optimisation algorithm well suited to the test function.

The metric N_{worst} in (4) is the size of the random search optimisation that must be performed, that when repeated M times, will obtain a worst optima of Y_{worst}. If this metric is larger than N_{median}, then the spread of the inferior solutions from the optimisation process (i.e. variance of inferior solutions) is smaller than the spread that would be obtained by a random search process. This is a desirable feature of optimisation algorithms as it suggests that if only a single run of the optimiser can be performed, there is confidence that a good solution will be identified. If N_{worst} is smaller than N_{median}, the optimiser is prone to premature convergence on poor solutions (highly undesirable).

Any situations that give N_{median} lower than the actual number of evaluations used indicate that a random search would have most likely provided better results than from the optimiser.

3 Multi-Objective Equivalent Random Search

The extension to multi (and many) objective problems is straightforward. To assess the quality of M non-dominated surfaces generated from the optimisation algorithm under test, each objective vector in each non-dominated set can be combined using an aggregation function to allow a set of single-objective metrics to be calculated. For assessing

Pareto sets, the weighted min-max aggregation function in equation 5 is suitable, but alternative metrics may be used if desired (e.g. for assessing objective surfaces).

The weighted min-max score of k objectives is calculated using equation 5,where w_i is the weight of the ith objective, O_i. Weighted min-max is able to generate points on both convex, concave and discontinuous Pareto sets.

$$Y = \max_{i=1}^{k}(w_i O_i) \tag{5}$$

As the weight vector is changed, the aggregated objective surface is modified and the cumulative probability distribution is modified. If a large random search has been performed of the objective space, then the results can be transformed by the aggregation function and sorted to form a CDF. Although the vectors will not be truly independent, one large random sampling of the objective space may be re-cycled for calculating the CDFs for any weight vector set (equation 7 shows an example analytic CDF).

The multi-objective assessment is performed by first generating a set of H weight vectors (typically $H = 100$ or more), giving $W_j : j = 1 \ldots H$, that span the true Pareto surface (or the non-dominated surface of the large random sampling). Each of the vectors W_j corresponds to a full set of weights, $W_j = [w_{1j}\ w_{2j}\ \ldots w_{kj}]$.

For each of the $j \in H$ weight vectors, all the $n \in M$ non-dominated surfaces are scanned in turn, aggregating using W_j. The best performing aggregated point from each of the M non-dominated surfaces is gathered, Y_{nj}, resulting in M best points for each of the H test weight vectors.

Thus each of the sets of M non-dominated surfaces can be assessed using the single objective theory. If we take the first weight vector W_1 for example, we can take the worst and median of the $Y_{n1} : n \in M$ aggregated values, and process using the CDF corresponding to the vector W_1 with equations 2 and 4 and therefore obtain the performance in the direction of the weight vector W_1. The process can be repeated for all of the H weight vectors, yielding vectors of results for $\boldsymbol{N}_{median}$, $\boldsymbol{N}_{worst}$ and their associated confidence intervals. Sorting the vectors $\boldsymbol{N}_{median}$ etc. will create CDFs of the performance across the entire Pareto surface.

The median of the $\boldsymbol{N}_{median}$ vector can be used as a good indicator of general performance, but for the most accurate representation, the overall 95% limits on the $\boldsymbol{N}_{median}$ vector should also be reported (the 'outer' confidence interval), along with the analytic 95% confidence limits on the median of $\boldsymbol{N}_{median}$ (the 'inner' confidence interval). As the Pareto surface is being analysed using an ensemble of aggregations, the 'single objective' problem that is being analysed is being changed as we scan the Pareto set with the weight vectors. Thus it is likely that the optimiser under test may perform differently on different regions of the Pareto set (typically the edges of the Pareto surface are different to the central region) and a spread of ERS values that is wider than the analytic error will be observed. The spread (especially the lower limit) can be very informative about the reliability of the optimiser at identifying solutions. The 'outer' confidence limits are calculated from this spread and relate closely to the distribution of solutions across the Pareto set, as any gaps in coverage will result in a low ERS value for the lower 'outer' confidence limit. The multi-objective ESR metrics are be denoted by the quintet of results: $[N^-_{median_{outer}}\ \ N^-_{median_{inner}}\ \ N_{median}\ \ N^+_{median_{inner}}\ \ N^+_{median_{outer}}]$, abbreviated to $[N^{--}_M\ N^-_M\ N_M\ N^+_M\ N^{++}_M]$.

A similar set of results can be provided for the worst case performance too: $[N_W^{--}\ N_W^{-}\ N_W\ N_W^{+}\ N_W^{++}]$. The outcome is 10 numbers that summarise the equivalent random search sizes that would be required to mimic the performance distribution of the optimiser under test.

4 Example Analytic Density Function

The equation for the cumulative density function under the weighted min-max aggregation function has been derived for a simple multi-objective test function. Equation 6 details the function, and the objective space is depicted pictorially in Fig. 1.

$$\begin{aligned} O_1 &= \sqrt[v]{x} \\ O_2 &= \sqrt[v]{y} \\ 1 \leq O_1 + O_2 & \quad 0 \leq x, y \leq 1 \end{aligned} \tag{6}$$

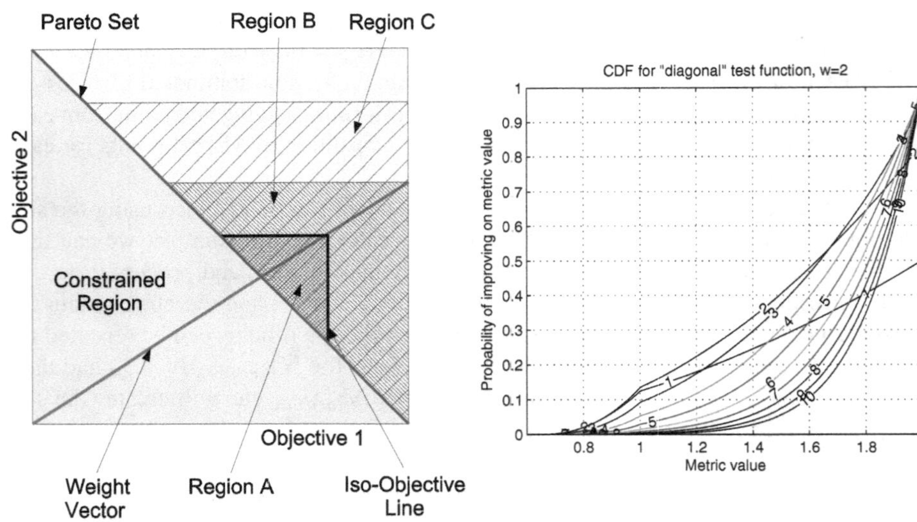

Fig. 1. Objective space and Cumulative Probability Density function for the "diagonal" function

In Fig. 1, the Pareto surface is simply a diagonal line across the objective space which is defined by the constraint boundary of the feasible region $O_1 + O_2 \geq 1$. To calculate the cumulative density function $D(Y)$, the two objectives are combined using equation 5 to form the metric Y. If the points in objective space that result in a constant metric value of Y are plotted, an *iso-objective* contour results and a typical example is shown in blue on Fig. 1. If the distribution of points in the objective space is uniform (when $v = 1$), then $D(Y)$ is simply the ratio of the area of the superior feasible region bounded by the iso-objective line defined by Y (region A in the figure), to the total area of the objective space. If the distribution of the objectives is not uniform, then $D(Y)$ is the area integral of the probability density of the objectives bounded by the constraints and the iso-objective contour defined by Y.

In the example shown in Fig. 1, $D(Y)$ will grow as a square-law relationship until the iso-objective line reaches the boundary of region B, then will progress on a compound law thereafter (e.g. as seen in region C). The resulting equation for $D(Y)$ is given in equation 7, where $w = \max(w_1, w_2)$, $\min(w_1, w_2) = 1$, w_1 and w_2 are the weights applied to objective 1 and 2 respectively and v is a shape parameter that describes the density of the Pareto set. An integer shape parameter in the range $[2, 10]$ provides a useful range of difficulty for the optimisation process.

$$D(Y) = \begin{cases} \frac{Y^{2v}}{w^v} - Y^v(1-Y)^v - v \sum\limits_{r=0}^{v} \binom{v}{r} \frac{(-1)^r}{v+r} \left[\left(\frac{Y}{w}\right)^{v+r} - (1-Y)^{v+r} \right] & Y < 1, \\ \frac{Y^v}{w^v} - v \sum\limits_{r=0}^{v} \binom{v}{r} \frac{(-1)^r}{v+r} \left(\frac{Y}{w}\right)^{v+r} & Y \geq 1. \end{cases} \tag{7}$$

Figure 1 shows the cumulative density function for equation 6 and $w = 2$, for v over a range [1,10]. The 'knee' in the CDF when $Y = 1$ is visible clearly. At low values for v, there are a large number of constrained solutions and the density of the solutions at the Pareto surface is high. With a high density of solutions, the random search performs well and the optimisers have difficulty improving on the random solutions. At high values of v, there are very few constrained solutions, but the Pareto set density is low and the random search is not so good. There is more scope for improvements by the optimisation algorithms. A good general-purpose optimiser will perform satisfactorily across a wide range of Pareto set densities.

5 Performance Trials of Optimisers

To illustrate the metric, two alternative optimisation strategies have been tested against the objective function in equation 6 with a shape parameter of $v = 5$ to provide a Pareto set with a reasonably low density. As a baseline, random search has been used to confirm that the MOERS metric is truly relative to the analytic random search process. The second optimiser is NSGA-II using software downloaded from the algorithm authors website [1]. In order to allow independent verification, the Matlab software for the MOERS metric used to generate the results in this section is available at [3].

Figure 2 shows the different metrics as assessed from NSGA-II [2] on the objective function in equation 6 (with a shape parameter of $v = 5$) using 5000 actual objective calculations, $H = 200$ weight vectors and $M = 100$ repeated trials. On the figure, the horizontal solid line indicates $log_{10}(5000) = 3.7$, the upper varying solid line is the median equivalent random search size ($\boldsymbol{N}_M$) and the lower varying solid line is the worst-case equivalent random search size ($\boldsymbol{N}_W$). The dashed lines indicate the upper and lower bound of the analytic (inner) 95% confidence intervals ($\boldsymbol{N}_M^+$, $\boldsymbol{N}_M^-$ and $\boldsymbol{N}_W^+$, $\boldsymbol{N}_W^-$). The horizontal dashed lines indicate the locations of N_M^{++} and N_M^{--} and N_W^{++} and N_W^{--} (outer confidence limits).

The corresponding equivalent random search metrics are shown in table 1. Table 2 shows the *Log Search Ratio* (LSR) which is the logarithm of the ratio of the ERS metric over the actual number of evaluations used. A LSR of zero would indicate that the optimiser is equivalent to a random search.

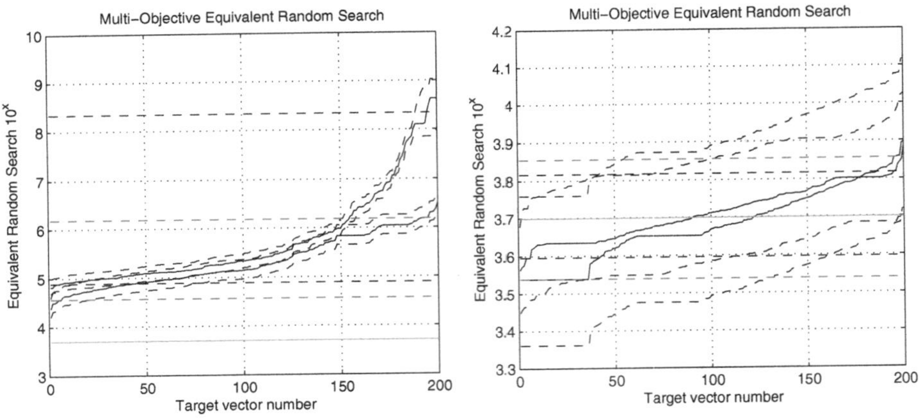

Fig. 2. Multi objective equivalent random search metric for NSGA-II (left) and random search (right) on test function equation 6

Table 1. Equivalent random search for NSGA-II with equation 6 and 5000 evaluations

Metric	N^{--}	N^{-}	N	N^{+}	N^{++}
N_{worst}	36914	93682	**140460**	233808	1534218
N_{median}	78128	157795	**217641**	306711	217931129
$\log_{10}(N_{worst})$	4.57	4.97	**5.15**	5.37	6.19
$\log_{10}(N_{median})$	4.89	5.20	**5.34**	5.49	8.34

Table 2. Log Search Ratio for NSGA-II with equation 6 and 5000 evaluations

Metric	LSR^{--}	LSR^{-}	LSR	LSR^{+}	LSR^{++}
LSR_{worst}	0.87	1.27	**1.45**	1.67	2.49
LSR_{median}	1.19	1.50	**1.64**	1.79	4.64

It is clear from Fig. 2 that there is a definite improvement over the analytic random search with the optimisation algorithm as all metrics are above the horizontal solid line (and therefore all LSR values are positive). The shallow slope of $\boldsymbol{N}_M$ and $\boldsymbol{N}_W$ on the left of the graph indicates that there are no large gaps in the Pareto set in any of the 100 trials. The $\boldsymbol{N}_W$ and $\boldsymbol{N}_M$ curves are near coincident for the worst 150 weight vectors, indicating that the CDF of the spread of the optima is the same shape as would be expected from a random search (a good feature). The results for $\boldsymbol{N}_W$ in the right-hand 50 weight vectors however are lower than the $\boldsymbol{N}_M$ results and suggests that the worst case results are spread much further than the $\boldsymbol{N}_M$ equivalent random search would provide. This indicates that the behaviour is becoming erratic over a few small regions of the Pareto surface and the algorithm is converging to local solutions. The good median performance shown on the right-hand-side is due to the random search not being good at finding the extremes of the Pareto set for the test problem. NSGA-II however, obtains a good spread of results right across the Pareto set. Hence the best of the H median ERS vectors are at the edges of the Pareto set, and the worst at the centre. An ideal algorithm would have $\boldsymbol{N}_W$ consistently higher than $\boldsymbol{N}_M$ demonstrating a very robust optimiser whose bad results are still very good. Overall the assessment is that NSGA-II is performing well, a random search would need approximately 43 times as many points ($10^{1.64}$) to achieve equivalent optima.

Table 3. Log Search Ratio for random search with equation 6 and 5000 evaluations

Metric	LSR^{--}	LSR^{-}	LSR	LSR^{+}	LSR^{++}
LSR_{worst}	-0.16	-0.21	**-0.03**	0.19	0.16
LSR_{median}	-0.10	-0.11	**0.01**	0.15	0.12

Figure 2 and table 3 shows the results of performing a 5000 point random search on equation 6. The search was repeated $M = 100$ times and is assessed over $H = 200$ weight vectors. The horizontal solid line shows the actual number of points used and it is clear that the metrics all lie within the anticipated 95% confidence intervals predicted from the median values of the ensemble of weight vectors. The random search test is very useful as it confirms the correctness of the analytic equations.

The two optimisation processes have been tested further with 10 different maximum number of evaluations in the range [800, 500000]. At each configuration $M = 100$ trials were performed in order to allow the MOERS metrics to be calculated with useful confidence intervals. The MOERS results were converted to the Log Search Ratio so that a direct comparison with the performance against the analytic random search can be made as the algorithm computational allowance is increased.

Figure 3a shows a graph of [LSR_M^{--} LSR_M^{-} LSR_M LSR_M^{+} LSR_M^{++}] for a range of different search sizes with NSGA-II. It is clear that the performance relative to the

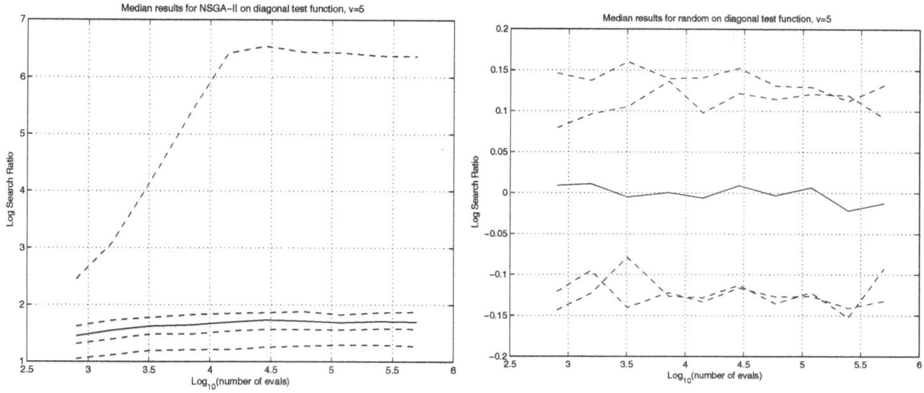

Fig. 3. Plot of Log search ratio of NSGA-II and random search for different search sizes on equation 6

analytic random search improves as the number of evaluations allowed increases, but eventually, the performance 'saturates'. Different optimisers saturate at different levels and the saturation is an indication of intrinsic optimisation capacity on the function under test.

Figure 3b shows a graph of $[LSR_M^{--}\ LSR_M^{-}\ LSR_M\ LSR_M^{+}\ LSR_M^{++}]$ for a range of different search sizes and the random search algorithm. It is clear that the Log Search Ratio is a good approximation to zero, i.e. the actual number of points used matches the analytic prediction that was based on the $M = 100$ non-dominated sets that were analysed. It is also clear that LSR_M^{--} is very similar to LSR_M^{-}, and LSR_M^{+} is very similar to LSR_M^{++}, demonstrating that the analytic confidence intervals are accurate.

6 Conclusions

This paper has introduced a new metric for assessing the performance of multi-objective optimisation algorithms. The metric uses an analytic random search as the reference, allowing performance to be *quantified*. The metric requires multiple independent runs of the optimiser and assesses both median and worst performance, and provides analytic confidence intervals on the results. The metric is both repeatable and accurate.

References

1. K. Deb. NSGA-II code in C. http://www.iitk.ac.in/kangal/codes/nsga2/nsga2-v1.1.tar.
2. K. Deb, S. Agrawal, A. Pratap, and T. Meyarivan. A fast elitist non-dominated sorting genetic algorithm for multi-objective optimization: NSGA-II. In M. Schoenauer, K. Deb, G. Rudolph, X. Yao, E. Lutton, J. J. Merelo, and H.-P. Schwefel, editors, *Parallel Problem Solving from Nature – PPSN VI*, pages 849–858, Berlin, 2000. Springer.
3. E. J. Hughes. MOERS example software. http://code.evanhughes.org.
4. E. J. Hughes. Assessing robustness of optimisation performance for problems with expensive evaluation functions. In *World Congress on Computational Intelligence*, Vancouver, Canada, July 2006. IEEE. to appear.
5. J. Knowles and D. Corne. On metrics for comparing non-dominated sets. In *Congress on Evolutionary Computation (CEC 2002)*, volume 1, pages 711–716, Hawaii, 2002.
6. T. Okabe, Y. Jin, and B. Sendhoff. A critical survey of performance indices for multi-objective optimization. In *Congress on Evolutionary Computation (CEC'2003)*, volume 2, pages 878–885, Canberra, Australia, Dec. 2003.
7. E. Zitzler, L. Thiele, M. Laumanns, C. M. Fonseca, and V. G. da Fonseca. Performance assessment of multiobjective optimizers: An analysis and review. In *IEEE Transactions on Evolutionary Computation*, volume 7, pages 117–132, April 2003.

Compressed-Objective Genetic Algorithm

Kuntinee Maneeratana[1], Kittipong Boonlong[1], and Nachol Chaiyaratana[2]

[1] Department of Mechanical Engineering, Chulalongkorn University
Phaya Thai Road, Pathum Wan, Bangkok 10330, Thailand
kuntinee.m@chula.ac.th, kittipong_toy@yahoo.com
[2] Research and Development Center for Intelligent Systems,
King Mongkut's Institute of Technology North Bangkok
1518 Piboolsongkram Road, Bangsue, Bangkok 10800, Thailand
nchl@kmitnb.ac.th

Abstract. A strategy for solving an optimisation problem with a large number of objectives by transforming the original objective vector into a two-objective vector during survival selection is presented. The transformed objectives, referred to as preference objectives, consist of a winning score and a vicinity index. The winning score, a maximisation criterion, describes the difference of the number of superior and inferior objectives between two solutions. The minimisation vicinity index describes the level of solution clustering around a search location, particularly the best value of each individual objective, is used to encourage the results to spread throughout the Pareto front. With this strategy, a new multi-objective algorithm, the compressed-objective genetic algorithm (COGA), is introduced. COGA is subsequently benchmarked against a non-dominated sorting genetic algorithm II (NSGA-II) and an improved strength Pareto genetic algorithm (SPEA-II) in six scalable DTLZ benchmark problems with three to six objectives. The results reveal that the proposed strategy plays a crucial role in the generation of a superior solution set compared to the other two techniques in terms of the solution set coverage and the closeness to the true Pareto front. Furthermore, the spacing of COGA solutions is very similar to that of SPEA-II solutions. Overall, the functionality of the multi-objective evolutionary algorithm (MOEA) with preference objectives is effectively demonstrated.

1 Introduction

Various techniques have been proposed for solving multi-objective problems. Among these techniques, the genetic algorithm has been established as one of the most widely used methods [1,2,3,4,5,6,7,8]. Due to the parallel search nature of the algorithm, the approximation of multiple optimal solutions—the Pareto optimal solutions, comprising of non-dominated individuals—can be effectively executed. The performance of the algorithm always degrades as the search space or problem size gets bigger. As an increase in the number of conflicting objectives also significantly raises the difficulty level [9], the non-dominated solutions may deviate from the true Pareto front and effects the coverage of the Pareto front by the solutions.

T.P. Runarsson et al. (Eds.): PPSN IX, LNCS 4193, pp. 473–482, 2006.

A number of strategies have been successfully integrated into genetic algorithms to solve these problems, including a direct modification of selection pressure [1,2,3] and elitism [4,5,6,7,8]. Although they have been proven to significantly improve the search performance of genetic algorithms, virtually all reported results deal with only few objectives. In reality, the possibility that a candidate solution is not dominated always increases with objective numbers, leading to an explosion in the total number of non-dominated solutions. This difficulty stems from the way that a non-dominated solution is defined. During a comparison between two candidate solutions, a solution x would not dominate another solution y unless all objectives from x satisfy the domination condition. In a problem with a large number of objectives, the chance that two solutions cannot dominate one another is inevitably high. A genetic algorithm must be able to pick out a well chosen solution set from a vast number of non-dominated solutions in order to successfully approximate the Pareto front.

In order to properly approximate such Pareto fronts with a managable solution number, a number of non-dominated solutions must be excluded from the search target. This paper presents a new technique which assigns different preference levels to non-dominated solutions. It is hypothesised that a set containing highly preferred solutions would reflect a close approximation of the true Pareto front. Two conflicting criteria will be used in the preference assignment. These criteria will serve as the 'preference objectives' by which the survival decision for the non-dominated solution will be made through a direct application of the standard multi-objective domination concept to the preference objectives. This can be viewed as a transformation from an m-objective problem to a two-objective problem during the survival competition between two non-dominated solutions. Since existing MOEAs are highly capable of solving two-objective problems, this approach should be universally applicable to any of these algorithms.

In this paper, the impact of preference objectives and the newly proposed compressed-objective genetic algorithm (COGA) will be demonstrated via scalable DTLZ problems [9]. As the objective numbers of these benchmarks are expandable while the problem characteristic is maintained, the performance of the proposed strategy with various objective numbers, ranging from three to six, can be systematically evaluated. Meanwhile, the associated number of decision variables is proportional to the objective numbers. Thus, the organisation of this paper is as follows. In section 2, descriptions of the preference objectives and their application to a multi-objective problem are given. COGA is discussed in section 3. Next, the scalable multi-objective benchmark problems and performance evaluation criteria are outlined in section 4, followed by the results and discussions in section 5. Finally, the conclusions are drawn in section 6.

2 Preference Objectives

When two non-dominated solutions are competing for survival, the solution with better 'preference objectives' has a higher chance of being selected. Here, two conflicting preference objectives and their ranking are introduced.

2.1 Preference Objective Definitions

Winning Score. The winning score is calculated from the numbers of superior and inferior objectives between a pair of two non-dominated solutions. Let sup_{ij} be the number of objectives in the solution i that is superior to the corresponding objectives in the solution j while inf_{ij} be the number of objectives in i that is inferior to j. For a population containing N non-duplicated non-dominated individuals, the winning score for the ith solution or WS_i is given by

$$WS_i = \sum_{j=1}^{N} w_{ij} \qquad \text{where } w_{ij} = sup_{ij} - inf_{ij} \ . \tag{1}$$

Obviously, $w_{ji} = -w_{ij}$ and $w_{ii} = 0$. With this assignment, non-dominated solutions with high winning scores should be close to the true Pareto front but they tend to cluster around the best values of individual objectives instead of spreading throughout the Pareto front.

Vicinity Index. In order to retard the winning score bias towards best values of individual objectives, the vicinity index is introduced. For simplicity, the objective vector is normalised such that the range of its element is between zero and one. Let $\{e_{i1}, e_{i2}, \ldots, e_{im}\}$ be the m-dimensional normalised objective vector of a solution i, the vicinity index for i or VI_i and the associated vicinity function v_{ij} are defined as

$$VI_i = \sum_{j=1}^{m} v_{ij} \ , \tag{2}$$

$$v_{ij} = \frac{(1 - e_{ij})}{\overline{V}_j} \text{ with } \overline{V}_j = \sum_{k=1}^{N} \frac{(1 - e_{kj})\,\rho_{kj}}{N} \text{ for minimising objective } j \ ,$$

$$v_{ij} = \frac{e_{ij}}{\overline{V}_j} \text{ with } \overline{V}_j = \sum_{k=1}^{N} \frac{e_{kj}\rho_{kj}}{N} \text{ for maximising objective } j \ . \tag{3}$$

The divisor $\overline{V}_j$ is included to ensure that each objective contributes equally to VI_i. In addition, the summation $\sum v_{kj}$ from $k = 1$ to N is equal to N for any objective j. The value of v_{ij} is high when a solution i is clustered around the best value of an objective j; v_{ij} is reduced to zero when e_{ij} is farthest away form the biased best value of j. Hence, VI_i is a minimisation objective. The ρ_{ij} denotes the density of e_{ij} and is estimated over N solutions from the set that contains $e_{1j}, e_{2j}, \ldots, e_{Nj}$ such that

$$\rho_{ij} = \frac{1}{h_j} \sum_{k=1}^{N} K\left(\frac{e_{ij} - e_{kj}}{h_j/N}\right) = \sum_{k=1}^{N} K\left(\frac{e_{ij} - e_{kj}}{1/N}\right) \ , \tag{4}$$

where K is a Gaussian kernel with $K(u) = e^{-0.5u^2}/\sqrt{2\pi}$ and h_j is the range of the normalised objective which is equal to 1.0. The inclusion of solution density is important since the density of solutions in the vicinity of the winning score bias towards best values of individual objective raises with increasing number of objectives. The multiplication by ρ_{ij} lessens this bias by further increasing the vicinity index, resulting in lower ranking of clustered solutions and higher possibility of solution truncation.

2.2 Rank Assignment by Preference Objectives

With the winning score, a maximisation objective, and the vicinity index, a minimisation objective, a rank can be assigned to each non-dominated solution based upon the preference level. A non-dominated solution x is preferable to another non-dominated y if and only if one of the following conditions is satisfied.

a) The winning score of x is higher than that of y and the vicinity index of x is less than that of y ($WS_x > WS_y \wedge VI_x < VI_y$).
b) The winning scores of x and y are equal and the vicinity index of x is less than that of y ($WS_x = WS_y \wedge VI_x < VI_y$).
c) The winning score of x is higher than that of y and the vicinity indices of x and y are equal ($WS_x > WS_y \wedge VI_x = VI_y$).

Similar to [3], the rank of the non-dominated solution of interest is assigned by the number of non-dominated solutions that are more 'preferable' than the individual of interest. The preference objectives and the resulting rank will be used only during the selection and truncation processes in the search algorithm.

3 Compressed-Objective Genetic Algorithm (COGA)

3.1 Main Algorithm

1. Generate an initial population P_0 and an empty archive A_0. Initialise the generation counter ($t = 0$).
2. Merge the population P_t and the archival individuals in A_t together. Then select non-duplicated non-dominated individuals, obtained from objective space, from the merged population and place them in the archive A_{t+1}.
3. If the number of selected non-duplicated non-dominated individuals is less than or equal to the archive size, go to step 4. Otherwise, truncate the individual set using the operator described in sub-section 3.2.
4. Calculate the rank of each archival individual according to sub-section 2.2.
5. Assign the fitness value to each individual i in the archive such that

$$\text{fitness}_i = |A_{t+1}| + \frac{d_i}{\sqrt{m+1}} - \text{rank}_i \ , \tag{5}$$

where $|A_{t+1}|$ denotes the number of archival individuals, m is the number of objectives and d_i is the Euclidean distance between the individual i and its nearest neighbour in normalised objective space. If i is an extreme solution with extreme objective values, the value of d_i is infinite.

6. Perform binary tournament selection with replacement on archival individuals in order to fill the mating pool.
7. Apply crossover and mutation operation within the mating pool. Then place the offspring in the population P_{t+1} and increase the generation counter by one ($t \leftarrow t+1$).
8. Go back to step 2 until the termination condition is satisfied. Report the final archival individuals as the output solution set.

Although the archive may not be fully filled at the beginning of the run, the available number of non-dominated individuals tends to increase rapidly, especially in problems with large numbers of objectives as the chance that two individuals cannot dominate one another is heightened. Thus, a truncation operator for maintaining individuals in the archive is introduced next.

3.2 Truncation Operator for the Archive

The truncation for the archive with size Q is based upon the preference level and the spread of solutions in the objective space. It can be described as follows.

1. Calculate ranks of N archival individuals according to the preference level.
2. All E extreme solutions are placed in the archive. Set the numbers of selected solutions $L = E$ and remaining solutions $R = N - E$. Then, calculate the Euclidean distance d_i^{RL} between the individual i in R and its nearest neighbour in L.
3. Select $(Q - L)$ solutions with highest values of d_i^{RL} from R. From this set, the candidate with the highest rank is moved to the archive. If there is more than one solution of the highest rank, the suitability is decided by the high value of d_i^{RL}.
4. Increase the counter for the number of selected solutions ($L \leftarrow L+1$) and decrease the counter for the number of remaining solutions ($R \leftarrow R-1$). Update the d_i^{RL} for the remaining individual i.
5. Go back to step 3 until the number of selected individuals is equal to the required archive size.

4 Scalable Benchmarks and Performance Evaluation

The proposed algorithm will be benchmarked against six test cases, DTLZ1–DTLZ4, DTLZ6 and DTLZ7 [9]. They are scalable minimisation with n decision variables and m objectives. The relationship between the number of decision variables and the number of objectives is defined by $n = m + k - 1$, where the value of k is set to ten in this paper, while the number of objectives is between three and six. DTLZ1 has a linear Pareto front with multiple local fronts. DTLZ2 has a spherical Pareto front. DTLZ3 and DTLZ4 both have spherical Pareto fronts but DTLZ3 contains multiple local fronts while the DTLZ4 solutions are non-uniformly distributed in the search space. DTLZ6 has a curve Pareto front and contains multiple local fronts. DTLZ7 has multiple discrete Pareto fronts.

Table 1. Parameter setting for the algorithms in all problems

Parameter	Setting and Value
Chromosome coding	Real-value representation
Selection method	Tournament selection
Crossover method	SBX recombination with probability = 1 [11]
Mutation method	Variable-wise polynomial mutation with probability = 1/number of decision variables [11]
Population size	100
Archive size (COGA, SPEA-II)	100
Number of generations	600
Number of repeated runs	30

As the optimality of non-dominated solutions should be assessed by comparing (a) among themselves, (b) with the solutions obtained from a different algorithm and (c) with the true Pareto optimal solutions [10], three measurement criteria are used: the solution set coverage (C), the average distance between the non-dominated solutions to the true Pareto optimal solutions (M_1) and the neighbour-series spacing (S_{ns}). The C is evaluated by comparing domination or equality between two sets of solutions while the remaining two minimisation criteria are calculated from objective vectors of the solutions. The C and M_1 are taken from [10] while S_{ns} is adapted from [11]. For the $d_i^{0,1}, d_i^{1,2}, ..., d_i^{q-1,q}$ distance series between two individuals, $d_i^{0,1}$ denotes the distance between individual i and its nearest neighbour; $d_i^{1,2}$ denotes the distance between the previously identified neighbouring solution and its nearest neighbour taken from the solution set that excludes individual i; and so on. The S_{ns} is defined by

$$S_{ns} = \left(\sum_{i=1}^{N} \frac{1}{q} \sum_{j=1}^{q} |d_i^{j-1,j} - \overline{d}| \right) \Big/ N \qquad \text{when } \overline{d} = \left(\sum_{i=1}^{N} d_i^{0,1} \right) \Big/ N \ , \tag{6}$$

where N is the number of non-duplicated non-dominated solutions and q is the neighbouring series size, which is arbitrarily set to 10% of the population. In the original spacing [11], the index is obtained from a pair-wise nearest neighbouring distance, implying that a low index may not reflect a good solution distribution since a lumped solution set can produce a low spacing value. Since S_{ns} interests in the pair-wise distances that expand outwards from the individual of interest, it should provide a better distribution measurement.

5 Optimisation Results and Discussions

In this section, results of the specified DTLZ problems from COGA will be benchmarked against those from NSGA-II [6] and SPEA-II [7]. The parameter settings are given in Table 1. After all repeated runs, the final non-dominated solutions are retrieved from either individuals in the last generations (NSGA-II) or the archive (SPEA-II and COGA). The performance indicators—M_1, C and S_{ns}—are displayed in Table 2, Fig. 1 and Table 3, respectively.

From M_1 in Table 2, COGA outperforms NSGA-II and SPEA-II in all problems. Performances of NSGA-II and SPEA-II are comparable when the number of considered objectives is less than five. Once the number of objectives exceeds four, the performance of NSGA-II is noticeably better than that of SPEA-II.

Moving onto the solution set coverage C in Fig. 1, the comparative values of results from algorithms A and B can be obtained from the difference in their coverage values $C(A, B) - C(B, A)$, from which a higher values indicates better results from A as compared against B. COGA is shown to be better than NSGA-II and SPEA-II in DTLZ1, DTLZ3 and DTLZ6 problems with three and four objectives. For problems with five and six objectives, the results reveal that COGA is the most suitable technique. With the use of real-value chromosome, the possibility of two algorithms to produce solutions with exactly the same decision variable set is highly unlikely. This implies that the coverage index is obtained mainly from solutions taken from the compared algorithm that dominate solutions of interest. In other words, the low C indices from all algorithm pairs in three- and four-objective DTLZ2, DTLZ4 and DTLZ7 problems, which are problems with either spherical or discrete Pareto fronts, are caused by the fact that the majority of solutions from all three algorithms do not dominate each other. The solution sets obtained from COGA clearly dominate the so-

Table 2. Comparisons of average (Avg) and standard deviation (SD) values of M_1. The boldface indicates the best average values.

M_1	Algorithm	3 Objectives		4 Objectives		5 Objectives		6 Objectives	
		Avg	SD	Avg	SD	Avg	SD	Avg	SD
DTLZ1	NSGA-II	0.534	0.588	298.2	111.8	834.1	60.20	1105	52.46
	SPEA-II	0.404	0.579	364.4	48.03	943.3	66.15	1224	40.56
	COGA	**0.033**	0.044	**35.52**	25.89	**346.6**	65.82	**568.9**	65.72
DTLZ2	NSGA-II	0.010	0.002	0.041	0.006	0.415	0.085	1.761	0.155
	SPEA-II	0.008	0.001	0.071	0.022	1.342	0.110	2.241	0.052
	COGA	**0.006**	0.001	**0.020**	0.004	**0.055**	0.016	**0.180**	0.047
DTLZ3	NSGA-II	0.401	0.584	352.8	71.60	920.5	38.59	1247	80.11
	SPEA-II	0.834	1.109	320.7	47.37	1035	77.25	1660	62.16
	COGA	**0.041**	0.043	**79.30**	30.67	**450.1**	52.33	**663.5**	63.61
DTLZ4	NSGA-II	0.009	0.002	0.045	0.019	0.936	0.191	1.847	0.092
	SPEA-II	0.009	0.002	0.113	0.024	1.547	0.081	2.248	0.064
	COGA	**0.005**	0.001	**0.017**	0.003	**0.125**	0.048	**0.566**	0.108
DTLZ6	NSGA-II	0.194	0.041	9.098	0.481	13.94	0.300	19.35	0.309
	SPEA-II	0.179	0.031	7.579	0.378	15.32	0.139	20.29	0.180
	COGA	**0.101**	0.008	**5.647**	0.333	**10.08**	0.357	**16.98**	0.510
DTLZ7	NSGA-II	0.016	0.003	0.100	0.010	0.243	0.044	0.451	0.087
	SPEA-II	0.016	0.003	0.106	0.011	0.367	0.052	0.946	0.136
	COGA	**0.011**	0.002	**0.060**	0.007	**0.139**	0.033	**0.237**	0.034

lution sets from NSGA-II and SPEA-II in three- and four-objective DTLZ1, DTLZ3 and DTLZ6 problems, which contain multiple local Pareto fronts, in order to achieve high C indices. Nonetheless, in all benchmarks with five and six objectives, COGA is capable of producing solution sets that cover solution sets generated by NSGA-II and SPEA-II, implying a significant deterioration in their search capability once the number of objectives increases.

From the spacing measurement by the S_{ns} index in Table 3, NSGA-II yields the worst results in all problems. COGA and SPEA-II produce better solutions but the performance of SPEA-II is marginally better than COGA, especially in problems with high objective numbers. The reason for this SPEA-II superiority is most likely to stem from the use of k-nearest neighbour technique during solution pruning in which extreme solutions may be eliminated for problems with three-or-more objectives. In contrast, the pruning technique in COGA always maintains the existence of extreme solutions at hand; the build-up of extreme solutions in close proximity can lead to the deterioration in the S_{ns} values.

It should be noted that the vicinity index does not always in conflict with the winning score; ranks solutions with a high values of winning score should be high and solutions with the highest winning score is certain to be of the highest rank. In COGA runs, it is possible that strong conflicts between the two preference objectives may exist in a few solutions whose ranks may be

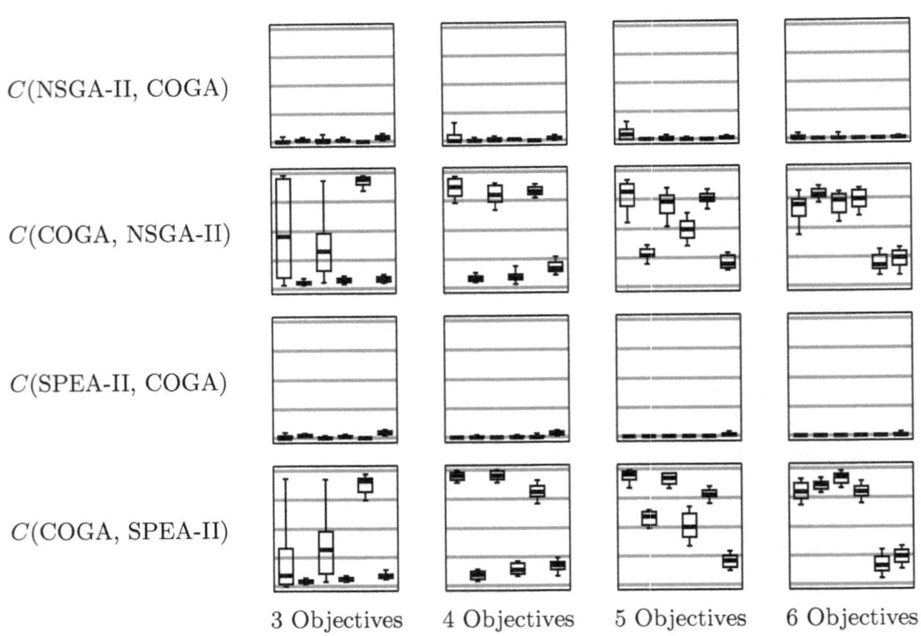

Fig. 1. Box plots of $C(A, B$ which is covered by $A)$. In each rectangle, the leftmost plot refers to DTLZ1 while the rightmost to DTLZ7. The scale is 0 (no coverage) at the bottom and 1 (total coverage) at the top. In each plot, the thick horizontal line indicates the average values.

Table 3. Comparisons of average (Avg) and standard deviation (SD) values of S_{ns}. The boldface indicates the best average values.

S_{ns}	Algorithm	3 Objectives		4 Objectives		5 Objectives		6 Objectives	
		Avg	SD	Avg	SD	Avg	SD	Avg	SD
DTLZ1	NSGA-II	0.0398	0.0081	0.0491	0.0076	0.0758	0.0098	0.0953	0.0094
	SPEA-II	**0.0200**	0.0072	**0.0374**	0.0051	**0.0324**	0.0038	**0.0282**	0.0036
	COGA	0.0206	0.0036	0.0376	0.0061	0.0498	0.0061	0.0511	0.0073
DTLZ2	NSGA-II	0.0528	0.0036	0.0776	0.0058	0.1002	0.0071	0.1225	0.0096
	SPEA-II	**0.0184**	0.0015	**0.0263**	0.0024	**0.0365**	0.0057	**0.0321**	0.0039
	COGA	0.0251	0.0029	0.0370	0.0047	0.0404	0.0063	0.0517	0.0095
DTLZ3	NSGA-II	0.0411	0.0088	0.0402	0.0037	0.0790	0.0077	0.1101	0.0071
	SPEA-II	0.0272	0.0091	**0.0370**	0.0065	**0.0414**	0.0065	**0.0381**	0.0043
	COGA	**0.0246**	0.0036	0.0422	0.0046	0.0477	0.0049	0.0591	0.0058
DTLZ4	NSGA-II	0.0511	0.0046	0.0748	0.0064	0.0926	0.0071	0.1107	0.0073
	SPEA-II	**0.0182**	0.0022	**0.0268**	0.0033	**0.0351**	0.0043	**0.0333**	0.0040
	COGA	0.0242	0.0020	0.0328	0.0043	0.0369	0.0048	0.0421	0.0060
DTLZ6	NSGA-II	0.0257	0.0025	0.0716	0.0054	0.1010	0.0060	0.1183	0.0068
	SPEA-II	0.0146	0.0023	**0.0291**	0.0036	**0.0258**	0.0030	**0.0287**	0.0028
	COGA	**0.0132**	0.0016	0.0309	0.0041	0.0404	0.0045	0.0480	0.0053
DTLZ7	NSGA-II	0.0410	0.0039	0.0828	0.0055	0.1158	0.0065	0.1262	0.0115
	SPEA-II	**0.0205**	0.0024	**0.0379**	0.0049	**0.0407**	0.0063	**0.0492**	0.0056
	COGA	0.0224	0.0026	0.0486	0.0041	0.0465	0.0061	0.0527	0.0065

inappropriately assigned. Thus, the relationship between objectives, for instance conflict, harmony and independence [12], should be further investigated. But since most solutions do not involve such strong conflicting characteristics, their ranks are considered acceptable. This reasoning concurs with the resulting solutions in which COGA results is generally superior to the two other algorithms in which all non-dominated solutions have the same rank. In addition, solutions in some problems may bias towards certain sections of the Pareto front due to the truncation based only on ranks. In such cases, the truncation in sub-section 3.2 already takes the spreads of solutions into consideration.

6 Conclusions

COGA is introduced in this paper. Basically, large number of objectives in a problem can be transformed into two-objectives, a maximising winning score and a minimising vicinity index, for selection and truncation. COGA is formulated and benchmarked against NSGA-II [6] and SPEA-II [7] using six scalable DTLZ problems with three to six objectives [9]. The results reveal that COGA is superior to NSGA-II and SPEA-II in terms of the solution set coverage and the average distance from the non-dominated solutions to the true Pareto front. In addition, the spacing index of the solutions generated by COGA is very close to that from SPEA-II. These results clearly indicates the strong potential of preference objective implementation into MOEAs.

Acknowledgements. This work was supported by the Research Grant for New Scholar (RGNS) from the Commission on Higher Education and Thailand Research Fund (TRF) with Prof. P. Dechaumphai as the project mentor.

References

1. Horn, J., Nafpliotis, N.: Multiobjective optimization using the niched Pareto genetic algorithm. IlliGAL Report No. 93005, Illinois Genetic Algorithms Laboratory, University of Illinois at Urbana-Champaign, IL (1993)
2. Srinivas, N., Deb, K.: Multi-objective function optimization using non-dominated sorting genetic algorithms. Evol. Comput. **2**(3) (1994) 221–248
3. Fonseca, C.M., Fleming, P.J.: Multiobjective optimization and multiple constraint handling with evolutionary algorithms–Part 1: A unified formulation. IEEE Trans. Syst. Man Cybern. A Syst. Hum. **28**(1) (1998) 26–37
4. Zitzler, E., Thiele, L.: Multiobjective evolutionary algorithms: A comparative case study and the strength Pareto approach. IEEE Trans. Evol. Comput. **3**(4) (1999) 257–271
5. Deb, K., Goel, T.: Controlled elitist non-dominated sorting genetic algorithms for better convergence. Lect. Notes Comput. Sc. **1993** (2001) 67–81
6. Deb, K., Pratap, A., Agarwal, S., Meyarivan, T.: A fast and elitist multiobjective genetic algorithm: NSGA-II. IEEE Trans. Evol. Comput. **6**(2) (2002) 182–197
7. Zitzler, E., Laumanns, M., Thiele, L.: SPEA2: Improving the strength Pareto evolutionary algorithm for multiobjective optimization. In: Giannakoglou, K., Tsahalis, D., Periaux, J., Papailiou, K., Fogarty, T. (eds.): Evolutionary Methods for Design, Optimisation and Control. CIMNE, Barcelona, Spain (2002) 95–100
8. Chaiyaratana, N., Piroonratana, T., Sangkawelert, N.: Effects of diversity control in single-objective and multi-objective genetic algorithms. J. Heuristics (2007) in press
9. Deb, K., Thiele, L., Laumanns, M., Zitzler, E.: Scalable test problems for evolutionary multi-objective optimization. In: Abraham, A., Jain, L.C., Goldberg, R. (eds.): Evolutionary Multiobjective Optimization: Theoretical Advances and Applications. Springer, London, UK (2005) 105–145
10. Zitzler, E., Deb, K., Thiele, L.: Comparison of multiobjective evolutionary algorithms: Empirical results. Evol. Comput. **8**(2) (2000) 173–195
11. Deb, K.: Multi-objective Optimization Using Evolutionary Algorithms. Wiley (2001)
12. Purshouse, R.C., Fleming, P.J.: Conflict, harmony, and independence: Relationships in evolutionary multi-criterion optimisation. Lect. Notes Comput. Sc. **2632** (2003) 16–30

A New Proposal for Multiobjective Optimization Using Particle Swarm Optimization and Rough Sets Theory

Luis V. Santana-Quintero[1], Noel Ramírez-Santiago[1], Carlos A. Coello Coello[1], Julián Molina Luque[2], and Alfredo García Hernández-Díaz[3]

[1] CINVESTAV-IPN, Electrical Engineering Department, Computer Science Section, México D.F. 07300, México
lvspenny@hotmail.com, santiago@computacion.cs.cinvestav.mx, ccoello@cs.cinvestav.mx

[2] University of Malaga, Department of Applied Economics (Mathematics), Spain
julian.molina@uma.es

[3] Pablo de Olavide University, Department of Quantitative Methods, Seville, Spain
agarher@upo.es

Abstract. This paper presents a new multi-objective evolutionary algorithm which consists of a hybrid between a particle swarm optimization approach and some concepts from rough sets theory. The main idea of the approach is to combine the high convergence rate of the particle swarm optimization algorithm with a local search approach based on rough sets that is able to spread the nondominated solutions found, so that a good distribution along the Pareto front is achieved. Our proposed approach is able to converge in several test functions of 10 to 30 decision variables with only 4,000 fitness function evaluations. This is a very low number of evaluations if compared with today's standards in the specialized literature. Our proposed approach was validated using nine standard test functions commonly adopted in the specialized literature. Our results were compared with respect to a multi-objective evolutionary algorithm that is representative of the state-of-the-art in the area: the NSGA-II.

1 Introduction

In this paper, we propose a new multi-objective evolutionary algorithm (MOEA) which consists of a hybrid between a particle swarm optimization (PSO) approach and rough sets theory. The main aim of this work is to design a MOEA that can produce a reasonably good approximation of the true Pareto front of a problem with a relatively low number of fitness function evaluations (no more than 5000 fitness function evaluations). PSO is a bio-inspired metaheuristic that was proposed by James Kennedy and Russell Eberhart in the mid-1990s [1], and which is inspired on the choreography of a bird flock. In PSO, each solution is represented by a particle. Particles group in "swarms" (there can be either one swarm or several in one population) and the evolution of the swarm to the optimal solutions is achieved by a velocity equation. This equation is composed of

T.P. Runarsson et al. (Eds.): PPSN IX, LNCS 4193, pp. 483–492, 2006.

three elements: a velocity inertia, a cognitive component and a social component. Depending on the topology adopted (i.e., one swarm or multiple swarms), each particle can be affected by either the best local and/or the best global particle in its swarm. PSO has been found to be a very successful optimization approach both in single-objective and in multi-objective problems [1,2]. However, so far, the high convergence rate of PSO has not been properly exploited by researchers, since most of the current multi-objective PSOs (MOPSOs) perform 20,000 fitness function evaluations or more in test functions such as the ones adopted in this paper. The main reason for this is that despite its high convergence rate, PSO normally has difficulties to achieve a good distribution of solutions with a low number of evaluations. That is why we adopted rough sets theory (which can be useful at finding solutions within the neighborhood of a reference set) in this paper in order to have a local optimizer whose computational cost is low.

2 Particle Swarm Optimization

In the PSO algorithm, the particles (including the *pbest*) are randomly initialized at the beginning of the search process. Next, the fittest particle from the swarm is identified and assigned to the *gbest* solution (i.e., the global best, or best particle found so far). After that, the swarm flies through the search space (in k dimensions, in the general case). The flight function adopted by PSO is determined by equation (1), which updates the position and fitness of the particle (see equation (2)). The new fitness is compared with respect to the particle's *pbest* position. If it is better, then it replaces the *pbest* (i.e., the personal best, or the best value that has been found for this particle so far). This procedure is repeated for every particle in the swarm until the termination criteria is reached.

$$v_{i,k} = w \cdot v_{i,k} + c_1 \cdot U(0,1)(pbest_{i,k} - x_{i,k}) + c_2 \cdot U(0,1)(gbest_k - x_{i,k}); \quad (1)$$

$$x_{i,k} = x_{i,k} + v_{i,k} \quad (2)$$

where c_1 and c_2 are constants that indicate the attraction from the *pbest* or *gbest* position, respectively; w refers to the velocity inertia of the previous movement; $x_i = (x_{i1}, x_{i2}, ..., x_{ik})$ represents the $i - th$ particle. U(0,1) denotes a uniformly random number generated in the range (0,1).

There are plenty of proposals to extend PSO for dealing with multiple objectives (see for example [2,3]). A survey of MOPSOs is beyond the scope of this paper, but interested readers may refer to [4].

3 Rough Sets Theory

Rough sets theory is a new mathematical approach to imperfect knowledge that was originally proposed by Pawlak [5]. The main idea of this approach is explained next. Let's assume that we are given a set of objects S called the universe and an indiscernibility relation $R \subseteq S \times S$, representing our lack of knowledge about elements of S (in our case, R is simply an equivalence relation based on a grid over the feasible set; this is, just a division of the feasible set in (hyper)-rectangles). Let X be a subset of S. We want to characterize the set X with respect to R. The way rough sets theory expresses vagueness is employing a boundary region of the set X. If the boundary region of a set is empty it means that the set is *crisp*; otherwise, the set is *rough* (inexact). A nonempty boundary region of a set means that our knowledge about the set is not enough to define the set precisely. Then, each element in S is classified as *certainly* inside X if it belongs to the lower approximation or *partially* (*probably*) inside X if it belongs to the upper approximation. The *boundary* is the difference of these two sets, and the bigger the boundary the worse the knowledge we have of set X. On the other hand, the more precise is the grid implicity used to define the indiscernibility relation R, the smaller the boundary regions are. But, the more precise is the grid, the bigger the number of elements in S, and then, the more complex the problem becomes. Our aim is to use rough sets to explore the neighborhood of a set of reference solutions (the nondominated solutions found by our PSO-based MOEA), so that we can spread such solutions along the Pareto front. For this sake, it is required to design a grid and decide which elements of S (that we will call *atoms* and will be just rectangular portions of decision variable space) are inside the Pareto optimal set and which are not. Once we have the *efficient atoms*, we will intensify the search over these atoms. Note however, that the precision of the grid has an impact on both the computational cost (the more precise the grid, the higher its cost) and on effectiveness (the less precise the grid, the less knowledge we can obtain from it). Evidently, in our approach, we will try to generate a grid that is not so computationally expensive but that offers a reasonably good knowledge about the Pareto optimal set. Once this grid is built, it becomes relatively straightforward to generate more points on the *efficient atoms*, as these atoms are built in decision variable space. Note however, that the use of rough sets requires not only a set of nondominated solutions, but also another one of dominated solutions that are close to being nondominated. This second set is required in order to intensify the search. Thus, our MOEA will be modified in order to keep this second set, which is not normally required in evolutionary multiobjective optimization.

4 Pareto-adaptive ϵ-Dominance

Our approach also adopts a variant of ε-dominance [6] that we call *pa*ε-dominance. The details of *pa*ε-dominance are omitted due to space constraints (see [7] for further information), but its main difference with respect to the original proposal is that in this case the hyper-grid generated adapts the sizes of the boxes to certain geometrical characteristics of the Pareto front (e.g., almost horizontal or vertical portions of the Pareto front) as to increase the number of solutions retained in the grid. Thus, this scheme maintains the good properties of ε-dominance but improves on its main weaknesses.

5 Our Proposed Approach

Our proposed approach, called PSOMORSA (Particle Swarm Optimization for Multiobjective Optimization with Rough Sets), is divided in two phases, and each of them consumes a fixed number of fitness function evaluations. During Phase I, our PSO-based MOEA is applied for 2000 fitness function evaluations. During Phase II, a local search procedure based on rough sets theory is applied for another 2000 fitness function evaluations, in order to improve the solutions (i.e., spread them along the Pareto front) produced at the previous phase. Each of these two phases is described next in more detail.

5.1 Phase I: Particle Swarm Optimization

Our proposed PSO-based approach adopts a very small population size ($P = 5$ particles). The leader is determined using a very simple criterion: the first N particles (N is the number of objectives of the problem) are guided by the best particle in each objective, considered separately. The remainder $P - N$ particles are adopted to build an approximation of the ideal vector. Then, we identify the individual which is closest to this ideal vector and such individual becomes the leader for the remainder $P - N$ particles. The purpose of these selection criteria is twofold: first, we aim to approximate the optimum for each separate objective, by exploiting the high convergence rate of PSO in single-objective optimization. The second purpose of our selection rules is to encourage convergence towards the "knee" of the Pareto front (considering the bi-objective case). We found that the use of rough sets can generate the entire Pareto front even if only one nondominated solution is available in the Pareto front, and in disconnected Pareto fronts it is required only one nondominated solution per each discontinuos segment of the Pareto front.

Algorithm 1 shows the pseudocode of Phase I from our proposed approach. First, we randomly generate 5 individuals. In the $getLeaders()$ function, we identify the best particles in each objective and the closest particle to the ideal vector. Those particles (the leaders) are stored in the set L. Then the $getLeader(\boldsymbol{x})$ function returns the position of the leader from the set L. Then, we perform the flight in order to obtain a new particle. If this solution is beyond the allowable bounds for a decision variable, then we adopt the $BLX - \alpha$ recombination operator [8], and a new vector solution $Z = (z_1, z_2, ..., z_d)$ is generated, where $z_i \in [c_{min} - I\alpha, c_{max} + I\alpha]$; $c_{max} = max(a, b)$, $c_{min} = min(a, b)$, $I = c_{max} - c_{min}$, $\alpha = 0.5$, $a = L_g$ (the leader of the particle) and $b = pbest$ (i.e., the personal best of the particle). Note that the use of a recombination operator is not a common practice in PSO, and some people may consider our approach as a PSO-variant because of that. PSO does not use a specific mutation operator (the variation of the factors of the flight equation may compensate for that). However, it has become common practice in MOPSOs to adopt some sort of mutation (or turbulence) operator that improves the exploration capabilities of PSO [2,3]. The use of a mutation operator is normally simpler (and easier) than varying the factors of the flight equation and therefore its extended use. We adopted Parameter-Based Mutation [9] in our approach with $p_m = 1/n$. Our proposed approach

Algorithm 1: Algorithm for the Phase I of our approach

```
begin
    Initialize Population (P) with randomly generated solutions;
    getLeaders();
    repeat
        for i = 1 to P do
            g = getLeader(i);
            for d = 1 to k do
                /* L_{g,d} is the leader of particle i */;
                v_{i,d} = w · v_{i,d} + c_1 · U(0,1)(p_{i,d} − x_{i,d}) + c_2 · U(0,1)(L_{g,d} − x_{i,d});
                x_{i,d} = x_{i,d} + v_{i,d};
            end
            if x_i ∉ search space then
                x_i = BLX − α(x_i);
            end
            if U(0,1) < p_m then
                x_i = Mutate(x_i);
            end
            if x_i is nondominated then
                for d = 1 to k do
                    p_{i,d} = x_{i,d};;
                end
            end
        end
        getLeaders();
        Add nondominated solutions into secondary population
    until MaxIter ;
end
```

also uses an external archive (also called secondary population). In order to include a solution into this external archive, it is compared with respect to each member already contained in the archive using the $pa\epsilon$-dominance grid [7]. And a third population (called DS) stores the dominated points needed for Phase II. Every removed point from the secondary population (also called ES) is included into the third population. If this third population reaches a size of 100 points, a $pa\epsilon$-dominance grid will be created in order to ensure a good distribution of dominated points.

5.2 Phase II: Local Search Using Rough Sets

The Rough Sets Phase departs from the two sets obtained from Phase I (ES, which contains the nondominated solutions, and DS, which contains the dominated solutions). The main loop of the second phase is the following:

1. From the set ES, we choose $NumEff$ points previously unselected. If we do not have enough unselected points, we choose the rest randomly from the set ES.
2. We choose from the set DS, $NumDom$ points previously unselected (complete randomly as before).
3. Do a Rough Sets iteration, to approximate the boundary between the Pareto front and the rest of the feasible set. This information is used to intensify the search in the area where the nondominated points reside, while refusing the finding of more points in the dominated area.

The dominated and nondominated points are both stored in the set *Items* and the rough sets iteration is the following:

1. **Range Initialization:** For each decision variable i, we compute and sort (from the smallest to the highest) the different values contained in *Items*. Then, we have the set $Range_i$, for each i. By combining all these sets we produce a (non-uniform) grid in decision variable space.
2. **Compute Atoms:** We compute $NumEff$ rectangular atoms centered in the $NumEff$ efficient points selected. To build a rectangular atom associated to a nondominated point $x^e \in Items$ we compute the following upper and lower bounds for each decision variable i:
   - Lower Bound i: Middle point between x_i^e and the previous value in the set $Range_i$.
   - Upper Bound i: Middle point between x_i^e and the following value in the set $Range_i$.

   In both cases, if there are no previous or subsequent values in $Range_i$, we consider the absolute lower or upper bound of variable i. This setting allows the method to explore closer to the feasible set boundaries.
3. **Generate Offspring:** Inside each atom we randomly generate $Offspring$ new points. Each of these points is sent to the set ES (we use the $pa\epsilon$-dominance grid for that sake) to check if it must be included as a new nondominated point. If any point in ES is dominated by this new point, it is sent to the set DS.

6 Analysis of Results

In order to validate our proposed approach, we compare results with respect to the NSGA-II [9], which is a MOEA representative of the state-of-the-art in the area. The first phase of our approach uses three parameters: population size (P), leaders number (N), mutation probability (P_m), plus the traditional PSO parameters (w, c_1, c_2). On the other hand, the second phase uses three more parameters: number of points randomly generated inside each atom ($Offspring$), number of atoms per generations ($NumEff$) and the number of dominated points considered to generate the atoms ($NumDom$). Finally, the minimum number of nondominated points needed to generate the $pa\epsilon$-dominance grid is set to 100 for all problems. Our approach was validated using 9 test problems: 5 problems from the **ZDT** set [10] and 4 from the **DTLZ** set [11]. The detailed description of these test functions was omitted due to space restrictions (see [10,11] for further information). However, all of these test functions are unconstrained, minimization and have between 10 and 30 decision variables. In all cases, the parameters of our approach were set as follows: $P = 5$, $N = k + 1$ (k = number of objective functions), $P_m = 1/n$ (n = number of decision variables), $w = 0.3$, $c_1 = 0.1$, $c_2 = 1.4$, $Offspring = 1$, $NumEff = 2$ and $NumDom = 10$. The NSGA-II used the following parameters: crossover rate = 0.9, mutation rate = 1/n, $\eta_c = 15$, $\eta_m = 20$, population size = 100 and maximum number of generations = 40. The population size of the NSGA-II is the same as the size of

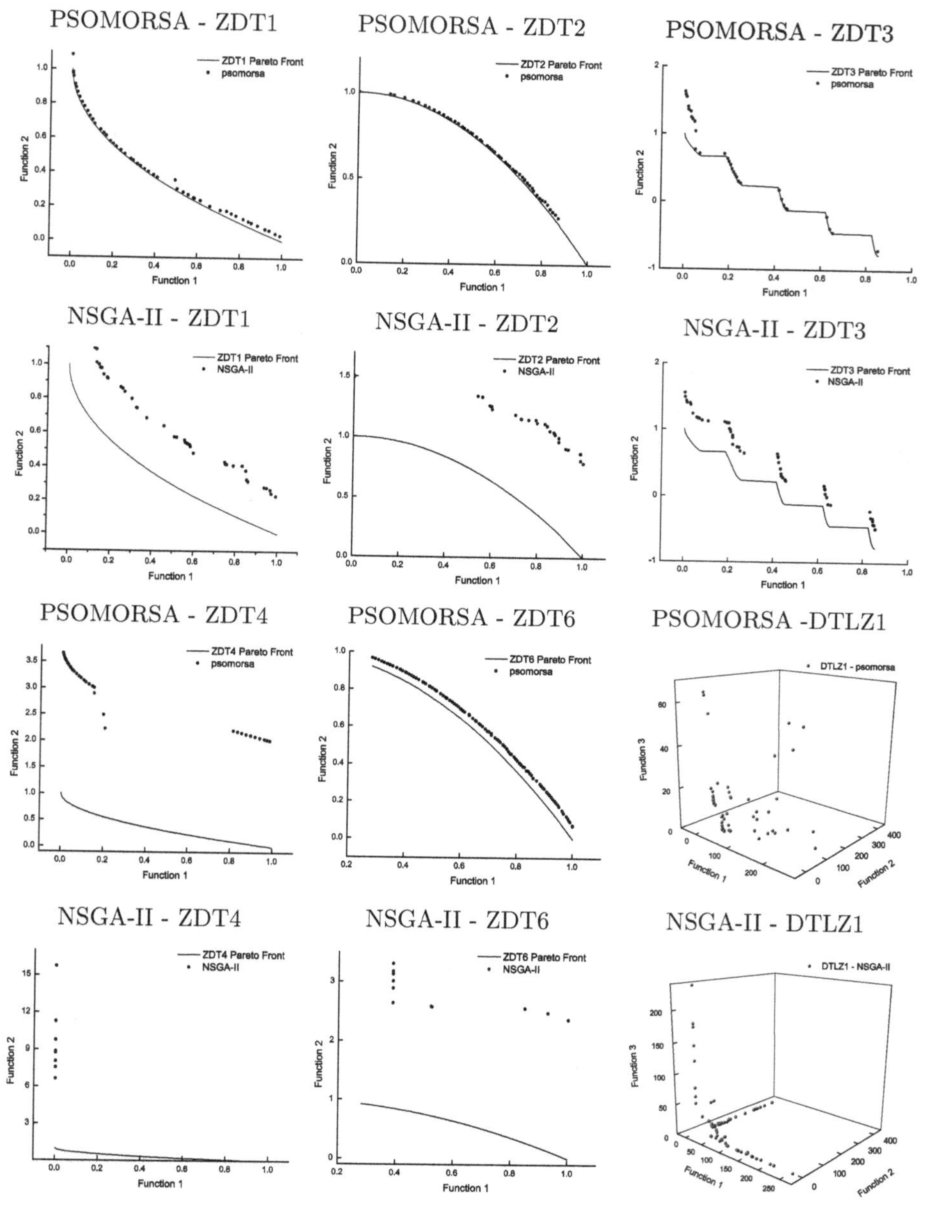

Fig. 1. Pareto fronts generated by PSOMORSA and NSGA-II for ZDT's and DTLZ1

the grid of our approach. In order to allow a fair comparison of results, both approaches adopted real-numbers encoding and performed 4,000 fitness function evaluations per run. Three performance measures were adopted in order to allow a quantitative assessment of our results: (1) Inverted Generational Distance (**IGD**), which is a variation of a metric proposed by Van Veldhuizen [12] in

Table 1. Comparison of results between our approach (called PSOMORSA) and the NSGA-II for the nine test problems adopted

Function	IGD				S				SC			
	PSOMORSA		NSGA-II		PSOMORSA		NSGA-II		PSOMORSA		NSGA-II	
	Mean	σ	Mean	σ	Mean	σ	Mean	σ	Mean	σ	Mean	σ
ZDT1	**0.0009**	0.0005	0.0097	0.0019	**0.4827**	0.1306	0.5603	0.0483	**0.0222**	0.0312	0.9332	0.0355
ZDT2	**0.0036**	0.0057	0.0223	0.0064	**0.6176**	0.2199	0.7130	0.1114	**0.0038**	0.0127	0.8784	0.1645
ZDT3	**0.0043**	0.0014	0.0155	0.0020	0.7761	0.0656	**0.7441**	0.0456	**0.0608**	0.0656	0.9062	0.0555
ZDT4	**0.1265**	0.0371	0.4297	0.1304	**0.9590**	0.0424	0.9718	0.0412	**0.0342**	0.0557	0.3065	0.1560
ZDT6	**0.0009**	0.0003	0.0420	0.0041	**0.7336**	0.1271	0.8706	0.0817	**0.0012**	0.0066	0.9333	0.2034
DTLZ1	**0.5157**	0.1217	0.7318	0.2062	0.9983	0.0015	**0.9972**	0.0011	0.3208	0.1945	**0.3142**	0.1839
DTLZ2	**0.0004**	0.0001	**0.0004**	0.0000	0.5676	0.0747	**0.3188**	0.0440	**0.1418**	0.1485	0.1913	0.1131
DTLZ3	**1.1681**	0.3063	1.4228	0.2690	0.9990	0.0012	**0.9986**	0.0012	0.5220	0.2600	**0.1545**	0.1019
DTLZ4	0.0221	0.0038	**0.0096**	0.0025	0.7682	0.1055	**0.6676**	0.1250	0.8537	0.1626	**0.0084**	0.0272

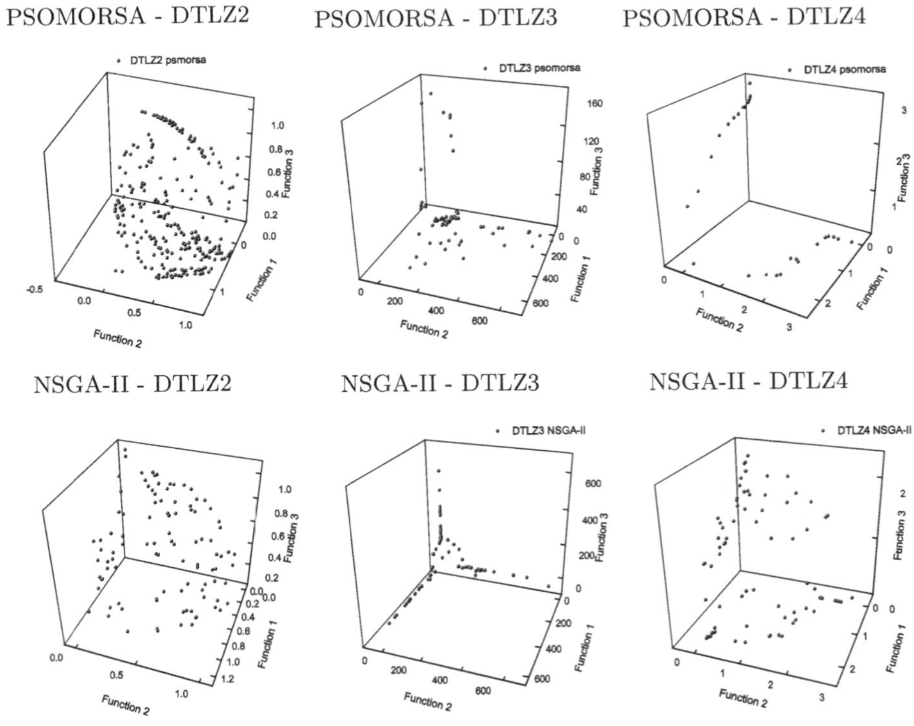

Fig. 2. Pareto fronts generated by PSOMORSA and NSGA-II for DTLZ2, DTLZ3 and DTLZ4

which the true Pareto is used as a reference; Spread (**S**), proposed by Deb et al. [13], which measures both progress towards the Pareto-optimal front and the extent of spread; and (3) Two Set Coverage (**SC**), proposed by Zitzler et al. [10], which performs a relative coverage comparison of two sets. For each test problem, 30 independent runs were performed and the results reported in Table 1 correspond to the mean and standard deviation of the performance metrics

(IGD, S and SC). We show in boldface the best mean values per test function. It can be observed that in the ZDT's test problems our approach produced the best results with respect to both IGD and SC in all cases. Remarkably, our approach also outperformed the NSGA-II with respect to the spread metric in all but one case (ZDT3). In the DTLZ's test problems, the NSGA-II outperformed our approach in one case with respect to IGD, in all cases with respect to Spread and in 3 (out of 4) cases with respect to SC. Figures 1 and 2 show the graphical results produced by the PSOMORSA and NSGA-II for all the test problems adopted. The solutions displayed correspond to the median result with respect to the IGD metric. The true Pareto front (obtained by enumeration) is shown with a continuous line and the approximation produced by each algorithm is shown with circles. In Figures 1 and 2, we can clearly see that in problems ZDT1, ZDT2, ZDT3, ZDT4 and ZDT6, the NSGA-II is very far from the true Pareto front, whereas our PSOMORSA is very close to the true Pareto front after only 4,000 fitness function evaluations (except for ZDT4). Graphically, the results are not entirely clear for the DTLZ test problems. However, if we pay attention to the scale, it will be evident that, in most cases, our approach has several points closer to the true Pareto front than the NSGA-II. Nevertheless, due to the better spread of the NSGA-II, there are a few points that dominate several of the solutions produced by our approach and therefore the superiority of the NSGA-II with respect to the SC and S metrics. The poor performance of our approach in the DTLZ's test problems is caused in the PSO selection process because we select one particle that helps to optimize the third objective function and the ideal vector is optimized with two other particles, causing that the convergence rate gets lower than expected in problems with three or more objectives.

7 Conclusions and Future Work

We have introduced a new hybrid between a MOEA based on PSO and a local search mechanism based on rough sets theory. This hybrid aims to combine the high convergence rate of PSO with the good neighborhood exploration performed by the rough sets algorithm. Our proposed approach produced results that are competitive with respect to the NSGA-II in problems whose dimensionality goes from 10 up to 30 decision variables, while performing only 4,000 fitness function evaluations. Although our results are still preliminary, they are very encouraging, since they seem to indicate that our proposed approach could be a viable alternative for solving real-world problems in which the cost of a single fitness function evaluation is very high (e.g., in aeronautics). As part of our future work, we intend to improve the performance of the PSO approach adopted. Particularly, the selection of the appropriate leader is an issue that deserves further study.

Acknowledgments. The third author acknowledges support from CONACyT through project number 45683-Y.

References

1. Kennedy, J., Eberhart, R.C.: Swarm Intelligence. Morgan Kaufmann Publishers, California, USA (2001)
2. Coello Coello, C.A., Toscano Pulido, G., Salazar Lechuga, M.: Handling Multiple Objectives With Particle Swarm Optimization. IEEE Transactions on Evolutionary Computation **8**(3) (2004) 256–279
3. Mostaghim, S., Teich, J.: Strategies for Finding Good Local Guides in Multi-objective Particle Swarm Optimization (MOPSO). In: IEEE Swarm Intelligence Symposium Proc., Indianapolis, Indiana, USA, IEEE Service Center (2003) 26–33
4. Reyes-Sierra, M., Coello Coello, C.A.: Multi-Objective Particle Swarm Optimizers: A Survey of the State-of-the-Art. International Journal of Computational Intelligence Research **2**(3) (2006) 287–308
5. Pawlak, Z.: Rough sets. International Journal of Computer and Information Sciences **11**(1) (1982) 341–356
6. Laumanns, M., Thiele, L., Deb, K., Zitzler, E.: Combining convergence and diversity in evolutionary multi-objective optimization. Evolutionary Computation **10**(3) (2002) 263–282
7. Hernández-Díaz, A.G., Santana-Quintero, L.V., Coello, C.A.C., Molina, J.: Pareto-adaptive ε-dominance. Technical Report EVOCINV-02-2006, Evolutionary Computation Group at CINVESTAV, Sección de Computación, Departamento de Ingeniería Eléctrica, CINVESTAV-IPN, México (2006)
8. Eshelman, L.J., Schaffer, J.D.: Real-coded Genetic Algorithms and Interval-Schemata. In Whitley, L.D., ed.: Foundations of Genetic Algorithms 2. Morgan Kaufmann Publishers, San Mateo, California (1993) 187–202
9. Deb, K., Pratap, A., Agarwal, S., Meyarivan, T.: A Fast and Elitist Multiobjective Genetic Algorithm: NSGA–II. IEEE Transactions on Evolutionary Computation **6**(2) (2002) 182–197
10. Zitzler, E., Deb, K., Thiele, L.: Comparison of Multiobjective Evolutionary Algorithms:Empirical Results. Evolutionary Computation **8**(2) (2000) 173–195
11. Deb, K., Thiele, L., Laumanns, M., Zitzler, E.: Scalable Test Problems for Evolutionary Multiobjective Optimization. In Abraham, A., Jain, L., Goldberg, R., eds.: Evolutionary Multiobjective Optimization. Theoretical Advances and Applications. Springer, USA (2005) 105–145
12. Veldhuizen, D.A.V.: Multiobjective Evolutionary Algorithms: Classifications, Analyses, and New Innovations. PhD thesis, Department of Electrical and Computer Engineering. Graduate School of Engineering. Air Force Institute of Technology, Wright-Patterson AFB, Ohio (1999)
13. Deb, K.: Multi-Objective Optimization using Evolutionary Algorithms. John Wiley & Sons (2001) ISBN 0-471-87339-X.

Incorporation of Scalarizing Fitness Functions into Evolutionary Multiobjective Optimization Algorithms

Hisao Ishibuchi, Tsutomu Doi, and Yusuke Nojima

Department of Computer Science and Intelligent Systems, Graduate School of Engineering, Osaka Prefecture University, 1-1 Gakuen-cho, Naka-ku, Sakai, Osaka 599-8531, Japan
hisaoi@cs.osakafu-u.ac.jp, doi@ci.cs.osakafu-u.ac.jp
nojima@cs.osakafu-u.ac.jp
http://www.ie.osakafu-u.ac.jp/~hisaoi/ci_lab_e

Abstract. This paper proposes an idea of probabilistically using a scalarizing fitness function in evolutionary multiobjective optimization (EMO) algorithms. We introduce two probabilities to specify how often the scalarizing fitness function is used for parent selection and generation update in EMO algorithms. Through computational experiments on multiobjective 0/1 knapsack problems with two, three and four objectives, we show that the probabilistic use of the scalarizing fitness function improves the performance of EMO algorithms. In a special case, our idea can be viewed as the probabilistic use of an EMO scheme in single-objective evolutionary algorithms (SOEAs). From this point of view, we examine the effectiveness of our idea. Experimental results show that our idea improves not only the performance of EMO algorithms for multiobjective problems but also that of SOEAs for single-objective problems.

1 Introduction

Evolutionary multiobjective optimization (EMO) is one of the most active research areas in the field of evolutionary computation. EMO algorithms have been successfully applied to various application areas [2]. Most EMO algorithms use Pareto ranking to evaluate the fitness of each solution. Pareto ranking-based EMO algorithms, however, do not work well on many-objective problems (e.g., see [5], [6], [8], [12], [16]). This is because solutions rarely dominate other solutions in the presence of many objectives. Hughes [6] showed that multiple runs of single-objective evolutionary algorithms (SOEAs) outperformed a single run of EMO algorithms in their applications to many-objective problems. Similar results were also reported in [8], [12]. Whereas EMO algorithms do not work well on many-objective problems, usually they work very well on two-objective problems. In some cases, EMO algorithms can outperform SOEAs even when they are used to solve single-objective problems. It was reported in some studies [13], [18] that better results were obtained by transforming single-objective problems into multi-objective ones.

These experimental results suggest that SOEAs and EMO algorithms have their own advantages and disadvantages. In this paper, we hybridize them into a single algorithm in order to simultaneously utilize their advantages. More specifically, we

T.P. Runarsson et al. (Eds.): PPSN IX, LNCS 4193, pp. 493 – 502, 2006.

propose an idea of probabilistically using a scalarizing fitness function for parent selection and generation update in EMO algorithms. Following this idea, we implement a hybrid algorithm using NSGA-II [3] and a weighted sum fitness function. The weighted sum fitness function is probabilistically used for parent selection and generation update in NSGA-II. We introduce two probabilities to specify how often the weighted sum fitness function is used for parent selection and generation update.

We use NSGA-II because it is one of the most frequently-used EMO algorithms in the literature. The use of the weighted sum fitness function is due to its simplicity. Of course, other scalarizing fitness functions can be used in our hybrid algorithm. A scalarizing fitness function-based EMO algorithm was proposed by Hughes [5] in a general form. The weighted sum fitness function was successfully used in multiobjective genetic local search (MOGLS) algorithms [7], [9], [10]. High performance of MOGLS of Jaszkiewicz [10] was reported [1], [11], [14]. The weighted sum fitness function was also used in a two-stage EMO algorithm of Mumford [14].

The main feature of our hybrid algorithm is the probabilistic use of the weighted sum fitness function. When the probability of its use is very low, our hybrid algorithm is almost the same as NSGA-II. The increase in the probability of its use intensifies the flavor of weighted sum-based algorithms. Another feature is the flexibility in the specification of the weight vector in the weighted sum fitness function. We can use a set of uniformly distributed weight vectors for multiobjective optimization as well as a single weight vector for single-objective optimization. In this paper, we first explain our hybrid algorithm in Section 2. Then we examine its performance as single-objective and multiobjective algorithms in Section 3 and Section 4, respectively.

2 Implementation of a Hybrid Algorithm

In this section, we implement a hybrid algorithm by incorporating a weighted sum fitness function into NSGA-II [3]. We introduce two probabilities P_{PS} and P_{GU}, which specify how often the weighted sum fitness function is used for parent selection and generation update, respectively.

Let us consider the following k-objective maximization problem:

$$\text{Maximize } \mathbf{f}(\mathbf{x}) = (f_1(\mathbf{x}), \ldots, f_k(\mathbf{x})) \text{ subject to } \mathbf{x} \in \mathbf{X}, \tag{1}$$

where $\mathbf{f}(\mathbf{x})$ is the k-dimensional objective vector, $\mathbf{x}$ is the decision vector, and $\mathbf{X}$ is the feasible region in the decision space. When the following relation holds between two feasible solutions $\mathbf{x}$ and $\mathbf{y}$, $\mathbf{x}$ is said to be dominated by $\mathbf{y}$ (i.e., $\mathbf{y}$ is better than $\mathbf{x}$):

$$\forall i,\ f_i(\mathbf{x}) \le f_i(\mathbf{y}) \quad \text{and} \quad \exists j,\ f_j(\mathbf{x}) < f_j(\mathbf{y}). \tag{2}$$

When there is no feasible solution $\mathbf{y}$ in $\mathbf{X}$ that dominates $\mathbf{x}$, $\mathbf{x}$ is referred to as a Pareto-optimal solution. Usually multiobjective optimization problems have a large number of Pareto-optimal solutions. The set of objective vectors corresponding to all Pareto-optimal solutions is referred to as Pareto front.

2.1 Description of NSGA-II as a General Evolutionary Algorithm

NSGA-II of Deb et al. [3] is an elitist EMO algorithm with the $(\mu+\lambda)$-ES generation update mechanism. The outline of NSGA-II can be written as follows:

[NSGA-II]

```
Step 1: P = Initialize(P)
Step 2: While the stopping condition is not satisfied, do
Step 3:              P' = Parent Selection(P)
Step 4:              P'' = Genetic Operations(P')
Step 5:              P = Generation Update(P∪P'')
Step 6: End while
Step 7: Return Non-dominated(P)
```

In NSGA-II, each solution in the current population is evaluated using Pareto ranking and a crowding measure in the following manner for parent selection in Step 3. First the best rank (i.e., Rank 1) is assigned to all the non-dominated solutions in the current population. Solutions with Rank 1 are tentatively removed from the current population. Next the second best rank (i.e., Rank 2) is assigned to all the non-dominated solutions in the remaining population. Solutions with Rank 2 are tentatively removed from the remaining population. In this manner, ranks are assigned to all solutions in the current population. Solutions with smaller rank values are viewed as being better than those with larger rank values. A crowding measure is used to compare solutions with the same rank. Roughly and informally speaking for two-objective problems, the crowding measure of a solution is the Manhattan distance between its two adjacent solutions in the objective space (for details, see [2], [3]). When two solutions have the same rank, one solution with a larger value of the crowding measure is viewed as being better than the other with a smaller value.

A prespecified number of pairs of parent solutions are selected from the current population by binary tournament selection to form a parent population P' in Step 3. An offspring solution is generated from each pair of parent solutions by crossover and mutation to form an offspring population P'' in Step 4. The current population and the offspring population are merged to form an enlarged population. Each solution in the enlarged population is evaluated by Pareto ranking and the crowding measure as in the parent selection phase. A prespecified number of the best solutions are chosen from the enlarged population as the next population P in Step 5.

2.2 Weighted Sum Fitness Function

The weighted sum fitness function of the k objectives in (1) is written as follows:

$$fitness(\mathbf{x}) = w_1 \cdot f_1(\mathbf{x}) + w_2 \cdot f_2(\mathbf{x}) + \ \ldots \ + w_k \cdot f_k(\mathbf{x}), \tag{3}$$

where w_i is a non-negative weight value.

One important issue is the specification of the weight vector $\mathbf{w} = (w_1, w_2, \ldots, w_k)$. We examine the following three versions in our hybrid algorithm.

Version I: The weight vector is always specified as $\mathbf{w} = (1, 1, ..., 1)$. That is, we always use the following scalarizing fitness function:

$$fitness(\mathbf{x}) = f_1(\mathbf{x}) + f_2(\mathbf{x}) + \ ... \ + f_k(\mathbf{x}) . \tag{4}$$

Version II: A different weight vector is randomly chosen from the $(2^k - 1)$ binary vectors excluding the zero vector (0, 0, ..., 0). For example, a weight vector is randomly chosen from the three binary vectors (1, 1), (1, 0) and (0, 1) in the case of $k = 2$ (i.e., two-objective problems). We have 7 and 15 non-zero binary vectors for three-objective and four-objective problems, respectively.

Version III: A different vector is randomly chosen from a set of non-negative integer vectors satisfying the following relation: $w_1 + w_2 + \ ... \ + w_k = d$ where d is a prespecified integer. In this paper, d is specified as $d = 4$ (Other values should be examined in the future study). In the case of two-objective problems, a weight vector is randomly chosen from the five integer vectors (4, 0), (3, 1), (2, 2), (1, 3) and (0, 4). For three-objective problems, we have 15 integer vectors: (4, 0, 0), (3, 1, 0), (2, 2, 0), ..., (0, 1, 3), (0, 0, 4). For four-objective problems, we have 35 integer vectors: (4, 0, 0, 0), (3, 1, 0, 0), ..., (0, 0, 0, 4). The same idea of the weight vector specification was used in [12], [14], [15].

2.3 Hybrid Algorithm

Our hybrid algorithm is the same as NSGA-II except for parent selection in Step 3 and generation update in Step 5. When a pair of parent solutions are to be selected from the current population, the weighted sum fitness function and the NSGA-II fitness evaluation mechanism are used with the probabilities P_{PS} and $(1 - P_{PS})$, respectively. When another pair of parent solutions are to be selected, the probabilistic choice between the two fitness evaluation schemes is performed again. As in NSGA-II, we always use binary tournament selection independent of the chosen fitness evaluation scheme. It should be noted that we use a randomly chosen weight vector in Version II and Version III of our hybrid algorithm.

As in the parent selection phase, we probabilistically use the weighted sum fitness function in the generation update phase. When one solution is to be chosen from the enlarged population and added to the next population, the weighted sum fitness function and the NSGA-II fitness evaluation mechanism are used with the probabilities P_{GU} and $(1 - P_{GU})$, respectively. When another solution is to be chosen, the probabilistic choice between the two fitness evaluation schemes is performed again.

One extreme case of our hybrid algorithm with $P_{PS} = P_{GU} = 0.0$ is exactly the same as the pure NSGA-II since the weighted sum fitness function is never used. Another extreme case with $P_{PS} = P_{GU} = 1.0$ is a weighted sum-based genetic algorithm with the $(\mu + \lambda)$-ES generation update mechanism. In this case, Version I algorithm is a single-objective genetic algorithm (SOGA) since the scalarizing fitness function in (4) is always used. Version II and Version III algorithms with $P_{PS} = P_{GU} = 1.0$ are EMO algorithms, which are somewhat similar to VEGA of Schaffer [17].

3 Single-Objective Optimization by Our Hybrid Algorithm

In this section, we examine the performance of our hybrid algorithm as a single-objective optimization algorithm for maximizing the sum of the k-objectives (i.e., the scalarizing fitness function in (4)). We use Version I of our hybrid algorithm where the scalarizing fitness function in (4) is used with the probabilities P_{PS} and P_{GU} for parent selection and generation update, respectively. As test problems, we use three 500-item knapsack problems with two, three and four objectives in [19]. These test problems are denoted as 2-500, 3-500 and 4-500, respectively. Our hybrid algorithm is applied to each test problem using the following parameter specifications:

Population size: 200 (i.e., $\mu = \lambda = 200$),
Crossover probability: 0.8 (uniform crossover),
Mutation probability: 0.002 (bit-flip mutation),
Probability P_{PS}: 0.0, 0.1, 0.2, 0.3, 0.4, 0.5, 0.6, 0.7, 0.8, 0.9, 1.0,
Probability P_{GU}: 0.0, 0.1, 0.2, 0.3, 0.4, 0.5, 0.6, 0.7, 0.8, 0.9, 1.0,
Termination condition: 2000 generations.

We examine the 11×11 combinations of the 11 values of P_{PS} and P_{GU}. Our hybrid algorithm with each combination of P_{PS} and P_{GU} is applied to each test problem 50 times. Average results over 50 runs are summarized in Fig. 1 for the 2-500 problem. In this figure, the performance of the pure SOGA with $P_{PS} = P_{GU} = 1.0$ at the top-right corner is improved by probabilistically using the NSGA-II fitness evaluation mechanism for generation update (i.e., by decreasing P_{GU} from $P_{GU} = 1.0$ to $P_{GU} < 1.0$). It is interesting to observe that even the pure NSGA-II with $P_{PS} = P_{GU} = 0.0$ at the bottom-left corner outperforms the pure SOGA with $P_{PS} = P_{GU} = 1.0$. This observation supports the idea of using EMO algorithms for single-objective optimization to escape from local optima [13], [18].

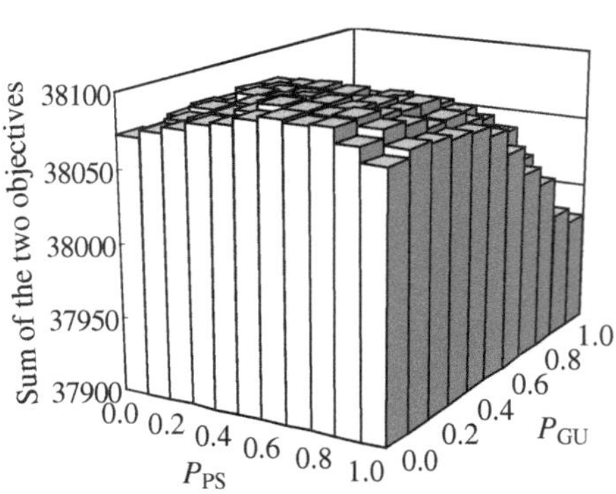

Fig. 1. Experimental results by Version I of our hybrid algorithm on the 2-500 problem

In order to further examine the performance of the three algorithms (i.e., our hybrid algorithm and its two extreme cases: NSGA-II and SOGA), each algorithm is applied to the 2-500 knapsack problem 100 times. In our hybrid algorithm, P_{PS} and P_{GU} are specified as $P_{PS} = 0.5$ and $P_{GU} = 0.0$. Fig. 2 shows the histograms of the obtained 100 values of the scalarizing fitness function in (4) by each algorithm. From Fig. 2 (and also from Fig. 1), we can see that NSGA-II and our hybrid algorithm outperform SOGA even when they are evaluated as single-objective optimization algorithms for maximizing the sum of the two objectives of the 2-500 problem.

The performance of SOGA is also improved by probabilistically using the NSGA-II fitness evaluation mechanism for the knapsack problems with three and four objectives (i.e., 3-500 and 4-500). Experimental results are shown in Fig. 3. The search ability of the pure SOGA with $P_{PS} = 1.0$ and $P_{GU} = 1.0$ at the top-right corner is improved by using the NSGA-II fitness evaluation mechanism for generation update (i.e., by decreasing P_{GU}). The pure NSGA-II with $P_{PS} = 0.0$ and $P_{GU} = 0.0$ at the bottom-left corner, however, cannot find good solutions with respect to the scalarizing fitness function. From the comparison between Fig. 1 and Fig. 3, we can see that the convergence ability of NSGA-II is degraded by increasing the number of objectives. This observation coincides with some studies on the performance of Pareto ranking-based EMO algorithms for many-objective optimization [6], [8], [12], [16].

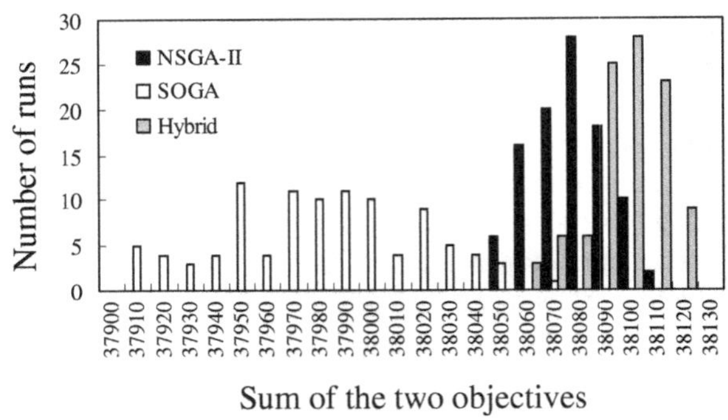

Fig. 2. Histograms of the obtained 100 values of the scalarizing fitness function by each of NSGA-II, SOGA and our Version I hybrid algorithm with $P_{PS} = 0.5$ and $P_{GU} = 0.0$

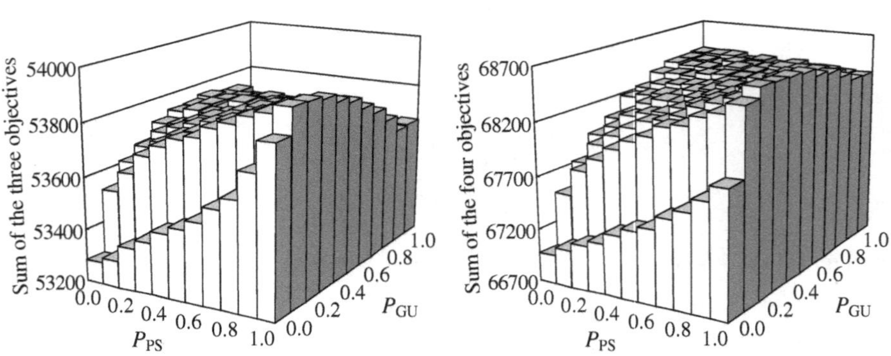

Fig. 3. Experimental results of our Version I hybrid algorithm

4 Multi-objective Optimization by Our Hybrid Algorithm

In this section, we examine the performance of our hybrid algorithm as a multi-objective optimization algorithm. As in the previous section, we use the three 500-item knapsack problems as test problems. Version II and Version III of our hybrid algorithm are applied to each test problem using the same parameter specifications as in the previous section. Each version of our hybrid algorithm is applied to each test problem 50 times using each of the 11×11 combinations of P_{PS} and P_{GU}.

In each run of our hybrid algorithm (i.e., Version II and Version III), we calculate the hypervolume measure (e.g., see Deb [2]) after the 2000th generation. Average results over 50 runs are summarized in Figs. 4-6.

The choice of a performance measure is very difficult. Whereas we only use the hypervolume (due to the page limitation), it is not necessarily the best choice [8]. We may need other performance measures in addition to the hypervolume. For example, Jaszkiewicz [12] proposed an idea of using achievement scalarizing functions. For the 2-500 problem, we also show the 50% attainment surface [4] later.

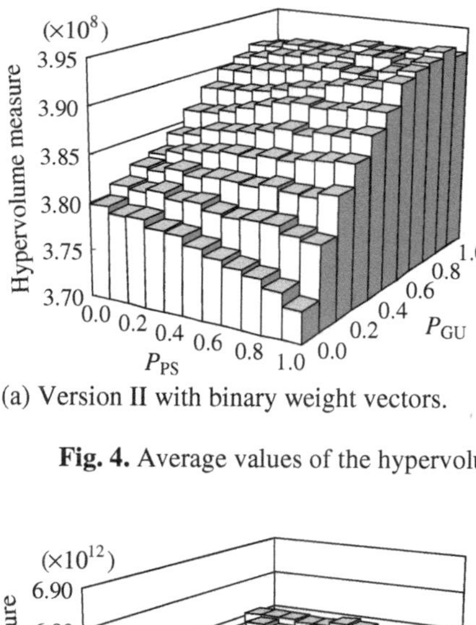

(a) Version II with binary weight vectors.

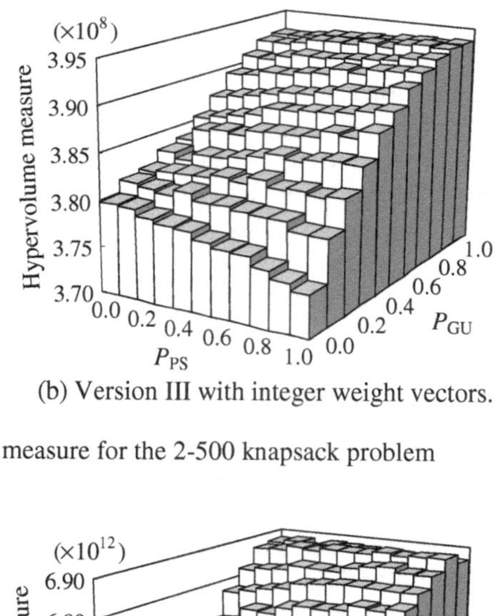

(b) Version III with integer weight vectors.

Fig. 4. Average values of the hypervolume measure for the 2-500 knapsack problem

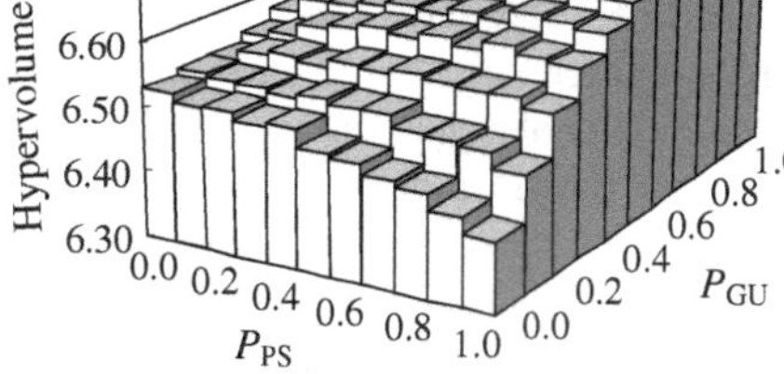

(a) Version II with binary weight vectors.

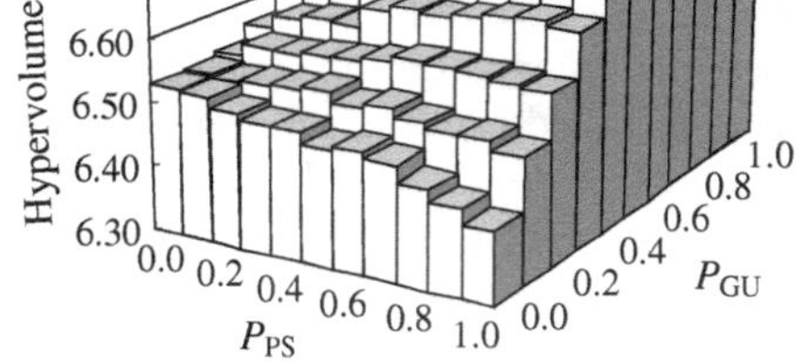

(b) Version III with integer weight vectors.

Fig. 5. Average values of the hypervolume measure for the 3-500 knapsack problem

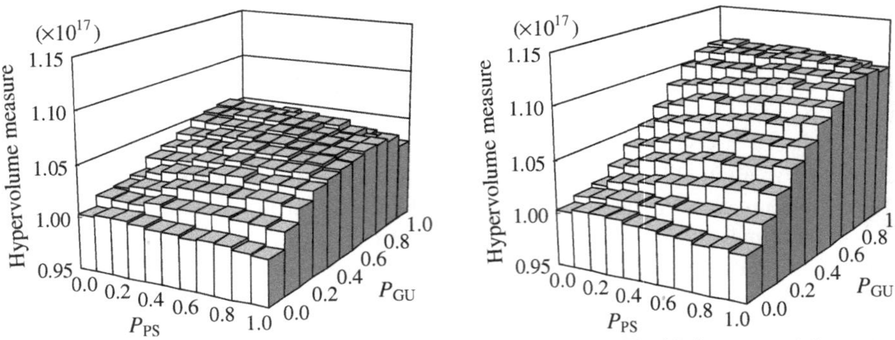

(a) Version II with binary weight vectors.

(b) Version III with integer weight vectors.

Fig. 6. Average values of the hypervolume measure for the 4-500 knapsack problem

In Figs. 4-6, the performance of the pure NSGA-II at the bottom-left corner with $P_{PS} = P_{GU} = 0.0$ is improved by probabilistically using the weighted sum fitness function for generation update (i.e., by increasing P_{GU} from $P_{GU} = 0.0$ to $P_{GU} > 0.0$). Good results are also obtained when the weighted sum fitness function is used with high probabilities for both parent selection and generation update (i.e., around the top-right corner). An interesting observation is that the use of the weighted sum fitness function only for parent selection (i.e., $P_{PS} > 0.0$ and $P_{GU} = 0.0$: experimental results along the bottom row) clearly degrades the performance of NSGA-II especially for the 2-500 problem in Fig. 4 and the 3-500 problem in Fig. 5.

In all the six plots in Figs. 4-6, good results are obtained by the weighted sum-based EMO algorithm at the top-right corner with $P_{PS} = P_{GU} = 1.0$. Its performance, however, can be further improved by appropriately specifying the two probabilities P_{PS} and P_{GU}. For example, better results are obtained in Fig. 6 around the top-left corner with a small value of P_{PS} and a large value of P_{GU} than the top-right corner with $P_{PS} = P_{GU} = 1.0$. For all the three test problems, better results are obtained from Version III with integer weight vectors than Version II with binary vectors.

In Fig. 7, we show the 50% attainment surface [4] over 50 runs of our hybrid algorithm on the 2-500 knapsack problem for some combinations of P_{PS} and P_{GU} including the two extreme cases (i.e., the pure NSGA-II and the pure weighted sum-based EMO algorithm). We use our Version II hybrid algorithm in Fig. 7 with the three binary weight vectors (1, 1), (1, 0) and (0, 1). As a result, the 50% attainment surface has three peaks in the case of the pure weighted sum-based EMO algorithm as shown by the dotted line labeled as "Weighted sum" in Fig. 7. Whereas NSGA-II can find better solutions than the center peak of the pure weighted sum-based EMO algorithm, it cannot find extreme solutions around the other two peaks. Depending on the specifications of the two probabilities P_{PS} and P_{GU}, our hybrid algorithm finds different solution sets. In Fig. 7 (a), the 50% attainment surface by our hybrid algorithm with $P_{PS} = 1.0$ and $P_{GU} = 0.9$ is similar to but clearly better than that of the pure weighted sum-based EMO algorithm. On the other hand, the 50% attainment surface by our hybrid algorithm with $P_{PS} = 0.5$ and $P_{GU} = 0.5$ in Fig. 7 (b) is similar to but has larger diversity than that of NSGA-II.

From Fig. 7, we can see that the probabilistic use of the weighted sum fitness function increases the diversity of obtained non-dominated solutions. Such an increase in the diversity leads to the improvement in the hypervolume measure for the 2-500 problem in Fig. 4. Not only the diversity improvement but also the convergence improvement, however, contributes to the improvement in the hypervolume measure in Fig. 5 for the 3-500 problem and Fig. 6 for the 4-500 problem. Actually, the convergence performance of NSGA-II is improved by the probabilistic use of the weighted sum fitness function in all the four combinations of the two versions (i.e., Version II and Version III) and the two test problems (i.e., 3-500 and 4-500). Such improvement has already been demonstrated for the case of our Version I hybrid algorithm in Fig. 3 for the 3-500 and 4-500 problems.

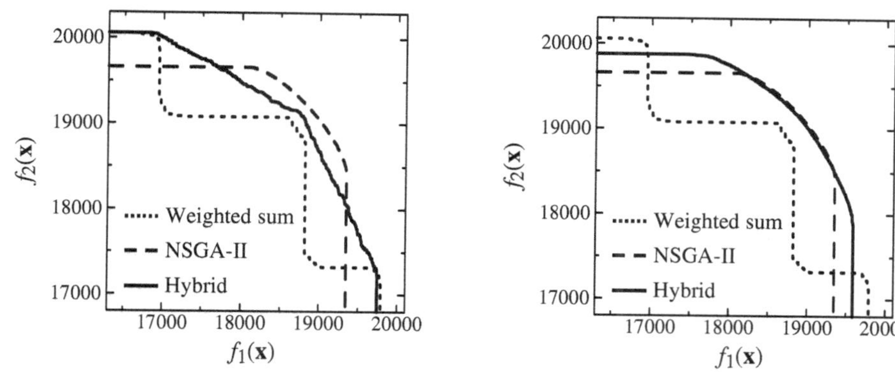

(a) $P_{PS} = 1.0$ and $P_{GU} = 0.9$. (b) $P_{PS} = 0.5$ and $P_{GU} = 0.5$.

Fig. 7. 50% attainment surface over 50 runs by our Version II hybrid algorithm for the 2-500 problem. Experimental results by the two extreme cases (i.e., the pure NSGA-II and the pure weighted sum-based EMO algorithm) are also shown for comparison.

5 Conclusions

In this paper, we proposed an idea of probabilistically using a scalarizing fitness function for parent selection and generation update in EMO algorithms. Following the proposed idea, we implemented a hybrid algorithm by incorporating the weighted sum fitness function into NSGA-II. When our hybrid algorithm was used for single-objective optimization, it outperformed SOGA. That is, the probabilistic use of the NSGA-II fitness evaluation mechanism improved the performance of SOGA. On the other hand, when our hybrid algorithm was used for multiobjective optimization, it outperformed NSGA-II in terms of the hypervolume measure. That is, the probabilistic use of the weighted sum fitness function improved the performance of NSGA-II. Future work includes the comparison of our hybrid algorithm with other approaches to many-objective optimization problems (e.g., [5], [6], [12], [14]).

This work was partially supported by Japan Society for the Promotion of Science (JSPS) through Grand-in-Aid for Scientific Research (B): KAKENHI (17300075).

References

1. Colombo, G., Mumford, C. L.: Comparing Algorithms, Representations and Operators for the Multi-objective Knapsack Problem. Proc. of 2005 Congress on Evolutionary Computation (2005) 2241-2247
2. Deb, K.: Multi-Objective Optimization Using Evolutionary Algorithms. John Wiley & Sons, Chichester (2001)
3. Deb, K., Pratap, A., Agarwal, S., Meyarivan, T.: A Fast and Elitist Multiobjective Genetic Algorithm: NSGA-II. IEEE Trans. on Evolutionary Computation 6 (2002) 182-197
4. Fonseca, C. M., Fleming, P. J.: On the Performance Assessment and Comparison of Stochastic Multiobjective Optimizers. Lecture Notes in Computer Science, Vol. 114: Parallel Problem Solving from Nature - PPSN IV. Springer, Berlin (1996) 584-593
5. Hughes, E. J.: Multiple Single Objective Sampling. Proc. of 2003 Congress on Evolutionary Computation (2003) 2678-2684
6. Hughes, E. J.: Evolutionary Many-objective Optimization: Many Once or One Many? Proc. of 2005 Congress on Evolutionary Computation (2005) 222-227
7. Ishibuchi, H., Murata, T.: A Multi-Objective Genetic Local Search Algorithm and Its Application to Flowshop Scheduling. IEEE Trans. on Systems, Man, and Cybernetics - Part C: Applications and Reviews 28 (1998) 392-403
8. Ishibuchi, H., Nojima, Y., Doi, T.: Comparison between Single-objective and Multi-objective Genetic Algorithms: Performance Comparison and Performance Measures. Proc. of 2006 Congress on Evolutionary Computation (2006) (in press)
9. Ishibuchi, H., Yoshida, T., Murata, T.: Balance between Genetic Search and Local Search in Memetic Algorithms for Multiobjective Permutation Flowshop Scheduling. IEEE Trans. on Evolutionary Computation 7 (2003) 204-223
10. Jaszkiewicz, A.: Genetic Local Search for Multi-Objective Combinatorial Optimization. European Journal of Operational Research 137 (2002) 50-71
11. Jaszkiewicz, A.: On the Performance of Multiple-Objective Genetic Local Search on the 0/1 Knapsack Problem - A Comparative Experiment. IEEE Trans. on Evolutionary Computation 6 (2002) 402-412
12. Jaszkiewicz, A.: On the Computational Efficiency of Multiple Objective Metaheuristics: The Knapsack Problem Case Study. European Journal of Operational Research 158 (2004) 418-433
13. Knowles, J. D., Watson, R. A., Corne, D. W.: Reducing Local Optima in Single-Objective Problems by Multi-Objectivization. Lecture Notes in Computer Science, Vol. 1993: Evolutionary Multi-Criterion Optimization - EMO 2001. Springer, Berlin (2001) 269-283
14. Mumford, C. L.: A Hierarchical Solve-and-Merge Framework for Multi-Objective Optimization. Proc. of 2005 Congress on Evolutionary Computation (2005) 2241-2247
15. Murata, T., Ishibuchi, H., Gen, M.: Specification of Genetic Search Directions in Cellular Multi-Objective Genetic Algorithms. Lecture Notes in Computer Science, Vol. 1993: Evolutionary Multi-Criterion Optimization - EMO 2001, Springer, Berlin (2001) 82-95
16. Purshouse, R. C., Fleming, P. J.: Evolutionary Many-Objective Optimization: An Exploratory Analysis. Proc. of 2003 Congress on Evolutionary Computation (2003) 2066-2073
17. Schaffer, J. D.: Multiple Objective Optimization with Vector Evaluated Genetic Algorithms. Proc. of 1st International Conference on Genetic Algorithms and Their Applications (1985) 93-100
18. Watanabe, S., Sakakibara K.: Multi-Objective Approaches in a Single-Objective Optimization Environment. Proc. of 2005 Congress on Evolutionary Computation (2005) 1714-1721
19. Zitzler, E., Thiele, L.: Multiobjective Evolutionary Algorithms: A Comparative Case Study and the Strength Pareto Approach. IEEE Trans. on Evolutionary Computation 3 (1999) 257-271

Solving Multi-objective Optimisation Problems Using the Potential Pareto Regions Evolutionary Algorithm

Nasreddine Hallam, Graham Kendall, and Peter Blanchfield

School of Computer Science and IT, The Univeristy of Nottingham

Abstract. In this paper we propose a novel multi-objective evolutionary algorithm that we call Potential Pareto Regions Evolutionary Algorithm (PPREA). Unlike state-of-the-art algorithms, which use a fitness assignment method based on Pareto ranking, the approach adopted in this work is new. The fitness of an individual is equal to the least improvement needed by that individual in order to reach non-dominance status.

This new algorithm is compared against the Nondominated Sorting Genetic Algorithm (NSGA-II) on a set of test suite problems derived from the works of researchers from MOEA community.

1 Introduction

Many specialised algorithms have been devised to tackle multi-objective problems. In recent years, a new wave of algorithms has emerged as the major 'stakeholder' in this field of research. The most attractive feature of these algorithms is their capability to search for a set of solutions in a single run by considering a population of potential solutions. These are Multi-Objective Evolutionary Algorithms (MOEAs).

Recently, elitist-MOEAs (archive-based MOEAs) have dominated the field of MOEAs. Essentially, they are the standard MOEAs supplied with an elitist archive as proposed by (Zitzler and Thiele 1999; Knowles and Corne 1999). These algorithms have proven to be successful in solving complex real world problems (Burke et al 2006).

In this work a novel MOEA, called Potential Pareto Regions Evolutionary Algorithm (PPREA), is formulated and developed. This algorithm is based on the new approach of Potential Pareto Regions (PPRs) (Hallam 2005).

This paper is organised as follows. Section 2 briefly describes the related work. NSGA-II being the most popular MOEA is briefly presented. Section 3 describes and proposes the novel MOEA. Section 4 is an empirical study of the PPREA. The latter is tested against NSGA-II on a set of suitably chosen test problems. Lastly, concluding remarks are given in section 5.

2 Related Work

The literature is rich of successful MOEAs. Strength Pareto Evolutionary Algorithm (SPEA2) of (Zitzler et al. 2001) and Nondominated Sorting Genetic

T.P. Runarsson et al. (Eds.): PPSN IX, LNCS 4193, pp. 503–512, 2006.

Algorithm (NSGA-II) of (Deb et al. 2001) are the most widely used. In our comparative study, we choose NSGA-II as it is simple to implement. Therefore, this algorithm is briefly explained in this section.

Following criticisms (see Knowles and Corne 1999 ; Zitzler and Thiele 1999), a new improved NSGA, coined NSGA-II, has been designed and tested by (Deb et al. 2001) specifically to address those criticisms.

The improvements brought to NSGA were mainly concerning three basic points:

elitism NSGA-II implements an elitist strategy to improve convergence.
speed NSGA-II employs a fast nondominance sorting approach based on a better book-keeping technique.
diversity NSGA-II uses a density preservation technique that is better than the niching and fitness sharing technique.

3 Potential Pareto Regions Evolutionary Algorithm (PPREA): A New MOEA

The theoretical foundation of the proposed algorithm is briefly described. Potential Pareto Regions Evolutionary Algorithm (PPREA) is designed based on a new fitness assignment scheme and a new diversity preservation technique. These two are detailed in (Hallam 2005, Hallam et al. 2005).

3.1 Definitions and Key Concepts (Hallam 2005)

Definition 1. *A PPR is hyper-area delimited by two immediate neighbouring nondominated points of the archive.*

These PPRs are dynamic regions in the objective space within which any generated vector solution is automatically nondominated with regard to all the current solutions of the archive.

Let A_t be the archive of the current population and $MaxArchiveSize$ its maximum size.

Let $z_t = Gen(t)$ be a solution generated by the function Gen at iteration t.

Let PPR^{xy} be a PPR delimited by two (neighbouring) nondominated solutions x and y of A_t. For the proof of the following lemmas, one can refer to (Hallam 2005).

Lemma 1. *If there exist a PPR which contains z_t, then z_t is incomparable to any point in the archive ($z_t \in PPR^{xy} \Rightarrow \forall a \in A_t \ , \ z_t \sim a$).*

Then, constructing the chain of PPRs is done by determining the set of PPRs. For this purpose, the $z^i, i = 1, |A_t| - 1 \ \wedge \ z^i \in A_t$ are arranged in a way that $z_{i,k} > z_{i+1,k}$ for a given k. Without loss of generality we set k to 1.

Definition 2. *SPPR is the set of the PPRs ordered according to 'neighbourhood' order.* $SPPR = \{PPR^{z_i z_{i+1}} \mid z_i, z_{i+1} \in A_t \ \wedge \ z_{i,k} > z_{i+1,k} \ , \ i = 1..|A_t| - 1\}$

After determining the set $SPPR$, the task is to find a closest PPR to each point in the objective space. This is done thanks to the following lemma (depicted in Fig. 1). This also forms the basis of the fitness assignment scheme. Let $Dom(A_t, g)$ be the set of all points in the archive dominating g ($g \notin A_t$). Let us define the set of those PPRs dominating a point b.

Definition 3. *$DomPPR(g)$ is the set of those PPRs whose at least one of their end-points is in $Dom(A_t, g)$. $DomPPR(b) = \{R^{xy} \mid x \in Dom(A_t, g) \vee y \in Dom(A_t, g)\}$.*

Lemma 2. *a. The minimum distance of a point g to SPPR is the minimum distance to one of the PPRs in $DomPPR(g)$.*
b. For every two consecutive points in $Dom(A_t, g)$, the minimum distance from the point g to their PPR is from the point to the upper right corner of that region.
c. If the $Dom(A_t, g)$ is a singleton $\{d\}$, then the minimum two distances from the point b to the two PPRs of d, (PPR^{-d} and PPR^{d-}), are respectively $(g_1 - d_1)$ and $(g_2 - d_2)$.

3.2 PPREA: The Algorithm

MOEAs differ only in the fitness assignment scheme and the archive update process. Sampling, crossover, mutation, and re-insertion are basically the same. It has been shown in (Burke and Silva 2006) that the choice of a fitness evaluation method does have an influence on the performance of a multi-objective optimiser. On the other hand, diversity is as important as the fitness assignment scheme not only for diversifying the solutions, but also on guiding the search process (see Silva and Burke 2004).

Algorithm 1 PPREA: The algorithm - (Hallam 2005)

Input: N (Population size),
MaxArchiveSize, M (maximum number of generations)
Ouput: A (The archive)
Step 0: Initialisation
generate an initial Population Pop_0, Set t = 0 and
create the empty archive (external set) $A_t = \emptyset$
Step 1: FITNESS ASSIGNMENT: Calculate the fitness values of all individuals in Pop_t

Step 2: A_{t+1} = ARCHIVE UPDATE(A_t)
Step 3: Termination.
if $t > M$ or another stopping condition is met **then**
  $A = filterFront(A_{t+1})$ and Stop.
end if
Step 4: Mating Selection (tournament selection)
Step 5: $Q_{t+1} = Variation(A_{t+1})$: Produce offspring using Crossover and Mutation
$Pop_{t+1} = A_{t+1} \cup Q_{t+1}, t = t + 1$ and GO TO Step 1.

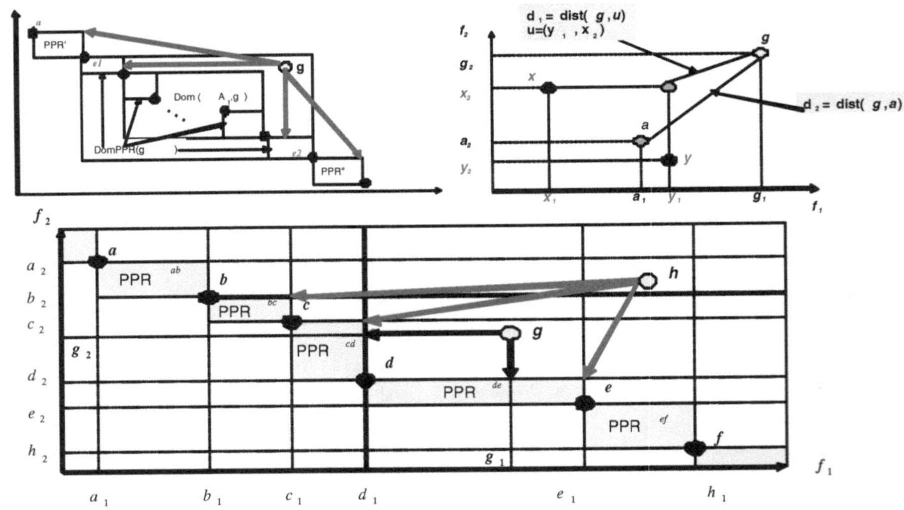

Fig. 1. Illustration of Lemma 2

Fitness Assignment. Minimisation is adopted in PPREA . Individuals of the archive are assigned negative values, while the remaining individuals are assigned positive values. The nondominated extremums of the archive are assigned a fitness value that is (in absolute value) twice the size of the largest PPR, whereas the rest of the archive members are assigned values equal (in absolute value) to the sum of the sizes of the two adjacent PPRs.

The dominated individuals are assigned fitness values equal to their respective Euclidean distances to the nearest PPR as calculated in lemmas 2. This is called the Expected Improvement which, besides being the cornerstone of the fitness assignment scheme, is also used as the building block of a quality performance indicator (Hallam 2005).

Archive Update. Whenever the size of the current Pareto front is less than $MaxArchiveSize$, then the empty slots need to be populated with adequate individuals from the rest of the population. These individuals should be fit and not concentrated in one or few sub-spaces.

The rest of the population is re-arranged into a set of lists. Recall that non-dominated individuals are sorted according to the first objective. Then each of these individuals is assigned a list of those points that it dominates. These lists are sorted in an ascending order according to the distances to the PPR of the corresponding nondominated point (fitness of the dominated individuals). Then, the filling process is a cyclic removal of the best individuals from each list. While the archive is not full, we take from each list the first individual and insert it into the archive. If the archive is still not full, we take the second individual from each list and insert it into the archive, and so forth.

The other situation is when the size of the archive containing nondominated individuals is greater than $MaxArchiveSize$. The nondominated points in excess and found in the most crowded regions must be removed. Thus, the removal process is iterative. First the smallest PPR is found. Thereafter, if one of the individuals of this PPR is an extremum, then the other individual is removed; otherwise, from the two individuals, we remove the one whose other adjacent PPR is the smallest.

4 Numerical Testing and Analysis

The PPREA is tested and compared with NSGA-II – one of the most successful MOEA in the literature. In other experimental comparative studies (Zitzler et al. 2001), SPEA2 has been shown to be as effective as NSGA-II. We choose (for the comparative study) NSGA-II as it is more efficient (fast in execution) and simple to implement.

The test functions used in the experiments reported herein are excatly those used by (Deb et al. 2001) when first they proposed NSGA-II. The popularity of their algorithm has in fact started after it has excelled in outperforming other MOEAs on these test problems. Due to space limit, the reader is referred to (Deb et al. 2001) for a complete and detailed listing of these test suite functions. Also, only the results of the ZDTs test functions are shown in this paper. Reference (Hallam 2005) contains an exhaustive emperical study of PPREA and its comparison with NSGA-II.

Table 1. ZDT1's Test Results (100, 250, 500, and 1000 generations)

Gen	100		250	
MOEA	PPREA	NSGA-II	PPREA	NSGA-II
SizeFrontMOEA	124	78	544	350
ParetoSize	86		687	
InsidePareto	11	75	520	167
OutsidePareto	113	3	137	186
PercentFromPareto	12.79	87.20	75.69	24.30
PercentFromFRONT	8.87	96.15	95.58	47.71
AvergaeEI	0.022	0.0009	0.06	0.002
StdvEI	0.012	0.001	0.034	0.015
AverageTimeExec	0.7	0.6	1.7	1.6
Generation	500		1000	
MOEA	PPREA	NSGA-II	PPREA	NSGA-II
SizeFrontMOEA	938	964	910	908
ParetoSize	1847		1804	
InsidePareto	909	938	904	900
OutsidePareto	148	215	154	223
PercentFromPareto	49.21	50.78	50.11	49.88
PercentFromFRONT	96.90	97.30	99.34	99.11
AvergaeEI	0.048	0.003	0.054	0.002
StdvEI	0.038	0.017	0.038	0.005
AverageTimeExec	3.4	3.3	7	6.8

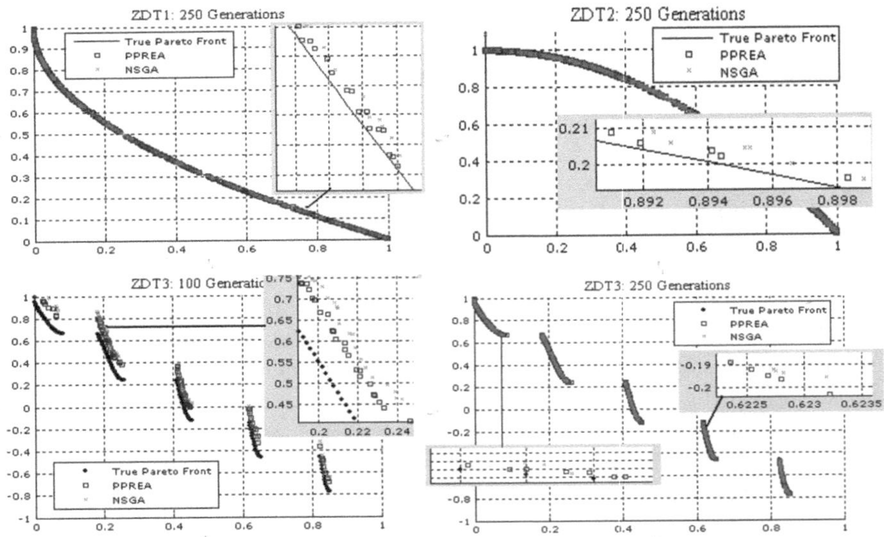

Fig. 2. Convergence Results for ZDT1, ZDT2 and ZDT3 Test Functions

Per algorithm and test function, the outcomes of ten runs were unified. A front is filtered from the unified set. In order to get a glimpse on the pace of the convergence, we used the following maximum number of generations (100, 250, 500, and 1000). Furthermore, each simulation run was carried out independently of the test function using the following parameters:

- Size of the population and the archive is 100
- Individual representation Real
- Simulated Binary Crossover (SBX) with probability 0.9 and a Polynomial Mutation probability $1/numberOfVariables$. The distribution indices for the SBX and the mutation are set to 20 ($\eta_m = \eta_c = 20$).

Measuring the Performance. A Common Pareto Front (CPF) is filtered from both algorithms: $CPF = ND(PPREA \cup NSGA - II)$. Two main performance values are then computed. The percentage of a front in the common archive (which is the error ratio), and the average of the cumulative Expected Improvement (see Hallam 2005) of its residual set with regards to SPPR . Also, the set of vector solutions of each MOEA that are in the CPF is also derived: $MOEA_{Pareto} = MOEA \cap CPF$. Let $MOEA \in \{PPREA, NSGA - II\}$

For each simulation run, the following results are reported:

- The sizes of the CPF and the two fronts returned by each MOEA.
- The number of vector solutions of each MOEA *inside* and *outside* the CPF.
- The % of each front covering the CPF: $\frac{|MOEA_{Pareto}|}{|CPF|}$.
- The % of each MOEA Pareto covering the front returned by the MOEA in question: $\frac{|MOEA_{Pareto}|}{|MOEA|}$.

Table 2. ZDT2's Test Results (100, 250, 500, and 1000 generations) A = PPREA, B= NSGA-II

Generation	100		250	
MOEA	A	B	A	B
SizeMOEA	36	42	431	442
ParetoSize	41		679	
In Pareto	36	5	365	314
Out Pareto	0	37	66	165
%Pareto	87.80	12.19	53.75	46.24
%FRONT	100	11.90	84.68	71.04
AvergaeEI	0	0.088	0.0008	0.063
StdvEI	0	0.038	0.001	0.121
AvgTimExe	0.7	0.6	1.8	1.5

Table 3. ZDT3's Test Results (100, 250, 500, and 1000 generations)

Generation	100		250	
MOEA	A	B	A	B
SizeMOEA	98	91	429	463
ParetoSize	101		677	
In Pareto	97	4	379	298
Out Pareto	1	87	51	252
% Pareto	96.03	3.96	55.98	44.01
% Front	98.97	4.39	88.34	64.36
AvergaeEI	0.0002	0.015	0.0008	0.020
StdvEI	0	0.023	0.001	0.040
AvgTimExe	0.7	0.6	1.8	1.6

Table 4. ZDT4's Test Results (100, 250, 500, and 1000 generations)

Generation	100		250	
MOEA	A	B	A	B
SizeMOEA	94	98	283	403
ParetoSize	102		476	
In Pareto	94	8	253	223
Out Pareto	0	90	30	270
% Pareto	92.15	7.84	53.15	46.84
% Front	100	8.16	89.39	55.33
AvergaeEI	0	0.10	0.002	0.045
StdvEI	0	0.038	0.001	0.065
AvgTimExe	0.6	0.4	1.6	1.3
Generation	500		1000	
MOEA	A	B	A	B
SizeMOEA	654	514	759	603
ParetoSize	864		1129	
In Pareto	616	248	690	439
Out Pareto	144	446	213	610
% Pareto	71.29	28.70	61.11	38.88
% Front	94.18	48.24	90.90	72.80
AvergaeEI	0.002	0.024	0.001	0.02
StdvEI	0.002	0.052	0.002	0.047
AvgTimExe	3.3	2.7	6.8	5.7

Table 5. ZDT6's Test Results (100, 250, 500, and 1000 generations)

Generation	100		250	
MOEA	A	B	A	B
SizeMOEA	97	104	669	721
ParetoSize	133		1140	
In Pareto	83	50	616	524
Out Pareto	14	54	67	251
% Pareto	62.40	37.59	54.03	45.96
% Front	85.56	48.07	92.07	72.67
AvergaeEI	0.003	0.004	0.005	0.007
StdvEI	0.002	0.003	0.015	0.012
AvgTimExe	0.6	0.5	1.6	1.4

- The average and standard deviation of the Expected Improvement (EI) of each MOEA.
- The average Execution Time of each MOEA.

ZDT1's Test Results. Referring to Table 1, NSGA-II is clearly outperforming PPREA at Generation 100 test (early stage). However, PPREA clearly outperforms NSGA-II at Generation 250 test (see the top-left figure in Fig. 2).

ZDT2's Test Results. Refer to Table 2, and the top-right figure in Fig. 2. At Generation 100 test, PPREA is almost totally outperforming NSGA-II. Notice also that the vector solutions of the front returned by PPREA are *all* in the

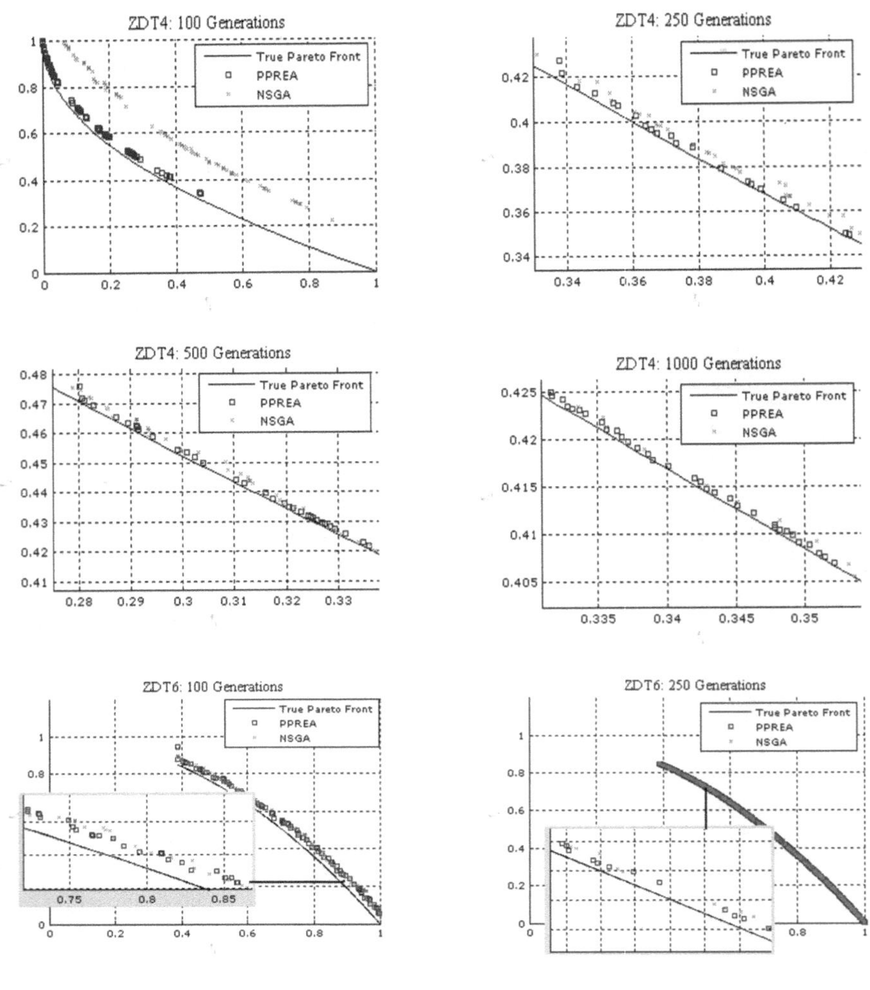

Fig. 3. Convergence Results for ZDT4 and ZDT6 Test Functions

CPF. In Generation 250 and Generation 1000 tests, PPREA is also clearly outperforming NSGA-II. In Generation 500 test, both algorithms seem to fairly share the CPF.

ZDT3's Test Results. One can see from Table 3 that PPREA is monopolising the CPF in the Generation 100 test. Only 1 vector solution returned by PPREA is outside the CPF (but still very close to it ($AverageEI = 0.0002$), compared to 87 vector solutions returned by NSGA-II out of 91 being outside the CPF (see the two bottom figures in Fig. 2). PPREA outperforms (to some extent) NSGA-II in Generation 250 test. In the remaining simulation tests, PPREA and NSGA-II fairly share the CPF. However, the vectors solutions returned by PPREA and left behind the CPF are much closer on average to the CPF than those of NSGA-II. See also the two bottom figures in Fig 2.

ZDT4's Test Results. ZDT4 is known to be a difficult multi-modal test problem. It has one true Pareto-optimal front and a huge number of local Pareto fronts (21^9). PPREA is proving to be much more effective in solving this problem than NSGA-II in that, it is clearly outperforming NSGA-II (see Table 4).

From the 1st four figures in Fig. 3, one can see that the fronts returned by NSGA-II are clearly behind those returned by PPREA .

ZDT6's Test Results. Referring to Table 5, one can notice that even though the front returned by PPREA is smaller in size than that of NSGA-II, PPREA still outperforms NSGA-II in terms of taking bigger shares from the CPF, and of being the closest to the CPF as well. The last two figures in Fig. 3 shows some snapshots of the two fronts returned by the two contending MOEAs.

5 Concluding Remarks

A novel MOEA called PPREA (Potential Pareto Regions Evolutionary Algorithms) has been proposed based on a new fitness scheme and a new diversity technique.

NSGA-II of (Deb et al. 2001) has gained a worldwide popularity among MOEAs researchers. It is the most cited and the most used MOEA in the past couple of years. The new MOEA proposed in this work is compared against NSGA-II using the same test suite functions in which NSGA-II has excelled.

In some of the test results, PPREA clearly monopolised more of the Common Pareto Front (CPF) than NSGA-II did. In other test results, both algorithms *equitably* contributed to the CPF. However, the vector solutions returned by PPREA and left behind are much closer to the CPF than are those returned by NSGA-II. This result is anticipated since the very concept of PPREA is designed around the Expected-Improvement selection scheme which tend to drive the whole population towards the actual Pareto regions.

References

1. Deb K, Pratap, A., Agarwal, S., and Meyarivan, T. (2001). A Fast and Elitist Multiobjective Genetic Algorithm: NSGA-II. *IEEE Transactions on Evolutionary Computation*, vol 6(2), pp.182-197.
2. Burke, E.K. and Landa Silva, J.D. (2006). The influence of the Fitness Evaluation Method on the Performance of Multiobjctive Optimisers, European Journal of Operational Research, Volume 169 issue 3, pp 875-897.
3. Burke, E.K., Landa Silva, J.D., and Soubeiga, E. (2005). Multi-objective Hyper-heuristic Approaches for Space Allocation and Timetabling, in: Ibaraki T., Nonobe K., Yagiura M. (eds.), *Meta-heuristics: Progress as Real Problem Solvers*, Springer, pp.129-158.
4. Hallam, N., (2005). State-of-the-art Multi-Objective Evolutionary Algorithms: Diversity Preservation and Archive Update Analysis, and Proposal of a New Evolutionary Algorithm, *PhD thesis submitted to the University of Nottingham.*
5. Hallam N., Blanchfield P., and Kendall G. (2005). Handling Diversity in Evolutionary Multiobjective Optimisation. In *Proceedings of 2005 IEEE Congress on Evolutionary Computation (CEC'05)*, pp. 2233-2240, Edinburgh, Scotland.
6. Knowles, J. D. and Corne, D. W. (1999). The Pareto archived evolution strategy: A new baseline algorithm for multi-objective optimization. *IEEE International Conference on Evolutionary Computation*, pp. 98-105.
7. Landa Silva, J.D. and Burke, E.K. (2004). Using Diversity to Guide the Search in Multi-objective Optimisation, In: Coello Coello C.A., Lamont G.B. (eds.), *Applications of Multi-Objective Evolutionary Algorithms, Advances in Natural Computation*, Vol. 1, World Scientific, pp. 727-751.
8. Zitzler, E. and Thiele, L. (1999). Multiobjective evolutionary algorithms: A comparative case study and the strength Pareto approach. *IEEE Transactions on Evolutionary Computation*, 3(4), pp. 257-271.
9. Zitzler, E., Laumanns, M., and Thiele, L. (2001). SPEA2: Improving the strength pareto evolutionary algorithm. *Technical report*, Swiss Federal Institute of Technology.

Pareto Set and EMOA Behavior for Simple Multimodal Multiobjective Functions

Mike Preuss, Boris Naujoks, and Günter Rudolph

Universität Dortmund, Lehrstuhl für Algorithm Engineering
44221 Dortmund, Germany
{mike.preuss, boris.naujoks, guenter.rudolph}@uni-dortmund.de
http://ls11-www.cs.uni-dortmund.de

Abstract. Recent research on evolutionary multiobjective optimization has mainly focused on Pareto fronts. However, we state that proper behavior of the utilized algorithms in decision/search space is necessary for obtaining good results if multimodal objective functions are concerned. Therefore, it makes sense to observe the development of Pareto sets as well. We do so on a simple, configurable problem, and detect interesting interactions between induced changes to the Pareto set and the ability of three optimization algorithms to keep track of Pareto fronts.

1 Introduction

In recent years, *evolutionary multiobjective optimization* (EMO) [1,2] has developed from a marginal into one of the most actively pursued areas within *evolutionary computation* (EC). Many new algorithms and measures have been suggested, and, with them, concepts like Pareto set and Pareto front have entered the common EC vocabulary [3]. Increasing interest in multiobjective techniques has even evoked new theoretical approaches that employ multiple objectives to simplify an originally singleobjective problem [4]. However, most of the current EMO research concentrates on processes observed in the objective space, which consists of the possibly obtainable value combinations of the considered objective functions. Undoubtedly, approximating the Pareto front well is the final aim of EMO algorithms (EMOAs), and the Pareto set distribution may be of minor interest for estimating their performances. Nevertheless, for improving these algorithms, as well as for attaining guidelines on which of the solutions contained in the approximated Pareto set shall eventually be implemented in a real-world situation, a well-founded understanding of Pareto set distributions is supposed to be a major advantage.

Research on singleobjective algorithms largely focuses on population behavior in the decision space, or simplified models thereof, e.g. using basins of attraction as means of abstraction [5]. Especially for multimodal problems, numerous techniques have been invented to prevent the populations from converging to a single point too soon. Some of these, as crowding [6], are also applied in EMOAs. But diversity maintenance is only sought in objective space, to ensure good coverage

T.P. Runarsson et al. (Eds.): PPSN IX, LNCS 4193, pp. 513–522, 2006.

of the Pareto front. However, for at least one of the objective functions being multimodal, it is clear that this coverage cannot normally be achieved when the whole population is clustered around one local minimum of this function. We thus conjecture that a) there are situations—and these are not uncommon—where the Pareto set does not share the aspired nice properties of the received Pareto front the user normally focusses the attention on, and b) that diversity maintenance is not only needed in objective but also in decision space for successfully treating *multiobjective optimization problems* (MOPs): The product designer is mainly interested in a thorough covering of the Pareto front for maximum wide scope in selecting solutions according to the (conjectured) customers' desires. This is the situation which contemporary EMOAs are designed for. But the product engineer is mainly interested in a thorough covering of the Pareto set since it is important to know if a certain design can be realized by different parameters of the production process: Solutions may differ in sensitivity or in shorter tooling times and the like. Evidently, contemporary EMOAs are not geared toward product engineers yet.

These both sides of one medal (Pareto front in the objective space, Pareto set in the decision space) and the conjunction between them has not been studied in detail before. Only few theoretical results for special classes of search spaces and multiobjective functions were presented before, cf. Ehrgott [7]. But the handled cases are restricted in a way that no generalization can be foreseen. Some effort has been made in the development of test functions not only with regard to a nice behaving Pareto front, but also with aspired properties in the decision space, cf. Okabe et al. [8]. Zhou et al. [9] propose a specialized EA to implicitly handle and profit from regularities in the objective as well as in the decision space. Such regularities stem from the test functions proposed by Okabe et al. [8] and cannot be expected generally.

2 Aims and Methods

Our approach is constructive; on a minimalist bimodal bicriteria test problem, we study structural changes of true Pareto set and Pareto front on a set of targeted modifications. These are derived both analytically and empirically, the latter employing grid-based and stochastic enumerators. Furthermore, we observe how different EMOAs cope with the original problem and the changes. More detailed, we try to answer the following questions:

- How do Pareto set distributions change when the problem is modified? Are there unexpected outcomes?
- Are different EMOAs able to cover Pareto set and Pareto front well?
- Are there consistent similarities/dissimilarities in the behavior of different EMOAs due to problem modifications that hint to distinct capabilities of these?

3 A Simple Test Problem: TWO-ON-ONE

To deepen the insight in behavior and structure of Pareto sets mapping onto Pareto fronts, we define the plainest bimodal/unimodal test problem we could think of. It consists of a polynomial function f_1 of degree four with two optima, and the sphere function f_2, which is of degree two:

$$f = (f_1, f_2) : \mathbb{R}^2 \to \mathbb{R}^2 : f_1(x_1, x_2) = x_1^4 + x_2^4 - x_1^2 + x_2^2 - cx_1x_2 + dx_1 + 20,$$
$$f_2(x_1, x_2) = (x_1 - k)^2 + (x_2 - l)^2$$

The level (niveau) of the optima of f_1 can be adjusted smoothly via parameter d. With d positive, the optimum in the positive x_1 domain is lifted up in comparison to the optimum in the negative x_1 domain. Consequently, the former becomes a local optimum, while the latter remains a global optimum (asymmetric optima). With parameter $c = 0$, both minimizers are located on the x_1 axis, but for increasing c, their connecting line is rotated counterclockwise, until its gradient is nearly 1.

The function f_2 is unimodal, the location of its minimizer determined by parameters k and l. For $k = l = 0$ it is located in the origin, right between the minimizers of the bimodal function f_1. By variation of k and l the minimizer is moved away from the connecting line of the minimizers of f_1. Next to changing the Pareto front, this also effects the Pareto set.

Table 1. Parameter setting for the five cases of TWO-ON-ONE, c was set to 10

Cases		1	2	3	4	5
Parameters	d	0	0	0.25	0.25	0.25
	k	0	1	0	1	0
	l	0	0	0	0	1

In order to allow for a theoretical analysis of the problem, five parameter settings have been fixed (Table 1, Figure 1). These result in different placements of the minimizers in search space, two for the symmetric case (both optima of f_1 identical), three for the asymmetric case (optima distinct). While all these settings are expected to lead to ordinary (generic) Pareto fronts, the Pareto sets are expected to look more complex.

The coordinates of the minimizers of f_1 can be determined analytically to

$$(x^*_{1_{1,2}}, x^*_{2_{1,2}}) = \left(\pm\frac{1}{2}\sqrt{(\sqrt{101}+1)}, \pm\frac{1}{20}(\sqrt{101}-1)\sqrt{(\sqrt{101}+1)} \right).$$

In cases 1 and 2, both optima of f_1 are on the same level, ensured by $d = 0$. In 1, the minimizer of the sphere function is located in the origin, where f_1 has a saddle point. In 2, the optimum is moved right on the x_1 axis by one unit.

Cases 3 and 4 repeat the same configuration, with asymmetric optima of f_1; the global optimum resides in the negative x_1 and x_2 domain, and the local

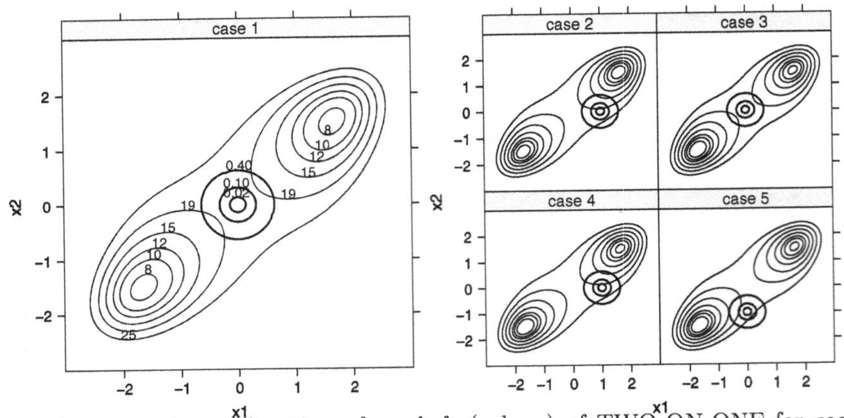

Fig. 1. Superposition of functions f_1 and f_2 (sphere) of TWO-ON-ONE for cases 1 to 5. The optima of f_1 are symmetrical (equal fitness) in cases 1 + 2, asymmetrical in 3+4+5, with the right minimizer shifted slightly upwards and the left one downwards.

optimum in the positive domain. It is expected that the Pareto set now establishes a connection between the global optima of f_1 and of f_2. This is due to the solutions in the global optimum of f_1 being mapped to the extremal part of the Pareto front. Consequently, solutions from the local optimum of f_1 may be lost.

The same situation is expected for case 5, which is similar, except for a movement of the minimizer of f_2 towards the global minimizer of f_2, whereas in case 4, it is brought nearer to the local minimizer.

4 Experimental Investigation of Pareto Sets

Our expectation is that for all symmetrical cases, the Pareto sets consist of two curves, connecting either peak with the minimizer of the sphere function f_2. For the asymmetric cases, it seems reasonable that Pareto sets contain only points on a curve between the global minimizers of f_1 and f_2. But this expectation stems from thought experiments rather than empirical or analytical facts.

We employ two simple tools, a grid based and a stochastic enumerator, for obtaining a first, rough impression of structure and location of the Pareto sets. Either one samples points from a given interval and keeps a list of the Pareto-optimal solutions found. Tried points are either taken from a pre-specified grid or determined randomly. As we shall see, it sometimes makes sense to use both, as the obtained results can subtly differ.

Experiment 1: Determine Pareto sets and fronts of TWO-ON-ONE.

Pre-experimental planning: First experiments were performed with a grid-based enumerator only. They revealed an unexpectedly wide Pareto set (Fig. 2, left). We thus additionally sampled by means of a stochastic enumerator.

Task: Find location of the Pareto sets, detect deviations from the expected.

Setup: For each of the 5 cases specified in Table 1, we sample points in the interval $x_1, x_2 \in [-3, 3]$. The grid-based enumeration consists of $300 \times 300 = 90,000$ points each, the stochastic enumeration of $500,000$ points each. The difference is intended as we hope for a better resolution with the latter method, to shed light on the bar-shaped artifacts. All non-dominated points are archived.

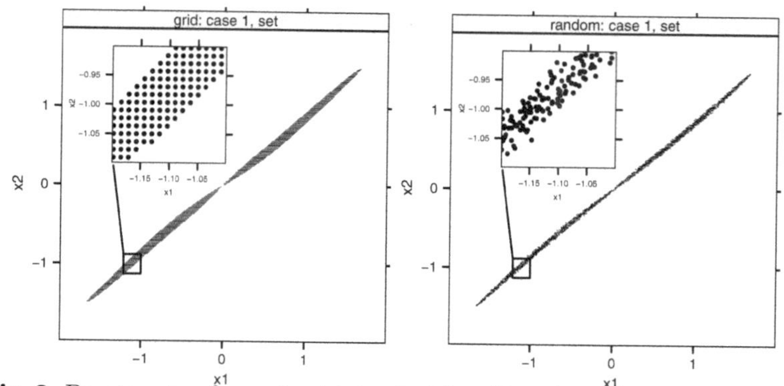

Fig. 2. Pareto sets of case 1, obtained with grid and stochastic enumerator

Experimentation/Visualization: Figures 2 and 3 show the most interesting of the obtained Pareto sets and fronts. All others largely comply with the previously stated expectations and are omitted due to space limitations.

Observations: The figures clearly show that neither grid nor stochastic sampling produces a clear-cut picture of the true Pareto sets. Roughly, case 1 yields a smeared areal, propeller-like structure (Fig. 2) instead of the expected single curve. However, the Pareto set appears narrower under stochastic enumeration.

For case 4 (sphere function f_2 moved towards local optimum of f_1), the Pareto front splits into two parts at $f_1 \approx 8$, as visualized in Fig. 3. Accordingly, the Pareto set breaks up into two distinct fragments. Note that no connection exists between the location of the sphere and the global optimum of f_1. At the left edge of its right part, the grid-based approximated Pareto set reveals a strange curl which is not visible in the stochastically approximated Pareto set. Pareto fronts of cases 4 and 5 both contain pieces of very low point densities, at $17 < f_1 < 19$ in the former, and $15 < f_1 < 17$ in the latter case.

Discussion: We regard the obtained Pareto set approximations for case 1 as rather misleading, and analytical investigation in §5 supports this view. However, considering the amount of sampled points ($90\,k$ and $500\,k$), and taking into account that the latter (stochastically approximated) Pareto set is much tighter, one may conclude even from our empirical data that the true Pareto set indeed is most likely located on a curve and non-areal. The enumerators are probably misguided by the huge difference in gradients of f_1 and f_2 in direction of the connecting line between the two optima of f_1 and orthogonal to it. Following from that, any EMOA will experience the same situation: Practically identical values of the objective functions can have a large set of preimages and thus spread in search space.

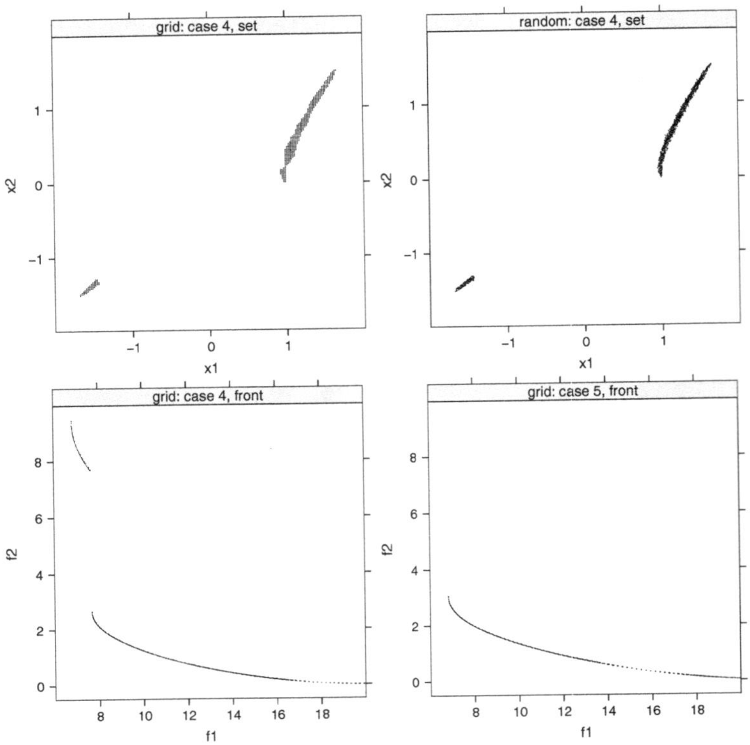

Fig. 3. Surprising Pareto sets and fronts for cases 4 and 5

Results obtained for case 4 show that contrary to our expectation, by far the larger Pareto set portion resides in the range between the local optimum of f_1 and the optimum of f_2. Only where function values for f_1 are better than may be attained at the local optimum, points from the left fragment can enter the Pareto set, resulting in a stepped Pareto front. The curl found near $x_1 = 1$ seemingly corresponds to the low density part of the Pareto front which must be located in proximity of the sphere center as values for f_2 are near 0. The stochastic Pareto set approximation is again tighter than the grid-based one, leading to the conjecture that the true Pareto set is non-areal as in case 1.

Two more conclusions may be drawn from the case 4 results. Firstly, search space distances between optima of separate objective functions play a major role for the composition of Pareto sets, and secondly, it is necessary to keep the population of EMOAs spread over several local optima of the treated objective functions during an optimization run.

5 Analytical Derivation of Pareto Sets

The Pareto set for case 1 can be derived analytically but its analytic expression is too complex and space-consuming to be presented here. Instead, we suggest the linear approximation

$$\left(x_1, \frac{\sqrt{101}-1}{10}x_1\right) \quad \text{for} \quad x_1 \in \left[-\frac{1}{2}\sqrt{\sqrt{101}+1}, \frac{1}{2}\sqrt{\sqrt{101}+1}\right]$$

whose deviation from the true convex-concave curve is less than 0.045 for all x_1 above. In any case, the Pareto set is a 1-dimensional connected set and not an areal set of higher dimension as the output of the grid or stochastic enumerator might suggest (see fig. 2).

As can be seen from the symmetry $f(x_1, x_2) = f(-x_1, -x_2)$ the entire Pareto front can be built solely by positive (or negative) points of the Pareto set. Thus, it may happen that an EMOA approximating the Pareto front quite well with regard to the S-metric has found only points in the decision space with, say, positive components. As a consequence, a good value for the S-metric tells only half the story.

The Pareto sets of the other cases are also amenable to an analytic solution but the expressions are far away from being manageable easily. This observation is quite counter-intuitive given the pretended simple expressions and structural design of the objective functions.

6 Behavior of EMOAs on TWO-ON-ONE

Whereas Pareto sets and fronts of problem TWO-ON-ONE have been explored in §4 and determined analytically in §5, we now turn to the behavior of different EMOAs in a second experiment. Note that it is not intended to argue in favor of or against any algorithm here, but rather to detect possible differences.

Algorithms. We invoke two standard techniques next to a new development within the field. The Pisa framework[1] is used to conduct the referred optimization runs. Here, the TWO-ON-ONE problem has been implemented as a variator, which can be optimized with respect to different objectives and multiple selectors. Among the set of available selectors, NSGA-II and SPEA2 are chosen, because these appear to be the currently most well-known and commonly used algorithms in the field [1,2]. Additionally, the more recent SMS-EMOA [10,11] is tested within this framework. The SMS-EMOA was designed for featuring a performance measure, namely the hypervolume or S-metric, as secondary ranking criterion in a NSGA-II like manner. The additional effort for a third algorithm in the study seems to be justified, because the SMS-EMOA was found to spread solutions more nicely over Pareto-fronts than the other two algorithms. This aspired behavior is purchased by a runtime of $O(\mu \log \mu + \mu^{(d/2+1)} \log \mu)$ of the SMS-EMOA, with μ denoting the population size and d the number of objectives (cp. Beume [12]). In contrast, the runtime of NSGA-II and SPEA2 is quadratic in the population size and polynomial in the number of objectives.

[1] PISA - Platform and Programming Language Independent Interface for Search Algorithms, ETH Zurich, `www.tik.ee.ethz.ch/pisa/`

Measures. To detect differences in algorithm behaviors on the most interesting cases, we define two simple measures. For case 1, we measure if the resulting population P is fairly distributed over the left and right wings of the Pareto set by taking the fraction on the less crowded wing into account:

$$\text{fair}(P) = \frac{1}{2} - \frac{\min(|\{\text{individual} \in P : x_1 < 0\}|, |\{\text{individual} \in P : x_1 \geq 0\}|)}{|P|} \quad (1)$$

For case 4, we are interested in the fraction of points in proximity of the global optimum of f_1, corresponding to the search points in the left half of the search space:

$$\text{left}(P) = \frac{|\{\text{individual} \in P : x_1 < 0\}|}{|P|} \quad (2)$$

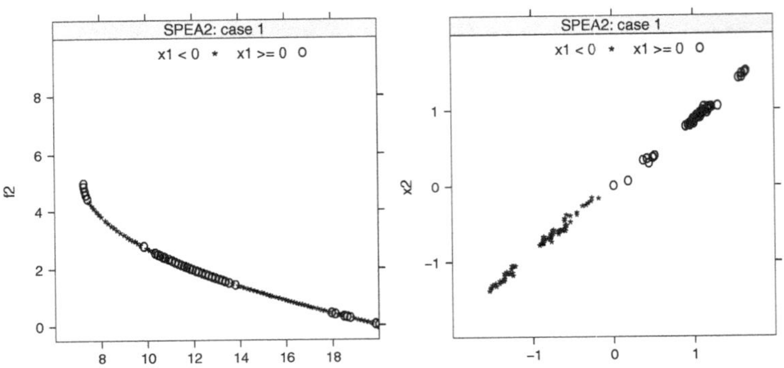

Fig. 4. Pareto front (left) and Pareto set (right) of a single SPEA2 run on case 1

Experiment 2: Search Space Behavior of EMOAs on function TWO-ON-ONE.

Pre-experimental planning: First runs indicated that results on cases 2, 3, and 5 are comparable for all three algorithms. We thus focused on cases 1 and 4. For case 1 it was found that at least 50 runs are necessary to get a detailed picture of differences in measure fair(P), for case 4, 20 runs seemed sufficient.

Task: Detect differences in the obtained Pareto sets and fronts that may be related to test problem properties. We employ bootstrap permutation tests with 49,999 replicates and significance level 5% for the measured data.

Setup: The decision space was limited to $f_1, f_2 \in [-50, 50]$, thereby enclosing the region around the optima of f_1 and f_2, and a certain amount of space the algorithms have to bypass to get there. All three algorithms, NSGA-II, SPEA2, and SMS-EMOA, are run with a population size of 100 for 30,000 evaluations, otherwise utilizing default parametrizations. For case 1 and 4, 50 and 20 runs are performed, respectively.

Experimentation/Visualization: Figure 4 depicts a typical outcome for case 1. More extreme population distributions with almost all individuals on one wing

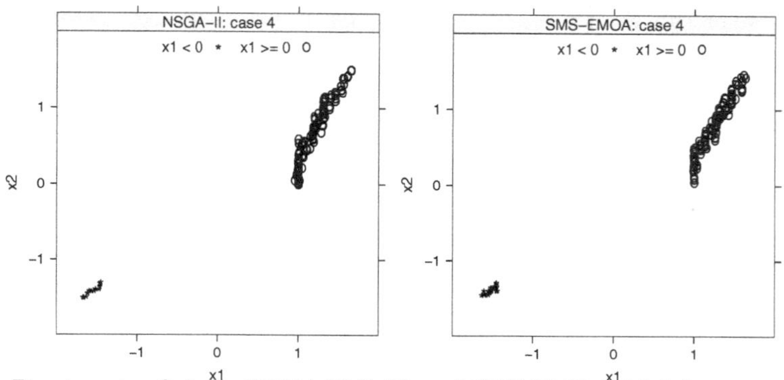

Fig. 5. Pareto sets of single NSGA-II (left) and SMS-EMOA (right) runs on case 4

of the Pareto set also happen. In figure 5, resulting Pareto sets for two different algorithms are presented, again, typical runs are chosen.

Observations: Figure 4 demonstrates that for symmetric optima, the Pareto front often contains large chunks of points originating from the proximity of different minimizers. Accordingly, the approximated Pareto sets show corresponding clouds of points, unevenly distributed over the true Pareto set. For case 4, Figure 5 shows that the algorithms are able to spread their populations over both important parts of the Pareto set. However, the shape of the clouds near the global minimizer of f_1 is different: NSGA-II often forms lines of points in that region, whereas the SMS-EMOA rather builds areal structures.

Discussion: For case 1, hypothesis testing reveals a slight difference (p-value 0.071) between NSGA-II and SMS-EMOA and a strong one (p-value 0.030) between NSGA-II and SPEA2. SMS-EMOA and SPEA2 may be considered behaving relatively similar (p-value 0.427). NSGA-II covers both wings of the Pareto set more evenly on average, its *fair*-measure is 0.110, compared to 0.149 and 0.152 for SPEA2 and SMS-EMOA, respectively.

All three algorithms cope surprisingly well with case 4. Here, hypothesis tests hint to a similarity between SMS-EMOA and NSGA-II (p-value 0.468) and sharp distinction between SPEA2 and SMS-EMOA, and SPEA2 and NSGA-II, both p-values 0.001. As indicated by the histograms, NSGA-II and SMS-EMOA both place more points near the global optimizer, their *left*-measures are 0.169 and 0.167, respectively. SPEA2 only puts 13.1% of its final population there. Unfortunately, we are currently not able to explain what makes the algorithms behave differently in this respect.

7 Summary and Outlook

The main message of the work presented here is our belief in the fact that a neat covering of the Pareto front is not sufficient for meeting the needs of all clients that may use EMOAs. Therefore, future versions of EMOAs should also take into account a proper covering of the Pareto set. Evidently, contemporary EMOAs cannot deliver this kind of behavior. For this purpose we need an effective measure for assessing the quality of a solution set in decision space—similarly to the S-metric in objective space.

To follow this avenue we have to deepen our understanding of EMOA behavior in the decision space, which may be quite counter-intuitive as our seemingly simple test problem has revealed. Obviously, EMOAs are easily confronted with strangely shaped approximate Pareto sets as the ones obtained from our empirical approaches to determine the true Pareto set. We attribute this behavior to scaling issues between orthogonal gradients and discretized computer representation of real values, but this assessment can only be preliminary. The important point is that EMOAs have no means of detecting 'real' Pareto set shapes, they have to cope with their inexact counterparts. These problems are currently not reflected in algorithm design. Furthermore, we are convinced that a thorough analysis of the interaction between Pareto front and Pareto set will eventually lead to new insights, new search operators, and even better EMOAs.

References

1. Deb, K.: Multi-Objective Optimization using Evolutionary Algorithms. Wiley, Chichester, UK (2001)
2. Coello Coello, C.A., Van Veldhuizen, D.A., Lamont, G.B.: Evolutionary Algorithms for Solving Multi-Objective Problems. Kluwer, New York (2002)
3. Coello, C.A.C.: Evolutionary multi-objective optimization: a historical view of the field. IEEE Computational Intelligence Magazine **1**(1) (2006) 28–36
4. Neumann, F., Wegener, I.: Minimum spanning trees made easier via multi-objective optimization. In Beyer, H.G., ed.: Genetic and evolutionary computation conference (GECCO), ACM Press, New York (2005) 763–769
5. Preuss, M., Schönemann, L., Emmerich, M.: Counteracting genetic drift and disruptive recombination in $(\mu \overset{+}{,} \lambda)$-ea on multimodal fitness landscapes. In Beyer, H.G., ed.: Genetic and evolutionary computation conference (GECCO), ACM Press, New York (2005) 865–872
6. De Jong, K.A.: An analysis of the behavior of a class of genetic adaptive systems. PhD thesis, University of Michigan (1975)
7. Ehrgott, M.: Multicriteria Optimization. 2 edn. Springer, Berlin (2005)
8. Okabe, T., Jin, Y., Olhofer, M., Sendhoff, B.: On Test Functions for Evolutionary Multi-objective Optimization. In Yao, X., et al., eds.: Parallel Problem Solving from Nature (PPSN), Springer, Berlin (2004) 792–802
9. Zhou, A., Zhang, Q., Jin, Y., Tsang, E., Okabe, T.: A model-based evolutionary algorithm for bi-objective optimization. In: Congress on Evolutionary Computation (CEC), IEEE Press, Piscataway NJ (2005) 2568–2575
10. Emmerich, M., Beume, N., Naujoks, B.: An EMO algorithm using the hypervolume measure as selection criterion. In Coello, C.A.C., et al., eds.: Evolutionary Multi-Criterion Optimization (EMO), Springer, Berlin (2005) 62–76
11. Naujoks, B., Beume, N., Emmerich, M.: Multi-objective optimisation using S-metric selection: Application to three-dimensional solution spaces. In: Congress on Evolutionary Computation (CEC), IEEE Press, Piscataway NJ (2005) 1282–1289
12. Beume, N.: Hypervolumen-basierte Selektion in einem evolutionären Algorithmus zur Mehrzieloptimierung. Diploma thesis, University of Dortmund (2006)

About Selecting the Personal Best in Multi-Objective Particle Swarm Optimization

Jürgen Branke and Sanaz Mostaghim

Institute AIFB, University of Karlsruhe, Germany
{branke, smo}@aifb.uni-karlsruhe.de

Abstract. In particle swarm optimization, a particle's movement is usually guided by two solutions: the swarm's global best and the particle's personal best. Selecting these guides in the case of multiple objectives is not straightforward. In this paper, we investigate the influence of the personal best particles in Multi-Objective Particle Swarm Optimization. We show that selecting a proper personal guide has a significant impact on algorithm performance. We propose a new idea of allowing each particle to memorize all non-dominated personal best particles it has encountered. This means that if the updated personal best position be indifferent to the old one, we keep both in the personal archive. Also we propose several strategies to select a personal best particle from the personal archive. These methods are empirically compared on some standard test problems.

1 Introduction

Particle swarm optimization (PSO) has established itself as an efficient optimization algorithm in a variety of contexts, see e.g., [13]. PSO is a population based technique, similar in some respects to evolutionary algorithms, except that potential solutions (particles) move, rather than evolve, through the search space. The rules, or particle dynamics, which govern this movement, are inspired by models of swarming and flocking [8].

PSO consists of several candidate solutions called particles, each of which has a position and a velocity, and experiences linear spring-like attractions towards two attractors: (a) The best position attained by that particle so far (local guide), and (b) The best of the particle attractors in a certain neighborhood (global guide), where best is in relation to evaluation of an objective function at that position.

In recent years, more and more attempts have been made to extend PSO to multi-objective problems, see e.g. [11,1]. These methods, called Multi-objective Particle Swarm optimization methods (MOPSO), follow the same principals as the single objective PSO, with the main differences being the selection of local and global guides. Finding the global guide has been studied extensively as the first step in converting PSO in MOPSO [11,14]. It has been shown that how to select the global guide has a great impact on the obtained solutions, i.e. on their convergence and diversity. However, an issue that has (at least to our knowledge) not been thoroughly investigated so far is the choice of each particle's personal best (local guide).

In this paper, we propose and compare several different strategies regarding the local guide. Specifically, we propose to allow each particle to keep an archive of non-dominated personal best solutions. Then, we propose and investigate several strategies

T.P. Runarsson et al. (Eds.): PPSN IX, LNCS 4193, pp. 523–532, 2006.

to select the local guide from this archive. We show that this selection strategy has a significant impact on the algorithm performance by applying it to several test problems.

The paper is structured as follows. In the following section, multi-objective problems and and multi-objective particle swarm optimization are briefly introduced. In Section 2, we propose several strategies in updating the personal best particle and introduce the personal archive. Section 3 is dedicated to the experiments, the analysis and evaluations. Finally, the paper concludes with a summary.

1.1 Multi-Objective Problem

Typically a Multi-Objective Problem (MOP) involves several objectives which have to be optimized simultaneously, i.e. the objective function is multi-dimensional $f : \mathbb{R}^n \rightarrow \mathbb{R}^m$:

$$\min_{x \in S \subset \mathbb{R}^n} f_i(x) \quad \text{for } i = 1 \ldots m$$

We denote the image of S by $Z \subset \mathbb{R}^m$ and call it the objective space, the elements of Z are called objective vectors. Since we are dealing with MOPs, there is not generally one global optimum but a set of so-called **Pareto optimal solutions**. A decision vector $x_1 \in S$ is called **Pareto-optimal** if there is no other decision vector $x_2 \in S$ that **dominates**[1] it. An objective vector is called Pareto-optimal if the corresponding decision vector is Pareto-optimal. In the case that the two solutions x_1 and x_2 do not dominate each other, we say that they are indifferent to each other.

1.2 Multi-Objective Particle Swarm Optimization (MOPSO)

In MOPSO, a set of N particles may be considered as a population P_t in generation t. Each particle i has a position defined by $x_i = \{x_i^1, x_i^2, \cdots, x_i^n\}$ and a velocity defined by $v^i = \{v_i^1, v_i^2, \cdots, v_i^n\}$ in the search space S. In generation $t+1$, a new velocity and position for each particle i is generated by updating the old ones as follows:

$$\begin{aligned} v_i^{j,t+1} &= wv_i^{j,t} + c_1R_1(p_i^{j,t} - x_i^{j,t}) + c_2R_2(p_g^{j,t} - x_i^{j,t}) \\ x_i^{j,t+1} &= x_i^{j,t} + v_i^{j,t+1} \end{aligned} \tag{1}$$

where $j = 1, \cdots, n$, w is called the inertia weight of the particle, c_1 and c_2 are two positive constants, and R_1 and R_2 are random values in the range $[0, 1]$. In Equation (1), p_g^t denotes the position of the global best particle and p_i^t denotes the position of the personal best of particle i. In single objective PSO, these are typically the best solution found so far by any particle, and the best solution found so far by the particle i itself, and they are updated in every iteration. In the case of multiple objectives, however, the notion of "best" is not so easily defined.

Thus, the main challenge in MOPSO is to pick suitable personal guide (p_i) and global guide (p_g) to move the particles through the space. In general, a good MOPSO method

[1] x_1 is said to dominate x_2 if x_1 is not worse than x_2 in all of the objectives and it is strictly better than x_2 in at least one objective.

must obtain solutions with (a) a good convergence, and (b) a good diversity and spread along the Pareto-optimal front. Most research so far in the area of MOPSO has concentrated on the selection of p_g for each individual. The choice of p_g aims at moving the particles towards the Pareto-optimal front, but also has to ensure diversity along the front. Usually, all non-dominated solutions found are stored in an external archive, and p_g is selected from this archive. Typical strategies include random selection [3], selecting a solution that dominates many particles [1], or the sigma-method explained in more detail below. A recent survey on MOPSO can be found in [14].

The issue of selecting local best has been mostly ignored in the literature so far. The following section discusses this issue more thoroughly. For a more extensive treatment of MOPSO and PSO techniques in general, the reader is referred to [2,5,6].

2 Selecting the Personal Best

In this section, we propose different strategies for updating the personal guide for each particle in the population. In MOPSO, if the new position x_i dominates the current personal guide p_i, clearly p_i will be replaced by x_i. In the case that p_i dominates x_i, p_i will be kept. However, it is not straightforward what to do if x_i and p_i are indifferent to each other. The simplest and most natural strategies are certainly to keep only one value for p_i and update it as:

1. **Oldest:** p_i is updated only if it is dominated by x_i. If p_i and x_i are indifferent to each other, nothing will happen and the oldest non-dominated position will be kept in the memory. We expect this method to have a negative effect on particle diversity, because the particle is attracted towards the first of the obtained non-dominated positions.
2. **Newest:** p_i is updated to x_i except if it dominates x_i, i.e. we always keep the newest non-dominated position in the memory. In contrary to **Oldest**, the particle will not be dragged back to previously explored regions. It is not influenced by a personal guide as long as it keeps finding non-dominated solutions. Hence a better diversity of solutions than with **Oldest** is expected.

However, one could easily make a more informed choice:

3. **Sum:** Keep the solution which is better regarding the sum of objective values. If one solution is much better in one criterion, but only slightly worse in the other, it is probably preferable over all. This concept is illustrated in Figure 1 (a) and is expected to lead to faster convergence. A similar approach has been proposed in [7].

Instead of selecting one solution as the personal best and discarding the other, an alternative approach would be to keep track of more than one personal best, and remember **all** the non-dominated solutions visited in the past. Of course, then the question arises as to which of the stored personal best particles should be used to update the particle's velocity. It must be noted that the personal archive must be updated in each generation, i.e., it must be kept domination-free. Here, we propose the following ideas:

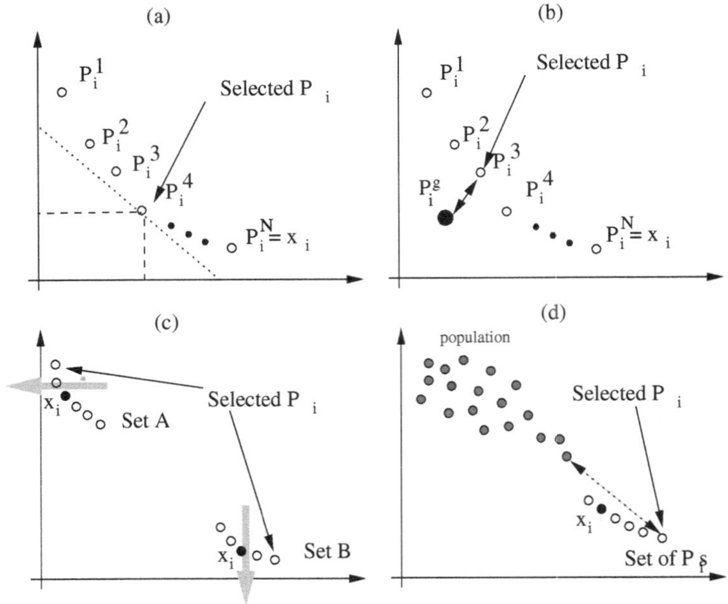

Fig. 1. Illustration of some selection concepts in objective space: (a) **Sum**, (b) **Global**, (c) **WSum**, and (d) **Diversity**

4. **Random:** The simplest strategy is to select a non-dominated p_i from the personal archive at random.
5. **WSum:** The **Sum** approach introduced above weights all of the criteria equally. For **WSum**, in order to better maintain diversity, we will now assign a higher weight to those criteria in which the particle is already relatively good. In particular, if $f_j(x_i)$ is the j-th fitness value of particle i, the weighted sum for the particle's personal best is calculated as

$$F = \sum_j \frac{f_j(x_i)}{\sum_k f_k(x_i)} f_j(p_i) \tag{2}$$

   The personal best with the smallest weighted sum is used for the update. This is illustrated in Figure 1 (c) with two sets (A and B) of personal archives for two different particles, denoted by x_i. If x_i is very close to one of the coordinate axis, it means that the particle tends to go more in this direction, so we select the p_i closest to this axis. In the case that x_i is somewhere in the middle of the objective space, the selected personal archive member would be a good compromise between the objectives. This method may help maintain a better spread of solutions.
6. **Global:** One might argue that the personal best should not be too far from the global best assigned to the particle. To test this conjecture, in this strategy we use the personal best which is closest in objective space to the assigned global best. This method may increase the convergence rate. This helps the particle to faster follow the global best particle, c.f. Figure 1 (b).

7. **Diversity:** The personal guide can also be used to increase diversity. Here, we use the personal best which has the largest minimal distance to any other particle, i.e. which is most isolated from the other particles. This is illustrated in Figure 1 (d). This method forces the particle to explore the regions which are far from the particles in the population.
8. **All:** Instead of using only one personal guide to influence the particle, we can also extend Equation 1 and use a smaller force towards all of the particle's personal bests.

$$v^i_{j,t+1} = wv^i_{j,t} + c_1R_1\left(\frac{\sum_{k=1}^{N_p}(p^k_{j,t} - x^i_{j,t})}{N_p}\right) + c_2R_2(p^{i,g}_{j,t} - x^i_{j,t}) \quad (3)$$

where N_p is the number of particles in the personal archive. As [9] has shown, using the location of several other solutions for update can indeed be helpful.
9. **None:** With this strategy, we test whether a personal best is at all beneficial in a multi-objective setting by simply replacing the personal best by the global best (i.e. the particle now experiences two forces to the global best).

Because some methods of the above methods are sensitive to the scaling of the objectives, we test them with non-normalized (default) and normalized objective values. The methods using normalized objectives are denoted by **Sum-N**, **Global-N**, **Diversity-N** and **WSum-N**.

3 Empirical Results

In principle, our strategies to select the personal best can be combined with any of the existing MOPSO approaches. In the following, we use the sigma-method which was proposed in [11] and which has been shown to compare favorably to other methods. The sigma method uses an archive of non-dominated solutions found. It operates on normalized objective values, scaled to the unit square (or hypercube):

$$f_i' = \frac{f_i - f_i^{min}}{f_i^{max} - f_i^{min}}$$

with f_i^{min}, f_i^{max} being the minimal and maximal value of objective i of any particle or archive member. As global guide for each particle, it chooses the archive member which is closest to the line connecting the particle's current position to the origin. This idea is illustrated in Figure 2 (a) for 2 dimensions. The sigma method also uses a turbulence factor [10] which introduces diversity into the swarm by randomizing the coordinates of a fraction of the particles within the area covered by the particles, i.e., within $[x_i^{min}, x_i^{max}]$ where x_i^{min} and x_i^{max} are the minimal and maximal coordinates for decision variable x_i over all particles in the population and the archive.

The MOPSO algorithm used the following parameter settings found reasonable based on some preliminary runs: inertia weight $w = 0.4$, turbulence factor $tf = 0.1$, population size 50, maximum archive size 100, and 300 generations. For more details about the influence of the parameters, please refer to [10].

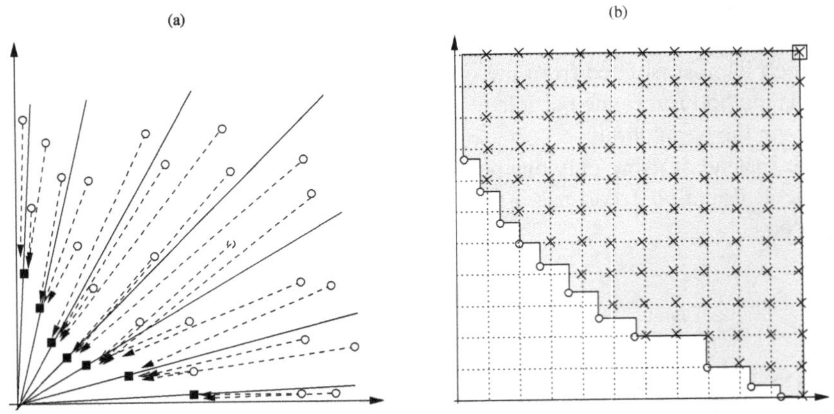

Fig. 2. Objective space: (a) Selecting the global best guide using sigma method. o and ■ denote the population members and non-dominated solutions respectively. (b) Hyper-volume metric: the number of dominated grid points (x) by the obtained non-dominated solutions o show the hyper-volume value.

3.1 Test Functions

We used some standard test functions from the multi-objective optimization literature. These test functions are two-objective optimization problems selected from [15,4,12] and are shown in Table 1. These test functions have different properties that make them more or less suitable. For ZDT1 and ZDT3, based on the method to generate these functions, all Pareto-optimal solutions differ in only one variable, while all other variables lie at the boundary of the search space (namely, $x_i = 0$ for all i except $i = 1$). This makes it relatively simple to explore the Pareto front once a single solution has been found, as only one variable has to be varied. Furthermore, because all other variables are on the boundary of the search space, it is very important how the optimizer handles boundaries. In our case, we simply set a particle to the boundary if the boundary is exceeded, which makes it particularly easy to find such solutions. Test functions OKA1 and OKA2 are relatively difficult test function, although they only have 2 resp. 3 parameters [12]. Test function FF doesn't suffer from the above difficulties and is, in our opinion, the most representative.

3.2 Evaluations

In order to achieve statistical significance, we run each method for 300 runs with different initial seeds. The algorithms are evaluated based on the hyper-volume metric. Hyper-volume is a measurement which takes into account the diversity as well as the convergence of solutions [15]. Figure 2 (b) shows the way we calculate the hyper-volume. We build a grid between a reference point (□) and the origin in the objective space. The grid points dominated by the solutions (x) are counted as the hyper-volume. High values of hyper-volume show a high quality in terms of the diversity and convergence of

Table 1. Test functions

Test	Function	Constraints
OKA1	$x_1' = \cos(\frac{\pi}{12})x_1 - \sin(\frac{\pi}{12})x_2$	$n = 2$
	$x_2' = \sin(\frac{\pi}{12})x_1 + \cos(\frac{\pi}{12})x_2$	$x_1 \in [6\sin(\frac{\pi}{12}),\ 6\sin(\frac{\pi}{12}) + 2\cos(\frac{\pi}{12})]$
	$f_1(x) = x_1'$	$x_2 \in [-2\sin(\frac{\pi}{12}),\ 6\cos(\frac{\pi}{12})]$
	$f_2(x) = \sqrt{2\pi} - \sqrt{\lvert x_1' \rvert} + 2\lvert x_2' - 3\cos x_1' - 3 \rvert^{\frac{1}{3}}$	
OKA2	$f_1(x) = x_1$	$x_1 \in [-\pi,\ \pi]$
	$f_2(x) = 1 - \frac{1}{4\pi^2}(x_1 + \pi)^2 +$	$x_2, x_3 \in [-5, 5]$
	$\lvert x_2 - 5cos(x_1) \rvert^{\frac{1}{3}} + \lvert x_3 - 5sin(x_1) \rvert^{\frac{1}{3}}$	$n = 3$
ZDT1	$g(x_2, \cdots, x_n) = 1 + 9(\sum_{i=2}^{n} x_i)/(n-1)$	$x_i \in [0,\ 1]$
	$h(f_1, g) = 1 - \sqrt{f_1/g}$	$n = 30$
	$f_1(x_1) = x_1$	$i = 1, 2, \ldots, n$
	$f_2(x) = g(x_2, \cdots, x_n) \cdot h(f_1, g)$	
ZDT3	$g(x_2, \cdots, x_n) = 1 + 9(\sum_{i=2}^{n} x_i)/(n-1)$	$x_i \in [0,\ 1]$
	$h(f_1, g) = 1 - \sqrt{f_1/g} - (f_1/g)\sin(10\pi f_1)$	$n = 30$
	$f_1(x_1) = x_1$	$i = 1, 2, \ldots, n$
	$f_2(x) = g(x_2, \cdots, x_n) \cdot h(f_1, g) + 1$	
FF	$f_1(x) = 1 - exp(-\sum_i (x_i - \frac{1}{\sqrt{n}})^2)$	$n = 10$
	$f_2(x) = 1 - exp(-\sum_i (x_i + \frac{1}{\sqrt{n}})^2)$	$x_i \in [-4,\ 4]$

the obtained solutions. This method depends on the number of grid lines. We select a relatively high resolution (200×200).

3.3 Observations

Tables 2 shows the results obtained at the end of the run (iteration 300). It shows whether one method is better than another based on a two-sided t-Test with significance level 95%. A "+" sign means that the method in the row is significantly better than the method in the column, a "-" sign denotes the reverse, and if the difference is not significant, we list a "o". The results are sorted from best to worst for each test problem.

The first observation from the obtained results is that the methods **None** (13), **All** (4) and **Sum** (2) are generally among the worst methods. At least for **None** this is not surprising, as it removes the good property of local searching and only incorporates the global searching of MOPSO.

Comparing **Global** (7) to **Global-N** (8), **WSum** (11) to **WSum-N** (12), and **Diversity** (9) to **Diversity-N** (10), we realize that normalization is not always helpful. For instance, **Diversity-N** is consistently outperformed by **Diversity**, presumably because we require to have access to the real distances in the objective space to generate diversity. For **Global**, the normalized version is always better, and for **WSum** and **Sum** the results are mixed. **Diversity** (9) delivers consistently good results and therefore is our recommended method.

Among the other methods, methods **Random** (1) and **Newest** (5) are recorded as simple methods in terms of implementation. However, **Random** outperforms **Newest** in all cases, demonstrating the advantage of an archive.

Table 2. Comparing the hyper-volume of different methods. "+", "-", and "o" signs mean that the method in the row is significantly better, worse, and indifferent than the method in the column

Mapping of methods to numbers:

1	Random	2	Sum	3	Sum-N	4	All	5	Newest	6	Oldest	7	Global
8	Global-N	9	Diversity	10	Diversity-N	11	WSumt	12	WSum-N	13	None		

OKA1		9	6	1	8	10	5	11	3	4	12	2	7	13
Diversity	9	o	+	+	+	+	+	+	+	+	+	+	+	+
Oldest	6	-	o	+	+	+	+	+	+	+	+	+	+	+
Random	1	-	-	o	o	+	+	+	+	+	+	+	+	+
Global-N	8	-	-	o	o	+	+	+	+	+	+	+	+	+
Diversity-N	10	-	-	-	-	o	+	+	+	+	+	+	+	+
Newest	5	-	-	-	-	-	o	o	+	+	+	+	+	+
WSum	11	-	-	-	-	-	o	o	+	+	+	+	+	+
Sum-N	3	-	-	-	-	-	-	-	o	+	+	+	+	+
All	4	-	-	-	-	-	-	-	-	o	o	o	+	+
WSum-N	12	-	-	-	-	-	-	-	-	o	o	o	+	+
Sum	2	-	-	-	-	-	-	-	-	o	o	o	+	+
Global	7	-	-	-	-	-	-	-	-	-	-	-	o	+
None	13	-	-	-	-	-	-	-	-	-	-	-	-	o

OKA2		9	6	13	10	8	1	12	5	11	7	3	2	4
Diversity	9	o	+	+	+	+	+	+	+	+	+	+	+	+
Oldest	6	-	o	o	o	+	+	+	+	+	+	+	+	+
None	13	-	o	o	o	+	+	+	+	+	+	+	+	+
Diversity-N	10	-	o	o	o	+	+	+	+	+	+	+	+	+
Global-N	8	-	-	-	-	o	o	o	o	o	o	+	+	+
Random	1	-	-	-	-	o	o	o	o	o	o	o	+	+
WSum-N	12	-	-	-	-	o	o	o	o	o	o	o	+	+
Newest	5	-	-	-	-	o	o	o	o	o	o	o	+	+
WSum	11	-	-	-	-	o	o	o	o	o	o	o	+	+
Global	7	-	-	-	-	o	o	o	o	o	o	o	+	+
Sum-N	3	-	-	-	-	-	o	o	o	o	o	o	o	+
Sum	2	-	-	-	-	-	-	-	-	-	-	o	o	o
All	4	-	-	-	-	-	-	-	-	-	-	-	o	o

ZDT1		12	9	1	5	8	11	10	13	6	7	2	4	3
WSum-N	12	o	o	+	+	+	+	+	+	+	+	+	+	+
Diversity	9	o	o	+	+	+	+	+	+	+	+	+	+	+
Random	1	-	-	o	o	+	+	+	+	+	+	+	+	+
Newest	5	-	-	o	o	o	o	+	+	+	+	+	+	+
Global-N	8	-	-	-	o	o	o	o	+	+	+	+	+	+
WSum	11	-	-	-	o	o	o	o	+	+	+	+	+	+
Diversity-N	10	-	-	-	-	o	o	o	+	+	+	+	+	+
None	13	-	-	-	-	-	-	-	o	o	+	+	+	+
Oldest	6	-	-	-	-	-	-	-	o	o	o	+	+	+
Global	7	-	-	-	-	-	-	-	-	o	o	+	+	+
Sum	2	-	-	-	-	-	-	-	-	-	-	o	o	+
Sum-N	3	-	-	-	-	-	-	-	-	-	-	o	o	o
All	4	-	-	-	-	-	-	-	-	-	-	-	o	o

ZDT3		11	9	12	1	8	10	2	5	6	13	7	4	3
WSum	11	o	o	+	+	+	+	+	+	+	+	+	+	+
Diversity	9	o	o	+	+	+	+	+	+	+	+	+	+	+
WSum-N	12	-	-	o	o	+	+	+	+	+	+	+	+	+
Random	1	-	-	o	o	o	+	+	+	+	+	+	+	+
Global-N	8	-	-	-	o	o	o	o	o	+	+	+	+	+
Diversity-N	10	-	-	-	-	o	o	o	o	+	+	+	+	+
Sum	2	-	-	-	-	o	o	o	o	+	+	+	+	+
Newest	5	-	-	-	-	o	o	o	o	+	+	+	+	+
Oldest	6	-	-	-	-	-	-	-	-	o	o	+	+	+
None	13	-	-	-	-	-	-	-	-	o	o	o	+	+
Global	7	-	-	-	-	-	-	-	-	-	o	o	+	+
Sum-N	3	-	-	-	-	-	-	-	-	-	-	-	o	o
All	4	-	-	-	-	-	-	-	-	-	-	-	o	o

FF		12	3	2	9	8	1	5	10	6	11	4	7	13
WSum-N	12	o	+	+	+	+	+	+	+	+	+	+	+	+
Sum-N	3	-	o	+	+	+	+	+	+	+	+	+	+	+
Sum	2	-	-	o	+	+	+	+	+	+	+	+	+	+
Diversity	9	-	-	-	o	+	+	+	+	+	+	+	+	+
Global-N	8	-	-	-	-	o	+	+	+	+	+	+	+	+
Random	1	-	-	-	-	-	o	+	+	+	+	+	+	+
Newest	5	-	-	-	-	-	-	o	+	+	+	+	+	+
Diversity-N	10	-	-	-	-	-	-	-	o	o	+	+	+	+
Oldest	6	-	-	-	-	-	-	-	o	o	+	+	+	+
WSum	11	-	-	-	-	-	-	-	-	-	o	+	+	+
All	4	-	-	-	-	-	-	-	-	-	-	o	+	+
Global	7	-	-	-	-	-	-	-	-	-	-	-	o	+
None	13	-	-	-	-	-	-	-	-	-	-	-	-	o

For further analysis, we plot the hyper-volume values over the generations in Figure 3 for the different test functions. For reasons of clarity, not all methods are included in every plot. We observe that the ranking of the different methods, and in particular, the superiority of **Diversity** and **WSum**, is largely consistent throughout the run. For the OKA1 and OKA2 test functions, **Diversity** highly outperforms the other methods. In particular for OKA2, MOPSO seems to have a difficulty to find a well distributed set of non-dominated solutions. Most methods have only between one and four different non-dominated solutions in the archive at the end of the run, a clear lack of diversity. So it is not surprising that the method designed to foster diversity (**Diversity**) works so much better, finding an average of 7.28 different non-dominated solutions.

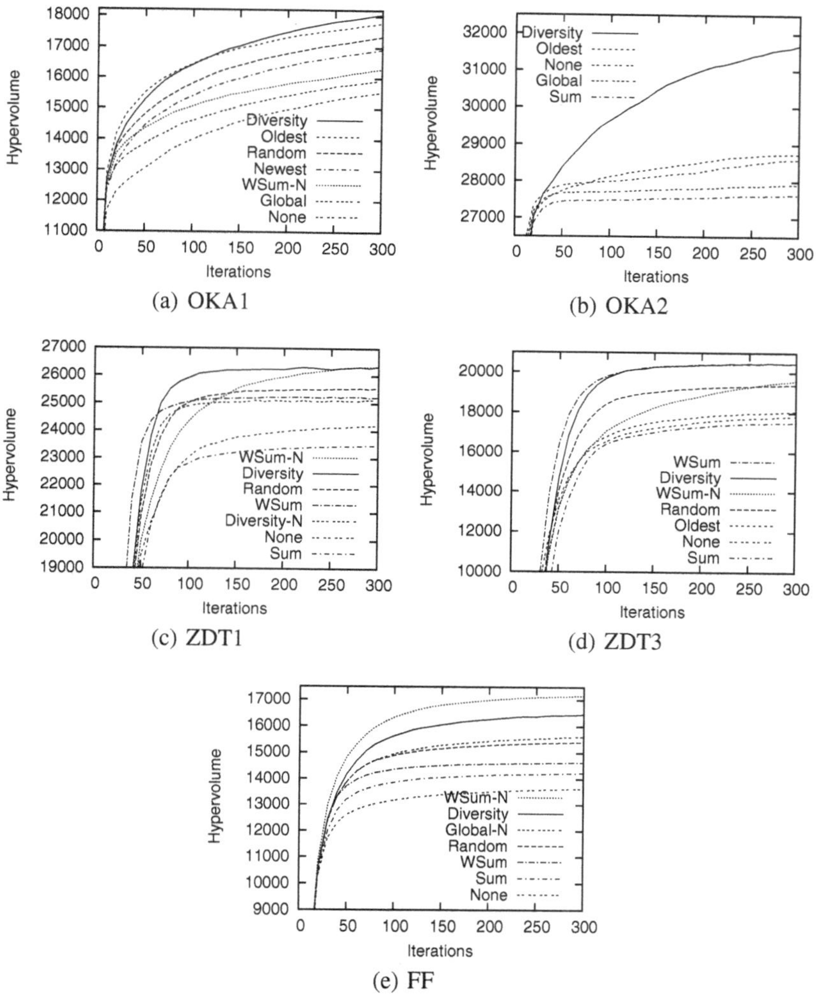

Fig. 3. Hyper-volume of different methods for 300 generations (scaled axis)

For the FF test function, **WSum** works best. **WSum** converges very quickly in particular on the ZDT test functions, while **WSum-N** often converges slowly in the beginning, but yielding good results at the end of the run.

4 Conclusion

We addressed the issue of how to select the personal best in a multi-objective setting. To this end, we proposed to allow each particle to store all non-dominated solutions encountered in a personal archive and proposed several methods to select the personal best from this archive. We empirically compared these methods by applying them to different test problems. The results show that by keeping the personal archive we obtain significantly better results than the traditional methods. In the future, we will investigate the new methods on problems with a higher number of objectives. Also, we will study the influence of a combination of the proposed methods, and the relationship between the selection of the global guide and the personal guide in order to increase the spread and convergence of the solutions.

References

1. J. E. Alvarez-Benitez, R. M. Everson, and J. E. Fieldsend. A MOPSO algorithm based exclusively on pareto dominance concepts. In C. Coello-Coello et al., editors, *Evolutionary Multi-Criterion Optimization*, volume 3410, pages 459–73. Springer, 2005.
2. M. Clerc and J. Kennedy. The particle swarm: Explosion, stability, and convergence in a multi-dimensional complex space. *IEEE Transactions on Evolutionary Computation*, 6(1):58–73, 2002.
3. C. A. Coello Coello and M. S. Lechuga. Mopso: A proposal for multiple objective particle swarm optimization. In *Congress on Evolutionary Computation*, pages 1051–1056. IEEE, 2002.
4. K. Deb, L. Thiele, M. Laumanns, and E. Zitzler. Scalable multi-objective optimization test problems. In *Congress on Evolutionary Computation*, pages 825–830. IEEE, 2002.
5. R. C. Eberhardt and Y. Shi (eds). Special issue on particle swarm optimization. *IEEE Transactions on Evolutionary Computation*, 8(3), 2004.
6. R. C. Eberhart and Y. Shi. *Swarm Intelligence*. Morgan Kaufmann, 2001.
7. S. Janson and D. Merkle. A new multi-objective particle swarm optimization algorithm using clustering applied to automated docking. In *Workshop on Hybrid Metaheuristics*, number 3636 in LNCS, pages 128–141. Springer, 2005.
8. J. Kennedy and R.C. Eberhart. Particle swarm optimization. In *IEEE International Conference on Neural Networks*, pages 1942–1948, 1995.
9. R. Mendes, J. Kennedy, and Jos e Neves. The fully informed particle swarm: Simpler, maybe better. *IEEE Transactions on Evolutionary Computation*, 8(3):204–210, 2004.
10. S. Mostaghim. *Multi-objective Evolutionary Algorithms: Data structures, Diversity and Convergence*. Shaker, 2005.
11. S. Mostaghim and J. Teich. Strategies for finding good local guides in multi-objective particle swarm optimization. In *Swarm Intelligence Symposium*, pages 26–33. IEEE, 2003.
12. T. Okabe, Y. Jin, M. Olhofer, and B. Sendhoff. On test functions for evolutionary multi-objective optimization. In *Parallel Problem Solving from Nature*, volume 3242 of *LNCS*, pages 792–802. Springer, 2004.
13. K.E. Parsopoulos and M.N. Vrahatis. Recent approaches to global optimization problems through particle swarm optimization. *Natural Computing*, 1(2-3):235–306, 2002.
14. M. Reyes-Sierra and C. Coello Coello. Multi-objective particle swarm optimizers: A survey of the state-of-the-art. *International Journal of Computational Intelligence Research*, 2006.
15. E. Zitzler. *Evolutionary Algorithms for Multiobjective Optimization: Methods and Applications*. Shaker, 1999.

Are All Objectives Necessary? On Dimensionality Reduction in Evolutionary Multiobjective Optimization

Dimo Brockhoff and Eckart Zitzler

Computer Engineering and Networks Laboratory, ETH Zurich, 8092 Zurich, Switzerland
{brockhoff, zitzler}@tik.ee.ethz.ch

Abstract. Most of the available multiobjective evolutionary algorithms (MOEA) for approximating the Pareto set have been designed for and tested on low dimensional problems (≤ 3 objectives). However, it is known that problems with a high number of objectives cause additional difficulties in terms of the quality of the Pareto set approximation and running time. Furthermore, the decision making process becomes the harder the more objectives are involved. In this context, the question arises whether all objectives are necessary to preserve the problem characteristics. One may also ask under which conditions such an objective reduction is feasible, and how a minimum set of objectives can be computed. In this paper, we propose a general mathematical framework, suited to answer these three questions, and corresponding algorithms, exact and heuristic ones. The heuristic variants are geared towards direct integration into the evolutionary search process. Moreover, extensive experiments for four well-known test problems show that substantial dimensionality reductions are possible on the basis of the proposed methodology.

1 Motivation

The field of multiobjective evolutionary algorithms (MOEA) has been rapidly growing over the last decade, and most of the publications deal with two- or three-dimensional problems [1]; however, studies addressing high-dimensional problems are rare [2,3]. The main reason is that problems with a high number of objectives cause additional challenges wrt low-dimensional problems. Current algorithms, developed for problems with a low number of objectives, have difficulties to find a good Pareto set approximation for higher dimensions [4]. Even with the availability of sufficient computing resources, some methods are practically not useable for a high number of objectives; for example, algorithms based on the hypervolume indicator [5] have running times exponential in the number of objectives [6,7]. Moreover, the decision maker's choice of an appropriate trade-off solution from a set of alternative solutions, generated by a MOEA, becomes difficult or infeasible with many objectives. In this context, several questions arise. On the one hand, one may ask whether it is possible to omit some of the objectives while preserving the problem characteristics, under which conditions such an objective reduction is feasible, and how a minimum set of objectives can be computed. On the other hand, if one allows changes in the problem structure while omitting objectives, one may ask how to quantify such structural changes and how to compute a minimum

T.P. Runarsson et al. (Eds.): PPSN IX, LNCS 4193, pp. 533–542, 2006.

set of objectives according to such a qualitative measure. These research topics have gained only little attention in the literature so far. In some studies [8,9,10], the issue of objective conflicts has been discussed; however, the issue under which conditions, *in general*, objectives can be omitted and how a minimum objective subset can be computed has not been addressed. Deb and Saxena [11] proposed a method for reducing the number of objectives, based on principal component analysis. Roughly speaking, their method aims at keeping those objectives that can explain most of the variance in the objective space. However, it is not clear (i) how the objective reduction alters the dominance structure and (ii) what the quality of a generated objective subset is (no minimum guarantee).

In a previous work [12], we have tackled the above questions for the case that the problem structure must not be changed. In particular, we have presented the minimum objective subset problem (MOSS) which asks which objective functions are essential, have introduced a general notion of conflicts between objective sets, and have proposed an exact algorithm and a greedy heuristic for the $\mathcal{NP}$ hard MOSS problem. In practice, though, one may be interested in "allowing errors", i.e., slight changes of the dominance structure, in order to obtain a smaller minimum set of objectives. This continuative study addresses this issue. The key contributions are

- a generalized notion of conflicting objective sets extending [12],
- the introduction of a measure for variations of the dominance structure
- the definition of the problems δ-MOSS and k-EMOSS, as an extension of the MOSS problem to the objective reduction with allowed problem structure variations,
- an exact algorithm, capable to solve both, the δ-MOSS and the k-EMOSS problem, as well as heuristics for both problems,
- experimental results on four different high-dimensional problems, and
- a comparison between our approach and Deb and Saxena's method [11].

As such, this paper provides a basis for online dimensionality reduction in evolutionary multiobjective algorithms.

2 A Measure for Changes of the Dominance Structure

Without loss of generality, in this paper we consider a minimization problem with k objective functions $f_i : X \to \mathbb{R}$, $1 \leq i \leq k$, where the vector function $f := (f_1, \ldots, f_k)$ maps each solution $\mathbf{x} \in X$ to an objective vector $f(\mathbf{x}) \in \mathbb{R}^k$. Furthermore, we assume that the underlying dominance structure is given by the weak Pareto dominance relation which is defined as follows: $\preceq_{\mathcal{F}'} := \{(\mathbf{x}, \mathbf{y}) \mid \mathbf{x}, \mathbf{y} \in X \wedge \forall f_i \in \mathcal{F}' : f_i(\mathbf{x}) \leq f_i(\mathbf{y})\}$, where $\mathcal{F}'$ is a set of objectives with $\mathcal{F}' \subseteq \mathcal{F} := \{f_1, \ldots, f_k\}$. For better readability, we will sometimes only consider the objective functions' indices, e.g., $\mathcal{F}' = \{1, 2, 3\}$ instead of $\mathcal{F}' = \{f_1, f_2, f_3\}$. We say $\mathbf{x}$ *weakly dominates* $\mathbf{y}$ *wrt the objective set* $\mathcal{F}'$ ($\mathbf{x} \preceq_{\mathcal{F}'} \mathbf{y}$) if $(\mathbf{x}, \mathbf{y}) \in \preceq_{\mathcal{F}'}$. Two solutions $\mathbf{x}, \mathbf{y}$ are *incomparable* if neither weakly dominates the other one. A solution $\mathbf{x}^* \in X$ is called *Pareto optimal* if there is no other $\mathbf{x} \in X$ that dominates $\mathbf{x}^*$ wrt the set of all objectives. The set of all Pareto optimal solutions is called *Pareto (optimal) set*, for which an approximation is sought.

In [12] we have proposed a method that computes for a given solution set $A \subseteq X$ a minimum subset $\mathcal{F}'$ of objectives with $\mathcal{F}' \subseteq \mathcal{F} := \{f_1, \ldots, f_k\}$ such that the dominance structure is preserved. In other words, for $\mathcal{F}'$ holds that $\mathbf{x} \preceq_{\mathcal{F}'} \mathbf{y} \Longleftrightarrow \mathbf{x} \preceq_{\mathcal{F}} \mathbf{y}$ for all $\mathbf{x}, \mathbf{y} \in A$. This is illustrated in the following example.

Example 1. *Fig. 1 shows the parallel coordinates plot, cf. [9], of three solutions* $\mathbf{x}_1$ *(solid line),* $\mathbf{x}_2$ *(dashed) and* $\mathbf{x}_3$ *(dotted) that are pairwise incomparable. At a closer inspection, the objective functions* f_1 *and* f_3 *indicate redundancy in the problem formulation, as the corresponding relations* $\preceq_{f_1}$ *and* $\preceq_{f_3}$ *are the same:* $\mathbf{x}_3 \preceq_{f_1} \mathbf{x}_1 \preceq_{f_1} \mathbf{x}_2$ *as well as* $\mathbf{x}_3 \preceq_{f_3} \mathbf{x}_1 \preceq_{f_3} \mathbf{x}_2$*. The approach of [12], therefore, computes the set* $\{f_1, f_2, f_4\}$ *as a minimum objective set which preserves the dominance structure, i.e.,* $\mathbf{x} \preceq_{\{f_1, f_2, f_4\}} \mathbf{y}$ *if and only if* $\mathbf{x} \preceq_{\mathcal{F}} \mathbf{y}$*, because all solutions are also pairwise incomparable wrt to* $\{f_1, f_2, f_4\}$*. That there is, for this example, no objective subset with less than three objectives, preserving the dominance structure, can be easily checked by hand.*

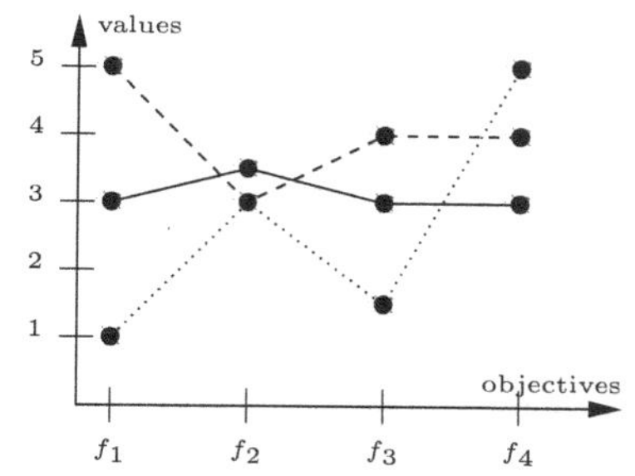

Fig. 1. Parallel coordinates plot for three solutions and four objectives

In practice, one is often interested in a further objective reduction at the cost of slight changes in the dominance structure. This poses the question how such a structural change can be quantitatively measured and how one can compute a minimum objective set for a given threshold on the degree of change.

Example 2. *Consider, once again, Fig. 1 and the objective subset* $\mathcal{F}' := \{f_3, f_4\}$*. We observe that by reducing the set of objectives to* $\mathcal{F}'$*, the dominances change: on the one hand* $\mathbf{x}_1 \preceq_{\mathcal{F}'} \mathbf{x}_2$*; on the other hand* $\mathbf{x}_1 \not\preceq_{\mathcal{F}} \mathbf{x}_2$*. In this sense, we make an error: the objective values of* $\mathbf{x}_1$ *had to be smaller by an additive term of* $\delta = 0.5$*, such that* $\mathbf{x}_1 \preceq_{\mathcal{F}} \mathbf{x}_2$ *would actually hold. This* δ *value can be used as a measure to quantify the difference in the dominance structure induced by* $\mathcal{F}'$ *and* $\mathcal{F}$*. By computing the* δ *values for all solution pairs* $\mathbf{x}, \mathbf{y}$*, we can then determine the maximum error. The meaning of the maximum* δ *value is that whenever we wrongly assume that* $\mathbf{x} \preceq_{\mathcal{F}'} \mathbf{y}$*, we also know that* $\mathbf{x}$ *is not worse than* $\mathbf{y}$ *in all objectives by an additive term of* δ*. For* $\mathcal{F}' := \{f_3, f_4\}$*, the maximum error is* $\delta = 0.5$*; for* $\mathcal{F}' := \{f_2, f_4\}$*, the maximum* δ *is 4.*

In the following, we formalize the definition of error, according to the above example. The background for that is provided by the (additive) ε-dominance relation[1] [13] and a generalization of the notion of conflicts between objective sets, defined in [12].

Definition 1. *Let* $\mathcal{F}_1$ *and* $\mathcal{F}_2$ *two objective sets. We define* $\mathcal{F}_1 \sqsubseteq^{\delta} \mathcal{F}_2 :\Longleftrightarrow \preceq_{\mathcal{F}_1} \subseteq \preceq^{\delta}_{\mathcal{F}_2}$.

Definition 2. *Let* $\mathcal{F}_1$ *and* $\mathcal{F}_2$ *two objective sets. We call*

- $\mathcal{F}_1$ δ-nonconflicting *with* $\mathcal{F}_2$ *iff* $(\mathcal{F}_1 \sqsubseteq^{\delta} \mathcal{F}_2) \wedge (\mathcal{F}_2 \sqsubseteq^{\delta} \mathcal{F}_1)$;
- $\mathcal{F}_1$ δ-conflicting *with* $\mathcal{F}_2$ *iff* $\neg$ ($\mathcal{F}_1$ *δ-nonconflicting with* $\mathcal{F}_2$).

---

[1] $\preceq^{\varepsilon}_{\mathcal{F}'} := \{(\mathbf{x}, \mathbf{y}) \mid \mathbf{x}, \mathbf{y} \in X \wedge \forall i \in \mathcal{F}' \subseteq \mathcal{F} : f_i(\mathbf{x}) - \varepsilon \leq f_i(\mathbf{y})\}$.

The above definition of δ-nonconflicting objective sets is useful for changing a problem formulation by considering a different objective set. If a multiobjective optimization problem uses the objective set $\mathcal{F}_1$ and one can prove that $\mathcal{F}_1$ is δ-nonconflicting with another objective set $\mathcal{F}_2$, one can easily replace $\mathcal{F}_1$ with $\mathcal{F}_2$ and can be sure that in the new formulation, for any $\mathbf{x}, \mathbf{y} \in X$, $\mathbf{x}$ either weakly dominates $\mathbf{y}$ wrt $\mathcal{F}_2$ or $\mathbf{x}$ ε-dominates $\mathbf{y}$ wrt $\mathcal{F}_2$ if $\mathbf{x}$ weakly dominates $\mathbf{y}$ wrt $\mathcal{F}_1$ and $\varepsilon = \delta$. In the special case of an objective subset $\mathcal{F}' \subseteq \mathcal{F}$, δ-nonconflicting with all objectives $\mathcal{F}$, the definition fits the intuitive measure of error in Example 2. If an objective subset $\mathcal{F}' \subset \mathcal{F}$ is δ-nonconflicting with the set $\mathcal{F}$ of all objectives, $\mathbf{x}$ δ-dominates $\mathbf{y}$, i.e., $\forall i \in \mathcal{F} : f_i(\mathbf{x}) - \delta \leq f_i(\mathbf{y})$, whenever $\mathbf{x}$ weakly dominates $\mathbf{y}$ wrt the reduced objective set $\mathcal{F}'$. We, then, can omit all objectives in $\mathcal{F} \setminus \mathcal{F}'$ without making a larger error than δ in the omitted objectives.

Based on the above conflict definitions, we will now formalize the notion of δ-minimal and δ-minimum objective sets including the corresponding notion for $\delta = 0$ in [12] and, furthermore, present a condition under which an objective reduction is possible.

Definition 3. *Let $\mathcal{F}$ be a set of objectives and $\delta \in \mathbb{R}$. An objective set $\mathcal{F}' \subseteq \mathcal{F}$ is denoted as*

- δ-minimal wrt $\mathcal{F}$ *iff (i) $\mathcal{F}'$ is δ-nonconflicting with $\mathcal{F}$, (ii) $\mathcal{F}'$ is δ'-conflicting with $\mathcal{F}$ for all $\delta' < \delta$, and (iii) there exists no $\mathcal{F}'' \subset \mathcal{F}'$ that is δ-nonconflicting with $\mathcal{F}$;*
- δ-minimum wrt $\mathcal{F}$ *iff (i) $\mathcal{F}'$ is δ-minimal wrt $\mathcal{F}$, and (ii) there exists no $\mathcal{F}'' \subset \mathcal{F}$ with $|\mathcal{F}''| < |\mathcal{F}'|$ that is δ-minimal wrt $\mathcal{F}$.*

A δ-minimal objective set is a subset of the original objectives that cannot be further reduced without changing the associated dominance structure with an error of at most δ. A δ-minimum objective set is the smallest possible set of original objectives that preserves the original dominance structure except for an error of δ. By definition, every δ-minimum objective set is δ-minimal, but not all δ-minimal sets are at the same time δ-minimum.

Definition 4. *A set $\mathcal{F}$ of objectives is called* δ-redundant *if and only if there exists $\mathcal{F}' \subset \mathcal{F}$ that is δ-minimal wrt $\mathcal{F}$.*

This definition of δ-redundancy represents a necessary and sufficient condition for the omission of objectives while the obtained dominance relation preserve the most of the initial dominance relation according to the definition of error in Example 2.

3 Identifying Minimum Objective Subsets

After the definition of an objective subset's error regarding its dominance structure, we present the two problems δ-`MOSS` and `k-EMOSS`, dealing with the two questions, mentioned in the introduction: On the one hand, the computation of an objective subset of minimum size, yielding a (changed) dominance structure with given error, and, on the other hand, the computation of an objective subset of given size with the minimum error. Furthermore, we present an exact algorithm, capable of solving both the δ-`MOSS` and the `k-EMOSS` problem, and afterwards approximation algorithms for each of the two problems, that are fast and designed for the integration into the search process.

3.1 The δ-MOSS and k-EMOSS Problems

Based on Sec. 2, the problem MINIMUM OBJECTIVE SUBSET (MOSS), proposed in [12], can be characterized as follows. Given a multiobjective optimization problem, a given instance consists of the set A of solutions, the generalized weak Pareto dominance relation $\preceq_{\mathcal{F}}$, and for all objective functions $f_i \in \mathcal{F}$ the single relations $\preceq_i$, where $\bigcap_{1 \leq i \leq k} \preceq_i = \preceq_{\mathcal{F}}$. We then ask for a 0-minimum objective set $\mathcal{F}' \subseteq \mathcal{F}$ wrt $\mathcal{F}$. This problem can easily be generalized to the following problem, when allowing an error δ.

Definition 5. *Given a multiobjective optimization problem, the problem δ- MINIMUM OBJECTIVE SUBSET (δ-MOSS) is defined as follows.*

Instance: *The objective vectors $f(\mathbf{x}_1), \ldots, f(\mathbf{x}_m) \in \mathbb{R}^k$ of the solutions $\mathbf{x}_1, \ldots, \mathbf{x}_m \in A \subseteq X$ and a $\delta \in \mathbb{R}$.*

Task: *Compute a δ-minimum objective subset $\mathcal{F}' \subseteq \mathcal{F}$ wrt $\mathcal{F}$.*

Note, that the limitation of the instances to the whole search space description is not essential here. Since the objective values are only known for a small set of solutions in practice, and not for the entire search space, Pareto set approximations, e.g., given by a MOEA's population, can also be the underlying set A of solutions. Note also, that the set A and the relations $\preceq_i$, $\preceq_{\mathcal{F}}$ are only given implicitly in a δ-MOSS instance. Nevertheless, δ-MOSS is a generalization of MOSS and therefore $\mathcal{NP}$ hard, cf. the accompanying technical report [14]. As a variation of the δ-MOSS problem, we introduce the problem of finding an objective subset of size $\leq$ k with minimum error according to $\mathcal{F}$.

Definition 6. *Given a multiobjective optimization problem, the problem MINIMUM OBJECTIVE SUBSET OF SIZE k WITH MINIMUM ERROR (k-EMOSS) is defined as follows.*

Instance: *The objective vectors $f(\mathbf{x}_1), \ldots, f(\mathbf{x}_m) \in \mathbb{R}^k$ of the solutions $\mathbf{x}_1, \ldots, \mathbf{x}_m \in A \subseteq X$ and a $k \in \mathbb{R}$.*

Task: *Compute an objective subset $\mathcal{F}' \subseteq \mathcal{F}$ which has size $|\mathcal{F}'| \leq$ k and is δ-nonconflicting with $\mathcal{F}$ with the minimal possible δ.*

3.2 Algorithms

An Exact Algorithm. Algorithm 1, as a generalization of the exact algorithm for the MOSS problem [12], solves both the δ-MOSS and the k-EMOSS problem exactly in exponential time. Thus, it can only solve small problem instances in reasonable time. The basic idea is to consider all solution pairs $(\mathbf{x}, \mathbf{y})$ successively and store in S_M all minimal objective subsets $\mathcal{F}'$ together with the minimal δ' value such that $\mathcal{F}'$ is δ'-nonconflicting with the set $\mathcal{F}$ of all objectives when taking into account only the solution pairs in M, considered so far.

The algorithm uses a subfunction $\delta_{\min}(\mathcal{F}_1, \mathcal{F}_2)$, that computes the minimal δ error for two solutions $\mathbf{x}, \mathbf{y} \in X$, such that $\mathcal{F}_1$ is δ-nonconflicting with $\mathcal{F}_2$ wrt $\mathbf{x}, \mathbf{y}$. Due to space limitations, we cannot show here, how this minimal δ can be computed in time $O(k \cdot m^2)$ and refer to [14]. Furthermore, Algorithm 1 computes the union $\sqcup$ of two sets of objective subsets with simultaneous deletion of not δ'-minimal pairs $(\mathcal{F}', \delta')$:

Algorithm 1. An exact algorithm for δ-MOSS and k-EMOSS.

1: Init:
2: $M := \emptyset, \quad S_M := \emptyset$
3: **for all** pairs $\mathbf{x}, \mathbf{y} \in A$, $\mathbf{x} \neq \mathbf{y}$ of solutions **do**
4: $S_{\{(\mathbf{x},\mathbf{y})\}} := \emptyset$
5: **for all** objective pairs $i, j \in \mathcal{F}$, not necessary $i \neq j$ **do**
6: compute $\delta_{ij} := \delta_{\min}(\{i\} \cup \{j\}, \mathcal{F})$ wrt $\mathbf{x}, \mathbf{y}$
7: $S_{\{(\mathbf{x},\mathbf{y})\}} := S_{\{(\mathbf{x},\mathbf{y})\}} \sqcup (\{i\} \cup \{j\}, \delta_{ij})$
8: **end for**
9: $S_{M \cup \{(\mathbf{x},\mathbf{y})\}} := S_M \sqcup S_{\{(\mathbf{x},\mathbf{y})\}}$
10: $M := M \cup \{(\mathbf{x}, \mathbf{y})\}$
11: **end for**
12: Output for δ-MOSS: $(s_{\min}, \delta_{\min})$ in S_M with minimal size $|s_{\min}|$ and $\delta_{min} \leq \delta$
13: Output for k-EMOSS: (s, δ) in S_M with size $|s| \leq$ k and minimal δ

Algorithm 2. A greedy algorithm for δ-MOSS.

1: Init:
2: compute the relations $\preceq_i$ for all $1 \leq i \leq k$ and $\preceq_{\mathcal{F}}$
3: $\mathcal{F}' := \emptyset$
4: $R := A \times A \setminus \preceq_{\mathcal{F}}$
5: **while** $R \neq \emptyset$ **do**
6: $i^* = \underset{i \in \mathcal{F} \setminus \mathcal{F}'}{\operatorname{argmin}} \{ |(R \cap \preceq_i) \setminus (\preceq^0_{\mathcal{F}' \cup \{i\}} \cap \preceq^\delta_{\mathcal{F} \setminus (\mathcal{F}' \cup \{i\})})| \}$
7: $R := (R \cap \preceq_{i^*}) \setminus (\preceq^0_{\mathcal{F}' \cup \{i^*\}} \cap \preceq^\delta_{\mathcal{F} \setminus (\mathcal{F}' \cup \{i^*\})})$
8: $\mathcal{F}' := \mathcal{F}' \cup \{i^*\}$
9: **end while**

$$\begin{aligned} S_1 \sqcup S_2 := \{ (\mathcal{F}_1 \cup \mathcal{F}_2, \max\{\delta_1, \delta_2\}) \mid & (\mathcal{F}_1, \delta_1) \in S_1 \wedge (\mathcal{F}_2, \delta_2) \in S_2 \\ \wedge \nexists (\mathcal{F}_1', \delta_1') \in S_1, (\mathcal{F}_2', \delta_2') \in S_2 : & \left(\mathcal{F}_1' \cup \mathcal{F}_2' \subset \mathcal{F}_1 \cup \mathcal{F}_2 \wedge \max\{\delta_1', \delta_2'\} \leq \max\{\delta_1, \delta_2\} \right) \\ \wedge \nexists (\mathcal{F}_1', \delta_1') \in S_1, (\mathcal{F}_2', \delta_2') \in S_2 : & \left(\mathcal{F}_1' \cup \mathcal{F}_2' \subseteq \mathcal{F}_1 \cup \mathcal{F}_2 \wedge \max\{\delta_1', \delta_2'\} < \max\{\delta_1, \delta_2\} \right) \} \end{aligned}$$

The correctness proof of Algorithm 1—as well as the proof of its running time of $O(m^2 \cdot k \cdot 2^k)$—can also be found in [14]. Note, that the exact algorithm can be easily parallelized, as the computation of the sets $S_{\{(\mathbf{x},\mathbf{y})\}}$ are independent for different pairs $(\mathbf{x}, \mathbf{y})$. It also can be accelerated if line 9 of Algorithm 1 is tailored to either the δ-MOSS or the k-EMOSS problem by including a pair $(\mathcal{F}', \delta')$ into $S_{M \cup \{(\mathbf{x},\mathbf{y})\}}$ only if $\delta' \leq \delta$, and $|\mathcal{F}'| \leq$ k respectively.

A Greedy Algorithm for δ-MOSS. Algorithm 2, as an approximation algorithm for δ-MOSS, computes an objective subset $\mathcal{F}'$, δ-nonconflicting with the set $\mathcal{F}$ of all objectives in a greedy way. Starting with an empty set $\mathcal{F}'$, Algorithm 2 chooses in each step the objective f_i which yields the smallest set $\preceq_{\mathcal{F}'} \cap \preceq_i$ without considering the relationships in $\preceq^0_{\mathcal{F}' \cup \{i\}} \cap \preceq^\delta_{\mathcal{F}}$ until $\mathcal{F}'$ is δ-nonconflicting with $\mathcal{F}$. For the correctness proof of Algorithm 2 and the proof of its running time of $O(\min\{k^3 \cdot m^2, k^2 \cdot m^4\})$ we once again refer to [14]. Note, that Algorithm 2 not necessarily yields a δ-minimal or even δ-minimum objective set wrt $\mathcal{F}$.

Algorithm 3. A greedy algorithm for k-EMOSS.

Init:
  $\mathcal{F}' := \emptyset$
while $|\mathcal{F}'| < \mathrm{k}$ **do**
  $\mathcal{F}' := \mathcal{F}' \cup \underset{i \in \mathcal{F} \setminus \mathcal{F}'}{\operatorname{argmin}} \{\delta_{\min}(\mathcal{F}' \cup \{i\}, \mathcal{F}) \text{ wrt } A\}$
end while

A Greedy Algorithm for k-EMOSS. Algorithm 3 is an approximation algorithm for k-EMOSS. It supplies always an objective subset of size k but does not guarantee to find the set with minimal δ. The greedy algorithm needs time $O(m^2 \cdot k^3)$ since at most $\mathrm{k} \leq k$ loops with k calls of the $\delta_{\min}$ subfunction are needed. One call of the $\delta_{\min}$ function needs time $\Theta(m^2 \cdot k)$ and all other operations need time $O(1)$ each. Note, that Algorithm 3 can be accelerated in a concrete implementation as the while loop can be aborted if either $|\mathcal{F}'| = \mathrm{k}$ or $\delta_{min}(\mathcal{F}', \mathcal{F}) = 0$.

4 Experiments

In the following experiments, we apply the suggested algorithms to Pareto set approximations, generated by a MOEA, in order to investigate (i) whether the proposed dimensionality reduction method yields noticeable smaller sets of objectives, (ii) how the greedy algorithms perform, compared to the exact counterparts, and (iii) how our approach compares to the method proposed by Deb and Saxena. The experimental results indicate that our method is not only useful to analyze the output of MOEAs but also qualified for using it within an evolutionary algorithm. The Pareto set approximations, used in the experiments, are generated with the IBEA algorithm [15] on a linux computer (SunFireV60x with 3060 MHz). Due to space limitations, we refer to [14] for a detailed description of the experimental setups.

Are All Objectives Necessary? This issue has been studied for 9 different 0-1-knapsack problem instances [16] and 3 instances for three different continuous test problems, namely DTLZ2, DTLZ5, and DTLZ7 [4]. The Pareto set approximations, generated by IBEA, contain up to 300 solutions for these problems. The results in Table 1 show for all instances that an objective reduction is possible without changing the dominance structure between the solutions, except for the 5-objective-instances and the knapsack instances with 500 items. The results also show that, the more objectives an instance possesses, the more objectives are omissible. If we allow changes of the dominance structure within the dimensionality reduction, further objectives can be omitted. However, the influence of a greater error on the resulting objective set size depends significantly on the problems. For example, only small errors yield fundamentally smaller objective sets for the DTLZ7 instances, while even a large error produces no further reduction for all DTLZ2 and DTLZ5 instances. Similar results for the δ-MOSS problem apply for another study, regarding the dominance structure on the whole search space for a small knapsack instance, cf. Fig. 2. By examining the k-EMOSS problem for the 18 instances in Table 1, we see similar results in a different manner. The smaller the chosen size of the resulting objective sets, the larger the error in the corresponding dominance structure.

Table 1. Sizes (for δ-MOSS) and relative errors (for k-EMOSS) of objective subsets for different problems, computed with the greedy algorithms. For δ-MOSS, the δ value is chosen relatively to the maximum spread of the IBEA population after 100 generations; in the case of k-EMOSS the specified size k of the output subset is noted relatively to the problem's number of objectives.

	δ-MOSS				k-EMOSS		
	0%	10%	20%	40%	30%	60%	90%
knapsack: 100 items, 5 objectives, 100 solutions	5	5	5	5	0.926	0.516	0.486
knapsack, 100 items, 15 objectives, 200 solutions	11	10	10	9	0.818	0.348	0.000
knapsack, 100 items, 25 objectives, 300 solutions	13	13	13	11	0.597	0.000	0.000
knapsack: 250 items, 5 objectives, 100 solutions	5	5	5	4	0.859	0.697	0.280
knapsack, 250 items, 15 objectives, 200 solutions	11	11	10	9	0.762	0.342	0.000
knapsack, 250 items, 25 objectives, 300 solutions	12	12	12	11	0.575	0.000	0.000
knapsack: 500 items, 5 objectives, 100 solutions	5	5	5	4	0.748	0.504	0.237
knapsack, 500 items, 15 objectives, 200 solutions	15	15	14	10	0.643	0.435	0.278
knapsack, 500 items, 25 objectives, 300 solutions	25	23	17	13	0.472	0.320	0.138
DTLZ2: 5 objectives, 100 solutions	5	5	5	5	0.991	0.970	0.920
DTLZ2: 15 objectives, 200 solutions	13	13	13	13	0.942	0.891	0.000
DTLZ2: 25 objectives, 300 solutions	18	18	18	18	0.832	0.782	0.000
DTLZ5: 5 objectives, 100 solutions	5	5	5	5	0.952	0.906	0.896
DTLZ5: 15 objectives, 200 solutions	11	11	11	11	0.860	0.803	0.000
DTLZ5: 25 objectives, 300 solutions	13	13	13	13	0.820	0.000	0.000
DTLZ7: 5 objectives, 100 solutions	5	5	1	1	0.135	0.134	0.132
DTLZ7: 15 objectives, 200 solutions	10	1	1	1	0.078	0.070	0.000
DTLZ7: 25 objectives, 300 solutions	11	1	1	1	0.050	0.000	0.000

Does the Exact Algorithm Outperform the Greedy One? Fig. 2 shows both the resulting objective set sizes and the running times for the exact and the greedy algorithm on the δ-MOSS problem for the 0-1-knapsack problem with four different numbers of objectives and 7 items. The small number of items allows the examination of the whole search space instead of a Pareto set approximation. For all four choices of the objective set size and all allowed errors δ, the exact algorithm yields smaller objective subsets than the greedy algorithm, while the running times, however, are considerably smaller for the greedy algorithm. Note in this context, that Fig. 2 shows a log scale plot for the running times. Also note, that the running time of the greedy algorithm decreases with higher δ which is not self-evident but significant, e.g., in a Wilcoxon rank sum test. Altogether, the results confirm the above observation, the more error is allowed, the more objectives can be omitted. This effect strengthens with instances of higher dimension.

Is Our Method Comparable to the Dimensionality Reduction Method by Deb and Saxena? Last, we compare our approach to the method of Deb and Saxena [11] on k-EMOSS for a knapsack instance with 20 objectives. Table 2 shows the absolute and relative[2] δ errors for the objective subsets computed with the method of Deb and Saxena, the exact and the greedy algorithm. With more objectives, the δ error gets smaller for all methods. But since Deb and Saxena's method is not especially developed for k-EMOSS, the resulting objective sets causes larger errors in the dominance structure than the corresponding sets computed with the greedy algorithm.

[2] The relative error δ_{rel} is the absolute error δ_{abs} divided by the spread of the IBEA population, where we define the maximal spread S of a population P as the maximal difference of the solutions' objective values: $S = \max_{f_i \in \mathcal{F}} \max_{\mathbf{x},\mathbf{y} \in P}\{|f_i(\mathbf{x}) - f_i(\mathbf{y})|\}$.

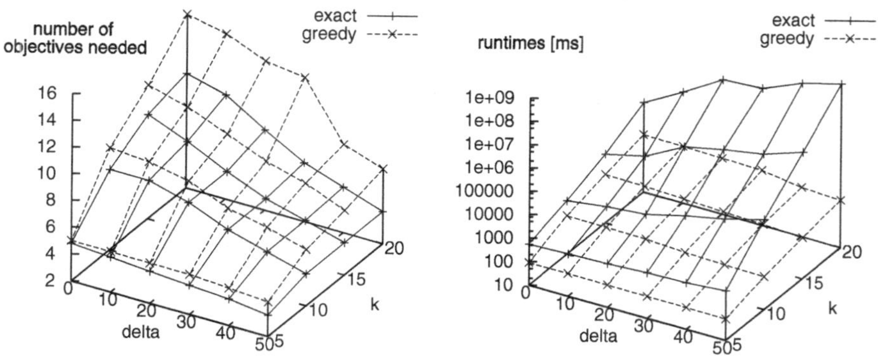

Fig. 2. Analysis of the whole search space for the knapsack problem with 7 items and comparison between the exact algorithm (solid lines) and the greedy algorithm (dashed lines). The sizes of the computed objective subsets are shown in the left plot and the running times of the two algorithms in the right one. Each data point is the average of five independent knapsack instances.

Table 2. Comparison between the approach of Deb and Saxena [11] with the exact and greedy algorithm for `k-EMOSS` on a Pareto set approximation of a knapsack instance with 20 objectives. Due to space limitations, we refer to [14] for details.

	Deb and Saxena		exact algorithm		greedy algorithm	
# obj	δ_{abs}	δ_{rel}	δ_{abs}	δ_{rel}	δ_{abs}	δ_{rel}
1	-	-	552	0.9154	552	0.9154
2	603	1.0000	485	0.8043	508	0.8425
3	546	0.9055	447	0.7413	462	0.7662
4	546	0.9055	363	0.6020	418	0.6932
5	-	-	289	0.4793	369	0.6119
6	-	-	129	0.2139	356	0.5904
7	466	0.7728	0	0.0000	324	0.5373
8	466	0.7728	0	0.0000	287	0.4760
9	357	0.5920	0	0.0000	0	0.0000
≥ 11	0	0.0000	0	0.0000	0	0.0000

5 Conclusions

In this paper we covered the problem of objective reduction in multiobjective optimization. We presented a necessary and sufficient condition for the possibility of an omission of objectives with a small change in the dominance structure. Besides that, we defined a measure of the dominance structure's variation when omitting a certain objective set and gave a general notion of conflicts between objective sets. We introduced the problem of finding a minimum objective subset, maintaining the given dominance structure with a given error and the problem of finding an objective subset with given size, changing the dominance structure least. In addition, we proposed an exact algorithm and fast heuristics for both problems. The capability of this objective reduction method was shown in experiments for outcomes of an MOEA on four different test problems and in comparison with a recently published dimensionality reduction approach.

The presented approach is useful for reducing the number of objectives *after* a MOEA run to simplify the decision maker's process, and we are currently working on the adequate integration of the presented dimensionality reduction method into an existing MOEA to reduce the number of objectives adaptively *during* an EA run.

References

1. Coello Coello, C.A., Van Veldhuizen, D.A., Lamont, G.B.: Evolutionary Algorithms for Solving Multi-Objective Problems. Kluwer Academic Publishers, New York (2002)
2. Paechter, B., Rankin, R.C., Cumming, A., Fogarty, T.C.: Timetabling the classes of an entire university with an evolutionary algorithm. In: PPSN V Proceedings, Springer (1998) 865–874
3. Coello Coello, C.A., Hernández Aguirre, A.: Design of Combinational Logic Circuits through an Evolutionary Multiobjective Optimization Approach. Artificial Intelligence for Engineering, Design, Analysis and Manufacture **16**(1) (2002) 39–53
4. Deb, K., Thiele, L., Laumanns, M., Zitzler, E.: Scalable test problems for evolutionary multi-objective optimization. In Abraham, A., Jain, R., Goldberg, R., eds.: Evolutionary Multiobjective Optimization: Theoretical Advances and Applications. Springer (2005) 105–145
5. Emmerich, M., Beume, N., Naujoks, B.: An emo algorithm using the hypervolume measure as selection criterion. In: EMO 2005 Proceedings, Springer (2005) 62–76
6. Knowles, J., Corne, D.: Properties of an adaptive archiving algorithm for storing nondominated vectors. IEEE Transactions on Evolutionary Computation **7**(2) (2003) 100–116
7. While, L.: A new analysis of the lebmeasure algorithm for calculating hypervolume. In: EMO 2005 Proceedings, Springer (2005) 326–340
8. Deb, K.: Multi-objective optimization using evolutionary algorithms. Wiley, Chichester, UK (2001)
9. Purshouse, R.C., Fleming, P.J.: Conflict, harmony, and independence: Relationships in evolutionary multi-criterion optimisation. In: EMO 2003 Proceedings, Springer, Berlin (2003) 16–30
10. Tan, K.C., Khor, E.F., Lee, T.H.: Multiobjective Evolutionary Algorithms and Applications. Springer, London (2005)
11. Deb, K., Saxena, D.K.: On finding pareto-optimal solutions through dimensionality reduction for certain large-dimensional multi-objective optimization problems. Kangal report no. 2005011, Kanpur Genetic Algorithms Laboratory (KanGAL) (2005)
12. Brockhoff, D., Zitzler, E.: On Objective Conflicts and Objective Reduction in Multiple Criteria Optimization. TIK Report 243, ETH Zurich, Zurich, Switzerland (2006) submitted to Operations Research 2006.
13. Zitzler, E., Thiele, L., Laumanns, M., Foneseca, C.M., Grunert da Fonseca, V.: Performance assessment of multiobjective optimizers: An analysis and review. IEEE Transactions on Evolutionary Computation **7**(2) (2003) 117–132
14. Brockhoff, D., Zitzler, E.: Dimensionality Reduction in Multiobjective Optimization with (Partial) Dominance Structure Preservation: Generalized Minimum Objective Subset Problems. TIK Report 247, ETH Zurich, Zurich, Switzerland (2006)
15. Zitzler, E., Künzli, S.: Indicator-based selection in multiobjective search. In: PPSN VIII Proceedings, Springer (2004) 832–842
16. Zitzler, E., Thiele, L.: Multiobjective evolutionary algorithms: A comparative case study and the strength pareto approach. IEEE Transactions on Evolutionary Computation **3**(4) (1999) 257–271

Solving Hard Multiobjective Optimization Problems Using ε-Constraint with Cultured Differential Evolution

Ricardo Landa Becerra and Carlos A. Coello Coello

Evolutionary Computation Group at CINVESTAV-IPN (EVOCINV)
Electrical Eng. Department, Computer Science Dept.
Av. IPN No. 2508 Col. San Pedro Zacatenco, México D.F. 07300, México
rlanda@computacion.cs.cinvestav.mx
ccoello@cs.cinvestav.mx

Abstract. In this paper, we propose the use of a mathematical programming technique called the ε-constraint method, hybridized with an evolutionary single-objective optimizer: the cultured differential evolution. The ε-constraint method uses the cultured differential evolution to produce one point of the Pareto front of a multiobjective optimization problem at each iteration. This approach is able to solve difficult multiobjective problems, relying on the efficiency of the single-objective optimizer, and on the fact that none of the two approaches (the mathematical programming technique or the evolutionary algorithm) are required to generate the entire Pareto front at once. The proposed approach is validated using several difficult multiobjective test problems, and our results are compared with respect to a multi-objective evolutionary algorithm representative of the state-of-the-art in the area: the NSGA-II.

1 Introduction

Evolutionary multiobjective optimization consists of using evolutionary algorithms to solve problems with two or more (often conflicting) objective functions. This research area has become very popular in the last few years [1]. Concurrently, more challenging problems have been integrated into the most recent benchmarks, some of which require a considerably high number of objective function evaluations to be solved, or can even make current algorithms to fail in their efforts to generate the true Pareto front [2].

The ε-constraint method is a mathematical programming technique, which transforms a multiobjective optimization problem into several constrained single-objective problems. This method has not been used too often in evolutionary computation, due to the fact that it does not generates a set of nondominated solutions in a single run, as most evolutionary algorithms do. Moreover, it has been found that this method is relatively expensive when solving "easy" multiobjective problems, because of the several single-objective optimizations executed.

In this paper we propose the use of the ε-constraint method together with an efficient evolutionary approach which solves constrained single-objective

T.P. Runarsson et al. (Eds.): PPSN IX, LNCS 4193, pp. 543–552, 2006.

optimization problems. The optimizer consists of a differential evolution-based cultural algorithm, which improves the optimization process by means of domain information extracted during the evolutionary search.

The rest of the paper is organized as follows: in Section 2, the ε-constraint method is presented in some detail. Section 3 briefly describes the cultured differential evolution approach, which is the single-objective optimizer adopted in this work. Section 4 describes our proposed approach. Section 5 contains our results, and a comparative study with respect to the NSGA-II. Finally, Section 6 provides our conclusions and some possible paths for future research.

2 The ε-Constraint Method

This is a multiobjective optimization technique, proposed by Haimes et al. [3], for generating Pareto optimal solutions. It makes use of a single-objective optimizer which handles constraints, to generate one point of the Pareto front at a time. For transforming the multiobjective problem into several single-objective problems with constraints it uses the following procedure (assuming minimization for all the objective functions):

$$\begin{aligned}&\text{minimize } f_l(\mathbf{x})\\&\text{subject to } f_j(\mathbf{x}) \leq \varepsilon_j \text{ for all } j = 1, 2, \ldots, m,\ j \neq l,\\&\qquad\qquad \mathbf{x} \in S\end{aligned}$$

where $l \in \{1, 2, \ldots, m\}$ and S is the feasible region, which can be defined by any equality and/or inequality constraint. The vector of upper bounds, $\varepsilon = (\varepsilon_1, \varepsilon_2, \ldots, \varepsilon_m)$, defines the maximum value that each objective can have. In order to obtain a subset of the Pareto optimal set (or even the entire set, in case this set is finite), one must vary the vector of upper bounds along the Pareto front for each objective, and make a new optimization process for each new vector. The generation of different points of the Pareto front using different values of the upper bound is illustrated in Figure 1.

For any nonlinear multiobjective optimization problem, the solution of an ε-constraint problem yields a weakly Pareto optimal solution [3]. A true Pareto optimal solution can be obtained either if the solution is unique, or if the optimizations are done for all the objectives before reporting the solution [4]. However, to improve the speed of the generation of solutions, only one optimization per point can be performed to obtain an approximation of the Pareto optimal set.

To the best of our knowledge, the only attempt to hybridize the ε-constraint method with an evolutionary algorithm is the approach called CMEA [5]. This approach performs the intermediate optimizations using a standard evolutionary algorithm. To reduce the computational cost of each independent optimization, the final population of one optimization process is used as the initial population for the next one; however, the authors noted the lack of diversity of the approach and proposed a high mutation rate at the beginning of each process.

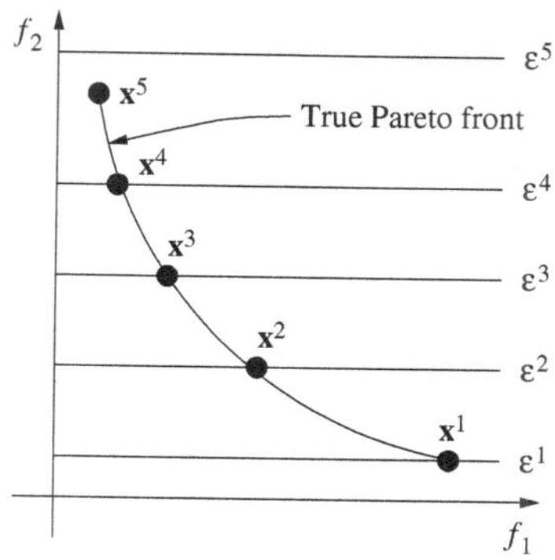

Fig. 1. Generating different solutions with the ε-constraint method

The authors provide no further details about the mechanism adopted to handle the constraints in the single-objective optimizer.

In [6], the authors proposed an extension of CMEA for three-objective problems. However, the algorithm does not seem able to find the extreme points of the Pareto front itself, since they are provided *a priori* by the user. Regarding the number of fitness function evaluations needed for CMEA to obtain good results, in [6], the authors mention that they perform 500,000 evaluations for the three-objective knapsack problem.

3 Cultured Differential Evolution

The cultured differential evolution is a cultural algorithm [7] based on differential evolution [8], designed to solve nonlinear constrained optimization problems. In previous experiments [9], this algorithm exhibited a very good performance, obtaining competitive results when compared to other state-of-the-art evolutionary optimization techniques, but requiring only a fraction of their fitness function evaluations. This is because of the use of domain knowledge, extracted during the evolutionary process, to efficiently guide the search. Next, we will briefly describe this approach.

Cultural algorithms are made of two main components: The *population space* consists of a set of possible solutions to the problem, and can be modeled using any population based technique. The *belief space* is the information repository in which the individuals can store their experiences for the other individuals to learn them indirectly; it may be composed by several *knowledge sources*. Our proposed approach uses differential evolution in the population space [8]. A pseudo-code of our approach is shown in Algorithm 1.

In the initial steps of the algorithm, a population of $popsize$ individuals, $\mathbf{x}^j, j = 1, \ldots, popsize$, is created; each individual contains the n parameters of the problem, $\mathbf{x}^j = (x_1^j, \ldots, x_n^j)$. An initial belief space is also created. For the offspring generation, the variation operator of differential evolution is modified by the

Algorithm 1. Pseudo-code of the cultured differential evolution

Generate initial population of size *popsize*
Initialize the belief space
repeat
  for each individual j in the population **do**
    Randomly select a knowledge source k_s from the belief space
    Generate a random integer $i_{rand} \in (1, n)$
    for each parameter i **do**
      $$x_i^{j'} = \begin{cases} influence(k_s) & \text{if } rand(0,1) < CR \text{ or } i = i_{rand} \\ x_i^j & \text{otherwise} \end{cases}$$
    end for
    Replace $\mathbf{x}^j$ with the child $\mathbf{x}^{j'}$, if $\mathbf{x}^{j'}$ is better
  end for
  Update the belief space
until the termination condition is achieved

$influence()$ function of a knowledge source, but the parameters CR and F of the standard differential evolution are also required. To determine if a child is better than its parent, and, therefore, if it can replace it, we use the following rules: 1. A feasible individual is better than an infeasible one. 2. If both are feasible, the individual with the best objective function value is better. 3. Otherwise, the individual with less amount of constraint violation is considered better. The amount of constraint violation is measured using the expression: $viol(\mathbf{x}) = \sum_{c=1}^{C} \frac{g_c(\mathbf{x})}{g_{maxc}}$ where $g_c(\mathbf{x})$ with $c = 1, \ldots, C$ are the constraints of the problem, and g_{maxc} is the largest violation found for the constraint $g_c(\mathbf{x})$ so far.

In our approach, the belief space is divided into 4 knowledge sources:

Situational Knowledge: consists of the best exemplar found along the evolutionary process. Its infuence function modifies the direction of the variation operator to follow the leader.

Normative Knowledge: contains the intervals for the decision variables where good solutions have been found, to move new solutions towards them, through the use of its influence function.

Topographical Knowledge: It consists of a set of cells, and the best individual found on each cell. The topographical knowledge has an ordered list of the best cells, based on the fitness value of the best individual on each of them. Its influence function moves newly generated individuals towards the best cells.

History Knowledge: was originally proposed for dynamic objective functions [10]. It records in a list, the location of the best individual found before each environmental change. In our approach, instead of detecting changes of the environment, we use it to escape from local optima.

At the beginning, all the knowledge sources have the same probability to be applied, but during the evolutionary process, the probability of applying each knowledge source is updated according to its success rate.

4 Hybridizing the ε-Constraint Method with CDE

There are two main possibilities of how we can vary the ε values: one is to have an approximation of the dimensions of the Pareto front, and then divide it into a number of intervals depending of the number of solutions that we want as outcome. The other, proposed by Laumanns et al. [11] is to execute an initial optimization without constraints, and then use the result of this first step to set the values for ε. If the Pareto front is discrete, this approach is particularly suitable, because it can find the entire Pareto optimal set, as proved in [11].

As our proposed approach is designed to deal with real-valued problems, it is most likely to have a continuous Pareto front, so we chose the first approach (from the two previously mentioned) to obtain ε. The ε_j must vary from the best to the worst value for the objective j, *i.e.* the search must move from the ideal to the nadir objective vector. The estimation of the ideal objective vector involves individual optimizations of one objective at a time. On the other hand, the estimation of the nadir objective vector is a more difficult task [4]. Currently, there are no efficient and reliable methods to estimate the nadir point, for an arbitrary problem. Only for the two-objective case, there exists a simple method that can provide a good estimation, which is called the *payoff table*. Due to this limitation, the proposed approach is currently working only for two-objective problems. However, there are very hard two-objective problems in the literature, which are very difficult to solve efficiently by any of the current multi-objective evolutionary algorithms (MOEAs). Some details about the estimation of the dimensions of the Pareto front, in the proposed approach, are shown in the first steps of Algorithm 2.

The single-objective optimizer, in which our method is based, is the cultured differential evolution previously described. Let's now assume that it is available as the procedure $cde(f_l, \varepsilon, g)$, which performs the optimization process of the ε-constraint method during g generations and returns the best point found. If the procedure is called without any ε values ($cde(f_l, g)$), the optimization is performed removing the constraints of the form $f_j(\mathbf{x}) \leq \varepsilon_j$. The pseudo-code of the ε-constraint with CDE (ε-CCDE) is shown in Algorithm 2.

In Algorithm 2, the lower and upper bounds, lb and ub, are increased by a tolerance t; this is done since the results of the *cde* procedure are only approximations, and it is possible to find a better point outside of them. We use $t = 0.05(ub - lb)$. The ε values are updated with a δ, which is dependent of the number of points in the Pareto front desired by the user or the decision maker, p. It is obtained as follows: $\delta = \frac{ub-lb}{p}$ This way, we aim that the final points are equally spaced in their projection over the f_2 axis. g is an input parameter of the algorithm, but it is very important, because together with p and the population size of the *cde* procedure, *popsize*, define the total number of fitness function evaluations required for the approach. The number of fitness function evaluations is approximately $p \cdot g \cdot popsize$.

Algorithm 2 shows f_1 as the objective to be optimized, and f_2 as the constraint. However, one can interchange the roles of the objectives if the problem looks harder to solve in the original setting. In the experiments shown in this

Algorithm 2. ε-Constraint with CDE.

$P = \emptyset$
$ub = f_2(cde(f_1, 2g))$
$lb = f_2(cde(f_2, 2g))$
$ub = ub + t$, $lb = lb - t$
$\varepsilon = lb$
while $\varepsilon \leq ub$ **do**
  $\mathbf{x} = cde(f_1, \varepsilon, g)$
  if $\mathbf{x}$ is nondominated with respect to P **then**
    $P = P - \{\mathbf{y} \in P \mid \mathbf{x} \succ \mathbf{y}\}$
    $P = P \cup \{\mathbf{x}\}$
  end if
  $\varepsilon = \varepsilon + \delta$
end while

paper, the original setting was always preserved, and f_1 was always taken as the objective to optimize, to allow a fair comparison. In order to improve the performance of each optimization process, the algorithm shares a percentage of the population, in the initial population of the next process. This helps because the problems to be solved are very similar, and the only change is the upper bound of the objective functions that are treated as constraints. When all the population is shared, the loss of diversity leads to premature convergence. In practice, we found that a small percentage (around 10%) of the population to be shared is enough to improve convergence without losing diversity.

5 Comparison of Results

In order to validate the performance of the proposed approach, some test functions have been taken from the specialized literature. One may think that the several single-objective optimizations required may give rise to a prohibitively high computational cost, which is unnecessary considering that a modern MOEA may produce a similar approximation of the Pareto front at a much more affordable computational cost. There are problems, however, where this is not the case, and in which a modern MOEA cannot converge to the true Pareto front even if we do not restrict the number of evaluations performed. It is precisely in those cases for which we believe that our approach can be a viable alternative.

In order to validate our hypothesis we looked specifically for hard multiobjective problems within the existing benchmarks. Our search led us to the use of DTLZ8 and DTLZ9 (from [12]), with 20 decision variables, as suggested by their designers. The main difficulty of these two problems lies on the satisfaction of their constraints. We also looked at a more recent benchmark proposed by Huband et al. [2], where we found harder problems (WFG1, WFG2, WFG3 and WFG9). Each of them has 24 variables. WFG1 is strongly biased toward small values of the first 4 variables, WFG2 and WFG3 are non-separable, but WFG2 has also a disconnected Pareto front, and WFG9 is a deceptive problem.

We decided to compare results with respect to the NSGA-II [13], since this is an approach representative of the state-of-the-art in the area.

5.1 Experimental Setup

We ran both algorithms during 50,000 fitness function evaluations each (except for two problems). We aimed to obtain a set of 50 points as a result of each run, so we adapted the parameters according to that. For the ε-CCDE, the parameters adopted were: $p = 50$, $g = 48$, with 10% of the population shared between optimizations (this 10% is chosen at random). For the *cde* procedure we used $popsize = 20$, $F = 0.7$, $CR = 0.5$. The population size of NSGA-II was set to 52, and the number of generations to 962. The rest of the parameteres were set as recommended by its authors: probability of crossover = 0.9, probability of mutation = 0.0333, the value of the distribution index for crossover = 15, and the value of the distribution index for mutation = 20.

Only for WFG1, the total number of fitness function evaluations was increased to 250,000, because this is a really difficult problem. The parameters adopted in this case were: $g = 120$ and $popsize = 40$. The number of generations of the NSGA-II was changed in this case to 4808. Even with this large number of iterations, the NSGA-II was not able to reach the true Pareto front. On the other hand, for WFG2, the total number of fitness function evaluations was decreased to 25,000, because this problem is less difficult than the others. The NSGA-II ran in this case for 481 generations, and our approach adopted $popsize = 10$.

In Figure 2, we show the results of a single run for each test problem. Since a visual comparison of the results may be inaccurate, we also used some performance measures to allow a quantitative comparison of results.

5.2 Performance Measures

To assess the performance of the proposed approach, we adopted the two set coverage (CS) metric [14], which is an indicator of how much a set covers (or dominates) another one. A value of $CS(X,Y) = 1$ means that all points in X dominate or are equal to Y. If $CS(X,Y) = 0$, there are no points in X that dominate some point in Y. We executed our ε-CCDE 30 times per problem, and then executed the NSGA-II 30 times with the same random seeds, and we performed 30 one-to-one comparisons. The results are summarized in Table 1.

In all the problems in Table 1, the ε-CCDE obtained better average values. However, the improvement is not always the same. In WFG1, all the points of ε-CCDE always dominate the points produced by the NSGA-II, because the latter cannot properly converge. On the other hand, in DTLZ8 and 9, both algorithms could make most of their points to converge to the true Pareto front. But, as it can be seen from the application of the next performance measure, the ε-CCDE was able to generate points nearer to the ends of the true Pareto front.

Our second performance measure was the binary coverage (Q_c) [15], which is an indicator of the ability of an algorithm to obtain solutions near the extrema of the Pareto front, measuring the largest possible angle between two vectors of the

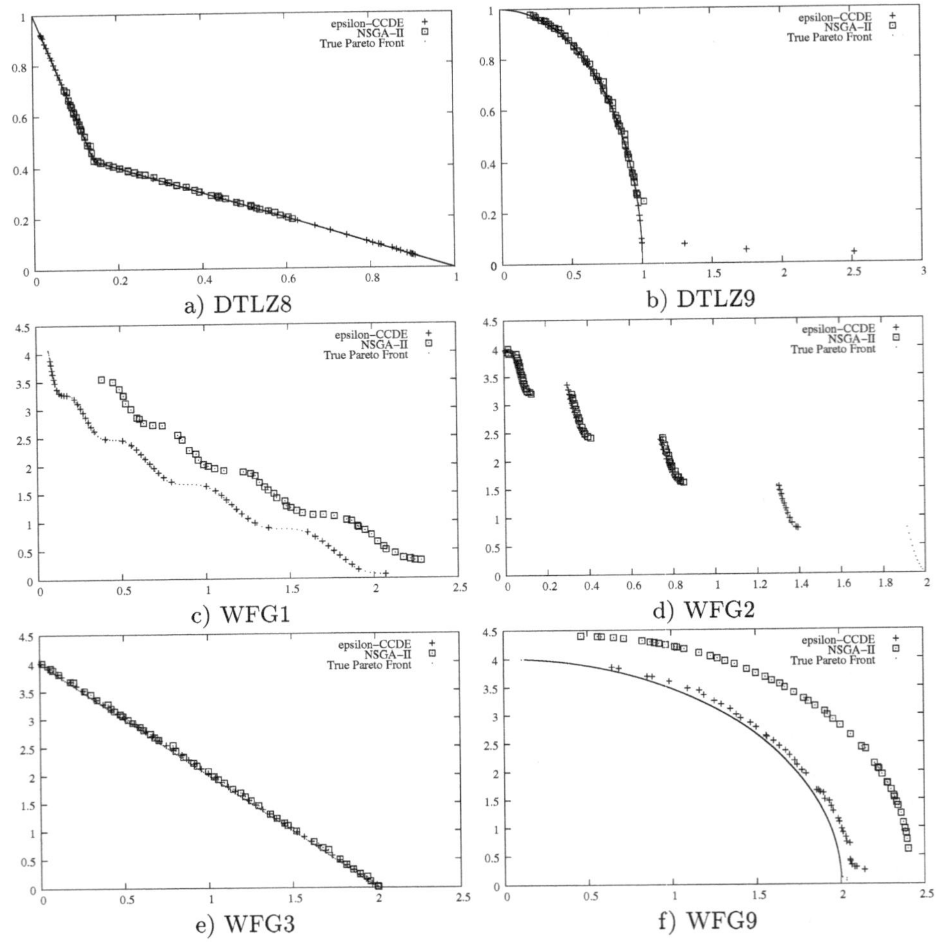

Fig. 2. Results produced by our ε-CCDE and the NSGA-II on the six test problems adopted

Table 1. Mean and standard deviation of the CS measure (a larger value is better for the first algorithm)

Test Problem	CS(ε-CCDE, NSGA-II) mean (std. dev.)	CS(NSGA-II, ε-CCDE) mean (std. dev.)
DTLZ8	0.1415 (0.0521)	0.0185 (0.0184)
DTLZ9	0.1849 (0.0715)	0.1334 (0.0805)
WFG1	1.0000 (0.0000)	0.0000 (0.0000)
WFG2	0.8509 (0.1771)	0.0362 (0.0614)
WFG3	0.3987 (0.2691)	0.0908 (0.1368)
WFG9	0.6415 (0.3669)	0.0995 (0.2114)

output of an algorithm. This is a second criterion when proper convergence has been achieved. A value of $Q_c(X,Y) > 0$ means that X obtained points nearer to the extrema of the Pareto front (it covers a larger angle). In Table 2, we show the results (note that $Q_c(Y,X) = -Q_c(X,Y)$).

Table 2. Mean and standard deviation of the binary coverage measure (a larger value is better for the first algorithm)

Test Problem	$Q_c(\varepsilon\text{-CCDE}, \text{NSGA-II})$ mean (std. dev.)
DTLZ8	0.2496 (0.0536)
DTLZ9	0.1204 (0.1180)
WFG1	0.2112 (0.0634)
WFG2	0.0677 (0.2172)
WFG3	-0.0299 (0.0253)
WFG9	-0.0913 (0.1154)

This time, our approach obtained the largest values for DTLZ8, DTLZ9 and WFG1. For WFG3 and WFG9, this metric indicates that the NSGA-II can cover a larger portion of the Pareto front. However, it is important to keep in mind that this is a secondary criterion, which becomes relevant only when convergence has been achieved. In this case, and based on the two set coverage measure, our ε-CCDE achieved a better convergence than the NSGA-II.

6 Conclusions and Future Work

In this paper, we explored the use of the ε-constraint method hybridized with an efficient evolutionary single-objective optimizer, when solving hard multiobjective optimization problems. Our results show that the proposed approach can solve problems that a highly competitive MOEA (the NSGA-II) cannot. Also, there are some problems where the NSGA-II can converge properly, but it cannot reach the ends of the true Pareto front, while our proposed approach obtained a better spread of solutions in such cases. This approach may be recommended when other algorithms cannot achieve a proper convergence, or when it is known that the problem is deceptive or is strongly biased.

As part of our future work, we aim to extend our approach for $m > 2$ objectives. This task requires that we implement a mechanism to estimate the ideal and nadir objective vectors for more than 2 objectives.

Acknowledgments. The first author acknowledges support from CONACyT through a scholarship to pursue graduate studies at CINVESTAV-IPN. The second author acknowledges support from CONACyT through project number 45683-Y.

References

1. Coello Coello, C.A., Van Veldhuizen, D.A., Lamont, G.B.: Evolutionary Algorithms for Solving Multi-Objective Problems. Kluwer Academic Publishers, New York (2002) ISBN 0-3064-6762-3.
2. Huband, S., Barone, L., While, L., Hingston, P.: A Scalable Multi-objective Test Problem Toolkit. In Coello Coello, C.A., et al., eds.: Evolutionary Multi-Criterion Optimization. Third International Conference, EMO 2005, Guanajuato, México, Springer. LNCS Vol. 3410 (2005) 280–295
3. Haimes, Y.Y., Lasdon, L.S., Wismer, D.A.: On a Bicriterion Formulation of the Problems of Integrated System Identification and System Optimization. IEEE Transactions on Systems, Man, and Cybernetics **1**(3) (1971) 296–297
4. Miettinen, K.M.: Nonlinear Multiobjective Optimization. Kluwer Academic Publishers, Boston, Massachusetts (1999)
5. Ranjithan, S.R., Chetan, S.K., Dakshima, H.K.: Constraint Method-Based Evolutionary Algorithm (CMEA) for Multiobjective Optimization. In Zitzler, E., et al., eds.: First International Conference on Evolutionary Multi-Criterion Optimization. Springer-Verlag. LNCS No. 1993 (2001) 299–313
6. Kumar, S.V., Ranjithan, S.R.: Evaluation of the Constraint Method-Based Evolutionary Algorithm (CMEA) for a Tree-Objective Optimization Problem. In Langdon, W., et al., eds.: Genetic and Evolutionary Computation Conference (GECCO'2002), San Francisco, California, Morgan Kaufmann Publishers (2002) 431–438
7. Reynolds, R.G.: An Introduction to Cultural Algorithms. In Sebald, A.V., Fogel, L.J., eds.: Third Annual Conference on Evolutionary Programming. World Scientific, River Edge, New Jersey (1994) 131–139
8. Price, K.V.: An introduction to differential evolution. In Corne, D., et al., eds.: New Ideas in Optimization. McGraw-Hill, London, UK (1999) 79–108
9. Landa Becerra, R., Coello Coello, C.A.: Optimization with Constraints using a Cultured Differential Evolution Approach. In Beyer, H.G., et al., eds.: Genetic and Evolutionary Computation Conference (GECCO'2005). Volume 1., Washington, D.C., U.S.A., ACM Press (2005) 27–34
10. Saleem, S.M.: Knowledge-Based Solution to Dynamic Optimization Problems using Cultural Algorithms. PhD thesis, Wayne State University, Detroit, Michigan (2001)
11. Laumanns, M., Thiele, L., Zitzler, E.: An efficient, adaptive parameter variation scheme for metaheuristics based on the epsilon-constraint method. European Journal of Operational Research **169** (2006) 932–942
12. Deb, K., Thiele, L., Laumanns, M., Zitzler, E.: Scalable Test Problems for Evolutionary Multiobjective Optimization. In Abraham, A., et al., eds.: Evolutionary Multiobjective Optimization. Theoretical Advances and Applications. Springer, USA (2005) 105–145
13. Deb, K., Pratap, A., Agarwal, S., Meyarivan, T.: A Fast and Elitist Multiobjective Genetic Algorithm: NSGA–II. IEEE Transactions on Evolutionary Computation **6**(2) (2002) 182–197
14. Zitzler, E., Deb, K., Thiele, L.: Comparison of Multiobjective Evolutionary Algorithms: Empirical Results. Evolutionary Computation **8**(2) (2000) 173–195
15. Farhang-Mehr, A., Azarm, S.: Minimal Sets of Quality Metrics. In Fonseca, C.M., et al., eds.: Evolutionary Multi-Criterion Optimization. Second International Conference, EMO 2003, Faro, Portugal, Springer. LNCS. Volume 2632 (2003) 405–417

A Fast and Effective Method for Pruning of Non-dominated Solutions in Many-Objective Problems

Saku Kukkonen[1] and Kalyanmoy Deb[2]

[1] Department of Information Technology
Lappeenranta University of Technology
P.O. Box 20, FIN-53851 Lappeenranta, Finland
saku.kukkonen@lut.fi
[2] Kanpur Genetic Algorithms Laboratory (KanGAL)
Indian Institute of Technology Kanpur
Kanpur, PIN 208 016, India
deb@iitk.ac.in

Abstract. Diversity maintenance of solutions is an essential part in multi-objective optimization. Existing techniques are suboptimal either in the sense of obtained distribution or execution time. This paper proposes an effective and relatively fast method for pruning a set of non-dominated solutions. The proposed method is based on a crowding estimation technique using nearest neighbors of solutions in Euclidean sense, and a technique for finding these nearest neighbors quickly. The method is experimentally evaluated, and results indicate a good trade-off between the obtained distribution and execution time. Distribution is good also in many-objective problems, when number of objectives is more than two.

1 Introduction

Pruning a set of non-dominated solutions is a common and essential part of multi-objective evolutionary algorithms (MOEAs) such as the strength Pareto evolutionary algorithm (SPEA2) [1] and the elitist non-dominated sorting genetic algorithm (NSGA-II) [2]. An idea is to prune a non-dominated set to have a desired number of solutions in such a way that the remaining solutions have as good diversity as possible, meaning that the spread of extreme solutions is as high as possible, and the relative distance between solutions is as equal as possible. The best way to obtain a good distribution would be using some clustering algorithm. However, this is computationally expensive, since clustering algorithms usually take time $O(MN^2)$ to prune a set of size N with M objectives [3]. The complexity makes clustering techniques inapplicable to large population sizes, especially as pruning is usually done after each generation. The pruning technique of SPEA2 is based on finding the kth nearest neighbor of solutions, and has complexity of clustering because of a naive implementation.

In NSGA-II, the pruning of non-dominated solutions takes time $O(MN \log N)$ based on the *crowding distance*. The pruning method of NSGA-II provides good

T.P. Runarsson et al. (Eds.): PPSN IX, LNCS 4193, pp. 553–562, 2006.

diversity in the case of two objectives, but when the number of objectives is more than two, the obtained diversity declines drastically [4]. The reason for the bad performance is the fact that the crowding distance fails to approximate the crowding of the solutions when the number of the objectives is more than two [5].

Pruning of non-dominated solutions can be seen as a multi-objective optimization problem in itself: the method should provide as good diversity as possible and be as fast as possible. It has been considered that these objectives are conflicting. However, this paper proposes a new algorithm with two different crowding estimation techniques for pruning non-dominated solutions in such a way that the obtained diversity is good also in the case of more than two objectives, and the consumed time is considerably less than in clustering.

2 Proposed Pruning Method

The basic idea of the proposed pruning method is to eliminate the most crowded members of a non-dominated set one by one, and update the crowding information of the remaining members after each removal. This idea is trivial but it contains two problems: how to efficiently determine the crowding of members and how to efficiently update the crowding information of remaining members after removal. Straightforward approaches for these computations are in time complexity class $O(MN^2)$, which makes them inapplicable to large population sizes. Therefore two approaches for crowding estimation based on the nearest neighbors of solution candidates are introduced, and then a technique for finding these nearest neighbors *quickly* is introduced.

2.1 Crowding Estimation Based on Nearest Neighbors

2-NN. Probably the simplest crowding estimation technique is to measure the distance between a solution and its nearest neighbor solution, and use this distance to estimate crowding. The solution having the smallest distance is considered as the most crowded. When the Euclidean (L_2) distance metric is used for distance calculations, there will always be two solutions having the same smallest distance to the nearest neighbor due to the symmetry property of the metric. Instead of selecting randomly one of the two solutions, the solutions can be ordered according to the distance to the second nearest neighbor. The solution having smaller distance to second nearest neighbor is more crowded. If the distance to the nearest and second nearest neighbors is marked with $L_2^{\mathrm{NN}_1}$ and $L_2^{\mathrm{NN}_2}$, respectively, then a distance vector $d_{2-\mathrm{NN}} = [L_2^{\mathrm{NN}_1}, L_2^{\mathrm{NN}_2}]$ is attached to each solution. In the case of real-coded variables and continuous objective functions, this provides a crowding measure, which usually establishes unambiguous ordering of solutions having the same smallest distance to the nearest neighbor.

***M*-NN.** A bit more developed idea is to use the k nearest neighbors for crowding estimation in such a way that distances to the k nearest neighbors are *multiplied* together, and the solution having the smallest product is considered the most crowded. The product of distances, which is here called the *vicinity distance*, is a simple measure, but it already manages to contain information about vicinity and location. The idea is extended in such a way that the number of nearest neighbors for crowding estimation calculations is kept the same as the number of objectives, i.e., $k = M$. More formally vicinity distance is defined $d_{M-\mathrm{NN}} = \prod_{i=1}^{M} L_2^{\mathrm{NN}_i}$, where $L_2^{\mathrm{NN}_i}$ is distance to the ith nearest neighbor according to L_2 distance metric.

2.2 Efficient k Nearest Neighbor Search

Finding the k nearest neighbors (k-NN) is a widely used operation in vector quantization (VQ), and many efficient algorithms have been proposed during the last three decades. The exact k-NN search technique used here is known as the *equal-average nearest neighbor search (ENNS) algorithm* [6, 7], and it uses the following theorem for the Euclidean (L_2) distance measure to reduce the amount of distance calculations:

$$\left| \frac{1}{M}\sum_{i=1}^{M} x_i - \frac{1}{M}\sum_{i=1}^{M} y_i \right| \le \frac{L_2(\boldsymbol{x},\boldsymbol{y})}{\sqrt{M}} \Leftrightarrow \left(\sum_{i=1}^{M} x_i - \sum_{i=1}^{M} y_i \right)^2 \le M L_2(\boldsymbol{x},\boldsymbol{y})^2 \ . \quad (1)$$

Thus, if the sums of elements of given vectors $\boldsymbol{x}$ and $\boldsymbol{y}$ are known, an upper bound for the Euclidean distance between them can be calculated. It is more convenient to use the squared Euclidean distance, since the actual distance values are not needed for finding neighbors, and calculating the square root is an expensive operation computationally. The geometrical interpretation of (1) is that vectors $\boldsymbol{x}$ and $\boldsymbol{y}$ are projected to a central axis of a hypercube (a projection vector starting from origin and going through point $(1, 1, \ldots, 1)$) and then the difference of projection values is at most equal to the Euclidean distance between vectors divided by the square root of the number of elements in the vectors. It has been proved that (1) holds also for any other projection vector $\boldsymbol{p}$ than the central axis of a hypercube, and (1) transforms into form [8]:

$$(p_x - p_y)^2 \le L_2(\boldsymbol{x},\boldsymbol{y})^2 \ , \quad \text{where} \quad p_x = \frac{\boldsymbol{p}\cdot\boldsymbol{x}}{|\boldsymbol{p}|} \quad \text{and} \quad p_y = \frac{\boldsymbol{p}\cdot\boldsymbol{y}}{|\boldsymbol{p}|} \ . \quad (2)$$

It is useful to select the projection axis to represent the direction in which the vectors have the largest variance, and such axis can be obtained using, e.g., principal component analysis (PCA) [8]. However, data analysis is not necessarily needed in the case of a set of non-dominated solutions, since there already exists information on how the vectors/solutions are distributed. When all the objectives are to be minimized (or maximized), there exists such kind of monotonicity between objective values that when values of $M-1$ objectives increase, then the objective value of the remaining objective decreases. Thus, there is a negative correlation between objective values, and the projection axis can be chosen to go through points $(0, 0, \ldots, 0, 1)$ and $(1, 1, \ldots, 1, 0)$ if the objective values have been normalized to the value range [0, 1]. The projection axis chosen in this way in the case of two and three objectives has been illustrated in Fig. 1 for sets of non-dominated solution points. Projections of the points are also illustrated.

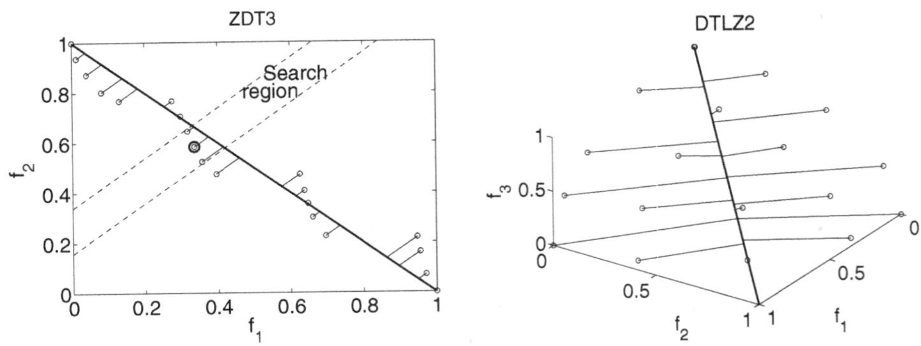

Fig. 1. Selected projection axis in the case of two and three objectives when k-NN search based on (2) is used

The ENNS technique can be used to find the nearest neighbors for solutions in such a way that first the projected values of the vectors are calculated, and these values are sorted. Then, for each solution vector, the distance to the solution having the nearest projected value is set as the best minimum distance found so far. The distances to other neighbor solutions according to the projected value are also calculated, and the minimum distance value is updated accordingly, as long as there exist neighbors for which (2) holds. This technique can be extended easily for finding the k nearest neighbors using k-th smallest distance instead of the minimum distance to reject distant solutions with (2) [8].

Besides ENNS, a technique called partial distortion search (PDS) algorithm [9] is used to speed up the execution further. It interrupts the distance calculation if a partial sum of elements exceeds a known minimum distance value. This technique adds one extra comparison but decreases the number of mathematical calculations speeding up the execution.

2.3 The Proposed Algorithm

The proposed pruning algorithm is based on the crowding estimation and k-NN search techniques presented above, and minimization of all objectives is assumed. For efficient maintenance of crowding information of remaining solutions after removal of the most crowded solution, a priority queue such as a heap [10, pp. 140–152] is used. The proposed algorithm is:

PRUNING OF NON-DOMINATED SET
input: a non-dominated set $\mathcal{F}$ (objectives are minimized),
  the size n of a desired pruned set
output: elements of a heap $\mathcal{H}$

1 find minimum ($f_i^{\min}$) and maximum ($f_i^{\max}$) values of each objective i of the members of $\mathcal{F}$ and normalize members according to the formula $f_i = (f_i - f_i^{\min})/(f_i^{\max} - f_i^{\min})$
2 for each member of $\mathcal{F}$, change Mth objective f_M to value $1 - f_M$ and calculate a sum of objective values, m
3 for each member of $\mathcal{F}$, find nearest neighbors (cf. Sect. 2.2) and calculate distance measure d (cf. Sect. 2.1) for crowding estimation
4 for members of $\mathcal{F}$ having a minimum or maximum objective value, assign $d = \infty$
5 create an ascending heap $\mathcal{H}$ from the members of $\mathcal{F}$
6 while $|\mathcal{H}| > n$
7   remove an element (root node) with a minimum d value from $\mathcal{H}$ and update $\mathcal{H}$
8   for the neighbors of the removed element
9   calculate a new d value
10   replace old d value in $\mathcal{H}$ with the new one and update $\mathcal{H}$

The first operation of the algorithm in line 1 is the normalization of objective values of the obtained non-dominated set. Different objectives might have very different value ranges, and using unnormalized values would distort the obtained distribution. The time complexity of the normalization is $O(MN)$. The normalization can lead to an infinite value if minimum and maximum values for some objective are same. Then this objective can be discarded from calculations. The second line of the algorithm re-maps the M-th objective value f_M to value $1 - f_M$ so that the original form (1) of ENNS can be used directly. The complexity of the operations in line 2 is $O(MN)$. Finding the M nearest neighbors (in the case of M-NN crowding measure) for all the members of given set in line 3 is known as the *all-M-nearest-neighbor problem*, and it can be done in time $O(MN \log N)$ [11]. Line 4 takes time $O(M)$ and makes sure that members having extreme objective values are removed last. Creating a heap in line 5 takes time $O(N \log N)$. The while-loop in lines 6–10 is executed at most N times (on average $N/2$ times). Removing a minimum element from the heap and updating the heap to have correct structure in line 7 takes time $O(\log N)$. If the M-NN crowding measure is used, each member of a non-dominated set has on average M neighbors, whose crowding values are affected if the member is removed (these neighbors can be found easily if neighborhood information is also stored when the nearest neighbors have been searched in line 3). Therefore, the for-loop in lines 8–10 is executed M times on average. The calculation of a new crowding value in line 9 means finding the M nearest neighbors. This can be done in time $O(M \log N)$ for a static set of vectors. Now, the set of vectors is changing (reducing) and the actual time complexity depends on how the vectors are distributed. Finally, replacing the crowding value to the heap, and updating the heap to have the correct structure in line 10 takes time $O(\log N)$.

This analysis leads to a complexity class estimate $O(M^2 N \log N)$ for the whole pruning algorithm. However, when the k-NN method presented earlier in this section is used in lines 3 and 9, the actual time complexity depends on how members of the non-dominated set are distributed on the selected projection axis. As the pruning method is used extensively, the most interesting thing is to know the expected complexity in practice. This, as well as the performance of the method according to the obtained diversity, is evaluated experimentally in the following.

3 Experiments

The proposed pruning method with the two introduced crowding estimation techniques was implemented in the Generalized Differential Evolution 3 (GDE3) [12], which was then used to solve test problems. Also, pruning based on the crowding distance as in NSGA-II was implemented in GDE3. GDE3 is an extension of Differential Evolution (DE) [13] for constrained multi-objective optimization. Roughly speaking, the evolutionary part of the algorithm is DE and the multi-objective part is from NSGA-II [2]. This combination has been shown to give benefit over NSGA-II with rotated problems [14]. Furthermore, GDE3 has other improvements over NSGA-II, and an interested reader is advised to see references [12, 5].

NSGA-II and SPEA2 were used for comparison[1], and the diversity of the obtained results was measured using spacing, maximum spread, and hypervolume [15, pp. 327–333]. The spacing (S) measures the standard deviation of distances from each vector to the nearest vector in the obtained non-dominated set. A smaller value for S is better, and for an ideal distribution $S = 0$. The maximum spread (D) measures the length of the diagonal of a minimal hyperbox, which encloses the obtained non-dominated set, and a larger value tells about a larger spread between extreme solutions. The hypervolume (HV) calculates the volume of the objective space between the solutions and a reference (nadir) point, and a larger value is better. The hypervolume measures both diversity and convergence, but reflects more of convergence in its value.

Due to space limitations, only a small part of results are shown. The complete set of results (including figures and more test problems) can be found in [16], where also the code for the proposed pruning method is provided.

3.1 Bi-objective Problems

Bi-objective test problems, ZDT1, ZDT3, and ZDT6 [15, pp. 356–360] were solved using population size 100 and 1000 generations. Tests were repeated 100 times and mean & standard deviation values are reported in Table 1. According to the spacing value, the proposed pruning method provides the best diversity, and the M-NN crowding estimation technique is slightly better. Differences in the maximal spread and hypervolume values are minimal compared to the differences in the spacing values. The proposed pruning method takes about two times longer to

[1] Code for NSGA-II was obtained from the web site www.iitk.ac.in/kangal and for SPEA2 from the web site www.tik.ee.ethz.ch/pisa.

Table 1. Mean and standard deviation values of spacing (S), maximum spread (D), hypervolume (HV), and CPU times for ZDT test problems measured from 100 independent runs. GDE3 is implemented with pruning methods based on the crowding distance (CD) and described crowding estimation techniques (2-NN & M-NN).

Problem	Method	S	D	HV	Total time (s)	Pruning time (s)
ZDT1	NSGA-II	$6.9175e-03 \pm 5.6118e-04$	$\mathbf{1.4146e+00} \pm 2.2506e-03$	$3.6604e+00 \pm 2.3269e-04$	$2.4076e+00 \pm 1.0456e-02$	$1.5600e-01 \pm 3.8006e-02$
	GDE3, CD	$6.4240e-03 \pm 5.5946e-04$	$1.4113e+00 \pm 1.4634e-03$	$3.6610e+00 \pm 1.2739e-03$	$1.4877e+00 \pm 1.3246e-02$	$\mathbf{1.0530e-01} \pm 3.1669e-02$
	GDE3, 2-NN	$2.8501e-03 \pm 2.8597e-04$	$1.4114e+00 \pm 1.5524e-03$	$3.6615e+00 \pm 1.7195e-03$	$\mathbf{1.3560e+00} \pm 6.5134e-03$	$2.3340e-01 \pm 3.6048e-02$
	GDE3, M-NN	$\mathbf{2.6305e-03} \pm 2.8921e-04$	$1.4115e+00 \pm 1.5376e-03$	$3.6616e+00 \pm 1.1364e-03$	$1.3570e+00 \pm 7.4536e-03$	$2.3260e-01 \pm 4.1013e-02$
	SPEA2	$3.2063e-03 \pm 2.9122e-04$	$1.4142e+00 \pm 7.2339e-05$	$\mathbf{3.6619e+00} \pm 3.6100e-05$	$1.1756e+01 \pm 7.0249e-02$	$7.6469e+00 \pm 1.9474e-01$
ZDT3	NSGA-II	$4.9342e-03 \pm 4.5888e-04$	$\mathbf{1.9676e+00} \pm 1.0790e-03$	$4.8146e+00 \pm 1.3933e-04$	$2.3584e+00 \pm 9.3980e-03$	$1.5770e-01 \pm 3.7196e-02$
	GDE3, CD	$4.3573e-03 \pm 4.1398e-04$	$1.9639e+00 \pm 1.7943e-03$	$4.8151e+00 \pm 1.0630e-04$	$1.3838e+00 \pm 5.4643e-03$	$\mathbf{8.5400e-02} \pm 2.9074e-02$
	GDE3, 2-NN	$1.7614e-03 \pm 1.9583e-04$	$1.9600e+00 \pm 3.6983e-02$	$4.8117e+00 \pm 3.6699e-02$	$1.2235e+00 \pm 5.9246e-03$	$1.6420e-01 \pm 4.5797e-02$
	GDE3, M-NN	$\mathbf{1.6415e-03} \pm 1.6563e-04$	$1.9639e+00 \pm 1.5796e-03$	$\mathbf{4.8154e+00} \pm 2.5151e-05$	$\mathbf{1.2194e+00} \pm 5.4717e-03$	$1.6510e-01 \pm 4.3797e-02$
	SPEA2	$3.0892e-03 \pm 3.4177e-04$	$1.9673e+00 \pm 1.0494e-04$	$2.8151e+00 \pm 6.1957e-05$	$1.1500e+01 \pm 7.2117e-02$	$7.3613e+00 \pm 2.2574e-01$
ZDT6	NSGA-II	$8.3199e-03 \pm 6.6005e-04$	$1.0463e+00 \pm 1.2942e-04$	$2.9204e+00 \pm 2.8917e-04$	$1.3882e+00 \pm 8.2118e-03$	$1.4790e-01 \pm 3.3584e-02$
	GDE3, CD	$6.6047e-03 \pm 6.5536e-04$	$1.1648e+00 \pm 2.5260e-02$	$3.0209e+00 \pm 1.3448e-01$	$\mathbf{1.2147e+00} \pm 5.7753e-03$	$\mathbf{9.6869e-02} \pm 3.4866e-02$
	GDE3, 2-NN	$2.7362e-03 \pm 3.0119e-04$	$1.1656e+00 \pm 2.0350e-02$	$3.0265e+00 \pm 1.0448e-01$	$1.2347e+00 \pm 5.7656e-03$	$2.3490e-01 \pm 3.5971e-02$
	GDE3, M-NN	$\mathbf{2.6386e-03} \pm 2.8531e-04$	$1.1632e+00 \pm 3.1709e-02$	$3.0114e+00 \pm 1.8180e-01$	$1.2309e+00 \pm 6.2109e-03$	$2.3240e-01 \pm 3.6985e-02$
	SPEA2	$3.1010e-03 \pm 3.0937e-04$	$\mathbf{1.1685e+00} \pm 3.6318e-05$	$\mathbf{3.0412e+00} \pm 1.5286e-04$	$1.1662e+01 \pm 5.7654e-02$	$7.5451e+00 \pm 2.0404e-01$

execute than the pruning method based on the crowding distance. However, the time needed for pruning is less than 20% from total CPU time needed[2].

3.2 Tri-objective Problems

The proposed pruning method was also tested on a set of tri-objective test problems, DTLZ1, DTLZ4, and DTLZ7 [4], using population size 300 and 1000 generations. Results after one run are shown in [16], and numerical results for the problems from 100 repetition runs are shown in Table 2. The improvement over the pruning method based on the crowding distance is clearly visible in [16], and, visually, the proposed pruning method provides similar results compared to SPEA2. Also the spacing metric in Table 2 indicates the same, this time the 2-NN crowding estimation technique being slightly better in most cases compared to M-NN. As in the case of bi-objective problems, the maximal spread and hypervolume values have only small differences. The proposed pruning method is now at worst about eight times slower than the pruning method based on the crowding distance. The pruning time is intelligibly less for the 2-NN than for the M-NN crowding estimation technique, and it is also less for DTLZ7, which does not have continuous Pareto-front.

[2] The total CPU time for the proposed pruning method is smaller compared to GDE3 with the crowding distance because of overall speedups in the program code. GDE3 uses a naive $O(MN^2)$ non-dominated sorting implementation instead of faster $O(N \log^{M-1} N)$ implementation [3].

Table 2. Mean and standard deviation values of spacing (S), maximum spread (D), hypervolume (HV), and CPU times for DTLZ test problems measured from 100 independent runs. GDE3 is implemented with pruning methods based on the crowding distance (CD) and described crowding estimation techniques (2-NN & M-NN).

Problem	Method	S	D	HV	Total time (s)	Pruning time (s)
DTLZ1	NSGA-II	$2.7301e-02 \pm 3.6882e-03$	$8.0296e-01 \pm 4.8071e-02$	$9.6937e-01 \pm 2.0890e-03$	$\mathbf{9.3375e+00} \pm 6.6284e-02$	$6.3347e-01 \pm 1.2919e-01$
	GDE3, CD	$2.3927e-02 \pm 1.1410e-03$	$9.0238e-01 \pm 1.7048e-01$	$9.6748e-01 \pm 3.4917e-02$	$1.3648e+01 \pm 1.1168e-01$	$\mathbf{6.2460e-01} \pm 6.3444e-02$
	GDE3, 2-NN	$1.0591e-02 \pm 7.4208e-04$	$8.8532e-01 \pm 1.2251e-01$	$9.7272e-01 \pm 2.3476e-02$	$1.6237e+01 \pm 1.0560e-01$	$3.5605e+00 \pm 8.7404e-02$
	GDE3, M-NN	$1.1260e-02 \pm 6.8360e-04$	$\mathbf{9.1129e-01} \pm 1.9040e-01$	$9.6780e-01 \pm 3.6437e-02$	$1.7627e+01 \pm 1.6803e-01$	$5.1749e+00 \pm 1.0265e-01$
	SPEA2	$\mathbf{8.7750e-03} \pm 2.0557e-03$	$8.6981e-01 \pm 2.1762e-02$	$\mathbf{9.7622e-01} \pm 3.9209e-05$	$1.2211e+02 \pm 1.2821e-01$	$7.6808e+01 \pm 1.7632e-01$
DTLZ4	NSGA-II	$3.1285e-02 \pm 1.5006e-03$	$1.7385e+00 \pm 1.0485e-02$	$7.3842e+00 \pm 1.5108e-02$	$1.5752e+01 \pm 8.6729e-02$	$7.7610e-01 \pm 6.4790e-02$
	GDE3, CD	$2.8450e-02 \pm 1.2669e-03$	$1.7321e+00 \pm 1.0347e-06$	$7.4252e+00 \pm 2.9245e-03$	$\mathbf{1.3813e+01} \pm 5.8934e-02$	$\mathbf{6.4060e-01} \pm 6.9614e-02$
	GDE3, 2-NN	$1.4207e-02 \pm 1.6561e-03$	$1.7289e+00 \pm 3.1785e-02$	$7.4330e+00 \pm 1.0168e-01$	$1.6918e+01 \pm 4.9857e+00$	$4.1224e+00 \pm 4.9245e+00$
	GDE3, M-NN	$1.5221e-02 \pm 1.1413e-03$	$1.7321e+00 \pm 1.6773e-07$	$\mathbf{7.4437e+00} \pm 2.2990e-04$	$1.8109e+01 \pm 1.1213e-01$	$5.1986e+00 \pm 1.7774e-01$
	SPEA2	$\mathbf{1.2543e-02} \pm 2.4636e-03$	$\mathbf{1.7465e+00} \pm 7.0831e-02$	$7.3918e+00 \pm 1.9807e-01$	$1.3105e+02 \pm 1.0151e+00$	$8.7409e+01 \pm 1.2951e+00$
DTLZ7	NSGA-II	$2.3073e-02 \pm 1.6451e-03$	$3.5925e+00 \pm 4.8045e-02$	$1.3493e+01 \pm 2.4877e-02$	$1.4823e+01 \pm 1.4667e-01$	$7.7070e-01 \pm 1.0215e-01$
	GDE3, CD	$2.3658e-02 \pm 2.6283e-03$	$\mathbf{3.6179e+00} \pm 7.8436e-03$	$1.3545e+01 \pm 1.9480e-02$	$\mathbf{1.2066e+01} \pm 2.2497e-02$	$\mathbf{5.5920e-01} \pm 6.4834e-02$
	GDE3, 2-NN	$\mathbf{9.1687e-03} \pm 1.1766e-03$	$3.6153e+00 \pm 3.0744e-03$	$1.3586e+01 \pm 5.3207e-03$	$1.2809e+01 \pm 2.9450e-01$	$2.2352e+00 \pm 1.0391e-01$
	GDE3, M-NN	$9.7859e-03 \pm 8.8586e-04$	$3.6155e+00 \pm 2.6746e-03$	$\mathbf{1.3588e+01} \pm 3.7791e-03$	$1.3540e+01 \pm 3.3633e-02$	$3.0734e+00 \pm 6.1664e-02$
	SPEA2	$1.5140e-02 \pm 8.2394e-04$	$3.6067e+00 \pm 7.1954e-03$	$1.3577e+01 \pm 1.1132e-02$	$1.3342e+02 \pm 6.7649e-02$	$8.8697e+01 \pm 1.0649e-01$

3.3 Measured Pruning Time Complexity

The time complexity of the proposed pruning method was verified experimentally in the case of two and three objectives using ZDT1 and DTLZ1. The measured pruning times for various population sizes are shown in Fig. 2.

In the bi-objective case (ZDT1), the proposed pruning method takes about twice the time of the pruning method based on the crowding distance, and complexity classes of the methods are same. Intelligibly, there is no notable difference between the observed pruning times with the 2-NN and M-NN crowding estimation techniques.

In the tri-objective case (DTLZ1), the execution time of the proposed pruning method with the M-NN crowding estimation technique is at worst ten times more than the time with the pruning method based on the crowding distance, and the pruning time with the 2-NN crowding estimation technique is less than with the M-NN crowding estimation technique. It seems that the proposed pruning method scales well with the population size.

The difference between the measured pruning times in bi- and tri-objective cases is larger than the estimated complexity class $O(M^2 N \log N)$ predicts. The reason for this is probably the fact that the search of the nearest neighbors in the case of two objectives is relatively easy because of the monotonic relation between solutions in the objective space. On the other hand, the difference between the 2-NN and M-NN crowding estimation techniques in the tri-objective case is relatively small, although the difference should be in proportion to M^2.

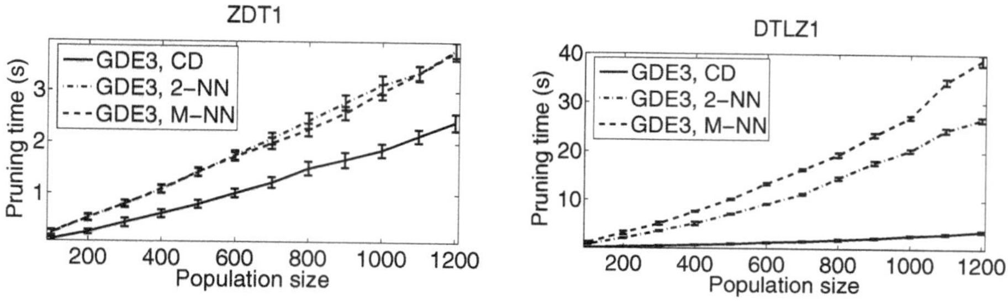

Fig. 2. Average and standard error of pruning times measured from 100 runs of solving ZDT1 and DTLZ1 by GDE3 with pruning methods based on the crowding distance (CD) and described crowding estimation techniques (2-NN & M-NN)

A probable reason for this is that there are constant calculations, which decrease the proportional difference of measured times.

Estimation of the actual complexity class would require more problems with different Pareto-fronts and a larger number of objectives. However, the measured pruning times appear logarithmic and considerably smaller than that of the pruning method in SPEA2 [5].

4 Conclusions

A pruning method with two different crowding estimation techniques for pruning a set of non-dominated solutions has been proposed. The method is based on crowding estimation using nearest neighbors of solutions and a fast technique for finding the nearest neighbors.

According to the experimental results, the proposed pruning method provides a better distribution than the pruning method based on the crowding distance. Especially in the case of tri-objective problems, the obtained diversity is significantly better. The obtained distribution is observed to be similar to the distribution obtained with SPEA2. The execution time needed for the proposed pruning method is more than for the pruning method based on the crowding distance but significantly less than for the pruning method in SPEA2.

Based on the results, the proposed method provides near optimal distribution, which does not need improvement. The execution time might be still reduced even thought it is currently reasonable. Evaluating the performance in the case of more than three objectives, remain as future work.

References

1. Zitzler, E., Laumanns, M., Thiele, L.: SPEA2: Improving the strength pareto evolutionary algorithm for multiobjective optimization. In: Proceedings of the Third Conference on Evolutionary and Deterministic Methods for Design, Optimization and Control with Applications to Industrial and Societal Problems (EUROGEN 2001), Athens, Greece (2002) 95–100

2. Deb, K., Pratap, A., Agarwal, S., Meyarivan, T.: A fast and elitist multiobjective genetic algorithm: NSGA-II. IEEE Transactions on Evolutionary Computation **6**(2) (2002) 182–197
3. Jensen, M.T.: Reducing the run-time complexity of multiobjective EAs: The NSGA-II and other algorithms. IEEE Transactions on Evolutionary Computation **7**(5) (2003) 503–515
4. Deb, K., Thiele, L., Laumanns, M., Zitzler, E.: Scalable Test Problems for Evolutionary Multiobjective Optimization. In: Evolutionary Multiobjective Optimization. Springer-Verlag, London (2005) 105–145
5. Kukkonen, S., Deb, K.: Improved pruning of non-dominated solutions based on crowding distance for bi-objective optimization problems. In: Proceedings of the 2006 Congress on Evolutionary Computation (CEC 2006), Vancouver, BC, Canada (2006) Accepted for publication.
6. Guan, L., Kamel, M.: Equal-average hyperplane partioning method for vector quantization of image data. Pattern Recognition Letters **13**(10) (1992) 693–699
7. Ra, S.W., Kim, J.K.: A fast mean-distance-ordered partial codebook search algorithm for image vector quantization. IEEE Transactions on Circuits and Systems-II **40**(9) (1993) 576–579
8. Baek, S., Sung, K.M.: Fast K-nearest-neighbour search algorithm for nonparametric classification. IEE Electronics Letters **36**(21) (2000) 1821–1822
9. Bei, C.D., Gray, R.M.: An improvement of the minimum distortion encoding algorithm for vector quantization. IEEE Transactions on Communications **COM-33**(10) (1985) 1132–1132
10. Cormen, T.H., Leiserson, C.E., Rivest, R.L.: Introduction to Algorithms. Prentice-Hall (1990)
11. Vaidya, P.M.: An $O(n \log n)$ algorithm for the all-nearest-neigbors problem. Discrete & Computational Geometry **4** (1989) 101–115
12. Kukkonen, S., Lampinen, J.: GDE3: The third evolution step of Generalized Differential Evolution. In: Proceedings of the 2005 Congress on Evolutionary Computation (CEC 2005), Edinburgh, Scotland (2005) 443–450
13. Price, K.V., Storn, R., Lampinen, J.: Differential Evolution: A Practical Approach to Global Optimization. Springer-Verlag, Berlin (2005)
14. Inorio, A., Li, X.: Solving rotated multi-objective optimization problems using Differential Evolution. In: Proceedings of the 17th Australian Joint Conference on Artificial Intelligence (AI 2004), Cairns, Australia (2004) 861–872
15. Deb, K.: Multi-Objective Optimization using Evolutionary Algorithms. John Wiley & Sons, Chichester, England (2001)
16. Kukkonen, S.: A fast and effective method for pruning of non-dominated solutions in many-objective problems, results (2006) [Online] Available: http://www.it.lut.fi/ip/evo/pruning , 15.6.2006.

Multi-level Ranking for Constrained Multi-objective Evolutionary Optimisation

Philip Hingston[1], Luigi Barone[2], Simon Huband[1], and Lyndon While[2]

[1] Edith Cowan University, Mt Lawley, WA, Australia
[2] The University of Western Australia, Crawley, WA, Australia

Abstract. In real-world optimisation problems, feasibility of solutions is invariably an essential requirement. A natural way to deal with feasibility is to cast it as an additional objective in a multi-objective optimisation setting. In this paper, we consider two possible ways to do this, using a multi-level scheme for ranking solutions. One strategy considers feasibility first, before considering objective values, while the other reverses this ordering. The first strategy has been explored before, while the second has not. Experiments show that the second strategy can be much more successful on some difficult problems.

1 Introduction

Evolutionary algorithms have shown to be a powerful optimisation tool, solving complex problems that are difficult to specify analytically, are highly non-linear, possibly dynamic, have multiple competing objectives, and arbitrary constraints on feasibility. Real-world problems often have these messy, difficult features. In particular, optimisation in the real-world often involves trade-offs (e.g. costs against quality), and an infeasible solution is clearly of no use in the real-world.

Especially in the case where the feasible region of the search space is not known a priori, an effective search method must be able to traverse infeasible regions. Researchers have realised that a natural way to do this with a multi-objective algorithm is to assign an "infeasibility" value to a solution, and to treat it as an additional objective. The idea is that in the early stages of the search, a "nearly feasible" region containing good quality solutions is roughly identified, and then further refinement eliminates infeasible solutions and sharpens the performance in the other objectives.

In this paper, we investigate two ways to implement this idea by using a multi-level ranking scheme for selection in a multi-objective evolutionary algorithm. One variant ranks solutions primarily on the other objectives, and uses feasibility to resolve ties between mutually non-dominating solutions. The other variant ranks solutions primarily on feasibility, and breaks ties using the other objectives. On the face of it, each approach would appear to have its benefits.

2 Constrained Multi-objective Optimisation

In its most general form, we consider a constrained multi-objective optimisation problem of the form:

T.P. Runarsson et al. (Eds.): PPSN IX, LNCS 4193, pp. 563–572, 2006.

$$\begin{gathered}\text{minimise } f_i(\mathbf{x}),\ i = 1, ..., n,\\ \text{subject to } g(\mathbf{x}) = 0,\\ \text{where each } f_i : S \to \Re,\ g : S \to \Re^+\end{gathered}$$

That is, we seek to optimise multiple real-valued objectives f_i over some search space S, subject to feasibility constraints, expressed as a requirement that a certain non-negative real-valued function g maps to zero. Informally, this infeasibility function represents "how infeasible" a solution is. In a real-world problem, it may be that neither f_i nor g can be written down explicitly; for example, they may be outcomes of a complex simulation. Other formulations of constrained optimisation can readily be transformed into this formalism.

Many approaches have been used to tackle infeasibility in such problems, including adding penalty terms into objectives, use of specially designed operators, repair methods, co-evolutionary methods, and multi-objective methods [1,2]. In this paper, we are interested in multi-objective methods that employ a ranking scheme (usually based on Pareto dominance) to perform selection.

Perhaps the simplest way to modify ranks for constrained optimisation is to consider constraint violations or the infeasibility function as additional objective(s), and to rank solutions using Pareto dominance. A recent example of this approach is IS-PAES [5].

In Deb et al. [6], the authors propose ranking using *constraint-domination*:

1. all feasible solutions are better than all infeasible ones;
2. more feasible ones are better that less feasible ones; and
3. among feasible solutions, Pareto dominance determines ranking.

A number of variations of this idea have been proposed and explored. Jiménez and Verdegay propose a similar scheme, except that feasible solutions are ranked using a niched-Pareto GA [7]. Ray et al. [8] used a scheme involving non-dominated sorting based on constraints alone, objectives alone, and both together. In Kimbrough et al. [9], the authors introduce an algorithm that uses separate populations for feasible and infeasible solutions. Taking this a step further, Venkatraman and Yen [10] separate the search into two phases — one to determine the feasible region, and a second to optimise objectives. Another variation is to use randomness in the selection process to obtain a balance between feasibility and objectives [11,12,13].

3 A Multi-level Ranking Approach

In this paper, we propose and test a generalisation of the ranking scheme first introduced in our earlier application-based paper on ore-processing circuit design [14]. In that work, we presented a real-world optimisation problem — designing an ore-processing circuit — subject to a number of feasibility conditions. The problem of feasibility was successfully handled by modifying the ranking mechanism used in the evolutionary algorithm. The feasibility conditions were combined into a single feasibility (or "error") function, which was considered as an additional objective in the multi-objective optimisation problem. Evolutionary selection was based on rank, but rank was determined as follows:

1. solutions are first ranked using Goldberg's Pareto ranking (including the additional error objective);
2. for solutions with the same rank, the most feasible one is better.

For solutions with the same rank and feasibility, the older solution is preferred. Note that the most feasible solution is always assigned a rank of 0.

A significant difference between this scheme and constraint domination is that infeasible solutions can be deemed better than feasible ones, and that less feasible ones can be deemed better than more feasible ones. Priority is placed on objective values. We call this rule the *objective-first* ranking rule.

It is natural then to consider its dual, the *feasibility-first* ranking rule:

1. solutions are first ranked using infeasibility function values;
2. solutions with the same infeasibility value are ranked against each other using Pareto ranking.

This set of rules is essentially the same as Deb's constraint domination [6].

Intuitively, feasibility-first ranking concentrates initially on approaching the feasible region, and then on refining objective values as long as feasibility is preserved. By contrast, objective-first ranking concentrates initially on objective values. Later in the search, when the trade-off relationship is roughly determined, attention is concentrated on feasibility, so long as objective value dominance is preserved. By allowing infeasible solutions to remain in the population longer, the objective-first ranking scheme allows the search more time to explore the infeasible regions of the search space — the hope being that good feasible solutions may be seeded from the good infeasible solutions in these regions.

So which is actually the better strategy? We investigate this question in this paper by testing each approach on a number of benchmark problems.

4 Experiments

In order to explore these different approaches, we implemented two rank-based multi-objective evolutionary algorithms that differ only in the order in which objectives and feasibility are considered in determining rank. We tested these algorithms on a number of synthetic test problems from the literature as well as the real-world problem described in our earlier work [14].

The multi-objective evolutionary algorithm we use is a hybrid of our ESP algorithm [15] and NSGA-II [16]. For all the test problems, the following common settings were used:

- Parent population size: 100
- Child population size: 100
- Number of generations: 500
- Recombination: uniform crossover, with probability 0.8
- Mutation probability: 0.5 for each parameter
- Mutation method: for real-valued parameters, NSGA-II's polynomial mutation, with distribution index = 50, constrained to a given range. See Huband et al. [14], for details of the mutation method for the other parameters in the real-world problem.

The objectives-first ranking scheme is the same ranking scheme as in our earlier work [14], with the addition of a diversity mechanism to ensure a fair comparison with the feasibility-first scheme:

1. solutions are first ranked using Goldberg's Pareto ranking;
2. for solutions with the same rank, the most feasible one is better;
3. for solutions with the same Pareto rank and feasibility, the one that best promotes diversity is better.

As before, for solutions that are still tied, the older solution was preferred. For diversity, we used Deb's crowding measure, as is used in NSGA-II [16].

The feasibility-first ranking scheme is:

1. solutions are first ranked using infeasibility function values;
2. solutions with the same infeasibility value are ranked against each other using Pareto ranking;
3. for solutions with the same Pareto rank and feasibility, the one that best promotes diversity is better.

Again, Deb's crowding measure is used as the diversity preservation mechanism.

4.1 Benchmark Problems

To test the differences between the feasibility-first and objectives-first ranking schemes, we chose a number of commonly used benchmark problems from the literature and conducted experiments using both schemes. For brevity and space restrictions, in this paper, we report on selected example problems only.

The first problem, TNK, is due to Tanaka et al. [17]:

$$\begin{array}{ll} \text{minimise} & f_1(\mathbf{x}) = x_1 \\ \text{minimise} & f_2(\mathbf{x}) = x_2 \\ \text{subject to} & c_1(\mathbf{x}) \equiv x_1^2 + x_2^2 - 1 - 0.1\cos(16\arctan(\frac{x_1}{x_2})) \geq 0 \\ \text{and} & c_2(\mathbf{x}) \equiv (x_1 - 0.5)^2 + (x_2 - 0.5)^2 \leq 0 \\ \text{where} & x_1,\ x_2 \in [0, \pi] \end{array}$$

Defining:

$$e_1(\mathbf{x}) = \begin{cases} -c_1(\mathbf{x}) & \text{if } c_1(\mathbf{x}) < 0 \\ 0 & \text{otherwise} \end{cases} \quad \text{and} \quad e_2(\mathbf{x}) = \begin{cases} c_2(\mathbf{x}) & \text{if } c_2(\mathbf{x}) > 0 \\ 0 & \text{otherwise} \end{cases}$$

we can combine the two constraints to give us the infeasibility function:

$$g(\mathbf{x}) = e_1(\mathbf{x}) + e_2(\mathbf{x}).$$

The second problem, OSY, is from Osyczka and Kundu [18]:

$$\begin{array}{ll} \text{minimise} & f_1(\mathbf{x}) = -(25(x_1 - 2)^2 + (x_2 - 1)^2 + (x_3 - 1)^2 + (x_4 - 4)^2 + (x_5 - 1)^2) \\ \text{minimise} & f_2(\mathbf{x}) = x_1^2 + x_2^2 + x_3^2 + x_4^2 + x_5^2 + x_6^2 \\ \text{subject to} & c_1(\mathbf{x}) \equiv x_1 + x_2 - 2 \geq 0 \\ \text{and} & c_2(\mathbf{x}) \equiv 6 - x_1 + x_2 \geq 0 \\ \text{and} & c_3(\mathbf{x}) \equiv 2 - x_2 + x_1 \geq 0 \\ \text{and} & c_4(\mathbf{x}) \equiv 2 - x_1 + 3x_2 \geq 0 \\ \text{and} & c_5(\mathbf{x}) \equiv 4 - (x_3 - 3)^2 - x_4 \geq 0 \\ \text{and} & c_6(\mathbf{x}) \equiv (x_5 - 3)^2 + x_6 - 4 \geq 0 \\ \text{where} & x_1,\ x_2,\ x_6 \in [0, 10],\ x_3,\ x_5 \in [1, 5],\ \text{and } x_4 \in [0, 6] \end{array}$$

In a similar fashion to the TNK problem above, we again combined the constraints together to obtain an infeasibility function that measures the amount by which the constraints are violated.

Noting that both of the benchmark problems above admit solutions which are simultaneously both globally Pareto optimal and feasible, we implemented another problem that does not have this property. We call this problem REV:

$$\begin{array}{ll} \text{minimise} & f_1(\mathbf{x}) = (x_1 - 5)^2 + x_2^2 \\ \text{minimise} & f_2(\mathbf{x}) = (x_1 + 5)^2 + x_2^2 \\ \text{subject to} & c_1(\mathbf{x}) \equiv x_2 \geq 10 \\ \text{where} & x_1 \text{ and } x_2 \in [-20, 20] \end{array}$$

4.2 The Comminution Circuit Design Problem

The real-world problem (RWP) we used in this investigation is the problem of designing a comminution circuit to improve the performance of ore processing plants in the mining industry. The term *comminution* describes a collection of physical processes that can be applied to a stream of ore to reduce the sizes of the particles in the stream — the purpose being to transform raw ore into a more usable or more saleable product or to prepare it for further processing. A *comminution circuit* consists of a collection of ore processing units (e.g. *crushers* that crush particles and *screens* that separate particles depending on size) connected together, similar to an electrical circuit. As billions of tons of material is crushed annually, optimisation of crushing operations offers the potential for enormous economic and environmental benefits [19]. We present an overview of problem here — complete details are available in Huband et al. [14].

This problem involves the optimisation of a comminution circuit to transform an ore stream generated from some primary crushing stage into a product stockpile suitable for further processing. To reduce the demands of this later processing, particles produced by the circuit need to be as small as possible. This can be achieved by forcing crushers to produce small-sized particles, but this reduces the capacity of the crushers, requiring a greater number of parallel machines to handle the same load of ore particles as with coarser crushers. This comes at a cost: the more parallel machines used in the comminution circuit, the greater the overall financial cost (setup, operating, and maintenance costs) of the circuit. Obviously, overall cost is to be minimised, so a compromise is needed and hence the problem is multi-objective: minimise the size of the particles in the resultant product stockpile, while minimising the total cost of the circuit.

Each of the ore processing units contained in the comminution circuit has various attributes that can be adjusted that affect the performance and cost of the unit. However, not all combinations of these design parameters produce valid comminution circuits. For example, if too many particles or too large-sized particles are re-directed to a crusher, the crusher may "overflow" or "jam", rendering the machine useless. Clearly these situations need to be avoided, and hence the problem is constraint-based. Cast in these terms, the comminution circuit design problem is the problem of finding feasible combinations of design control parameters that minimise both the size of the particles in the product stockpile and overall financial cost of the circuit.

5 Results and Discussion

For each of the four test problems, we executed our algorithm 35 times with each ranking scheme. To judge the quality of the non-dominated fronts found, from these 35 runs, we calculated the average hypervolume achieved after 500 generations for each ranking scheme. Hypervolume is a measure of the amount of objective space that is dominated by a set of solutions ([20,21]). Supplementing these, we show plots of 50% attainment surfaces after 500 generations for each ranking scheme (the attainment surface is a kind of median solution extracted from a set of fronts [22]). Lastly, as the two ranking schemes place different emphasis on feasibility versus objectives, we show how many infeasible solutions are present in each generation.

Fig. 1 plots these results for the benchmark problems defined above. In all cases, the hypervolume and plots of 50% attainment surfaces include only the feasible solutions from their respective population. Hypervolume calculations were performed relative to a reference point determined for each test problem (TNK: (1.3, 1.3), OSY: (0, 220), REV: (625, 625), and RWP: (13, 1.1)).

The first row of Fig. 1 plots the results for the TNK test problem. The average hypervolumes achieved by the objectives-first ranking scheme was almost identical to that for the feasibility-first scheme. In the plot of the 50% attainment surfaces, the two variants are again almost indistinguishable — both variants have located the Pareto optimal curve rather well. However, the third column shows that the objectives-first scheme maintains infeasible solutions in the population longer than the feasibility-first scheme. We see that there are no infeasible solutions in the population after 10 generations in the feasibility-first scheme, whereas there are still some infeasible solutions until about generation 170 in the objectives-first case. Indeed, the average number of infeasible solutions actually rises after an initial drop ("local" optimisation finds other rank 0 solutions near the existing infeasible rank 0 solutions), before gradually declining over time. This is promising in terms of delaying the convergence to the feasible region, potentially allowing more chance to explore nearby high quality, but infeasible solutions.

Results for the OSY benchmark problem (the second row of Fig. 1) show that the problem seems to be significantly more difficult than TNK. Examination of the results for this problem show the superiority of the objectives-first ranking scheme over the feasibility-first scheme. The average hypervolume of the objectives-first ranking scheme is 3% larger, and the 50% attainment surface produced by the objectives-first scheme shows a greater coverage of the Pareto optimal front than the feasibility-first scheme (the leftmost portion of the Pareto front has mostly been missed by the feasibility-first variant). The plot of the average number of infeasible solutions shows a similar pattern to the one seen for TNK, with the objectives-first scheme maintaining infeasible solutions in the population much longer than the feasibility-first scheme.

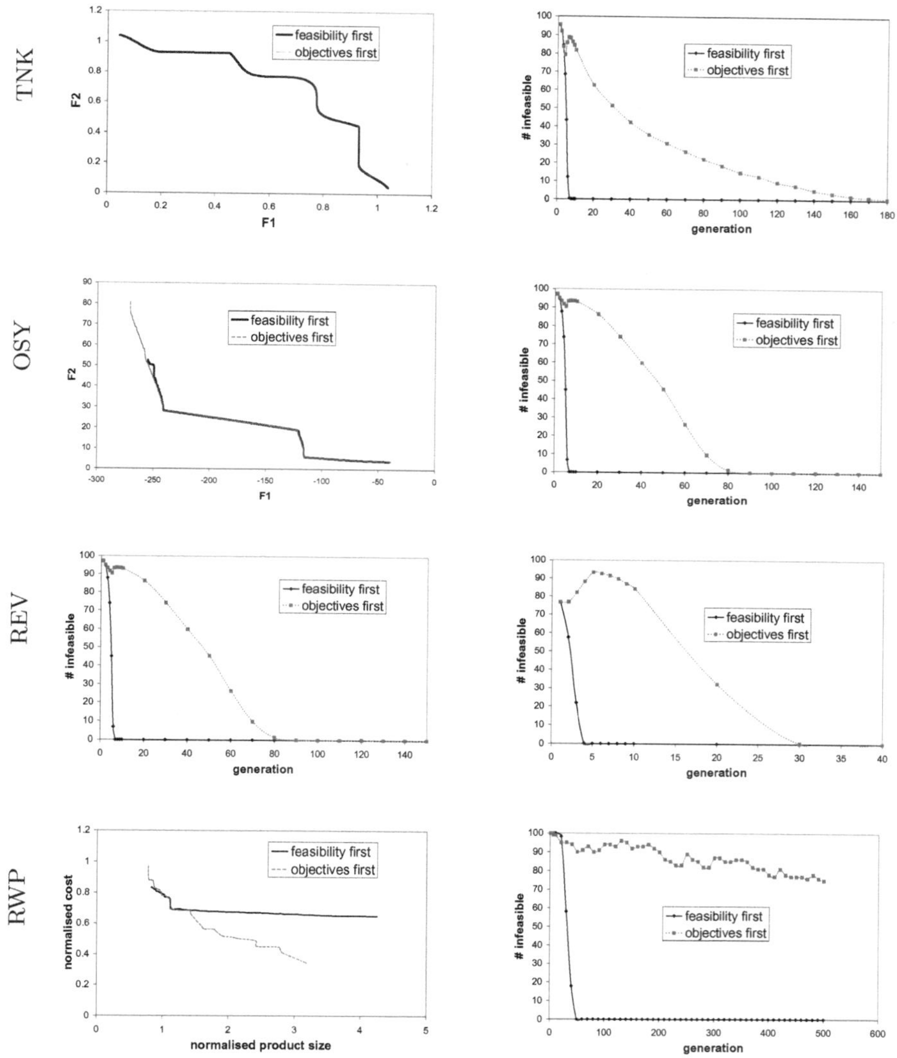

(a) 50% attainment surfaces

(b) Average number of infeasible solutions

Fig. 1. A comparison of the different ranking schemes on each test problem

Recall that the REV problem is a problem where the globally Pareto optimal front is not contained in the feasible region of the search space. As both schemes preference feasible solutions — the feasibility-first scheme directly, the objectives-first scheme preferences the more feasible solutions out of the equally Pareto ranked (including feasibility as an objective) solutions — both ranking schemes produce very similar results on this relatively simple problem. Indeed, the average hypervolume and 50% attainment surface plots are virtually indistinguishable. Note however that the number of infeasible solutions in the objectives-first scheme remains high for some time; only towards the end of the run does selection pressure drive out the infeasible solutions from the population.

The real-world problem is difficult. Each fitness evaluation is a complex simulation that tracks material as it passes through the comminution circuit, is acted upon by the various processing units, and is possibly recycled, requiring iterative mass-balancing calculations. Indeed, each run of the evolutionary algorithm can take many hours to complete. For this reason, we have limited these experiments to 15 runs of each algorithm, and 500 generations per run (a run may require several thousand generations to reach convergence). Nevertheless, the average hypervolume was 42.5% better for objectives-first, showing that the rate of convergence is superior when we use the objectives-first ranking scheme.

The 50% attainment surface comparison plot (see also Fig. 2 for plots of 50% attainment surfaces versus generations) confirms this — we see that the objectives-first variant is able to locate solutions with a normalised cost that is significantly better than that found using the feasibility-first scheme. We conjecture that the feasibility-first scheme misses a portion of the search space due to it prematurely discarding nearly-feasible solutions in regions that could have seeded good feasible solutions with time. The average number of infeasible solutions plot shows the effect of maintaining infeasible solutions in the population longer is much more pronounced than in the simpler synthetic test problems.

(a) feasibility-first (b) objectives-first

Fig. 2. The 50% attainment surfaces after 50, 100, and 500 generations for the different ranking schemes on the real-world test problem

6 Conclusions and Future Work

Through this work, we have introduced a new ranking scheme for constrained multi-objective evolutionary algorithms. Our new scheme places greater importance on objective values than existing approaches (capturing infeasibility as just another objective — one to be minimised), thus allowing infeasible solutions to remain in the search population longer, effectively allowing the evolutionary search more of an opportunity to approach good solutions from infeasible regions of the search space. In this paper, we have presented a comparison of our new technique with its more widely-used dual (feasibility-first). The initial experiments reported in this paper support the hypothesis that our new approach is indeed a successful strategy, especially on more difficult problems.

More analysis and experimentation is however needed. In order to focus as much as possible on the ranking scheme, we have tested it within the context of a single, fairly simple multi-objective evolutionary algorithm. It remains to be seen whether the benefits will be great when used in other, more sophisticated algorithms. Further experiments are needed on a larger range of test problems with different levels of difficulty in terms of both the underlying problem, and the extra complications introduced by feasibility conditions. Even further analysis is needed to better understand in what circumstances it is better to maintain infeasible solutions in the population. However, our results to this point suggest a significant improvement is possible over existing methods for some problems.

Acknowledgments. This work was supported by an Australian Research Council Linkage Grant and by Rio Tinto Ltd.

References

1. Fonseca, C.M., Fleming, P.J.: Multiobjective optimization and multiple constraint handling with evolutionary algorithms – Part I: A unified formulation. IEEE Transactions on Systems, Man and Cybernetics, Part A **28**(1) (1998) 26–37
2. Coello Coello, C.A.: Theoretical and numerical constraint handling techniques used with evolutionary algorithms: A survey of the state of the art. Computer Methods in Applied Mechanics and Engineering **191**(11-12) (2002) 1245–1287
3. Goldberg, D.E.: Genetic Algorithms in Search, Optimization & Machine Learning. Addison-Wesley (1989)
4. Fonseca, C.M., Fleming, P.J.: Genetic algorithms for multiobjective optimization: Formulation, discussion and generalization. In: Proceedings of the Fifth International Conference on Genetic Algorithms. (1993) 416–423
5. Hernández Aguirre, A., Botello Rionda, S., Coello Coello, C.A., Lizárraga Lizárraga, G., Mezura-Montes, E.: Handling constraints using multiobjective optimization concepts. International Journal for Numerical Methods in Engineering **59**(15) (2004) 1989–2017
6. Deb, K., Pratap, A., Meyarivan, T.: Constrained test problems for multi-objective evolutionary optimization. In: Proceedings of the First International Conference on Evolutionary Multi-Criterion Optimization. (2001) 284–298
7. Jiménez, F., Verdegay, J.L.: Constrained multiobjective optimization by evolutionary algorithms. In: Proceedings of the International ICSC Symposium on Engineering of Intelligent Systems (EIS'98). (1998) 266–271
8. Ray, T., Kang, T., Chye, S.K.: Multiobjective design optimization by an evolutionary algorithm. Engineering Optimization **33**(4) (2001) 399–424
9. Kimbrough, S.O., Lu, M., Wood, D.H., Wu, D.: Exploring a two-market genetic algorithm. In: Proceedings of the Genetic and Evolutionary Computation Conference (GECCO' 02). (2002) 415–421

10. Venkatraman, S., Yen, G.G.: A genetic framework for constrained optimization using genetic algorithms. IEEE Transactions on Evolutionary Computation **9**(4) (2005) 424–435
11. Runarsson, T.P., Yao, X.: Stochastic ranking for constrained evolutionary optimization. IEEE Transactions on Evolutionary Computation **4**(3) (2000) 284–294
12. Mezura-Montes, E., Coello Coello, C.A.: A simple multimembered evolution strategy to solve constrained optimization problems. IEEE Transactions on Evolutionary Computation **9**(1) (2005) 1–17
13. Runarsson, T.P., Yao, X.: Search biases in constrained evolutionary optimization. IEEE Transactions on Systems, Man and Cybernetics, Part C **35**(2) (2005) 233–243
14. Huband, S., Barone, L., Hingston, P., While, L., Tuppurainen, D., Bearman, R.: Designing comminution circuits with a multi-objective evolutionary algorithm. In: Proceedings of the 2005 Congress on Evolutionary Computation (CEC'05). (2005) 1815–1822
15. Huband, S., Hingston, P., While, L., Barone, L.: An evolution strategy with probabilistic mutation for multi-objective optimization. In: Proceedings of the 2003 Congress on Evolutionary Computation (CEC'03). (2003) 2284–2291
16. Deb, K., Pratap, A., Agarwal, S., Meyarivan, T.: A fast and elitist multiobjective genetic algorithm: NSGA-II. IEEE Transactions on Evolutionary Computation **6**(2) (2002) 182–197
17. Tanaka, M., Watanabe, H., Furukawa, Y., Tantrio, T.: GA-based decision support system for multicriteria optimization. In: Proceedings of the International Conference on Systems, Man and Cybernetics 2. (1995) 1556–1561
18. Osyczka, A., Kundu, S.: A new method to solve generalized multicriteria optimization problems using the simple genetic algorithm. Structural Optimization **10** (1995) 94–99
19. Western australian iron ore industry 2002. Department of Mineral and Petroleum Resources, Western Australia Government (2002) Available from: `http://www.mpr.wa.gov.au/`.
20. Zitzler, E.: Evolutionary Algorithms for Multiobjective Optimization: Methods and Applications. PhD thesis, Swiss Federal Institute of Technology (ETH) (1999)
21. While, L., Hingston, P., Barone, L., Huband, S.: A faster algorithm for calculating hypervolume. IEEE Transactions of Evolutionary Computation **10**(1) (2006) 29–38
22. Fonseca, C.M., Fleming, P.J.: On the performance assessment and comparison of stochastic multiobjective optimizers. In: Proceedings of the Fourth International Conference on Parallel Problem Solving from Nature (PPSN IV). (1996) 584–593

Module Identification from Heterogeneous Biological Data Using Multiobjective Evolutionary Algorithms

Michael Calonder, Stefan Bleuler, and Eckart Zitzler

Computer Engineering and Networks Laboratory (TIK), ETH Zurich, Switzerland
michael.calonder@alumni.ethz.ch, {bleuler, zitzler}@tik.ee.ethz.ch

Abstract. This paper addresses the problem of identifying gene modules on the basis of different types of biological data such as gene expression and protein-protein interaction data. Given one or several genes of interest, the aim is to find a group of genes—containing the prespecified genes—that are maximally similar with respect to all data types and sets under consideration. While existing studies follow an aggregation approach to tackle the problem of data integration in module identification, we here propose a multiobjective evolutionary method that provides several advantages: (i) no overall similarity measure needs to be defined, (ii) the interactions and conflicts between the data sets can be explored, and (iii) arbitrary data types can be integrated. The usefulness of the presented approach is demonstrated on different biological scenarios, also in comparison to standard clustering.

1 Motivation

With the advent of different high-throughput measurement technologies it is possible to investigate biological mechanisms on a systems level. While each type of measurements quantifies a different aspect of the cellular behavior such as gene expression, protein-protein interactions or metabolic fluxes, most existing computational analysis methods are designed for a single specific type of measurements. However, many important biological questions cannot be addressed by the analysis of just one type of measurements as they provide a limited view of the biological system under investigation. In such cases, a combined analysis of multiple data types is crucial to reveal the underlying mechanisms and accordingly a lot of research is currently devoted to this topic. Data integration represents a major challenge as the relation between the different data types are often complex.

In this work, we focus on a central part of the computational analysis of high-throughput data, namely *module identification*, i. e., the identification of groups of genes that share a similar biological function or regulation mechanism. Several methods exist for the identification of modules on multiple types of biological data. In [1], Hanisch et al. propose a co-clustering approach of biological networks and gene expression data in which a combined distance function is defined

T.P. Runarsson et al. (Eds.): PPSN IX, LNCS 4193, pp. 573–582, 2006.

which is used in hierarchical clustering. This approach works with arbitrary networks but was tested on a metabolic network. A different approach proposed in [2] combines distances on the Gene Ontology graph with gene expression data and applies a memetic algorithm for identifying high scoring clusters. A further data type that has been used in a joint analysis is sequence data; the method presented in [3] aggregates three types of distances, namely similarity of gene expression, operon membership, and intergenic distance, into one distance function and applies hierarchical clustering. All these approaches aggregate the similarities on the different data types into one similarity measure. This strategy has two main drawbacks: i) it is often difficult to define a suitable aggregation function as similarity relates to completely different properties in the different data types such as distance on a protein-protein interaction graph and similarity of gene expression patterns; ii) the resulting modules do not give information about the relation of the data types, e. g., it is not possible to determine whether accepting a slightly worse similarity on one data type could increase the similarity on the other data types substantially.

In this paper, we present a multiobjective optimization approach to the problem of module identification based on multiple data types. In particular we pursue the query gene concept as presented in citeOSMV2003b,IFBS2002a for single data types; here a module containing a specified gene is sought. In this respect our approach is designed for a different problem than the only multiobjective approach to module identification previously published which is targeted to partitioning and does not deal with multiple data types citeHK2004a. The advantages of the proposed approach over the aforementioned data integration methods are:

- The method does not require any aggregation function as each data type is associated with a distinct objective function.
- It allows to explore the trade-offs between different data types.
- The framework is applicable to arbitrary data types and similarity measures.

The application of this framework to combinations of three different data types, namely protein-protein interaction networks, metabolic pathways and gene expression data in Arabidopsis and yeast reveals that the amount of conflict between two data types depends heavily on both the specific data types as well as the query genes chosen. Thus, visualizing the trade-off provides additional insight compared to aggregation strategies. Furthermore the proposed multiobjective method can produce better results than multiple runs of a single objective optimizer and the classical k-means algorithm on the considered data set.

2 Optimization Framework

2.1 Model

Given a small set of user defined query genes Q and a target size $s_{\min}$ for the resulting modules, the goal is to identify the best module containing the query gene(s) with respect to the n data sets $D_1, ..., D_n$. The quality of a module for a specific data set D_i can be defined in multiple ways: a straight forward method is to calculate the mean distance to the query genes. An alternative score is given by the mean distance of the module genes to the module centroid. While the former places the query genes in the "middle" of the module the latter allows query genes to be placed on the "border" of a tight module. Note that in the case of a single data set and correspondingly a single objective function ($k = 1$) the former score provides a trivial way of identifying the optimal module by sorting the genes according to their distance to the query genes. In contrast, in the case of multiple data sets ($k > 1$) genes that are close on one data set will in general not also be close on the other data set(s). This results in a multiobjective optimization problem where the score on each data set represents one objective.

Formally, a *module* is defined as a subset of genes $G \subseteq \{1, \ldots, m\}$. Note that the binary search space $\mathcal{X} = 2^{1,\ldots,m}$ of all possible modules is exponential in m, $|\mathcal{X}| = 2^m$. The optimization task consists of solving a minimization problem over several objective functions subject to a size constraint $s_{\min}$,

$$\begin{array}{ll} \arg\min_{G \subseteq \{1,\ldots,m\}} & \mathbf{f} = \begin{pmatrix} \text{dist}(G, D_1) \\ \ldots \\ \text{dist}(G, D_n) \end{pmatrix}, \\ \text{subject to} & |G| \geq s_{\min} \in \{2, 3, \ldots, m\} \end{array}$$

where $\text{dist}(G, D_k)$ is the mean distance from all genes to the query gene(s) on data set k.

2.2 Biological Data Types and Distance Measures

In general, arbitrary types of biological data can be used as long as it is possible to define a useful measure of distance between genes based on them. In this work, we analyze three different types of biological data: gene expression (GE), protein-protein interaction (PPI) and metabolic pathway data. This section introduces these data types and describes how distances are measured on these data.

Gene Expression Data. Gene expression reflects the current activity of genes. The expression levels of all genes are measured under different conditions or at different time points resulting in a $m \times n$-matrix, E, where m is the number of considered genes and n the number of experimental conditions. In general, genes that exhibit highly similar expression patterns are thought to have a similar biological function. The most common approach for calculating similarity of expression is to define a distance function on the gene expression vectors, and a variety of distance measures has been proposed. Here we apply a distance metric based on ranking of the gene expression values which provided good results in previous studies [4,5] and in preliminary comparisons to Euclidean distance and Pearson correlation. Formally the distance measure is defined as

$$\text{dist}(G, D_k) = \frac{1}{|Q|} \frac{1}{|G|} \sum_{\substack{q \in Q \\ g \in G}} \left[\frac{1}{n} \sum_{0 \leq i \leq n} \left(r_{gi}^{(k)} - r_{qi}^{(k)} \right)^2 \right] \qquad (1)$$

where Q is the set of query genes and $r_{ij}^{(k)}$ is an element of the k-th row-wise ranked expression matrix. Ranks are scaled to be in $[0, 1]$.

Protein-Protein Interaction Data. Another widely used high-throughput measurement technology provides information about pairwise physical interaction of proteins. In general each protein can be associated to the gene that codes for it. Correspondingly, the interactions between proteins can be regarded as linking the corresponding genes. This yields a symmetrical interaction matrix $I \in \mathbb{R}^{m \times m}$ where m denotes the number of genes. In principal one could use a distance measure for pairs of rows as in (1). However from a biological point of view it is more informative to consider another distance metric similar to the one used in [1]. I can be represented by a graph: there is one node per gene and an edge if I is indicating an interaction. The straightforward measure for the distance between two genes on the graph is the number of hops that lie between them, or the maximum occurring distance if they are not connected. For the PPI data, the distance function is defined as

$$\text{dist}(G, D_k) = \frac{1}{|Q|}\frac{1}{|G|}\sum_{\substack{q \in Q \\ g \in G}} S(g, q), \tag{2}$$

$$S(g, q) = \begin{cases} \sigma_{gq} & \text{if } g \text{ and } q \text{ are connected} \\ \max\limits_{q \in Q, g \in G} \sigma_{gq} + 1 & \text{else} \end{cases},$$

where σ_{gq} is the shortest path from g to q in the interaction graph.

Metabolic Pathway Maps. A second type of biological networks consists of a map of metabolic pathways which for many organisms are well studied. By linking enzymes that are active in neighboring reactions, this reaction network can be transformed into a network of enzymes which in turn can be regarded as a network of the corresponding genes. Similar arguments as for the PPI apply here and accordingly the distance on the metabolic pathways can be defined like in the case of PPI data.

3 Implementation of the Evolutionary Algorithm

In the following we will describe the architecture and implementation of a general EA for this optimization problem. As we will see the representation and most of the operators are generic while the initialization and the mutation operator are more specific to the proposed optimization problem.

Each individual represents one module. For reasons of simplicity we use a binary representation with a bit string of length m where a bit is set to 1 if the corresponding gene is included in the module. We apply uniform crossover and a repair mechanism that adds the closest gene (in the average over all data sets) that is not yet in the module until the constraint is met.

For the initial population, it is desirable to have modules of different size. A simple strategy, for example, which sets each bit to 1 with a probability of

0.5 produces a set of modules containing different genes but all modules will have similar sizes. Instead, we choose the size of the modules deterministically such that the they are equally distributed between 2 and m genes. The genes themselves are chosen randomly.

A standard mutation operator as independent bit mutation is not well suited for this problem as only a small fraction of the bits are 1, e. g., 15 out of 22000 and thus many more genes are added to the module than removed. To prevent this we apply a fair single bit mutation where a randomly chosen bit is flipped from 1 to 0 and one randomly chosen bit is flipped from 0 to 1 thus leaving the module size unchanged.

Fitness assignment and selection in this multiobjective scenario is handled by an indicator-based selection method, namely IBEA, a recent method that compared favorably to other state-of-the-art multiobjective evolutionary algorithms [6]. We implemented this problem setting in PISA [7], an interface separating the problem specific parts of an EA from the problem independent parts. All algorithms have been implemented in C++ and are available on `www.tik.ee.ethz.ch/sop/mo_module/`.

4 Results

Several extensive experiments have been carried out in order to evaluate the performance of the proposed algorithm and the capabilities of the proposed methodology in general by applying it to different biological data. As to the first aspect, we have investigated whether a local search strategy improves the overall performance and how the multiobjective approach compares to a scalarization approach with multiple independent runs. Concerning the second aspect we studied the characteristics of the trade-off fronts resulting from different data type combinations, and in addition compared the outcomes with the ones of a classical clustering algorithm, namely k-means.

4.1 Experimental Setup

For the simulation runs we have used three different combinations of data types: two diverse time course gene expression data sets on Arabidopsis provided by the ATGenExpress consortium (containing 6 and 11 time points and 22746 genes each), the first of these gene expression data sets in combination with a manually curated metabolic pathway map [8] (986 genes) and a yeast gene expression data set [9] (3665 genes) in combination with PPI data [10].

Figure 1 (left) summarizes the parameter settings we used for this study. All simulations were run on one Intel Xeon 3.06 GHz CPU with 2 GB RAM.

4.2 Performance of the Proposed Algorithm

Local Search. We addressed the question whether the incorporation of a local search heuristic could improve the performance of the EA. The local search

Parameter	*Value*
min # genes $s_{\min}$	15
use local search	false
mutation rate p_m	0.1
mutation type	fair single bit
crossover rate p_c	0.1
tournament size	2
population size	100
# generations	100

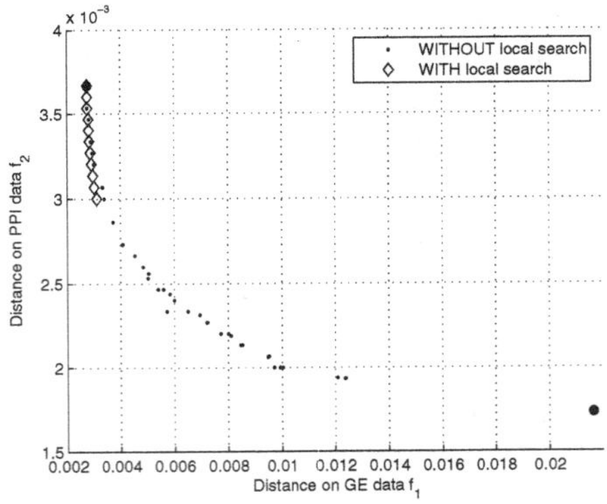

Fig. 1. (left) Default parameter settings for this study. (right) A run with the local search enabled (◊) or disabled (·), respectively. The two bold dots (•) indicate the extreme values.

proceeds in two steps: first it reduces the size of the module until the minimum number of genes constraint is reached. Then it adds those genes which are closest to the query gene(s) based on the average distance over all objectives and do not increase the mean dissimilarity value of the module at the same time. For a minimum number of genes constraint of 15, this is typically zero to three genes. The effect of the local search is clearly visible in Figure 1 (right): obviously, a preferred search direction is introduced by averaging over the different objectives. This inhibits the EA in settling individuals in the lower f_2 region. This behavior is reflected in a much faster convergence for the optimization runs with local search than without local search. Since we do not want to impose such strong preference for a specific direction, we consider such a local search inappropriate for this type of problem.

Comparison to Chebyshev Scalarization. For the purpose of validation of the multiobjective approach we set up several single-objective runs that follow the idea of a Chebyshev scalarization. To generate an approximation of the Pareto set, the single-objective optimizer was run subsequently for 21 weight combinations (5% steps) that were uniformly distributed over the range of all possible weight combinations. The results of these runs were combined into a single non-dominated front. For both the single- and multiobjective runs the number of generations was held constant, i. e., the run time of the single-objective approach was accordingly longer[1]. The input data for this evaluation was the GE/PPI pairing. The simulation was run for 5 randomly chosen query genes (one query gene per run) and 10 different random number generator seeds were used for each query gene. Figure 2 shows the result for two different query genes. On the left, the two algorithms produced comparable fronts. In contrast, the right plot shows a rare case for a query gene where both algorithms encounter

[1] The multiobjective EA took about 16 sec to complete where the single-objective EA needed about 18 times longer (289 sec).

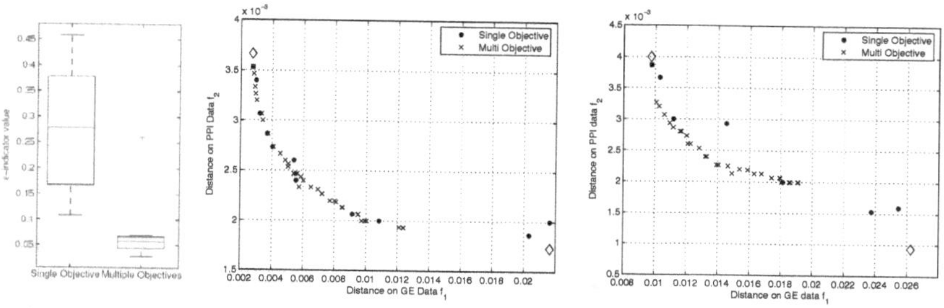

Fig. 2. (left) Scalarization vs. multiobjective optimization. Box plot of ϵ-indicator values. (middle and right) Scalarization versus multiobjective optimization. Representative fronts for two selected query genes. Results of one multiobjective run and a series of single objective runs with different weights. The two diamonds indicate theoretically possible extreme values.

problems in advancing towards low f_2 values. This problem is alleviated when the number of generations is increased. The outcomes for the other query genes are somewhere in between these extrema. We would expect the Chebyshev approach to find nearly as many non-dominated points as there are weight combinations, namely 21. This is obviously not the case and we find the multiobjective EA yielding many intermediate points of the Pareto set approximation that the single-objective algorithm did not find. In order to do a statistical assessment, we use the ε-indicator to compare the quality of the fronts, cf. [6]. Roughly speaking, this measure calculates a reference front by collecting all non-dominated solutions from both fronts and then determines the distance by which each front needs to be shifted such that no solution from this front is dominated by the reference front anymore. Based on the Kruskal-Wallis test, the ε values for the multiobjective approach are significantly lower than those of the Chebyshev approach for all query genes with a p-value of 10^{-6} or less. This provides evidence for a superiority of the multiobjective approach over the single-objective algorithm with respect to the ε-indicator, cf. Figure 2 (left). The high variance in the single-objective case results from the above mentioned difficulties to advance into the lower f_2 region which mainly appeared in the single-objective approach. The outlier in the multiple objective case corresponds to the run of Figure 2 (right).

4.3 Application to Different Biological Scenarios

Exploring the Trade-Offs. For all of the three pairings of input data (GE/GE, GE/PPI, GE/metabolic) we quantify the trade-offs and show that they widely vary for the different data by comparing them against each other. All runs in this section comply with the default configuration of Figure 2 (left) and each simulation was run for a single query gene. Five query genes were randomly chosen for this analysis and ten runs with different seeds were performed for each query gene, leading to a total of 50 runs.

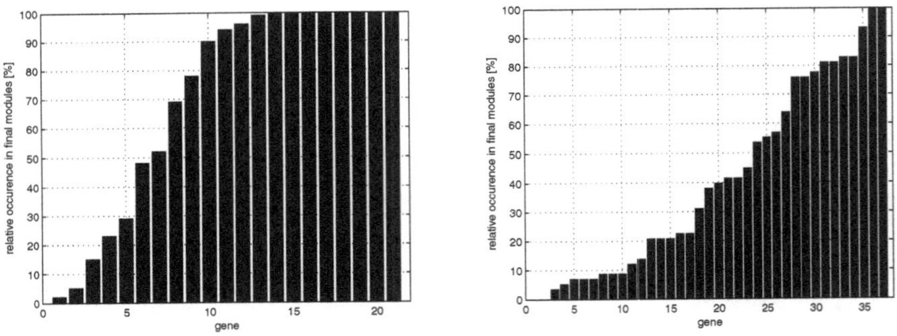

Fig. 3. Comparing the trade-off of GE/GE (left) vs. GE/PPI data (right). The plots show in how many of the non-dominated modules each gene is contained, e. g. in the left case, Gene number 10 occurs in about 90% of all modules that the algorithm found.

a) GE vs. GE data (Arabidopsis). For this pairing we found only little trade-off; the front closest to the origin in Figure 4 corresponds to this case. In none of the runs we encountered more conflict than indicated by this plot. The absence of conflict is also reflected in the diversity of the modules: Figure 3 (left) shows that more than half of all genes occur in 90% of the modules.
b) GE vs. PPI data (Yeast). In the case of a GE/PPI pairing we found a much stronger trade-off between the two objectives, compared to the preceding case. Figure 4 again depicts the resulting front (the middle one). This can be clearly verified from Figure 3 (right) that reveals a much larger diversity among the modules: less than 10% of the genes occur in 90% of the modules.
c) GE vs. metabolic data (Arabidopsis). Between these two data types we observed the largest trade-off, as shown in Figure 4 (left).

   Figure 4 (right) shows the statistical distribution of the hyper-volume indicator [11] for each of the three fronts on the left and 10 different random generator seeds [2]. Again, this clearly documents that we find the most conflict in GE/metabolic data pairs as the plot on the left would imply. These differences demonstrate clearly the advantage of the multiobjective approach compared to an aggregation based method where only one point on the front is generated.

Comparison to k-means. We substantiate the usefulness of an evolutionary approach compared to a standard clustering method by comparing the proposed algorithm to the well-known k-means algorithm.

For a test data set we selected the GE/PPI pairing and proceed in four steps: first, we ran k-means only on the GE data. Second, we selected randomly a query gene. For the cluster that contains the query gene we calculated *both* objective values, on the GE and PPI data and received the k-means "front", consisting of only one point. Third we used the same query gene as input to the EA and

[2] The objective values are scaled to $[1, 2]$ and the reference point is $(2.1, 2.1)$.

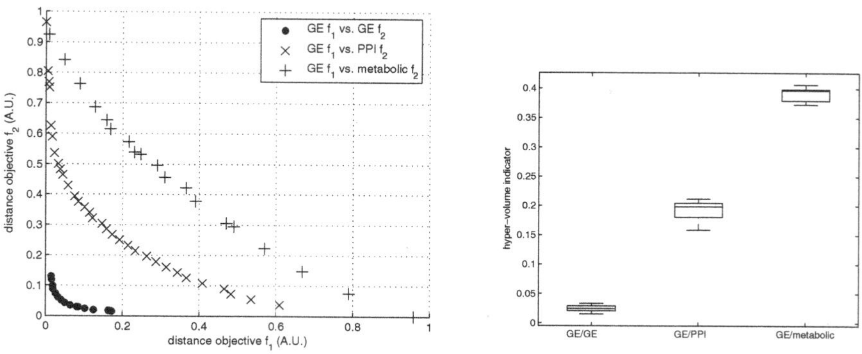

Fig. 4. (left) Comparing representative fronts of the different data type combinations for one query gene. (right) Related boxplot for the hyper-volume indicator for five query genes and ten seeds each.

set the minimum number of genes to the size of the k-means cluster. Finally we compared the front produced by the EA to the one point resulting from the k-means algorithm and repeated this procedure 50 times, varying seeds and query genes. Note that the ε value indicates whether at least one EA module dominates the k-means cluster, i. e., it is better in both objectives.

Using the two-sided Wilcoxon signed rank test we showed that the EA performs significantly better in this respect than k-means with a p-value of $1.1 \cdot 10^{-9}$. Thus, k-means is not able to produce results that compare well to the evolutionary approach, not even when comparing on the GE objective only.

5 Conclusion

Several approaches exist for co-clustering of multiple biological data types [1,2,3]. All these approaches are based on an aggregation function that combines distance measures on the different data types into one distance measure, thereby fixing the relative importance of the different data types and obscuring potential conflict between the data types. In order to overcome these shortcomings, we have presented a flexible framework for module identification that is based on multiobjective optimization which does not need any aggregation function to be defined and additionally makes potential conflicts between data types visible. The second main difference is that our approach provides a way to guide the search by specifying one or a few query genes which are contained in the resulting modules.

The effectiveness of the suggested approach was demonstrated on gene expression, protein-protein interaction and metabolic pathway data sets from Arabidopsis and yeast. Comparisons to a scalarization approach and to the k-means algorithm clearly show the advantage of the multiobjective optimization. The simulation results also revealed that the amount of conflict between two data types varies largely depending on the data sets and the specific query genes. This demonstrates that by defining a single aggregation function important information about the resulting modules may be missed.

Interesting future steps in this line of work include additional comparisons to existing algorithms such as [1] and [12] and more elaborated measures of similarity on biological graphs. Weighted edges that represent the probability or strength of an interaction can be easily included in order to adapt the method to specific biological problems.

References

1. Hanisch, D., Zien, A., Zimmer, R., Lengauer, T.: Co-clustering of biological networks and gene expression data. Bioinformatics **18**(Suppl. 1) (2002) S145–S154
2. Speer, N., Spieth, C., Zell, A.: A memetic co-clustering algorithm for gene expression profiles and biological annotation. In: CEC04, IEEE (2004) 1631–1638
3. Steinhauser, D., et al.: Hypothesis-driven approach to predict transcriptional units from gene expression data. Bioinformatics **20**(12) (2004) 1928–1939
4. Bleuler, S., Zitzler, E.: Order preserving clustering over multiple time course experiments. In: EvoWorkshops 2005. Number 3449 in LNCS, Springer (2005) 33–43
5. Prelić, A., et al.: A systematic comparison and evaluation of biclustering methods for gene expression data. Bioinformatics **22**(9) (2006) 1122–1129
6. Zitzler, E., Künzli, S.: Indicator-based selection in multiobjective search. In: PPSN VIII. LNCS, Springer (2004)
7. Bleuler, S., Laumanns, M., Thiele, L., Zitzler, E.: PISA — a platform and programming language independent interface for search algorithms. In: EMO03. LNCS, Springer (2003) 494–508
8. Wille, A., et al.: Sparse graphical gaussian modeling of the isoprenoid gene network in arabidopsis thaliana. Genome Biol **5**(11) (2004)
9. Gasch, A.P., et al.: Genomic expression programs in the response of yeast cells to environmental changes. Mol Biol Cell **11**(12) (2000) 4241–57
10. Salwinski, L., et al.: The database of interacting proteins: 2004 update. Nucleic Acids Res **32**(Database issue) (2004) D449–51
11. Zitzler, E.: Evolutionary Algorithms for Multiobjective Optimization: Methods and Applications. PhD thesis, Swiss Federal Institute of Technology (ETH) Zürich, Switzerland (1999)
12. Owen, A.B., et al.: A gene recommender algorithm to identify coexpressed genes in c. elegans. Genome Res **13**(8) (2003) 1828–1837

A Multiobjective Differential Evolution Based on Decomposition for Multiobjective Optimization with Variable Linkages

Hui Li and Qingfu Zhang

Department of Computer Science, University of Essex
Wivenhoe Park, Colchester CO4 3SQ, United Kingdom
{hlil, qzhang}@essex.ac.uk

Abstract. Although a number of multiobjective evolutionary algorithms have been proposed over the last two decades, not much effort has been made to deal with variable linkages in multiobjective optimization. Recently, we have suggested a general framework of multiobjective evolutionary algorithms based on decomposition (MOEA/D) [1]. MOEA/D decomposes a MOP into a number of scalar optimization subproblems by a conventional decomposition method. The optimal solution to each of these problems is a Pareto optimal solution to the MOP under consideration. An appropriate decomposition could make these individual Pareto solutions evenly distribute along the Pareto optimal front. MOEA/D aims at solving these scalar optimization subproblems simultaneously. In this paper, we propose, under the framework of MOEA/D, a multiobjective differential evolution based decomposition (MODE/D) for tackling variable linkages. Our experimental results show that MODE/D outperforms several other MOEAs on several test problems with variable linkages.

1 Introduction

In many real-world applications, there are several objectives to be optimized. Often, these objectives conflict with each other. There is no single solution that can optimize all objectives at the same time. Pareto optimal solutions are optimal trade-offs among the objectives. Over the past two decades, a number of multiobjective evolutionary algorithms (MOEAs) have been proposed [2][3]. MOEAs are able to find a set of representative Pareto optimal solutions in a single run.

Like their counterparts for scalar optimization, most MOEAs employ a selection operator to direct their search into promising areas in the decision space. Since Pareto domination is not a complete ordering, conventional selection operators, which were originally developed for scalar optimization, cannot be directly applied to multiobjective optimization. Furthermore, the task of most MOEAs is to produce a set of solutions which are uniformly distributed in the Pareto front. A selection operator in MOEAs should not encourage the search to converge to a single point. Therefore, it is not a trivial job to assign a relative fitness

T.P. Runarsson et al. (Eds.): PPSN IX, LNCS 4193, pp. 583–592, 2006.

value to each individual solution for reflecting its utility in selection in MOEAs. Fitness assignment has been subject to much research over the last two decades [2]. Some techniques such as fitness sharing and crowding have been frequently used within fitness assignment for maintaining the diversity of search [4][5].

Most existing MOEAs treat the MOP under consideration as a whole. They use Pareto domination for ranking solutions during their search. Their selection operators are often very complicated and time-consuming, and it is hard to balance the diversity and convergence. Note that a Pareto optimal solution for a MOP, under mild condition, could be an optimal solution of a scalar optimization problem in which the objective is an aggregation of all the f_i's. Therefore, approximation of the Pareto front of a MOP can be decomposed into a number of scalar objective optimization subproblems. In [1], we proposed a general multiobjective evolutionary algorithm based on decomposition (MOEA/D). MOEA/D explicitly decomposes a MOP into N scalar optimization subproblems. Each scalar optimization subproblem has its best solution found so far in the current population. Each subproblem is optimized in MOEA/D by using information from its neighboring subproblems. It has been proved that MOEA/D has a lower complexity than NSGA-II, the most popular MOEA, at each generation.

Although variable linkages exist in many applications, not much effort has been devoted to how to deal with variable linkages in MOEAs. As shown in [6], recombination operators play a key role in tackling variable linkages. In this paper, under the framework of MOEA/D, we design a multiobjective differential evolution based on decomposition (MODE/D) for continuous MOPs with variable linkages. MODE/D maintains a population which contains the best solution found so far to each of the subproblems. The DE operator is used for generating new trail solutions. We define a neighborhood relationship among all the subproblems such that neighboring subproblems have similar optimal solutions. Consequently we obtain a neighborhood relationship among all the individual solutions in the current population. The DE recombination operator is restricted to neighboring solutions since otherwise it may generate poor solutions for MOPs with variable linkages.

The remainder of this paper is organized as follows. Section II introduces basic definitions in MOPs. The proposed algorithm is then described in Section III. Section IV presents multiobjective test problems with variable linkages. Experimental results are given in Section V. The final section concludes the paper.

2 Multiobjective Optimization

We consider a multiobjective optimization problem of the form:

$$\begin{aligned} \text{minimize } & F(x) = (f_1(x), f_2(x), \ldots, f_m(x))^T \\ \text{s.t.} & \quad x \in X \end{aligned} \tag{1}$$

where $x = (x_1, \ldots, x_n)$ is called decision vector, $X \subset R^n$ is the decision space, $f_i : R^n \to R, i = 1, \ldots, m$ $(m \geq 2)$ are objective functions. $F(x)$ is the objective vector. The objective space Y consists of the set of all objective vectors. The optimal solutions of (1) can be defined in terms of Pareto optimality [7].

Let $a = (a_1, \ldots, a_m)^T$, $b = (b_1, \ldots, b_m)^T \in R^m$ be two vectors, a is said to *dominate* b, denoted by $a \prec b$, if $a_i \leq b_i$ for all $i = 1, \ldots, n$, and $a \neq b$. A point $x^\star \in X$ is called *(globally) Pareto optimal* if there is no $x \in X$ such that $F(x) \prec F(x^\star)$. The set of all Pareto optimal points, denoted by PS, is called the *Pareto set*. The set of all Pareto objective vectors, $PF = \{y \in R^m | y = F(x), x \in PS\}$, is called the *Pareto front* [7].

3 Algorithm

MODE/D is an MOEA/D which uses DE operator to generate new solutions. In our implementation of MODE/D in this paper, the weighted Tchebycheff approach is used to decompose the MOP (1). In this approach, the scalar optimization problem is in the form

$$g^{te}(x|\lambda, z^*) = \max_{i \in \{1,\ldots,m\}} \lambda_i \left| f_i^* - f_i(\mathbf{x}) \right| \tag{2}$$

where $\lambda = (\lambda_1, \ldots, \lambda_m)$ is the scalar weight vector,

$$\sum_{i=1}^{m} \lambda_i = 1$$

and $\lambda_i \geq 0$ for all $i = 1, \ldots, m$. $z^* = \{f_1^*, \ldots, f_m^*\}$ is the ideal point, i.e.,

$$f_i^* = \min\{f_i(x) | x \in X\}$$

for each $i = 1, 2, \ldots, m$.

Under some mild conditions, for each Pareto optimal solution x^* there exists a weight vector λ such that x^* is the optimal solution of (2), and each optimal solution of (2) is a Pareto optimal solution of (1).

MODE/D first selects N evenly distributed weight vectors $\lambda^1, \lambda^2, \ldots, \lambda^N$. Then the MOP (1) is decomposed into N optimization subproblems, where the objective in j-th subproblem is $g^{te}(x|\lambda^j, z^*)$. MODE/D aims at minimizing these subproblems in a single run. Note that g^{te} is continuous of λ, the optimal solution of $g^{te}(x|\lambda^i, z^*)$ should be close to that of $g^{te}(x|\lambda^j, z^*)$ if λ^i and λ^j are close to each other. Therefore, any information about these g^{te}'s with weight vectors close to λ^i should be helpful for optimizing $g^{te}(x|\lambda^i, z^*)$.

At each iteration, MODE/D maintains:

- a population of N points $x^1, \ldots, x^N \in X$, where x^i is the current solution to the i-th subproblem;
- a population of objective vectors $FV^1, \ldots, FV^N$, where FV^i is the F-value of x^i, i.e., $FV^i = F(x^i)$;
- a temporary reference point $z = (z_1, \ldots, z_m)^T$, where z_i is the smallest value found so far for objective f_i;

MODE/D works as follows:

Input:
- MOP (1);
- a stopping criterion;
- N : the number of the subproblems considered in MOEA/D;
- an uniform spread of N weight vectors: $\lambda^1, \ldots, \lambda^N$;
- K : the number of the weight vectors in the neighborhood of each weight vector;

Output: $x^1, \ldots, x^N$ and $FV^1, \ldots, FV^N$.

Step 1 Initialization
Step 1.1 For each $i = 1, \ldots, N$, set $B(i) = \{i_1, \ldots, i_K\}$ where $\lambda^{i_1}, \ldots, \lambda^{i_K}$ are the K closet weight vectors to λ^i.
Step 1.2 Randomly generate an initial population $x^1, \ldots, x^N$. Set $FV^i = F(x^i)$;
Step 1.3 For each $j = 1, \ldots, m$, $z_j = \min_{i \in \{1,\ldots,N\}} f_j(x^i)$.
Step 2 Reproduction Randomly choose a solution x^r and then randomly select three indexes a, b, c from $B(r)$. A new solution $y = (y_1, \ldots, y_n)^T$ is generated in the following way.
For each $i = 1, \ldots, n$

$$y_i = \begin{cases} x_i^a + R \cdot (x_i^b - x_i^c) & \text{if rand} < CR \\ x_i^r, & \text{otherwise} \end{cases} \tag{3}$$

where R and CR are two control parameters.
Step 3 Update of Reference Point z**:** For each $j = 1, \ldots, m$, if $f_j(y) < z_j$, then set $z_j = f_j(y)$.
Step 4 Update of Neighboring Solutions: For each $j \in B(r)$, if $g^{te}(y|\lambda^j, z) \leq g^{te}(x^j|\lambda^j, z)$, then set $x^j = y$ and $FV^j = F(y)$.
Step 5 Stopping Criteria If stopping criteria are satisfied, then stop and output $x^1, \ldots, x^N$ and $FV^1, \ldots, FV^N$. Otherwise go to **Step 2**.

In **step 1**, the neighborhood $B(i)$ is defined as the set of the indexes of K nearest weight vectors to λ^i. The initial population consists of N solutions randomly chosen from the decision space. The ideal point $z^* = (f_1^*, \ldots, f_m^*)$ in (2) is replaced with a reference point $z = (z_1, \ldots, z_m)$. In **step 2**, four neighboring solutions x^r, x^a, x^b, x^b undergo the DE operator for producing a new trail solution y. The reference vector z is updated by y in **step 3**. In **step 4**, the neighboring solutions of x^r are replaced by y if they are worse than y with respect to its associated g^{te}.

4 Multiobjective Test Problems with Variable Linkage

Various features of MOPs might cause difficulties for MOEAs, such as non-convexity, multi-modality, discontinuity, and non-uniformality. Deb et al [8][9] constructed a number of test problems using the following model:

$$\text{Minimize } F(x) = \{f_1(x_1), f_2(x)\} \qquad (4)$$
$$\text{s.t. } f_2(x) = g(x_2, \ldots, x_n)h(f_1(x_1), g(x_2, \ldots, x_n))$$

where $f_1 : R \to R$, $g : R^{n-1} \to R$, and $h : R^n \to R$ are three real functions. The main features of test problems of (4) can be controlled by setting f_1, g, and h with specific properties.

As Deb et al noticed [6], several widely-used test instances induced from the above models don't not have variable linkages. More precisely, the *PS*s of these test instances are linear and parallel to coordinate axes. Therefore, it is relatively easy for MOEAs to find *PS*.

Recently, some researchers have studied the multiobjective test problems with variable linkages [6] [10][11]. In this paper, two OKA test instances [10] are used.

- OKA-1

$$f_1(x) = x_1$$
$$f_2(x) = \pi - x_1 + |x_2 - 5\cos(x_1)| \qquad (5)$$

where $x_1 \in [-\pi, \pi]$ and $x_2 \in [-5, 5]$. The *PS* of OKA-1 is $\{(x_1, x_2)|x_2 = 5\cos(x_1), x_1 \in [-\pi, \pi])\}$ and the *PF* is $\{(f_1, f_2)|f_2 = \pi - f_1, f_1 \in [-\pi, \pi])\}$

- OKA-2

$$f_1(x) = \eta(x_1)$$
$$f_2(x) = \pi - \eta(x_1) + |x_2 - 5\cos(x_1)| \qquad (6)$$
$$\eta(x_1) = \begin{cases} x_1^{\frac{1}{3}} & \text{if } x_1 \geq 0 \\ -x_1^{\frac{1}{3}} & \text{if } x_1 < 0 \end{cases}$$

where $x_1 \in [-\pi^3, \pi^3]$ and $x_2 \in [-5, 5]$. The *PS* of OKA-1 is $\{(x_1, x_2)|x_2 = 5\cos(x_1), x_1 \in [-\pi, \pi])\}$ and the *PF* is $\{(f_1, f_2)|f_2 = \pi - f_1, f_1 \in [-\pi, \pi])\}$

Inspired by the construction of OKA test instances, we propose the following two variants of ZDT1 and ZDT2:

- ZDT1-L

$$f_1(x) = x_1$$
$$g(x) = 1 + \frac{1}{n-1}\sum_{i=2}^{n} |x_1 - sin(0.5x_i\pi))|$$
$$h(x) = 1 - \sqrt{f_1/g}$$

where $x \in [0, 1]^n$. The *PS* of ZDT1-L is $\{x|x_1 = sin(0.5x_i\pi), i = 2, \ldots, n\}$.

- ZDT2-L

$$f_1(x) = x_1$$
$$g(x) = 1 + \frac{1}{n-1}\sum_{i=2}^{n} |x_1 - sin(0.5x_i\pi)|$$
$$h(x) = 1 - (f_1/g)^2$$

where $x \in [0, 1]^n$. The *PS* of ZDT2-L is $\{x|x_1 = sin(0.5x_i\pi), i = 2, \ldots, n\}$.

There are nonlinear variable linkages in ZDT1-L and ZDT2-L. Obviously, the *PF*s of ZDT1-L and ZDT2-L are the same as those of ZDT1 and ZDT2 in the objective space.

In [6], Deb et al proposed using linear or nonlinear variable transformation to construct test instances with variable linkages. Their approach is more complicated than ours.

5 Experimental Results

5.1 Performance Metrics

In MOEAs, various performance metrics can be used to measure convergence and diversity [12]. In our experiments, we use set coverage ($\mathcal{C}$-metric) and generational distance ($\mathcal{D}$-metric) to assess the performance of the algorithms.

Let A and B be two approximations to the *PF* of a MOP, $C(A, B)$ is defined as the percentage of the solutions in B that are dominated by at least one solution in A, i.e.,

$$C(A,B) = \frac{|\{u \in B | \exists v \in A : v \text{ dominates } u\}|}{|B|}$$

$C(A, B)$ is not necessarily equal to $1 - C(B, A)$. $C(A, B) = 1$ means that all solutions in B are dominated by some solutions in A, while $C(A, B) = 0$ implies that no solution in B is dominated by a solution in A.

Veldhuizen proposed a distance-based metric, called generational distance, as follows.

$$\mathcal{D}_p(A, P^*) = \frac{1}{|A|}\left(\sum_{i=1}^{|A|} d_i(a_i, P^*)^p\right)^{1/p} \tag{7}$$

where P^* is the reference set of representative Pareto optimal solutions and $d_i(a_i, P^*) = \min_{r \in P^*}\left\{\sqrt{\sum_{k=1}^{m}(f_k(a_i) - f_k(r))^2}\right\}$. $\mathcal{D}_1$ represents the average distance from A to P^* when $p = 1$. $\mathcal{D}_1$ only measures the closeness between A and P^*.

We also can calculate the average Euclidean distance from P^* to A, denoted by $\mathcal{D}_2 = \mathcal{D}_1(P^*, A)$.

In our experiments, uniformly distribution points in *PF* are selected to form the reference set P^*.

5.2 Experimental Settings

We compared MODE/D with NSGA-II/SBX [11], NSGA-II/DE [13], and GDE3 [14] in our experiments.

The population size is set to be 100 for all the algorithms. In NSGA-II/SBX, The distribution index used in SBX and polynomial mutation is set to be 20, the mutation rate is set to be $1.0/n$, where n is the number of decision variables.

The DE operator is the same in NSGA-II/DE, GDE3 and MODE/D. R is set to be 0.5 and CR is 0.95. The size K of neighborhood in MODE/D is set to be 20 for all test instances.

For OKA-1 and OKA-2, all algorithms are run for 25,000 function evaluations. For ZDT1-L and ZDT2-L, n is set to be 10. We allow all the algorithms 50,000 function evaluations. All algorithms were implemented in C++. Each algorithm has been independently run for 20 times for each test instance on PC (Pentium (R) 2.4GHZ, 1.00 GB of RAM).

5.3 Results

Table 1 and 2 show the best, mean, and standard deviation of the $\mathcal{D}$-metric values between the obtained solutions and reference set P^*. In terms of the best and mean of $\mathcal{D}_1$-metric values in Table 1, MODE/D outperforms other three algorithms on OKA-1, OKA-2 and ZDT1-L. It is also evident that both GDE3 and NSGA-II/SBX can find a set of solutions with zero distance to the reference set. This is because GDE3 and NSGA-II/SBX reach the *PF*. Table 2 shows the best, mean and standard deviation of the $\mathcal{D}_2$-metric values from the reference set to the obtained solutions. In terms of this metric, MODE/D performs better than other three algorithms on all test problems. This also suggests that the diversity of the solutions found by MODE/D is better than those in other three algorithms.

Table 1. $\mathcal{D}_1$-metric values of four algorithms

D1-metric	MODE/D			GDE3			NSGA-II/DE			NSGA-II/SBX		
Test Problems	best	mean	std	best	mean	std	best	mean	std	best	mean	std
OKA-1	0.0051	0.0058	0.0004	0.0138	0.0166	0.0034	0.0195	0.0263	0.0052	0.0185	0.0581	0.0877
OKA-2	0.0090	0.0128	0.0034	0.0141	0.0175	0.0019	0.0177	0.0358	0.0202	0.0162	0.0355	0.0272
ZDT1-L	0.0028	0.0036	0.0007	0.0083	0.0099	0.0010	0.0072	0.0090	0.0009	0.0093	0.0118	0.0024
ZDT2-L	0.0033	0.0050	0.0009	0	0.0049	0.0100	0.0114	0.0161	0.0056	0	0.0669	0.1292

Table 2. $\mathcal{D}_2$-metric values of four algorithms

D2-metric	MODE/D			GDE3			NSGA-II/DE			NSGA-II/SBX		
Test Problems	best	mean	std	best	mean	std	best	mean	std	best	mean	std
OKA-1	0.0229	0.0231	0.0002	0.0283	0.0298	0.0009	0.0373	0.0421	0.0021	0.1070	0.1959	0.0976
OKA-2	0.0262	0.0295	0.0017	0.0299	0.0335	0.0022	0.0429	0.0520	0.0069	0.1019	0.1734	0.0363
ZDT1-L	0.0054	0.0195	0.0124	0.0099	0.0116	0.0009	0.0099	0.0113	0.0011	0.2769	0.7322	0.1353
ZDT2-L	0.0065	0.0178	0.0156	0.0331	0.5005	0.2241	0.0166	0.0243	0.0053	0.1034	0.3090	0.2054

Figure 1 illustrates the distributions of the nondominated solutions in the run with the lowest D-metric value. It is clear from Figure 1 that MODE/D performs better than other algorithms in terms of maintaining diversity. Intuitionally, NSGA-II/SBX is outperformed by other three DE-based MOEAs in both convergence and diversity for all test instances.

The box plot of $\mathcal{C}$-metric values between the MOEAs considered is visualized in Figure 2. As we can see, MODE/D performs slightly better than GDE3 on

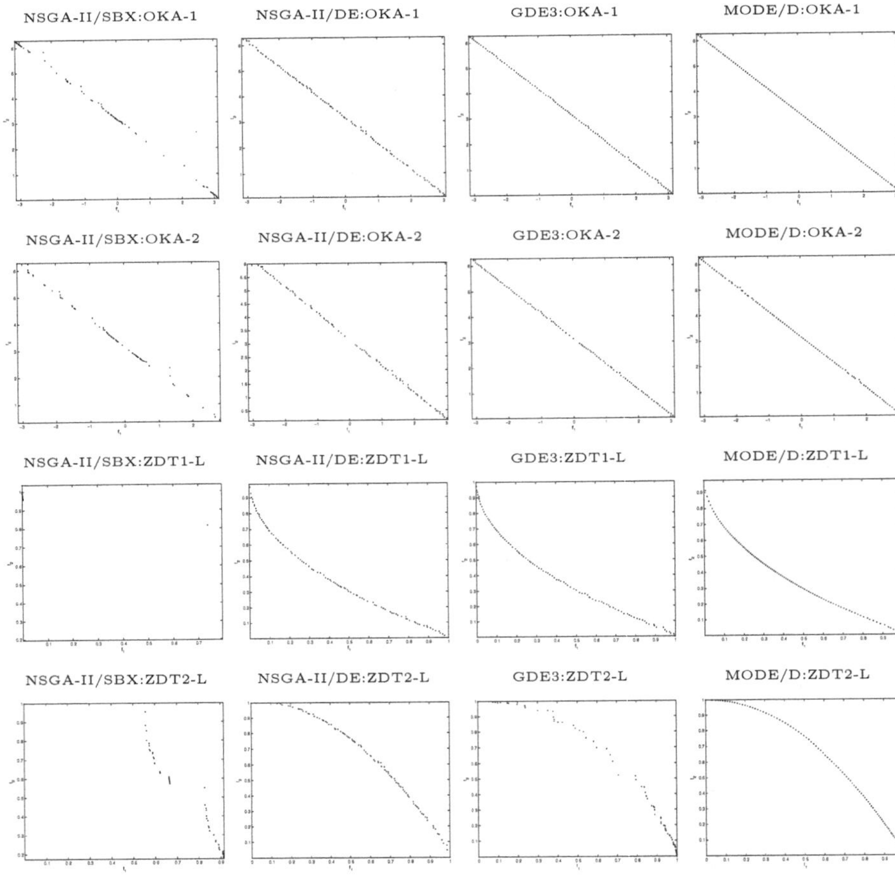

Fig. 1. Plots of the nondominated solutions in the run with the lowest D-values found by NSGA-II/SBX, NSGA-II/DE, GDE3, and MODE/D

OKA-1 and OKA-2. For ZDT1-L and ZDT2-L, MODE/D outperforms the other three MOEAs. In terms of $\mathcal{C}$-metric, NSGA-II/SBX is outperformed by the other three DE-based MOEAs. Therefore, a reproduction operator plays a key role in MOEAs for dealing with variable linkages.

6 Conclusions

In this paper, we proposed a multiobjective differential evolution approach based on decomposition (MODE/D) for MOPs with linkage. MODE/D is a MOEA/D with a DE operator. The experimental results show that, overall, MODE/D clearly outperforms NSGA-II/SBX, NSGA-II/DE, and GDE3. Our results suggest that MOEA/D is a promising method for solving MOPs. It is also clear that one needs to consider reproduction operators for tackling variable linkages

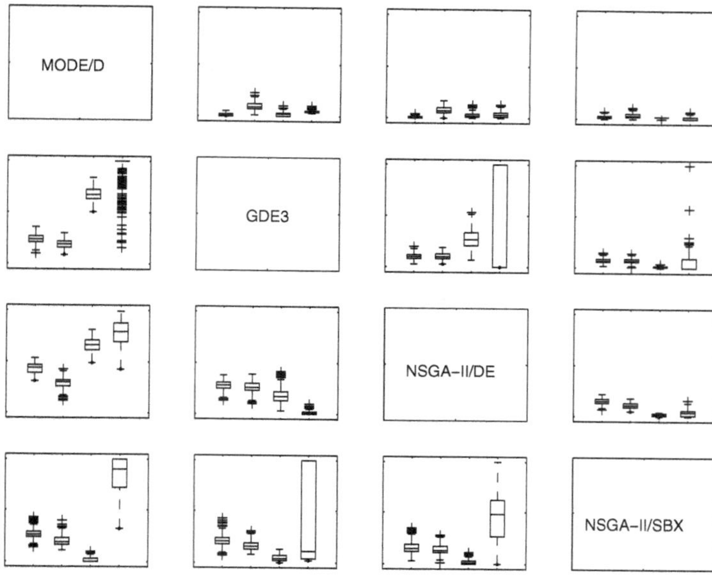

Fig. 2. The box plots of $\mathcal{C}$-metric of MODE/D, GDE3, NSGA-II/DE, and NSGA-II/SBX. Four box plots from left to right in each chart relate to OKA-1, OKA-2, ZDT1-L, and ZDT-L, respectively.

in MOPs. Future work includes study of the effect of parameters and schemes for adaptively adjusting weight vectors in MODE/D.

References

1. Zhang, Q., Li, H.: A multiobjective evolutionary algorithm based on decomposition. Technical Report CSM-450, Department of Computer Science, University of Essex (2006)
2. Deb, K., Kalyanmoy, D.: Multi-Objective Optimization Using Evolutionary Algorithms. John Wiley & Sons, Inc. (2001)
3. Coello, C.A.C.: Recent trends in evolutionary multiobjective optimization. In: Evolutionary Multiobjective Optimization: Theoretical Advances And Applications. Springer-Verlag, London (2005) 7–32
4. Bosman, P.A.N., Thierens, D.: The balance between proximity and diversity in multiobjective evolutionary algorithms. IEEE Trans. Evolutionary Computation **7**(2) (2003) 174–188
5. Knowles, J.D., Corne, D.: Properties of an adaptive archiving algorithm for storing nondominated vectors. IEEE Trans. Evolutionary Computation **7**(2) (2003) 100–116
6. Deb, K., Sinha, A., Kukkonen, S.: Multi-objective test problems, linkages, and evolutionary methodologies. Technical Report KanGAL Report No. 2006001, KanGAL, Indian Institute of Technology Kanpur (2006)

7. Miettinen, K.: Nonlinear Multiobjective Optimization. Kluwer Academic Publishers (1999)
8. Deb, K.: Multi-objective genetic algorithms: Problem difficulties and construction of test problems. Evolutionary Computation **7**(3) (1999) 205–230
9. Zitzler, E., Deb, K., Thiele, L.: Comparison of multiobjective evolutionary algorithms: Empirical results. Evolutionary Computation **8**(2) (2000) 173–195
10. Okabe, T., Jin, Y., Olhofer, M., Sendhoff, B.: On test functions for evolutionary multi-objective optimization. In: PPSN'2004. Lecture Notes in Computer Science, Springer (2004) 792–802
11. Deb, K., Agrawal, S., Pratap, A., Meyarivan, T.: A fast and elitist multiobjective genetic algorithm: NSGA-II. IEEE Trans. Evolutionary Computation **6**(2) (2002) 182–197
12. Zitzler, E., Thiele, L., Laumanns, M., Fonseca, C.M., da Fonseca, V.G.: Performance assessment of multiobjective optimizers: an analysis and review. IEEE Trans. Evolutionary Computation **7**(2) (2003) 117–132
13. Iorio, A., Li, X.: Solving rotated multi-objective optimization problems using differential evolution. In: Australian Conference on Artificial Intelligence. Lecture Notes in Computer Science, Cairns, Australia, Springer (2004) 861–872
14. Kukkonen, S., Lampinen, J.: GDE3: The third evolution step of generalized differential evolution. In: CEC'2005, Edinburgh, Scotland, IEEE Service Center (2005) 443–450

Digital Images Enhancement with Use of Evolving Neural Networks

Yuri Tsoy[1] and Vladimir Spitsyn[2]

Computer Engineering Department, Tomsk Polytechnic University, Russia
[1] qai@mail.ru
[2] spitsyn@ce.cctpu.edu.ru

Abstract. An approach to image enhancement through artificial neural network's (ANN) processing is proposed. The structure and weights of ANN are tuned with use of evolutionary concept. Each image is processed in pixel-by-pixel manner using pixels' local characteristics that are calculated approximately to increase the processing speed but preserving satisfactory calculations' error. The two-step procedure for image enhancement is proposed: (1) local level processing using ANN; (2) global level autoleveling algorithm. The results for the proposed two-step image enhancement procedure are presented and compared with that of some alternative approaches.

1 Introduction

The images enhancement problem is very challenging due to high calculations' complexity, problem of image quality evaluation and the others. The ultimate goal: creation of the universal algorithm or approach to images enhancement, – seems unreachable because of great variety of practical domains involving different demands to the image quality. The latter consideration in fact gives a chance for researchers to invent new methods of images enhancement to attack this problem.

By now many approaches to images enhancement have been proposed [1, 2]. Some of them are quite simple (e.g. contrast stretching or gamma correction [1]) while others are rather sophisticated (e.g. Multi-Scale Retinex (MSR) algorithm [3] adopting model of human vision).

In general the problem of per-pixel image processing can be presented as the following transform function (or its parameters) search problem:

$$I^* = T(I, \mathbf{\Omega}), \tag{1}$$

where I^* and I – pixel's intensity after and before the processing respectively; $\mathbf{\Omega}$ – vector of features that define specific local/global characteristics for each pixel on the image under processing.

In this paper we introduce new method for images enhancement through approximation of transform function T given its general behavior. The function is approximated with use of ANN which is trained evolutionary (neuroevolutionary approach) to process images in pixel-by-pixel manner.

T.P. Runarsson et al. (Eds.): PPSN IX, LNCS 4193, pp. 593 – 602, 2006.

The paper is organized as follows. In the Section 2 the developed evolutionary algorithm for ANN design and training is described briefly. The idea of the introduced images enhancement method is presented in the Section 3. Simplified formulae for local characteristics calculations are given in the Section 4. The 5th section contains experimental settings specifications and some results of images processing. Conclusion is given in the Section 6.

2 Brief Description of the Neuroevolutionary Algorithm

Developed neuroevolutionary (NE) algorithm NEvA [4] implements simultaneous design and training of ANNs through evolution of networks' structures along with the connections' weights. In this paper only a brief description is presented but interested reader can refer to [4].

Each ANN is genetically encoded as the list of its connections. The weight of each connection is presented with 19-bit integer mapped over the range [-26,2144; +26,2143] with the step of 0,0001. Truncation selection is used for parental subpopulation formation. Original crossover and mutation operators, which respect structures of the ANNs undergoing recombination and mutation, are used. Nodes with sigmoid activation functions: $o = (1 - \exp(-aS))^{-1}$, where S is a weighted sum of input signals, a – constant parameter, are considered.

The population size adapts to the properties of evolution during the algorithm run using simple resizing strategy. The strategy arises from the experimental observation [5] that if the average fitness is increasing (the fitness maximization task is considered) than the population size is worth decreasing and vice versa, in case of the average fitness's stabilization or decrease the population should be expanded. This resizing mechanism is also remarkable because it is in a good agreement with biological evidence that dynamics of genotypic diversity behaves in converse way with respect to evolution speed for population of simple organisms [6, 7].

3 Image Enhancement Through Neural Processing

We will use local-adaptive approach to images enhancement. The notion of the approach under consideration is that each pixel is processed independently according to the set of local and global image characteristics (e.g. local and global mean intensity). In this paper we adopt pixel-by-pixel brightness processing with use of ANN paradigm.

In contrast to well-known approaches where the entire image is mapped onto the ANN's input for processing (e.g. Fukushima's neocognitron [8], Hopfiled's nets [9] and Kohonen's maps [10]) we train ANN that processes only one pixel at a time. Thus the requirements to the operating memory size necessary to store the information about ANN are weaken and, moreover, we are free to process images of arbitrary dimensions. It's worth noting that it is still possible to joint single pixel processing ANNs into 2D arrays of ANNs so this approach is flexible enough for implementation on parallel processing structures.

We consider general transformation presented in the eq. (1) in the following way:

$$L^{*}(x,y)=T\left(L(x,y),\ D_{(x,y)},\ m_{(x,y)}\right), \tag{2}$$

where $L^{*}(x,y)$ and $L(x,y)$ – processed and initial brightness of (x,y) pixel respectively; $m_{(x,y)}$ and $D_{(x,y)}$ – respectively mean brightness and brightness deviation in local neighborhood of (x,y) pixel. Thus the ANN approximating T function should have three input nodes and one output node.

Since visual quality of image is very hard to evaluate because of subjective nature of human's perception there is always some uncertainty in information for image processing caused by observer. Besides, different images should be processed in different ways with respect to the context information. So chosen local parameters (brightness and its local statistics) tend to be misleading and noisy and these obstacles drive to the conclusion that the trained ANN should "know" how to process images in some abstract, general case. To satisfy these speculations we train ANNs to approximate the function that is slightly different from the T function (2). Specifically we train ANN to perform the following transformation:

$$L^{*}(x,y)=T\left(m_{(x,y)},\ D_{(x,y)},\ m^{G}\right), \tag{3}$$

where m^{G} is the global mean brightness calculated for the entire image. Thus we are trying to train ANN to deal with averaged parameters values instead of specific ones.

For the processing of the color image we, firstly, transform image in the grey-scale representation, then the image is processed and after that the color information is restored as follows:

$$Z_i^{*}(x,y)=\frac{L*(x,y)}{L(x,y)}Z_i(x,y), \tag{4}$$

where $Z_i^{*}(x,y)$ and $Z_i(x,y)$ – restored after processing and initial i^{th} color component of (x,y) pixel respectively. The primary motivation is to preserve the ratio of different color components in order to avoid color distortion after processing.

According to the eq. (2) ANN processes pixels with use of local statistics so it seems reasonable to apply the global level image enhancement technique for more efficient and competitive image post-processing. The well-known autoleveling algorithm, implemented in many image processing software packages, was chosen to perform the global level enhancement thanks to its efficiency and processing speed. Thus we introduce the two-step image enhancement procedure:

1. Local level processing using evolutionary trained ANN.
2. Global level processing using autoleveling algorithm.

3.1 ANN Functioning Evaluation

During the training we evaluate each ANN with respect to the visual quality of the processed images. The formalization of the image quality is approximate and inspired by the [11]. We modified the formula from [11] in the following way:

$$f = \frac{N*M - \mu}{N*M} + \frac{256 - \exp(H)}{192}, \quad (5)$$

$$H = -\sum_{i=1}^{256} l_i \log l_i, \quad (6)$$

where N and M – are width and height of the image respectively, l_i – the portion of the processed pixels with the ith brightness level. The value of f function is considered as the error of the correspondent ANN and the goal of evolutionary design and training of ANNs is to minimize value of the function f.

The first summand in (5) is necessary to maximize the number of pixels on the edges thus making the processed image more detailed. The more pixels are present on the edges separating the different brightness areas, the more contrast the processed image is. The second summand in (5) prevents processed images from degradation to binary images, where only pixels of black and white colors are present, although the intensity of the edge pixels is maximized.

From the formula (5) it can be seen that quality of the processed image considers two factors that are of rather general nature:

1. Total number of pixels on the edges μ.
2. Total number of different brightness levels.

The evaluation of the ANN functioning is calculated for the output signals sequence of the length $N*M$. The formula (5) presents rather rough evaluation of the image quality because it considers only contrast property and brightness distribution (histogram) of the processed image. Nevertheless it will be shown further that such an evaluation is competent enough for evolutionary training of ANN for images processing.

It is also possible to train ANN using several images. In this case the evaluation for each ANN is calculated as the average evaluation of each processed image. After the training procedure is finished the resulting ANN can be applied for processing of the images that were not included in the training set of images. Thus the "classic" methodology of ANN's training and use is preserved. This feature allows to save processing time due to absence of necessity to retrain the ANN for each new image.

4 Approximate Calculation of the Local Statistics

According to the introduced approach, use of trained ANN considers use of local mean and deviation (2) so the time to image processing depends dramatically on the speed of calculation of statistics for certain neighborhood. It is clear that the more the neighborhood size, the more computational power is required because more pixels are considered during calculations.

In what follows we introduce the way to obtain approximate formulae for local mean and deviation for the rectangular neighborhood on the arbitrary 2D map.

Given the brightness distribution $L=\{l_{ij} \mid i=1..M, j=1..N\}$, where l_{ij} is the brightness of the pixel located on the intersection of the ith row and the jth column, we will assume that *L* defines joint distribution for the 2D random quantity (*X*, *Y*) where *X* and *Y* posses values from the ranges [1; *N*] and [1; *M*] respectively. Thus we have

$$p_{xy}(i,j)=\frac{l_{ij}}{\sum_i\sum_j l_{ij}}, \tag{7}$$

where $p_{xy}(i,j)$ is the joint frequency distribution in the point with rectangular coordinates (*j* ; *i*). Then the distributions for random quantities *X* and *Y* are calculated as follows:

$$\begin{aligned} p_x(j) &= \sum_i p_{xy}(i,j), \\ p_y(i) &= \sum_j p_{xy}(i,j), \end{aligned} \tag{8}$$

We assume that neighborhood for each pixel has a rectangular shape and is limited by points (j_1 ; i_1) and (j_2 ; i_2) where $i_2 \geq i_1$ and $j_2 \geq j_1$. Using the notion of conditional probability and supposing that brightness distributions corresponding to the neighboring rows are correlated (i.e. the case of rather smooth brightness distribution on the image is considered) we have:

$$\sum_{i=i_1}^{i_2}\sum_{j=j_1}^{j_2} p_{xy}(i,j)=\sum_{i=i_1}^{i_2} p_y(i)\sum_{j=j_1}^{j_2} p_x(j\mid i)\approx \lambda_y \sum_{j=j_1}^{j_2} p_x(j\mid y_\lambda)\sum_{i=i_1}^{i_2} p_y(i), \tag{9}$$

$$\lambda_y=\frac{\sum_{i=i_1}^{i_2} p_y(i)}{(i_2-i_1+1)\,p_y(y_\lambda)}, \tag{10}$$

where y_λ is some row number within the range [i_1 ; i_2] and λ_y is treated as the proportionality coefficient. After some algebra we obtain:

$$\sum_{i=i_1}^{i_2}\sum_{j=j_1}^{j_2} p_{xy}(i,j)\approx \lambda_y^2 (i_2-i_1+1)\sum_{j=j_1}^{j_2} p_{xy}(y_\lambda, j). \tag{11}$$

Using the same assumptions it is easy to calculate approximately the 1st and the 2nd starting moments and then obtain approximate formulae for local mean $\tilde{m}_{(x,y)}$ and deviation $\tilde{D}_{(x,y)}$:

$$\tilde{m}_{(x,y)} = \frac{\lambda_y^2}{(j_2 - j_1 + 1)} \sum_{j=j_1}^{j_2} p_{xy}(y_\lambda, j), \tag{12}$$

$$\tilde{D}_{(x,y)} = \frac{\lambda_y^2}{j_2 - j_1 + 1} \left(\sum_{j=j_1}^{j_2} p_{xy}(y_\lambda, j) \left(\beta_y p_{xy}(y_\lambda, j) - \tilde{m}_{(x,y)} \right) \right), \tag{13}$$

$$\beta_y = \frac{\sum_{i=i_1}^{i_2} p_y^2(i)}{(i_2 - i_1 + 1) p_y^2(y_\lambda)}. \tag{14}$$

Note that coefficients λ_y and β_y in (10) and (14) respectively are presented as the division of some averaged value on the some particular value. So assuming rather small neighborhood size we can make the following substitution $\lambda_y = 1$ and $\beta_y = 1$ which leads to the further simplification of formulae (12) and (13):

$$\tilde{m}_{(x,y)} = m_{(x)}(y_\lambda) = \frac{\sum_{j=j_1}^{j_2} p_{xy}(y_\lambda, j)}{(j_2 - j_1 + 1)}, \tag{15}$$

$$\tilde{D}_{(x,y)} = D_{(x)}(y_\lambda) = \frac{\sum_{j=j_1}^{j_2} p_{xy}^2(y_\lambda, j)}{j_2 - j_1 + 1} - m_{(x)}^2(y_\lambda). \tag{16}$$

Thus it is possible to calculate approximately local mean and deviation for 2D rectangular region via analysis of an arbitrary row within the neighborhood using assumptions about correlation of distributions in consequent rows and considering rather small neighborhood size. Note that the analogical formulae can be deduced for the arbitrary column inside the local region.

In order to avoid loss of information caused by calculation of local statistics for 2D region using 1D array, which corresponds to arbitrary row or column of pixels, we will use the following formulae:

$$\tilde{m}_{(x,y)} = \frac{m_{(x)}(y_\lambda) + m_{(y)}(x_\kappa) + m^G}{3}, \tag{17}$$

$$\tilde{D}_{(x,y)} = \frac{D_{(x)}(y_\lambda) + D_{(y)}(x_\kappa)}{2}, \tag{18}$$

where $x_\kappa \in [j_1; j_2]$.

To summarize the result presented in this section we note that the computational complexity required for calculation of local statistics is simplified from $O(n^2)$ to $O(n)$. Our additional experiments showed that given the set of synthetic and real images the peak signal-to-noise ratio for approximate formulae (17) and (18) lies within the range of 20..30 dB, which is quite satisfactory taking into consideration speculations from the Section 3 that it is not obligatory to deal with exact statistics due to subjective nature of perception and wide variety of images. The speedup of calculations using the approximate formulae is up to about 20 times for the 65x65 neighborhood.

5 Experiments

5.1 Experimental Settings

Following the notion of the local-adaptive image processing we will train ANNs to approximate the transformation (2). In order to avoid possible processing bias and to reduce uncertainty, ANNs deal with transformation (3) during the training, where statistics $m_{(x,y)}$ and $D_{(x,y)}$ are calculated exactly for the smallest possible neighborhood 3x3.

To calculate number of edge pixels necessary for evaluation (5) of ANN processing we use fast variant of Sobel's edge detector described in [12]. Since the evaluation (5) is inexact there is no need to minimize it until 0 is reached. It was noted that quite satisfactory results are obtained when the objective function is within the approximate range [1,4; 1,9]. We use $f = 1{,}5$ as a stop criterion.

Evolution time for population of ANNs is limited with 25 generations. Initial population size is 50 organisms and adapts during the run of the NEvA algorithm which is briefly described in the Section 2.

Two images depicted in the figure 1 are used for training. Images' dimensions are small to increase the training speed and are equal to 128x128 pixels (fig. 1a) and 128x160 pixels (fig. 1b).

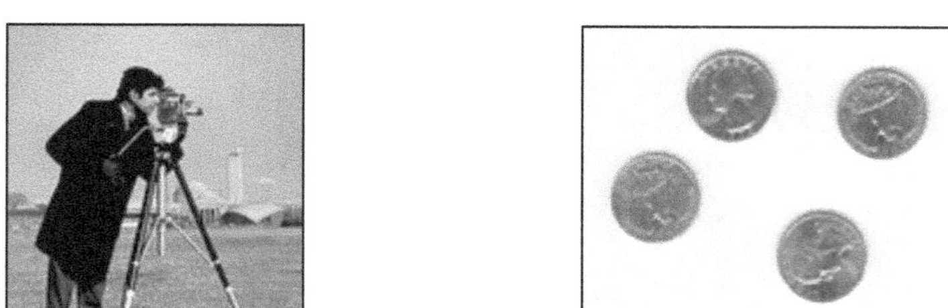

a) b)

Fig. 1. Images used for training. Black frames are added advisedly to ease the perception and not present on the original images.

After the training is finished the best network is picked up to perform processing of the test images that were not introduced during the training. Neighborhood size for the test processing is 5x5 and local statistics are calculated approximately using formulae (17) and (18).

5.2 Results

The training process took about 80 seconds on Pentium IV – 3 GHz CPU. Resulting example network is presented on the fig. 2.

Some examples of image processing using ANN on the fig. 2 are shown on the fig. 3-4. Processing of each image took approximately 1 sec. Note that another trained ANN, which is different from the network on the fig. 2, is likely to give another results of images' enhancement and, possibly, different processing time.

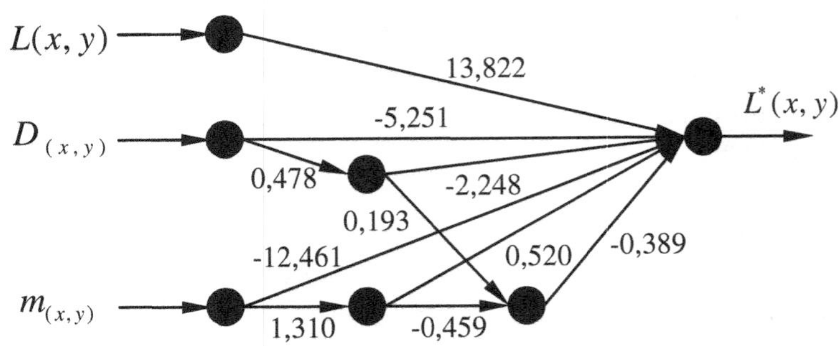

Fig. 2. Sample resulting network obtained in result of evolutionary training using images shown on the fig. 1

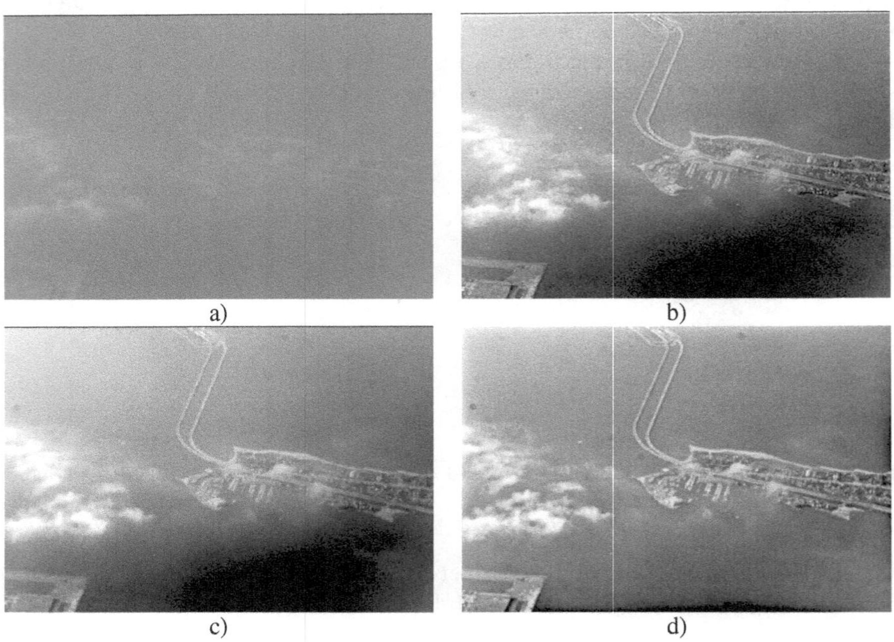

Fig. 3. Comparison of the two-step ANN+autoleveling processing (b) with standalone autoleveling (c) and MSR processing (d). Original image (a) is taken from [3].

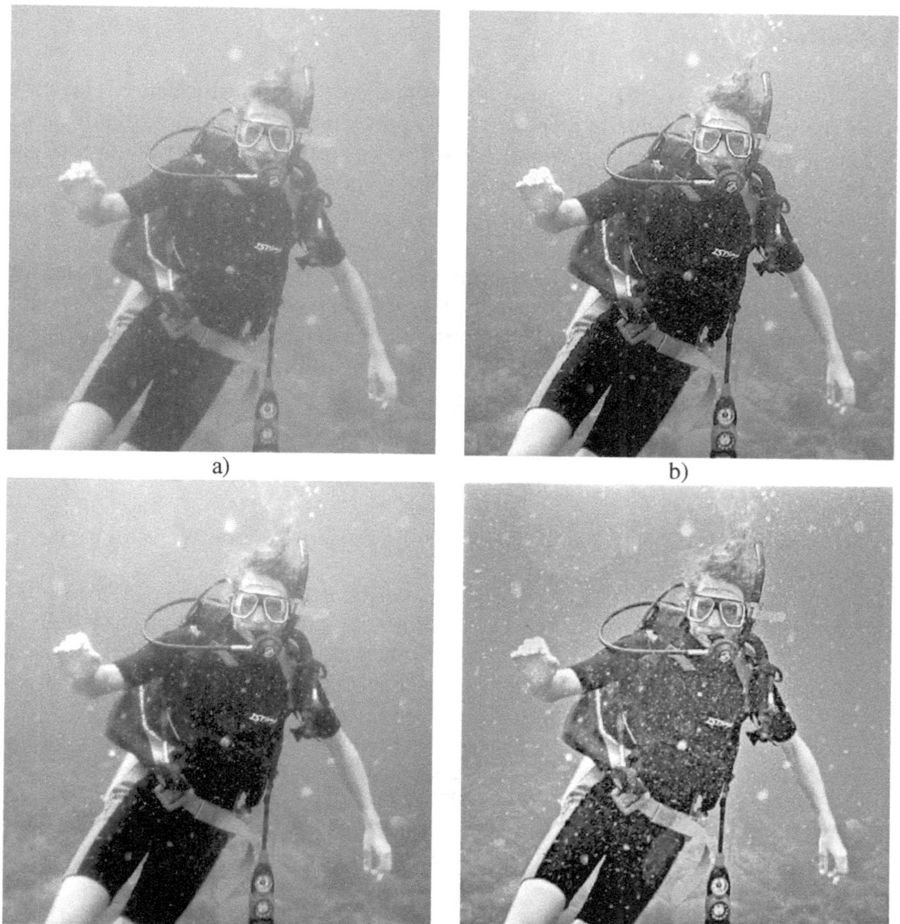

Fig. 4. Comparison of the two-step ANN+autoleveling processing (b) with standalone autoleveling (c) and MSR processing (d). Original image (a) is taken from [3].

Comparison with standalone autoleveling algorithm and processing using MSR algorithm was made. In most cases the results of the proposed two-step ANN+autoleveling approach had subjectively better or equal quality than the results of processing with autoleveling algorithm only. When compared to MSR processing the introduced two-step procedure allowed to obtain comparable results with slight superiority of the MSR algorithm. Nevertheless, the processing using two-step procedure seems to be faster because MSR uses Fourier transformation and each pixel is processed with respect to 3 neighborhoods with radiuses equal to 15, 80 and 250 pixels[1] [13].

[1] There are no results for image processing time for the MSR algorithm in the literature but Fourier transformation together with multi-scale processing is to be computationally expensive.

6 Conclusion

Since there are no exact guidelines how to approximate transformation (1), use of ANN seems promising due to their universal approximation properties. In this paper it is shown that use of evolving neural networks with rather rough evaluation of their quality is an efficient way to obtain a neuro-solution for fast and effective image processing. To make calculations faster approximate formulae (17) and (18) for local statistics are introduced.

First results of experiments show competence and efficiency of the proposed two-step processing procedure: (1) local level processing with use of ANN; (2) global level processing using autoleveling algorithm. The further research is aimed to the improvement of the ANNs evaluation and extension of possible domains of application of the neural image processing.

References

1. Gonzalez, R.C., Woods, R.E. Digital Image Processing. Addison-Wesley, Reading MA, (1992)
2. Jahne, B. Digital Image Processing. Springer-Verlag, Berlin Heidelberg New York (2002)
3. Woodell, G.A., Jobson, D.J., Rahman, Z., Hines, G.D. Enhancement of Imagery in Poor Visibility Conditions // Sensors, and Command, Control, Communicati-ons, and Intelligence (C3I) Technologies for Homeland Security and Homeland Defense IV, Proc. SPIE 5778 (2005)
4. Tsoy, Y.R., Spitsyn, V.G. Using Genetic Algorithm with Adaptive Mutation Mechanism for Neural Networks Design and Training. Optical Memory and Neural Networks, Vol. 13, No. 4. Allerton Press, Inc., New York (2004) 225-232
5. Tsoy, Y.R., Spitsyn, V.G. Analysis of Genetic Algorithm with Dynamic Population Sizing. Proc. of the V Int. Conf. on Artificial Intelligent Systems (AIS'05). Dyvnomorskoe, Russia (2005)
6. Papadopoulos, D., Schneider, D., Meier-Eiss, J., Arber, W., Lenski, R.E., Blot, M. Genomic Evolution during a 10000-generation Experiment with Bacteria. Proc. Natl. Acad. Sci. USA, Vol. 96 (1999) 3807-3812
7. Schuster, P. Molecular Insights into Evolution of Phenotypes. In: Crutchfield, J.P., Schuster, P. (eds.): Evolutionary Dynamics – Exploring the Interplay of Accident, Selection, Neutrality, and Function. Oxford Univ. Press (2002)
8. Fukushima, K., Miyake, S. Neocognitron: A New Algorithm for Pattern Recognition Tolerant of Deformations and Shifts in Position. Pattern Recognition, Vol. 15, No. 6 (1982) 455–69
9. Hopfield, J.J. Neural Networks and Physical Systems with Emergent Collective Computational Abilities. Proc. Natl. Acad. Sci. USA, Vol. 79, No. 8 (1982) 2554-2558
10. Kohonen, T. The Self Organizing Map. Proc. of IEEE, Vol. 78 (1990) 1464-1479
11. Munteanu, C., Rosa, A. Gray-Scale Image Enhancement as an Automatic Process Driven by Evolution. IEEE Trans. on Systems, Man, and Cybernetics – part B: Cybernetics, Vol. 34, No. 2 (2004)
12. Lindley, C.A. Practical Image Processing in C: Acquisition, Manipulation, Storage. John Wiley & Sons, Inc., New York (1991)
13. Rahman Z., Jobson D. J., Woodell G. A., Hines G. D. Image Enhancement, Image Quality and Noise. Proc. of SPIE Photonic Devices and Algorithms for Computing VII (2005)

Environments Conducive to Evolution of Modularity*

Vineet R. Khare[1], Bernhard Sendhoff[2], and Xin Yao[1]

[1] Natural Computation Group, School of Computer Science,
The University of Birmingham, Birmingham B15 2TT, UK
{V.R.Khare, X.Yao}@cs.bham.ac.uk
http://www.cs.bham.ac.uk/research/NC/
[2] Honda Research Institute Europe GmbH, Carl-Legien-Straße 30,
63073 Offenbach/Main, Germany
Bernhard_Sendhoff@de.hrdeu.com
http://www.honda-ri.de

Abstract. Modularity has been recognised as one of the crucial aspects of natural complex systems. Since these are results of evolution, it has been argued that modular systems must have selective advantages over their monolithic counterparts. Simulation results with artificial neuro-evolutionary complex systems, however, are indecisive in this regard. It has been shown that advantages of modularity, if judged on a static task, in these systems are very much dependent on various factors involved in the training of these systems. We present a couple of dynamic environments and argue that environments like these might be partly responsible for the evolution of modular systems. These environments allow for a better, more direct use of structural information present within modular systems hence limit the influence of other factors. We support these arguments with the help of a co-evolutionary model and a fitness measure based on system performance in these dynamic environments.

1 Introduction

There are modular systems all around us in nature. The most cited example is the human brain, which is modular on several levels [1]. Macroscopically, we can observe specialised areas for certain tasks, like for visual (V1-V2-V4-ITL (inferior temporal lobe)) or auditory processing. On a mesoscopic level the structural re-occurring element is the column, and even on the microscopic level neurons can be grouped into structurally distinct classes, e.g. pyramidal neurons. This structural organisation is a results of evolution by natural selection. Often debated are the reasons for evolution of these modular systems. Models that try to explain the evolution of modularity can be divided into two categories [2]. Models in the first category have direct relationship between modularity and selective advantage. In this category some of the reasons presented for the evolution of

* This work is partly funded by Honda Research Institute Europe GmbH.

T.P. Runarsson et al. (Eds.): PPSN IX, LNCS 4193, pp. 603–612, 2006.

modularity are evolvability, phenotypic robustness against environmental perturbations, ease of learning etc. The other category includes model that do not assume a direct relationship but explain modularity as a side effect of dynamics of evolution.

This paper is concerned with models that relate the selective advantage of modularity with the effectiveness of learning in individuals. Hence these models deal with interaction between genetic modularity and learning. It has been argued [3] that during their lifetimes individuals need to learn more than one tasks simultaneously and having a modular structure helps in avoiding conflicting messages from these tasks. In Artificial Neural Network (ANN) literature this has been shown with the help of modular neural networks (MNNs) - as they outperform fully-connected structures. The classic example being the "what" and "where" vision tasks. Attempts have also been made to illustrate that this advantage of MNNs can lead to their evolution, using neuro-evolutionary methods. In [3] it was shown that modularity can be evolved on the basis of this advantage. In this work an ANN's architecture was genetically determined and evolved by mutation and selection, while its fitness was dependent on how well it performs on these "what" and "where" vision tasks, after training with backpropagation. This modular (non) interference based advantage, however, is not universal and depends on various factors involved in the training of the network. In [4] it was shown that this advantage depends crucially on the choice of cost function used for training and a proper choice can lead to superior non-modular structures. Our earlier experiments show that this also depends on the choice of mode of training (batch or incremental) and learning algorithm [5]. These results indicate that (a) it is possible to deal with modular interference with non-modular structures and (b) either the tasks and simulations considered are too simplistic to extract the benefits of modularity in complex systems or, simply, learning efficacy is not the reason behind the evolution of modularity.

For this work we take a different approach and consider a couple of dynamic environments, unlike the static environments considered in these models. We show that because of the nature of tasks in these environments the structural information within a MNN can be exploited more directly (Sect. 2) and hence limits the effect of other parameters. We then use a co-evolutionary model (Sect. 3) to show that modularity can be evolved in conditions earlier shown to be unappreciative towards the evolution of modularity. We discuss various experiments and results in Sect. 4 and finally conclude in Sect. 5. We would like to emphasize at this point that the aim of this work is not to design optimal systems for these dynamic environments, but to use these environments to contribute to the understanding of evolution of modularity in nature.

2 Dynamic Environments

Here we consider two different kinds of environments. In the first one an individual is not just expected to learn a given task but is also expected, afterwards, to adapt to a related task, which shares some of its characteristics with the original task.

In the other scenario an individual is expected to learn more and more complex task incrementally. While adapting to a related task the individual is expected to learn a function of form $g(f_1, f_2)$ and then adapt to $g'(f_1, f_2)$ and while adapting to a more complex task a function is expected to learn $g(f_1, f_2, f_3)$ after learning $g(f_1, f_2)$. Let us assume a MNN with matching topology, after learning the first function in phase-one, is required to adapt to the second function (Fig. 1) in phase-two. For incrementally complex tasks, individuals are allowed to grow. In this section we look at how modular and non-modular systems adapt in these environments. As examples of these we consider boolean functions (see Sect. 2.1 and 2.2). The goal here is not to solve these simple boolean problems, but to use these to gain a deeper understanding of when modularity is useful.

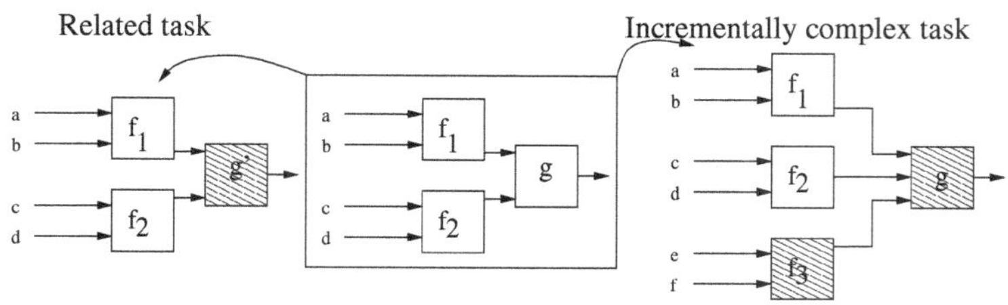

Fig. 1. A modular neural network adapting from $g(f_1, f_2)$ (center) to a related task $g'(f_1, f_2)$ (left) or to a more complex task $g'(f_1, f_2, f_3)$ (right). Shaded modules are to be labelled as "new."

In Fig. 1, modules f_1 and f_2 specialize in corresponding sub-functions during phase-one. To utilise the structural information present in the MNN we must be able to use these two modules in phase-two. However, when we try to learn the next function the modules very quickly lose their specialization[1] and the advantage is lost. When we change the function the corresponding error derivatives are large initially, which results in big changes in parameters of the networks in all the modules, hence we loose the specialization. One of the solutions to this problem is to fix the parameters in the two modules and keep them fixed during the training in phase-two. A less restrictive approach is where we do not fix these parameters but try to control the changes in their magnitude at the beginning of phase-two. If we prevent big changes in these parameters at the beginning, that will give the combination module a chance to adapt to the already specialised modules. Also, in absence of definite information about the relationship between the two functions the second approach is desirable because if they are not related then using the second approach the network can still learn the second function, which might not be possible using the first.

Modified-IRPROP Algorithm: To implement the second approach we need a parameter, associated with each of the weight parameters, controlling the

[1] This is similar to the problem of catastrophic forgetting [6] in neural networks which refers to the complete and sudden loss of a network's knowledge, of what it has learnt earlier, in the process of learning a new set of patterns.

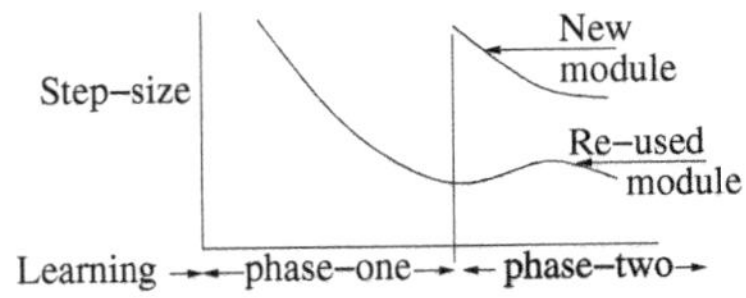

Fig. 2. Typical changes in the absolute values of step-sizes associated with parameters in various modules during adaptation to a related task

magnitude of changes in these weight parameters. In *Improved Resilient Backpropagation* (IRPROP) [7]) we already have such a parameter called step-size. During training with IRPROP the absolute value of this parameter decreases over time and at later stages of training we have very small values of step-sizes in the network. At the beginning of phase-two of learning the modules that we want to preserve are labelled as "re-used" and others as a "new" modules. We then use step-sizes at the end of phase-one to initialise the step-sizes for the subsequent learning phase for all parameters in "re-used" modules, while "new" modules get their step-sizes initialised normally. This, we argue, is a very natural way of handling learning in modular systems, whereby old modules keep their old characteristics (step-size in this case) while the new modules start with new ones. Using this scheme of initialisation, step-sizes corresponding to the two differently labelled modules exhibit typical behaviours, shown in Fig. 2. In phase-two, step-sizes associated with "new" module start from a high (constant) value, while step-sizes associated with "re-used" module start at very low values, increase first then finally start decreasing again. This indicates some adjustments in "re-used" modules, but not the undesirable catastrophic changes discussed earlier. To illustrate this effect let us now consider an example of each of these tasks.

2.1 Adaptability Towards Related Tasks

To understand the role of modularity in an ANN in such a dynamic environment let us consider an example. For *XOR-OR problem* after learning the *Composite XOR* function $((\overline{a \oplus b}) \oplus (\overline{c \oplus d}))$ in phase-one a network has to adapt to *Composite OR* function $((\overline{a \oplus b}) + (\overline{c \oplus d}))$ in phase-two. Here a, b, c and d are boolean variables and $+$ and $\oplus$ represent OR and XOR functions, respectively. The two boolean functions share common sub-functions and the combination functions OR (g) and XOR (g') are different.

Now for this problem let us compare a fully-connected and a modular structure using the modified-IRPROP, the normal IRPROP and incremental steepest-descent algorithms. In addition we also use cross entropy and mean-squared error functions for these comparisons. Fully-connected structure is an RBF network and the modular network is a combination of three smaller RBF networks, each representing one module in Fig. 1. Number of hidden units are chosen so as to make the number of free parameters the same in both networks. For all these experiments, phase-two training starts with the weight parameters learnt after phase-one and both phases consist of 100 epochs. Table 1 lists cross entropy or

Table 1. Comparison of adaptability towards related tasks: Cross entropy (CE) or normalised root-mean-squared errors (NRMSE) on training set at the end of phase-two, averaged over 30 runs, for the two structures trained using different learning algorithms. Bold entries in a column represent the significantly better (paired t-test, significance level $\alpha = 0.05$) result in that column.

Algorithm →	**steepest descent**	**IRPROP**		**modified-IRPROP**	
Error Function →	NRMSE	NRMSE	CE	NRMSE	CE
Structure ↓					
fully-connected	0.48	0.19	0.06	0.19	0.06
modular	**0.31**	0.24	0.04	**0.07**	**0.02**

normalised root-mean-squared errors (depending on the error function used) on training set at the end of phase-two, averaged over 30 runs, for the two structures trained using different learning algorithms. Training set errors are used as there are only 16 possible data points for the problem. Modular structure adapts much better than a fully-connected structure if we use incremental steepest descent learning algorithm. With IRPROP both structures adapt equally well. With modified-IRPROP, however, modular structure is much better because we are able to use the modular specialisations in the second task.

2.2 Adaptability Towards Incrementally Complex Tasks

To compare the adaptability of a fully-connected structure and a modular structure to tasks which incrementally become more and more complex[2], let us consider the following three-stage example. In stage-one, the task is to learn f_1, in stage-two the task is to learn $g(f_1, f_2)$ and finally in stage-three the task is to learn $g(f_1, f_2, f_3)$, where $f_1 = \overline{a \oplus b}$, $f_2 = \overline{c \oplus d}$, $f_3 = \overline{e \oplus f}$ and the combination function g is OR. Again a, b, c, d, e and f are boolean variables and $\oplus$ represents XOR. For stage one and two all possible data points (4 and 16, respectively) are used for training and for stage three 50 out of total 64 are used for training and the rest for testing. For stage one there is no modularity in the problem hence we start with two fully-connected RBF networks. In stage-two one of these networks is grown in a modular way, whereby the new inputs go into a separate module, and the other is grown by simply adding more hidden units in the network. These two structures are again grown in a similar fashion in stage-three. In any of these stages the total number of parameters in the two structures is kept same. Figure 3 shows the learning curves for these two structures with mean-squared error function. For stages one and two training error is plotted while for stage three test error is plotted. From these we can see that the modular structure is able to use the structural information within and performs better than a fully-connected structure. This difference in performance

[2] This is similar to the idea of lifelong learning [8] in robot control tasks, whereby an agent is expected to reduce the difficulty of learning i-th control task by using already acquired knowledge from other tasks.

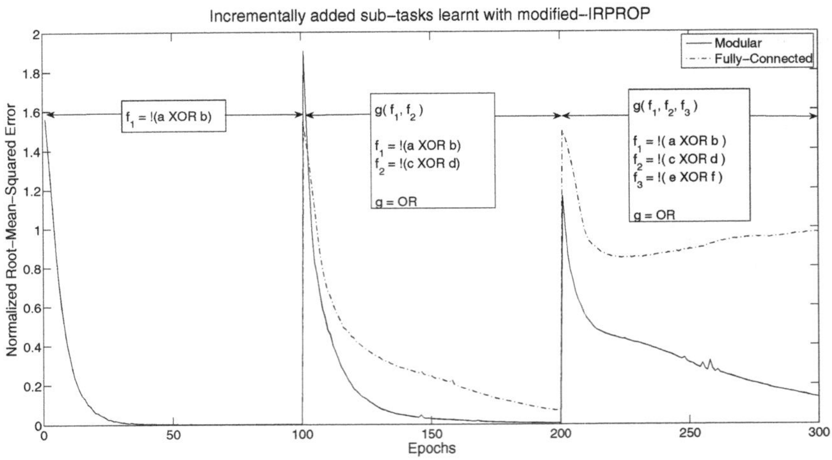

Fig. 3. Average NRMSE of 30 independent runs at different epochs, for the modified-IRPROP learning of modular and IRPROP learning of fully-connected structure

increases with increase in the number of sub-tasks within the overall task. This is observed irrespective of the error function used for training.

3 Evolution of Modularity

Here we consider the two dynamic environments again but the second one is made more realistic by making an individual learn incrementally complex task, not in its lifetime but, after every few generations. Previously we observed that making better use of structural information present in a MNN helps it adapt better in these environments. Our aim here is to illustrate how this better adaptability can lead to the evolution of modularity. For this purpose we use an extension of our *co-evolutionary modules and modular neural networks* (CoMMoN) *model* [9,5]. CoMMoN has a module population or *ModPop* and a MNN population or *SysPop* co-evolving together (Fig. 4). *ModPop* consists of RBF networks and *SysPop* consists of MNNs which are made up of one or more modules from *ModPop*. If an MNN has more than one module, it uses a *Combining-module* (another RBF network) to combine the outputs of these modules. Evolution at *ModPop* level searches for good building blocks and at *SysPop* level it searches for good combinations of these. Within this general co-evolutionary framework, both the structure and parameterisation of MNNs is evolved.

Modules differ from each other in terms of the input connections they have out of all possible inputs for the problem (*AllInps*). Initially they are assigned these inputs randomly. Centers and widths of hidden units in a module are initialised using K-Means Clustering on the training data points, considering only the inputs which are connected to the module. Weights and bias values are initialised randomly using uniform distribution. In *SysPop*, first each MNN is

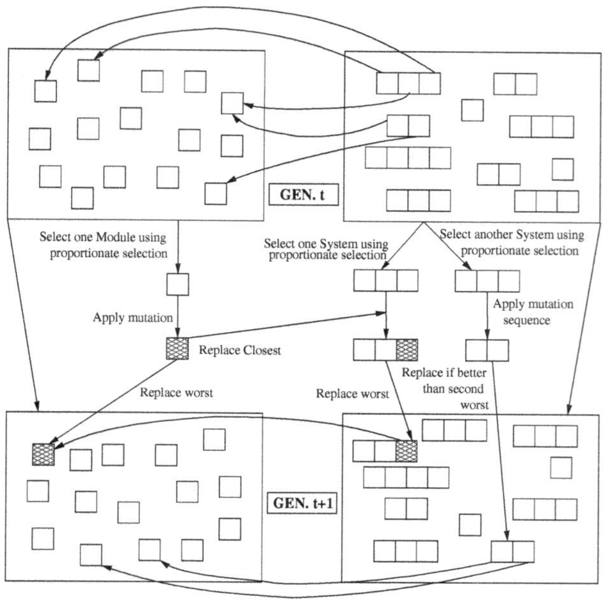

Fig. 4. Steady-state CoMMoN Model : Generation t to generation $t+1$

assigned a random number of modules between 1 and 4 uniformly. If there are more than one modules then a *Combining-module* is added and initialised in a fashion similar to the initialisation of modules in *ModPop*, only the inputs to this module are obtained as the outputs of other modules in the MNN. After initialisation, each MNN is trained using modified-IRPROP and one of the two error functions (cross entropy or mean-squared error) and its fitness is evaluated using the same error function. These fitnesses are then used to evaluate fitness of modules in *ModPop* (Sect. 3.1). In each generation a module from *ModPop* is chosen using proportionate selection. It is then mutated by changing its input positions (each input position is flipped with probability $p_m = 1/AllInps$) and its parameters are reinitialised to obtain *ModChild.* This *ModChild* replaces the worst individual in *ModPop.* A couple of individuals for *SysPop* are then chosen with replacement, using proportionate selection. The first individual is mutated using a mutation sequence (Sect. 3.2) and, if the offspring is fitter than the second worst individual in *SysPop*, it replaces that individual. This mutation is used to make the best use of innovation at the module level. The second system is mutated by swapping the module most similar (based on hamming distance between input connections) to *ModChild* in this individual with *ModChild* and replaces the worst individual in *SysPop.*

3.1 Fitness Assignment

In the first dynamic environment, where individuals (MNNs) need to adapt to a related task, fitness of a MNN is derived from both tasks. We calculate the mean-squared errors (or cross entropy) at the end of each phase of training and sum the inverse of the two values to evaluate an individual. In the second task mean-squared error (or cross entropy) for the current task is used. Fitness for modules in *ModPop* is derived from various MNNs in *SysPop*. We use the sum of fitnesses of best few MNNs (25% of all MNNs in *SysPop*) in which a module participates to evaluate its fitness.

3.2 Mutation Sequence

To encourage simpler structures against more complex structures, the following sequence of mutations (similar to the one used in EPNet [10]) is applied on MNNs in *sysPop*. A particular type of mutation is used only when the preceding type could not produce an offspring which, after partial training, was better than the second worst individual in *SysPop*. The steps involved, in that order, are (a) deletion : a module from the MNN or a node from *Combining-module* is deleted with equal probability, (b) swap: a module in the MNN is swapped with another module from *ModPop*, (c) addition: either a randomly chosen module from *ModPop* is added to the MNN or a new node is added to the *Combining-module*, with equal probability.

4 Simulation Results and Discussion

To observe the evolution of modularity we use a structural modularity index or SMI. It indicates how far a given structure is from the modular solution. If the current task has three sub-tasks, for each module in the network this index is defined as: $\text{SMI}_{mod} = \frac{1}{N}(n_1 - n_2 - n_3)$, where n_1, n_2 and n_3 are the number of inputs corresponding to the three sub-tasks, $n_1 \geq n_2 \geq n_3$ and N is the total number of inputs in the problem. If there are only two sub-tasks then n_3 is always zero. The SMI of the MNN is calculated by summing m_{mod}s corresponding to all sub-tasks. If a structure has more than one module for a sub-task then only one is taken into consideration while calculating SMI and this module is the one that (structurally) matches the corresponding sub-task best. Figure 5 illustrates SMI calculations for two MNNs. A structure that matches the problem topology has an SMI value of 1.0 and a fully-connected structure has an SMI value of 0.0.

Various parameters used in experiments for both environments are listed in Table 2. In the first instance where we use adaptability towards related tasks (example from Sect. 2.1) as the fitness measure the best MNN in *SysPop* in all 20 runs (10 each using cross entropy and mean-squared error) at the end of 1000 generations always have an SMI value of 1.0. Although, four runs produce MNNs with an extra module.

To test the adaptability towards incrementally complex tasks the co-evolutionary model is given 1000, 2000 and 3000 generations to adapt to a task in the three stages (Sect. 2.2), respectively. In each stage the collective inputs (all six) are provided and only the target values are changed in between stages. Hence in stage-one (between generation 0 and 999) the task requires feature selection, in

Table 2. Parameter values used for experimentation

Partial training per generation	20 epochs
ModPop size	120
SysPop size	30
Maximum modules per MNN	4
Maximum hidden units in *Combining-network*	8
Hidden units in modules	5

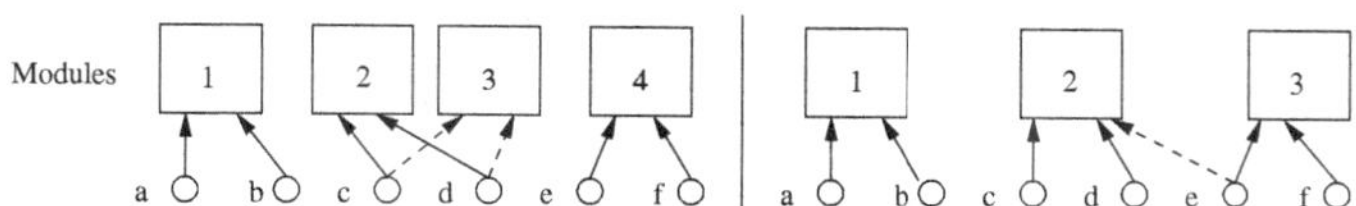

Sub–task	!(a XOR b)	!(c XOR d)	!(e XOR f)	!(a XOR b)	!(c XOR d)	!(e XOR f)
Module	1	2 or 3	4	1	2	3
SMI_{mod}	1 / 3	1 / 3	1 / 3	1 / 3	1 / 6	1 / 3
SMI		1			5 / 6	

Fig. 5. Errors in connections between modules and inputs in two of the solutions obtained using adaptability towards incrementally complex problem (stage-three) alongside corresponding SMI values. Structure on the left has an extra module and the one on the right has an extra connection.

stage-two onwards both feature selection and decomposition is required. We use cross entropy in 10 runs and mean-squared error in the other 10 runs as error functions for training and fitness values for evolution. Irrespective of the error function used we obtain modular solutions at the end of both second and third stages. Although the resulting solutions do not match the problem topology exactly. Average SMI values for the best solutions at the end of stage-three for cross entropy and mean-squared error runs are 0.83 and 0.88. Also, t-test ($\alpha = 0.05$) on the two sets of values reveals that the two are not significantly different from each other. A couple of deviations from the exact problem-topology matching structure observed in these results are shown in Fig. 5. Both sets of results indicate that selective advantage based on individuals' ability to adapt in these two environments can results in evolution of modularity. This is observed using both mean-squared error and cross entropy error functions, which indicates the limited influence of the choice of error functions used.

5 Conclusions

Examples of dynamic environments are presented in which the structural information built in a MNN can be better exploited. This is done using the modified-IRPROP algorithm and it results in better adaptability of MNNs than fully-connected structures, independent of various factors involved in training. Error function and training algorithm (which have been shown to be crucial in learning a static task) are both shown to have limited influence in these environments. Also, with the help of a co-evolutionary model we have shown that in these dynamic environments a selective advantage based on these improved adaptabilities can result in the evolution of modularity, irrespective of these factors.

Previous studies have not been able to show a clear cut advantage of having modularity in neural networks. We argue that the advantage of modularity in neural networks is much more visible in dynamic environments like the ones considered here. Even with such simple dynamic tasks we have been able to show how adaptability benefits from modularity in neural networks. Another, even broader, implication of this work is the partial explanation for the abundance of modularity in natural complex systems. It is argued that dynamic environments like these might be partly responsible for such an abundance.

References

1. Hrycej, T.: Structure of the Brain. In: Modular Learning in Neural Networks. A Modularized Appproach to Neural Network Classification. Wiley, New York (1992) 59–82
2. Wagner, G.P., Mezey, J., Calabretta, R.: Natural Selection and the Origin of Modules. In Callebaut, W., Rasskin-Gutman, D., eds.: Modularity. Understanding the Development and Evolution of Natural Complex Systems. The MIT Press: Cambridge, MA (2005) 33–49
3. Ferdinando, A.D., Calabretta, R., Parisi, D.: Evolving Modular Architectures for Neural Networks. In French, R.M., Sougné, J.P., eds.: Proceedings of the Sixth Neural Computation and Psychology Workshop, Liege, Belgium, Springer Verlag (2001) 253–264
4. Bullinaria, J.A.: To Modularize or Not To Modularize? In Bullinaria, J., ed.: Proceedings of the 2002 U.K. Workshop on Computational Intelligence (UKCI-02), Birmingham (2002) 3–10
5. Khare, V.R., Yao, X., Sendhoff, B.: Multi-network Evolutionary Systems and Automatic Decomposition of Complex Problems. International Journal of General systems (2006) to appear in the special issue on 'Analysis and Control of Complex Systems'.
6. French, R.M.: Catastrophic Interference in Connectionist Networks: Can It Be Predicted, Can It Be Prevented? In Cowan, J.D., Tesauro, G., Alspector, J., eds.: Advances in Neural Information Processing Systems. Volume 6., Morgan Kaufmann (1994) 1176–1177
7. Igel, C., Hüsken, M.: Empirical Evaluation of the Improved Rprop Learning Algorithm. Neurocomputing **50**(C) (2003) 105–123
8. Thrun, S.B., Mitchell, T.M.: Lifelong Robot Learning. Robotics and Autonomous Systems **15** (1995) 25–46
9. Khare, V.R., Yao, X., Sendhoff, B., Jin, Y., Wersing, H.: Co-evolutionary Modular Neural Networks for Automatic Problem Decomposition. In: The 2005 IEEE Congress on Evolutionary Computation, CEC 2005, Edinburgh, Scotland, UK, IEEE Press (2005) 2691–2698
10. Yao, X., Liu, Y.: A New Evolutionary System for Evolving Artificial Neural Networks. IEEE Transactions on Neural Networks **8**(3) (1997) 694–713

Arms Races and Car Races

Julian Togelius and Simon M. Lucas

Department of Computer Science
University of Essex
Colchester CO4 3SQ, UK

Abstract. Evolutionary car racing (ECR) is extended to the case of two cars racing on the same track. A sensor representation is devised, and various methods of evolving car controllers for competitive racing are explored. ECR can be combined with co-evolution in a wide variety of ways, and one aspect which is explored here is the relative-absolute fitness continuum. Systematical behavioural differences are found along this continuum; further, a tendency to specialization and the reactive nature of the controller architecture are found to limit evolutionary progress.

1 Introduction

Evolutionary car racing (ECR) is about using evolutionary algorithms to create and tune controllers, sensors or other parameters for racing cars, in simulation or physical reality. Only a few attempts to evolve controllers or aspects of controllers have so far been made, all quite recently [1][2][3][4]; see [5] for a complete review. Our own work has focused on investigating various controller architectures and sensor representations, and finding ways of developing neurocontrollers with general driving skills that can proficiently race a variety of tracks, as well as specialized controllers that perform very well on particular tracks. We have also argued that car racing is a promising environment for evolving complex and relatively general intelligence, as the task of navigating a basic track is relatively simple to learn, but gradually can be made more and more complex almost without limits, requiring path planning, anticipation, opponent modelling, etc.

All published research on ECR so far has dealt with the case of a solo-racing, or one car on a track a time. This paper addresses the more complex case of two cars competing against each other on the same track at the same time, and includes the possibility of car-car collisions. We will explore different methods of evolving neurocontrollers and sensor setups for successfully competing against another car, and we hope that our results will be useful both for game developers looking to automatically create racing game AI, and computational intelligence researchers seeking to use games and game-like environments to evolve ever more general and complex intelligence.

1.1 Co-evolution

In our previous research, a controller's fitness was defined as the progress a controlled car had made around a track within a pre-specified time, and so depended

T.P. Runarsson et al. (Eds.): PPSN IX, LNCS 4193, pp. 613–622, 2006.

only on the controller itself and a few small random factors. Competing against another controller fundamentally changes the problem, so that fitness becomes dependent on the behaviour of both the assessed controller and its competitor. Evolution with such fitness functions is commonly called co-evolution, and has been used in evolutionary computation both to improve evolvability and to study evolutionary dynamics [6][7].

ECR allows the application and exploration of several uncommon forms of co-evolution. According to Dawkins and Krebs, biological co-evolution can be either intraspecific or interspecific and either symmetric or asymmetric [8]; in evolutionary computation terms, the co-evolution can be either between two populations, or individuals in one population, and between contestants using the same or different fitness functions. ECR allows all these types of co-evolution, which is interesting since most competitive co-evolutionary robotics experiments we know of build on predator-prey scenarios, and thus fall in the asymmetric interspecific category [9][10][11].

A second way in which ECR allows uncommon modes of co-evolution is through the existence of a well defined solo fitness function: any controller can be tested both for absolute solo fitness, which means the distance covered when racing without competition, absolute competitive fitness, which is the same thing when having to take the behaviour of another car into account (including the possibility of collisions), and relative fitness, which is defined as how far in front of or behind the competitor a controlled car finishes. Further, absolute competitive fitness and relative fitness can be blended seamlessly. We believe that these characteristics make ECR ideal for exploring co-evolution.

1.2 Scope of This Paper

The first set of questions we will try to answer concern the extension of the car racing model and evolutionary approach to two cars: how well will controllers evolved for solo racing do with competition? Will it be possible to co-evolve controllers that do better? Is our controller architecture and sensor setup appropriate for this? Will we be able to evolve human-competitive drivers, and if not, what are the problems with our method?

The second set of questions address co-evolution. Will there be a difference in fitness, and in behaviour, if we evolve for absolute, relative or mixed absolute and relative fitness? What sort of difference will be observed? For example, will controllers evolved for relative fitness turn out to drive more aggressively? Will there be a difference in sensor setups?

2 Methods

2.1 Simulation Environment

The experiments reported in this article were done in a slightly updated version of the simulator used in [5]. The 2-dimensional simulator is intended to, qualitatively if not quantitatively, model a standard radio-controlled (R/C) toy car (approximately 17 centimeters long) in an arena with dimensions approximately 3*2 meters, where the track is delimited by solid walls. The simulation has the dimensions 400*300 pixels, and the car measures 20*10 pixels.

A track consists of a set of walls, a chain of waypoints, and a set of starting positions and directions. Cars are added to a track in one of the starting positions, with corresponding starting direction, both the position and angle being subject to random alterations. The waypoints are used for fitness calculations.

The dynamics of the car are based on a reasonably accurate mechanical model, taking into account the small size of the car and bad grip on the surface, but is not based on any actual measurements [12][13]. While the dynamics of the car itself are fairly straightforward, the collision handling has been subject to much tuning and exception-handling in order to get a behaviour that feels right for the human player and cannot easily be exploited in an unintended way by the evolutionary algorithm. A collision between two cars is basically handled as a fully elastic collision, but the orientations of the cars are also disturbed, depending on which parts of the cars collided.

2.2 Sensors

The car experiences its environment through four types of sensors: the speed sensor, the waypoint sensor, a number of wall sensors, and a number of car sensors. The speed sensor is simply the speed of the car. The waypoint sensor gives the difference between the car's current orientation and the angle to the next waypoint (but not the distance to the waypoint). When pointing straight to a waypoint, this sensor thus outputs 0, when the waypoint is to the left of the car it outputs a positive value, and vice versa.

The wall sensors are modelled on "range-finders" similar to sonars or IR sensors, where each sensor has an angle (relative to the orientation of the car) and a range, between 0 and 200 pixels. The output of the wall sensor is zero if no wall is encountered along a line with the specified angle and range from the centre of the car, otherwise it is a fraction of one, depending on how close to the car the sensed wall is. The car sensors work exactly like the wall sensors, with the crucial difference that the output depends on whether and how far along the line another car is detected. A small amount of noise is applied to all sensor readings, as it is to starting positions and orientations.

2.3 Controller Architecture

The controllers in the experiments below are based on neural networks. More precisely, we are using multilayer perceptrons with three neuronal layers (two adaptive layers) and *tanh* activation functions. A network has at least three inputs: one fixed input with the value 1, one speed input in the approximate range [0..3], and one input from the waypoint sensor, in the range [$-\Pi..\Pi$]. In addition to this, it has eight inputs from wall and car sensors, in the range [0..1]. All networks have two outputs, which are interpreted as driving commands for the car. Both the neural network and sensor configuration of a controller are directly encoded together in the genome as an array of real numbers.

2.4 Co-evolutionary Algorithm

For the co-evolutionary algorithm, a modified $(\mu + \lambda)$ evolutionary strategy with $\mu = 50$ and $\lambda = 50$ without self-adaptation) was used. (This algorithm is based on the EAs used in [3] and [5]. It is possible that the addition of crossover and/or self-adaptation could make evolution more efficient, but we chose to leave these out for the sake of conceptual simplicity and minimizing the number of parameters to tune.) The difference between the co-evolutionary algorithm used here and a standard evolutionary strategy is in the fitness calculation. There are two types of primitive fitness defined: absolute and relative fitness. The absolute fitness of a controller C is calculated as the number of waypoints it has passed, divided by the number of waypoints in the track, plus an intermediate term representing how far it is on its way to the next waypoint. An absolute fitness of 1.0 thus means having completed one full track within the alloted time. In the evolutionary experiments reported below, each car was allowed 700 time-steps (enough to do two to three laps on most tracks in the test set). Relative fitness is defined as the difference in absolute fitness between C and the car it is competing against. Both the absolute and relative fitness values for a given controller was calculated as the mean of three trials of the controller on each of the tracks.

When the primitive fitnesses of all the controllers have been calculated, they are normalized, so that they are all in the range [-1..1]. The final fitness value of each controller is then calculated by blending the two primitive fitness values: $fitness = p*absfit+(1-p)*relfit$ where p is the proportion of absolute fitness, a constant set at the beginning of the evolutionary run. It could be argued that only evolution with completely relative fitness constitutes co-evolution.

There are three mutation operators: Gaussian mutation of all neural connection weights, Gaussian mutation of all sensor parameters (angles and lengths), or sensor type mutation. Each time the mutation method of a controller is called, numbers drawn from a Gaussian distribution with a standard deviation of 0.1 are added to both neural connection weights and sensor parameters. With a probability of 0.4, a sensor type mutation is also performed, meaning that one of the sensors has its type changed from car to wall or wall to car.

At the start of an evolutionary run, all controllers have four wall sensors and four car sensors, pointing in random directions and with random ranges, and the neural connection weights are initialized to small random values.

2.5 Competition Tracks

In order for the competitions to be more challenging, and to prevent the controllers from adopting strategies that would only work on a single track, three different tracks were used to evaluate every trial (see figure 1). While we have previously shown [5] that controllers can be evolved that proficiently race a diverse collection of tracks, this seems to require a lengthy process of incremental evolution if the tracks are both clockwise and counter-clockwise. But if all the tracks have the same direction, like the three tracks chosen for the present experiments, it is possible to evolve a good controller for these tracks using standard evolution.

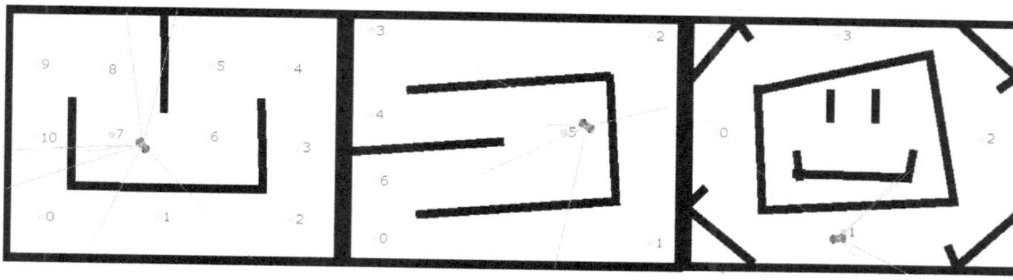

Fig. 1. The three tracks used in the experiments, including waypoints. Each track also shows a sample car with evolved sensors (discussed in section 3.2).

3 Experiments

3.1 Giving Solo-Evolved Controllers Some Competition

10 separate solo-evolutionary runs were made according to the setup described in the Methods section above. Each evolutionary run lasted for 200 generations. (The mean fitness was zero at generation 0 of every evolutionary or co-evolutionary run in this paper; fitness growth graphs have been omitted to conserve space.)

On average, the best individual of the last generation of each of the evolutionary runs had fitness 2.49 (with standard deviation $\sigma = 0.23$), and used 5.7 ($\sigma = 0.67$) wall sensors and 2.3 (σ=0.67) car sensors. The best run resulted in a best controller with fitness 2.67, and the best controller of the worst run had fitness 1.89. Most of the evolved sensor setups consisted in a relatively even spread of medium-range wall sensors pointing forward and diagonally forward, and the few car sensors pointing backward.

One of these controllers, with fitness 2.61 (0.13), was selected for further testing. When put in a competition with another car controlled by a copy of the same controller, average fitness dropped to 1.23 (0.6). Behavioural analysis shows that the two cars collide repeatedly at the beginning of almost every trial, as they don't have any method of detecting and reacting to each other's presence. Depending on starting conditions, the outcome of the competitions vary, but usually one or both of the cars is either driven to collide with the wall, or spun around so that it starts driving the track the wrong way. A car that starts going the wrong way is usually, but not always, unable to turn around and start driving in the correct direction again; a car that crashes into the wall usually gets stuck. This is because of the controller design rather the game mechanics, as it is perfectly possible for a human player to back away from the wall and continue driving in the right direction. In many trials, however, one of the cars managed to escape the collisions in the right direction and proceeded to make its way smoothly around the track.

From this experiment, it can be seen that the problem of racing two cars concurrently is sufficiently different from the problem of solo-racing that the performance of a solo-evolved controller is catastrophically compromised when tested in competition conditions.

3.2 Co-evolving Controllers: The Absolute-Relative Fitness Continuum

50 evolutionary runs were made, each consisting of 200 generations. They were divided into five groups, depending on the absolute/relative fitness mix used by the selection operator of the co-evolutionary algorithm: ten evolutionary runs were performed with absolute fitness proportions 0.0, 0.25, 0.5, 0.75 and 1.0 respectively. These were then tested in the following manner: the best individuals from the last generation of each run were first tested for 50 trials on all three tracks without competitors, and the results averaged for each group. Then, all five controllers in each group were tested for 50 trials each in competition against each controller of the group. Finally, the number of wall and car sensors were averaged in each group. See table 1 for results.

Table 1. The results of co-evolving controllers with various proportions of absolute fitness. All numbers are the mean of testing the best controller of ten evolutionary runs for 50 trials. Standard deviations in parentheses.

Proportionabsolute	0.0	0.25	0.5	0.75	1.0
Absolute fitness solo	1.99 (0.31)	2.09 (0.33)	2.11 (0.35)	2.32 (0.23)	2.23 (0.23)
Absolute fitness duo	0.99 (0.53)	0.95 (0.44)	1.56 (0.45)	1.44 (0.44)	1.59 (0.45)
Relative fitness duo	0 (0.75)	0 (0.57)	0 (0.53)	0 (0.55)	0 (0.47)
Wall/car sensors	5.8 / 2.2	5.6 / 2.4	5.2 / 2.8	4.2 / 3.8	6.4 / 1.6

Analysis. It is clear that, when driving without competitors, the co-evolved controllers on average have lower absolute fitness than the solo-evolved controllers. Behavioural inspection suggests that the co-evolved controllers drive more carefully, seldom accelerating to top speeds, and take corners more conservatively. A similar but smaller difference in absolute solo-fitness seems to exist between the groups of co-evolved controllers, with controllers evolved more for absolute fitness performing better than controllers evolved more for relative fitness. The controllers within a group perform similarly, and the lower fitness comes from driving slower around the track rather than crashing into walls or losing direction.

The difference between controllers co-evolved with different fitness mixes becomes clearer when we measure performance in competition with other controllers from the same group, where controllers evolved mostly for absolute fitness generally get about half a lap farther than those evolved mostly for relative fitness. Behavioural analysis confirms that this is because the cars more often collide at the start of a trial, often forcing one or both of the cars to crash against the wall or spin around and lose track of which direction it is going. Often, the controllers evolved with low (0 or 0.25) proportions of absolute fitness actively look for trouble by trying to collide. (See figure 2).

There seems to be little consistency in evolved sensor setups, samples of which can be seen in figure 1 (wall sensors are blue; car sensors are pink; each car is travelling forwards in direction of the waypoints). We found one controller in the group evolved purely for relative fitness that had only wall sensors and no car sensors, and another one in the group evolved for purely absolute fitness! There is no obvious tendency towards fewer or more car sensors at either end of the fitness mix, and the data is too scarce to prove any more subtle tendency. When looking at all 50 controllers together, every controller has at least three wall sensors, and there is always at least one pointing mostly forward. On average, the cars have twice as many wall sensors as car sensors, and when car sensors are present, there seems to be at least one pointing mostly backward; overall, more car sensors point backward than forward.

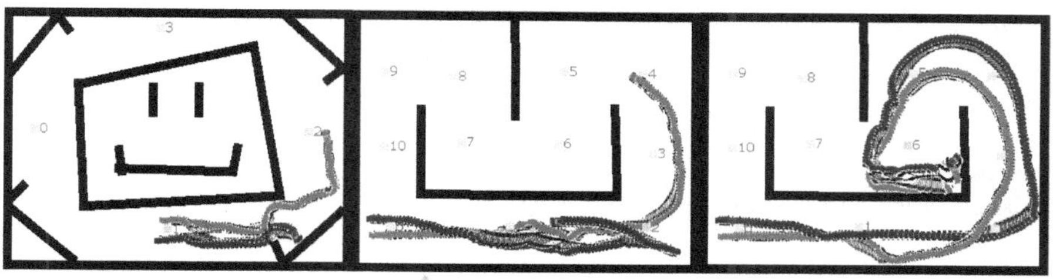

Fig. 2. Traces of the first 100 or so time-steps of three runs that included early collisions. From left to right: red car pushes blue car to collide with a wall; red car fools blue car to turn around and drive the track backwards; red and blue car collide several times along the course of half a lap, until they force each other into a corner and both get stuck. Note that some trials see both cars completing 700 time-steps driving in the right direction without getting stuck.

Fitness mix groups versus each other. In order to find out how the controllers evolved with various fitness mixtures performed against each other, we tested all the five controller groups against each other. The slightly surprising results was that the groups performed on average equally well against each other, though with considerable intra-group variation. The absolute fitnesses of the controllers in these encounters were quite low, on average 0.96, which suggest that all controllers are quite ill prepared to race against controllers from another fitness mix group.

3.3 Co-evolved Versus Solo-Evolved Controllers

The 50 controllers co-evolved with various fitness mixes in the section above were now tested against the 10 solo-evolved controllers from section 3.1. For each group, the ten co-evolved controllers competed for 10 trials with each of the 10 solo-evolved controllers. See table 2 for results.

Analysis. Observe that there is a small (mostly) but consistent fitness advantage for the solo-evolved controllers over the co-evolved ones. (Both co-evolved and solo-evolved controllers performed significantly worse in these competitions

Table 2. Co-evolved versus solo-evolved controllers

Proportionabsolute	0.0	0.25	0.5	0.75	1.0
Co-evolved	1.41 (0.52)	0.99 (0.44)	1.32 (0.58)	1.23 (0.65)	1.41 (0.45)
Solo-evolved	1.68 (0.56)	1.95 (0.62)	1.74 (0.57)	1.38 (0.65)	1.51 (0.63)

than when tested in solo racing conditions.) The cause of this fitness difference is not completely obvious after looking at a large number of these competitions, but it appears that the solo-evolved controllers (which gain higher fitness than the co-evolved ones in solo trials) simply outrun the co-evolved controllers in many cases, and so avoid many of the collisions, and further corroborate the hypothesis that the controllers tend to be very specialized to compete against controllers similar to themselves. This could be seen either as a shortcoming of the evolutionary algorithm, or as the desired state of things; it could be argued that the co-evolved controllers should have strategies general enough to take on any opponent, or that a their more careful driving style should always make them slower than a solo-evolved controller.

3.4 Evolution with a Static Target

To investigate whether the tendency to specialization in co-evolved controllers could be used to create controllers that could out-compete the solo-evolved controllers from section 3.1, we modified a copy of the co-evolutionary algorithm to work with a static target. In this configuration, each controller is evaluated by racing three races against randomly selected controllers out of the ten solo-evolved controllers. It should be noted that this is not co-evolution at all, as the target controllers do not evolve. The car controlled by the target controller could instead be seen as an interactive feature of the environment.

The experiments we run with this configuration failed to generate any controllers with better fitness than the target controller. This was despite attempts at evolving from scratch, starting from a general controller, or starting from a clone of the target controller, and using various mixtures of absolute and relative fitness. Our interpretation of this is that the solo-evolved controller drives the tracks as fast as can be done given its sensing and processing limitations, and that the same limitations hinder the co-evolved controllers from doing any better.

3.5 Human-Competitiveness of Evolved Controllers

A random selection of controllers were tested by competing with a car controlled by one of the authors via the keyboard. It was found that the solo-evolved controllers were generally good contenders, driving at about the same skill level or slightly better than the author, as long as collisions were avoided. However, it was found to be quite easy to learn how to collide with the computer controlled car in such a way that it got stuck on a wall, and then continue to win the race.

Most of the co-evolved controllers were pretty simple to beat by just accelerating hard at the beginning of a race and keep driving, as their slower driving wouldn't allow them to catch up.

4 Conclusion

Our main positive finding concerns the effects of changing the type of fitness function. A very clear effect was that controllers evolved more for relative fitness acted more aggressively, but covered less distance both when running solo and when competing with other controllers from the same population, than controllers evolved more for absolute fitness. We could not find any systematic difference between the sensor setups evolved with the various fitness mixtures, but observed a general tendency to point car sensors backwards rather than forward, and the opposite tendency for wall sensors - it seems to be more important to watch your back than to know whats happening in front of you.

A finding that is relevant to the overarching quest to scale up ECR and evolutionary robotics in general is that competitive ECR is a much more complex problem than solo ECR. This can be seen both from the drastic degradation of fitness when solo-evolved controllers are put in competitive environments, and from our great difficulty in evolving controllers that can reliably outperform the solo-evolved ones. It can also be seen from the total inability of all evolved controllers to backtrack upon a frontal collision with a wall, and the relatively poor ability of most evolved controllers to find the correct direction after having been spun around. This points to the need for more complex sensors and neural networks.

However we set up the evolutionary runs, they seem to suffer from over-specialization, where the controllers in a population only learn to race each other. This result is in broad agreement with what has been found in co-evolutionary predator-prey experiments[9][10]. So even though ECR allows us to explore a larger space of variants of competitive co-evolution, it seems that we at present are stuck with the same basic obstacles to evolving generally good competitive behaviour.

4.1 Future Research

One obvious extension of the controller architecture would be to add state to the presently stateless controller; this could be done by adding recurrent connections to the network. The controller could also be given the ability to grow or "complexify" itself as needed during the evolutionary run[11]. This could also be the case for the sensors; we believe that either more sensors of the present kind or some alternate sensor representation will be needed to give the controller the information needed to compete well.

The evolutionary algorithm could be enhanced with the addition of a "hall of fame", where the controllers of a generation compete not only against each other but also against the best controllers of previous generations[7][9][10]. It would be interesting to use evolutionary multi-objective optimization to evolve fronts of pareto-optimal tradeoffs between relative and absolute fitness.

References

1. Floreano, D., Kato, T., Marocco, D., Sauser, E.: Coevolution of active vision and feature selection. Biological Cybernetics **90** (2004) 218–228
2. Tanev, I., Joachimczak, M., Hemmi, H., Shimohara, K.: Evolution of the driving styles of anticipatory agent remotely operating a scaled model of racing car. In: Proceedings of the IEEE Congress on Evolutionary Computation. (2005) 1891–1898
3. Togelius, J., Lucas, S.M.: Evolving controllers for simulated car racing. In: Proceedings of the IEEE Congress on Evolutionary Computation. (2005) 1906–1913
4. Stanley, K.O., Kohl, N., Sherony, R., Miikkulainen, R.: Neuroevolution of an automobile crash warning system. In: Proceedings of the Genetic and Evolutionary Computation Conference (GECCO-2005). (2005)
5. Togelius, J., Lucas, S.M.: Evolving robust and specialized car racing skills. In: Proceedings of the IEEE Congress on Evolutionary Computation (to appear). (2006)
6. Hillis, W.D.: Co-evolving parasites improve simulated evolution as an optimization procedure. Physica D **42** (1990) 228–234
7. Rosin, C.D., Belew, R.K.: New methods for competitive coevolution. Evolutionary Computation **5:1** (1996)
8. Dawkins, R., Krebs, J.R.: Arms races between and within species. Proceedings of the Royal Society of London , series B **205** (1979) 489–511
9. Nolfi, S., Floreano, D.: Co-evolving predator and prey robots: Do 'arm races' arise in artificial evolution? Artificial Life **4** (1998) 311–335
10. Bason, G., Bergfeldt, N., Ziemke, T.: Brains, bodies, and beyond: Competitive co-evolution of robot controllers, morphologies and environments. Genetic Programming and Evolvable Machines **6** (2005) 25–51
11. Stanley, K., Miikkulainen, R.: Competitive coevolution through evolutionary complexification. Journal of Artificial Intelligence Research **21** (2004) 63–100
12. Bourg, D.M.: Physics for Game Developers. O'Reilly (2002)
13. Monster, M.: Car physics for games. http://home.planet.nl/ monstrous/tutcar.html (2003)

BeeHiveAIS: A Simple, Efficient, Scalable and Secure Routing Framework Inspired by Artificial Immune Systems

Horst F. Wedde, Constantin Timm, and Muddassar Farooq

Informatik III, University of Dortmund,
44221 Dortmund, Germany
{wedde, timm, farooq}@ls3.cs.uni-dortmund.de

Abstract. The major contribution of this paper is a novel security framework, which is inspired by the principles of Artificial Immune Systems (AIS), for Nature inspired routing protocols in general and for *BeeHive* in particular. We have designed an empirical validation framework to demonstrate that the new framework provides the same security level as *BeeHiveGuard*, a digital signature based cryptography framework. But the processing and communication costs of the new framework are significantly smaller as compared to *BeeHiveGuard*.

1 Introduction

Nature inspired routing protocols are becoming an active area of research because agents in such algorithms enable a node to take decentralized routing decisions without any knowledge of global network topology. The algorithms can also adapt to changes in the network, or traffic patterns. *AntNet* [1], *BeeHive* [11] and *Distributed Genetic Algorithm (DGA)* [5] are well known Nature inspired routing algorithms. However, the impact of the malicious nodes, which manipulate the identity of the agents and their routing information, on the behavior of routing algorithms has received little attention in the community. In our earlier work [12], we have shown that the malicious nodes can significantly alter the routing behavior of *BeeHive* and a preliminary work by Zhong and Evans [13] has shown similar shortcomings in *AntNet*.

In [12], we proposed a digital signature based cryptography solution, *BeeHiveGuard*. The important conclusion of the work is that a classic cryptography based security framework is inappropriate for securing Nature inspired routing protocols because of its exceptionally large processing and control (portion of the bandwidth occupied by the agents) overheads.

The other relevant corollary of the work is: Nature inspired routing protocols could not be deployed in real world routers without designing and developing a simple, efficient and scalable security framework for them that must have acceptable processing and control overheads. The major contribution of the current paper is that it proposes a simple, efficient and scalable security framework on the basis of principles of AIS. The results of our extensive experiments show

T.P. Runarsson et al. (Eds.): PPSN IX, LNCS 4193, pp. 623–632, 2006.

that *BeeHiveAIS* is able to successfully counter the attacks of malicious nodes and provides the same security level as provided by *BeeHiveGuard*, but with significantly smaller processing and control overheads.

The rest of the paper is organized as follows. In Section 2 we provide a brief description of those features of AIS that proved helpful in designing and developing our new security framework, *BeeHiveAIS*, which is described in Section 3. In Section 4, we first introduce our verification methodology for *BeeHiveAIS* and then discuss the results of extensive experiments. Finally, we conclude the paper with an outlook to our future research.

2 Artificial Immune Systems (AISs)

AISs [2,3] are inspired by the principles of human immune system. The features of AIS that are particularly relevant to providing security in routing protocols are: self-identity, anomaly detection and learning. The self-identity enables an AIS to understand normal behavior of the agents in a routing protocol and to generate corresponding self-antigens. The AIS then generates a repository of antibodies, which can detect an anomalous behavior due to malicious agents (non-self antigens). The antigens and antibodies must be in a shape space format [6,7] to facilitate the definition of affinity between them, which is often a mathematical distance function. The negative selection algorithm [4] takes a randomly chosen set of antibodies and adds only those to the repository of effective antibodies whose affinity with the self-antigens is not above a certain threshold value. This generation process for the antibodies is known as *thymus model* [2,3], which enables an AIS to do anomaly detection through self/non-self differentiation.

The security framework based on AIS provides a number of benefits: small processing overhead due to a simple anomaly detection algorithm, no significant increase in control overhead because the agents need not carry any signatures, and finally the size of the database required to store antibodies is reasonably small. These benefits of AIS make it perfectly suitable for securing agent-based adaptive routing protocols in an efficient manner in real time.

3 BeeHiveAIS

We comprehensively analyzed the normal behavior of the *BeeHive* algorithm to design our AIS security framework for it. We concluded that if all routers in the network are operational then the flooding pattern of the *bee agents* is stable. If a router can learn this then it can detect any tampering of the agent identity. A second important observation was that the propagation delay in most of the cases was significantly higher than the queuing delay. As a result, the goodness of a neighbor for reaching a certain destination varied, most of the time, within a small window from its average goodness value. If a router can estimate this window then it can counter tampering of routing information (propagation and queuing delays). Another important observation was that reducing the update frequency of routing tables below a certain value does not enhance the performance of the algorithm. Last but not least a deterioration in the goodness of a neighbor for a certain destination without a deterioration in the goodness of other neighbors is a strong hint for an attack by a malicious node (under a high traffic load the goodness of all neighbors for reaching a certain destination are expected to deteriorate). This systematic study of *BeeHive* proved useful in designing a simple, efficient and scalable security framework, *BeeHiveAIS*.

3.1 AIS Model

The security framework, *BeeHiveAIS*, consists of three distinct phases: initialization, learning and protection. During initialization phase, the AIS model learns the normal flooding pattern of the *bee agents*, which is eventually responsible for the creation of *foraging zones* and *foraging regions* [9,11], which are organizational units (subdivisions) of the network topology. This phase lasts about 30 seconds. Then starts the learning phase, in which data traffic is injected into the network and the AIS assumes that no malicious nodes are present in the network. The major objective is to learn the normal behavior of the *BeeHive* algorithm in order to build a repository of the self-antigens, from which a database of the antibodies to counter different types of threats is generated. This phase lasts 50 seconds after the data traffic has been injected into the network. Finally, the protection phase starts in which the AIS detects the security threats of the malicious nodes and then counters them through the antibodies.

The block level diagrams of the important functions in *learning* and *protection* phases are shown in Figures 1 and 2 respectively. The important AIS concepts utilized in *BeeHiveAIS* are cataloged in Table 1. The purpose of type 1 self-antigens is to reduce the probability of tampering the agent specific data by a malicious node. This is achieved through self-antigens that consist of tuples like "source address, neighbor, hops". The antibodies are randomly generated and if their affinity, measured by Hamming distance, with the self-antigens is above a threshold value then they are discarded (negative selection). These antibodies/antigens are in a symbolic shape space with the elements of above-mentioned tuples as genes. The random generation of antibodies serves our purpose because in shape space an antibody generator has limited possibilities. Currently, if an antigen is matched to an antibody during the protection phase then the *bee agent* that triggered the match is dropped.

The type 2 self-antigens reduce the probability of manipulating the propagation and queuing delays by a malicious node. The antibodies/antigens of type 2 are in a real valued shape space and their affinity is measured by the Manhattan distance [2,3]. These self-antigens consist of average goodness values, which are gathered for a certain destination through a certain neighbor over a sliding window of the delays of five subsequent *bee agents*. In addition, the self-antigens also contain a flag which determines whether the change in goodness value is due to the presence of a malicious node or due to the change in traffic patterns. As a result, upper and lower threshold goodness values are assigned to a neighbor for reaching a destination. The creation process for the antibodies is similar to

Table 1. Mapping of concepts from AIS to *BeeHiveAIS*

AIS		*BeeHiveAIS*
Self Cells		Well-behaving nodes
Nonself Cells		Misbehaving nodes
Self-Antigens	type 1	Correct incoming direction and region of a bee agent
	type 2	Correct propagation and queuing delays tendencies
Antigens	type 1	Incorrect incoming direction and region of a bee agent
	type 2	Incorrect propagation and queuing delays tendencies
Antibody	type 1	Pattern that can detect antigens of type 1
	type 2	Pattern that can detect antigens of type 2

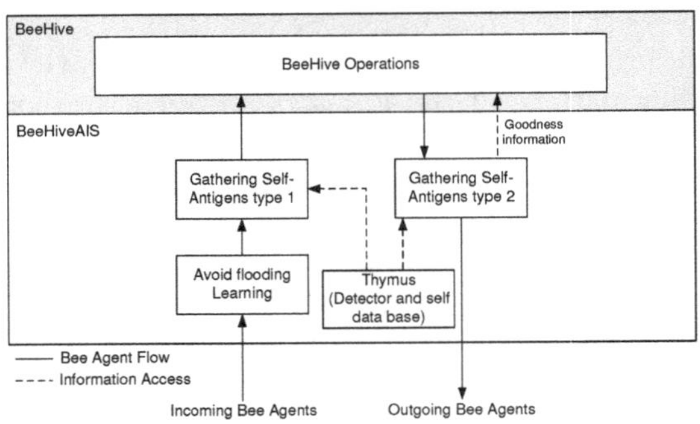

Fig. 1. *BeeHiveAIS* - Learning Phase

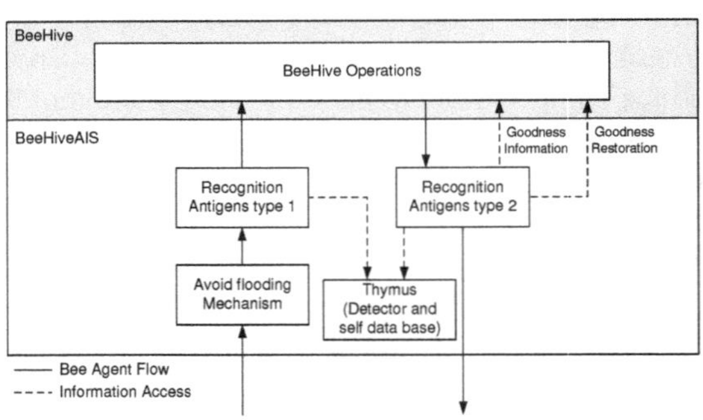

Fig. 2. *BeeHiveAIS* - Protection Phase

the one explained for type 1. A bee agent is dropped if an antibody matches an antigen: the reported goodness value of a neighbor is either above or below the upper or lower learned threshold values respectively. In this case the goodness value of the neighbor is set to the average goodness value. Our analysis show that in NttNet, the Japanese Internet Backbone (see Figure 3), 936 bytes are needed to store type 1 antibodies and 3130 bytes are needed to store type 2 antibodies. This sums to 4006 or 4 Kbytes which is acceptable [8].

Finally, an auxiliary feature has been added into AIS, which limits the update frequency of the routing tables to a certain value. If a *bee agent* arrives before the expected time then it is dropped to counter the Denial of Service (DoS) attack, which can result due to substantial reduction in the bee launching interval.

4 Experiments and Results

We selected NttNet, shown in Figure 3, to empirically validate correctness of our security framework. The experiments demonstrate that the presence of malicious nodes, launching a number of different attacks, can significantly alter the routing behavior of *BeeHive* protocol. We extended the performance evaluation framework proposed in [10] in order to calculate the relevant performance and cost values of the algorithms [9]. Our verification principle is: *BeeHiveAIS must provide the same security level as BeeHiveGuard does, but with significantly smaller processing and control overheads. Moreover, the relevant performance values of the secure algorithm must be within an acceptable difference of BeeHive (without any attack).*

We equipped each node with a traffic scope that measures *routing affinity*, which is the ratio of the packets routed through the node to the total number of packets generated in the network. The traffic scope generates the traffic chart, showing the routing affinity of a node for a selected algorithm (see Figure 4). Due to cyclic paths this ratio can exceed a value of 1. If a malicious node cannot significantly increase its *routing affinity* by launching different attacks, then we can safely conclude that the security framework did achieve its objective. The important symbols used in this paper are cataloged in Table 2 and their definitions and significance are explained in [9,10].

Table 2. Symbols used in this paper

$BHive$	BeeHive (without any attack)	$BHive(a)$	BeeHive (under attack)
$BHG(a)$	*BeeHiveGuard* (under attack)	$BHAIS(a)$	*BeeHiveAIS*(under attack)
T_{av}	Average throughput (Mbits/sec)	p_d	Packet delivery ratio (%)
$MSIA$	Mean of session inter-arrival times (sec)	$MPIA$	Mean of packet inter-arrival times (sec)
R_{ent}	Routing table entries	R_o	Control overhead
S_c	Session completion ratio (%)	S_o	Suboptimal overhead
t_d	Average packet delay (msec)	T_o	Total overhead
t_{90d}	90th percentile of packet delays (msec)	h_{ex}	Average extra hop count per data packet
S_d	Average session delay (msec)	A_a	Average agent processing cycles
S_{90d}	90th percentile of session delays (msec)	P_{loop}	Percentage of packets that followed a cyclic path
J_d	Average jitter value (msec)		

The network traffic is session oriented with MSIA=2.6 sec and MPIA=0.005 sec, session size=2130000 bits. MSIA and MPIA are taken from negative exponential distributions. The reported results are an average of the values obtained from 10 independent runs, each lasting for 1000 seconds. The detailed statistical analysis of the results is presented in [8]. We report, in this paper, four relevant

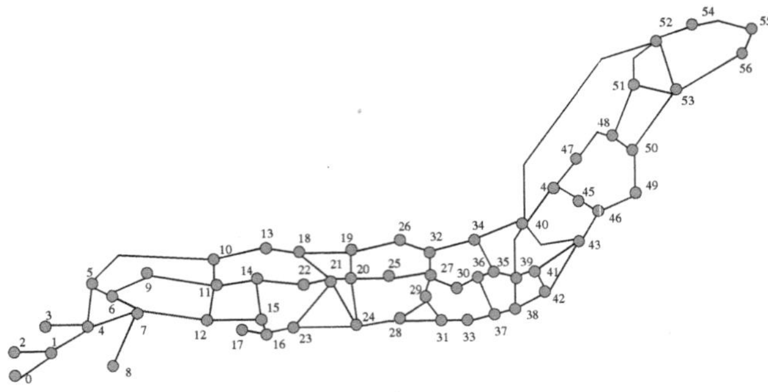

Fig. 3. NttNet

types of security threats that malicious nodes can launch in a network: impersonating, tampering of routing information, a combined super attack and DoS attack.

Impersonating. In this scenario, Node 35 transferred data to Node 55. Node 25, which does not lie on a desirable route from Node 35 to Node 55, impersonated the Node 55 (Node 25 launched *bee agents* by faking the source address of Node 55). As a result, Node 25 is expected to significantly disrupt the routing behavior of *BeeHive*. Figure 4 and Table 3 confirm this hypothesis. The attacker node, Node 25, is able to significantly enhance its routing affinity by attracting a large numbers of packets towards itself even though it does not lie on the route (note that the packets from Node 35 can reach Node 55 either through the path "34-40-52-53-56-55" or through the path "34-40-52-54-55"). As a result, 60% data packets are dropped due to looping in cyclic paths (see Table 3).

Table 3. NttNet - Data from Node 35 to Node 55 - Attacker: Node 25 ("35-55-25")

Algorithm	p_d	P_{loop}	S_c	R_o	A_a	t_d	t_{90d}	S_d	S_{90d}	J_d	T_{av}	h_{ex}	S_o	T_o	R_{ent}
(1)BHive	99.9	0	99.8	0.167	30683	0.027	0.028	2.62	2.77	0.004	0.844	0.443	0.038	0.206	65.9
(2)BHive(a)	41.4	29.9	9.51	0.232	25009	2.29	5.49	2.62	2.77	0.904	0.336	26.5	0.918	1.149	69.4
(3)BHG(a)	99.9	2.11	99.7	4.15	8801801	0.031	0.036	2.63	2.77	0.006	0.82	2.52	0.213	4.36	73.3
(4)BHAIS(a)	99.9	0	99.7	0.197	52433	0.027	0.028	2.62	2.77	0.004	0.812	0.443	0.037	0.234	65.8
(3)-(1) in %	-	-	-	2385	28586	-	-	-	-	-	-	-	461	-	
(4)-(1) in %	-	-	-	18	71	-	-	-	-	-	-	-	2.6	-	

One can easily conclude from Figure 4 and Table 3 that *BeeHiveAIS* and *BeeHiveGuard* are able to successfully counter the attack of Node 25. The additional processing and control overheads of *BeeHiveGuard* are 28586% and 2385% respectively as compared to *BeeHive*. It is important to note that the increase in processing and control overheads of *BeeHiveAIS* are only 71% and 18% respectively as compared to *BeeHive*. This is certainly attributable to the AIS utilized by *BeeHiveAIS*, which requires no additional information to be transmitted in the *bee agents* for correct functionality of its simple anomaly detection model. In *BeeHiveGuard* about 2% data packets enter cyclic paths. But this is due to

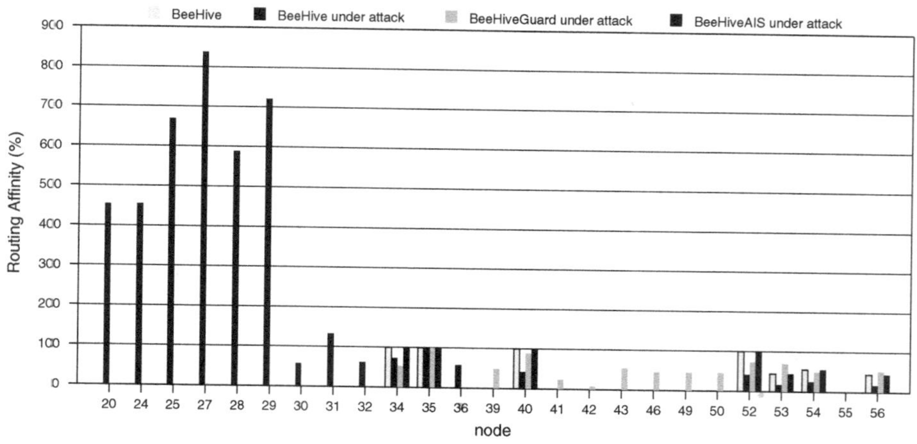

Fig. 4. NttNet - Data from Node 35 to Node 55 - Attacker: Node 25 ("35-55-25")

the fact that extremely large size *bee agents*, carrying digital signatures, in *BeeHiveGuard* altered their reachability pattern. As a result, data packets can reach Node 55 also through Node 43. Note that the performance values of *BeeHiveAIS* are comparable to *BeeHive* (without any attack).

Tampering of routing information. In this attack, a malicious node tries to manipulate the routing information, propagation and queuing delays, carried by the *bee agents*. As a result, a node can artificially alter the goodness of different nodes to its benefits. In this scenario, Node 55 transferred data to Node 48 and Node 54 manipulated the routing information to enhance its routing affinity.

Table 4. NttNet - Data from Node 55 to Node 48 - Attacker: Node 54 ("55-48-54")

Algorithm	p_d	P_{loop}	S_c	R_o	A_a	t_d	t_{90d}	S_d	S_{90d}	J_d	T_{av}	h_{ex}	S_o	T_o	R_{ent}
(1)BHive	99.9	0	99.8	0.167	30487	0.018	0.024	2.61	2.76	0.005	0.799	0.533	0.043	0.212	66.1
(2)BHive(a)	99.9	0.001	99.8	0.167	29933	0.019	0.027	2.62	2.76	0.006	0.803	0.763	0.063	0.231	66.1
(3)BHG(a)	99.9	0.006	99.6	3.5	8850628	0.018	0.025	2.62	2.76	0.005	0.826	0.573	0.048	3.55	70.2
(4)BHAIS(a)	99.9	0	99.6	0.167	53144	0.018	0.024	2.61	2.76	0.005	0.801	0.534	0.043	0.211	65.6
(3)-(1) in (%)	-	-	-	1996	28931	-	-	-	-	-	-	-	12	-	
(4)-(1) in (%)	-	-	-	0	74	-	-	-	-	-	-	-	0	-	

It is evident from Figure 5 that in *BeeHive* Node 54 is successful in its attack because it is able to enhance its routing affinity by 40%, and as a consequence, decreasing the routing affinity of Node 56 from 60% to less than 20%. One can easily conclude from Figure 5 and Table 4 that *BeeHiveAIS* and *BeeHiveGuard* are able to successfully neutralize the impact of this attack. However, the processing and control overheads of *BeeHiveAIS* are significantly smaller than *BeeHiveGuard*. The reasons for this substantial difference are already described in the impersonating attack. The performance values of *BeeHiveAIS* are approximately the same as of *BeeHive* (without any attack).

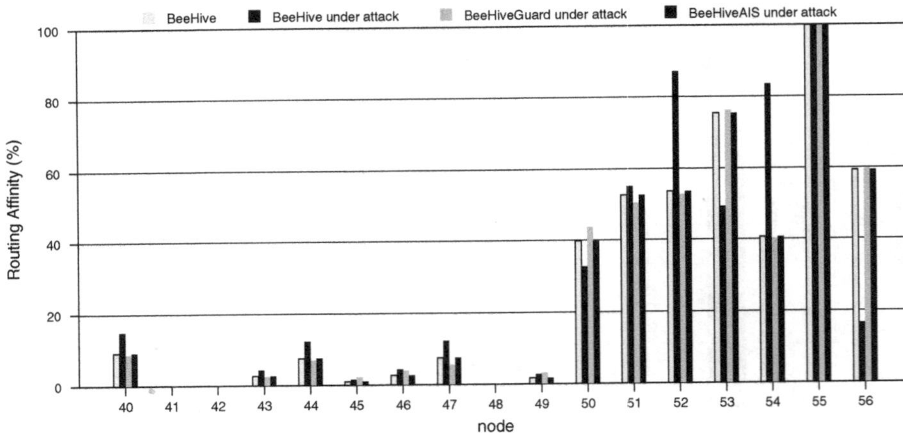

Fig. 5. NttNet - Data from Node 55 to Node 48 - Attacker: Node 54 ("55-48-54")

A combined super attack. The motivation behind this experiment was to study the impact of a combined super attack collectively launched by a number of nodes (Nodes 21,24,40 and 43), each node selecting a different type of the attack, in the network. Node 40 and 43 simply set the delay values of each *bee agent* passing through them to zero. In this attack all nodes acted as a source or destination node of a traffic session.

Table 5. NttNet - Normal traffic - 4 Nodes Attack ("all-all-4")

Algorithm	p_d	P_{loop}	S_c	R_o	A_a	t_d	t_{90d}	S_d	S_{90d}	J_d	T_{av}	h_{ex}	S_o	T_o	R_{ent}
(1)BHive	99.6	3.35	93.2	0.293	31972	0.121	0.426	2.74	3.1	0.026	46.5	1.83	8.77	9.06	78.4
(2)BHive(a)	97.8	7.15	80.2	0.472	36152	0.238	0.831	2.84	3.43	0.06	45.7	2.58	12.1	12.6	84
(3)BHG(a)	98.7	5.7	83.7	7.87	9118316	0.204	0.731	2.81	3.38	0.041	46.2	2.03	9.66	17.5	80.2
(4)BHAIS(a)	99.2	4.45	88.5	0.333	65302	0.162	0.551	2.77	3.18	0.034	46.5	1.91	9.18	9.51	77.3
(3)-(1) in (%)	-	-	-	2586	28420	-	-	-	-	-	-	-	10	-	
(4)-(1) in (%)	-	-	-	14	104	-	-	-	-	-	-	-	4.68	-	

One can see in Figure 6 that in *BeeHive* the nodes, which launched the attack, are able to significantly enhance their routing affinity. The impact of the attacks of Node 43 and Node 21 is more as compared to the other two nodes. It is also important to note that *BeeHiveAIS* and *BeeHiveGuard* are able to successfully counter the attacks in Node 24, Node 40 and Node 43. However, their countermeasures are not completely successful in Node 21. It is worth mentioning that Node 21 occupies a pivotal position in NttNet, hence it is not easy to counter all side effects caused by tampering of its routing information. Nevertheless *BeeHiveAIS* provides the same security level as provided by *BeeHiveGuard* but at significantly smaller processing and control overheads (see Table 5). Again the performance values of *BeeHiveAIS* are closest to *BeeHive* (without any attack) and are significantly better as compared to *BeeHiveGuard* (under attack).

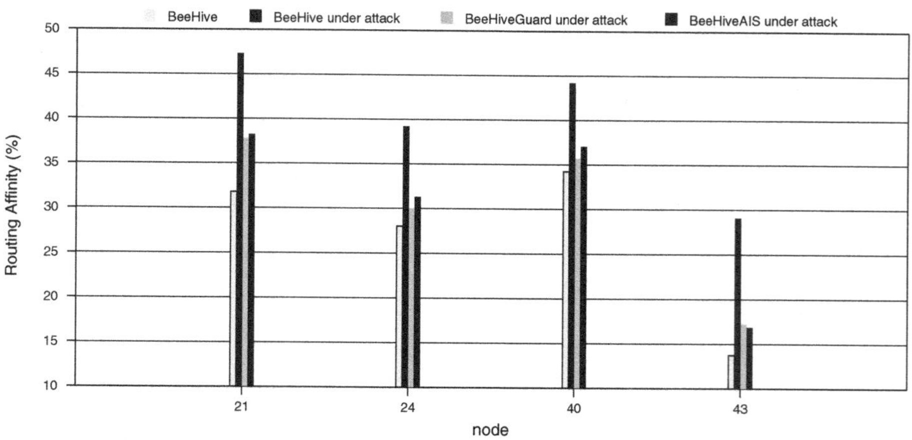

Fig. 6. NttNet - Normal traffic - 4 Nodes Attack ("all-all-4")

DoS attack. This attack can be launched by substantially reducing the bee launching interval of the *bee agents* in order to saturate the priority queues. As a result, a router is always busy processing the *bee agents* (due to their higher priority) and never gets the chance to do its actual task of packet switching. This attack was launched by 19 nodes in the network. In this scenario all nodes acted as a source or destination node of a traffic session.

Table 6. NttNet - Normal traffic - 19 Nodes launch DoS Attack ("all-all-19")

Algorithm	p_d	P_{loop}	S_c	R_o	A_a	q_{av}	t_d	t_{90d}	S_d	S_{90d}	J_d	T_{av}	h_{ex}	S_o	T_o
(1)BHive	99.6	3.35	93.2	0.293	31972	0.012	0.121	0.426	2.74	3.1	0.026	46.5	1.83	8.77	9.06
(2)BHive(a)	67.5	1.73	39.8	34.6	22379	0.296	1.56	4.84	2.88	3.85	0.183	31.3	1.55	5.01	39.6
(3)BHAIS(a)	99.2	2.87	87.6	6.69	46570	0.021	0.193	0.629	2.8	3.24	0.04	46	1.74	8.25	14.9
(3)-(1) in (%)	-	-	-	2183	46	-	-	-	-	-	-	-	-	5.93	

One can conclude from Table 6 that this attack has the strongest impact on the performance values of *BeeHive*. However, *BeeHiveAIS* is able to successfully counter the attack and its performance values are approximately same as of *BeeHive* (without any attack). The difference in control overhead stems from the fact that a neighbor node of the malicious node in *BeeHiveAIS* has to still process a significantly higher number of *bee agents* before dropping them. *BeeHiveGuard* simply crashed in this scenario.

5 Conclusion

We proposed a new AIS based security framework, *BeeHiveAIS*, which provides the same security level as that of a classic digital signature based cryptography framework. We designed and developed an empirical validation framework for the secure routing algorithms. The results of our extensive experiments show that *BeeHiveAIS* is able to successfully counter a number of serious attacks launched by malicious nodes. But its processing and control overheads are approximately 200 and 20 times respectively smaller than *BeeHiveGuard*. *BeeHiveAIS* needs only 4 KBytes of memory, in NttNet, to store a repository of antibodies. Our future efforts are focused to evaluate its scalability on large topologies.

References

1. G. Di Caro and M. Dorigo. AntNet: Distributed stigmergetic control for communication networks. *JAIR*, 9:317–365, Dec 1998.
2. Dipankar Dasgupta, editor. *Artificial Immune Systems and their Applications*. Springer-Verlag, 1998.
3. L. N. de Castro and J. Timmis. *Artificial Immune Systems: A new computational intelligence approach*. Springer-Verlag, 2002.
4. S. Forrest, A. S. Perelson, L. Allen, and R. Cherukuri. Self-nonself discrimination in a computer. In *Proceedings of the IEEE Symposium on Research in Security and Privacy*, pages 202–212. IEEE Computer Society Press, 1994.
5. S. Liang, A. N. Zincir-Heywood, and M. I. Heywood. Intelligent packets for dynamic network routing using distributed genetic algorithm. In *Proceedings of Genetic and Evolutionary Computation Conference*. GECCO, July 2002.
6. A.S. Perelson and G. F. Oster. Theoretical studies of clonal selection: Minimal antibody repertoire size and reliability of self-nonself discrimination. *Journal of Theoretical Biology*, 81:645–670, 1993.
7. R. H. Schwartz and J. Banchereau. Immune tolerance. *The Immunologist 4*, pages 211–218, 1996.
8. C. Timm. Design and development of a security framework for nature inspired routing algorithms. master thesis. Technical report, Informatik III, School of Computer Science, Universität Dortmund, 2006.
9. H. F. Wedde and M. Farooq. Beehive: An efficient, scalable, adaptive, fault-tolerant and dynamic routing algorithm inspired from the wisdom of the hive. Technical Report TR-801, Computer Science Department, University of Dortmund, 2005.
10. H. F. Wedde and M. Farooq. A performance evaluation framework for nature inspired routing algorithms. In *Applications of Evolutionary Computing, LNCS 3449*, pages 136–146. Springer Verlag, March 2005.
11. H. F. Wedde, M. Farooq, and Y. Zhang. BeeHive: An efficient fault-tolerant routing algorithm inspired by honey bee behavior. In *Ant Colony Optimization and Swarm Intelligence, LNCS 3172*, pages 83–94. Springer Verlag, Sept 2004.
12. H. F. Wedde, C. Timm, and M. Farooq. Beehiveguard: A step towards secure nature inspired routing algorithms. In Rothlauf et al., editor, *Proocedings of the EvoWorkshops 2006*. Springer Verlag, April 2006.
13. W. Zhong and D. Evans. When ants attack: Security issues for stigmergic systems. Technical report, Department of Computer Science, University of Virginina, CS-2002-3, 2002.

Critical Temperatures for Intermittent Search in Self-Organizing Neural Networks

Peter Tiňo

School Of Computer Science, University Of Birmingham
Birmingham B15 2TT, UK

Abstract. Kwok and Smith [1] recently proposed a new kind of optimization dynamics using self-organizing neural networks (SONN) driven by softmax weight renormalization. Such dynamics is capable of powerful intermittent search for high-quality solutions in difficult assignment optimization problems. However, the search is sensitive to temperature setting in the softmax renormalization step of the SONN algorithm. It has been hypothesized that the optimal temperature setting corresponds to symmetry breaking bifurcation of equilibria of the renormalization step, when viewed as an autonomous dynamical system called iterative softmax (ISM). We rigorously analyze equilibria of ISM by determining their number, position and stability types. Moreover, we offer *analytical* approximations to the critical symmetry breaking bifurcation temperatures that are in good agreement with those found by numerical investigations. So far the critical temperatures have been determined only via numerical simulations. On a set of N-queens problems for a wide range of problem sizes N, the analytically determined critical temperatures predict the optimal working temperatures for SONN intermittent search very well.

1 Introduction

Since the pioneering work of Hopfield [2], adaptation of neural computation techniques to solving difficult combinatorial optimization problems has proved useful in numerous application domains [3]. In particular, a self-organizing neural network (SONN) was proposed as a general methodology for solving 0-1 assignment problems in [4]. The methodology has been successfully applied in a wide variety of applications, from assembly line sequencing to frequency assignment in mobile communications (see e.g. [5]).

Searching for 0-1 solutions in general assignment optimization problems can be made more effective when performed in a continuous domain, with values in the interval $(0, 1)$ representing partial (soft) assignments. Typically the softmax function is employed to ensure that elements within a set of positive parameters sum up to one. When endowed with a physics-based Boltzmann distribution interpretation, the softmax function contains a free parameter (temperature, or inverse temperature). As the system cools down, the assignments become more and more crisp.

T.P. Runarsson et al. (Eds.): PPSN IX, LNCS 4193, pp. 633–640, 2006.

Recently, interesting observations have been made regarding the appropriate values of the temperature parameter when solving assignment problems with SONN endowed with softmax renormalization of the weight parameters [1]. There is a critical temperature T_* at which SONN is capable of powerful intermittent search through a multitude of high quality solutions represented as meta-stable states of the SONN dynamics. It has been suggested that the critical temperature may be closely related to the symmetry breaking bifurcation of equilibria in the autonomous softmax dynamics [6]. Kwok and Smith numerically studied global dynamical properties of SONN in the intermittent search mode and argued that such models display characteristics of systems at the edge-of chaos [7].

In this contribution we attempt to shed more light on the phenomenon of critical temperatures and intermittent search in SONN. In particular, since the critical temperature is closely related to bifurcations of equilibria in autonomous iterative softmax systems (ISM), we rigorously analyze the number, position and stability types of fixed points of ISM. Moreover, we offer analytical approximations to the critical temperature, as a function of ISM dimensionality. So far, critical temperatures have been determined only via numerical simulations. Due to space limitations, we cannot prove fully all the statements presented in this study. Detailed proofs can be found in [8].

2 SONN with Softmax Weight Renormalization

Consider a finite set of elements $j \in \mathcal{J} = \{1, 2, ..., N\}$ that need to be assigned to elements $i \in \mathcal{I} = \{1, 2, ..., M\}$, so that a global cost (potential) $Q(\mathcal{A})$ of an assignment $\mathcal{A} : \mathcal{J} \to \mathcal{I}$ is minimized. Partial cost of assigning $j \in \mathcal{J}$ to $i \in \mathcal{I}$ is denoted by $V(i, j)$. The "strength" of assigning j to i is represented by the "assignment weight" $w_{i,j} \in (0, 1)$. The SONN consists of the following steps:

1. Initialize assignment weights $w_{i,j}$, $j \in \mathcal{J}$, $i \in \mathcal{I}$, to random values around 0.5.
2. Choose at random an input item $j_c \in \mathcal{J}$ and calculate partial costs $V(i, j_c)$, $i \in \mathcal{I}$, of all possible assignments of j_c.
3. The "winner" element $i(j_c) \in \mathcal{I}$ is the one that minimizes $V(i, j_c)$, i.e. $i(j_c) = \text{argmin}_{i \in \mathcal{I}} V(i, j_c)$.
   The "neighborhood" $\mathcal{B}_L(i(j_c))$ of size L of the element $i(j_c)$ consist of L elements $i \neq i(j_c)$ that yield the smallest partial costs $V(i, j_c)$.
4. Assignment weights of nodes $i \in \mathcal{B}_L(i(j_c))$ get strengthened, those outside $\mathcal{B}_L(i(j_c))$ are left unchanged:

$$w_{i,j_c} \leftarrow w_{i,j_c} + \eta(i)(1 - w_{i,j_c}), \quad i \in \mathcal{B}_L(i(j_c)),$$

   where

$$\eta(i) = \exp\left\{-\frac{|V(i(j_c), j_c) - V(i, j_c)|}{|V(k(j_c), j_c) - V(i, j_c)|}\right\},$$

   and $k(j_c) = \text{argmax}_{i \in \mathcal{I}} V(i, j_c)$.

5. Weights $\mathbf{w}_i = (w_{i,1}, w_{i,2}, ..., w_{i,N})^T$ for each element $i \in \mathcal{I}$ are normalized using softmax
$$w_{i,j} \leftarrow \frac{\exp(\frac{w_{i,j}}{T})}{\sum_{k=1}^{N} \exp(\frac{w_{i,k}}{T})}.$$
6. Repeat from step 2 until all elements $j \in \mathcal{J}$ have been selected (one epoch).

Even though the soft assignments $w_{i,j}$ evolve in continuous space, when needed, a 0-1 assignment solution can be produced by imposing $\mathcal{A}(j) = i$ if and only if $j = \text{argmax}_{k \in \mathcal{J}} w_{i,k}$.

A frequently studied (NP-hard) assignment optimization problem in case of SOP is the N-queen problem: place N queens onto an $N \times N$ chessboard without attacking each other. In this case $\mathcal{J} = \{1, 2, ..., N\}$ and $\mathcal{I} = \{1, 2, ..., N\}$ index the columns and rows, respectively, of the chessboard. Partial cost $V(i, j)$ evaluates the diagonal and column contributions[1] to the global cost Q of placing a queen on column j of row i (see [1] for more details).

Kwok and Smith [1] argue that step 5 of the SONN algorithm is crucial for intermittent search by SONN for globally optimal assignment solutions. In particular, they note that temperatures at which symmetry breaking bifurcation of equilibria of the renormalization procedure in step 5 occurs correspond to temperatures at which optimal (both in terms of quality and quantity of found solutions) intermittent search takes place.

3 Iterative Softmax

Denote the $(N-1)$-dimensional simplex in $\mathbb{R}^N$ by S_{N-1}, i.e.

$$S_{N-1} = \{\mathbf{w} = (w_1, w_2, ..., w_N)^T \in \mathbb{R}^N \mid w_i \geq 0, i = 1, 2, ..., N, \text{ and } \sum_{i=1}^{N} w_i = 1\}.$$

Given a parameter $T > 0$ (the "temperature"), the softmax maps S_{N-1} into its interior

$$\mathbf{w} \mapsto \mathbf{F}(\mathbf{w}; T) = (F_1(\mathbf{w}; T), F_2(\mathbf{w}; T), ..., F_N(\mathbf{w}; T))^T, \tag{1}$$

where

$$F_i(\mathbf{w}; T) = \frac{\exp(\frac{w_i}{T})}{Z(\mathbf{w}; T)}, \text{ and } Z(\mathbf{w}; T) = \sum_{k=1}^{N} \exp(\frac{w_k}{T}). \tag{2}$$

The softmax map $\mathbf{F}$ induces on S_{N-1} a discrete time dynamics

$$\mathbf{w}(t+1) = \mathbf{F}(\mathbf{w}(t); T), \tag{3}$$

sometimes referred to as *Iterative Softmax* (ISM). Unless stated otherwise, we study systems for $N \geq 2$.

[1] In the sense of directions on the chessboard.

4 Fixed Points of Iterative Softmax

Recall that $\mathbf{w}$ is a fixed point (equilibrium) of the ISM dynamics driven by $\mathbf{F}$, if $\mathbf{w} = \mathbf{F}(\mathbf{w})$. It is easy to see that the maximum entropy point $\overline{\mathbf{w}} = (N^{-1}, N^{-1}, ..., N^{-1})^T \in S_{N-1}$ is a fixed point of ISM (3) for temperature setting T. In addition, there is a strong structure in the fixed points of ISM - coordinates of any fixed point of ISM can take on only two distinct values.

Theorem 1. *Except for the maximum entropy fixed point* $\overline{\mathbf{w}} = (N^{-1}, ..., N^{-1})^T$, *for all the other fixed points* $\mathbf{w} = (w_1, w_2, ..., w_N)^T$ *of ISM (3) it holds:* $w_i \in \{\gamma_1(\mathbf{w}; T), \gamma_2(\mathbf{w}; T)\}$, $i = 1, 2, ..., N$, *where* $\gamma_1(\mathbf{w}; T) > N^{-1}$ *and* $\gamma_2(\mathbf{w}; T) < N^{-1}$.

We will often write the larger of the two fixed-point coordinates as $\gamma_1(\mathbf{w}; T) = \alpha N^{-1}$, $\alpha \in (1, N)$.

Theorem 2. *Fix* $\alpha \in (1, N)$ *and write* $\gamma_1 = \alpha N^{-1}$. *Let* ℓ_{min} *be the smallest natural number greater than* $(\alpha - 1)/\gamma_1$. *Then, for* $\ell \in \{\ell_{min}, \ell_{min}+1, ..., N-1\}$, *at temperature*

$$T_e(\gamma_1; N, \ell) = (\alpha - 1)\left[-\ell \cdot \ln\left(1 - \frac{\alpha - 1}{\ell \gamma_1}\right)\right]^{-1}, \tag{4}$$

there exist $\binom{N}{\ell}$ *distinct fixed points of ISM (3), with* $(N - \ell)$ *coordinates having value* γ_1 *and* ℓ *coordinates equal to*

$$\gamma_2 = \frac{1 - \gamma_1(N - \ell)}{\ell}. \tag{5}$$

5 Fixed Point Stability in Iterative Softmax

Theorem 3. *Consider a fixed point* $\mathbf{w} \in S_{N-1}$ *of ISM (3) with one of its coordinates equal to* $N^{-1} \leq \gamma_1 < 1$. *Define*

$$T_s(\gamma_1) = \begin{cases} T_{s,2}(\gamma_1) = \gamma_1, & \text{if } \gamma_1 \in [N^{-1}, 1/2) \\ T_{s,1}(\gamma_1) = 2\gamma_1(1 - \gamma_1), & \text{if } \gamma_1 \in [1/2, 1). \end{cases} \tag{6}$$

Then, if $T > T_s(\gamma_1)$, *the fixed point* $\mathbf{w}$ *is stable.*

Theorem 4. *Consider a fixed point* $\mathbf{w} \in S_{N-1}$ *of ISM (3) with one of its coordinates equal to* $N^{-1} \leq \gamma_1 < 1$. *Let* $N - \ell$ *be the number of coordinates of value* γ_1. *Then if*

$$T \leq T_u(\gamma_1; N, \ell) = \gamma_1\ (2 - N\gamma_1)\frac{N - \ell}{N\ell} + \frac{1}{N} - \frac{1}{N\ell}, \tag{7}$$

$\mathbf{w}$ *is not stable.*

An illustrative summary of the previous results for equilibria $\mathbf{w} \neq \overline{\mathbf{w}}$ is provided in figure 1. The ISM has $N = 17$ units. Coordinates of such fixed points can only take on two possible values, the larger of which we denote by γ_1. The number of coordinates with value γ_1 is denoted by N_1. Temperatures $T_s(\gamma_1)$ (6) above which equilibria with larger coordinate equal to γ_1 are guaranteed to be stable are shown with solid bold line. For $N_1 = N - \ell \in \{1, 2, 3, 4\}$, we show the temperatures $T_u(\gamma_1; N, \ell)$ (7) bellow which equilibria with larger coordinate equal to γ_1 are guaranteed to be unstable with solid normal lines. Temperatures $T_e(\gamma_1; N, \ell)$ (4) at which equilibria with the given number N_1 of coordinates of value γ_1 exist (dashed lines) are also marked according to stability type of the corresponding fixed points. The stability types were determined by eignanalysis of Jacobians of the ISM map $\mathbf{F}$ at the fixed points. Stable and unstable equilibria existing at temperature $T_e(\gamma_1; N, \ell)$ are shown as stars and circles, respectively. All the unstable equilibria are of saddle type. Horizontal dashed line shows a numerically determined temperature by Kwok and Smith [1] at which attractive equilibria of 17-dimensional ISM lose stability and the maximum entropy point $\overline{\mathbf{w}}$ remains the only stable stable fixed point. Position where $T_s(\gamma_1)$ crosses $T_e(\gamma_1; N, \ell)$ for $N_1 = 1$ is marked by bold circle. Note that no equilibrium with more than one coordinate greater than N^{-1} is stable.

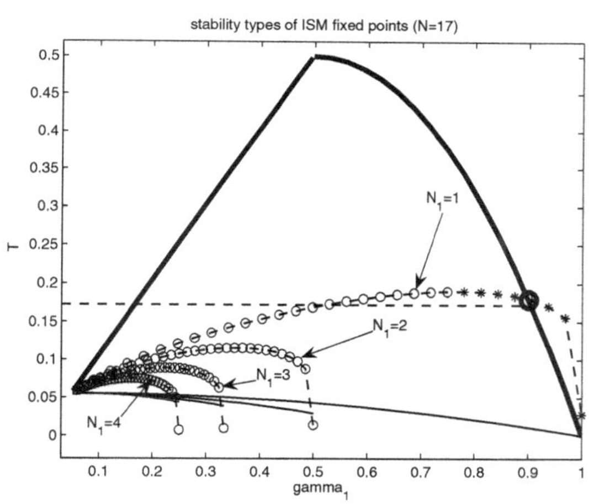

Fig. 1. Stability types for equilibria $\mathbf{w} \neq \overline{\mathbf{w}}$ of ISM with $N = 17$ units as a function of the larger coordinate γ_1 and temperature T. For a more detailed explanation, see the text.

6 Critical Temperatures for Intermittent Search in SONN

It has been hypothesized that ISM provides an underlying driving force behind intermittent search in SONN with softmax weight renormalization [6,1]. Kwok and Smith [1] argue that the critical temperature at which the intermittent search takes place corresponds to the "bifurcation point" of the *autonomous* ISM dynamics when the existing equilibria lose stability and only the maximum entropy point $\overline{\mathbf{w}}$ survives as the sole stable equilibrium. The authors numerically determined such bifurcation points for several ISM dimensionalities N. It was reported that bifurcation temperatures decreased with increasing N. Based on our analysis, the bifurcation points correspond to the case when equilibria near vertexes of the simplex S_{N-1} (equilibria with only one coordinate of large value γ_1) lose stability. We will call such fixed points *one-hot equilibria*. Based on the bound $T_s(\gamma_1)$ (6) and temperatures $T_e(\gamma_1; N, N-1)$ (4) at which equilibria of ISM exist, such a bifurcation point can be approximated by a bold circle in figure 1.

We present an analytical approximation to the critical temperature $T_*(N)$ at which the bifurcation occurs by expanding $T_e(\gamma_1; N, N-1)$ (4) around γ_1^0 as a second-order polynomial $T^{(2)}_{N-1}(\gamma_1)$. Based on figure 1 (and similar figures for other ISM dimensionalities N), a good choice for γ_1^0 is e.g. $\gamma_1^0 = 0.9$. Approximation to the critical temperature is then obtained by solving

$$T^{(2)}_{N-1}(\gamma_1) = T_s(\gamma_1)$$

for $\gamma_1 = \alpha/N$, and then plugging the result $\gamma_1^{(2)}$ back to bound (6), i.e. calculating $T_s(\gamma_1^{(2)})$.

We have

$$T_e(\gamma_1; N, N-1) = \frac{N\gamma_1 - 1}{(N-1)\ln\left(\frac{(N-1)\gamma_1}{1-\gamma_1}\right)}, \tag{8}$$

$$T'_e(\gamma_1; N, N-1) = \frac{N}{(N-1)\ln\left(\frac{(N-1)\gamma_1}{1-\gamma_1}\right)} - \frac{N\gamma_1 - 1}{(N-1)\gamma_1(1-\gamma_1)\ln^2\left(\frac{(N-1)\gamma_1}{1-\gamma_1}\right)} \tag{9}$$

and

$$T''_e(\gamma_1; N, N-1) = \frac{N\gamma_1^2 - 2\gamma_1 + 1 - 2\ln^{-1}\left(\frac{(N-1)\gamma_1}{1-\gamma_1}\right)}{(N-1)\gamma_1^2(1-\gamma_1)^2\ln^2\left(\frac{(N-1)\gamma_1}{1-\gamma_1}\right)}. \tag{10}$$

By solving

$$A\gamma_1^2 + B\gamma_1 + C = 0, \tag{11}$$

where

$$\begin{aligned} A &= \frac{1}{2}T''_e(\gamma_1^0; N, N-1) + 2, \\ B &= T'_e(\gamma_1^0; N, N-1) - \gamma_1^0\, T''_e(\gamma_1^0; N, N-1) - 2, \\ C &= T_e(\gamma_1^0; N, N-1) - \gamma_1^0\, T'_e(\gamma_1^0; N, N-1) + \frac{1}{2}(\gamma_1^0)^2\, T''_e(\gamma_1^0; N, N-1) \end{aligned}$$

and retaining a solution $\gamma_1^{(2)}$ that is compatible with the requirement that $\mathbf{w} \in S_{N-1}$, we obtain an analytical approximation $T_*^{(2)}(N)$ to the critical temperature $T_*(N)$:

$$T_*^{(2)}(N) = 2\gamma_1^{(2)}(1 - \gamma_1^{(2)}). \tag{12}$$

A cheaper approximation to $T_*^{(1)}(N)$ to $T_*(N)$ can be obtained by first-order expansions of both $T_s(\gamma_1)$ and $T_e(\gamma_1; N, N-1)$.

To illustrate the approximations $T_*^{(1)}(N)$ and $T_*^{(2)}(N)$ of the critical temperature $T_B = T_*(N)$, numerically found bifurcation temperatures for ISM systems with dimensions between 8 and 30 are shown in figure 2 as circles. The approximations based on quadratic and linear expansions, $T_*^{(2)}(N)$ and $T_*^{(1)}(N)$, are plotted with bold solid and dashed lines, respectively. Also shown are the temperatures $1/N$ above which the maximum entropy equilibrium $\overline{\mathbf{w}}$ is stable. At bifurcation temperature, $\overline{\mathbf{w}}$ is already stable and equilibria at vertexes of simplex S_{N-1} lose stability. The analytical solutions $T_*^{(2)}(N)$ and $T_*^{(1)}(N)$ appear to approximate the bifurcation temperatures well.

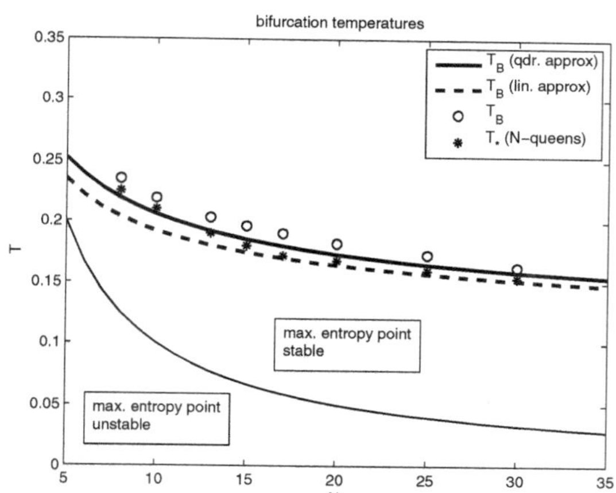

Fig. 2. Analytical approximations of the bifurcation temperature $T_B = T_*(N)$ for increasing ISM dimensionalities N. The approximations based on quadratic and linear expansions, $T_*^{(2)}(N)$ and $T_*^{(1)}(N)$, are plotted with bold solid and dashed lines, respectively. Numerically found bifurcation temperatures are shown as circles. The best performing temperatures for intermittent search in the N-queens problems are shown as stars.

We also numerically determined optimal temperature settings for intermittent search by SONN in the N-queens problems. Following [1], the SONN parameter β was set to $\beta = 0.8$[2]. The optimal neighborhood size increased with the problem size N from $L = 2$ (for $N = 8$), through $L = 3$ ($N = 10, 13$), $L = 4$ ($N = 15, 17, 20$), to $L = 5$ ($N = 25, 30$)[3]. Based on our extensive experimentation, the best performing temperatures for intermittent search in the N-queens

[2] Our experiments confirmed finding by Kwok and Smith that the choice of β is in general not sensitive to N.

[3] The increase of optimal neighborhood size L with increasing problem dimension N is in accordance with findings in [1].

problems are shown as stars. Clearly, as suggested by Kwok and Smith, there is a marked correspondence between the bifurcation temperatures of ISM equilibria and the best performing temperatures in intermittent search by SONN. The *analytically* obtained approximations critical temperatures predict the optimal working temperatures for SONN intermittent search very well. So far the critical temperatures have been determined only via extensive numerical simulations.

7 Conclusions

Self-organizing neural networks driven by softmax weight renormalization are capable of powerful intermittent search for high-quality solutions in difficult assignment optimization problems [1]. We have rigorously analyzed equilibria of the underlying renormalization process and derive *analytical* approximations to their critical bifurcation temperatures necessary for optimal SONN performance. The approximations are in good agreement with the temperature values found by numerical investigations.

References

1. Kwok, T., Smith, K.: Optimization via intermittency with a self-organizing neural network. Neural Computation **17** (2005) 2454–2481
2. Hopfield, J.: Neural networks and physical systems with emergent collective computational abilities. Proceedings of the National Academy of Science USA **79** (1982) 2554–2558
3. Smith, K.: Neural networks for combinatorial optimization: a review of more than a decade of research. INFORMS Journal on Computing **11** (1999) 15–34
4. Smith, K.: Solving the generalized quadratic assignment problem using a self-organizing process. In: Proceedings of the IEEE Int. Conf. on Neural Networks. Volume 4. (1995) 1876–1879
5. Smith, K., Palaniswami, M., Krishnamoorthy, M.: Neural techniques for combinatorial optimization with applications. IEEE Transactions on Neural Networks **9** (1998) 1301–1318
6. Kwok, T., Smith, K.: Performance-enhancing bifurcations in a self-organising neural network. In: Computational Methods in Neural Modeling: Proceedings of the 7th International Work-Conference on Artificial and Natural Neural Networks (IWANN'2003). Volume Lecture Notes in Computer Science, vol. 2686., Singapore, Springer-Verlag, Berlin (2003) 390–397
7. Langton, C.: Computation at the edge of chaos: Phase transitions and emergent computation. Physica D **42** (1990) 12–37
8. Tiňo, P.: Equilibria of iterative softmax and critical temperatures for intermittent search in self-organizing neural networks. Technical Report CSRP-06-07, University of Birmingham, School of Computer Science, http://www.cs.bham.ac.uk/~pxt/PAPERS/tino.tr06.pdf (2006)

Robust Simulation of Lamprey Tracking

Matthew Beauregard and Paul J. Kennedy

Faculty of IT, University of Technology, Sydney, PO Box 123,
Broadway, NSW 2007, Australia
paulk@it.uts.edu.au

Abstract. Biologically realistic computer simulation of vertebrates is a challenging problem with exciting applications in computer graphics and robotics. Once the mechanics of locomotion are available it is interesting to mediate this locomotion with higher level behavior such as target tracking. One recent approach simulates a relatively simple vertebrate, the lamprey, using recurrent neural networks to model the central pattern generator of the spine and a physical model for the body. Target tracking behavior has also been implemented for such a model. However, previous approaches suffer from deficiencies where particular orientations of the body to the target cause the central pattern generator to shutdown. This paper describes an approach to making target tracking more robust.

1 Introduction

Increasingly, digital media professionals are incorporating biologically realistic representations of artificial animals into films and computer games. Whilst representations of bodies, fur and skin have become increasingly realistic, it is challenging to model life–like movement and life–like behaviors such as tracking of targets. Vertebrate locomotion is a complex process that is difficult to imitate in simulated environments. Arms, legs, and spinal columns have many degrees of freedom that must be controlled in a co–ordinated way for stable locomotion to occur. However, life–like locomotion on its own is only the first step towards generating biologically realistic behavior. Other higher actions, beginning with target tracking and foraging, must be simulated on top of the locomotion to produce life–like behavior. Many of these types of behavior have been explored previously in the robotics and Artificial Life domains (eg. [1]), but usually with simple models of locomotion. The form of locomotion affects the higher level behavior. For example, swimming in a simulated fish involves movement of the head from side to side. Consequently, the inputs from simple models of eyes tracking an object in the environment change as the simulated animal's head moves. Target tracking must take this into account for robust behavior.

This paper examines target tracking behavior that has been implemented with specific inputs to a complex simulated fish spinal cord. Two previous approaches to tracking are described. However, these approaches suffer in that they do not sufficiently take into account head movements of the simulated animal and, consequently, are not robust in all situations. We describe a modification that makes the tracking more robust to movements of the target.

T.P. Runarsson et al. (Eds.): PPSN IX, LNCS 4193, pp. 641–650, 2006.

Digital characters in computer graphics are often composed of a skin (collection of surfaces) associated with a skeletal configuration or "armature" at various places. As the armature moves, the skin deforms with the resulting effect showing the character moving. Computation of movement of bones is often done with inverse kinematics [2]. Sequences of poses are compiled by an animator and replayed (with interpolation of the in between movement) to show the character performing actions. This gives precise control, allowing movements and deformations that are not physically possible in the real world. However, if the aim is life–like movement, these techniques may be tedious to apply.

A complementary approach is to model the anatomy of the animal in greater detail. The challenge is that detailed actual physiology of animals, at the neural level, is mostly unknown and very complex. One successful approach has been to start with simpler animals, for which knowledge of the neural pathways is available. The animal is modelled as a body and a spine consisting of connected oscillating clusters of recurrent neural networks. A (greatly) simplified model of simulated brain and eyes transmits impulses through the spine to motoneurons, which control tension in muscles along the body. The tension in the muscles subsequently applies forces to joints, which together with forces from an environment determine the position of the body. A system of differential equations represents the configuration of the spine and body. These are numerically integrated to determine the movement of body segments for particular neural and environmental inputs over time. Once locomotion from a simulated spine has been attained, target tracking can be implemented by modulating inputs to the spine from the eyes and simplified brain to produce locomotion towards targets.

One simple vertebrate that has been well studied is the lamprey, which is a jawless eel–shaped fish. It is primitive in an evolutionary sense with its major distinguishing feature being a large rounded sucker surrounding the mouth [3]. The spinal cord is a continuous column of neurons made up of around 100 clusters. Each cluster projects motoneurons to the surrounding muscles [4]. Lampreys swim by propagating a wave along the body from head to tail by phased muscular contraction. In the normal case, the wavelength of this travelling wave is constant and approximately corresponds to the length of the body; its frequency determines the speed of swimming. The lamprey has been studied over several decades (see [5] for a clear introduction and other papers in the same volume e.g. [6] for more details). A variety of simulations has been implemented and our model is based on one of these with minor modifications (see Section 2). Target tracking behavior appears to have been added to these previous simulations almost as an afterthought, mainly to illustrate the locomotion behavior. This is understandable given the significant amount of effort required just to build and simulate the model of locomotion. However, it is a shame because modulating biologically realistic locomotion systems with target tracking signals adds subtle and interesting complexities that must be addressed to maintain robustness and stability of the behavior. Section 3 reviews previous approaches to target tracking for lamprey models and section 4 describes our more robust approach.

2 Model

Ijspeert [4] groups neural models of the lamprey into three classes: biophysical, connectionist and mathematical. Biophysical models investigate the detailed low–level neurobiology (on the order on dozens of cells). Connectionist models are less realistic and are interested in connections *between* neurons. Mathematical models are more abstract and view the controller as a chain of oscillators with a focus on the couplings between them. Connectionist models are similar to dynamical recurrent neural networks and compute the mean firing rate of neurons. Our work takes the continuous time *leaky integrator* models used in [7] and [4] as a starting point. In contrast to these models, the neural and physical aspects of our simulation are combined into a single model, rather than two separate but interacting models. This gives significant improvements in simulation speed [8]. The rest of this section describes in detail the complex neural and physical model and where our model differs from [7] and [4]. Detailed knowledge is required to appreciate the effect of modulating inputs for target tracking and to allow replication of our work.

2.1 Neural Model

Biologically the lamprey spinal cord is a continuous column of neurons without clear boundaries but it can be considered as roughly 100 discrete but interconnected oscillators (or segmental networks). The combined assembly is known as a central pattern generator (CPG). The main types of neuron involved are: motoneurons (MN) projecting to muscles, excitatory interneurons (EIN) projecting to ipsilateral neurons (ie. those on the same side of the segment), lateral inhibitory interneurons (LIN) projecting to ipsilateral neurons, contralateral inhibitory interneurons (CIN) projecting to contralateral neurons (ie. the other side of the segment) and excitatory brain stem (BS) neurons that project from the brain. The controller consists of 100 segmental networks. Each model neuron represents a population of functionally similar neurons. Actual connections between segments are not well known, so Ekeberg in [7] chooses a simplified, symmetric coupling (except for connections from the CINs which are longer tailward). Parameters for both inter– and intrasegmental connections and extents are given in Table 1 and most of the connections for one segment are shown in Fig. 1. In order to limit output from neurons and to compensate neurons in segments near ends of the body (and have fewer intersegmental inputs), synaptic weights are scaled by dividing by the number of input segments. Ekeberg [7] also suggested supplying extra excitation to the first few segments of the spinal column in order to help generate a phase–lagged oscillation down the spine. However, we found in simulations [8] that this is not necessary and reduced the speed of the lamprey swimming. Accordingly, extra excitation was not applied in our model. As mentioned in [4], if the excitation levels for each side of the lamprey neural model are set independently and differently, the lamprey turns. This observation forms the basis for an approach to modulating the lamprey neural assembly with outputs from simple eyes to result in target tracking behavior.

Table 1. Neural connection configuration. From [4] with additions from [7] and separately–controllable left– and right–side excitation. Negative weights indicate inhibitory connections. Extents of connections to neighbor segments are given in brackets (headward and tailward, respectively).

To ↓	From: EIN_L	CIN_L	LIN_L	EIN_R	CIN_R	LIN_R	BS_L	BS_R
EIN_L	0.4 [2, 2]	-	-	-	-2 [1, 10]	-	2	0
CIN_L	3 [2, 2]	-	-1 [5, 5]	-	-2 [1, 10]	-	7	0
LIN_L	13 [5, 5]	-	-	-	-1 [1, 10]	-	5	0
MN_L	1 [5, 5]	-	-	-	-2 [5, 5]	-	5	0
EIN_R	-	-2 [1, 10]	-	0.4 [2, 2]	-	-	0	2
CIN_R	-	-2 [1, 10]	-	3 [2, 2]	-	-1 [5, 5]	0	7
LIN_R	-	-1 [1, 10]	-	13 [5, 5]	-	-	0	5
MN_R	-	-2 [5, 5]	-	1 [5, 5]	-	-	0	5

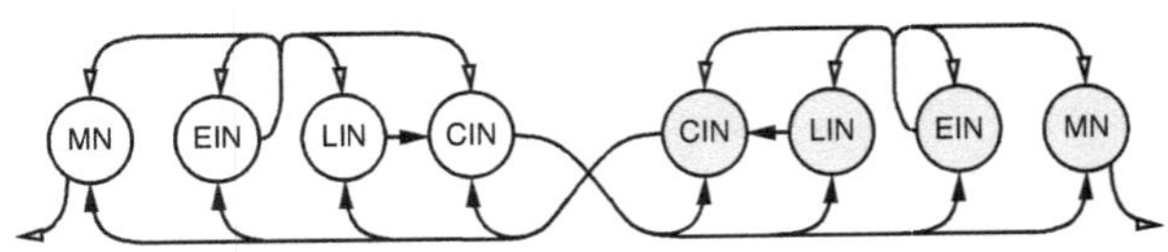

Fig. 1. Schematic of neural connections for one segment. Filled arrows are inhibitory.

Each neuron is modeled as a leaky integrator with a saturating transfer function. Let u be the mean firing frequency of the population of neurons, ξ_+ and ξ_- the delayed 'reactions' to excitatory and inhibitory input and ϑ the frequency adaptation (decrease in firing rate over time given a constant input) observed in some real neurons. Let w be the synaptic weights of excitatory and inhibitory presynaptic neuron groups ψ_+ and ψ_-, τ_D the time constant of dendritic sums, τ_A the time constant of frequency adaptation, μ a frequency adaptation constant, Θ the threshold and Γ the gain. It is not possible to directly measure values of these parameters, so values (Table 2) are hand–tuned to produce output matching physiological observations. The neuron is modeled as

$$\begin{aligned}
\dot{\xi}_+ &= \frac{1}{\tau_D}\left(\sum_{i\in\psi_+} u_i w_i - \xi_+\right)\\
\dot{\xi}_- &= \frac{1}{\tau_D}\left(\sum_{i\in\psi_-} u_i w_i - \xi_-\right)\\
\dot{\vartheta} &= \frac{1}{\tau_A}(u-\vartheta)\\
u &= 1 - e^{(\Theta-\xi_+)\Gamma} - \xi_- - \mu\vartheta \text{ if positive}\\
&\quad\; 0, \text{ otherwise.}
\end{aligned} \tag{1}$$

Table 2. Neuron parameters. From [7]. Symbols are explained in the text.

Neuron type	Θ	Γ	τ_D	μ	τ_A
EIN	-0.2	1.8	30 ms	0.3	400 ms
CIN	0.5	1.0	20 ms	0.3	200 ms
LIN	8.0	0.5	50 ms	0.0	-
MN	0.1	0.3	20 ms	0.0	-

2.2 Physical Model

As with the neural model, the physical lamprey body is modeled similarly to [7] and [4]. It is represented by ten links with nine joints between them each with one degree of freedom. Ten neural segments act on one body segment or link. Each link is modeled as a right elliptic cylinder with the major axes of the ellipses aligned vertically. All links have length l of 30 mm, height 30 mm with the width starting at a maximum of 20 mm at the head and decreasing towards the tail. Muscles appear on both sides of the body, attached to the centers of each segment. Muscles are modeled with a spring–and–damper arrangement, where the force exerted by the muscle is set using the spring constant. Local body curvature varies linearly with muscle length. The body and the neural network are linked by having motoneuron excitation drive the muscular spring constants. The body is represented in our model in two dimensions as rectangles with joints at the midpoints of their sides. The position of a link i is described by (x_i, y_i, φ_i), where x_i and y_i are the co–ordinates of the rectangle centre and φ_i is the angle of a line through the centre and the joint with respect to the x–axis (see Fig. 2). Constraint forces are used to keep body links together. The physical parameter values for the links are the same as those in [4].

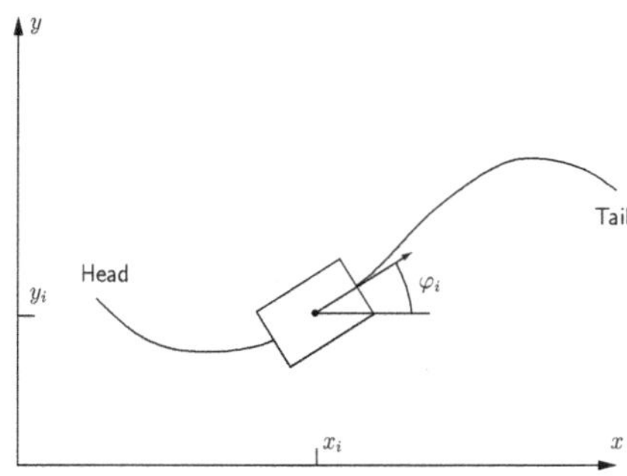

Fig. 2. Co–ordinates describing the position of a link. From [7].

Movement of the body results from the interaction of three forces: torques T generated by the muscles, forces W_i from the water and constraint forces F_i and F_{i-1} that keep the body links together. These forces determine the acceleration of the links according to Newton's law of motion. Change in position for links $i \in \{1, \ldots, N\}$ is determined by numerical integration of the equations of motion.

$$\begin{aligned} m_i \ddot{x}_i &= W_{i,x} + F_{i,x} - F_{i-1,x} \\ m_i \ddot{y}_i &= W_{i,y} + F_{i,y} - F_{i-1,y} \\ I_i \ddot{\varphi}_i &= T_i - T_{i-1} - (F_{i-1,x} + F_{i,x}) \frac{l_i}{2} \sin \varphi_i \\ &\quad + (F_{i-1,y} + F_{i,y}) \frac{l_i}{2} \cos \varphi_i \end{aligned} \tag{2}$$

As described above, muscles are modeled as springs directly connected to sides of links. Force exerted by each spring on its associated joint is determined not only by the local curvature of the body but also linearly by the output of the motoneurons in the associated segments. Let M_L and M_R be the left and right motoneuron activity and assign parameters α (=3 N mm), β (=0.3 N mm), γ (=10) and δ (=30 N mm ms). As in [7] the torque is defined as

$$T_i = \alpha (M_L - M_R) + \beta (M_L + M_R + \gamma) (\varphi_{i+1} - \varphi_i) + \delta (\dot{\varphi}_{i+1} - \dot{\varphi}_i) .$$

Speed of motion through water in our case is sufficiently high that we only account for inertial water force which is proportional to the square of the speed:

$$W = \rho v^2 \frac{A}{2} C$$

where ρ is the fluid density, v object speed, A area parallel to movement and C drag coefficient. The abbreviation $\lambda = \rho \frac{A}{2} C$ is made in [7], together with the simplification $W = W_\perp + W_\| = v_\perp^2 \lambda_\perp + v_\|^2 \lambda_\|$ and values of $\lambda_\perp$ and $\lambda_\|$ for links.

Body segments are constrained such that for adjacent segments, joints for the facing sides must be in the same position (ie., the links stay joined together). The joint position is expressed in terms of x_i, y_i and φ_i for $i \in \{1, \ldots, n-1\}$, so

$$\begin{aligned} x_i + \frac{l_i}{2} \cos \varphi_i &= x_{i+1} - \frac{l_{i+1}}{2} \cos \varphi_{i+1} \\ y_i + \frac{l_i}{2} \sin \varphi_i &= y_{i+1} - \frac{l_{i+1}}{2} \sin \varphi_{i+1} \end{aligned} \tag{3}$$

Equations (2) and (3) form a differential–algebraic equation (DE) system [7] typical of non–minimal coordinate systems that can be numerically integrated.

The models described above were implemented in C++ and rendered graphically in Python using PyOpenGL [9]. For details of the implementation and approaches to increasing simulation speed, together with typical model behavior see [8]. A 10 s simulation takes 620 s to run on an AMD 1800 CPU. After a start up period the steady state swimming speed and characteristics observed in our model are similar to those observed by [4].

3 Approaches Towards Target Tracking

Even a simple, hard–coded oscillator can generate appropriate neural outputs for straight–line swimming. However, for applications such as target tracking, the pattern generator must be able to accept and respond to changing conditions in the environment while still emitting a stable oscillation pattern. It must have inputs that cause it to change its outputs in relevant ways, and be able to accept a wide range of varying inputs without the oscillation collapsing and a subsequent stop of locomotion. In summary, the CPG must be robust to changes in the environment whilst producing reasonable behavior.

Ijspeert describes two different approaches to making the lamprey swim towards a target [4,10]: (i) simple bearing–based tracking and (ii) exponentiated bearing–based tracking. Both approaches build on the observation that the lamprey can be made to turn by supplying different levels of excitation to the left and right halves of each segment (see Figure 3). Two notional "retinas" supply excitation that varies according to the relative bearing of the target. Neither case considers the distance to the target.

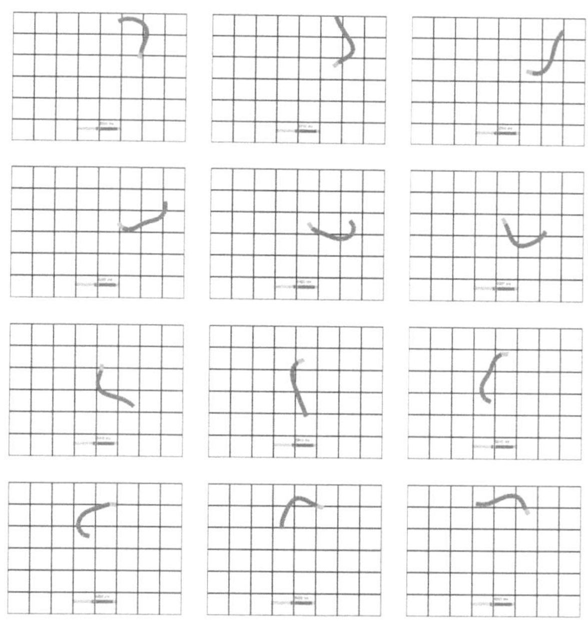

Fig. 3. Circling behavior with $BS_L = 0.1$ and $BS_R = 0.8$. Gridlines 100 mm apart.

3.1 Simple Bearing–Based Tracking

In this arrangement [4], retina output varies linearly with bearing to the target. The lamprey is considered to have a "dead zone" in that it does not respond to targets bearing more than 150° from the head axis. Any bearing more acute than this is linearly transformed into an excitation between 0 and 1 for the side of the body on which the target lies, and no excitation on the opposite side.

This model of vision is somewhat effective, but suffers from two major weaknesses. The most obvious is the dead zone: if the target is located out of the field of view, brainstem excitation drops to 0 resulting in a shutdown of the pattern generators. Even if the randomly moving target eventually reappears, the lamprey may not be able to restart its swimming. The spinal cord needs specific startup conditions or phased oscillation will not occur.

More subtle is the effect of linearly mapping the bearing to excitation. As the bearing to the target approaches 0°, so does the excitation from the brainstem. The more the lamprey turns to face the target, the less excitation is supplied, often resulting in shutdown. The case illustrated in [4] is a favorable one where the target crosses the lamprey's field of view repeatedly, so that the lamprey spends very little time unexcited. However, not all random movements of the target will be so fortunate.

3.2 Exponentiated Bearing–Based Tracking

A more complicated tracking system for a salamander simulation is developed in [10]. Here, the retinas are considered to have axes offset from the head's major axis. (The offset is not given but would be about ±30°.) Excitation again ranges between 0 and 1 but is calculated as $R = e^{-\alpha \Delta\phi^2}$ where $\alpha = 0.0005$ and $\Delta\phi$ is the angle between the axis and the target. In effect, excitation is 67% for a target directly ahead of the lamprey, marginal (10%) at 90° away and nil at 150°. Retina output depends only on the bearing of the target from the major axis of the head, with an angular offset.

Observations of experiments with this tracking arrangement demonstrate that it performs far better than the linear mapping. The CPG receives levels of excitation sufficient to sustain pattern generation for almost the full range of bearings within the "dead zone" seen in linear mapping, and in particular a target directly in front of the lamprey causes enough excitation for effective pursuit. However the problem of the lamprey becoming becalmed when it reaches orientations where the target is in the dead zone remains.

4 Bearing-Based Tracking with Foraging

The previous section relates two methods of implementing tracking behavior to modulate the inputs to a lamprey simulation. However, these approaches suffer from the problem that the lamprey can become becalmed in some situations.

Our solution to the becalming problem is to apply a foraging algorithm when the target disappears from the field of view. This is implemented by sending the lamprey into a fast circling action when the target disappears from view. One input to the spine (arbitrarily the right–side) is set to 0.8 and the other to 0.1 until the target is recovered. These values result in a fast, tight circling motion without being so excessively high as to swamp the CPG. In combination with the exponentiated tracking arrangement the lamprey becomes able to effectively track targets exhibiting a wide variety of random behaviour: straight, circling or weaving motion, and holding stationary or almost stationary (Figure 4).

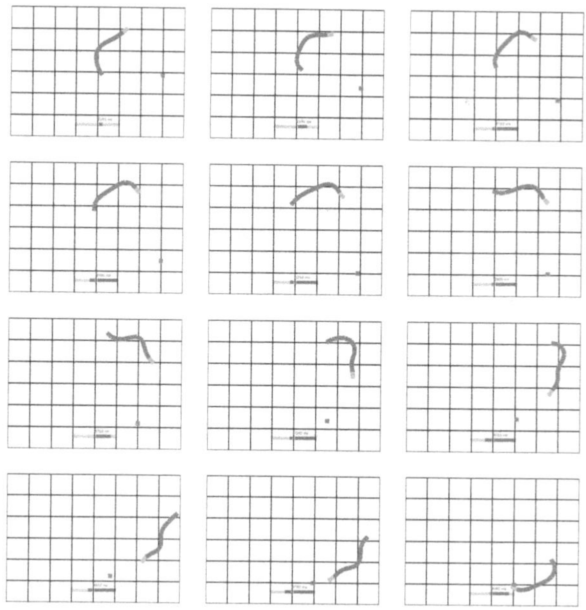

Fig. 4. Target-tracking behavior. Gridlines are 100 mm apart.

4.1 Observations

Although exhaustive tests have not been conducted, in general the CPG withstands the constantly–changing brainstem inputs remarkably well. It should be noted that apart from the variation in input caused by the random movements of the target, the lamprey's head moves from side to side during normal swimming, causing a 6 Hz oscillation in the brainstem activation. That the CPG generally continues to function even when subjected to an oscillatory signal of the same frequency but not the same phase is testament to its stability.

This resistance is not perfect. In runs with a fixed target the lamprey will from time to time cease forward motion and propagate waves in place, or even briefly move in reverse. These effects are short–lived, with the pause lasting around 700 ms before being overcome by the natural phase delay of the CPG. In runs with a randomly moving target this effect is much rarer, though still in evidence. The random component in excitation levels that results from the random motion makes the particular confluence of oscillations described above less likely to occur. Random target motion also reduces the likelihood of triggering the permanent becalming conditions described with the previous approaches.

Finally, it should be noted that the arrangement of two sensors tied to two physical systems is distinctly reminiscent of Braitenberg's famous vehicles [11]. The lamprey exhibits the source–seeking, AGGRESSIVE behaviour of Vehicle 2b, despite being wired as a Vehicle 2a. This is of course because increased activity on a given side of the lamprey propels it towards that direction, while increased activity in the motor of a Braitenberg vehicle propels it away.

5 Conclusion

Simulation of lifelike locomotion has applications to computer graphics and robotics. Once locomotion is achieved it is interesting to simulate higher level behavior such as target tracking. Previous approaches to target tracking in neural simulations of a lamprey suffer from deficiencies where the lamprey loses neural input and is becalmed in some configurations. We present an approach to overcoming this problem based on an underlying foraging behavior and show simulation results. There are several opportunities for farther work, including identification of quantitative measures of the behavior despite the long simulation times involved. We are interested in determining whether other patterns of foraging than tight circling, such as slow random movements, also solve the problem. Also, we plan to explore other higher level behaviors and apply similar models to other skeletal configurations and armatures within computer graphics animation packages.

References

1. Pfeifer, R., Scheier, C.: Understanding Intelligence. MIT Press (1999)
2. Foley, J.D., van Dam, A., Feiner, S.K., Hughes, J.F.: Computer graphics: principles and practice. 2nd in C edn. Addison–Wesley (1996)
3. Janvier, P.: Tree of Life: Hyperoartia. URL: http://tolweb.org/tree?group=Hyperoartia (1997)
4. Ijspeert, A.J.: Design of artificial neural oscillatory circuits for the control of lamprey- and salamander-like locomotion using evolutionary algorithms. PhD thesis, Department of Artificial Intelligence, University of Edinburgh (1998)
5. Lansner, A., Ekeberg, Ö., Grillner, S.: Realistic modeling of burst generation and swimming in lamprey. In Stein, P.S.G., Grillner, S., Selverston, A.I., Stuart, D.G., eds.: Neurons, Networks and Motor Behaviour. The MIT Press (1997) 165–172
6. Wallén, P.: Spinal networks and sensory feedback in the control of undulatory swimming in lamprey. In Stein, P.S.G., Grillner, S., Selverston, A.I., Stuart, D.G., eds.: Neurons, Networks and Motor Behaviour. The MIT Press (1997) 75–81
7. Ekeberg, Ö.: A combined neuronal and mechanical model of fish swimming. Biological Cybernetics **69** (1993) 363–374
8. Beauregard, M., Kennedy, P.J.: Fast simulation of animal locomotion: lamprey swimming. To appear in Symposium on Professional Practice at 19th IFIP World Computer Congress, Santiago, Chile, 20–25 August 2006 (2006)
9. Fletcher, M.C., Liebscher, R.: PyOpenGL – the Python OpenGL binding. URL: http://pyopengl.sourceforge.net/ (2005)
10. Ijspeert, A., Arbib, M.: Visual tracking in simulated salamander locomotion. Proceedings of the Sixth International Conference of The Society for Adaptive Behavior (SAB2000), Paris, France, 11–15 September 2000 (2000)
11. Braitenberg, V.: Vehicles. The MIT Press (1984)

Evolutionary Behavior Acquisition for Humanoid Robots

Deniz Aydemir and Hitoshi Iba

Graduate School of Frontier Sciences, Department of Frontier Informatics
Tokyo University, Tokyo, Japan
{deniz, iba}@iba.k.u-tokyo.ac.jp
http://www.iba.k.u-tokyo.ac.jp/english/

Abstract. This paper describes and analyzes a series of experiments to develop a general evolutionary behavior acquisition technique for humanoid robots. The robot's behavior is defined by joint controllers evolved concurrently. Each joint controller consists of a series of primitive actions defined by a chromosome. By using genetic algorithms with specifically designed genetic operators and novel representations, complex behaviors are evolved from the primitive actions defined. Representations are specifically tailored to be useful in trajectory generation for humanoid robots. The effectiveness of the method is demonstrated by two experiments: a handstand and a limbo dance behavioral tasks (leaning the body backwards so as to pass under a fixed height bar).

1 Introduction

The recent remarkable progression of robotics research makes highly precise and advanced robots available today. Despite the availability of sophisticated robots, acquisition of behavioral tasks remains as a big hurdle in the field. Currently, several approaches are prominent in evolutionary behavior acquisition. [1], [2], [3] investigate appropriate neural network architectures using genetic algorithms for the adjustment of network parameters. Authors of these papers try to evolve behavioral tasks mainly based on navigation in a constructed environment for the wheeled robot Khepera. Although the results from these experiments are promising in terms of conceptual findings, there exist very few applications of the neuro-evolutionary techniques for more complex and high mobility robots such as humanoid robots. Another approach in evolutionary behavior acquisition is evolutionary gait optimization undertaken by the authors [4], [5]. These experiments involve optimization of a readily available controller for a previously specified behavior, such as quadruple walking. Main drawback here is the assumption that a hand designed controller is readily available. In this paper, we take a slightly different approach than the techniques discussed above. Rather than optimizing a hand designed controller or trying to evolve primitive behaviors conceptualized with neural networks, we consider the behavior acquisition task as a combinatorial optimization task where the task at hand is decomposable into primitive actions, and the goal is to find the optimum sequence (behavioral sequence) of those primitive actions which constitute the desired complex behavior. In this regard, evolving feedback controllers is beyond the scope and aim of this paper. Before

T.P. Runarsson et al. (Eds.): PPSN IX, LNCS 4193, pp. 651 – 660, 2006.

delving into details of the devised GA architecture we would like to discuss the difficulties and restrictions regarding the humanoid robots.

2 Peculiarities of Humanoid Robots

Balancing requirements for biped humanoid robots are governed by complex equations and are mostly specific to the generated motion patterns. One general approach in controlling the balance of a walking biped humanoid robot is Zero Moment Point (ZMP) [7]. ZMP computation requires the precise knowledge of robot dynamics, center of mass location and inertia of each link involved in the motion pattern. Another approach which requires relatively limited knowledge of robot dynamics is Inverted Pendulum Model (IPM). However, IPM is inapplicable in cases where the foot must be placed in specified locations during the phase of a motion (Fig.1a.) In order to resolve this issue, hybrid approaches, combining ZMP and IPM methods are also proposed [8]. The main difficulties with these approaches are the need for the precise knowledge of robot dynamics which is not available all the time, and the customization or in some cases redesign of the dynamics models for each individual motion. Moreover, ZMP based approaches are not directly applicable in situations where the robot's feet have no contact with the ground as demonstrated in the handstand task (Fig. 1b) or in case of interacting with a third object such as kicking a ball (Fig. 1c).

(a) (b) (c)

Fig. 1. Typical examples where traditional methods fall short. (a) Walking on specified locations (b) Handstand task (c) Ball kicking.

There exist also motion generation techniques based on Interactive Evolutionary Computation (IEC) for people who have no specialized knowledge of humanoid robots [9]. However, IEC methods suffer from the subjective evaluation criteria incurred by the human factor involved and still require the developer to account for the inverse kinematics equations governing the balancing issues between the key frames of a motion [10]. Addressing these issues, we devise a general learning scheme based on genetic algorithms which requires only minimum knowledge of humanoid robot dynamics and the balancing requirements of a particular motion pattern. With the proper selection of a primitive action, the genetic algorithm implicitly accounts for the balancing requirements and the acquisition of desired behavior, where traditional methods would require custom balancing methods based on ZMP and/or IMP along with complicated forward and inverse kinematics computation. The proposed method has the following advantages over the traditional methods.

- Alleviates the need for ZMP, IMP based balancing methods
- Does not require inverse and forward kinematics calculations
- Does not require a precise knowledge of the robot dynamics and joint interactions
- Originality and creativity in behaviors achieved through evolutionary process

In the upcoming section we present our approach for finding an effective and compact representation to be used in the evolutionary algorithm for the humanoid robot joint controllers.

3 GA Architecture

3.1 Problem Representation

The representation of a joint controller makes use of two significant trajectory path characteristics. Trajectory paths are continuous and mostly sinusoidal in nature. Considering these two properties, a joint controller is represented as a sequence of allele pairs denoting the transition point and type of motions in terms of primitive actions. In physical terms, transition points correspond to places where the derivation of a trajectory curve changes, i.e. the point where the direction of a motion alternates or stops. When composed of primitive actions, a transition point is defined as a change in the primitive action type belonging to a behavioral sequence. For example, for the chromosome in Fig. 2, gene locations 3rd, 6th, 9th positions represent the transition points for a 10 unit time motion of a particular trajectory.

(0,1) (3,0) (6,1) (9,0)

Fig. 2. A chromosome using absolute timings for transition points in joint trajectories, and a binary field to denote the type of transition

Based on this definition, transition points of primitive actions in the behavioral sequence and the type of transition (positive, negative or still) is represented as a gene in the form of an allele pair (t_τ, p_i). This defines a set of primitive actions starting from time t_τ bounded by the next gene pair's transition time field $t_{\tau+1}$ in the chromosome. Parameter p_i denotes the type of transition based on the previous p_{i-1} value except for the initial p_0. The first transition type value p_0 exceptionally defines the type of the first primitive action, regardless of the previous transition type value. Since a binary field is used for the transition type field, each joint involved in a behavior must initiate a rotation either with a positive or negative slope, i.e. initially no joint is allowed to stay still. The main advantage of this representation is the fact that using absolute timings for transition points alleviates the need to keep the genes in sorted order. So the order of genes is irrelevant of their interpretation and the representation is not susceptible to fixed locus assumption [12]. Another advantage is the relatively easy handling of boundary conditions for the primitive action timings. As the transition timing is bounded by the experiment time, there is no processing necessary to adjust the transition points. Finally, restricting the problem representation to only sinusoidal nature motions effectively reduces the search space explored by the evolutionary algorithm.

3.2 Mutation Operator

The mutation operator is the customized version of the single point mutation which is applicable to allele pair locations. With a given probability p_{mut} , a specific transition point is perturbed with discrete values ranging from a negative lower bound to a positive upper bound. The pseudo code given below describes this variation process for the transition time field of a gene. *N* denotes the maximum value the transition time field can take. As for boundary conditions, each chromosome is thought to be circular. A modulus operation is applied after the perturbation of the gene location containing the transition point which removes the edge effects.

Pseudocode for range mutation operator.

```
Range_mut( offspring, pmut, lower, upper )
  L = length( offspring )
  for( i = 0 to L do )
    prob = random( 0, 1 )
    if( prob > pmut  )
      var = random_int( lower, upper )
      offspring[i].time =
        ( offspring[i].time + var + N ) mod N
    endif
  done
```

3.3 Postprocessing of a Chromosome

Since chromosomes accommodate absolute timings for trajectory transition points, the very first gene defining the rotation of a joint for the initial time step may disappear through the evolution process due to the genetic operations applied. Similarly, duplicate genes can occur inside a chromosome due to the same reason. The strategy employed for ensuring the existence of the initial gene is to find the gene with a minimum transition time field inside the chromosome and reset the field to zero. To eliminate the duplicate genes, simply repeat the genetic operation causing duplicates until we get distinct transition time fields for each allele pair inside the chromosome.

3.4 Fitness Evaluation

Scoring of individuals is done using these components as shown in eq.(1) and (2). In eq.(1), waist, chest and ankle altitudes are simply summed up to evaluate the fitness of individuals for the handstand behavior. Following this calculation, individuals having a waist altitude greater than their ankle altitudes are given a penalty proportional to the waist altitude gained. This penalty is used to eliminate the individuals trying to gain fitness by only raising their chest and waist altitudes in the early generations.

Table 1. Components of the fitness evaluation for the handstand task

Variable Name	Value
waist_alt	Waist Altitude(cm)
chest_alt	Chest Altitude(cm)
ankle_alt	Ankle Altitude(cm)

$$Fitness = waist\_alt + chest\_alt + ankle\_alt\,. \tag{1}$$

$$Fitness = Fitness - waist\_alt.\ (if\ waist\_alt > ankle\_alt\ )\,. \tag{2}$$

For the limbo dance behavior, components used in the fitness evaluations are listed in Table 2. First of all, a target point in the three dimensional space is chosen just behind the humanoid robot specified by the coordinates *target_x, target_y and target_z.* The Euclidian distance between this target point and the center of the arm ankle segment of the humanoid robot is calculated as given in eq.(3). Accommodating this calculated distance and a constant *k1,* a minimization procedure of the Euclidian distance between the robots arm and the target point is undertaken in eq.(4). Constant *k2 in* eq.(4) is used such that, *k2 > elapsed * k3,* to separate fall situations from the stable ones.

Table 2. Components of the fitness evaluation for the limbo dance task

Variable Name	Expression
arm_pos_x	X coordinate of arm ankle
arm_pos_y	Y coordinate of arm ankle
arm_pos_z	Z coordinate of arm ankle
target_x	X coordinate of target position
target_y	Y coordinate of target position
target_z	Z coordinate of target position
elapsed	Elapsed simulation time

$$Euclid\_dist = \text{Distance}(\ arm\_pos, target\ )\,. \tag{3}$$

$$Fitness = (\ k1 - Euclid\_dist\ ) + k2\,. \tag{4}$$

$$Fitness = elapsed * k3\ (\ if\ fall\ )\,. \tag{5}$$

4 Experiments and Results

We performed two experiments in order to show the applicability and generality of our approach. The first behavior attempted is a handstand behavior and the second is limbo dance behavior.

4.1 Robot Simulation Environment

We use the simulation environment available from Open Architecture Humanoid Robotics Platform (OpenHRP) which consists of a simulator and motion control library of humanoid robots [13]. Humanoid robot HOAP-1 manufactured by Fujitsu Automaton Limited is used for the experiments. HOAP-1 has 20 degrees of freedom (DOF). Robot is about 6kgs in weight and 48cms in height.

4.2 Handstand Behavior

The main goal in the handstand task is to properly raise the legs while balancing the whole body on the hands and optionally the forehead. Joints evolved for this behavior are waist, arm and knees. Main parameters and experiment settings are shown in Table 3. Since the trajectories are long and require less precision, the primitive action is allowed to have a coarse granularity. A chromosome is designed for each degree of freedom for all joint types as given in Fig.1. However, instead of designing a pair of chromosomes for symmetrical joints, one joint is represented by a single chromosome and the symmetrical reflection is taken for the symmetric joint on the other side of the body. This effectively reduces the required number of chromosomes by half.

Table 3. Genetic algorithm parameters and experiment settings for the handstand task

Parameter	Value
Population size	100
Generation size	50
Chromosome Length	30
Selection	Roulette wheel
Range mutation probability	0.1
Crossover probability	0.9
Primitive action	0.27radian/s (open loop)

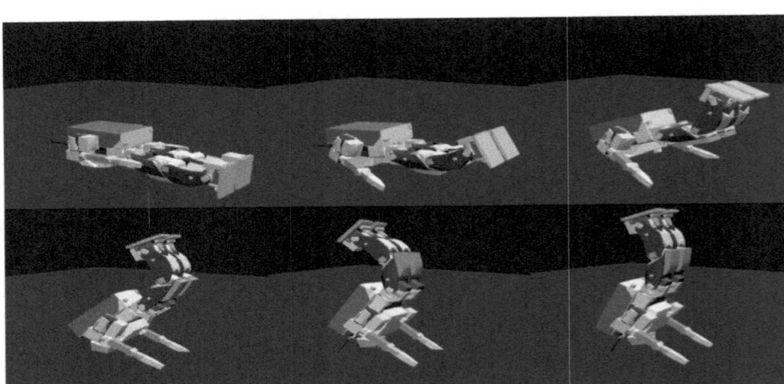

Fig. 3. Significant moments from the handstand behavior experiment of the best individual evolved. Initial position and screenshots from the 4th, 8th, 12th, 16th, 20th seconds are displayed.

The acquired handstand behavior can be said to have several human like properties. First of all, the robot wide opens its arms to properly balance itself starting from the middle top frame in Fig. 3. Next, in the down left frame, again using the arm joint, the robot attains more height by closing the arm joints. Lastly, the robot bends its knees while raising its legs, possibly not to fall, and then finally stretches its knees to attain more altitude, in the down right frame.

4.3 Limbo Dance Posture

The main objective of the dance is to lower the upper body along with hips and knees to walk under a fixed height horizontal bar. For the humanoid robot, the task is simplified to achieving the necessary posture to pass under the bar.

(a) Simulation

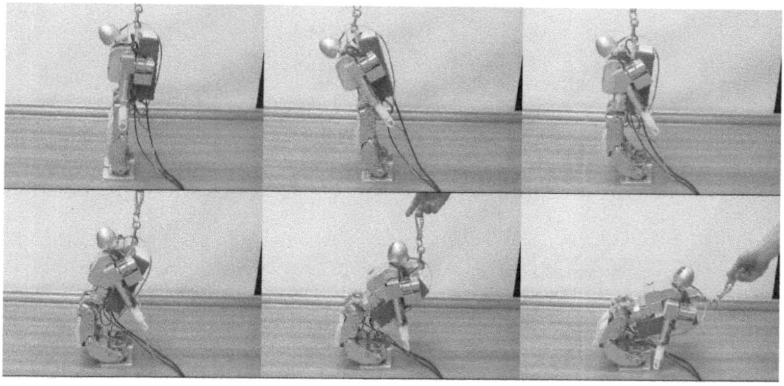

Fig. 4. Simulation and real experiment results for the limbo dance task

For the limbo dance behavior, a counter intuitive and an unpredictable result arose. One would expect the humanoid robot to initially bend its upper body backwards to achieve the necessary limbo posture. However, as can be seen in top middle frame in Fig. 4, the robot initially bends its body forward, evidently to compensate for the improper balancing caused by the rotation of knee joints. This behavior may as well be attributed to the fact that the battery pack attached to the back of the humanoid robot forbids an initial backward lean and initially mandates a forward lean to shift the center of mass forward in order to keep the balance in the following steps of this behavioral sequence. Despite this unexpected constraint, the humanoid robot successfully learns the complex behavior governing the interactions among the knee, ankle and waist joints, using this exceptional balancing strategy to achieve the necessary limbo posture in a stable manner.

5 Discussion

Empirical results regarding the handstand and limbo dance behavior suggest that both the evolutionary architecture and in particular the problem representation look promising as a possible solution to address problems in complex behavior acquisition for humanoid robots. Experiments showed that the method is applicable to different behavior acquisition tasks with minor changes. Moreover, the behaviors acquired by the humanoid robot surprisingly bears resemblance to human designed controllers and at some points surpasses the ideas and the predictions existent in a hand designed program. This became especially apparent in the limbo dance behavior when the robot unexpectedly started with a forward body lean to keep its balance although the objective of the behavior is to attain a backward lean.

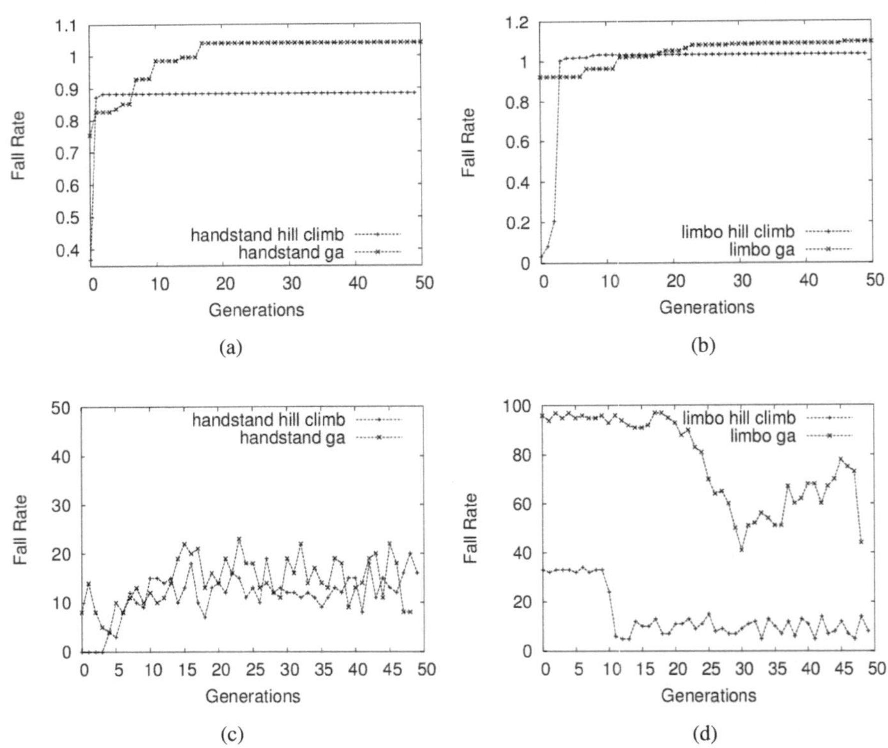

Fig. 5. Best fitness values for (a) handstand task and (b) limbo dance task. Fall rates for (c) limbo dance task and (d) handstand task.

Comparative results are also provided with a next ascent hill climbing algorithm in Fig. 5. Solutions obtained with the hill climbing algorithm tend to have low fall rates when compared to the genetic algorithm used as shown in Fig. 5c and 5d. However, results in Fig. 5a show that next ascent hill climbing method is incompetent for the handstand task and the solutions improve only up to 3rd generation, finally ending up with a stable but premature posture. As for the limbo dance task, hill climbing algorithm shows better performance until the 20th generation with a low fall rate. However, after this point the genetic algorithm generates better solutions than the hill climbing algorithm, with the best individual having 5cm higher fitness value as shown in Fig. 5b.

6 Conclusion and Future Research

In this paper we presented a general approach in evolutionary behavior acquisition for high mobility robots. The empirical results show clearly that evolutionary algorithms with problem specific representations possess the potential of achieving more than a satisfactory level of success in high level behavior acquisition tasks for humanoid robots. The experiments have also demonstrated that genetic algorithms can be used to evolve complex behaviors without the need for understanding the detailed dynamics and physics of the humanoid robot and the desired behavior. Another significant result is the observed creativity and the originality in the behaviors which are comparable to human designed controllers. For future work, we are planning to include the action granularity and dynamics parameters of the joints into the learning process to evolve more complex behaviors. Furthermore, we would like to conduct experiments for planning tasks such as [14] using the behaviors learned here as primitives and transferring the simulation results on the real robot for the handstand task as well.

References

1. I. Harvey, P. Husbands, and D. Cliff, "Issues in Evolutionary Robotics," Proceedings of the Second International Conference on Simulation of Adaptive Behavior (SAB92), MIT Press, Cambridge, MA (1993) 364-373
2. I. Harvey, P. Husbands, D. Cliff, A. Thompson, and N. Jakobi, "Evolutionary robotics: The Sussex approach," Robotics and Autonomous Systems (1997) 205–224.
3. S. Nolfi, "Evolving non-Trivial Behaviors on Real Robots: A garbage collecting robot," Robotics and Autonomous Systems (1997) 187-198
4. S. Chernova, M. Veloso, "An Evolutionary Approach To Gait Learning For Four-Legged Robots," Robots, In Proceedings of IROS, Sendai Japan (2004)
5. T. Rofer, "Evolutionary Gait-Optimization Using a Fitness Function Based on Proprioception," Lecture Notes in Artificial Intelligence, Springer (2005) 310–322
6. S. Nolfi, "Evolutionary Robotics: Exploiting the full power of self-organization," Connection Science, (1998) 10(3–4)
7. K. Nishiwaki, S. Kagami, Y. Kuniyoshi, M. Inaba, and H. Inoue, "Online generation of humanoid walking motion based on a fast generation method of motion pattern that follows desired zmp," Proceedings of the 2002 IEEE/RSJ Intl. Conference on Intelligent Robots and Systems, EPFL, Lausanne, Switzerland (2002) 2684–2689

8. S. Kajita, F. Kanehim, and K. Kaneko, "Biped Walking Pattern Generation by using Preview Control of Zero-Moment Point," Proc. on the ICR.4 (2003) 1620-1626
9. H. Takagi "Interactive Evolutionary Computation: System optimization based on human subjective evaluation," IEEE Int'l Conf. on Intelligent Engineering System (1998) 1-6
10. T. Yanase, and H. Iba, "Evolutionary Motion Design for Humanoid Robots," In Proc. of the Genetic and Evolutionary Computation Conference (2006) (To appear)
11. G. P. Wagner and L. Altenberg, "Complex adaptations and the evolution of evolvability," Evolution (1996), vol. 50, no. 3, 967–976
12. D. E. Goldberg, K. Deb, H. Kargupta, and G. Harik, "Rapid, accurate optimization of difficult problems using fast messy genetic algorithms," in Proc. 5th Int. Conf. on Genetic Algorithms. San Mateo, CA: Morgan Kaufmann (1993) 56–64.
13. F. Kanehiro, S. Kajita, and H. Hirukawa "OpenHRP: Open Architecture Humanoid Robotics Platform," The International Journal of Robotics Research (2004) vol. 23, No. 2 155-165
14. S. Kamio and H. Iba, "Random Sampling Algorithm for Multi-agent Cooperation Planning," Proc. of IEEE/RSJ International Conference on Intelligent Robotics and Systems (2005) 1676-1681.

Modelling Group-Foraging Behaviour with Particle Swarms

Cecilia Di Chio[1], Riccardo Poli[1], and Paolo Di Chio[2]

[1] Department of Computer Science,
University of Essex, UK
{cdichi, rpoli}@essex.ac.uk
[2] Dipartimento di Sistemi e Istituzioni per l'Economia,
University of L'Aquila, Italy
pdc@ec.univaq.it

Abstract. Despite the many features that the behaviour of the standard particle swarm algorithm shares with grouping behaviour in animals (e.g. social attraction and communication between individuals), this biologically inspired technique has been mainly used in classical optimisation problems (i.e. finding the optimal value in a fitness landscape). We present here a novel application for particle swarms: the simulation of *group-foraging* in animals. Animals looking for food sources are modelled as particles in a swarm moving over an abstract food landscape. The particles are guided to the food by a smell (or *aura*), which surrounds it and whose intensity is proportional to the amount of food available. The results show that this new extended version of the algorithm produces qualitatively realistic behaviour. For example, the simulation shows the emergence of group-foraging behaviour among particles.

1 Introduction

The particle swarm optimisation (PSO) algorithm is a function optimisation tool based on the simulation of a simplified social model, the *particle swarm* [4]. The algorithm uses a population (*swarm*) of candidate solutions (*particles*) that fly over the fitness landscape looking for optima. In the original version, the particles are driven by two forces which attract them to the best location encountered both by any other member of the swarm and by themselves.

Despite its socio-biological background, the field of applications for PSOs has mainly been the optimisation of nonlinear functions. In [3], we introduced a new way to use PSOs for the simulation of ecological processes, so far largely restricted to the field of individual-based modelling in ecology (for a review, see [2]). In particular, we looked at a classical problem in behavioural ecology: the *group-foraging* problem. With this paper, we extend our previous work by introducing more realistic features for the food sources. In particular, food sources are surrounded by an *aura*, which can be interpreted as the smell the food releases, and which attracts the particles to the source. Our objective is not only to study the emergence of grouping behaviour among particles, but also to understand which is the most successful design and the best parameter settings for

T.P. Runarsson et al. (Eds.): PPSN IX, LNCS 4193, pp. 661–670, 2006.

the particle swarm algorithm to allow this emergence. Our research is part of a multidisciplinary project called *XPS*[1]. One of the goals of XPS is to extend the particle swarm algorithm with strategies from biology. Modelling group-foraging is just a first step towards the simulation of more general and complex group-behaviour in animals. We necessarily have to start simulating simple behaviours, but we intend to progressively add complexity, and eventually obtain a model as complete as possible of animal social behaviour.

The paper is structured as follows. In section 2 we give a brief introduction to the field of behavioural ecology and the problem of group-foraging. Section 3 describes our approach to the problem: the Food Particle Swarm (FPS) algorithm. In section 4 we summarise the settings for the experiments and present and discuss the results of our simulations. We conclude in section 5.

2 Behavioural Ecology and the Group-Foraging Problem

Behavioural ecology is the branch of evolutionary biology which studies the ecological and evolutionary basis for animal behaviour, i.e. what are the "historical" reasons for certain animal behaviour and what is the role an animal's behaviour plays in allowing it to adapt to its environment. Among the more complex and intriguing animal behaviours, group-living is certainly one of the most studied, being such a widespread phenomenon in the animal kingdom [5]. Two general requirements for grouping behaviour are: (1) individuals have to be close to each other in space and time (e.g. the elective group size concept developed by Pitcher (see [5]) requires that the animals are close enough to each other in order to allow a continuous exchange of information), and (2) animals must show *social attraction* (i.e. they have to "actively" seek to be close to each other, instead of simply meeting at a certain point because of the attraction to environmental conditions at that point).

Animals show grouping behaviour for different reasons. One of these is *foraging* (i.e. in behavioural ecology, all those interactions that occur between a predator and its prey, being it animal or plant) [5]. Some of the most likely hypotheses for *group-foraging behaviour* are: (1) aggregations find more food (e.g. bigger preys, larger patches) more quickly than individuals do, and so animals in a group feed more effectively; (2) animals in bigger groups can allocate more time to feed and less to look for predators [7]; (3) by observing the behaviour of other members of a group, animals can gain useful information (e.g. individuals use information on the position of others to obtain food from sources that are otherwise difficult to find) [5].

Foraging efficiency is usually a matter of *trade-off* between competing priorities, e.g. energy gained versus energy spent, energy gained versus risk of predation, energy gained versus losses to rivals, etc.[6]. Theoretical models predict that, while joining a group will not increase an individual's ability to find food, the time spent to obtain food is reduced. The trade-off for the reduction in

[1] XPS stands for eXtended Particle Swarm. Details of the project can be found at http://xps-swarm.essex.ac.uk.

searching time is that a smaller share of food will be available, the only exception being when the resource is so abundant that consumption by one individual does not decrease the availability for others. Animals that perform better at increasing the benefits of foraging and decreasing its costs will propagate their genes more effectively than those whose foraging behaviour is less effective [1].

3 The Food Particle Swarm (FPS) Algorithm

As mentioned above, group-foraging is a fairly complex behaviour, and modelling it is a difficult task. Therefore, in this work we focus on an abstraction of the group-foraging problem, where: we do not take the presence of predators into account; food sources are surrounded by an aura attracting the animals to them; animals can neither reproduce nor die; animals can communicate with each other; they can "smell" food, and this is the only way that they can detect the presence of a food source (e.g. they cannot see the food).

A group of animals looking for food is modelled with a swarm of particles "flying" over a 2D landscape scattered with sources of food. Each source is represented as a circular *patch*. The intensity of the aura surrounding the patches is proportional to the amount of food available and is an exponentially decreasing function of the distance from the source, while its spread is proportional to the size of the patch. Therefore, the larger the amount of food and the closer the patch, the "taller" the aura. Also, the bigger the patch, the wider the aura. Food patches are distributed at random on the landscape. To reflect different conditions that may happen in nature, we will consider four configurations (Figure 1):

1. a single small source but with a large amount of food, whose tall aura covers a small portion of the landscape;
2. a single large source but with a small amount of food, whose short aura covers most of the landscape;
3. a small number of medium sources covering a restricted portion of the landscape;
4. a large number of small sources, sparsely scattered on the landscape.

The particles move over the food landscape according to the rules of the extended version of the particle swarm algorithm introduced in [3]. The equations controlling acceleration, velocity, and position of the particles are as in the standard PSO (equations (1)-(3)), but with an extra control which allows the particles to stop on the patch. Namely:

$$f_i = \phi_1 R_1(x_{s_i} - x_i) + \phi_2 R_2(x_{p_i} - x_i); \tag{1}$$

$$v_i(t) = \begin{cases} 0 & \text{if food is on patch} \\ \mathit{Random} & \text{if food is just finished} \\ k((\omega v_i(t-1)) + \Delta t f_i) & \text{otherwise} \end{cases} \tag{2}$$

$$x_i(t) = x_i(t-1) + \Delta t v_i(t). \tag{3}$$

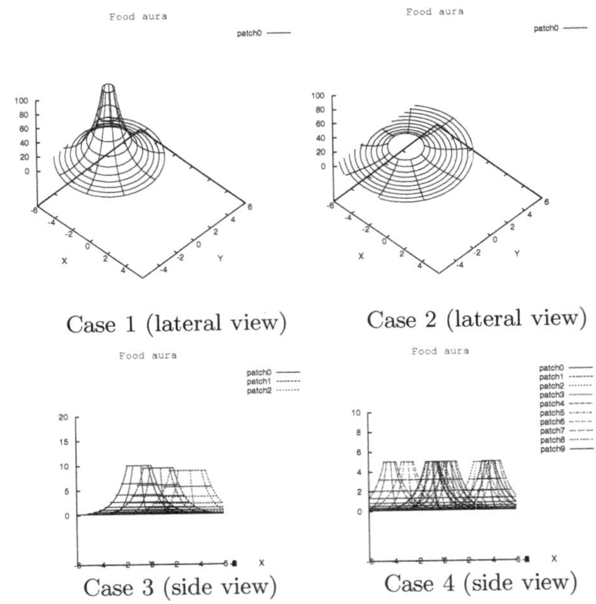

Fig. 1. Food patch distribution classes and aura intensity

where: ϕ_1 and ϕ_2 are the *social interaction* and the *individual learning* rate respectively; R_1 and R_2 are two random variables uniformly distributed in $[0, 1]$; x_i, x_{s_i}, and x_{p_i} are the current position of the particle, the best position found by the swarm, and the best position found by the particle respectively; k and ω are the constriction coefficient and the inertia weight respectively; Δt is a factor to decrease the step the particles take when they move to obtain "smoother" trajectories for the particles (i.e. a more refined search).

Particles are attracted to the food by its aura. They follow the gradient until they reach the surface of the patch, where they stop and start feeding. The food eaten by the particles increases their fitness. Unlike in nature, the fitness of our abstract animals is also increased when they approach food patches, i.e. the intensity of the aura contributes to the fitness. The first situation mirrors the biological nature of the problem, while the latter is inspired by the optimisation nature of the algorithm (where patches of food can be consider optima to be found). Formally:

$$fit_i(t) = \begin{cases} fit_i(t-1) + FE & \text{if particle is on patch} \\ FA * e^{-\left(dis - \frac{FS}{2}\right)} & \text{otherwise} \end{cases} \tag{4}$$

where: FE is the amount of food eaten by the particle; FA is the amount of food available on the patch; dis is the distance between the particle and the surface of the patch; FS is the size of the patch.

Food patches with aura

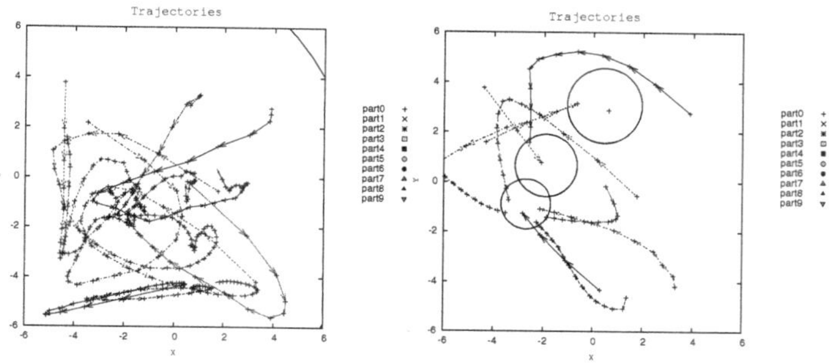

1 patch 3 patches

Fig. 2. Trajectories in FPS on different landscapes (200 iterations, $\Delta t = 0.25$)

The first particle that reaches a patch and starts eating will have the highest fitness, and therefore will become the best of the swarm. Other particles will then be attracted to the same patch not only by its aura, but also by the presence of the particle already feeding on it. When the food available is entirely consumed, the particles leave the patch with random velocity and start foraging again. While feeding, the amount of food available on the patch decreases, and so does its aura. Eventually, there will no longer be any food left on the patch, and the aura will be completely dissolved. If a particle is at the intersection of two or more auras, it will follow the one with highest intensity. If the particles are too far from any patch, or if the food is no longer available, the effect of the aura is considered irrelevant and their fitness is set to zero. This causes x_{s_i} to be equal to x_{p_i} and, as a consequence, the particles start oscillating close to these positions.

4 Results

The goal of this research is to produce a model of abstract animals and their foraging environment through which to observe the emergence of group-foraging behaviour. In terms of simulation, this means that the particles have to both gather together on the food sources (i.e. form *clusters* when feeding), and eat as much food as they can find (i.e. achieve a high fitness). Different foraging abilities and swarm sizes have been tested to investigate which settings produce a more "natural" behaviour, with various patch distributions[2] to observe how these behaviours change (Figure 2). Table 1 summarises both the algorithm and the landscape parameters.

All the parameters except Δt are related to the nature of the group-foraging problem. Δt is instead an algorithmic "artifact" which needs to be small for the continuous force equation to be discretised effectively (e.g. the default step of

[2] The four alternative patch distributions reflect the qualitative patterns explained in section 3.

Table 1. Independently varied parameter settings

Parameter	Value
Number of iterations	200, 500
Number of particles (N)	10, 30
Δt	0.1, 0.25, 0.5, 1.0
Number of food patches (F)	1, 1, 3, 10
Patch size & food amount	$F =$ 1: size 1, food 100
	$F =$ 1: size 3, food 10
	$F =$ 3: size from 2 to 3, food from 9 to 10
	$F = 10$: size 1, food 5

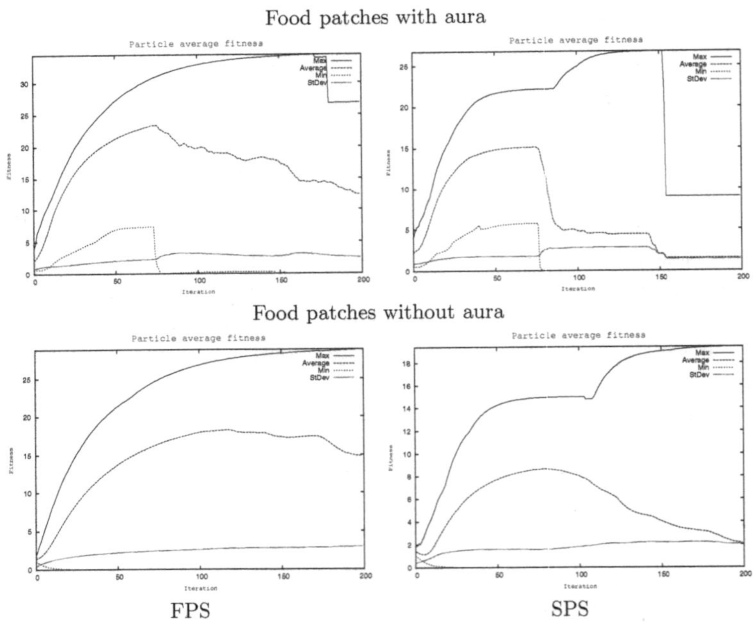

Fig. 3. Fitness in FPS and SPS on different landscapes (200 iterations, $\Delta t = 0.25$); means over 100 independent runs

the standard particle swarm algorithm ($\Delta t = 1$) makes the particles move with excessively large jumps which can cause them to miss the food patches).

Since the initial position of the particles on the landscape could influence the behaviour of the simulation, we repeated the experiments 100 times with different random number generator seeds. For completeness, we have run some comparative tests with the standard version of the particle swarm algorithm (SPS) on this newly defined landscape. We also report here some of the most significant results obtained in [3], to show how the introduction of the concept of

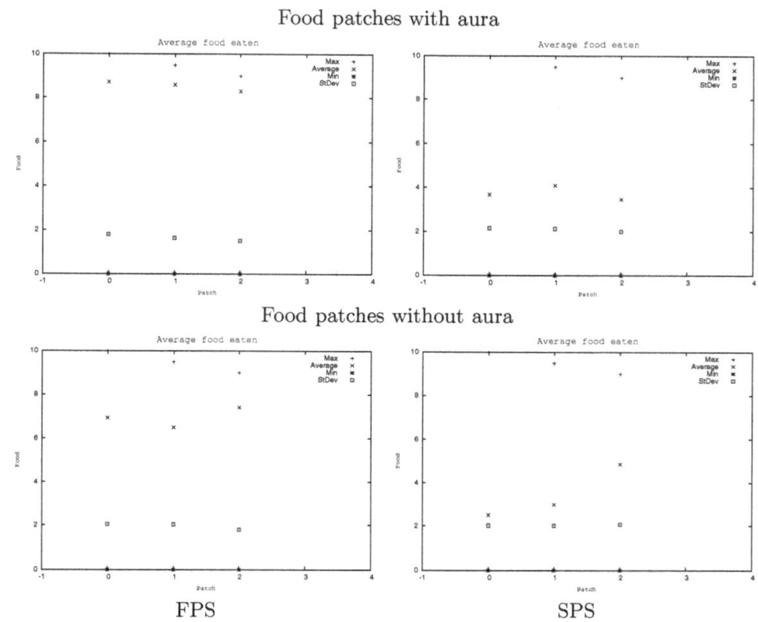

Fig. 4. Amount of food eaten in FPS and SPS on different landscapes (200 iterations, $\Delta t = 0.25$); means over 100 independent runs

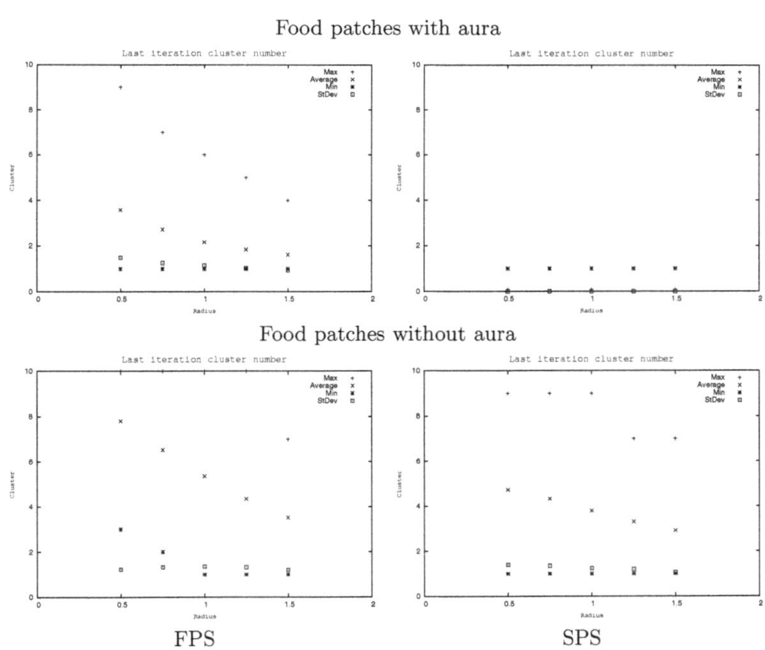

Fig. 5. Clustering in FPS and SPS on different landscapes (200 iterations, $\Delta t = 0.25$, threshold $= 0.5, 1.0, 1.5$); means over 100 independent runs

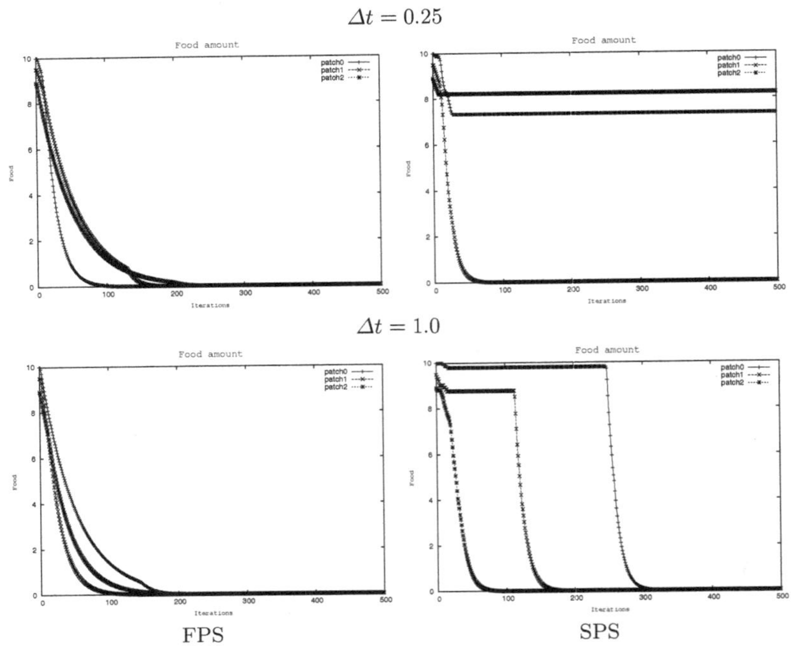

Fig. 6. Amount of food eaten in FPS and SPS (500 iterations)

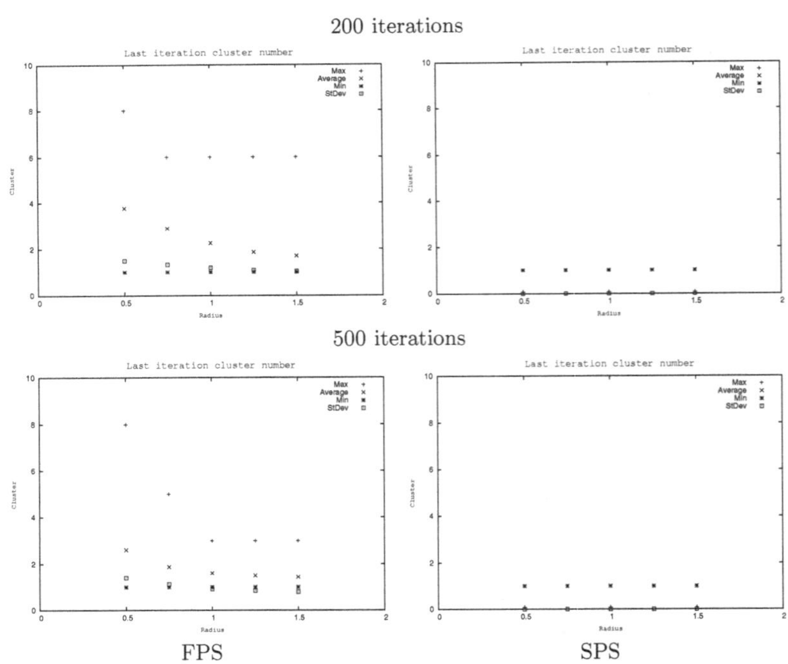

Fig. 7. Clustering in FPS and SPS ($\Delta t = 0.25$, threshold $= 0.5, 1.0, 1.5$)

aura has improved the behaviour of the model. Given the large number of combinations of parameters we used in the experiments, it is impossible to present all the results obtained in the limited space available. We consider here only the more significant ones, run with 10 particles, 3 patches, and $\Delta t = 0.25$ and 1.0. We have checked differences between the FPS and the SPS versions, in both types of landscape (i.e. with or without aura), with respect to number of patches visited (i.e. the ability of the particles to find food), fitness value (i.e. the amount of food eaten by each particle), and clustering (i.e. the ability of the particles to gather together). The clustering technique uses the following definition.

Definition 1. *Two particles p_1 and p_2 are in the same cluster if there exists an ordered set of particles $\{p_{(0,1)}, p_{(0,2)}, \cdots, p_{(0,n)}\}$, with $p_{(0,1)} = p_1$ and $p_{(0,n)} = p_2$, such that $d\left(p_{(0,k)}, p_{(0,k+1)}\right) \leq r$, where r is the cluster threshold.*

The results highlight that the introduction of the aura is beneficial both in terms of amount of food eaten (Figures 3 and 4) and of number of clusters (Figure 5).

The results confirm that, in FPS, there are a larger number of particles that are able to visit more patches, and therefore to eat a greater quantity of food (Figure 6). From the figures it is also evident how, with a larger value for Δt, particles in the SPS model succeed in finding all the patches, but they require more time than the particles moving according to the FPS algorithm. The experiments reveal that particles in the SPS model cluster more than they do in the FPS simulation. Our hypothesis is that this is due to the "stop-eat-restart" behaviour of particles in the FPS model: the random re-initialisation of velocities can cause trajectories to be directed differently, resulting in a lesser ability to aggregate. This phenomenon tends in any case to decrease with time (Figure 7). On average, despite the fact that particles in the SPS algorithm show a better grouping behaviour (for smaller iterations), the ones in the FPS model are able to find a greater number of patches and eat a larger quantity of food.

5 Conclusion

The standard particle swarm algorithm shares features like social attraction and communication between individuals with group-foraging in animals. It is therefore surprising that its main field of application has only been function optimisation. By using the particle swarm algorithm as a simulation tool, we want to change this and take advantage of this biologically inspired technique.

We have shown how it is possible to obtain a version of the particle swarm model well suited for the foraging problem by modifying the standard algorithm. Here the landscape is no longer static (food can be eaten), and the fitness is now related both to the proximity to food (the optimisation problem of finding food) and internal energy (the biological problem of eating enough). From the experiments, we have seen that these changes extend the standard particle swarm model into one which produces qualitatively realistic behaviour.

This work is part of an initial investigation, whose final goal is the simulation of more complex group behaviour in animals. With [3], we introduced a simulation for a simple abstraction of the group-foraging problem. In this paper, we have further extended this study by refining the definition of the landscape, through the introduction of the concept of an aura surrounding the patches of food. Future investigations will focus on introducing other realistic features for the food sources (e.g. allowing the patches to deteriorate and regenerate, *ephemeral* patches) and for the particles (e.g. allowing them to reproduce and die). In fact, as stated in [8], *"it is possible that many of the different collective patterns are generated by small variations in the rules followed by individual group members"*.

References

1. J. Alcock, *Animal Behavior*, Sinauer Associates, 1998
2. D.L. DeAngelis and W.M. Mooij, *Individual-Based Modeling of Ecological and Evolutionary Processes*, Annual Reviews in Ecology, Evolution and Systematics, 2005
3. C. Di Chio, R. Poli and P. Di Chio, *Extending the Particle Swarm Algorithm to Model Animal Foraging Behaviour*, ANTS2006 - Fifth International Workshop on Ant Colony Optimization and Swarm Intelligence, 2006.
4. J. Kennedy and R.C. Eberhart, *Swarm Intelligence*, Morgan Kaufmann Publishers, 2001.
5. J. Krause and G.D. Ruxton, *Living in Groups*, Oxford University Press, 2002.
6. D. MacFarland, *Animal behaviour*, Longman, 1999.
7. J.K Parrish and W.M. Hamner, *Animal Groups in Three Dimensions*, Cambridge University Press, 1997.
8. D.J.T. Sumpter, *The principles of collective animal behaviour*, Philosophical Transactions of the Royal Society of London: Series B, 2006.

Neuroevolution with Analog Genetic Encoding

Peter Dürr, Claudio Mattiussi, and Dario Floreano

Laboratory of Intelligent Systems, Institute of Systems Engineering, Ecole Polytechnique Fédérale de Lausanne, CH-1015 Lausanne, Switzerland
`http://lis.epfl.ch`

Abstract. The evolution of artificial neural networks (ANNs) is often used to tackle difficult control problems. There are different approaches to the encoding of neural networks in artificial genomes. Analog Genetic Encoding (AGE) is a new implicit method derived from the observation of biological genetic regulatory networks. This paper shows how AGE can be used to simultaneously evolve the topology and the weights of ANNs for complex control systems. AGE is applied to a standard benchmark problem and we show that its performance is equivalent or superior to some of the most powerful algorithms for neuroevolution in the literature.

1 Introduction

The use of artificial neural networks (ANNs) in control systems is a widely covered research topic. The complexity of control tasks often makes it difficult to design ANNs manually. Therefore, it is a common approach to use evolutionary algorithms for this kind of problem. Not only the synaptic weights, but also the structure of the network can be subject to neuroevolution. Thus one of the challenges is to find an appropriate genotype-phenotype mapping for both the topology and the weights. In the literature we find different methods to accomplish this. The most straightforward approach is *direct encoding* (e.g. used by [1,2,3,4]) where the genome is composed of a list of genes, each representing either a neuron or a link between two neurons. Genomes of this type can be decoded very easily, but their length grows rapidly with increasing complexity of the network. Another popular approach is *developmental encoding*, as shown in [5,6,7,8,9], which is based on the use of a genome that directs a developmental process leading to the construction of the network. This allows a more compact representation of complex networks, but the developmental process, linking the genome to the developed network, typically makes it difficult to find suitable genetic operators. Somewhat different is the *implicit encoding*. Derived from the observation of biological genetic regulatory networks (GRNs) (see [10] for more details), implicit encoding is a very interesting approach, which is quite popular as a representation for GRNs [11] but is not very commonly used on ANNs.

Analog Genetic Encoding (AGE) [10,12] is an implicit method, which - so far - has only been applied to very simple problems of neuroevolution. The goal of this paper is to show that it is possible to solve more complex problems using AGE and that it outperforms other established methods. The double pole balancing

T.P. Runarsson et al. (Eds.): PPSN IX, LNCS 4193, pp. 671–680, 2006.

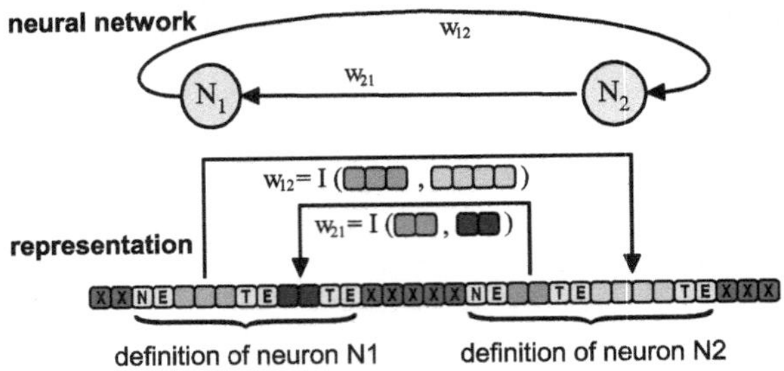

Fig. 1. AGE provides a solution to the encoding of networks in digital genomes. The genome contains genes encoding the devices that form the network.

without velocity information, which has been used as a standard problem in various publications (e.g. [13,14,15]), has been selected as benchmark. The results allow a direct comparison to the above-mentioned methods, thus showing the high performance of AGE, quantitatively and qualitatively.

2 Analog Genetic Encoding (AGE)

2.1 The Challenge

The evolution of an artificial neural network requires the encoding of the network in a genome. In the general case, an arbitrary network of hidden neurons, connected to a given number of fixed input and output neurons has to be evolved. The analog genetic encoding as presented in [10,12] provides a very plausible approach to this problem. The basic idea of AGE is to define a genetic representation that allows the interpretation illustrated in Figure 1.

2.2 Device Representation

The genome is constituted by a sequence of characters from a finite genetic alphabet. Here, the 26 characters of the ASCII uppercase alphabet are used (see [10] for justification). The experimenter defines the kind of devices that can appear in the network. (Here a single type of dynamic neuron is used.) For each device type, a specific *device token* has to be defined. Each device token signals the start of a gene, that is a fragment of the genome which encodes an instance of the corresponding neuron. Furthermore, a *terminal token* is defined, whose role is to delimit the sequence of characters that must be associated with a terminal of the corresponding device. These are the so-called *terminal sequences*. A neuron is hence encoded by a device token, followed by a number of terminal sequences, each delimited by a terminal token[1].

[1] Tokens are typically short sequences of letters. The tokens used in the experiment can be found in Figure 2 (hidden neurons) and Figure 3 (input and output neurons).

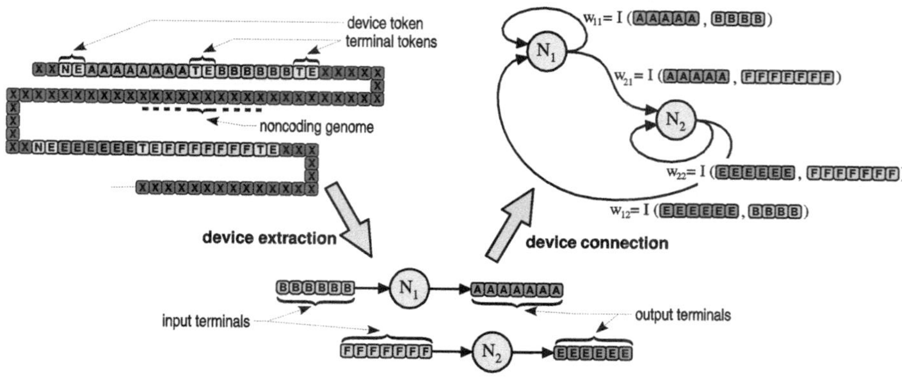

Fig. 2. Neurons can be represented as symbolic devices with two associated terminal sequences: one for the output terminal and one for the input terminal. The device extraction process obtains them from the genome by assigning the sequences of characters between the device token ("NE") and the terminal tokens ("TE") to the respective terminal. The terminal sequences of the different neurons are then used to determine the synaptic weights of the network. The interaction map $I(s_1, s_2)$ assigns a weight to a pair of sequences, so that we can for example calculate $w_{11} = I(s_{11}, s_{12})$. The entire weight matrix can be calculated by doing this for all pairs of terminal sequences in the network.

2.3 Device Extraction

Given a list of device tokens and a terminal token, a list of devices can be decoded from a genome by simply extracting the devices one by one. To this end, the genome is scanned in search of device tokens and if one is found, the fragment of genome following the token is scanned for the necessary terminal tokens. Then the sequences of characters between the device token and the terminal token (or between two terminal tokens respectively) are assigned to the corresponding terminal of the neuron. If a device token in the genome is not followed by the required number of terminal sequences, the gene is considered invalid and the decoding continues with the next device token in the genome.

2.4 Device Connection

To determine the synaptic weights between the neurons, a so-called *interaction map* $I(s_1, s_2) = N(L(s_1, s_2))$ is needed. This function assigns a synaptic weight value to any given pair of terminal sequences. The inner function $L(s_1, s_2)$ is called *sequence interaction map* and returns a distinct interaction score i for each pair of terminal sequences s_1 and s_2. For these experiments, the value of the sequence interaction map corresponds to the value of the local alignment score[2] between the two sequences s_1 and s_2 (see [16]). The parameters of the

[2] The local alignment score is a function which operates on pairs of sequences of arbitrary length and has some very desirable properties from an evolutionary point of view, which are more extensively discussed in [10,16].

local alignment function (the circulant *substitution matrix* and the *indels vector*) used here are:

	A	B	C	D	E	F	G	...	U	V	W	X	Y	Z
A	5	2	1	0	-1	-2	-5	...	-5	-2	-1	0	1	2
B	2	5	2	1	0	-1	-2	...	-5	-5	-2	-1	0	1

⋮

and

	A	...	Z
-	-3	...	-3

The *network-specific interaction map* $N(i)$ transforms the (integer) sequence interaction values to the (floating point) values of the synaptic weight between the terminals. Here a logarithmic quantization $N : [1, 37] \longrightarrow [0.001, 1000]$ was used, mapping interaction scores from $i_{min} = 1$ to $i_{max} = 37$ to weights in an interval from $w_{min_P} = 0.001$ to $w_{max} = 1000$. Interaction scores lower than i_{min} lead to a weight $w_{min} = 0$, scores above i_{max} lead to a weight of w_{max}.

We can calculate the whole weight matrix of the network by applying the interaction map to all pairs of input and output terminals. Since no inhibitory neurons are used, the two outputs of a neuron provide a positive and negative output of its state. If there are n neurons, the entries w_{ij} of the weight matrix W are accordingly defined as

$$w_{ij} = N(L(i_{s_{input}}, j_{s_{output+}})) - N(L((i_{s_{input}}, j_{s_{output-}}))$$

for $i = [1, n]$ and $j = [1, n]$.

2.5 External Connections

Based on the same principle, it is very easy to incorporate the connections to the external input and output neurons. For each type of signal a separate, external neuron type with a distinct token is defined (see Figure 3). The connection weights from the external neurons to the hidden neurons can be calculated using the same method as above.

2.6 Genetic Operators

Artificial (and natural) evolution relies on the reorganization of the genome. Contrary to other methods, the AGE genome is very robust to such operations, since it is of variable length and there is no special protection needed to keep the genome decodable. There is actually no distinction between tokens, coding and non-coding regions of the genome. In the experiments, the following operators where used:

- *Character deletion, insertion, and substitution.* A character is removed, inserted or substituted in the genome.
- *Fragment deletion, transposition and duplication.* Two points of the genome are chosen and the intervening fragment is deleted, transferred or copied to another point of the genome.

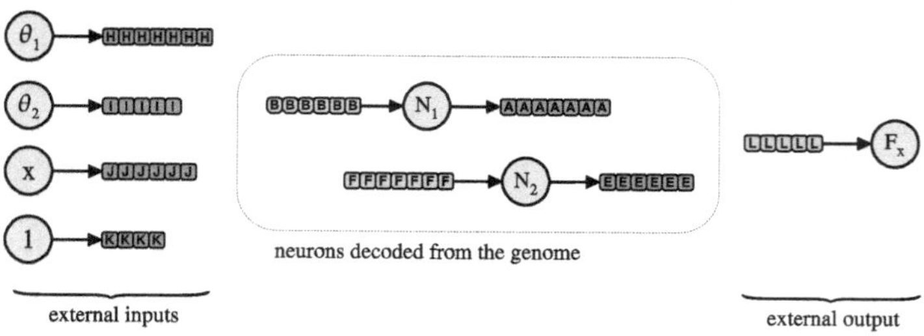

Fig. 3. The external input and output neurons are encoded as separate devices (exactly like the hidden neurons in Figure 2). For each sensor input, the motor output and a bias input, a device type with an associated token is used to decode the respective neurons from the genome. The tokens used for the external inputs are "AA", "AB", "PA" and "BB", the token for the output is "OA".

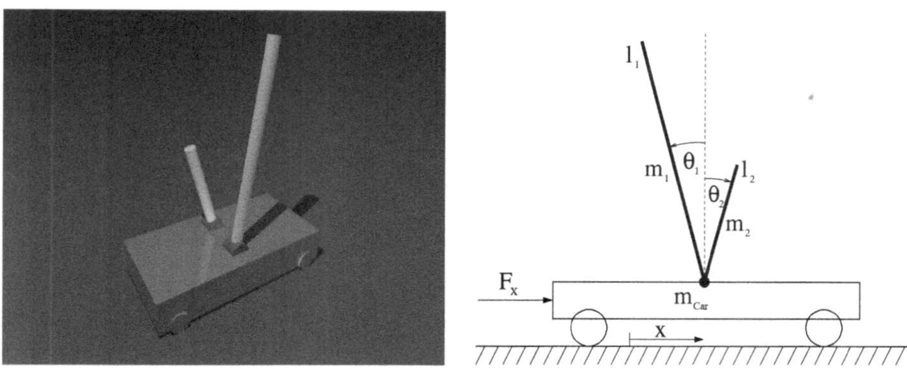

Fig. 4. The double pole balancing problem (DPNV). Two poles mounted on a car have to be balanced, using measurements of the pole angles and the position of the car.

- *Device insertion.* The descriptor of a device (e.g. a hidden neuron) is inserted in the genome. The terminal sequences are randomly generated.
- *Homologous Crossover.* Fragments of the genome are recombined using homologous crossover (see [10] for more details).
- *Genome duplication.* The whole genome is duplicated.
- *Generation of an initial population.* The initial population is created by generating individuals with a random genome and inserting a given number of different neurons with random terminal sequences.

3 Double Pole Balancing as a Benchmark Test

In order to compare the different approaches in neuroevolution on a practical rather than a purely theoretical level, a benchmark test is needed. The double pole balancing problem without velocity information (DPNV) is quite challenging compared to the fairly simple single pole balancing problems[3], while it is still easy to understand and simple enough to be simulated without huge computational efforts. Stanley and Miikkulainen [15] compare the results of the only neuroevolution methods which have reportedly solved the DPNV problem by evolving topology and weights of neural networks: Gruaus *Cellular Encoding* (CE, [13]), Gomez and Miikkulainens *Enforced Sub Populations* (ESP, [14]), and Stanley and Miikkulainens *Augmenting Topologies* (NEAT, [15])[4].

3.1 The Controlled System

The double pole balancing setup (see Figure 4), consists of a car with mass $m_{Car} = 1[kg]$ and one degree of freedom x, on which two poles of different lengths $l_1 = 1[m]$ and $l_2 = 0.1[m]$ are mounted. The poles have the masses $m_1 = 1[kg]$ and $m_2 = 0.1[kg]$. Based on the measured values of the joint angles θ_1 and θ_2 and the position of the car x, the controller is required to balance both of the poles by applying a force F_x (with a maximal magnitude of $F_{max} = 10[N]$). Assuming rigid body dynamics and neglecting friction, the system can be described by the equations of motion as in [18]. The numerical simulation of the system is based on a 4th-order Runge-Kutta integration of these equations with a time step of $\Delta t = 0.01s$.

3.2 Fitness Assignment

In their original publication, Gruau, Whitley and Pyeatt [13] suggest the following approach for the assessment of candidate solutions. In order to avoid demanding calculations for every fitness evaluation, they split the definition of the fitness value from the decision to judge a solution successful by applying a simple fitness function to every individual in the population and an extensive test series on the best individual of the population. Although it saves a lot of computation time, this is very questionable, since it is not a priori clear that individuals with a high fitness will perform well in the extensive test. But since the benchmark data collected by [14] and [15] relies on this measure, the same approach is used here.

The Fitness Function. In order to assign a fitness value to an individual, a numerical simulation is carried out over a maximum of 1000 timesteps, starting from given initial conditions ($\theta_1(0) = 0.0785$, $\dot{\theta}_1(0) = \theta_2(0) = \dot{\theta}_2(0) = x(0) = \dot{x}(0) = 0$). For each timestep the position of the car and the pole angles are observed and the simulation continues only as long as they stay in a given range:

[3] They can typically be solved in a few generations with simple evolutionary algorithms, or with random search in the parameter space.

[4] In [17] Igel shows that it is possible to outperform these methods by using an evolution strategy (CMA-ES) to optimize the weights of a fixed topology ANN. But since in general evolution of both weights and topology is needed, his results are not really comparable to those presented here.

$$-\theta_1^{Max} \leq \theta_1 \leq \theta_1^{Max} \tag{1}$$
$$-\theta_2^{Max} \leq \theta_2 \leq \theta_2^{Max} \tag{2}$$
$$-x^{Max} \leq x \leq x^{Max} \tag{3}$$

where $\theta_1^{Max} = \theta_2^{Max} = 36°$ and $x^{Max} = 2.4[m]$. The fitness value F is defined as

$$F = 0.1f_1 + 0.9f_2 \qquad with \tag{4}$$
$$f_1 = \frac{t}{1000} \tag{5}$$
$$f_2 = \begin{cases} 0 & if \quad t < 100, \\ \frac{0.75}{\sum_{i=t-100}^{t}\left(|x^i|+|\dot{x}^i|+|\theta_1^i|+|\dot{\theta}_1^i|\right)} & otherwise. \end{cases} \tag{6}$$

where t is the number of time steps the system remains inside the boundaries (1), (2) and (3).

The Generalization Score. The best individual (i.e. the one with the highest fitness value F) of every generation is tested for its ability to balance the system for a longer time period. If a potential solution passes this test by keeping the system balanced for 100'000 timesteps, the so called *generalization score* (GS) of this particular individual is calculated. This score measures the potential of a controller to balance the system starting from different initial conditions. It is calculated with a series of experiments, running over 1000 timesteps, starting from 625 different initial conditions. The initial conditions are chosen by assigning each value of the set $\Omega = [0.05\ 0.25\ 0.75\ 0.95]$ to each of the states x, $\dot{x}$, θ_1 and $\dot{\theta}_1$, scaled to the range of the variables (as specified in the following section). The short pole angle θ_2 and its angular velocity $\dot{\theta}_2$ are set to zero. The GS is then defined as the number of successful runs from the 625 initial conditions and an individual is defined as a solution if it reaches a generalization score of 200 or more.

3.3 The Artificial Neural Network

Neuron Model. The neurons used here are simple continuous time recurrent neurons as in [19]. The time constant is set to $\tau = 0.001[s]$. The resulting network state equation

$$\tau\dot{\mathbf{y}} = -\mathbf{y} + \mathbf{W}\sigma\left(\mathbf{y} + \theta\right) + \mathbf{I} \tag{7}$$
$$where \qquad \sigma(x) = \frac{1}{1+e^{-x}} \tag{8}$$

is integrated with a separate embedded Runge-Kutta-Fehlberg (4,5) method. For this benchmark problem, the bias vector θ is set to zero and an external input with the constant output of 1.0 is connected to the network. To match the conditions of the original experiment [13], the input neurons are fed with scaled measurement values ($\theta_{1_{neur}} = \frac{\theta_1}{0.52}$, $\theta_{2_{neur}} = \frac{\theta_2}{0.52}$ and $x_{neur} = \frac{x}{4.8}$). The outputs of the motor output neuron ranging from -1 to 1 are scaled to forces from $-F_{max}$ to F_{max}.

3.4 Genetic Algorithm

The genetic algorithm used in the experiment is a standard generational GA with the AGE specific genetic operators as explained above and tournament selection. The mating pool size is 30 and there is an elite of size 1, thus the total population size is 31. The tournament size is set to 2. The probability of homologous recombination is 0.1 with 5 characters required to be similar for recombination to take place. The probabilities of nucleotide substitution, insertion and deletion are set to 0.001, the probabilities of fragment duplication, insertion and deletion to 0.01. Random devices are inserted with a probability of 0.01 with terminals of length 20.

In order to improve the performance of the algorithm, the GA is restarted whenever it gets stuck (i.e. when no improvement in the fitness of the best individual is observed after 15 generations). This choice was inspired by experiments with NEAT reported in [20], where subpopulations, which do not improve within 15 generations are removed. To avoid bootstrapping problems, the GA is initialized with a large initial population of 1000 individuals, each with a random genome of 500 to 800 characters. Each individual in the initial population gets a complete set of input, output and bias neurons plus one or two hidden neurons with randomly generated terminal sequences.

4 Results

Table 1 shows the results of AGE compared to the other methods, which have reportedly solved the DPNV so far. Both the number of fitness evaluations and the generalization score are about equal or better than the results obtained by NEAT. The average number of function evaluations needed by AGE is smaller than the best results previously reported in the literature. It seems that AGE is able to produce better solutions in a smaller number of generations. The example solution in Figure 5 (which obtained a GS of 525) shows that simple structures can obtain relatively high generalization scores. Initialized with only one or two hidden neurons, AGE tends to exploit these small structures and finds elegant solutions.

An odd property of the DPNV benchmark with the split fitness is that high fitness scores do not automatically lead to good generalization properties. In the

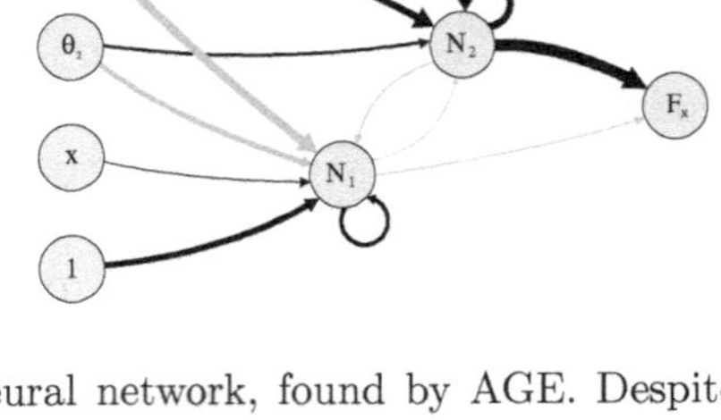

Fig. 5. An example neural network, found by AGE. Despite its simple structure, it generalizes really well (with a GS of 525).

Table 1. The results of the double pole balancing with no velocity information (DPNV). CE is cellular encoding [13], ESP is enforced subpopulations [14], NEAT is augmenting topologies [15]. All results are averaged over 20 evolutionary runs. AGE has to be restarted about 10 times on average to obtain a solution.

Method	Evaluations	Standard Deviation	Generalization
CE	840000	n.a.	300
ESP	169466	n.a.	289
NEAT	33184	21790	286
AGE	25065	19499	317

experiment, some populations with relatively high fitness of the best individual got stuck without producing a solution which could pass the long run test, whereas other populations with relatively low fitness could produce good solutions very quickly. The fact that the fitness function and the generalization test do not correlate well indicates that a better fitness function should be chosen for future benchmark experiments.

5 Conclusion

The results obtained in the standard benchmark double pole balancing problem with no velocity information show that it is possible to use analog genetic encoding to evolve neural networks for a difficult control task. They also indicate that AGE outperforms the best algorithms existing in the literature for the evolution of ANN topology and weights, producing compact, high quality solutions within a small number of fitness evaluations.

Acknowledgments. The implementation of the benchmark problem relies directly on source code by Kenneth O. Stanley. Thanks to Daniel Marbach for his collaboration on the implementation of AGE and a lot of inspiring discussions. Thanks to Sara Mitri for her valuable comments and further thanks to the anonymous reviewers for their helpful remarks.

References

1. Maniezzo V.: Genetic evolution of the topology and weight distribution of neural networks. IEEE Transactions on Neural Networks, vol. 5, no. 1 (1994) 39–53
2. Pujol J., Poli R.: Evolving the topology and the weights of neural networks using a dual representation. Applied Intelligence, vol. 8, no. 1 (1998) 73–84
3. Kobayashi K., Ohbayashi M.: A new indirect encoding method with variable length gene code to optimize neural network structures. Proceedings of the International Joint Conference on Neural Networks, vol. 6(1999) 4409–4412
4. Stanley K., Miikkulainen R.: Evolving neural networks through augmenting topologies. Evolutionary Computation, vol. 10, no. 2 (2002) 99–127

5. Cangelosi A., Parisi D., Nolfi S.: Cell division and migration in a genotype for neural networks. Network: Computation in Neural Systems, vol. 5, no. 4 (1994) 497–515
6. Gruau F.: Automatic definition of modular neural networks. Adaptive Behaviour, vol. 3, no. 2, (1995) 151–183
7. Nolfi S., Parisi D.: Genotypes for neural networks. The Handbook of Brain Theory and Neural Networks, M. Arbib, Ed. Cambridge, MA: MIT Press (1995) 431–434.
8. Eggenberger P.: Creation of neural networks based on developmental and evolutionary principles. Proceedings of the International Conference on Artificial Neural Networks, Lausanne, Switzerland (1997)
9. Astor J., Adami C.: A developmental model for the evolution of artificial neural networks. Artificial Life, vol. 6, no. 3 (2000) 189–218
10. Mattiussi, C.: Evolutionary synthesis of analog networks. Ph.D. dissertation n.3199, EPFL, Lausanne (2005)
11. Bongard, J.: Evolving modular genetic regulatory networks. Proceedings of the IEEE 2002 Congress on Evolutionary Computation, CEC2002. Piscataway, NJ: IEEE Press (2002) 1872–1877
12. Mattiussi, C., Floreano, D.: Evolution of analog networks using local string alignment on highly reorganizable genomes. Proceedings of the 2004 NASA/DoD Conference on Evolvable Hardware (2004) 30–37
13. Gruau,F., Whitley, D., Pyeatt, L.: A comparison between cellular encoding and direct encoding for genetic neural networks. Genetic Programming 1996: Proceedings of the First Annual Conference (1996) 81–89
14. Gomez, F. J., Miikkulainen, R.: Solving non-markovian control tasks with neuroevolution. Proceedings of the International Joint Conference on Artificial Intelligence (1999) 1356–1361
15. Stanley, K.O., Miikkulainen, R.: Evolving neural networks through augmenting topologies. Evolutionary Computation 10(2) (2002) 99–127
16. Gusfield, G.: Algorithms on strings, trees, and sequences. Cambridge: Cambridge University Press (1997).
17. Igel C.: Neuroevolution for reinforcement learning using evolution strategies. Congress on Evolutionary Computation 2003 (CEC 2003) 2588–2595
18. Wieland, A.P.: Evolving neural network controllers for unstable systems. Proceedings of the International Joint Conference on Neural Networks (1991) 667–673
19. Beer, R.D.: On the dynamics of small continuous-time recurrent neural networks. Adaptive Behavior 3(4) (1995) 469–509
20. Stanley K.O.: Efficient evolution of neural networks through complexification. Ph.D. dissertation, University of Texas at Austin (2004)

A Two-Level Clustering Method Using Linear Linkage Encoding

Emin Erkan Korkmaz

Computer Engineering Department
Yeditepe University
34755, İstanbul, Turkey
ekorkmaz@cse.edu.tr
http://cse.yeditepe.edu.tr/~ekorkmaz

Abstract. *Linear Linkage Encoding* (LLE) is a representational scheme proposed for *Genetic Algorithms* (GA). LLE is convenient to be used for grouping problems and it doesn't suffer from the redundancy problem that exists in classical encoding schemes. Any number of groups can be represented in a fixed length chromosome in this scheme. However, the length of the chromosome in LLE is determined by the number of elements to be grouped just like the other encoding schemes. This disadvantage becomes dominant when LLE is applied on large datasets and the encoding turns out to be an infeasible model. In this paper a two-level approach is proposed for LLE in order to overcome the problem. In this method, the large dataset is divided into a group of subsets. In the first phase of the process, the data in the subsets are grouped using LLE. Then these groups are used to obtain the final partitioning of the data in the second phase. The approach is tested on the clustering problem. Two considerably large datasets have been chosen for the experiments. It is not possible to obtain a satisfactory convergence with the straightforward application of LLE on these datasets. The method proposed can cluster the datasets with low error rates.

1 Introduction

Researchers have been interested in applying *Genetic Algorithms* (GA) to grouping problems [1]. The chromosomes in GA are encoded strings. The representation of different number of groups in this linear structure is the most important issue related to the subject. *Linear Linkage Encoding* (LLE) is a newly proposed encoding scheme for GA and is quite convenient to be used for grouping problems [2,3]. In this paper, a two-level grouping process is proposed for LLE.

LLE uses links to determine the groups in a partition and has been applied to the clustering problem in [2,3]. LLE is clearly a better encoding scheme compared to the two previously used representations, *Group Number Encoding*(NE) and *Permutation with Separators*[4]. Both of these classical representations have the effect of numbering the groups in a partition. Hence, it is possible to have

T.P. Runarsson et al. (Eds.): PPSN IX, LNCS 4193, pp. 681–690, 2006.

more than one chromosome representing the same partitioning. This is a factor decreasing the efficiency of GA. LLE does not suffer from the redundancy that exists in these representation models. What is more, these classical encoding schemes can only be used for the k-grouping problem where the number of groups should be known beforehand. LLE can encode any number of groups in a fixed length chromosome and can be used for the general grouping problem. LLE has clearly a better performance compared to the other two encoding schemes [2,3].

All of the three representations mentioned above reserve a gene in the chromosome for each element in the dataset to be grouped. Hence, the length of the chromosomes used in the GA search is equal to the number of elements to be grouped. The performance of GA rapidly decreases with increasing chromosome length. When a large dataset is used, no convergence can be achieved even if LLE is used as the encoding scheme.

This paper proposes a two-level approach so that GA using LLE can be applicable to large datasets, too. The method used divides a given dataset into a group of subsets randomly. In the first phase of the process, the standard approach is used to partition each subset. In the second phase, the groups obtained from the subsets are used to form the final partitioning of data. This approach has been tested on *Dermatology* [5] and *Breast Cancer*[6] data. The number of instances and the dimensions of the datasets are considerably large compared to the datasets previously used with LLE. It has been observed that the straightforward application of LLE is infeasible on both datasets. When the new approach is used, it becomes possible to partition both datasets with high accuracy.

A grouping problem can be defined as the task of partitioning a set of items into a collection of mutually disjoint subsets [1]. *Bin packing*, *graph coloring* and *data clustering* are some examples to grouping problems. The new approach proposed in this paper is tested on the clustering problem. Clustering is a grouping problem which is considered as one of the most challenging problems in unsupervised learning. Various approaches has been proposed to solve the problem. An efficient method is the hierarchical clustering where a tree hierarchy is built from the elements to be clustered. In this structure, sibling nodes partition the cluster denoted by their common parent [7,8].

A different approach used in the area is to search for the solution by dividing initial dataset into subsets. Checking all possible partitions would be an exponential algorithm. A heuristic or an optimization method is needed to find the best partitioning. GA has been used by the researchers to search for the optimal grouping of data [9,10,11]. K-medoids [8,12] and K-means [13] are two other well known examples of this framework.

As mentioned above, the classical representations used for applying GA on the problem, have disadvantages. A proper encoding scheme is proposed in [2]. The details of the classical and this new encoding scheme can be found in the next section. Then, in section 3, the newly proposed approach is presented. Section 4 includes the experimental results obtained on the datasets. Lastly, in section 5, the conclusions and future work is provided.

2 Encoding Schemes

In *Group Number Encoding* [4], each gene of a chromosome is reserved for an object and the value of the gene denotes the cluster that contains the object. *Permutation with Separators* encoding [4] uses certain integers to denote the boundaries of the groups. This time, the gene values refer to the objects to be grouped. For instance, the gene values before the first separator will denote the object ids of the first group in the partition.

Let $\mathcal{O} = \{a, b, c, d, e, f\}$ be the set of objects to be grouped. The chromosome $[2, 1, 3, 2, 1, 2]$ will denote the partition $\{(b, e), (a, d, f), (c)\}$ according to number encoding. The value 2 in the first gene denotes that object a is in the second group. b will be in the first group due to the value 1 in the next gene and so on. The chromosome $[2, 5, -1, 1, 4, 6, -1, 3]$ is a chromosome of permutation with separators encoding. Here, -1 is used to denote group boundaries. The chromosome represents the same partitioning of data. The values of 2 and 5 denote that objects b and e are in the first group and the objects after the separator are in the second group and so on. It is easy to construct different chromosomes which represent the same partitioning of data. For instance, $[3, 2, 1, 3, 2, 3] \Longrightarrow \{(c), (b, e), (a, d, f)\}$ and $[3, -1, 2, 5, -1, 1, 4, 6] \Longrightarrow \{(c), (b, e), (a, d, f)\}$ are such examples where only the ordering of the groups are different. The drawbacks of this traditional encoding are presented in [1], and it is pointed out in [14] that this encoding is against the minimal redundancy principles set for encoding scheme design.

2.1 Linear Linkage Encoding (LLE) Scheme

The idea used in LLE is to represent each cluster as a linked-list of objects. Again a different gene is reserved for each object [2]. The value of each gene is interpreted as a link from an object to another object of the same cluster. Two objects are considered to be in the same group, if either object can be reached from the other one using one or more links.

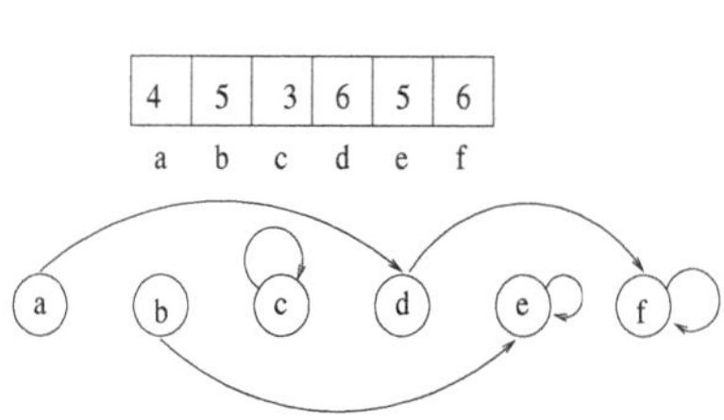

Fig. 1. An Example Chromosome in LLE and the linked list structure it represents

In figure 1 an example chromosome and the link structure it preserves is given. The chromosome represents the partitioning $\{(b, e), (a, d, f), (c)\}$. Note that any number of groups can be represented in a fixed length chromosome in this encoding scheme.

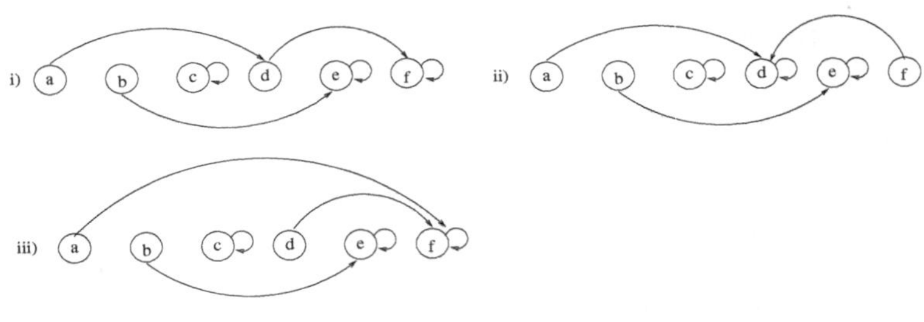

Fig. 2. Redundancy in LLE Scheme

In fact, redundancy exists with the initial definition provided above. For example in figure 2, all of the examples represent the partition $\{(b, e), (a, d, f), (c)\}$

The redundancy can be prevented by adding the following two constraints to the definition of LLE.

- No backward links are allowed.
- No two genes in the chromosome have the same value except one of them is an ending node.

The two constraints remove the initial redundancy totally. Thus, one to one mapping between the chromosomes in LLE and the possible partitioning schemes is achieved, reducing the search space considerably [2].

2.2 Multi Objective GA for LLE Clustering

LLE can encode any number of groups in a fixed length chromosome. The encoding has been tested on the clustering problem in this work and in [2,3] using a multi-objective GA. The *Total Within Cluster Variation* (TWCV) has been widely used as the fitness measure when GA is applied to a clustering problem. TWCV is a measure of variation in clusters of a given partition[2]. A good partitioning of data would have a small TWCV value. Let $\boldsymbol{X} = \{\boldsymbol{X_1}, \boldsymbol{X_2}, ..., \boldsymbol{X_n}\}$ be the set of objects to be clustered, where each object has d attributes; $\boldsymbol{X_i} = (x_{i1}, x_{i2}, ...x_{id})$. If K clusters exist in the optimal partitioning of the data, the clustering problem is defined as finding out a mapping

$$\mu_K^{'} : \boldsymbol{X} \mapsto 1, 2, ..., K \tag{1}$$

where TWCV in $\mu_K^{'}$ is minimal. TWCV is defined as the summation of the total variation in the clusters. TWCV of a partitioning μ_K is defined as

$$V(\mu_K) = \sum_{k=1}^{K} \sum_{i=1}^{n} w_{ik} \sum_{j=1}^{d} (x_{ij} - c_{kj})^2 \tag{2}$$

where x_{ij} is the jth property of the ith object and c_{kj} is the jth property of the kth cluster center. w_{ik} is a control term which has the value one if object i is in cluster k and zero otherwise [15]. The cluster center attributes are defined to be the average attribute values of the objects in that cluster, hence

$$c_{kj} = \frac{\sum_{i=1}^{n} w_{ik}.x_{ij}}{\sum_{i=1}^{n} w_{ik}} \tag{3}$$

In the general clustering problem, the optimal number of clusters is unknown. The search is carried out on all possible number of clusters in a parallel fashion. It is more probable for TWCV to decrease as the number of clusters increases. [2]. Hence, GA using TWCV as the sole fitness measure would tend to find partitions containing larger number of clusters. Therefore, a second objective is needed to balance the bias introduced by TWCV.

The second fitness value is set as the number of clusters in a partition. Hence, the multi-objective GA used in this study tries to decrease both TWCV and the number of clusters in a partition at the same time. The *Niched Pareto Genetic Algorithm* presented in [16] is used to minimize these two objectives for the problem. Hence, at the end of the search a Pareto optimal set is obtained which consists of the minimal TWCV values found for all possible number of clusters that can exist in the partitioning of data.

3 Using LLE on Large Datasets

Application of GA to the grouping problem has a basic drawback which exists in all of the three encoding schemes presented here. In these representations, a different gene is reserved for each element of the dataset. Hence, the length of the chromosomes used in GA search is equal to the size of the dataset to be grouped and the performance of GA decreases dramatically on large datasets.

LLE has been compared with the classical encoding schemes on the clustering problem in [2,3]. *Iris* and *Ruspini* datasets are used in the experiments. The results clearly denote that LLE has a superior performance, as expected. However, the datasets have only 150 and 75 instances, respectively. These are relatively small sizes compared to many other clustering datasets.

In this study, two large medical datasets have been chosen to test the performance of LLE. These are *Dermatology* and *Breast Cancer* Datasets [5]. These datasets are quite large compared to the datasets used in [2,3]. Hence, the GA search has to be carried out on larger chromosomes. It has been observed that the straightforward application of GA cannot obtain any convergence in a practical amount of time on these datasets. The GA run turns into an infeasible search method even if LLE is used as the encoding scheme.

The method proposed to overcome the problem divides a given dataset into a number of disjoint subsets, randomly. The clustering of each subset is achieved using LLE. Hence, a separate GA run is used for each subset. In the second phase of the process, a meta level clustering is carried out to combine the clusters formed in the first phase and to obtain the final partitioning of data. More formally, the set of objects defined as $\boldsymbol{X}$ in the previous section is divided into s disjoint subsets where for each subset; $\boldsymbol{S_i} \subseteq \boldsymbol{X}$ and $|\boldsymbol{S_i}| = \frac{n}{s}$, $1 \leq i \leq s$. The subset length is also the length of the chromosomes that will be used in each GA search. Note that, at the end of each GA run, a Pareto front will be obtained for a subset. The Pareto front includes the best groupings found for all possible number of clusters. Let the size of subsets be l, then l different mappings will be the output of each GA run ($\forall q \exists \mu_q^{'} : 1 \leq q \leq l, \mu_q^{'} : \boldsymbol{S_i} \mapsto 1, 2, ..., q$). Now an element in the Pareto front of each subset has to be chosen in order to form the set of elements that will be clustered in the second phase of the algorithm. The Pareto fronts obtained are plotted and the elbow criterion is used to determine the optimal number of clusters in the data. Here, the same number of clusters can be chosen for all subsets, because the subsets are formed randomly from the initial dataset and the optimal partitioning of them would have the same number of clusters. Hence, the optimal partitioning or a partitioning where the number of clusters is larger than the optimum, can be chosen for the second phase. However, there is a trade off in this decision. If the size of the clusters used are small, then the accuracy will be better. On the other side, if the number of clusters in the chosen partitioning is too large, then the total number of elements to be clustered in the second phase will increase.

Let's assume that the partitioning chosen for each subset has c clusters. These clusters will form the elements to be grouped in the second phase of the process. Since, s different subsets are used, the total number of elements to be clustered in the second phase will be $c * s$. This is at the same time the chromosome size of the second phase.

The objects subject to clustering are the elements of the initial dataset in the first phase of the process. The attributes of the elements are used to calculate the TWCV of the clusters formed. A cluster in the second phase is a combination of the clusters from the first phase. The average attribute values of the center points in these clusters are used in order to determine the variation of the the meta clusters in the second phase.

A multi objective GA is used in the second phase, too. Hence, the search will combine different number of clusters of the first phase in different groups and a new Pareto optimal set will be obtained this time for the whole set. This new Pareto front can be considered as the output of the algorithm. The algorithm presented above can be summarized as follows. Let size of the dataset to be clustered be n.

i Divide the dataset into s disjoint subsets randomly, yielding subsets with size n/s.
ii For each subset, run the multi-objective GA.
iii Determine a fixed element in the Pareto front and extract the partitions represented by this element for each subset.
iv Apply the multi-objective GA on the set of clusters obtained in the first level.

4 Experimental Results

Dermatology dataset contains the clinical features of *erythemato-squamous* diseases and consists of 366 instances. 34 different clinical features are recorded for each instance. The instances belong to 6 different types of erythemato-squamous disease. The diagnosis of the disease is a real problem in Dermatology. The feature values alter minimally for instances having different disease types [5].

Breast Cancer dataset consists of 699 instances obtained from University of Wisconsin Hospitals. The data has 10 different clinical features and contains two classes. Each class denotes the presence of either *Benign* or *Malignant* tumor. The determination of these breast tumors is a complex problem for oncologists.

The instances in both datasets are labeled according to their class ids. Therefore, the datasets are suitable to be used with supervised (classification) techniques. The best observed accuracy when a classification technique is used is reported as 96.9% for the Dermatology dataset and 97% for the Breast Cancer[17]. It is a more difficult problem to cluster the datasets in an unsupervised manner, since no training phase is used in this approach. To the author's knowledge, no significant success is obtained by a clustering method on the Dermatology Dataset. The best accuracy observed with a clustering method is reported as 96.63% for the Breast Cancer data in [18].

Table 1. Genetic parameters used for the experiments on *Dermatology* and *Breast Cancer* datasets

Parameter	**Dermatology**	**Breast Cancer**
Number of Experiments	30	30
Number of Generations	5000	3000
population size	250	200
Nitch Radius	5	5
Crossover Rate	0.8	0.8
Mutation Rate	0.01	0.01
Number of subsets	3	7
Number of clusters used for the second phase	10	4

In table 1, the genetic parameters used for the experiments are given. Almost the same parameters are used for both datasets. The size of the population and the number of generations are larger for the dermatology dataset. Note that Dermatology dataset is divided into three subsets in the first phase of the process. On the other side, seven subsets are used for Breast Cancer data. Hence, a subset size around 100 instances is achieved for both datasets.

As mentioned above, the optimal number of clusters is six for the Dermatology dataset. In table 2, the best partitioning that contains six clusters, is given. The class ids of the instances are shown in the table. The erroneous instances are the ones which have a different class id from the majority of the cluster elements. For instance, clusters $1, 3, 4$ and 5 have gathered the instances of the same id perfectly. All of the erroneous instances belong to the second and the last clusters. The number of misplaced elements is 28 among 366 instances. This corresponds to a clustering accuracy of 92.4%.

There are two clusters in the optimal partitioning of Breast Cancer data. The number of instances is quite large in this dataset. Hence the actual clusters

Table 2. Clusters Found for Dermatology Dataset

Cluster 1	Cluster 2	Cluster 3	Cluster 4	Cluster 5	Cluster 6
6.0 6.0 6.0 6.0	2.0 2.0 2.0 2.0	3.0 3.0 3.0 3.0 3.0 3.0	5.0 5.0 5.0 5.0 5.0	1.0 1.0 1.0 1.0 1.0 1.0 1.0 1.0	4.0 4.0 4.0 4.0 4.0
6.0 6.0 6.0 6.0	2.0 2.0 **4.0** 2.0	3.0 3.0 3.0 3.0 3.0 3.0	5.0 5.0 5.0 5.0 5.0	1.0 1.0 1.0 1.0 1.0 1.0 1.0 1.0	**2.0** 4.0 4.0 1.0 4.0
6.0 6.0 6.0 6.0	2.0 2.0 **4.0** 2.0	3.0 3.0 3.0 3.0 3.0 3.0	5.0 5.0 5.0 5.0 5.0	1.0 1.0 1.0 1.0 1.0 1.0 1.0 1.0	4.0 4.0 4.0 4.0 4.0
6.0 6.0 6.0 6.0	2.0 2.0 2.0 2.0	3.0 3.0 3.0 3.0 3.0 3.0	5.0 5.0 5.0 5.0 5.0	1.0 1.0 1.0 1.0 1.0 1.0 1.0 1.0	4.0 4.0 4.0 4.0 4.0
6.0 6.0 6.0 6.0	**4.0** 2.0 2.0 2.0	3.0 3.0 3.0 3.0 3.0 3.0	5.0 5.0 5.0 5.0 5.0	1.0 1.0 1.0 1.0 1.0 1.0 1.0 1.0	4.0 4.0 4.0 4.0 4.0
	4.0 2.0 2.0 2.0	3.0 3.0 3.0 3.0 3.0 3.0	5.0 5.0 5.0 5.0 5.0	1.0 1.0 1.0 1.0 1.0 1.0 1.0 1.0	4.0 4.0 4.0 **2.0** 4.0
	2.0 2.0 2.0 2.0	3.0 3.0 3.0 3.0 3.0 3.0	5.0 5.0 5.0 5.0 5.0	1.0 1.0 1.0 1.0 1.0 1.0 1.0 1.0	4.0 **2.0** 4.0 4.0 4.0
	2.0 2.0 2.0 2.0	3.0 3.0 3.0 3.0 3.0 3.0	5.0 5.0 5.0 5.0 5.0	1.0 1.0 1.0 1.0 1.0 1.0 1.0 1.0	**2.0** **2.0** **2.0** 4.0 **2.0**
	2.0 2.0 2.0 2.0	3.0 3.0 3.0 3.0 3.0 3.0	5.0 5.0 5.0 5.0 5.0	1.0 1.0 1.0 1.0 1.0 1.0 1.0 1.0	**2.0** **2.0** **2.0** 4.0 **2.0**
	2.0 2.0 **4.0** 2.0	3.0 3.0 3.0 3.0 3.0 3.0	5.0 5.0 5.0 5.0 5.0	1.0 1.0 1.0 1.0 1.0 1.0 1.0 1.0	4.0 **2.0** 4.0 **2.0** 4.0
	2.0 2.0 2.0 2.0	3.0 3.0 3.0 3.0 3.0 3.0	5.0 5.0	1.0 1.0 1.0 1.0 1.0 1.0 1.0 1.0	4.0 **2.0** **2.0** **2.0** 4.0
	2.0 2.0 2.0 **4.0**	3.0 3.0 3.0 3.0 3.0 3.0		1.0 1.0 1.0 1.0 1.0 1.0 1.0 1.0	**2.0** **2.0** 4.0 4.0 **2.0**
	4.0 **4.0**			1.0 1.0 1.0 1.0 1.0 1.0 1.0 1.0	4.0
				1.0 1.0 1.0 1.0 1.0 1.0 1.0	

found are not presented here. The number of misplaced instances in the best partitioning found for this set is 21. The success rate is 97% which is exactly the best rate reported by the supervised techniques.

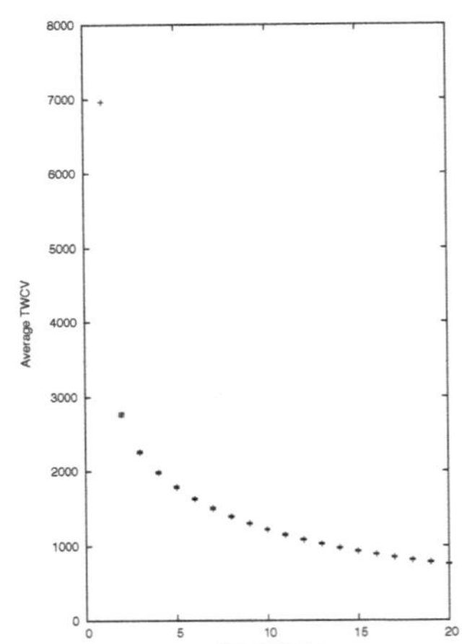

Fig. 3. Average best TWCVs in the Pareto front of the first phase for Breast Cancer data. Number of runs is 30

Note that a Pareto front is generated in both phases of the method. It is important to analyze if the TWCV values point out the optimal number of clusters according to elbow criterion. In figure 3, average best TWCVs in the Pareto front of the first phase are presented for Breast Cancer Dataset. In the figure, the increase in TWCV value is quite steady until the partition where the number of clusters is two. There is a big leap, between one and two clusters. This clearly points out that the optimal partitioning of data has two clusters.

The same analysis is presented in figure 4 for the dermatology dataset. Here, the sharp increase in TWCV starts between 5 and 4 clusters, denoting that 5 might be the optimal number of clusters for the data. However, there are 6 classes in the original dataset. This is due to the fact that the classes labeled as

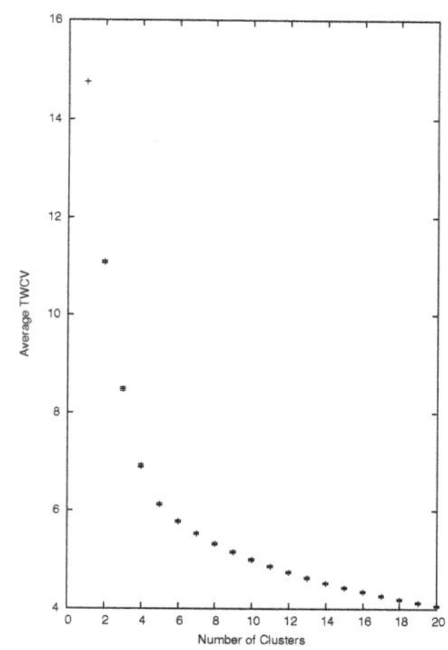

Fig. 4. Average best TWCVs in the Pareto front of the first phase for Dermatology data. Number of runs is 30

2 and 4 in the data are too close to each other. TWCV value doesn't increase much even if these two classes are combined into the same cluster. Note that all of the erroneous examples belong to these classes in table 2.

5 Conclusion

In this paper, a two-level approach is proposed to overcome the difficulty of using GA in grouping large datasets. The method is applied to the clustering problem and two large datasets have been chosen for experimentation. The results are promising and are even competitive with the results of supervised techniques. The future work will include testing the method on other well known datasets. On the other side, more efficient genetic operators suitable to be used with LLE might be developed in order to increase the performance further.

References

1. Falkenauer, E.: Genetic Algorithms and Grouping Problems. John Wiley&Sons (1998)
2. Du, J., Korkmaz, E., Alhajj, R., Barker, K.: Novel clustering approach that employs genetic algorithm with new representation scheme and multiple objectives. Lecture Notes in Computer Science **3181** (2004) 219
3. Du, J., Korkmaz, E., Alhajj, R., Barker, K.: Alternative clustering by utilizing multi-objective genetic algorithm with linked-list based chromosome encoding. Lecture Notes in Computer Science **3587** (2005) 346
4. Jones, D.A., Beltramo, M.A.: Solving partitioning problems with genetic algorithms. In Belew, Richard K.; Booker, L.B., ed.: Proceedings of the 4th International Conference on Genetic Algorithms, San Diego, CA, Morgan Kaufmann (1991) 442–449

5. Blake, C.L., Merz, C.J.: UCI repository of machine learning databases. http://www.ics.uci.edu/~mlearn/mlrepository.html, university of california, irvine, dept. of information and computer sciences (2000)
6. Mangasarian, O.L., Wolberg, W.H.: Cancer diagnosis via linear programming. SIAM News **23** (1990) 1–18
7. Jain, A.K., Dubes, R.C.: Algorithms for Clustering Data. Prentice Hall International (1988)
8. Kaufman, L., Rousseeuw, P.J.: Finding Groups in Data. John Wiley & Sons (1990)
9. Cole, R.M.: Clustering with genetic algorithms. Master's thesis, Nedlands 6907, Australia (1998)
10. Bezdek, J., Boggavarapu, S.: Genetic algorithm guided clustering. Proc. 1st IEEE Conf. on Evolutionary Computation (1994) 34–39
11. Maulik, U., Bandyopadhyay, S.: Genetic algorithm-based clustering technique. Pattern Recognition **33** (2000) 1455–1465
12. Ng, R., Han, J.: Efficient and effective clustering method for spatial data mining. In: Proc. of 1994 Int'l Conf. on Very Large Data Bases (VLDB'94). (1994) 144–155
13. Dhillon, I., Fan, J., Guan, Y.: Efficient clustering of very large document collections. In Grossman, R., Kamath, C., Naburu, R., eds.: Data Mining for Scientific and Engineering Applications. Kluwer Academic Publishers (2001)
14. Radcliffe, N.J.: Forma analysis and random respectful recombination. In Belew, Richard K.; Booker, L.B., ed.: Proceedings of the 4th International Conference on Genetic Algorithms, San Diego, CA, Morgan Kaufmann (1991) 222–229
15. Krishna, K., Murty, M.: Genetic k-means algorithm. IEEE Transactions on Systems, Man, and Cybernetics - PartB: Cybernetics **29**(3) (1999) 433–439
16. Horn, J., Nafpliotis, N., Goldberg, D.E.: A Niched Pareto Genetic Algorithm for Multiobjective Optimization. In: Proceedings of the First IEEE Conference on Evolutionary Computation. Volume 1., New Jersey (1994) 82–87
17. Torrez, F.: (Machine learning datasets, universite charles de gaulle,groupe de recherche sur l'apprentissage automatique, cedex, france)
18. Fred, A.L.N.: Clustering based on dissimilarity first derivatives. In: 2nd International Workshop on Pattern Recognition in Information Systems, PRIS. (2002) 257–266
19. Ruspini, E.: Numerical methods for fuzzy clustering. Inform. Sci. **2**(3) (1970) 19–150

A New Swarm Intelligence Coordination Model Inspired by Collective Prey Retrieval and Its Application to Image Alignment

G. Da San Martino[1], F.A. Cardillo[2], and A. Starita[2]

[1] Dept. of Pure and Applied Mathematics, University of Padova, Italy
dasan@math.unipd.it
[2] Dept. of Computer Science, University of Pisa, Italy

Abstract. Swarm Intelligence is the emergent collective intelligence of groups of simple agents acting almost independently. Algorithms following this paradigm have many desirable properties: flexibility, decentralized control, robustness, and fault tolerance. This paper presents a novel agent coordination model inspired by the way ants collectively transport large preys. In our model a swarm of agents, each having a different destination to reach, moves with no centralized control in the direction indicated by the majority of agents keeping its initial shape. The model is used to build an algorithm for the problems of image alignment and image matching. The novelty of the approach and its effectiveness are discussed.

1 Introduction

Swarm Intelligence (SI) is the property of a system where the behaviour of simple quasi-independent agents, interacting locally with their environment, cause intelligent global behaviour to emerge. Since intelligent behaviour should emerge from collaboration rather than from individual abilities, each agent is designed to be very simple. The agents should have a limited knowledge of the environment, which they should be able to modify only locally, and should be designed according to the reactive paradigm [1].

A feature distinguishing Swarm Intelligence from classical multi-agent systems is the concept of stigmergy. While in classical multi-agent systems, the agents communicate directly between each other, in the SI paradigm the agents communicate by modifying a shared environment. The alterations of the environment, amplified through a feedback process, may lead the system to self-organize. The state reached by the system should correspond to an optimal solution of the problem. A system with such characteristics is non-linear. The next state of the system does not depend solely on the current state of every agent. The prediction must be based also on the relationships among the various agents. Such complexity makes difficult for an agent to determine the action leading to the desired macroscopic behaviour.

Despite some interesting works [2,3,4], there is a lack of general theories and programming methodologies in the SI field. The difficulties have induced

T.P. Runarsson et al. (Eds.): PPSN IX, LNCS 4193, pp. 691–700, 2006.

researchers to look for inspiration at biological phenomena. Ant Colony Optimization (ACO) and Particle Swarm Optimization (PSO) are optimization techniques inspired to coordination mechanisms used by, respectively, ants gathering for food [5] and birds flocking [6]. Other examples of biologically-inspired algorithms can be found in [7,8,9,10].

This paper presents a new agent coordination model named Democratic Collective Transportation (DCT). The model is inspired by ants collectively transporting large preys to the nest. In fact, some species of ants are able to transport a heavy prey by coordinating their forces through the prey itself. In our new model, the constraint that all agents try and move the prey toward the same destination (the nest) is removed: each agent has a desired destination. The group moves the prey toward the direction chosen by the majority of agents with no centralized control. Based on the introduced model, an algorithm for the Image Alignment problem has been devised. It is a population-based optimization algorithm but, unlike ACO and PSO, only one solution, obtained through a self-organizing mechanism, is generated at each iteration.

The paper is organized as follows. Section 2 describes the biological model. Section 3 presents the new model. Section 4 describes an algorithm for image alignment based on the presented coordination model and discusses its results. Section 5 presents some concluding remarks.

2 Collective Prey Retrieval

In order to overcome the limits imposed by their small size and limited capabilities, many species of ants have evolved by developing collaborative strategies. The carriage of a large prey into the nest is an example of such process. Some species of ants have specialized workers able to cut the prey into small pieces that a single ant can carry, while other species are able to collectively transport large preys. Experimental results show that the latter strategy, called collective transportation, is the most efficient one [5]. The species with the most interesting strategies are *Pheidole crassinoda, Myrmica rubra and Myrmica lugubris.* They exhibit the same behavioural patterns in solitary and group transport [11]. An high level description of collective prey retrieval is summarized below:

1. When an ant finds a prey, it tries to carry it.
2. If the ant does not succeed in moving the prey, it tries to drag it in various directions (realignment behavior).
3. If the prey does not move, the ant grasps the prey differently, then tries and drag it in various directions.
4. If the prey still does not move, the ant starts recruiting nest mates. First, it releases a secretion in the air in order to attract nearby ants (short range recruitment). If the number of recruited ants is not enough to move the prey, the ant goes back to the nest leaving a pheromone trail on the ground. Such trail will lead other ants to the prey (long range recruitment). The recruitment phase stops as soon as the group is able to move the prey.

Resistance to traction represents a positive feedback mechanism. As specified at point 4, recruitment stops when resistance to traction ends and the prey starts moving.

While moving toward the nest, coordination among the ants occurs through the prey itself. The change of the force applied by a single ant modifies the stimuli perceived by the other ants (which react accordingly). Such coordination strategy is an example of stigmergy.

3 A New Coordination Mechanism Based on Collective Prey Retrieval

The new coordination model introduced in this paper is an extension of the last phase of the collective prey retrieval strategy: the coordination of forces during the transportation of the object to the nest. It introduces two significant differences with respect to the model described in section 2:

- in collective prey retrieval, each ant tries and carry the prey to the same destination (the nest). In our model each agent has its own destination for the prey. The group must move in the direction indicated by the majority of its agents.
- In section 2 the prey is considered a rigid body. A force applied to a rigid body is perceived instantaneously by all the carrying ants. The inclusion of a similar propagation mechanism in a model would lead to an unacceptable level of complexity: either the agents or the preys should be equipped with a broadcasting mechanism. In the democratic transportation model, the application of a force by an agent is immediately notified to its neighbouring agents only and is perceived by all the other agents after some instants. Such delayed propagation roughly corresponds to considering the prey as a non-rigid body. We show how such modification still allows the coordination of the agents, while keeping simple both the prey and the agent models.

3.1 Model Description

In order to obtain the democratic collective transportation model described in section 3, the biological model (section 2) is to be modified as follows:

1. each agent constantly applies a force on the prey toward his preferred destination V_p.
2. The intensity of the applied force is inversely proportional to the angle between V_p and the direction V_g chosen by the majority of the agents.
3. The direction V_g of the majority of the ants is estimated by each agent by simply looking at the movements of the prey in the previous time steps.

In the following we outline the functions needed for a formal description of the democratic collective transportation model.

p denotes a generic agent of the system. The agents are grouped in a set P. $p(t)$ is the position of agent p at time t. Each p has 0 initial velocity and moves according to F_n and F_p.

$\mathbf{F_n}$ propagates the individual forces applied to the item being transported to neighbouring agents. F_n is obtained constraining each agent to keep the initial distance from its neighbours at every time step:

$$F_n(p) = c \cdot \sum_{q \in P} \left(\frac{q(t) - p(t)}{\|q(t) - p(t)\|} \right) \cdot (\|q(t) - p(t)\| - \|q(0) - p(0)\|) \cdot \delta(p, q) \ , \quad (1)$$

with $0 \leq c \leq 1$. The first factor of eq. (1) is the versor from agent p to agent q. The second factor is the gap between the current and the initial distance between p and q. Function δ indicates whether p and q are to be considered neighbours: $\delta(p, q) = 1$ if $q \in neigh(p)$ and 0 otherwise. Function $neigh(p)$ determines the initial disposition of the agents. The function $neigh$, used in our work, is defined as:

$$neigh(p) = \left\{ q \in P : 0 < \|p(0) - q(0)\|_2 \leq \sqrt{2} \right\} \ . \quad (2)$$

$\mathbf{F_p}$ controls the velocity of the agents p moving in their preferred directions. F_p can be expressed as:

$$F_p(p(t)) = \begin{cases} 0 & \text{if} \quad F_p(p(t-1)) + V_p \cdot A < 0 \\ \mathrm{Max}_{F_p} & \text{if} \quad F_p(p(t-1)) + V_p \cdot A > \mathrm{Max}_{F_p} \\ F_p(p(t-1)) + V_p \cdot A & \text{otherwise} \end{cases} \ . \quad (3)$$

At time $t = 0$, $F_p(p(0)) = 0$. The term A in equation 3 represents the increment in modulus of F_p at time t:

$$A = \lambda(V_p \cdot \hat{V_g}(p)) \ . \quad (4)$$

It is worth noting that F_p and V_p have the same orientation and the same direction. Since V_p and $\hat{V_g}(p)$ are versors, the parameter λ represents the maximum value of A. The increment of the modulus of F_p is inversely proportional to the angle between the direction chosen by the agent, i.e. the versor V_p, and the direction chosen by the majority of agents, i.e. the versor V_g.

In order to obtain the exact value of V_g, we should know the state of each agent in any iteration, but such assumption violates SI principles. An estimate $\hat{V_g}$ of V_g can be obtained by using local information only, namely comparing the current position of an agent to its position at time $t - k$:

$$\hat{V_g}(p) = \frac{p(t) - p(t-k)}{\|p(t) - p(t-k)\|} \ . \quad (5)$$

In order for eq. (5) to be consistent for every t, it is assumed that $p(-1) = p(-2) = \ \ldots \ = p(-k) = 0$. In the first k iterations each p receives a positive feedback from the system.

The position of agent p at time t is expressed as follows:

$$p(t) = p(t-1) + F_n\left(p(t)\right) + F_p\left(p(t)\right) \ . \quad (6)$$

In order to ease the description, we will identify agents with the points of the transported item.

3.2 Model Validation

The democratic collective transportation model has been validated through a series of simulations. In order to prove the correctness of the model, we show that, in such model, each agent, after some iterations, starts following the direction chosen by the majority of the agents, independently by its initial direction.

The simulation is divided into two stages. At the beginning of the first stage, all the agents are still. The versors V_p are randomly selected and each agent starts moving. During the first $\frac{N}{2}$ iterations, where N is the total number of iterations of the simulation, the V_ps remain unchanged. At iteration number $\frac{N}{2}+1$, when the agents are moving along the direction of the majority of them, their V_ps are reselected. In this case, it is more difficult for a moving agent to modify its parameters and start following the majority.

The main issue for the model concerns the estimates of the majority direction $\hat{V_g}$ made by the agents. In order to verify such estimates, we used the following error measure:

$$E = \sum_{\forall p \in P} \left(1 - \hat{V_g}(p) \cdot V_g\right) \ . \tag{7}$$

Figure 1 shows the results of a single simulation. In that case the simulation was run for $N = 80$ iterations with a population of 900 agents and parameters set as follows: $c = 0.49$, $\lambda = 0.06$, $k = 3$, $\mathrm{Max}_{F_p} = 0.24$.

As the bottom right box of figure 1 shows, the sum of the errors rapidly decreases to 0 (the peak at iteration 40 is caused by the second selection of the preferred destinations). The slope of E depends on the percentage of agents willing to move in the direction of the majority. The slope of E does not depend on the number of agents: we ran simulations with up to 10000 agents obtaining similar results.

4 An Algorithm for Image Alignment and Matching

In this section we propose an algorithm for Image Alignment based on the democratic collective transportation model.

Image alignment is defined as the problem of finding an optimal spatial alignment of two images of the same scene/object taken in different conditions. For example, two images of the same object taken at different times or from different points of view or with different modalities [12]. Image alignment is the problem of finding an optimal transformation ω minimizing dissimilarities between an input image I_{input} and a target image I_{target}. The degree of dissimilarity is measured by a cost function f:

$$\omega_{min} = \mathrm{argmin}_{\omega \in \Omega} \left\{ f(\omega(I_{input}), I_{target}) \right\} \ . \tag{8}$$

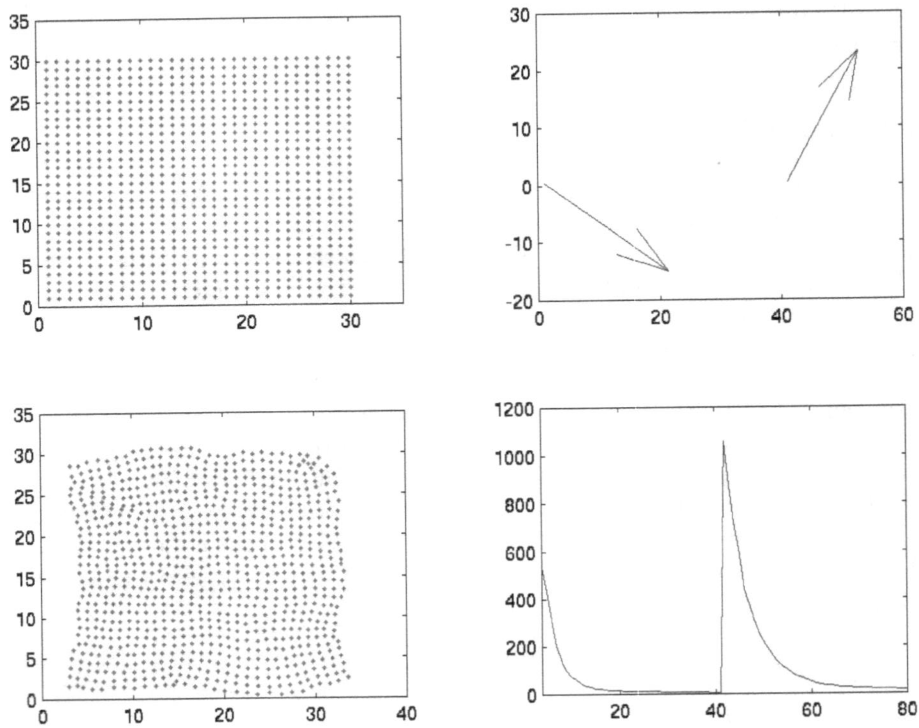

Fig. 1. A simulation of the democratic collective transportation model. From left to right, top to bottom: initial positions of the agents, qualitative idea of the direction chosen by the majority of the agents (from iteration one to 40: South-East, from iteration 41 to 80: North-East), final positions of the agents, plot of the error rate E, representing the error made by the agents in guessing the direction of the majority.

In some cases the differences between the two images should not be corrected since they might contain relevant information. For example, the diagnosis obtained by some image-based medical examinations relies on the differences between two images acquired at different times. Any registration algorithm should correct all the differences caused by misalignment and should preserve all the other ones. A detailed description of the image alignment problem and an overview of classical and new approaches can be found in [13,12].

As eq. (8) suggests, image alignment can be seen as an optimization problem, where Ω is a family of functions differing only for a set of parameters. Classical optimization techniques as well as popular swarm intelligence methods, such as Particle Swarm Optimization [14] and Ant Colony Optimization [15], have been applied to the image alignment problem. Such methods require a global cost function (or error function) to drive the system toward an optimal choice for the parameters of ω. The algorithm we propose does not use a global cost function: each agent has its local cost function.

4.1 Description of the Algorithm

Before describing in full details the algorithm, we will sketch its relationship with the introduced model:

1. I_{input}, the image to be registered, is considered the object that has to be moved.
2. Pixels of I_{input} are considered as points (and therefore agents) moving in a bi-dimensional space. Each agent has 8 neighbours corresponding to the neighbourhood of the pixel in I_{input}.
3. An application of a force on the object to be transported causes the pixel in I_{input} to move.
4. Each agent p has a set $Dest(p)$ of possible destinations, corresponding to the coordinates of the points in I_{target} that are similar, according to eq. (10), to p.
5. Each agent selects a point q in $Dest(p)$ and tries to move toward q.

The functions of the model are modified as follows:

p is a generic agent of the system. Pixels of I_{target} are grouped in a set O. At $t = 0$ the agents form a grid of points. A function $Color$ maps the agents to the gray values of the corresponding pixels in I_{input}.

$\mathbf{F_p}$ modifies I_{input} in order to make it as similar as possible to I_{target}. The idea is to let regions of I_{input} with a high gradient be attracted by corresponding regions of I_{target}. The only difference with the democratic transportation model concerns the V_p definition. Each $p \in P$ has an associated set of pixels $Dest(p)$, composed by the pixels of I_{target} which are similar to p according to eq. (10):

$$Dest(p) = \{q \in O | sim(p,q) \geq d_{sim}\} \quad , \tag{9}$$

where d_{sim} is the similarity threshold. The similarity function used is:

$$sim(p,q) = |Color(p) - Color(q)| + \|\nabla p - \nabla q\|^2 \quad , \tag{10}$$

where ∇p is the gradient of the image I at coordinates (p_x, p_y). Each p tries to reach a position corresponding to an element of $Dest(p)$ stored in $CurrentDestination(p)$. $CurrentDestination(p)$ is modified every g iterations according to probability density ρ defined as:

$$\rho(p,q) = \left((1 + \|p(t) - q\|) \cdot \sum_{o \in Dest(p)} \frac{1}{1 + \|p(t) - o\|} \right)^{-1} \quad . \tag{11}$$

By reselecting $CurrentDestination(p)$ every g iterations, the system explores more solutions. Since in the selection process closest destinations are preferred, when a good solution has been found each agent tends, with high probability, to go back to the same point.

V_p is the versor with direction from p to its current destination:

$$V_p = \frac{CurrentDestination(p) - p(t)}{\|CurrentDestination(p) - p(t)\|} \quad .$$

The dynamic of the algorithm pushes the majority of I_{input} pixels in the direction of their current preferred destination. With high probability I_{input} will move to a position "satisfying" the majority of the agents. In this paper we hypothesize that this position is the one with the highest probability to correctly align the image.

4.2 Results and Discussion

The algorithm has been tested on Magnetic Resonance images of the human brain. We ran several test using different images and different degree of noise. In each case the target image was obtained by 1) removing the background in the original image, 2) translating the filtered image to South-East and 3) by adding noise. The typical results of such experimentations are shown in fig. 2, which contains the output of three tests on 116 x 137 images. In the first row a 45% salt & pepper noise was added to I_{input}. In the second row a 16% speckle noise was added. In the last row a 16% speckle noise and a 35% salt & pepper noise were added. The last image in each row represents the final result of the algorithm. In every case the swarm needed few seconds on an AMD 1800+, with 1 GB of RAM, to compute the correct registration. The algorithm still finds the correct transformation on larger images, even if it takes longer. The results show that the algorithm corrects the differences caused by the translation.

In fig. 3 the results of a different experimentation are shown. In this case the goal was to locate a small image in a larger one. In this case also the algorithm is able to correctly locate the input image.

The algorithm described in this paper is different from classical population based optimization techniques such as genetic algorithms (GA), ACO, and PSO. In GA, ACO, and PSO at each iteration every agent proposes a complete solution to the problem. The best solutions are then selected and influence the creation of the solutions in subsequent iterations. Such approaches require a global cost function able to evaluate how good each proposed solution is. In the approach described in this paper, only one solution is generated at every iteration. There is no need of a global cost function: each agent uses a local cost function which is much simpler than common global cost functions. The system is able to discard the contribution of those agents whose cost function would lead to a poor solution and to promote those agents whose cost function would increase the quality of the solution.

5 Conclusions and Future Work

In this paper we presented a new agent coordination model based on the collective prey retrieval strategy of some species of ants. In the model a swarm of agents, each having a different destination to reach, is able, with no centralized control, to move in the direction indicated by the majority of the agents keeping, at the same time, the initial shape of the swarm.

From this coordination model an algorithm for Image Alignment and Matching in which simple agents collaborate to move an input image toward a target

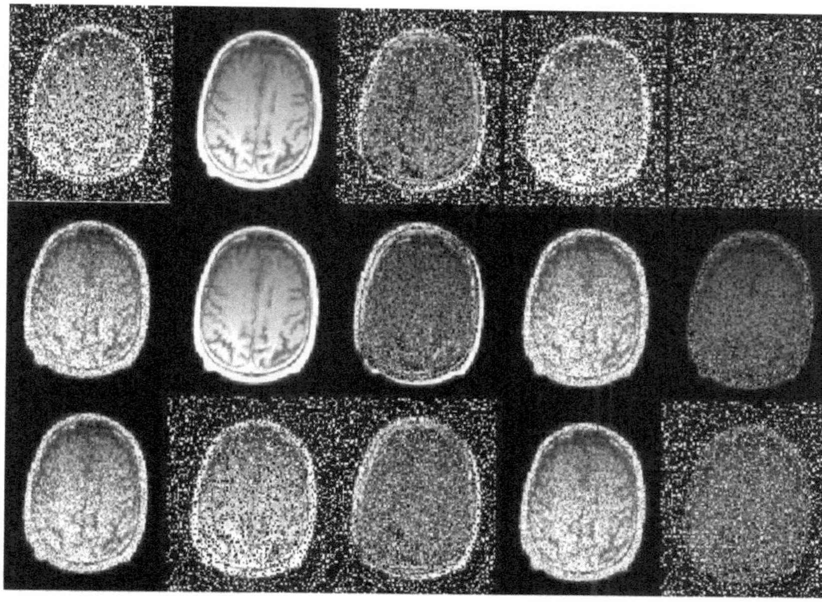

Fig. 2. Example of the execution of the algorithm. For every row, from left to right: I_{input}, I_{target}, differences between I_{input} and I_{target}, the output of the algorithm (the aligned image), the difference between I_{target} and the output of the algorithm.

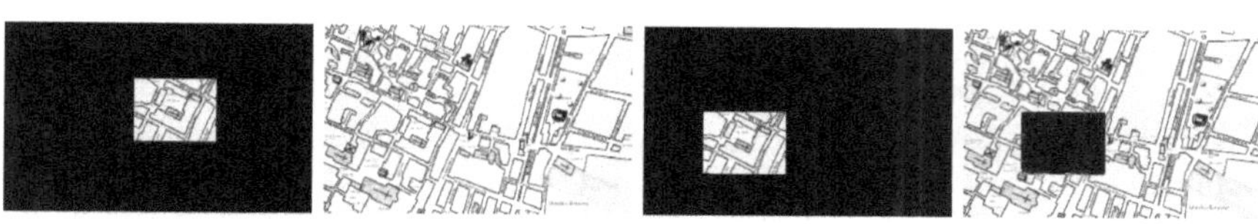

Fig. 3. Example of application of our algorithm to the Image Matching problem. In this case the goal is to find the location of the patch I_{input} in I_{target}. From left to right: I_{input}, I_{target}, the output of the algorithm, the differences between I_{target} and the estimated location of I_{input} in I_{target}. The black box means that the algorithm was able to correctly locate the patch over I_{target}.

one has been devised. According to the current results, the algorithm is tolerant to noise, but we need to further investigate its dynamic behaviour by using a larger set of test images.

The algorithm is able to correct translations only, but the results obtained so far induce us to further investigate the capabilities of our approach. The short-term goal is to extend the algorithm in order to match rotated images and to compare its performance against standard approaches. The long-term goal is to introduce new interactions that should enable the image alignment with elastic deformations and other types of noise.

References

1. Brooks, R.A.: Intelligence without representation, Dedham, Endicott House (1987)
2. Birattari, M., Caro, G.D., Dorigo, M.: Toward the formal foundation of ant programming. In: Ant Algorithms. (2002) 188–201
3. Leonardi, L., Mamei, M., Zambonelli, F.: Co-fields: Towards a unifying model for swarm intelligence. (2002)
4. Parunak, H., Brueckner, S.: Engineering swarming systems, Methodologies and Software Engineering for Agent Systems, F. Bergenti and M.P. Gleizes, eds., Amsterdam: Kluwer, 341-376 (2004)
5. Bonabeau, E., Dorigo, M., Theraulaz, G.: Swarm intelligence: from natural to artificial systems. Oxford University Press, Inc. (1999)
6. Kennedy, J., Eberhart, R.C.: Swarm intelligence. Morgan Kaufmann Publishers Inc. (2001)
7. Ramos, V., Almeida, F.: Artificial ant colonies in digital image habitats - a mass behaviour effect study on pattern recognition (2000)
8. Bourjot, C., Chevrier, V., Thomas, V.: Web Intelligence and Agent System. In: A new swarm mechanism based on social spiders colonies: from web weaving to region detection. Volume 1. (2003) 47–64
9. Lumer, E., Faieta, B.: Exploratory database analysis via self-organization. Unpubished manuscript (1995)
10. Kondacs, A.: Biologically-inspired self-assembly of two-dimensional shapes using global-to-local compilation. In: IJCAI. (2003) 633–638
11. Kube, R.C., Bonabeau, E.: Cooperative transport by ants and robots. Robotics and Autonomous Systems **30**(1/2) (2000) 85–101 ISSN: 0921-8890.
12. Zitová, B., Flusser, J.: Image registration methods: a survey. Image Vision Comput. **21**(11) (2003) 977–1000
13. Maintz, J., Viergever, M.: A survey of medical image registration. Medical Image Analysis **2**(1) (1998) 1–36
14. Wachowiak, M.P., Smolíkova, R., Zheng, Y., Zurada, J.M., Elmaghraby, A.S.: An approach to multimodal biomedical image registration utilizing particle swarm optimization. IEEE Trans. Evolutionary Computation **8**(3) (2004) 289–301
15. Meshoul, S., Batouche, M.: Ant colony system with extremal dynamics for point matching and pose estimation. In: ICPR (3). (2002) 823–826

Exploring the Effect of Proximity and Kinship on Mutual Cooperation in the Iterated Prisoner's Dilemma

Colin Frayn, Andy Pryke, and Siang Yew Chong

Cercia, School of Computer Science, University of Birmingham, Edgbaston, Birmingham, UK, B15 2TT
{C.M.Frayn, A.N.Pryke, S.Y.Chong}@cs.bham.ac.uk
http://www.cercia.ac.uk

Abstract. The iterated prisoner's dilemma (IPD) has been used as a model for investigating cooperation in nature. Here, we present an analysis of the evolution of reciprocal cooperation in a dynamically simulated environment in which individual agents are free to move in space, interacting with their nearest neighbors in fixed-length IPD games. Agents aim to avoid those against whom they score poorly, and to seek out those against whom they score highly. Individuals are modeled using finite state machines, allowing us to extend previous work on kin group markers. Though they have no direct effect on an individual's strategy, such markers do lead to the emergence of coherent, mutually-cooperating sub-populations.

1 Introduction

The IPD was first popularized as an effective model for cooperative strategies over 20 years ago[1]. Initial studies focused on a simple 2-player iterated game in which individuals were allowed either to cooperate or defect on each turn. Axelrod's famous open tournament ([2][3]) showed that the most successful individual when competing against varied opponents tends to be one that remains cooperative until the opponent defects, at which point it punishes and then forgives. E.g. 'tit-for-tat', which always does in each round exactly what the opponent did in the previous round. Most importantly, Axelrod showed that cooperative strategies could be successful in certain scenarios, depending on the nature of the opponents.

IPD remains a highly studied topic, with modern hardware allowing far more complex simulations involving a larger number of interacting individuals, with increasingly complex interactions. It has also been extended to cover further avenues of research:

- Adding a spatial component in order to investigate the effect of physical proximity on cooperation. [4][5][6][7]
- Increasing the number of players per game above 2, to the generalized N-player game [8][9][10][11].
- Adding noise, giving the possibility of miscommunication [12][13][14].
- Increasing the number of response levels to include intermediate possibilities, as well as allowing a continuous spectrum of cooperation [15][16][17].

T.P. Runarsson et al. (Eds.): PPSN IX, LNCS 4193, pp. 701 – 710, 2006.

This paper focuses on further extending the concept of spatial dynamics applied to the IPD game: a field that has so far only been studied simplistically. We embed a population of agents within a continuous, 3D environment, allowing individuals to interact stochastically with their physical neighbors. In addition, we incorporate the research on ethnic marking of McElreath et al. [18], which allows individuals to learn different strategies for dealing with different subgroups of opponents based on an externally visible 'tag'.

The goal of this work is to demonstrate a new simulation mechanism, which can provide a more accurate conformity to real-world situations. We have designed an environment which allows individual agents to behave more realistically, each aiming to maximize its own personal fitness by clustering with its most beneficial neighbors, and avoiding those that are harmful to it.

We introduce two techniques used to extend the investigation of the IPD. The first, to the best of our knowledge, has never been applied to this problem. The second is very rarely applied but we believe that it is extremely well suited.

1.1 Force-Based Clustering and Visualization

The technology of force-based clustering and visualization (FBC) has been used for some time to address the visualization of large and opaque datasets in an intuitive, interactive manner. Though it is literally a 'nature-inspired' technique, it was inspired by physics rather than biology; in this case the interaction of physical forces between mutually attractive bodies. A real-world analogy is clusters of stars, which have been modeled in astrophysics for many years using N-body codes. The technique is an unsupervised dimension reduction algorithm, directing the emergence of structure and substructure based on arbitrary measures of mutual affinity and without requiring the original data to possess particular statistical properties.

In this application to the IPD, we use a population of single points within a 3D space, each point representing a single evolutionary agent. These agents are linked to every other agent by means of a continuous simulated force with a strength related to the degree of affinity of those two individuals. The details of this force calculation are laid out in section 2.1.

1.2 Finite-State Machines

A finite-state machine is a class of control system for a simple decision-making process, acting in a deterministic manner based on certain inputs from its environment and a hidden internal state. This state can be thought of as analogous to an emotion, in the sense that it influences the way in which this individual interacts with its peers, even given identical (external) inputs, yet it is not externally visible.

A machine is precisely described by its current state, and a transition vector detailing tuples of (target state, action) for every (current state, environmental input) combination. In this case, there are exactly four possible inputs for each state, corresponding to the last result in the IPD game. Those states correspond to "mutual cooperation", "mutual defection" and "one player cooperates and one defects," the last occurring in two symmetrical ways.

The genome for a finite-state machine is therefore comprised of three components. Firstly, the state transition vector detailing which action to take in every possible situation. Secondly, the initial state for the individual, and thirdly the action to take on the first move before any environmental input is obtained.

We also introduce the concept of kin tags, which are stored as a single integer within the genome. The effect of kin tags is to set the initial state in which an individual's opponent commences each interaction. When competing against an opponent with a tag of 'x', an individual starts off in internal state 'x'. Because of this, the number of internal states is constrained to be greater than or equal to the total number of different kin groups in the initial population. Initial kin tags are evenly distributed.

2 Experiment Design

The experiments were designed to explore a subset of the parameter space of the proposed simulation environment. The simulated framework consists of two separate, parallel components: the dynamical simulation based on force-based clustering, and the evolutionary simulation that runs in parallel and uses a nearest-neighbor interaction fitness measure.

2.1 Dynamical Framework

The dynamical framework uses the force-based clustering method as explained above. This simulation runs continuously, allowing individuals to cluster closely with those opponents with whom they perform most successfully in the IPD games. In order to do this, a matrix is stored detailing the 'affinity' of each individual for every other. This is calculated once at the beginning of the simulation, and is then updated whenever a new individual is introduced in the evolutionary component of the simulation.

Affinity is given by the following formula:

$$\textbf{Affinity (P1, P2)} = \textbf{Score of P1 vs. P2 in fixed-length IPD} . \qquad (1)$$

Affinity is converted linearly into a scalar force by considering a standard Hooke's law spring model in which the force in a spring is related to the degree to which it is extended or compressed relative to its 'natural' length. In an equivalent sense, we convert Affinity (1) to a force between two individuals by the following relation:

$$\textbf{Force(P1,P2)} = -\,\textbf{k} * (\,\textbf{D} - \textbf{S} * (\textbf{M} - \textbf{Affinity(P1,P2)}\,)\,) . \qquad (2)$$

Where **k** is a force scale factor, **D** is the Euclidean distance between the two individuals, **S** is a distance scale factor and **M** is the maximum score that any individual could obtain in a game. In the standard game, **M** is equal to the Traitor's payoff (conventionally 5 points) multiplied by the number of games. Thus an individual scoring maximally against another will attempt to get as close as possible to that other individual as the force reduces to **–kD**. The opponent to that individual, having scored zero points, will attempt to stay at an equilibrium distance of **S*M** units.

Note that Affinity(A,B), and hence Force(A,B), is not symmetrical. If individual A scores well against individual B, then it will attempt to remain close to that same individual. However, in this case B may have scored poorly, so B will attempt to remain further away from A in order to avoid future interactions with A. Because of this, A will 'chase' B rather like in a predator-prey interaction.

The time complexity of FBC scales proportionally to the square of the number of points in the simulation, N, so we are constrained to relatively small population sizes of a few hundred for such an experiment with a reasonable generation count.

2.2 Evolutionary Framework

The evolutionary framework is totally separate from the dynamical framework, and follows a standard evolutionary algorithm design with a population of N=500 and elitism of N-1. The evolutionary update happens in parallel to the dynamical update, with a fixed rate.

In each evolutionary update, three steps are performed as in a standard evolutionary algorithm. Firstly every individual is assessed to calculate its fitness. Secondly, the weakest individual is killed off. Thirdly, a new individual is inserted into the population based on the crossover of two parents, selected biased by high fitness.

Fitness Evaluation

Fitness evaluation occurs in a geographical niche, with each individual playing a fixed number of fixed-round IPD games against selected neighbors. These neighbors are selected using a distance-based tournament selection. That is to say, in order to assess the fitness of individual **P**, a group of **Q** individuals is chosen from the rest of the population. From that group, the one which is physically closest to **P** is selected, and plays a fixed-round IPD game against **P**. This process is repeated a fixed number of times (we used **Q**=6 and 10 iterations for all the simulations in this paper) and the total scores are summed. This overall total score is assigned as the individual's fitness.

It is important to note the distinction between the fitness measure and the affinity matrix. The affinity is calculated between every pair of individuals and remains the same as long as those two individuals do not change. The fitness is recalculated each round, is unique for each individual, and is based on this stochastic neighborhood competition measure.

Selection and Crossover

After the fitness of every individual has been calculated then the weakest individual (or a randomly selected weakest individual, in the case of a tie) is selected and removed from the population. This individual is then replaced by a single offspring created by a continuous random crossover between two parents selected by n=2 tournament selection from the entire population, based on fitness. Mutation is applied to every offspring, uniformly replacing a single, randomly selected state transition.

We chose to use N-1 elitism, replacing only one individual each generation, in order to retain the dynamic stability of the simulation. If too many discrete changes are made at one time then the simulation becomes highly unstable, and must be given time to settle back down to equilibrium. A further study would investigate the use of tournament selection in order to select this worst individual, rather than the deterministic 'worst score' method. There is also room to vary the tournament size for neighbor selection. We leave these options for future work.

There is a potential interaction between the dynamical timescale of the clustering algorithm and the timescale for a generation update within the evolutionary code. The ideal scenario would be to allow the dynamical algorithm time to settle to a steady state between updates, though in practice this would make simulations prohibitively slow, and such a steady state does not always exist, once predator-prey chases are considered. In this initial work, we have not comprehensively investigated this interplay. We appreciate that the configuration of these two timescales may well affect the number of generations within which an outcome is achieved. However, our preliminary qualitative investigations suggest that any reasonable variation in these two timescales does not affect the outcome of the simulation in essence.

3 Results

We present brief results for four separate selected experiments run using the dynamical-evolutionary framework. These highlight real differences in the way the system of co-evolving agents reacts to variations in the simulation parameters detailed above, and are the result of approximately 5.6 trillion individual games of IPD.

3.1 Evolution of Cooperation

The evolution of cooperation within a dynamical evolutionary framework was qualitatively assessed during the course of the simulations. Figure 1 shows the results of a control run, consisting of 3000 generations with 3 kin groups and 4 internal states. No communication errors were considered.

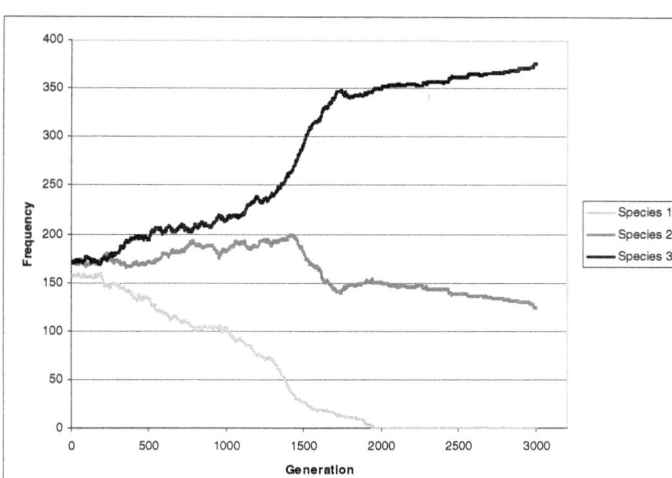

Fig. 1. Frequency of each kin group over the course of 3000 generations in one example simulation. Groups 2 & 3 dominate the population at generation 3000, mutually cooperating.

Qualitatively, the different kin groups could be visualized on screen using our 3D visualization package as the evolution proceeded. We found that the kin groups began to cluster together after a few hundred generations. This clustering became clearer as the sub-groups began to diverge and cooperate with themselves. Most simulations ended up with one or more groups dominating the environment and cooperating with all other survivors.

We also found other intriguing situations where a component of one kin group acted as a predator on one of the others. In such cases, two or three surviving groups existed in a stable, mutually-cooperating mix. However, a minority of one of the surviving groups would exist by cooperating with all groups except one, against which it would act as a predator (i.e. occasionally defect). Because this predatory subpopulation had the same kin tag as one of the cooperative populations, the other individuals never evolved a hostility towards them. If the predators had been identified by a separate marker then their 'prey' would have evolved a hostility towards them and hence the predators would have died out. This mimicry seems to be a remarkably successful adaptation and mirrors that found in nature, e.g. with camouflaged predators, cuckoos laying eggs in the nests of other birds, and carnivorous plants trapping feeding insects.

Genomic diversity remained high throughout the simulations. This is because certain states and transitions are never used. So the genome has freedom in those loci to change to any other value without affecting the phenotype (behavior). The genotypic diversity was calculated as the variance within a kin group of any genome locus from the group-average. The range of each locus was 8 points in total and the average diversity at the end of a control simulation was 5.91±0.44, which means that the average gene in an average individual was still sqrt(5.91) = 2.43 points away from the mean. This shows that almost all loci were essentially still random even after the simulation had settled down to mutual cooperation. Further work should investigate how this may correspond to the existence of 'junk DNA' in animals.

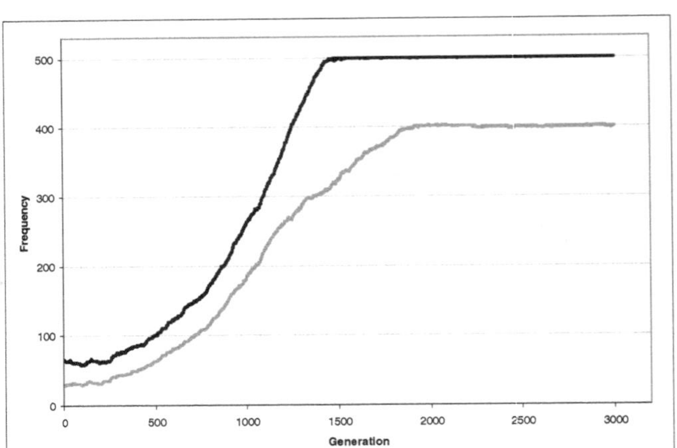

Fig. 2. Variation of 'niceness' over time, with kin (upper line) and non-kin for the same simulation as in figure 1

Figure 2 shows how Kin (K) and Non-Kin (NK) niceness varies with generation. K-niceness is defined as number of individuals in the simulation who will always cooperate with members with the same kin tag as long as that opponent also cooperates. NK niceness is defined identically, except applied to individuals with different tags. Note that, in order to avoid discontinuities, it is possible for an individual to be classed as nasty even if it only defects against a kin group that has gone extinct.

3.2 Variation of Kin Groups

Varying the number of kin groups provided a remarkably clean relationship with the K- and NK- niceness measures. When there are more kin groups, it takes longer to learn reciprocal altruism. In this simulation, the number of states is set equal to the number of groups. Re-running this test with a fixed number of states (7) and varying the number of groups reduced the overall levels of 'niceness', but retained the general form of the relationship. These results are shown in figure 3.

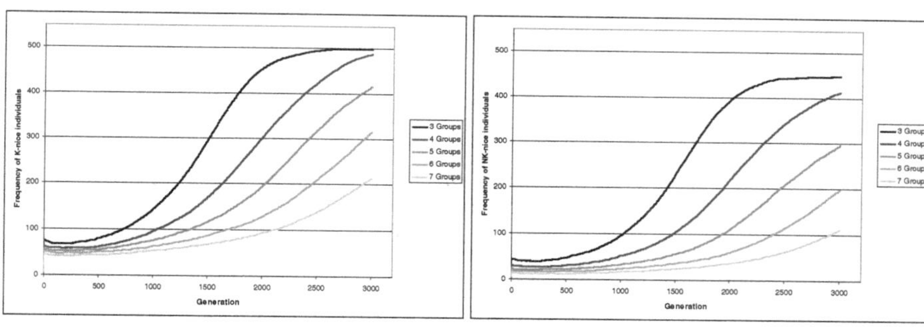

Fig. 3. Variation of Kin (K) and Non-Kin (NK) niceness as a function of generation and the number of kin groups. State complexity = kin group count.

3.3 Variation of State Complexity

When keeping the number of kin groups constant at three, we varied the state complexity of all individuals within the population, changing the number of internal states between three and seven. Figure 4 shows the effect this has on the extinction rate of kin groups. It is evident that a more complex state machine implies that individuals are more likely to cooperate with non-kin rather than force them to extinction. The main reason for this is simply that coherent 'nasty' (first-to-defect) strategies are more difficult to evolve than 'nice' ones. With mutually cooperating individuals, only the 'cooperate' state transitions need be correct. However, with 'nasty' individuals, the state transitions followed in any one game tend to be far more complex, and all these transitions need to be optimized in order to gain a reasonable score.

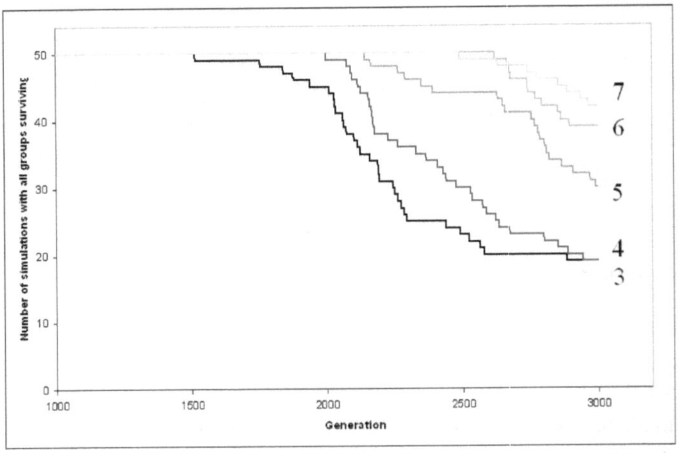

Fig. 4. Frequency of simulations in which all 3 kin groups survive, as a function of generation and state complexity (labeled on the right-hand side)

3.4 Introduction of Errors

Investigating the introduction of errors into the assessment of group identification and action communication has already been shown to affect the degree of cooperation that arises in the IPD [12][13][14]. Here we introduced noise in two areas. Firstly, in the communication of the action that an individual performs ('cooperate' or 'defect'). Secondly, in the identification of an opponent's kin tag. Figure 5 shows that increased error rates lead to a greater degree of cooperation between kin groups. Clearly, the more likely it is that an opponent's identity may have been incorrectly ascertained, the wiser it is to cooperate with that individual, in case it is kin.

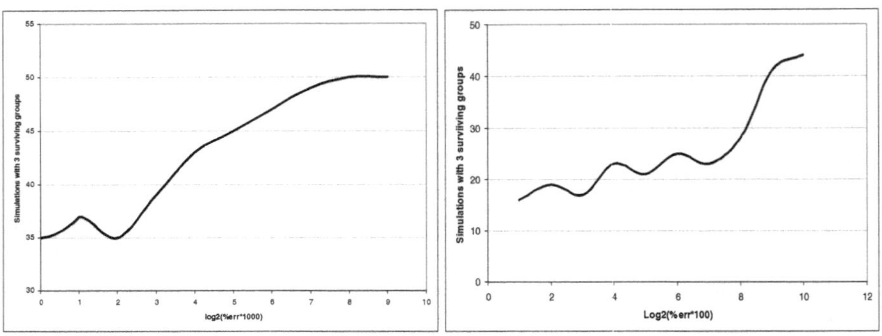

Fig. 5. The effect of errors in the number of surviving kin groups. Here are plotted the number of simulations (out of the maximum of 50) in which all three kin groups survive for 3000 generations, versus the logarithm of the level of error introduced. On the left is the result of an error in kin identification, and on the right is an error in communication of an individual action.

4 Conclusions

We have introduced a novel method for investigating the IPD within a dynamical evolutionary framework. Our conclusions are as follows:

(1) We confirm the prediction made by McElreath [18] that individuals prefer to cooperate with, and remain near, their own kin compared with others.
(2) Increasing state complexity or kin diversity increases the degree of inter-group cooperation and leads to less frequent extinctions.
(3) Semi-stable predatory niches with mimicry do exist within this environment.
(4) The introduction of errors increases the degree of inter-group cooperation.

For further extensions to this project, we would like to investigate the following:

(1) Introducing more realistic (harsh) payoff matrices for predatory individuals.
(2) Investigating the effect of tournament size on localized cooperation.
(3) Introducing kin tags that vary with some phenotypic (behavioral) features.
(4) Investigating how 'niceness' varies as a function of proximity to individuals with different kin tags.
(5) Varying the crossover mechanism to account for the fact that crossover of individuals with different kin tags will create an unbalanced offspring.
(6) Modeling incomplete knowledge in affinity matrix, by assuming cooperation until proven otherwise by direct interaction.

References

1. Axelrod, R., The Evolution of Cooperation, Basic Books New York (1984)
2. Axelrod, R., Effective Choice in the Prisoner's Dilemma, The Journal of Conflict Resolution, Vol. 24, No. 1 (1980) 3-25
3. Axelrod, R., More Effective Choice in the Prisoner's Dilemma, The Journal of Conflict Resolution, Vol. 24, No. 3 (1980) 379-403
4. Nowak, M. A., Bonhoeffer, S., May, R. M.: Spatial Games and the Maintenance of Cooperation, Proc. National Acad. Sci., Vol. 91 (1994) 4877-4881
5. Ifti, M., Killingback, T., Doebli, M.: Effects of Neighbourhood Size and Connectivity on the Spatial Continuous Prisoner's Dilemma, Journal of Theoretical Biology, Vol. 231 (2004) 97-106
6. Frean, M.R., Abraham, E.R.: A Voter Model of the Spatial Prisoner's Dilemma, IEEE Trans. Evol. Comp., Vol. 5 No. 2 (2001) 117-121
7. Isibuchi, H., Namikawa, N.: Evolution of Iterated Prisoner's Dilemma Game Strategies in Structured Demes Under Random Pairing in Game Playing, IEEE Trans. Evol. Comp. Vol. 9 No. 6 (2005) 552-561
8. Seo, Y.G., Cho, S.B., Yao, X.: Exploiting Coalition in Co-Evolutionary Learning, Proc. CEC (2000) 1268-1275
9. Seo, Y.G., Cho, S.B., Yao, X.: Emergence of Cooperative Coalition in NIPD game with Localization of Interaction and Learning, Proc. CEC (1999) 877-884
10. Yao, X.: Evolutionary Stability in the N-person Iterated Prisoner's Dilemma, BioSystems, Vol. 37 No. 3 (1996) 189-197

11. Yao, X., Darwen, P.: An Experimental Study of N-Person Iterated Prisoner's Dilemma Games, Informatica, Vol. 18 No. 4 (1994) 435-350
12. Fogel, D. B.: Evolving Behaviors in the Iterated Prisoner's Dilemma, Evolutionary Computation, Vol. 1, No. 1 (1993) 77-97
13. Julstrom, B. A.: Effects of Contest Length and Noise on Reciprocal Altruism, Cooperation, and Payoffs in the Iterated Prisoner's Dilemma, Proc. 7th ICGA (1997) 386-293
14. Axelrod, R., Dion, D.: The Further Evolution of Cooperation, Science, Vol. 242, No. 4884 (1988) 1385-1390
15. Harrald, P.G., Fogel, D.B.: Evolving Continuous Behaviors in the Iterated Prisoner's Dilemma, BioSystems, 37 (1996) 135-145
16. Darwen, P., Yao, X.: Co-Evolution in Iterated Prisoner's Dilemma with Intermediate Levels of Cooperation: Application to Missile Defense, IJCIA, Vol. 2 No. 1 (2002) 83-107
17. Chong, S.Y., Yao, X.: Behavioral Diversity, Choices, and Noise in the Iterated Prisoner's Dilemma, IEEE Trans. Evol. Comp., Vol. 9, No. 6, (2005), 540-551
18. McElreath, R., Boyd, R., Richerson, P.J.: Shared Norms and the Evolution of Ethnic Markers, Current Anthropology, Vol. 44 (2003) 122-130

Investigating the Emergence of Multicellularity Using a Population of Neural Network Agents

Ehud Schlessinger[1], Peter J. Bentley[2], and R. Beau Lotto[1]

[1] Institute of Ophthalmology, University College London, 11-43 Bath Street, London
{e.schlessinger, lotto}@ucl.ac.uk
[2] Department of Computer Science, University College London, Malet Place, London
P.Bentley@cs.ucl.ac.uk

Abstract. This paper expands Mosaic World, an artificial life model, in order to directly test theories on the emergence of multicellular life. Five experiments are conducted and demonstrate that both the presence of predation and accidental aggregation are sufficient conditions for the transition to multicellularity. In addition, it is shown that division of labour is a major benefit for aggregation, and evolves even if aggregates 'pay' for abilities they do not use. Analysis of evolved results shows multiple parallels to natural systems, such as differentiation in constituent members of an aggregate, and life-like, complex ecosystems.

1 Introduction

Explaining the transition from single cells to multicellular organisms is one of the key challenges faced by evolutionary theory. A multicellular organism is comprised of more than one cell that are in physical contact; these cells are specialised (or differentiated) to perform specialised tasks - and their activities are coordinated, at least with regards to some key functions. Multicellular life, which is believed to have independently arisen multiple times in the different kingdoms [3], is evident even in the most ancient fossils dating some 3.5 billion years [18]. Multicellularity can be achieved in two ways: through aggregation and through cell division accompanied by adhesion.

Although it is accepted that for this transition to repeatedly take place it must offer some advantages, no one knows for certain the conditions that led to the original emergence of multicellularity, nor how it emerged. One view is that the transition to multicellularity occurred by accident, caused by a mutation that prevented offspring cells from separating [3], and that at first there were no advantages. In this scenario, the benefits came later, thus causing the selection of the organism. Another theory suggests that predation pressure was one of the causes leading to the emergence of multicellularity, as multicellular organisms would be more resistant to phagotrophy (ingestion of whole prey) [19]. This theory was tested by exposing a unicellular organism, Chlorela vylgas, to a predator. Within few generations the multicellular version of the organism, a rare mutant, evolved and was nearly immune to predation [5].

The possible advantages associated with multicellularity are numerous. One is the enhanced efficiency of dividing labour between cells [11]. This can provide advantages in feeding (e.g. efficient feeding through cooperation) and dispersion (e.g. a

T.P. Runarsson et al. (Eds.): PPSN IX, LNCS 4193, pp. 711 – 720, 2006.

larger fruiting body improves spore dispersion) [3]. The larger size may improve protection from environmental disturbances [1] and enable greater storage capacity of inorganic nutrients [9]. It also enables a greater division of labour – more cell types that offer greater specialisation [4]. Perhaps, most importantly, sheer size itself can be advantageous with regards to predation: the prey may be too large for the predators to eat and organisms may be able to move faster so could better catch prey or escape predation (e.g., in water environments [2]).

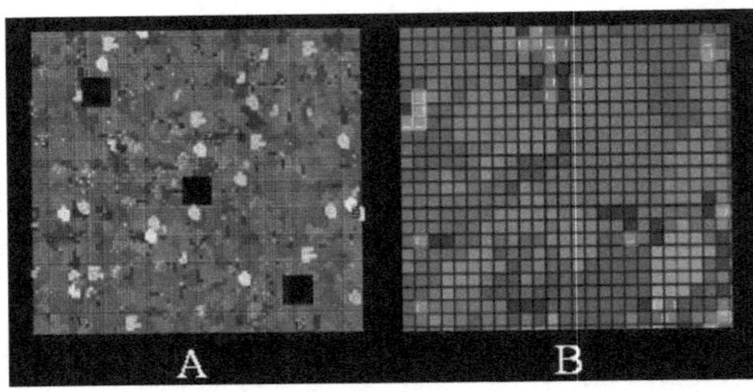

Fig. 1. (A) A screenshot of Mosaic World. (B) A close-up of Mosaic World.

It is important to emphasise that a group of individual cells (i.e. a colony) is not a multicellular organism. The first necessary step for this transition is that the individual cells stop competing and start cooperating; in other words, the individual cells start sacrificing their fitness for the fitness of the group [12]. Only then can cell differentiation begin and the organism becomes multicellular [10]. It is crucial that functions that limit internal conflict emerge [13]. According to some, successful complex multicellular organisms must be comprised of genetically identical members [20].

It is difficult to study events such as the emergence of multicellularity for obvious practical reasons. This is where artificial life models can greatly help. Indeed, several researchers have modelled aspects of the emergence of multicellular life: for example, Rothermich and Miller investigated the emergence of multicellularity by modelling cells using Cartesian genetic programming [15]. Bull used versions of the abstract NKC model to examine the conditions under which multicellularity is likely to occur [7]. Furusawa and Kaneko studied the origin of multicellularity using artificial chemistry [8]. Bryden modelled the macrocyst stage in slime mould in order to understand why an organism might decide to aggregate [6].

In this paper, we expand Mosaic World, a multi-agent system [16] [17]. Although originally created to understand the principles that underlie colour vision, its extensive model of evolutionary agents in a complex environment lends itself perfectly to gaining insights into the emergence of multicellularity. Specifically, we wish to explore the factors that may have provided an advantage for multicellular life when it first appeared in nature. Mosaic World is inhabited by a population of agents that sense their environment, consume food, reproduce and die. In this study, we have expanded their capabilities to include aggregation: they can now literally become multicellular organisms – reproduce as one, and divide tasks among members.

2 System

Mosaic World comprises a 2D grid of 'coloured' surfaces and is modelled after key characteristics of natural scenes. Its environment is inhabited by a population of virtual agents, 'critters', that try to survive. Survival requires consuming positive resources, and avoiding negative ones. Critters must also keep from falling from the world. There is no explicit fitness function in this model: by reproducing both sexually and asexually, the critters themselves maintain their population. Critters are instantiated with a given amount of health, and die if it drops below zero. If all critters die, a new population is generated where 80% are random critters and the rest are mutated clones of critters that showed general promising survival skills earlier in the run. By evolving the genome of the critter that determines all critter aspects and behaviour, the critter population becomes increasingly better at survival (for a more thorough discussion of Mosaic World and its critters see [16])

Critters can sense their environment through specialised sensors (called receptors), and must learn to generate behaviour accordingly. All critters are created with the ability to perform several actions, but must also learn how (and when) to perform them: moving, turning, sexual and asexual reproduction, resource consumption and predation. Each of these behaviours costs energy, so a critter must learn to balance its energy gain with its energy consumption. Additionally, every critter has a metabolism which determines the rate of energy it loses over time. The metabolic rate is determined according to the actions the critter has the capacity of performing. This attempts to model the notion that in nature, different types of cells have different energy costs (e.g. [14]) – although the costs used do not capture the mechanisms of biology in detail, the model does – in our view – present the critters with the same fundamental ecological challenges that is faced in the evolution of natural systems.

Even though at first all critters are created with the capacity to perform all actions except predation, by losing some of these capabilities (through evolution), the critters can decrease their metabolic rate – however, even a critter with no capacity to do anything still loses energy at a slow rate. Critters that lose the capacity to perform a certain action cannot perform it. The basic metabolic rate for a critter is 10 units per time step, reproduction adds 30 units, consumption adds 30 units, moving/turning adds 30 units, and predation adds 30 units. E.g. a critter that can only reproduce and move, but not eat, loses 70 energy units per time step, which is 70% of the rate of a critter that can also eat. There are two ways of gaining energy. The first is by consuming surfaces – a surface's value is determined from its colour (using a value function, see [16]). The second is by hunting for prey. However, an organism must be larger than its prey, and so, a standard critter cannot be anything other than an herbivore, and has no use for the capacity of predation.

Every critter has a brain, which is comprised of a control module (a gating network), and up to 8 secondary modules. The control module receives stimuli and determines which of the modules to activate at any given time step. Previously we have shown that this mechanism facilitates modular specialisation and increases critter performance [17]. Each of the modules is a modified 3D feed-forward neural network, and is comprised of multiple 2D layers. The visual layer, which corresponds to a standard input layer, contains receptors (input units with novel additions) which receive stimuli from the environment. Each of the secondary modules has three extra receptors: a health monitor which receives the percentage of the critter's remaining health, an aggregate monitor which indicates whether the critter is a part of an aggregate, and if it is, the aggregate's size, and a neighbour indicator, which receives a positive signal if another critter is on the same surface as this critter. The hidden layer contains standard hidden units. The output layer contains output units, which determine the critter's behaviour: turning, speed of movement, reproduction (sexually or asexually), resource consumption, predation, join or split from an aggregate.

In terms of evolution, every aspect of the critter brain is evolvable: weight values, module topology (number of hidden units, connectivity, etc) and other attributes (e.g. critter colour), as well as the actual number of modules (for a full description, see [16]). In addition, the critter can evolve (or devolve) its capacity to perform all actions: the capacity to consume surfaces, the capacity to move/turn, the capacity to prey, and the capacity to reproduce; as mentioned, this affects its metabolic rate.

Crossover takes place during sexual reproduction. Several modules (randomly determined) are cloned from one parent, and the rest are cloned from the other. The control module is recombined by 'slicing' all layers of the modules of both parents at a random point, cloning a part from each and combining these to form the brain of the offspring. In addition, the resulting brain is mutated at this point.

Mutation takes place during both sexual and asexual reproduction. The last active secondary module (as determined by the control module) and the control module are subject to several types of mutations; (i) Mutation operators that change receptor attributes. (ii) Mutation operators that change module topology (iii) Mutation operators that change the weight values. Additionally, the brain has its set of mutations (add module, delete module, duplicate module), a mutation that changes the critter's colour and a mutation that change the critter's behavioural capacities (6% per action).

2.1 Aggregation in Mosaic World

In order to investigate the emergence of multicellularity, mechanisms for critter aggregation have been added. An aggregate can comprise up to 25 adjacent critters in any form within a 5x5 square, and is subject to all the costs and limitations that critters incur. Two goals were aimed for: first, the usage of neural networks and sensors within critters is intended as a functionally equivalent model of gene regulatory networks and cellular receptors. Also, by making the aggregation methods optional, we enable evolution to discover the utility (or not) of aggregation - there is no bias towards multicellularity or differentiation and no requirement for critters to aggregate.

Aggregates can use all abilities of their constituent members: if no members have the capacity to perform certain actions, the aggregate cannot perform them. Decisions for reproduction, preying on critters/smaller aggregates, and splitting are determined 'democratically'; an aggregate performs these only if at least half its members wish to. Members that have lost the capacity to perform an action do not participate in this decision process. When critters form an aggregate, their genomes merge (see fig. 2). The aggregate genome is the combined genomes of its members, with an additional gene indicating the member's position in the aggregate. The genome defines all the traits of the aggregate, and by definition, of its comprising critters.

Aggregates pool the energy of their constituent members; an aggregate's current and maximum health levels are the combined total of its members' current and maximum health levels. Similarly, an aggregate's metabolism is the combined metabolic rates of its members. Aggregates enjoy the combined sensing capabilities of all their comprising members: every individual critter senses the environment, and can affect the behaviour of the aggregate. In addition, every member that has the capacity to consume can still decide whether to consume a surface or not, although it is still subject to the same limitations faced by critters (i.e. it cannot consume while moving, which depends on other members of the aggregate as well). The energy gained (or lost) is added to the aggregate's energy pool.

Location in aggregate [2,2]				Location in aggregate [2,3]			
Eating true	Movement false	Predation true	Reproduction false	Eating false	Movement true	Predation false	Reproduction true
-Begin control module Receptor (location [0,2], peak [430nm], tuning [0.25], on) Hidden (location [0,0]) Hidden (location [0,1]) * Weight (Rec[0,2], Hid[0,0], val[0.83], on]				-Begin control module Receptor (location [0,0], peak [400nm], tuning [0.003], on) Receptor (location [0,1], peak [470nm], tuning [0.01], on) Receptor (location [-1,0], peak [550nm], tuning [0.02], on) Receptor (location [0,-1], peak [630nm], tuning [0.09], on) Receptor (location [1,1], peak [690nm], tuning [0.5], on)			

Fig. 2. Sample aggregate (size 2) genome; most genes for critters are not shown (see [16])

An aggregate's movement is determined by its members, and is effectively their combined movements. Since aggregate members can turn inside an aggregate, an aggregate's overall movement depends on its members' individual orientations. Consequentially, the movement of an aggregate is difficult to coordinate. The movement and turning energy costs are identical to those of an ordinary critter – this models multicellular organisms using flagellates for swimming [2]. An aggregate does not fall from the world as long as its central member is still on it.

Aggregates can prey on critters and smaller aggregates. An aggregate must be larger than its prey to consume it, and must physically overlap at least 75% of it. Preying may not kill the target: only some of its energy is transferred to the aggregate (80% of full capacity). Preying also incurs an energy cost that depends on an aggregate's size.

Aggregates can only reproduce asexually. To reproduce, an aggregate must not move for a given number of time-steps and must also transfer a percentage (20%) of its maximum health to its offspring. All reproduction attempts incur an energy cost relative to the aggregate's size regardless of their success. When an aggregate reproduces, all its members are cloned and mutated (similarly to standard sexual reproduction). The members' spatial position is also copied, thus, cloning the aggregate's shape as well. There are three types of mutations, which may affect the metabolic rate of the offspring. The *clone element* mutation causes one of the offspring's members (randomly determined) to be cloned twice at a given probability (4%). The new member is attached randomly to an existing member. The *delete element* mutation (4%) causes an offspring's member (randomly selected) not to be copied. The picked member must not be the only connection between two parts of the aggregate (it cannot split the aggregate in two). The *shift element* mutation (4%) causes an offspring's member (randomly picked) to change position (altering the aggregate's shape).

There are two ways for critters to form an aggregate; each is used in different experiments. **Aggregation by choice** enables critters to aggregate with other willing critters and aggregates that are in immediate contact with it. A critter may be in 'join' mode, where it adheres to any willing organism it is in contact with, 'neutral' mode where it does not initiate aggregation, but adheres to any other organism that attempts to adhere to it, and 'split' mode where it never aggregates. **Accidental aggregation** causes a percentage (4%) of every reproduction to result in a small (size 2) aggregate – this models an offspring that does not separate from its parents during reproduction. In this setting, aggregates cannot split or grow during their lifetime.

Aggregates cannot increase their size by joining other organisms; however, a critter attempting to join an aggregate succeeds and adds its energy to the aggregate (with a corresponding increase in its metabolic rate). Aggregates can also decide to split – this causes the aggregate to split to its individual members. When an aggregate splits, every critter receives the appropriate part of the full genome.

3 Experiments

Five experiments were run with the aims of: (i) obtaining data that will directly test existing theories for the emergence of multicellularity in nature; (ii) examining whether evolved aggregates share characteristics common to natural multicellular systems (i.e. differentiation); and (iii) analysing the evolved ecosystems and discerning whether there is any consistent correspondence between the structure of the aggregate and its ecosystem. In each experiment, the environmental conditions are set to emulate conditions suggested to have affected the emergence of multicellularity. The data collected measures the percentage of runs in which aggregation occurred. Additionally, a representative aggregate is taken from all runs (where applicable) and its genome analysed; this data, together with the population statistics is used to characterise the type of ecosystem that was evolved. Behavioural analysis of aggregates is done by presenting the selected aggregates 500 random surfaces at two levels of consumption ('full' and 'eaten') while recording their actions; this enables characterising the behaviour of members of the aggregate and understanding the task they perform.

All experiments require a random population of evolving individual critters to be placed in a test world, and end after 400,000 time steps. Once finished, the critter population is stored and analysed. Each experiment is repeated at least 10 times.

Hypothesis 1: predation is sufficient to cause the emergence of multicellularity.
Three experiments examine the hypothesis and attempt to discern what aspect influences multicellularity: the *ability to prey* or *the presence of predators.* In all runs, the aggregation mode is 'aggregation by choice'.
Experiment 1: 'predation' is disabled - aggregates must be herbivores.
Experiment 2: conditions identical to exp. 1, however, every 1000 time steps, 7 sterile predators are placed in the population. These predators cannot reproduce, split, or consume surfaces, and die unless they can catch prey. Furthermore, they are very small (size 2), and so can only eat critters but not other aggregates.
Experiment 3: 'predation' is enabled - evolved aggregates may prey on organisms.

Hypothesis 2: accidental aggregation is a sufficient condition to cause the emergence of multicellularity.
Experiment 4: the aggregation mode is set to 'accidental aggregation'. 'Predation' is disabled so it would not affect aggregation. This experiment explores whether

statistics alone - random occurrence of aggregation - is enough to initiate multicellularity without any guiding selection pressure.

Hypothesis 3: member differentiation is important to multicellular organisms. Experiment 5: the ability of aggregates to evolve the capacities for different behaviours is turned off – in other words, the aggregates' differentiation is disabled – they are always capable of performing all actions. A secondary effect of this condition is that evolved aggregates have multiple redundancies of all behavioural capacities, consequentially, a very high metabolic rate. The aggregation mode is set to 'aggregation by choice', and 'predation' is enabled (to encourage multicellularity).

4 Results

Table 1 shows the percentage of runs that evolved aggregates for every experiment. As the data shows, preventing evolution of predators when critters 'choose' to aggregate results in no aggregates evolving (exp. 1). However, the presence of predators is enough to encourage some aggregate formation (exp. 2). When predators can be evolved, aggregates form very frequently (exp. 3). Furthermore, accidental aggregation is sufficient to cause aggregation quite frequently even when predators cannot evolve. Last, although differentiation is disabled, multicellularity still occurred according to exp. 5, albeit less than when differentiation is enabled (exp. 3).

Table 1. Percentage of runs that evolved aggregates for every experiment

#	Experiment	% with Aggregates
1	Aggregation by choice, predation disabled	0.00%
2	Aggregation by choice, predation disabled, sterile predators present	30.00%
3	Aggregation by choice, predation enabled	76.92%
4	Accidental aggregation, predation disabled	60.00%
5	Aggregation by choice, predation enabled, differentiation disabled	60.00%

During the analysis of the representative aggregates and ecosystems, it became apparent that there are recurring patterns. Three types of aggregates and four types of ecosystems that repeatedly emerged are summarised in fig. 3 with details of a run that exemplified them. Since the number of shapes and structures the aggregates evolved was large, 4 aggregates were picked for close analysis (fig. 3). Aggregates A,B,C were picked from exp. 1. Aggregate D was picked from exp. 5 (no differentiation).

Aggregate A: Critters in aggregation: 6. Classification: relatively unoptimised carnivore. Metabolic rate: 270 units. Critter tasks: critters (C2)(C4) Splitting. (C3) Eating, reproducing, moving/turning, splitting, preying. (C5) Eating, reproducing, preying. (C1)(C6) No task ('fat cell').

Aggregate B: Critters in aggregation: 6. Classification: optimised herbivore. Metabolic rate: 210. Critter tasks: critters (C3) Eating, moving/turning. (C5) Eating, splitting. (C6) Eating, reproducing, splitting. (C1)(C2)(C4) No task.

Aggregate C: Critters in aggregation: 3. Classification: 'coral' carnivore with complete division of labour. Metabolic rate: 90. Critter tasks: critters (C1) Reproducing. (C3) Preying. (C2) No task

Aggregate D: Critters in aggregation: 9. Classification: carnivore. Metabolic rate: 1170. According to genome, members can do all tasks. However, the behavioural test revealed that although every member can perform all tasks, effectively each only performs some tasks: critters (C1) Eating, preying, reproducing, turning. (C2)(C6) Eating, preying, reproducing. (C5) Eating, preying, reproducing, moving, turning, splitting. (C3)(C4)(C7)(C8)(C9) Eating, preying.

Types of aggregates:
Herbivore: an aggregate that consumes surfaces and cannot prey.
Carnivore: an aggregate that can only prey and cannot consume surfaces.
'Coral' Carnivore: a carnivore that cannot move and only eats prey that moves into its area.

Types of ecosystems:
Herbivorous Aggregates: this ecosystem is dominated by herbivorous aggregates - there are few or no unaggregated critters. E.g. exp. 1, run 5: total of 248 herbivorous aggregates, 16 critters.
Coexistence - Herbivorous Aggregates and Critters: this ecosystem contains stable amounts of herbivorous aggregates and unaggregated critters. E.g. exp. 4, run 4: total of 20 herbivorous aggregates, 227 critters.
Predator/Prey: this ecosystem contains stable amounts of carnivorous aggregates and unaggregated critters. E.g. exp 1, run 11: total of 45 carnivorous aggregates, 158 critters.
Predator ('Corals')/Prey: this ecosystem contains stable amounts of 'coral' carnivorous aggregates and unaggregated critters. E.g. exp 1, run 2: 280 'coral' carnivorous aggregates, 149 critters.

Fig. 3. Types of aggregates and ecosystems that were repeatedly evolved during experiments

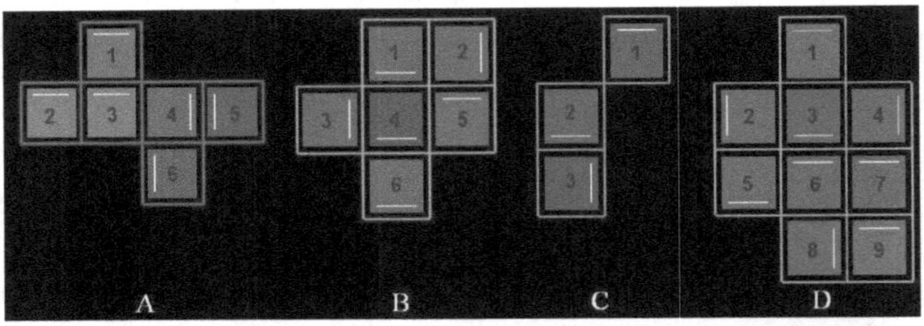

Fig. 4. Four representative aggregates. Note: every member has an orientation (the white line).

Table 2. Average size of aggregate per type of ecosystem (classified using fig. 3)

Type of Ecosystem	Ave. Size of Aggregate
Herbivorous Aggregates	2.22
Coexistence: Herbivorous Aggregates and Critters	3.04
Predator/Prey	5.64
Predator/Prey ('Corals')	2.06

Table 2 shows the average size of aggregates per type of ecosystem (using the definitions of fig. 3). It seems that the type of ecosystem greatly affects the size of the aggregate: carnivores are significantly larger than herbivores and 'coral' carnivores. In addition, herbivorous aggregates that coexist with critters are larger than herbivorous aggregates that dominate their ecosystem.

5 Discussion

Our results suggest several conclusions. First, it is clear that in our system, when there is no threat of predators and aggregation is 'by choice', there is not enough selection pressure for critters to form aggregates – individual critters are more adequate as they need less energy and can more easily reproduce. However, the threat of predation is enough to cause critter aggregation, primarily in order to gain protection from predation, but also to obtain a new energy source: prey. In addition, leaving aggregation to random chance by enabling accidental aggregation is sufficient to induce multicellularity: although at first aggregates are inefficient in comparison to critters, eventually evolution learns to exploit the benefits multicellularity offers. Last, in runs where the aggregates could not differentiate, the percentage of multicellularity was somewhat lower, supporting the notion that differentiation is important. More so, of particular interest is the fact that evolution found a way to implicitly differentiate: although the aggregate's members had the capacity to perform all behaviours, *and the aggregate 'paid' the metabolic rate cost for these capabilities,* most members still chose **not to** perform certain tasks (e.g., aggregate D in fig. 4). This result clearly supports the idea that differentiation is a major benefit for aggregation.

Even from only viewing the 4 representative aggregates, it is possible to state that many shapes and specialisations were evolved, ranging from complete redundancy to a complete division of labour. A common pattern was to evolve several 'eater' members (as each member eats independently), a single 'mover' member (to minimise coordination issues), and several prey/reproduce/split members (allows several critters to affect the overall behaviour of the aggregate - e.g. fig. 4, A, B). Also, members without any capabilities were often evolved and were apparently used as 'fat cells'; their only purpose was to grant the aggregate a larger maximum health capacity.

Of particular relevance is that there was a consistency in the different types of evolved ecosystems. Furthermore, different types of aggregates appear to require different structures (indicated by the consistency in average size). This is unsurprising: herbivores eat often while carnivores have to catch their prey so are not likely to eat as frequently, thus, require larger energy storage. Another explanation is the predation ability: larger predators can eat more types of organisms, and are harder to eat. The emergence of 'coral' carnivores was intriguing: in these ecosystems, there were enough critters that 'corals' would rarely starve and had no need to move. As 'corals' reproduced in the vicinity of their parent, reef-like structures consistently emerged.

Our system has investigated perhaps the earliest, most primitive form of multicellularity using the notions of aggregation for growth and fission for reproduction. This can be seen as analogous to the hypothesised symbiosis that resulted in mitochondria becoming incorporated into modern cells [11]. Multicellular organisms comprising more complex cells are capable of developmental growth via mitosis and differentiation, and reproduction via a specialised gamete cell, resulting in all cells sharing identical genes and thus all genes benefiting from the collaboration. This work can be seen as the first evolutionary step towards this ultimate form of multicellularity.

6 Conclusions

The results of our experiments support the theories examined in the paper: both the presence of predation and accidental aggregation are sufficient to initiate the transition to multicellularity. The model also shows that differentiation is indeed a major benefit for aggregates and it will evolve even if aggregates obtain it by not using capabilities they had 'paid for' with an expensive metabolism. Last, our evolved results shared many parallels with natural systems, from the emergence of a division of labour within an aggregate, to the life-like dynamics of the evolved ecosystems.

References

1. Bell, G.: The origin and early evolution of germ cells as illustrated by the Volvocales. In: The Origin and Evolution of Sex, pp. 221-256. Alan R. Liss, New York (1985)
2. Bonner, J.T.: The origin of multicellularity. Integrative Biology 1:27–36.2 (1998)
3. Bonner, J.T.: First Signals: The Evolution of Multicellular Development. Princeton, NJ: Princeton University Press (2001)
4. Bonner, J.T.: Perspective: the size-complexity rule. Evolution 58:1883–1890 (2004)
5. Boraas, M.E., Seale D.B, Boxhorn J.E.: Phagotrophy by a flagellate selects for colonial prey: A possible origin of multicellularity. Evolutionary Ecology 12: 153-164 (1998)
6. Bryden, J.: Slime Mould and the Transition to Multicellularity: The Role of the Macrocyst Stage. Proc. of European Conference on Artificial Life (ECAL), Canterbury, UK (2005)
7. Bull, L.: On the Evolution of Multicellularity and Eusociality. Art. Life 5(1):1-15 (1999)
8. Furusawa, C., Kaneko, K.: Emergence of Multicellular Organism with Dynamic Differentiation and Spatial Pattern, Artificial Life, 4 79-93 (1998)
9. Kirk, D.L.: Volvox, pp. 30–60. New York: Cambridge Univ. Press. 381 pp (1998)
10. Kirk, D.L.: A twelve-step program for evolving multicellularity and a division of labor. BioEssays 27.3 299-310 (2005)
11. Maynard Smith, J., Szathmary, E.: The Major Transitions in Evolution (Oxford) (1995)
12. Michod, R.E. Darwinian Dynamics, Evolutionary Transitions in Fitness and Individuality. Princeton University Press, Princeton, NJ. (1999)
13. Michod, R.E., Roze, D.: Cooperation and conflict in the evolution of multicellularity. Heredity 81:1-7 (2001)
14. Rolfe, D.F.S, Brown G.C.: Cellular energy utilization and molecular origin of standard metabolic rate in mammals. Physiol Rev 77:731-758 (1997)
15. Rothermich, J., Miller J.F.: Studying the Emergence of Multicellularity with Cartesian Genetic Programming in Artificial Life, in UK Workshop on Comp. Intelligence (2002)
16. Schlessinger, E., Bentley, P.J., Lotto, R.B.: Evolving Visually Guided Agents in an Ambiguous Virtual World. Proc. of Genetic and Evolutionary Computation Conference (GECCO), Washington, DC (2005)
17. Schlessinger, E., Bentley, P.J., Lotto, R.B.: Modular Thinking: Evolving Modular Neural Networks for Visual Guidance of Agents. To appear in Proc. of Genetic and Evolutionary Computation Conference (GECCO 2006), July 8-12, 2006, Seattle, WA (2006)
18. Schopf, J.W.: Microfossils of the early archean apex chert: new evidence of the antiquity of life. Science 260:640–46 (1993)
19. Stanley, S.M.: An ecological theory for the sudden origin of multicellular life in the Late Precambrian. PNAS 70, 1486-1489 (1973)
20. Wolpert, L., Szathmáry, E.: Multicellularity: evolution and the egg. Nature 420, 745 (2002)

Building of 3D Environment Models for Mobile Robotics Using Self-organization

Jan Koutník[1], Roman Mázl[2], and Miroslav Kulich[2]

[1] Neural Computing Group, Department of Computer Science and Engineering,
Faculty of Electrical Engineering,
Czech Technical University in Prague, Karlovo nam. 13, 121 35 Prague 2, Czech Republic
koutnij@fel.cvut.cz
http://ncg.felk.cvut.cz
[2] Center of Applied Cybernetics,
Faculty of Electrical Engineering,
Czech Technical University in Prague, Technická 1, 166 27 Prague 6, Czech Republic
{mazl, kulich}@labe.felk.cvut.cz

Abstract. In this paper, we present a new parallel self-organizing technique for three dimensional shape reconstruction for mobile robotics. The method is based on adaptive input data decomposition, parallel shape reconstruction in decomposed clusters using Kohonen Self-Organizing Map, which creates mesh representation of the input data. Afterwards, the sub-maps are joined together and the final mesh is re-optimized. Our method overcomes a problem of fitting one mesh to complex non-continuous shapes like building interiors. The method allows to process unordered data collected by mobile robots. The method is easily paralelizable and gives promising results.

1 Introduction

The problem of surface reconstruction appears in many applications of mobile robotics as well as in geometric model acquisition in computer graphics and computer vision. Our objective is to build environment models from the real measured data of building interiors. The data has been collected using mobile robot equipped with laser range-finder. The data set is a set of unorganized points.

There exist a lot of methods for the 3D reconstruction, see e.g. [1,2]. The problem of the reconstruction can be expressed as a procedure of learning the topology from the data set and reduction of the data set cardinality. Artificial neural networks are commonly used for solution of this task. We already implemented and tested Neural Gas algorithm for reconstruction of two dimensional environmental map [3]. Nice application of the Kohonen Self-Organizing Map (SOM) [4] can be found in [5], where a top-down approach (improving already known topology of the data using SOM networks) in reconstruction instead of bottom-up (building connection among nearest points) is used. The Kohonen SOM is a suitable approach to learning the topology. The SOM network itself is usually a two-dimensional mesh, which self-organizes to cover the data during the learning phase. The surface data are two-dimensional, thus a usage of SOM is a good approach. Another approach based on Kohonen SOM can be found in recent work [6].

T.P. Runarsson et al. (Eds.): PPSN IX, LNCS 4193, pp. 721–730, 2006.

The main problem of the presented solutions is that a single SOM is normally used for the reconstruction. The topology of the SOM is normally a rectangular mesh, which stretches during the learning phase. In most applications usage of a rectangular mesh is a correct approach but usage of such mesh for representation of a complex surface in three dimensions does not give precise results.

Imagine that you let the SOM network to reconstruct the human body surface. The resulting shape will be a strange clothing which will not perfectly fit the body and it will not be easy to wear it. Our approach is similar to a work of a tailor which has to sew a perfect fit dress from a stretch fabric. The input space (a human body) is divided to several parts (legs, trunk, arms etc.) and the tailor cuts the correct shapes from the two-dimensional fabric. The parts are sewn together and the dress is ready. The stretch material allows some deformations to fit the body when used. Our algorithm works similarly.

This paper is organized as follows. Section 2 describes how the data sets were obtained. Section 3 describes proposed reconstruction algorithm. Section 4 shows experimental results. Section 5 contains a discussion of the results. Section 6 concludes the work and section 7 mentions several improvements that will be made in near future.

2 Data Acquisition

All experimental data has been gathered using the G2 mobile robot developed in the Gerstner laboratory, see figure 1. The G2 robot is non-holonomic differential drive robot for indoor usage able to reach the maximal velocity about 0.5 m/s. The robot motion is established by two stepper motors.

2.1 Orthogonally Mounted Range-Finders

The former approach of data gathering uses the G2 mobile robot with two orthogonally mounted SICK LMS 200 laser range-finders as can be seen in figure 1.

The first laser range-finger has been mounted horizontally, while the second laser range-finder has been mounted in vertical position pointing up perpendicularly to the horizontal measurement half-plane of the first laser. The horizontal laser measures data in parallel half-plane to the floor in order to ensure proper 2D localization of the robot in space. The data obtained from the horizontal laser as well as the robot trajectory during acquisition of experimental data are shown in figure 2.

The knowledge of the current position of the mobile robot allows registration of the spatial data from the vertical laser. The measured data from the vertical laser describes depth of surrounding environment while the robot moves. This configuration in fact replaces expensive 3D scanners for spatial point retrieval.

2.2 Data Registration

Knowledge of the correct position of the robot (the place from where the data has been measured) is the essential condition for future data processing. The localization issues are one of the central topic in mobile robotics, an overview can be found e.g. in [7] or [8].

Fig. 1. Hardware setup of the G2 mobile robot

Our solution of the localization problem is based on modified scan matching technique utilizing the ICP (Iterative Closest Point) algorithm [9,10,11]. The modification is targeted on improvements of outlier point rejection and on combination of the scan matching technique with a global point based map of the environment. The usage of the simultaneously built map increases precision and reliability of the scan matching technique during a localization process.

Two different approaches to the registration of 3D data has been used, since we have two sensor setup of the robot. The first setup employs a 2D version of ICP localization algorithm that processes only laser scans incoming from the horizontal range-finder while the robot is continuously traversed through the environment and gathers data from the vertical laser range-finder. It means that registration of the vertical spatial scan is just determined by the proper localization of the whole mobile robot using horizontal range-finder. The precision of localization is approx. 5cm.

The second sensor setup with the sweeping laser assumes the stop-and-go style of mobile robot movements since a complete 3D scan has to be measured from one position. The current raw 3D scan position is estimated using a robot odometry. The final fine alignment of the 3D scans in 6DOF ensures the 3D version of ICP algorithm, where a kD-tree approach was used for searching for corresponding pair points. The calculation of a transformation for 3D rotation and translation minimizing the mutual scan misalignments is realized by a quaternion approach. All computation details can be found in [12]. With a knowledge of the sensor position a set of the 3D laser scan can be merged together in order to obtain a huge 3D point cloud of spatial points that describes a shape of a surrounding environment.

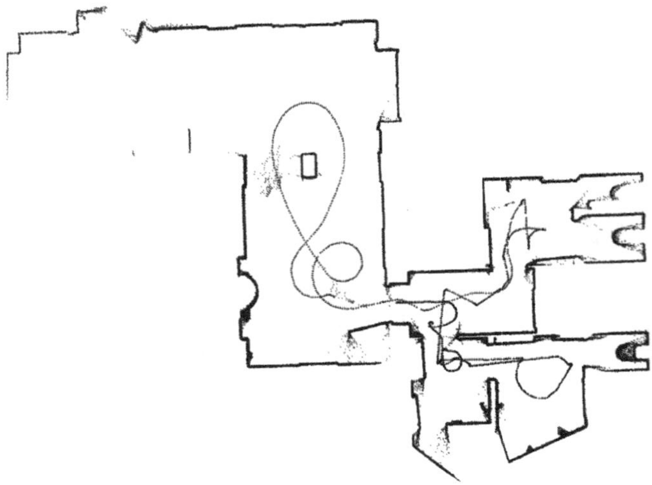

Fig. 2. Data collected from the horizontal laser and trajectory of the robot

3 Algorithm for 3D Reconstruction

We designed a hybrid algorithm that embeds either non-topological clustering techniques like Neural Gas and K-Means algorithms for initial data preprocessing and topological clustering algorithm – Kohonen SOM for building of wired model of the data. The main idea behind is that several SOMs are executed in parallel and process clustered input data. We introduce a joining phase, which combines the SOM output together into large SOM, which is partly re-optimized. Thus, the algorithm has following four phases:

1. *initial clustering,*
2. *building of sub-maps,*
3. *joining phase,*
4. *re-optimization.*

3.1 Initial Clustering

The basic idea is to divide the input data into subsets to ease usage of SOM algorithm for the subsets. We used algorithms, which preserve the distribution of the data in the input space. This approach has two advantages. First, as mentioned in introductory part of this paper, the data needs to be clustered to allow proper approximation of the data by two-dimensional mesh. Second, such clustering rapidly reduces the real time complexity of the method. It allows the second phase to run in parallel. The complexity of SOM algorithm rapidly grows with the map size due adaptation of neighboring neurons in the map. Sequential execution of SOMs with the same sum of neurons is even faster than execution of one big SOM.

The clustering has another property exploited by the method. The SOMs in the second phase are put only in the parts of the input space where the data exists. If one starts to approximate the whole input space with one big SOM, the SOM neurons will appear in the space where no data are present. Such approach does not allow to process two isolated objects in the scene like boxes and obstacles, which appear in the robot workspace. Our approach eliminates this drawback.

We used Neural Gas (NG) [13] and K-Means [14] algorithms. The unsupervised clustering algorithm splits data into clusters. Afterwards, in the second sub-map building phase, the individual SOMs are used for topological approximation of the data in the clusters separately.

First, we employed the Neural Gas (NG) algorithm for data clustering. The complexity of the NG is $O(n * d * m * k * log(k))$ where n is the cardinality of the data set, d is a dimension of the input data (3), m is number of iterations over the data set and k is required number of clusters (number of neurons in NG). The NG algorithm requires the neurons to be sorted after each presentation of the input vector, which is expressed by $k * log(k)$.

The most crucial element is the number of iterations. NG algorithm requires about 40000 iterations to get proper clustering. Our data sets have typically more than 100 thousands of data vector, which makes the NG algorithm unusable due it's big time complexity.

The K-Means (KM) algorithm has complexity $O(n * d * m * k)$ but it requires to be m much less than in the case of the NG. Practically, the NG algorithm takes several hours but the KM ends in few minutes (measured on 2 GHz Opteron processor).

There is virtually no difference between clusters obtained with NG and KM algorithm. Thus we use computationally optimal K-Means in following experiments.

3.2 Building of Sub-maps

After the initial clusters are created, the SOM is built from data subsets. We use well known iterative Kohonen SOM algorithm described in [4].

The neurons in the SOM are organized in either rectangular or hexagonal map. We use the rectangular mesh. Two distances are defined within the algorithm. The first one, the Euclidean distance, is measured between weights of the neuron (vector stored in the neuron) and an input vector. The second distance is measured in the SOM map. Closest neighbors have the distance defined to be one, distance of other neurons is defined by the shortest path between the neurons in the map. In the learning phase, so called Best Matching Unit (BMU) is selected among all neurons. It is a neuron with closest Euclidean distance to the input vector. The neuron weights are updated to be closer to the input vector. Weights of the neurons in the neighborhood are updated as well. Closest neurons are updated more than far neurons. The amount of learning is expressed by a function of distance in the map.

This property makes the SOM to be suitable for our approach. The SOM algorithm places a mesh in three dimensional data in order to bet best coverage of the input data. In contradiction to first phase of the algorithm, the clustering, we need the network to be topological.

The advantage is that the sub-maps can be created in parallel. The clustering algorithms in the first phase creates clusters with approximately similar cardinality. Thus the SOM algorithms in the second phase take relatively same computational time. We do not have to solve other parallelization issues like load balancing etc. Only the initial distribution of the load is needed.

3.3 Joining Phase

In the joining phase, all the SOMs created in the previous phase are merged together. We use a simple nearest neighbor algorithm where for each neuron in the SOM boundary a candidate in other SOM boundaries is searched. If the candidate has an Euclidean distance lower than a specified threshold, the connection between the two neurons is built. The threshold is a mean distance to closest neighbors of the candidates in their SOM maps ($\bar{d}$) multiplied by a constant (θ) as depicted in figure 3.

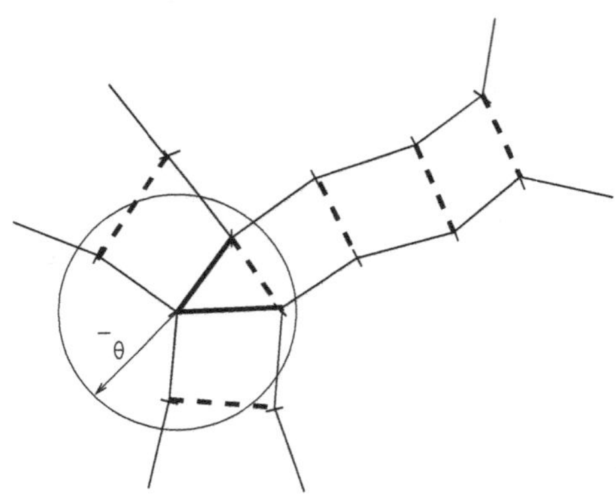

Fig. 3. Joining phase. The map boundaries alre depicted with solid line. Two connections are built for neuron a to neurons b and c, whose distance to neuron a is lower than the threshold ($\bar{d}\theta$). Dashed lines express connections between other neurons constructed by the same algorithm.

The connections obtained in the joining phase are exploited in the last re-optimization phase. The joining phase creates large SOM from the particular SOMs. The added connections are taken as normal connections in the standard SOM algorithm. The resulting SOM has not a planar topology.

3.4 Re-optimization

It the last phase the final SOM is re-optimized. The key point is that the final SOM is not a planar structure. It has a desired structure corresponding to the data distribution in the input space. Our implementation of the SOM allows us to work with such SOM maps which are not strictly rectangular. The neighborhood neurons are stored in list of neighbors. The joining phase processes these lists and adds neurons from the joined SOMs.

The SOM algorithm used in this phase contains a little modification. It is not necessary to re-optimize the whole map. If so, the problems with the time complexity will arise again. Thus we re-optimize only that neurons, which are close to boundaries of the joined sub-maps. The neurons that will not be re-optimized as well as the corresponding data are removed from the calculation before the re-optimization starts. This speeds up the algorithm.

The final SOM algorithm optimizes joins of the maps. It precises the joining, makes approximation of edges to be sharper and better fit the input data.

4 Experimental Results

As the experimental data set we used a set of points measured in the first floor of our building. Figure 2 shows the trajectory of the robot and the data collected from the horizontal laser in purpose of better understanding to reconstructed three-dimensional model shown in figure 4. All phases of the algorithm were performed on the data. The data contained approximately 126 thousands of points, in the first phase 100 clusters were created, the sub-maps contained 10x5 neurons. The algorithm run takes about 2 hours on the 2 GHz Opteron processor for the complete data set when executed sequentially. Physical parallelization of the second phase would save at least one hour of computational time. Other parameters were setup the same in all experiments. All SOM maps iterated 10000 times over all input data, the initial learning rate was setup to 0.5

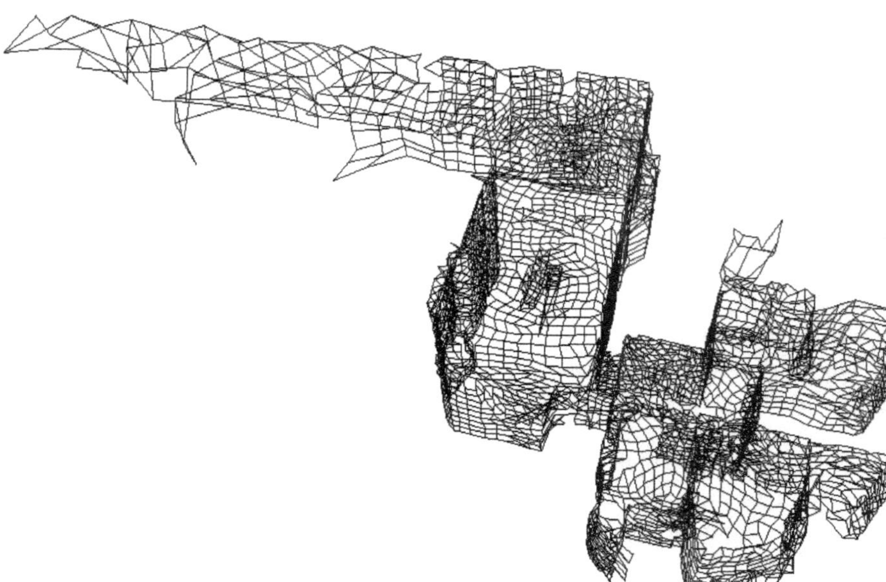

Fig. 4. Final algorithm result – the reconstructed three-dimensional interior from the vertical laser data. The rooms with a lower ceiling on the right-hand side are toilets. The L-shape corridor is on the left-hand side. The front wall of the corridor contain low density of input points as can be seen also in the horizontally scanned data.

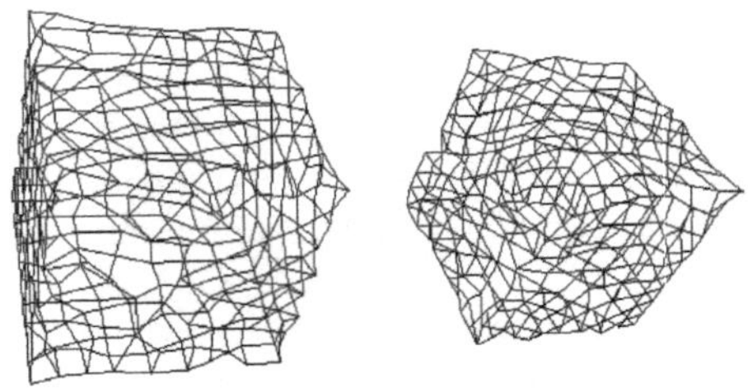

Fig. 5. Reconstruction from the data sampled to two isolated cube shapes. Our algorithm arranged 6 sub-maps to each cube.

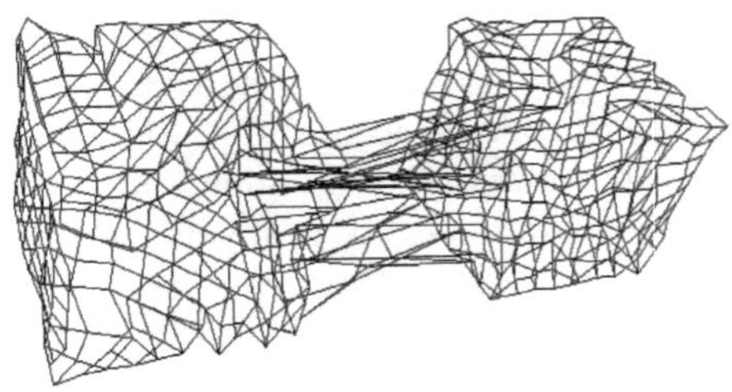

Fig. 6. Reconstruction from the data sampled to two isolated cube shapes using a single SOM map. It can be seen, that the cubes were not isolated. Even if the neurons are placed to the data clouds the connections between map still exist and disrupt the final reconstruction. Reconstruction of at least two objects in the scene fails using a single connected structure.

and diminished to 0.005 linearly during the learning. The neighborhood was initially setup to the longest path in the map and diminished to 1. The joining parameter θ was experimentally setup to 1.8.

The algorithm works also if the data do not consist of continuous shapes. We created an artificial data set with two artificially generated cubes, each consisting of 726 points. We used 12 clusters and SOM sub-maps of 10x5 neurons. We can see that each cube was easily encapsulated into 6 sub-maps joined together and re-optimized. The result is shown in figure 5.

Figure 6 shows the reconstruction using a single SOM consisting of same amount of neurons as in previous example. The SOM had 20x30 neurons. Single SOM could not split itself into two parts. Usage of one SOM for complex data reconstruction could not be satisfactory. The computational complexity of such large mesh caused the algorithm to run approximately 30 minutes in comparison to 6 minutes of run of our algorithm including re-optimization of the final map.

5 Discussion

The clustering and decomposition of the input space to clusters using K-Means and reconstruction in clusters using Self-Organizing Map seems to be promising combination of algorithms for the problem of three-dimensional shape reconstruction. As can be seen in figures 4 and 5, there are still some holes in the joined maps. This is caused because the optimal join of the neighboring sub-maps is not straightforward. The grids of the maps can be mutually rotated and a search for the correct join is also an optimization problem. Our method provides a wired model. If we want to obtain a solid model a triangulation has to be performed. A triangulation of the sub-maps is easy, each rectangle is split into two triangles. Triangulation of the joins is not that obvious. Currently, the joins are exploited as a *logical* connections between SOMs. Such joins allows the final map to be more complex than a planar rectangular mesh only. The triangulation of stripes between the maps requires embedding of another algorithm for triangulation of stripes.

We currently use a nearest neighbor algorithm to produce the joins between sub-maps. The algorithm is simple and produces joins that are used in the final re-optimization phase. The threshold for joining the neighbors on the map borders was experimentally found to be 1.8 times an average Euclidean distance between joined neurons and their neighbors. If the constant is lower than 1.8 the sub-maps are not enough joined. If the constant is higher, the map contains crossed joins, the final SOM algorithm deforms the joined parts of the sub-maps and the further triangulation would not be easy.

The final re-optimization precises the final mesh. The time complexity of the final phase is reduced by a selection of the input data and neurons that are on the sub-maps' boundaries.

6 Conclusion

In this paper we introduced a combination of self-organizing techniques that gives satisfactory results in the task of reconstruction of shapes from the unordered data sets. The algorithm was tested on data obtained from a laser range-finder sensor mounted on a mobile robot. It was shown that a usage of only one algorithm, either Neural Gas or Self-Organizing Map, does not lead to good results for reconstruction of complex and non-continuous shapes. The idea of the initial decomposition, building of separate sub-maps using topological Kohonen Self-Organizing Map, joining and re-optimization gives nice and stable results. The method reduces the complexity of the data and produces a wired model of the environment where the robot is situated. The algorithm allows to create model of more than one isolated objects found in the input data. The second phase of the algorithm can be effectively parallelized. The reconstruction can be built using collaboratively scanning robots, since the algorithm allows processing of unorganized data sets.

7 Future Work

Future research will focus on improvements of the current algorithm. The K-Means clustering algorithm will be replaced with an algorithm which preserves the flat clusters so the clusters will represent the walls found in the data sets. A usage of triangular shape SOM map is expected instead of the rectangular topology. The batch version of SOM training algorithm can rapidly diminish the computational time as well. The map itself will create the triangulation needed for solid displaying of the reconstructed shape.

Finally, an optimizing algorithm for generation of joins will be embedded instead of simple and computationally inexpensive nearest neighbor joining algorithm.

Acknowledgment. This work has been supported by the Ministry of Education of the Czech Republic under Projects No. 1M0567 and MSM6840770012. The implementation of the algorithms was performed by CTU student Tomáš Jaroš.

References

1. Sequeira, V., Ng, K.C., Wolfart, E., Gonçalves, J., Hogg, D.: Automated 3d reconstruction of interiors with multiple scan-views. In: Proceedings of SPIE, Electronic Imaging '99, IS & T/SPIE's 11th Annual Symposium, San Jose, CA, USA (1999)
2. Christian Früh, A.Z.: An automated method for large-scale, ground-based city model acquisition. International Journal of Computer Vision **60**(1) (2004) 5–24
3. Štepán, P., Kulich, M.: Buildings maps for autonomous mobile robots. In: Field and Service Robotics. Helsinki: FSA-Finnish Society of Automation. Volume 1. (2001) 321–326
4. Kohonen, T.: Self-Organizing Maps. 3rd edn. Springer-Verlag (2001)
5. Yu, Y.: Surface reconstruction from unorganized points using self-organizing neural networks (1999)
6. Farid Boudjema, Philippe Biela Enberg, J.G.P.: Dynamic adaptation and subdivision in 3d-som: Application to surface reconstruction. In: 7th IEEE International Conference on Tools with Artificial Intelligence (ICTAI'05). (2005) 425–430
7. Thrun, S., Burgard, W., Fox, D.: Probabilistic Robotics. The MIT Press (2005)
8. Siegwart, R., Nourbakhsh, I.R.: Introduction to Autonomous Mobile Robots (Intelligent Robotics and Autonomous Agents). The MIT Press (2004)
9. Lu, F., Milios, E.: Robot pose estimation in unknown environments by matching 2D range scans. In: CVPR94. (1994) 935–938
10. Besl, P., McKay, N.: A method for registration of 3-d shapes. IEEE Transactions on Pattern Analysis and Machine Intelligence **2**(14) (1992) 239–256
11. Mázl, R., Přeučil, L.: Methods for mobile robot localization. In: 5th International Scientific - Technical Conference Process Control 2002, ŘÍP 2002, University of Pardubice (2002)
12. Surmann, H., Nchter, A., Hertzberg, J.: An autonomous mobile robot with a 3d laser range finder for 3d exploration and digitalization of indoor environments. Journal Robotics and Autonomous Systems **45**(3-4) (2003) 181– 198
13. Fritzke, B.: Growing cell structures—a self-organizing network in *k* dimensions. In Aleksander, I., Taylor, J., eds.: Artificial Neural Networks, 2. Volume II., Amsterdam, Netherlands, North-Holland (1992) 1051–1056
14. Christopher, B.: Neural networks: A pattern recognition perspective (1996)

January: A Parallel Algorithm for Bug Hunting Based on Insect Behavior

Peter Lamborn[1] and Michael Jones[2]

[1] Mississippi State University
[2] Brigham Young University

Abstract. January[1] is a group of interacting stateless model checkers designed for bug hunting in large transition graphs that represent the behavior of a program or protocol. January is based upon both individual and social insect behaviors, as such, dynamic solutions emerge from agents functioning with incomplete data. Each agent functions on a processor located on a network of workstations (NOW). The agents' search pattern is a semi-random walk based on the behavior of the grey field slug (*Agriolimax reticulatus*), the house fly (*Musca domestica*), and the black ant (*Lassius niger*). January requires significantly less memory to detect bugs than the usual parallel approach to model checking. In some cases, January finds bugs using 1% of the memory needed by the usual algorithm to find a bug. January also requires less communication which saves time and bandwidth.

1 Introduction

The main contribution of this paper is a cooperative parallel algorithm based on insect behavior for use in error discovery, or bug hunting, in the context of model checking. The algorithm is based on both individual and social insect behaviors.

Model checking is the problem of verifying that property X is satisfied, or modeled, by a transition system M. A key feature of model checking is that both X and M are defined using a formal, i.e. mathematically precise, language (for a thorough introduction to model checking see [3]). The transition system typically describes a circuit, program or protocol under test and the property defines some desirable property of M. For example, in a wireless protocol the transition system might describe the protocol behavior at the transaction level and the property might require that a repeated request is eventually granted. In this case, an error would occur when a device can be ignored indefinitely.

While model checking can be used to produce a proof that the M models X, model checking is most valuable in practice when it can be used to inexpensively locate errors that are too expensive to find using other testing methods. The process of using a model checker to find errors rather than proofs of correctness is often called semi-formal verification, bug hunting or error discovery.

[1] Named after January Cooley, a contemporary artist famous for painting insects.

T.P. Runarsson et al. (Eds.): PPSN IX, LNCS 4193, pp. 731–740, 2006.

Model checking can be divided into explicit and symbolic methods. Explicit methods involve the creation of a directed graph which contains explicit representations of transition system states. Symbolic methods result in a boolean characteristic function, encoded as a binary decision diagram (BDD), which describes the reachable states implicitly. Explicit methods are better suited for transition systems with asynchronous interleaving semantics (like protocols and programs) while symbolic methods are better suited for transition systems with true concurrency (like circuits). In this paper, we focus on the problem of explicit model checking for systems with asynchronous interleaving semantics and address error discovery rather than proofs of correctness.

The problem of locating an error in a transition graph using explicit model checking algorithms can be reduced to the problem of traversing a large, irregular, directed graph while looking for target vertexes in the graph. In this formulation of the problem, graph vertices are often refereed to as *states*, meaning "states of the transition system encoded by the transition graph." The transition graph is generated on-the-fly during the search process and a predicate is used to determine if a newly generated state is one of the targets. A hash table is used during the search and analysis process to avoid duplicate work and to detect termination. The size of the hash table is the limiting factor in the application of explicit model checking to large problems.

The objective of parallel explicit model checking is to increase the amount of memory available for the hash table by aggregating the memory resources of several processing nodes. The first parallel explicit model checking algorithm, and indeed the one from which most others were derived, was created by Stern and Dill [8]. This algorithm, which we will call the *Dill* algorithm, uses a hash function to partition the state graph into n pieces, where n is the number of processing nodes. The objective of this algorithm is to partition duplicate state detection by partitioning the states between nodes. A state must then be sent across the network every time a parent and child state do not hash to the same node. Since states can have multiple parents, more states can be sent through the network than actually exist in the model. This process allows the use of more memory than might be available on a single node, but is limited by network throughput and terminates ungracefully when memory is exhausted on one processing node.

Randomized model checking uses random walk methods to explore the model. Randomized model checking has been found to locate bugs quickly with low memory and communication demands [7, 11, 9]. Randomized model checking is effective because it generates many low-quality (in terms of the probability of finding errors) states quickly rather than a few high-quality states slowly. While random walk is useful for some problems, it can over-visit certain areas of the state graph while under-visiting others. The novelty of the January algorithm is that it improves on prior randomized algorithms by using seach strategies adapted from slug and fly behavior to increase the probability that the entire graph is visited.

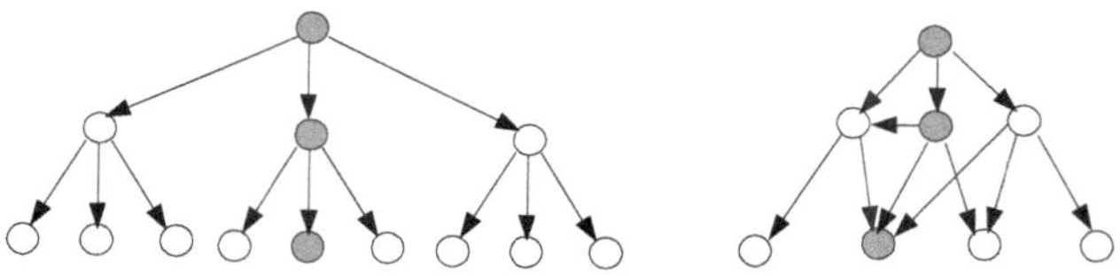

Fig. 1. Gray states show straight paths through two different transition graphs. For this example, "to go straight" means to pick the middle branch.

In this paper, we present a parallel algorithm that avoids the overhead of a partitioned hash table as used by the Dill algorithm but replaces randomized behavior with significantly more effective behavior based on both individual and group insect behavior. The rationale for including insect behavior is that, relative to their perceptual abilities, insects solve relatively difficult search problems when locating food. Similarly our search agents have a limited perception of the space they are searching.

The January algorithm is an improvement of our previous error discovery algorithm based on social honeybee behavior [6]. The January algorithm builds on the bee-based error discovery algoirhtm by improving individual search behavior. The January algorithm also employs a group cooperation scheme based on negative reinforcement through pheremonal communication in ant colonies. The group cooperation scheme appeared ill-suited for this application. However, future work involving the standard ant colony optimization (ACO) may improve reported error lengths.

2 Biological Foundations

The January algorithm is an amalgamation of three insect behaviors: negative reinforcement in the grey field slug (*Agriolimax reticulatus*), positive reinforcement in the house fly (*Musca domestica*), and pheromonal communication in black ant colonies (*Lassius niger*). Negative reinforcement helps a search agent avoid searching in the same area for too long. Positive reinforcement helps the agent spend more time in areas that have received little search attention and pheromonal communication helps agents avoid over-visiting an area by marking paths that have been extensively searched by another agent.

Search behaviors in animals are often described in terms of the turning rate or the relative straightness of the path. To relate animal behavior to explicit model checking, we first define what it means to go straight while traversing a transition graph and describe how to control turning rate during graph traversal.

In graph traversal, we define straight to mean that the same branch is selected repeatably. If all possible branches are numbered 1 to n, then a straight path always selects the kth branch, where $1 \leq k \leq n$. Turning involves a different choice of branch i at each step, where $1 \leq i \leq n$. Figure 1 contains two examples of straight paths created by consistently choosing the second branch. States in the straight path are colored gray.

The relative straightness of the path is controlled with a normal distribution. A normal distribution was selected because it can be described and manipulated using just the mean and variance. The mean corresponds to the index of the straight branch in the graph. The variance corresponds to the turning rate. Large variances coincide with a higher turning rate and small variances lead to a relatively straight path.

2.1 Negative Reinforcement

When the grey field slug (*Agriolimax reticulatus*) repeatedly recrosses its own slime trail, that area is deemed less desirable for further searching. When this occurs, the slug decreases its turning rate so that further travel takes the slug to a new foraging site [2]. This behavior is useful in state generation because it causes agents to seek out areas that have not been previously explored while storing only the recent trail of visited states rather than the entire set of all previously visited states.

To implement this behavior, we simulate the slime trail using states in an individual agent's search trace and use those states to detect recrossing. The search trace is the sequence of states that lead to the agent's current state. Recrossing is detected by encountering a state that already exists in the trace.

2.2 Positive Reinforcement

When the house fly (*Musca domestica*) encounters small amounts of sugar, the sugar triggers a more thorough search behavior [12]. The more thorough search increases the probability that an individual fly will locate more sugar in close proximity. In state generation, this behavior is adapted to concentrate the search in places that are either more likely to lead to an error.

In our search encountering "sugar" is simulated by a user-defined triggering function which recognizes changes in a key variable toward a predefined value. Most often, the trigger function is related to the predicate used to determine if a given state is an error state.

A more thorough search is conducted by performing a breadth first search (BFS) for a short time. All states explored during BFS remain in the trace of active states that led to the current state. Keeping the trace of states visited during BFS increases the probability that one of those states will be expanded after backtracking. The January algorithm backtracks periodically to avoid becoming caught in a strongly connected component.[2] The agent backtracks out of areas when it repeatedly encounters states with a large number of revisits. When the agent backtracks, it will remove the k most recent entries of the stack. The $k+1$th most recent state will become the start of a new guided depth-first search.

The new search can occur at any point because the algorithm can backtrack to any point. However, a new search is more likely to start from states left by

[2] A search trapped in a strongly connected component would be similar to an insect trapped in a sink basin with vertical walls.

the BFS, simply because the BFS leaves a large amount of states in the trace. These leads to more searching in the exciting parts of the state space.

2.3 Pheromonal Communication

The third behavior in January is loosely based on the group interactions of the black ant (*Lassius niger*). Ants ¡¡¡¡¡¡ biological-foundations.tex communicate with pheromones and have many types of pheromones that allow a broad spectrum of communication [10]. January simulates a discouragement pheromone. During search, the agents selectively place a discouragement marker. When other agents see this marker, they avoid that area and search elsewhere. It should be noted that January does not use ant colony optimization (ACO) [4]. ACO is based upon an excitatory pheromone and has been used successfully in several optimization problems.

January differs from ACO by using a discouraging pheromone. The agents use messages to mark spaces they have thoroughly searched. If agent i explores state s several times, it warns other agents about state s by sending them a message. Other agents will know the first time they visit state s that it is well-covered. This inhibits the ant from searching in the same areas. Agents encountering the pheromone switch to a straighter search pattern (as described in 2.1) to find an unsearched area.

3 The January Algorithm

Figure 2 contains pseudocode for the January algorithm.

The state s taken from the top of the search stack (line 4) is either a new undiscovered state or a revisitation of a known state. If state s is already in the trace (line 7), then the state is being revisited and the variance is decreased (line 8). This is negative reinforcement based on revisitation, as described previously. The lower variance causes the agent to move straighter and leave the current area.

Alternatively, if the state is new, the agent will evaluate the state to see if it is exciting (line 12). Positive reinforcement occurs if the state is "exciting" relative to states seen recently. The positive reinforcement causes the search to become a BFS (line 14) for a short time, putting states onto the stack for future exploration. Also, the variance of the normal distribution is increased (line 13).

Each revisited state could cause a backtrack. Backtracking occurs when the variance is sufficiently small (line 15). This is an indirect way of measuring the number of states that have been revisited recently. Backtracking is performed by popping states off the stack. The number of states popped will at a minimum be the number of revisits on the state triggering the backtrack (line 16).

Revisited states may be broadcast to other agents. The agent broadcasts the state to other agents based on the agent's threshold and the number of times the state has been revisited (line 9). The threshold is based on the states previously broadcast and received. Broadcasting a state with a larger number of

```
1  boolean January
2    mean=random() % numrules;
3    while ~stack.empty()
4      s=stack.top();
5      if CheckInvariants(s) then
6        return true; // found an error
7      if revisit(s) then //negative reinforcement
8        variance=variance*shrinkingFactor; //less turning
9        if s.numRevists > broadcastThredhold then
10         broadcast(s);
11         broadcastThreshold=s.numRevisits;
12     else if exciting(s) then // positive reinforcement
13       variance=variance*increaseFactor; // more turning
14       if findError(BFS(s)) then return true; //found error in BFS
15     if variance < backTrackThreshold then
16       backtrackAtLeast(s.numRevisits);
17       variance=INITIALVARIANCE;
18       mean=random() % numrules;
19     rand=random();
20     choice=round(Normal(mean,variance,rand));
21     s=generateChild(s,choice);
22     mean=choice;
23     if ~stack.full() then stack.push(s) else backtrack();
24     while states_to_receive
25       RecieveState (state*r)
26       addRevistsTo(r);
27       if r.numRevisits < broadcastThreshold then
28         broadcastThreshold–;
29   return false;
```

Fig. 2. Pseudocode for the January algorithm

revisits than were recently broadcast raises the threshold (line 11). This keeps the network traffic down, and causes only the most important information to be broadcast.

4 Results

The January algorithm has been implemented as an extension of the Hopper model checker [5], parallelized using MPI [1] and tested on a cluster of Linux workstations. This section describes the experimental methods and results. Results are given for a collection of large and small model checking problems. In this context, "large" means requires more than 2 GB of memory to store the reachable states of the transition graph. Each test was repeated ten times and the average time is reported.

Table 1. Memory threshold ratio of the January and Dill algorithms on 16 models that each contain at least one bug. A ratio less than 1.0 indicates that the January algorithm required less memory than the Dill algorithm.

Model	Memory Ratio	Model	Memory Ratio
2-peterson	0.03	sort5	0.13
bullsandcows	0.01	td	0.03
down	<0.01	adash1211e	0.50
lin	0.31	adash1212e	0.13
mutex2	0.28	atomixe	0.03
queens4	<0.01	dense-deep8	<0.03
rubikcube_2x2	0.04	jordan2	<0.03
sets	0.03	10-peterson	<0.03

Results for three algorithms are included. The January algorithm is the algorithm described in the previous section. The *UnCoop* algorithm is the January algorithm, but with no communication between nodes. Comparing January with UnCoop allows us to determine the cost and benefits of the cooperation scheme in January. The Dill algorithm is a parallel model checking algorithm that uses a partitioned hash table to store all of the reachable states. The Dill algorithm is the standard parallel explicit model checking algorithm.

Because the order of message reception affects the search order in the Dill algorithm, some of the ten tests using the Dill algorithm may detect an error while others terminated due to exceeding memory allocation. Data for these problems are referred to as "Dill-Partial" in our graphs.

The tests were performed on a IBM Linux Cluster in the Fulton Supercomputing Center at Brigham Young University. The cluster contains 256 2.4 GHz Intel Zeon processors and an optical Myrinet interconnect.

In summary, January consistently finds errors in transition graphs when the amount of memory available is insufficient for the Dill algorithm to find the same error. The January algorithm also sends fewer messages between nodes than the Dill algorithm. However, when the amount of memory is sufficient for the Dill algorithm to find errors, the Dill algorithm consistently finds errors more quickly.

4.1 Memory Threshold

We define the memory threshold for a specific problem and algorithm as the minimal amount of memory, measured in bytes, required by that algorithm to find an error in the given problem. We measure memory use for all three algorithms as the size of the table of visited states plus the size of the queue of states waited to be expanded. In all cases the threshold for January is less than the threshold for Dill on the same model. Table 1 shows the ratio of memory thresholds as the ratio the memory threshold for January compared to that of

Dill. While there is not widespread agreement on the composition of a good test suite for the anlaysis of bug discover tools, the problems listed in Table 1 are part of a benchmark suite we have created for the analysis of explicit model checking algorithms[3].

January always requires less memory to find the error than Dill's algorithm. January never requires more than half the memory of Dill. In many cases, such as the down and queens4 models, the ratio is quite small, with January requiring less than 1% of the memory of Dill. The savings in memory is the most clear advantage of January.

4.2 Comparison on a Large Problem

Larger models are more challenging for the Dill algorithm. More memory is required and more messages are passed. They are also more interesting problems to solve. Figure 3 shows January and Dill on the atomixe model with 1 to 32 processing nodes. The atomixe problem is a large problem with 2,966,400 states.

The atomixe model provides a good example of January's lower memory requirements. Atomixe is a model of a one player game. The goal is to rearrange atoms into a target molecule. The "error" in this problem is a winning position in the atomix game. Every node added to the system increases the memory available to Dill's algorithm. It is not until the 32 node test that the Dill algorithm had enough memory to detect the error. January performs well even when only provided with one node.

Also, the Dill algorithm with 32 nodes used large amounts of communication. Although Dill finished soon after January, Dill sent more than 35 times the number of messages. January uses less communication as well as less memory.

In the atomixe problem, cooperation was an advantage, that is, the uncooperative implementation of January is slower than the cooperative version. UnCoop takes longer to finish and explores significantly more states in the process. In the lower graph, messages reported to be sent by UnCoop refers to the number of times that UnCoop would have sent a message, but did not.

All models listed in table 1 went through the same analysis as atomixe but for brevity are not presented here. On these models Dill finishes with the fastest time when it finishes at all. Also, when it finishes, Dill has the fewest number of states explored, but the largest number of messages sent.

Only 3 of the 16 models show an advantage for cooperation. On 11 of 16 models tested cooperation seemed to have no effect at all. On a two models cooperation actually impeded the search in terms of time and efficiency. Based on this evidence we conclude that our form of cooperation does not affect outcomes on most models. Although any given state generated by January is less likely to be an error state than a state generated by Dill's algorithm, the state generation speed of January is sufficiently faster to find errors in less time in general.

[3] The suite is available at http://vv.cs.byu.edu/emc_benchmarks/murphi/.

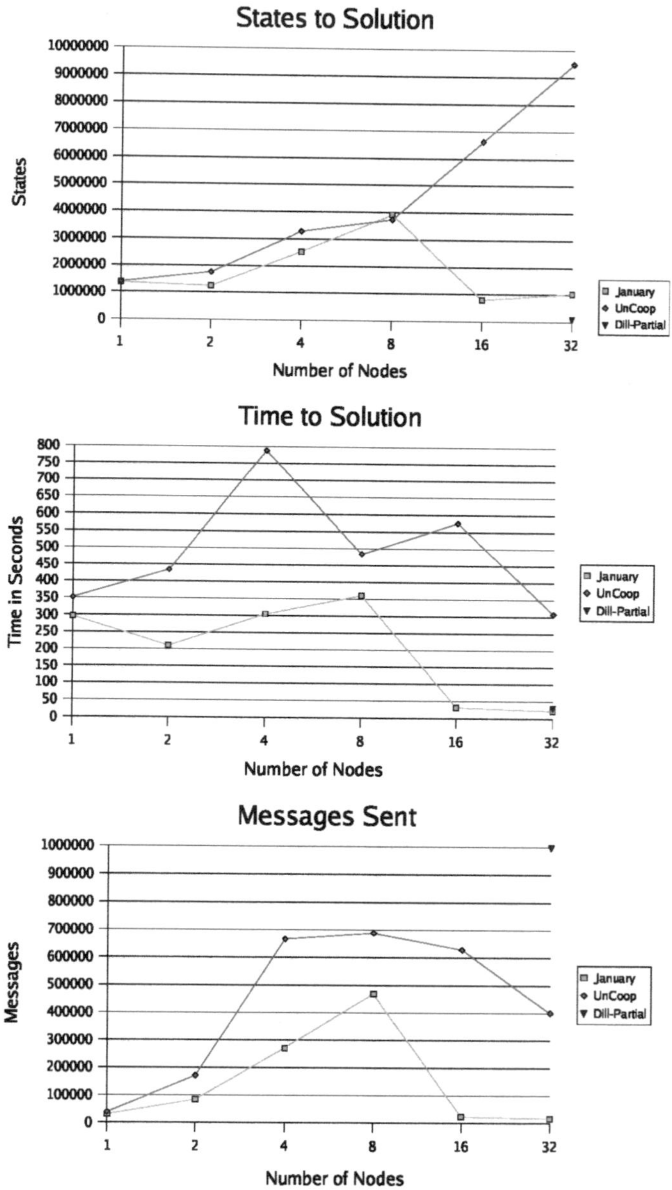

Fig. 3. Comparison of the cooperating January, uncooperating January and Dill's algorithm on the atomixe problem. On this problem, cooperation in January is advantageous and Dill's algorithm terminates only when given 32 processing nodes. Note that there is only a single data point, rather than a line, for Dill's algorithm.

5 Conclusions

The January algorithm locates errors using less memory and network bandwidth than the Dill algorithm. In many cases, the January algorithm can locate an error when the Dill algorithm fails using only a fraction of the resources required by the Dill algorithm. However, when the Dill algorithm has enough memory to store enough of the graph to find an error, the Dill algorithm finds the error is much less time (albeit using more network bandwidth). In all instances, the threshold of memory required for the Dill algorithm to discover the goal is higher than the threshold for January. This statement is true even for the models in which Dill did well. When the amount of memory allowed was lowered, Dill's algorithm prematurely terminated at an amount of memory that January still performed well at.

Our ant-based cooperation scheme appeared to have little or no effect on the efficiency of error discovery compared to seach without cooperation. However, future work may determine that a variant of ACO allows the discovery of shorter error traces with little additional effort.

References

1. MPICH 1.2.5. Mpich 1.2.5. http://www-unix.mcs.anl.gov/mpi/mpich/, 1993.
2. R.R. Baker. *The Evolutionary Ecology of Animal Migration.* Hodder and Stoughton, London, 1978.
3. E. M. Clarke, O. Grumberg, and D. Peled. *Model Checking.* MIT Press, 2000.
4. Marco Dorigo and Thomas Stutzle. *Ant Colony Optimization.* Bradford Books. MIT Press, first edition, 2004.
5. M. D. Jones and E. Mercer. Explicit state model checking with Hopper. In *International SPIN Workshop on Software Model Checking (SPIN'04)*, number 2989 in LNCS, pages 146–150, Barcelona, Spain, March 2004. Springer.
6. Michael D. Jones and Jacob Sorber. Parallel search for LTL violations. *Software Tools for Technology Transfer*, 7(1):31–42, 2005.
7. Hemanthkumar Sivaraj and Ganesh Gopalakrishnan. Random walk based heuristic algorithms for distributed memory model checking. In *Proceedings of Workshop on Parallel and Distributed Model Checking 2003*, 2003.
8. Ulrich Stern and D. L. Dill. Parallelizing the Murϕ verifier. In Orna Grumburg, editor, *Computer-Aided Verification, CAV '97*, volume 1254 of *Lecture Notes in Computer Science*, pages 256–267, Haifa, Israel, June 1997. Springer-Verlag.
9. Israel A. Wagner, Michael Lindenbaum, and Alfred M. Bruckstein. Robotic exploration, brownian motion and electrical resistance. In *Randomization and Approximation Techniques in Computer Science*, pages 116–130, 1998.
10. Ronald D. Weeks, Jr. Chemical ecology in the red imported fire ant (*Solenopsis invicta* buren) (hymenoptera: Formicidae). Technical report, Colorado State University, Fort Collins, CO 80523, 1998.
11. C. West. Protocol validation in complex systems. In *Symposium Proceedings on Communications Architecture and Protocols*, pages 303–312, 1989.
12. J. White, T.R. Tokbin, and W.J. Bell. Local search in the housefly, musca domestica after feeding on sucrose. In *J. Insect Physiol.*, pages 477–88, 1984.

A Generalized Graph-Based Method for Engineering Swarm Solutions to Multiagent Problems*

R. Paul Wiegand[1], Mitchell A. Potter[1], Donald A. Sofge[1], and William M. Spears[2]

[1] U.S. Naval Research Lab
{wiegand, mpotter, sofge}@aic.nrl.navy.mil
[2] University of Wyoming
wspears@cs.uwyo.edu

Abstract. We present two key components of a principled method for constructing modular, heterogeneous swarms. First, we generalize a well-known technique for representing swarm behaviors to extend the power of multiagent systems by specializing agents and their interactions. Second, a novel graph-based method is introduced for designing swarm-based behaviors for multiagent teams. This method includes engineer-provided knowledge through explicit design decisions pertaining to specialization, heterogeneity, and modularity. We show the representational power of our generalized representation can be used to evolve a solution to a challenging multiagent resource protection problem. We also construct a modular design by hand, resulting in a scalable and intuitive heterogeneous solution for the resource protection problem.

1 Introduction

Natural examples of emergent complexity from collections of simple components have led to the development of a number of methods that provide *swarm intelligence*—collective capabilities from simple autonomous agents [1]. Application of swarm methods to discrete and real-valued optimization problems include ant colony optimization [2] and particle swarm optimization [3] respectively, while other swarm methods have been applied to the area of collective robotics [4]. Designing swarms in simple situations is primarily a matter of replicating agents with the same behaviors, but more challenging problems require varying degrees of heterogeneity, where agents may *share* key behaviors and may also be capable of specialization. However, few swarm methods address issues of heterogeneity and modularity.

Historically, problems in Artificial Intelligence have been approached using methods that involve representing and incorporating domain knowledge. Unfortunately, such methods are difficult to implement, due to the amount of human engineering required. This is especially true for multiagent problems, where the number of interactions between agents becomes prohibitive. In response, swarm-based solutions to multiagent problems have been knowledge-poor. This raises other issues, especially with respect to scalability and intuition. What is missing is a principled and practical method for finding a middle ground: incorporating *some* human knowledge into the system, while providing as much representational flexibility as possible.

* This work was performed under Office of Naval Research Work Orders N0001406WX20006 and N0001406WX30002.

T.P. Runarsson et al. (Eds.): PPSN IX, LNCS 4193, pp. 741–750, 2006.

We present a method for designing swarm-based behaviors for multiagent teams that achieves this objective. While our method is general, this paper will focus on one particular swarm control paradigm, *physicomimetics*. Specifically, we will illustrate how physicomimetics can be generalized to include heterogeneity explicitly as part of the swarm design process, and will introduce a graph-based method to design heterogeneous, modular swarms. Our method allows engineers to embed knowledge about the domain into the system to constrain agent interactions for improved scalability, as well as to maintain intuition about the system's operation.

The paper first presents background information on physicomimetics, then describes our generalizations to this framework. An example of how this can be used to develop heterogeneous solutions is given. We follow by describing our graph-based design method and use it to construct a heterogeneous, modular solution by hand. The result is a very scalable solution that was intuitively designed and easily understood. We finish by discussing how our work relates to other swarm engineering methods, then provide some concluding remarks, including intended future endeavors.

2 Physicomimetics

Physicomimetics provides a framework for the control of multiple agents [5]. Agents are treated as point-mass (m) particles. Each particle has a position, $\mathbf{x}$, and velocity, $\mathbf{v}$. We use a discrete time simulation, with time-step Δt. At each time step, the particle is repositioned based on the velocity and the size of the step, $\Delta \mathbf{x} = \mathbf{v}\Delta t$. The change in velocity of the particles is determined by the artificial forces operating on the particles, $\Delta \mathbf{v} = \mathbf{F}\Delta t/m$, where $\mathbf{F}$ is the aggregate force on the particle as a result of interactions with other particles and the environment. Each particle also has a coefficient of friction, $c_f \in [0,1]$. Velocity in the next step becomes $(\mathbf{v} + \Delta\mathbf{v})c_f$, stabilizing the system [6,7].

There are two constraints: the magnitude of the force cannot exceed F_{max} and the magnitude of the velocity cannot exceed V_{max}. These restrict acceleration and velocity of particles in the model. Also, since there is an emphasis on *local* interactions, there are further restrictions on the range of effect particles have on other particles.

The simplicity of this framework creates a number of benefits. First, a variety of force laws can be employed to different effect. Moreover, the parameters of the above model, coupled with the force law parameters, provide engineers with mechanisms to adjust the behaviors of agents. Finally, since physicomimetics is based on physics, practical analyses are possible using traditional physics techniques such as force balance equations, conservation of energy and potential energy [6,8].

A slight variation of the well-known Newtonian force law will be used in this paper. The range of effect of the force is C, while R is the desired *range of separation* between agents. The gravitational constant is G, and there are two parameterized exponents: one for distance, d, and one for mass, a. The distance between two particles i and j is r_{ij}. The magnitude of the force between particles i and j is computed as follows.

$$F_{ij} = \begin{cases} -G\frac{(m_i m_j)^a}{r_{ij}^d} & \text{if } r_{ij} \in [0, R) \\ G\frac{(m_i m_j)^a}{r_{ij}^d} & \text{if } r_{ij} \in [R, C] \\ 0 & \text{otherwise} \end{cases} \tag{1}$$

This force law repels particles closer than R and attracts particles past that distance but within the range of effect. The gradient of the force can be controlled using d, and a can raise or lower the importance of mass on the force. In total, there are two parameters associated with each particle (m and c_f) and five parameters associated with their interactions (G, C, R, a, and d). Distance variable r_{ij} is an observed phenomenon.

3 Generalizing Physicomimetics

3.1 Differentiating Particle Types and Their Interactions

In heterogeneous multiagent systems, different types of agents will have different behavioral profiles. When heterogeneity is necessary, the first step is to explicitly consider different particle types during the swarm design process — each type having its own mass and coefficient of friction. Differentiating particle types provides some degree of specialized behaviors. For example, we can generate a variety of ring formations of arbitrary radii by creating two different particle types: one with a relatively small mass and one with a relatively large mass. However, only a limited subset of ring behaviors are possible when all particles are homogeneous.

In addition to differentiating particles, interactive forces between the types of particles can vary. When heterogeneity is important, the second step a swarm engineer should consider is specializing the different interactions between those types. With the combination of different types of interactions and different particle types, a wide range of complex heterogeneous behaviors are now possible. Moreover, by controlling how many particle types there are, and how many agents there are of each particle type, engineers can explicitly control the *level of heterogeneity* in cooperative teams.

In the simplest cases, the same force law is imposed for all interactions, but the parameters differ. For example, Spears *et al.* [6] showed that, while one can generate hexagonal lattice formations using traditional Newtonian physics, to produce square lattices one must differentiate particles[1] and vary the parameters of their interactions.

Force interactions between different particle types may also be asymmetric. That is, particle type A may affect particle type B differently than B affects A. This idea was leveraged by the online evolutionary learning system applied by [9,10] to an obstacle avoidance problem. In this case, particles representing agents reacted to each other differently than those representing the goal or the obstacles, yet the particles representing the goal and obstacles remained fixed.

More generally, the underlying force law itself can vary for different interactions. There is a physical metaphor for this — particles in the natural world affect one another via a variety of forces and one often dominates. An example of where this might be useful is the game capture the flag. Those agents retrieving the opponent flag might be better off using a force law that takes advantage of fluid-like effects for movement and obstacle avoidance, while those protecting the home flag may be better off using something more appropriate for strong structural formations [10].

---

[1] In the referenced work, they used the artificial label "spin" to differentiate particles.

3.2 An Example Problem

To begin exploring the advantages and limitations of our generalized physicomimetic framework, we introduce a simple resource protection problem. A centrally-located, immobile resource is encircled by a defense perimeter. Nine protector agents are deployed from the vicinity of the resource. Two slightly faster intruder agents appear in random locations just outside the perimeter and begin attack runs at the resource, attempting to avoid protectors during the run. If an intruder is destroyed, hits the resource, or is chased out of the perimeter, it is removed from the simulation, and a new intruder will begin a new run from just outside the perimeter after a short random waiting period.

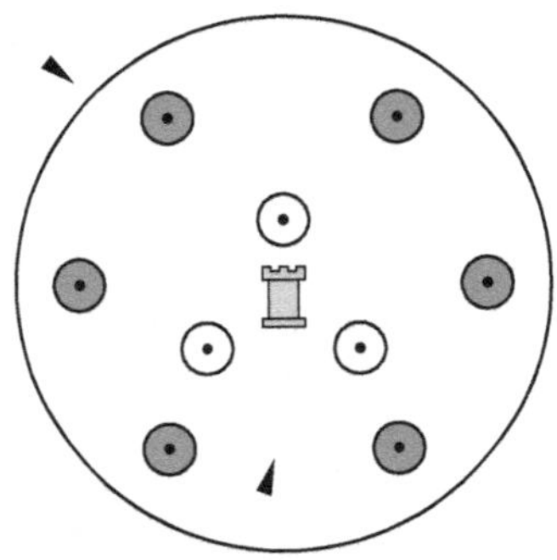

Fig. 1. Example resource protection problem. Castle marks resource to be protected, outer circle marks defense perimeter, gray and white circles with dots indicate protectors (two types), and the triangles indicate intruders (one type).

The problem is multiobjective. Ultimately, we want to reduce the extent of incursions into the defense perimeter, but also we want to avoid damage to the resource. Thus we define two objectives: the average per-step incursion distance of intruders into the perimeter and the ratio of resource hits taken over the total number of intruder runs at the resource. While these two objectives overlap a great deal, they are not the same — particularly when there are multiple intruders as is the case here.

As a result of its multiobjective nature, the resource protection problem is a good one for exploring questions about heterogeneity. By changing aspects of the problem, such as the relative importance of the two objectives, the number of intruders, or the types of possible intruder behaviors, we can begin to address questions about how heterogeneous teams of protectors can help, and what level of heterogeneity is useful in what circumstances. Specifically, we will consider solutions that allow for two different types of protectors (6 of one and 3 of the other) defending against a single type of intruder. The intuition here is to allow the system to deal with each objective separately byproviding it with different protective mechanisms for each objective. For example, it might be useful to have one set of protectors on the frontier chasing away intruders as soon as they enter the perimeter, while also having a few protectors back by the resource to prevent last-minute strikes.

3.3 Optimizing a General Physicomimetic Solution

Solutions to the resource protection problem can be represented using generalized physicomimetics; intruders and protectors use this model in all cases in this paper. Additionally, since their behaviors will be significantly influenced by the resource itself, it is also useful to model this as a separate particle type.

If we allow all possible instantiations, the parameter space is quite large, but we can reduce it somewhat. Since the central resource does not move, we need not worry about its coefficient of friction or interactions from other types of particles. Additionally, we limit the intruders to a single pre-defined strategy and focus on optimizing a solution for the protectors. Still, protector behaviors require eight interactions (one from each of the four types affecting each of the two protector types) and a total of 46 parameters (8 interactions with 5 parameters each + 4 for the mass of each type + 2 for the c_f of the protectors). If we were to add another protector type, there would be 6 more interactions and 32 more parameters. Indeed, the number of parameters scales quadratically with the number of particle types.

In spite of these simplifications, the size and complexity of the parameter space make it intractable for us to solve this by hand. Instead, we turned to evolutionary computation to help learn the parameters for the problem. Evolution was performed with a simple ES$(2 + 10)$. The physicomimetic parameters were encoded as real values in the range $[0.0, 1.0]$ and mapped to the ranges shown in Table 1. An adaptive Gaussian mutation was used, where $\sigma \in [0.005, 0.2]$, initialized at 0.2. The ES optimized two equally weighted measures: the average incursion distance of intruders into a defense perimeter of radius 150, scaled to the range $[0.0, 1.0]$, and the hit ratio of the intruders on the resource. These measures were evaluated using five discrete-time, 350×350 continuous space simulations of the problem run for 1000 steps each. This time is sufficient to allow approximately 20 intruder attack runs per simulation. The simulation was implemented with MASON, a multiagent simulation library [11].

Table 1. Legal physicomimetic parameter ranges for resource protector agents

C_{uv}	R_{uv}	G_{uv}	d_{uv}	a_{uv}	m_u	c_{f_u}
$[0, 350]$	$[0, C]$	$[0, 2400]$	$[-5, 5]$	$[0, 5]$	$[0.1, 50.0]$	$[0, 1]$

We performed 10 independent evolutionary runs, each for 100 generations, and tested the final best parameter set for an additional 100 simulations. The resulting average scaled incursion distance measure and 95% confidence interval for this solution was 0.120 ± 0.0016, and it allowed 4 hits on the resource over the 100 simulations. As hoped, the ES took advantage of the generalized physicomimetic framework byevolving a heterogeneous solution in which 6 protectors formed an outer ring to block incoming intruders as far away from the resource as possible, while 3 protectors formed a tight cluster around the resource to block any intruders making it through the outer defense. However, the inner ring of defenders was too close to the resource to be physically plausible. The majority of the other evolutionary runs produced physically implausible solutions as well. Furthermore, all the evolved solutions had an unnatural jitter that would not be acceptable if deployed.

A more carefully considered EA might have produced more natural and physically plausible solutions in this case. Additionally, it is clear that some kind of representational constraints are necessary if one wishes to increase the level of heterogeneity: the parameter space scales quadratically as the number of particle types increases. Such considerations are attempts to implicitly add domain knowledge into the algorithm. We detail an approach that addresses the scale-up problem while allowing the engineer more control over the final solution by *explicitly* incorporating domain knowledge in the design process. Our approach is meant to *complement* the learning algorithm, though for our example problem it is sufficient to allow us to develop solutions by hand.

4 Engineering Physicomimetic Solutions Using Directed Graphs

Our goal is to systematically design formation-oriented, collaborative multiagent teams capable of true heterogeneity and modularity. While generalized physicomimetics is capable of *representing* such solutions, it isn't clear how to *design* them.

It isn't a trivial problem. The parameter space of generalized physicomimetics, in which any level of heterogeneity of team members is possible, is very large. Every agent could be represented by a different particle type. Hence, due to pair-wise interactions, the parameter space can grow quadratically with the number of types. Moreover, since there can be strong non-linear influences between these parameters, designing solutions will become increasingly intractable as the level of heterogeneity increases. Finally, with this system it is unclear how to share successful partial solutions.

We provide a principled and practical method of engineering solutions using generalized physicomimetics by noticing two key facts: We do not always need every possible interaction, and we can often reuse an interaction's parameters. Reasoning about the types of interactions is necessary for designing successful heterogeneous, swarm-based multiagent solutions. Digraphs are natural and useful tools for this type of reasoning.

4.1 A Graph-Based Force Interaction Model

Let each type of particle be a node in a digraph and each interaction be a directed edge in that graph. An edge is associated with a force law as follows: for two particle types, u and v, a directed edge $(u, v, \mathcal{F}_{uv})$ denotes an interaction where particles of type u *impart* a force on particles of type v according to the force law defined by $\mathcal{F}_{uv}$. Fig. 2 illustrates a graph for a two-agent example.

These digraphs can have isolated nodes and cycles. Omitted edges imply there is no direct interaction between the particle types represented by those nodes in the graph.

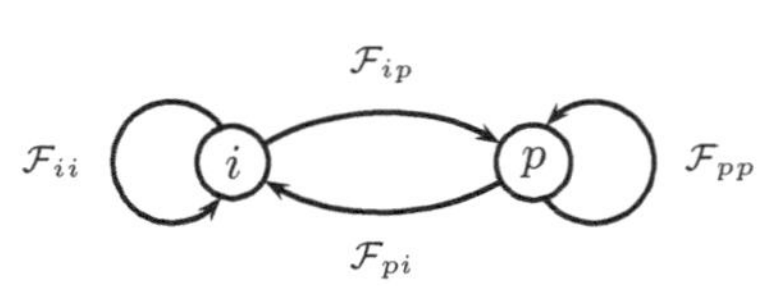

Fig. 2. An example force interaction digraph. There are two particle types, (i) and (p), and there are separate force laws between every possible pair of particle types.

4.2 Modularity Via Condensed Subgraphs

In swarm engineering, the concept of modularity is particularly important. Here, we address two different views of modularity: modularity of design and behavioral modules.

When designing something complex, engineers often decompose systems, build components separately, and then combine them. We employ a similar idea for constructing complex multiagent simulations. Using our graph-based approach, we break the graph into relevant subgraphs, and then consider them in conjunction with one another. It is helpful to categorize agents by developing subgraphs that *profile* how agents of a group interact with other agents in the system. This constitutes *modular design*.

In addition to modular design, there may be times when modularizing *behaviors* (sharing subsets of behaviors) in a heterogeneous multiagent team is important. One way to introduce modularity to generalized physicomimetics is to allow particles to share force laws and parameters. We do this by allowing the engineer to *condense* a subgraph by consolidating particle types into a single node.

Some simple notational elements can be added to the digraph to aid with these sorts of design issues. This is illustrated in the next section.

4.3 A Simple Graph-Based Solution

Our generalized physicomimetic solution to the resource protection problem was versatile, but yielded a large parameter space that was quadratic with respect to the number of protector types. Careful analysis, however, reveals obvious ways that engineer-guided knowledge can limit the space in order to craft a solution to the problem by hand.

We begin our design by considering the agent types: an arbitrary number of protector types ($p_1, p_2, \ldots$), one intruder type (i), and a resource type (r). Next we consider the types of interactions that we believe will be necessary. Since intruders cannot distinguish types of protectors, we can condense some of the intruder behaviors. Moreover, if we consider each protector type as nearly independent, we need provide only limited interactions between types of protectors — just enough to avoid hitting one another. Both of these pieces of knowledge lead to fairly obvious reductions in the model.

We designed the interactions using three subgraphs (see Figure 3), profiling protectors (all types) separately from intruders (one type). The first subgraph represents a module of behaviors for the intruder, while the second two represent two modules of behaviors for the protector types. The notation p_* in a node means all protector types are represented by that node. Links connecting such nodes represent identical force laws between the nodes. Additionally, rather than drawing many subgraphs for each type of protector, we abbreviate the design using the p_j notational convenience. Our designsolution for the interactions can be seen below. We omit the $\mathcal{F}$ labels in the graph since they are implied by the existence of the edge and identified by the nodes they connect.

Notice that we must resolve a notational conflict. The middle subgraph shows a specific edge between a particle protector type and itself, while the third subgraph shows a general edge between any two protector types. A specific edge has precedence over a general one, so the way to read the graph is as follows. Every interaction between different protector types is identical, except for the interaction of the protector type with itself — that is specified explicitly and is different for each type.

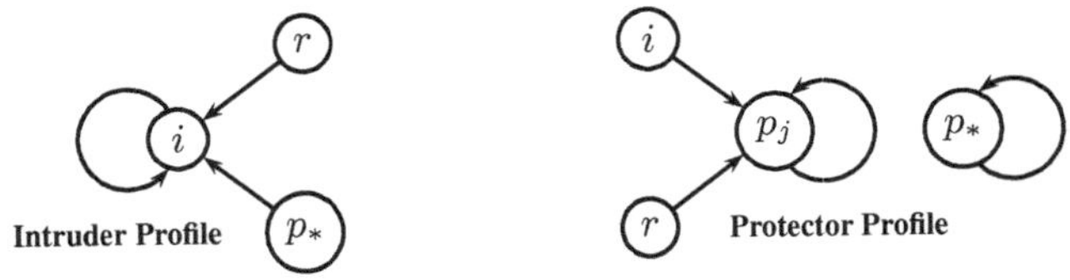

Fig. 3. Force interaction models for the resource protection problem. The graph on the left represents all the interactions affecting the intruders. Note this does not depend on the protector type. The two on the right represent those affecting the protector types. Each type of protector can react to its own type and to intruders in a different way, but they react identically to all other protectors.

We have designed our subgraphs in such a way as to capture both senses of modularity. The first and third subgraphs *condense* reactions toward any kind of protector, creating reusable modules. The second subgraph provides a design-level modularity. By using this visualization, we can compute the number of required parameters for the protector profile. Each interaction requires five parameters (G, C, R, a, and d). If there are P protector types, then $3P+1$ edges (interactions) must be defined, requiring $5(3P+1)$ parameters. Each protector type requires two more parameters (m and c_f), resulting in $2P$ additional parameters. Hence, for P protector types, $17P+5$ parameters must be optimized. This means there will be a constant number of new parameters (17) with the addition of each protector type: a linear scaling of parameters.

With the above interaction design, it was easy to construct a solution to the resource protection problem by hand. Beginning with the first protector type, we adjusted the parameters such that these agents form a large ring around the resource. They attempt to maintain formation, but will chase off or destroy intruders that come close to them. The rest of the ring will redistribute if a protector is pulled away in pursuit of an intruder. Next we designed the second protector type to stay close to the resource, but aggressively pursue intruders that are moderately far from them. These protectors are pulled back to the resource if they get too far away, but are given a fair amount of latitude to pursue enemies that are in close quarters. In this case, combining these two behaviors was trivial — we merely sought to keep them out of the way of one another. The combined behaviors are smooth, easily understood, and physically plausible.

The parameter values for the above solution are shown below. We ran this model of 100 independent simulations; the resulting average scaled incursion distance and confidence interval was 0.199 ± 0.004. Of the 100 trials, 94 of them resulted in runs where no intruder ever struck the resource. The remaining six admitted just a single strike each.

Table 2. Model parameters for hand-coded solution to the resource protection problem

	$i \to p_1$	$r \to p_1$	$p_1 \to p_1$	$i \to p_2$	$r \to p_2$	$p_1 \to p_2$	$p_* \to p_*$
C	80	350	250	150	350	300	20
R	5	100	110	5	15	200	20
G	2400	600	1200	2400	0.05	1200	1200
d	2	2	1.5	2	-0.5	2	2
a	0	1	1	0	0	1	1

	i	p_1	p_2	r
m	1.0	1.0	1.0	60.0
c_f	0.15	0.15	0.15	-

5 Related Swarm Engineering Work

Swarm engineering, the process of designing, building, and validating swarm behaviors, has sparked much interest of late. In a recent survey of case studies applying conventional engineering approaches for dependability to swarm design, Winfield *et al.* [12] point out the need for better tools for swarm engineering.

In response to such needs, Kazadi [13] developed a formalism of *swarm intelligence* and described an approach to engineering the behavior of swarms according to that formalism. Chang [14] describes this approach as a *middle-meeting method* that combines both top-down macroscopic with bottom-up microscopic swarm design techniques. While the method provides guidance to the swarm designer in decomposing the swarm engineering problem, low-level behaviors must still be created by the designer.

In work contemporaneous with the initial development of physicomimetics, Reif and Wang [15] develop a method called *social potential fields* as a way to program large teams of robots. Like generalized physicomimetics, their method models the agents as particles, provides for multiple types of agents, and generates behaviors through interactions of forces between agents. Reif and Wang propose a hierarchical methodology for determining the set of potential force laws, laying out a step-by-step procedure for developing system behaviors with different levels of interactions.

Both Kazadi and Reif and Wang proffer methodologies for designing interactions between agents. However, both methods largely leave it to the designer to determine how to discover or create behaviors that achieve the *global goal* (Kazadi) or *required behaviors* (Reif and Wang). Our work complements these approaches to force law design by presenting an intuitive graph-based means for designing such behaviors while incorporating some human knowledge into the design process.

6 Conclusions and Future Work

This paper presented two key components of a principled method for constructing swarms in a modular way, capable of both shared and specialized behaviors using physicomimitics. We responded to the growing need to find a middle ground between open-ended, knowledge-poor representations and brittle, knowledge-rich representations by illustrating how *some* engineer-guided knowledge can be incorporated into a multiagent system. Our intent is to provide one view on how to practically develop complex swarm-based solutions in a principled way.

First, we clarified how physicomimetics can be generalized to extend the power of multiagent systems by specializing particles and their interactions. We advocate making such choices explicitly a part of the design process in constructing swarm-based systems. This gives one control over the ability of the system to produce specialized, coordinated behaviors. We illustrated these points using a challenging multiagent resource protection problem. The representational power of the generalized physicomimetic solution is more than sufficient to solve the problem; however, the scale of the parameter space necessitated heuristic optimization. This resulted in specialized squads of agents that effectively protected a central resource from intrusion, but sacrificed predictability and physical plausibility.

Second, we presented a graph-based method for designing interaction models in physicomimetic systems. This method allows engineers to construct graphs that clearly define what interactions are possible. By using our technique for condensed subgraphs, engineers can think more modularly about the design process and produce reusable behavioral modules, giving the engineer the ability to directly control the scalability of the system. We illustrated this method by hand designing a heterogeneous, modular solution to the aforementioned resource protection problem. Our solution is easy to understand, physically plausible, and performs quite well on the task.

Our next step is to apply our method to design swarm-based solutions to well-known multiagent problems, such as the art gallery problem, multi-asset surveillance, and problems from the search and rescue domain. We are also interested in combining our graph-based design method with heuristic optimization methods, designing the force interaction models by hand and eliciting the model parameters algorithmically.

References

1. Bonabeau, E., Dorigo, M., Theraulaz, G.: Swarm Intelligence. Oxford University Press (1999)
2. Dorigo, M., Stützle, T.: Ant Colony Optimization. The MIT Press (2004)
3. Kennedy, J., Eberhart, R.C.: Swarm Intelligence. Morgan Kaufmann Publishers (2001)
4. Kube, C.R., Zhang, H.: Collective Robotics: From Social Insects to Robots. Adaptive Behavior **2** (1994) 189–218
5. Spears, W., Gordon, D.: Using Artificial Physics to control agents. In: IEEE International Conference on Information, Intelligence, and Systems, IEEE (1999) 281–288
6. Spears, W., Spears, D., Hamann, J., Heil, R.: Distributed, physics-based control of swarms of vehicles. Autonomous Robots **17** (2004) 137–162
7. Howard, A., Mataric, M., Sukhatme, G.: Mobile sensor network deployment using potential fields: A distributed, scalable solution to the area coverage problem. In: Sixth International Symposium on Distributed Autonomous Robotics Systems. (2002)
8. Spears, W., Spears, D., Heil, R.: A formal analysis of potential energy in a multiagent systems. In: Lecture Notes in Artificial Intelligence. Volume 3228., Springer (2004)
9. Hettiarachchi, S., Spears, W., Kerr, W., Zarzhitsky, D., Green, D.: Distributed agent evolution with dynamic adaptation to local unexpected scenarios. In: Second GSFC/IEEE Workshop on Radical Agent Concepts, Springer (2006)
10. Hettiarachchi, S., Spears, W.: Moving swarm formations through obstacle fields. In: International Conference on Artificial Intelligence. Volume 1., CSREA Press (2005) 97–103
11. Luke, S., Balan, G.C., Panait, L., Cioffi-Revilla, C., Paus, S.: MASON: A java multi-agent simulation library. In: Agent 2003 Conference on Challenges in Social Simulation. (2003)
12. Winfield, A., Harper, C., Nembrini, J.: Towards dependable swarms and a new discipline of swarm engineering. In: 2004 SAB Swarm Robotics Workshop. (2004) 133–148
13. Kazadi, S.: On the Development of a Swarm Engineering Methodology. In: IEEE Conference on Systems, Man, and Cybernetics, IEEE (2005) 1423–1428
14. Chang, K., Hwang, J., Lee, E., Kazadi, S.: The Application of Swarm Engineering Technique to Robust Multi-chain Robot System. In: IEEE Conference on Systems, Man, and Cybernetics, IEEE (2005) 1429–1434
15. Reif, J.H., Wang, H.: Social Potential Fields: A Distributed Behavioral Control for Autonomous Robots. Robotics and Autonomous Systems **27** (1999) 171–194

Probabilistic Adaptive Mapping Developmental Genetic Programming (PAM DGP): A New Developmental Approach

Garnett Wilson and Malcolm Heywood

Faculty of Computer Science, Dalhousie University, 6050 University Ave., Halifax, Nova Scotia, Canada B3H 1W5
{gwilson, mheywood}@cs.dal.ca

Abstract. Developmental Genetic Programming (DGP) algorithms have been introduced where the search space for a problem is divided into genotypes and corresponding phenotypes that are connected by a mapping (or "genetic code"). Current implementations of this concept involve evolution of the mappings in addition to the traditional evolution of genotypes. We introduce the latest version of Probabilistic Adaptive Mapping DGP (PAM DGP), a robust and highly customizable algorithm that overcomes performance problems identified for the latest competing adaptive mapping algorithm. PAM DGP is then shown to outperform the competing algorithm on two non-trivial regression benchmarks.

1 Introduction

Traditionally in genetic programming, direct evaluation of the genotype is sufficient to define the corresponding phenotype. Broadly speaking, developmental genetic programming (DGP) can refer to any methodology that explicitly sets out to separate the genotype space from the phenotype (or solution) space. In the literature, the term has been used to encompass systems such as the one presented in this work that inserts a mapping (encoding) to establish a relationship between the two spaces. The term also describes systems that involve considerably more constructs between the two spaces, such as proteins and embryos. This research concerns itself with the issue of mappings, or biological codes, to relate the genotype and phenotype spaces in the spirit of Banzhaf and Keller [1-4]. This separation enables a DGP to investigate all areas of a genotype (search) space without being constrained by demands on the validity of the phenotype. The mappings utilized in initial research efforts were fixed [1], [2], but the benefit and potential for evolving the mappings themselves has since been recognized. The first implementation to explore this possibility was described by Keller and Banzhaf [3], while an alternate type of adaptable mapping and an associated algorithm were later introduced by Margetts and Jones [5]–[7]. With the use of evolved mappings, a DGP must evolve both a set of genotypes and a set of mappings that apply to them. For this additional effort, the DGP is provided with the ability to adapt its mappings so that the function set for a solution is tailored to its unique problem space, and it is given the capability to freely explore the genotype search space. To do so, adaptive mappings provide the basis for determining what bit string

T.P. Runarsson et al. (Eds.): PPSN IX, LNCS 4193, pp. 751 – 760, 2006.

combinations and lengths in the genotype correspond to the function set, or even if a member of the function set should be represented at all.

Section 2 of this work examines the original evolved mapping structure and algorithm [3] and the adaptive DGP algorithm and mapping mechanism [5]–[7]. Section 3 defines the latest version of the Probabilistic Adaptive Mapping DGP (PAM DGP) algorithm based on significant performance enhancing modifications since [8]. Sections 4 and 5 describe two regression benchmark problems and the performance of PAM DGP and the current standard adaptive mapping algorithm on those problems. Conclusion and Future Work follow in Section 6.

2 Previous DGP Mapping Structures and Algorithms

Mappings between genotypes and phenotypes are denoted *global* when all genotypes are mapped onto phenotypes using the same encoding [3]. Genetic codes are evolvable when they are *individual*, meaning that each individual is a pairing of its own genetic code with its own genotype. Redundant encodings of members of the function and terminal set are used to allow the search to emphasize certain symbols and disregard others that are of little or no use in the problem solution. That is, symbols having a larger number of encodings, or possessing more prevalent ones, are expected to be more important and to be reflected in phenotypes more often. Upon initialization, each genotype is coupled with a randomly generated genetic code, or codon-symbol mapping. The mapping was traditionally symbiotically mated with the genotype individual throughout the tournament, and it was mutated, reproduced, or selected along with the genotype that carried it [3], [4]. Mappings were thus static.

Mapping schemes to improve the symbol emphasis component of DGP search were examined by Margetts and Jones in [5], [6]. In [5], [7], they introduce an alternative encoding scheme where binary strings of dynamically determined length are used. The *adaptive mapping* representations themselves and the associated algorithm of Margetts and Jones is hereafter denoted the Adaptive Mapping DGP. In their implementation, each mapping has its own assignment of binary sequences to symbols based on Huffman encoding. This ensures that the most frequent bit sequences correspond to the most frequent symbols, with shorter bit sequences allocated to more frequent symbols and vice versa. Given n separate symbols in the phenotype, each individual in the population of mappings consists of binary strings composed of n sections. Each section is a number of bits b representing a frequency. Each section of b binary bits is converted to a real valued frequency in the interval [0, 1] using a normalized function (called countingOnes) that sums all the ones in a given binary string [6]. (The countingOnes function was chosen on the basis that it resulted in a more refined search during the later exploitation phase of search.) For each symbol in the function set, its associated frequency and the entire genotype binary string are passed to Huffman's algorithm to determine the particular sequence of bits in the genotype (codon) that expresses it. The mapping process is shown below in Figure 1.

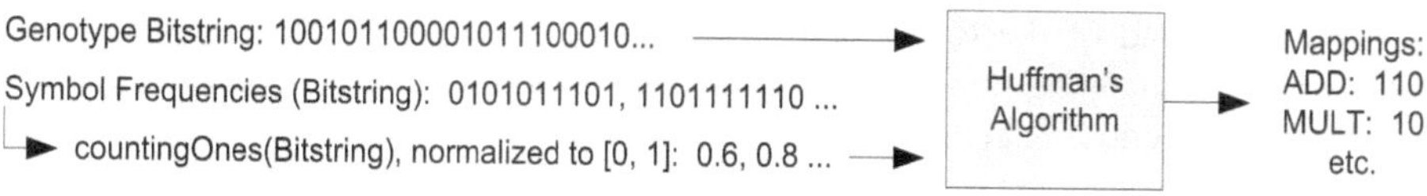

Fig. 1. Mapping representation using Huffman's encoding in Adaptive Mapping DGP

The Adaptive Mapping DGP algorithm uses two populations: a population of mappings and a population of genotypes. The populations co-evolve so that a search is conducted for both a genotype and a corresponding mapping simultaneously. In order to evaluate a particular genotype, the member of the mapping population with the current highest fitness is selected to produce the phenotype for fitness evaluation. To evaluate a mapping individual, the current best member of the genotype population is used. Mappings are thus dynamically assigned to genotypes. Members of each population are initialized by being evaluated with random members of the other. A steady state tournament is used with members of each population evaluated alternately.

We recently demonstrated that the Adaptive Mapping DGP methodology was shown (empirically) to cause itself to regularly disrupt the progress it makes toward a solution [8]. The two populations were shown to end up struggling to match their search to each other's best individual while at the same time causing the best individual in each other's population to change, thus always losing search context. We propose a new DGP algorithm called "Probabilistic Adaptive Mapping DGP" (PAM DGP) that both avoids the context change of the Adaptive Mapping DGP algorithm and explores more of the possible genotype and mapping combinations. An initial version of PAM DGP was presented in [8]. Considerable performance enhancements are presented here, including better protection of high fitness contexts (genotype-phenotype pairings) to prevent context loss and a procedure for introduction of noise to probabilistic selection to avoid local optima in the search space. The improved algorithm consistently outperforms Adaptive Mapping DGP on the MAX problem (whereas the previous attempt only outperformed on particular constraints) and has solved a considerably more difficult regression problem (Two Boxes). All results in this work compare the refined version of PAM DGP, as presented below, to the Adaptive Mapping DGP of Margetts and Jones [5]-[7].

3 Probabilistic Adaptive Mapping DGP (PAM DGP)

PAM DGP evolves one population of genotypes and one population of mappings, a feature common to previous statically [3], [4], and dynamically mapped [5]–[7] DGP algorithms. The individuals in the PAM DGP mapping population employ adaptive mappings using Huffman encoding as described above. PAM DGP uses a probability table to define the genotype-mapping relationship between the two populations. Each individual in the genotype population is allotted a corresponding point on the x axis of the table, and each individual in the adaptive mapping population is allotted a corresponding point on the y axis. The table is initialized so that each column, one corresponding to each genotype point on the x axis, sums to unity. All blocks in each column are thus initialized to the same probability.

For each round of the tournament, a member of the genotype population and a member of the mapping population are selected using the probability table. Roulette wheel selection chooses a position in the table, with four separate genotype individuals selected in each tournament round. The genotypes are ranked by fitness after being interpreted in the context of the mapping they are associated with by the index on the table. The tournament is steady state, so the best 2 genotype individuals (the parents) are left untouched while the last two genotype individuals become children. The children become copies of the parents and are subjected to mutation and crossover with associated likelihood probability thresholds. The mappings associated with the ranked genotypes receive the ranking of their connected genotypes during competition in a tournament round. The mappings associated with the top two genotype parents are ranked as the top two mappings and kept as the parent mappings, while the mappings associated with the last two ranked genotype children become copies of the mapping parents and are subject to mutation and crossover. Since there is only a guarantee during selection that separate genotypes will be selected, some mapping individuals may appear more than once in the ranked list for a tournament round. A mapping appearing twice or more in the ranking list may (and will likely) have a different fitness each time, in virtue of being associated with a different genotype at each placement in the ranked list.

When crossover occurs, it is explicitly protected against being applied to a single mapping individual. The algorithm also features elitism in that it protects the genotype individual and the mapping that produces the current highest fitness. Note that unless both members of that pairing are explicitly protected, either member of the pairing can be selected as a child by being coupled with an alternate member of the other population during roulette wheel selection on the probability table. The position on the table associated with the two winning genotype-mapping combinations is updated according to (1), while the losing combinations are updated according to (2)

$$P(g,m)_{new} = P(g,m)_{old} + \alpha(1 - P(g,m)_{old}) \tag{1}$$

$$P(g,m)_{new} = P(g,m)_{old} - \alpha(P(g,m)_{old}) \tag{2}$$

where g is the genotype index, m is the mapping index, α is the learning rate (or how much emphasis is placed on current values as opposed to previous search), and $P(g,m)$ is the probability in location $[g, m]$ of the table. Equations (1) and (2) ensure that all columns in the probability table sum to unity after being updated.

Roulette wheel selection for the probability table operates by adding the probabilities across the rows associated with mapping individuals. Allowing the roulette wheel to travel across rows, instead of the genotype-associated columns, gives a more direct influence to the mapping population in the algorithm i.e., the wheel must pass through all probabilities associated with each mapping before moving onto the next mapping in the table. This balances the fact that ranking of genotypes otherwise guides the search and determines mapping selection during a tournament round.

After a period of search depending on the learning rate, it was discovered that the probability table can prematurely converge on particular genotype-mapping pairings while other locations in the table have no (or practically no) probability associated to them. In order to allow the algorithm to continue to explore all genotype-mapping combinations and the underlying binary sequences they make available to the search space, noise is introduced. This is accomplished by examining each (genotype-associated) column when it is updated to see if any location in that column has exceeded a user-defined threshold n. If it has, each member of the column has a uniform probability $P(1 - n)$ of having a standard Gaussian probability adjustment in the interval [0, 1] added to its current value. (In rarer cases where the Gaussian value is outside the interval [0, 1], it is simply re-chosen until it falls in the interval.) The values in the column are then re-normalized so that they sum to unity. Summary of the algorithm and pseudocode are given below in Figures 2 and 3, respectively.

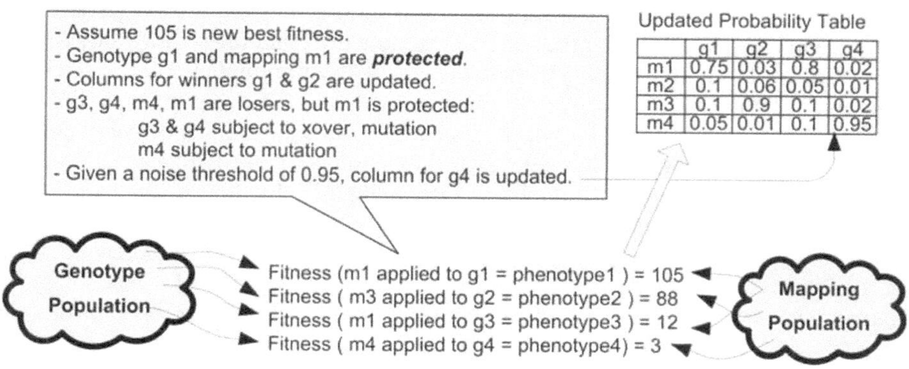

	g1	g2	g3	g4
m1	0.75	0.03	0.8	0.02
m2	0.1	0.06	0.05	0.01
m3	0.1	0.9	0.1	0.02
m4	0.05	0.01	0.1	0.95

Fig. 2. Example of execution for the PAM DGP algorithm

```
Initialize size P mapping & genotype populations
Initialize each value in P x P probTable = 1/P
while (tournamentNotDone && solutionNotFound)
   Use probTable mapping rows for roulette selection
   Rank selectedGenotype & associatedMapping pairings
   Verify or set current bestGenotype & bestMapping
   Apply update to probTable according to Eq. (1) & (2)
   if (element of winning genotype column > threshold)
      for (each column element)
         Add Gaussian noise value to element
      Normalize column contents to unity
   for 2 loserGenotypes & 2 loserMappings
      if (respective mutation thresholds are met)
         if (loserIndividual ≠ bestIndividual)
            mutate(loserIndividual = copy of parent)
      if (respective xover threshold is met)
         if (both loserIndividuals ≠ bestIndividual)
            xover(loserIndividuals = copy of parents)
```

Fig. 3. Pseudocode for the PAM DGP algorithm

4 Maximum Output Problem

The Maximum Output (MAX) problem, as described in [5], [7], is to create a program that returns the largest value possible within a specified program size limit. An ideal solution to the problem is a program that repeatedly duplicates a large number and multiplies it by itself, effectively squaring the number repeatedly as many times as possible. As in the work describing the Adaptive Mapping DGP [5], [7], the MAX problem is implemented in PAM DGP with a linear (bit string) stack-based version of GP. Each individual is a stack-based machine composed of a general-purpose stack and an output register. A program that changes the state of the machine is a list of instructions from the function set in Table 1 below. When an instruction in the program is processed sequentially, the required arguments are taken from the stack, they are presented to the function, and the return value (if any) is pushed back onto the stack. If there are insufficient arguments on the stack, the function does nothing.

In PAM DGP, the dimensions of the probability table are the respective population sizes. Parameterization of the algorithm thus involves considering a trade-off between the amount of initial genotype and mapping material you want available for the search and the sparseness of the probability table. The smallest population under which the tournament can still be conducted was found to work best for the MAX problem. PAM DGP thus uses a population of 8 (4 genotypes and 4 mappings). A tournament is stopped when the maximum round limit of 1250 is reached or the success criterion is met. The MAX problem was considered solved when an individual generated the double value of "Infinity" by the Java 2 RE, build 1.5.0_05, on a 1.25 GHz PowerPC G4 running Mac OS X Version 10.4.4. Algorithm parameters are summarized in Table 1 for both DGP algorithms.

The number of solutions out of 50 independent trials is given below in Table 2. Restricting the standard adaptive DGP to a population of 8 to match PAM DGP hindered its performance, so its population was increased to 50 (25 individuals in each

Table 1. Maximum Output parameterization of Adaptive Mapping and PAM DGP

Tournament Style	Steady State, 4 individuals for each round
Maximum Rounds	1250 (5000 individuals processed)
Experiments	50 independent runs
Function Set	+, *, const, dup, pop, stack3Register, register2Stack
Genotype structure	Stack-based with register; 50, 100, 150, 200, 250 bits
Mapping structure	Adaptive, 70 bits (10 bits per function set member)
Geno., map mutation	Point mutation, threshold = 0.01
Geno., map crossover	Equal-sized blocks, threshold = 0.9
Population size	4 or 25 individuals in each population
Fitness	Output register content after evaluation.
Objective	Generate largest number possible.
Termination	Infinity (success) or maximum rounds.
Learning rate	0.1 (only applicable to PAM DGP)
Noise threshold	0.95 (only applicable to PAM DGP)

Table 2. Number of Maximum Output solutions in 50 independent experiments

Bits	PAM DGP, Pop. 8	Adaptive, Pop. 8	Adaptive, Pop. 50
50	0	0	0
100	10	0	1
150	38	0	6
200	47	9	22
250	48	21	28

population). On equal basis of respective optimal population sizes, PAM DGP dramatically outperforms the standard (Table 2).

The mean best fitness for each tournament round over all 50 experiments is plotted below in Figure 4 for both algorithms using their respective optimal populations. (250 bits represents a trend similar to 200 and was omitted for brevity.) Fitness measure for any experiment not yet achieving success at a round is used to determine the mean (infinity cannot be plotted). PAM DGP (solid line) outperforms the standard adaptive mapping algorithm consistently throughout all tournament rounds. The algorithm is also more robust, as far fewer fitness spikes are present.

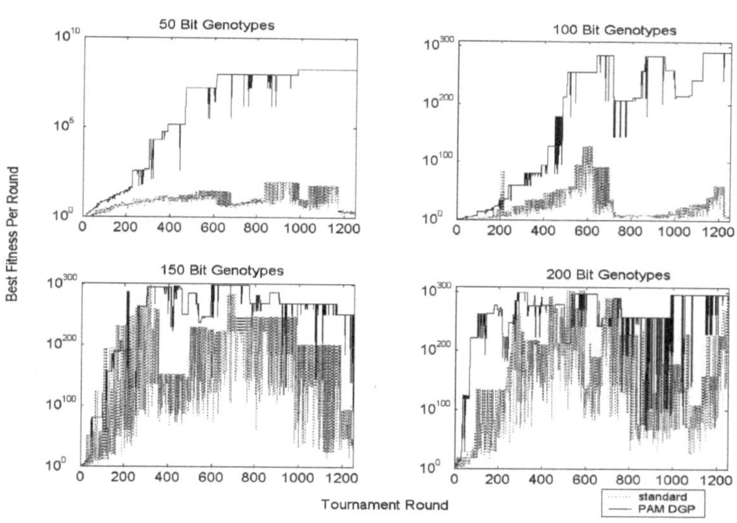

Fig. 4. Mean best MAX problem fitness per round over 50 independent runs for PAM DGP, population 8, and Adaptive Mapping algorithm, population 50

The operator content of the solutions as a percentage of total operators is shown in Table 3 along with p-values. There is no significant difference at the 0.95 or 0.99 confidence intervals for 5 out of 7 operators, where PAM DGP used less constants and more multiplication. Since the best solutions only require repeated duplication/multiplication following initial presence of a constant, the difference in symbols would only give PAM DGP more ideal solutions.

Table 3. Mean operators as percentage of total solution over 50 trials for 200 bit, Population 8 MAX Problem for PAM DGP and Adaptive Mapping with associated p-values

	CONST	POP	DUP	S2R	R2S	PLUS	TIMES
PAM DGP	0.0292	0.0314	0.232	0.166	0.121	0.203	0.218
Adaptive	0.0471	0.0371	0.241	0.166	0.115	0.205	0.189
p-value	0.000249	0.275	0.575	0.986	0.591	0.882	0.00771

5 Two Boxes Problem

The Two Boxes problem is to relate six independent variables (L_0, W_0, H_0, L_1, W_1, and H_1) through the equation for the difference in volume of two boxes ($L_0W_0H_0$ - $L_1W_1H_1$) [9]. Ten fitness cases are created using uniform sampling of integers over the interval [1, ..., 10]. Fitness is measured as the summed absolute error over all fitness cases, where in each case an absolute error ≤ 0.01 counts as a hit. The success criterion is to produce 10 hits. Each instruction in a genotype's bit sequence is parsed by processing the number of bits associated with a function, followed by a single bit determining whether to load a value from the fitness cases or from a register, with the next two bits determining one of four registers as the target and the last two bits specifying a register as the source. Emphasis of functional operators is achieved by mappings varying bit lengths and combinations used to start each instruction.

The parameterization is modified to better suit a considerably harder regression problem, with the salient differences being a separation of genotype/mapping crossover rates and mutation type and rates. An increased mutation rate was used in the genotypes to allow exploration against the backdrop of more persistent (due to low operator rates) mappings. Point mutation is used in the mappings to ensure a number of frequencies per operator are explored; whereas an instruction-level mutation operator that performs XOR on the instruction with a randomly generated bit mask (the instruction chosen with uniform probability) is used for the genotype mutation operator. Both algorithms perform best with a population of 50 individuals (25 genotypes and 25 mappings) in this problem, benefiting from the additional genetic material with which to perform a search. The alternative settings for this problem demonstrate the high customizability of PAM DGP and provide an example of its performance on a hard problem using a larger population (and larger probability table) than the MAX problem. Parameterizations specific to the Two Boxes problem are shown in Table 4 (Table 1 details the common parameters).

Neither algorithm provided a solution with a population of 8, with only PAM DGP providing one solution during 50 trials with a population of 50. Mean best fitness produced in each trial is shown below in Figure 5. For both starting populations, PAM DGP outperforms the adaptive mapping algorithm, producing lower cumulative errors. Overall fitness performance of PAM DGP is also not affected by raising population size to handle harder problems with more obscure solutions, such as the Two Boxes problem. This conclusion is supported at the 99% confidence interval. (PAM DGP performance is not statistically different for either population size.)

Table 4. Two Boxes parameterization of Adaptive Mapping and PAM DGP

Maximum Rounds	50 000
Function Set	+, *, %, / (protected against underflow/overflow)
Terminal Set	L_0, W_0, H_0, L_1, W_1, H_1
Genotype structure	Instruction sequence with 4 registers; 320 bits
Mapping structure	Adaptive, 40 bits (10 bits per function set member)
Genotype mutation	XOR instruction-level mutation, threshold = 0.5
Mapping mutation	Point mutation, threshold = 0.1
Genotype crossover	Equal-sized blocks, threshold = 0.9
Mapping crossover	Equal-sized blocks, threshold = 0.1
Fitness Cases	10 sets of 6 integers in [1, ..., 10], output value
Fitness	Summed absolute error.
Objective	Fit equation to $L_0W_0H_0 - L_1W_1H_1$
Hits	Number of fitness cases with absolute error ≤ 0.01
Termination	10 hits (success) or maximum rounds.

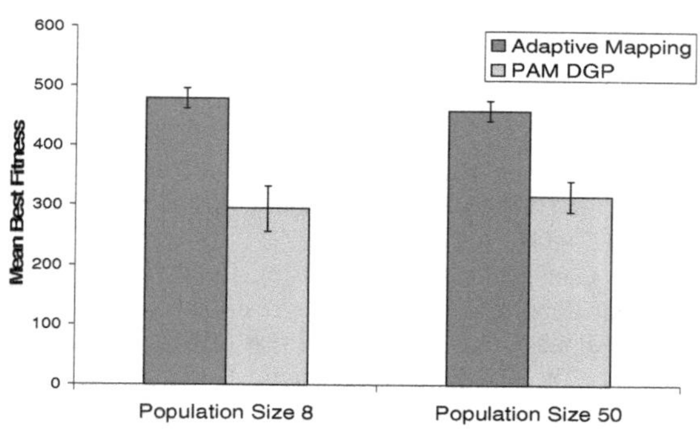

Fig. 5. Mean best fitness achieved (after maximum rounds or a solution) for PAM DGP and Adaptive Mapping algorithm for 50 trials. Error bars reflect t-distribution.

The operator content of the solutions as a percentage of total operators is shown in Table 5 below along with p-values for population 50. There is no significant difference at the 0.95 or 0.99 confidence intervals for all operators, indicating that both algorithms were equal in their ability to choose useful function set symbols and that overall the algorithms chose similar solution content.

Table 5. Mean operators as percentage of total solution over 50 trials for the Two Boxes Problem, population 50, for PAM DGP and Adaptive Mapping with associated p-values

	MULT	SUB	ADD	DIVIDE
PAM DGP	0.285	0.285	0.204	0.258
Adaptive	0.303	0.250	0.213	0.234
p-value	0.482	0.161	0.637	0.262

6 Conclusion and Future Work

This paper presents the latest version of a new developmental GP algorithm, PAM DGP, which outperforms the previous Adaptive Mapping DGP algorithm on a number of metrics for two non-trivial regression problems. PAM DGP is specifically designed not to suffer from sporadic fitness gains and losses due to changes in context, and it considers more context combinations of genotypes and mappings during its search than the Adaptive Mapping algorithm. PAM DGP was also shown to select just as beneficial, if not more efficient, function set choices than the Adaptive Mapping algorithm. Moreover, this is the first time that regression problems as difficult as the Two Boxes problem have been considered using an adaptive DGP paradigm. Future work will examine alternative mapping structures in the PAM DGP framework and performance on other benchmark and real world problems.

Acknowledgements. The authors gratefully acknowledge the support of a NSERC PGS-B and Honorary Izaak Walton Killam scholarship (Garnett Wilson), and the CFI New Opportunities and NSERC research grants (Dr. M. Heywood).

References

1. Banzhaf, W.: Genotype-Phenotype Mapping and Neutral Variation. In Davidor, Y., Schwefel, H.-P., Manner, R., eds.: Proceedings of Parallel Problem Solving from Nature III. Springer-Verlag (1994) 322–332
2. Keller, R., Banzhaf, W.: Genetic Programming using Genotype-Phenotype Mapping from Linear Genomes in Linear Phenotypes. In Koza, J., *et al.*, eds.: Genetic Programming 1996: Proceedings of the First Annual Conference. MIT Press (1996) 116-122
3. Keller, R., Banzhaf, W.: The Evolution of Genetic Code in Genetic Programming. In Banzhaf, W., *et al.*, eds.: Proceedings of the Genetic and Evolutionary Computation Conference—GECCO 1999. Morgan Kaufman (1999) 1077-1082
4. Keller, R., Banzhaf, W.: Evolution of Genetic Code on a Hard Problem. In Spector, L., *et al.*, eds: Proceedings of the Genetic and Evolutionary Computation Conference—GECCO 2001. Morgan Kaufman (2001) 50-56.
5. Margetts, S.: Adaptive Genotype to Phenotype Mappings for Evolutionary Algorithms. Ph. D. thesis, Cardiff University, Wales, Great Britain, 2001
6. Margetts, S., Jones, A.: Phlegmatic Mappings for Functional Optimisation with Genetic Programming. In Whitley, L., *et al.*, eds.: Proceedings of the Genetic and Evolutionary Computation Conference—GECCO 2000. Morgan Kaufman (2000) 82-89
7. Margetts, S., Jones, A.: An Adaptive Mapping for Developmental Genetic Programming. In Miller, J., *et al.*, eds.: Proceedings of the Fourth European Conference on Genetic Programming—EuroGP 2001. Springer-Verlag (2001) 97-107
8. Wilson, G., Heywood, M.: Probabilistic (Genotype) Adaptive Mapping Combinations for Developmental Genetic Programming. In Proceedings of the IEEE Congress on Evolutionary Computation—CEC 2006. IEEE Press (2006) (upcoming)
9. Koza, J.: Genetic Programming II: Automatic Discovery of Reusable Programs. MIT Press, Cambridge (1994)

A Distance-Based Information Preservation Tree Crossover for the Maximum Parsimony Problem

Adrien Goëffon, Jean-Michel Richer, and Jin-Kao Hao

LERIA - University of Angers, 2 bd Lavoisier, 49 045 Angers Cedex 01, France
{goeffon, richer, hao}@info.univ-angers.fr

Abstract. The Maximum Parsimony problem aims at reconstructing a phylogenetic tree from DNA sequences while minimizing the number of evolutionary changes. Known to be NP-complete, the MP problem has many applications. This paper introduces a Distance-based Information Preservation (DiBIP) Tree Crossover. Contrary to previous crossover operators, DiBIP uses a distance measure to characterize the semantic information of a phylogenetic tree and ensures the preservation of distance related properties between parents and offspring. The performance of DiBIP is assessed with a mimetic algorithm on a set of 28 benchmark instances from the literature. Comparisons with 3 state-of-the-art algorithms show very competitive results of the proposed approach with improvement of some previously best results found.

1 Introduction

Phylogeny can be defined as the reconstruction of the evolutionary history of a set of species identified by sequences of molecular or morphological characters [5]. The evolutionary relationships between species are represented by a tree whose leaves are labeled by the given species. Hillis *et al.* in [11] identify many applications of phylogeny like genetic evolution, taxonomy and classification, or virus detection. The general problem of inferring the most probable phylogenetic tree according to a given criterion is computationally hard.

In the past much work has been devoted to the problem of phylogeny reconstruction following 3 main approaches. *Distance methods* rely on a matrix of distances observed between species and have polynomial-time algorithms. But they are known to lack sometimes robustness.

Probabilistic methods are based on an evolution model of characters. The Maximum Likelihood (ML) provides a general framework that consists in inferring the most probable phylogeny that maximizes the likelihood of observed species. Although ML is popular for phylogenetic inference because it is considered as a robust method, it is more computationally expensive than other methods.

Cladistic methods are based on a matrix of given characters. The most well-known method of this class relies on the Maximum Parsimony (MP) criterion. Such a method aims at building a binary tree that minimizes a cost function which corresponds to the number of evolutionary changes. The cost of a tree can be computed in polynomial time. However the problem of searching for an optimal tree is NP-complete [7]. Given

T.P. Runarsson et al. (Eds.): PPSN IX, LNCS 4193, pp. 761–770, 2006.

this fact, various heuristic algorithms have been proposed, including local search [10,8], evolutionary algorithms [14,3,15], GRASP [16] and supertrees [1].

In this paper, we are interested in solving effectively the MP problem. For this purpose, we propose a new crossover scheme, called Distance-Based Information Preservation (DiBIP) Tree Crossover. DiBIP is fundamentally different from existing crossover operators. It ensures the transmission of useful information from parents to offspring. Benchmarking results are reported and compared with some best known and performing algorithms for the MP problem.

2 The Maximum Parsimony Problem

Given a multiple alignment of a set S of n sequences of length k characters, the aim of the Maximum Parsimony problem is to find a phylogenetic tree that minimizes the number of changes (mutations) between sequences. Each leaf of the tree is associated to one of the n species and the cost (number of mutations) of the overall tree can be estimated by building sequences of parsimony from the leaves to the root of the tree. More precisely we have the following definitions:

Definition 1 (Sequence of parsimony). *Given 2 sequences S_1 and S_2 of length k such that $S_1 =< x_1, \cdots, x_k >$, $S_2 =< y_1, \cdots, y_k >$ with $\forall i \in \{1..k\}, x_i, y_i$ belong to the power set $\mathcal{P}(\Sigma)$, where Σ is the set of possible characters, the sequence of parsimony of S_1 and S_2, noted $F(S_1, S_2) =< z_1, \cdots, z_k >$ is obtained by (see Fitch [6]):*

$$\forall i, 1 \leq i \leq k, z_i = \begin{cases} x_i \cup y_i, \text{if } x_i \cap y_i = \emptyset \\ x_i \cap y_i, \text{otherwise} \end{cases}$$

The cost of the sequence of parsimony is defined by:

$$\phi(F(S_1, S_2)) = \sum_{i=1}^{k} c_i \quad \text{where} \quad c_i = \begin{cases} 1, \text{if } x_i \cap y_i = \emptyset \\ 0, \text{otherwise} \end{cases}$$

Definition 2 (Binary Tree of Parsimony). *Let S be a set of n aligned sequences of length k where each character of the sequence is expressed over a given alphabet Σ. Let $T = (V, E)$ be a binary tree, where $V = \{v_1, \ldots, v_r\}$ is the set of nodes and $E \subseteq \{(u, v)/u, v \in V\}$ is the set of edges. T is called a binary tree of parsimony of S if there exist $r = 2 \times n - 1$ nodes partitioned in 2 subsets:*

- *a set of internal nodes I composed of $n - 1$ nodes each having 2 descendants and being labeled by a (hypothetical) sequence of parsimony of the 2 descendants,*
- *a set of leaves L composed of n nodes with no descendant, bijectively labeled by the sequences of S.*

Definition 3 (Cost of a Tree of Parsimony). *Let T be a binary tree of parsimony of a set of sequences S. The cost (or score) of T, $\phi(T)$ is equal to $\sum \phi(S_w), \forall w \in I$.*

Definition 4 (Maximum Parsimony Problem). *Given a set S of n sequences of length k, expressed over an alphabet Σ, find the most parsimonious tree T of S such that the score of parsimony of T is minimum.*

For a set of sequences S, there are $\prod_{i=3}^{|S|}(2i - 3)$ possible parsimony trees. The MP problem is thus a highly combinatorial search problem.

3 Crossover Operators for MP and Trees

The literature describes several evolutionary algorithms for phylogenetic reconstruction: for instance [13,12] for the ML problem, [14,2,3,15] for the MP problem and [4] for distance-based phylogenetic approaches. Notice that conventional subtree crossover operators used in tree-based genetic programming are not directly applicable here.

Tree crossover operators designed for inferring phylogenetic trees often follow the subtree cutting-and-regrafting strategy. Generally, given 2 parents trees, a subtree is first selected from one parent (donor parent). Then the leaves of this subtree are deleted from the other parent (receiver parent), leading to an intermediate tree. The final child tree is obtained by reconnecting the subtree from the donor parent to a merge point of the intermediate tree. Obviously, exchanging the donor and receiver parents can lead to a second child. Fig. 1 shows an example with fourteen species, where the subtree $(B, (L, N))$ is taken from parent 1 and reinserted in parent 2 between the root and the subtree $((F, J), M)$ after deleting the 3 leaves (B, L and N) from parent 2.

With such a crossover strategy, only partial information is transmitted from parents to offspring. For instance, in the above example, a subtree with 3 leaves (out of fourteen) of the donor tree is passed on to the child. In one sense, only a small portion of information of the donor is transmitted while a large portion of information related to the eleven other species of the donor tree is lost during the crossover operation. In

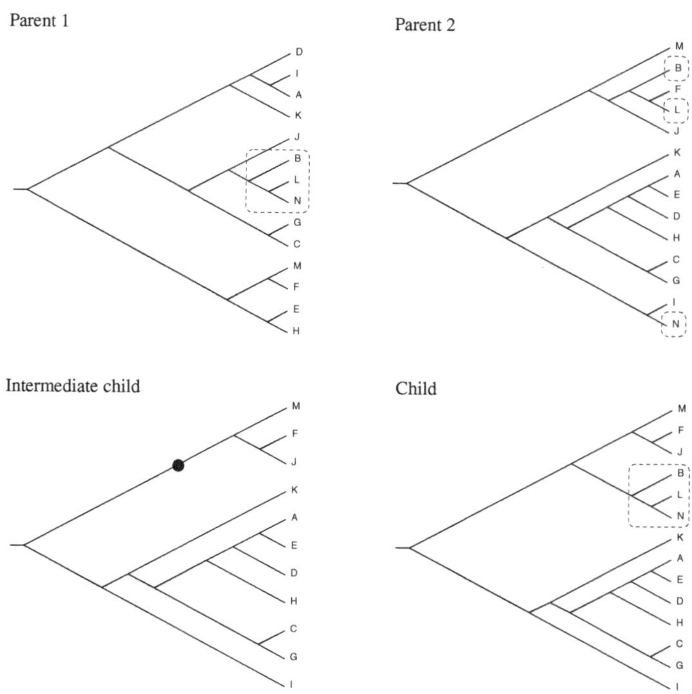

Fig. 1. Example of commonly used crossover

the next section, we introduce a Distance-Based Information Preservation crossover scheme, which ensures a global combination and transmission of information during crossover operations.

4 Distance-Based Information Preservation (DiBIP) Crossover

4.1 General Scheme

Our Distance-Based Information Preservation (DiBIP) crossover scheme aims to preserve representative properties of parents in terms of *distance* between species. The general approach can be summarized as a three-steps procedure: 1) calculate a distance matrix for each parent tree, 2) combine the matrices of the 2 parents to get a third matrix, 3) create a child tree from the previous third matrix.

In order to give a formal description of the DiBIP crossover scheme, we first introduce some notations.

- T_1 and T_2 represent 2 trees used for the crossover operation;
- δ_T is a distance metric to measure the distance of each pair of species of a tree T;
- $\Delta : \mathcal{T} \rightarrow \mathcal{D}$ is a tree-to-distance operator to obtain a distance matrix from a tree;
- $\oplus : \mathcal{D} \times \mathcal{D} \rightarrow \mathcal{D}$ is a matrix operator to combine 2 distance matrices to produce a new distance matrix;
- $\Lambda : \mathcal{D} \rightarrow \mathcal{T}$ is a distance-to-tree operator to construct a tree from a given distance matrix.

Given these notations, the general DiBIP crossover scheme can be described with the procedure shown in Algorithm 1.

Algorithm 1 The general DiBIP crossover scheme

Input: $T_1, T_2, \delta_T, \Delta, \oplus, \Lambda$
Output: A child tree T^*

1. Apply the tree-to-distance operator Δ to each parent tree T_i (i=1,2) to obtain the corresponding distance matrix $D_i = \Delta(T_i)$ (i=1,2);
2. Apply the matrix operator $\oplus$ to D_1 and D_2 to obtain D^*: $D^* = D_1 \oplus D_2$;
3. Apply the distance-to-tree operator Λ to D^* to obtain a child tree: $T^* = \Lambda(D^*)$.

This general scheme gives rise to several comments. First, the distance measure should be ideally correlated to the evolutionary changes between species. For instance, 2 species separated in the tree by a small number of evolutionary changes should have a smaller distance than 2 species separated by a large number of changes. A minimal requirement for the distance measure would make the measure topology dependent. In this sense, the length of the elementary path between 2 species is such a possible example. On the other hand, the conventional Hamming distance is not applicable here because this metric is totally independent of tree topologies.

Second, since we want to preserve representative properties of the parents during the crossover operation, a valid matrix operator $\oplus$ should meet some specific requirements meaningful to the MP problem and help to transmit good properties shared by both parents to the child. For instance, if a pair of species (a,b) is closer than another pair (c,d) in both parents, then this distance property should be conserved by the crossover process and transmitted to the resulting child. More generally, let (a,b) and (c,d) be 2 pairs of species, D_1 and D_2 the distance matrix of 2 trees T_1 and T_2, and $\lhd \in \{<, =, >\}$ a relation, then the following condition, called relation preservation property, should be verified:

$$(D_1(a,b) \lhd D_1(c,d)) \wedge (D_2(a,b) \lhd D_2(c,d)) \Rightarrow (D^*(a,b) \lhd D^*(c,d))$$

For example, let us consider the operation $\oplus$ such that for a pair of species (i,j), $(D_1 \oplus D_2)(i,j) = \alpha . \min\{D_1(i,j), D_2(i,j)\} + (1-\alpha) . \max\{D_1(i,j), D_2(i,j)\}$ with $\alpha \in [0,1]$. It is easy to verify that this defines indeed a valid $\oplus$ operator. Moreover, this definition offers in fact many possibilities and seems particularly relevant to the MP problem. For instance, the arithmetic average ($\alpha = 0.5$) and the max operator max ($\alpha = 0$) are 2 special cases. At last, let us mention that the arithmetic addition $+$ is another simple valid $\oplus$ operator.

Finally, one may notice that Λ is not Δ^{-1} and the distance matrix $\Delta(T^*)$ is in general different from D^*.

To summarize, the proposed DiBIP crossover scheme is fundamentally different from conventional tree crossover operators. From this scheme, one can derive a concrete DiBIP crossover operator by defining a distance metric δ_T and instantiating the following 3 operators: Δ, $\oplus$ and Λ.

4.2 Application of the DiBIP Crossover to the MP Problem

In order to show how the above DiBIP crossover scheme is applied to the MP problem, we devise a concrete DiBIP operator by making the following choices. The distance measure δ_T between 2 species i and j is defined by the length of the elementary path between the respective ascendants of i and j, minus 1 if the path contains the root of the tree T. Since the position of the root has no effect on the parsimony score, this element must not affect the distance matrix. Fig. 2 shows a tree and the resulting distance matrix according to δ_T.

As to the matrix operator $\oplus$, we simply used the addition $+$ such that $D(i,j) = D_1(i,j) + D_2(i,j)$. Notice that this operator satisfies the relation preservation property mentioned in the previous section. Finally, the distance-to-tree operator Λ is a

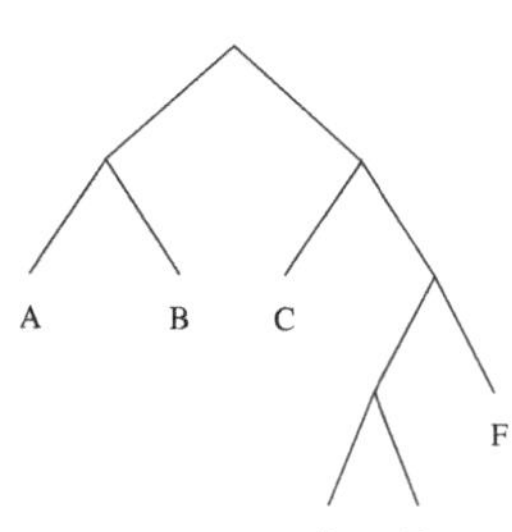

	A	B	C	D	E
B	0				
C	1	1			
D	3	3	2		
E	3	3	2	0	
F	2	2	1	1	1

Fig. 2. Distances measured using the length of elementary path between 2 species

non-deterministic variant of the well-known UPGMA method [17]. Fig. 3 shows an application of this crossover operator. One notices that the closeness of species in both parents is conserved in the child. This observation applies equally to distant species.

4.3 Complexity of the DiBIP Crossover Operator

For a given tree T, $\Delta(T)$ can be done in $\Theta(n^2 \log_2(n))$ time with n being the number of the leaves (species). This calculation is performed only once for each inferred tree even if the same tree can be used several times by the crossover operation. This is simply done by recording the corresponding distance matrix. The matrix addition using $+$ as well as the distance-to-tree operation with UPGMA have time complexity of $\Theta(n^2)$. Consequently, the crossover operator has a total time complexity of $\Theta(n^2 \log_2(n))$.

Parent 1 : T_1

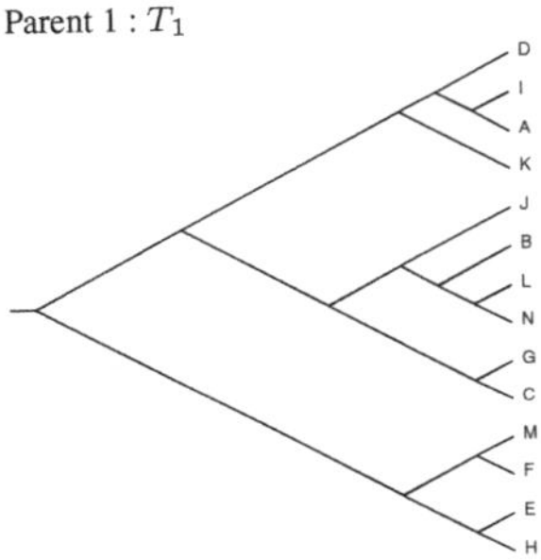

Parent 2 : T_2

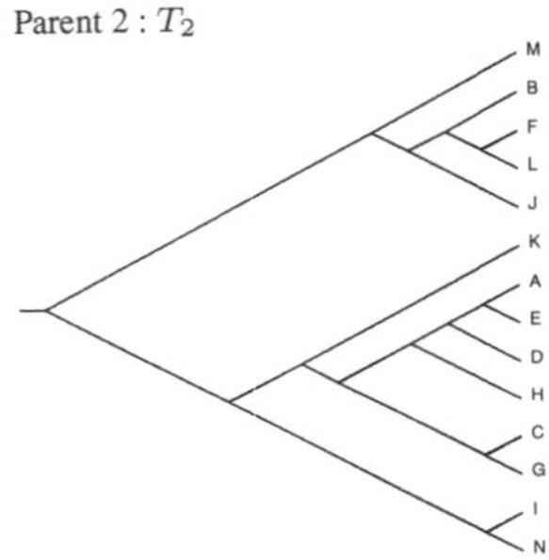

$D_1 = \Delta(T_1)$

	A	B	C	D	E	F	G	H	I	J	K	L	M	N
A	-	**B**												
B	6	-	**C**											
C	5	3	-	**D**										
D	1	5	4	-	**E**									
E	5	5	4	4	-	**F**								
F	5	5	4	4	2	-	**G**							
G	5	3	0	4	4	4	-	**H**						
H	5	5	4	4	0	2	4	-	**I**					
I	0	6	5	1	5	5	5	5	-	**J**				
J	5	1	2	4	4	4	2	4	5	-	**K**			
K	2	4	3	1	3	3	3	3	2	3	-	**L**		
L	7	1	4	6	6	6	4	6	7	2	5	-	**M**	
M	5	5	4	4	2	0	4	2	5	4	3	6	-	**N**
N	7	1	4	6	6	6	4	6	7	2	5	0	6	-

$D_2 = \Delta(T_2)$

	A	B	C	D	E	F	G	H	I	J	K	L	M	N
A	-	**B**												
B	8	-	**C**											
C	4	6	-	**D**										
D	1	7	3	-	**E**									
E	0	8	4	1	-	**F**								
F	9	1	7	8	9	-	G							
G	4	6	0	3	4	7	-	**H**						
H	2	6	2	1	2	7	2	-	**I**					
I	6	4	4	5	6	5	4	4	-	**J**				
J	7	1	5	6	7	2	5	5	3	-	**K**			
K	4	4	2	3	4	5	2	2	2	3	-	**L**		
L	9	1	7	8	9	0	7	7	5	2	5	-	**M**	
M	6	2	4	5	6	3	4	4	2	1	2	3	-	**N**
N	6	4	4	5	6	5	4	4	0	3	2	5	2	-

$D^* = D_1 \oplus D_2$

	A	B	C	D	E	F	G	H	I	J	K	L	M	N
A	-	**B**												
B	14	-	**C**											
C	9	9	-	**D**										
D	2	12	7	-	**E**									
E	5	13	8	5	-	**F**								
F	14	6	11	12	11	-	**G**							
G	9	9	0	7	8	11	-	**H**						
H	7	11	6	5	2	9	6	-	**I**					
I	6	10	9	6	11	10	9	9	-	**J**				
J	12	2	7	10	11	6	7	9	8	-	**K**			
K	6	8	5	4	7	8	5	5	4	6	-	**L**		
L	16	2	11	14	15	6	11	13	12	4	10	-	**M**	
M	11	7	8	9	8	3	8	6	7	5	5	9	-	**N**
N	13	5	8	11	12	11	8	10	7	5	7	5	8	-

Child : $T^* = \Lambda(D^*)$

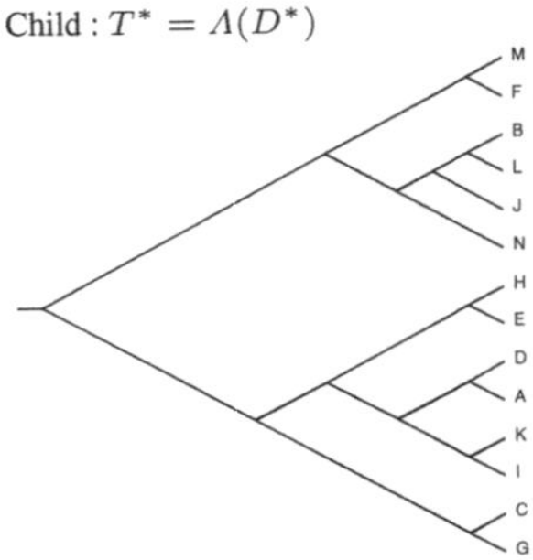

Fig. 3. Application of the DiBIP Tree Crossover

5 A Hybrid Genetic Local Search Algorithm for the MP Problem

5.1 General Procedure

HYDRA (for HYbrid Distance Recombination Algorithm) is a mimetic algorithm that combines a genetic algorithm using the DiBIP crossover operator and a local search algorithm called DPN (*Descent with Progressive Neighborhood*) [9]. The HYDRA algorithm (see Algorithm 2) starts by randomly generating an initial population where each individual is an inferred phylogenetic tree (*GeneratePopulation*). Then, the algorithm enters an iterative process. At each step 2 individuals (parents) are chosen in the population (*ChooseParents*) and recombined (*DiBIP* crossover) to obtain a new individual (child). The DPN local search algorithm is applied to improve the child during l iterations. The improved child is finally added to the population under insertion conditions. This process is repeated until the stop condition is met, usually when a maximum number of iterations Max_{iter} has been reached or when the computation time exceeds a maximum duration Max_{time}.

Algorithm 2 Hybrid genetic local search algorithm (HYDRA) for the MP problem

Input: A : an alignment of sequences, N : the size of the GA population, l : the number of local search iterations
Output: The most parsimonious tree found

P = *GeneratePopulation*(A,N)
While *not StopCondition()* **do**
  (T_1, T_2) = *ChooseParents*(P)
  T = *DiBIP*(T_1, T_2)
  T = *DPN*(T,l)
  P = *Replace*(P,T)
return the best tree found

The function *ChooseParents* operates with a tournament selection strategy. Two groups of 20% of the individuals are constituted. Two individuals that represent the best individuals of each group are selected for the crossover operation. The *Replace* function inserts the child tree T into the population P and removes from P the older individual (insertion condition). Notice that other selection strategies and insertion conditions may be defined.

5.2 Local Search: Descent with Progressive Neighborhood

The DPN procedure used in HYDRA for local improvement is a basic descent algorithm using a Progressive Neighborhood [9]. DPN considers a large size neighborhood at the beginning of the search which progressively shrinks when the search goes on. The basic neighborhood used in DPN is the well-known SPR (*Subtree Pruning and Regrafting*) neighborhood which cuts a subtree and reinserts it elsewhere. To control gradually the size of the neighborhood, DPN introduces a parameter $d_{\max}$ which fixes the maximum allowed distance between the root of the detached subtree and the position where it is reconnected. In practice, $d_{\max}$ is set to a maximum value at the beginning of the search in order to allow any SPR move. Then this value is progressively reduced until it becomes equal to 1 which corresponds to the much smaller neighborhood NNI (*Nearest Neighbor Interchange*).

6 Experimentations

6.1 Competing Algorithms and Benchmarks

In this section, we compare the mimetic HYDRA algorithm based on the DiBIP crossover operator with 3 highly effective MP algorithms: an evolutionary algorithm [15], the GRASP+VND [16] method and the software TNT [10]. GRASP+VND is a combined application of 2 well-known metaheuristics GRASP and VND to the MP problem. TNT (Tree analysis using New Technology) is probably the fastest and one of the most effective parsimony analysis program. TNT uses many search strategies such as tree recombinations, local search and supertrees.

The benchmark instances used here come from [15] and [16] and represent 28 instances: 8 obtained from real data and 20 randomly generated instances (TST 01 to 20). For these instances, the best results found in the literature are reported in [15,16].

6.2 Computational Results

HYDRA uses a population of size $N = 30$, a maximum of 50,000 iterations for each DPN run and ends after 300 seconds. The algorithm is coded in C++ and compiled with *gcc* using the optimization flag `-O3`. It is run sequentially onto a cluster of 10 nodes, each having a Xeon 2 GHz BiProcessor with 1 Gb of RAM. Like in [15], the HYDRA algorithm is run 10 times for each instance.

Results are printed on Tables 1 and 2, where ϕ_b, ϕ_m and *CO* respectively represent the best score obtained, the average score and the average number of crossover operations over 10 runs. For random instances, *diff* is the improvement of the score obtained in comparison to the best known scores. The reported results of [15,16] are taken from these 2 papers while the results of TNT are obtained by us using the default parameters.

Table 1. Results on real instances

Instance			Hydra			[15]		[16]	TNT
Name	n	k	ϕ_b	ϕ_m	*CO*	ϕ_b	ϕ_m	ϕ_b	ϕ_b
GRIS	47	93	**172**	172.0	*4012*	**172**	172.0	**172**	**172**
ANGI	49	59	**216**	216.0	*1658*	**216**	216.0	**216**	217
TENU	56	179	**682**	682.0	*812*	**682**	682.0	**682**	**682**
ETHE	58	86	**372**	372.0	*2392*	**372**	372.4	**372**	373
ROPA	75	82	**325**	326.2	*1519*	**325**	325.8	**325**	327
GOLO	77	97	**496**	496.0	*2068*	**496**	496.2	**496**	501
SCHU	113	146	**759**	759.0	*669*	**759**	759.2	**759**	761
CARP	117	110	**548**	548.9	*815*	**548**	548.6	**548**	550
Average computation time (s)			300			1000		33789	< 1

Table 2. Results on random instances

Instance			Hydra			[15]		[16]	TNT	
Name	n	k	ϕ_b	ϕ_m	*CO*	ϕ_b	ϕ_m	ϕ_b	ϕ_b	*diff*
TST01	45	61	**545**	547.1	*2548*	549	549.6	551	554	-4
TST02	47	151	**1354**	1358.7	*775*	1358	1363.6	1364	1380	-4
TST03	49	111	**834**	837.3	*1012*	838	840.6	845	849	-4
TST04	50	97	**590**	591.2	*1064*	592	595.0	598	603	-2
TST05	52	75	**789**	792.6	*1458*	790	794.0	797	805	-1
TST06	54	65	**597**	599.3	*1491*	603	605.4	609	612	-6
TST07	56	143	**1271**	1275.5	*548*	1276	1280,6	1291	1300	-5
TST08	57	119	**853**	857.2	*666*	863	867.4	870	889	-11
TST09	59	93	**1146**	1149.5	*906*	1150	1154.2	1152	1167	-4
TST10	60	71	**721**	723.7	*1168*	725	728.6	733.0	740	-4
TST11	62	63	**544**	546.2	*1237*	**544**	546,8	553	564	0
TST12	64	147	**1218**	1224.1	*408*	1229	1233.0	1243	1250	-11
TST13	65	113	**1523**	1526.4	*660*	1526	1530.6	1532	1538	-3
TST14	67	99	**1167**	1171.7	*683*	1174	1177,4	1177	1194	-7
TST15	69	77	**757**	760.1	*792*	765	766.4	774	783	-8
TST16	70	69	**532**	535.5	*865*	545	547.6	551	552	-13
TST17	71	159	**2460**	2467.1	*360*	2468	2470.8	2468	2485	-8
TST18	73	117	**1529**	1533.8	*473*	1542	1548.2	1554	1571	-13
TST19	74	95	**1019**	1021.6	*601*	1028	1033.0	1036	1037	-9
TST20	75	79	**665**	668.5	*720*	676	678.8	682	693	-11
Average computation time (s)			300			1000		1982	< 1	

From Tables 1 and 2, one observes that for the 8 real instances HYDRA consistently obtains the previously best results reported in [15,16] but with much shorter computation time. Also observe the robustness of HYDRA which, for 6 of 8 instances, has found the best score for each run. The effectiveness of HYDRA is better observed on the set of random instances. Indeed, for 19 instances out of 20, the previously published best scores are improved.

Let us mention that when the number of runs is increased to 100, HYDRA obtains still better results for 11 of the 20 random instances (up to 5 units). HYDRA is also compared with its local search component DPN alone, showing clearly better results on the tested instances (not shown here).

7 Conclusion

In this paper, we have introduced the Distance-Based Information Preservation (DiBIP) crossover, a new crossover scheme for inferring phylogenetic trees. The key idea is to use a distance matrix to characterize each inferred tree. Consequently, 2 trees can be easily combined by an operation on 2 distance matrices. Contrary to existing crossover mechanisms, the DiBIP crossover scheme offers a simple and natural way to ensure a global information combination and transmission during the cross-overing operation.

The practical usefulness of the DiBIP crossover scheme for the Maximum Parsimony problem is assessed within a mimetic algorithm. Comparisons with 3 state-of-the-art algorithms on a set of 28 (real and randomly generated) benchmark instances show very competitive results of our approach. Indeed, for the real instances, the best known score are systematically found rapidly and consistently. The most remarkable results concern the random instances for which we can improve 19 (out of 20) best scores known today within 5 minutes of CPU time.

Acknowledgments. This work is partially supported by the French Ouest Genopole®. We thank the reviewers of the paper for their careful reading and useful comments and Dr. Celso C. Ribeiro for providing us with the dataset used in the paper.

References

1. O. R. P. Bininda-Emonds (Ed.). Phylogenetic Supertrees: Combining Information to Reveal the Tree of Life. Springer, 2004.
2. C. B. Congdon. Gaphyl: An Evolutionary Algorithms Approach For The Study Of Natural Evolution. *Proceedings of the 6th Joint Conference on Information Science*, 2002.
3. C. B. Congdon and K. J. Septor. Phylogenetic trees using evolutionary search: Initial progress in extending gaphyl to work with genetic data. *Proc. of the 2003 Congress on Evolutionary Computation*, pp.320-326, IEEE press, 2003.
4. C. Cotta and P. Moscato. Inferring Phylogenetic Trees Using Evolutionary Algorithms. *Lecture Notes in Computer Science*, 2439:720-729, Springer, 2002.
5. J. Felsenstein. Inferring phylogenies. *Sinauer Associates*, 2003.
6. W. Fitch. Towards defining course of evolution: minimum change for a specified tree topology. *Systematic Zoology* 20:406-416, 1971.
7. L. R. Foulds and R. L. Graham. The Steiner problem in phylogeny is NP-complete. *Advances in Applied Mathematics* 3:43-49, 1982.
8. A. Goëffon, J.-M. Richer and J.-K. Hao. Local search for the maximum parsimony problem. *Lecture Notes in Computer Science* 3612:678-683, Springer, 2005.
9. A. Goëffon, J.-M. Richer and J.-K. Hao. Progressive Tree Neighborhood applied to the Maximum Parsimony Problem. Submitted to *IEEE Transactions on Computational Biology and Bioinformatics*, 2006.
10. P. A. Goloboff, J. S. Farris and K. Nixon. TNT: Tree Analysis Using New Technology, 2003.
11. D. Hillis, C. Moritz and B. Mable. Molecular Systematics, Sinauer, Boston, 1996.
12. P. O. Lewis. A genetic algorithm for maximum-likelihood phylogeny inference using nucleotide sequence data. *Molecular Biolology and Evolution*, 15(3):277-283, 1998.
13. H. Matsuda. Protein Phylogenetic Inference Using Maximum Likelihood With A Genetic Algorithm *Prof. of Pacific Symposium on Biocomputing*, pp.512-536, 1996.
14. A. Moilanen. Searching for Most Parsimonious Trees with Simulated Evolutionary Optimization. *Cladistics* 15(1):39-50, 1998.
15. C. C. Ribeiro and D. S. Vianna. A genetic algorithm for the phylogeny problem using an optimized crossover strategy based on path-relinking. *Proc. of 2nd Bresil Workshop on Bioinformatics*, pp.97-102, 2003.
16. C. C. Ribeiro and D. S. Vianna. A GRASP/VND heuristic for the phylogeny problem using a new neighborhood structure. *International Transactions in Operational Research* 12:1-14, 2005.
17. Sneath, P. H. A., and R. R. Sokal. 1973. Numerical taxonomy. W. H. Freeman and Co., San Francisco, California

Solving SAT and HPP with Accepting Splicing Systems

Remco Loos[1], Carlos Martín-Vide[1], and Victor Mitrana[1,2]

[1] Research Group in Mathematical Linguistics, Rovira i Virgili University
Pça. Imperial Tarraco 1, 43005, Tarragona, Spain
[2] Faculty of Mathematics and Computer Science, University of Bucharest
Str. Academiei 14, 70109, Bucharest, Romania
{remcogerard.loos, carlos.martin, vmi}@urv.net

Abstract. In this paper, we present a different look on splicing systems, namely as problem solvers. After defining the concept of accepting splicing system we discuss how these systems can be used as problem solvers. Then we construct an accepting splicing system able to uniformly solve SAT in time $O(m+n)$ for a formula of length m over n variables. We also propose a uniform solution based on accepting splicing systems to HPP that runs in time $O(n)$, where n is the number of vertices of the instance of HPP.

1 Introduction

A rather vividly investigated model of molecular computation based on the cutting and recombination of DNA strands induced by restriction enzymes is the *splicing system*. One of the basic mechanism by which genetic material is merged is recombination. DNA sequences are recombined under the effect of enzymatic activities. Formalizing this process as a string rewriting operation, it can be used to define computing systems. In 1987, T. Head introduced the *splicing* operation as a language theoretical approach of the recombinant behavior of DNA under the influence of restriction enzymes and ligases [5]. Roughly speaking, the main idea of the splicing operation is that two sequences are cut at specific sites, and the first substring of one sequence is pasted to the second segment of the other and vice versa. A new model of computation - called splicing system or H system - based on the splicing operation has been considered. Most research in this area has been focused on defining different types of splicing systems and investigating their computational power from a language generating point of view. Many variants of H systems have been invented and investigated (regulated H systems, distributed H systems, H systems with multisets, etc.) Under certain circumstances, H systems are computationally complete and universal (see [10] for an overview). This result suggests the possibility to consider H systems as theoretical models of programmable universal DNA computers based on the splicing operation.

Recently, a few new approaches to splicing have emerged. We briefly discuss two of them. First, two slightly different types of splicing systems have been introduced in [4] and [7]. Their common feature is that they do not differ from

T.P. Runarsson et al. (Eds.): PPSN IX, LNCS 4193, pp. 771–777, 2006.

basic splicing systems in terms of elements. Rather, the difference lies in the definition of the way the splicing rules are applied and the way the generated language is defined. Both new definitions are in fact generalizations of the usual definition, in the sense that we obtain a definition equivalent to the usual one by imposing certain restrictions on the splicing system. Both types of systems have been shown to be computationally complete. Second, several works like [1], and the references therein, address two fundamental questions concerning splicing systems: *recognition*, which asks for an algorithm able to decide whether or not a given regular language is a splicing language, and *synthesis*, which asks for an effective procedure to construct a splicing system able to generate a given splicing language.

An important result in splicing theory is the so-called *Regularity Preserving Lemma* proved first in [2], as a consequence of a more general result, and then in [11] by a direct argument. It states that H systems with a regular initial language and a finite set of rules generate only regular languages. To obtain computational completeness, a regular (thus infinite) set of rules is needed, as shown in [9]. In this paper, we present a different look on splicing systems, namely as problem solvers. We define the concept of problem solving H system starting from the another concept introduced here, namely accepting splicing system. It is rather strange that though the theory of splicing systems is mature and well developed, an accepting model based on the splicing operation has not considered so far, in spite of the fact that in practice we deal more with accepting processes than with generating ones. We are not interested here by the computational power and complexity of these accepting devices, but we propose efficient solutions - working in linear time - to two well-known NP-complete problems. Both solutions are based on accepting splicing systems with a finite initial language and a regular set of rules.

2 Basic Definitions and Notation

We start by summarizing the notions used throughout the paper. An *alphabet* is a finite and nonempty set of symbols. The cardinality of a finite set A is written $card(A)$. Any finite sequence of symbols from an alphabet V is called a *word* over V. The set of all words over V is denoted by V^* and the empty word is denoted by ε. The length of a word x is denoted by $|x|$ while $alph(x)$ denotes the minimal alphabet W such that $x \in W^*$.

A splicing rule over V is a string $u_1\#u_2\$u_3\#u_4$, with $u_1, u_2, u_3, u_4 \in V^*$, and $\$, \#$ special symbols not in V.

For a splicing rule $r = u_1\#u_2\$u_3\#u_4$ and a pair of words $x, y \in V^*$, we write

$$\sigma_r(x, y) = \{w \in V^*\} \cup \{z \in V^*\} \text{ if } x = x_1u_1u_2x_2,\ y = y_1u_3u_4y_2, \\ z = x_1u_1u_4y_2,\ w = y_1u_3u_2x_2,$$

for some $x_1, x_2, y_1, y_2 \in V^*$. This definition is extended to a set of splicing rules R and a language L by

$$\sigma_R(L) = \bigcup_{r\in R} \bigcup_{w_1,w_2\in L} \sigma_r(w_1, w_2).$$

A *splicing system* or *H system* is a construct

$$H = (V, A, R),$$

where V is an alphabet, $A \subseteq V^*$ is the initial language, and R is a set of splicing rules over V. For a splicing language $H = (V, A, R)$ we set

$$\begin{aligned}
&\sigma_R^0(A) = A,\\
&\sigma_R^{i+1}(A) = \sigma_R^i(A) \cup \sigma_R(\sigma_R^i(A)), i \geq 0,\\
&\sigma_R^*(A) = \bigcup_{i\geq 0} \sigma_R^i(A).
\end{aligned}$$

When the set of splicing rules is clear, we omit the subscript. Then, the language generated by H is defined as $L(H) = \sigma_R^*(A)$. Adding a terminal alphabet T we get an *extended splicing system* $H = (V, T, A, R)$, which generates the language $T^* \cap \sigma_R^*(A)$.

For H systems with a finite set of rules and a finite initial language, i.e. A and R are both finite sets, it is shown in [11] that they generate only regular languages. When one allows the set of splicing rules to be described by regular expressions, we obtain computationally complete systems [9].

The framework for studying time complexity for (generating) splicing systems has been introduced in [8]. The time complexity $Time(\Gamma, w)$ of a word w with respect to an extended splicing system $\Gamma = (V, T, A, R)$ is the minimal i such that $w \in \sigma_R^i(A)$. Relating the time complexity of a word to its length, we can define complexity classes for H systems. We say that for a function $T(n)$, $H(T(n))$ is the set of all languages L for which there exists an extended splicing system Γ such that for all $w \in L(\Gamma)$ it holds that $Time(\Gamma, w) \leq T(|x|)$.

We now introduce the definitions and terminology for accepting splicing systems. An accepting splicing system is a quadruple

$$\Gamma = (V, A, R, \underline{YES}),$$

where $\underline{YES} \in V$ and $H_\Gamma = (V, A, R)$ is a splicing system. Let $\Gamma = (V, A, R, \underline{YES})$ be an accepting splicing system; we say that Γ halts on a word $w \in V^*$ if one of the following conditions holds:

(*i*) $\underline{YES} \in \sigma_R^k(A \cup \{w\})$ for some integer k,
(*ii*) $\sigma_R^k(A \cup \{w\}) = \sigma_R^{k+1}(A \cup \{w\})$ and $\underline{YES} \notin \sigma_R^k(A \cup \{w\})$ for some integer k.

In both cases we say that Γ halts on w in k steps. We say that Γ decides the language L iff Γ halts on every word $w \in L$ such that condition (i) is satisfied.

Let $\Gamma = (V, A, R, \underline{YES})$ be a splicing system that halts on every word in V^*; for a word $w \in V^*$ we set

$$\begin{aligned}
Time(\Gamma, w) &= \min\{k \mid \Gamma \text{ halts on } w \text{ in } k \text{ steps}\}\\
Time_\Gamma(n) &= \max\{Time(\Gamma, w) \mid |w| = n\}.
\end{aligned}$$

We say that Γ decides L in time $T(n)$ if Γ decides L and $Time_{\Gamma}(n) \leq T(n)$ for all $n \geq 1$.

We now propose a way of using accepting splicing systems as problem solvers. A possible correspondence between decision problems and languages can be done via an encoding function which transforms an instance of a given decision problem into a word, see, e.g., [3]. We say that a decision problem P is solved in time $O(f(n))$ by accepting splicing systems if there exists a family $\mathcal{H}$ of accepting H systems such that the following conditions are satisfied:

1. The encoding function of any instance p of P having size n can be computed by a deterministic Turing machine in time $O(f(n))$.

2. For each instance p of size n of the problem one can effectively construct, in time $O(f(n))$, an accepting splicing system $\Gamma(p) \in \mathcal{H}$ which decides, again in time $O(f(n))$, the word encoding the given instance. This means that the word is decided if and only if the solution to the given instance of the problem is "YES". This effective construction is called an $O(f(n))$ time solution to the considered problem.

If an accepting splicing system $\Gamma(n)$ decides the language of words encoding all instances of the same size n, then the construction of $\mathcal{H}$ is called a uniform solution. Intuitively, a solution is uniform if for problem size n, we can construct a unique H system solving all instances of size n taking the (reasonable) encoding of instance as "input".

3 A Linear Time Uniform Solution to SAT

In this section we illustrate the use of accepting splicing systems as problem solvers by showing that accepting H systems with regular sets of rules and finite initial languages can uniformly solve SAT in linear time.

A *Boolean expression* is an expression composed of variables, parentheses and the operators $\bar{\cdot}$, $\wedge$ and $\vee$. The variables can take values 0 (false) and 1 (true). An expression is satisfiable if there is some assignment of variables such that the expression is true. The *satisfiability problem*, commonly denoted as *SAT*, is to determine, given a Boolean expression, whether it is satisfiable. SAT is a well known NP-complete problem (see e.g. [6] for more details). A Boolean expression is said to be in *conjunctive normal form (CNF)* if it is of the form $E_1 \wedge E_2 \wedge ... E_k$, where each E_i, called a *clause*, is of the form $\alpha_{i1} \vee \alpha_{i2} \vee ... \vee \alpha_{ir_i}$, where each α_{ij} is a literal, that is either x or $\bar{x}$, for some variable x. Here, we assume that all boolean formulas are in CNF.

Theorem 1. *SAT can be uniformly solved in linear time by splicing systems with regular sets of rules.*

Proof. For all formulas over n variables, we construct an accepting splicing system $\Gamma = (V, A, R, \underline{YES})$, where

$$V = \{x_1, x_2, \ldots, x_n\} \cup \{\bar{x}_1, \bar{x}_2, \ldots, \bar{x}_n\} \cup \{\langle\!\langle_0, \langle\!\langle_1, \rangle\!\rangle, X, W, \underline{YES}, \vee, \wedge, \bot, (,), \top\} \cup \{[x_i = b] \mid 1 \leq i \leq n, b \in \{0,1\}\}$$

$$A = \{X\#[x_i = b]\rangle\!\rangle \mid 1 \leq i \leq n, b \in \{0,1\}\} \cup \{\langle\!\langle_0\bot, \langle\!\langle_1\bot, \top\bot, W\underline{YES}\},$$

and the set of splicing rules is defined as follows:

(1) $\{)\#\rangle\rangle\$X\#[x_1 = a]\rangle\rangle \mid a \in \{0,1\}\} \cup$
$\{[x_i = a]\#\rangle\rangle\$X\#[x_{i+1} = b]\rangle\rangle \mid 1 \leq i \leq n-1, a, b \in \{0,1\}\}$,

(2) $\{\langle\langle_0(\#z\$\langle\langle_0\# \perp \mid z \in \{x_1, x_2, \ldots, x_n\} \cup \{\bar{x}_1, \bar{x}_2, \ldots, \bar{x}_n\}\} \cup$
$\{\langle\langle_0 x_i\#\alpha\$\langle\langle_1\# \perp \mid \alpha \in V^*[x_i = 1]V^*, 1 \leq i \leq n\} \cup$
$\{\langle\langle_0 \bar{x}_i\#\alpha\$\langle\langle_1\# \perp \mid \alpha \in V^*[x_i = 0]V^*, 1 \leq i \leq n\} \cup$
$\{\langle\langle_0 x_i\#\alpha\$\langle\langle_0\# \perp \mid \alpha \in V^*[x_i = 0]V^*, 1 \leq i \leq n\} \cup$
$\{\langle\langle_0 \bar{x}_i\#\alpha\$\langle\langle_0\# \perp \mid \alpha \in V^*[x_i = 1]V^*, 1 \leq i \leq n\} \cup$
$\{\langle\langle_1 Y\#Z\$\langle\langle_1\# \perp \mid Y, Z \in \{x_i \mid 1 \leq i \leq n\} \cup \{\bar{x}_i \mid 1 \leq i \leq n\} \cup \{\vee\}\} \cup$
$\{\langle\langle_1 Y\#)\$\langle\langle_0\# \perp \mid Y \in \{x_i \mid 1 \leq i \leq n\} \cup \{\bar{x}_i \mid 1 \leq i \leq n\}\} \cup$
$\{\langle\langle_0 \vee\#(\$\langle\langle_0\# \perp\}$,

(3) $\{\langle\langle_0\#)\$\top\# \perp\}$,

(4) $\{\varepsilon\#\langle\langle_0[x_1 = b]\$W\#\underline{YES} \mid b \in \{0,1\}\}$.

Clearly, given n the splicing system Γ can be constructed in $O(n)$ time. Now, given an instance of SAT over n variables, that is a formula $\phi = C_1 \wedge C_2 \wedge \cdots \wedge C_m$ for some $m \geq 1$, we define the word encoding this instance as $\langle\langle_0\phi\rangle\rangle$.

We discuss how the splicing system Γ works on $w = \langle\langle_0\phi\rangle\rangle$, where ϕ is a word over the alphabet $\{x_1, x_2, \ldots, x_n\} \cup \{\bar{x}_1, \bar{x}_2, \ldots, \bar{x}_n\} \cup \{\vee, \wedge, (,)\}$. First we assume that ϕ is satisfiable, that is there exists an assignment of variable that satisfies each clause. Let $x_i = b_i$, $b_i \in \{0,1\}$, $1 \leq i \leq n$, be such an assignment. By using the splicing rules in the set (1) the word w is transformed into $\langle\langle_0\phi[x_1 = b_1][x_2 = b_2]\ldots[x_n = b_n]\rangle\rangle$. This process takes n splicing steps. Then, the rules of (2) remove the current leftmost symbol of the formula ϕ at every step. Since each clause is a disjunction, for each $1 \leq k \leq m$, there exists $1 \leq i_k \leq n$ such that $x_{i_k} = b_{i_k}$ satisfies the clause C_k. Moreover, we assume that x_{i_k} is the leftmost variable appearing in C_k that satisfies C_k. When x_{i_k} is the current leftmost symbol of the formula, a rule of type $\langle\langle_0 x_i\#\alpha\$\langle\langle_1\# \perp$ applies, removing $\langle\langle_0 x_{i_k}$ and replacing it by $\langle\langle_1$, which we interpret as a marker that the current clause is satisfied. The process resumes with $\langle\langle_0$ for every clause. Therefore, after $|\phi|$ splicing steps, Γ generates the word $\langle\langle_0[x_1 = b_1][x_2 = b_2]\ldots[x_n = b_n]\rangle\rangle$. In the next splicing step, by using the rule $\varepsilon\#\langle\langle_0[x_1 = b_1]\$W\#\underline{YES}$ in the set (4), one gets $\underline{YES}$.

On the other hand, it is easy to note that if Γ decides a word $\langle\langle_0\phi\rangle\rangle$ (if this happens, then it happens in $O(n + |\phi|)$ time), then the rule in the singleton (3) can never be used in the computation of Γ on the word $\langle\langle_0\phi\rangle\rangle$. It follows that every clause is satisfiable, therefore ϕ is satisfiable. From these explanations it follows that Γ decides every word $\langle\langle_0\phi\rangle\rangle$ in linear time if and only if ϕ is satisfiable.

Now, to conclude the proof, let us argue that Γ halts on every word $\langle\langle_0\phi\rangle\rangle$ where ϕ is not satisfiable. Then for every possible assignment, there is a clause that is not satisfied by the assignment. Let C_{s_i} be the first clause of ϕ which is not satisfied by the assignment $1 \leq i \leq 2^n$. When reaching the closing bracket of C_{s_i}, rule (3) applies, introducing the symbol $\top$, after which no rule can be applied. In the worst case, $C_{s_i} = C_m$ so that $\sigma_R^k(A \cup \{\langle\langle_0\phi\rangle\rangle\}) = \sigma_R^{k+1}(A \cup \{\langle\langle_0\phi\rangle\rangle\})$ for $k \leq n + |\phi|$. □

4 A Linear Time Uniform Solution to HPP

The Hamiltonian path problem (HPP) is to decide whether or not a given directed graph has a Hamiltonian path. A Hamiltonian path in a directed graph is a path which contains all vertices exactly once. It is known that HPP is an NP-complete problem.

Theorem 2. *HPP can be uniformly solved in linear time by splicing systems with regular sets of rules.*

Proof. Let us consider a directed graph $G = (X, E)$, with $X = \{x_1, x_2, \ldots, x_n\}$ for which we are looking for a Hamiltonian path starting with x_1. We construct the accepting splicing system $\Gamma = (V, A, R, \underline{YES})$ with

$$V = \{x_1, x_2, \ldots, x_n\} \cup \{[1], [2], \ldots, [n]\} \cup \{(,), Y, <, \underline{YES}, >\},$$
$$A = \{Yx_1[1], \underline{YES} <\} \cup \{Yx_i[j] \mid 2 \leq i, j \leq n\},$$

and the set R defined as follows:

(1) $\{)\# > \$Y\#x_1[1]\} \cup \{\alpha x_t[j]\# > \$Y\#x_k[j+1] \mid 1 \leq t \neq k \leq n,$
$1 \leq j \leq n-1, \alpha \in V^*(x_t, x_k)V^* \setminus V^*x_kV^*\},$

(2) $\{\underline{YES}\# < \$[n] > \#\varepsilon\}$.

The instance $G = (X, E)$ of HPP is encoded into the word

$$w = (x_1, x_{i_1}^{(1)})(x_1, x_{i_2}^{(1)}) \ldots (x_1, x_{i_{k_i}}^{(1)})(x_2, x_{i_1}^{(2)})(x_2, x_{i_2}^{(2)}) \ldots (x_2, x_{i_{k_i}}^{(2)}) \ldots$$
$$(x_n, x_{i_1}^{(n)})(x_n, x_{i_2}^{(n)}) \ldots (x_n, x_{i_{k_i}}^{(n)}) >,$$

over V^*, where $(x_j, x_{i_1}^{(j)}), (x_j, x_{i_2}^{(j)}), \ldots, (x_j, x_{i_{k_i}}^{(j)})$ are all edges going out from the node x_j, for some $1 \leq j \leq n$.

Clearly, given n the splicing system Γ can be constructed in $O(n)$ time. The rules of (1) extend w, constructing a path starting in x_1 and appending an edge at each step, provided w contains an edge from the current node x_i to some node $x_j, j \neq i$. It is easy to note that if there exists a Hamiltonian path in G, say $x_1, x_{s_2}, x_{s_3}, \ldots, x_{s_n}$, then the word

$$wx_1[1]x_{s_2}[2]x_{s_3}[3] \ldots x_{s_n}[n] >$$

is generated by Γ in n splicing steps, hence $\underline{YES}$ is obtained in the next splicing step. On the other hand, the only possibility to get $\underline{YES}$ is to apply the splicing rule (2) to a pair of words formed by the axiom $\underline{YES} <$ and a word of the form $wx_1[1]x_{s_2}[2]x_{s_3}[3] \ldots x_{s_n}[n] >$. By the form of the splicing rules in the set (1), the word $wx_1[1]x_{s_2}[2]x_{s_3}[3] \ldots x_{s_n}[n] >$ is obtained only if $x_1, x_{s_2}, x_{s_3}, \ldots, x_{s_n}$ is a Hamiltonian path in G.

If G has no Hamiltonian path, then Γ halts on w after at most n splicing steps without generating $\underline{YES}$, which concludes the proof. □

5 Conclusions and Further Research

In this paper, we introduced the concept of accepting splicing systems and proposed a way of using these devices as problem solvers. We showed how two NP-complete problems can be uniformly solved with accepting H systems in linear time. Further research might be aimed at investigating whether using other types of accepting H systems we can get similar results, for it looks like the regular rules are a very powerful tool, and it does not seem obvious to get the same kind of efficiency without them. However, since such a system with infinitely many rules is hard to imagine from a biochemical point of view, it would be interesting to use types of accepting H systems which are better motivated biochemically. For instance, one could consider systems as introduced in [7]. These are *finite* systems, which differ from usual systems by the fact that strings can disappear by applying a rule to them.

References

1. P. Bonizzoni, G. Mauri, Regular splicing languages and subclasses, *Theoret. Comput. Sci.*, 340:349–363, 2005.
2. K. Culik II, T. Harju, Splicing semigroups of dominoes and DNA, *Discrete Appl. Math.*, 31:261-277, 1991.
3. M. Garey, D. Johnson, *Computers and Intractability. A Guide to the Theory of NP-completeness*, Freeman, San Francisco, CA, 1979.
4. T. Harju, M. Margenstern, *Splicing systems for universal Turing machines*, Proc. 10th Internat. Meeting on DNA Based Computers (DNA10, Milan; C. Ferretti et al., eds), Lecture Notes in Computer Science3384, Springer-Verlag, 151-160, 2005
5. T. Head, Formal language theory and DNA: an analysis of the generative capacity of specific recombinant behaviours, *Bull. Math. Biology* 49:737–759, 1987.
6. J. E. Hopcroft, J. D. Ullman, *Introduction to Automata Theory, Languages and Computation*, Addison-Wesley, Reading MA, 1979
7. R. Loos, An alternative definition of splicing, *Theoret. Comput. Sci.*, to appear
8. R. Loos, M. Ogihara, A complexity theory for splicing systems, submitted (2006)
9. Gh. Paun, Regular extended H systems are computationally universal, *J. Automata, languages, Combinatorics*, 1(1):27–36, 1996.
10. Gh. Paun, G. Rozenberg, A. Salomaa, *DNA computing - New computing paradigms*, Springer-Verlag, Berlin, 1998
11. D. Pixton, Regularity of Splicing Languages, *Discrete Appl. Math.*, 69, 101-124, 1996

Some Steps Towards Understanding How Neutrality Affects Evolutionary Search

Edgar Galván-López and Riccardo Poli

University of Essex, Colchester, CO4 3SQ, UK
{egalva, rpoli}@essex.ac.uk

Abstract. The effects of neutrality on evolutionary search have been considered in a number of interesting studies, the results of which, however, have been contradictory. We believe that this confusion is due to several reasons. In this paper, we shed some light on neutrality by addressing these problems. That is, we use the simplest possible definition of neutrality, we consider one of the simplest possible algorithms, we apply it to two problems (a unimodal landscape and a deceptive landscape), which we analyse using fitness distance correlation, performance statistics and, critically, tracking the full evolutionary path of individuals within their family tree.

1 Introduction

Natural selection is a powerful theory which can explain the existence of adaptation in nature. However, it is unlikely that natural selection is the only force that directs evolution. Indeed, at molecular scale there is support for the idea that most evolutive variations are neutral [10]. This Neutral theory does not affirm that during evolution the genes are not making something useful, rather it suggests that different forms of the same gene are indistinguishable in their effects. The theory argues that mutations occurring during evolution are neither advantageous nor disadvantageous to the survival and reproduction of individuals, but that such random genetic drift should be considered in the study of the evolutionary process.

Some EC researchers have found neutrality to be beneficial for the evolutionary process while others have found it either useless or worse. We believe there are various reasons of these contradictory results and, by addressing them, we can start clarifying the effects of neutrality. The aims of this study are: (a) to understand how population flows in the search space are affected by the presence of neutrality in the evolutionary process, and (b) to identify under what circumstances neutrality may improve performance.

The paper is organised as follows. In the next section, we review previous work on neutrality. In Section 3 we describe our approach. In Section 4 the fitness distance correlation is computed for landscapes with neutrality. Section 5 provides details on the experimental setup used. In Sections 6 and 7 we present and discuss the results of experiments with unimodal and deceptive landscape problems and draw some conclusions.

T.P. Runarsson et al. (Eds.): PPSN IX, LNCS 4193, pp. 778–787, 2006.

2 Previous Work

Harvey and Thompson studied some effects of neutral networks in an evolvable hardware problem [7]. They defined the concept of potentially useful junk that refers to loci in a genotype that are functionless within the current context, but which may become functional with different values elsewhere in the genotype. They argued that with neutrality it is possible to reach a global optimum without worrying about premature convergence.

Banzhaf [2] proposed an approach where a genotype-phenotype mapping was used in the context of constrained optimisation problems. He argued that, very often, constraining the solution space leads to local optima which are difficult to escape from with traditional methods. He used high variability of neutral variants to escape from local optima on saddle surfaces.

Barnett [3] proposed a variant of NK landscapes which he called NKp landscapes. The idea was to introduce a parameter, p, which could vary the degree of neutrality present in the landscape and study the effects of neutrality in the evolutionary process. He claimed that with the presence of neutral networks with certain properties, it is possible to avoid to get stuck in local optima.

Shipman *et al.* [12] explored the benefits of neutrality in the context of a mapping based on an abstraction of genetic regulatory networks — a random boolean network. The mapping used in their experiments provided a very large degree of neutrality. They concluded that neutral drift allowed the discovery of many more phenotypes than would be the case with a direct encoding without redundancy. In [13] they proposed four different redundant mappings to study how neutrality influences the search. They found that redundancy was useful in three of their mappings and concluded that some kind of neutrality is crucial.

Smith *et al.* [14] analysed how evolvability was affected by the presence of neutral networks. For this purpose they used a system with an extremely complex genotype-to-fitness mapping. They concluded that the existence of neutral networks in the search space does not necessarily provide advantages because the population does not evolve any faster with neutrality. In [15] the same authors looked at the dynamics of the population rather than just the fitness, and argued that neutrality did not perform a useful role in an evolutionary robotic task.

Yu and Miller [18] showed that neutrality improves the evolutionary search process for a Boolean benchmark problem. They used Miller's Cartesian GP to measure explicit neutrality in the evolutionary process. They argued that mutation on active genes is adaptive because it exploits accumulated beneficial mutations, while mutation on inactive genes has a neutral effect on a genotype's fitness, yet it provides exploratory power by maintaining genetic diversity. Furthermore, in [19] they showed that neutrality was helpful and that there is a relationship between neutral mutations and success rate in a Boolean function induction problem. However, Collins [5] claimed that the conclusion that, in this problem, neutrality is beneficial is flawed. In [20] Yu and Miller also investigated neutrality using the simple OneMax problem. They used a theoretical approach and showed that neutrality is advantageous because it provides a buffer to absorb destructive mutations.

Igel and Toussaint [8] claimed that neutrality is necessary for self-adaptation and classified self-adaptation to classical and generalized self-adaptation. Both definitions are inspired from the genotype-phenotype mapping. They argued that neutrality could have benefit when the mapping is done in such a way that desirable phenotypes are represented more often than other ones.

3 Approach

We believe that the confusion regarding neutrality has several sources:(a) many studies have based their conclusions on performance statistics (e.g., on whether or not a system with neutrality could solve a particular problem faster than a system without neutrality) rather than a deep analysis of population dynamics, (b) studies often consider problems, representations and search algorithms that are relatively complex and, so, results represent the composition of multiple effects (e.g., bloat or spurious attractors in genetic programming), (c) there is not a single definition of neutrality and different studies have added neutrality to problems in radically different ways, and, (d) the features of a problem's landscape change when neutrality is artificially added, but rarely an effort has been made to understand exactly how.

In this paper, we shed some light on neutrality by addressing these problems. Firstly, we use the simplest possible definition of neutrality: a neutral network of constant fitness, identically distributed in the whole search space. Neutrality is "plugged into" the original non-redundant representation by adding an extra bit to the representation: when the bit is 1 the individual is on the neutral network (and, so, its fitness has a pre-fixed constant value), when the bit is 0, the fitness of the individual is determined by the coding bits as usual. Secondly, we consider one of the simplest possible algorithms (a mutation-only, binary genetic algorithm). Thirdly, we analyse population flows from and to the neutral network and the basins of attraction of the optima. Fourthly, we compare the percentage of success to find the optimum solution and the difficulty of the problem using fitness distance correlation. Finally, we use two problems with significantly different landscape features: a unimodal landscape (OneMax) where we expect neutrality to always be detrimental and a deceptive landscape (a trap function with different degrees of difficulty), where there are conditions where neutrality is more helpful than others.

In the presence of the form of neutrality discussed previously, the landscape is therefore divided into two areas of identical size: the *neutral layer* and the *normal layer*. However, we still only have one global optimum. So, the addition of neutrality comes at a cost since we are expanding the size of the search space without correspondingly expanding the solution space. Thus, we should expect to see benefits of neutrality (e.g., improved performance) only when neutrality modifies the search bias of an algorithm-problem pair in such a way to make it much more likely to (eventually) sample the global optimum. If this does not happen, or worse, if the original search bias is modified in such a way to make it harder to reach the global optimum, then we can be certain that neutrality will not help.

Neutrality is often reported to help in multimodal landscapes. So, in the case of our multimodal deceptive problem, should we expect a uniform neutral network to increase performance? And what sort of population dynamics should we expect? For analysis purposes, we further divide the normal and neutral layers into two regions depending on which of the two basins of attraction a string belongs to. We will term the resulting four areas "global neutral", "local neutral", "global normal" and "local normal".

Let us now consider whether a uniform neutral network could provide a performance improvement in the case of a trap landscape. We must first consider whether or not the neutral layer acts as an attractor or a repellent and for what proportion of the local and global areas. If, for example, the neutral layer has a very low fitness, then it should become harder for individuals to use it as a "tunnel" between the large basin of attraction of the local optimum and the narrow basin of attraction of the global optimum. In this case, the neutral layers would provide no advantage and, given that it doubles the search space, we should see a marked decrease in performance. If, instead, the neutral layers had a relatively high fitness, we should expect to see more individuals moving towards it. This means that there could be a flow of individuals from one basis of attraction to the other. This, however, would not in itself provide a performance improvement w.r.t. the case where no neutrality is used, because the flow is bidirectional and, so, individuals already in the global area may end up performing a random walk which leads them outside it. In addition, because the search space is still twice as big as the original while the solution spaces has still size 1, in order to beat the performance of the no-neutrality case, neutrality would need to provide a very significant "improvement" in search bias. These considerations have motivated our analysis and experiments. These are described in more detail in the following sections.

4 Fitness Distance Correlation

The fitness distance correlation (*fdc*) [9] measures the hardness of a landscape according to the correlation between the distance from the optimum and the fitness of solutions. The definition of *fdc* is quite simple: given a set $F = \{f_1, f_2, ..., f_n\}$ of fitness values of n individuals and the corresponding set $D = \{d_1, d_2, ..., d_n\}$ of distances to the nearest optimum, we compute the correlation coefficient r, as:

$$r = \frac{C_{FD}}{\sigma_F \sigma_D},$$

where:

$$C_{FD} = \frac{1}{n}\sum_{i=1}^{n}(f_i - \overline{f})(d_i - \overline{d})$$

is the covariance of F and D, and σ_F, σ_D, $\overline{f}$ and $\overline{d}$ are the standard deviations and means of F and D, respectively.

According to [9] a problem can be classified in one of three classes, depending of the value of r: (1) **misleading** ($r \geq 0.15$), in which fitness tends to increase with the distance from the global optimum, (2) **difficult** ($-0.15 < r < 0.15$), for which there is no correlation between fitness and distance, and (3) **easy** ($r \leq -0.15$), in which fitness increases as the global optimum approaches.

There are some known weakness in the *fdc* as a measure of problem hardness [1,11]. However, it is fair to say that the method has been generally very successful [9,4,17,16]. The distance used in the calculations is, for binary search spaces, the Hamming distance.

In this work we will use *fdc* to evaluate problem difficulty with and without neutrality. Since we only consider problems where the fitness function is a function of unitation, we can rewrite C_{FD} in a more useful form.

For a search space of binary strings of length l, if we sample the whole search space in order to compute C_{FD}, we have:

$$C_{FD_f} = \frac{1}{2^l} \sum_{u=0}^{l} \binom{l}{u} (f(u) - \overline{f}_f)(u - \overline{u}_f)$$

where:

$$\overline{f}_f = \frac{\sum_{u=0}^{l} \binom{l}{u} f(u)}{2^l}$$

$$\overline{u}_f = \frac{l}{2}$$

where u represent the unitation class of strings.

As mentioned in the previous section, the form of neutrality we consider here is one where an extra bit is added to the representation. When the bit is set we say that an individual is in the neutral layer and its fitness is the constant value f_{layer}. So, when neutrality is present the size of the landscape is 2^{l+1}. Now C_{FD} is given by:

$$C_{FD_{neu}} = \frac{1}{2^{l+1}} \sum_{u=0}^{l} \binom{l}{u} \left[(f(u) - \overline{f}_{neu})(u - \overline{u}_{neu}) + (f_{layer} - \overline{f}_{neu})(u + 1 - \overline{u}_{neu}) \right]$$

where:

$$\overline{f}_{neu} = \frac{\frac{\sum_{u=0}^{l} \binom{l}{u} f(u)}{2^l} + f_{layer}}{2}$$

$$\overline{u}_{neu} = \frac{l+1}{2}$$

These calculations indicate that the introduction of neutrality does not necessarily imply a reduction of *fdc*. So, whether or not a problem is easier with neutrality depends on landscapes features and on f_{layer}.

5 Experimental Setup

We have used two problems to analyse neutrality. The first one is the OneMax problem which consist in maximizing the number of ones of a bitstring. Seen as a function of unitation the problem is represented by $f(u) = u$.

Table 1. Parameters

Parameter	*Value*
Length of the genome	10, 14 (+1 for neutrality)
Population Size	80
Generations	100
Mutation Rate (per bit)	0.02
Independent Runs	1,000

The second problem is a trap function, which is a deceptive function of unitation [6]. For this example, we have used the function:

$$f(X) = \begin{cases} \frac{a}{z}(z - u(X)) & \text{if } u(X) \leq z, \\ \frac{b}{k-z}(u(X) - z) & \text{otherwise} \end{cases}$$

where a is the deceptive optimum, b is the global optimum, and z is the slope-change location. Basically the idea is that there are two optima, a and b, and by varying the parameters k and z, we can make the problem easier or harder.

For the OneMax problem we have used chromosomes of length $l = 10$ while for the trap function we have used chromosomes of length $l = 14$, $k = 14$, $z = \{8, 9, 10, 11, 12, 13\}$, $a = 39$, $b = 40$, and sample size 4,000 to calculate *fdc*.

The experiments were conducted using a GA with fitness proportionate selection and bit-flip mutation. Runs were stopped when the maximum number of generations was reached. The parameters used are given in Table 1.

6 Results and Analysis

6.1 Performance Comparison

In this section, we describe empirical evidence which corroborates the discussion presented above. Let's start by analysing the results for the OneMax problem. In Table 2 we show the *fdc*, the number of generations required to reach the optimum solution and the percentage of success in finding the optimum. As expected the problem is more difficult in the presence of neutrality. However, the degree of difficulty varies f_{layer}. *fdc* is a good heuristic measure of difficulty as one can see by comparing the *fdc* against the percentages of successes for different values on the neutral layer. In the case considered here ($l = 10$) the maximum achievable fitness is 10, and so a neutral layer with fitness 9 turns the search into a set of parallel random walks. It is not surprising then that, performance decreases so much with neutrality.

Now, let's consider the second problem - the trap problem. In this problem, the length of the genome is 14. As shown in Table 3, the bigger the value of the slope-change location z the harder the problem. When the neutral layer is present, regardless the value of f_{layer}, the number of generations required to reach the global optimum is bigger than when it is not present. This is easy to explain if we consider that the search space without neutrality is of size 2^l

Table 2. Statistical information on the OneMax problem

f_{layer}	fdc	Avg. Generations	% of Success
Not present	-1	8.07	100
6	-0.4922	10.68	100
7	-0.3010	12.72	100
8	-0.1604	21.73	94.7
9	-0.0650	35.02	34.2

Table 3. Statistical information on the trap problem

Value of z	fdc			Avr. Generations			% of Success		
	No neutral layer	f_{layer} 30	f_{layer} 38	No neutral layer	f_{layer} 30	f_{layer} 38	No neutral layer	f_{layer} 30	f_{layer} 38
8	0.42	0.35	0.33	10.81	40.25	29.60	38.7	19.8	1.7
9	0.74	0.45	0.40	8.65	31.26	24.50	17.5	12.1	1.3
10	0.90	0.51	0.45	6.83	12.45	22.60	7.7	1.3	1.9
11	0.96	0.55	0.45	3.85	16.75	17.20	1.7	1.1	1.2
12	0.99	0.57	0.48	0.25	6.20	7.55	0.2	0.7	0.7
13	0.99	0.59	0.49	-	7.90	24.30	0	0.6	0.9

whereas with the presence of it is 2^{l+1}. When $8 \leq z \leq 11$, the percentage of runs that reached the optimum solution is bigger when neutrality is not present. However, the opposite happens when $12 \leq z \leq 13$. Moreover, when neutrality is not present the solution is either found after few generations or is not found at all. This does not hold when neutrality is present, as can be seen in Table 3. This means that there are complex dynamics going on between layers and regions of the landscapes, and that only by understanding these one can understand the effects of neutrality. We investigate them in the next section.

6.2 Family Tree

In a particular generation each individual can be in one of four areas: normal layer close to the global value, normal layer close to the local value, neutral layer close to the global value and neutral layer close to the local value. However, so far we have not studied where an individual in a specific layer came from. Fortunately, in a mutation based genetic algorithm each individual has only one parent. This makes it possible to track the origin of a sample point, and, in fact, the full evolutionary path of an individual within its family tree. This has allowed us to collect detailed statistics of population flows from one layer and region to another. To perform a full analysis we need to look at $2^4 = 16$ different parent/offspring transitions: a parent could be in any of four areas and his offspring could be in any of the same four areas.

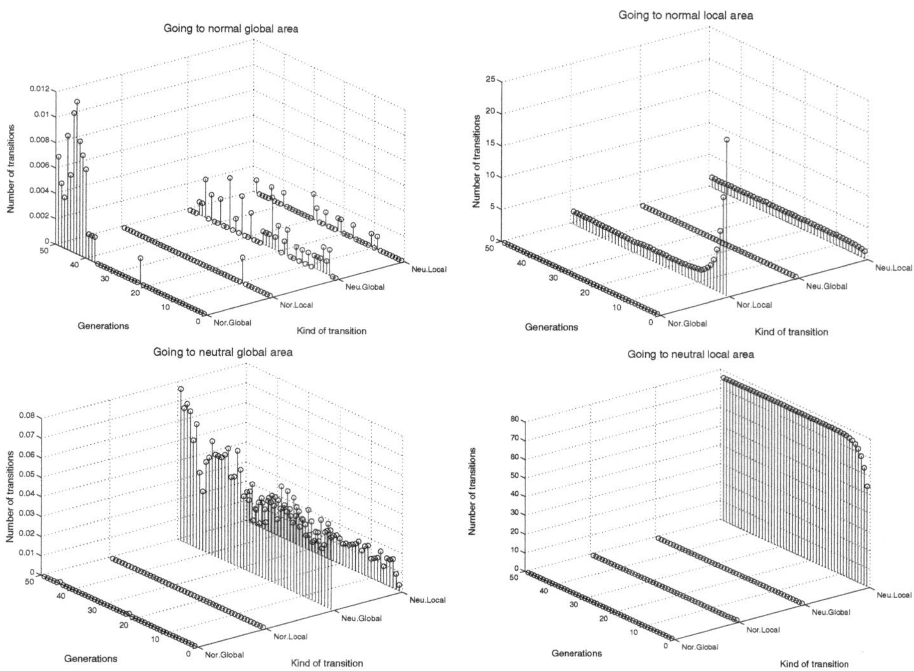

Fig. 1. Number of transitions to the normal global area (top left), normal local area (top right), neutral global area (bottom left) and neutral local area (bottom right), when the fitness of the neutral layer is 38

In Figure 1 we show the result of the analysis of family trees for the trap function using $f_{layer} = 38$, $l = 14$ and $z = 13$. In all plots we can observe that the majority of offspring in an area came from parents already in that area. These are not the only sources, however, as shown in Figure 1 where can see that a small proportion of individuals in the neutral layer near the global optimum actually comes from neutral local area, indicating the presence of tunnelling.

7 Conclusions

There is considerable controversy on whether or not neutrality helps or hinders evolutionary search. In this paper we have highlighted some possible reasons for this situation. A particularly serious problem is that many studies are only based on performance statistics, rather than more in-depth investigations, and there is considerable variability in the problems, algorithms and representations used for benchmarking purposes. Also, there is neither a single definition of neutrality nor a unified approach to add neutrality to a representation. In this paper, we have made an effort to address these problems. We used *fdc* to assess if a problem gets easier or harder in the presence of neutrality. We complemented this with statistical information (e.g. average number of generations required to solve a problem). We also recorded parent-offspring flows from and to the neutral network and the basins of attraction of the optima.

We argue that neutrality *may* be beneficial in some cases, but when it comes at the cost of an increased size of the search space without a corresponding expansion of the solution space, then any benefits it may bring via search bias, tunnelling ability, etc. may be insufficient to compensate for the additional search effort required by a reduced density of solutions. It is clear that the modifications in the original search bias of an algorithm produced by the addition of neutrality (at least of the form we have discussed here) are not always beneficial. We brought, for instance, the example of a unimodal landscape, where, as confirmed also experimentally, it is very hard to imagine any advantages in adding neutrality. Neutrality-induced bias, may, however, be very beneficial (so much so to fully overcome the inefficiencies due to an extended search space) in certain circumstances, like, for example, when the population is initialised in the wrong part of the search space. This is particularly common when dealing with infinitely large search spaces (e.g., the space of variable length strings and the space of computer programs), where it is impossible to initialise the population uniformly at random across the whole search space. This may be a further reason why certain studies have reported significant benefits when using neutrality (albeit of forms very different from the one used here).

We have shown that it is very difficult to infer the effects (or benefits) of neutrality without getting under the bonnet and looking at the population flows induced by the presence of neutrality. For example, as we have shown, in exactly the same conditions, a neutral network of low fitness changes the behaviour of a genetic algorithm in very different ways than a high-fitness neutral network.

Acknowledgments

The first author thanks to CONACyT for support to pursue graduate studies at University of Essex. The authors would like to thank the anonymous reviewers for their valuable comments.

References

1. L. Altenberg. Fitness distance correlation analysis: An instructive counterexample. In *Proceedings of the Seventh International Conference on Genetic Algorithms*, pages 57–64, San Francisco, CA, USA, 1997. Morgan Kaufmann Publishers Inc.
2. W. Banzhaf. Genotype-phenotype-mapping and neutral variation – A case study in genetic programming. In Y. D. *et al.*, editor, *Parallel Problem Solving from Nature III*, volume 866 of *LNCS*, pages 322–332. Springer-Verlag, 9-14 Oct. 1994.
3. L. Barnett. Ruggedness and neutrality: The nkp family of fitness landscapes. In R. A. *et al.*, editor, *Artificial Live VI: Proceedings of the Sixth International Conference on Artificial Life*, pages 18–27. MIT Press, 1998.
4. M. Clergue, P. Collard, M. Tomassini, and L. Vanneschi. Fitness distance correlation and problem difficulty for genetic programming. In W. B. L. *et al.*, editor, *GECCO 2002: Proceedings of the Genetic and Evolutionary Computation Conference*, pages 724–732, New York, 9-13 July 2002. Morgan Kaufmann Publishers.

5. M. Collins. Finding needles in haystacks is harder with neutrality. In H.-G. B. *et al.*, editor, *GECCO 2005: Proceedings of the 2005 conference on Genetic and evolutionary computation*, volume 2, pages 1613–1618, Washington DC, USA, 25-29 June 2005. ACM Press.
6. D. E. Goldberg. Construction of high-order deceptive functions using low-order walsh coefficients. *Ann. Math. Artif. Intell.*, 5(1):35–47, 1992.
7. I. Harvey and A. Thompson. Through the labyrinth evolution finds a way: A silicon ridge. In *Proceedings of the First International Conference on Evolvable Systems: From Biology to Hardware (ICES)*, pages 406–422. Springer-Verlag, 1996.
8. C. Igel and M. Toussaint. Neutrality and self-adaptation. In *Natural Computing*, pages 117–132, 2003.
9. T. Jones and S. Forrest. Fitness distance correlation as a measure of problem difficulty for genetic algorithms. In *Proceedings of the 6th International Conference on GA*, pages 184–192, San Francisco, CA, USA, 1995. Morgan Kaufmann Publishers Inc.
10. M. Kimura. Evolutionary rate at the molecular level. In *Nature*, volume 217, pages 624–626, 1968.
11. R. J. Quick, V. J. Rayward-Smith, and G. D. Smith. Fitness distance correlation and ridge functions. In *PPSN V: Proceedings of the 5th International Conference on Parallel Problem Solving from Nature*, pages 77–86. Springer-Verlag, 1998.
12. R. Shipman, M. Schackleton, and I. Harvey. The use of neutral genotype-phenotype mappings for improved evolutionary search. *BT. Technology Journal*, 18(4):103–111, October. ISSSN 2000.
13. R. Shipman, M. Schakleton, M. Ebner, and R. Watson. Neutral search spaces for artificial evolution: A lesson from life. In M. B. *et al.*, editor, *Artificial Life: Proceedings of the Seventh International Conference on Artificial Evolution*, pages 162–169. MIT Press, 2000.
14. T. Smith, P. Husbands, and M. O'Shea. Neutral networks and evolvability with complex genotype-phenotype mapping. *Lecture Notes in Computer Science*, 2159:272–282, 2001.
15. T. Smith, P. Husbands, and M. O'Shea. Neutral networks in an evolutionary robotics search space. In *Congress on Evolutionary Computation: CEC 2001*, pages 136–145. IEEE Press, 2001.
16. M. Tomassini, L. Vanneschi, P. Collard, and M. Clergue. A study of fitness distance correlation as a difficulty measure in genetic programming. *Evolutionary Computation*, 13(2):213–239, Summer 2005.
17. L. Vanneschi, M. Tomassini, P. Collard, and M. Clergue. Fitness distance correlation in structural mutation genetic programming. In C. R. *et al.*, editor, *Genetic Programming, Proceedings of EuroGP'2003*, volume 2610 of *LNCS*, pages 455–464, Essex, 14-16 Apr. 2003. Springer-Verlag.
18. T. Yu and J. Miller. Neutrality and the evolvability of boolean function landscape. In *Fourth European Conference on GP*, pages 204–211. Springer-Verlag, 2001.
19. T. Yu and J. F. Miller. Needles in haystacks are not hard to find with neutrality. In J. A. F. *et al.*, editor, *Genetic Programming, Proceedings of the 5th European Conference, EuroGP 2002*, volume 2278 of *LNCS*, pages 13–25, Kinsale, Ireland, 3-5 Apr. 2002. Springer-Verlag.
20. T. Yu and J. F. Miller. The role of neutral and adaptive mutation in an evolutionary search on the onemax problem. In E. Cantú-Paz, editor, *Late Breaking Papers at the Genetic and Evolutionary Computation Conference (GECCO-2002)*, pages 512–519, New York, NY, July 2002. AAAI.

Performance of Evolutionary Algorithms on Random Decomposable Problems

Martin Pelikan[1], Kumara Sastry[2], Martin V. Butz[3], and David E. Goldberg[2]

[1] Missouri Estimation of Distribution Algorithms Laboratory (MEDAL), 320 CCB; University of Missouri in St. Louis; One University Blvd., St. Louis, MO 63121
pelikan@cs.umsl.edu

[2] Illinois Genetic Algorithms Laboratory (IlliGAL), 107 TB; University of Illinois at Urbana-Champaign; 104 S. Mathews Ave., Urbana, IL 61801
kumara@illigal.ge.uiuc.edu, deg@uiuc.edu

[3] Department of Cognitive Psychology; University of Würzburg; Röntgenring 11, 97070 Würzburg, Germany
mbutz@psychologie.uni-wuerzburg.de

Abstract. This paper describes a class of *random additively decomposable problems* (rADPs) with and without interactions between the subproblems. The paper then tests the hierarchical Bayesian optimization algorithm (hBOA) and other evolutionary algorithms on a large number of random instances of the proposed class of problems. The results show that hBOA can scalably solve rADPs and that it significantly outperforms all other methods included in the comparison. Furthermore, the results provide a number of interesting insights into both the difficulty of a broad class of decomposable problems as well as the sensitivity of various evolutionary algorithms to different sources of problem difficulty. rADPs can be used to test other optimization algorithms.

1 Introduction

There are three important approaches to testing optimization algorithms:

(1) *Testing on the boundary of the design envelope using artificial test problems.* For example, concatenated traps [1,2] represent a class of artificial test problems that can be used to test whether the optimization algorithm can automatically decompose the problem and exploit the discovered decomposition effectively.
(2) *Testing on classes of random problems.* For example, to test algorithms for solving maximum satisfiability (MAXSAT) problems, large sets of random formulas in conjunctive normal form can be generated and analyzed [3].
(3) *Testing on real-world problems or their approximations.* For example, the problem of designing military antennas can be considered for testing [4].

The primary purpose of this paper is to introduce a class of random additively decomposable problems (rADPs), which can be used to test optimization algorithms that address nearly decomposable problems. There are three main goals in the design of the proposed class of problems:

T.P. Runarsson et al. (Eds.): PPSN IX, LNCS 4193, pp. 788–797, 2006.

(1) *Scalability.* It should be straightforward to control problem size and difficulty in order to test scalability.
(2) *Known optimum.* It should be possible to efficiently discover the global optimum of any problem instance so that it can be verified whether the global optimum was found.
(3) *Easy generation of random instances.* It should be possible to generate a large number of instances of the proposed class of problems.

The paper then applies several genetic and evolutionary algorithms to a large number of random rADP instances. Specifically, we consider the hierarchical Bayesian optimization algorithm (hBOA), genetic algorithms (GAs) with standard variation and mutation operators, the univariate marginal distribution algorithm (UMDA), and the stochastic hill climber (HC). The results show that hBOA significantly outperforms other algorithms included in the comparison. Furthermore, the results provide a number of interesting insights into both the difficulty of decomposable problems as well as the sensitivity of various evolutionary algorithms to different sources of problem difficulty in decomposable problems.

The paper starts by introducing the class of rADPs in section 2. Section 3 presents and discusses experimental results. Finally, section 4 summarizes and concludes the paper.

2 Random Additively Decomposable Problems (rADPs)

This section describes the class of random additively decomposable problems (rADPs) of bounded difficulty with and without overlap. Candidate solutions are represented by binary strings of fixed length, but the proposed class of problems can be generalized to fixed-length strings over any finite alphabet in a straightforward manner. The goal is to *maximize* the objective function (fitness function).

The section first presents the general form of additively decomposable problems (ADPs). Then, the section discusses ADPs of bounded order with and without interactions between subproblems. Finally, the section describes how to generate random instances of the proposed class of decomposable problems.

2.1 Additively Decomposable Problems (ADPs)

The fitness function for an n-bit ADP can be written as the sum of subfunctions defined over subsets of string positions:

$$f(X_1, X_2, \ldots, X_n) = \sum_{i=1}^{m} f_i(S_i),$$

where n is the number of bits in a candidate solution, X_i is the variable corresponding to the ith bit of a candidate solution, m is the number of subproblems or subfunctions, f_i is the ith subproblem, and $S_i \subset \{X_1, \ldots, X_n\}$ is the subset of variables (string positions) corresponding to the ith subproblem.

Clearly, any fitness function can be written in the above form because any problem can be trivially decomposed into one subproblem containing all variables. The difficulty of ADPs depends on the order of subproblems, the subproblems themselves, and their interaction through string positions contained in multiple subproblems. It is important to note that many difficult problems, including NP-complete problems, can be defined using subproblems of relatively short order that interact in a complex structure, while many easy problems may contain interactions of high order. For example, the problem of finding ground states of Ising spin glasses can be additively decomposed into subproblems of order 2, but the problem is NP-complete as a result of complex interactions between the different subproblems that lead to strong frustration effects [5,6]. On the other hand, if we consider a simple onemax problem (maximize the sum of bits) and reinforce the global optimum by adding 1 to its fitness, any decomposition of the problem must use a subproblem that contains all variables, but for most algorithms the problem is still as easy as the original onemax or even easier.

The remainder of this section defines the proposed class of rADPs, shows how to generate random instances of the described class of problems, and outlines an efficient method to solve these problem instances.

2.2 Defining ADPs with Overlap

Here we describe a class of ADPs where the overlap is relatively simple and the optimum can be verified using an efficient procedure based on dynamic programming. The order of all subproblems is fixed to a constant k and the amount of overlap is specified by a parameter $o \in \{0, 1, \ldots, k-1\}$ called *overlap*.

The first subproblem is defined in the first k string positions. The second subproblem is defined in the last o positions of the first subproblem and the next $(k - o)$ positions. All the remaining subproblems are assigned string positions analogically, always defining the next subproblem in the last o positions of the previous subproblem and the next $(k-o)$ positions. For example, for $k = 3, o = 1$, and $m = 3$ subproblems, the first subproblem is defined in positions $(1, 2, 3)$, the second subproblem is defined in positions $(3, 4, 5)$, and the third subproblem is defined in positions $(5, 6, 7)$. Note that each string position is contained in one or two subproblems and that for m subproblems with overlap o, the overall number of bits is $n = k + (m - 1)(k - o)$. Separable problems of order k are a special case of decomposable problems of order k with no overlap, that is, $o = 0$. Other approaches that control overlap in ADPs can be found in references [7,8,9].

To ensure that the subproblems are not always located in consequent string positions, the string can be reordered according to a randomly generated permutation. See Fig. 1 to visualize the aforementioned class of decomposable problems.

Assuming that the problem is decomposable according to the above definition and that we know the subsets S_1 to S_m and the subfunctions f_1 to f_m, it is possible to solve any problem instance using a deterministic algorithm based on dynamic programming in $O(2^k n)$ fitness evaluations. The algorithm iterates

(a) Tight linkage. (b) Loose linkage.

Fig. 1. Examples of ADPs with 4 subproblems of 4 bits each and 1-bit overlap. Each string position (bit) is displayed as a rectangle and the string positions corresponding to one subproblem are filled with the same color. The string positions that are located in more subproblems are split along the diagonal.

through all subproblems, starting with one of the two subproblems that overlap with only one other subproblem via o string positions. Each next iteration considers one of the unprocessed subproblems that interacts with the last processed subproblem via o string positions. For example, consider the aforementioned problem with $n = 7$, $k = 3$, and $o = 1$, where the subproblems are defined in the following subsets of positions: $(1, 2, 3)$ for subproblem f_1, $(3, 4, 5)$ for f_2, and $(5, 6, 7)$ for f_3. The dynamic programming algorithm could consider the subproblems in either of the following permutations: (f_1, f_2, f_3) or (f_3, f_2, f_1).

The dynamic programming algorithm starts by creating a matrix $G = (g_{i,j})$ of size $(m - 1) \times 2^o$, where $g_{i,j}$ for $i \in \{1, 2, \ldots, m-1\}$ and $j \in \{0, 1, \ldots, 2^o - 1\}$ encodes the maximum fitness contribution of the first i subproblems according to the considered permutation of subproblems under the assumption that the o bits that overlap with the next subproblem (that is, with the $(i + 1)$th subproblem) are equal to j using integer representation for these o bits. For example, for the above example problem of $n = 7$ bits and permutation (f_1, f_2, f_3), $g_{2,0}$ represents the best fitness contribution of f_1 and f_2 (ignoring f_3) under the assumption that the 5th bit is 0; analogically, $g_{2,1}$ represents the best fitness contribution of f_1 and f_2 under the assumption that the 5th bit is 1.

The algorithm starts by considering all 2^k instances of the k bits in the first subproblem, and records the best found fitness for each combination of values of the o bits that overlap with the second subproblem; the resulting values are stored in the first row of G (elements $g_{1,j}$ for $j \in \{0, \ldots, 2^o - 1\}$). Then, the algorithm goes through all the remaining subproblems except for the last one, starting in the second subproblem, and ending in the $(m - 1)$th subproblem. For ith subproblem, all 2^k instances of the k bits in this subproblem are examined. For each instance, the algorithm first looks at the column j' of G that corresponds to the o bits of ith subproblem that overlap with the previous subproblem. Then, the algorithm computes the fitness contribution of the first i subproblems assuming that the first $(i - 1)$ subproblems are set optimally and the ith subproblem is set to the considered instance of k bits; this fitness contribution is computed as the sum of $g_{i-1,j'}$ and the fitness contribution of the considered instance of the ith subproblem. The values in the ith row of G are then computed from the fitness contributions computed as described above.

In the last step, all 2^k instances of the last subproblem are considered and their fitness contributions are computed analogically to other subproblems, using the $(m - 1)$th row of G and the fitness contributions of the mth subproblem. The maximum of these values is the best fitness value we can obtain. The values that lead to the optimum fitness can be found by examining all choices made when choosing the best combination of bits in each subproblem.

2.3 Generating Random Problems

To generate random instances of the class of ADPs defined above, the user must specify the number m of subproblems, the order k of decomposition, and the overlap o. After specifying m, k, and o, for each subproblem f_i, the 2^k values that specify f_i are generated randomly; overall, there are $2^k m$ values to generate. Finally, the permutation of string positions is generated to eliminate the assumption of tight linkage.

In this work, we generate all 2^k values of each subfunction from a uniform distribution over interval $[0, 1)$. The permutation is also generated from a uniform distribution so that each permutation has the same probability. Of course, other distributions can be considered for both the subfunctions and the permutations; for example, the 2^k values for each subfunction can be distributed according to a Gaussian distribution and the permutations can be biased to enforce loose linkage.

3 Experiments

This section presents and discusses experimental results.

3.1 Test Problems

We performed experiments on a number of instances of rADPs with and without overlap that were generated as described above. All problems were solved using the presented deterministic algorithm so that we could ensure that all algorithms would find the actual global optimum. However, the compared algorithms were not provided any information about the global optimum, the locations of the subproblems, the order of decomposition, or the overlap.

All problems tested in this paper have the same order of subproblems, $k = 4$. Three values of the overlap parameter were considered, specifically, $o = 0$, $o = 1$, and $o = 2$. To examine scalability of the compared algorithms, problems of various sizes n were examined for every value of o; the number of subproblems can be computed from n and o as $m = (n - o)/(k - o)$. For each combination of values of k, o, and n, 1000 random problem instances were generated and tested.

3.2 Compared Algorithms

The paper considers genetic algorithms (GA) with standard crossover operators, the univariate marginal distribution algorithm (UMDA) [10], stochastic hill climbing (HC), and the hierarchical Bayesian optimization algorithm (hBOA) [11].

In GA, bit-flip mutation and either two-point or uniform crossover operator were used. hBOA and UMDA are estimation of distribution algorithms

(EDAs) [12,10,13,14] where standard variation operators are replaced by building and sampling a probabilistic model of promising solutions; hBOA uses Bayesian networks with local structures to model candidate solutions, whereas UMDA uses a simple univariate model based on single-bit probabilities. In stochastic hill climbing, bit-flip mutation is used as the perturbation operator. In GA, UMDA and hBOA, restricted tournament replacement is used to ensure effective diversity maintenance.

Performance of all algorithms is expressed in terms of the number of evaluations until the global optimum has been found because in difficult real-world problems, fitness evaluation is usually the primary source of computational complexity. Furthermore, in all compared algorithms, the computational overhead excluding evaluations can be upper bounded by a low-order polynomial of the number of evaluations [15].

For hBOA, UMDA and GA, for every problem instance the minimum population size to ensure convergence to the optimum in 10 out of 10 independent runs is found using the bisection method [15]. The upper bound on the number of generations for hBOA, UMDA and GA is set according to the existing theory [16]; specifically, the number of generations for hBOA is upper bounded by n whereas it is upper bounded by $5n$ for all other algorithms. In GA, the probability of applying two-point and uniform crossover is set to $p_c = 0.6$, whereas the probability of flipping each bit in mutation is set to $p_m = 1/n$.

In HC, the only parameter set by the user is the probability of flipping each bit in bit-flip mutation. Here we set the mutation rate to the optimum mutation rate for order-k separable problems provided in [17] as $p_m = k/n$. The HC is ran 10 times and each run is terminated when the global optimum is found.

3.3 Results

Fig. 2 compares the performance of hBOA, GA, UMDA, and HC on random problems with $o = 0$ and $o = 2$. Fig. 3 visualizes the effects of the overlap parameter o on the performance of hBOA, GA, and HC. We omit the results for UMDA because UMDA could solve only smallest problem instances. Fig. 4 shows how the performance of the two best methods (hBOA and GA with uniform crossover) varies across the class of random decomposable problems by showing not only the results for the entire set of 1000 random problems, but also those for the most difficult 50%, 25%, 12.5%, 6.25%, and 3.125% problem instances (the difficulty is measured by the number of evaluations until convergence).

3.4 Discussion

The results indicate a low-order polynomial growth of the number of function evaluations required by hBOA to solve random instances of the proposed class of problems for any value of o; specifically, the number of evaluations can be approximately upper bounded by $O(n^{1.85})$ for $o = 0$, $O(n^{1.92})$ for $o = 1$, and $O(n^{2.02})$ for $o = 2$. The low-order polynomial performance can be observed even if one considers only the most difficult problem instances.

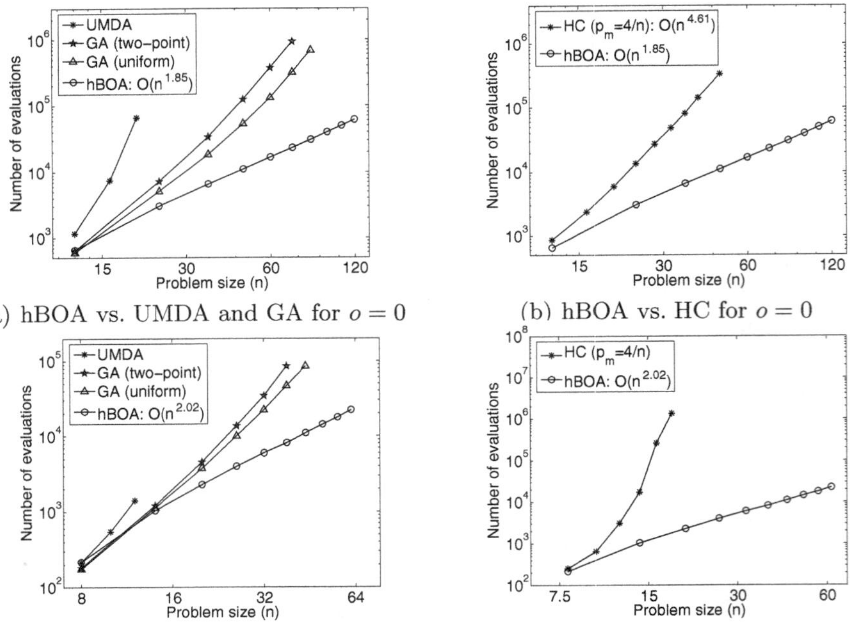

(a) hBOA vs. UMDA and GA for $o = 0$

(b) hBOA vs. HC for $o = 0$

(c) hBOA vs. UMDA and GA for $o = 2$

(d) hBOA vs. HC for $o = 2$

Fig. 2. Comparison on random decomposable problems

On the other hand, the results indicate that GA with standard crossover and mutation operators requires exponential time because it is not capable of combining promising solutions effectively as argued in [18,19] for deceptive problems; the reason for this behavior is that standard recombination operators can effectively combine only short-order, tight schemata [20,21] and this may often be insufficient if the short-order, tight schemata do not lead to the optimum. The performance of hBOA, GA and UMDA gets slightly worse with overlap although all algorithms perform similarly for different values of overlap.

Mutation by itself is also inefficient and its performance is much worse than the performance of hBOA even on separable problems where there is no overlap. Overlap further affects mutation, making this operator work much less efficiently even with the overlap of only $o = 1$; the effects of overlap are much stronger for HC than for the recombination-based methods hBOA, GA and UMDA.

4 Summary and Conclusions

This paper presented a class of random additively decomposable problems (rADPs) with and without overlap. The proposed class of problems differs from other comparable problem classes in several important ways. First of all, unlike in concatenated traps, onemax, and many other artificial decomposable test problems, here each subproblem of a specific problem instance is expected to be unique

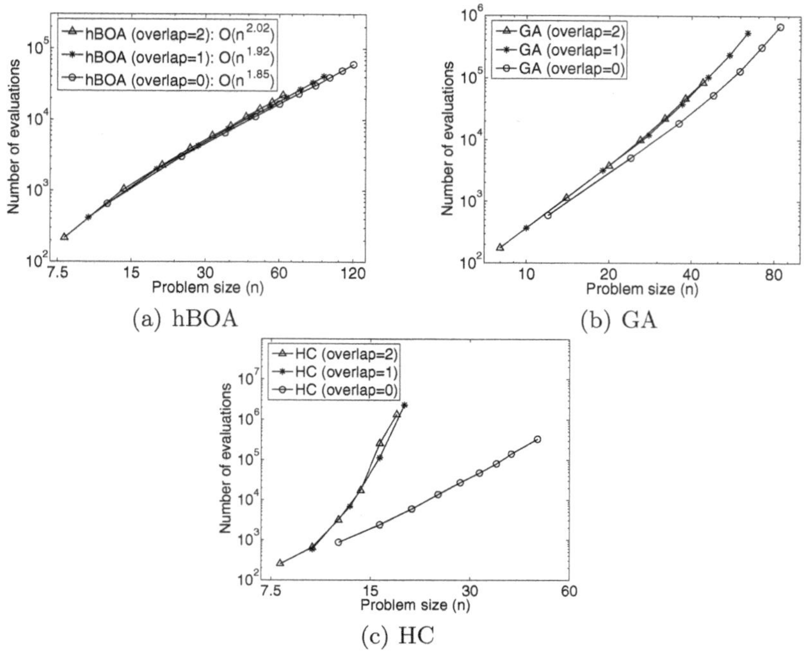

Fig. 3. The effects of overlap on the performance of hBOA, GA, and HC

and both the difficulty of subproblems as well as the signal-to-noise ratio are expected to vary from one subproblem to another. Second, unlike in Ising spin glasses, MAXSAT and many other difficult problems, all problem instances are relatively easy to solve given all problem-specific knowledge or effective variation operators that can automatically identify and exploit problem decomposition. Despite that, the generated problems are still difficult enough to make many standard, ineffective variation operators fail. It is also important that in the proposed class of problems, problem difficulty and the order of interactions between subproblems can be controlled in a straightforward manner. Since it is widely believed that many real-world problems are nearly decomposable and the proposed class of problems covers many potential problems of this form, the proposed class of random problems can be used to provide valuable information about the performance of various optimization algorithms in many real-world problems and to design automated methods for setting algorithm-specific parameters in a robust manner.

The paper applied a number of evolutionary algorithms to random instances of the proposed class of problems. Specifically, the paper considered the hierarchical BOA (hBOA), the genetic algorithm (GA) with standard crossover and mutation operators, the univariate marginal distribution algorithm (UMDA), and the hill climbing (HC) with bit-flip mutation. The results showed that the best performance is achieved with hBOA, which can solve all variants of random decomposable problems with only $O(n^{2.02})$ function evaluations or faster. GA, UMDA and HC perform much worse than hBOA, usually requiring a number of evaluations that appears to grow exponentially fast. The results also provided

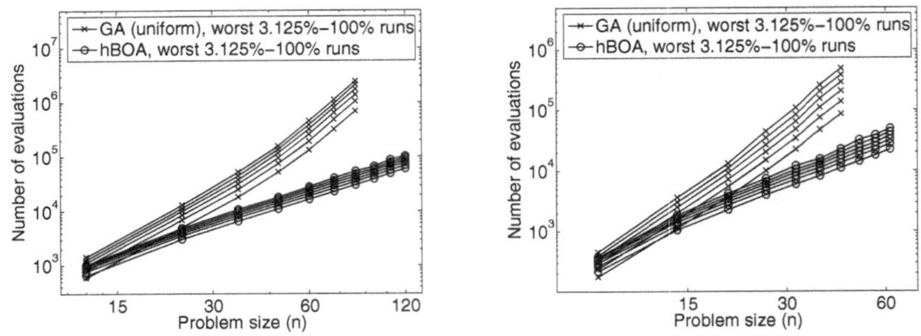

(a) No overlap (b) Overlap $o = 2$

Fig. 4. hBOA on most difficult 100%, 50%, 25%, 12.5%, 6.25%, and 3.125% instances

insight into the sensitivity of recombination and mutation operators to overlap in decomposable problems; specifically, recombination-based methods appear to be much less sensitive to overlap than the methods based on local search operators. Although deception is not enforced for any subproblem, linkage learning remains important. Finally, the difficulty of random decomposable problems does not seem to vary much within the same setting of n, k, and o.

The source code of the proposed problem generator and other related functions in ANSI C is provided online at MEDAL web page, `http://medal.cs.umsl.edu/`.

Acknowledgments. This work was supported by the National Science Foundation under CAREER grant ECS-0547013, ITR grant DMR-03-25939 (at Materials Computation Center, UIUC), and ITR grant DMR-0121695 (at CPSD), by the Air Force Office of Scientific Research, Air Force Materiel Command, USAF, under grant FA9550-06-1-0096, by the Dept. of Energy under grant DEFG02-91ER45439 (at Frederick Seitz MRL), by the European Commission contract No. FP6-511931, and by the University of Missouri in St. Louis through the High Performance Computing Collaboratory sponsored by Information Technology Services, and the Research Award and Research Board programs. Some experiments presented in this work were done using the hBOA software developed by Martin Pelikan and David E. Goldberg at the University of Illinois at Urbana-Champaign.

References

1. Ackley, D.H.: An empirical study of bit vector function optimization. Genetic Algorithms and Simulated Annealing (1987) 170–204
2. Deb, K., Goldberg, D.E.: Analyzing deception in trap functions. IlliGAL Report No. 91009, University of Illinois at Urbana-Champaign, Illinois Genetic Algorithms Laboratory, Urbana, IL (1991)
3. Cheeseman, P., Kanefsky, B., Taylor, W.M.: Where the really hard problems are. Proceedings of the International Joint Conference on Artificial Intelligence (IJCAI-91) (1991) 331–337

4. Santarelli, S., Goldberg, D.E., Yu, T.L.: Optimization of a constrained feed network for an antenna array using simple and competent genetic algorithm techniques. Proceedings of the Workshop Military and Security Application of Evolutionary Computation (MSAEC-2004) (2004)
5. Barahona, F., Maynard, R., Rammal, R., Uhry, J.: Morphology of ground states of a two dimensional frustration model. J. Phys. A **15** (1982) 673
6. Papadimitriou, C.H.: The Euclidean travelling salesman problem is NP-complete. Theoretical Computer Science **4** (1977) 237–244
7. Gao, Y., Culberson, J.: Space complexity of EDA. Evolutionary Computation **13**(1) (2005) 125–143
8. Gao, Y., Culberson, J.: On the treewidth of NK landscapes. Genetic and Evolutionary Computation Conference (GECCO-2003) **II** (2003) 948–954
9. Weinberger, E.D.: Local properties of kauffman's N-k model: A tunably rugged enegy landscape. Physical Review A **44**(10) (1991) 6399–6413
10. Mühlenbein, H., Paaß, G.: From recombination of genes to the estimation of distributions I. Binary parameters. Parallel Problem Solving from Nature (1996) 178–187
11. Pelikan, M., Goldberg, D.E.: Escaping hierarchical traps with competent genetic algorithms. Proceedings of the Genetic and Evolutionary Computation Conference (GECCO-2001) (2001) 511–518 Also IlliGAL Report No. 2000020.
12. Baluja, S.: Population-based incremental learning: A method for integrating genetic search based function optimization and competitive learning. Tech. Rep. No. CMU-CS-94-163, Carnegie Mellon University, Pittsburgh, PA (1994)
13. Pelikan, M., Goldberg, D.E., Lobo, F.: A survey of optimization by building and using probabilistic models. Computational Optimization and Applications **21**(1) (2002) 5–20 Also IlliGAL Report No. 99018.
14. Larrañaga, P., Lozano, J.A., eds.: Estimation of Distribution Algorithms: A New Tool for Evolutionary Computation. Kluwer, Boston, MA (2002)
15. Pelikan, M.: Hierarchical Bayesian optimization algorithm: Toward a new generation of evolutionary algorithms. Springer-Verlag (2005)
16. Thierens, D., Goldberg, D.E., Pereira, A.G.: Domino convergence, drift, and the temporal-salience structure of problems. Proceedings of the International Conference on Evolutionary Computation (ICEC-98) (1998) 535–540
17. Mühlenbein, H.: How genetic algorithms really work: I.Mutation and Hillclimbing. In Männer, R., Manderick, B., eds.: Parallel Problem Solving from Nature, Amsterdam, Netherlands, Elsevier Science (1992) 15–25
18. Thierens, D.: Analysis and design of genetic algorithms. PhD thesis, Katholieke Universiteit Leuven, Leuven, Belgium (1995)
19. Goldberg, D.E.: The design of innovation: Lessons from and for competent genetic algorithms. Volume 7 of Genetic Algorithms and Evolutionary Computation. Kluwer Academic Publishers (2002)
20. Holland, J.H.: Adaptation in natural and artificial systems. University of Michigan Press, Ann Arbor, MI (1975)
21. Goldberg, D.E.: Genetic algorithms in search, optimization, and machine learning. Addison-Wesley, Reading, MA (1989)

Evolving Binary Decision Diagrams with Emergent Variable Orderings

Richard M. Downing

University of Birmingham, Edgbaston, UK
R.M.Downing@cs.bham.ac.uk

Abstract. Binary Decision Diagrams (BDDs) have become the data structure of choice for representing discrete functions in some design and verification applications: They are compact and efficient to manipulate with strong theoretical underpinnings. However, and despite many appealing characteristics, BDDs are not a representation commonly considered for evolutionary computation (EC). The inherent difficulties associated with evolving graphs combined with the variable ordering problem poses a significant challenge which is yet to be overcome. This work addresses this challenge and presents a new approach to evolving BDDs that exhibits good variable orderings as an emergent property.

1 Introduction

The variable ordering problem is prominent in all BDD[1] applications, not just EC. If a good variable ordering can be found the BDD representation of a function will often be simple and efficient to manipulate [3]. However, the variable ordering problem is NP-complete in both optimal and approximate solutions [2,13]. Furthermore, Krause [9] has argued theoretically that synthesising even an approximating function in the BDD representation is hard, and further suggested that the variable ordering must be optimised during the synthesis procedure.

The EA presented here optimises the variable ordering alongside function. It is elegant in its construction and can exhibit near optimal orderings as an emergent property. Most of the previous approaches to evolving BDDs have employed only a static variable ordering and have therefore been limited to functions for which a good variable ordering is known in advance [15,12,6,14,4]. For most practical applications, however, good variable orderings cannot be known in advance so the variable ordering must be optimised along with functional fitness. Only Droste [7] has addressed this previously with a distributed hybrid approach, combining his earlier BDD-based GP with existing heuristics for variable reordering.

The important aspects of BDDs are reviewed in section 2, and the algorithm for evolving them introduced in section 3. The relationship between evolvability and variable ordering is then investigated, and it is shown in section 4 that better variable orderings are associated with greater evolvability. That result is then used in section 5 to account for the emergence of good variable orderings demonstrated therein.

[1] The term BDD is used here as the generic sense; there are many variants.

T.P. Runarsson et al. (Eds.): PPSN IX, LNCS 4193, pp. 798–807, 2006.

2 Binary Decision Diagrams

BDDs [1,10] are similar in principle to the more familiar decision tree, and can be considered a generalisation of binary decision trees. A BDD is a rooted directed acyclic graph representing a function of the form $f(V) : \mathbb{B}^n \longrightarrow \mathbb{B}$. Each non-terminal is labelled with a Boolean variable $v \in V$ and has a *then* child and an *else* child, reflecting the fact that each non-terminal represents an *if-then-else* operation on v. Terminals are labelled from $\mathbb{B}$. Given an assignment of values for V, the output is determined by traversing the BDD from the root to a terminal following the child indicated by each vertice's variable label value.

An *ordered* BDD (OBDD) [3] imposes a total ordering on the appearance of non-terminal labels along any path with π, the variable ordering. Thus, $\pi = [v_1, v_2, \ldots, v_n]$, an ordered list of variables, and $i < j$ must hold for each v_i followed by v_j along any path. It is not necessary that all $v \in \pi$ appear in a path. In this paper the notation $[v_1, v_2, \ldots, v_n]$-OBDD is used to specify the ordering associated associate with an OBDD, or simply π-OBDD to emphasise the significance of the ordering without specifying it.

Redundancy in an OBDD can be removed in two ways:

1. **Remove redundant tests.** A nonterminal α that has both outgoing edges pointing to the same vertex β is redundant. Redirect all α's incoming edges to β.
2. **Remove duplicate vertices.** If nonterminals α and β have identical sub-structure and variable label, then β can be removed with its incoming edges redirected to α.

A *reduced* OBDD (ROBDD) is an OBDD that cannot have its complexity reduced further by the reductions described above. Bryant [3] has shown ROBDDs to be *canonical forms*; meaning that each function has a unique ROBDD representation for any given π, allowing easy equivalence and satisfiability checking.

It is OBDDs and ROBDDs that are of most practical use. In section 5, the space of all OBDDs for all π are taken as the genotype space. The redundancy of having many OBDD equivalent representations has been found to enhance the search [4,5] through the neutrality concept [8]. In section 4, subspaces of genotype space, restricted by categories of π, will also be used.

The variable ordering, π, can have a dramatic impact on the *complexity* of resulting π-ROBDD: In this paper, the complexity of an π-(R)OBDD is the number of nonterminals it contains. For example, figure 1 shows the effect of reversing π for the 6-bit multiplexer problem. For the n-bit multiplexer, the complexity of ROBDD is known to grow linearly for the best π and exponentially for the worst. Furthermore, as n increases, the fraction of π leading to ROBDDs exponential in complexity is said to converge to 1 [7]. While some functions are insensitive to the π in this respect, many are expected to have similar properties to the multiplexer. Thus, for applications employing ROBDDs, the problem of finding a good π is of crucial significance.

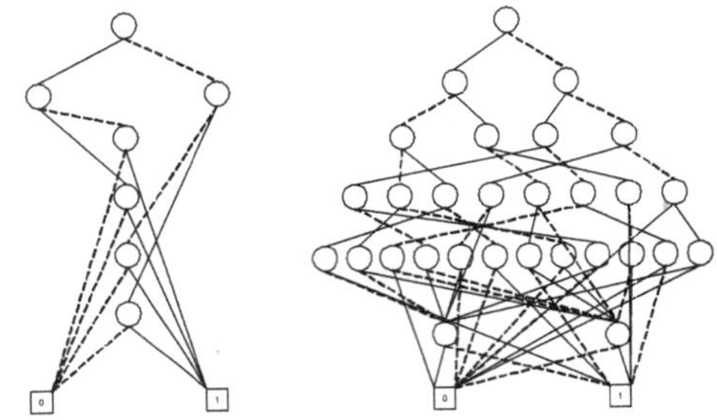

Fig. 1. The influence of variable ordering on ROBDD complexity. The two ROBDDs represent the 6-bit multiplexer function. The ROBDD on the left has ordering $[0, 1, 2, 3, 4, 5]$ (control bits = 0,1), the one on right has the reverse ordering, $[5, 4, 3, 2, 1, 0]$.

All heuristic approaches to dynamic variable ordering are built on the procedure for swapping adjacent variables without affecting function; see [11] for an efficient implementation method. Variable swapping has complexity proportional to the number of nodes associated with the two adjacent variables, so can generally be done in reasonable time.

3 Evolving BDDS Using Implicit Neutrality

The EA for evolving BDDs is now introduced. It is derived and extended from that introduced in the paper entitled *Evolving Binary Decision Diagrams using Implicit Neutrality* [4]. The highly significant extension introduced here is that of dynamic variable ordering. From hereon this EA will be referred to by the acronym EBDDIN after the title of the paper that introduced it and in recognition of the underlying principle evident in the approach. This principle is that of exploiting the neutrality implicit in the OBDD representation, and is thus differentiated from methods typically employed for introducing neutrality through the absence of any explicit mapping from one representation to another. Exploiting this implicit neutrality offers considerable inherent benefits within the context of OBDDs [4,5].

The following atomic mutations are defined, five explicitly neutral and one functionally modifying. The neutral atomic mutations are derived from established OBDD theory; the functionally modifying atomic mutation is a natural and intuitive one for any graph-based representation.

Definition 1. *Let* **N1** *be the neutral mutation of removing a redundant test.*

Definition 2. *Let* **N1′** *be the neutral mutation of inserting a redundant test, the inverse of* **N1**.

Definition 3. *Let* **N2** *be the neutral mutation of removing a redundant non-terminal (merging two equivalent non-terminals).*

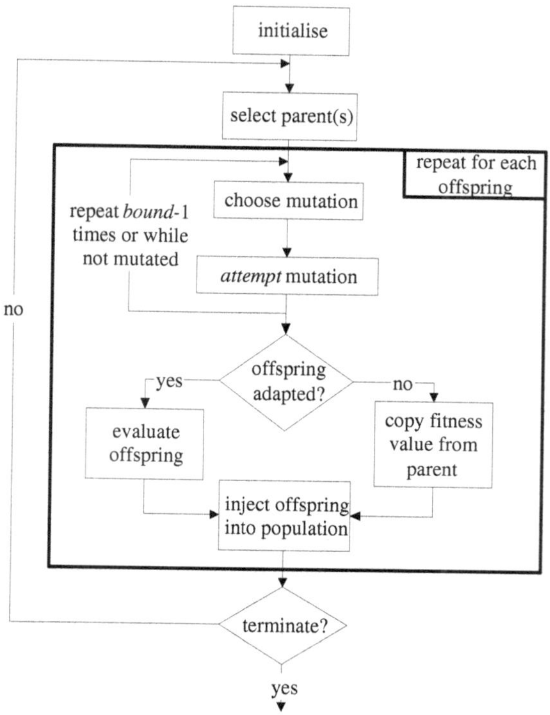

Fig. 2. Algorithm flowchart. The *bound* (mutation bound) parameter is an integer specifying the number of attempts at choosing and applying an atomic mutation. If the selected vertex (or vertices) is not amenable to the chosen mutation operation, the mutation attempt is deemed a failure. If all 'bound' mutation attempts are either failures or are neutral, the fitness value can be copied over from the parent.

Definition 4. *Let* **N2′** *be the neutral mutation of inserting a redundant non-terminal, the inverse of* **N2** *(splitting).*

Definition 5. *Let* **N3** *be the neutral mutation of swapping adjacent variables while maintaining overall function.*

Definition 6. *Let* **A1** *be the 'potentially' adaptive (or functionally modifying) mutation of changing one of the children of a non-terminal, to another vertex, potentially orphaning a sub-graph.*

The general structure of the breeding algorithm is depicted in figure 2. The choice of selection scheme is somewhat arbitrary: Tournament selection and both $(\mu + \lambda)$ and (μ, λ) ES schemes have all been found to work well in practice. The atomic mutations are applied to randomly selected vertices or variables in a way that respects the requirement of total variable ordering demanded for all paths through an OBDD. The mutations are atomic in the sense that they are each considered minimal changes. More severe changes are achieved by stringing together atomic mutations, the maximum number of which is specified by the *bound* parameter.[2] In practice, about one quarter of all mutation attempts fail, so the actual number of atomic changes between parent and offspring genotype lies somewhere between 1 and the bound inclusive when clones are prohibited.

There are many BDD packages available but they are typically restricted to working with OBDDs in their reduced form only, and not amenable to the methods described herein. For this reason the author's own experimental OBDD implementation package was employed for all experiments described in this paper. However, only implementation independent performance measures are used in the evaluation of these experiments.

4 Evolvability and Variable Ordering

The aim of this section is to establish the relationship between evolvability and the ROBDD complexities induced by π. The complexity of ROBDD induced by a given π for a given problem is referred to in this paper as the *Implied Solution Complexity* (ISC) of π, or of an π-(R)OBDD. For example, the ISC of $\pi = [0, 1, 2, 3, 4, 5]$ for the 6-bit multiplexer problem (6-mux) is 7; this is the number of nonterminals in the $[0, 1, 2, 3, 4, 5]$-ROBDD solution to 6-mux (see figure 1): The reverse ordering has an ISC of 29. Similarly, any $[0, 1, 2, 3, 4, 5]$-(R)OBDD has an ISC of 7 for 6-mux, regardless of its actual fitness for 6-mux.

So, the objective here is to investigate how differing π, categorised by their ISC values, influence evolvability. To achieve this, the algorithm is run *without* dynamic variable ordering (i.e., no N3 mutations) for selected ISC categories. The Average Evaluations to a Solution (AES) performance measure is then taken as an indication of the degree of evolvability associated with each ISC category. The actual π under each ISC category are generated randomly. The results are plotted in figure 3. As can be seen clearly, for all problems tested, the trend associated with increasing ISC is increasing AES (poorer evolvability). Furthermore, the trend of increasing AES is greater than linear in ISC, and appears to be approaching exponential. What is concluded from these results is that better π, that is, π having lower ISC values, are associated with much greater evolvability.

Knowing that evolvability is associated with low ISC values, however, appears of little use if there is no prior knowledge about which π have low ISC values. For functions such as the multiplexer and adder, optimal π are well-known so a good π can be fixed in advance of running the EA. However, in general, it is not possible to tell in advance which π have low ISC.

5 Emergence and Variable Ordering

In this section it is argued that good π are an emergent property of the extended EBDDIN with dynamic variable ordering. What is meant by 'emergence' in this

[2] In [4] the *bound* parameter was referred to as *rate*, but is changed here due to potential ambiguity with per-gene mutation that is specified with a probability.

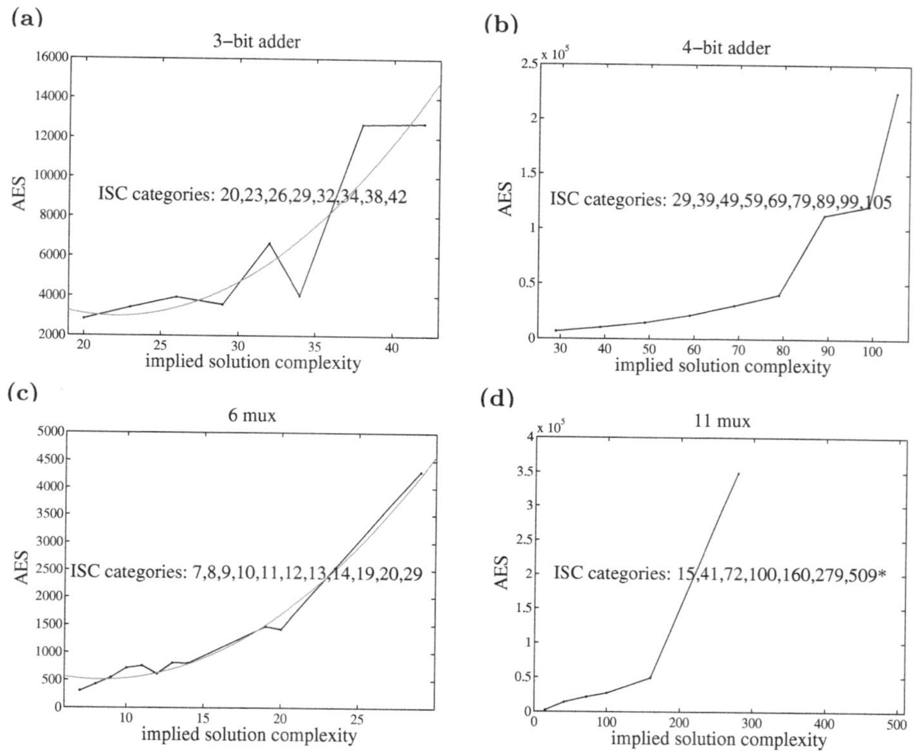

Fig. 3. Evolvability comparison of variable orderings for selected problems. Variable orderings are categorised by their ISC value and sample categories selected to span the entire range for each problem. 100 runs are perfomed for each ISC category. All four graphs exhibit the trend of rapidly increasing AES against increasing ISC value.
* In (d) no AES value could be obtained for 509 due to to the extremely poor evolvability of this category.

respect is that there is no explicitly introduced incentive in EBDDIN for inducing individuals with below average ISC value. That is, there is no aspect of the fitness function, secondary size-related fitness objective, or mutation-related incentive that explicitly encourages propagation of π with low ISC. Indeed, only the N3 mutation, the swapping of adjacent variables, can influence ISC directly, and the location point for N3 in the genotype is always chosen randomly by variable. Good π arise solely as the logical consequence of being associated with subspaces of genotype space that are more evolvable. That is, individuals possessing π with lower ISC values propagate more readily due to the fact that they are more likely to produce fitter offspring.

The problems investigated here are the 11-mux (11 inputs, 1 output), 20-mux (20 inputs, 1 ouput) and the 4-bit adder with carry out (8 inputs, 5 outputs). The fitness functions employed on both problems are negated counts of erroneous output bits, so maximum fitness = 0. Optimal ISC is 15, 32 and 29 respectively, and

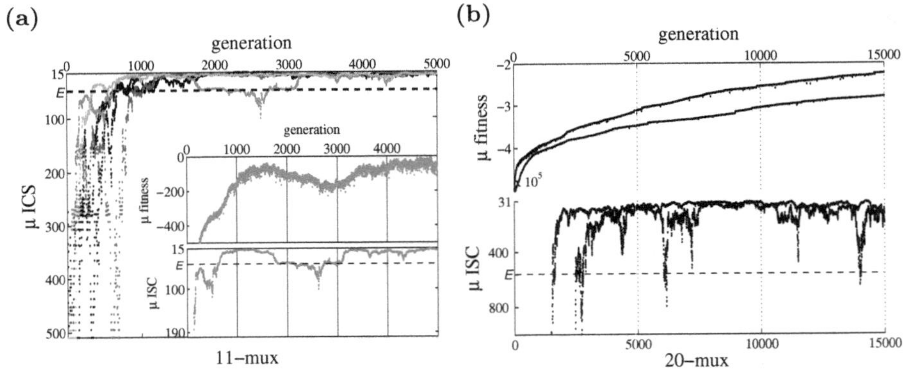

Fig. 4. The emergence of good π. The population mean (μ) ISC and fitness values are plotted. The population is initialised to random OBDDs having worst π. (a) The main figure shows ISC values for five independent runs on 11-mux. Inset: the single run that undergoes temporary ISC relapse is shown below fitness as an indication of the correlation between ISC and fitness. Within 1000 generations all runs pass expected ISC, E, and stabilise near the optimal of 15. (b) Two runs are shown for 20-mux with fitness alongside ISC. Both runs approach optimal ISC, and remain fairly stable there, while fitness remains in the very early stages of optimisation.

worst ISC is 509, 131,069 and 105 respectively; expected ISC, E, established by frequency sampling, is approximately 49, 564, 72 respectively. A $(10, 16)$ ES is employed for the mux-n problems, and a $(15, 50)$ ES for the adder, so no parents are carried to subsequent generations; no clones are bred either.[3] A mutation bound of 1, the minimal, is used for all experiments, as this has been found likely to be the most favourable [5]. The populations are initialised to worst π for mux-n, and randomly for the adder. The results are shown in figures 4 and 5: Note that the vertical scales for ISC are inverted so that correlation with fitness is more easily interpreted, and ISC may be plotted only within the range of primary interest. An interpretation of the results is presented in the remainder of this section.

For both mux problems (figure 4), expected ISC is exceeded, and near optimal ISC reached, early on in each run. It is near the optimal where ISC appears most stable. However, there are periods where ISC undergoes temporary relapse, but is soon recovered. In the inset of figure 4(a) this can be seen in more detail, a correlation between ISC and fitness apparent. An increase in ISC appears to be followed by a drop in fitness or slowing in fitness increase, while a drop in ISC appears to be followed by an increase in fitness or rate of increase. While a drop in ISC is accounted for by inherent selection for evolvability, the converse, an increase in ISC (drop in evolvability), can only be the result of random genetic drift, where mutants with high fitness but high ISC (low evolvability) saturate the population temporarily; this behaviour is not unexpected in a small population. In addition, for 20-mux, it can be seen that the near optimal ISC is

[3] These parameters are not optimised.

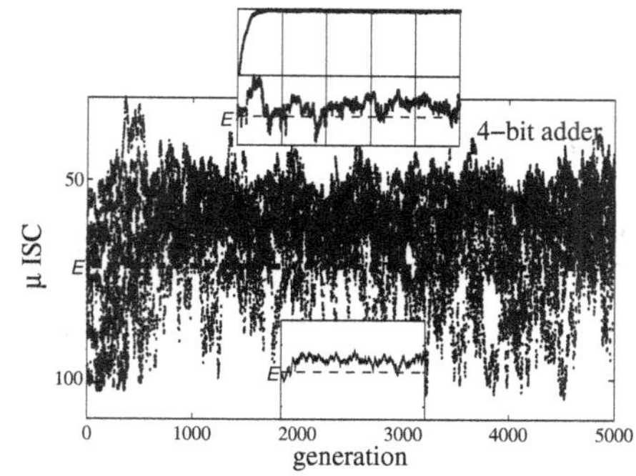

Fig. 5. 10 runs on the 4-bit adder problem are shown with population initialised to random π. The top inset shows the a single run as ISC below fitness, and a less prominent correlation than for 11-mux. The bottom inset shows the average of all runs. ISC exceeds the expected and stabilises within 1000 generations, but the gain is, respectively, more modest than for 11-mux.

reached long before fitness is optimised, the population genotype appearing to forge itself into one most evolvable for the fitness function.

The results for the adder also exhibit the emergence of π with better than expected ISC (figure 5). The population is this time initialised to random π rather than worst. While better than expected ISC is reached in around 500 generations, ISC appears to remain erratic within a wide range of values whose average is a long way off the optimal of 29, but better than the expected of 72. One run (top inset) does approach the optimal ISC early on, but this is quickly lost and never recovered like it was in for 11-mux. However, in contrast to the single run shown for 11-mux, optimal fitness is maintained during this loss evolvability: This is perhaps accountable, in part, to the larger population which counters the loss of parents in subsequent populations.

The apparent difference in the emergence of low ISC π between mux and the adder problem is now discussed. The terrain of ISC values under the N3 mutation is likely to be significant here. Both mux and adder problems are known to have many local optima under direct ISC optimisation using N3. However, the fact that the objective of the fitness function used here is optimised function, not optimised ISC, allows genetic drift to move the search away from the trappings of what would otherwise be ISC local optima. To give an indication of the comparative ISC terrain, optimal ISC were perturbed for 11-mux and the 4-bit adder, and the corresponding increases in ISC recorded. The results are shown in Table 1. 11-mux is clearly much more robust to perturbations than 4-bit adder, which suggests a much smoother ISC terrain for the former. The range of ISC values is 15-509 and 29-105 respectively, which enhances confidence in this conclusion. The frequences of ISC values may also be a factor. Thus, for the adder, the population appears to become ISC-localised due to rugged ISC terrain, which is difficult to navigate under the present scheme. A wider range of range of operators for variable reordering may help smooth the ISC terrain, but this has not been tested.

Table 1. ISC robustness to N3 perturbations. The column headers indicate the number of successive perturbations applied to a π with optimal ISC. The values below reflect the corresponding increase in ISC for the two problems, averaged of 1000.

# perturbations	1	5	10	15
11-mux	0.0960	0.4860	1.0350	1.4980
4-bit adder	3.0960	11.3100	17.9850	22.7310

6 Conclusion

The extended EBDDIN with dynamic variable ordering offers a straightforward approach to BDD synthesis where good variable orderings are not known in advance. Near optimal variable orderings can emerge due to the fact that they induce a greater capacity to evolve under this approach: This readily observable property demonstrates the evolution of evolvability, a property which is of significant interest to the EC community. Applications for the synthesis of BDDs representing both fully and incompletely specified functions are expected to benefit, as is the study of evolvability and its emergence.

More work needs to be done before EBDDIN, and BDDs in general, find favour within the EC community. However, in this and previous work, some of the potential has begun to be uncovered.

Acknowledgements. Ata Kaban, Peter Hancox and Stefan Droste.

References

1. Sheldon B. Akers. Binary Decision Diagrams. *IEEE Transactions on Computers*, C-27(6):509–516, June 1978.
2. B. Bollig and I. Wegener. Improving the variable ordering of OBDDs is NP-complete. *IEEE Transactions on Computers*, 45(9):993–1002, 1996.
3. Randall E. Bryant. Symbolic boolean manipulation with ordered binary-decision diagrams. *ACM Computing Surveys*, 24(3):293–318, September 1992.
4. Richard M. Downing. Evolving Binary Decision Diagrams using implicit neutrality. In David Corne, Zbigniew Michalewicz, Marco Dorigo, Gusz Eiben, David Fogel, Carlos Fonseca, Garrison Greenwood, Tan Kay Chen, Guenther Raidl, Ali Zalzala, Simon Lucas, Ben Paechter, Jennifier Willies, Juan J. Merelo Guervos, Eugene Eberbach, Bob McKay, Alastair Channon, Ashutosh Tiwari, L. Gwenn Volkert, Dan Ashlock, and Marc Schoenauer, editors, *Proceedings of the 2005 IEEE Congress on Evolutionary Computation*, volume 3, pages 2107–2113, Edinburgh, UK, 2-5 September 2005. IEEE Press.
5. Richard M. Downing. Neutrality and gradualism: encouraging exploration and exploitation simultaneously with Binary Decision Diagrams. In *(to appear in) Proceedings of the 2006 IEEE Congress on Evolutionary Computation*, Vancouver, Canada, 2006.

6. Stefan Droste. Efficient genetic programming for finding good generalizing boolean functions. In John R. Koza, Kalyanmoy Deb, Marco Dorigo, David B. Fogel, Max Garzon, Hitoshi Iba, and Rick L. Riolo, editors, *Genetic Programming 1997: Proceedings of the Second Annual Conference*, pages 82–87, Stanford University, CA, USA, 13-16 July 1997. Morgan Kaufmann.
7. Stefan Droste, Dominic Heutelbeck, and Ingo Wegener. Distributed hybrid genetic programming for learning boolean functions. In Marc Schoenauer, Kalyanmoy Deb, Günter Rudolph, Xin Yao, Evelyne Lutton, Juan Julian Merelo, and Hans-Paul Schwefel, editors, *Parallel Problem Solving from Nature - PPSN VI 6th International Conference*, volume 1917 of *LNCS*, pages 181–190, Paris, France, 16-20 September 2000. Springer Verlag.
8. Motoo Kimura. *The neutral theory of molecular evolution.* Cambridge University Press, 1983.
9. Matthias Krause, Petr Savický, and Ingo Wegener. Approximations by OBDDs and the variable ordering problem. In *Proc. 26th International Colloquium on Automata, Languages and Programming (ICALP)*, volume 1644 of *LNCS*, pages 493–502, 1999.
10. C.Y. Lee. Representation of Switching Circuits by Binary-Decision Programs. *Bell Systems Technical Journal*, 38:985–999, July 1959.
11. R. Rudell. Dynamic variable ordering for ordered binary decision diagrams. In *Proceedings of the International Conference on CAD (ICCAD)*, pages 42–47, 1993.
12. Hidenori Sakanashi, Tetsuya Higuchi, Hitoshi Iba, and Yukinori Kakazu. Evolution of binary decision diagrams for digital circuit design using genetic programming. In *International Conference on Evolvable Systems*, pages 470–481, 1996.
13. D. Sieling. On the existence of polynomial time approximation schemes for OBDD-Minimization. *LNCS*, 1373:205–215, 1998.
14. P. van Remortel, T. Lenaerts, and B. Manderick. pages 249–254, Pasadena, California, 19-21 July. Jet Propulsion Laboratory, California Institute of Technology, IEEE Computer Society.
15. Masayuki Yanagiya. Efficient genetic programming based on binary decision diagrams. In *1995 IEEE Conference on Evolutionary Computation*, volume 1, pages 234–239, Perth, 29 November - 1 December 1995. IEEE Press.

Life History Evolution of Virtual Plants: Trading Off Between Growth and Reproduction

Stefan Bornhofen and Claude Lattaud

Laboratoire d'Intelligence Artificielle de Paris 5
LIAP5 - CRIP5, Université de Paris 5
45, rue des Saints-Pères
75006 Paris, France

Abstract. This paper presents studies on the life history evolution of plants carried out by experimenting with a multi-agent platform of generic virtual plants. The conducted simulations address the trade-off between resource allocation to vegetative and reproductive structures. The trade-off is pointed out by evolutionary runs selecting for one of the two traits. It is further shown that the introduction of an age at maturity is an effective measure to enhance both life history traits. A third series of experiments highlights that competition in plant communities has an impact on the trade-off. Depending on the competitive pressure, plants evolve more investment of resources into growth than into reproduction. The results corroborate some hypotheses of life history theory.

1 Introduction

Life history is a term that refers to the pattern of survival, growth and reproduction exhibited by an organism [1]. One major challenge of life history theory is to study the variation in traits such as growth rate, age and size at maturity, reproductive effort, number and size of offspring and life span observed in nature, and to explain them as evolutionary adaptations to environmental conditions [20]. A fundamental component of the theory is the concept of trade-offs. Its framework is expressed in the "principle of allocation" which states that resources can only be allocated to one life history function and that investment in one activity is at the expense of the others [2]. As an example related to this paper, reproductive allocation reduces survival and growth rate and therefore is likely to decrease future reproduction. Understanding trade-offs is a key point in life history theory which, according to the evolutionary ecologists Stephen Stearns, like "no other field brings you closer to the underlying simplicities that unite and explain the diversity of living things and complexities of their life cycles." [20]. However, Stearns recently stated that "we have a lot of evidence that trade-offs exist; we have very little understanding of the mechanisms that cause them" [21].

Hypotheses relating to evolution are often difficult to verify due to its slow pace. This is why, for validation and analysis, mathematical models have been formulated [17]. Yet the computational power of modern computers offers the possibility to conceive individual based models and test evolutionary hypotheses

T.P. Runarsson et al. (Eds.): PPSN IX, LNCS 4193, pp. 808–817, 2006.

by simulating corresponding processes in silico [14]. For plants and their communities, there exists a large number of computer models, but they are most often specifically adapted to represent given plant species or plant community scenarios and not intended for evolutionary dynamics. This paper introduces a model of generic virtual plants designed for the study of plant evolution. The conducted experiments address the life history trade-off between resource allocation to vegetative and reproductive structures, and reveal age at maturity and competition to be two influential elements.

The next section gives an overview of the state of the art in the modeling of plants. In section three the virtual plant model and its simulation platform are presented. The conducted experiments are described and discussed in section four. Section five concludes the paper with reflections on the approach.

2 State of the Art

The origins of the computer modeling of plants can be traced back to the 1960s, when Ulam simulated the development of branching patterns using cellular automata [24]. Since then a huge amount of work has been devoted to this research field. As study objectives can differ from one plant model to another, there exists a variety of approaches. According to the traditional classification suggested by Kurth [10], physiological and morphological models can be distinguished.

Physiological models, also called process-based models, reflect metabolic activities inside a plant. Their architectural structure remains low detailed, as the individual plant is merely decomposed into a fixed number of compartments such as root, stem and crown, exchanging substances in terms of mass variables. The attention is primarily turned to carbon balance, due to its importance for plant growth, by modeling photosynthesis, carbon allocation and respiration. However other influential substances such as soil nutrients can equally be taken into account. Because of their manageable architecture and their small number of parameters, physiological models are convenient for plant representations on a rather coarse scale [11].

Morphological models describe plant architecture by making use of its modular structure. They consider the plant as a composition of repeated modules like leaf, fruit or fine root which dynamically appear and disappear during the plant development according to a number of growth rules. Probably the most widely used representation of plant morphology is the L-system formalism [16]. L-systems are formal grammars with the possibility of recursive applications in a parallel rewriting process. Starting from an initial axiom ω , a set of rules P is iteratively applied in order to form a string of characters from an alphabet A. The string represents the plant, whereas each character represents an elementary module. Positional information of the modules can be integrated by using a bracketed notation. The translation of the string into a geometric structure is achieved by graphical interpretation using turtle geometry [16]. Figure 1 illustrates a sample L-system and the resulting plant after several iterations.

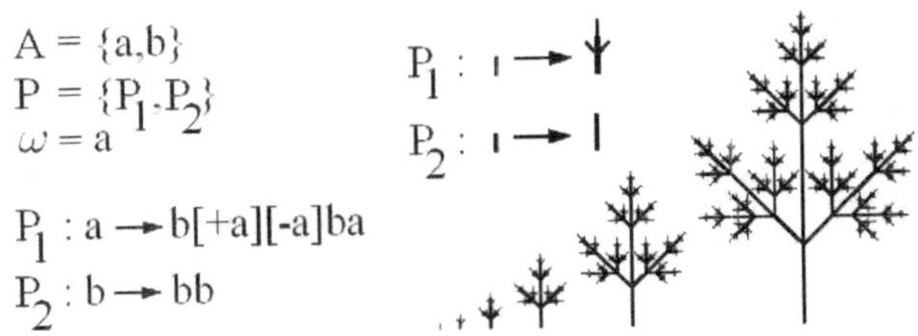

Fig. 1. Example of an L-system

Morphological and physiological processes of plant development are profoundly interwoven [12], and in the last decade many models emerged as the coupling of both aspects. They typically depict a 3D description of the plant where the organs interact with local environmental conditions and with one another according to the plant topology. Because of their complete picture of plant development, these models are also termed "virtual plants" [18]. Plant communities can be represented as a number of virtual plants which develop concurrently in a multi-agent approach [5]. Interaction results from the modifications that each individual contributes to the physical environment. In particular, the available resources become an object of competition between neighboring plants.

3 The Plant Model

The following section presents a model for the study of evolutionary dynamics in plant communities. Based on a simple concept of generic virtual plants, it is able to carry out simulations of evolving plant communities while emphasizing the most important morphological and physiological aspects of a single plant. Thus individual responses to resource disposition and other environmental constraints can be observed.

3.1 The Environment

The physical environment is a continuous 3D space composed of the soil and the sky, homogeneously divided into a number of voxels each of which holds local environmental information. Light and minerals are resources of prime importance for the growth of natural plants [25]. The sky voxels provide light which is captured by the leaves in order to produce carbon via photosynthesis. If an object is situated aboveground, it casts shadows. In such case, the light intensity of all sky voxels following the angle of incidence is decreased. Soil voxels contain minerals which are assimilated by the fine roots. Diffusion, a passive movement from regions of high concentration to regions of low concentration, leads to mineral balance between neighboring voxels. All the assimilated minerals of a virtual plant are eventually redeposited in the soil so that their total amount within the environment is constant. The minerals of dead roots are put in the corresponding soil voxels and those of the aerial compartment in a mold layer which gradually penetrates the upmost soil layer.

3.2 The Virtual Plant

A virtual plant is divided into an aboveground and belowground component called shoot and root respectively. Their morphologies are each expressed by an L-system whose alphabet is detailed in figure 2. The geometric shape of the plant modules is based on sphyls (cylinders with spherical ends). In the scope of this paper, only deterministic context free L-systems, also called D0L-systems [16], are applied. The predecessor character of the first rule is A, of the second rule B and so on. The shoot and root morphologies of a virtual plant seedling both start with the single non-terminal character A. A small amount of initially available biomass allows the young plant to develop its first modules, but subsequently it has to rely on the acquisition of resources.

The physiological processes of a plant are based on a two-substrate version of the transport-resistance model [22]. Shoot and root hold separate substrate pools for carbon and minerals. Photosynthesis charges the shoot carbon pool, and root assimilation supplies the root mineral pool. Growth occurs through the conversion of carbon and minerals into biomass, deducting a certain loss to litter. The exchange between the carbon and mineral pools is represented as a function of substrate concentration difference divided by a resistance. Thornley suggested that all physiological models of plant development should start with this irreducible framework [23].

Produced biomass is distributed to the apexes and, in the shoot, reproductive modules according to a sink strength. Once an apex reaches the required cost for the production of a successor string, the appropriate production rule is applied. When a reproductive module attains a specified biomass, a seed is dispersed in the neighborhood of the plant. After a limited span of life the plant dies and its resources are restored to the environment.

Character	Compartment	Geometry	Function
l	shoot	sphyl	captures virtual light to photosynthesize carbon
f	shoot	sphere	reproductive module producing seeds
b	shoot	sphyl	creates a branching structure
r	root	sphyl	assimilates nutrients in the soil
c	root	sphyl	creates a branching structure
A ... Z	shoot/root	none	represent predecessors of the production rules
[,]	shoot/root	none	indicate a ramification
+ - < > $ &	shoot/root	none	represent 3D rotations by fixed angles

Fig. 2. The L-system alphabet

```
Shoot chromosome                      Transport-           Root chromosome
growth = 10.00                        resistance           growth = 10.00
litter = 0.00                         parameters           litter = 0.00
assimilation = 1.00                                        assimilation = 1.00
inhibition = 100.00                   Additional           inhibition = 100.00
...                                   physiological        ...
maxAge = 30.00                        parameters           maxAge = 30.00
durationBloom = 0.00                                       ...
biomassSeed = 1.00                    L-system             rotateX = 0.3925
...                                   parameters and       rotateY = 0.3925
rotateX = 0.3925                      production rules     rotateZ = 0.3925
rotateY = 0.3925                                           lRule = (A,[<c[B]$$A][[B]$$A])
rotateZ = 0.3925                                           lRule = (B,>r)
lRule = (A,[>b[B]A]$$$$$[>b[B]A]$$$$$$[>b[B]A])
lRule = (B,>>l)
```

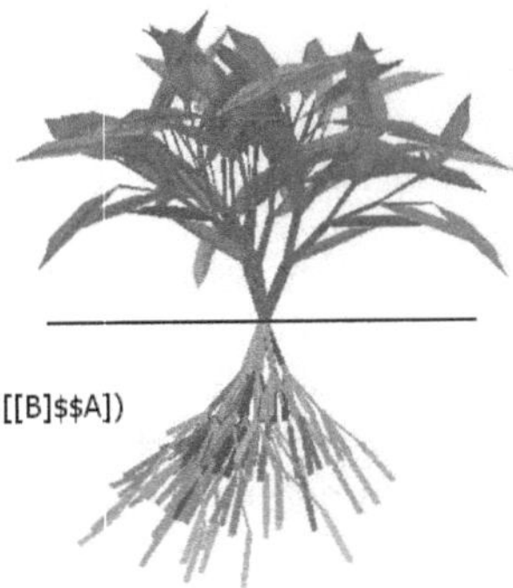

Fig. 3. Sample shoot and root genotypes of a bush

3.3 The Genotype

The development of the virtual plants is ruled by a set of "genetic information" recorded in a genotype. It contains the variables of the transport-resistance model such as growth and litter rates or resource assimilation and inhibition, as well as twelve additional real-valued physiological parameters like age limit, duration of bloom and seed biomass. Moreover, it specifies the parameters and production rules of the root and shoot L-systems. Figure 3 displays a portion of this genotype for a simple bush. Depending on the object of the study, some of its elements may be fixed and others subjected to evolution. For the purpose of investigating the allocation to reproductive and vegetative structures, the evolving elements in the genotype are limited to the L-system production rules. Evolution may affect the trade-off between the two life history traits by insertion and deletion of reproductive (f) and vegetative modules ($l, b, A, B, ...$) in the production rules of the shoot L-system. All other parameters are predefined and fixed in order not to obscure the results by too large a genetic search space. Mutations are introduced by several genetic operators each of which is associated with a probability. They are chosen such that any set of production rules can be constructed by evolution. The three operators

- Delete rule (a rule of the L-system is deleted)
- Insert rule (an empty rule is appended)
- Duplicate rule (a rule is duplicated and appended)

modify the number of rules. Five other operators act on the successor strings. Only minor changes, i.e. character by character, are possible between successive generations. For example, if the production $A \rightarrow blfA$ is selected to be mutated, some of the possible mutations are

- Delete character (a character is deleted): $A \rightarrow blf$
- Insert character (a character is inserted): $A \rightarrow b\&lfA$
- Permute character (two adjacent characters are switched): $A \rightarrow bflA$
- Duplicate character (a character is duplicated): $A \rightarrow blffA$
- Mutate character (a character is replaced by a new one): $A \rightarrow b[A]fA$

4 Results

The model of section three has been implemented as a simulation platform. It is developed in C++ and uses the OGRE library [15] for graphical representations. This section presents the results of three different sets of experiments, aiming at the identification of evolutionary mechanisms in the life history trade-off between allocation to reproductive and vegetative structures.

4.1 Experimental Setup

In every experiment, virtual plants are evolved by a typical evolutionary algorithm [9]. A run starts with an initial population of genotypes with the minimal production rules $A \rightarrow l$ and $A \rightarrow r$. In the phase of development the genotypes are translated into a population of phenotypes. To do so, a seed of each genotype is placed in a sufficiently large environment and grown for a fixed amount of time. Selection then chooses a proportion of individuals by measuring the phenotypes in terms of a predefined notion of fitness. The selected individuals survive and give birth to the next generation of mutated genotypes. In the literature, there exist various selection methods for evolutionary algorithms. The tournament selection applied here is inspired by competition in nature and arranges "tournaments" to compare the fitness between a few randomly chosen individuals [6]. The best performing individual of every tournament is retained. This approach additionally offers the advantage to easily adjust selection pressure by changing the tournament size.

The probability of each genetic operator is defined as 0.1. This value may be overrated compared to natural evolution, but has been chosen to accelerate the process. The populations are typically composed of 40 plants grown for 30 time units. Survival ratio is set to $\frac{1}{4}$ and tournament size to 10 individuals. This setup was determined experimentally and turned out to produce conclusive results in a reasonable amount of time. A run over 500 generations would take about two hours on a modern PC.

4.2 Revealing the Trade-Off

The first experiment is intended to point out the trade-off between allocation to reproductive and vegetative structures. A straightforward method to show an evolutionary trade-off is the comparison between breedings with selection for one of the two considered traits. Therefore, two series of evolutionary runs were conducted. In the first twenty runs, the virtual plants were selected for reproductive output, defined as the overall produced seed biomass during their lifetime [19]. In the second twenty runs, the individuals were bred for their amount of vegetative biomass at the end of the simulation.

The performance of the evolved plants with respect to both life history traits is shown in figure 4. Depending on the course of evolution, the runs result in different local fitness maxima. The plants selected for seed biomass only grow to a fraction of size of those selected for vegetative biomass. Reproduction is not

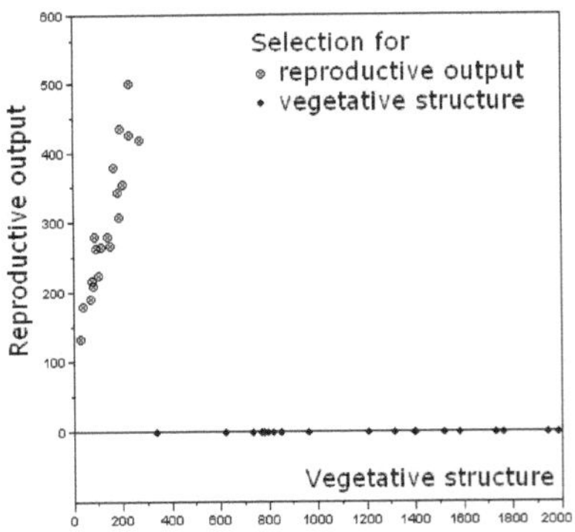

Fig. 4. Selection for reproductive and vegetative structure

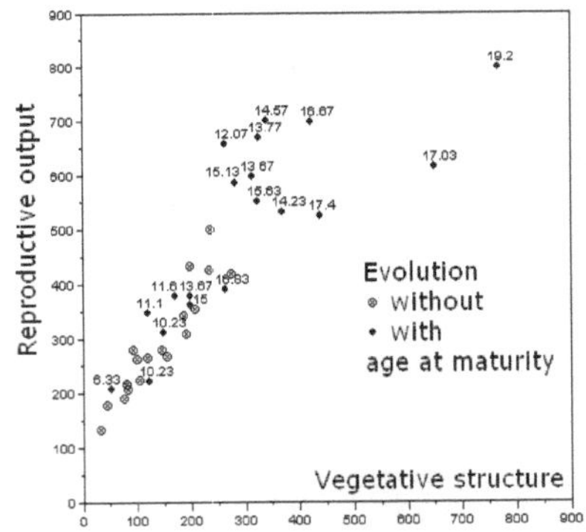

Fig. 5. Evolution with and without age at maturity (the indicated numbers correspond to the evolved parameter values)

completely exclusive of growth because fertility depends on resource acquisition, which is again correlated with plant size. In contrast, plants evolved for growth do not produce any reproductive output because seeds are disadvantageous resource sinks. Besides indicating the trade-off, the simulation notably highlights the advantage of computer models to accelerate evolutionary experiments which would simply take too long, if performed in nature.

4.3 Reproductive Maturity

A closer look at the genotypes evolved for seed biomass reveals that the shoot L-system of well performing individuals is arranged such that reproductive modules do not appear in all production rules, but develop only via the application of several preceding rules. By this means, the plant starts reproduction with a certain delay. Early investment into reproductive structure leads to the exhaustion of resources and incurs a cost in growth and therefore future fecundity. Therefore, natural plants most often possess a threshold size which has to be attained before reproduction is possible. Just as observed in the simulation, this can be due simply to the requirement to produce the necessary structures [4].

The result of the first experiment suggests that a preliminary growth period without any allocation to seed biomass may enhance the final reproductive output. Age and size at maturity are considered as key parameters in the life history of most organisms [20]. The second series of experiments goes further and investigates if and to what extent a physiologically controlled age at maturity can influence the trade-off. To model this life history trait, an additional, real-valued genetic parameter has been introduced into the genotype and subjected to evolution. With this parameter, the allocation of biomass into reproductive modules is only activated when the plant attains the indicated age. A new series of twenty runs selecting for reproductive output was conducted. Figure 5 compares the performance of the previous plants to those featuring an age at maturity. It can

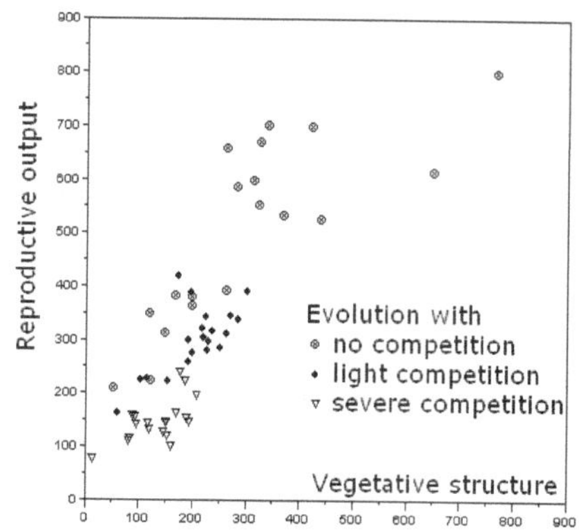

Fig. 6. Competitive pressure influencing the trade-off

Fig. 7. Evolved morphologies of isolated and competing plants

be observed that the new parameter allows to evolve significantly better values with respect to both life history traits. Moreover, well growing plants defer their age at maturity in order to make the most out of the exponential character of their juvenile growth period. It can be concluded that the introduction of an age at maturity is an effective measure to enhance both considered traits. Many natural plants indeed start reproduction only after a period of juvenile stage [3].

4.4 Competition

Thanks to their isolated breeding, the plants of the previous experiments did not encounter any interference from neighboring individuals. Consequently, evolution optimized resource allocation without considerations of competitiveness. However, except for some colonizing species, natural plants rarely encounter such open environments but grow in crowded communities where resources are more limiting. A third series of experiments therefore addressed the impact of competition on the studied allocation trade-off. This time, the plants of a population were not grown individually but simultaneously, randomly placed in an environment with limited space and resources. Afterwards, the reproductive output of all individuals was determined and the ten best performing plants were kept to produce a new population of genotypes.

Figure 6 compares the isolated breeding with evolutionary runs at two degrees of competition. Light competition occurs in an environment which confronts the plants with few interferences from neighbors. Severe competition is induced by quartering the size of the terrain. Due to the limitation of resources, the competing plants generally develop less vegetative and reproductive structures. Moreover, they decrease their reproductive effort, defined as the proportion of the total resource budget devoted to reproductive processes [8]. Depending on the competitive pressure, the plants need to invest more resources into growth. Figure 7 illustrates this conclusion by opposing the best performing specimen evolved in isolation to a group of competing individuals. Light becomes a particularly limiting factor, so that the plants need to adopt high and tall shapes stretching out to the sky in the effort to outcompete their neighbors. This result agrees with Harper's hypothesis that, as individual success is based on the capture of resources, competing plants need to sacrifice fecundity in order to develop competitive ability [7].

5 Conclusion

Trade-offs play a central role in life history theory [20]. To contribute to the understanding of the evolutionary mechanisms involved, three series of experiments have been presented in this paper. They addressed the trade-off in plants between resource allocation to reproductive and vegetative structures, conducted with a multi-agent platform of generic virtual plants. The plants, growing in a 3D environment, are based upon the fusion between a two-substrate transport-resistance model and an L-system formalism.

The trade-off was pointed out by evolutionary runs selecting for one of the two life history traits. The introduction of a physiological parameter representing an age at maturity was shown to be an effective measure to enhance both traits. A third series of experiments highlighted that competition in plant communities has an impact on the trade-off. Depending on the competitive pressure, plants evolved more allocation into growth than into reproduction, sacrificing fecundity in order to gain access to the available resources. These simulations showed that age at maturity and competition are two influential elements in the life history evolution of plants and revealed some of their implications. The results are obtained without intentional parametric bias and demonstrate the emergence of life-like traits in artificial systems.

Combining process-based with structural models, virtual plants allow to represent plant development with respect to physiological as well as morphological aspects and notably to embrace the interrelations between them. This may yield new insights on the evolution of life history traits which are intrinsically tied to both aspects. Moreover, virtual plants complement the mathematical approaches with the possibility of producing a number of results for the same general type of computation, by adding a stochastic component, which may be relevant for inherently statistical hypotheses of evolutionary biology. Even if biological hypotheses cannot be actually proved by computer modeling, they can be partially confirmed or, in the opposite case, suggested to be modified or rejected [14].

As a major extension, the model will be enriched with abiotic parameters such as water, temperature and gravity. By this means, further experiments may address questions which need to consider more environmental factors influencing the evolution of plants.

References

1. Begon, M., Harper, J.L., Townsend, C.R.: Ecology: Individuals, Populations and Communities (2nd ed). Blackwell Scientific Publications, Cambridge (1990)
2. Cody, M.L.: A general theory of clutch size. Evolution **20** (1966) 174–184

3. Dana, M. N., Lerner, B. R.: A guide to flowering and why plants fail to bloom. Purdue University Cooperative Extension Service Publication HO-173-W (2002)
4. Fenner, M., Thompson, K.: The ecology of seeds. Cambridge University Press, Cambridge (2005)
5. Ferber, J.: Les systèmes multi-agents. InterEdition, Paris (1995)
6. Goldberg D. E.: Genetic Algorithms in Search, Optimization, and Machine Learning. Addison-Wesley, Reading Massachusetts (1989)
7. Harper, J.L.: A Darwinian approach to plant ecology. Journal of Ecology **55** (1967) 247–270
8. Hirshfield, M.F., Tinkle,D.W.: Natural selection and the evolution of reproductive effort. Proc. of the National Academy of Sciences USA **72** (1975) 2227–2231
9. Holland. J.: Adaptation in Natural and Artificial Systems. University of Michigan Press, Ann Arbor (1975)
10. Kurth W.: Morphological models of plant growth: Possibilities and ecological relevance. Ecological Modelling **75** (1994) 299–308
11. Landsberg, J.J., Gower, S.T., Applications of Physiological Ecology to Forest Management. Academic Press, London (1997)
12. Le Roux, X., Lacointe, A., Escobar-Gutiérrez, A., Le Dizès, S.: Carbon-based models of individual tree growth: A critical appraisal. Ann. For. Sci. **58** (2001) 469–506
13. Lewontin, R.C.: Selection for colonizing ability. In The Genetics of Colonizing Species (H.G. Baker, G.L. Stebins, eds), London, Academic Press (1965) pp. 79–94
14. Niklas, K.J.: Computer-simulated plant evolution. Scien. Am. **254** (1986) 78–86
15. OGRE Internet home page: http://www.ogre3d.org (last accessed in April, 2006)
16. Prusinkiewicz, P., Lindenmayer, A.: The Algorithmic Beauty of Plants. Springer-Verlag, Berlin (1990)
17. Roff, D.A.: The Evolution of Life Histories: Theory and Analysis. Chapman and Hall, New York (1992)
18. Room, P., Hanan, J., Prusinkiewicz, P.: Virtual plants: new perspectives for ecologists, pathologists and agricultural scientists. Trends in Plant Science **1** (1996) 33–38
19. Samson, D.A., Werk, K.S.: Size-dependent effects in the analysis of reproductive effort in plants. The American Naturalist **127** (1986) 667–680
20. Stearns, S.C.: The Evolution of Life Histories. Oxford Univ. Press, UK (1992)
21. Stearns, S.C.: Life history evolution: successes, limitations, and prospects. Naturwissenschaften **87** (2000) 476–486
22. Thornley J.H.M.: A balanced quantitative model for root:shoot ratios in vegetative plants. Annals of Botany **36** (1972) 431–441
23. Thornley, J.H.M.: Modelling shoot:root relations: the only way forward? Annals of Botany **81** (1998) 165–171
24. Ulam, S.: On some mathematical properties connected with patterns of growth of figures. In Proc. of Symposia on Appl. Math., Am. Math. Soc. **14** (1962) 215–224
25. Westoby, M., Falster, D.S., Moles, A.T., Vesk, P.A., Wright, I.J.: Plant ecological strategies: some leading dimensions of variation between species. Annual Review of Ecology and Systematics **33** (2002) 125–159
26. Williams, G.C.: Natural selection, the cost of reproduction, and a refinement of Lack's principle. Am. Nat. **100** (1966) 687–690

Finding State-of-the-Art Non-cryptographic Hashes with Genetic Programming

César Estébanez, Julio César Hernández-Castro,
Arturo Ribagorda, and Pedro Isasi

Universidad Carlos III de Madrid
Avda. de la Universidad, 30, 28911, Leganés (Madrid). Spain
{cesteban, jcesar, arturo}@inf.uc3m.es, isasi@ia.uc3m.es

Abstract. The design of non-cryptographic hash functions by means of evolutionary computation is a relatively new and unexplored problem. In this paper, we use the Genetic Programming paradigm to evolve collision free and fast hash functions. For achieving robustness against collision we use a fitness function based on a non-linearity concept, producing evolved hashes with a good degree of Avalanche Effect. The other main issue, efficiency, is assured by using only very fast operators (both in hardware and software) and by limiting the number of nodes. Using this approach, we have created a new hash function, which we call *gp-hash*, that is able to outperform a set of five human-generated, widely-used hash functions.

1 Introduction

1.1 Definitions

Hash functions take a message as input and produce an output referred to as a *hash*. More precisely, a hash function h maps bitstrings of arbitrary finite length to strings of fixed length. For a domain D and range R with $h : D \rightarrow R$ and $|D| > |R|$ the function is many-to-one, implying that the existence of collisions (pairs of different inputs with identical outputs) is unavoidable. In the following, the term hash function will refer to non cryptographic hash functions for table and database lookup, mostly used with hash tables [9], not to be confused with the related but quite different cryptographic hash functions usually found in computer security for digital signature and integrity checking. In any case, hash functions should be very efficient (fast) and relatively collision-free (that is, even if we know collisions *should* exist, finding them should be nontrivial).

1.2 A Fitness Function for Hashes

A good way for assuring the quality of a hash function could be to measure the randomness of the hash values produced. There are a number of tests that can be used for this purpose, such as entropy, serial correlation coefficient, average, etc.

One could use any combination of these test as a fitness function for generating highly-random hash functions. However, the common problem to this approach

T.P. Runarsson et al. (Eds.): PPSN IX, LNCS 4193, pp. 818–827, 2006.

is that the hash functions obtained need not to pass any other tests than those that form part of the fitness function. Thus, the functions may produce nearly optimal values for all the tests included in the fitness function but quickly fail other, not related, previously unseen tests, even very simple ones.

In this work, however, we propose a completely different approach: instead of measuring output randomness, we measure input/output non-linearity. This change is quite important, because randomness has not a clear definition: it depends on the observer, the tests used, etc. There are multiple definitions for the concept which not satisfy all authors and which, more importantly, make it very difficult, if not impossible, to obtain an undisputed and efficient measure. However, some aspects of non-linearity can be measured by means of a property called Avalanche Effect. In this work, we use this property in the fitness function of a Genetic Programming algorithm for evolving hashes. In this way, we find hash functions that have a very non-linear behavior. Here we show that this generated hash functions can be faster and perform better than other well-known widespread-used hash functions such as FNV Hash [1].

This idea of using evolutionary techniques for generating non-cryptographic hash functions is relatively new: there is only a few works in this topic [7,4,3], and none of them uses a similar approach to ours.

This paper is organized as follows: Section 2 introduces the previously mentioned Avalanche Effect and a stricter variant of it. Section 3 describes our approach and some implementation issues. Section 4 reports the experiments carried out, and the obtained results. Finally, Section 5 draws the main conclusions of the paper.

2 The Avalanche Effect

Nonlinearity can be measured in a number of ways or, what is equivalent, has not a complete unique and satisfactory definition. Fortunately, this is of no concern to us as we do not pretend to measure non-linearity but a very specific mathematical property named avalanche effect because it tries to reflect, to some extend, the intuitive idea of high-nonlinearity: a very small difference in the input producing a high change in the output, thus an avalanche of changes.

Mathematically, $F : 2^m \rightarrow 2^n$ has the avalanche effect if it holds that

$$\forall x, y | H(x, y) = 1, \quad Average\Big(H\big(F(x), F(y)\big) \Big) = \frac{n}{2}$$

So if F is to have the avalanche effect, the Hamming distance between the outputs of a random input vector and one generated by randomly flipping one of the bits should be, on average, $n/2$. That is, a minimum input change (one single bit) produces a maximum output change (half of the bits) on average.

This definition also tries to abstract the more general concept of output independence from the input (and thus our proposal and its applicability to the generation of good hash functions). Although it is clear that this independence is impossible to achieve (a given input vector always produces the same output) the ideal F will resemble a perfect random function where inputs and outputs are statistically unrelated. Any such F would have perfect avalanche effect, so it is natural to try to obtain such functions by optimizing the amount of avalanche. In fact, we will use an even more demanding property that has been called the Strict Avalanche Criterion [5] which, in particular, implies the Avalanche Effect, and that could be mathematically described as:

$$\forall x, y | H(x, y) = 1, \quad H\big(F(x), F(y)\big) \approx B\left(\frac{1}{2}, n\right)$$

It is interesting to note that this implies the avalanche effect, because the average of a Binomial distribution with parameters $1/2$ and n is $n/2$, and that the amount of proximity of a given distribution to a certain distribution (in this case a $B(1/2, n)$) could be easily measured by means of a chi-square goodness-of-fit test. That is exactly the procedure we will follow.

3 Implementation Issues

We have used the lilgp genetic programming library [2] as the base for our system. Lil-gp provides the core of a GP toolkit so the user only needs to adjust the parameters to fit his particular problem. In this section we detail the changes needed in order to configure our system.

3.1 Function Set

Firstly, we need to define the set of functions: This is critical for our problem, as they are the building blocks of the functions we would obtain. Being efficiency one of the paramount objectives of our approach, it is natural to restrict the set of functions to include only very efficient operations, both easy to implement in hardware and software. Another, but minor, objective was to produce portable algorithms; so the inclusion of the basic binary operations such as **vrotd** (right rotation), **vroti** (left rotation), **xor** (addition mod 2), **or** (bitwise or), **not** (bitwise not), and **and** (bitwise and) are an obvious first step. Other operators as the **sum** (sum mod 2^{32}) are necessary in order to avoid linearity, being itself quite efficient.

The inclusion of the **mult** (multiplication mod 2^{32}) operator was not so easy to decide, because, depending on the particular implementations, the multiplication of two 32 bit values could cost up to fifty times more than an **xor** or an **and** operation (although this could happen in certain architectures, its nearly a worst case: 14 times [6] seems to be a more common value), so it is relatively inefficient, at least when compared with the rest of the operators used. In fact, we did not include it at first, but after extensively experimentation, we conclude that its inclusion was beneficial because, apart from improving non-linearity it at least doubled and sometimes tripled the amount of avalanche we were trying to maximize. That's the reason why we finally introduced it in the function set.

Similarly, after many experiments, we concluded that the functions **vroti** and **vrotd** were absolutely interchangeable and that using them at the same time was not necessary nor useful, so we arbitrarily decided to remove **vroti** and left **vrotd**. Anyway, with **vrotd** we have a similar problem than with **mult**: compared to other operators, in some architectures **vrotd** is very inefficient so we tried to eliminate this operator and include the $\gg$ (regular right shift) instead. But the problem is that $\gg$ was not able of producing as much non-linearity as **vrotd** and the efficiency gains of the obtained hash functions were not as good as for ignoring the loss of Avalanche Effect.

3.2 Terminal Set

The set of terminals in our case is easy to establish. Firstly, it is mandatory for the hash function to operate with the previous generated hash value. Thus, one of the terminals of the GP system will represent the previous calculated hash value. It will be called **hval**. In our approach, the length of the output v is fixed to 32 bits, so **hval** will be a 32 bits unsigned integer value.

The bitlength of the input (the m value), however, is not that easy to set. Initially, we tried different approaches which did not generated good results, specially in terms of efficiency, so we finally set the input length to 32 bits. In this case, input-related terminals were reduced to a single 32-bit unsigned long value, **a0**. Some experiments confirmed that, as expected, the best obtained 128-to-32-bits hashes were never able to outperform the best 32-to-32 hashes. The later were more efficient, and they usually reached a much higher level of Avalanche Effect.

Finally, we included Ephemeral Random Constants (ERC's) [10] for completing the terminal set. In our problem, ERC's are 32-bits random-values that can be included in the hash function as constants to operate with. The idea behind this operator was to provide a constant value that, independently from the input, could be used by the operators of the function to increase non-linearity, and idea suggested by [12].

3.3 Fitness Function

The fitness of every individual is calculated as follows: First, we use the Mersenne Twister generator [11] to generate two 32-bit random values. Those values are assigned to **hval** and **a0**[1]. As we already know, each individual represents a candidate hash function, so we run the hash function being evaluated with the randomly generated values of **a0** and **hval**. The hash value produced (we call it $hash_1$) is stored. Then, we randomly flip one single bit of one of the two input values, **a0** or **hval**, and we run again the hash function, obtaining a new hash value ($hash_2$). Now, we compute the Hamming distance between $hash_1$ and $hash_2$. This process is repeated a number of times (8192 was experimentally proved to be enough) and each time a Hamming distance among 0 and 32 is obtained and stored. For a perfect Avalanche Effect, the distribution of this

[1] This stands for the 32-to-32-bits hashing. For other input sizes, we only need to use additional **a*** input values.

Hamming distances should adjust to the theoretical Bernoulli probability distribution $B(1/2, 32)$. Therefore, fitness of each individual is calculated by adding two factors: first the measure of how close to 16 ($16/32 = 1/2$) is the mean of the calculated Hamming distances; and second, the chi-square (χ^2) statistic that measures the distance of the observed distribution of the Hamming distances from the theoretical Bernoulli probability distribution $B(1/2, 32)$. Thus, we try to minimize the following fitness expression:

$$Fitness = (16 - mean)^2 + \chi_c^2$$

where χ_c^2 is a corrected value of χ^2, which is calculated as follows:

$$\chi_c^2 = \chi^2 * 10^{-8}$$

where

$$\chi^2 = \sum_{h=0}^{h=32} \frac{(O_h - E_h)^2}{{E_h}^2}$$

and

$$E_k = 8192 * Pr\big(B(1/2, 32) = k\big)$$

We should note that we are computing the value of the χ^2 statistic without the commonly used restriction of adding up only the values when $E_k > 5.0$, for amplifying the effect of a bad output distribution, thus, the sensibility of our measure.

It was necessary to correct the χ^2 statistic because its values were much bigger than the values of the expression $(16-mean)^2$. Without this correction, the mean measure was negligible and the fitness was guided only by the χ^2.

3.4 Tree Size Limitations

When using genetic programming approaches, it is necessary to put some limits to the depth and to the number of nodes the resulting trees could have. We tried various approaches here, both limiting the depth and not limiting the number of nodes and vice versa. The best results where consistently obtained using this latter option, so we fixed the number of maximum nodes to 25 and did not put a limit (other that the number of nodes itself) to the tree depth. This is also a very important step for assuring the efficiency of the resulting algorithm.

4 Experimentation and Results

The experimentation carried out was extensive. In the GP system part, we tried with many different configurations of the terminal and function sets, the fitness function and the GP parameters, as mentioned in Section 3. Even so, in this

Section we will only show the experiments that produced the most interesting results, in order to save space and do not distract the reader from the important results.

Experiments were carried out in two phases. In the first stage, we use GP to evolve individuals (GP will try to find an individual that minimizes the fitness function described in previous sections). For each configuration and set of parameters described in Section 3 we executed ten GP runs. Using the information provided by the best individuals of each configuration, we selected the parameters that produced better results. This set of parameters is shown in Table 1.

Table 1. Experimentally-found best GP parameters

Parameter	Value
G (Max.Gen.)	2000
M (Pop.Size)	100
Max nodes	25
Terminal and Function set	and or not vrotd xor sum mult a0 hval ERC

Using these parameters, we obtained a large set of candidate individuals. Among them, we selected the best one and called it *gp-hash*. This individual is the best hash function our GP system was able to produce. A description of *gp-hash* can be seen in Figure 1, and its pseudocode in C in Figure 2.

```
(mult 0x6CF575C5
     (vrotd (vrotd (vrotd (vrotd (vrotd
(vrotd (vrotd (vrotd (vrotd (vrotd
(vrotd (vrotd (vrotd (vrotd (vrotd
(vrotd (vrotd (vrotd (mult 0x6CF575C5
      (sum hval a0)))))))))))))))))))))
```

Fig. 1. Individual of the generated *gp-hash* function

The second stage starts at this point: We have generated a hash function by means of optimizing the Avalanche Effect, restricting its size and using only the most efficient operators, believing that in this way we would obtain a very fast and relatively collision free hash function. In this stage, we want to check if we have really achieved our objective. In order to do so, we decided to compare *gp-hash* with a set of 5 human-generated non cryptographic hash functions: CRC32, oneAtATimeHash, alphaNumHash, FNVHash [1] and BobJenkinsHash [8]. All of them are state-of-the-art, widely-used hash functions, but within this group FNVHash is well-known to be specially fast and collision free. This justifies its wide adoption in dozens of applications, from NFS implementations (e.g., FreeBSD 4.3, IRIX, Linux (NFS v4)) to Domain Name Servers, not forgetting

```
magic_number = 0x6CF575C5
AUX = magic_number * (hval + a0)
rotate_18_positions_right (AUX)
hash = magic_number * AUX
return hash
```

Fig. 2. C pseudocode of the generated *gp-hash* function

high performance EMail servers, text based referenced resources for video games on the PS2, Gamecube and XBOX, etc.

As the two most important features of a non-cryptographic hash function are its speed and its collision robustness, these will be the two variables that we will test. The former describes how fast the function can hash variable-length bitstrings, and the later is the capability of generating a large amount of hashes while producing as few collisions as possible. So we carried out two different tests: one to compare the speed of the six hash functions, and another one to compare their collision robustness. Both tests were ran in an AMD Athlon XP2000+ with 256 Mb of RAM and a Gentoo Linux Operating System.

4.1 Speed Test

The speed test was designed as follows: All the hash functions are coded in C (none is optimized) and inserted into a speed benchmark. Each run of this benchmark is divided in 32 phases, which we call "executions". In every execution, each function must hash 10^6 random-generated strings. The time took for every function is stored. This process is repeated ten times, and after that, the average time for each function is calculated and stored. Then the execution ends. In the first execution, the length of the random-generated strings is 32 bits. In the second one, this size is multiplied by 2, in the third is multiplied by 3, and so on. Finally, in execution 32, the string size is $32 * 32 = 1024$. This way, when all the executions ends, we have the average time that each hash function needed to hash 10^6 strings of a length varying from 32 to 1024 bits. A summary of these results can be seen in Table 2. Values of the table are average time (in seconds). The headers of the columns are the string size (in bits) of the experiment. Figure 3 shows the graphical representation of the results. It is clear from the results of this experiment that *gp-hash* is faster than the other hash functions, for every string length.

4.2 Collision Test

With the collision test we wanted to know how many hashes (in average) a function can produce before generating the first collision. Furthermore, we also wanted to know how the number of collisions growths when the number of hashes growths. Thus, we created a battery of ten different tests. For each hash function, each test is divided in ten executions. In each execution we store the number of hashes before producing the first collision, and finally we calculate the average

Table 2. Summarized results of the speed test

	32	64	128	256	512	1024
CRC32	0.039	0.068	0.127	0.229	0.435	0.847
oneAtATime	0.059	0.1	0.195	0.367	0.708	1.399
alphaNum	0.033	0.06	0.094	0.222	0.427	0.831
FNVHash	0.039	0.072	0.143	0.267	0.517	1.017
gp-hash	**0.032**	**0.05**	**0.088**	**0.175**	**0.357**	**0.703**
BobJenkins	0.09	0.087	0.164	0.23	0.439	0.82

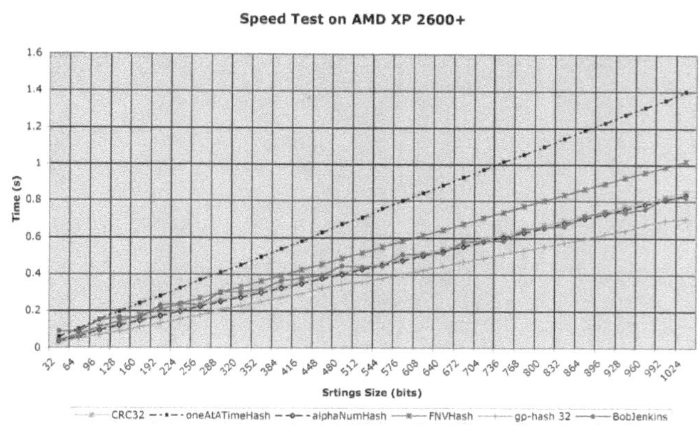

Fig. 3. Results of the speed test

of the ten executions. The second test is similar, but when a first collision is produced, we continue producing hashes and storing values. When a second collision is produced, we store the number of hashes generated. In the third test, we store the number of hashes needed for generate three collisions, and so on.

Results of the complete battery of tests can be seen in Table 3. The chart in Figure 4 shows the way in which the number of collisions growths when the number of hashes also growths. The behavior of all hash functions is almost linear, and it can be seen that *gp-hash* and the other functions have very similar collision-per-hash rates, except oneAtATimeHash which produces significantly worse ratios.

5 Conclusions and Future Work

The results obtained by *gp-hash* in both the speed and collision tests show that this automatically-generated hash function is faster that all the other functions tested when used in the standard AMDXP 2000+ architecture, while its collision rate is absolutely competitive or even slightly better that the rest of the human-designed hash functions, except for one of them (oneAtATimeHash)

Table 3. Summarized results of the collision tests

Hash function	Test 1	Test 2	Test 4	Test 6	Test 8	Test 10
hline CRC32	**323648.38**	541053.83	1033888.5	1445630.91	2033342.26	2583637.81
oneAtATimeHash	71380.66	132346.52	272675.61	407190.86	547254.59	659462.41
alphaNumHash	247355.25	523988.1	1040997.09	**1587157.6**	2079883.36	2657898.19
FNVHash	239840.3	578113.04	**1049437.85**	1559196.5	**2165332.38**	2590886.49
gp-hash	273480.69	**584374.64**	1028586.79	1522586.03	2054192.25	**2670056.92**
BobJenkins	276244.12	554777.21	935246.5	1582715.73	2015192.26	2600531.72

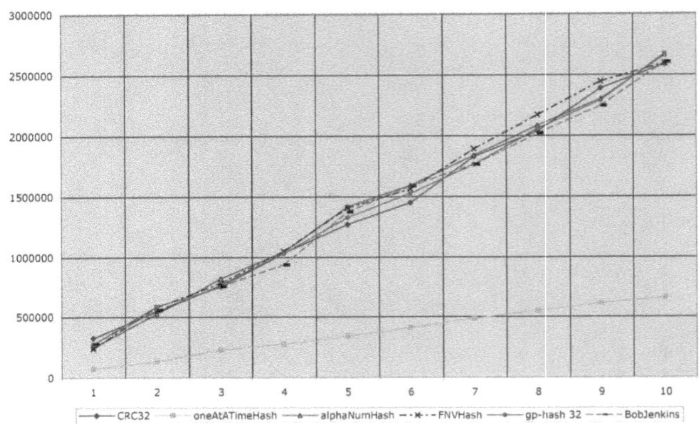

Fig. 4. Results of the collisions test

which performs significantly worse than the rest. So, we can conclude that our proposed system is able to produce competitive hash functions that can outperform other well-known, expert-designed and commonly used hash functions.

Gp-hash, the hash function produced in our experiments and proposed here as an alternative, is slightly faster than FNV Hash (a widespread-used, very fast hash function with many important real-life applications) and adjusts better to the optimal probability distribution $B(1/2, 32)$, or, which is the same, is more non-linear than FNV.

It is important to remark that *gp-hash* was designed in an automatic way. Except for the fitness function, *gp-hash* was generated using no information about the objective, the usage or even the nature of a hash function. Nevertheless, the other hash functions used in the experiments were generated by practiced humans, with years of experience and a vast knowledge about the topic. Even so, *gp-hash* is faster than the rest and able of generating approximately the same number of collisions per hash than the others, in fact winning (the only with FNV who repeats this honor) twice at Table 3. So we have generated an artificial algorithm which can compete on equal terms with those produced by human experts or even beat them.

Acknowledgments

This article has been financed by the Spanish founded research MCyT project OP:LINK, Ref:TIN2005-08818-C04-02.

References

1. Fowler, noll, vo. fnv hash web page, http://www.isthe.com/chongo/tech/comp/fnv/.
2. The lil-gp genetic programming system is available at http://garage.cps.msu.edu/software/lil-gp/lilgp-index.html.
3. P. Berarducci, D. Jordan, D. Martin, and J. Seitzer. GEVOSH: Using grammatical evolution to generate hashing functions. In R. Poli, S. Cagnoni, M. Keijzer, E. Costa, F. Pereira, G. Raidl, S. C. Upton, D. Goldberg, H. Lipson, E. de Jong, J. Koza, H. Suzuki, H. Sawai, I. Parmee, M. Pelikan, K. Sastry, D. Thierens, W. Stolzmann, P. L. Lanzi, S. W. Wilson, M. O'Neill, C. Ryan, T. Yu, J. F. Miller, I. Garibay, G. Holifield, A. S. Wu, T. Riopka, M. M. Meysenburg, A. W. Wright, N. Richter, J. H. Moore, M. D. Ritchie, L. Davis, R. Roy, and M. Jakiela, editors, *GECCO 2004 Workshop Proceedings*, Seattle, Washington, USA, 26-30 June 2004.
4. E. Damiani, V. Liberali, and A. G. B. Tettamanzi. Evolutionary design of hashing function circuits using an FPGA, Sept. 17 1998.
5. R. Forré. The strict avalanche criterion: spectral properties of boolean functions and an extended definition. In *CRYPTO '88: Proceedings on Advances in cryptology*, pages 450–468. Springer-Verlag New York, Inc., 1990.
6. G. Hinton, D. Sager, M. Upton, D. Boggs, D. Carmean, A. Kyker, and P. Roussel. The microarchitecture of the pentium 4 processor. *Intel Technology Journal*, Q1 2001. http://developer.intel.com/technology/itj/q12001/articles/art_2.htm.
7. D. Hussain and S. Malliaris. Evolutionary techniques applied to hashing: An efficient data retrieval method. In D. Whitley, D. Goldberg, E. Cantu-Paz, L. Spector, I. Parmee, and H.-G. Beyer, editors, *Proceedings of the Genetic and Evolutionary Computation Conference (GECCO-2000)*, page 760, Las Vegas, Nevada, USA, 10-12 July 2000. Morgan Kaufmann.
8. B. Jenkins. A hash function for hash table lookup. *Dr.Dobbs Journal*, September 1997.
9. D. Knuth. *The Art of Computer Programming*. Addison Wesley, 1998.
10. J. R. Koza. *Genetic Programming: On the Programming of Computers by Means of Natural Selection.* MIT Press, Cambridge, MA, USA, 1992.
11. Matsumoto and Nishimura. Mersenne twister: A 623-dimensionally equidistributed uniform pseudo-random number generator. *ACMTMCS: ACM Transactions on Modeling and Computer Simulation*, 8, 1998.
12. D. J. Wheeler and R. M. Needham. TEA, a tiny encryption algorithm. *Lecture Notes in Computer Science*, 1008:363–369, 1995.

Offspring Generation Method Using Delaunay Triangulation for Real-Coded Genetic Algorithms

Hisashi Shimosaka[1], Tomoyuki Hiroyasu[2], and Mitsunori Miki[2]

[1] Graduate School of Engineering, Doshisha University,
1-3 Tatara Miyakodani Kyotanabe, Kyoto, Japan
hisashi@mikilab.doshisha.ac.jp

[2] Department of Engineering, Doshisha University
tomo@is.doshisha.ac.jp, mmiki@mail.doshisha.ac.jp

Abstract. To design crossover operators with high search ability in real-coded Genetic Algorithms, it will be efficient to utilize both information regarding the parent distribution and the landscape of the objective function. Here, we propose a new offspring generation method using Delaunay triangulation. The proposed method can concentrate offspring in regions with a satisfactory evaluation value, inheriting the parent distribution. Through numerical examples, the proposed method was shown to be capable of deriving the optimum with a smaller population size and lower number of evaluations than Simplex Crossover, which uses only information of the parent distribution.

1 Introduction

Genetic Algorithms (GAs) are optimization methods that simulate the heredity and evolution of living organisms. Real-Coded GA (RCGA), which uses real number vector representation of chromosomes, is utilized for global optimization of nonlinear functions. In RCGAs, offspring can be generated by dealing directly with the parent distribution in design space. Various crossover operators have been proposed in RCGAs some of which have also been shown to have efficient search ability[1,2,3,4,5]. A well-known set of guidelines for design of these crossover operators is the functional specialization hypothesis[6]. In this hypothesis, it is important that a crossover operator generates offspring with the same distribution as the parents. Then, a generation alternation model changes the distribution and evolves the population. Based on this hypothesis, it is commonly believed that crossover operators with high search ability can be designed easily in RCGAs. In addition, the offspring generation that correctly inherits the parent distribution is an important design guideline in Probabilistic Model-Building GA (PMBGA)[7,8].

On the other hand, some of offspring generation methods with higher search ability in real-coded PMBGAs estimate the parent distribution using the joint normal kernels distribution or the histogram distribution[9,10,11]. These methods implicitly construct the probabilistic model similar to the landscape of the

T.P. Runarsson et al. (Eds.): PPSN IX, LNCS 4193, pp. 828–838, 2006.

objective function. Therefore, in RCGAs as in real-coded PMBGAs, crossover operators with higher search ability can be designed by utilizing not only the parent distribution but also the landscape of the objective function. In Simplex Crossover (SPX)[4,5], which is one of the crossover operators for RCGAs, offspring generation range is first defined from the parent distribution. Then, large numbers of offspring are generated uniformly within the defined range. In the offspring generation of SPX, it is possible that the search ability will be increased by concentrating offspring in regions with a satisfactory evaluation value within the defined region.

From these backgrounds, in this paper, to concentrate offspring in regions with a satisfactory evaluation value, we propose a new offspring generation method using the Delaunay triangulation. The next section first presents an outline of the Delaunay triangulation. Then, we discuss the details of SPX, which forms the foundation of the proposed method. Finally, we describe the proposed offspring generation method in detail. In the numerical examples in this paper, the effectiveness of the proposed method is discussed by comparison with the search ability of SPX.

2 Voronoi Diagram and Delaunay Triangulation

2.1 Voronoi Diagram

The Voronoi diagram[12] decides how to divide the space between the region of each point and its boundary as in Equation 1, when a point set $P = \{\boldsymbol{p}_1, \boldsymbol{p}_2, \boldsymbol{p}_3, ..., \boldsymbol{p}_m\}$ is given in an n-dimensional space. In Equation 1, $d(\boldsymbol{p}_i, \boldsymbol{p}_j)$ expresses the distance function between $\boldsymbol{p}_i$ and $\boldsymbol{p}_j$. Generally, the Euclid distance is used as the distance function.

$$V(\boldsymbol{p}_i) = \{\boldsymbol{p} | \boldsymbol{p} \in \mathrm{R}^n, d(\boldsymbol{p}, \boldsymbol{p}_i) < d(\boldsymbol{p}, \boldsymbol{p}_j), j \neq i\} \tag{1}$$

Fig. 1 shows an example of the Voronoi diagram with 8 points in a 2-dimensional space. Each point that generates the Voronoi diagram is called a Voronoi generator, and each region divided by Voronoi generators is known as a Voronoi region. The region $V(\boldsymbol{p}_i)$ that includes the point $\boldsymbol{p}_i$ shows that, at any arbitrary location in the regions, the point $\boldsymbol{p}_i$ is the closest point in the point set.

2.2 Delaunay Triangulation

The Delaunay triangulation can be created by connecting neighboring Voronoi generators in a Voronoi diagram. Fig. 2 shows an example of the Delaunay triangulation created from the Voronoi diagram shown in Fig. 1. Each triangle that consists of $(n+1)$ Voronoi generators in an n-dimensional space is called a Delaunay triangle. One of the typical applications that can create the Voronoi diagram and the Delaunay triangulation is Qhull[13,14]. In this study, Qhull was used for creating the Delaunay triangulation.

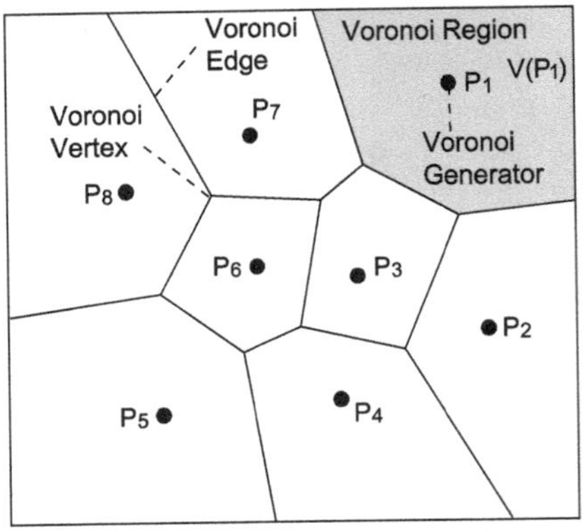

Fig. 1. Voronoi diagram

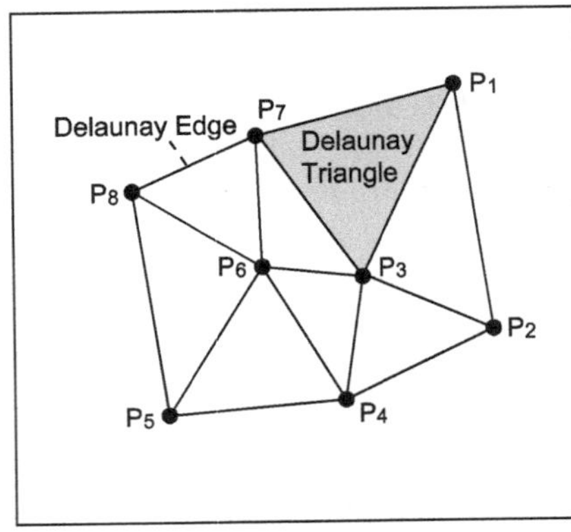

Fig. 2. Delaunay triangulation

3 Simplex Crossover

Simplex Crossover (SPX) is a typical crossover based on the functional specialization hypothesis. In an n-dimensional design space, SPX generates offspring as follows:

1. Select $(n+1)$ parents $\boldsymbol{P}_0, \boldsymbol{P}_1, \ldots, \boldsymbol{P}_n$ from the population by random sampling.
2. Calculate their center of mass $\boldsymbol{G}$ as

$$\boldsymbol{G} = \frac{1}{n+1} \sum_{i=0}^{n} \boldsymbol{P}_i \tag{2}$$

3. Calculate $\boldsymbol{x}_k$ and $\boldsymbol{C}_k$, respectively, as

$$\boldsymbol{x}_k = \boldsymbol{G} + \epsilon(\boldsymbol{P}_k - \boldsymbol{G}) \qquad (k = 0, \ldots, n) \tag{3}$$

$$\boldsymbol{C}_k = \begin{cases} \boldsymbol{0} & (k = 0) \\ \boldsymbol{r}_{k-1} - \boldsymbol{x}_k + \boldsymbol{C}_{k-1} & (k = 1, \ldots, n) \end{cases} \tag{4}$$

$$\boldsymbol{r}_k = (u(0,1))^{\frac{1}{k+1}} \qquad (k = 0, \ldots, n-1) \tag{5}$$

where ϵ is the expansion rate, a control parameter of SPX and $u(0,1)$ is uniform random number $\in$ [0,1].
4. Generate offspring $\boldsymbol{C}$ as

$$\boldsymbol{C} = \boldsymbol{x}_n + \boldsymbol{C}_n \tag{6}$$

Fig. 3 shows the offspring generation range in SPX. Generally, SPX generates large numbers of offspring, which are distributed uniformly on the gray range in Fig. 3. Then, a generation alternation model chooses a few better offspring and substitutes them into the population. ϵ is the expansion rate and a positive

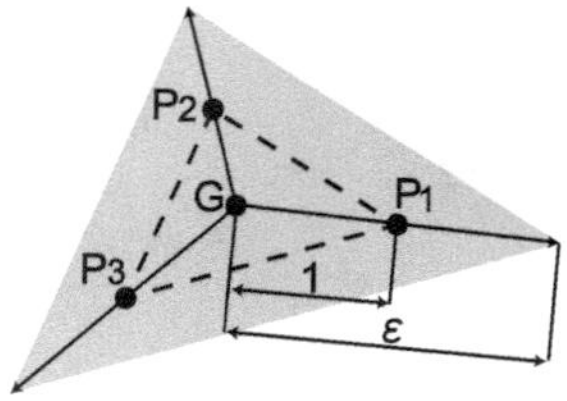

Fig. 3. Offspring generation range in SPX

parameter of SPX. The expansion rate has a marked effect on the search of SPX. However, SPX also recommends the value $\epsilon_{spx} = \sqrt{n+2}$, which is based on the functional specialization hypothesis[5].

4 Offspring Generation Method Using Delaunay Triangulation

SPX and other crossover operators based on the functional specialization hypothesis generate offspring with the same distribution as the parents. On the other hand, crossover operators with higher search ability can be designed by utilizing not only the parent distribution but also the landscape of the objective function. Therefore, in this paper, a new offspring generation method using the Delaunay triangulation is proposed. The proposed method enables the generation and concentration of offspring in regions with a satisfactory evaluation value, inheriting the parent distribution.

4.1 Procedure of Offspring Generation Using Delaunay Triangulation

Fig. 4 shows an overview of the proposed method. In an n-dimensional design space, the proposed method generates N_{off} offspring from $(n+1)$ parents as follows:

1. Select $(n+1)$ parents $\boldsymbol{P}_0, \boldsymbol{P}_1, \ldots, \boldsymbol{P}_n$ from the population by random sampling.
2. Using SPX, first $(N_{off} \times R_{spx})$ offspring are generated.
3. Repeat the following items $N_{delaunay}$ times.
4. Create the Delaunay triangulation from the offspring coordinates.
5. Evaluate offspring and calculate the evaluation value of each Delaunay triangle. In this item, offspring evaluated in the past should not be re-evaluated. The evaluation value of a triangle is the summation of the evaluation value of the offspring, which form its triangle.
6. Select $(N_{off} \times (1 - R_{spx})/N_{delaunay})$ Delaunay triangles in decreasing order of evaluation value of triangles and generate offspring on the center of mass of each triangle.

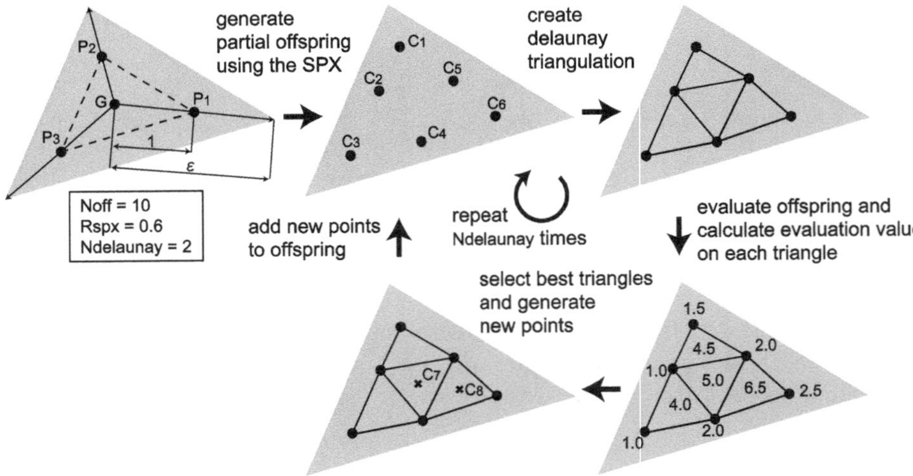

Fig. 4. Offspring generation procedure in the proposed method

The important parameters of the proposed method are the expansion rate ϵ of SPX that defines the offspring generation range, the R_{spx} that determines the number of first offspring generated by SPX, and the $N_{delaunay}$ that determines the number of iterations of offspring generation using the Delaunay triangulation. The number of evaluations for each generation alternation in the proposed method is N_{off}, which is the same number in the offspring generation of the original SPX.

4.2 Offspring Distributions

Fig. 5 shows the offspring distributions when 500 offspring ($N_{off} = 500$) are generated from 3 parents $(n+1)$ in 2-dimensional design space $(n = 2)$ of 3 test functions. The expansion rate ϵ is 1.0. Then, offspring are generated within the 3 parents. In addition, R_{spx} is defined as 0.5 and $N_{delaunay}$ is also defined as 2. Therefore, the first 250 offspring ($N_{off} \times R_{spx}$) are generated by SPX and the last 250 offspring are generated by 2 Delaunay triangulations. Each triangulation generates 125 offspring ($N_{off} \times (1 - R_{spx})/N_{delaunay}$). The number of generators that is the same as the number of generated offspring is 250 in the first triangulation and 375 in the second triangulation.

As shown in Fig. 5, the distributions of all offspring are different according to the landscape of each objective function. However, the distributions of the first 250 offspring generated by SPX are uniform and the same regardless of the landscape of each objective function. On the other hand, the last 250 offspring generated by the Delaunay triangulations are concentrated in regions with a satisfactory evaluation value. In particular, the last 125 offspring generated by the second Delaunay triangulation are concentrated more in regions with better evaluation value. Therefore, $N_{delaunay}$ can control the concentration level of offspring.

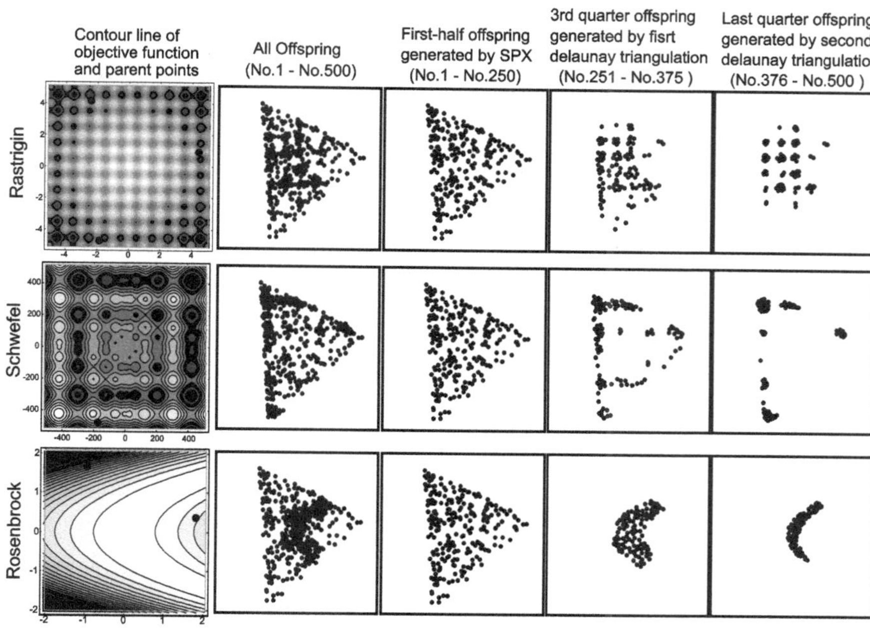

Fig. 5. Distributions of offspring generated by the proposed method

5 Numerical Examples

As described in Subsection 4.1, the three parameters, ϵ, R_{spx}, and $N_{delaunay}$, have marked effects on offspring generation in the proposed method. In these parameters, the expansion rate ϵ that is used for generating offspring in SPX is the most important because it defines the offspring generation range. As explained in Section 3, SPX recommends the value $\epsilon_{spx} = \sqrt{n+2}$, which is based on the functional specialization hypothesis. However, ϵ_{spx} designates that offspring are generated using a uniform distribution. Therefore, ϵ_{spx} is not effective in the proposed method. In the numerical examples described in this paper, we first discuss the most appropriate expansion rate, ϵ, in the proposed method. Then, the effectiveness of the proposed method is clarified through comparison of its search ability with that of SPX.

5.1 Target Problems

In these numerical examples, Sphere, Rosenbrock, Ill-Scaled Rosenbrock, and Ridge functions shown in Equation 7-10 are used as single-peak test functions. Of these functions, the Rosenbrock, Ill-Scaled Rosenbrock, and Ridge functions have correlations among design variables. The Ill-Scaled Rosenbrock function also has a non-uniform scale on the coordinate system. On the other hand, Rastrigin, Griewank, and Schwefel functions shown in Equation 11-13 are used as multi-peak test functions. In addition, the Rotated Rastrigin function, which is obtained by rotating each coordinate axis of the Rastrigin function by $(\pi/3)$, and the Rastrigin-2.0 function, which is obtained by translating each coordinate axis with 2.0, are also used. Of these functions, the Rotated Rastrigin and Griewank functions have correlations among design variables. In the Schwefel function, local optima exist separately on the edge of the design space. Therefore, to maintain the diversity of the population, a larger population size is generally required as compared with other functions. In all functions, the region with an evaluation value of less than 1.0×10^{-6} is considered optimal.

$$F_{Sphere}(x) = \sum_{i=1}^{n} (x_i)^2 \qquad (-5.12 \leq x_i \leq 5.12) \quad (7)$$

$$F_{Rosenbrock}(x) = \sum_{i=2}^{n} (100(x_1 - x_i^2)^2 + (1 - x_i)^2) \qquad (-2.048 \leq x_i \leq 2.048) \quad (8)$$

$$F_{Ill-Scaled-Rosenbrock}(x) = \sum_{i=2}^{n} (100(x_1 - (ix_i)^2)^2 + (1 - ix_i)^2) \qquad (-2.048/i \leq x_i \leq 2.048/i) \quad (9)$$

$$F_{Ridge}(x) = \sum_{i=1}^{n} \left(\sum_{j=1}^{i} x_j\right)^2 \qquad (-64 \leq x_i \leq 64) \quad (10)$$

$$F_{Rastrigin}(x) = 10n + \sum_{i=1}^{n} (x_i^2 - 10\cos(2\pi x_i)) \qquad (-5.12 \leq x_i \leq 5.12) \quad (11)$$

$$F_{Griewank}(x) = 1 + \sum_{i=1}^{n} \frac{x_i^2}{4000} - \prod_{i=1}^{n} \left(\cos\left(\frac{x_i}{\sqrt{i}}\right)\right) \qquad (-512 \leq x_i \leq 512) \quad (12)$$

$$F_{Schwefel}(x) = 418.9828873n + \sum_{i=1}^{n} x_i \sin\left(\sqrt{|x_i|}\right) \qquad (-512 \leq x_i \leq 512) \quad (13)$$

5.2 Experimental Methodology

The generation alternation model in these numerical examples is the Minimal Generation Gap (MGG)[15]. The MGG model has desirable convergence properties for maintaining the diversity of the population, and shows better performance than other conventional models. However, MGG was designed with the number of parents set to 2. Therefore, we extended MGG as follows:

1. In an n-dimensional design space, select $(n+1)$ parents from the population by random sampling.
2. Generate N_{off} offspring by applying the proposed method or SPX.
3. Select 2 parents from the $(n+1)$ parents by random sampling without replacement.
4. Substitute the best individual and another randomly selected individual with rank-based roulette-wheel selection among the 2 parents selected in Item 3 and the offspring into the population.

No mutation method is applied. The initial population is generated randomly within the domain of definition with a uniform distribution. However, no explicit treatment of the domain of definition is considered during the GA search in all test functions except the Schwefel function, in which there are better regions than optimum outside the domain of definition. Therefore, in the offspring generation using SPX in the Schwefel function, when an offspring is generated outside the domain of definition, it is re-generated until it is located inside the domain of definition.

5.3 Discussion of the Expansion Rate

In this example, we discuss the appropriate expansion rate in the proposed method. Experimental conditions are defined as follows:

- Number of dimensions (n): 2, 4, 6, 8
- Population size:
  $n \times 10$ (all single-peak functions and the Schwefel function),
  $n \times 25$ (all multi-peak functions except the Schwefel function)
- Number of offspring (N_{off}): $n \times 10$
- Number of trials: 20. Maximum number of evaluations: 2.0×10^6
- Parameters of the proposed method: $R_{spx} = 0.5$, $N_{delaunay} = 2$

Tables 1 and 2 show the number of times that the optimum was achieved in the proposed method when the expansion rate ϵ is defined as $\epsilon_{spx} \times 1.0$ to $\epsilon_{spx} \times 2.5$. The $\epsilon_{spx} = \sqrt{n+2}$ is the recommended value of SPX. Table 1 shows that the proposed method whose ϵ is defined as greater than $\epsilon_{spx} \times 2.0$ can perform an effective search in single-peak functions. In addition, the proposed method can derive the optimum regardless of the correlations among design variables and the scale of the coordinate system. Table 2 also shows that the proposed method whose ϵ is defined as greater than $\epsilon_{spx} \times 2.0$ can perform effective searches in multi-peak functions. However, in the higher-dimensional Schwefel function and the 4-dimensional Griewank function, the proposed method whose ϵ is defined as $\epsilon_{spx} \times 2.5$ cannot derive the optimum, because the population cannot converge on the optimum or a certain local optimum. Therefore, the most appropriate expansion rate is $\epsilon_{spx} \times 2.0$ in the proposed method.

Table 1. Number of times that the optimum was achieved (single-peak functions)

Expansion Rate	$\epsilon_{spx} \times 1.0$				$\epsilon_{spx} \times 1.5$				$\epsilon_{spx} \times 2.0$				$\epsilon_{spx} \times 2.5$			
Number of Dimensions	2	4	6	8	2	4	6	8	2	4	6	8	2	4	6	8
Sphere	20	20	19	18	20	20	20	20	20	20	20	20	20	20	20	20
Rosenbrock	11	0	0	0	20	20	20	3	20	20	20	20	20	20	20	20
Ill-Scaled Rosenbrock	13	1	0	0	20	20	20	4	20	20	20	20	20	20	20	20
Ridge	20	20	16	1	20	20	20	20	20	20	20	20	20	20	20	20

Table 2. Number of times that the optimum was achieved (multi-peak functions)

Expansion Rate	$\epsilon_{spx} \times 1.0$				$\epsilon_{spx} \times 1.5$				$\epsilon_{spx} \times 2.0$				$\epsilon_{spx} \times 2.5$			
Number of Dimensions	2	4	6	8	2	4	6	8	2	4	6	8	2	4	6	8
Rastrigin	20	19	18	19	20	20	20	19	20	20	20	20	20	20	20	20
Rotated Rastrigin	20	19	18	19	20	20	20	20	20	20	20	20	20	20	20	20
Rastrigin-2.0	20	6	1	0	20	20	14	16	20	20	20	20	20	20	20	20
Griewank	17	7	8	5	20	16	17	19	20	19	20	20	20	0	20	20
Schwefel	5	2	0	0	15	5	2	2	19	15	18	17	18	19	3	0

5.4 Comparison of the Searching Abilities Between the Offspring Generation Method Using Delaunay Triangulation and SPX

Through the comparison of searching abilities between the proposed method and SPX, we discuss the effectiveness of the proposed method. The number of dimensions (n) is 8 and other experimental conditions are same as the previous ones. However, to derive the same number of times that the optimum is achieved with the proposed method in SPX, the population size of SPX is defined as 120 ($n \times 15$) in single-peak functions, 200 ($n \times 25$) in multi-peak functions except the Schwefel function and 880 ($n \times 110$) in the Schwefel function. These sizes are larger than the population sizes of the proposed method. With regard to the expansion rate, $\epsilon_{spx} = \sqrt{n+2}$ is applied in SPX and $\epsilon_{spx} \times 2$ is applied in the proposed method. In this example, the average number of evaluations when the optimum is achieved is compared.

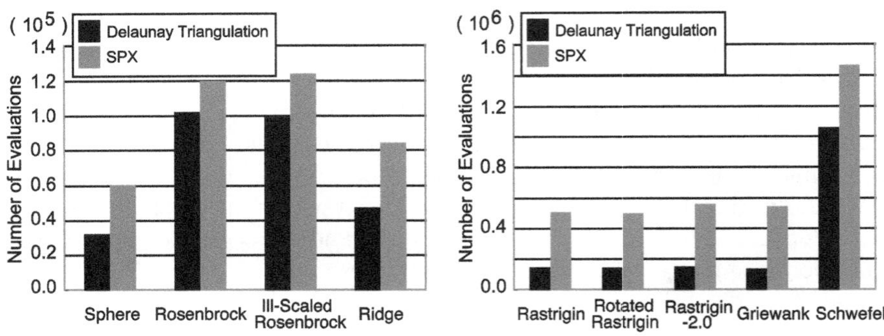

Fig. 6. Average number of evaluations when the optimum was achieved in the proposed method and SPX

Fig. 6 shows the average number of evaluations when the optimum was achieved in both methods. The number of times that the optimum was achieved in both methods was 17 in the Schwefel function and 20 in other functions. As shown in Fig. 6, in all test functions, the proposed method can derive the optimum with a lower number of evaluations than SPX. Especially, with the exception of the Schwefel function, the proposed method requires only about the one-third or one-quarter number of evaluations in multi-peak functions.

These results indicated that the proposed method has the following features. First, the proposed method can derive the optimum with a smaller population size than SPX. This feature is due to concentration of offspring in regions with a satisfactory evaluation value in the proposed method. In addition, as the proposed method requires a smaller population size than SPX, the optimum can be derived with a lower number of evaluations by converging the population earlier than SPX, combining local optima in the design space.

6 Conclusions and Future Work

The crossover operators based on the functional specialization hypothesis generally use only the information of the parent distribution and generate offspring with the same distribution as the parents. On the other hand, we feel that crossover operators with better search ability can be designed by utilizing not only the parent distribution but also the landscape of the objective function. Therefore, we proposed a new offspring generation method using the Delaunay triangulation. In the proposed method, the Delaunay triangulation is used with SPX. Then, the proposed method enables offspring to be concentrated in regions with a satisfactory evaluation value, inheriting the parent distribution. Comparison of search ability between the proposed method and SPX indicated that the proposed method can derive the optimum with smaller population size and lower number of evaluations than SPX.

In future work, we will apply the proposed method to higher-dimensional functions. As Qhull uses a large amount of memory, the proposed method cannot create the Delaunay triangulation with about 100 generators in more than 10-dimensional design space. Therefore, some processes that remove unneeded generators before the Delaunay triangulation creation will be added to the proposed method.

References

1. Eshleman, L. and Schaffer, J. D.: Real-Coded Genetic Algorithms and Interval-Schemata. Foundations of Genetic Algorithms 2 (1993)
2. Ono, I. and Kobayashi, S.: A Real Coded Genetic Algorithm for Function Optimization Using Unimodal Normal Distributed Crossover. Proc. of the 7th International Conference on Genetic Algorithms (1997)
3. Kita, H., Ono, I. and Kobayashi, S.: Multi-parental Extension of the Unimodal Normal Distribution Crossover for Real-coded Genetic Algorithm. Proc. of the 1999 Congress on Evolutionary Computation (1999).
4. Tsutsui, S., Yamamura, M. and Higuchi, T.: Multi-parent Recombination with Simplex Crossover in Real-Coded Genetic Algorithms. GECCO'99 (1999).
5. Higuchi, T., Tsutsui, S. and Yamamura, M.: Theoretical Analysis of Simplex Crossover for Real-Coded Genetic Algorithms. PPSN VI (2000).
6. Kita, H. and Yamamura, M.: A Functional Specialization Hypothesis for Designing Genetic Algorithms. Proc. of the IEEE International Conference on Systems, Man and Cybernetics (1999).
7. Pelikan, M., Goldberg, D. E., and Lobo, F.: A Survey of Optimization by Building and Using Probabilistic Models. Technical Report 99018, IlliGAL (1999).
8. Larranaga, P. and Lozano, J. A.: Estimation of Distribution Algorithms. A New Tool for Evolutionary Computation. Kluwer Academic Publishers (2001).
9. Bosman, P. and Thierens, D.: Continuous Iterated Density Estimation Evolutionary Algorithms Within The IDEA Framework. Proc. of OBUPM Workshop at the GECCO-2000, pp.197-200 (2000).
10. Tsutsui, S., Pelikan, M. and Goldberg, D. E: Evolutionary Algorithm Using Marginal Histograms in Continuous Domain. Technical Report 2001019, IlliGAL (2001).

11. Yuan, B. and Gallagher, M.: Playing in Continuous Spaces: Some Analysis and Extension of Population-based Incremental Learning. Proc. of the 2003 Congress on Evolutionary Computation, pp.443-450 (2003).
12. Okabe, A., Boots, B. and Sugihara, K.: Spatial Tesselation Concept and Applications of Voronoi Diagrams. John Wiley & Sons, New York (1992).
13. C. Bradford Barber and David P. Dobkin and Hannu Huhdanpaa: The Quickhull Algorithm for Convex Hulls. ACM Transactions on Mathematical Software, Volume 22, Number 4, pp.469–pp.483 (1996).
14. Qhull code for Convex Hull, Delaunay Triangulation, Voronoi Diagram, and Half-space Intersection about a Point: http://www.qhull.org/
15. Satoh, H., Ono, O. and Kobayashi, S.: Minimal Generation Gap Model for GAs considering Both Exploration and Exploitation. Proc. of IIZUKA'96 (1996).

An Investigation of Representations and Operators for Evolutionary Data Clustering with a Variable Number of Clusters

Julia Handl and Joshua Knowles

Manchester Interdisciplinary Biocentre, University of Manchester, UK
j.handl@postgrad.manchester.ac.uk, j.knowles@manchester.ac.uk

Abstract. This paper analyses the properties of four alternative representation/operator combinations suitable for data clustering algorithms that keep the number of clusters variable. These representations are investigated in the context of their performance when used in a multiobjective evolutionary clustering algorithm (MOCK), which we have described previously. To shed light on the resulting performance differences observed, we consider the relative size of the search space and heuristic bias inherent to each representation, as well as its locality and heritability under the associated variation operators. We find that the representation that performs worst when a random initialization is employed, is nevertheless the best overall performer given the heuristic initialization normally used in MOCK. This suggests there are strong interaction effects between initialization, representation and operators in this problem.

1 Introduction

Data clustering [7] is an unsupervised classification problem in which a set of data items is partitioned into a number of disjoint subsets or 'clusters', based on proximity information. The number of clusters, k, inherent to the data is usually unknown *a priori*, so clustering algorithms that investigate solutions with different numbers of clusters may be preferred to algorithms requiring a fixed value of k to be specified by the user. In this work, we consider alternative combinations of representations and variation operators that are suitable for exploring solutions with a variable number of clusters. We analyse the different choices within a multiobjective clustering evolutionary algorithm, MOCK, described previously [6], and attempt to understand the performance differences observed in terms of key properties of the representations and operators.

The effects of representations and operators on evolutionary search are a perennial topic in the literature, though few firm rules or conclusions of practical significance exist. Important factors, nonetheless, are thought to be: the size of the search space induced by a representation; whether phenotype space is entirely covered and/or reachable; whether the mapping from genotype to phenotype is injective, or 'degenerate' [11][1]; whether particular (groups of) phenotypes are over-represented [11,12,13]; and the 'heritability' and 'locality' of

[1] Meaning that several genotypes may map to the same phenotype.

T.P. Runarsson et al. (Eds.): PPSN IX, LNCS 4193, pp. 839–849, 2006.

the representation under crossover and mutation, respectively [12]. We consider each of these aspects in the analysis of the alternative representations studied here, and reflect on how much they tell us about performance.

The organization of the paper is as follows. Section 2 briefly recalls the principles behind the multiobjective clustering algorithm, MOCK, and the requirements it imposes on possible representations and operators. We also briefly revisit other work that considers representations for evolutionary data clustering. Section 3 provides the details of the representations and operators that are studied and the parameter setting used. Section 4 presents both theoretical and empirical findings of the study, and Section 5 concludes.

2 Previous Work

Basic principles of MOCK. In our previous work, we have described a multiobjective evolutionary algorithm (MOEA) for clustering, called MOCK (for Multiobjective clustering with automatic k-determination, [6]). MOCK is based on the elitist multiobjective evolutionary algorithm, PESA-II, described in detail in [2]. It minimizes two clustering objectives, *overall deviation* and *connectivity*: overall deviation is computed as the overall sum of the distances between each data item and its corresponding cluster centre,

$$Dev(C) = \sum_{C_k \in C} \sum_{i \in C_k} \delta(i, \mu_k),$$

where C is the set of all clusters, μ_k is the centroid of cluster C_k and $\delta(.,.)$ is the chosen distance function (here, the Euclidean distance); quite differently, connectivity evaluates the degree to which neighbouring data-points have been placed in the same cluster and is computed as,

$$Conn(C) = \sum_{i=1}^{N} \left(\sum_{j=1}^{L} x_{i,nn_{ij}} \right), \quad \text{where } x_{r,s} = \begin{cases} \frac{1}{j} & \text{if } \nexists C_k : r \in C_k \wedge s \in C_k \\ 0 & \text{otherwise,} \end{cases}$$

and where nn_{ij} is the jth nearest neighbour of datum i, N is the size of the clustered data set, and L is a parameter determining the number of neighbours that contribute to the connectivity measure.

When these two objectives are minimized, an approximate Pareto front is obtained with solutions arranged along the front by the number of clusters, k. (This arrangement occurs because the objectives have opposite biases with respect to the number of clusters [6]). The shape of the Pareto front gives important clues as to which is the actual 'best solution' and MOCK uses an automatic heuristic strategy to select the best solution, hence determining or estimating k automatically. Using this strategy, MOCK seems to provide solutions of a more consistently high quality compared to some other clustering algorithms, when a range of data sets is considered [6]. However, the final solution returned by MOCK's selection strategy depends crucially on obtaining a good overall Pareto front, and one that covers a range of values of k. This means that any representation used must facilitate finding solutions over a wide range of different numbers of clusters. Moreover, the representation must encourage effective exploration of the search space for another reason: although overall deviation is a relatively easy objective to minimize, connectivity (like most objectives capturing spatial separation or local connectedness [6]) provides relatively poor guidance in some areas of the search space.

MOCK's representation, operators and initialization. The representation employed in MOCK in [6] is the locus-based adjacency scheme proposed in [10]. In this graph-based representation, each individual g consists of N genes $g_1, \ldots, g_N$, where N is the size of the clustered data set, and each gene g_i can take allele values j in the range $\{1, \ldots, N\}$. A value of j assigned to the ith gene, is then interpreted as a link between data items i and j: in the resulting clustering solution they will be in the same cluster. The decoding of this representation requires the identification of all connected components, and all items belonging to the same connected component are assigned to one cluster. This decoding step can be done in linear time.

MOCK's initialization is based on (i) minimum spanning trees (MSTs) and (ii) the k-means algorithm [9]. For a given data set, the complete MST is computed using Prim's algorithm. Individuals corresponding to different clustering solutions are then obtained by breaking up the MST, using either a measure of 'interestingness' of individual links or the partitionings prescribed by the k-means solutions. This has the effect of generating solutions with a range of cluster numbers that already provide a good and well-spread approximation to the Pareto front [6].

MOCK's variation operators are uniform crossover and a mutation operator that allows data items to be linked to one of their L nearest neighbours only. Hence, $\forall i, g_i \in \{nn_{i1}, \ldots, nn_{iL}\}$, where nn_{il} denotes the lth nearest neighbour of data item i.

Alternative representations. For single-objective clustering tasks, a variety of different EA representations for clustering solutions have been explored in the literature (see [1]), ranging from a straightforward representation (with the ith gene coding for the cluster membership of the ith data item), to more complex representations, such as matrix-based or permutation-based representations. Falkenauer's grouping GA [3] also provides a general template for the implementation of evolutionary algorithms for grouping problems, although an application of the approach to straightforward data clustering has not been demonstrated, to our knowledge, previously, and under Falkenauer's template, this would require the design of several clustering-specific operators. Much previous work has also explored the use of existing clustering heuristics (most notably the k-means algorithm) as the cluster generator in a hybrid coding scheme (see [8]). This restricts the search space 'seen' by the evolutionary algorithm to the set of local optima that can be identified by the clustering heuristic used, and is therefore unsuitable for the use in multiobjective clustering where trade-off solutions (not identifiable by existing single-objective clustering heuristics) are to be found.

3 Representations/Operators Studied

The four different combinations of representations/operators investigated in this paper are as follows.

Baseline: A straightforward clustering representation, with one gene for every data item and its allele value specifying the cluster membership. An upper limit on the maximum number of clusters is imposed. Uniform crossover and a standard mutation operator (random change of cluster membership for a single data item) are used.

VIENNA: Representation identical to the Baseline representation. No crossover, but the mutation operator introduced in [5] is used. When a gene undergoes mutation to a different allele value (i.e. cluster), a number g of other genes are simultaneously 'moved' with it into the same target cluster (and the genotype is updated accordingly). The particular data items that undergo this move are the g nearest neighbours to the data item coded for by the initially mutated gene. The integer g itself is chosen, independently at each mutation event, uniformly at random in $0, \ldots, N/2$.

Falkenauer: Following the principles in [3], the genome of every individual consists of two sections, the first being identical to the above Baseline representation, and the second being a list of the groups (i.e. the set of allele values making up the first part). Two-point crossover operates directly on the second section, and the first section is updated, subsequently. We have developed a crossover operator that uses heuristic information to repair the first section: all unassigned data items are assigned the cluster membership of their nearest data items. We have also designed three mutation operators for the splitting, merging and the exchange of data items between groups, respectively. The splitting mutation operates on a randomly selected group: two items from this 'parent' cluster are randomly selected and used as 'seeds' for the two 'daughter' clusters. All remaining data items are then assigned to the cluster whose seed they are closer to. The merging mutation simply joins two randomly selected clusters. The swapping mutation swaps the cluster membership of two randomly selected data items.

MOCK: MOCK's standard representation and operators (see Section 2).

These different representations and operators are 'plugged' into our existing multiobjective clustering algorithm, that is, the optimization algorithm (PESA-II) and the objectives used remain constant throughout the experiments. MOCK's heuristic initialization scheme is also used for all representations/operators, but we additionally conduct experiments with random initialization in order to assess the impact of this initialization scheme. Here, the random initialization schemes used for the different representations vary slightly, as we aim to use the initialization that intuitively seems the most 'natural' for each of the representations used. For the adjacency-based representation, a random initialization is obtained by linking each data item to one of its randomly selected L nearest neighbours

Table 1. Parameter settings for the four algorithms. In those representations using crossover, a crossover probability of 0.7 is used. The mutations in the Baseline representation and VIENNA, and Falkenauer's swapping mutation are applied with a probability of $\frac{1}{N}$, where N is data set size. For MOCK, the biased mutation probability $p_m = \frac{1}{N} + (\frac{l}{N})^2$ introduced in [6] is used. The merge and split mutations in Falkenauer's representation are applied to a given individual with a probability of 0.2 each.

Parameter	*setting*
Number of generations	1000
External population size	1000
Internal population size	10
Resolution of hypergrid per dimension	10
#(Initial solutions)	100
Objective functions	Overall deviation and connectivity ($L = 10$)

of the data set. For the other three representations we first (randomly) determine the number of clusters, and then (randomly) assign cluster numbers to the individual data items.

Apart from representation-specific variations, the parameter settings are kept constant throughout the experiments and are summarized in Table 1.

4 Analysis

4.1 Empirical Performance Analysis

The data sets used in our empirical performance analysis have been previously described in [6] and are obtained using a generator for Gaussian clusters. For eight different combinations of cluster number and dimension, 10 different instances are generated, giving 80 data sets in all. In our experiments, these groups of 10 instances are referred to as xd-yc, where x is the dimensionality and y is the number of clusters in the data set.

In order to assess the algorithms' performance at solving the clustering task, two different measures are employed. Firstly, the quality of the best solution present in the Pareto front is analyzed. Here, the quality of a clustering solution is established using an external validation technique (which compares to the known correct partitioning), the Adjusted Rand Index (see [6]). It returns values in the interval $[\sim 0, 1]$ and is to be maximized.

Secondly, the quality of the Pareto fronts obtained is assessed using the hypervolume indicator (a.k.a. the S measure [15]), a standard measure from the literature. This indicator assesses the size of the region dominated by a sample set of points, and is to be maximized. Here, the Pareto front of all runs combined is normalized to lie in (0,1),(1,0); this normalization is then applied to each Pareto front. To compute each hypervolume, the point (2,2) is used to bound the dominated region, and the hypervolumes are divided by 4.0 to normalize them to a maximum value of 1.0.

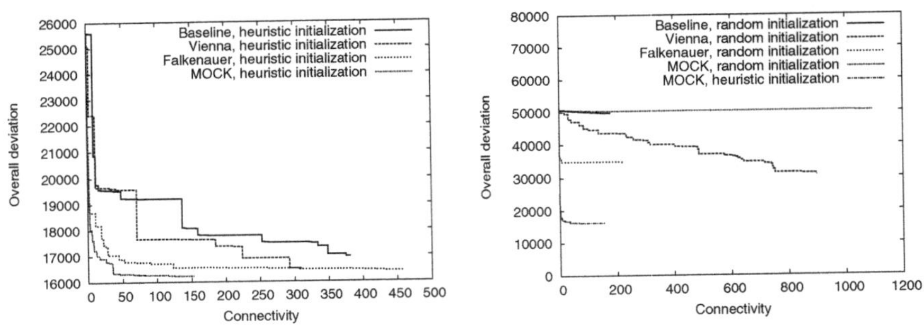

Fig. 1. Illustration of the differences between the approximation sets returned by the four algorithms on one of the 10d-40c data sets. (Left) With heuristic initialization. (Right) With random initialization. Results are for the first run of each algorithm.

Table 2. Mean values of the Adjusted Rand Index (wrt the known correct partitioning) of the best solution in the approximation sets identified by the four MOEAs, and the hypervolume of the entire approximation sets. Bold font indicates the statistically best performer (and ties) under a paired Wilcoxon test (overall $\alpha = 0.05$).

	Adjusted Rand Index				Hypervolume Indicator			
Data set	MOCK	Falkenauer	VIENNA	Baseline	MOCK	Falkenauer	VIENNA	Baseline
2d-4c	**0.988905**	0.98401	0.965744	0.853658	**0.98123**	0.972678	0.963554	0.953729
2d-10c	**0.948349**	0.91774	0.858553	0.800329	**0.985935**	0.97792	0.959744	0.949203
2d-20c	**0.949477**	0.935117	0.877584	0.862006	**0.989509**	0.982987	0.968587	0.96579
2d-40c	**0.875799**	0.81649	0.775303	0.771587	**0.987412**	0.976384	0.954132	0.949916
10d-4c	**0.995852**	**0.996396**	0.96457	0.898749	**0.968248**	0.95513	0.941786	0.933688
10d-10c	**0.969794**	0.955316	0.893811	0.859238	**0.978902**	0.970791	0.949533	0.94131
10d-20c	**0.997959**	**0.997976**	0.970049	0.961713	**0.983116**	0.978429	0.96757	0.966485
10d-40c	**0.99129**	0.983576	0.943561	0.937465	**0.997303**	0.988787	0.971748	0.968548

Table 2 summarizes the performance of the four algorithms under these two different measures. The results indicate clear performance differences between the algorithms. MOCK emerges as the strongest overall performer. In terms of the Adjusted Rand Index, it is closely followed by Falkenauer's representation, however, the results of the hypervolume reveal a significantly better convergence of MOCK towards the Pareto front. Both MOCK and Falkenauer's representation outperform VIENNA and the Baseline method. Figure 1 provides some representative examples of the approximation sets obtained by the four algorithms on a complex data set, and contrasts these results with the performance of the algorithms when random initialization is used. With the latter, all four algorithms perform very poorly, with MOCK suddenly being one of the worst performers. These results suggest that MOCK's good performance derives from a synergy between its initialization, representation and operators. This also seems apparent from the results obtained when comparing crossover innovation during a run of each MOEA, with the same for random solutions (see Section 4.4).

4.2 Size of the Search Space

In its original formulation, the size of the search space of the adjacency-based representation is bounded by N^N. However, the introduction of the nearest-neighbour mutation reduces the upper bound of the size of the search space seen by mutation to L^N, where, in our case, $L = 10$.

The Baseline representation and VIENNA result in a search space of $(k_{max})^N$ each, where k_{max} is the upper limit on the number of clusters, which, in this work, has been set to $k_{max} = 50$. For Falkenauer's representation, the search space is of size $(k_{max})^N \times k_{max}!$.

4.3 Heuristic Bias

A representation is said to be biased if it leads to an over-representation of certain phenotypes: hence, when sampling the search space without any selection pressure, these phenotypes will have a larger probability of being generated [12]. Here, the presence of a bias is analyzed with respect to two different phenotypic properties: (i) the number of clusters of the solution; and (ii) the clustering quality of the solution.

In the Baseline representation and VIENNA, every phenotype is encoded by $\binom{k_{max}}{k} \times k!$ different genotypes. Furthermore, the number of phenotypes $S(N,k)$ with a fixed number k of clusters is given by the Stirling number of the second kind. Consequently, the number of genotypes coding for a clustering solution with a fixed number of clusters k is given by

$$R_{Baseline}(N,k) = \binom{k_{max}}{k} \times \sum_{i=1}^{k} (-1)^{k-i} \binom{k}{i} i^N.$$

For very small data sets ($n = 1, \ldots, 9$), the resulting distributions are illustrated in Figure 2 (right). The bias of Falkenauer's representation is closely related and is given as

$$R_{Falkenauer}(N,k) = R_{Baseline}(N,k) \times k!.$$

Hence, all three of these representations have a strong bias towards large numbers of clusters. On the other hand, it is clear that the adjacency-based representation suffers from a strong bias towards small numbers of clusters. In particular, for a data set of size N, the number of different genotypes coding for solutions with a fixed number of clusters k corresponds to the integer sequence A060281 [14] and is computed as [4],

$$R_{MOCK}(N,k) = \sum_{i=k-1}^{N-1} \binom{N-1}{i} N^{N-1-i} [z^{k-1}](z+1)\ldots(z+i),$$

where $[z^{k-1}]$ is a coefficient operator, and means that only the coefficients of the terms with the specified powers of z contribute to the sum. For very small data sets ($n = 1, \ldots, 9$), the resulting distributions are illustrated in Figure 2 (left).

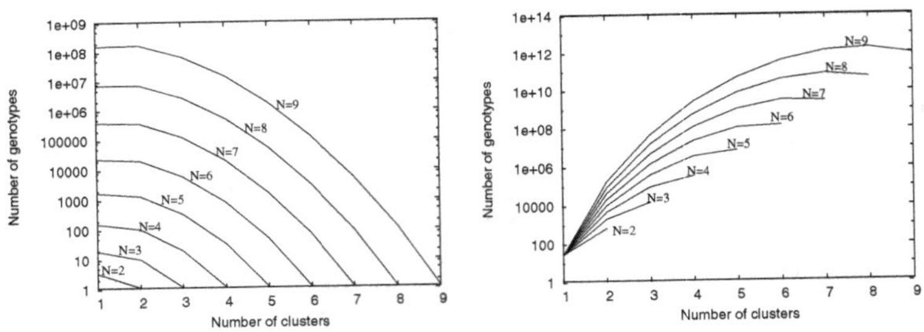

Fig. 2. Number of genotypes coding for a clustering solution for a fixed number of clusters for $N = 1, \ldots, 9$ data items. (Left) Adjacency-based representation. Note that, for increasing N, the maximum of the curve moves from $k = 1$ to $k = 2$, and this slow shifting to the right can be observed to continue for growing N. (Right) Baseline/VIENNA representation.

These calculations are confirmed by random sampling of the search space with neither selection pressure nor the use of specialized heuristic operators (results not shown). Figure 3, illustrates the selection pressure *implicitly* introduced through the use of specialized operators for clustering. The most striking results are MOCK's convergence to high numbers of clusters (caused by the nearest neighbour restriction in the mutation operator), the quick loss of diversity in Falkenauer's and the Baseline method (caused by the use of crossover) and the continuing exploration behaviour exhibited by VIENNA (due to the use of a large-scale mutation operator with strong heuristic bias).

4.4 Locality and Heritability

An analysis of locality and heritability of the operators can help to further understand the performance differences observed between the algorithms. This analysis only requires the definition of a distance in phenotype space [12], which is easily defined for the clustering task. A binary version of the Adjusted Rand Index is used to compare the similarity of two given clustering solutions. Note that, due to the use of a similarity (rather than a distance) measure, the following definitions are slightly different from those introduced in [12].

In order to assess heritability under crossover, crossover innovation CI is defined as the phenotypic similarity between an offspring and its phenotypically closer parent:

$$CI = \max(s_P(x^c, x^{p1}), s_P(x^c, x^{p2})),$$

where x^{p1} and x^{p2} are the phenotypes of the two parents and x^c is the phenotype of the offspring, and $s_P(,)$ is the similarity measure chosen.

Accordingly, the locality of the mutation operator is defined as the mutation innovation MI, which is the phenotypic similarity between solution x and its mutant:

$$MI = s_P(x, x^m).$$

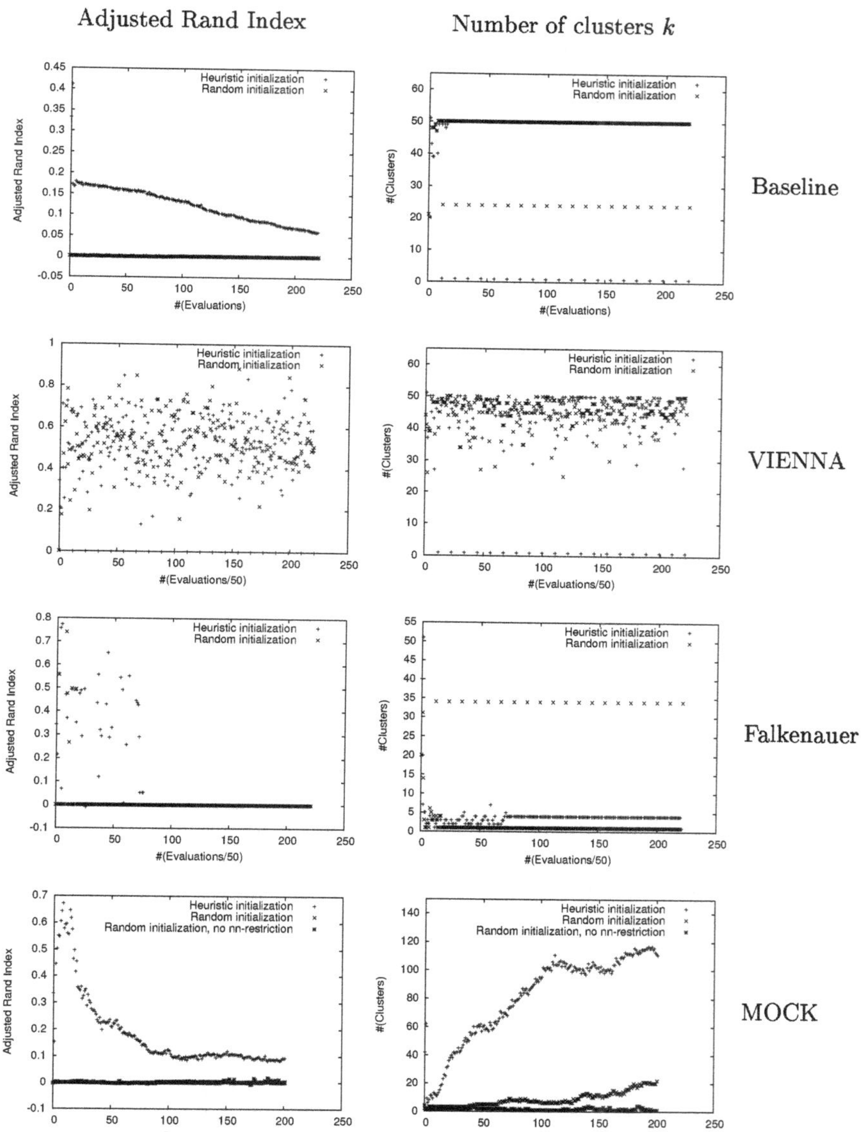

Fig. 3. Evolution of the number of clusters and the Adjusted Rand Index during a typical run of the MOEAs without selection pressure on one of the 2d-4c data sets

Figure 4 compares the distributions of crossover innovation and mutation innovation throughout the runs of the four MOEAs, and for randomly generated solutions. These plots illustrate that the reasons for the quick convergence of Falkenauer's representation in the absence of explicit selection pressure lie in the crossover operator's poor performance as a variation operator (it frequently creates identical copies of one parent). In contrast to this, MOCK's crossover

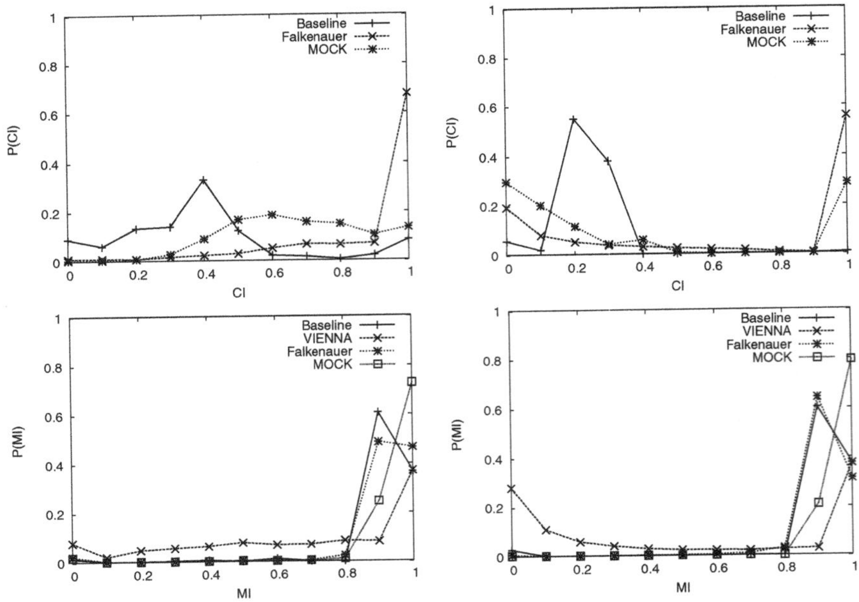

Fig. 4. (Top left) Crossover innovation in a normal run of the algorithms on a 2d-4c data set. (Top right) Crossover innovation for randomy generated solutions. (Bottom left) Mutation innovation in a normal run of the algorithm on a 2d-4c data set. (Bottom right) Mutation innovation for randomly generated solutions.

operator generates a large number of potentially interesting solutions (in the range $[0.4, 0.9]$), which may be the reason for its superior performance. Importantly, however, it fails to do so when random initialization is used, underlining once again that this representation relies crucially on the use of a powerful initialization scheme.

5 Conclusion

In this paper, four alternative representation/operator combinations for data-clustering with variable-k, have been investigated. We have focused on their use in the multiobjective clustering algorithm, MOCK, where it is necessary to be able to represent both compact clusters *and* locally-connected clusters equally well, and represent these for a large range of values of k. The analysis has revealed that, in this context, the simple adjacency-based representation, when combined with uniform crossover and nearest-neighbour mutation, performs very well, but only if a specialized initialization scheme is used. The more complicated scheme following Falkenauer is good if random initialization is used. Some of these results were reflected in the crossover innovation plots. The effects of the different representations' heuristic biases in phenotype space were also apparent under random selection, but these were overcome by the effects of standard selection and especially the use of the heuristic nearest-neighbour mutation.

Acknowledgments. We would like to thank Vladeta Jovovic and Neil Sloane for pointing us to A060281 in the online encyclopedia of integer sequences. JH acknowledges support of a doctoral scholarship from the German Academic Exchange Service (DAAD) and the Gottlieb Daimler- and Karl Benz-Foundation, Germany. JK is supported by a David Phillips Fellowship from the Biotechnology and Biological Sciences Research Council (BBSRC), UK.

References

1. R. M. Cole. Clustering with genetic algorithms. Master's thesis, University of Western Australia, Australia, 1998.
2. D. W. Corne, J. D. Knowles, and M. J. Oates. PESA-II: Region-based selection in evolutionary multiobjective optimization. In *Proceedings of the Genetic and Evolutionary Computation Conference*, pages 283–290. ACM Press, New York, NJ, 2001.
3. E. Falkenauer. *Genetic Algorithms and Grouping Problems*. John Wiley and Son Ltd, New York, NJ, 1998.
4. I. P. Goulden and D. M. Jackson. *Combinatorial Enumeration*. John Wiley and Sons, Inc., New York, NJ, 1983. (Page 192, 3.3.28).
5. J. Handl and J. Knowles. Evolutionary multiobjective clustering. In *Proceedings of the Eighth International Conference on Parallel Problem Solving from Nature*, pages 1081–1091. Springer-Verlag, Berlin, Germany, 2004.
6. J. Handl and J. Knowles. An evolutionary approach to multiobjective clustering. *IEEE Transactions on Evolutionary Computation*, 2006. (In press).
7. A. K. Jain and R. C. Dubes. *Algorithms for Clustering Data*. Prentice Hall, Englewood Cliffs, NJ, 1988.
8. P. C. H. Ma, K. C. C. Chan, X. Yao, and D. K. Y. Chiu. An evolutionary clustering algorithm for gene expression microarray data analysis. *IEEE Transactions on Evolutionary Computation*, 2006. (In press).
9. L. MacQueen. Some methods for classification and analysis of multivariate observations. In *Proceedings of the Fifth Berkeley Symposium on Mathematical Statistics and Probability*, pages 281–297. University of California Press, Berkeley, CA, 1967.
10. Y.-J. Park and M.-S. Song. A genetic algorithm for clustering problems. In *Proceedings of the Third Annual Conference on Genetic Programming*, pages 568–575. Morgan Kaufmann, San Francisco, CA, 1998.
11. N. J. Radcliffe and P. D. Surry. Fitness variance of formae and performance prediction. In *Foundations of Genetic Algorithms 3*, pages 51–72. Morgan Kaufmann Publishers, San Mateo, CA, 1995.
12. G. R. Raidl and J. Gottlieb. Empirical analysis of locality, heritability and heuristic bias in evolutionary algorithms: A case study for the multidimensional knapsack problem. *Evolutionary Computation*, 13(4):441–475, 2005.
13. F. Rothlauf and D. E. Goldberg. Redundant representations in evolutionary computation. *Evolutionary Computation*, 11(4):381–415, 2003.
14. N. J. A. Sloane. Series A060281 in The On-Line Encyclopedia of Integer Sequences.
15. E. Zitzler. *Evolutionary algorithms for multiobjective optimization: methods and applications*. PhD thesis, Swiss Federal Institute of Technology (ETH), Zurich, Switzerland, 1999.

Lamar: A New Pseudorandom Number Generator Evolved by Means of Genetic Programming

Carlos Lamenca-Martinez, Julio Cesar Hernandez-Castro, Juan M. Estevez-Tapiador, and Arturo Ribagorda

Computer Science Department, Carlos III University of Madrid
{clamenca, jcesar, jestevez, arturo}@inf.uc3m.es

Abstract. Pseudorandom number generation is a key component of many Computer Science algorithms, including mathematical modeling, stochastic processes, Monte Carlo simulations, and most cryptographic primitives and protocols. To date, multiple approaches that use Evolutionary Computation (EC) techniques have been proposed for designing useful Pseudorandom Number Generators (PRNGs) for certain non-cryptographic applications. However, none of the proposals have been secure nor efficient enough to be of interest for the much more demanding crypto world. In this work, we present a general scheme, which uses Genetic Programming (GP), for the automatic design of crypto-quality PRNGs by evolving highly nonlinear and extremely efficient functions. A new PRNG named Lamar and obtained using this scheme is proposed, whose C code and preliminary security analysis are provided.

1 Introduction

There are two types of random number generators: True Random Number Generators (TRNGs), also known as Random Number Generators (RNGs), that get their randomness from natural sources; and Pseudorandom Number Generators (PRNGs), based on deterministic algorithms that expand short keys into sequences of seemingly random bits.

Hardware implementations of TRNGs, like the chaotic system proposed in [32], are generally costly and slow, so their use is limited to only a few cases like the generation of seeds for PRNGs in cryptographic applications. That is why there is a constant need for powerful and efficient PRNGs, to be implemented in hardware and software.

Designing new, better, and more efficient PRNGs is an important open problem in Computer Science and, in particular, in computer security and cryptography. Apart from that, they play a major role in areas such as mathematical modeling, stochastic processes, and Monte Carlo simulation.

Unfortunately, it is not possible to prove randomness, because there is no efficient and deterministic definition of this rather abstract idea. Some basic

T.P. Runarsson et al. (Eds.): PPSN IX, LNCS 4193, pp. 850–859, 2006.

concepts that help in detecting evidence against the randomness hypothesis can be consulted in [11]. In 2001, the National Institute of Standards and Technology (NIST) proposed a comprehensive suite of randomness tests for the evaluation of PRNGs used in cryptographic applications [25]. One of the most stringent sets of randomness tests is Diehard [14], developed in 1996 by Marsaglia who, in 2002, extended and improved it by including the new tests presented in [15]. On the other hand, ENT [30] is a relatively light but very quick battery of tests. Nevertheless, none of these tests suites ensure, when successfully passed, that a given generator is useful for all kinds of applications. Systematically passing the NIST and Diehard batteries of tests provides, however, evidence in favor of a good degree of output randomness, probably adequate to make the algorithm suitable even for the most demanding application a PRNG can have: cryptography.

Multiple techniques based on EC (being Cellular Automata, CA, the most successful approach due to its output complexity and parallel nature) have been proposed for designing useful PRNGs for certain non-cryptographic applications. Nevertheless, the results typically do not pass a battery of very demanding statistical tests or, in the few cases when they do, it is at a high computational cost, resulting in very slow and completely worthless schemes for real-world high-throughput applications.

In this work, we present a general GP scheme for the automatic design of crypto-quality PRNGs by evolving highly nonlinear and extremely efficient functions. As an example, we propose Lamar, a new PRNG obtained using this approach, whose C code and preliminary security analysis are provided.

2 State of the Art

Many EC paradigms have been used for designing non-cryptographic PRNGs: Genetic Algorithms, GAs [6]; GP [5,12]; CA [31]; Cellular Programming [28], etc. However, none of the proposals were secure nor efficient enough to be of interest for the much more demanding crypto applications. With a different approach, some works [3,18] study the behavior of EC algorithms to measure the quality of PRNGs and, although this is a quite interesting research line, it is still wide open and waiting for mature results.

Randomness is not the only requirement for crypto-quality PRNGs, but just one more in a long list of very demanding properties. That is why very few works have used EC for developing cryptographic primitives. In [22], GAs are applied to generate boolean functions with excellent cryptographic properties, particularly a high degree of nonlinearity. A key-exchange protocol developed by means of neural networks was presented in [10]. We should also mention [27], where a new block cipher relying on a reversible CA was proposed. CAs have also been used in the design of stream ciphers [21] and hash functions [8,20]. Nevertheless, many of the previous schemes have been broken [2]. Despite these discouraging results, a steady flow of new EC-based cryptographic primitives (especially PRNGs and symmetric ciphers) exists, although they are looked upon suspiciously by the vast majority of the crypto community.

3 Avalanche Effect

Nonlinearity, as randomness, has not a complete, unique, and satisfactory definition. Fortunately, we will just try to measure a very specific mathematical property named the Avalanche Effect. This property reflects, to some extent, the intuitive idea of high nonlinearity: a very small difference in the input produces an avalanche of changes in the output, hence its name. Formally, let $H(x, y)$ be the Hamming distance between x and y. It is said that $F : \{0,1\}^m \to \{0,1\}^n$ has the Avalanche Effect property when:

$$\forall x, y | H(x, y) = 1, \quad Average\Big(H(F(x), F(y))\Big) = \frac{n}{2}$$

That is, a minimum random input change (one single bit) produces a maximum output change (half of the bits), on average. This definition also tries to reflect the general concept of independence between input and output (a good reason for being the base for our proposal, and an intuitive explanation for its applicability to the generation of PRNGs). An ideal F will resemble a perfect random function and will have a perfect Avalanche Effect. So, it seems natural to look for such functions by optimizing the amount of Avalanche Effect.

We will use, in fact, an even more demanding property: the Strict Avalanche Criterion [4], which can be mathematically described as:

$$\forall x, y | H(x, y) = 1, \quad H(F(x), F(y)) \sim B\Big(n, \frac{1}{2}\Big)$$

That is, the Hamming distances, after changing one single input bit, follow a Binomial distribution with parameters n and $1/2$. It is interesting to note that this property implies the Avalanche Effect, because the mean of such a random variable is $n/2$.

4 Experimentation Issues

We have used the `lil-gp` library [1] for our experimentation. Next, we describe the parameters the user has to adjust in order to define a particular problem.

4.1 Function Set

As functions are the building blocks of the individuals we will obtain, the correct definition of this set is critical to our problem. We decided to include only very efficient operations, easy to implement both in hardware and software and common in other implementations of PRNGs and stream ciphers. Hence, the inclusion of basic operations such as **vrotd** (one-bit right rotation), **vroti** (one-bit left rotation), **xor** (addition mod 2), **and** (bitwise and), **or** (bitwise or), and **not** (bitwise not) is an obvious choice. The **sum** (sum mod 2^{32}) operator is also useful, in order to avoid linearity.

We did not include **mult** (multiplication mod 2^{32}) at first because, depending on the implementation, the multiplication of two 32-bit values can be up to fifty times costlier than an **and** operation [7]. After extensive experimentation, we concluded that its inclusion was beneficial. Furthermore, there are some widely-used cryptographic primitives that use multiplication, like RC6 [24].

In some architectures, **vrotd** and **vroti** are also quite inefficient. We tried to solve this by including $\gg$ (one-bit right shift) and $\ll$ (one-bit left shift) too. These four operators were also implemented in a binary form (**vrotdk**, **vrotik**, **rotdk**, and **rotik**, respectively), where the argument k represents the number of positions that the first argument must be *moved*.

Although some operators were never used in any of the best individuals found (for example, the **not** and the **and** operators never showed up), when we included *all of them* in the function set, the results were notably better. That is why we decided to let the evolution discard the useless ones.

4.2 Terminal Set

The terminals will be eight 32-bit unsigned integers (a_0, a_1, a_2, a_3, a_4, a_5, a_6, a_7) for representing a 256-bit input. We also included Ephemeral Random Constants (ERCs), which are constant values (in our problem, 32-bit random values) that the GP system uses to generate better individuals. The idea behind this is providing a constant value, independently of the input.

4.3 Fitness Function

We wanted the PRNG to be efficient, complex, and robust because our objective is including it in the scheme of a stream cipher. To achieve this, we used:

$$Fitness = 10^9/\chi^2 \tag{1}$$

where χ^2 is the χ^2 goodness-of-fit test statistic that measures the proximity of the computed Hamming distances distribution to the sought theoretical $B(n, 1/2)$. It was necessary to amplify the fitness function (multiplying by 10^9) because the initial values of the χ^2 statistic were extremely high, making the fitness negligible at the beginning of the evolution process.

Summarizing, the fitness of each individual is computed as follows: we use the Mersenne Twister generator [17] to randomly generate the tuple (a_0, a_1, a_2, a_3, a_4, a_5, a_6, a_7). The output O_0 corresponding to this input is stored. Then, we randomly flip one single bit of this 256-bit input and obtain its output O_1. Now, we store the Hamming distance between these two output values, $H(O_0, O_1)$. This process is repeated a number of times ($2^{14} = 16384$ was experimentally proved to be enough) and, each time, a Hamming distance between 0 and 32 is obtained. Therefore, the fitness of each individual is computed by using the χ^2 goodness-of-fit test statistic that measures the distance between the observed distribution of the Hamming distances and their theoretical distribution under perfect Strict Avalanche Criterion hypothesis ($B(32, 1/2)$). Thus, our GP system tries to minimize this statistic in order to maximize *Fitness* (1).

4.4 Tree Size Limitations

When using GP, the depth and/or the number of nodes of the individuals should be limited. We tried both limiting the depth and not limiting the number of nodes, and vice versa. The best results were obtained by using the latter option, that is, we allowed the PRNG to use up to 100 nodes for trying to ensure a high degree of Avalanche Effect and robustness, while keeping a relatively small size, compatible with efficiency.

4.5 Results

We ran 20 experiments with different seeds for generating the initial population ($seed_i = (\pi * 100000)^i \pmod{1000000}$), a population size of 150 individuals, a crossover probability of 0.8, a reproduction probability of 0.2, and an ending condition of reaching 250 generations. These parameters were experimentally found to be adequate for our purposes.

Next, we show the tree corresponding to the best individual found over these experiments. This PRNG has an Avalanche Effect of 15.9631 (randomly flipping one input bit, the 32-bit output changes in 15.9631 bits on average, being 16.00 the optimal value) and presents a χ^2 goodness-of-fit test statistic of 12.6614 for a χ^2 probability distribution with 32 degrees of freedom; it means that, with probability 0.999112, the computed Hamming distances come from a Binomial distribution $B(32, 1/2)$.

```
=== BEST-OF-RUN ===
              generation: 153
                   nodes: 100
                   depth: 27
                    hits: 159631
TOP INDIVIDUAL: -- #1 --
                    hits: 159631
             raw fitness: 6237837.6345
    standardized fitness: 6237837.6345
        adjusted fitness: 6237837.6345
TREE:
 (sum (sum a5 (xor a6 a1)) (sum (vrotd 928a463)
 (mult (sum a5 (mult (sum a7 (sum a5 (mult
 (xor a3 (xor (vrotdk (xor (xor (rotdk (xor (xor
 (rotdk (sum a5 (mult (xor (rotdk (sum a3 (mult
 (xor (xor a6 a2) (xor (vroti (xor a6 a1)) a4))
 928a463)) (vrotd 928a463)) (roti a1)) 928a463))
 928a463) a1) (mult a3 a6)) 928a463) a1) (mult a3
 (roti a1))) 928a463) (sum (rotd (vroti (xor (xor
 (rotdk (sum a5 (mult (xor (rotdk (sum a5 (mult
 (xor a0 (xor (xor a3 a1) a7)) 928a463)) (vrotd
 928a463)) a0) 928a463)) (vrotd 928a463)) a0) a2)))
 (xor a6 a2)))) 928a463))) 928a463)) 928a463)))
```

5 Security Analysis

In this section, the results of testing the statistical and cryptographic properties of Lamar are presented.

5.1 Statistical Properties

We have performed a preliminary security analysis of our PRNG, consisting in examining the statistical properties of its output over a low-entropy input. In our case, we have set the 256-bit input to a simple incremental counter starting at zero ($a_i^n = i + 8 * (n-1)$).

Following this scheme, we have generated a file of 250MB to be analyzed with three batteries of statistical tests: ENT, Diehard, and NIST. The results obtained with ENT and Diehard are presented in Tables 1 and 2, respectively. In the latter, when several p-values were produced in the same test, we summarized them by a Kolmogorov-Smirnov p-value (marked with *), being necessary it to be greater than 0.05 to be considered successful. Lamar also passed the very demanding – because it is oriented to cryptographic applications– NIST statistical battery. We have computed 100 p-values for every test in the statistical suite; the proportion of successful ones is presented in Table 3. If this proportion is lower than 0.96, it is considered that the whole test failed. From these results, we can conclude that the output successfully passed all the randomness tests, even with the output being obtained from an extremely low-entropy input.

Table 1. Results obtained with ENT

Test	Result
Entropy	7.999999 bits/byte
Compression Rate	0%
χ^2 Statistic	258.29 (50%)
Arithmetic Mean	127.4984
Monte Carlo π Estimation	3.141524737 (0.00%)
Serial Correlation Coefficient	-0.000060

5.2 PRNG Quality Evaluation

To compare how Lamar performs against several different PRNGs, we used Johnson's scoring scheme [9]: we initialized (a_0, a_1, a_2, a_3, a_4, a_5, a_6, a_7) with 32 different random 256-bit values obtained from `http://randomnumber.org`, got 32 different 10MB files, and then assigned scores based on the results of the Diehard tests. The terminal updating during this process was made in a feedback manner, that is:

$$a_i^{n+1} = a_{i+1}^n \quad \forall i = 0, ..., 6$$
$$a_7^{n+1} = O^n_{(a_0,a_1,a_2,a_3,a_4,a_5,a_6,a_7)}$$

The PRNGs we have compared to ours are of several different kinds: Linear Congruential Generators (rand [11], rand1k [19], pm [23]), Multiply with Carry Generators (mother [13]), Additive and Substractive Generators (add [11], sub [23]), Compound Generators (shsub [11], shpm [23], shlec [23]), Feedback Shift Register Generators (tgfsr [16], fsr [26]), and Tausworthe Generators (tauss [29]).

Table 2. Test results obtained with the Diehard suite

Test	p-value	Test	p-value
Birthday Spacings	0.909*	Count the 1s in a Stream of Bytes	0.894001
GCD	0.816*	Count the 1s in Specific Bytes	0.857*
Overlapping Permutations	0.976*	Parking Lot Test	0.476150
Ranks of 31×31 and 32×32 Matrices	0.964*	Minimum Distance Test	0.789136
Ranks of 6×8 Matrices	0.354932	Random Spheres Test	0.676330
Monkey Tests on 20-bit Words	0.759*	The Squeeze Test	0.756284
Monkey Test OPSO	0.236*	Overlapping Sums Test	0.245735
Monkey Test OQSO	0.613*	Runs Up and Down Test	0.379
Monkey Test DNA	0.793*	The Craps Test	0.985*
Overall p-value		**0.360260**	

Table 3. Proportion results obtained with the NIST suite

Test	Proportion	Test	Proportion
Frequency	1.0000	Random-excursions	1.0000, 0.9718
Block-frequency	1.0000		0.9859, 0.9859
Cumulative-sums	1.0000, 1.0000		1.0000, 1.0000
Runs	1.0000		1.0000, 1.0000
Longest-run	0.9900	Random-excursions-variant	1.0000, 1.0000, 1.0000
Rank	0.9900		1.0000, 1.0000, 0.9718
FFT	0.9700		0.9859, 0.9859, 1.0000
Overlapping-templates	1.0000		1.0000, 1.0000, 1.0000
Universal	0.9900		0.9859, 0.9718, 0.9859
Apen	0.9900		0.9859, 0.9859, 0.9718
Linear-complexity	1.0000	Serial	0.9900, 0.9900

Each of the Diehard tests produces one or more p-values. We categorize them as good, suspect or rejected. We classify a p-value as rejected if $p \geq 0.998$, and as suspect if $0.95 \leq p < 0.998$; all other p-values are considered to be good. We assign two points for every rejection, one point for every suspect classification, and no points for the rest. Finally, we add up these points to produce a global Diehard score for each PRNG, and compute the average over the 32 evaluations: low scores indicate good PRNG quality. The information relating to the different PRNGs was taken from [18,19].

The results are presented in Table 4, where the behavior of a random variable X following the distribution of the scores ($X = 0$ with probability 0.95, $X = 1$ with probability 0.048, and $X = 2$ with probability 0.002) is also included. We note that Lamar is outstandingly better than the rest of the analyzed PRNGs: the lowest scores correspond to shsub (17.125) and fsr (17.90625), significantly greater than Lamar's (11.78125). On the other hand, the average scores increase up to 50.59375 (pm), 66.53125 (rand), and even 291.78125 (rand1k). As these are non-cryptographic PRNGs, this behavior could have been foreseen.

To measure the proximity between Lamar and the true random variable X, a χ^2 test has been computed, which is also shown in Table 4. As a result, we can affirm the behavior of Lamar can not be distinguised from that of a random variable at a significance level of $\alpha = 0.99$.

Table 4. PRNG Diehard Scores

PRNG	Total Score	Mean	
rand	2129	66.53125	
rand1k	9337	291.78125	
pm	1619	50.59375	
mother	602	18.8125	
add	577	18.03125	
sub	655	20.46875	
shsub	548	17.125	
shpm	799	24.96875	
shlec	751	23.46875	
fsr	573	17.90625	
tgfsr	584	18.25	
tauss	935	29.21875	
Lamar	**377**	**11.78125**	**χ^2 Test p-value**
Random Variable	**371.072**	**11.596**	**0.021**

6 Conclusions and Future Work

In this work, we have proved that the GP paradigm can be successfully applied to the design of competitive PRNGs. The most relevant aspect of our scheme is the selection of the fitness function, where nonlinearity and efficiency are the paramount objectives. We have opted to use the Strict Avalanche Criterion as the key property of the explored mathematical functions, and used only very efficient operators to construct them.

The proposed PRNG has successfully passed several batteries of very demanding statistical tests, which were not part of the fitness function; being this, by itself, quite an interesting result. Although passing these tests does not ensure a certain security level, it guarantees, to some extent, that neither trivial weaknesses nor implementation bugs exist. Moreover, Lamar has been compared to several PRNGs by measuring their statistical quality from Diehard results, and we have proved ours is the best and that there is no evidence to ensure Lamar is different from a random variable.

Future work will use Lamar as the building block of a stream cipher. For this, a deeper security analysis is needed, particularly against basic cryptanalytic attacks. We have tried to incorporate robustness in Lamar by construction, even though further testing is required. Additionally, speed tests should be performed to measure the exact efficiency of the proposed generator. In particular, it could be interesting to compare the efficiency of Lamar, which is expected to be good by design, with the current state-of-the-art stream ciphers, including RC4 and all its variants.

References

1. The `lil-gp` GP system. http://garage.cps.msu.edu/software/lil-gp/.
2. F. Bao. Cryptanalysis of a partially known cellular automata cryptosystem. *IEEE Trans. on Computers*, 53(11):1493–1497, 2004.

3. E. Cantú-Paz. On random numbers and the performance of genetic algorithms. In *Proc. of GECCO'02*, volume 2, pages 311–318. Morgan Kaufmann, 2002.
4. R. Forré. The strict avalanche criterion: Spectral properties of boolean functions and an extended definition. In *Proc. of CRYPTO'88*, LNCS, pages 450–468. Springer-Verlag, 1990.
5. J.C. Hernandez-Castro, P. Isasi, and A. Seznec. On the design of state-of-the-art PRNGs by means of genetic programming. In *Proc. of the IEEE CEC'04*, pages 1510–1516. IEEE Press, 2004.
6. J.C. Hernandez-Castro, A. Ribagorda, P. Isasi, and J.M. Sierra. Finding near optimal parameters for linear congruential PRNGs by means of evolutionary computation. In *Proc. of GECCO'01*, pages 1292–1298. Morgan Kaufmann, 2001.
7. G. Hinton et al. The microarchitecture of the pentium 4 processor. *Intel Technology Journal Q1*, 2001.
8. S. Hirose and S. Yoshida. A one-way hash function based on a two-dimensional cellular automaton. In *Proc. of the 20th Symposium on Information Theory and its Applications*, volume 1, pages 213–216. Matsuyama, 1997.
9. B.C. Johnson. Radix-b extensions to some common empirical tests for PRNGs. *ACM Trans. on Modeling and Comp. Sim.*, 6(4):261–273, 1996.
10. I. Kanter, W. Kinzel, and E. Kanter. Secure exchange of information by synchronization of neural networks. *Europhysical Letters*, 57(141), 2002.
11. D.E. Knuth. *The Art of Computer Programming, Volume 2: Seminumerical Algorithms.* Addison-Wesley, 3rd edition, 1998.
12. J.R. Koza. Evolving a computer program to generate random number using the genetic programming paradigm. In *Proc. of the 4th Int. Conference on Genetic Algorithms*, pages 37–44. Morgan Kaufmann, 1991.
13. G. Marsaglia. Yet another RNG. Posted to sci.stat.math, 1994.
14. G. Marsaglia. *The Marsaglia Random Number CDROM Including the DIEHARD Battery of Tests of Randomness.* http://stat.fsu.edu/pub/diehard, 1996.
15. G. Marsaglia and W.W. Tsang. Some difficult-to-pass tests of randomness. *Journal of Statistical Software*, 7(3), 2002.
16. M. Matsumoto and Y. Kurita. Twisted GFSR generators. *ACM Trans. on Modeling and Comp. Sim.*, 2(3):179–194, 1992.
17. M. Matsumoto et al. Mersenne twister: A 623-dimensionally equidistributed uniform PRNG. *ACM Trans. on Modeling and Comp. Sim.*, 8(1):3–30, 1998.
18. M.M. Meysenburg and J.A. Foster. The quality of PRNGs and simple genetic algorithm performance. In *Proc. of the 7th Int. Conference on Genetic Algorithms*, pages 276–281. Morgan Kaufmann, 1997.
19. M.M. Meysenburg and J.A. Foster. Randomness and GA performance, revisited. In *Proc. of GECCO'99*, volume 1, pages 425–432. Morgan Kaufmann, 1999.
20. M. Mihaljevic, Y. Zheng, and H. Imai. A cellular automaton based fast one-way hash function suitable for hardware implementation. volume 1431 of *LNCS*, pages 217–233. Springer-Verlag, 1998.
21. M.J. Mihaljevic. An improved key stream generator based on the programmable cellular automata. In *Proc. of ICICS'97*, volume 1334 of *LNCS*, pages 181–191. Springer-Verlag, 1997.
22. W. Millan, A. Clark, and E. Dawson. An effective genetic algorithm for finding boolean functions. In *Proc. of ICICS'97*, 1997.
23. W.H. Press, S.A. Teukolsky, W.T. Vetterling, and B.P. Flannery. *Numerical Recipes in C.* Cambridge University Press, 2nd edition, 1992.
24. R.L. Rivest, M.J.B. Robshaw, R. Sidney, and Y.L. Yin. The RC6 block cipher, v1.1, August 20 1998.

25. A. Rukhin et al. A statistical test suite for random and pseudorandom number generators for cryptographic applications. NIST special publication 800-22, http://csrc.nist.gov/rng/, 2001.
26. B. Schneier. *Applied Cryptography.* John Wiley and Sons, 1994.
27. M. Seredynski and P. Bouvry. Block cipher based on reversible cellular automata. *Next Generation Computing Journal*, 23(3):245–258, 2005.
28. M. Sipper and M Tomassini. Generating parallel random number generators by cellular programming. *Int. Journal of Modern Physics C*, pages 181–190, 1996.
29. S. Tezuka and P. L'Ecuyer. Efficient and portable combined Tausworthe Random Number Generators. *ACM Trans. on Modeling and Comp. Sim.*, 1(2):99–112, 1991.
30. J. Walker. *ENT Randomness Tests.* http://www.fourmilab.ch/random/, 1998.
31. S. Wolfram. Random sequence generation by cellular automata. *Advances in Applied Mathematics*, 7:123–169, 1986.
32. M.E. Yalcin, J.A.K. Suykens, and J. Vandewalle. True random bit generation from a double-scroll attractor. *IEEE Trans. on Circuits and Systems-I: Regular Papers*, 51(7):1395–1404, 2004.

Appendix: C Source Code

Finally, a C implementation of the Lamar PRNG is included, where `unsigned long` variables represent unsigned integers of 32 bits.

```
unsigned long lamar (unsigned long a0, unsigned long a1, unsigned long a2, unsigned long a3,
                     unsigned long a4, unsigned long a5, unsigned long a6, unsigned long a7)
{  unsigned long nonce, aux1, aux2, aux3;

   aux1 = ((vroti(a6 ^ a1) ^ a2 ^ a4 ^ a6) * 0x928a463) + a3;
   aux2 = rotdk(aux1, vrotd(0x928a463)) ^ (a1<<1);
   aux1 = (0x928a463 * aux2) + a5;
   aux2 = rotdk(aux1, 0x928a463) ^ a1 ^ (a3 * a6);
   aux1 = rotdk(aux2, 0x928a463) ^ a1 ^ ((a1<<1) * a3);
   aux2 = ((a0 ^ a1 ^ a3 ^ a7) * 0x928a463) + a5;
   aux3 = ((rotdk(aux2, vrotd(0x928a463)) ^ a0) * 0x928a463) + a5;
   aux2 = rotdk(aux3, vrotd(0x928a463)) ^ a0 ^ a2;
   aux3 = (a2 ^ a6) + (vroti(aux2)>>1);
   aux2 = vrotdk(aux1,0x928a463) ^ a3 ^ aux3;
   aux1 = ((aux2 * 0x928a463) + a5 + a7) * 0x928a463;
   aux2 = (a6 ^ a1) + a5 + vrotd(0x928a463);
   nonce = ((aux1 + a5) * 0x928a463) + aux2;
   return(nonce);  }
```

Evolving Bin Packing Heuristics with Genetic Programming

E.K. Burke, M.R. Hyde, and G. Kendall

School of Computer Science and Information Technology
The University of Nottingham
Nottingham, NG8 1BB
United Kingdom (UK)
mvh@cs.nott.ac.uk
http://cs.nott.ac.uk/~mvh

Abstract. The bin-packing problem is a well known NP-Hard optimisation problem, and, over the years, many heuristics have been developed to generate good quality solutions. This paper outlines a genetic programming system which evolves a heuristic that decides whether to put a piece in a bin when presented with the sum of the pieces already in the bin and the size of the piece that is about to be packed. This heuristic operates in a fixed framework that iterates through the open bins, applying the heuristic to each one, before deciding which bin to use. The best evolved programs emulate the functionality of the human designed 'first-fit' heuristic. Thus, the contribution of this paper is to demonstrate that genetic programming can be employed to automatically evolve bin packing heuristics which are the same as high quality heuristics which have been designed by humans.

1 Introduction

The aim of this work is to explore how a genetic programming system might evolve good heuristics that can pack bins. The goal is to automatically generate good heuristics which can operate over a range of instances and, perhaps more importantly, do not require human intervention or parameter tuning. The aim is therefore to show that a genetic programming system is capable of generating heuristics which have the functionality of human-designed heuristics. In this work we use a basic genetic programming system which does not incorporate any of the more advanced techniques such as re-usable code, loops, or memory, all of which are explained in [1] and [2] for the interested reader.

1.1 Genetic Programming

Genetic programming [3] evolves a population of computer programs which are represented as tree structures. After each program (or individual) has been executed, its performance is assessed and a fitness rating is given to it. The genetic operators of crossover and reproduction are applied to individuals in the population in proportion to their relative fitness.

T.P. Runarsson et al. (Eds.): PPSN IX, LNCS 4193, pp. 860–869, 2006.

1.2 Hyper-heuristics

One of the aims of a hyper-heuristic [4,5] is to "raise the level of generality at which optimisation systems can operate" [5]. To this end, hyper-heuristics are heuristics which choose "between a set of low-level heuristics, using some learning mechanism" [6].

Of course, the No Free Lunch theorem [7,8] shows that all search algorithms have the same average performance on all problems defined on a given finite search space. However, it is important to recognise that this theorem is *not* saying that it is not possible to build search methodologies which are *more* general than is possible today. Indeed, research into hyper-heuristics is motivated by the assertion that in many real world problem solving environments, there are users who are interested in *"good-enough soon-enough cheap-enough"* solutions to their optimisation problems [5].

Some examples of hyper-heuristic methods are briefly explained here. Two hyper-heuristic methods have been tested on the one-dimensional bin-packing problem, a learning classifier system [9] and a genetic algorithm [10]. In [11], an ant algorithm hyper-heuristic chooses a sequence of low-level heuristics for the project presentation scheduling problem. A tabu search hyper-heuristic is applied in [12] to a nurse scheduling problem and a university course timetabling problem. A choice function has also been employed as a hyper-heuristic, to rank the low-level heuristics and choose the best [13]. A multi-objective hyper-heuristic is applied to space allocation and timetabling in [14]. A graph based hyper-heuristic is used for timetabling in [15]. Case based heuristic selection is applied on a timetabling problem in [16]. Finally, in [17], a simulated annealing hyper-heuristic is used to determine shipper sizes.

1.3 Using Genetic Programming as a Hyper-heuristic

This paper invesigates the role of genetic programming as a hyper-heuristic. The genetic programming system chooses between a set of low level building blocks to construct a heuristic which performs well in the environment given to it. In this case the building blocks are the function and terminal set shown in table 2, and the environment is the data set given to the system.

In previous work (e.g. [12]), hyper-heuristics have had their low-level heuristics given to them by the human programmer, and so the number and quality of heuristics that the hyper-heuristic has available is limited to those which a human can provide. The aim of this research is to show that even more of the decision process can be automated. For example, the human programmer would normally choose the low-level heuristics, from the space of all heuristics. This paper aims to show that by using a genetic programming system as a hyper-heuristic, *any* heuristic can be chosen from the space of all heuristics that can be constructed with the function and terminal set. The human programmer therefore need only supply the *potential* components of a heuristic.

2 The Bin Packing Problem

The one-dimensional bin-packing problem involves a set of integer-size pieces L, which must be packed into bins of a certain capacity C, using the minimum number of bins possible. In other words, the set of integers must be divided into the smallest number of subsets so that the sum of the sizes of the pieces in a subset does not exceed C [18].

2.1 The Problem

Twenty instances of the bin packing problem are used in this research, taken from benchmark data studied by Falkenauer in [19] and now maintained by Beasley in the OR-Library of Brunel University [20]. In each instance, there are 120 pieces, all uniformly distributed in (20, 100). These pieces are packed into bins of capacity 150 for every instance.

In this paper, the 'on-line' bin packing problem is studied. That is, we do not know in advance how many pieces there are or the size of those pieces. Our system must simply pack the pieces into the bins in the order they arrive, and the pieces cannot be moved once they have been placed in a bin [21]. This situation is likely to arise in the real world. For example when items come off a production line and are placed into containers, or packages of different sizes are packed into trucks at a depot, and only a certain number of trucks can be at the depot at any one time [21].

2.2 Existing Heuristics

The bin packing problem is known to be NP-Hard [22] so heuristics are commonly used to generate solutions that are of high enough quality for practical purposes, as a polynomial-time exact algorithm is unlikely to be found for the general case [21]. A number of examples of heuristics used in the online bin packing problem are described below:
Best Fit [23]: Puts the piece in the fullest bin that has room for it. Opens a new bin if the piece does not fit in any existing bin
Worst Fit [21]: Puts the piece in the emptiest bin that has room for it. Opens a new bin if the piece does not fit in any existing bin.
Almost Worst Fit [21]: Puts the piece in the second emptiest bin if that bin has room for it. Opens a new bin if the piece does not fit in any open bin.
Next Fit [24]: Puts the piece in the right-most bin and opens a new bin if there is not enough room for it.
First Fit [24]: Puts the piece in the left-most bin that has room for it and opens a new bin if it does not fit in any open bin.

3 The Genetic Programming Hyper-heuristic

3.1 Evolving the Choice of Bin

Our system evolves a control program that decides whether to put a given piece into a given bin. An individual in the population is assessed by rating the result created when the algorithm in Fig. 1 is run, where L = the list of all the pieces, and A = the array of bins. Note that when making the choice of whether to put the current piece in the current bin, each individual in the population is not constrained by whether it is legal to do so. For example, putting every piece in the first bin is permitted. However, this will lead to an illegal solution with a high penalty. For this reason, when the *best-of-run* individual produces a legal solution, it is because the system will have evolved an understanding of the rules, not because of artificial constraints imposed by humans.

```
For each piece p in L
  For each bin i in A
    output = evaluate(p, fullness of i, capacity of i)
    If (output > 0)
      place piece p in bin i
      break
    End If
  End For
End For
```

Fig. 1. Pseudo code showing the overall program structure

Initialisation Parameters. Table 1 shows the parameters of the run. No optimality is claimed for these parameters. They were chosen from a range of possible initialisation parameters, after a series of experiments, because they result in a good solution in reasonable time. The population size of 1000 was chosen because it gives a good range of solutions in the initial population, and it allows for reasonable run times. The maximum depth of the initial trees is a relatively low value because the maximum depth obtainable during the run is not limited. The 'Grow' method of initialising the trees [25] is used here because it creates an initial population of diverse structures. Using 50 as the maximum number of generations is a standard parameter used in [3], where generation 0 is the initial random population.

Fitness measure. The fitness measure is shown in equation 1, where:
B = Number of bins used, n = Number of pieces,
S_k = Size of piece k, and C = Bin capacity

$$Fitness = B - \frac{\sum_{k=1}^{n} S_k}{C} \tag{1}$$

This means that a fitness of zero is the perfect result, because the pieces are packed into the smallest number of bins possible. A fitness of 1000 is assigned to any illegal solution (an arbitrarily high number compared to the range of fitness values that a legal solution can have).

Genetic Operators. At the end of each generation, the reproduction operator is used on 10% of the individuals, and the crossover operator is used on 90% of

Table 1. Initialisation parameters of each genetic programming run

Population size	1000
Maximum depth of initial trees	4
Method of initialising the trees	Grow
Maximum generations	50

the individuals. These are standard parameters taken from [3]. In the crossover operator, any node in the tree can be selected with equal probability to be the crossover point. 'Fitness proportional selection' is used [3] (also known as 'roulette wheel selection'). Each individual is selected for the genetic operators with probability proportional to its normalised fitness. Reselection is permitted, so the original individuals involved in the genetic operations are put back in the population and can be used if selected again.

Function and Terminal Set. In the diagrams below, the functions and terminals are represented by symbols. The symbols are shown in table 2 along with an explanation of their function within the program. 'S', 'F' and 'C' are parameters given to the individuals in the population before they are evaluated.

Table 2. The functions and terminals used in the experiments and descriptions of the values they return

Symbol	Arguments	Description
+	2	Add
-	2	Subtract
*	2	Multiply
%	2	Protected divide function. Division by zero will return 1
<	2	Tests if the first argument is less than or equal to the second argument. Returns 1 if true, -1 if false
A	1	Returns the absolute value of the argument
F	0	Returns the sum of the pieces already in the bin
C	0	Returns the bin capacity
S	0	Returns the size of the current piece

4 Results

4.1 Evolved Small Trees

Figs. 2-5 show four *best-of-run* individuals (referred to as trees A-D) from four different runs, which illustrate that very simple programs can be found by the genetic programming system, and that the system is versatile enough to produce many different ways of expressing the same heuristic, including some ways that would perhaps not be thought of immediately by a human programmer given the same task. They all result in a legal solution because a piece is never put in a bin when it is larger than the space left in the bin.

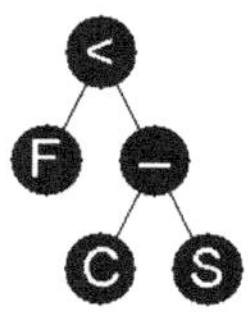

Fig. 2. Tree A

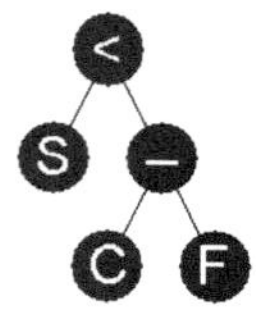

Fig. 3. Tree B

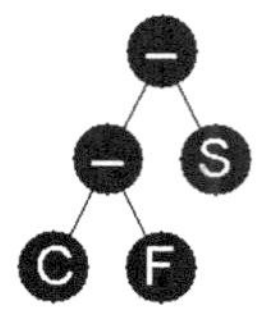

Fig. 4. Tree C

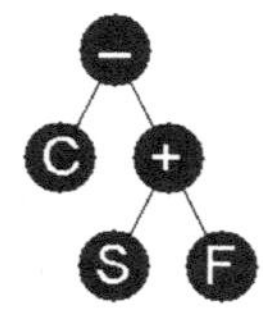

Fig. 5. Tree D

All four individuals perform much the same function. However, trees C and D are slightly different to A and B. Trees A and B both return a negative number if the piece size is greater than the space left in the bin, and a positive number if not. Therefore, they implement the first-fit heuristic. Trees C and D perform the same way, apart from the case when the piece size is the *same* as the space left in the bin. Zero is returned in this case, which means the greater-than-zero condition, shown in the pseudo code (Fig. 1), is not met and the piece is not placed in the bin. So C and D are individuals that do not implement the first-fit heuristic, but their functionality is highly similar.

The question can be asked why trees C and D were the *best-of-run* individuals in their run when it seems easy for the system to produce trees which copy the functionality of trees A and B. The answer to this question is that if a tree like C or D is found first in its run then it is stored as the *best-of-run* individual so far. Trees like A and B *were* produced in the run but with the data sets used here they did not produce a solution which used less bins, so tree C or D remained as the best individual in the run so far.

The reason a better result is not gained by using trees A and B is because the bin capacity is large and the piece sizes are such that it is uncommon for a bin to be filled exactly, so the fact that the piece will not be put in the bin if it exactly fills the bin barely affects the assignment of pieces to bins. Therefore the solutions produced by both heuristics are almost the same, and they receive the same fitness.

This plateau in the search space also means that code-bloat [26] was not an issue in the runs which produced Figs. 2-5. They were found in the early generations when the average tree size was small, they were stored as the best so far, and then were not surpassed by individuals found in later generations. Code-bloat does exist in our genetic programming system, but the average and maximum complexity of the trees only increases in later generations. Therefore, if a first-fit heuristic is found early in the run, it is more likely to be a simple and easy to understand tree than if it is found in a later generation.

4.2 More Complex Trees

In this section, we present two more examples of trees created during different runs which are more complex than the four individuals presented in section 4.1. These individuals are of interest because they are quite far removed from any

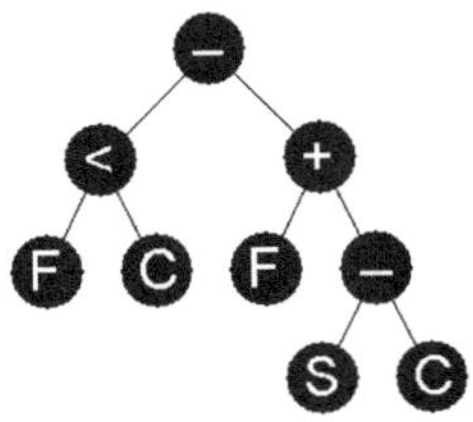

Fig. 6. Tree Structure 1

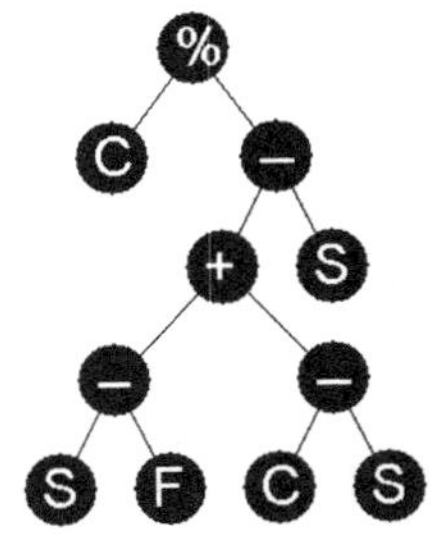

Fig. 7. Tree Structure 2

program that a human programmer would create for the same task. Both are *best-of-run* individuals.

Tree Structure 1. Fig. 6 has the same functionality as the first-fit heuristic. The tree works this way because F is always less than or equal to C. So 1 will always be returned by the left branch. In general, if the following equation is satisfied, then this means that the piece fits in the bin,

$$(F + (S - C)) <= 0$$

The right hand branch will return 0 or less if this is the case, therefore the result returned by the whole tree will be 1 or greater and the piece will be put in the bin.

Tree Structure 2. Fig. 7 shows a tree which also implements the first-fit heuristic. In Fig. 7, the tree's right hand branch (from the first subtract node downwards) can be simplified to:

$$(C - F) - S$$

This branch will therefore return 0 or greater if the piece fits or else it will return a negative number. Since C is always a positive integer number, C divided by a positive number returns a positive number, and so the piece is placed in the bin in such a case. On the other hand, C divided by a negative number returns a negative number and so if a negative number is returned by the right hand branch then the piece is not placed in the bin.

The most interesting feature of Fig. 7, however, is the way that the 'protected divide' node at the top fixes the problem that Figs. 4 and 5 have. Recall that in those trees, when the piece fits exactly, 0 is returned, and therefore the 'greater-than-zero' condition of Fig. 1 is not satisfied and the piece is not placed in the bin. The protected divide function at the root of Fig. 7 means that when the piece fits exactly, 1 is returned as it is a division by zero. So the problems in Figs. 4 and 5 have been solved in Fig. 7.

This functionality was not the reason why the protected divide function was defined in this way. The reason was to represent the closure of the function set, as explained in [3]. This is, therefore, an example of how the evolutionary process can use combinations of functions and terminals in ways not originally envisaged by the human programmer that supplied them.

4.3 Comparison with First-Fit and Other Heuristics Found

Over the 20 benchmark binpacking instances, our best evolved heuristic matches the performance of the first-fit heuristic (a well known human designed heuristic). This paper concentrates on reporting the best of the heuristics found. However, a worse heuristic was found in approximately 3 percent of the runs. For example, a heuristic with 17 nodes was found which puts a piece in a bin if its size is greater than the fullness multiplied by 2. Another heuristic with 17 nodes was found which never fills a bin higher than 148.

5 Conclusions and Future Work

It has been shown that a heuristic invented by a human, namely the first fit heuristic, can also be evolved by genetic programming. We evolved the heuristic without any human input except for the specification of the building-block nodes that it manipulates to make the tree structures of each individual in the population.

The selection pressure exerted by the fitness-proportional selection progressively eliminated those individuals that produced illegal solutions and used more individuals that produced legal solutions to construct the next generation. In this way the average fitness of the population improved over successive generations and better individuals were more likely to be created by the crossover genetic operator.

One potential area of future work is to increase the range of functions and terminals available to the genetic programming system. This will concentrate on expanding the potential complexity of evolved programs. Specifically, work will concentrate on expanding two new aspects of the system. Firstly, each individual must be given the array of bins as input, not just the piece size, bin fullness, and bin capacity. Secondly, automatically defined loops and automatically defined storage have to be included, which are explained in [2].

Plateaus in the search space are common when using the fitness function in this paper. We will investigate the use of other fitness functions which can differentiate between two solutions where the number of bins used is the same. An example is given in [27], where, if the number of bins used in both situations is equal, a solution with some full bins and some almost empty bins is considered superior to a solution where all bins are packed to a constant level.

We will test the genetic programming system over more binpacking benchmark instances to investigate if different heuristics are evolved under different conditions.

We will also investigate the effects of code-bloat as the population size is reduced from 1000. The average complexity of the population increases with the generation number, and we predict that as the population size is decreased, the *best-of-run* individuals will be larger and harder to understand because the system will need more generations to find the same standard of program.

References

1. Koza, J.R.: Genetic Programming II: Automatic Discovery of Reusable Programs. The MIT Press, Cambridge, Massachusetts (1994)
2. Koza, J.R., Bennett III, F.H., Andre, D., Keane, M.A.: Genetic Programming III: Darwinian Invention and Problem solving. Morgan Kaufmann (1999)
3. Koza, J.R.: Genetic Programming: on the Programming of Computers by Means of Natural Selection. The MIT Press, Boston, Massachusetts (1992)
4. Ross, P.: Hyper-heuristics. In Burke, E.K., Kendall, G., eds.: Search Methodologies: Introductory Tutorials in Optimization and Decision Support Techniques. Kluwer, Boston (2005) 529–556
5. Burke, E.K., Hart, E., Kendall, G., Newall, J., Ross, P., Schulenburg, S.: Hyper-heuristics: An emerging direction in modern search technology. In Glover, F., Kochenberger, G., eds.: Handbook of Meta-Heuristics. Kluwer (2003) 457–474
6. Soubeiga, E.: Development and Application of Hyperheuristics to Personnel Scheduling. PhD thesis, Univesity of Nottingham, School of Computer Science (2003)
7. Wolpert, D.H., Macready, W.G.: No free lunch theorems for optimization. IEEE Transactions on Evolutionary Computation **4** (1997) 67–82
8. Whitley, D., Watson, J.P.: Complexity theory and the no free lunch theorem. In Burke, E.K., Kendall, G., eds.: Search Methodologies: Introductory Tutorials in Optimization and Decision Support Techniques. Kluwer, Boston (2005) 317–339
9. Ross, P., Schulenburg, S., Marin-Blazquez, J.G., Hart, E.: Hyper heuristics: Learning to combine simple heuristics in bin packing problems. In: Proceedings of the Genetic and Evolutionary Computation Conference 2002 (GECCO '02). (2002) 942–948
10. Ross, P., Marin-Blazquez, J.G., Schulenburg, S., Hart, E.: Learning a procedure that can solve hard bin-packing problems: A new ga-based approach to hyper-heurstics. In: Proceedings of the Genetic and Evolutionary Computation Conference 2003 (GECCO '03), Chicago, Illinois (2003) 1295–1306
11. Burke, E.K., Kendall, G., Landa Silva, J.D., O'Brien, R.F.J., Soubeiga, E.: An ant algorithm hyperheuristic for the project presentation scheduling problem. In: Proceedings of the Congress on Evolutionary Computation 2005 (CEC'05). Volume 3., Edinburgh, U.K. (2005) 2263–2270
12. Burke, E.K., Kendall, G., Soubeiga, E.: A tabu-search hyper-heuristic for timetabling and rostering. Journal of Heuristics **9** (2003) 451–470
13. Cowling, P., Kendall, G., Soubeiga, E.: A hyperheuristic approach to scheduling a sales summit. In Burke, E.K., Erben, W., eds.: Proceedings of the 3rd International Conference on the Practice and Theory of Automated Timetabling (PATAT 2000), Konstanz, Germany (2000) 176–190
14. Burke, E.K., Landa Silva, J.D., Soubeiga, E.: Multi-objective hyper-heuristic approaches for space allocation and timetabling. In Ibaraki, T., Nonobe, K., Yagiura, M., eds.: Meta-heuristics: Progress as Real Problem Solvers, Selected Papers from the 5th Metaheuristics International Conference (MIC 2003). Springer (2005) 129–158

15. Burke, E.K., McCollum, B., Meisels, A., Petrovic, S., Qu, R.: A graph-based hyper heuristic for educational timetabling problems. European Journal of Operational Research (In Press, to appear 2006, Available online 21 November 2005)
16. Burke, E.K., Petrovic, S., Qu, R.: Case based heuristic selection for timetabling problems. Journal of Scheduling **9** (2006) 99–113
17. Dowsland, K., Soubeiga, E., Burke, E.K.: A simulated annealing hyper-heuristic for determining shipper sizes. Accepted for European Journal of Operational Research (In Press, to appear 2006, Available online 29 November 2005)
18. Martello, S., Toth, P.: Knapsack Problems: Algorithms and Computer Implementations. John Wiley and Sons, Chichester (1990)
19. Falkenauer, E.: A hybrid grouping genetic algorithm for bin packing. Journal of Heuristics **2** (1996) 5–30
20. Beasley, J.E.: Binpacking benchmark data, at the brunell university or-library. Available at: http://people.brunel.ac.uk/~mastjjb/jeb/orlib/binpackinfo.html (Last modified: 07-09-2004) [Accessed 1st March 2006].
21. Coffman Jr, E.G., Galambos, G., Martello, S., Vigo, D.: Bin packing approximation algorithms: Combinatorial analysis. In Du, D.Z., Pardalos, P.M., eds.: Handbook of Combinatorial Optimization. Kluwer (1998)
22. Garey, M.R., Johnson, D.S.: Computers and Intractability: A Guide to the Theory of NP-Completeness. W.H. Freeman and Company, San Fransisco (1979)
23. Rhee, W.T., Talagrand, M.: On line bin packing with items of random size. Math. Oper. Res. **18** (1993) 438–445
24. Johnson, D., Demers, A., Ullman, J., Garey, M., Graham, R.: Worst-case performance bounds for simple one-dimensional packaging algorithms. SIAM Journal on Computing **3** (December 1974) 299–325
25. Koza, J.R., Poli, R.: Genetic programming. In Burke, E.K., Kendall, G., eds.: Search Methodologies: Introductory Tutorials in Optimization and Decision Support Techniques. Kluwer, Boston (2005) 127–164
26. Bernstein, Y., Li, X., Ciesielski, V., Song, A.: Multiobjective parsimony enforcement for superior generalisation performance. In: Proceedings of the Congress for Evolutionary Computation 2004 (CEC'04), Portland, Oregon (2004) 83–89
27. Falkenauer, E., Delchambre, A.: A genetic algorithm for bin packing and line balancing. In: Proceedings of the IEEE 1992 Int. Conference on Robotics and Automation, Nice, France (1992) 1186–1192

The Importance of Neutral Mutations in GP

Edgar Galván-López[1] and Katya Rodríguez-Vázquez[2]

[1] University of Essex, Colchester, CO4 3SQ, UK
egalva@essex.ac.uk
[2] IIMAS-UNAM, Circuito Escolar s/n, Ciudad Universitaria
Del. Coyoacán, México, D.F. 04510, Mexico
katya@uxdea4.iimas.unam.mx

Abstract. Understanding how neutrality works in EC systems has drawn increasing attention. However, some researchers have found neutrality to be beneficial for the evolutionary process while others have found it either useless or worse. We believe there are various reasons for these contradictory results: (a) many studies have based their conclusions using crossover and mutation as main operators rather than using only mutation (Kimura's studies were done analysing only mutations) and, (b) studies often consider problems and representation with larger complexity. The aim of this paper is to analyse how neutral mutations tend to behave in GP and establish how important they are. For this purpose we introduce an approach which has two advantages: (a) it allows us to specify neutrality and, (b) this makes possible to understand how neutrality affects the evolutionary search process.

1 Introduction

In late 1960s, Motoo Kimura observed that mutations were present more often than previously thought. Evolutionary Computation (EC) systems are mostly inspired from the theories of genetic inheritance and natural selection. However, Neutral theory [8] has interested some researchers who want to understand it so that they can incorporate it in their EC systems to solve complex problems. This theory suggests that a mutation from a gene to another is neutral if this modification does not affect the phenotype.

Kimura's theory seems to contradict the Darwinian theory but this is not right. The Darwinian theory judges genes by their phenotypic expression whereas Kimura's theory argues that mutations occurring during evolution are neither advantageous nor disadvantageous to the survival and reproduction of individuals. Such random genetic drift should be considered into the study of the evolutionary process which is an issue neglected by the EC community.

Some researchers have made effort to understand how neutrality works in EC systems in order to add elements to the evolutionary process to evolve complex problem solutions. In Genetic Programming (GP) [9], neutrality if often identified with redundancy and introns. Both have being widely studied in the EC community [1,10,12,13,14].

T.P. Runarsson et al. (Eds.): PPSN IX, LNCS 4193, pp. 870–879, 2006.

Functional redundancy refers to the fact that many different individuals, at the phenotype level, represent the same function. For instance the following two genotypes represent the XOR function:

(NOR (AND (NOT (NOT A)) B) (NOT (OR A B)))
(NOR ((NAND (NAND A B) (OR A B)) (NOT (OR A B))))

Introns refers to code that is part of an individual but that semantically does not affect the program's behaviour. A good example of an intron could be found in a typical individual generated for the artificial ant problem [6]. Suppose that in the root node there is an IF instruction, which means that either the left or right subtree will not be executed, so, any change in the subtree which is not executed will have no effect on the behaviour of such individual.

The problem with functional redundancy and introns is that both emerge and vary during the evolutionary process and for this reason it is very difficult to measure and study the effects of neutrality.

The aim of this paper is to analyse how neutral mutations behave in GP and establish how important they are. For this reason, we introduce a new approach to study the effects of neutrality. This method has two advantages: (a) it allows us to specify neutrality, (b) this makes possible to understand how explicit neutrality[1] affects the evolutionary search process.

The paper is organized as follows. In Section 2, previous work on neutrality is presented. Section 3, the approach used to carry out our research is described. Section 4 provides details on the experimental setup used and results are presented. In Section 5 conclusions are drawn.

2 Previous Work

As we will see in the next paragraphs, neutrality theory has been explored in Genetic Algorithms. However, neutrality could be easier to find in GP due to its representations.

Harvey and Thompson [5] studied some effects of neutral networks in an evolvable hardware problem. In their work, they defined the concept of potentially useful junk that refers to loci in a genotype that are functionless within the current context, but with different values elsewhere in the genotype they may become functional. Harvey and Thompson argued that it is possible to reach a global optimum without worrying about premature convergence if one uses neutrality in the evolutionary process.

Banzhaf [2] proposed an approach where a genotype-phenotype mapping was used in the context of constrained optimisation problems. Banzhaf argued that, very often, constraining the solution space leads to local optima which are difficult to escape from with traditional methods. He used high variability of neutral variants to escape from local optima on saddle surfaces. Keller and Banzhaf extended this work in [7].

[1] Term coined by Yu and Miller [19], which means that neutrality can be added to the evolutionary process.

Shipman *et al.* [15] explored the benefits of neutrality in the context of a mapping based on an abstraction of a genetic regulatory network — a random Boolean network. The mapping used in their experiments provided a very large degree of neutrality. From the experimental results they concluded that neutral drift allowed the discovery of many more phenotypes than would be the case with a direct encoding without redundancy. In [16] they proposed four different redundant mappings to study their effect in the evolutionary process and see how neutrality influences the search. They argued that redundancy was useful in three of their mappings. They concluded that some kind of redundancy (neutrality) is crucial.

Smith *et al.* [17] analysed the effects of the presence of neutral networks on the evolutionary process. They observed how evolvability was affected by the presence of such neutral networks. For this purpose they used a system with an extremely complex genotype-to-fitness mapping. They concluded that the existence of neutral networks in the search space, which allows the evolutionary process to escape from local optima, does not necessarily provide any advantage. This is because the population does not evolve any faster due to inherent neutrality. In [18] they focused their research on looking at the dynamics of the population rather than looking at just the fitness, and argued that neutrality did not perform a useful role in an evolutionary robotic task.

Yu and Miller [19] showed that neutrality improves the evolutionary search process for a Boolean benchmark problem. They used Miller's Cartesian GP [11] to measure explicit neutrality in the evolutionary process. They have explained that mutation on a genotype that has part of its genes active and others inactive may produce different effects: mutation on active genes is adaptive because it exploits accumulated beneficial mutations, while mutation on inactive genes has a neutral effect on a genotype's fitness, yet it provides exploratory power by maintaining genetic diversity. Yu and Miller extended this work in [20] showing that neutrality was helpful and that there is a relationship between neutral mutations and success rate in a Boolean function induction problem. However, Collins [4] claimed that the conclusion that, in this problem, neutrality is beneficial is flawed.

Yu and Miller [21] also investigated neutrality using the simple OneMax problem. They attempted a theoretical approach in this work. With their experiments, they showed that neutrality is advantageous because it provides a buffer to absorb destructive mutations.

Chow [3] proposed a method that uses individuals which contains multiple chromosomes instead of a single chromosome. The idea of his approach was to apply genetic operators which do not maintain a one-to-one mapping between a genotypic bit and a phenotypic bit. Chow tested his approach in well known deceptive problems with good results.

As it can be seen from the brief summaries provided above, some researchers have found neutrality to be beneficial to evolutionary process while others have found it either useless or worse. We believe there are various reasons of why contradictory results on neutrality have been reported. In the next section we will describe in detail the proposed approach.

3 Graph-GP Representation

We believe that contradictory results regarding neutrality have several reasons:

- many studies have based their conclusions using crossover and mutation as main operators rather that using only mutation,
- studies often consider problems, representations and search algorithms that are relatively complex and so results represent the composition of multiple effects (e.g., bloat or spurious attractors in GP).

In this paper, we make an effort to clarify these problems. That is,

- We use the traditional representation as suggested by Koza, with the difference to allow explicit neutrality,
- We analyse performance with and without the presence of neutrality, using only the mutation operator.

The inspiration of using GP to study some effects of neutrality in the evolutionary process comes from many facets of their properties.

Programs are represented in GP as parse tree, rather than as lines of code. For instance, the expression `AND(a AND (b OR b), a OR a)` could be expressed as shown in Figure 1(a). The set of internal nodes used in GP parse trees is called *function set*, $F = \{f_1, \cdots, f_{NF}\}$. The function set could include almost any kind of programming construct: arithmetic operators, Boolean functions, looping instructions, etc. The set of terminal nodes is called *terminal set* $T = \{t_1, \cdots, t_{NT}\}$. This set can include variables, constants, random constants, etc.

For our experiments, $F = \{AND, OR, NOT\}$, while $T = \{a, b, c, \cdots\}$ representing input wires. Moreover, we have added an extra element in the function set, p. This p symbol works as follows: (a) Once an individual has been created as usual, we use a probability to replace a function with a p symbol which is a function of arity 2, which means that only functions of arity 2 can be replaced by p symbol. However, this is not a restriction because p can be defined of any arity, (b) If an individual contains this p symbol, this will point to code somewhere in the program, so when p is executed, the subtree rooted at that node is ignored, (c) If p symbol points to a function symbol, the p symbol effectively represents the sub-tree rooted at that function, and, (d) If p symbol points to a terminal symbol, the p symbol simply represents that node.

As can be seen, when p symbol is executed, the subtree rooted at that node is ignored, and so plays the role of inactive code[2]. When the mutation is applied in the inactive code, the individual will change at the genotype level but it will not change at the phenotype level. Figure 1(b) illustrates the concept.

The mutation operator is applied as usual on a per node basis. The only difference is that when a mutation is applied to the p symbol, we reassign the position to which it is pointing to. The fitness function that we used for circuit design is the raw fitness, where we assign the fitness to the individual according to the number of correct output bits.

---

[2] However, it is worth pointing out that this inactive code can be activated if p point to this code.

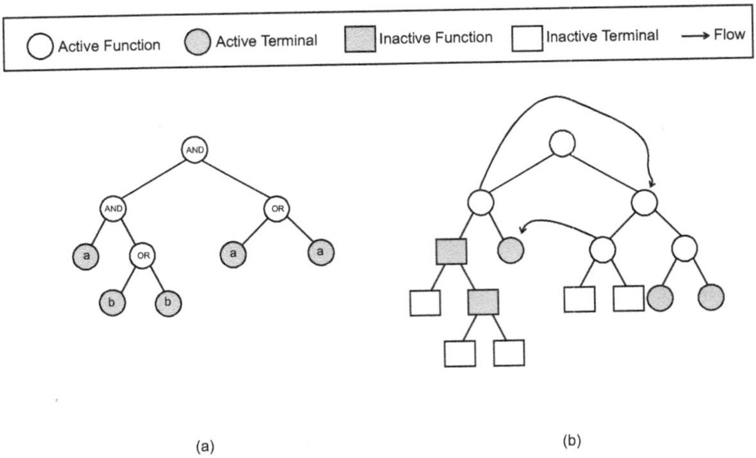

Fig. 1. (a) Parse-tree representation, and, (b) Graph-GP representation created with our approach

Table 1. Summary of Parameters

Parameter	*Value*
Depth	6, 7, 8, 9, 10
Population Size	200
Generations	400
Mutation Rate per node	0.02, 0.03, 0.04, 0.05, 0.06
P Rate per node	0.00, 0.01, 0.02, 0.03, 0.04

4 Experiments

4.1 Experimental Setup

In this section we use the 6-bit Multiplexer Boolean function to evaluate the proposed approach. To obtain meaningful and conclusive results, we performed 20 independent runs for each of different mutation rates and different p rates. We will show the results and analyse them in the following section. Moreover, runs were stopped when the maximum number of generations was reached. The parameters we have used are shown in Table 1 (these parameters were defined after a series of preliminary experiments). Initialization of the population was made with the full method. Crossover operator was not used in any of our experiments.

4.2 Results and Analysis

Due to space limitations we will focus our attention on results generated with depth 8. However, it is worth pointing out that results with depths 6, 7, 9 and 10 are very similar to those found with depth 8.

From Figure 2 we can see the success rates found by our approach with different p and mutation rate values. The highest success rate found was 100%

Table 2. Results found with our approach in the 6-bit Multiplexer. P and Mutation rate values are shown in the first and second column, respectively. Average of Fitness, Standard Deviation (σ) and Median are shown in the third, fourth and fifth column, respectively. Finally, Feasible Circuits (Success Rate) and Average of Generations (this refers to the average number of generations that are necessary to reach the feasible zone) are shown in the last two columns.

% P	*% Mutation*	*Avr. of Fit.*	*Standard Deviation*	*Median*	*F. Circuits*	*Avr. of Gen.*
0.01	0.02	64	0	64	100%	80.6
0.01	0.03	63.6	1.23	64	90%	155.66
0.01	0.04	62.65	2.98	64	70%	138.62
0.01	0.05	62.4	1.7	62.5	55%	146.65
0.01	0.06	62.25	1.37	62	30%	203.5
0.02	0.02	63.15	1.76	64	75%	91.46
0.02	0.03	62.5	2.42	64	65%	136.66
0.02	0.04	62.4	2.01	63	50%	141.5
0.02	0.05	60.95	3.24	61	35%	163.71
0.02	0.06	60.35	3.5	60	35%	243.14
0.03	0.02	63.5	2.86	64	85%	122.7
0.03	0.03	63.6	1.05	64	85%	109.64
0.03	0.04	62.3	2	62.5	45%	179.5
0.03	0.05	62	2.68	63	50%	237.5
0.03	0.06	60.7	3.51	61.5	30%	157.56
0.04	0.02	61.5	4.05	64	65%	109.65
0.04	0.03	61.3	4.17	64	60%	117
0.04	0.04	62.4	3.27	64	65%	132.45
0.04	0.05	61.9	2.95	63	45%	220.54
0.04	0.06	60.2	3.29	60	30%	164

with $p = 0.01$ and mutation rate $= 0.02$. Keeping constant this p value and increasing the mutation rate values, the success rate tends to decrease.

Similar behaviour can be observed with different p rate values. Therefore, we can conclude that regardless the value of p is, the higher the mutation rate is, the lower the success rate will be.

At this point, one question arises: what happen if we do not allow the presence of the p element in our individuals? To answer this question we need to take a look to Figure 2. In no case the system was able to reach a success rate of 100% in the absence of the p symbol. Moreover, the performance of the GP system without the presence of p is poor comparing when it is present. Actually, the performance of the GP system when p is not present in the individuals is, the worst for all mutation rates, except when mutation rate is 0.03.

Table 2 shows additional details on our results. The last column reports the average number of generations that are necessary to reach the feasible region[3].

[3] The feasible region is the area of the search space containing circuits that match all the outputs of the problem's truth table.

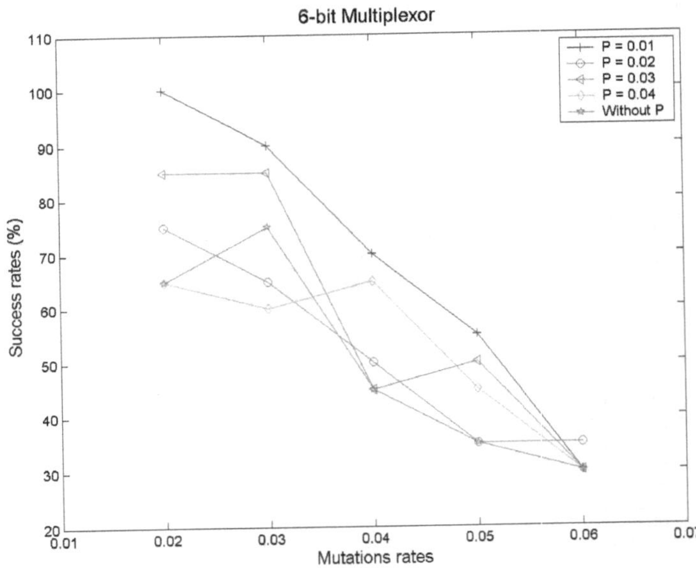

Fig. 2. Success rate results. P refers to the p rates used in our experiments.

We can see that the lower the value of p is, the smaller the number of generations that are required to solve the problem.

The experimental results also show how the individuals in the population tends to behave in the presence of p in their structures. Figure 3 summarizes such a behaviour on 4 different p rates. The highest success rates were found when mutation rates were set with the lowest value (0.02), regardless of the p rates.

At the beginning of the evolutionary process, the number of individuals affected by neutral mutations is high but it tend to decrease after few generations. In other words, individuals with p elements in their structures tend to disappear at the beginning of the process. We think this happened because at the beginning of the evolutionary process the solution needs to be protected by allowing the presence of p in their structures. However, further analysis need to be done to know why this happen.

Around generation 50 - 60 it is when the number of individuals affected by neutral mutations becomes stable. As can be observed in all plots in Figure 3, the best performance is achieved when the number of individuals affected by neutral mutations is in the range of 90 - 100 (notice that this range is close to half of the population). On the other hand, the worst performance was found when the number of individuals affected by neutral mutations is below 80.

From this analysis, it is clear that the presence of p in the individuals can make the solution avoid get stuck in local optimum. However, a balance between p rate and mutation rate is needed in order to improve the exploration of the search space.

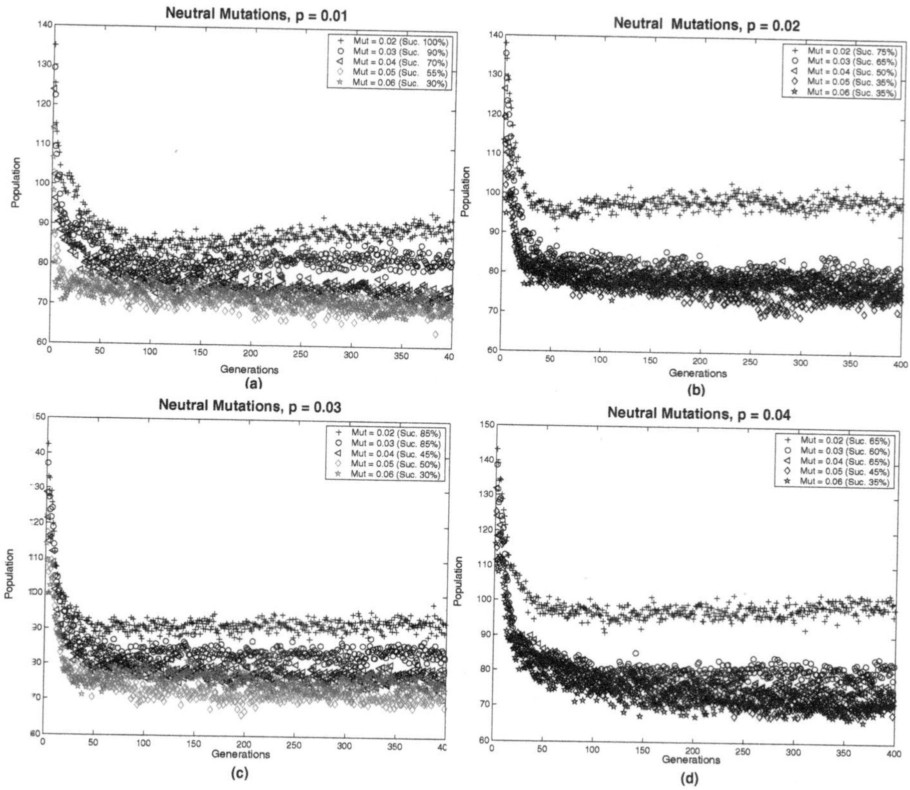

Fig. 3. Number of individuals affected by neutral mutations. $p = 0.01$ (a), $p = 0.02$ (b), $p = 0.03$ (c), $p = 0.04$ (d).

5 Conclusions

In late 1960s, Motoo Kimura observed that mutations were present more often than previously thought. He explained this phenomenon with the concept of Neutrality which established that the majority of mutations that are present during the evolutionary process do not have impact at the phenotype level. This paper makes an analysis of some effects of neutrality in GP. Moreover, we have shown that neutrality is an important research area to be considered in the evolutionary process. With the approach described in this paper, we have been able to analyse some effects of neutrality.

From results found for the benchmark Boolean problem, we conclude that: (a) Neutral Mutations help to the evolutionary process to reach feasible regions, (b) Regardless the value of p, with higher mutation rates the success rates are low, (c) Neutral Mutations do not allow to get stuck in local optima, and (d) With low probability of p and low probability of mutation, the evolutionary process tends to behave in a consistent way and shows better overall performance.

Further work need to be done about the effects of p symbol in tree's structures. The amount of neutrality and the mutation rate present in the evolutionary process play an important role during the evolutionary process. In the future we will investigate the reasons behind the fine balance between these two elements that is required to aid evolution. We also would like to know why the presence of p in individuals' structure tends to decrease in the evolutionary process and with the use of family trees we can be able to clarify this point. In a mutation based algorithm each individual has only one parent. This makes it possible to track the origin of a sample point, and, in fact, the full evolutionary path of an individual within its family tree.

Acknowledgments. The first author thanks to CONACyT for support to pursue graduate studies at University of Essex. The second author gratefully acknowledges support from CONACyT through project 40602-A. The authors would like to thank the anonymous reviewers for their valuable comments.

References

1. P. Angeline. Genetic Programming and Emergent Intelligence. In K. E. Kinnear, Jr., editor, *Advances in Genetic Programming*, pages 75–98. MIT Press, 1994.
2. W. Banzhaf. Genotype-phenotype-mapping and neutral variation – A case study in genetic programming. In Y. D. *et al.*, editor, *Parallel Problem Solving from Nature III*, volume 866 of *LNCS*, pages 322–332. Springer-Verlag, 9-14 Oct. 1994.
3. R. Chow. Evolving genotype to phenotype mappings with a multiple-chromosome genetic algorithm. In K. D. *et al.*, editor, *GECCO 2004: Proceedings of the 2004 Conference on Genetic and Evolutionary Computation*, volume 1, pages 1006–1017, Seattle WA, USA, 26-30 June 2004. Springer-Verlag.
4. M. Collins. Finding needles in haystacks is harder with neutrality. In H.-G. B. *et al.*, editor, *GECCO 2005: Proceedings of the 2005 conference on Genetic and evolutionary computation*, volume 2, pages 1613–1618, Washington DC, USA, 25-29 June 2005. ACM Press.
5. I. Harvey and A. Thompson. Through the labyrinth evolution finds a way: A silicon ridge. In *Proceedings of the First International Conference on Evolvable Systems: From Biology to Hardware (ICES)*, pages 406–422. Springer-Verlag, 1996.
6. D. Jefferson, R. Collins, C. Cooper, M. Dyer, M. Flowers, R. Korf, C. Taylor, and A. Wang. Evolution as a Theme in Artificial Life: The Genesys/Tracker System. In C. G. L. *et al.*, editor, *Artificial Life II*, volume X of *Santa Fe Institute Studies in the Sciences of Complexity*, pages 549–578. Addison-Wesley, Febrary 1992.
7. R. E. Keller and W. Banzhaf. Genetic programming using genotype-phenotype mapping from linear genomes into linear phenotypes. In J. R. K. *et al.*, editor, *Genetic Programming 1996: Proceedings of the First Annual Conference*, pages 116–122, Stanford University, CA, USA, 28–31 July 1996. MIT Press.
8. M. Kimura. Evolutionary rate at the molecular level. In *Nature*, volume 217, pages 624–626, 1968.
9. W. Langdon and R. Poli. *Foundations of Genetic Programming*. Springer, 2002.
10. S. Luke. Code Growth is Not Caused by Introns. In D. Whitley, editor, *Late Breaking Papers at the 2000 Genetic and Evolutionary Computation Conference*, pages 228–235, Las Vegas, Nevada, USA, 8 July 2000.

11. J. F. Miller and P. Thomson. Cartesian genetic programming. In R. P. *et al.*, editor, *Genetic Programming, Proceedings of EuroGP'2000*, volume 1802 of *LNCS*, pages 121–132, Edinburgh, 15-16 Apr. 2000. Springer-Verlag.
12. P. Nordin and W. Banzhaf. Complexity Compression and Evolution. In L. Eshelman, editor, *Genetic Algorithms: Proceedings of the Sixth International Conference (ICGA95)*, pages 310–317, Pittsburgh, PA, USA, 1995. Morgan Kaufmann.
13. P. Nordin, W. Banzhaf, and F. Francone. Introns in Nature and in Simulated Structure evolution. In D. L. *et al.*, editor, *Bio-Computation and Emergent Computation*, Skovde, Sweden, 1-2 Sept. 1997. World Scientific Publishing.
14. P. Nordin, F. Francone, and W. Banzhaf. Explicitly Defined Introns and Destructive Crossover in Genetic Programming. In J. P. Rosca, editor, *Proceedings of the Workshop on Genetic Programming: From Theory to Real-World Applications*, pages 6–22, Tahoe City, California, USA, 9 July 1995.
15. R. Shipman, M. Schackleton, and I. Harvey. The use of neutral genotype-phenotype mappings for improved evolutionary search. *BT. Technology Journal*, 18(4):103–111, October. ISSSN 2000.
16. R. Shipman, M. Schakleton, M. Ebner, and R. Watson. Neutral search spaces for artificial evolution: A lesson from life. In M. Bedau, S. Rasmussen, J. McCaskill, and N. Packard, editors, *Artificial Life: Proceedings of the Seventh International Conference on Artificial Evolution*, pages 162–169. MIT Press, 2000.
17. T. Smith, P. Husbands, and M. O'Shea. Neutral networks and evolvability with complex genotype-phenotype mapping. *Lecture Notes in Computer Science*, 2159:272–282, 2001.
18. T. Smith, P. Husbands, and M. O'Shea. Neutral networks in an evolutionary robotics search space. In *Congress on Evolutionary Computation: CEC 2001*, pages 136–145. IEEE Press, 2001.
19. T. Yu and J. Miller. Neutrality and the evolvability of boolean function landscape. In *Fourth European Conference on GP*, pages 204–211. Springer-Verlag, 2001.
20. T. Yu and J. F. Miller. Needles in haystacks are not hard to find with neutrality. In J. A. F. *et al.*, editor, *Genetic Programming, Proceedings of the 5th European Conference, EuroGP 2002*, volume 2278 of *LNCS*, pages 13–25, Kinsale, Ireland, 3-5 Apr. 2002. Springer-Verlag.
21. T. Yu and J. F. Miller. The role of neutral and adaptive mutation in an evolutionary search on the onemax problem. In E. Cantú-Paz, editor, *Late Breaking Papers at the Genetic and Evolutionary Computation Conference (GECCO-2002)*, pages 512–519, New York, NY, July 2002. AAAI.

New Order-Based Crossovers for the Graph Coloring Problem

Christine L. Mumford

Cardiff University, School of Computer Science
C.L.Mumford@cs.cardiff.ac.uk
http://www.cs.cardiff.ac.uk/

Abstract. Huge color class redundancy makes the graph coloring problem (GCP) very challenging for genetic algorithms (GAs), and designing effective crossover operators is notoriously difficult. Thus, despite the predominance of population based methods, crossover plays a minor role in many state-of-the-art approaches to solving the GCP. Two main encoding methods have been adopted for heuristic and GA methods: direct encoding, and order based encoding. Although more success has been achieved with direct approaches, algorithms using an order based representation have one powerful advantage: every chromosome decodes as a feasible solution. This paper introduces some new order based crossover variations and demonstrates that they are much more effective on the GCP than other order based crossovers taken from the literature.

1 Introduction

The graph coloring problem (GCP) is a well studied combinatorial optimization problem. It involves finding a minimum set of colors for the vertices of a given graph, so that no two adjacent vertices have the same color. Interest in the GCP is broadly based and the field is highly competitive. In 1993 the GCP was the subject of a Discrete Mathematics and Theoretical Computer Science (DIMACS) implementation challenge, [13], in which the best algorithms of the day were pitted against each other on a collection of large and very difficult benchmark instances. Since 1993 enthusiasm for the GCP has not diminished, and new approaches continue to be developed. As an archetypal set partitioning problem, the GCP provides a useful testbed for techniques applicable more widely to real world problems such as timetabling [2] and frequency assignment [18] and many others.

The GCP is NP-hard, thus heuristic and metaheuristic methods are appropriate techniques for solving the problem. Two main encoding methods can be identified: direct encoding, and order based encoding. With direct encoding arbitrary colors are assigned and heuristics used to recolor the vertices in an attempt to improve the solution. On the other hand, order based approaches organize vertices as permutation lists, and rely on a greedy decoder to assign the colors in a methodical way. Although algorithms using a direct approach have enjoyed more success recently, order based techniques have one powerful advantage: every permutation decodes as a feasible solution. Direct approaches work to minimize and eventually eliminate conflicts but do not guarantee legal solutions.

T.P. Runarsson et al. (Eds.): PPSN IX, LNCS 4193, pp. 880–889, 2006.

The main contribution of the present paper is to introduce two new and effective order based crossover/local search combinations: *Merge Independent Sets (MIS)* and *Permutation One Point (POP)*. The success of the new operators is demonstrated by comparing their performance on DIMACS benchmarks with that of well known order based crossovers for the GCP taken from the literature.

2 Summary of Related Work

As mentioned above, the most successful current approaches to solving the GCP use a direct representation with conflict minimization as the goal: i.e., given k colors, a coloring is sought which minimizes the number of adjacent vertices bearing the same color. Most commonly, a genetic (or population based) algorithm (GA) is used in combination with some form of local search. However, because graph coloring is essentially a set partitioning problem with arbitrary color labels assigned to the individual sets, crossover has proven a huge challenge. Indeed, several population based approaches do not incorporate crossover at all, [11,16]. For others, crossover plays only a limited role, [3,9]. Exceptional among recent conflict minimization techniques is the hybrid coloring algorithm of Galinier and Hao [10]. In this case a novel crossover operator, which attempts to propagate complete color classes from parents to offspring, makes a significant contribution to the success of the approach. Furthermore, competitive results have been reported on large DIMACS benchmarks.

Although rather less successful than direct encoding methods, order based techniques for the GCP have a very long history. These methods rely on a simple greedy algorithm to transform a permutation of vertices into a legal coloring, and it is thus the role of good ordering (or reordering) heuristics to present the greedy algorithm with a suitable permutation that it can transform into a high quality solution. The simplest and fastest such techniques generate an ordering in one go, usually by ensuring that the more heavily constrained vertices are placed before those that are less constrained [15,19]. A somewhat more sophisticated technique, known as *DSatur*, [6] operates by first assigning colors to heavily constrained vertices with colors already assigned to adjacent vertices. Unfortunately, despite their attractiveness in terms of speed and simplicity, none of the above mentioned simple ordering techniques produces very good results on large benchmarks.

Rather more successful than "one go" ordering heuristics based on vertex degree, are the iterative reordering heuristics of Culberson and Luo, [5]. These methods do not need to rely on vertex degrees or saturation. Instead, beginning with an arbitrary permutation and greedy allocation of colors, Culberson and Luo's heuristics operate by grouping and rearranging color classes along the permutation list. Of particular significance is a rare property possessed by each of Culberson and Luo's reordering heuristics for the GCP: it is impossible to get a worse coloring by rearranging the color classes, and it is possible that a better coloring (using fewer colors) may result. Capitalizing on this property, the authors applied a random mix of various reordering heuristics repeatedly to individual problems, and watched the solutions gradually improve. They called their algorithm *iterated greedy*. Disappointingly, however, in spite of its elegance, the iterated greedy technique achieves only moderate success on large graph benchmarks, and may need to run a very long time.

We now move on to consider order based GAs for the GCP. In one of the earliest and best known studies of this type Davis developed new order based crossover and mutation operators especially for the GCP, [14]. However Davis' work predates the DIMAC challenge and he used a very specialized type of graph (with weighted edges) to test his algorithms. Realizing difficulties in designing effective crossover operators for the GCP, Eiben *et al*, [7] developed an order based evolutionary algorithm with mutation only. Once more, though, the approach was tested only on a very specialized type of graph coloring problem: the three color problem. More recently, Anderson and Ashlock [1] have introduced a crossover called "merging crossover" (MOX) which shows some promise for the GCP, although, once again, the authors did not present results for literature benchmarks.

Finally, a technique known as the *grouping genetic algorithm (GGA)* is worthy of a mention. This algorithm was originally developed for the bin packing problem, but later adapted by Eiben *et al* [7], and probably more successfully by Erben [8], for graph coloring. Like the hybrid algorithm of Galinier and Hao, the GGA relies on a special crossover to propagate complete color classes, wherever possible. The algorithm differs from that of Galinier and Hao, however, in its representation. Although the colors for the vertices are recorded in a direct manner, the chromosomes are augmented with a *grouping part*, and it is only this latter part that takes part in exchanges. Some good results on some notoriously difficult GGPs have been reported by Erben in [8], though not for the DIMACS benchmarks. The present author is heavily indebted to many of the above mentioned researchers for their insight, and many of their ideas have been incorporated into the present work.

3 The GA Framework

A simple steady-state GA is used as a framework for our comparative study, which concentrates only on crossover operations. There are few parameters to set using this approach: no global fitness function is used and crossover occurs at 100 % with no mutation. At the start of the procedure a population of N random permutations is generated. If the GCP instance has n vertices, then each chromosome will consist of a permuted list of the integers $\{1, 2, 3, \ldots n\}$. Once the initial population is created, the individual members have to be evaluated, according to the performance measure described later. Within the main generation loop, each member of the population is selected in turn and paired in crossover with a second individual selected (uniformly) at random. The performance measure of the resulting single offspring is then compared with that of its weaker parent. If the new offspring is better than its weaker parent it replaces it in the population, otherwise it dies. The GA is run for a fixed number of generations, where a generation is defined as N trials of crossover, one led by each member of the population in turn.

The number of colors (chromatic number) is probably not the best measure of progress to use, given that many colorings will produce identical values. We will adopt the progress measure used by Culberson and Luo [5]: $\sum_1^n c_i + nc$. In this equation the *coloring sum* (i.e., $\sum_1^n c_i$, where c is the color assigned to vertex i) is added to the term nc, where n is the number of vertices and c the number of colors. The main idea is to encourage large color classes to grow even larger at the expense of the smaller classes, in the hope that eventually some classes will lose their remaining vertices and disappear altogether. We shall see later that the two operations taken from Culberson and Luo, [5], *sort independent sets* followed by *largest first*, ensure that the color sets are presented in a favorable sequence for minimizing the coloring sum. The term nc is added to ensure that improved colorings are always reflected in the measure of progress.

3.1 The Representation and Greedy Decoder

Chromosomes consist of permutations of the n vertices, and the greedy decoder colors each vertex in sequence, using the first available color from an ordered set (i.e., each color is identified by an integer label, $0, 1, 2, 3, \ldots$). Figure 1 a) and 1 b) illustrate this process using a small graph with 12 vertices and 14 edges, Figure 1 b) giving a typical random permutation of the vertices from Figure 1 a) and also the resulting greedy coloring. Note: an efficient version of the greedy algorithm has been implemented using linked lists to keep track of vertices already assigned to color classes, as advised in [5]. The remaining parts of Figure 1 illustrate the stages of the optional local search procedure described below.

3.2 The Local Search

The local search uses Culberson and Luo's [5] "largest first" and "sort independent set" heuristics. Its purpose in the present study is twofold: firstly to reduce the value of the performance measure, and secondly to improve the correlation of the chromosomes in the population. Figure 1 c) shows the permutation list sorted in non-descending sequence of color label, and 1 d) gives the chromosome following the application of the "largest first" heuristic: i.e., the list is rearranged in non-ascending sequence of color class size. Following the advice given in [5], the sequence of color classes of identical size is reversed. Note that the application of "largest first" will normally reduce the value of the performance measure. In Figure 1 f) vertices are randomly "shuffled" within (but not between) independent sets. Finally, the greedy algorithm is applied to the new arrangement in f) and the result is shown in 1 g). Interestingly, vertices 4 and 1 are reassigned lower color labels, further reducing the magnitude of the performance measure. In the present study the local search loop is iterated 5 times.

3.3 The Crossover Operators Used for the Comparative Study

A genetic algorithm with order based chromosomes requires a crossover technique that preserves building blocks [12] appropriate for the GCP. Of particular

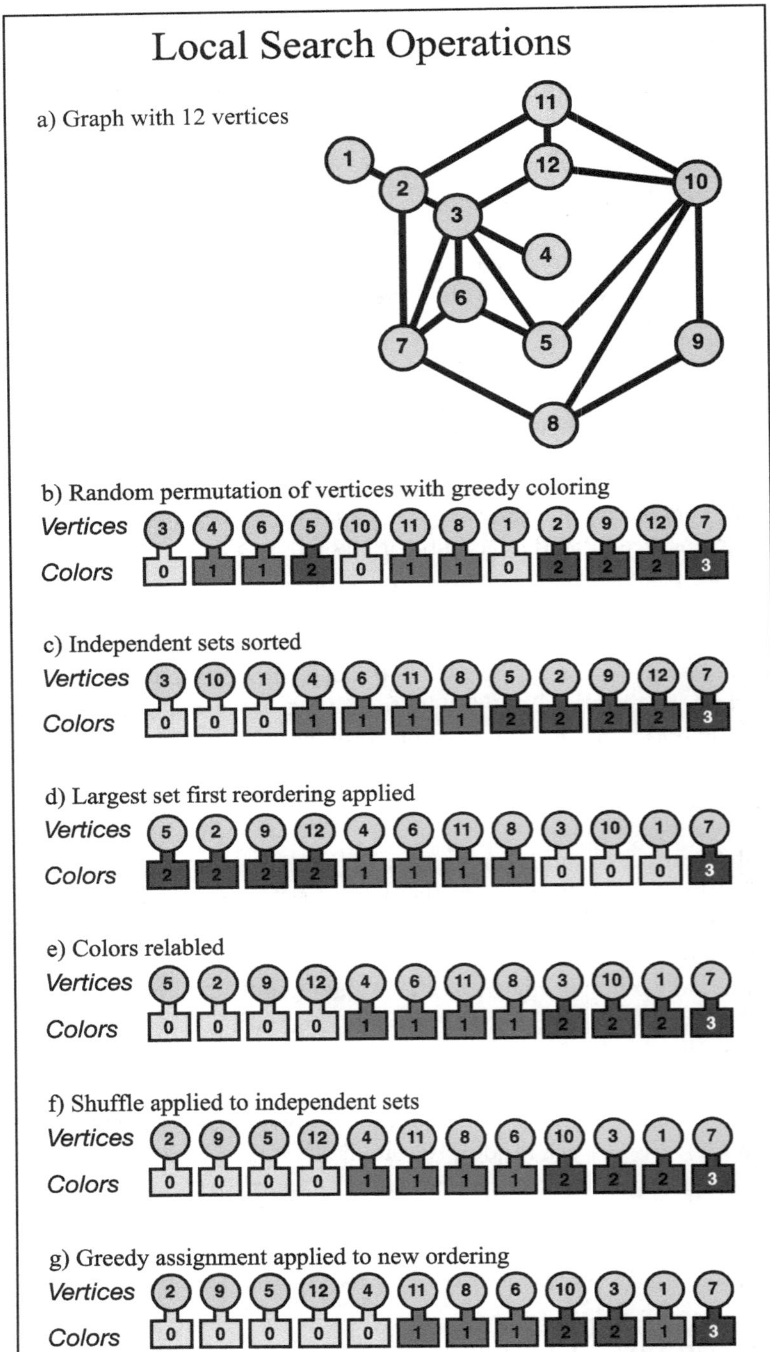

Fig. 1. Various operations by Culberson and Luo, [5], used in the local search procedure

relevance for the greedy decoder, is that some items precede others in the permutation list. Historically the operators *cycle crossover (CX)* [17] and *uniform order based crossover (UOBX)* [14] seem worthy of consideration. CX is good at preserving absolute positions of vertices, and every vertex in the offspring list will occur in exactly the same position in one or other of its parents. CX has proven effective in the related frequency assignment problem [18]. UOBX was developed by Davis with the GCP in mind and is good at preserving relative positions and orderings.

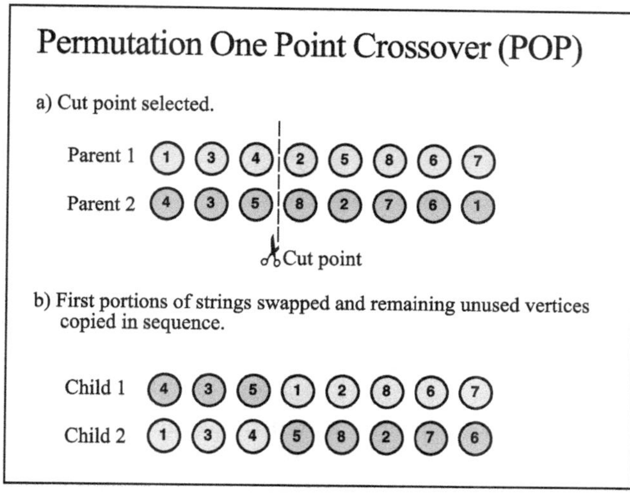

Fig. 2. POP Crossover

Some variations of the well known *order crossover (OX)* [17] are also tried here. The basic idea is taken from the simple one point crossover of the "standard" bit string GA, which simply selects two parents and a cut point. The first portion of parent 1 up to the cut point becomes the first portion of offspring 2, in the normal way. However, the remainder of offspring 2 is obtained by copying the vertices absent from the first portion of the offspring in the same sequence as they occur in parent 2 (see Figure 2). The same idea was used in [4], although the crossover was not given a specific name. We will call this crossover *permutation order based crossover (POP)*. Further, we will identify two variants, POP1 and POP2, which differ slightly in the way the cut point is selected: for POP1 it is chosen at random and can appear anywhere in the list, but for POP2 the cut point is restricted to a boundary between two color classes. Of course the application of POP2 is dependent on having previously grouped the vertices into their color classes.

Merging crossover (MOX) was presented by Anderson and Ashlock, [1]. Initially two n element parents are randomly merged into a single $2n$ element list. The first occurrence of each value in the merged list gives the ordering of elements in the first child, and the second occurrence in the second child. MOX is

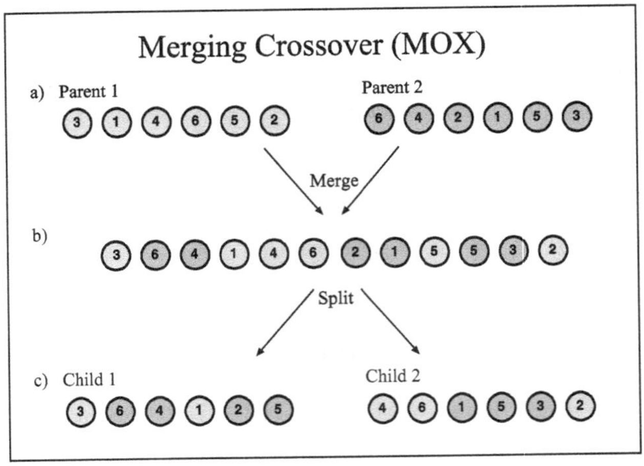

Fig. 3. MOX Crossover by Anderson and Ashlock, [1], used as a basis for the new MIS crossover

illustrated in Figure 3. Anderson and Ashlock point out the following property of MOX: if and element, a precedes another element b in both parents, then it follows that a will precede b in both children.

Merging independent sets (MIS) is a new crossover, adapted from MOX. It requires that the color sets are first grouped together in both of the parents, as illustrated in Figure 1 c). MIS then proceeds in the same way as MOX, but whole color sets are copied from the parents to the merged list in one go, rather than individual vertices. The merged list is split in exactly the same way as for MOX, with the first occurrence of each vertex appearing in the first offspring and the second occurrence in the second offspring. The idea of MIS is to better preserve the parents' color classes than MOX.

4 Results

Three sets of experiments were conducted to assess the viability of the various crossover operators for the GCP on the two benchmarks, DSJC500.5 and le450_15c. The first set of experiments used a basic order based approach without sorting the independent sets or applying the local search. Only CX, UOBX, MOX and POP1 could be compared here, because the other operators rely on sorted color classes. Local search did not form part of the second set of experiments either, although individual vertices were sorted into their color classes (as shown in Figure 1 c) to make it possible to test all the crossovers in our study. Finally, the third set of experiments included the full (5 iterations of) local search. Table 1 displays the results for all the crossovers, showing the best (i.e., lowest) value for the performance measure averaged over 10 replicate runs in each case. For all the runs a population of 250 was used and the GA run for 200 generations. Clearly the best results are obtained when local search is used

Table 1. Mean value for the performance measure over 10 replicate runs

Experiment	Instance	CX	UOBX	MOX	POP1	POP2	MIS
No sort and no LS	DSJC500.5	49090	48994	49171	**48120**	-	-
	le450_15c	17370	17322	17513	**17184**	-	-
Sorting and no LS	DSJC500.5	49115	49350	49182	47718	**47351**	48258
	le450_15c	18060	18075	18072	**17588**	17615	17939
Sorting and LS	DSJC500.5	43484	45453	41158	39217	39294	***37851***
	le450_15c	17399	17517	17513	***16370***	16615	17001

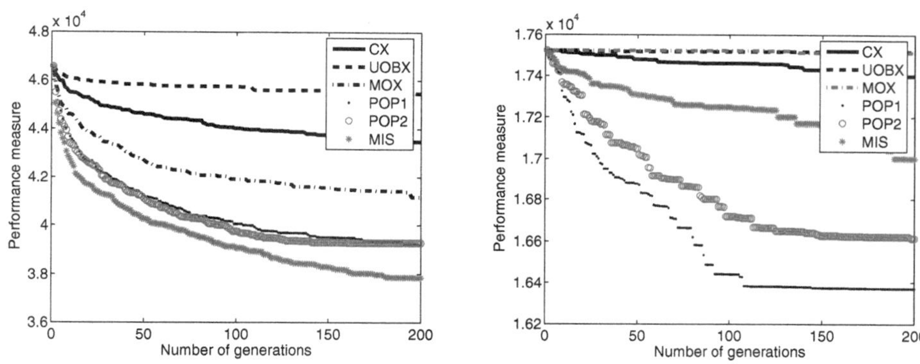

(a) DSJC500.5 (b) le450_15c

Fig. 4. Comparing order based crossovers with sorting of independent sets and local search. Typical best colorings obtained are 52 for DSJC500.5 and 26 for le450_15.c.

with MIS a clear winner on DSJC500.5 and POP1 on le450_15c. Figure 4 shows the best-so-far curves for the third set of experiments.

To complete the study, a final set of experiments were performed to indicate the potential of the new techniques on seven large DIMACS benchmarks. That MIS and POP1 perform well compared to the other order based crossover operators has already been established, but the results could surely be improved with longer runs and the introduction of a mutation operator. Table 2 shows the results obtained from ten replicate runs of a genetic simulated annealing algorithm (GSA) each for 5,000 generations with a population size of 300. The GSA is based on the simple GA described earlier, but a single mutation follows each crossover operation, and the resulting offspring replaces a parent according the standard simulated annealing formula. The chosen mutation consists of a simple inversion operation between two random cut points. MIS crossover is used for the DSJC instances and POP for the remainder. A GSA was chosen because it produced slightly more promising results than the other GA techniques tried so far by the author, although run times are long. However, this represents "work in progress" and there is much more to be done. In Table 2 results produced by the GSA are compared with those generated using a version of the algorithm with the crossover removed, but with mutation and local search intact. Results for

Table 2. Comparison of the GSA with Other Approaches

Instance	Order Based GSA				Mutation GSA			Iterated Greedy			DSat	Best known
	Time	Min	Mean	Max	Min	Mean	Max	Min	Mean	Max		
DSJC250.5	1618	**29**	29.5	30	31	31.2	32	**29**	29.5	30	37	*28*
DSJC500.5	6473	**50**	50.1	51	55	55.9	56	52	52.6	53	65	*48*
DSJC1000.5	25777	**86**	87.2	89	100	100.4	101	95	96.4	98	115	*83*
le450_15c	4007	*15*	15.1	16	25	25	25	23	23.5	24	23	*15*
le450_25c	4563	**29**	29.9	30	30	30	30	**29**	**29**	**29**	**29**	*26*
flat300_28	2081	**32**	32.2	33	35	35	35	**32**	33.1	34	42	*31*
flat1000_76	27204	**91**	92	93	99	99.6	100	95	95.6	96	114	*83*

iterated greedy and DSatur are also included for comparison. Runs of iterated greedy are replicated ten times, and the run times adjusted to match those of the GSA. Clearly, the GSA with crossover outperforms the mutation only version, reinforcing the valuable contribution made by the new crossover operators. The GSA also performs better than iterated greedy or DSatur on most of the instances. The final column in Table 2 gives the results reported by Galinier and Hao, and these are better than those produced by the GSA with the exception of le450_15c, where the results are matched.

5 Conclusions

The paper has presented two new order based crossover/heuristic combinations: *Merge Independent Sets (MIS)* and *Permutation One Point (POP)* for the GCP, and demonstrated their success in a simple genetic algorithm, comparing their performance with other crossovers on DIMACS benchmarks. The new crossovers appear to owe much of their success to an ability to respect color set boundaries, and this is made possible by utilizing some reordering heuristics taken from Culberson and Luo, [5]. In the experiments MIS seemed to work better than POP on problems where color classes vary in size, and POP proved more successful on the "flat" problems (le450_15c, le450_25c, flat300_28, and flat1000_76), which are specially formulated so that color class sizes are identical in the optimum solution. More extensive experiments showed that a genetic simulated annealing algorithm (GSA) worked much better with the new crossovers included than it did if they were excluded. The experiments also showed that the GSA is generally more effective than Culberson and Luo's iterated greedy algorithm, the source of the reordering heuristics used for MIS and POP. Thus, we have clear evidence that the crossovers provide much "added value" over and above mutation and local search. Current work is focussed on improving the results for the GCP, and also on adapting the techniques for other set partitioning problems, principally bin packing and timetabling. Choosing the most suitable performance measure (or fitness function) for an application is crucial, and preliminary experiments indicate that the function used by Erben [8] may work better on the GCP than the one developed by Culberson and Luo, especially if used in conjunction with a modified color class reordering heuristic instead of "largest first".

References

1. P. G. Anderson and D. Ashlock. Advances in ordered greed. 2004. Available from http://www.cs.rit.edu/~pga/abstracts.php.
2. E. Burke and S. Petrovic. Recent research directions in automated timetabling. *European Journal of Operational Research*, 140(2):266–280, 2002.
3. D. Costa, A. Hertz, and O. Dubuis. Embedding a sequential procedure within an evolutionary algorithm for coloring problems. *Journal of Heuristics*, 1:105–128, 1995.
4. C. Croitoru, H. Luchian, O. Gheorghieş, and A. Apetrei. A new genetic graph coloring heuristic. In *Proceedings of the Computational Symposium on Graph Coloring and its Generalizations*, pages 63–74, 2002.
5. J. Culberson and F. Luo. Exploring the k-colorable landscape with iterated greedy. In Johnson and Trick [13], pages 499–520.
6. D.Brélaz. New methods to color the vertices of graphs. *Communications of the ACM*, 24(4):251–256, 1979.
7. A. Eiben, J. V. der Hauw, and J. V. Hemert. Graph coloring with adaptive evolutionary algorithms. *Journal of Heuristics*, 4:25–46, 1998.
8. W. Erben. A grouping genetic algorithm for graph colouring and exam timetabling. In *PATAT 2000*, volume 2079 of *Lecture Notes in Computer Science*, pages 132–156. Springer, 2001.
9. C. Fleurent and J. A. Ferland. Genetic and hybrid algorithms for graph coloring. *Annals of Operations Research*, 63:437–461, 1996.
10. P. Galinier and J. K. Hao. Hybrid evolutionary algorithms for graph coloring. *Journal of Combinatorial Optimization*, 3(4):379–397, 1999.
11. C. A. Glass and A. Prügel-Bennett. A polynomially searchable exponential neighbourhood for graph colouring. *Journal of the Operational Research Society*, 56(3):324–330, 2005.
12. D. E. .Goldberg. *Genetic Algorithms in Search, Optimization, and Machine Learning*. Addison-Wesley, 1989.
13. D. S. Johnson and M. A. Trick, editors. volume 26 of *DIMACS Series in Discrete Mathematics and Theoretical Computer Science*. American Mathematical Society, 1996.
14. L.Davis. Order-based genetic algorithms and the graph coloring problem. In *Handbook of Genetic Algorithms*, chapter 6, pages 72–90. Van Nostrand Reinhold, New York, 1991.
15. D. Matula, G. Marble, and J. Isaacson. Graph coloring algorithms. In *Graph theory and computing*, pages 104–122. Academic Press, 1972.
16. C. Morgenstern. Distributed coloration neighborhood search. In Johnson and Trick [13], pages 335–357.
17. I. M. Oliver, D. J. Smith, and J. Holland. A study of permutation crossover operators on the traveling salesman problem. In *Genetic Algorithms and their Applications: Proceedings of the Second International Conference on Genetic Algorithms*, pages 224–230, 1987.
18. C. Valenzuela. A study of permutation operators for minimum span frequency assignment using an order based representation. *Journal of Heuristics*, 7(1):5–22, 2001. C.L. Valenzuela is now known as C. L. Mumford.
19. D. Welsh and M. Powell. An upper bound for the chromatic number of a graph and its application to timetabling problems. *The Computer Journal*, 10:85–86, 1967.

Assortative Mating Drastically Alters the Magnitude of Error Thresholds

Gabriela Ochoa[1] and Klaus Jaffe[2]

[1] INRIA – COMPLEX Team,
Domaine de Voluceau BP 105 78153 Le Chesnay Cedex – France
Gabriela.Ochoa.@inria.fr
[2] Laboratorio de Comportamiento,
Universidad Simón Bolívar, Caracas 89000, Venezuela
kjaffe.@usb.ve

Abstract. The *error threshold* of replication is an important notion of the *quasispecies* evolution model; it is a critical mutation rate (error rate) beyond which structures obtained by an evolutionary process are destroyed more frequently than selection can reproduce them. With mutation rates above this critical value, an error catastrophe occurs and the genomic information is irretrievably lost. Recombination has been found to reduce the magnitude of the error threshold in evolving viral quasispecies. Here, through a simulation model based on genetic algorithms, we incorporate assortative mating and explore its effect on the magnitude of error thresholds. We found, consistently on four fitness landscapes, and across a range of evolutionary parameter values, that assortative mating overcomes the shift toward lower error threshold magnitudes induced by recombination, on the other hand, dissortative mating drastically reduces the error threshold magnitude. These results have implications to both natural and artificial evolution: First, they support the hypothesis that assortative mating by itself may overcome some of the evolutionary disadvantages of sex in nature. Second, they suggest a critical interaction between mutation rates and mating strategies in evolutionary algorithms.

1 Introduction

Quasispecies theory was derived by Eigen and Schuster [3,5], to describe the dynamics of molecular evolution under the influence of mutation and selection. The theory was originally developed for studying pre-biotic evolution, but in a wider sense it describes any population of reproducing organisms. The *error threshold* of replication is an important notion of the quasispecies model; it is a critical mutation rate (error rate) beyond which structures obtained by an evolutionary process are destroyed more frequently than selection can reproduce them. With mutation rates above this critical value, an error catastrophe occurs and the genomic information is irretrievably lost [14,21]. Therefore, studying the factors that alter this threshold has important implications in the study of evolution. The quasispecies model, as stated originally, considered infinite asexual

T.P. Runarsson et al. (Eds.): PPSN IX, LNCS 4193, pp. 890–899, 2006.

populations (i.e no recombination) on a single peak (needle in a haystack) landscape. Later on, Nowak and Schuster [14] extended the calculations of the error threshold on this landscape to *finite* populations. Finite populations lose grip on the solitary spike of superior fitness more easily because of the added hazard of natural fluctuations. Another extension by Boerlijst et al. [1] included recombination; the authors studied two abstract simple landscapes: the isolated peak and a *plateau* landscape (see section 2) and found that recombination shifted error thresholds toward lower values, and made the transition sharper (for an explanation to this phenomenon, see section 3.1). Thus, recombination is advantageous only if the landscape is correlated and if the mutation rate is sufficiently small. Results obtained using infinite population models cannot be expected to automatically apply to the more realistic case of finite populations. To investigate this latter case, Ochoa and Harvey [16], reproduced the experiments in [1] but used a genetic algorithm (GA) [7] – and hence finite populations – instead of the quasispecies model as the underlying model of evolution. The empirical results mirrored qualitatively those produced by, Boerlijst et al. for infinite populations. Notably, error thresholds for finite populations were, in all scenarios, lower than for the infinite case. The work by Wright et al. [25,26] used the Vose [24] dynamical system model to show that a simple GA can exhibit bi-stability on a single peak and double peak fitness landscapes. They also found that recombination creates catastrophic errorthresholds transitions as mutation was increased, and confirmed that recombination decreased the mutation rate at which the error threshold occurred.

The work of Bonhoeffer and Stadler [2] described an empirical approach for locating thresholds on complex landscapes (see section 2.2). In [15] this method is borrowed and adapted. Instead of the quasispecies model a GA is used as the underlying model of evolution, thus a method for estimating error thresholds in GAs is devised. In addition , *consensus sequence plots* (see section 2.2) are suggested as tools for visualising the structure of fitness landscapes. A later contribution [19] confirmed the existence of the error threshold feature on a wider selection of complex landscapes including real-world domains, the study also considered the effect of modifying the most prominent evolutionary parameters on the magnitude of error thresholds.

The recombinating model by Boerlijst et al. considered random mating. In nature, however, mating is rarely random, and mate selection may be as important in guiding evolution as natural selection [10]. Theoretical studies of mate selection using agent-based simulations [20,9] suggest that some mating strategies confer higher fitness on individuals, and produce higher evolutionary stability than random mating. Assortative mating is a form of non-random mating common in nature, where individuals of similar phenotype mate more (or less) often than expected by chance. It is positive if similar organism mate more often, and negative (or dissortative) if dissimilar organisms mate more often.

In this paper we incorporate non-random mating through a GA-based simulation model, and study the effects of assortative mating on the magnitude of the error threshold. We argue that this study is relevant to both natural and artificial evolution. In evolutionary biology models,the mating strategy modelled has been shown to be fundamental in determining whether sexual reproduction emerges and is maintained in the simulated populations [8]. In evolutionary computation, the notion of error threshold has been related to the idea of having an "optimal" mutation rate, since this threshold is intuitively related to the idea of an optimal balance between *exploitation* and *exploration* [17,19]

2 Methods

We studied four fitness landscapes. First, the two simple landscapes proposed by Boerlijst et al. [1]: a single peak and a plateau landscape. The single peak landscape has much neutrality (almost all flat), but a correlation measure of the whole landscape indicates it is highly uncorrelated; the plateau is still simple, with much neutrality but slightly more correlated. Second, two families of more correlated and complex landscapes: Royal Staircase functions [23], and NK landscapes [11]. A description of these landscapes, along with the particular instances selected, is given below:

Single peak landscape: In this scenario, only one sequence F has an increased fitness. This single bit string has fitness $R_F = 5$, whereas all other sequences have fitness $R_i = 3.5$.

Plateau landscape: Here, the single peak landscape is modified so that the fitness of sequences close by the fittest string F is increased to $R_{H_1} = 4.8$, and $R_{H_2} = 4.6$, where H_1 is the set of all sequences with a Hamming distance of 1 from the fittest string F, and H_2 the set of all sequences with a Hamming distance of 2 from F.

Royal Staircase: The Royal Staircase family of functions was proposed for analysing epochal evolutionary search, it is a simple class of functions that allows neutrality to be modelled and tuned. Genotypes are specified by binary strings of length $L = MB$, where M is the number of blocks and B the number of bits per block. Any completely set block (with all bits set to 1) contributes a fitness component, but blocks that are only partially set (with one or more bits at zero) contribute no fitness. Royal Staircase functions are always unimodal, but we can increase the landscape neutrality by enlarging the size of the blocks. Modifying the number of blocks also alters the overall shape and ruggedness of the landscape. The selected instance ($M = 3$, $B = 14$) corresponds to a rugged, neutral, unimodal landscape.

***NK* landscape:** The NK family of landscapes is a problem-independent model for constructing multimodal landscapes that can gradually be tuned from smooth to rugged. In the model, N refers to the number of genes in the genotype (i.e. the string length) and K to the number of genes that influence a particular gene. By increasing the value of K from 0 to $N - 1$, NK landscapes can be tuned from smooth to rugged. The selected NK landscape instance ($N = 24$, $K = 10$) corresponds to a multimodal rugged landscape.

The default experiment setting used a generational GA with fitness proportional selection and a population of size 100. The genetic operations were uniform crossover [22] and the standard bit mutation. The GA was run in four modes: (a) using mutation only (*Asexual*), (b) using both mutation and recombination with random mating (*Random Mating*), (c) implementing assortative mating (*Assortative Mating*), and (d) implementing dissortative mating (*Dissortative Mating*). Assortative mating was implemented as follows: when selecting two individuals for a crossover, the first parent was selected as usual (based on fitness). For choosing the second parent, two potential partners were selected using the GA fitness-based selection method. Thereafter, the similarity between the two potential partners and the first parent was computed. For negative assortative (dissortative) mating, the genotype with less similarity was chosen. For positive assortative mating, the genotype closer to the first parent was selected as the second parent. We used Hamming distance as the similarity measure. Although in nature assortative mating is based on phenotypes, here we select a similarity measure based on genotypes given the simplicity of the model and landscapes as compared to nature. Furthermore, the phenotypic traits of organisms in nature are an expression of their genotypes.

2.1 Estimating Error Thresholds on Simple Landscapes

On the single peak and plateau landscape, we studied the steady state structure of the population, using the GA model described above, for a range of mutation rates. The structure of the population is characterised by the proportion of each error (or Hamming distance) class. We used the evolutionary parameters explored in [1]: string length of 15 and recombination rate of $r = 0.5$. In both landscapes there is a single optimum, F, we set it as the string of all 0s (000000000000000) with no loss of generality. Any other bit string is referred to as a 'mutant', and belongs to one of the Hamming distance classes H_i, where i is the Hamming distance to F. In the simulations, the initial population was generated differently for each landscape. For the single peak landscape, around 50% of the population was set on the peak and the rest was randomly generated. For the plateau landscape, 25% was set on the peak, 25% in the H_1 compartment, 25% in the H_2 compartment, and the rest was randomly generated. The per bit mutation rate p was varied from $p = 0.000$ up to $p = 0.05$, with a step size of 0.001. The number of generations per GA run was 1000. This value was empirically selected; the distribution of sequences was fairly stable by this point in all cases. Each experiment was run 50 times and the results were averaged.

2.2 Estimating Error Thresholds on Complex Landscapes

Bonhoeffer and Stadler (1993) studied the evolution of quasispecies on two correlated fitness landscapes (the Sherrington Kirkpatrick spin glass and the GraphBipartitioning landscape), and described an empirical approach for locating thresholds on complex landscapes. The approach is to calculate and plot theconsensus sequence at equilibrium for a range of mutation rates.The consensus sequence in a population is defined as the sequence of predominant symbols (bits) in each position; it is plotted as follows: if the majority of individuals has a '1' or '0' in a position i the field is plotted white or black, respectively. The field is plotted

Gray if the position is undecided. The *equilibrium state* is reached when the proportion of different sequences in the population is stationary. This happens when evolution is simulated for a large enough number of generations. In practise, it is considered that the equilibrium is reached when several parameters of the population (e.g. the maximal and average fitness) reach equilibrium. According to Bonhoeffer and Stadler (1993) the error threshold may be approached from *below* or *above* with both methods producing similar results. For approaching the error threshold from above, the simulation starts with a random population. Then the population is allowed to reach equilibrium at a constant predefined maximum for the mutation rate. Afterwards, the mutation rate is decreased by a fixed small step and the computation continues with the current population. This process is repeated until the mutation rate is 0.0. Therefore, the consensus sequence in the population is calculated and plotted at the end of each simulation cycle for each mutation step. The error threshold is characterised by the loss of the consensus sequence, i.e. the genetic information of the population. Beyond the error threshold the consensus sequence is no longer constant in time (see Figure 2).

Previous studies [18], confirmed that: (i) error thresholds approached from below and above produce similar results, (ii) the error threshold magnitude is independent of the particular initial population; and (iii) the error threshold is similar for different instances of an NK landscape with fixed N and K. Hence, the approach followed here is to approach error thresholds from above using a fixed random seed for generating the initial population in all cases; and for the NK landscape, selecting a single landscape instance. For the experiments reported here, the recombination rate was set to 1.0 when recombination is used. Mutation rates per locus ranged from from 0.05 to 0.0 with a step of 0.001. For each mutation rate the simulation lasted 10,000 generations, this number was found empirically to equilibrate the population maximal and average fitness.

2.3 Varying Evolutionary Parameters

In order to explore the robustness of the results, the most relevant evolutionary parameters were varied from the default setting described above, on two selected landscapes: the single peak and NK landscapes. In particular, we explored the effect of modifying the population size, chromosome length, and, on the single peak landscape, the relative fitness (or fitness difference) between the peak and the rest.

3 Results

Figure 1 show the steady state distribution of sequences on the plateau landscapes, for a range of mutation rates, and the four reproductive strategies. Similar plots (not reported here) were also produced for the single peak landscape. Sequences are classified in error classes: all sequences of i errors from the master are members of class i. The master sequence F (thick line) and error classes H_1 and H_2 are highlighted in the plots. The error threshold can be identified visually as the mutation rate just before the error classes become distributed as for a completely random population (i.e. the lines become parallel). Similar plots are commonly used to visualise error thresholds in quasispecies studies (see for instance [13], pp. 48). Assortative mating, on both the single peak and plateau landscapes, increases considerably the error threshold as compared to both random mating and no recombination. Moreover, assortative mating is advantageous for the population, because it increases the abundance of F, and makes the population more stable as the error threshold moves to higher values. Notice that on the plateau landscape (Figure 1) the proportion of the master sequence F for assortative mating is greater than twice the corresponding proportion for random mating, and about three times that proportion for the asexual population.

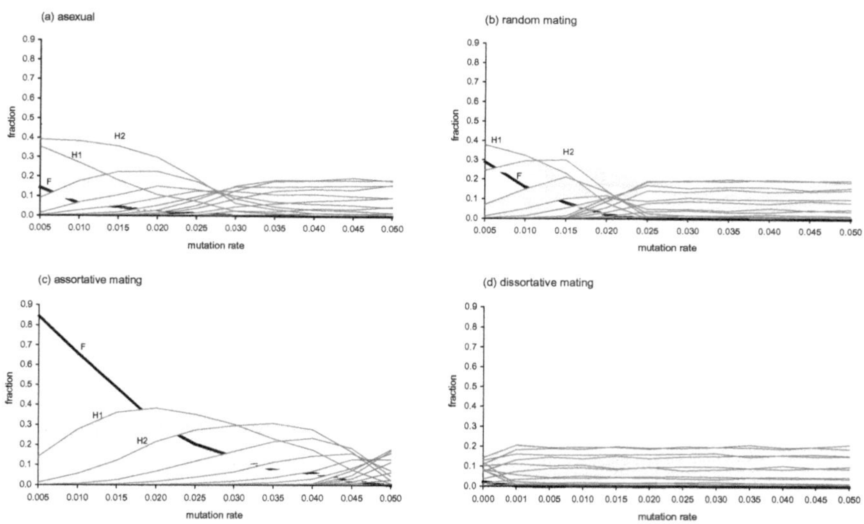

Fig. 1. Distribution of sequences for a range of mutation rates on the plateau landscape and the four reproductive strategies. Sequences are classified in error classes: all sequences of i errors from the master are members of class i. The master sequence F (thick line), error classes H_1 and H_2 are highlighted in the plots, and the other light lines correspond to the remaining error classes. The Y axis shows population fractions, and the X axis shows mutation rates (per bit). Error thresholds can be identified visually as the mutation rate just before the error classes become distributed as for a random population (the lines become flat).

Figure 2 shows the consensus sequence plots on the NK landscape. Similar plots were produced for the Royal Staircase Landscape. The plots show a clear error threshold; there is a distinguishable transition between an "ordered" (selection-dominated) regime, and a "disordered" (mutation-dominated) one. There is a stable consensus sequence for mutation rates below the error threshold. On the NK landscape (Figure 2), the consensus sequence in each case is

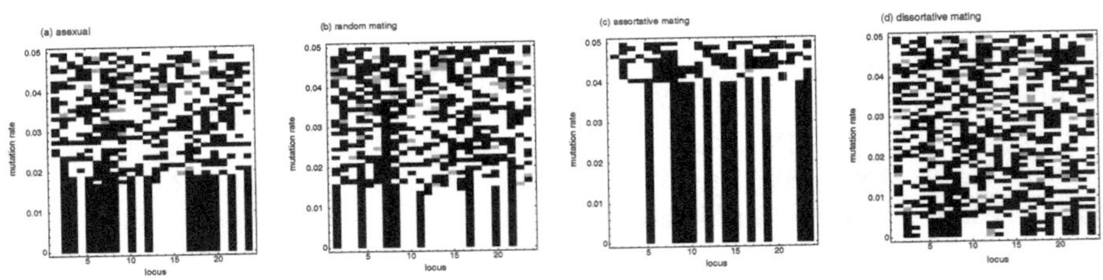

Fig. 2. Consensus sequence plots on the NK land scape and the four reproductive strategies. The horizontal axis shows the consensus bit for each locus, the vertical axis shows per bit mutation rates. The error threshold is characterised by the loss of the consensus sequence (one local optima for the NK Landscape).

Table 1. Approximate error thresholds on the four landscapes studied

	Single Peak	*Plateau*	*Royal Staircase*	*NK*
Asexual	0.017	0.030	0.018	0.018
Random Mating	0.010	0.018	0.004	0.015
Assortative Mating	0.032	0.045	0.024	0.040

different and corresponds to one of the many NK landscape's local optima; whereas on the Royal Staircase, the consensus sequence is always the single optimum in the landscape (the string of all 1s). Clearly assortative mating produces the highest error threshold, whereas asexual reproduction produces the lowest.

Table 1 summarises the approximate error thresholds values on the four landscapes studied, and the default evolutionary parameters. Results for dissortative mating were not included as they were generally null or close to zero. Additionally, tables 2 and 3, report the approximate error thresholds after altering the population size and chromosome length, respectively, on the single peak and NK landscapes. Results suggest that assortative mating increases considerably the error threshold as compared to random mating, these findings were found to be robust across a range of evolutionary parameter values. Error thresholds with assortative mating are even higher than for the populations without recombination. Figure 3, shows approximate error thresholds on the single peak landscape for a range of fitness difference values (between the peak and the rest), again assortative mating increases error threshold values as compared to random mating, the increase surpasses the error threshold of the asexual population for small and moderate fitness differences. For large fitness differences the asexual population has the higher error threshold. This is consistent with other authors observation that recombination may be advantageous for evolving populations, the critical requirement being that the locations of local optimal carry mutual information about where other good optima are located [1,11]. Finally, assortative mating was implemented selecting a mate from a pool of only two potential candidates, if the size of this pool is increased, empirical results confirmed that the effects on the error threshold are augmented (i.e. the error threshold is even higher).

Table 2. Approximate error thresholds on the Single Peak and NK landscapes for a range of population sizes

	Single Peak				*NK*			
	50	100	200	500	50	100	200	500
Asexual	0.013	0.017	0.019	0.021	0.013	0.018	0.020	0.028
Random Mating	0.009	0.010	0.011	0.011	0.012	0.015	0.015	0.016
Assortative Mating	0.028	0.032	0.034	0.035	0.031	0.040	0.052	0.059

Table 3. Approximate error thresholds on the Single Peak and NK landscapes for a range of chromosome lengths

	Single Peak				*NK*			
	10	15	30	60	16	20	24	28
Asexual	0.031	0.017	0.015	0.008	0.028	0.024	0.018	0.012
Random Mating	0.017	0.010	0.004	0.002	0.023	0.018	0.015	0.011
Assortative Mating	0.047	0.032	0.018	0.014	0.063	0.049	0.040	0.030

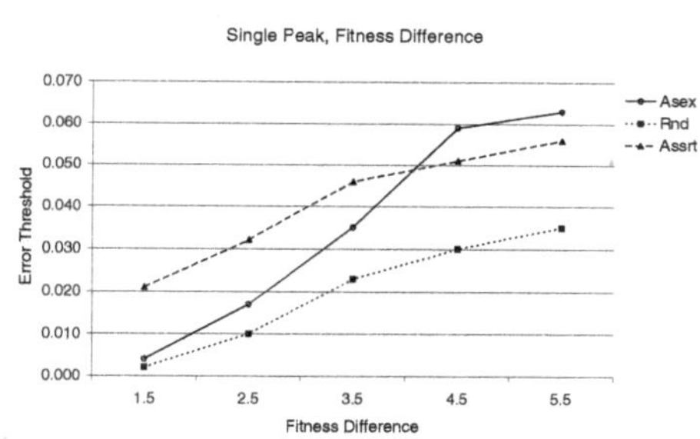

Fig. 3. Approximate error thresholds on the Single Peak landscape for several values of the fitness difference between the peak and the rest. The Y axis shows error thresholds, and the X axis shows fitness difference values.

3.1 Discussion

We explored the effect of including assortative mating on the magnitude of error thresholds on four different landscapes. Additionally, the robustness of the results was tested on a range of values of the most significant evolutionary parameters. Remarkably in all scenarios, recombination shifted the error threshold to lower mutation rates and it made the transition sharper. Near the error threshold, without recombination, the fittest sequence only makes up a small percentage of the total population [4]. Under such conditions, recombination acts as a diverging operator, driving the population beyond the error threshold. In this scenario assortative mating may be helpful for the evolving population by counteracting this diverging effect. Experiments including mate selection showed that assortative mating considerably increases the error threshold value, even beyond the corresponding value for asexual reproduction on correlated landscapes.

Moreover,assortative mating increases the abundance of the master sequence, and makes the population more stable in the presence of higher mutation rates.

As Kauffman [11] suggests, recombination appears to be a powerful strategy on a wide range of rugged fitness landscapes. The critical requirement appears to be that local optima carry mutual information about the location of other good or better optima. Thus, although our results suggest that assortative mating increases the value of sex as an evolutionary strategy, sex even with assortative mating may be sub-optimal under extreme conditions. Caution must be also taken when setting evolutionary parameters, as there seems to be a strong interection between mating strategies and mutation rate.

Regarding the implications to natural evolution, our results suggest that recombination with random mating reduces the population stability and abundance of the fittest individuals; and thus may hinder the average fitness of the whole population. However, assortative mating eliminates this negative effect of sex on evolutionary stability and is even capable of improving it over the asexual dynamics on correlated landscapes. This supports the conclusion by Jaffe [9] that assortative mating by itself may overcome some of the evolutionary disadvantages of sex, thus casting a new light on the dilemma posed by Fisher [6] of why sex exists.

References

1. M. C. Boerlijst, S. Bonhoeffer, and M. A. Nowak, *Viral quasi-species and recombination*, Proc. Royal Soc. London B **263** (1996), 1577–1584.
2. S. Bonhoeffer and P. Stadler, *Error thresholds on correlated fitness landscapes*, J. Theor. Biol. **164** (1993), 359–372.
3. M. Eigen, *Self-organization of matter and the evolution of biological macromolecules*, Naturwissenschaften **58** (1971), 465–523.
4. M. Eigen, J. McCaskill, and P. Schuster, *Molecular quasi-species*, J. Phys. Chem. **92** (1988), 6881–6891.
5. M. Eigen and P. Schuster, *The hypercycle: A principle of natural self-organization*, Springer-Verlag, 1979.
6. R. A. Fisher, *The genetic theory of natural selection*, Clarendon Press, Oxford, 1930.
7. J. H. Holland, *Adaptation in natural and artificial systems*, University of Michigan Press, Ann Arbor, 1975.
8. Klaus Jaffe, *On the adaptive value of some mate selection strategies*, Acta Biotheoretica **1** (1999), no. 47, 29–40.
9. ______, *Emergence and maintenance of sex among diploid organisms aided by assortative mating*, Acta Biotheoretica **2** (2000), no. 48, 137–147.
10. ______, *On sex, mate selection and evolution: an exploration*, Comments on Theoretical Biology **2** (2002), no. 7, 91–107.
11. Stuart A. Kauffman, *The origins of order*, Oxford University Press, Oxford, 1993.
12. J. Maynard Smith, *The evolution of sex*, Cambridge University Press, 1978.
13. J. Maynard Smith and E. Szathmary, *The major transitions in evolution*, Oxford University Press, 1995.

14. M. Nowak and P. Schuster, *Error thresholds of replication in finite populations: Mutation frequencies and the onset of Muller's ratchet*, J. Theor. Biol. **137** (1989), 375–395.
15. G. Ochoa, *Consensus sequence plots and error thresholds: Tools for visualising the structure of fitness landscapes*, Parallel Problem Solving from Nature - PPSN VI 6th International Conference, Lecture Notes in Computer Science, vol. 1917, Springer Verlag, 2000, pp. 129–138.
16. G. Ochoa and I. Harvey, *Recombination and error thresholds in finite populations*, Foundations of Genetic Algorithms 5 (W. Banzhaf and C. Reeves, eds.), Morgan Kauffman, 1998.
17. G. Ochoa, I. Harvey, and H. Buxton, *Error thresholds and their relation to optimal mutation rates*, Proceedings of the 5th European Conference on Advances in Artificial Life (ECAL-99) (Berlin) (Dario Floreano, Jean-Daniel Nicoud, and Francesco Mondada, eds.), LNAI, vol. 1674, Springer, September 13–17 1999, pp. 54–63.
18. Gabriela Ochoa, *Error thresholds and optimal mutation rates in genetic algorithms*, Ph.D. thesis, School of Cognitive and Computing Sciences, University of Sussex, UK, 2001.
19. ———, *Error thresholds in genetic algorithms*, Evolutionary Computation Journal **2** (2006), no. 14.
20. Gabriela Ochoa and Klaus Jaffe, *On sex, mate selection and the red queen*, J. Theor. Biol. **1** (1999), no. 199, 1–9.
21. J. Swetina and P. Schuster, *Self-replication with errors, a model for polynucleotide replication*, Phys. Rev. A [15] Stat. Phys. **45** (1992), 6038–6050.
22. Gilbert Syswerda, *Uniform crossover in genetic algorithms*, Proc. 3rd International Conference on Genetic Algorithms (George Mason University) (J. David Schaffer, ed.), Morgan Kaufmann, 1989, pp. 2–9.
23. E. van Nimwegen and J. P. Crutchfield, *Optimizing epochal evolutionary search: Population-size dependent theory*, Tech. Report Preprint 98-06-046, Santa Fe Institute, 1998.
24. Michael D. Vose, *The simple genetic algorithm: foundations and theory*, MIT Press, Cambridge, MA, 1999.
25. Alden H. Wright, Jonathan E. Rowe, and James R. Neil, *Analysis of the simple genetic algorithm on the single-peak and double-peak landscapes*, Proceedings of the 2002 Congress on Evolutionary Computation CEC2002, IEEE Press, 2002, pp. 214–219.
26. Alden H. Wright, Jonathan E. Rowe, Christopher R. Stephens, and Riccardo Poli, *Bistability in a gene pool GA with mutation*, Foundations of Genetic Algorithms 7 (Kenneth A. De Jong, Riccardo Poli, and Jonathan E. Rowe, eds.), Morgan Kaufmann, San Francisco, 2003, pp. 63–80.

Is Self-adaptation of Selection Pressure and Population Size Possible? – A Case Study

A.E. Eiben, M.C. Schut, and A.R. de Wilde

Department of Computer Science, Vrije Universiteit Amsterdam
{gusz, schut, ardwilde}@cs.vu.nl

Abstract. In this paper we seek an answer to the following question: Is it possible and rewarding to self-adapt parameters regarding selection and population size in an evolutionary algorithm? The motivation comes from the observation that the majority of the existing EC literature is concerned with (self-)adaptation of variation operators, while there are indications that (self-)adapting selection operators or the population size can be equally or even more rewarding. We approach the question in an empirical manner. We design and execute experiments for comparing the performance increase of a benchmark EA when augmented with self-adaptive control of parameters concerning selection and population size in isolation and in combination. With the necessary caveats regarding the test suite and the particular mechanisms used we observe that self-adapting selection yields the highest benefit (up to 30-40%) in terms of speed.

1 Introduction

Calibrating parameters of evolutionary algorithms (EAs) is a long-standing grand challenge in evolutionary computing (EC). In the early years of the field it was often claimed that Genetic Algorithms (GAs) are not very sensitive to the actual choice of their parameters. Later on this view has changed and the EC community now acknowledges that the right choice of parameter values is essential for good EA performance [8]. This emphasizes the importance of *parameter tuning*, where much experimental work is devoted to finding good values for the parameters *before* the "real" runs and then running the algorithm using these values, which remain fixed during the run. This approach is widely practiced, but it suffers from two very important deficiencies. First, the parameter-performance landscape of any given EA on any given problem instance is highly non-linear with complex interactions among the dimensions (parameters). Therefore, finding high altitude points, i.e., well performing combinations of parameters, is hard. Systematic, exhaustive search is infeasible and there are no proven optimization algorithms for such problems. Second, things are even more complex, because the parameter-performance landscape is not static. It changes over time, since the best value of a parameter depends on the given stage of the search process. In other words, finding (near-)optimal parameter settings is a dynamic optimization problem. This implies that the practice of using constant parameters that do not change during a run is inevitably suboptimal.

T.P. Runarsson et al. (Eds.): PPSN IX, LNCS 4193, pp. 900–909, 2006.

Such considerations have directed the attention to mechanisms that would modify the parameter values of an EA on-the-fly. Efforts in this direction are mainly driven by two purposes: the promise of a parameter-free EA and performance improvement. Over the last two decades there have been numerous studies on this subject [8,10]. The related methods – commonly captured by the umbrella term *parameter control* as opposed to parameter tuning – can further be divided into one of the following three categories. *Deterministic parameter control* takes place when the value of a strategy parameter is altered by some deterministic rule modifying the strategy parameter in a fixed, predetermined (i.e., user-specified) way without using any feedback from the search. Usually, a time-dependent schedule is used. *Adaptive parameter control* works by some form of feedback from the search that serves as input to a heuristic mechanism used to determine the change to the strategy parameter. The important point to note is that the heuristic updating mechanism is externally supplied, rather than being part of the "standard" evolutionary cycle. In the case of *self-adaptive parameter control* the parameters are encoded into the chromosomes and undergo variation with the rest of the chomosome. The better values of these encoded parameters lead to better individuals, which in turn are more likely to survive and produce offspring and hence propagate these better parameter values.

To keep our present investigation feasible we do not want to study on-the-fly adjustment of *all* parameters with *all* parameter control mechanisms. The choice about which combinations to consider is made by the following observations. Of the three options self-adaptation is of particular interest for two reasons. First, it fits the evolutionary framework very smoothly in the sense that the changes to the parameters are evolutionary changes, rather than heuristic ones (deterministic or adaptive control). Second, self-adaptation has a very strong reputation, i.e., overwhelming evidence of being capable of adequate parameter control as shown within Evolution Strategies [3,17]. This makes us choose for a self-adaptive approach. As for the parameters to be controlled it can be noted that the traditional mainstream of research concentrated on the control of the variation operators, mutation and recombination.

However, there is recent evidence, or at least strong indication, that "tweaking" other EA components can be more rewarding; see for instance [4] showing the relative advantage of controlling the population size, instead of other parameters. This makes us disregard variation parameters and concentrate on parameters for selection and population sizing. The literature on varying population size is rather diverse concerning technical solutions as well as the conclusions regarding how to manage population sizes successfully [2,9,12,14,6,13,16,18]. The picture regarding the control of selection pressure during a run is more coherent; most researchers agree that the selection pressure should be increasing as the evolutionary process goes on, perhaps a legacy of Boltzmann selection, [1,20,7,15,11]. In the present investigation we will introduce as little as possible bias towards increasing or decreasing the parameter values.

2 Self-adapting Selection Pressure and Population Size

Note that our choice for investigating self-adaptive selection and population sizing implies an interesting challenge. Namely, the parameters regarding selection and population issues (e.g., tournament size or population size) are of global nature. They concern the whole population and cannot be naturally interpreted on local level, i.e., they cannot be defined at the level of individuals like mutation step size in evolution strategies. Self-adaptive population and selection parameters seem to be a contradictory idea. The way we address this challenge is based on making global parameters being derived from local (individual level) parameters via an aggregation mechanism. In this way, the value of a global parameter is determined collectively by the individuals in the population. Technically, our solution is threefold:

1. We assign an extra parameter $p \in [p_{min}, p_{max}]$ to each individual representing the individuals "vote" in the collective decision regarding the given global parameter P.
2. We specify an aggregation mechanism calculating the value of P from the p values in the population.
3. We postulate that the extra parameter p is part of the individual's chromosomes, i.e., an extra gene, and specify mechanisms to mutate these genes.[1]

The aggregation mechanism is rather straightforward. Roughly speaking, the global parameter P will be the sum of the local votes of all individuals p_i calculated as follows:

$$P = \lceil \sum_{i=1}^{N} p_i \rceil \tag{1}$$

where $p_i \in [p_{min}, p_{max}]$, $\lceil\ \rceil$ denotes the ceiling function, and N is the (actual) population size.

Finding an appropriate way to mutate such parameters needs some care. A straightforward option would be the standard self-adaptation mechanism of σ values from Evolution Strategies. However, those σ values are not bounded, while in our case $p \in [p_{min}, p_{max}]$ must hold. We found a solution in the self-adaptive mechanism for mutation rates in GAs as described by Bäck and Schütz [5]. This mechanism is introduced for $p \in (0, 1)$ and it works as follows:

$$p' = \left(1 + \frac{1-p}{p} \cdot e^{-\gamma \cdot N(0,1)}\right)^{-1} \tag{2}$$

where p is the parameter in question and γ is the learning rate which allows for control of the adaptation speed. This mechanism has some desirable properties:

[1] Note that hereby the parameters in question will be subject to evolution: variation happens through the given mutation mechanisms, while selection is "inherited for free" from the selection upon the hosting individuals.

1. Changing $p \in (0,1)$ yields a $p' \in (0,1)$.
2. Small changes are more likely than large ones.
3. The expected change of p by repeatedly changing it equals zero (which is desirable, because natural selection should be the only force bringing a direction in the evolution process).
4. Modifying by a factor c occurs with the same probability as a modification by $1/c$.

3 Experimental Setup

The test suite[2] for testing GAs is obtained through the Multi-modal Problem Generator of Spears [19]. We generate landscapes of 1, 2, 5, 10, 25, 50, 100, 250, 500 and 1000 binary peaks whose heights are linearly distributed and where the lowest peak is 0.5. The chromosome of each individual consists of 100 binary genes, i.e., $\langle x_1, \ldots, x_{100} \rangle$ and 1 or 2 self-adaptive parameters p (representing the self-adaptation of selection and/or population size).

We use a simple GA, SGA, as benchmark and define 4 self-adaptive GA variants. GASAM is a GA with self-adaptive mutation used as a second benchmark; GASAP and GASAT are the GAs where only one parameter is self-adapted; in GASAPT two parameters are self-adapted simultaneously.

The setup of the SGA is as follows. The model we use is a steady-state GA. Every individual is a 100-bitstring. The recombination operator is uniform crossover; the recombination probability is 0.5. The mutation operator is bit-flip; the mutation probability is 0.01. The parent selection is 2-tournament and survival selection is delete-worst-two. The population size is 100. Initialization is random. The termination criterion is $f(x) = 1$ or 10,000 evaluations.

GASAMworks on individuals with chromosome $\langle x_1, \ldots, x_{100}, p \rangle$, where p is the self-adaptive mutation parameter. The algorithm works the same as SGA on the bit-part of the chromosome (bitflip), but uses equation 2 for mutation of p.

GASAP works on individuals with chromosome $\langle x_1, \ldots, x_{100}, p_1 \rangle$, where p_1 is the self-adaptive population size parameter. GASAP is different from SGA in that it uses the self-adaptive mechanism from equations 1 and 2 to determine the population size. In this particular case, p is scaled to (0,2) enabling the population to grow as well as shrink. For maintaining enough diversity a lower bound for the population size is enforced.

GASAT works on individuals with chromosome $\langle x_1, \ldots, x_{100}, p_2 \rangle$, where p_2 is the self-adaptive tournament size parameter. GASAT is different from SGA in that it uses the self-adaptive mechanism from equations 1 and 2 to determine the tournament size. For maintaining enough diversity a lower bound for the tournament size is enforced.

GASAPT works on individuals with chromosome $\langle x_1, \ldots, x_{100}, p_1, p_2 \rangle$, where p_1 is the self-adaptive population size parameter and p_2 is the self-adaptive tournament size parameter. GASAPT is a combination of GASAP and GASAT as described above.

[2] The test suite can be obtained from the web-page of the authors.

In all self-adaptive GAs we use $\gamma = 0.22$ according to the recommendation in [5]. The code of the problem instance generator, the particular instances, and all algorithm variants can be obtained from the authors' web-sites.

After 100 runs of each GA, the Success Rate (SR), the Average number of Evaluations to a Solution (AES) and its standard deviation (SDAES), and the Mean Best Fitness (MBF) and its standard deviation (SDMBF) are calculated[3]. The ranking of these measures in forming a judgment about competing EAs is, of course, essential. To this end, it is important that SR and MBF are strongly depend on the maximum number of fitness evaluations M in the termination criterion. In particular, experiments with a lower M typically result in a lower SR and MBF. For AES this link is less strong. It could happen that for a lower M the number of successful runs decreases, but if a run is successful it is of the same length as in the experiments with a higher M. In other words, for a lower M AES could remain the same, while SR and MBF are decreasing. As for us, the speed of an EA that counts most: a faster EA (i.e., an EA with lower AES) is more likely to deliver good performance even for lower values of M.

4 Experimental Results and Analysis

4.1 Experiments with the Self-adaptive Scheme

The results of the experiments with the benchmarks GAs and the self-adaptive variants are summarized in Tables 1 and 2 (right hand side, Max=10000 evaluations). Table 1 exhibits the results of the two benchmark EAs, the simple GA (SGA) and the GA with the original self-adaptive mutation GA (GASAM) from [5]. Further to these detailed Tables we offer a graphical representation of the outcomes in Figure 1 (left). Comparing the algorithms it occurs that the differences in terms of SR and MBF are not very big. The curves are crossing and lay rather close to each other. (Note the scale on the y-axis of the MBF graphs in Figure 1.) The AES results are much more discriminating between the GAs. With one exception, the curves are not crossing, implying a consistent ranking based on speed. Also the differences are significant: depending on the problem instance, the best GA outruns the worst one by a factor 1.5 to 3.

Based on the available data we can conclude that the GA with self-adaptive tournament size (GASAT) is the fastest, but the SGA is a close second. Somewhat surprisingly, the GA with self-adaptive mutation rate (GASAM) becoms very slow for the more rugged landscapes and diplays the worst performance in terms of AES. We have performed t-tests with 5% significance level to validate the differences. These tests confirmed that the differences were statistically significant.

4.2 Additional Experiments with an Alternative Scheme

In addition to the above tests with the self-adaptive GAs we have performed experiments with a modified scheme as well. The reason is that we do have

[3] For reasons of space, the standard deviation results were omitted. The results are used in the t-tests mentioned later in the paper.

some intuition about the direction of change regarding the parameters. In case of tournament size, if a new individual is better than its parents then it should try to increase selection pressure, assuming that stronger selection will be advantageous for him, giving a reproductive advantage over less fit individuals. In the opposite case, if it is less fit than its parents, then it should try to lower the selection pressure. In case of the population size, this logic might not be applicable, but we do try the idea for both cases. Formally, we keep the aggregation mechanism from equation 1 and use the following rule. If $\langle x, p\rangle$ is an individual, where x is the bitstring and p is the parameter value, to be mutated (either obtained by crossover or just to be reproduced solely by mutation), then first we create x' from x by the regular bitflips, then apply

$$p' = \begin{cases} p + \Delta p & if \quad f(x') \geq f(x) \\ p - \Delta p & otherwise \end{cases} \tag{3}$$

where

$$\Delta p = \left| p - \left(1 + \frac{1-p}{p} e^{-\gamma N(0,1)}\right)^{-1} \right| \tag{4}$$

with $\gamma = 0.22$.

This mechanism differs from "pure" self-adaptation because of the heuristic rule specifying the direction of the change. However, it could be argued that this mechanism is not a clean adaptive scheme (because the initial p values are inherited), nor a clean self-adaptive scheme (because the final p values are influenced by a user defined heuristic), but some hybrid form. In any case, the parameter values represented in a given population undergo regular evolutionary selection because good/bad values survive/disappear depending on the fitness of the hosting individual. For this reason we perceive and name this mechanism *hybrid self-adaptive* (HSA).

We perform extra experiments to see how this alternative usage of the Bäck and Schütz formula effects the performance of the algorithms. Implementing this idea for both the tournament size and the population size yields three new variants GAHSAT, GAHSAP and GAHSAPT with the obvious naming convention. Their results are given in Table 3 (right hand side, Max=10000 evaluations) and Figure 1 (right). They show that the hybrid self-adaptive scheme yields a better control of the tournament size than the pure self-adaptive one, in the sense that the new algorithm GAHSAT outruns GASAT, the winner of the first series of experiments, regarding AES. (Here again we confirmed with a t-test that the differences are significant.) For controlling the population size the effects are exactly the opposite (GASAP beats GAHSAP) and the same holds for the combined algorithm (GASAPT beats GAHSAPT).

At the moment we do not have an explanation for these differences. Nevertheless it is interesting to look at the development of tournament size during a successful run of GASAT or GAHSAT (not shown here because of the lack of space). Such curves show that the selection pressure is growing for quite some time and starts dropping after a while. Intuitively, this is sound, for in the beginning many offspring outperform their parents leading to an increase in their

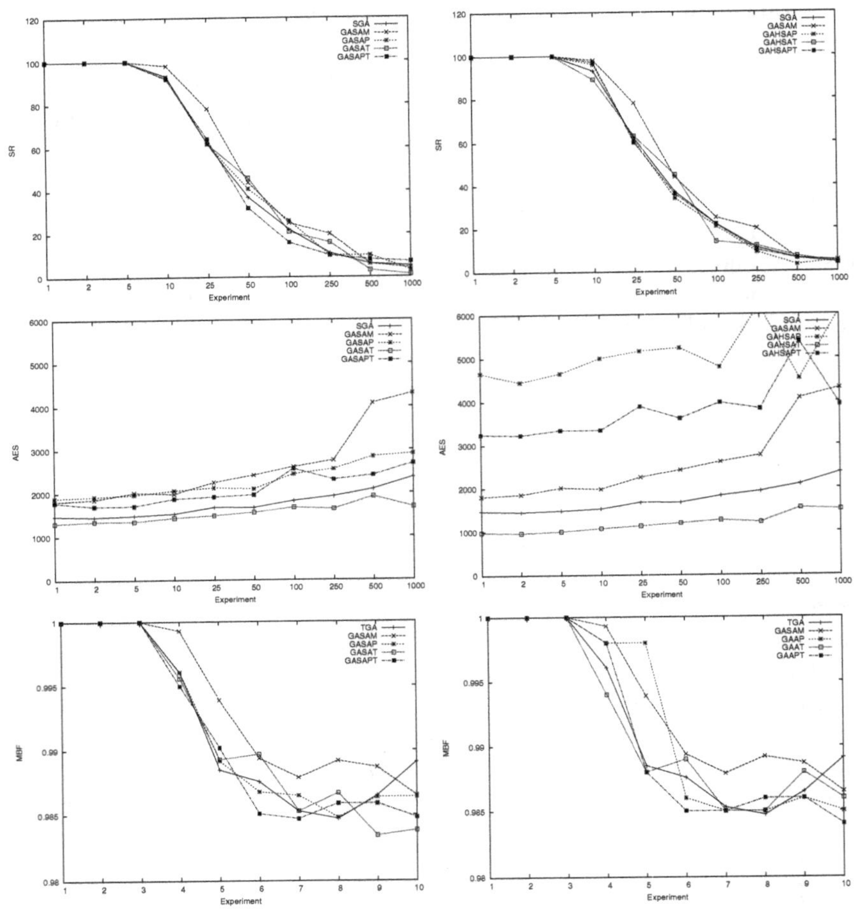

Fig. 1. SR, AES and MBF (from top to bottom) for self-adaptive algorithms (left) and hybrid self-adaptive algorithms (right) with max 10,000 fitness evaluations

"votes" for the global K. Later on, it becomes increasingly more seldom to produce children better than their parents, which in turn leads to decreasing K. This is also in line with the common view in EC that advocates increasing selection pressure, like in Boltzmann mechanisms. From this perspective we can interpret our results as a confirmation of this common view: the pure self-adaptive variant of the formula from [5] is unbiased w.r.t. the direction of the change and yet it results in increasing increasing tournament size. Last by not least, the overall winner of this contest among 8 GAs is GAHSAT.

The experiments with Max=10000 fitness evaluations give us *one* comparison. However, as our deliberation about the performance measures indicates such outcomes depend on the used maximum. To obtain a second assessment of our GAs we have repeated all experiments with Max=1500. These results are given in the left-hand sides of the tables. They show that the hybrid self-adaptive mechanism

Table 1. Experimental results of benchmark algorithms in terms of SR, AES and MBF with Max=1500 and Max=10000 fitness evaluations

	Max=1500 Evaluations						Max=10000 Evaluations					
	SGA			GASAM			SGA			GASAM		
Peaks	SR	AES	MBF	SR	AES	MBF	SR	AES	MBF	SR	AES	MBF
1	64	1353	0.9959	21	1405	0.9653	100	1478	1.0	100	1816	1.0
2	59	1361	0.9954	19	1398	0.9712	100	1454	1.0	100	1859	1.0
5	57	1376	0.9953	19	1421	0.9656	100	1488	1.0	100	2014	1.0
10	50	1370	0.9889	9	1375	0.9452	93	1529	0.9961	98	1982	0.9993
25	19	1422	0.9776	1	1166	0.9070	62	1674	0.9885	78	2251	0.9939
50	7	1391	0.9650	0	0	0.8677	37	1668	0.9876	44	2417	0.9894
100	3	1351	0.9590	0	0	0.8449	22	1822	0.9853	25	2606	0.9879
250	0	0	0.9432	0	0	0.7923	11	1923	0.9847	20	2757	0.9892
500	0	0	0.9265	0	0	0.7670	6	2089	0.9865	6	4079	0.9887
1000	0	0	0.9152	0	0	0.7565	5	2358	0.9891	4	4305	0.9865

Table 2. Experimental results of self-adaptive algorithms in terms of SR, AES and MBF with Max=1500 and Max=10000 fitness evaluations

	Max=1500 Evaluations									Max=10000 Evaluations								
	GASAP			GASAT			GASAPT			GASAP			GASAT			GASAPT		
Peaks	SR	AES	MBF	SR	AES	MBF	SR	AES	MBF	SR	AES	MBF	SR	AES	MBF	SR	AES	MBF
1	20	1364	0.9806	82	1252	0.9974	41	1322	0.9853	100	1893	1.0	100	1312	1.0	100	1787	1.0
2	27	1428	0.9804	77	1257	0.9974	48	1349	0.9872	100	1925	1.0	100	1350	1.0	100	1703	1.0
5	19	1411	0.9782	73	1244	0.9962	38	1273	0.9842	100	1966	1.0	100	1351	1.0	100	1710	1.0
10	6	1447	0.9672	59	1258	0.9887	31	1300	0.9757	93	2060	0.996	92	1433	0.996	92	1872	0.995
25	6	1416	0.9546	30	1262	0.9817	10	1394	0.9587	62	2125	0.989	62	1485	0.990	64	1915	0.990
50	1	1282	0.9452	13	1279	0.9751	6	1329	0.9519	41	2098	0.987	46	1557	0.990	32	1960	0.985
100	0	0	0.9317	7	1397	0.9687	1	1267	0.9426	26	2341	0.987	21	1669	0.985	16	2563	0.985
250	0	0	0.9279	1	1463	0.9644	0	0	0.9385	10	2554	0.985	16	1635	0.987	10	2307	0.986
500	0	0	0.9131	1	1451	0.9551	0	0	0.9312	10	2846	0.986	3	1918	0.983	8	2410	0.986
1000	0	0	0.9058	0	0	0.9520	0	0	0.9192	3	2908	0.986	1	1675	0.984	7	2685	0.985

Table 3. Experimental results of hybrid self-adaptive algorithms in terms of SR, AES and MBF with Max=1500 and Max=10000 fitness evaluations

	Max=1500 Evaluations									Max=10000 Evaluations								
	GAHSAP			GAHSAT			GAHSAPT			GAHSAP			GAHSAT			GAHSAPT		
Peaks	SR	AES	MBF	SR	AES	MBF	SR	AES	MBF	SR	AES	MBF	SR	AES	MBF	SR	AES	MBF
1	0	0	0.9273	96	925	0.9996	0	0	0.9508	100	4665	1.0	100	989	1.0	100	3250	1.0
2	0	0	0.9276	97	960	0.9997	0	0	0.9487	100	4453	1.0	100	969	1.0	100	3233	1.0
5	0	0	0.9222	91	982	0.9991	0	0	0.9512	100	4654	1.0	100	1007	1.0	100	3346	1.0
10	0	0	0.9200	82	1026	0.9940	0	0	0.9377	96	4998	0.998	89	1075	0.994	97	3343	0.998
25	0	0	0.9007	55	1065	0.9865	0	0	0.9200	61	5160	0.998	63	1134	0.988	60	3889	0.988
50	0	0	0.8989	37	1146	0.9849	0	0	0.9153	34	5233	0.986	45	1194	0.989	36	3612	0.985
100	0	0	0.8886	26	1152	0.9859	0	0	0.9062	21	4794	0.985	14	1263	0.985	22	3976	0.985
250	0	0	0.8789	11	1161	0.9832	0	0	0.8983	9	6211	0.985	12	1217	0.985	10	3834	0.986
500	0	0	0.8733	3	1437	0.9810	0	0	0.8864	3	4524	0.986	7	1541	0.988	6	5381	0.986
1000	0	0	0.8674	2	1140	0.9785	0	0	0.8768	5	6080	0.985	4	1503	0.986	4	3927	0.984

is disastrous for GAs where the population size is being modified, while the pure self-adaptive is not. Apparently, the logic that applies to tournament size does not apply to population size. Furthermore, we can see that the margin by which GAHSAT wins from the other becomes bigger than it was for Max=10000. This gives extra support to prefer this algorithm.

5 Conclusions

This investigation provided an answer to our original research question: Is self-adaptation of selection pressure and population size possible and rewarding in an evolutionary algorithm? The answer is double positive. First, we illustrated that it is possible to regulate global parameters (here: tournament size and population size) via aggregating locally specified values. Second, we showed that this can be very rewarding in terms of algorithm performance: the hybrid variant of self-adapting tournament size resulted in a superior GA and the regular self-adaptation variant became second best. Currently we are running additional experiments with constant selection pressure at various levels (tournament size = 2,4,8,16) and with increasing selection pressure (Boltzmann selection) for a broader comparison and more insights in the workings of GA(H)SAT.

Our work also "unearthes" the formula of Bäck and Schütz from [5]. This formula is interesting for its general applicability to mutate bounded parameters and the desirable properties as given in Section 2. The present investigation can also be considered as an assessment of the usefulness of this formula. Without much application specific adjustment we applied it to two parameters and observed that it can greatly improve algorithm performance (e.g., for tournament size). Meanwhile, we also established that it can be harmful (e.g., for population size). Future work is devoted to analyzing why the observed effects occur.

Considering the present investigation from the perspective of the challenge of freeing EAs from (some of) their parameters, our results constitute new evidence that self-adaptation of other than variation operators deserves more attention. We certainly hope that the results and the newly generated questions in this paper will inspire more work in this direction.

References

1. E.H.L. Aarts and J. Korst. *Simulated Annealing and Boltzmann Machines.* Wiley, Chichester, UK, 1989.
2. J. Arabas, Z. Michalewicz, and J. Mulawka. GAVaPS – a genetic algorithm with varying population size. In *Proceedings of the First IEEE Conference on Evolutionary Computation*, pages 73–78. IEEE Press, Piscataway, NJ, 1994.
3. T. Bäck. *Evolutionary Algorithms in Theory and Practice.* Oxford University Press, New York, 1996.
4. T. Bäck, A.E. Eiben, and N.A.L. van der Vaart. An empirical study on GAs "without parameters". In M. Schoenauer, K. Deb, G. Rudolph, X. Yao, E. Lutton, J.J. Merelo, and H.-P. Schwefel, editors, *Proceedings of the 6th Conference on Parallel Problem Solving from Nature*, number 1917 in Lecture Notes in Computer Science, pages 315–324. Springer, Berlin, 2000.
5. Th. Bäck and M. Schütz. Intelligent mutation rate control in canonical genetic algorithms. In Zbigniew W. Ras and Maciej Michalewicz, editors, *Foundations of Intelligent Systems, 9th International Symposium, ISMIS '96, Zakopane, Poland, June 9-13, 1996, Proceedings*, volume 1079 of *Lecture Notes in Computer Science*, pages 158–167. Springer, Berlin, Heidelberg, New York, 1996.

6. J. Costa, R. Tavares, and A. Rosa. An experimental study on dynamic random variation of population size. In *Proc. IEEE Systems, Man and Cybernetics Conf.*, volume 6, pages 607–612, Tokyo, 1999. IEEE Press.
7. Ambedkar Dukkipati, Narsimha Murty Musti, and Shalabh Bhatnagar. Cauchy annealing schedule: An annealing schedule for boltzmann selection scheme in evolutionary algorithms. In *Proceedings of the 2004 IEEE Congress on Evolutionary Computation*, pages 55–62.
8. A.E. Eiben, R. Hinterding, and Z. Michalewicz. Parameter control in evolutionary algorithms. *IEEE Transactions on Evolutionary Computation*, 3(2):124–141, 1999.
9. A.E. Eiben, E. Marchiori, and V.A. Valko. Evolutionary Algorithms with on-the-fly Population Size Adjustment. In X. Yao et al., editor, *Parallel Problem Solving from Nature, PPSN VIII*, number 3242 in Lecture Notes in Computer Science, pages 41–50. Springer, Berlin, Heidelberg, New York, 2004.
10. A.E. Eiben and J.E. Smith. *Introduction to Evolutionary Computing.* Springer, 2003.
11. Luis Gonzalez and James Cannady. A self-adaptive negative selection approach for anomaly detection. In *2004 Congress on Evolutionary Computation (CEC'2004)*, pages 1561–1568. IEEE Press, Piscataway, NJ, 2004.
12. G.R. Harik and F.G. Lobo. A parameter-less genetic algorithm. In W. Banzhaf, J. Daida, A. E. Eiben, M. H. Garzon, V. Honavar, M. Jakiela, and R. E. Smith, editors, *Proceedings of the Genetic and Evolutionary Computation Conference*, volume 1, pages 258–265, Orlando, Florida, USA, 1999. Morgan Kaufmann.
13. R. Hinterding, Z. Michalewicz, and T.C. Peachey. Self-adaptive genetic algorithm for numeric functions. In H.-M. Voigt, W. Ebeling, I. Rechenberg, and H.-P. Schwefel, editors, *Proceedings of the 4th Conference on Parallel Problem Solving from Nature*, number 1141 in Lecture Notes in Computer Science, pages 420–429. Springer, Berlin, 1996.
14. F.G. Lobo. *The parameter-less Genetic Algorithm: rational and automated parameter selection for simplified Genetic Algorithm operation.* PhD thesis, Universidade de Lisboa, 2000.
15. Eric Poupaert and Yves Deville. Acceptance driven local search and evolutionary algorithms. In L. Spector, E. Goodman, A. Wu, W.B. Langdon, H.-M. Voigt, M. Gen, S. Sen, M. Dorigo, S. Pezeshk, M. Garzon, and E. Burke, editors, *Proceedings of the Genetic and Evolutionary Computation Conference (GECCO-2001)*, pages 1173–1180. Morgan Kaufmann, 2001.
16. D. Schlierkamp-Voosen and H. Mühlenbein. Adaptation of population sizes by competing subpopulations. In *Proceedings of the 1996 IEEE Conference on Evolutionary Computation.* IEEE Press, Piscataway, NJ, 1996.
17. H.-P. Schwefel. *Evolution and Optimum Seeking.* Wiley, 1995.
18. R.E. Smith. Adaptively resizing populations: An algorithm and analysis. In S. Forrest, editor, *Proceedings of the 5th International Conference on Genetic Algorithms.* Morgan Kaufmann, San Francisco, 1993.
19. W.M. Spears. *Evolutionary Algorithms: the role of mutation and recombination.* Springer, Berlin, Heidelberg, New York, 2000.
20. Eckart Zitzler and Simon Künzli. Indicator-based selection in multiobjective search. In E.K. Burke X. Yao, J.A. Lozano, J. Smith, J.J.M. Guervos, J.A. Bullinaria, J.E. Rowe, P. Tino, A. Kaban, and H.-P. Schwefel, editors, *PPSN*, number 3242 in Lecture Notes in Computer Science, pages 832–842. Springer, Berlin, Heidelberg, New York, 2004.

A Particle Swarm Optimizer for Constrained Numerical Optimization

Leticia C. Cagnina[1], Susana C. Esquivel[1], and Carlos A. Coello Coello[2]

[1] LIDIC (Research Group). Universidad Nacional de San Luis - Ej. de Los Andes 950 - (5700) San Luis, Argentina
{lcagnina, esquivel}@unsl.edu.ar

[2] CINVESTAV-IPN (Evolutionary Computation Group), Computer Science Section, Av. IPN No. 2508, Col. San Pedro Zacatenco, Mexico D.F. 07300, Mexico
ccoello@cs.cinvestav.mx

Abstract. This paper presents a particle swarm optimizer to solve constrained optimization problems. The proposed approach adopts a simple method to handle constraints of any type (linear, nonlinear, equality and inequality), and it also presents a novel mechanism to update the velocity and position of each particle. The approach is validated using standard test functions reported in the specialized literature and it's compared with respect to algorithms representative of the state-of-the-art in the area. Our results indicate that the proposed scheme is a promising alternative to solve constrained optimization problems using particle swarm optimization.

1 Introduction

Constraints are usually adopted in any sort of real-world optimization problems (e.g., in engineering, in cutting and packing problems, in VLSI design, etc.). The unconstrained nature of evolutionary algorithms (EA) makes it necessary to design schemes to incorporate the constraints of a problem into the fitness function [2]. Despite the popularity of penalty functions, they have certain limitations from which the main one has to do with the difficulties to define accurate penalty factors that allow an EA an efficient exploration of the search space (particularly when dealing with problems in which the global optimum lies on the boundary between the feasible and the infeasible regions).

Constrained optimization problems have been extensively studied in Mathematical Programming. However, despite the existence of a considerable number of deterministic optimization algorithms, there is no single approach that can guarantee convergence for the general nonlinear programming problem, which is the one of interest to us [8].

In the last few years, several metaheuristics have been adopted for numerical optimization. One of such metaheuristics which has become increasingly popular is particle swarm optimization (PSO) [6]. PSO is based on the metaphor of how some species share information and then use it for moving to those places where the food is located. The population is a set of individuals named *particles*

T.P. Runarsson et al. (Eds.): PPSN IX, LNCS 4193, pp. 910–919, 2006.

which represent possible solutions within a multidimensional search space. The particles are characterized by a position, a velocity of exploration and a record of their past behavior. All of these are constantly updated in an iterative process. In this paper, we adopt PSO for solving constrained optimization problems.

The remainder of the paper is organized as follows. Section 2 provides the statement of the problem of our interest. In Section 3, we present a brief literature review. Section 4 describes our proposed approach. The experimental setup and the analysis of our results are presented in Section 5. Finally, our conclusions and some possible paths for future research are presented in Section 6.

2 Statement of the Problem

The problem of interest to us is the general *nonlinear programming problem* which is defined as the problem of finding $\boldsymbol{x}$ which optimizes the objective function:

$$f(\boldsymbol{x}) \text{ with } \boldsymbol{x} = (x_1, x_2, \ldots, x_D) \in \mathcal{F} \subseteq \mathcal{S} \subseteq \mathrm{I\!R}^D \ . \tag{1}$$

where $f(\boldsymbol{x})$ is subject to:

$$g_i(\boldsymbol{x}) \leq 0 \quad i = 1, 2, \ldots, n \ . \tag{2}$$

$$h_e(\boldsymbol{x}) = 0 \quad e = 1, 2, \ldots, m \ . \tag{3}$$

$x_d \in [l_d, u_d]$ with $d \in [1..D]$. l_d and u_d are the lower and upper bounds imposed on the decision variables. The g_i and h_e functions are defined on $\mathcal{S}$ (search space), and correspond to the inequality and equality constraint functions, respectively. A constraint delimits the search space splitting it into a feasible and an infeasible region. $\mathcal{S}$ is a D-dimensional rectangle defined by the lower and upper bounds of each variable x_d. All $\boldsymbol{x}$ satisfying all inequality and equality constraint functions determine the feasible solution space $\mathcal{F}$.

3 Literature Review

Despite the popularity of PSO as a numerical optimizer, there is relatively little work regarding its use in constrained optimization problems. Next, we will review the most representative research within this area.

Zhang et al. [11] presented a PSO algorithm with a *periodic* mode of handling constraints. This technique makes periodic copies of the search space when the algorithm starts the run. In that way, it avoids the disorganization that may arise when the mutation operator is applied to those particles lying on the boundary between the feasible and infeasible regions. The authors tested their algorithm with a low number of evaluations (28,000 and 140,000) in eight test functions. They performed 100 runs for each test function and compared the performance of their approach with respect to the results provided by conventional constraint-handling methods (i.e., penalty functions). However, no comparisons are provided with respect to state-of-the-art constraint-handling techniques.

Toscano Pulido and Coello Coello [10] added to a basic PSO a simple mechanism for tackling constraints based on how close are the particles from the feasible region. A *turbulence* operator was incorporated to improve the exploration of the search space. This operator changes the flight of particles to different zones. The algorithm was tested with a relatively large population size and a low number of iterations as to perform 340,000 evaluations of the objective function. Thirteen benchmark constrained functions from [9] were used to show the performance of this PSO. The authors concluded that their results were highly competitive.

Parsopoulos et al. [7] proposed a *Unified Particle Swarm Optimization* version and adapted it to handle constraints. They included a penalty function technique which uses the number of constraints that are violated and the degree of violation. The algorithm preserves the feasibility of the best solutions. They tested their version with four constrained engineering optimization problems with promising results.

4 Our Proposed Approach

In this section, we present our proposal of a Constrained Particle Swarm Optimizer (called **CPSO**). In CPSO, each particle consists of a n-dimensional real number vector (where n refers to the number of decision variables of the problem to be solved). Each dimension of a particle corresponds to a decision variable of the problem. The particles are evaluated using a fitness function which has some constraints. There are a several constraint-handling approaches that tend to add information about the distance from each individual to the feasible region into the fitness function in order to guide the search. One of the simplest methods (which was implemented in our algorithm) prefers to choose a feasible individual over an infeasible one. When the algorithm evaluates infeasible particles, it prefers the infeasible individuals that are closer to the feasible region. To determine the infeasibility degree, CPSO saves the largest violation obtained for each constraint. Then, when a particle is detected to be infeasible, the algorithm adds the amount of violation that corresponds to that particle (normalized with respect to the largest violation recorded so far). This approach was used in the PSO strategy to choose the best values: gbest, lbest and the best value reached by each particle. Thus, the equations to update velocity and position use the "best" feasible solution, or the infeasible solution which is closest to the feasible region (if there are feasible particles in the swarm).

Most constraint-handling techniques used in evolutionary algorithms tend to deal only with inequality constraints because equalities are very difficult to handle. To transform an equality constraint into an inequality we use:

$$|h_e(\boldsymbol{x})| - \epsilon \leq 0 \ . \tag{4}$$

where ϵ is the tolerance allowed. By adopting this transformation, our CPSO only deals with inequality constraints.

As in the basic PSO, our algorithm records the best position found so far for each particle (*gbest* approach) or in the neighborhood (*lbest* approach) if a neighborhood topology is implemented. These values are used to update the velocity and position of the particles. It is known that the *gbest* approach works well in many problems, but tends to converge to a local optimum in some cases [1]. For those cases, the *lbest* approach works better because it records the best value reached by a smaller group of particles, instead of considering the entire swarm.

We empirically found that a combination of the two approaches worked well in our CPSO. With *gbest*, the algorithm explores better and with *lbest*, we avoid stagnation. Thus, we modified the equation for computing the velocity (used to update the position of a particle) in the following way:

$$v_{id} = w(v_{id} + c_1 r_1 (p_{id} - part_{id}) + c_2 r_2 (p_{ld} - part_{id}) + c_3 r_3 (p_{gd} - part_{id})) \quad (5)$$

$$part_{id} = part_{id} + v_{id} \quad (6)$$

where v_{id} is the velocity of the particle i at the dimension d, w is the inertia factor [3] whose goal is to balance global exploration and local exploitation, c_1 is the personal learning factor, and c_2, c_3 are the social learning factors, r_1, r_2 and r_3 are three random numbers within the range [0..1], p_{id} is the best position reached by the particle i, p_{ld} is the best position reached by any particle in the neighborhood, p_{gd} is the best position reached by any particle in the swarm and $part_{id}$ is the value of the particle i at the dimension d.

To compute the p_{ld} value, we used a circle topology [4], in which each particle is connected to k neighbors. The neighbors are determined by the position of the particles in the structure. Figure 1 illustrates this concept.

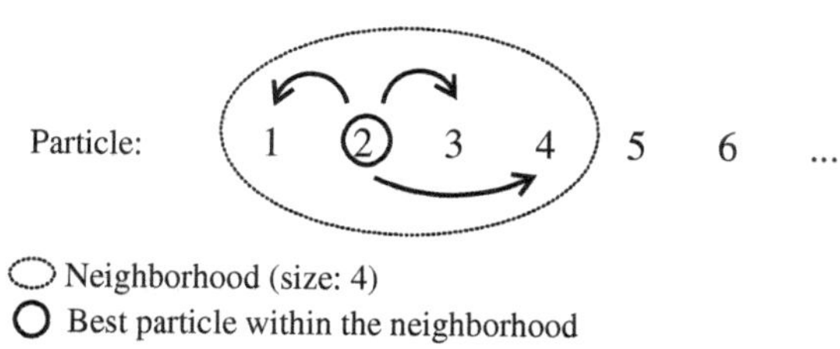

Fig. 1. Circle topology

It is well known that it is important to maintain the population's diversity to avoid stagnation (i.e., convergence to a local optimum). In order to meet this goal, we adopted a dynamic mutation operator, which was applied to each particle with a probability pm. This probability uses the total number of cycles and the current cycle number in the following equation:

$$pm = max\_pm - \frac{max\_pm - min\_pm}{max\_cycle} * current\_cycle \quad (7)$$

where max_pm and min_pm are the maximum and minimum values that pm can take, max_cycle is the number of cycles that the algorithm will iterate, and the $current\_cycle$ is the current cycle in the iterative process.

We empirically found that for some difficult functions, our CPSO could not find good values. The reason was its diversification of solutions which kept the approach from converging. In order to overcome this problem, we changed the common update equation (eq. (6)) of particles for the update equation presented by Kennedy [5] in the so-called *Gaussian Bare Bones PSO*. In that algorithm, the new position of each particle is randomly chosen from a Gaussian distribution with the mean selected as the average between the best position recorded for the particle and the best in its neighborhood. The standard deviation is the difference between these two values. Then, the position was updated using the following equation:

$$part_i = N\left(\frac{p_i + p_l}{2}, |p_i - p_l|\right) \quad (8)$$

where p_i is the position of the particle to be updated, N is the Gaussian random generator, p_i and p_l are the best position reached by the particle $part_i$ and the best position reached by any particle in the neighborhood of $part_i$. CPSO used this equation to update particles with a certain probability (a 50% probability was adopted to select between equation (6) and equation (8)). We choose those probabilities ($\langle 0.5, 0.5\rangle$) because we determined it was the best combination to be used to select between equations (6) and equation (8) for updating the particles. We performed a series of previous experiments (which are shown in Table 1) using the 3 functions in which CPSO had more difficulties to obtain good values: functions 2, 6 and 13. The notation $\langle r, s\rangle$ means that we selected equations (6) with a probability r and equation (8) with a probability s. Figure 2 shows the pseudo-code of our CPSO.

Table 1. Best Values obtained with *CPSO*, performing 340,000 evaluations with different probabilities of selection for the updating equations

Function	Best Known Value	$\langle 0.1, 0.9\rangle$	$\langle 0.5, 0.5\rangle$	$\langle 0.9, 0.1\rangle$
2	-0.803619	0.801825	-0.801388	-0.757889
6	-6961.814	-6962.046	-6961.825	-6827.984
13	0.053950	0.157094	0.054237	0.316460

5 Parameter Settings and Analysis of Results

The CPSO algorithm was tested using the thirteen constrained test functions adopted in [9]. We performed 30 independent runs for each function. Our results are compared with respect to the PSO-based approach which currently is the most competitive reported in the specialized literature for constrained optimization (i.e., the approach by Toscano Pulido and Coello Coello [10]). Additionally, we also compared our results with respect to Stochastic Ranking [9], which is a constraint-handling technique representative of the state-of-the-art in the area. Stochastic Ranking was validated performing 350,000 objective function evaluations per run. However, the approach from [10] performed 340,000 objective function evaluations per run. Thus, in order to allow a fair comparison, we performed experiments with only 340,000 objective function evaluations. The parameters of our approach are the following: swarm size = 10 particles, pm_min =

```
CPSO:
Swarm Initialization
    FOR i=1 TO number of particles DO
        FOR j=1 TO number of dimensions DO
            Initialize part_ij
            Initialize vel_ij
        END
    END
    Evaluate fitness
    Record pbest
    Record gbest
Swarm flights through the search space
    DO
        FOR i=1 TO number of particles DO
            Search the best leader in the
               neighborhood of part_i
               and record in lbest_i
            IF flip(0.5)
               FOR j=1 TO number of dimensions DO
                   Update vel_ij
                   Update part_ij using eq. (6)
               END
            ELSE
               gaussian update using eq. (8)
            END
        END
        Keeping particles
        Update pm
        Mutate every particle depending on pm
        Evaluate fitness(part_i)
        Record pbest
        Record gbest
    WHILE(current_cycle < max_cycle)
```

Fig. 2. Pseudo-code of our proposed CPSO

0.1, $pm\_max = 0.4$, neighborhood size = 4, the inertia factor w was set randomly with a value within the range [0.8,0.9], and learning factors c_1, c_2, and c_3 were randomly chosen within the range [1.8,1.9]. The parameter settings such as the probability of mutation, neighborhood size, inertia and learning factors were empirically derived after numerous experiments. As we stated in Section 3, we transformed the equality constraints into inequality constrains, using $\epsilon = 0.0001$. This tolerance causes that the algorithm identifies as feasible some constraints which are being slightly violated. That is the reason why some results reported in the present work are better than the reference solutions previously reported.

Table 2 displays the results obtained with 3 different algorithms: our version of *CPSO* with 340,000 evaluations, the algorithm presented by Toscano Pulido

Table 2. Best results obtained by our $CPSO$, PSO_{Tos} (with 340,000 objective function evaluations), and SR (with 350,000 objective function evaluations)

Function	Type	Best Known Value	$CPSO$	PSO_{Tos}	SR
1	Min	-15.000	*-15.000*	*-15.000*	*-15.000*
2	Max	-0.803619	-0.801388	-0.803432	*-0.803515*
3	Max	1.000	*1.000*	1.004	*1.000*
4	Min	-30665.539	-30665.659	-30665.500	*-30665.539*
5	Min	5126.498	*5126.497*	5126.640	*5126.497*
6	Min	-6961.814	-6961.825	-6961.810	*-6961.814*
7	Min	24.306	24.400	24.351	*24.307*
8	Max	0.095825	*0.095825*	*0.095825*	*0.095825*
9	Min	680.630	680.636	680.638	*680.630*
10	Min	7049.3307	*7052,8523*	7057.5900	7054.316
11	Min	0.750	0.749	0.749	*0.750*
12	Max	1.000	*1.000*	*1.000*	*1.000*
13	Min	0.053950	0.054237	0.068665	*0.053957*

Table 3. Best, Mean and Worst Values Obtained with $CPSO$, performing 340,000 objective function evaluations

Function	Best	Mean	Worst
1	-15.000	-15.0001	-134.2191
2	-0.801388	0.7653	0.0917
3	1.000	1.0000	1.0000
4	-30665.659	-30665.6564	-25555.6267
5	5126.497	5327.9569	2300.5443
6	-6961.825	-6859.0759	64827.5545
7	24.400	31.4854	4063.5252
8	0.095825	0.0958	-0.0006
9	680.636	682.3973	18484.7591
10	7052,8523	8533.6999	13123.4656
11	0.749	0.7505	0.4466
12	1.000	1.000	9386
13	0.054237	1.4139	0.9675

and Coello Coello [10] (PSO_{Tos}) and Stochastic Ranking (SR) [9]. The best result found for each function is marked with *italics*.

Comparing our best results with respect to PSO_{Tos} (Table 2), our approach was able to improve its best results in five test functions: 3, 5, 9, 10 and 13 (it is worth remarking that functions 10 and 13 are among the most difficult from the benchmark considered). PSO_{Tos} outperforms $CPSO$ in test functions 2 and 7. Additionally, in functions 4 and 6, our $CPSO$ did not reach the optimum values while PSO_{Tos} obtained values lower than the best reported values due to rounding errors on the constraints. Comparing our $CPSO$ with respect to SR,

Table 4. Best, Mean and Worst Values Obtained with PSO_{Tos}, performing 340,000 objective function evaluations

Function	Best	Mean	Worst
1	-15.000	-15.0000	-15.0000
2	-0.803432	0.790406	0.750393
3	1.004	1.0038	1.0024
4	-30665.500	-30665.5000	-30665.5000
5	5126.640	5461.0813	6104.7500
6	-6961.810	-6961.8100	-6961.8100
7	24.351	25.3557	27.3168
8	0.095825	0.0958	0.0958
9	680.636	680.8523	680.5530
10	7057.5900	7560.0478	8104.3100
11	0.749	0.7501	0.7528
12	1.000	1.0000	1.0000
13	0.068665	1.7164	13.6695

Table 5. Best, Mean and Worst Values Obtained with SR, performing 350,000 evaluations

Function	Best	Mean	Worst
1	-15.000	-15.0000	-15.0000
2	-0.803515	0.781975	0.726288
3	1.000	1.0000	1.0000
4	-30665.500	-30665.5000	-30665.5000
5	5126.539	5128.8810	5142.4720
6	-6961.814	-6875.9400	-6350.2620
7	24.307	24.3740	24.6420
8	0.095825	0.0958	0.0958
9	680.630	680.6560	680.7630
10	7054.3160	7559.1920	8835.6550
11	0.750	0.7500	0.7500
12	1.000	1.0000	1.0000
13	0.053957	0.0570	0.2169

we can observe that $CPSO$ obtained better values for function 10, equal values for five test functions (1, 3, 5, 8, 12) and SR found slightly better results for the rest of the problems (2, 4, 6, 7, 9, 11 y 13). However, it is important to note that both PSO algorithms obtained their results with a lower computational cost (measured in terms of the number of evaluations of the objective functions), since they performed 340,000 objective function evaluations, whereas Stochastic Ranking performed 350,000 objective function evaluations.

The mean and worst values obtained by PSO_{Tos} and SR (Tables 4 and 5) are both better that those of $CPSO$ (Table 3). We believe that this fact is due to the mechanism implemented to maintain the swarm's diversity. However, this mechanism provided a trade-off that we considered acceptable, since the best values found remained competitive despite the larger variability of results obtained. Note that in Table 3 some mean values (functions 2, 4, 5, 11 and 13) do not fall within the best and the worst values. This is because the worst values reached by $CPSO$ are not feasible while the best values are feasible. We believe the same occurs with PSO_{Tos} and SR (Tables 4 and 5) in some cases.

6 Conclusions and Future Work

We have introduced a new proposal to solve constrained optimization problems using particle swarm optimization. Our approach uses simple selection rules for handling the constraints of a problem, and adopts both the local and the global best models to update the particles of the swarm. Our best results are very competitive in most cases, even with respect to Stochastic Ranking (which is the best constraint-handling technique known to date) although they present a high variability in some cases. Additionally, in several cases our approach outperformed a previous PSO-based constraint-handling scheme.

As part of our future work, we aim to study alternative schemes to maintain diversity. Another goal is to improve the robustness of our approach, so that the variability of results significantly decreases, without degrading the quality of the best solutions currently found.

Acknowledgements. The third author acknowledges support from CONACyT through project number 45683-Y.

References

1. L. Cagnina, S. Esquivel, and R. Gallard. Particle swarm optimization for sequencing problems: a case study. In *Congress on Evolutionary Computation*, pages 536–541, Portland, Oregon, USA, 2004. http://www.lidic.unsl.edu.ar/publicaciones/info_publicacion.php?id_publicacion=200.
2. Carlos A. Coello Coello. Theoretical and Numerical Constraint Handling Techniques used with Evolutionary Algorithms: A Survey of the State of the Art. *Computer Methods in Applied Mechanics and Engineering*, 191(11-12):1245–1287, January 2002.
3. R. Eberhart and Y. Shi. A modified particle swarm optimizer. In *International Conference on Evolutionary Computation, IEEE Service Center*, Anchorage, AK, Piscataway, NJ, 1998.
4. J. Kennedy. Small world and mega-minds: effects of neighborhood topologies on particle swarm performance. In *1999 Congress on Evolutionary Computation*, pages 1931–1938, Piscataway, NJ, 1999. IEEE Service Center.
5. J. Kennedy. Bare bones particle swarms. In *IEEE Swarm Intelligence Symposium*, pages 80–87, 2003.
6. J. Kennedy and R. C. Eberhart. *Swarm Intelligence.* Morgan Kaufmann Publishers, California, USA, 2001.

7. K. E. Parsopoulos and M. N. Vrahatis. Unified particle swarm optimization for solving constrained engineering optimization problems. In *Lecture Notes of Computer Science*, pages 582–591, Springer-Verlag Berlin Heidelberg, 2005.
8. Singiresu S. Rao. *Engineering Optimization*. John Wiley & Sons, 3rd edition, 1996.
9. T. P. Runarsson and X. Yao. Stochastic ranking for constrained evolutionary optimization. In *IEEE Transactions on Evolutionary Computation*, volume 3, pages 284–294, 2000.
10. G. Toscano Pulido and C. A. Coello Coello. A constrained-handling mechanism for particle swarm optimization. In *Congress on Evolutionary Computation*, pages 1396–1403, Portland, Oregon, USA, 2004.
11. W. Zhang, X. Xie, and D. Bi. Handling boundary constraints for numerical optimization by particle swarm flying in periodic search space. In *Congress on Evolutionary Computation*, pages 2307–2311, Portland, Oregon, USA, 2004.

Self-regulated Population Size in Evolutionary Algorithms

Carlos Fernandes and Agostinho Rosa

LaSEEB-ISR-IST, Technical Univ. of Lisbon (IST)
{cfernandes, acrosa}@laseeb.org

Abstract. In this paper we analyze a new method for an adaptive variation of Evolutionary Algorithms (EAs) population size: the Self-Regulated Population size EA (SRP-EA). An empirical evaluation of the method is provided by comparing the new proposal with the CHC algorithm and other well known EAs with varying population. A fitness landscape generator was chosen to test and compare the algorithms: the Spear's multimodal function generator. The performance of the algorithms was measured in terms of success rate, quality of the solutions and evaluations needed to attain them over a wide range of problem instances. We will show that SRP-EA performs well on these tests and appears to overcome some recurrent drawbacks of traditional EAs which lead them to local optima premature convergence. Also, unlike other methods, SRP-EA seems to self-regulate its population size according to the state of the search.

1 Introduction

Although varying the population size of EAs during the run seems to be a rather natural and rewarding approach when implementing this type of algorithms, that particular parameter has not been widely studied as far as variation is concerned. Unlike other operators' parameters - like mutation rate for instance -, population size, with few exceptions, remained away from major efforts in finding parameter control methods. GAVaPS [1] (see next section) introduced some interesting concepts that gave rise to an optimist expectation about the performance of EAs with varying population size. But some aspects of the algorithm, namely population size self-regulation, could not be reproduced in other tests [5] [7]. The authors of GAVaPS suggested that the algorithm could adapt its population size according to the state of the search, balancing exploration and exploitation by increasing the population size on a first stage and then reducing the number of chromosomes on later stages. But, in further studies, a different behavior was observed. In [7], the authors noted that GAVaPS, when applied to a Royal Road problem, either grew its population size up to several thousand individuals or decreased it until extinction. These features were observed with different parameter values, that is, no combination of parameters was found to improve the stability of the population. In [5], GAVaPS also evolved into large populations when applied to Spears' multimodal problems, giving rise to a poor performance when compared to other EAs. Despite these disappointing general results of GAVaPS, some other studies indicate that varying the population size of EAs may

T.P. Runarsson et al. (Eds.): PPSN IX, LNCS 4193, pp. 920 – 929, 2006.

increase their performance on some problems (see [5], for instance). Also, although GAVaPS did not attain the expected impact, some of its concepts are very interesting and worth further exploring. With these issues in mind, we intended to develop a decentralized variation process that may lead to a self-regulated behavior of the population size, at least within a small subset of the parameters values, thus exploring more conveniently the search space and making use of the resources in a more rational way. The proposed process relies on the genetic diversity of the population during the run. Our results indicate that this may be a promising path to follow when developing EAs with varying population size.

2 Previous Research

According to Eiben and al. [4] parameter control mechanisms of EAs may be divided into three categories:

- Deterministic methods: parameter values are changed by some deterministic rule.
- Adaptive methods: values vary during the EA run depending on its behavior.
- Self-Adaptive methods: the values are codified within the chromosome and evolve together with the problem solutions.

In this paper we focus our attention on the variation of the population size of EAs during the run. Some techniques described below fall into the adaptive methods categories, while others, like RVPS [3] and PRoFIGA [5] are deterministic methods. Our proposal may also be classified as an adaptive method. However, the variation process in SRP-EA may also be viewed as a result of a varying crossover rate, which is indirectly controlled by the genetic diversity of the population.

The Genetic Algorithm with Varying Population Size (GAVaPS) [1] does not have an explicit selection mechanism. As in natural systems, population size is defined by the birth and death of individuals occurring at each iteration. A parameter called *lifetime* is introduced. It defines the number of generations in which each individual is allowed to remain *alive*, that is, a part of the population and the evolutionary process. After its creation, the chromosome is assigned to a specific lifetime, according to its fitness. Three lifetime calculation methods are proposed. The algorithm proceeds in a generational manner, at each time step increasing each individual's *age*. When an individual's age exceeds its lifetime, the chromosome is removed from the population. Since fittest individuals remain in the population for more generations, thus having a higher probability to be engaged in a reproduction process and generate offspring, GAVaPS' chromosomes have equal probability to be selected to reproduce, independently of their fitness value. This concept of lifetime/age provides the algorithm with the necessary selection pressure, which reduces the need for selection strategies: GAVaPS randomly pairs the chromosomes for crossover operations. The intensity of the pressure is controlled by two parameters, *minLT* and *maxLT*, that define, respectively, the minimum and maximum lifetime allowed for each chromosome. Higher difference between the two values leads to a more selective algorithm. However, this process may have a serious drawback since increasing the *maxLT* parameter will result in larger populations and, as stated above, an increasingly high population size is a characteristic of GAVaPS. The algorithm also introduces another parameter: reproduction rate (ρ). Its value defines the number of new chromosomes created in each generation t, depending on the size of the current population.

The Adaptive Population size Genetic Algorithm (APGA) [2] is very similar to GAVaPS. The only difference resides in reproduction rate, which in APGA has a fixed value of two individuals. This technique follows the reproduction strategy of the Steady-State GA and prevents the population from growing out of control has it often happens with GAVaPS. On the other hand, such a low reproduction rate results in populations with few individuals unless a high value for *maxLT* is used. But, even in the last case, the population size is very stable and apparently does not react to the evolution process and different search stages (see section 4). However, the algorithm performs well on some problems and clearly outperformed GAVaPS when applied to the Spears' multimodal problems [5]. Besides a low reproduction rate, APGA also uses an elitist strategy by keeping unchanged the age of the best individual.

The Population Resizing on Fitness Improvement GA (PRoFIGA) was proposed in [5] by Eiben, Marchiori and Valkó. The variation process of PRoFIGA is based on the improvement of the best fitness in the population. The process intends to balance exploration and exploitation by growing the population in earlier and exploratory stages and gradually decrease it in later stages of the search. When the population gets trapped in local optima, the process is supposed to generate another growing phase of the population, thus increasing diversity and escaping the local optima. The authors present a heuristic for size variation during the run that increases or decreases the population size according to whether or not the best fitness of the population has been improved and, if the later case is observed, for how long it has remained unchanged.

In the Random Variation of Population Size GA (RVPS) [3] the population size is randomly changed during the run. The authors concluded that in some cases the performance of RVPS is equivalent to the standard GA. So, when there are no hints about the optimal population size for some problem, it may be appropriate to randomly set and vary the population size of the GA.

Like PRoFIGA and RVPS, the Saw-Tooth Genetic Algorithm [8] is an example of a deterministic method used in the variation of the population size. In this algorithm the population size varies according to a predefined function with a saw-tooth shape. The authors concluded that the Saw-Tooth GA performed well on some particular test functions. However, besides a variable population size, the Saw-Tooth GA also uses a reinitialization mechanism to introduce genetic diversity in the population.

3 Our Proposal

The SRP-EA combines features of CHC [6] and GAVaPS and introduces a dynamic reproduction rate which is indirectly controlled by the genetic diversity of the population. CHC, which stands for *Cross generational elitist selection, Heterogeneous Recombination and Cataclysmic Mutation*, is a variation of the standard GA. It uses no mutation in the classical sense of the concept, but instead it goes through a process of macro-mutation when the best fitness of the population doesn't change after a certain number of generations. The genetic diversity is assured by a highly disruptive crossover operator (HUX) and a reproduction restriction which assures that selected pairs of chromosomes won't generate offspring unless their Hamming Distance is above a certain threshold. Then, each generation, *p/2* pairs of chromosomes are randomly selected from the population with size *p*. All pairs are submitted to the reproduction process. First, their Hamming Distance is computed. If the value is found to be above the threshold then the chromosomes generate two children with the HUX operator. When the process is concluded, the newly generated population of *p'* offspring replaces the worst *p'* chromosomes in the main population, therefore maintaining the size of the population. The threshold is usually set in the beginning of the runs to ¼ of the chromosome length, and decremented when no offspring is generated. When the algorithm gets stuck in local optima, a cataclysmic mutation is applied by replacing the entire population, except the best chromosome, with mutated copies of that individual. Usually, the mutation rate at this point is set to 0.35.

SRP-EA adapts the Hamming Distance restriction of CHC. Remember that the process leads to a changing reproduction rate meaning that in each generation the number of offspring is not necessarily the same. The difference is that in SRP-EA the new chromosomes do not replace the parents' population. Instead, offspring are added to the population, therefore increasing its size, while other individuals are removed via an age/lifetime process similar to the one found in GAVaPS and APGA. The process conduces to a variation in the size of the population and works as follows (SRP-EA pseudo-code is given in figure 1). First SRP-EA assigns a lifetime to each chromosome created (the three lifetime computation strategies of GAVaPS were adopted). Then, in each generation, the age (initially set to 0) of each chromosome is incremented. The chance of survival decreases with the age of the chromosome - the survival probability is set to *(lifetime-age)/maxLT* and when the age of a chromosome reaches its lifetime, the probability of survival reaches zero. There is a difference between the SRP-EA and GAVaPS, since in GAVaPS the individuals remain in the population during its lifetime, while in SRP-EA an individual may die before the age reaches its limit.

The *create new individuals* procedure increases the population size by generating offspring with a restriction based on the Hamming Distance between the parents. When two parents are selected and their Hamming Distance is above the threshold, the children are generated. If the Hamming Distance is below or equal to the threshold then the parents do not cross and the attempt is classified as *failure*. After the *p/2* mating attempts are concluded (where *p* is the size of the population), all newborn children are introduced in the population and the threshold is set to a new value according to the heuristic described in figure 1 (the process repeats until at least one mating attempt succeeds). Also, in the *kill older individuals* procedure, the threshold is increased by a predefined amount (*Inc*) if the number of newborn is higher than number of individuals that died in the present generation. This strategy, along with proper set of the *Dec* and *Inc* parameters, creates a self-regulated population, which increases in the beginning of the search, decreases with convergence, and sometimes reacts to local optima convergence. Notice that this emergent behavior is similar to the one that PRoFIGA intends to simulate by means of a set of deterministic rules. However, the correct way to set the parameter values necessary to attain the desired population behavior and consequent algorithm performance is still unclear, although the tests described in the next section have brought some light into the subject.

```
Procedure SRP-EA
  initialize and evaluate population          /*compute fitness and lifetime */
  while (not termination condition) {
     increase the age of each individual by 1
     create new individuals
     kill older individuals
     evaluate new individuals
     set lifetime of new individuals }   /*Using any kind of strategy*/

Procedure create new individuals
  do {
     mating_events = population_size/2
     for (i = 1 to mating_events) do{
        select two individuals      /*Any method may be used here*/
        if (hamming distance > threshold) crossover and mutate   /*Successful mating*/
     }
     if (failed matings> successful matings)  threshold = threshold-Dec
     else                                     threshold = threshold+Inc
  } while (successful matings = 0)

Procedure kill older individuals
     for all individuals except the best do {
        survival probability = (lifetime-age)/maxLT
        if (random [0, 1] > survival probability) kill individual }
     if (newborn > dead)  threshold = threshold+Inc
```

Fig. 1. SRP-EA pseudo-code

4 Test Bed Set and Results

To test the efficiency of the proposed method, a Genetic Algorithm with the reproduction procedure described above was tested on several Spears' multimodal problems [9]. In [5], the authors chose that function generator to study different EAs with varying population size.

For that reason, the Spears' problem may be a good benchmark to test the SRP-EA. Also, the generator creates problems with different sizes and degrees of multimodality making it a good tool to test some of the algorithms' characteristics. In the experiences described below we tried to follow the procedures described in [5].

Table 1. Algorithms' setup

Chromosome length L	100
Initial population size N	25, 50, 100, 200
Mutation rate p_m (in APGA and SRP-EA)	0.0025, 0.005, 0.01, 0.02
Crossover rate p_c (in APGA)	0.9
Selection	Random and 4-size tournament
Maximum number of evaluations in each run	10000
Initial threshold (in CHC and SRP-EA)	L/4
Inc, *Dec* (in SRP-EA)	Inc = Dec = 3
minLT (in APGA and SRP-EA)	1
maxLT (in APGA and SRP-EA)	7, 11, 20
Lifetime calculation (in APGA and SRP-EA)	Bilinear (see [1] for details)

The SRP-EA was tested and compared with the CHC and the APGA. In [5] the authors compared the APGA with a Simple Genetic Algorithm (SGA) and other algorithms with varying population size, like GAVaPS and PRoFIGA, and concluded that APGA outperformed those methods through a wide range of Spears' problem instances. For that reason we simplified our analysis and eliminated the results attained with other EAs from the figures below. Furthermore, we are mainly interested in adaptive control methods of the population size, so deterministic methods like the ones used in RVPS and PRoFIGA somehow fall off this paper's subject.

We ran the algorithms on 10 different types of landscapes, with the number of peaks (NP) ranging through 1, 2, 5, 10, 25, 50, 100, 250, 500 and 1000. The distribution of the peaks is linear and the lowest peak height was set to 0.5. Global optimum fitness is 1 in all instances of the problem. All configurations of the EAs created and evaluated no more than 10000 chromosomes in each run. The results were averaged over 100 runs. The initial population size (fixed in CHC) ranged through 25, 50, 100 and 200. Four different mutation rates were tested. The crossover rate of APGA was set to 0.9, following the test setups in [5], and a two point crossover operator was used, except in CHC where we used the HUX operator associated with the method. The value of *minLT* was set to 1 in APGA and SRP-EA, while *maxLT* varied through 7, 11 and 20. All algorithms use elitism. Table 1 resumes the setup.

Before we proceed to a more accurate study some general remarks must be stated.

- The APGA results shown in [5] were properly reproduced in our tests. Also, the configuration used by the authors revealed to be appropriate and, in general, other configurations didn't increase significantly the performance.
- While the tests with APGA and CHC revealed no clear improvement when using tournament instead of random selection, SRP-EA seems to perform better with a tournament selection strategy.
- As expected, CHC performed better with small populations (the algorithm is known to be more able to deal with problems that require small populations).
- Neither APGA nor SRP-EA had significant changes in the performance over the range of *maxLT* values.
- The values of *Inc* and *Dec* parameters were not achieved by means of an exhaustive search and optimization. However, a general inspection revealed that values between 1% and 10% of the chromosome length may lead to good results. Also, results indicate that setting *Inc* = *Dec* appears to be an adequate strategy.

The performance of the algorithms was analyzed under three criteria: the success rate of the algorithm (SR%), that is, the percentage of runs in which the global optimum is achieved; the average number of evaluations (AE) necessary to reach global optimum (considering successful runs); and the average of the best chromosome's fitness (AF) found in each run. Since one of the hypotheses about SRP-EA is its ability to balance exploration and exploitation by adapting the size of the population to the state of the search, therefore increasing the probability to reach optimum, we will focus our attention on the SR% criteria.

Figure 2 illustrates some of the above observations. The graphics depict the success rates achieved by some configurations of CHC and APGA compared with two configurations of SRP-EA which differ in the mutation rate. Success rates of the

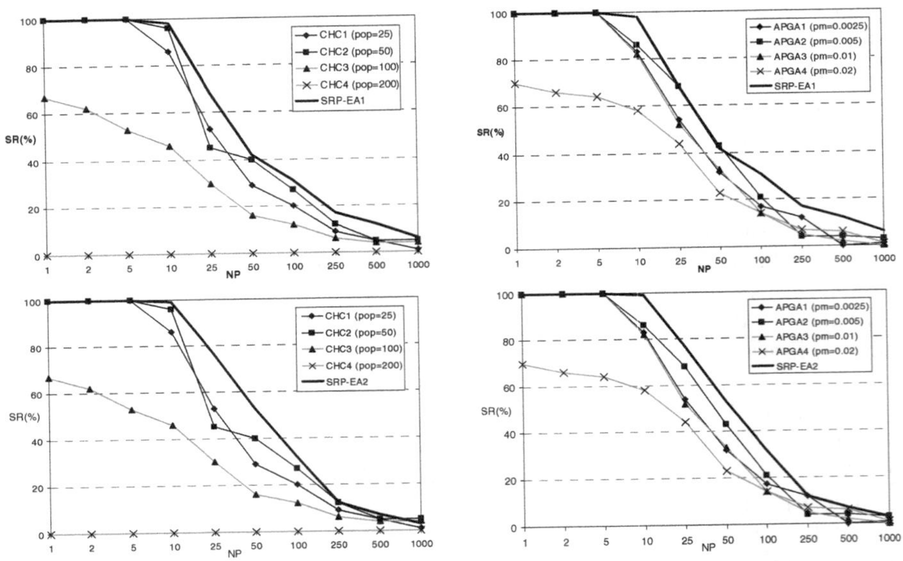

Fig. 2. CHC, APGA and SRP-EA success rates. SRP-EA parameters: N = 100, p_m= 0.005 (SRP-EA1), p_m = 0.0025 (SRP-EA2), $maxLT$ = 11, size 4 tournament; APGA: N = 100, p_c = 0.9 and $maxLT$ = 11.

algorithms are shown over the problem dimension range (number of peaks – NP). The graphics suggest that SRP-EA is more able to reach global optimum than APGA and CHC. Also, p_m = 0.0025 seems to favor SRP-EA performance in Spears' landscapes with higher number of peaks, while p_m = 0.005 works well on medium range problem dimension. Notice also, that CHC with a population of 200 individuals clearly fails in finding the optimal solutions and the same happens for APGA with p_m = 0.02.

When comparing the algorithms in terms of the best chromosome's fitness (AF), the results show that SRP-EA also attains, in general, higher values (see figure 3). However, the performance of SRP-EA pays a price in terms of number of evaluations to reach optima (AE). In figure 3 it is clear that SRP-EA performance comes with an increase in the number of evaluations. These results are not surprising since the population size variation process inherent to SRP-EA conduces to a large exploratory stage in the beginning of the search which increases the probability to reach global optimum but creates a large amount of new individuals, with obvious effects in the number of evaluations necessary to reach that optimum.

Choosing, for each NP, the best results of the algorithms over the complete space of parameter values of table 1 we obtain the curves represented in figure 4a. These results clearly illustrate the SRP-EA potential and its ability to find the global optima of Spears' landscapes.

One last test was conducted to examine the real influence of population variation in SRP-EA. As stated above, the population size variation of SRP-EA relies on a reproduction restriction that in nature is called assortative mating and tends to preserve genetic diversity. In some problems, that may be sufficient to increase convergence rate to global optimum. To try to quantify and distinguish the effects of genetic

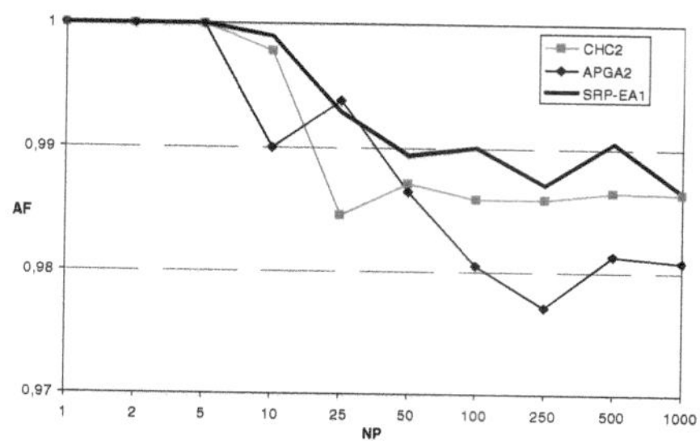

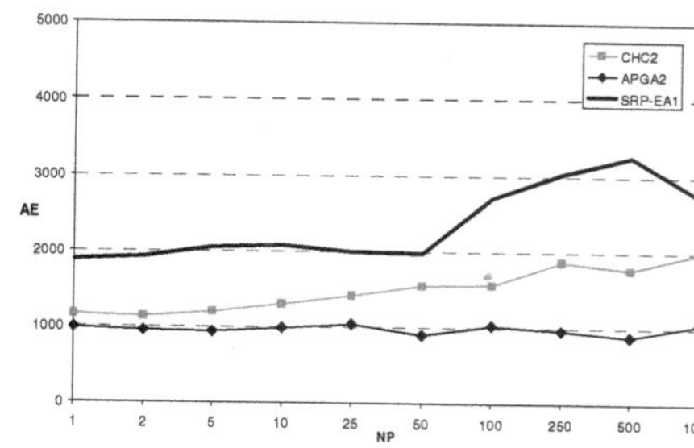

Fig. 3. Fitness of the best individual found and evaluations needed to reach the optima (results averaged over 100 runs) in CHC2, APGA2 and SRP-EA1

diversity maintenance and population size variation in SRP-EA, we created the Varying Assortative Mating EA (VAMEA), in which the procedure *kill older individuals* is replaced by a delete worst generational replacement as in CHC: like SRP-EA, *p'* individuals are created from *p/2* mating attempts (where *p* is the size of the population); then, the *p'* worst elements of the population are replaced by the offspring. This way, we remove the influence of the variation of population size and isolate the effects of the assortative mating found in the SRP-EA reproduction process. VAMEA was tested through the parameters' values range of table 1. Results are shown in figure 4b, where the curves represent the best results found for each NP (covering the complete set of parameter values shown in table 1). The differences found in the curves shape illustrate the role of the population variation mechanism. Although the assortative mating improves the success rates of the other genetic algorithms (as we can see by comparing the VAMEA curve in figure 4b with CHC and APGA curves in figure 4a), those rates experience even further improvement when the population variation process is introduced.

Although we tested SRP-EA with random selection of parents, following GAVaPS and APGA method, best results were achieved with tournament selection. APGA, on the other hand, didn't improve its results when changing the selection method. This outcome is not surprising for two reasons: 1) the way the chromosomes are eliminated from the population is different in SRP-EA, so the same *maxLT* value in SRP-EA and APGA conduces to a lower selection pressure in the first algorithm; 2) to amplify selection pressure in the algorithms, one must raise *maxLT* value; however, in SRP-EA, the increase in *maxLT* may lead to an excessive population growth and the consequent effort in terms of function evaluations (the population of APGA, with its "Steady-State like" reproduction, is almost immune to demographic explosion, even with large values of *maxLT*).

Before we conclude this section, a brief analysis of the population growth of the algorithms is required. Due to its fixed and low reproduction rate, the variation in the population size of APGA is very predictable and consists of small oscillations around an average value. Besides that, the population size seems to evolve without any feedback from the state of the search. Every APGA run over every instance of the problem showed the same behavior. The population size of SRP-EA evolves in a quite diverse manner. As we can see in figure 5, which represents the population growth and the evolution of the best fitness in two independent successful runs of the

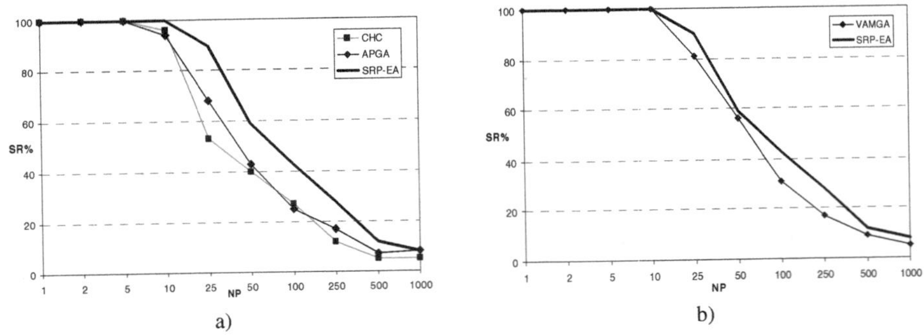

Fig. 4. Best success rates thorough the complete parameter space

algorithm on a NP=100 landscape, the population size clearly oscillates, sometimes even in severe way. There is a consistent demographic explosion in the beginning of the search which is quickly appeased. Then, the population stagnates in lower values but experience from time to time sudden increases in its size. Inspecting closely the curves below it can be seen that the sudden demographic growth is usually associated with stabilized or slowly growing phases of the best fitness value.

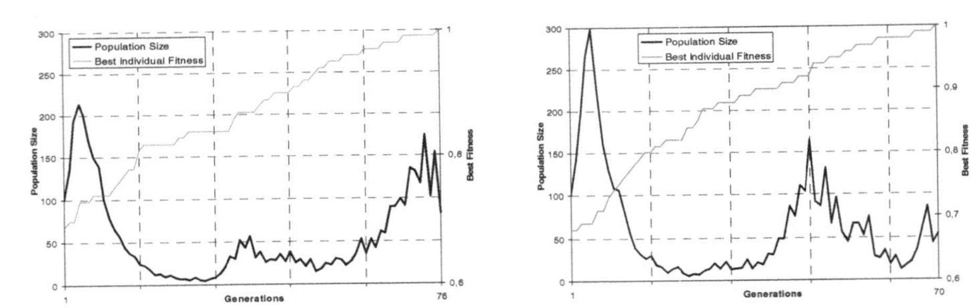

Fig. 5. Population growth and best fitness of SRP-EA in two independent runs. N = 100, p_m = 0.005 and *maxLT* =11. NP = 100.

5 Conclusions and Future Work

The results illustrated SRP-EA superior ability to find the global optima of Spears' landscapes when compared to CHC and APGA. That ability comes not only from the reproduction restriction based on the Hamming Distance between parents (which contributes with genetic diversity maintenance) but also from the population size variation itself. The dynamics of the population size seem to reflect the state of the search and the evolution of the quality of the solutions, in opposition to a more stable growth curve observed in APGA runs.

An in-depth analysis of the new parameters is needed in order to establish some rules that might reduce the complexity of the algorithm and also optimize its performance. Other distance criteria must also be inspected in order to reflect more properly the distribution of the population in the search space, avoiding overcrowded areas which do not contribute to maintain the genetic diversity, and redirecting the search to unexplored areas in an adaptive and non centralized manner. Finally, the application of SRP-EA to dynamic problems with on-line moving optima may be a proper field to evaluate the algorithm' potentialities and test its adaptive characteristics. Some preliminary tests already indicated that SRP-EA may be a useful tool to deal with dynamic problems.

Acknowledgement. The first author wishes to thank FCT, *Ministério da Ciência e Tecnologia*, his Research Fellowship SFRH/BD/18868/2004.

References

1. Arabas, J., Michalewicz, Z., Mulawka, J.: GAVaPS – A Genetic Algorithm with Varying Population Size. In: Proceedings of Evolutionary Computation Conference, IEEE Press, 1994.
2. Bäck, T., Eiben, A.E., van der Sart, N.A.L.: An empirical Study on Gas "without parameters". In Proceedings of the 6th Conference on Parallel Problem Solving from Nature, LNCS, pages 315-324, Springer, Berlin, 2000.
3. Costa, J., Tavares, R., Rosa, A.C.: An Experimental Study on Dynamic Random Variation of Population Size. In Proceedings of IEEE Systems, Man and Cybernetics Conference, Volume, pages 607-612, Tokyo, 1999. IEEE Press.
4. Eiben, A.E., Hinterding, R., Michalewicz, Z.: Parameter Control in Evolutionary Algorithms. IEEE Transaction on Evolutionary Computation, 3(2): 124-141, 1999.
5. Eiben, A.E., Marchiori E., Valkó, V.A.: Evolutionary Algorithms with On-the-Fly Population Size Adjustment. 8th Conference on Parallel Problem Solving from Nature, LNCS, pages 315-324, Springer, Birmingham, 2004.
6. Eschelman, L.J. The CHC Algorithm: How to Have Safe Search When Engaging in Non-traditional Genetic Recombination. In Proceedings of Foundations of Genetic Algorithms-1, pages 70-79, 1990.
7. Fernandes, C., Rosa, A.C.: A Study on Non-random Mating and Varying Population Size in Genetic Algorithms Using Royal Road Functions. In Proceedings of the IEEE Conference on Evolutionary Computation, pages 60-66, 2001.
8. Koumosis, V.K., Katsaras, C.P.: A Saw-Tooth Genetic Algorithm Combining the Effects of Variable Population Size and Reinitialization to Enhance Performance. In IEEE Transactions on Evolutionary Computation, 10(1), pages 19-28, 2006.
9. Spears, W.M.: Evolutionary Algorithms: the role of mutation and recombination. Springer, 2000.

Starting from Scratch: Growing Longest Common Subsequences with Evolution

Bryant A. Julstrom and Brenda Hinkemeyer

St. Cloud State University, St. Cloud, MN 56301 USA
julstrom@stcloudstate.edu, brenda@nikosha.net
http://www.stcloudstate.edu/~julstrom/

Abstract. An evolutionary algorithm (EA) usually initializes its population with random genotypes, which represent random solutions to the target problem instance. If the problem is one of constrained optimization, an initial population whose genotypes all represent empty solutions might allow the EA to grow valid solutions as much as search for them and thereby identify good solutions more quickly. This is the case in a genetic algorithm (GA) for the longest common subsequence problem, which seeks the length of a longest subsequence common to each of a set of given strings. The GA encodes sequences as binary strings that indicate subsequences of the shortest or first given string. In tests on a variety of problem instances, the GA always identifies an optimum subsequence, but on most instances, the GA reaches an optimum more quickly when its initial population encodes empty sequences than when its initial genotypes represent random sequences.

Keywords: Longest common subsequence, genetic algorithm, initially empty solutions.

1 Introduction

The longest common subsequence problem seeks the length of a longest string that is a subsequence of each of a set of given strings. A recent genetic algorithm (GA) for this problem [1], which Sect. 3 below summarizes, encodes candidate sequences as binary strings that indicate subsequences of the shortest or first given string. This GA initializes its population conventionally with random genotypes: each position in each genotype is assigned 0 or 1 with equal probability. In repeated trials on a variety of three-string problem instances with up to 6400 characters, the GA always found an optimum solution.

As Sect. 4 describes, however, the developments of subsequence length and fitness as the GA moved toward those optima suggest that the GA could achieve the same results more quickly if it started from scratch; that is, if all the genotypes in its initial population consisted entirely of 0s and thus represented empty sequences.

Section 5 explores this possibility. On a range of test instances over an alphabet of four characters, it compares the GA's performance with an initial population of random genotypes and with an initial population whose all-0 genotypes

T.P. Runarsson et al. (Eds.): PPSN IX, LNCS 4193, pp. 930–938, 2006.

represent empty sequences. On almost all of the test instances, the conjecture is confirmed. The GA continues to identify optimum solutions, but it requires significantly fewer generations to do so when the solutions its initial population represents are empty.

We begin by describing the longest common subsequence problem in detail.

2 The Problem

Deleting zero or more characters from a string S yields a subsequence of S. For example, if S = "CTTAGGCAA", then S itself, "TTGGAA", "AGCA", and the empty string are subsequences of S. The characters in a subsequence need not be contiguous in the original string, but the subsequence preserves their order. Given an alphabet Σ and a set of $K \geq 2$ strings S_1, S_2, ..., S_K over Σ, the Longest Common Subsequence (LCS) problem seeks the length of a longest subsequence found in all the strings.

For example, a longest common subsequence of the strings

$$\begin{aligned} S_1 &= \mathbf{C}\ \mathrm{G}\ \mathrm{T}\ \mathbf{G}\ \mathbf{G}\ \mathbf{T}\ \mathrm{A}\ \mathbf{A}\ \mathbf{T}\ \mathbf{C}\ \mathrm{A}\ \mathbf{C} \\ S_2 &= \mathrm{A}\ \mathrm{G}\ \mathbf{C}\ \mathrm{A}\ \mathbf{G}\ \mathrm{T}\ \mathbf{G}\ \mathbf{T}\ \mathbf{A}\ \mathbf{T}\ \mathbf{C}\ \mathbf{C} \\ S_3 &= \mathbf{C}\ \mathbf{G}\ \mathbf{G}\ \mathrm{G}\ \mathrm{C}\ \mathbf{T}\ \mathbf{A}\ \mathbf{T}\ \mathrm{G}\ \mathbf{C}\ \mathbf{C}\ \mathrm{G}, \end{aligned}$$

as indicated by the bold characters, is **C G G T A T C C**, with length eight. Note that a longest common subsequence need not be unique, either in the positions it occupies in the several strings or in its particular characters.

The decision version of the LCS problem fixes a positive integer ℓ and asks if there is a string w over Σ that is a subsequence of each string S_i and has length at least ℓ. Maier [2] showed that this problem is NP-complete for alphabets of any size $|\Sigma| \geq 2$. Polynomial-time algorithms exist for the decision problem if the target length ℓ or the number of strings is fixed, though these algorithms' times grow quickly as the strings' length or number grows. A dynamic programming algorithm for the optimization version of the problem is due to Irving and Fraser [3]. This algorithm requires time that is $O(n^K)$, where n is the length of the strings and K is the number of strings.

The LCS problem finds applications in areas such as DNA sequence matching [4] (which inspires the test instances of Sect. 5), search engines, molecule identification [5], data mining [6], file difference listing [7], plagiarism detection [8], author identification [9], text matching in specialized domains [10], syntactic rule identification [11], and comparing the performance of algorithms by measuring the similarity of their several solutions [12]. Researchers have described a variety of heuristic approaches to the problem [13, pp.145–184] [14].

3 The Genetic Algorithm

Hinkemeyer and Julstrom [1] recently described a genetic algorithm for the longest common subsequence problem. For an LCS instance of K strings S_1,

S_2, ..., S_K, the GA encodes candidate sequences as binary strings as long as the shortest string (or the first string, if all of the strings' lengths are the same) S_1: `c[i]` $= 1$ indicates that S_1`[i]` is in the subsequence; `c[i]` $= 0$ indicates that it is not. Figure 1 illustrates this mechanism.

$$S_1 = \mathbf{C}\ \mathrm{G}\ \mathrm{T}\ \mathbf{G}\ \mathbf{G}\ \mathbf{T}\ \mathrm{A}\ \mathbf{A}\ \mathbf{T}\ \mathbf{C}\ \mathrm{A}\ \mathbf{C}$$
$$S_2 = \mathrm{A}\ \mathrm{G}\ \mathbf{C}\ \mathrm{A}\ \mathbf{G}\ \mathrm{T}\ \mathbf{G}\ \mathbf{T}\ \mathbf{A}\ \mathbf{T}\ \mathbf{C}\ \mathbf{C}$$
$$S_3 = \mathbf{C}\ \mathbf{G}\ \mathbf{G}\ \mathrm{G}\ \mathrm{C}\ \mathbf{T}\ \mathbf{A}\ \mathbf{T}\ \mathrm{G}\ \mathbf{C}\ \mathbf{C}\ \mathrm{G},$$

$$\texttt{c[}i\texttt{]} = 1\ 0\ 0\ 1\ 1\ 1\ 0\ 1\ 1\ 1\ 0\ 1$$

Fig. 1. A genotype in the genetic algorithm and the subsequence that it represents. `c[i]` $= 1$ indicates that S_1`[i]` is in the subsequence, `c[i]` $= 0$ that it is not, where S_1`[·]` is the shortest (or first) of the target instance's strings.

The GA seeks to maximize genotypes' fitness. Its fitness function rewards longer sequences; strongly rewards a genotype for each given string in which its subsequence appears; rewards a genotype whose subsequence is as long as S_1; and very strongly penalizes a genotype whose subsequence is not found in all the given strings. A genotype's fitness cannot be positive unless the sequence it represents occurs in all the given strings.

The following sketch summarizes the fitness function. In it, v is a local variable in which `c[·]`'s fitness $f(\texttt{c}[\cdot])$ is developed, ℓ is the length of the subsequence `c[·]` represents (that is, the number of 1s in `c[·]`), m is the number of strings that the subsequence matches, S_1 is the shortest or first string, and K is the number of strings in the instance.

$$\begin{array}{l}
v \leftarrow \ell + 30 \times m \\
\text{if } \ell = |S_1| \\
\quad v \leftarrow v + 50 \\
\text{if } m = K \\
\quad v \leftarrow 3000 \times v \\
\text{else} \\
\quad v \leftarrow -1000 \times v \times (K - m) \\
\text{end if} \\
f(\texttt{c}[\cdot]) \leftarrow v
\end{array}$$

The GA's initial population consists of random genotypes: each symbol is 0 or 1 with equal probability. The GA chooses genotypes to be parents in tournaments without replacement, and each offspring genotype is generated by either one-point crossover or position-by-position mutation, never both. The GA is elitist; it preserves the best genotypes in the current generation unchanged into the next. If the population's best genotype has not improved for a specified number of generations, some of the population's members are replaced with new random genotypes.

In the tests of [1] and below, the GA's population contained 100 genotypes, and the size of its selection tournaments was two. The probability that crossover generated each offspring was 50%, the probability of mutation therefore the same. Within mutation, the probability that each entry would be reversed was $1/\ell$, where ℓ was the genotype length. The number of elite genotypes was one, and the non-elite members were randomly re-initialized if no improvement in the fittest genotype occurred for 100 generations. The GA ran until it found an optimum solution, which was always known.

In comparisons on a variety of three-string LCS instances with the dynamic programming algorithm of Irving and Fraser [3], the GA in general found optimum solutions almost as quickly on smaller instances ($100 \leq n \leq 400$) and much more quickly on larger instances ($800 \leq n \leq 6400$).

4 Starting from Scratch

The GA's fitness function encourages it to identify subsequences that match all the given strings and are as long as possible. It satisfied these two requirements in that order. The GA generated shorter and shorter sequences until one occurred in all the given strings, then found longer common subsequences until one was as long as possible.

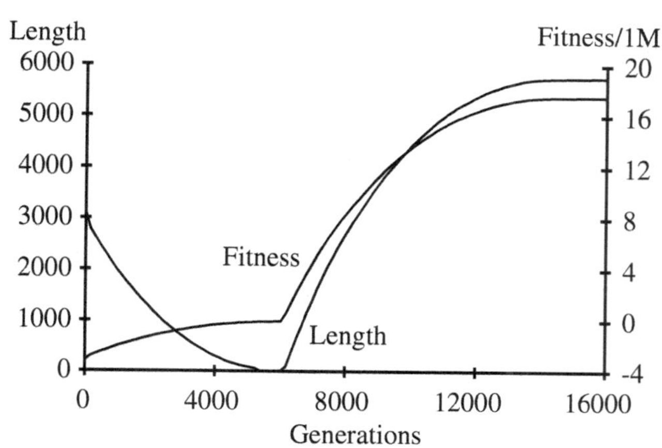

Fig. 2. Development of the length and fitness of the most fit subsequence in the GA's population on a set of three binary strings of length $n = 6400$ with LCS length $0.9n = 5760$ [1]

Figure 2 illustrates this behavior in a run of the GA on an instance with three binary strings of length $n = 6400$ and longest common subsequence length $= 0.9n = 5760$. The graph plots both the length and the fitness of the most fit genotype in the GA's population, through the algorithm's run. Fitness increases monotonically, as it must under elitism, but the length of the fittest sequence initially drops, and the sequence's fitness is negative. For about 6000 generations, the fittest sequence does not match all the instance's strings, and it gets shorter as the GA searches for a subsequence that occurs in all the instance's strings. Once such a subsequence is found, both length and fitness of the fittest subsequence increase, indicating that the GA is identifying longer and longer common subsequences.

In a typical run of the GA, the length of the sequence that the population's fittest genotype represents does not drop all the way to zero, but it does shrink to a small fraction of n. This suggests that the GA could achieve essentially the same results more quickly by starting with a population of genotypes that represent empty sequences; that is, at the "knee" of the two curves in Fig. 2. This would allow the GA to proceed to a good solution without processing the generations before the knee. Thus we propose a version of the GA whose initial population is entirely seeded with genotypes that represent empty sequences.

The resulting mechanism resembles genetic programming (GP) [15] [16], which evolves trees that represent programs from an initial population of relatively simple trees, and even more, the application of GP to the evolution of analog circuits [17] [18] [19, Sect.V]. In the latter, representations of more elaborate, more fit circuits evolve from an initial population of small, simple precursors.

The next section reports that the GA does reach optimum solutions faster when its initial population represents empty sequences, and that the speed-up is sometimes greater than Fig. 2 suggests.

5 Comparisons

Two versions of the GA, one with an initial population of random genotypes and a second with an initial population of all-zero genotypes that represent empty sequences, were compared on 24 instances of the LCS problem, each of three strings over an alphabet of four characters, as in DNA strings. These instances have lengths $n = 200$, 400, 800, 1600, 3200, and 6400, with maximum common subsequence lengths equal to 10%, 50%, 90%, and 100% of n.

When the LCS length is equal to n, it suffices to set the genotypes to all 1s and be done. The two versions of the GA were applied to these instances only to compare their performances.

One instance was generated for each combination of n and LCS length, in such a way that the lengths of their longest common subsequences are known. In particular, S_1 was chosen and a subsequence of it was specified. This subsequence then appeared in the other strings, whose remaining positions were filled in such a way that no longer subsequence was common to all the strings.

The GA was implemented in Java and executed on an AMD 3400+ processor with one Gbyte of memory running at 2.2 GHz under Windows XP. Both versions were run 30 independent times on each test instance; Table 1 summarizes the results of these trials. For each instance, the table lists n and the instance's LCS length as a fraction of n. For each version of the GA on each instance, it lists

Table 1. The trials of the GA, with random initial genotypes and with zeroed initial genotypes representing empty sequences on 24 LCS instances with "DNA" strings; $|\Sigma| = 4$. For each instance, the table lists the length n of its strings, the known length of a longest common subsequence as a percentage of n, the shortest and mean times in seconds that both versions of the GA required to find the longest length, and the standard deviations of those times.

Instance		Randomly init'ed. GA time (s)			Zeroed GA time (s)		
n	%	best	mean	stdev	best	mean	stdev
200	10%	1.047	1.298	0.139	0.219	0.286	0.054
	50%	2.016	2.345	0.206	1.297	1.545	0.128
	90%	1.297	1.942	0.306	1.359	1.568	0.099
	100%	0.844	1.028	0.106	1.468	1.676	0.119
400	10%	4.579	5.162	0.361	0.937	1.130	0.104
	50%	12.109	12.294	0.144	5.687	6.293	0.483
	90%	7.000	9.264	0.869	5.891	6.494	0.306
	100%	3.953	4.625	0.410	6.047	6.526	0.318
800	10%	19.875	21.779	1.193	3.765	4.395	0.280
	50%	37.625	41.700	2.284	22.547	25.643	1.769
	90%	35.157	39.507	2.159	24.172	26.355	1.280
	100%	16.516	18.897	1.273	1.126	26.427	1.126
1600	10%	83.610	92.017	5.633	16.156	17.481	0.564
	50%	164.765	180.656	10.059	93.156	107.344	8.845
	90%	148.890	166.621	10.371	99.859	109.563	4.792
	100%	72.781	78.786	4.346	101.859	110.758	4.772
3200	10%	347.609	382.175	23.236	67.219	71.439	2.054
	50%	687.438	736.156	32.872	390.438	442.359	27.655
	90%	645.781	703.531	28.021	422.250	472.437	28.918
	100%	288.547	323.813	18.164	426.000	459.509	21.396
6400	10%	1433.047	1566.138	68.087	269.000	282.212	5.827
	50%	2938.422	3208.825	157.626	1708.719	1869.030	103.683
	90%	2788.547	2983.347	137.954	1726.875	1833.085	54.564
	100%	1231.718	1392.686	92.700	1796.063	1878.862	71.007

the best and mean times in seconds that the algorithm required to identify a longest common subsequence and the standard deviations of these times.

The results confirm our conjecture. On the instances whose longest common subsequences are shorter than the given strings themselves, the zeroed GA identifies optimum sequences consistently and significantly more quickly than does the GA with an initial population of random genotypes. In particular, when the LCS length is $0.1n$, the zeroed GA takes, on average, only about 20% as long as does the randomly initialized GA. When the LCS length is $0.5n$, this average rises to about 60%, and for $0.9n$, to just less than 70%. Moreover, these proportions are relatively constant across the problem sizes. When the LCS length is $0.1n$, they range from about 18% to about 22%; for $0.5n$, from about 51% to about 66%; and for $0.9n$, from about 61% to about 81%. The zeroed GA does appear to begin its development and search at about the knees of the two curves in Fig. 3. On this problem, it is more efficient for the GA to grow candidate solutions from empty sequences than to begin with larger sequences which it must prune before it can develop longer common subsequences.

On the instances whose longest common subsequences have length $1.0n$, the zeroed GA loses its advantage. It reaches optimum solutions in about half again (144%) the time that the randomly initialized GA requires. In these instances, which as noted need not be addressed by heuristics like the two version of the GA, the problem becomes an ornate version of the ONE-MAX problem. All the strings are identical, the longest subsequence is S_1 ($= S_2 = S_3$) itself, the genotype that represents it is entirely 1s, and a genotype with more 1s is always more fit than a genotype with fewer 1s, regardless of their positions in the genotypes. The randomly initialized GA starts with a population whose genotypes have, on average, $(n/2)$ 1s while the zeroed GA begins with genotypes that have no 1s. The latter algorithm simply has farther to go than does the former to fill at least one genotype with 1s.

Notwithstanding this exceptional case, the results indicate the usefulness of a genetic algorithm starting from scratch—that is, with a population whose genotypes represent empty sequences—when it is applied to realistic instances of the longest common subsequence problem. They also raise the larger question of this device's possible application in EAs for other problems of constrained optimization.

The two versions of the GA differ only in how they initialize their populations. The zeroed GA might perform even better with initially large probabilities associated with mutation, which are gradually reduced as the algorithm runs. Such a strategy might encourage earlier development of longer common subsequences.

6 Conclusion

A genetic algorithm for the longest common subsequence problem encodes candidate sequences as binary strings that indicate subsequences of the shortest or first string in the target instance. This GA was effective on a variety of test instances, always finding an optimum subsequence, but its behavior in that search—shortening candidate sequences almost to empty, then growing longer and longer common subsequences—suggested that an initial population of genotypes that represent empty sequences would reduce the time the GA requires to find optimum subsequences.

Tests on a range of LCS instances with three strings over an alphabet of four symbols confirm this conjecture. On the instances whose longest common subsequences were shorter than the given strings, starting the GA with a population that encoded empty sequences shortened the time it required to identify an optimum subsequence by, on average, 30 to 80%, depending on the LCS's length, over starting with a population of random genotypes. Only when all of the strings were identical, and the LCS then equal to each of them, was this ranking reversed. In this case, the problem collapses to ONE-MAX, and when the GA begins with a randomly initialized population, it is closer to a genotype of 1s than when it begins with a population whose genotypes are all 0s.

These results suggest that this strategy—starting from scratch—might be generally useful in evolutionary algorithms for problems of constrained optimization.

References

1. Hinkemeyer, B., Julstrom, B.A.: A genetic algorithm for the longest common subsequence problem. In: Proceedings of the 2006 Genetic and Evolutionary Computation Conference, New York, The ACM Press (2006)
2. Maier, D.: The complexity of some problems on subsequences and supersequences. Journal of the ACM **25** (1978) 322–336
3. Irving, R., Fraser, C.: Two algorithms for the longest common subsequence of three (or more) strings. In: Proceedings of the 3rd Annual Symposium on Combinatorial Pattern Matching, New York, Springer-Verlag (1992) 214–229
4. Fogel, G., Chellapilla, K., Fogel, D.: Identification of coding regions in DNA sequences using evolved neural networks. In: Evolutionary Computation in Bioinformatics. Morgan Kaufmann, San Francisco, CA (2003)
5. Forrest, S., Javornik, B., Smith, R., Perelson, A.: Using genetic algorithms to explore pattern recognition in the immune system. Evolutionary Computation **1** (1993) 191–211
6. Pei, M., Goodman, E.D., Punch, W.F.: Pattern discovery from data using genetic algorithms. In: Proceedings of 1st Pacific-Asia Conference on Knowledge Discovery & Data Mining (PAKDD-97). (1997)
7. Shankar, P.: V Diff - A file comparer with visual output. On-line at `http://www.codeproject.com/cpp/vdiff.asp?df=100&forumid=14638&exp=0&select=825191` (2003) Retrieved October 25, 2004.
8. Clough, P.: Plagiarism in natural and programming languages: an overview of current tools and technologies. On-line at `http://www.dcs.shef.ac.uk/~cloughie/papers/Plagiarism.pdf` (2000) Retrieved October 13, 2004.
9. Grant, T., Baker, K.: Identifying reliable, valid markers of authorship: A response to Chaski. Forensic Linguistics **8** (2001) 66–79
10. Lovis, C., Baud, R.H.: Fast exact string pattern-matching algorithms adapted to the characteristics of the medical language. Journal of the American Medical Informatics Association **7** (2000) 378–391
11. Losee, R.: Learning syntactic rules and tags with genetic algorithms. Information Processing & Management **32** (1996) 185–197
12. Louis, S.: Learning to improve genetic algorithm performance on job shop scheduling. On-line at `http://www.cs.unr.edu/~sushil/papers/conference/newpapers/2002/gecco2002/cigarScheduling/cigarScheduling/cigarScheduling.html` (2002) Retrieved October 21, 2004.
13. Navarro, G., Raffinot, M.: Flexible Pattern Matching in Strings. Cambridge University Press, New York (2002)
14. Bergroth, L., Hakonen, H., Raita, T.: A survey of longest common subsequence algorithms. In: Proceedings of the Seventh International Symposium on String Processing and Information Retrieval. (2000)
15. Koza, J.R.: Genetic Programming: On the programming of computers by means of natural selection. The MIT Press, Cambridge, MA (1992)
16. Banzhaf, W., Nordin, P., Keller, R.E., Francone, F.D.: Genetic programming: An introduction. Morgan Kaufmann, San Francisco (1998)

17. Koza, J.R., Bennett, F.H., Andre, D., Keane, M.A.: Evolution using genetic programming of a low-distortion 96 decibel operational amplifier. In Bryant, B., Carroll, J., Oppenheim, D., Hightower, J., George, K.M., eds.: Applied Computing 1997: Proceedings of the 1997 ACM Symposium on Applied Computing, New York, ACM Press (1997) 207–216
18. Koza, J.R., Bennett, F.H., Andre, D., Keane, M.A., Dunlap, F.: Automated systhesis of analog electrical circuits by means of genetic programming. IEEE Transactions on Evolutionary Computation **1** (1997) 109–128
19. Koza, J.R., Bennett, F.H., Andre, D., Keane, M.A.: Genetic Programming III: Darwinian Invention and Problem Solving. Morgan Kaufmann, San Francisco (1999)

Local Meta-models for Optimization Using Evolution Strategies

Stefan Kern, Nikolaus Hansen, and Petros Koumoutsakos

Computational Science and Engineering Laboratory,
Institute of Computational Science,
ETH Zurich, Switzerland
{skern, hansenn, petros}@inf.ethz.ch

Abstract. We employ local meta-models to enhance the efficiency of evolution strategies in the optimization of computationally expensive problems. The method involves the combination of second order local regression meta-models with the Covariance Matrix Adaptation Evolution Strategy. Experiments on benchmark problems demonstrate that the proposed meta-models have the potential to reliably account for the ranking of the offspring population resulting in significant computational savings. The results show that the use of local meta-models significantly increases the efficiency of already competitive evolution strategies.

1 Introduction

The optimization of a large number of engineering processes, ranging from multidisciplinary design to manufacturing, can only be formulated as black-box problems. The fitness function in this context is usually computationally expensive and may involve noise and multiple optima. Evolutionary Algorithms (EAs) have been shown to cope successfully with noise and multimodality, and there is an ongoing effort to further extend their efficiency for expensive problems by incorporating local or global meta-models of the fitness function [1]. The use of meta-models based on *global* function approximation, even for moderate dimension, is hindered by the inhomogeneity of the data collected during the optimization. Several methods have been proposed to overcome this difficulty ranging from restricting the training data to the closest, most recently evaluated points [2] to sophisticated sequential update techniques [3,4]. Alternatively, *local* meta-models have been developed ranging from simple nearest neighborhood regression to local quadratic models [5,6,7].

Meta-models have been shown to improve the efficiency of EAs in many cases, but a number of open questions remain, including the choice of the meta-model complexity with regard to the underlying EA, as well as the balance between the use of the meta-model and the true objective. In this paper we address these open problems by investigating the use of *local* meta-models of varying complexity in conjunction with Covariance Matrix Adaptation (CMA-ES) [8,9,10]. The CMA-ES employs rank based selection, relaxing for the meta-model the requirement

T.P. Runarsson et al. (Eds.): PPSN IX, LNCS 4193, pp. 939–948, 2006.

of approximating the objective function. We propose a *local meta-model CMA-ES* (lmm-CMA) and investigate its performance on benchmark problems. We find that the lmm-CMA enhances significantly the performance of the standard CMA-ES.

The paper is organized as follows: In Sect. 2 we address model quality measures and the control of data points used as meta model support. Section 3 gives an introduction to Locally Weighted Regression as a class of meta models for EAs. In Sect. 4, the choice of complexity of the local model is investigated. In Sect. 5 we propose the lmm-CMA and determine the optimal bandwidth of the local model. In Sect. 6 the performance of the proposed lmm-CMA is examined on well known test-functions and compared to previous results. A summary and conclusions are presented in Sect. 7.

2 Meta-model Quality and Controlled Model Assistance

In meta-modeling the definition of optimal prediction needs to be consistent with the operators of the optimization algorithm [11]. Optimal prediction is usually associated with a minimum error in the quantitative approximation of the objective function by the meta-model. For rank-based EAs maintaining the fitness based ranking of the population is sufficient and therefore more appropriate.

Measuring meta-model quality. In this paper we use meta-model quality measures in order to: (i) investigate the optimal complexity of the local models to be learned, and (ii) control the adaptive use of the local models in the EA. In both cases we are interested in the deviation of the offspring ranking predicted by the meta-model $\hat{f}$ from the true ranking determined by the fitness function f in each generation g.

When the true fitness function values $y_i = f(\boldsymbol{x}_i)$ are known for the *complete* population of size λ, we propose a quality measure adopted from sorting that counts pair inversions in the approximate ranking. For an approximate ranking $\hat{F} = \langle \hat{y}_1, \ldots, \hat{y}_\lambda \rangle$, with $\hat{y}_i \leq \hat{y}_j, 1 \leq i < j \leq \lambda$, the normalized pair inversion count ρ_{inv} is defined as

$$\rho_{inv}(\hat{F}) = \frac{4}{\lambda(\lambda-1)} \left| \{(i,j) | 1 \leq i < j \leq \lambda \quad \text{and} \quad f(\boldsymbol{x}_{r(i)}) > f(\boldsymbol{x}_{r(j)})\} \right| , \qquad (1)$$

where $r(i)$ is the index mapping function determined by the model based ranking, i.e. $\hat{y}_i = \hat{f}(\boldsymbol{x}_{r(i)})$. The normalization factor $\lambda(\lambda-1)/4$ is the expected pair inversion count for a randomly ranked population which can be easily proven by induction; it holds $0 \leq \rho_{inv} \leq 2$. If not all individuals in one generation are evaluated, the measure (1) cannot be applied since the correct ranking of the population is only partially known.

Meta-model assisted ranking procedure. An elegant way to control model quality without knowing the correct ranking of the complete population is the *approximate ranking procedure* [7]: In every generation, the offspring are successively

approximate: build $\hat{f}(\boldsymbol{x}_k), k = 1, \ldots, \lambda$ based on evaluations in training set $\mathcal{S}$
rank: based on $\hat{f}$ generate ranking_0^μ of the μ best individuals
evaluate: n_{init} best individuals based on $\hat{f}$, add to $\mathcal{S}$
for $i := 1$ **to** $(\lambda - n_{\text{init}})/n_b$ **do**
  approximate: build $\hat{f}(\boldsymbol{x}_k), k = 1, \ldots, \lambda$ based on $\mathcal{S}$
  rank: based on $\hat{f}$ generate ranking_i^μ of the μ best individuals
  if $(\text{ranking}_{i-1}^\mu == \text{ranking}_i^\mu)$ **then** *(ranking of μ best remains unchanged)*
    break *(exit for loop)*
  else *(ranking of μ best individuals changed)*
    evaluate: n_b next best unevaluated points based on $\hat{f}$, add to $\mathcal{S}$
  fi
od
if $(i > 2)$ **then** $n_{\text{init}} = \min(n_{\text{init}} + n_b, \lambda - n_b)$
elseif $(i < 2)$ **then** $n_{\text{init}} = \max(n_b, n_{\text{init}} - n_b)$

Fig. 1. Approximate ranking procedure that is executed in every generation to determine the fraction of points evaluated on the fitness function. The procedure is not called until sufficiently many evaluations are stored in the training set $\mathcal{S}$ to build the model; initialization of $n_{\text{init}} = \lambda$.

evaluated and added to the training set of the fitness function model until the (deterministic) model based selection of the parents remains unchanged in two consecutive iteration cycles. This results in an adaptive control mechanism determining the number of evaluated individuals in every generation. The CMA-ES uses the ranked $\mu = \lambda/2$ best offspring to update its Gaussian mutation distribution [9]. We adapt the *approximate ranking procedure* to the requirements of CMA-ES: the predicted ranking in the μ first positions should not change for the meta-model iteration to stop. For large population sizes λ, often required to solve multimodal functions [9], the amount of information added in one iteration may result in insignificant changes even of a meta-model with bad ranking predictions. To overcome this deficiency we suggest to evaluate a batch of individuals in every meta-model iteration. We use a batch size n_b proportional to λ and choose $n_b = \max(1, \lfloor \lambda/10 \rfloor)$. The total cost of the meta model loop can be further reduced by introducing an adaptive parameter to specify the number of initial evaluations, n_{init}, performed before the model iteration loop is entered. The resulting meta-model assisted ranking procedure is outlined in Fig. 1.

3 Locally Weighted Regression

Locally weighted regression (LWR) [12] attempts to fit the training data (*here*: past evaluations of the fitness function stored in a database) only in a region around the location of the query. The local models are built consecutively as queries need to be answered and therefore are intrinsically designed for growing training data sets as they occur in the course of an optimization. In the following we give a brief introduction to LWR following the notation in [12].

For every offspring to be predicted an individual model is built. Given a set of points $(\boldsymbol{x}_j, y_j), j = 1, \ldots, m$, the training criterion C is minimized w.r.t. the parameters $\boldsymbol{\beta}$ of the local mode $\hat{f}$ at query point $\boldsymbol{q}$ and can be written as

$$C(\boldsymbol{q}) = \sum_{j=1}^{m} \left[(\hat{f}(\boldsymbol{x}_j, \boldsymbol{\beta}) - y_j)^2 K \left(\frac{d(\boldsymbol{x}_j, \boldsymbol{q})}{h} \right) \right], \tag{2}$$

where $K(.)$ is the kernel weighting function, $d(\boldsymbol{x}_j, \boldsymbol{q})$ the distance between data point $\boldsymbol{x}_j$ and $\boldsymbol{q}$, and h is the (local) bandwidth. We consider $\hat{f}$ linear in $\boldsymbol{\beta}$, i.e. $\hat{f}(\boldsymbol{x}, \boldsymbol{\beta}) = \tilde{\boldsymbol{x}}^T \boldsymbol{\beta}$ (cf. Table 1), and thus we can directly weight the training points and minimize (2) by solving the normal equations

$$\left((\boldsymbol{W}\tilde{\boldsymbol{X}})^T \boldsymbol{W}\tilde{\boldsymbol{X}} \right) \boldsymbol{\beta} = (\boldsymbol{W}\tilde{\boldsymbol{X}})^T \boldsymbol{W}\boldsymbol{y}, \tag{3}$$

where $\tilde{\boldsymbol{X}} = (\tilde{\boldsymbol{x}}_1, \ldots, \tilde{\boldsymbol{x}}_m)^T$, $\boldsymbol{y} = (y_1, \ldots, y_m)^T$, and $\boldsymbol{W} = \mathrm{diag}(\sqrt{K(d(\boldsymbol{x}_i, \boldsymbol{q})/h)})$. For a given model structure, K, d, and h remain to be chosen determining the locality and smoothness of the model.

For the calculation of $d(\boldsymbol{x}_j, \boldsymbol{q})$ we propose to utilize the metric of the search distribution of the EA. Evolution strategies as the CMA-ES adapt a multivariate Gaussian mutation distribution $\mathcal{N}(\boldsymbol{m}, \boldsymbol{C})$ to the (local) topography of the function, and the covariance matrix $\boldsymbol{C}$ naturally defines a metric that can be exploited in the calculation of d as fully weighted Euclidean distance

$$d(\boldsymbol{x}_j, \boldsymbol{q}) = \sqrt{(\boldsymbol{x}_j - \boldsymbol{q})^T \boldsymbol{C}^{-1} (\boldsymbol{x}_j - \boldsymbol{q})}. \tag{4}$$

Experiments using different kernel functions K showed insignificant variation in prediction performance. We use a bi-quadratic kernel function defined as

$$K(\zeta) = \begin{cases} (1 - \zeta^2)^2 & \text{if} \quad \zeta < 1 \\ 0 & \text{otherwise} \end{cases} \tag{5}$$

for the remainder of this paper. Because the density of the data points collected in the course of an optimization run changes considerably, an adaptive choice of the bandwidth h is essential. We use a *nearest neighbor bandwidth selection*, where h is set to the distance of the kth nearest neighbor data point to $\boldsymbol{q}$ and thus the volume increases and decreases in size according to the density of nearby data. In this way changes in scale of the distance function d are canceled by the choice of h, giving a scale invariant distribution of the weights to the data. The optimal choice of k is addressed in Sect. 5.

4 Choice of Model Complexity

A meta model can speed up the convergence of an EA if it is capable to provide information about the fitness function not yet incorporated in the search distribution. The choice of a suitable complexity for the local model involves two

Table 1. Locally polynomial models tested in the LWR framework

$\hat{f}_\mathrm{x} = \boldsymbol{\beta}_\mathrm{x}^T \tilde{\boldsymbol{x}}_\mathrm{x}$, $\tilde{\boldsymbol{x}}_\mathrm{x}$,		$\boldsymbol{\beta}_\mathrm{x}$	dim
$\hat{f}_\mathrm{wmean}$	$\tilde{\boldsymbol{x}}_w = 1$	$\boldsymbol{\beta}_w = \sum_{j=1}^m w_j f_j$,	1
$\hat{f}_\mathrm{linear}$	$\tilde{\boldsymbol{x}}_l = (x_1, \ldots, x_n, 1)^T$	$\boldsymbol{\beta}_l$: minimize (2),	$n+1$
$\hat{f}_\mathrm{dquad}$	$\tilde{\boldsymbol{x}}_d = (x_1^2, \ldots, x_n^2, x_1, \ldots, x_n, 1)^T$	$\boldsymbol{\beta}_d$: minimize (2),	$2n+1$
$\hat{f}_\mathrm{quad}$	$\tilde{\boldsymbol{x}}_q = (x_1^2, \ldots, x_n^2,$ $x_1x_2, \ldots, x_{n-1}x_n, x_1, \ldots, x_n, 1)^T$	$\boldsymbol{\beta}_q$: minimize (2),	$\frac{n(n+3)}{2} + 1$

Table 2. Test-functions and coordinate-wise initialization intervals

Name	Function	Init
Sphere	$f_\mathrm{Sphere}(\boldsymbol{x}) = \sum_{i=1}^n x_i^2$	$[-3, 7]^n$
Noisy Sphere	$f_\mathrm{NoisySphere}(\boldsymbol{x}) = f_\mathrm{Sphere}(\boldsymbol{x})\,(1 + \epsilon\mathcal{N}(0,1))$	$[-3, 7]^n$
Schwefel	$f_\mathrm{Schwefel}(\boldsymbol{x}) = \sum_{i=1}^n \left(\sum_{j=1}^i x_j\right)^2$	$[-10, 10]^n$
Ellipsoid	$f_\mathrm{Ellipse}(\boldsymbol{x}) = \sum_{i=1}^n \left(100^{\frac{i-1}{n-1}} y_i\right)^2$	$[-3, 7]^n$
Rosenbrock	$f_\mathrm{Rosenbrock}(\boldsymbol{x}) = \sum_{i=1}^{n-1} \left(100 \cdot (x_i^2 - x_{i+1})^2 + (x_i - 1)^2\right)$	$[-5, 5]^n$
Ackley	$f_\mathrm{Ackley}(\boldsymbol{x}) = 20 - 20 \cdot \exp\left(-0.2\sqrt{\frac{1}{n}\sum_{i=1}^n x_i^2}\right)$ $+e - \exp\left(\frac{1}{n}\sum_{i=1}^n \cos(2\pi x_i)\right)$	$[1, 30]^n$
Rastrigin	$f_\mathrm{Rastrigin}(\boldsymbol{x}) = 10n + \sum_{i=1}^n \left(y_i^2 - 10\cos(2\pi y_i)\right)$	$[1, 5]^n$

questions: (i) How good is the ranking prediction of a model, and (ii) how is the performance of the baseline optimization algorithm influenced by perturbations of the ranking introduced by erroneous models?

We investigate the performance loss for the CMA-ES caused by erroneous offspring rankings by running the strategy with artificially introduced ranking perturbations of given pair inversion count ρ_{inv} (1). The performance loss is computed as ratio between the number of function evaluations needed to reach the function value of $f_\mathrm{stop} = 10^{-10}$ with the erroneous and the correct ranking. A rank perturbation of fixed ρ_{inv} can be produced by uniformly sampling swaps of neighbors in the ranking and only conducting a swap if it increases ρ_{inv}. This procedure is repeated until the target ρ_{inv} is reached. Figure 2a shows the expected performance loss of the CMA-ES on f_Sphere, f_Ellipse, and $f_\mathrm{Rosenbrock}$ (see Table 2) for dimension $n = 5$ and 10 versus the pair inversion count ρ_{inv}. The data was obtained by averaging 20 runs with a uniformly random starting point from the interval given in Table 2. The performance loss shows only minor dependency on the function and the dimensionality.

We measured the quality of ranking predictions of constant, linear, and quadratic (with and without cross terms) local models as given in Table 1. The training data was obtained from independent runs of the CMA-ES. All four models where tested on 20 data sets for each of the three test-functions using fractions of $1, 1/2, 1/4$ and $1/8$ of the evaluated points, randomly chosen in every generation. The bandwidth parameter k was varied as 1, 2, and 4 times the number of free parameters of the model. Figure 2b gives the result for $\hat{f}_\mathrm{quad}$ on $f_\mathrm{Rosenbrock}$ in

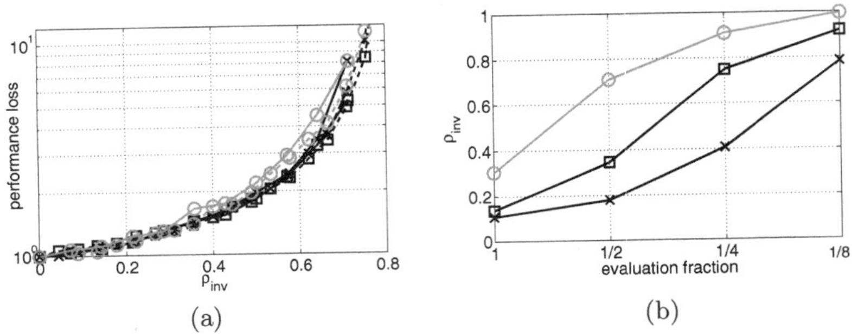

Fig. 2. (a) Mean performance loss of the CMA-ES with perturbed offspring ranking on f_{Sphere} ($\square$), f_{Ellipse} ($\times$), and $f_{\text{Rosenbrock}}$ ($\bigcirc$) for $n = 5$ (solid lines), and $n = 10$ (dashed lines). (b) Normalized pairwise inversion count of the predicted ranking versus evaluation fraction for $\hat{f}_{\text{quad}}$ on $f_{\text{Rosenbrock}}$ in 10D and bandwidth parameter $k = [1, 2, 4] \times \frac{n(n+3)+2}{2}$ (bottom to top).

10D, showing the loss in rank prediction quality as less function evaluations are used.

Combining the data of Fig. 2a & b, the speedup potential of a meta-model can be estimated[1] for a given evaluation fraction. Figure 3 depicts the speedup potential of the four investigated local models on f_{Sphere}, f_{Ellipse}, and $f_{\text{Rosenbrock}}$ with the optimal bandwidth parameter k. For none of the three functions $\hat{f}_{\text{wmean}}$ or $\hat{f}_{\text{linear}}$ a speedup factor of more than 1.5 is predicted; in 10D the results even predict a negative speedup for all three test-functions. $\hat{f}_{\text{dquad}}$ shows perfect speedup on f_{Sphere}, however already for randomly oriented misscaled convex quadratic functions the expected speedup does not exceed a factor of 2 in 10D. Only the full quadratic model $\hat{f}_{\text{quad}}$ is capable to predict reliable rankings to enhance convergence of CMA-ES on the non-quadratic $f_{\text{Rosenbrock}}$. The speedup potential is between 2 and 3 at an evaluation rate of about 1/3 to 1/4.

5 The lmm-CMA

The investigations in the previous section revealed that only *full quadratic* local models have the potential to significantly improve the convergence speed of the CMA-ES. We therefore enhance CMA-ES with a local quadratic meta-model using the adapted *approximate ranking procedure* presented in Fig. 1. The algorithm is referred to as lmm-CMA.

To complete lmm-CMA the optimal bandwidth for the locally weighted quadratic regression remains to be chosen. We investigate the influence of k for the k-th nearest neighbor bandwidth selection on the number of function evaluations of lmm-CMA to reach $f_{\text{stop}} = 10^{-10}$ on the non-quadratic $f_{\text{Rosenbrock}}$ for dimension $n = 2, 4, 8$, and 16. The parameter k is varied according to $k = \alpha\, k_{\min}$ with $\alpha =$

[1] Making the (optimistic) assumption that the use of the surrogate does not change the optimization path.

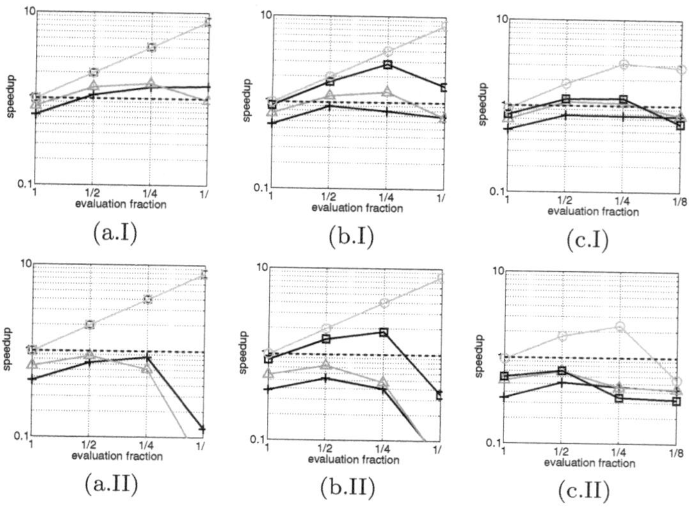

Fig. 3. Speedup potential of $\hat{f}_{\text{wmean}}$ (+), $\hat{f}_{\text{linear}}$ (Δ), $\hat{f}_{\text{dquad}}$ ($\square$), and $\hat{f}_{\text{quad}}$($\bigcirc$) on (a) f_{Sphere}, (b) f_{Ellipse}, and (c) $f_{\text{Rosenbrock}}$ in dimension (I) $n = 5$, and (II) $n = 10$

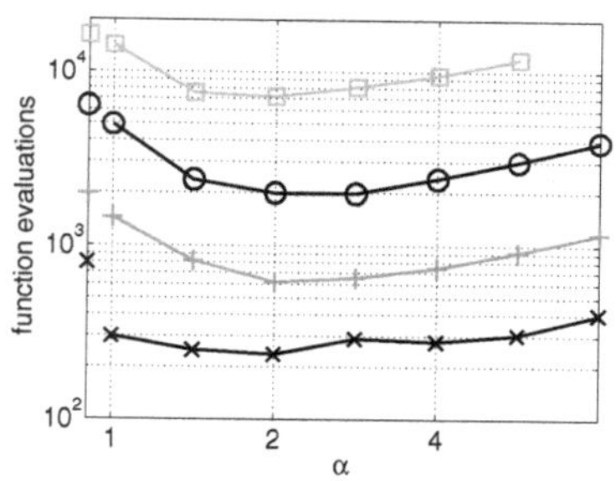

Fig. 4. Average number of function evaluations to reach f_{stop} of the lmm-CMA on $f_{\text{Rosenbrock}}$ for varying bandwidth parameter $k = \alpha \cdot (n(n+3)/2 + 1)$ and $n = 2$ ($\times$), 4 ($+$), 8 ($\bigcirc$), and 16 ($\square$). The points on the y-axis show the performance of the original CMA-ES. The optimal performance of lmm-CMA is observed for $\alpha = 2$.

$2^{i/2}, i = 0, \ldots, 6$, where $k_{\min} = \frac{n(n+3)}{2} + 1$ is the number of free parameters of the local quadratic model. Every data point is obtained by averaging 20 independent runs of lmm-CMA. The results in Fig. 4 show a unique minimum for $\alpha = 2$ independent of dimension. Therefore, we set $k = n(n+3) + 2$ for all experiments conducted in the following.

6 Performance of the lmm-CMA

The proposed lmm-CMA is investigated on a set of uni- and multimodal test-functions summarized in Table 2. The performance is assessed by averaging the number of function evaluations needed to reach $f_{\text{stop}} = 10^{-10}$ from 20 inde-

Table 3. Average number of function evaluations and standard deviations to reach f_{stop} of lmm-CMA versus CMA-ES, GPOP [2], and `fminunc`. For the multimodal functions, the numbers are divided by the probability to find the global optimum given in brackets. `fminunc` diverges on $f_{\text{NoisySphere}}$ (†) and has a vanishing probability to converge to the global optimum on f_{Ackley} and $f_{\text{Rastrigin}}$ for the given initialization region.

Function	n	λ	ϵ	lmm-CMA	CMA-ES	GPOP	`fminunc`
$f_{\text{Schwefel}}(\boldsymbol{x})$	2	6		81 ±5	391 ±42	40	**24** ±5
	4	8		145 ±7	861 ±53	110	**96** ±7
	8	10		**282** ±11	2035 ±93	440	428 ±22
	16	12		**626** ±17	5263 ±115	6000	1684 ±37
$f_{\text{Rosenbrock}}(\boldsymbol{x})$	2	6		263 ±87 (1.0)	799 ±119 (1.0)	180	**119** ±38 (1.0)
	4	8		674 ±103 (1.0)	1973 ±291 (.95)	700	**344** ±52 (.85)
	8	10		2494 ±511 (.90)	6329 ±747 (.85)	2500	**1057** ±119 (.95)
	16	12		7299 ±1154 (1.0)	16388 ±1414 (.95)	14000	**3628** ±226 (.90)
$f_{\text{NoisySphere}}(\boldsymbol{x})$	2	6	0.35	**184** ±24	372 ±39	-	†
	4	8	0.25	**503** ±56	855 ±93	-	†
	8	10	0.18	**1179** ±103	1645 ±84	-	†
	16	12	0.13	**2700** ±112	3073 ±94	-	†
$f_{\text{Ackley}}(\boldsymbol{x})$	2	5		**308** ±33 (.95)	728 ±51 (.95)	-	∞ (0.0)
	5	7		**1095** ±81 (1.0)	1767 ±74 (1.0)	-	∞ (0.0)
	10	10		**3029** ±106 (1.0)	3637 ±110 (1.0)	-	∞ (0.0)
	20	10		**8150** ±196 (1.0)	6155 ±409 (1.0)	-	∞ (0.0)
$f_{\text{Rastrigin}}(\boldsymbol{x})$	2	50		**1360** ±264 (.85)	1982 ±325 (.85)	-	∞ (0.0)
	5	140		**7320** ±1205 (.85)	8486 ±1160 (.85)	-	∞ (0.0)
	10	500		**29250** ±2769 (1.0)	40152 ±5409 (.95)	-	∞ (0.0)

pendent runs, randomly initialized in the given intervals. For the underlying CMA-ES we use the standard parameter settings given in [9] except for the population size λ: for the multimodal functions we choose the optimal λ from [9, Fig. 2]. In Table 3 the results are compared to the standard CMA-ES without meta-model support, the Gaussian Process Optimization Procedure (GPOP)[2] [2], and MATLAB's `fminunc`[3]. `fminunc` implements the BFGS Quasi-Newton method with a mixed quadratic and cubic line search procedure. In the present context of black-box optimization, gradients are estimated via finite difference approximation.

On the convex quadratic f_{Schwefel}, lmm-CMA improves CMA-ES by a factor of 5-8, and on $f_{\text{Rosenbrock}}$ the speedup is 2-3. Compared to `fminunc`, lmm-CMA is at most a factor of two slower (on $f_{\text{Rosenbrock}}$), but on f_{Schwefel} it performs even better for $n \geq 8$. The results of GPOP on f_{Schwefel} and $f_{\text{Rosenbrock}}$ are competitive for $n \leq 4$. However, for larger n the Gaussian Process Regression model gets less reliable and the performance deteriorates. Note that for small n

[2] In GPOP the optimal size of the training data set depends on the problem and the problem dimension. For the comparison we take the best data presented in [2].

[3] We set 'LargeScale'='off', 'TolFun'=1e-10, 'TolX'=1e-15, and 'MaxFunEvals'=1e6.

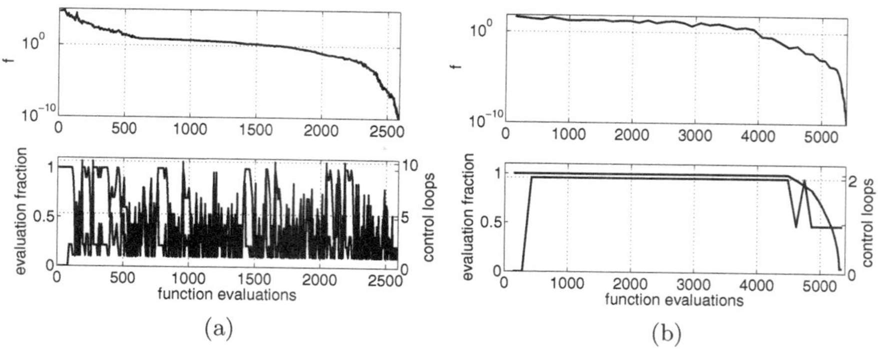

Fig. 5. Evolution of the evaluation fraction and the iteration loop count in the course of typical runs of lmm-CMA plotted aside the convergence of the fitness f on $f_{\text{Rosenbrock}}$, $n = 10$, (a), and $f_{\text{Rastrigin}}$, $n = 5$, (b)

the performance gain of lmm-CMA is limited by the n_b evaluations performed in every generation ($n_b = 1$ for $\lambda \leq 10$) and it generally scales well in n.

On $f_{\text{NoisySphere}}$ with fitness proportional Gaussian noise `fminunc` fails to converge due to the finite difference gradient estimation. In contrast, lmm-CMA and CMA-ES are able to cope with the noise levels as given in Table 3. The lmm-CMA shows a small advantage that vanishes with increasing dimension.

On the multimodal functions f_{Ackley} and $f_{\text{Rastrigin}}$ lmm-CMA is advantageous in small dimensions ($n \leq 10$), but the improvement compared to pure CMA-ES decays with increasing n. This might be an effect of suboptimal bandwidth selection of the local model for multimodal problems. Nevertheless, the results on $f_{\text{Rastrigin}}$ indicate that the adapted approximate ranking procedure works robustly with large populations.

Figure 5 exemplifies the evolution of the evaluation fraction and the iteration loop count in the course of typical runs of lmm-CMA. On $f_{\text{Rosenbrock}}$ the evaluation fraction varies throughout the whole search in the process of building local approximations of the non-quadratic function. The average evaluation fraction of $\sim \frac{1}{3}$ matches the predictions of Sect. 4 well. An interesting behavior can be observed on $f_{\text{Rastrigin}}$: In the initial (global) search phase, the local meta-models are not able to predict reliable rankings and thus are not used. However, as soon as the strategy finds the attraction region of the global optimum, the meta-model predictions get reliable and the local convergence is considerably accelerated.

7 Summary and Conclusion

The objective of this work was to enhance the performance of CMA-ES in the optimization of expensive fitness functions by incorporating local meta-models. We investigated the necessary model complexity using training data obtained from the CMA-ES. As a result, only *full quadratic* local models seem to have the potential to achieve a significant speed up. We demonstrate that locally weighted polynomial regression can preserve the ranking of the objective function enhancing significantly the performance of an already highly competitive ES on a number of benchmark problems.

The resulting lmm-CMA outperforms the standard CMA-ES on unimodal test functions by a factor between 2 and 8 scaling well with increasing dimension n. On noisy and multimodal functions, the speedup does not exceed a factor of 3 and vanishes with increasing dimension. Nevertheless, the meta-model does not jeopardize the performance even when the function cannot be modeled effectively. Therefore its main drawback remains the computational complexity of n^6 for building the meta-model and we hope to reduce the computational cost to n^4 in future implementations. Finally, we expect to be able to improve the performance in particular on multimodal and noisy functions by implementing a more sophisticated choice of the model bandwidth.

References

1. Jin, Y.: A comprehensive survey of fitness approximation in evolutionary computation. Soft Computing **9**(1) (2005) 3–12
2. Büche, D., Schraudolph, N.N., Koumoutsakos, P.: Accelerating evolutionary algorithms with Gaussian process fitness function models. IEEE Trans. Sys., Man Cyber. **35**(2) (2005) 183–194
3. Huang, D., Allen, T.T., Notz, W.I., Zeng, N.: Global optimization of stochastic black-box systems via sequential kriging meta-models. J. Glob. Opt. **34**(3) (2006) 441–466
4. Jin, Y., Olhofer, M., Sendhoff, B.: A framework fo evolutionary optimization with approximate fitness functions. IEEE Trans. Evol. Comput. **6**(5) (2002) 481–494
5. Branke, J., Schmidt, C., Schmeck, H.: Efficient fitness estimation in noisy environments. In Spector, J., ed.: Genetic and Evolutionary Computation, Morgan Kaufmann (2001) 243–250
6. Regis, R.G., Shoemaker, C.A.: Local function approximation in evolutionary algorithms for the optimization of costly functions. IEEE Trans. Evol. Comput. **8**(5) (2004) 490–504
7. Runarsson, T.P.: Constrained evolutionary optimization by approximate ranking and surrogate models. In Yao, X., et al., eds.: Parallel Problem Solving from Nature - PPSN VIII, LNCS 3242, Springer (2004) 401–410
8. Hansen, N., Ostermeier, A.: Completely derandomized self-adaptation in evolution strategies. Evol. Comput. **9**(2) (2001) 159–195
9. Hansen, N., Kern, S.: Evaluating the CMA evolution strategy on multimodal test functions. In Yao, X., et al., eds.: Parallel Problem Solving from Nature - PPSN VIII, LNCS 3242, Springer (2004) 282–291
10. Auger, A., Hansen, N.: A restart CMA evolution strategy with increasing population size. In: Proceedings of the IEEE Congress on Evolutionary Computation. (2005)
11. Jin, Y., Hüsken, M., Sendhoff, B.: Quality measures for approximate models in evolutionary computation. In Barry, A.M., ed.: GECCO 2003: Proceedings of the Bird of a Feather Workshop, Genetic and Evolutionary Computation Conference, AAAI (2003) 170–173
12. Atkeson, C.G., Moore, A.W., Schaal, S.: Locally weighted learning. Artificial Intelligence Review **11**(1-5) (1997) 11–73

Effects of Using Two Neighborhood Structures in Cellular Genetic Algorithms for Function Optimization

Hisao Ishibuchi, Tsutomu Doi, and Yusuke Nojima

Department of Computer Science and Intelligent Systems, Graduate School of Engineering, Osaka Prefecture University, 1-1 Gakuen-cho, Naka-ku, Sakai, Osaka 599-8531, Japan
hisaoi@cs.osakafu-u.ac.jp, doi@ci.cs.osakafu-u.ac.jp
nojima@cs.osakafu-u.ac.jp
http://www.ie.osakafu-u.ac.jp/~hisaoi/ci_lab_e

Abstract. We implement a cellular genetic algorithm with two neighborhood structures following the concept of structured demes: One is for interaction among individuals and the other is for mating. The effect of using these two neighborhood structures on the search ability of cellular genetic algorithms is examined through computational experiments on function optimization problems. Experimental results show that good results are obtained from the combination of a small interaction neighborhood and a large mating neighborhood. This relation in the size of the two neighborhood structures coincides with many cases of biological evolution in nature such as plants and territorial animals. It is also shown that the search ability of cellular genetic algorithms is deteriorated by the opposite combination of the two neighborhood structures.

1 Introduction

Cellular algorithms are one of the most popular models of spatially structured evolutionary algorithms [2], [3]. Since early studies in the late 1980s [6], [12] and the early 1990s [16], [17], cellular algorithms have been an active research area in the field of evolutionary computation (i.e., see [1]-[3], [5]). In cellular algorithms, each individual is spatially fixed in a cell of a lattice (typically a two-dimensional grid-world). A new offspring in a cell is generated from individuals in its neighboring cells. The main feature of cellular algorithms is the use of local selection based on a neighborhood structure. It was shown in the literature [7], [13], [14] that the size of the neighborhood structure has a large effect on the behavior of cellular algorithms.

A single neighborhood structure has been usually used in cellular algorithms in the literature. There are, however, many cases where biological evolution is based on two different neighborhood structures. For example, most plants have two neighborhood structures. Neighboring plants fight with each other for water and sunlight in an interaction neighborhood, which is much smaller than a mating neighborhood where they can disperse their pollen. Another example is territorial animals. The interaction neighborhood (i.e., territory) of a territorial animal is much smaller than its mating neighborhood. Evolution of altruism in the two neighborhood structures was actively studied under the name of structured demes in the late 1970s [4], [15], [18], [19].

T.P. Runarsson et al. (Eds.): PPSN IX, LNCS 4193, pp. 949 – 958, 2006.

The effect of the two neighborhood structures on the evolution of cooperative behavior was examined in spatial Iterated Prisoner's Dilemma (IPD) games [8]-[11]. In [9]-[11], an individual in each cell played against only its neighbors in the interaction neighborhood. A new individual in each cell was generated from its neighbors in the mating neighborhood. It was shown under random pairing that cooperative behavior was evolved only when the interaction neighborhood was very small and the mating neighborhood was small.

In this paper, we examine the effect of using the two neighborhood structures on the search ability of cellular genetic algorithms through computational experiments on function optimization problems. In Section 2, we implement a cellular genetic algorithm following the concept of structured demes. In our cellular genetic algorithm, a rank is assigned to each individual according to the ranking of its fitness among its neighbors in the interaction neighborhood. The selection of parents for generating a new individual in each cell is performed in the mating neighborhood. In Section 3, we examine the effect of using the two neighborhood structures through computational experiments using two-dimensional grid-worlds of various sizes. Experimental results show that good results are obtained when the mating neighborhood is larger than the interaction neighborhood. Finally we conclude this paper in Section 4.

2 Cellular Genetic Algorithms with Two Neighborhood Structures

In this section, we implement a cellular genetic algorithm with two neighborhood structures following the concept of structured demes [4], [15], [18], [19]. Our cellular genetic algorithm is similar to the spatial IPD model in [8]-[11].

2.1 Two-Dimensional Grid World with Two Neighborhood Structures

We use a two-dimensional grid-world where a single individual is spatially fixed in each cell. Thus the number of cells is the same as the number of individuals as in other studies on cellular genetic algorithms. We assume the torus structure of the two-dimensional grid-world. In computational experiments, we examine three specifications of the size of the two-dimensional grid-world: 11×11, 21×21 and 31×31.

As we have already explained, we use two neighborhood structures in our cellular genetic algorithm. One is for interaction among individuals. This neighborhood structure determines the neighbors against which each individual competes. We denote the interaction neighborhood of the ith cell as $N_{\text{Compete}}(i)$ in order to clearly show that the individual in the ith cell competes against its neighbors in $N_{\text{Compete}}(i)$. The other neighborhood structure is for mating. This neighborhood structure determines the neighbors from which an offspring is generated for each cell. We denote the mating neighborhood of the ith cell as $N_{\text{Select}}(i)$ in order to clearly show that parents are selected from the neighbors in $N_{\text{Select}}(i)$ to generate an offspring for the ith cell.

We show three neighborhood structures in Fig. 1. In each plot, open circles show the neighbors of the closed circle individual. In computational experiments, we examine five specifications of the neighborhood size for each of the interaction and mating neighborhood structures: 5, 9, 25, 49 and the unstructured case. The neighborhood

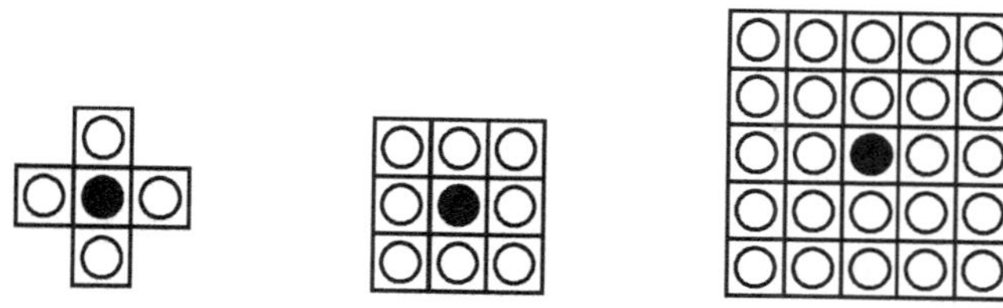

(a) 5 neighbors (b) 9 neighbors (c) 25 neighbors

Fig. 1. Three neighborhood structures. In each plot, open circles show the neighbors of the closed circle individual. The number of the neighbors includes the closed circle individual.

with 49 neighbors is defined by the 7×7 square as in Fig. 1 (b) and Fig. 1 (c). All individuals are included in the neighborhood in the unstructured case. A neighborhood structure with three neighbors is not used in this paper due to its single-dimensional property (see [9], [11] for the use of such a neighborhood structure).

2.2 Competition in the Interaction Neighborhood

In our cellular genetic algorithm, each individual competes against its neighbors in the interaction neighborhood. We assign a rank to each individual according to the ranking of its fitness among its neighbors in the interaction neighborhood.

Let us assume that our task is to find an optimal or near optimal solution of the minimization problem with the objective function $f(\mathbf{x})$. We denote the individual in the ith cell by $\mathbf{x}_i$. In order to assign a rank to $\mathbf{x}_i$, we sort the objective values of its neighbors (including $\mathbf{x}_i$ itself) in $N_{\mathrm{Compete}}(i)$ in ascending order. When multiple neighbors have the same objective value, we tentatively use random tiebreak to give them tentative rankings. Then a rank is assigned to $\mathbf{x}_i$ according to the ranking of its objective value. If $\mathbf{x}_i$ has the best objective value, rank 1 is assigned. If $\mathbf{x}_i$ has the second best objective value, rank 2 is assigned. When multiple neighbors including $\mathbf{x}_i$ have the same objective value, the average value of their rankings is assigned to $\mathbf{x}_i$. For example, when four neighbors including $\mathbf{x}_i$ have the second best objective value, rank 3.5 is assigned to $\mathbf{x}_i$ because their rankings are 2nd, 3rd, 4th, and 5th. In this manner, a rank is assigned to each individual according to the ranking of its objective value among its neighbors in the interaction neighborhood.

It should be noted that we do not have to sort all neighbors in $N_{\mathrm{Compete}}(i)$. The sorting of all neighbors in the above-mentioned procedure is just for the simplicity of explanation. We only need the ranking of the objective value of $\mathbf{x}_i$ and the number of its neighbors with the same objective value as $\mathbf{x}_i$ in $N_{\mathrm{Compete}}(i)$.

We handle all individuals with rank 1 as elites, which survive in their current cells to the next generation with no modifications. Such an elite is the best individual among its neighbors in the interaction neighborhood. If we use a small interaction neighborhood such as Fig. 1 (a) with five neighbors, the total number of elites is large. The number of elites decreases as the size of the interaction neighborhood increases.

2.3 Selection in the Mating Neighborhood

When the individual in the ith cell is an elite, it survives in the same cell. That is, the next generation has the same individual in the ith cell as the current generation. When the individual in the ith cell is not an elite, a new individual for the ith cell is generated from its neighbors in the mating neighborhood $N_{\text{Select}}(i)$. The standard binary tournament selection procedure is applied to the neighbors in $N_{\text{Select}}(i)$ to choose a pair of parents. A new individual for the ith cell is generated by crossover and mutation from the selected pair of parents. The point of our local selection scheme is that each individual is not evaluated by its raw objective value but its rank.

In computational experiments, we examine two versions of our local selection scheme. In the first version (Version I), two parents are selected from the neighbors as we have just explained. In the second version (Version II), the current individual in each cell is always used as one parent. Its mate is selected from its neighbors by the binary tournament selection procedure based on their ranks.

2.4 Cellular Genetic Algorithm

The outline of our cellular genetic algorithm can be written as follows:

Step 1: Randomly generate an initial population. A single individual is located in each cell of the two-dimensional grid-world.
Step 2: Assign a rank to each individual according to the ranking of its objective value among its neighbors in the interaction neighborhood. Individuals with rank 1 are handled as elite individuals.
Step 3: Replace the non-elite individual in each cell with an offspring generated by selection, crossover and mutation from its neighbors in the mating neighborhood. Elite individuals stay in their current cells with no modifications.
Step 4: Return to Step 2 if the prespecified stopping condition is not satisfied.

In computational experiments, the total number of generations is used as the stopping condition. The execution of our cellular genetic algorithm on each test problem is terminated at the 500th generation.

3 Computational Experiments

In this section, we examine the effect of using the two neighborhood structures on the search ability of our cellular genetic algorithm through computational experiments.

3.1 Conditions of Computational Experiments

As test problems, we use the following five minimization problems. The number of decision variables (i.e., n) is always specified as 10 in all the five test problems. That is, our test problems are 10-dimensional minimization problems.

F1 (Sphere Function):

$$f_1(x_j \mid 1 \le j \le n) = \sum_{j=1}^{n} x_j^2 , \quad x_j \in [-5.12,\ 5.11] . \tag{1}$$

F2 (Rastrigin Function):

$$f_2(x_j \mid 1 \le j \le n) = 10n + \sum_{j=1}^{n} \left[x_j^2 - 10\cos(2\pi x_j) \right], \quad x_j \in [-5.12,\ 5.11]. \tag{2}$$

F3 (Schwefel Function):

$$f_3(x_j \mid 1 \le j \le n) = 418.9829n + \left[\sum_{j=1}^{n} \left(-x_j \sin\left(\sqrt{|x_j|} \right) \right) \right], \quad x_j \in [-512,\ 511]. \tag{3}$$

F4 (Griewangk Function):

$$f_4(x_j \mid 1 \le j \le n) = \left[\sum_{j=1}^{n} \frac{x_j^2}{4000} \right] - \left[\prod_{j=1}^{n} \cos \frac{x_j}{\sqrt{j}} \right] + 1, \quad x_j \in [-512,\ 511]. \tag{4}$$

F5 (Rosenbrock Function):

$$f_5(x_j \mid 1 \le j \le n) = \sum_{j=1}^{n-1} \left[100(x_{j+1} - x_j^2)^2 + (1 - x_j)^2 \right], \quad x_j \in [-2.048,\ 2.047]. \tag{5}$$

Using a gray code, each decision variable x_j is coded as a binary string of length 10 (F1, F2, F3 and F4) or 12 (F5). We examine three specifications of the grid-world: 11×11, 21×21 and 31×31. In each grid-world, we examine five specifications of the neighborhood structure: 5, 9, 25 neighbors in Fig. 1, 49 neighbors in the 7×7 square, and the unstructured case. These five specifications are used for interaction and mating. That is, we examine 25 combinations of the two neighborhood structures.

Our cellular genetic algorithm is applied to each test problem using the following parameter specifications:

Population size: 121 (11×11), 441 (21×21), 961 (31×31),
Crossover probability (One-point crossover): 1.00,
Mutation probability (Bit-flip mutation): 0.05,
Termination condition: 500 generations.

3.2 Experimental Results: Version I

In this subsection, we report experimental results using our Version I algorithm where two parents are selected from the mating neighborhood to generate an offspring for each cell by crossover and mutation. In the next subsection, we report experimental results by our Version II algorithm where the current individual in each cell is used as one parent and its mate is selected from the mating neighborhood.

We examine the 25 combinations of the two neighborhood structures for the three grid-worlds. That is, we examine 75 different settings. Using each setting, we apply our Version I algorithm to each test problem 100 times. In each run, we record the best (i.e., smallest) objective value over all the examined individuals. Then the average of the best objective values is calculated over 100 runs.

Experimental results are shown in Figs. 2-6. In each figure, the left, center and right plots are results with the 11×11, 21×21 and 31×31 grid-worlds, respectively. In each plot, 121, 441 and 961 denotes the unstructured case (i.e., the total number of cells). The diagonal five bars from the bottom-left to the top-right corner of each plot correspond to the cases where the two neighborhood structures are the same (e.g., $|N_{\mathrm{Compete}}(i)| = |N_{\mathrm{Select}}(i)| = 5$ at the bottom-left corner). On the other hand, the other 20 off-diagonal bars correspond to the cases with two different neighborhood structures. In Figs. 2-5, we can observe the improvement in the search ability of our cellular genetic algorithm by the use of a small interaction neighborhood $N_{\mathrm{Compete}}(i)$ and a large mating neighborhood $N_{\mathrm{Select}}(i)$. On the contrary, the search ability of our cellular genetic algorithm is degraded by the opposite combination: a large interaction neighborhood $N_{\mathrm{Compete}}(i)$ and a small mating neighborhood $N_{\mathrm{Select}}(i)$. In Fig. 6, the effect of using the two neighborhood structures is not clear. The search ability is somewhat degraded around the bottom-right corner in Fig. 6 (especially Fig. 6 (c)).

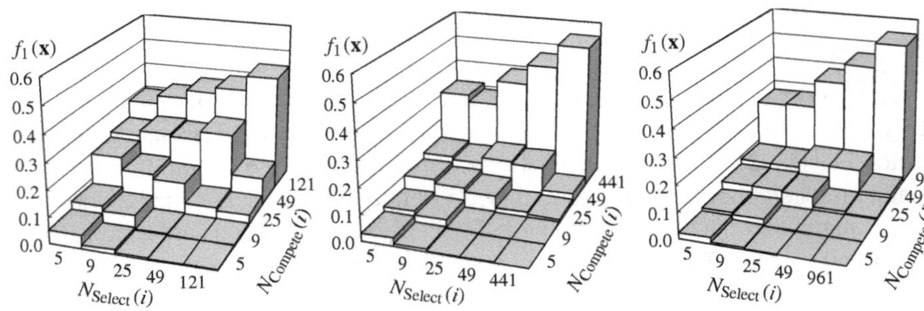

(a) 11×11 grid-world (b) 21×21 grid-world (c) 31×31 grid-world

Fig. 2. Experimental results by our Version I algorithm on F1 (Sphere Function)

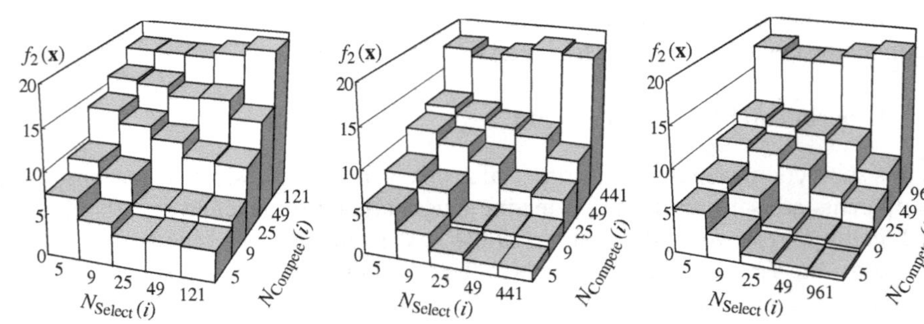

(a) 11×11 grid-world (b) 21×21 grid-world (c) 31×31 grid-world

Fig. 3. Experimental results by our Version I algorithm on F2 (Rastrigin Function)

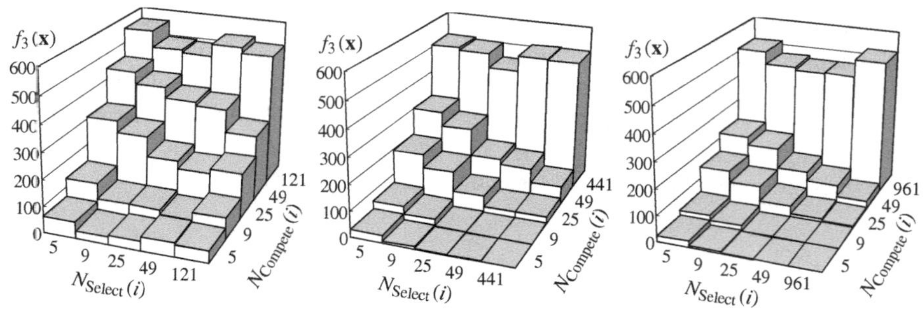

(a) 11×11 grid-world (b) 21×21 grid-world (c) 31×31 grid-world

Fig. 4. Experimental results by our Version I algorithm on F3 (Schwefel Function)

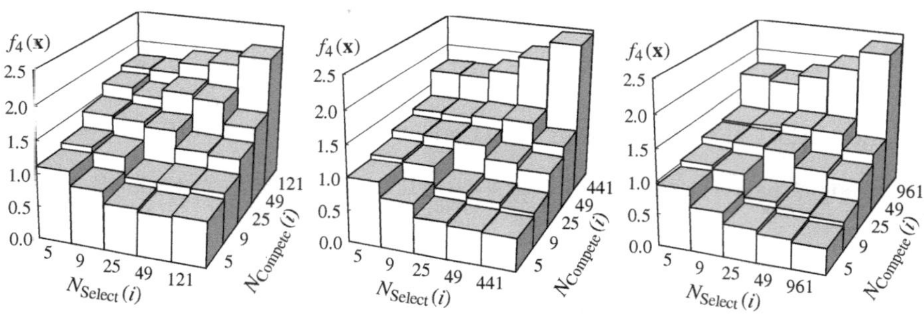

(a) 11×11 grid-world (b) 21×21 grid-world (c) 31×31 grid-world

Fig. 5. Experimental results by our Version I algorithm on F4 (Griewangk Function)

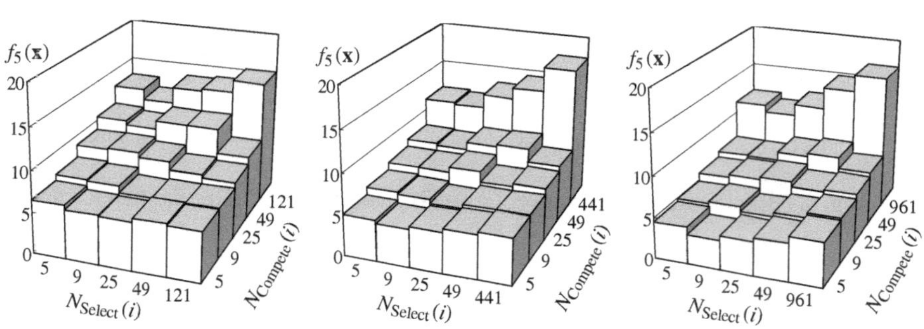

(a) 11×11 grid-world (b) 21×21 grid-world (c) 31×31 grid-world

Fig. 6. Experimental results by our Version I algorithm on F5 (Rosenbrock Function)

3.3 Experimental Results: Version II

In this subsection, we report experimental results using our Version II algorithm. In the same manner as Figs. 2-6, average results over 100 runs are shown in Figs. 7-11. From the comparison between Figs. 2-6 and Figs. 7-11, we can see that our Version II algorithm is inferior to our Version I algorithm (the scale of the vertical axis is not the same between the corresponding figures, e.g., see Fig. 2 and Fig. 7). Nevertheless, we can obtain almost the same observation from Figs. 7-11 as Figs. 2-6. That is, the search ability of our cellular genetic algorithm is improved around the bottom-right corner in Figs. 7-11 by the use of a small interaction neighborhood $N_{\text{Compete}}(i)$ and a large mating neighborhood $N_{\text{Select}}(i)$, and degraded by the opposite combination: a large interaction neighborhood and a small mating neighborhood.

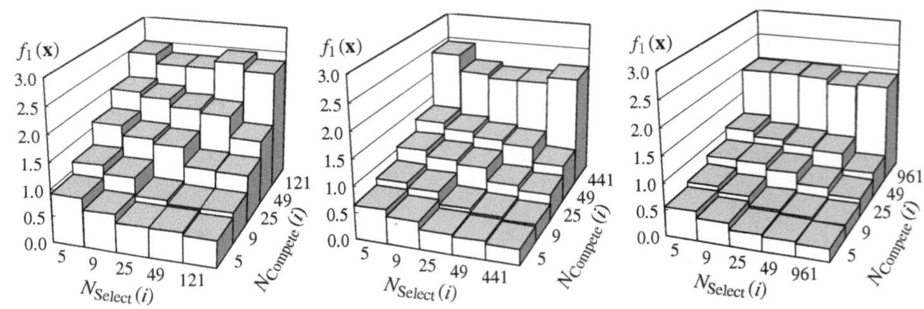

(a) 11×11 grid-world (b) 21×21 grid-world (c) 31×31 grid-world

Fig. 7. Experimental results by our Version II algorithm on F1 (Sphere Function)

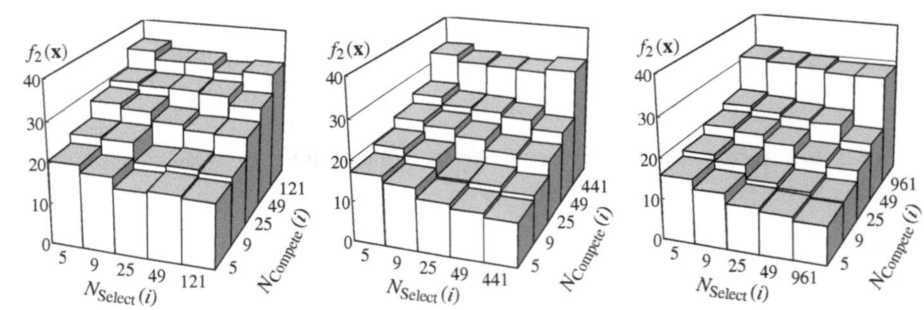

(a) 11×11 grid-world (b) 21×21 grid-world (c) 31×31 grid-world

Fig. 8. Experimental results by our Version II algorithm on F2 (Rastrigin Function)

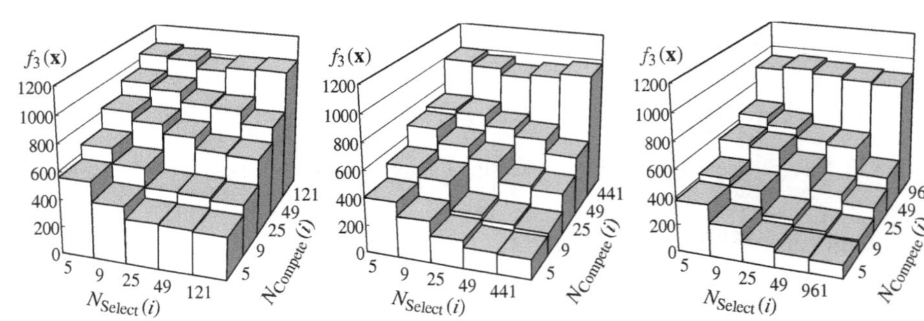

(a) 11×11 grid-world (b) 21×21 grid-world (c) 31×31 grid-world

Fig. 9. Experimental results by our Version II algorithm on F3 (Schwefel Function)

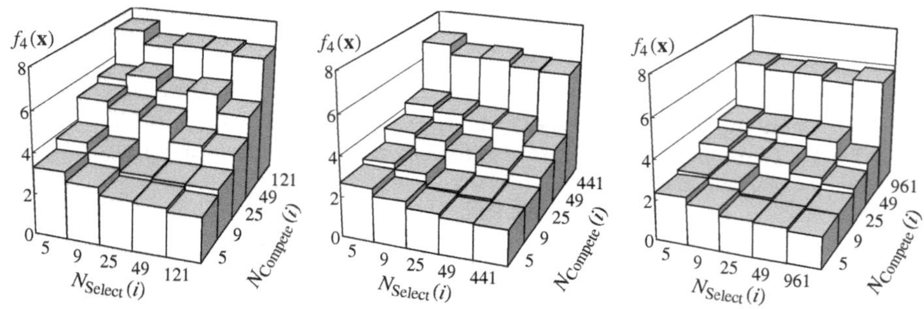

(a) 11×11 grid-world (b) 21×21 grid-world (c) 31×31 grid-world

Fig. 10. Experimental results by our Version II algorithm on F4 (Griewangk Function)

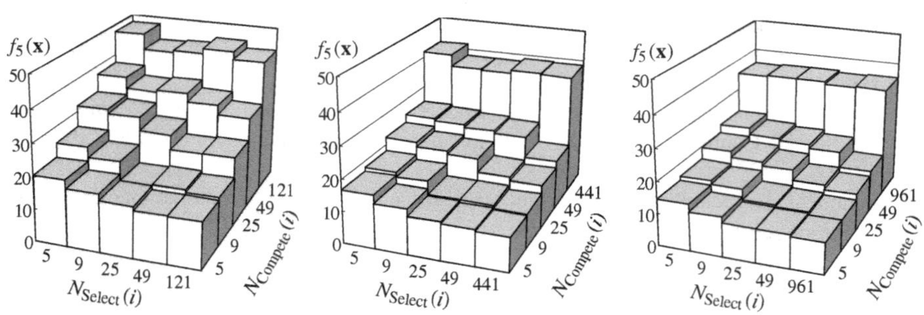

(a) 11×11 grid-world (b) 21×21 grid-world (c) 31×31 grid-world

Fig. 11. Experimental results by our Version II algorithm on F5 (Rosenbrock Function)

4 Conclusions

In this paper, we examined the effect of using two neighborhood structures on the search ability of cellular genetic algorithms: One is for interaction among individuals and the other is for mating. We first implemented a cellular genetic algorithm with the two neighborhood structures following the concept of structured demes. Then we examined the effect of the two neighborhood structures through computational experiments on function optimization problems. Experimental results showed that the search ability of our cellular genetic algorithm was improved by using a small interaction neighborhood and a large mating neighborhood. Such a combination of the two neighborhood structures coincides with many cases in nature such as plants and territorial animals. It was also shown that the opposite combination degraded the search ability of our cellular genetic algorithm. In our current implementation, the number of elite individuals depends on the size of the interaction neighborhood. In future work, we will compare different specifications of the neighborhood size under the same condition with respect to the number of elite individuals.

This work was partially supported by Japan Society for the Promotion of Science (JSPS) through Grand-in-Aid for Scientific Research (B): KAKENHI (17300075).

References

1. Alba, E., Dorronsoro, B.: The Exploration/Exploitation Tradeoff in Dynamic Cellular Genetic Algorithms. IEEE Trans. on Evolutionary Computation 9 (2005) 126-142
2. Alba, E., Tomassini, M.: Parallelism and Evolutionary Algorithms. IEEE Trans. on Evolutionary Computation 6 (2002) 443-462
3. Cantu-Paz, E.: Efficient and Accurate Parallel Genetic Algorithms. Springer, Berlin (2000)
4. Charlesworth, B.: A Note on the Evolution of Altruism in Structured Demes. The American Naturalist 113 (1979) 601-605
5. Giacobini, M., Tomassini, M., Tettamanzi, A. G. B., Alba, E.: Selection Intensity in Cellular Evolutionary Algorithms for Regular Lattices. IEEE Trans. on Evolutionary Computation 9 (2005) 489-505
6. Gorges-Schleuter, M.: ASPARAGOS: An Asynchronous Parallel Genetic Optimization Strategy. Proc. of 3rd International Conference on Genetic Algorithms (1989) 422-427
7. Gorges-Schleuter, M.: A Comparative Study on Global and Local Selection in Evolutionary Strategies. Lecture Notes in Computer Science, Vol. 1498: Parallel Problem Solving from Nature - PPSN V. Springer, Berlin (1998) 367-377
8. Ifti, M., Killingback, T., Doebelic, M.: Effects of Neighborhood Size and Connectivity on the Spatial Continuous Prisoner's Dilemma. Journal of Theoretical Biology 231 (2004) 97-106
9. Ishibuchi, H., Namikawa, N.: Evolution of Iterated Prisoner's Dilemma Game Strategies in Structured Demes under Random Pairing in Game Playing. IEEE Trans. on Evolutionary Computation 9 (2005) 552-561
10. Ishibuchi, H., Namikawa, N.: Evolution of Cooperative Behavior in the Iterated Prisoner's Dilemma under Random Pairing in Game Playing. Proc. of 2005 Congress on Evolutionary Computation (2005) 2637-2644
11. Ishibuchi, H., Namikawa, N., Ohara, K.: Effects of Spatial Structures on Evolution of Iterated Prisoner's Dilemma Game Strategies in Single-Dimensional and Two-Dimensional Grids. Proc. of 2006 Congress on Evolutionary Computation (2006) (in press)
12. Manderick, B., Spiessens, P.: Fine-Grained Parallel Genetic Algorithms. Proc. of 3rd International Conference on Genetic Algorithms (1989) 428-433
13. Sarma, J., De Jong, K.: An Analysis of the Effects of Neighborhood Size and Shape on Local Selection Algorithms. Lecture Notes in Computer Science, Vol. 1141: Parallel Problem Solving from Nature - PPSN IV. Springer, Berlin (1996) 236-244
14. Sarma, J., De Jong, K.: An Analysis of Local Selection Algorithms in a Spatially Structured Evolutionary Algorithm. Proc. of 7th International Conference on Genetic Algorithms (1997) 181-186
15. Slatkin, M., Wilson, D. S.: Coevolution in Structured Demes. Proc. of the National Academy of Sciences 76 (1979) 2084-2087
16. Spiessens, P., Manderick, B.: A Massively Parallel Genetic Algorithm: Implementation and First Analysis. Proc. of 4th International Conference on Genetic Algorithms (1991) 279-286
17. Whitley, D.: Cellular Genetic Algorithms. Proc. of 5th International Conference on Genetic Algorithms (1993) 658
18. Wilson, D. S.: Structured Demes and the Evolution of Group-Advantageous Traits. The American Naturalist 111 (1977) 157-185
19. Wilson, D. S.: Structured Demes and Trait-Group Variation. The American Naturalist 113 (1979) 606-610

A Selecto-recombinative Genetic Algorithm with Continuous Chromosome Reconfiguration

Jiří Kubalík, Petr Pošík, and Jan Herold

Department of Cybernetics, CTU Prague,
Technicka 2, 166 27 Prague 6, Czech Republic
{kubalik, posik}@labe.felk.cvut.cz, jan_herold@volny.cz

Abstract. A good performance of traditional genetic algorithm is determined by its ability to identify building blocks and grow them to larger ones. To attain this objective a properly arranged chromosome is needed to ensure that building blocks will survive the application of recombination operators. The proposed algorithm periodically rearranges the order of genes in the chromosome while the actual information about the inter-gene dependencies is calculated on-line through the run. Standard 2-point crossover, operating on the adapted chromosomal structure, is used to generate new solutions. Experimental results show that this algorithm is able to solve separable problems with strong intra building block dependencies among genes as well as the hierarchical problems.

1 Introduction

Standard selecto-recombinative genetic algorithms (GAs) work with fixed-length chromosomes with the gene order fixed during the whole evolution. A population of such chromosomes is evolved—they are recombined in order to generate the new ones. Through the evolutionary process, various high quality partial solutions called building blocks are generated that are needed to obtain the optimum solution. GA has to be able to identify essential building blocks and grow them to larger ones. Tightly linked building blocks have relatively high probability of surviving through successive generation, while building blocks with weak linkage are very likely to be disrupted by crossover operations. Thus, it is crucial that the genes belonging to the same building block are spatially grouped close to each other in order to maximize the efficiency of mixing the building blocks by recombination operators.

Many approaches have been proposed to deal with the linkage problem and to ensure appropriate building block mixing. They can be classified into the following categories:

- Linkage identification/learning techniques such as the messy GAs [1], linkage identification by non-monotonicity detection [6], linkage learning GA [2], dependency structure matrix driven GA [12], adaptive linkage model [5].
- Estimation of distribution algorithms also called probabilistic model building techniques include the bivariate marginal distribution algorithm [7], extended compact GA [3], Bayesian optimization algorithm [8].

T.P. Runarsson et al. (Eds.): PPSN IX, LNCS 4193, pp. 959–968, 2006.

A selecto-recombinative GA with continuous chromosome reconfiguration (CoCR), described in this paper, is based on an idea that given a chromosome structure that enables tight linkage of building blocks of the given problem, standard recombination operators can be used to efficiently grow the building blocks when recombining parental individuals. In order to attain this, CoCR updates pair-wise gene dependencies periodically during the evolutionary process and rearranges the chromosomal structure every generation according to the actual linkage information. The chromosome structure is generated by a heuristic procedure so that it reflects the most significant gene dependencies. Standard 2-point crossover, operating on the adapted chromosomal structure, is used to generate new solutions.

The rest of this paper is organized as follows. The next section describes the proposed algorithm. Section 3 and 4 describe the test problems and experimental setup used for our experiments. Then the results of experiments are presented and discussed. The work is summarized and possible future extensions are given in the last section.

2 CoCR Algorithm

An outline of CoCR algorithm is in Fig. 1. CoCR starts with a randomly generated order of genes in the chromosome. Then, the algorithm iterates in the main loop (1) generating subsequent populations of candidate solutions using a diversity preservation variant of selecto-recombinative GA while (2) continuously adapting the chromosome structure on the fly.

The pair-wise gene statistics are accumulated in *stats* every generation. All chromosomes of the processed population contribute to *stats*, no selection of high quality solutions is applied. The *stats* are accumulated for one epoch, consisting of *recalculation_step* number of generations, and then the gene dependencies are recalculated and stored in table *links_table*. *links_table* is a table of size $[n \times m]$, where for each gene $i \in \{0, n-1\}$ there is an ordered list of up to m genes that have the strongest epistasis with gene i. Each lists of the most epistatic genes is ordered in a descendant manner with respect to the strength of the epistasis. After the *links_table* has been updated the *stats* are erased.

The chromosome structure is reconfigured every generation using the actual gene dependencies in *links_table*. The gene order is calculated using the same gene dependencies information for each generation within one epoch. However, the actual linkage of genes in the chromosome might change slightly generation by generation since the heuristic procedure for the chromosome structure construction involves a stochastic component. This is an important aspect that makes the approach resistant against imperfectly identified epistasis among genes.

2.1 Identification of Pair-Wise Gene Dependencies

CoCR uses the Pearson's chi-square test for discovering the pair-wise gene dependencies in the same way as it was used in the BMDA [7]. It estimates the dependencies from the collected set of N chromosomes. For each gene i we define the

```
init(population)
init(chromosome_structure)
generations = 0
erase(stats)
repeat
    population ← selecto-recombinative_GA(population)
    generations = generations + 1
    accumulate_pairwise_stats(population,stats)
    if(generations mod recalculation_step = 0)
        links_table ← recalculate_links_table(stats)
        erase(stats)
    chromosome_structure ← construct_chromosome(links_table)
until(CoCR termination condition is met)
```

Fig. 1. An outline of CoCR algorithm

univariate marginal frequency $p_i(x_i)$ as the frequency of chromosomes that have ith gene set to x_i, where $x_i \in \{0,1\}$. For any two positions $i \neq j \in \{0,\ldots,n-1\}$ and any possible values $x_i, x_j \in \{0,1\}$ we define the bivariate marginal frequency $p_{i,j}(x_i,x_j)$ as the frequency of chromosomes that have genes i and j set to x_i and x_j, respectively. Then, for each pair of genes i and j, the Pearson's chi-square statistics can be defined by

$$X^2_{i,j} = \sum_{x_i,x_j} \frac{(Np_{i,j}(x_i,x_j) - Np_i(x_i)p_j(x_j))^2}{Np_i(x_i)p_j(x_j)},$$

where $Np_i(x_i)p_j(x_j)$ and $Np_{i,j}(x_i,x_j)$ is the expected and the observed frequency of the pair of values (x_i,x_j) on the positions i and j, respectively. If positions i and j are not independent for 95%, i.e. $X^2_{i,j} \geq 3.84$, then the value $X^2_{i,j}$ is recorded for both genes i and j and the strongest gene dependencies are retained in *links_table* for each gene. Note, that there may be some genes in *links_table* that have the list of the most related genes shorter than m if there were less than m dependencies identified for these genes.

2.2 Generation of the Chromosome Structure

The chromosome structure is constructed by means of a simple greedy algorithm (see Fig. 2) utilizing the information about the most significant epistases among genes (stored in *links_table*). The algorithm works in two steps - first the linkage groups are constructed, then the linkage groups are merged together to form the whole chromosome. It starts with a set of elementary linkage groups, where each gene represents one single group. Then it grows the linkage groups in the main loop (lines 3-11 in Fig. 2) using in turn the strongest links (i.e. the first column of *links_table*), then the second strongest links, etc., until all columns of *links_table* have been used or all the genes have been grouped in a single linkage group. In

```
init(linkage_groups)
i = 0
do
    unused ← {0,1,...,n − 1}
    do
        gene = select_random(unused)
        linkage_groups ← link(gene,links_table[gene, i])
        remove gene from unused
    while(unused ≠ {})
    i = i + 1
while(i < m) and (card(linkage_groups)>1)
chromosome_structure ← merge(linkage_groups)
return(chromosome_structure)
```

Fig. 2. An outline of `construct_chromosome` procedure

each i-th iteration of the main loop all links from the i-th column of *links_table* are used to grow the respective linkage groups. Note, that when processing ith column of *links_table* the links are picked from the list of unused links in a random order. Thus, each time the procedure is called different linkage groups can be generated, see Table 3.

A link between genes i and j is incorporated into the linkage groups so that the two linkage groups already assigned to i and j, respectively, are merged together. For example, let us assume that a link between genes 3 and 7 is to be added to the linkage groups, given the actual linkage groups assigned to gene 3 and 7 are LG_3 =(2–4–**7**–1) and LG_7 =(5–**3**–9), respectively. Merging LG_3 and LG_7 will yield a new linkage group $LG_3 = LG_7$ =(2–4–**7**–1–5–**3**–9).

After the linkage groups have been established they are merged together, again in a random order.

2.3 Genetic Algorithm with Allelic Diversity Preservation

It is crucial for proper functioning of the algorithm of identification of pair-wise dependencies to supply it with a diverse collection of chromosomes. Since the collection consists of the population contents collected over multiple generations the selecto-recombinative GA must be designed so that it can preserve the allelic diversity of the population at every generation.

In this work the genetic algorithm with limited convergence (GALCO) introduced by Kubalik et al. [4] is used to attain this goal. GALCO is based on the idea that the population is explicitly prevented from becoming homogenous by simply imposing limits on its convergence. This is done by specifying the maximum difference between the frequency of ones and zeros at any position of the chromosome calculated over the whole population. A steady-state evolutionary model and a special replacement operator are used to keep the desired distribution of ones and zeros during the whole run. An important point is that

GALCO is a type of a simple selecto-recombinative GA that uses the standard recombination operators and no explicit mutation operator.

3 Test Problems

There are four test problems, each of them composed of different fundamental building blocks of variable size.

DF3. This is a representative of deceptive problems, i.e. problems that are intentionally designed to make a GA converge towards local deceptive optimum. The problem is composed of 25 copies of a 4-bit fully deceptive function DF3 taken from [11]. DF3 has a global optimum in the string 1111 with fitness 30 and a deceptive attractor 0000 with low fitness 10, which is surrounded, in the search space, by four strings of just one 1 with fitness values 28, 27, 26, and 25. The whole 100-bit long chromosome has the global optimum of value 750.

DF3-intrl. This problem is an extension of the previous problem such that the whole chromosome is split into 12-bit blocks, where each of the blocks contributes to the fitness by the value $\sum DF3(b_j, b_{j+1}, b_{(j+2)mod12}, b_{(j+3)mod12})$, where $j \in \{0, 2, 4, 6, 8, 10\}$. In the optimal case, when all bits of the block are set to 1, the contribution of the block is $6 \times 30 = 180$. Here, a problem composed of eight blocks was used with the global optimum of value 1440.

H-IFF. A hierarchical-if-and-only-if function proposed in [10] is the representative of hierarchically decomposable problems. The hierarchical block structure of the function is a balanced binary tree. Leaf nodes, corresponding to single genes, contribute to the fitness by 1. Each inner node is interpreted as 1 if and only if its children are both 1's, and as 0 iff they are both 0's - in such cases the inner node contributes to the fitness by a positive value $2^{height(x)}$, where $height(x)$ is the distance from the node x to its antecedent leaves. Otherwise the node is interpreted as null and its contribution is 0. The function has two global optima - one consists of all 1's and the other one has all 0's. We have used 128-bit problem with global optima of value 1024.

H-TRAP. The structure of this problem is similar to the structure of H-IFF with the difference that each inner node has three children and the contribution of each building block at every level is given as $3^{height(x)} \times f_{trap}(u)$, see [9]. $f_{trap}(u)$ is a trap function returning 1.0 if all its three children nodes interpret as 1, f_{min} if the three children nodes interpret as 0, $f_{min}/2$ if one out of the three children interpret as 1, and 0.0 if two children interpret as 1. We set $f_{min} = 1.01$ at lower levels, and $f_{min} = 0.9$ at the top most level. Leaf nodes (0-th level nodes) do not contribute any value. The problem with 81 bits with the global optimum of the value 324.0 was used.

4 Experimental Setup

For each problem, 20 runs have been executed, from which the following statistics were calculated:

- *MeanBest.* Mean *best-of-run* value calculated over the 20 independent runs.
- *StDev.* Standard deviation of the *best-of-run* values.
- *#Success.* A number of runs, in which the optimum solution was found.
- *WhenFound.* The average number of fitness evaluations needed to get the optimum solution.

Graphs showing (1) the evolution of the building block compactness and (2) the evolution of the best-so-far solution are generated to demonstrate the co-evolution of the chromosome structure and the quality of solution through the evolutionary process. Both the best-so-far fitness and the building block compactness show median values out of the 20 values in each generation.

The building block compactness is calculated as the average defining length of fundamental building blocks under the given chromosome structure with respect to the ringed representation implied by the 2-point crossover. For DF3 and DF3-intrl problem it shows an average defining length of 25 4-bit and 8 12-bit deceptive building blocks, respectively. In case of H-IFF problem, building blocks of 16 adjacent genes are considered. In case of H-TRAP problem, building blocks of 27 adjacent genes are considered. Four algorithms were compared:

- CoCR-GALCO. GALCO is used as the selecto-recombinative GA. The maximal diversity of the evolved population is forced by setting the convergence limit to 1. This means that the number of ones is within the interval $(PopSize/2-1, PopSize/2+1)$ at every position in the chromosome in any stage of the run.
- CoCR-SGA. CoCR using a standard genetic algorithm with bit flipping mutation applied to 1 bit per chromosome.
- GALCO-tight and GALCO-loose. GALCO operating on the chromosome of ideally organized genes (the most compact building blocks) and randomly chosen gene order, respectively. The gene order is static through the whole evolutionary process.

All algorithms used the same configuration: population size 500, 2-point crossover applied with a probability 1.0, tournament selection (n=4). Both variants of CoCR algorithm used *recalculation_step* 10 generations.

5 Experimental Results

Table 1 compares the observed performance characteristics of the algorithms. Results of CoCR algorithms are achieved with the number of columns of *links_table* set to 2. This means, that for each gene i a list of up to two genes with the strongest epistasis with gene i (i.e. *links_table* with $m = 2$) is considered in the process of building the chromosome structure. The results show that the performance of CoCR-GALCO lies between GALCO-loose and GALCO-tight and outperforms CoCR-SGA on all test problems. This is in agreement with our expectations. An interesting observation is that CoCR-GALCO perfectly solves DF3-intrl problem composed of high-order building blocks and scores even on the hierarchical problems.

Table 1. Comparisons on DF3, DF3-intrl, H-IFF, and H-TRAP

		CoCR-GALCO	CoCR-SGA	GALCO-tight	GALCO-loose
DF3	*#Success*	20	0	20	0
	WhenFound	122658	-	115444	-
	MeanBest	750.0	728.8	750.0	708.9
	StDev	0.0	4.6	0	4.7
DF3-intrl	*#Success*	20	0	20	1
	WhenFound	108754	-	53881	498698
	MeanBest	1440.0	1305.0	1440.0	1392.4
	StDev	0.0	13.7	0.0	28.6
H-IFF	*#Success*	3	0	20	0
	WhenFound	115211	-	42564	-
	MeanBest	876.8	625.8	1024.0	626.8
	StDev	71.5	54.6	0.0	58.1
H-TRAP	*#Success*	10	0	20	0
	WhenFound	85152	-	26968	-
	MeanBest	293.6	197.6	324.0	199.6
	StDev	31.2	19.3	0.0	11.7

Fig. 3 also illustrates the inability of CoCR-SGA to evolve the proper chromosome structure with tight linkage. This is because SGA, using simple bit flipping mutation, is not able to maintain sufficiently high population diversity in comparison to GALCO. The less diverse the population is, i.e. the fewer unique chromosomes contribute to *stats*, the less information CoCR has for identification of the pair-wise gene dependencies used to derive the proper chromosome

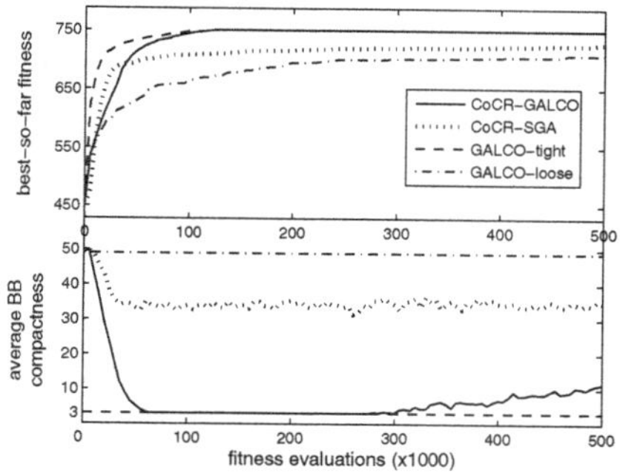

(a) DF3

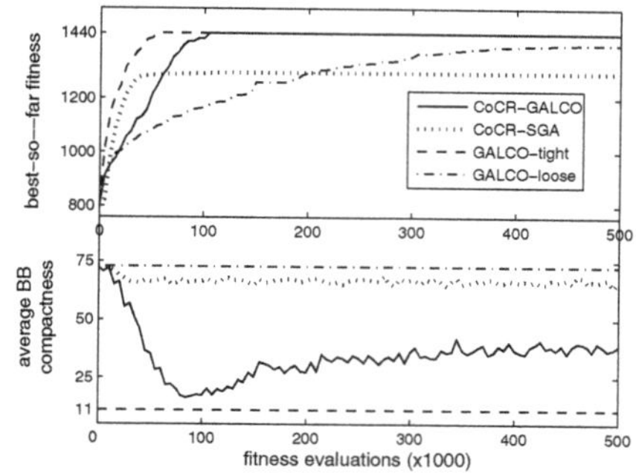

(b) DF3-intrl

Fig. 3. Mean convergence characteristics observed for different algorithms

Table 2. Results achieved for different sizes of *links_table*

	links_buffer	1	2	4	8
DF3	*#Success*	20	20	20	20
	WhenFound	141531	122658	122667	118522
	MeanBest	750.0	750.0	750.0	750.0
	StDev	0.0	0.0	0.0	0.0
DF3-intrl	*#Success*	9	20	20	20
	WhenFound	292447	108754	82501	85452
	MeanBest	1427.5	1440.0	1440.0	1440.0
	StDev	12.9	0.0	0.0	0.0
H-IFF	*#Success*	0	3	15	19
	WhenFound	-	115211	83714	61420
	MeanBest	763.2	876.8	992.0	1017.6
	StDev	52.9	71.5	56.9	28.6
H-TRAP	*#Success*	7	12	20	20
	WhenFound	105779	82303	42879	40234
	MeanBest	299.8	312.4	324.0	324.0
	StDev	21.3	18.7	0.0	0.0

structure. This is also the reason why the BB compactness eventually increases for CoCR-GALCO, as observed in Fig. 3 and Fig. 4. This happens when the optimal solution has already been found. As GALCO still tries to keep the population maximally diverse, it gets saturated with half-to-half the copies of the optimum and copies of the string that is a binary complement to the optimum. From such a two-valued set of strings any valid information about gene dependencies can not be obtained and the generated chromosome structure becomes partially randomized.

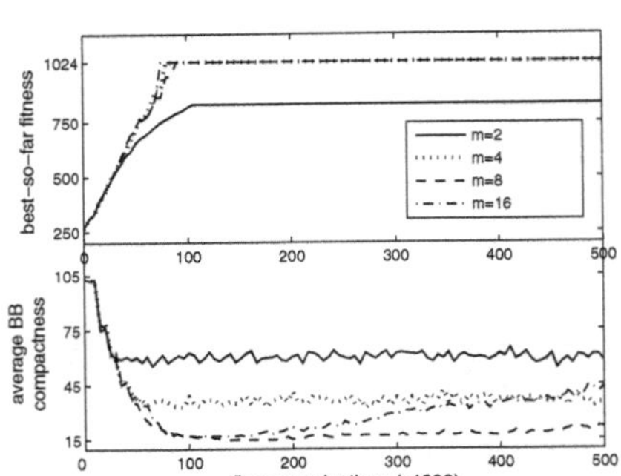

(a) H-IFF

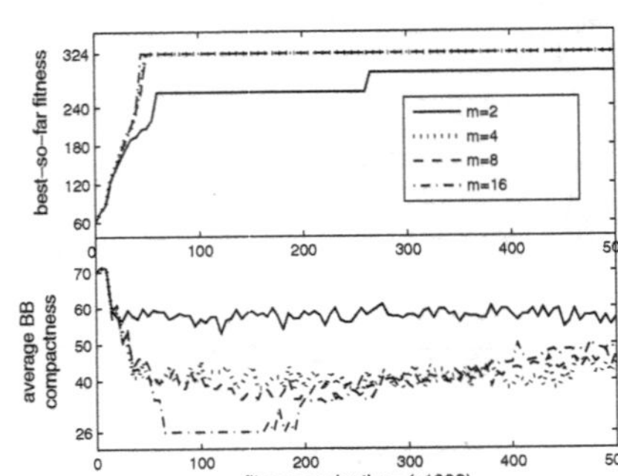

(b) H-TRAP

Fig. 4. Mean convergence characteristics observed for different sizes of *links_table*

Table 3. Chromosome structure evolution. An excerpt of one run when solving 32-bit H-IFF problem. Population size was 200. The optimal solution was found after 3264 fitness evaluations. G stands for the generation, BBC is the average BB compactness of given chromosome structure.

G	BBC	chromosome structure
1	26.0	10 21 7 25 15 4 24 27 30 16 12 18 20 26 22 9 2 19 23 17 11 8 31 29 0 1 3 6 13 5 28 14
2	27.0	1 20 14 25 17 21 7 0 22 3 5 6 28 9 27 13 12 31 4 26 11 15 10 8 29 16 19 24 2 18 23 30
3	26.5	1 14 16 25 7 4 26 20 22 30 5 21 24 12 27 31 19 10 2 15 11 8 17 29 0 9 3 6 18 28 23 13
4	28.0	21 1 7 23 2 30 3 27 25 4 12 31 22 29 13 28 8 10 15 24 9 17 11 26 5 20 19 6 16 18 0 14
5	25.0	13 7 23 3 4 8 10 0 25 12 27 11 17 29 9 28 30 6 1 24 31 22 20 26 19 21 5 18 16 15 2 14
16	9.0	26 27 25 24 21 20 23 22 3 2 0 1 4 5 6 7 8 9 10 11 13 12 14 15 16 18 17 19 29 28 30 31
17	7.0	4 5 6 7 3 2 0 1 19 18 17 16 22 23 20 21 26 27 25 24 31 30 29 28 11 10 8 9 12 13 14 15
18	9.0	3 2 0 1 28 29 30 31 7 6 5 4 11 10 8 9 13 12 14 15 19 17 16 18 21 20 22 23 26 27 25 24
19	7.0	23 22 20 21 25 24 26 27 31 30 28 29 10 11 9 8 15 14 12 13 4 5 6 7 1 0 2 3 19 18 17 16
20	9.0	28 29 30 31 12 13 15 14 7 6 5 4 0 1 2 3 10 11 8 9 18 19 17 16 23 22 21 20 26 27 25 24

Results in Table 2 and graphs in Fig. 4 show how the size m of *links_table* influences the performance of CoCR-GALCO. The general observation is that as the size m increases the better results in shorter time are achieved so that even the hierarchical problems are almost perfectly solved with $m = 8$. In other words, the more of the linkage information the construction algorithm can use the better results can be expected.

Table 3 illustrates the evolution of the chromosome structure for the 32-bit H-IFF problem. It shows that despite the last 5 generations were generated using the same linkage information stored in *links_table* they differ each other. This is due to the stochastic nature of the algorithm for generating the chromosome structure. Intuitively, such a variability may make the algorithm more robust when solving problems with complicated epistatic structure where the genes can not be arranged in a linear chromosome so that tight linkage of all strongly dependent genes are satisfied. In such cases, different chromosomes that neglect different dependencies can be generated each time.

6 Conclusions

The proposed CoCR algorithm identifies the pair-wise gene dependencies that are used to generate the proper chromosome structure on which standard recombination operators work. The chromosome structure changes every generation and the actual information about the inter-gene dependencies is calculated on-line through the run. The algorithm for construction of the chromosome structure uses a list of the most related genes to each gene. Thus, the generated chromosome can capture a structure of the problem with higher-order fundamental building blocks that can be efficiently processed then. Moreover, the chromosome reconfiguration that takes place every generation makes the algorithm more resistant against partial errors in the gene order. This was documented on problems with 12-bit building blocks as well as on hierarchical problems.

The results of the experiments suggest that this approach could be used for solving problems, where the epistatic structure is too complicated so that it is hard to find just one optimal arrangement of genes in the chromosome. The experiments presented in this paper illustrated the performance of the proposed algorithm on problems with uniformly scaled subfunctions. Future research should investigate applicability of this approach to problems with exponentially scaled subfunctions as well.

Acknowledgments. This research has been supported by the research program Information Society No. 1ET 101 210 513 "Relational machine learning for analysis of biomedical data", sponsored by Czech Academy of Sciences.

References

1. Goldberg, D.E., Korb, B. and Deb, K.: Messy genetic algorithms: Motivation, analysis and first results. Complex Systems 3(5), pp. 493–530, 1989.
2. Harik, G. and Goldberg, D. E.: Learning linkage. In *Foundations of Genetic Algorithms IV*, pp. 270–85. San Mateo: Morgan Kaufmann, 1997.
3. Harik, G.: Linkage learning via probabilistic modeling in the ECGA. IlliGAL Report N. 99010, University of Illinois at Urbana-Champaign, Urbana, IL, 1999.
4. Kubalik, J., Rothkrantz, L.J.M., Lazansky, J.: Genetic Algorithm with Limited Convergence. In Grana, M., Duro, R., d'Anjou, A., and Wang, P.P., (Eds.), Information Processing with Evolutionary Algorithms: From Industrial Applications to Academic Speculations. Springer-Verlag, ISBN: 1-85233-866-0, pp. 216-235. 2005.
5. Kwon, Y. K., Hong, S.D., Moon, B. R.: A Genetic Hybrid For Critical Heat Flux Function Approximation. In W. B. Langdon et al. (Eds.), Proceedings of GECCO 2002, Morgan Kaufmann Publishers, pp. 1119-1125, 2002.
6. Munetomo, M. and Goldberg, D. E.: Linkage identification by non-monotonicity detection for overlapping functions, Evolutionary Computation, Vol. 7, No. 4, pp. 377-398, 1999.
7. Pelikan, M., Muehlenbein, H.: The Bivariate Marginal Distribution Algorithm. In R. Roy, T. Furuhashi, and P. K. Chawdhry, (Eds.), Advances in Soft Computing - Engineering Design and Manufacturing, pp. 521-535, Springer-Verlag. 1999.
8. Pelikan, M., Goldberg, D. E., Cantu-Paz, E.: Linkage learning, estimation distribution, and Bayesian networks. Evolutionary Computation, 8(3), 314-341, 2000.
9. Pelikan, M., Goldberg, D. E.: Escaping hierarchical traps with competent genetic algorithms. In L. Spector et al. (Eds.), Proceedings of the GECCO–2001, pp. 511–518. Morgan Kaufmann, 2001.
10. Watson, R. A., Hornby, G. S., and Pollack, J. B.: Modeling Building-Block Interdependency. In *proceedings of Fifth International Conference PPSN V*, pp. 97–106. Springer, 1998.
11. Whitley, D.: Fundamental Principles of Deception in Genetic Search. In: *Foundations of Genetic Algorithms*. G. Rawlins (ed.), 221–241, Morgan Kaufmann, 1991.
12. Yu, T.-L., Goldberg, D. E.: Dependency Structure Matrix Analysis: Offline Utility of the Dependency Structure Matrix Genetic Algorithm. In K. Deb et al. (Eds.), Proceedings of GECCO 2004, pp. 355-366, Springer Berlin/Heidelberg, 2004.

Exploiting Expert Knowledge in Genetic Programming for Genome-Wide Genetic Analysis

Jason H. Moore and Bill C. White

Computational Genetics Laboratory, Department of Genetics, Dartmouth Medical School, Lebanon, NH, USA
{Jason.H.Moore, Bill.C.White}@Dartmouth.edu
http://www.epistasis.org

Abstract. Human genetics is undergoing an information explosion. The availability of chip-based technology facilitates the measurement of thousands of DNA sequence variation from across the human genome. The challenge is to sift through these high-dimensional datasets to identify combinations of interacting DNA sequence variations that are predictive of common diseases. The goal of this paper was to develop and evaluate a genetic programming (GP) approach for attribute selection and modeling that uses expert knowledge such as Tuned ReliefF (TuRF) scores during selection to ensure trees with good building blocks are recombined and reproduced. We show here that using expert knowledge to select trees performs as well as a multiobjective fitness function but requires only a tenth of the population size. This study demonstrates that GP may be a useful computational discovery tool in this domain.

1 Introduction

Genetic programming (GP) is an automated computational discovery tool that is inspired by Darwinian evolution and natural selection [1-7]. Genetic programming and its many variations have been applied successfully to a wide range of different problems including data mining and knowledge discovery [e.g. 8]. Despite the many successes, there are a large number of challenges that GP practitioners and theorists must address before this general computational discovery tool becomes a standard in the modern problem solver's toolbox. Yu et al. [9] list 22 such challenges. Several of these are addressed by the present study. First, is GP useful for the analysis of large and high-dimensional datasets? Second, what is the best way to use pre-processing? Finally, what is the best way to incorporate domain-specific knowledge? The goal of this paper is to explore the feasibility of using GP for genome-wide genetic analysis in the domain of human genetics.

1.1 The Problem Domain: Human Genetics

Biological and biomedical sciences are undergoing an information explosion and an understanding implosion. This is especially true in the domain of human genetics

T.P. Runarsson et al. (Eds.): PPSN IX, LNCS 4193, pp. 969–977, 2006.

where it is now technically and economically feasible to measure thousands of DNA sequence variations from across the human genome. For the purposes of this paper we will focus exclusively on the single nucleotide polymorphism or SNP which is a single nucleotide or point in the DNA sequence that differs among people. It is anticipated that at least one SNP occurs approximately every 100 nucleotides across the $3*10^9$ nucleotide human genome. An important goal in human genetics is to determine which of the many thousands of SNPs are useful for predicting who is at risk for common diseases. This 'genome-wide' approach is expected to revolutionize the genetic analysis of common human diseases.

The charge for computer science and bioinformatics is to develop algorithms for the detection and characterization of those SNPs that are predictive of human health and disease. Success in this genome-wide endeavor will be difficult due to nonlinearity in the genotype-to-phenotype mapping relationship that is due, in part, to epistasis or nonadditive gene-gene interactions. The implication of epistasis from a data mining point of view is that SNPs need to be considered jointly in learning algorithms rather than individually. The challenge of modeling attribute interactions has been previously described [10]. Due to the combinatorial magnitude of this problem, intelligent feature selection strategies are needed.

1.2 Concept Difficulty

Combining the difficulty of modeling nonlinear attribute interactions with the challenge of attribute selection yields for this domain what Goldberg [11] calls a *needle-in-a-haystack* problem. That is, there may be a particular combination of SNPs that together with the right nonlinear function are a significant predictor of disease susceptibility. However, individually they may not look any different than thousands of other SNPs that are not involved in the disease process and are thus noisy. Under these models, the learning algorithm is truly looking for a genetic needle in a genomic haystack. A recent report from the International HapMap Consortium [12] suggests that approximately 300,000 carefully selected SNPs may be necessary to capture all of the relevant variation across the Caucasian human genome. Assuming this is true (it is probably a lower bound), we would need to scan $4.5 * 10^{10}$ pairwise combinations of SNPs to find a genetic needle. The number of higher order combinations is astronomical. Is GP suitable for a problem like this? At face value the answer is no. There is no reason to expect that a GP or any other wrapper method would perform better than a random attribute selector because there are no building blocks for this problem when accuracy is used as the fitness measure. The fitness of any given classifier would look no better than any other with just one of the two correct SNPs in the model. Indeed, we have observed this in our preliminary work [13,14].

The goal of the present study was to develop and evaluate a GP approach to genetic analysis in the context of genome-wide data. Given the concept difficulty, we are generally interested in using expert knowledge to facilitate the generation and exploitation of good building blocks. We specifically address whether pre-processed expert knowledge is useful for selecting trees for recombination and reproduction.

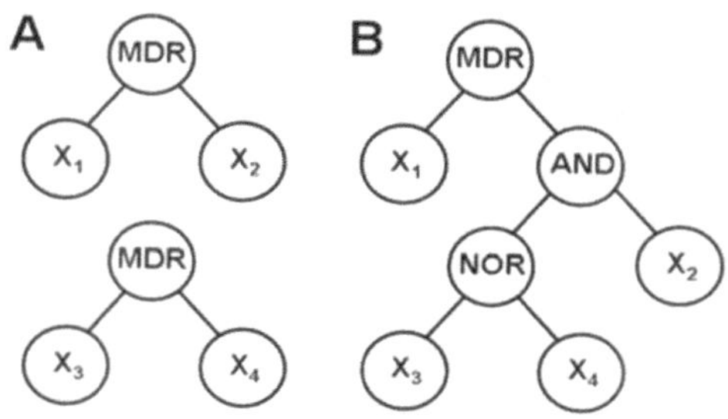

Fig. 1. Example GP trees for solutions (A). Example of a more complex tree that will be considered in future studies (B).

2 Genetic Programming Methods

Figure 1A illustrates an example GP tree for this problem. We have intentionally kept the initial solution representation simple with one function in the root node and two children to evaluate the best GP parameterization. More complex trees (e.g. Figure 1B) will be explored once we understand when and how the GP works with the simpler trees. We have selected the multifactor dimensionality reduction or MDR approach as an attribute constructor for the function set because it is able to capture interaction information (see Section 3). Each tree has two leaves or terminals consisting of attributes. The terminal set consists of 1000 attributes.

The fitness function used in this study was accuracy estimated using a naïve Bayes classifier. Each tree is resolved as a constructed attribute using the MDR function in the root node. It is this single constructed attribute with two levels that is assessed using the classifier. The classification accuracy of a tree is its fitness.

The goal of this study was to use expert knowledge to ensure good building blocks are exploited by the GP through selection. Here, we used pre-processed attribute quality from the Tuned ReliefF (TuRF) algorithm as our expert knowledge (see Section 4). The default selection method used a simple binary tournament. We modified this selection operator by first selecting the top 1% or 5% of trees according their maximum TuRF score. Each possible pair of these selected trees was recombined and the children passed on to the next population. For example, with a population size of 500 either 5 or 25 trees were selected. There are 5 choose 2 (10) and 25 choose 2 (300) possible recombination events. Thus, the new population consisted of either 10 or 300 recombined trees generated from those with the maximum TuRF scores. The remaining 490 or 200 individuals in the population were generated using the standard binary tournament operator. This new selection operator ensures that the best trees are selected and recombined as measured by pre-processed expert knowledge. Generating the remaining trees by binary tournament ensure that functional attributes not assigned a high quality by TuRF still have a chance of being evaluated.

For this study, we used a population size of 500 and ran the GP for 10 generations. We used a crossover probability of 0.9 and a mutation probability of 0. Since each tree has exactly two attributes, an initial population size of 500 trees will include 1,000 total attributes. Each initial population was generated such that each of the 1,000 attributes (i.e. terminals) was represented once and only once across the 500 trees. This ensures that all building blocks are represented. However, it is important to note that the probability of any one tree receiving both functional attributes (i.e. the solution) is 0.001 * 0.001 or 10^{-6}. Thus, it is unlikely that any one tree in the initial population will be the correct solution. The size of the search space is approximately 500,000 or 1000 choose 2. With a population size of 500 and 10 generations the GP is exploring a maximum of 1% of the search space. The GP was implemented in C++ using GAlib (http://lancet.mit.edu/ga/). The crossover operator was modified to ensure binary trees of depth one.

3 Multifactor Dimensionality Reduction (MDR) for Attribute Construction

Multifactor dimensionality reduction (MDR) was developed as a nonparametric and genetic model-free data mining strategy for identifying combination of SNPs that are predictive of a discrete clinical endpoint [15-17]. The MDR method has been successfully applied to detecting gene-gene interactions for a variety of common human diseases including, for example, adverse drug reactions [18]. At the heart of the MDR approach is an attribute construction algorithm that creates a new attribute by pooling genotypes from multiple SNPs. Constructive induction using the MDR kernel is accomplished in the following way. Given a threshold *T*, a multilocus genotype combination is considered high-risk if the ratio of cases (subjects with disease) to controls (healthy subjects) exceeds *T*, else it is considered low-risk. Genotype combinations considered to be high-risk are labeled G_1 while those considered low-risk are labeled G_0. This process constructs a new one-dimensional attribute with levels G_0 and G_1. It is this new single variable that is returned by the MDR function in the GP function set. The MDR method is described in more detail by Moore et al. [17]. Open-source software in Java and C are freely available from www.epistasis.org.

4 Expert Knowledge from Tuned ReliefF (TuRF)

Our goal was to provide an external measure of attribute quality that could be used as expert knowledge by the GP. Here, this external measure used was statistical but could just as easily be biological, for example. There are many different statistical and computational methods for determining the quality of attributes. Our goal was to identify a method that is capable of identifying attributes that predict class primarily through dependencies or interactions with other attributes. Kira and Rendell [19] developed an algorithm called Relief that is capable of detecting attribute dependencies. Relief estimates the quality of attributes through a type of nearest neighbor algorithm that selects neighbors (instances) from the same class and from the different class based on the vector of values across attributes. Weights (W) or quality estimates for each attribute (A) are estimated based on whether the nearest neighbor (nearest hit, H) of a randomly selected instance (R) from the same class and the nearest neighbor from the other class (nearest miss, M) have the same or different values. This process of adjusting weights is repeated for m instances. The algorithm produces weights for each attribute ranging from -1 (worst) to +1 (best). Kononenko [20] improved upon Relief by choosing *n* nearest neighbors instead of just one. This new ReliefF algorithm has been shown to be more robust to noisy attributes [21] and is widely used in data mining applications.

We have developed a modified ReliefF algorithm for the domain of human genetics called Tuned ReliefF (TuRF). We have previously shown that TuRF is significantly better than ReliefF in this domain [22]. The TuRF algorithm systematically removes attributes that have low quality estimates so that the ReliefF values if the remaining attributes can be re-estimated. We applied TuRF as described by Moore and White [22] to each dataset.

5 Data Simulation and Analysis

The goal of the simulation study is to generate artificial datasets with high concept difficulty to evaluate the power of GP in the domain of human genetics. We first developed 30 different penetrance functions (i.e. genetic models) that define a probabilistic relationship between genotype and phenotype where susceptibility to disease is dependent on genotypes from two SNPs in the absence of any independent effects. The 30 penetrance functions include groups of five with heritabilities of 0.025, 0.05, 0.1, 0.2, 0.3, or 0.4. These heritabilities range from a very small to a large genetic effect size. Each functional SNP had two alleles with frequencies of 0.4 and 0.6. Table 1 summarizes the penetrance values to three significant digits for one of the 30 models. The values in parentheses are the genotype frequencies. Each of the 30 models was used to generate 100 replicate datasets with a sample size of 1600. Each dataset consisted of an equal number of case (disease) and control (no disease) subjects. Each pair of functional SNPs was combined within a genome-wide set of 998 randomly generated SNPs for a total of 1000 attributes. A total of 3,000 datasets were generated and analyzed.

Table 1. Penetrance values for an example epistasis model

	AA (0.25)	*Aa* (0.50)	*aa* (0.25)
BB (0.25)	0.137	0.484	0.187
Bb (0.50)	0.482	0.166	0.365
bb (0.25)	0.193	0.361	0.430

For each set of 100 datasets we counted the number of times the correct two functional attributes were selected as the best model by the GP. This count, expressed as a percentage, is an estimate of the power of the method. That is, how often does GP find the right answer that we know is there?

6 Experimental Results

Figure 2 summarizes the average power for each method and each heritability level. Each bar in the barplots represents the power averaged over the five different models

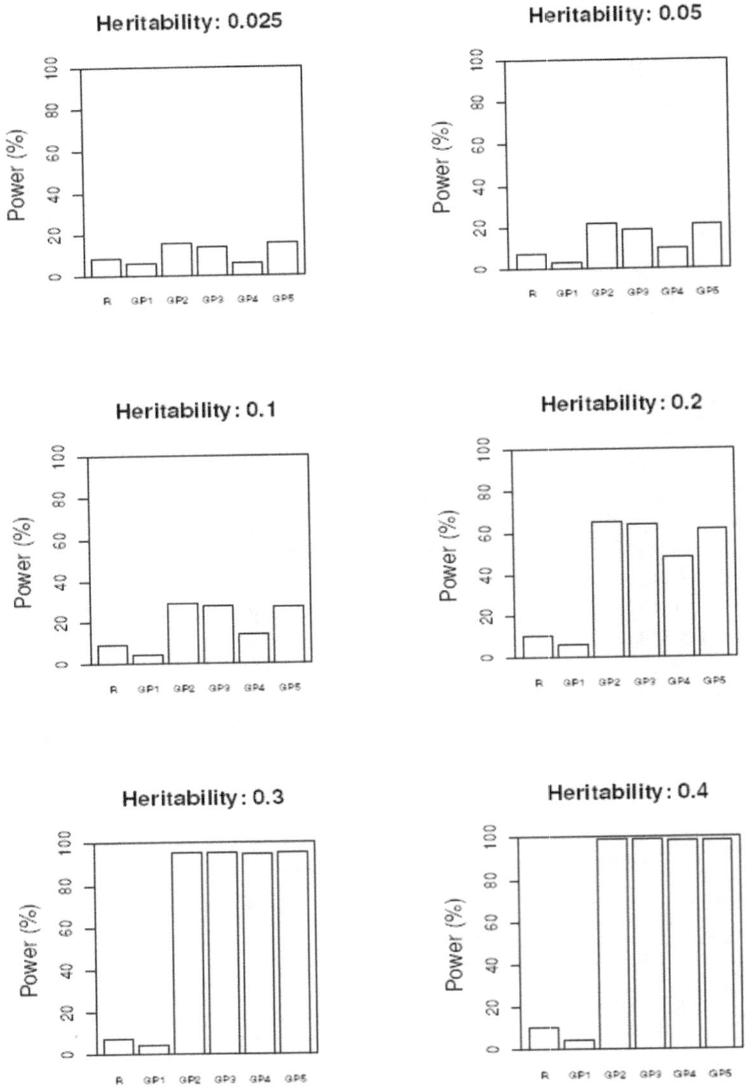

Fig. 2. Summary of the power of Random Search (R) and different GP strategies using random initialization with accuracy for fitness (GP1), random initialization with accuracy and TuRF for fitness (GP2), random initialization with TuRF weighted twice that of accuracy in the fitness function (GP3), systematic initialization with TuRF for selection (1%) and accuracy for fitness (GP4), and systematic initialization with TuRF for selection (5%) and accuracy for fitness (GP5)

for each of the heritabilities. Here, power represents the number of times out of 100 replicates the GP found the right two attributes (SNPs). The first bar (labeled R) represents the average power for a random search that evaluated 5,000 randomly generated trees. The next three bars represent 1) the power observed by Moore and

White [14] for GP using randomly initialized trees and accuracy as a fitness function (GP1), 2) the power observed by Moore and White [14] for GP using randomly initialized trees and a multiobjective fitness function weighting accuracy and TuRF score equally (GP2), and 3) the power observed by Moore and White [14] for GP using randomly initialized trees and a multiobjective fitness function weighting TuRF twice as much as accuracy. These previously published results used a GP with a population size of 5,000 evolved for 10 generations. These results clearly demonstrate the value of utilizing TuRF as expert knowledge in the fitness function.

How does using TuRF for selection compare with using TuRF as part of the fitness function? The last two bars represent the results from the present study. The bar labeled GP4 summarizes the average power of our modified selection method that selects 1% of the best trees as measured by TuRF for systematic recombination. The bar labeled GP5 summarizes the average power of our modified selection method that selects 5% of the best trees as measured by TuRF for systematic recombination. For the lower heritabilities GP5 had higher power than GP4. Interestingly, GP5 had approximately the same power as GP2 and GP3 that used TuRF in the fitness function. This is important because the results from the TuRF-based selection methods used a population size of 500 while the previous results were generated using a population size of 5,000 with the same number of generations. Thus, using expert knowledge for selection had the same power as using it for fitness but required 1/10 the population size (i.e. number of evaluations). This is a significant improvement in performance.

7 Discussion and Conclusion

There are several important conclusions from this study. First, expert knowledge provides the building blocks that are necessary to find the genetic needle in the genomic haystack. Second, using expert knowledge to guide selection may be preferable to using it in a fitness function in this domain.

Stochastic search algorithms such as GP are appealing for the genome-wide genetic analysis problem because the search space is astronomical and the fitness landscape is rugged, perhaps even resembling a needle in a haystack. Enumerative approaches aren't computationally feasible and hill-climbers will get lost in the local structure of the fitness landscape. Is a stochastic approach like GP useful for this type of problem? Is it better than a simple random search? Based on the results of our previous work [13,14] and the results of the present study, we would argue that GP is useful for the analysis of complex genetic datasets only when building blocks are present. When building blocks are not present or are poorly defined a GP may not perform any better than a random search. This is consistent with our previous experiments in this domain [13,14]. This is also consistent with the idea of a competent genetic algorithm (cGA) reviewed by Goldberg [11]. Goldberg argues that understanding and exploiting building blocks (schemata) is essential to the success of GAs and by extension to GP [23]. There are two important issues here. The first issue is to make sure the building blocks needed to construct good solutions are present. The second is to make sure the good building blocks are used and exploited during evolution. We used a systematic approach to ensure all attributes (i.e. the raw materials) are present in the initial population. We then used pre-processing of the quality of the attributes to establish building blocks that otherwise don't exist.

There are multiple different sources of information that could be used as expert knowledge in a GP. In this study, we used a statistical measure of attribute quality. However, future work needs to explore ways to include domain specific knowledge in the GP. There are a number of different public databases available to geneticists that could be mined for expert knowledge. For example, the PubMed database (http://www.ncbi.nlm.nih.gov/entrez/query.fcgi?db=PubMed) from the U.S. National Library of Medicine holds over 16 million citations from life science journal articles. There are a number of computational algorithms and tools available now for extracting information such as the co-occurrence of keywords from abstracts from the PubMed database [24]. If two genes co-occur frequently in journal abstracts then one could infer that there is a functional relationship. This type of information could be used to guide a GP search for combinations of SNPs that predict disease.

The availability of domain-specific expert knowledge raises the question of the best way to use it in a GP. This is a topic that has received some attention in recent years. Jin [25] covers the use of expert knowledge in population initialization, recombination, mutation, selection, reproduction, multi-objective fitness functions, and human-computer interaction, for example. We focused in this study exclusively on sensible (i.e. systematic) initialization and selection.

This study presents preliminary evidence suggesting that GP might be useful for the genome-wide genetic analysis of common human diseases that have a complex genetic architecture. These results raise numerous questions, some of which have been discussed here. It will be important to extend this study to higher-order genetic models. How well does GP do when faced with finding three, four, or more SNPs that interact in a nonlinear manner to predict disease susceptibility? How does extending the function set to additional attribute construction functions impact performance? How does extending the attribute set impact performance? Is using GP better than available or similar filter approaches? To what extent can GP theory help formulate an optimal GP approach to this problem? Does GP outperform other evolutionary or non-evolutionary search methods? This paper provides a starting point to begin addressing some of these questions.

Acknowledgements. This work was supported by National Institutes of Health (USA) grants LM009012, AI59694, HD047447, RR018787, and HL65234.

References

1. Koza, J.R. Genetic Programming: On the Programming of Computers by Means of Natural Selection. The MIT Press (1992).
2. Koza, J.R. Genetic Programming II: Automatic Discovery of Reusable Programs. The MIT Press (1994).
3. Koza, J.R., Bennett III, F.H., Andre, D., Keane, M.A. Genetic Programming III: Darwinian Invention and Problem Solving. Morgan Kaufmann (1999).
4. Koza, J.R., Keane, M.A., Streeter, M.J., Mydlowec, W., Yu, J., Lanza, G. Genetic Programming IV: Routine Human-Competitive Machine Intelligence. Springer (2003).

5. Banzhaf, W., Nordin, P., Keller, R.E., Francone, F.D. Genetic Programming: An Introduction : On the Automatic Evolution of Computer Programs and Its Applications. Morgan Kaufmann Publishers (1998).
6. Langdon, W.B. Genetic Programming and Data Structures: Genetic Programming + Data Structures = Automatic Programming!. Kluwer (1998).
7. Langdon, WB, Poli, R. Foundations of Genetic Programming. Springer (2002).
8. Freitas, A. Data Mining and Knowledge Discovery with Evolutionary Algorithms. Springer (2002).
9. Yu, T., Riolo, R., Worzel, B. Genetic programming: Theory and practice. In: Yu, T., Riolo, R., Worzel, B. (Eds.). Genetic Programming Theory and Practice III. Springer (2006).
10. Freitas, A., Understanding the crucial role of attribute interactions. Artificial Intelligence Review 16:177-199 (2001).
11. Goldberg, D.E. The Design of Innovation. Kluwer (2002).
12. Altshuler D, Brooks LD, Chakravarti A, Collins FS, Daly MJ, Donnelly P; International HapMap Consortium. A haplotype map of the human genome. Nature 437:1299-1320 (2005).
13. White, B.C., Gilbert, J.C., Reif, D.M., Moore, J.H. A statistical comparison of grammatical evolution strategies in the domain of human genetics. Proceedings of the IEEE Congress on Evolutionary Computing, 676-682 (2005).
14. Moore, J.H., White, B.C. Genome-wide genetic analysis using genetic programming: The critical need for expert knowledge. In: Genetic Programming Theory and Practice IV. Springer, in press (2006).
15. Ritchie, M.D., Hahn, L.W., Roodi, N., Bailey, L.R., Dupont, W.D., Parl, F.F., Moore, J.H. Multifactor dimensionality reduction reveals high-order interactions among estrogen metabolism genes in sporadic breast cancer. American Journal of Human Genetics 69, 138-147 (2001).
16. Moore, J.H. Computational analysis of gene-gene interactions in common human diseases using multifactor dimensionality reduction. Expert Review of Molecular Diagnostics 4, 795-803 (2004).
17. Moore, J.H., Gilbert, J.C., Tsai, C.-T., Chiang, F.T., Holden, W., Barney, N., White, B.C. A flexible computational framework for detecting, characterizing, and interpreting statistical patterns of epistasis in genetic studies of human disease susceptibility. Journal of Theoretical Biology, in press (2006).
18. Wilke RA, Reif DM, Moore JH. Combinatorial pharmacogenetics. Nature Reviews Drug Discovery 4:911-918 (2005).
19. Kira, K., Rendell, L.A. A practical approach to feature selection. In: Machine Learning: Proceedings of the AAAI'92 (1992).
20. Kononenko, I. Estimating attributes: analysis and extension of Relief. Machine Learning: ECML-94 (1994) 171-182.
21. Robnik-Šikonja, M., Kononenko, I. Theoretical and empirical analysis of ReliefF and RReliefF. Machine Learning 53 (2003) 23-69.
22. Moore, J.H., White, B.C. Tuning ReliefF for genome-wide genetic analysis. Submitted.
23. Sastry K., Goldberg, D.E. Probabilistic model building and competent genetic programming. In: Riolo, R., Worzel, B. (Eds.) Genetic Programming Theory and Practice. Kluwer (2003).
24. Jensen LJ, Saric J, Bork P. Literature mining for the biologist: from information retrieval to biological discovery. Nature Reviews Genetics 7:119-129 (2006).
25. Jin, Y. Knowledge Incorporation in Evolutionary Computation. Springer (2005).

Speeding Up Evolutionary Algorithms Through Restricted Mutation Operators

Benjamin Doerr[1], Nils Hebbinghaus[1], and Frank Neumann[2]

[1] Max-Planck-Institut für Informatik, 66123 Saarbrücken, Germany
[2] Institut für Informatik und Praktische Mathematik,
Christian-Albrechts-Universität zu Kiel, 24098 Kiel, Germany

Abstract. We investigate the effect of restricting the mutation operator in evolutionary algorithms with respect to the runtime behavior. For the Eulerian cycle problem; we present runtime bounds on evolutionary algorithms with a restricted operator that are much smaller than the best upper bounds for the general case. It turns out that a plateau that both algorithms have to cope with is left faster by the new algorithm. In addition, we present a lower bound for the unrestricted algorithm which shows that the restricted operator speeds up computation by at least a linear factor.

1 Introduction

Evolutionary algorithms (EAs) are randomized search heuristics, that have shown to be very successful in solving problems from combinatorial optimization as well as producing good solutions in real world applications. Especially in the case of real world applications often little is known about the structure of the problem and a standard evolutionary approach achieves good results.

In the case of combinatorial optimization problems frequently much more is known about the structure of a considered problem. Hence, EAs that are designed for the particular problem achieve better results than a standard evolutionary approach. Raidl et al. [9] have recently shown that NP-hard spanning tree problems can be solved much easier by using a mutation operator that chooses edges with a small weight much more often for inclusion in a mutation step than heavier edges. They have shown that minimum spanning trees can be computed by an evolutionary algorithm within a runtime bound that is of the same magnitude as the best deterministic algorithms such as Kruskal and Prim for the mentioned problem. This result also shows that a sophisticated mutation operator can speed up computations drastically compared with a standard evolutionary approach analyzed by Neumann and Wegener [8].

In this paper, we consider a restricted mutation operator for the Eulerian cycle problem and examine the effect of the restriction on the runtime of the algorithms. The analysis of EAs with respect to their runtime behavior has become very popular in recent years. Starting with results on the optimization of pseudo boolean objective functions a lot of results have been obtained by now. First results consider the behavior of this class of randomized search heuristics

T.P. Runarsson et al. (Eds.): PPSN IX, LNCS 4193, pp. 978–987, 2006.

on special functions that explain the behavior of evolutionary algorithms in different situations. One important issue is to analyze how evolutionary algorithms can cope with plateaus. Plateaus are regions in a search space where all search points have the same fitness. If such a plateau is large the search process frequently becomes difficult. Note that the number of different fitness values is often polynomial bounded in the input size whereas the number of search points is exponential. Then a pigeon hole argument implies that many search points have the same fitness. Plateaus have been for the first time examined by Jansen and Wegener [3] with respect to their impact on the runtime of an EA. They have investigated the effect of the structure of a plateau with respect to the runtime behavior of a simple evolutionary algorithm.

Since 2002 a lot of results concerning the runtime behavior of EAs on combinatorial optimization problems have been obtained. There are results on some of the best-known polynomial solvable problems such as sorting and shortest path (Scharnow, Tinnefeld, and Wegener [10]), maximum matchings (Giel and Wegener [1]), and minimum spanning trees (Neumann and Wegener [8]). In the case of NP-hard problems the first results have been achieved for the multi-objective minimum spanning tree problem (Neumann [6]) and a scheduling problem on two identical machines (Witt [11]).

For the Eulerian Cycle problem Neumann [7] has shown that a simple EA produces a Eulerian cycle of a Eulerian graph in expected number of $O(m^5)$ steps if a jump operator is used for mutation. In contrast to this the expected optimization time gets exponential if the mutation operator is changed to exchange operations. This is one of the first results on the runtime behavior of evolutionary algorithms that deal with the important representation of permutations. This kind of representation is important for many important NP-hard combinatorial optimization problems such as the traveling salesman problem (see e.g. Michalewicz and Fogel [5] for different evolutionary approaches to solve this problem) or a wide class of scheduling problems (see e.g. Mattfeld and Bierwirth [4]). The analysis of Neumann [7] shows that jumps lead for his model to a plateau of constant fitness that can be left in a polynomial number of steps. Whereas in the case of exchange operations this plateau changes to local optima with a large inferior neighborhood.

The aim of this paper is to show that a restricted jump operator can speed up computations of an evolutionary algorithms. EAs often do steps that only waste time. This is the price a general search heuristic usually pays in contrast to a specialized algorithm. Restricting the mutation operator to the considered problem can shorten the time until a desired step occurs. In addition such a restriction can change the behavior of an EA on a plateau. We will show that a restricted version of the jump operator leads to an EA that computes a Eulerian cycle of an Eulerian graph in an expected number of $O(m^3)$ steps. In addition we present an example graph which shows that our analysis is tight.

After having motivated our work, we introduce the model of the Eulerian cycle that will be analyzed in Section 2. In Section 3 we introduce restricted version of simple evolutionary algorithms that will be analyzed with respect to their runtime behavior. To show the advantages of these restriction we give lower bounds on the corresponding more general algorithms in Section 4 and present a runtime analysis of the restricted algorithms in Section 5. We finish with some conclusions.

2 Preliminaries

The Eulerian cycle problem can be seen as the first problem in graph theory. Proposed by Euler in 1736 as the famous Seven Bridges problem, its generalization can be described as follows and is known as the Eulerian cycle problem.

Given an undirected connected graph $G = (V, E)$ on n vertices and m edges, compute a cycle such that every edge is used exactly once. Euler proved that such a tour exists if and only if the degree of each vertex is even. Graphs that contain a Eulerian cycle are called Eulerian. In the remainder of this paper we assume that all graphs are Eulerian.

For every $n \in \mathbb{N}$ let us define $[n] := \{k \in \mathbb{N} : 1 \leq k \leq n\}$. We define the search space

$$S_m := \{\pi : [m] \to E \mid \pi \text{ is a bijection}\}.$$

S_m contains all permutations of the edges of G. Thus, a search point $\pi \in S_m$ corresponds to an order of the edges of G. Looking at the edges $\pi(1), \pi(2), \ldots, \pi(m)$ we can determine a longest path $p = \pi(1)\pi(2)\ldots\pi(l)$ for an appropriate $l \leq m$ such that it holds $\pi(i) \cap \pi(i+1) \neq \emptyset$ for all $i \in [l-1]$ and $\pi(l) \cap \pi(l+1) = \emptyset$. If $l = m$ the permutation π corresponds to a Eulerian tour. We formalize this in the following fitness function. For convenience we set $\pi(m+1) = \emptyset$ and choose $\pi(0)$ as a fixed one-element subset of $\pi(1) \setminus \pi(2)$. Define:

$$\text{path}(\pi) := 1 + \max\{\text{k} \in [\text{m}] \mid \forall \text{i} \in [\text{k}] : \pi(\text{i}) \subseteq \pi(\text{i}-1) \cup \pi(\text{i}+1)\}.$$

In the rest of this paper the path $\pi(1)\pi(2)\ldots\pi(\text{path}(\pi))$ will be named by p. The fitness function describes the processing order to use the edges for a tour starting with the edge on position 1. Another advantage of this fitness function is that it can be easily evaluated. If the resulting path is short most of the edges in the permutation do not have to be considered.

For the Eulerian cycle problem algorithms have been designed that compute a Eulerian cycle in linear time. To analyze randomized search heuristics we use the knowledge that has been put into these algorithms. The following algorithm proposed by Hierholzer [2] computes an Eulerian cycle of a given Eulerian graph G and contains ideas which will be later used in the analysis of our algorithms.

Algorithm 1 (Eulerian Cycle)

1. *Find a cycle C in G*
2. *Delete the edges of C from G*
3. *If G is not empty go to step 1.*
4. *Construct the Eulerian cycle from the cycles produced in step 1.*

Neumann [7] has shown that simple randomized search heuristics are able to compute a Eulerian cycle of a Eulerian graph in expected polynomial time if a mutation operator is used that uses jump operators. The expected optimization change drastically, i.e. from polynomial to exponential, if one chooses exchange operations instead of jumps.

3 Randomized Local Search and the (1+1) EA

Randomized local search (RLS) and the (1+1) EA are perhaps the simplest randomized search heuristics that can be considered. They work on a population of size 1 and only use mutation to produce one single new individual in each generation. We consider variants of RLS and the (1+1) EA that are similar to the ones discussed by Neumann [7] for the Eulerian cycle problem. The difference is that the algorithms considered here work with a more restricted mutation operator. EAs often waste time by doing many steps that are not accepted. Our aim is to show that such a restriction of the mutation operator can speed up computations and to show how the structure of a combinatorial optimization problem can change from the EAs point of view because of such a restriction. The algorithms considered use a restricted jump operator for mutation. Jump operators have also been discussed by Scharnow, Tinnefeld, and Wegener [10] for the sorting problem. In the case of restricted jumps a jump operation *jump*(i) executed on a permutation π produces a new permutation π' by putting the element on position i at position 1 and shifting the remaining elements to the right. This restricted operator differs from the general jump operator that chooses two positions i and j in the permutation and puts the element at position i at position j while shifting the elements between into the appropriate direction. For RLS in one mutation step exactly one jump operation is executed. The executed jump is chosen according to the uniform distribution. We can describe the restricted version of RLS as follows.

Algorithm 2 (Randomized Local Search (restricted) (RLS$_r$))
1. *Choose* $\pi \in S_m$ *uniformly at random.*
2. *Choose* $i \in [m]$ *uniformly at random and define* π' *by jumping the element at position* i *to position* 1 *and shifting the elements between position* 1 *and position* i *one position to the right.*
3. *Replace* π *by* π' *if* $\text{path}(\pi') \geq \text{path}(\pi)$.
4. *Repeat Steps 2 and 3 forever.*

Evolutionary algorithms use a mutation operator where more than one operation is possible in a mutation step. The (1+1) EA using the encoding of permutations is adopted from the well-known (1+1) ES (evolution strategy) and differs from RLS by the chosen mutation operator.

Algorithm 3 (Mutation operator of (1+1) EA$_r$)

2') *Define* π' *in the following way. Choose* s *according to a Poisson distribution with parameter* $\lambda = 1$ *and perform sequentially* $s + 1$ *restricted jump operations to produce* π' *from* π.

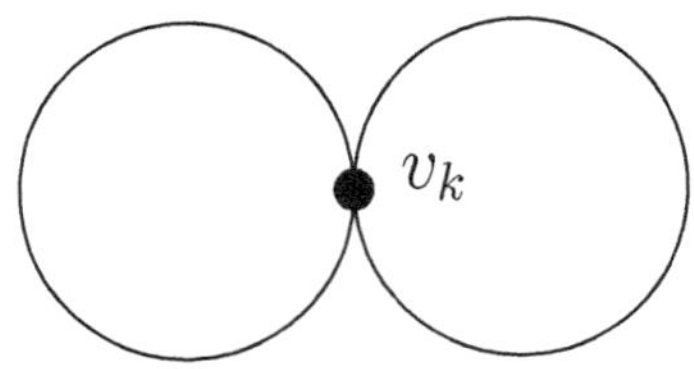

Fig. 1. Instance G_m: Two cycles of length $m/2$ sharing one vertex

In applications, we need a stopping criterion. For theoretical investigations it is a common use to investigate the number of fitness evaluations until an optimal solution has been achieved. This is called the runtime of the algorithm. Often the expectation of this value is considered which is called the expected optimization time of the considered algorithms.

The algorithms introduced here will be compared with variants called RLS and (1+1) EA that use the general jump operator. RLS and (1+1) EA have already been analyzed with respect to their runtime behavior on the Eulerian cycle problem. We will compare the results obtained for these algorithms with our results on the restricted versions.

4 A Lower Bound for RLS and the (1+1) EA

We consider RLS and the (1+1) EA with the general mutation operator in this section. Neumann [7] has proven that both algorithms need in expectation at most $O(m^5)$ steps until they compute a Eulerian cycle of a Eulerian graph. We now show that both algorithms need at least $\Omega(m^4)$ steps to find a Eulerian cycle.

Without loss of generality, let m be a multiple of 8. Consider the example graph G_m given in Figure 1, which consists of two cycles of length $m/2$ that are share exactly one vertex v_k.

Theorem 1. *The expected optimization time of RLS and the (1+1) EA on the graph G_m is lower bounded by $\Omega(m^4)$.*

Proof. Let us consider the situation for RLS where $|p| \geq 3$ for the first time. With probability $1 - o(1)$ all edges of p belong to only one of the two cycles of G_m. W. l. o. g. we may assume that p is contained in C. The first possibility that an edge of the other cycle C' can be integrated in the path p is given if v_k is the first vertex of p. Before one of the edges of C' adjacent to v_k is integrated in p, p cannot contain any other edge of C'. But with probability 1/3 (under the condition that the first small path is contained in C), the two edges of C adjacent to v_k are integrated in p before one of the two edges of C' adjacent with v_k is contained in p. If this is the case, there is a moment where the current path p is the cycle C. The expected time until C has been produced is upper bound by $O(m^3)$ as the path has to be lengthened at most $m/2$ times and the expected waiting time for such a mutation step is $O(m^2)$. Thus, with probability $1/3-o(1)$ there is a moment where p is one of the two cycles (w. l. o. g. C), and until that moment no edge of C' was contained in p. Let us denote the first vertex of the path p as x_0 and the other vertices of C clockwise as $x_1, x_2, \ldots, x_{\frac{m}{2}-1}$. We do this modulo $m/2$, in particular, by the vertex $x_{\frac{m}{2}}$ we mean the vertex x_0. Let $d \in \{0, 1, \ldots, \frac{m}{2} - 1\}$ be chosen such that $x_d = v_k$. By the symmetry of C and since the cycle C' can be ignored until this moment, with probability at least a half, $d \in \{\frac{m}{8}, \frac{m}{8} + 1, \ldots, \frac{3m}{8}\}$ and thus, the distance (measured in the number of edges) of x_0 to v_k is at least $m/8$. But for the next improvement of RLS v_k has to be the first vertex of p. Therefore, we are interested in the expected number of accepted steps until the first vertex of p is $x_d = v_k$.

Claim. The expected number of accepted steps until x_d is the first vertex of the path p is $d(\frac{m}{2} - d)$.

Proof. Let t_k be the expected number of accepted steps until the first vertex of p is x_k for the first time (after p has become the cycle C) for all $0 \le k \le \frac{m}{2} - 1$. Clearly, $t_0 = 0$. Because of the symmetry of C, t_k is also the expected number of accepted steps until the first vertex is x_0 for the first time, starting at the vertex x_k. Then, in the first step the first vertex of p changes from x_k to the adjacent vertices x_{k-1} or x_{k+1} each with probability $1/2$. Thus,

$$t_k = 1 + \tfrac{1}{2}t_{k-1} + \tfrac{1}{2}t_{k+1}$$

holds for all $0 \le k \le \frac{m}{2} - 1$. Note, that the vertices are named modulo $m/2$ and therefore $t_{\frac{m}{2}} = t_0 = 0$. This is a linear system of equations with $t_0, t_1, \ldots, t_{\frac{m}{2}-1}$ as variables. It is easy to see that this is a regular linear system of equations. Thus, it has a unique solution. One verifies that $t_k = k(\frac{m}{2} - k)$ for all $0 \le k \le \frac{m}{2} - 1$ solves this linear system of equations. This proves the claim. □

Since with probability at least a half $d \in \{\frac{m}{8}, \frac{m}{8} + 1, \ldots, \frac{3m}{8}\}$, the expected number of accepted steps until $x_d = v_k$ is the first vertex in the path p is at least of order $\Omega(m^2)$.

The (1+1) EA has the possibility of moving the start vertex of the path more than one position in one step. Let $k, \ell \in \mathbb{N}$. Denote by $p_{k\ell}$ the probability that the (1 + 1) EA moves the start vertex exactly k steps to the right (or left) conditional on that we perform ℓ jump operations. If $k + \ell < n/2$, this can only be achieved if each of the edges initially on position $n/2 - k + 1$ to $n/2$ is jumped to the front (not necessarily the first position). In particular, these edges have to be among the (randomly with repition chosen) 2ℓ edges that describe the ℓ jump operators. Hence, if $\ell = o(m)$, we have $p_{k\ell} \le (1 + o(1))\binom{m}{2\ell-k}\binom{m}{2\ell}^{-1} = 1/O(m^k)$, where we use the fact that things are only better if the 2ℓ edges are all different.

Now let $\ell_0 = K \log m$ for some sufficiently large constant K. Then the probability that the EA tries to perform more than ℓ_0 jump operations is less than $\exp(-\ell_0) = 1/O(m^K)$. Let us compute the probability p_t that the EA moves the start vertex by at least t to the right/left:

$$p_t = \sum_{\ell=t}^{\infty} \frac{1}{e(\ell+1)!)} \sum_{k=t}^{\infty} p_{k\ell} \leq 1/O(m^K) + \sum_{\ell=t}^{\ell_0} (e(\ell+1)!)^{-1} \sum_{k=t}^{\ell_0} p_{k\ell} \leq 1/O(m^t).$$

In particular, taking $t = 5$, we see that within $\Theta(m^4)$ rounds, with probability $1-o(1)$ the EA in each round moves the starting vertex of the cycle by less than 5. The only difference between RLS and the (1+1) EA is that the (1+1) EA can operate up to a factor of four faster.

Thus, RLS and the (1+1) EA need in expectation at least $\Omega(m^2)$ accepted mutation steps. Moreover, the expected waiting time of RLS and the (1+1) EA until such a mutation is accepted is $\Omega(m^2)$. Hence, both algorithms need $\Omega(m^4)$ steps to produce an optimal solution for the example graph G_m. □

5 Analysis of the Restricted Operator

The analysis in the previous section has shown that there are situations where RLS and the (1+1) EA need an expected number of $\Omega(m^4)$ steps to reach an improvement. We will investigate the corresponding algorithms RLS_r and the (1+1) EA_r that work with the restricted mutation operator and show that in each situation an improvement is found in an expected number of $O(m^2)$ steps. One reason for this improvement is that the plateau that has to be coped with changes its structure such that an inprovement is easier to obtain. On the other hand the expected waiting time for an accepted offspring can be reduced by a factor of m using the restricted mutation operator. This leads to an expected optimization time for RLS_r and the (1+1) EA_r which is upper bound by $O(m^3)$. Additionally, we show that there are graphs for which RLS_r and the (1+1) EA_r need in expectation a runtime of the same magnitude with probability close to 1.

Theorem 2. *The expected time until RLS_r and the (1+1) EA_r have computed a Eulerian cycle is bounded by $O(m^3)$.*

Proof. We distinguish two cases. In the first case the current path is not a cycle. Then there exists at least one edge that can jump to position 1 and lengthen the path. In the case that p represents a cycle C which is not a Eulerian cycle, the complement G^C of C in G is a subgraph whose components are all Eulerian. Let $d'(v)$ denote the degree of v in G^C for every vertex v that is in the cycle C and in the subgraph G^C For all vertices that are in the cycle C but not in the subgraph G^C we set $d'(v) := 0$. Since G is Eulerian, G^C has at least one vertex in common with C. Thus, there is at least one vertex v in C with $d'(v) \geq 2$. Let l be the length of the path p and let $e_i(p)$, $1 \leq i \leq l$, denote the ith edge of p. We call $v_1(p) := e_1(p) \setminus e_2(p)$ the starting point of the path p. If $d'(v_1(p)) = 0$, the only accepted jump is $jump(l)$. But after at most $l-1$ such jumps $d'(v_1(p)) \geq 2$. In such a situation there are $d'(v_1(p)) + 1$ accepted jumps. Besides $jump(l)$, all $d'(v_1(p))$ edges of G^C containing $v_1(p)$ can jump to the first position of p (shifting all the edges of p by one). Consequently, the probability that the path is lengthened is $\frac{d'(v_1(p))}{d'(v_1(p))+1} \geq \frac{2}{3}$. Hence, the expected number of jumps until the

Fig. 2. Example graph G'

path is improved is at most $\frac{3}{2}l \le \frac{3}{2}m$. Since in average at least every mth jump is accepted, this implies an expected time for an improvement of $O(m^2)$. The number of improvements is at most $m-1$, which completes the proof. □

To prove a matching lower bound, we consider the graph G' (see Figure 2) consisting of $m/4$ cycles C_i, $0 \le i \le m/4-1$ of length 4. C_i consists of the vertices $v_{3i}, v_{3i+1}, v_{3i+2}, v_{3(i+1)}$ and the edges $\{v_{3i}, v_{3i+1}\}, \{v_{3i}, v_{3i+2}\}, \{v_{3i+1}, v_{3(i+1)}\}$ and $\{v_{3i+2}, v_{3(i+1)}\}$. The number of vertices in G' is $3m/4+1$. Note that cycle C_i, $0 \le i \le m/4-2$, and C_{i+1} intersect in $v_{3(i+1)}$.

Theorem 3. *With probability $1-o(1)$, RLS$_r$ and the (1+1) EA$_r$ need $\Omega(m^3)$ steps to find a Eulerian cycle in G'.*

Proof. We call the vertices v_{3i}, $1 \le i \le m/4-1$, turning points of the graph G'. As in the proof of Theorem 2, we call $v_1(p) := e_1(p) \setminus e_2(p)$ the starting point of the path p, where e_1 denotes the first and e_2 the second edge of the path p. At the beginning of RLS$_r$ the path p consists of only a few edges. More precisely, the probability that the length of the path is shorter than for example $m/20$ is clearly $1-e^{-\Omega(m)}$. We now show the following claim.

Claim. Let the current path p_1 at a certain time t_1 in RLS$_r$ be not a cycle. And let $t_2 > t_1$ be the first time such that the current path p_2 is a cycle. Then

$$|\{0 \le i \le m/4-1 : C_i \cap p_1 = \emptyset \ne C_i \cap p_2\}| \le \frac{m}{40} \tag{1}$$

with probability $1-e^{-\Omega(m)}$.

Proof. Assume that (1) does not hold. Then at least $m/40$ times between t_1 and t_2 the starting point $v_1(p)$ was a turning point. In each of this situations the probability that the next edge that jumps at the first position of the path p is in the same cycle C_i as the edge that was in the first position of p before this jump is $1/3$. And with probability $2/3$ this two edges are in different cycles C_i and C_{i+1}. Since the path p is not closed until the time t_2, only up to two times between t_1 and t_2 the starting point $v_1(p)$ was a turning point and these two edges were in the same cycle. But at least $m/40$ times the starting point $v_1(p)$ was a turning point and those two edges were in different cycles. The probability for this is $e^{-\Omega(m)}$ which proves the claim. □

With probability $1 - e^{-\Omega(m)}$ the path p at the beginning of RLS$_r$ is shorter than $m/20$. That means, it contains edges of at most $m/40$ cycles. Using the claim, we get the following: when the path p is a cycle for the first time, it contains edges of at most $m/40 + m/40 = m/20$ cycles with probability $1 - e^{-\Omega(m)}$. Thus, the length of p is bounded by $m/5$ at this time with probability $1 - e^{-\Omega(m)}$. Another consequence of the claim is the following: Let l_1 be the length of the current path p at a certain time when p is a cycle. And let l_2 be the length of the current path p at the first time when the current path is a cycle again after p was not a cycle for a while. Then $l_2 - l_1 \leq m/10$ with probability $1 - e^{-\Omega(m)}$, since only edges from at most $m/40$ cycles C_i can jump into p (with probability $1 - e^{-\Omega(m)}$).

Therefore with probability $1 - e^{-\Omega(m)}$ there exists a moment when the current path p is a cycle of length at least $m/3$ and at most $m/3 + m/10 \leq m/2$. Hence, there are at least $m/8$ cycles left that have to be integrated. Each time when the starting point $v_1(p)$ is a turning point and only one edge e of the four edges adjacent to $v_1(p)$ is contained in p we have the following situation: the probability that the next edge that jumps at the first position of p is in the same cycle C_i as the edge e is $1/3$. Thus, this will occur in average in $1/3$ of the $m/8$ times. Using Chernoff bounds, with probability $1 - e^{-\Omega(m)}$ this happens at least $m/30$ times. After such an event, at least $m/6$ edges have to jump to the first position of the path p until the starting point $v_1(p)$ of p is a turning point, such that only one of the four edges adjacent to $v_1(p)$ is contained in p. Therefore, with probability $1 - e^{-\Omega(m)}$, at least $(m/6)(m/30) = m^2/180$ edges have to jump at the first position of the path p until the Eulerian cycle is found by RLS$_r$. Since the maximal degree of G' is 4, in average at most $3/m$ of all jumps is accepted. Thus, using the Chernoff bounds once more, the number of jumps until RLS$_r$ has found a Eulerian cycle is $\Omega(m^3)$ with probability $1 - e^{-\Omega(m)}$.

In contrast to RLS$_r$ more than one jump operation per mutation is possible in the mutation operator of the (1+1) EA$_r$. The probability that a jump is accepted is at most $3/m$ in the example graph G', since the maximum degree of G' is 4. Thus, with probability $1 - o(1)$ there is no accepted mutation with more than three jumps within $O(m^3)$ steps. Therefore, none of the circles can be integrated in one mutation with probability $1 - o(1)$. Hence, the only difference between RLS$_r$ and the (1+1) EA$_r$ is that (1+1) EA$_r$ is up to a factor of 3 faster than RLS$_r$. This shows the claim also for the (1+1) EA$_r$. □

6 Conclusions

In the case of combinatorial optimization problems often a lot is known about the structure of a given problem. This knowledge can lead to more sophisticated evolutionary algorithms. For the Eulerian cycle problem we considered a simple evolutionary algorithms that work with a restricted mutation operator. We have proven a bound of $\Theta(m^3)$ for the expected runtime of these restricted algorithms. This beats the up to now best upper bound on the more general versions of these algorithms by a factor m^2. We have also obtained a lower bound of $\Omega(m^4)$ for the unrestricted algorithm. This strengthens our claim that restricting the mutation operator can help to come up with faster evolutionary algorithms in some cases.

References

1. O. Giel and I. Wegener. Evolutionary algorithms and the maximum matching problem. In *Proc. of 20th STACS*, volume 2607 of *Lecture Notes in Computer Science*, pages 415–426, 2003.
2. C. Hierholzer. Über die Möglichkeit, einen Linienzug ohne Wiederholung und ohne Unterbrechung zu umfahren. In *Math. Ann*, volume 6, pages 30–32, 1873.
3. T. Jansen and I. Wegener. Evolutionary algorithms — how to cope with plateaus of constant fitness and when to reject strings of the same fitness. In *IEEE Trans. on Evolutionary Computation*, volume 5, pages 589–599, 2001.
4. D. C. Mattfeld and C. Bierwirth. An efficient genetic algorithm for job shop scheduling with tardiness objectives. In *European Journal of Operational Research*, volume 155, pages 616–630, 2004.
5. Z. Michalewicz and D. B. Fogel. *How to solve it.* Springer-Verlag, Berlin, 2004.
6. F. Neumann. Expected runtimes of a simple evolutionary algorithm for the multi-objective minimum spanning tree problem. In *Parallel Problem Solving from Nature - PPSN VIII*, volume 3242 of *Lecture Notes in Computer Science*, pages 80–89, Springer, Berlin, 2004.
7. F. Neumann. Expected runtimes of evolutionary algorithms for the Eulerian cycle problem. In *Proc. of the Congress on Evolutionary Computation 2004 (CEC 2004)*, volume 1, IEEE Press, pages 904–910, 2004.
8. F. Neumann and I. Wegener. Randomized local search, evolutionary algorithms, and the minimum spanning tree problem. In *Genetic and Evolutionary Computation Conference - GECCO 2004*, volume 3102 of *Lecture Notes in Computer Science*, pages 713–724, Springer, Berlin, 2004.
9. G. R. Raidl, G. Koller, and B. A. Julstrom. Biased mutation operators for subgraph-selection problems. In *IEEE Transactions on Evolutionary Computation*, 2006 (to appear).
10. J. Scharnow, K. Tinnefeld, and I. Wegener. Fitness landscapes based on sorting and shortest paths problems. In *Proc. of Parallel Problem Solving from Nature — PPSN VII*, volume 2939 of *Lecture Notes in Computer Science*, pages 54–63, Springer, Berlin, 2002.
11. C. Witt. Worst-case and average-case approximations by simple randomized search heuristics. In *Proc. of the 22nd Annual Symposium on Theoretical Aspects of Computer Science (STACS '05)*, volume 3404 of *Lecture Notes in Computer Science*, pages 44–56, Springer, Berlin, 2005.

Comparing the Niches of CMA-ES, CHC and Pattern Search Using Diverse Benchmarks

Darrell Whitley, Monte Lunacek, and Artem Sokolov

Computer Science, Colorado State University, Fort Collins, CO 80523

Abstract. This paper explores two questions: 1) On a relatively difficult and varied set of test problems, can we observe differences in evolutionary search algorithm performance related to problem features? 2) How do the evolutionary algorithms compare to *Pattern Search* algorithms, a more traditional optimization tool popular in the larger scientific community? The results suggest there are consistent differences in algorithm performance that can be related back to problem features. Some new ideas for the construction of benchmark problems are also introduced.

1 Introduction

There are two common complaints about the evaluation of evolutionary search algorithms: 1) test suites are too simple and 2) not enough comparisons include traditional optimization algorithms used in the larger scientific community. In this paper we compare *Generalized Pattern Search* and *Mesh Adaptive Direct Search* against CMA-ES, CHC and Local Search. The comparisons are not meant as a competition; and the results suggest that no one method is the best across all problems. However, the results do suggest that differences in performance that can be related to problem features.

We also attempt to use a more challenging set of test problems, including new versions of Griewangk and a synthetic version of the "static correction problem" from geophysics. This problem is nonlinear, multimodal, scalable and it has the nice property that one can visualize the solution. All test functions can be downloaded at: http://www.cs.colostate.edu/ genitor/functions.html

For most benchmark problems we include a rotated and shifted version of the problem: this ensures the problems are no longer separable and that the global optimum is not located at some fortuitous location in the search space. All of our problems have bound constraints on the input domain; thus, an algorithm that is invariant under rotation (e.g. CMA) will *not* produce the same results in expectation on the rotated version. One of the surprising results of this paper is how much a simple rotation of the search space can change algorithm performance.

Pattern Search Methods

The typical pattern search algorithm resembles local search. At every iteration k, the current solution x_k is compared to a finite set of points either on a next-descent or best-descent basis. The points are taken such that they belong to a mesh grid constructed

T.P. Runarsson et al. (Eds.): PPSN IX, LNCS 4193, pp. 988–997, 2006.

from a matrix of directions D and a step size Δ_k^m. Audet and Dennis [1] define the mesh at iteration k to be:

$$M_k = \bigcup_{x \in S_k} \{x + \Delta_k^m Dz : z \in \mathcal{N}^{n_D}\}$$

where S_k is the set of points that have been evaluated on prior to iteration k.

The directions are specified by the n_D columns of D and are chosen arbitrarily with the requirement that D spans $\mathcal{R}^n$, where n is the problem dimensionality. Δ_k^m denotes the granularity of the mesh; its value is increased after an improving move, and decreased otherwise.

Each iteration is a two steps process. The first optional `SEARCH` step evaluates a finite number of points anywhere on the mesh. The second step, referred to as `LOCAL POLL`, evaluates the objective function on several mesh points that lie in proximity to the current iterate x_k

We will use two forms of pattern search: **Generalized Pattern Search (GPS)** and **Mesh Adaptive Direct Search (MADS)**. GPS and MADS differ in their notion of "proximity." GPS enforces evaluation of points that conform to $x_k + \Delta_k^m Dy$, where $y \in \mathcal{N}^{n_D}$ and $\|y\|_\infty = 1$. MADS relaxes this by allowing $\|y\|_\infty \neq 0$ to be bound by some $\Delta_k^p \geq \Delta_k^m$ (for details see [10] [1]). We used the NOMAD package implementation of GPS and MADS and report results for the five standard NOMAD direction sets that we label as: gps_{2n}, gps_{n+1}, $mads_{2n}$, $mads_{n+1}$ and $unif_{N=1}$. All NOMAD parameters were kept at their default values.

The first n directions of gps_{2n} and gps_{n+1} are positive unit vectors along each dimension axis. Random nonnegative linear combinations (bound by the constraints above) of these make up the first n directions of $mads_{2n}$ and $mads_{n+1}$. The second half of the directions in gps_{2n} and $mads_{2n}$ is defined to be a symmetric reflection of the corresponding first half: $d^{n+i} = -d^i$ for $i = 1, 2, ..., n$. The sets gps_{n+1} and $mads_{n+1}$ are constructed to form an n-dimensional simplex. Therefore, the $(n+1)^{st}$ direction is taken to be $d^{n+1} = -\sum_{i=1}^{n} d^i$.

Typically, a pattern search algorithm is terminated when the step size falls below a certain threshold. A restart mechanism was added so that search would continue until some maximum number of function evaluations is reached.

CHC

CHC is a genetic algorithm that represents individuals as finite bit strings. CHC uses half uniform crossover (HUX), where exactly half of the non-matching bits are exchanged. CHC also uses *incest prevention* [2] such that parents are not allowed to recombine unless they are sufficiently different. Newly created offspring must compete with the parent population for survival via *truncation selection*. No mutation is used to alter one generation to the next. Instead, after CHC fails to find any offspring that improve on any of the parents, a restart mechanism called *cataclysmic mutation* replaces the entire population by repeatedly randomizing 35% of the bits of the best individual. CHC has proven to be very effective on both difficult benchmarks and real world applications.

Local Search

Local search is included for a baseline comparison. Local search as used here is a Gray coded *steepest ascent bit climber*; an L-bit neighborhood is defined by flipping each bit of the the current best solution. All neighborhood points are evaluated before accepting the best move. Local search restarts when no improving move is found.

CMA-ES

An *evolution strategy* is an iterative process where μ parents produce λ offspring based on distributions around the parents. *Evolution Strategy with Covariance Matrix Adaptation*, or CMA-ES [4], uses a covariance matrix to explicitly rotate and scale the mutation distribution that functions as strategy parameters. Hansen and Ostermeier define the reproduction phase from generation g to generation $g+1$ as:

$$x_k^{(g+1)} = \langle x \rangle_\mu^{(g)} + \sigma^{(g)} \mathbf{B}^{(g)} \mathbf{D}^{(g)} z_k^{(g+1)}$$

where $z_k^{(g+1)}$ are randomly generated from an $N(0, I)$ distribution. This creates a set of base points that are rotated and scaled by the eigenvectors ($\mathbf{B}^{(g)}$) and the square root of the eigenvalues ($\mathbf{D}^{(g)}$) of the covariance matrix C. The base points are translated to center around $\langle x \rangle_\mu^{(g)}$, the mean of the μ best parents.

CMA-ES also uses the evolutionary path of improving moves to update the covariance matrix. The evolution path updates after each generation using a weighted sum of the current path, $p_c^{(g)}$, and a vector that points from the mean of the μ best points in generation g to the mean of the μ best points in generation $g+1$. When a larger population (λ) is used, the best μ individuals may help describe the topology around the mean of the current generation. CMA-ES calculates the covariance of the steps that lead to μ best individuals.

$$\mathbf{Z}^{(g+1)} = \frac{1}{\mu} \sum \mathbf{B}^{(g)} \mathbf{D}^{(g)} z_i^{(g+1)} (\mathbf{B}^{(g)} \mathbf{D}^{(g)} z_i^{(g+1)})^T$$

Assuming $\mathbf{Z}^{(g+1)}$ is the covariance of the steps that lead to the μ individuals, and $\mathbf{P}^{(g+1)}$ is the covariance of the evolution path, the new covariance matrix, $\mathbf{C}^{(g+1)}$, is:

$$(1 - c_{cov}) \mathbf{C}^{(g)} + c_{cov} \left(\alpha_{cov} \mathbf{P}^{(g+1)} + (1 - \alpha_{cov}) \mathbf{Z}^{(g+1)} \right)$$

where c_{cov} and α_{cov} are constants that weigh the importance of each input.

We used an initial step size for σ of 25% of each function domain, which is consistent with other research involving multimodal test functions [3] [4].

2 The Test Functions

Both Salomon [9] and Whitley et al. [11] noted about 10 years ago that most functions used to evaluate evolutionary algorithms are *separable* [11] and can easily be solved to optimality by independently searching each dimension of the search space. Whitley et al. proposed new test functions. Salomon created new nonseparable problems by

Table 1. The test functions used in this paper. Functions F2 and F8F2 use $[-2.048, 2.047]$ as the domain. All other functions use $[-512, 511]$ as the domain.

Name	Function
F2	$f(x, y) = 100(x^2 - y)^2 + (1 - x)^2$
Rana	$f(x, y) = xsin(\sqrt{A})cos(\sqrt{B}) + (y+1)cos(\sqrt{A})sin(\sqrt{B});\ A = \|y+1-x\|, B = \|x+y+1\|$
F101	$f(x, y) = -xsin(\sqrt{\|x - (y + 47)\|}) - (y + 47)sin(\sqrt{\|(y + 47) + x/2\|})$
F8F2	$f(x, y) = 1 + \sum_{i=1}^{N} \frac{\mathrm{F2}(x,y)^2}{4000} - \prod_{i=1}^{N} cos(\mathrm{F2}(x, y)/\sqrt{(i)})$
Schwefel	$f(x_i\|_{i=1,N}) = \sum_{i=1}^{N} \left(-x_i \sin\left(\sqrt{\|x_i\|}\right)\right)$
G1	$f(x_i\|_{i=1,N}) = \sum_{i=1}^{N} \frac{x_i^2}{4000N} - -log\left[\left[\prod_{i=1}^{N}(cos(x_i) + 0.1)\right] + 1.0\right]$
G2	$f(x_i\|_{i=1,N}) = \sum_{i=1}^{N} \frac{x_i^2}{4000N} - -1.5^{N/4}\left[\prod_{i=1}^{N} \sqrt{cos(x_i/N + i) + 1.0}\right]^{1/4}$

rotating the existing test functions. This rotation make the problems nonlinear and also breaks symmetry in the search space that can make problems much easier to opimize.

Table 1 lists our test functions. Rosenbrock's "banana function" (F2) is well known. Schwefel's function is separable. F101 is designed to be similar to Schwefel's function but nonseparable. Rana is nonseparable (see Figure 1). F8F2 is a nonseparable composite function that passes the result from F2 to Griewangk's function [11]; this adds numerous local optima to F2 (see Figure 1). We also rotated each of these function 22.5 degrees in all dimensions. Each rotated function was also translated by 5% of the domain to further reduce symmetry.

We also *bounded* the domain after rotation; this means an algorithm such as CMA-ES does not produce the same results for the rotated and unrotated problem. Our experience is that real work optimization problems typically have constraints on the values that the domain parameter can assume: for example, in many science and engineering domains, parameter values below a specific value or larger than a specific value maybe not be physically plausible or may not be measurable. We also scaled each function by five percent to pull more local optima into the bounded search space. We used the following expansion method to convert each 2-D function (denoted F_{2D}) into 20 dimensional functions.

$$f(\boldsymbol{x}) = \sum_{i=1}^{n-1} F_{2D}(x_i, x_{i+1})$$

Included in the test functions are two new versions of Griewangk's function. The original Griewangk function is as follows [11]:

$$f(x_i|_{i=1,N}) = 1 + \sum_{i=1}^{N} \frac{x_i^2}{4000} - \prod_{i=1}^{N} (cos(x_i/\sqrt{i}))$$

The global optimum is at the origin. The search space is bowl shaped while local optima are created over the bowl through the oscillation of a cosine function. However,

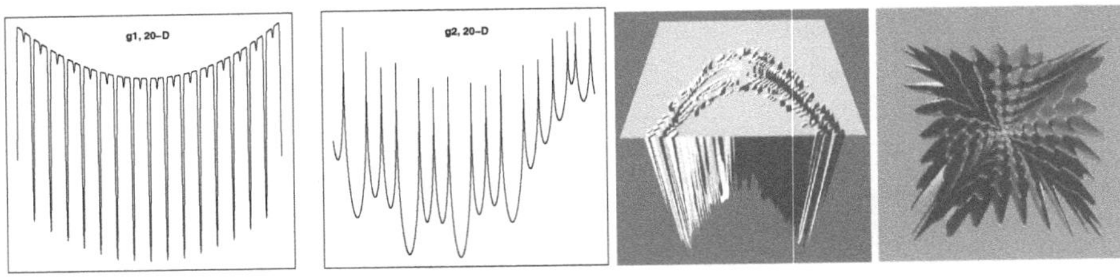

Fig. 1. The two rightmost figures are diagonal slices of G1 and G2. The 3rd figure is a clipped view of the local optima in F8F2. The leftmost figure is Rana's function.

the range of a cosine function is $[-1, 1]$ and as the number of dimensions increase, multiplication of the cosines destroys the local optima. Thus, higher dimensional versions of this problem become smooth with a strong global optimum. [11].

We used two modifications of the original Griewangk function denoted `G1` and `G2` that include a scaling factor that is added to the summation term to stabilize the function range across dimensions. In addition, the output from a cosine function is translated and/or scaled to offset the effect of multiplication. For `G1` and `G2` the global optimum does not have a consistent value as the number of dimensions is varied. The new forms of Griewangk are given in table 1. `G1` is characterized by taking a logarithm of the product term. Figure 1 shows slices of `G1` and `G2` at 20-D. The optima are now rather wide with thin barriers separating one from another. On `G2` the search space also loses its symmetry due to a phase shift.

Synthetic Static Corrections for Seismic Surveys

Seismic reflection surveys are used to construct subsurface images of geologic strata. A seismic signal contains information about the location of geological strata below the surface of the earth. However, differences in the materials at the earth's surface affect the arrival time of seismic signals: loose materials slow down signal arrival, packed materials speed up signal arrivals. The optimization problem is to find a *static correction* to the arrival time of each signal such that it correctly aligns signals to reveal subsurface geology. Misalignment of signals can result in numerous local optima (because the subsurface strata are misaligned); conventional optimization methods can easily be trapped in local optima. The images are also distorted by signal noise [7].

We introduce a synthetic static correction problem as a test function. The synthetic problem consists of a base matrix, which defines the structure of the simulated geologic strata. The base matrix M has i rows and j columns, where i indexes the ith strata and j indexes the jth signal. Entry $M(i,j)$ stores the depth of strata i as observed in signal j. (We can assume depth=time.) For example, consider the following $3x5$ base matrix:

$$\begin{pmatrix} -100 & -100 & -100 & -100 & -100 \\ -375 & -350 & -300 & -275 & -250 \\ -450 & -525 & -550 & -525 & -450 \end{pmatrix}$$

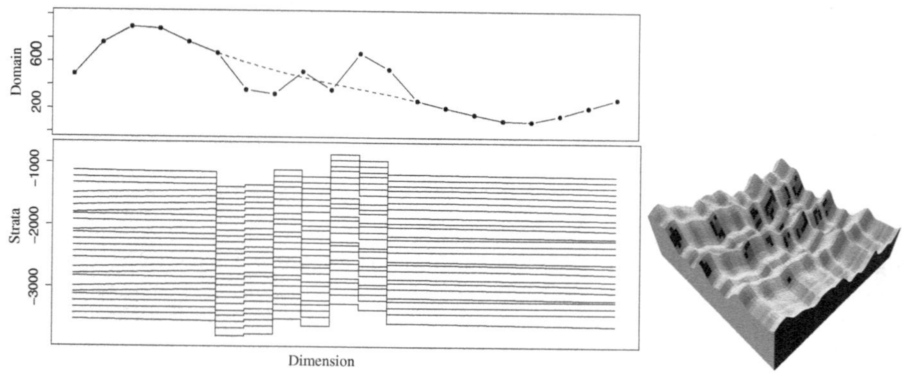

Fig. 2. The synthetic static corrections problem. In the leftmost figure, signals are indicated by column slices of the figure, and the known and proposed arrival times are shown across the top of the figure. If the solution is locally optima, moving any signal up or down (i.e., adjusting its arrival time in the Domain) will result in a poorer alignment of Strata. The rightmost figure shows there are many locally optimal alignments in a 2-D slice of the search space.

To simulate near surface variation of the earth we add a nonuniform **profile**, denoted p, to the problem. The profile has length equal to the problem dimension. Element p_j in the profile is added to each element of column j of matrix M: this effectively shifts signal j by p_j units and creates a new matrix $\mathcal{M}$. The optimization problem is to search for and retrieve vector p given the shifted matrix $\mathcal{M}$. Finding p will undo the shifts and restore the original matrix M and thereby align the geological strata.

Our simplified version of static corection assumes that the strata in M are structured and well behaved, while the shifts in matrix $\mathcal{M}$ are not regular. Fitness is usually calculated by computing the cross-correlation (e.g. the dot product) between all pairs of shifted signals. In the current experiments, we use simplified signals, such that the vector is 0 except when near the location of a strata. Within a distance of delta of the strata, the vector is 1. Figure 2 illustrates the simplied signals. When the total depth (length of the vectors) is greater than the number of signals (denoted by N), evaluation time is greater than $O(N^3)$. In our simplified model the dot-product is the same as overlap and we do not actually have to construct signals, which allows for evaluation in $O(N^2)$ time. If one wishes to model ambient noise the full evaluation must be used.

Figure 2 shows a 20 dimensional problem, including the profile vector (upper left: Domain), and the deviation of the current solution from the profile (lower left: Strata). The signals are shown as offset column slices. Figure 2 also shows a slice of first two dimensions of a 20 dimensional problem with a delta of $+/-50$ units (rightmost). Real static correction problems generally have 100's of variables.

This problem has several nice features: it is scalable, it can be made noisy, and more complex geology and signals can be used to make the problem more difficult; yet, it is easy to visualize misalignments in the solution.

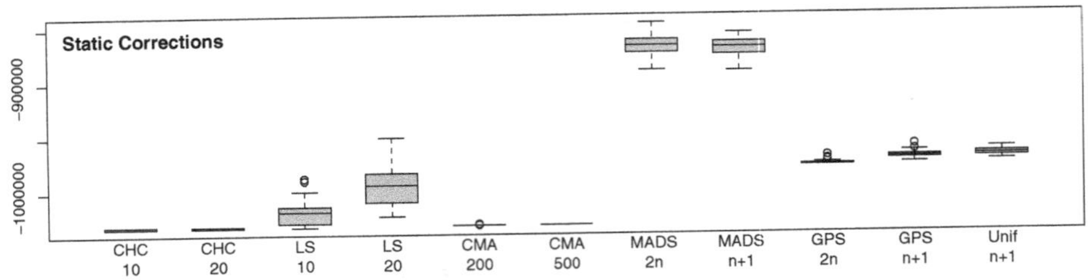

Fig. 3. The midline in the gray box is the median, while the gray box represents 25 percent of the sample above and below the median. The bars outside the gray box generally represent the max and min values, except when there are outliers, which are shown as small circles. The y-axis represents the value of the evaluation function.

3 Empirical Tests and Results

All test functions are 20 dimensional. Local search and CHC were run using 10-bits and 20-bits of precision. CHC used a population size of 50. We ran CMA-ES with rank-μ-updates and a population size of 200 and 500 [3]. We distinguish each algorithm based on its parameters; CHC-10, CHC-20, LS-10, LS-20, CMA-200, CMA-500. The Pattern Search algorithms are MADS-2n, MADS(n+1), GPS-2n, GPS(n+1) and Unif(n+1). Each algorithm was run for 50 trials; restarts ensured that each trial ran for exactly 100,000 evaluations. The results are presented in Figures 3, 4 and 5.

Rotating the functions generally reduced observed differences in algorithm performance. Most rotated problems are harder, except for Rosenbrock's F2 which becomes easier because the rotation aligns the "banana" with the search space coordinates.

CHC and Local Search, which use a bit representation, are very sensitive to the alignment of the search space. There exists versions of CHC that use a real valued representation that might yield better performance under rotation [5]. Nevertheless, CHC is highly competitive on F8F2 and F101 and Schwefel even after the functions are rotated. Salomon [9] found the Breeder Genetic Algorithm [8] performed poorly after rotation and he concluded from this that recombination was of limited value as a search operator: our results suggest this conclusion is too sweeping. The real problem seems to be that the Breeder Genetic Algorithm overly exploits separability.

Differences in Problem Structure. In another paper we have defined a *dispersion* metric that automatically identifies those functions where the local optima are globally clustered near one another [6]. Such functions includes the variants of Griewangk (G1 and G2) and the rotated and unrotated Rosenbrock's function. The Static Corrections problem used here also has globally clustered local optima; other variants of the Static Corrections problem need to be tested. CMA-ES does well on those problems where the best local optima are clustered together in a single "funnel."

The Pattern Search methods performed poorly on the functions with globally clustered local optima where CMA did well; however, GPS(2n) and MADS(N+1) did well on the rotated versions of Rana, Schwefel, F101 and F8F2. CHC performed best on the unrotated functions. This suggests that the Pattern Search algorithms are biased toward exploration at the expense of exploiting localstructure.

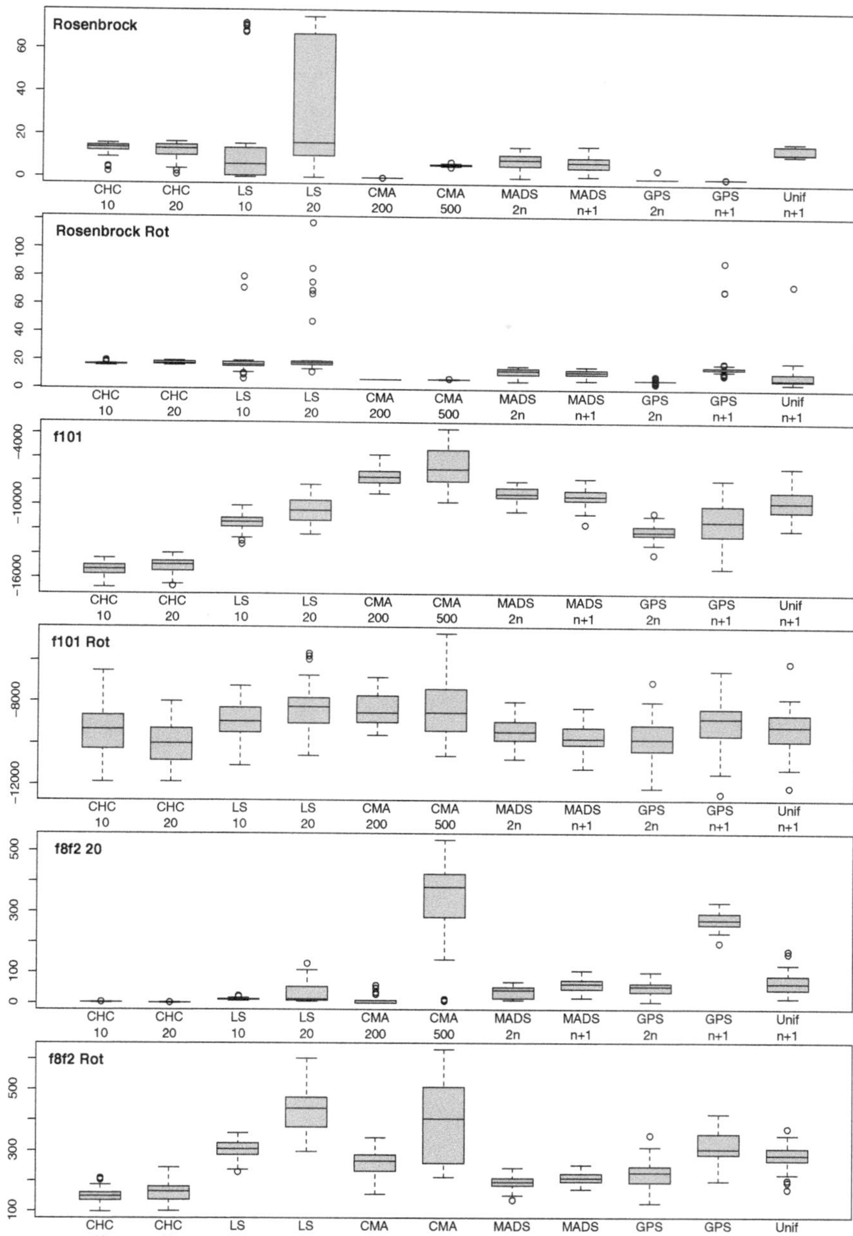

Fig. 4. The midline in the gray box is the median, while the gray box represents 25 percent above and below the median. The bars outside the gray box generally represent the max and min values, except when there are outliers, which are shown as small circles. The y-axis represents the value of the evaluation function.

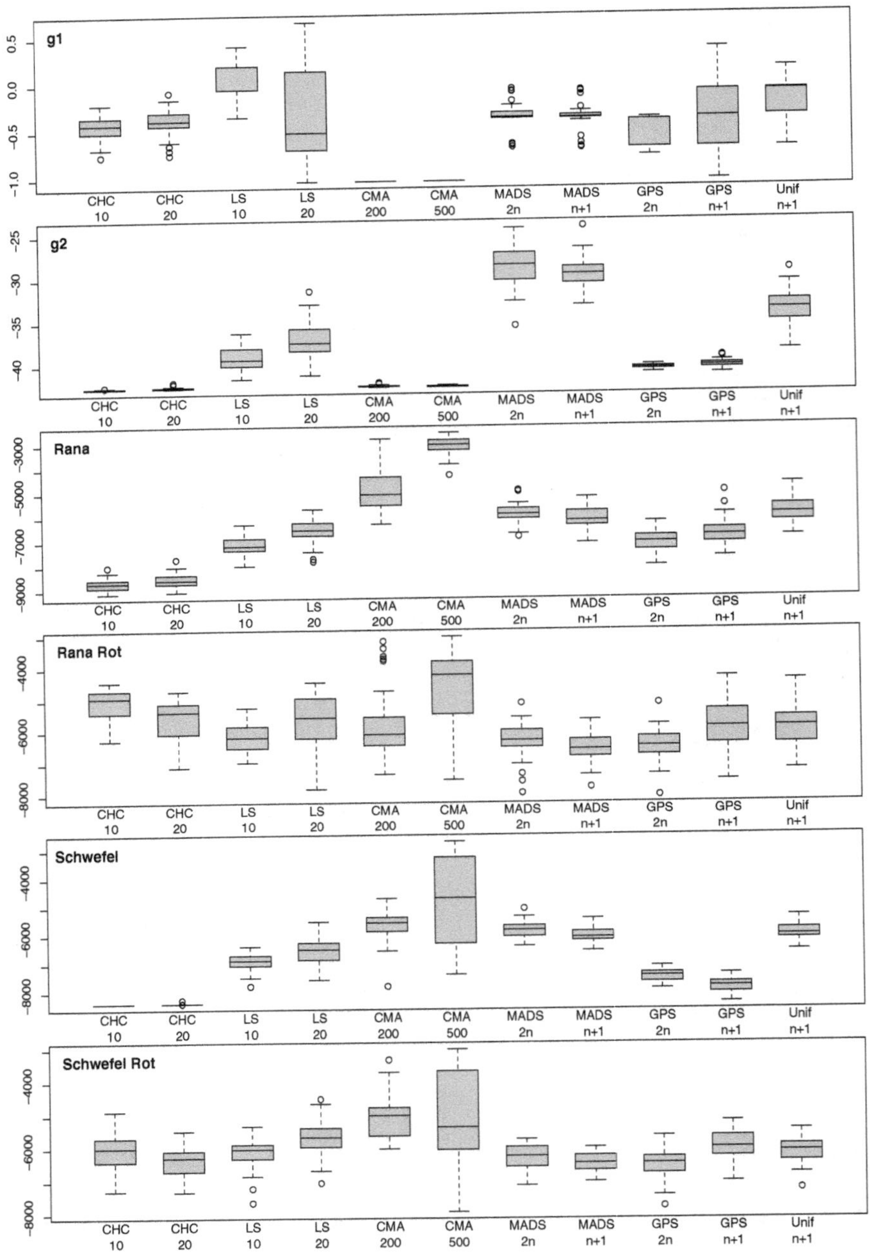

Fig. 5. The midline in the gray box is the median, while the gray box represents 25 percent above and below the median. The bars outside the gray box generally represent the max and min values, except when there are outliers, which are shown as small circles. The y-axis represents the value of the evaluation function.

4 Conclusions

No single algorithm dominates the others, and that different algorithms have better performance on different types of problems. Yet these kinds of differences are rarely reported in the literature. Perhaps the main significance of these results is that the community still has not been able to develop a clear understanding of how different algorithms exploit different types of problem features.

Acknowledgments. This material is based upon work supported by the National Science Foundation under Grant No. 0117209, by the Air Force Office of Scientific Research, USAF, under grant number F49620-03-1-0233 and Sandia National Labs.

References

[1] C. Audet and J.E. Dennis Jr. Mesh adaptive direct search algorithms for constrained optimization. *SIAM Journal on Optimization*, 17(1):188–217, 2006.
[2] L. J. Eshelman. The CHC adaptive search algorithm. In *Foundations of Genetic Algorithms*, pages 265–283. Morgan Kaufmann, 1991.
[3] N. Hansen and S. Kern. Evaluating the cma evolution strategy on multimodal test functions. In *PPSN*. Springer, 2004.
[4] N. Hansen and A. Ostermeier. Completely derandomized self-adaptation in evolution strategies. *Evolutionary Computation*, 9(2):159–195, 2001.
[5] J.D. Schaffer and L. Eshelman. Real-Coded Genetic Algorithms and Interval Schemata. In *Foundations of Genetic Algorithms 2*. Morgan Kaufmann, 1993.
[6] M. Lunacek and D. Whitley. The dispersion metric and cma algorithm. In *GECCO*. ACM Press, 2006.
[7] K. Mathias, D. Whitley, T. Kusuma, and C. Stork. An Empirical Evaluation of Genetic Algorithms on Noisy Objective Functions. In *Genetic Algorithms for Pattern Recognition*, pages 65–86. CRC Press, 1996.
[8] H. Mühlenbein and D. Schlierkamp-Voosen. Predictive Models for the Breeder Genetic Algorithm. *Evolutionary Computation*, 1(1):25–49, 1993.
[9] R. Salomon. Re-evaluating genetic algorithm performance under coordinate rotation of benchmark functions. *BioSystems*, 39:263–278, 1996.
[10] A. Torczon. On the convergence of pattern search algorthims. *SIAM Journal on Optimization*, 7(1):1–25, 1997.
[11] D. Whitley, S. B. Rana, J. Dzubera, and K. E. Mathias. Evaluating evolutionary algorithms. *Artificial Intelligence*, 85(1-2):245–276, 1996.

Model Complexity vs. Performance in the Bayesian Optimization Algorithm

Elon S. Correa[1] and Jonathan L. Shapiro[2]

[1] Computing Laboratory, University of Kent, Canterbury, Kent, CT2 7NF, United Kingdom
esc4@kent.ac.uk

[2] School of Computer Science, University of Manchester, Manchester, M13 9PL, United Kingdom
jls@cs.man.ac.uk

Abstract. The Bayesian Optimization Algorithm (BOA) uses a Bayesian network to estimate the probability distribution of promising solutions to a given optimization problem. This distribution is then used to generate new candidate solutions. The objective is to improve the population of candidate solutions by learning and sampling from good solutions. A Bayesian network (BN) is a graphical representation of a probability distribution over a set of variables of a given problem domain. The number of topological states that a BN can create depends on a parameter called maximum allowed indegree. We show that the value of the maximum allowed indegree given to the Bayesian network used by the BOA strongly affects the performance of this algorithm. Furthermore, there is a limited set of values for this parameter for which the performance of the BOA is maximized.

1 Introduction

The Bayesian Optimization Algorithm (BOA) [13,14] is a search procedure based on statistical information. It uses a Bayesian network to estimate the probability distribution of promising solutions to a given optimization problem. This distribution is then used to generate new candidate solutions. The objective is to improve the population of candidate solutions by learning and sampling from good solutions.

A Bayesian network (BN) is a graphical representation of a probability distribution over a set of variables of a given problem domain [9,11]. This graphical representation is a directed acyclic graph in which nodes represent the variables of the problem and arcs represent conditional probabilistic dependencies among the nodes. The network structure encodes probabilistic dependencies among domain variables and a joint probability distribution quantifies the strength of these dependencies.

Perhaps the most challenging task in dealing with Bayesian networks is learning their structures. Learning the structure of a BN is an NP-hard problem [3,4]. Many algorithms developed to this end use a scoring metric and a search procedure. The scoring metric evaluates the goodness-of-fit of a structure to the data. The search procedure generates alternative structures and selects the best

T.P. Runarsson et al. (Eds.): PPSN IX, LNCS 4193, pp. 998–1007, 2006.

one based on the scoring metric. To reduce the search space of networks, only candidate networks in which each node has at most k inward arcs (parents) are considered - k is a parameter determined by the user. We shall refer to this parameter as the "maximum allowed indegree" (the maximum number of parents that a variable can have) of the Bayesian network.

The number of topological states that a Bayesian network can create depends on its maximum allowed indegree k. We define the complexity of a Bayesian network as the number of topological states that it can create. The more topological states the Bayesian network can create the more complex it is. Thus, the complexity of the model of the BOA can be measured by the maximum allowed indegree of its Bayesian network. The larger this maximum allowed indegree value is the more complex the model used by the BOA is as well. Statistically speaking, model complexity is an inherent characteristic of the model that enables it to fit a wide range of probability distributions.

We show that the value of the maximum allowed indegree given to the Bayesian network used by the BOA strongly affects the performance of this algorithm. There is a limited set of values for the parameter that controls the complexity of the model in the BOA (i.e., for the maximum allowed indegree of the BN) for which the performance of this algorithm is maximized. For values of the parameter outside of this set, the BOA loses performance in terms of the quality of the solutions returned by the algorithm. Empirical experiments suggest that the numbers on this set are in a sequence of consecutive numbers.

The paper is organized as follows. Section 2 briefly describes the BOA. Sections 3 presents the test problems used in this work. Section 4 reports computational results. Section 5 discusses future work and presents conclusions.

2 The Bayesian Optimization Algorithm

The Bayesian Optimization Algorithm [14] works as follows: (1) randomly generate a population of candidate solutions for the problem being solved; (2) evaluate these solutions and select the best ones; (3) use this set of selected solutions to build a Bayesian network; (4) use this Bayesian network to sample new solutions;

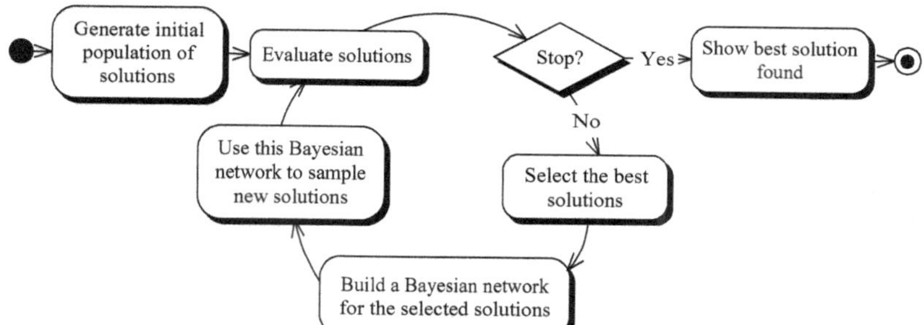

Fig. 1. BOA's working process

(5) repeat steps 2, 3 and 4 until a given stopping criterion is met. Fig. 1 depicts the working process of the BOA.

By choosing the maximum allowed indegree value for the Bayesian network that the BOA uses, one determines the complexity of BOA's probabilistic model.

3 Test Problems

The test problems used to evaluate the performance of the BOA are the following.

3.1 The 1D Spin-Glass Problem

The 1D spin-glass problem can be written as:

$$f_{1DSpinGlass}(X) = \sum_{i=1}^{\ell-1} w_{i,i+1}(x_i - \frac{1}{2})(x_{i+1} - \frac{1}{2}), \tag{1}$$

where the weights $w_{i,i+1}$ are uniformly distributed in the interval [-10, 10], ℓ is the length of the string and $x_i \in \{0, 1\}$ [1]. $X = \{x_1, x_2, ..., x_\ell\}$ is a random binary string and represents a candidate solution to the problem. The objective is to find the binary string X that maximizes $f_{1DSpinGlass}(X)$.

3.2 The Satisfiability Problem

The satisfiability (SAT) was one of the first problems shown to be NP-hard [5]. The problem is to determine, for a formula of the propositional calculus, if there is an assignment of truth values to its variables for which that formula evaluates to true [7,8]. It can be defined as follows: given a set of m clauses $\{C_1, C_2, ..., C_m\}$ on ℓ Boolean variables $v = (v_1, v_2, ..., v_\ell)$ with $v_i \in \{0, 1\}$, and a Boolean formula in conjunctive normal form, determine an assignment of truth values to v so that the Boolean formula evaluates to true. Corresponding to each variable v_i are two literals, v_i and its logical negation $\neg v_i$.

A clause C_i is a set of literals in disjunction in which all variables must be different from each other. In the Max-3-SAT problem, every clause C_i has exactly three literals. For example: $C_1 = (\neg v_3 \vee v_1 \vee v_7)$, for $i = 1$ and $\ell \geq 7$. Note that $C_1 = (\neg v_3 \vee v_1 \vee v_7)$ represents only one of the possible combination of the variables for a generic clause C_1. The objective is to determine an assignment to v that maximizes the number of satisfied clauses in:

$$f(v) = C_1 \wedge C_2 \wedge ... \wedge C_m. \tag{2}$$

A clause is satisfied when its truth value is true. A well-known feature of SAT problems is phase transition [15]. The phase transition area for SAT problems is known as the hardest area for determining whether a SAT problem is satisfiable. Experimental studies have shown that, for randomly generated 3-SAT problems, this phase transition area occurs when the ratio between the number of clauses and the number of variables of the problem is roughly 4.25 [10]. All the instances of 3-SAT problems used in this work are in the phase transition area. Therefore, they are hard 3-SAT instances to optimize.

3.3 Concatenated Functions

A concatenated function is the sum of n, $n > 1$, more elementary functions f_k of k variables. It can be expressed as:

$$f_{kConcatenated}(X) = \sum_{i=1}^{n} f_k(s_i), \tag{3}$$

where every s_i is a non-overlapping subset of X containing exactly k variables. For instance, given $f_3(x_1, x_2, x_3)$ the sum of two f_3 functions would result in:

$$f_{3Concatenated}(x_1, x_2, x_3, x_4, x_5, x_6) = \overbrace{f_3(\underbrace{x_1, x_2, x_3}_{s_1}) + f_3(\underbrace{x_4, x_5, x_6}_{s_2})}^{n=2}. \tag{4}$$

Trap Function of Order 5: The fitness of a trap function of order 5 is given by the equation:

$$f_{trap5}(u) = \begin{cases} 4 - u, \text{ if } u < 5, \\ 5, \quad \text{otherwise.} \end{cases} \tag{5}$$

where u is the number of ones on a five digits binary string [12, p. 17]. For our tests we use a concatenation of several blocks of the trap function of order 5. The fitness value of this function is given by the sum of the fitness value of each of the 5-bit blocks that compose the function.

4 Computational Results

Results reported here are averaged over 100 or 200 independent runs performed for every combination of maximum allowed indegree value, population size and problem size. We use the K2 metric to evaluate the goodness-of-fit of the Bayesian network to the data. The value of the K2 scoring metric is given by the formula:

$$K2(X|par(X)) = \prod_{j=1}^{q} \frac{(r-1)!}{(N_j^{'} + r - 1)!} \prod_{i=1}^{r} N_{ij}!, \tag{6}$$

where the variable X is a child node on the graph and $par(X)$ is the set of its parents. r represents the number of possible values that X can take and q represents the number of distinct instantiations of its parent nodes ($par(X)$). $N_j^{'}$ represents the number of cases in which variable X is instantiated to its ith value and its parents are instantiated to their j^{th} value combination ($N_j^{'} = \sum_{i=1}^{r} N_{ij}$) [2]. For the K2 metric see also [6]. At every generation the BN starts as an empty graph. It is then constructed from scratch to fit the distribution of a set of solutions selected through a truncation selection method. In truncation selection solutions are sorted by their fitness value. A percentage of the solutions with the best fitness value is then selected. Perhaps better performance could be achieved through other selection methods. Determining best performance, however, is not the purpose of our experiments. It is to investigate the effect of the complexity of the model in the performance of the BOA. The percentage of solutions selected is always 50%. At each generation the number of new solutions generated is equal to 50% of the population size. After generating new solutions, an elitist replacement scheme is used. At every generation, the worst 50% of the solutions in the current population is replaced by the new ones.

4.1 Experiments on the Trap Function of Order 5

Here the maximum allowed indegree set to the BOA varies from 0 to 18. Problems of size 50, 100 and 150 were tested for the following population sizes 4000, 8000 and 16000 respectively. Fig. 2 shows the percentage of blocks solved in the best solution found at each run for the concatenated trap function of order 5.

This percentage goes from 0%, for the maximum allowed indegree of 0, to 100%, for the maximum allowed indegree of 4, and then falls back to 0%, for the maximum allowed indegree of 15.

The shape of the curves in Fig. 2 suggests that there is a limited set of values for the parameter that controls the complexity of the model in the BOA for which its performance is maximized. For values of the parameter outside of this set, the algorithm loses performance in terms of the quality of the solutions returned by the algorithm. This behavior holds true for other functions as well.

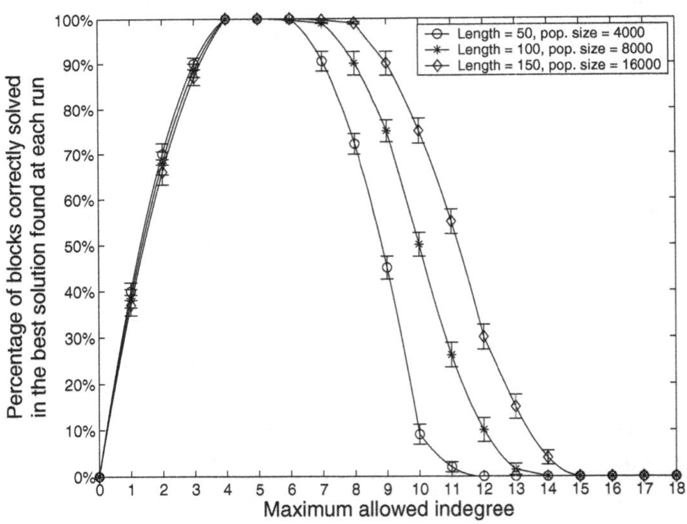

Fig. 2. The BOA applied to the concatenated trap function of order 5. Maximum allowed indegree versus the percentage of blocks solved in the best solution found at each run. The results are averaged over 200 independent runs.

4.2 MAX-3-SAT Problem

This experiment uses an instance of the Max-3-SAT problem with 50 variables and 218 clauses, all satisfiable. This instance of the problem was randomly gener-

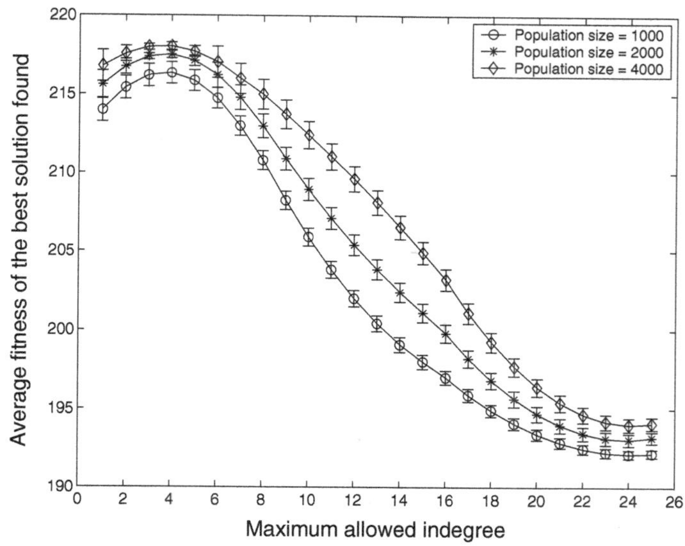

Fig. 3. The BOA applied to a Max-3-SAT problem of size 50. Maximum allowed indegree versus the average value, over 100 independent runs, of the best fitness found. The stopping criterion used was the convergence of all individuals in the population to a unique fitness value.

ated and is in the "phase transition". Fig. 3 plots the maximum allowed indegree versus the average value of the best fitness found at each run for the Max-3-SAT problem. The results are averaged over 100 independent runs. Three different population sizes were used, 1000, 2000 and 3000. The maximum allowed indegree varies from 0 to 25.

Again, the results indicate that when the complexity of the probabilistic model of the BOA is too high, the quality of the best solutions found by the algorithm decreases. The more complex the model is the more likely it is to detect spurious correlations on the data. Consequently, the diversity of the new solutions generated through this model also decreases as shown in Fig. 4.

Fig. 4 shows the average number of new unique configurations of the solutions to the problem generated per run. This number is computed as follows: at each generation, we count and record the number of strings whose configuration is present in the current population but was not present in the antecedent population. At the end of the run these numbers are summed up and the result is divided by the number of generations performed on that run. The curves in Fig. 4 represent the sum of the values obtained at the end of each run divided by the number of runs. The results suggest that the more complex the model is, the less diversity the population of solutions generated by the BOA tends to have. The diversity from one population to another goes to almost zero when the maximum allowed indegree is equal to 25. There seems to be a tradeoff between identifying enough correlations inside the partial solutions of the problem and not identifying an excessive number of correlations outside the partial solutions of the problem (spurious correlations). The

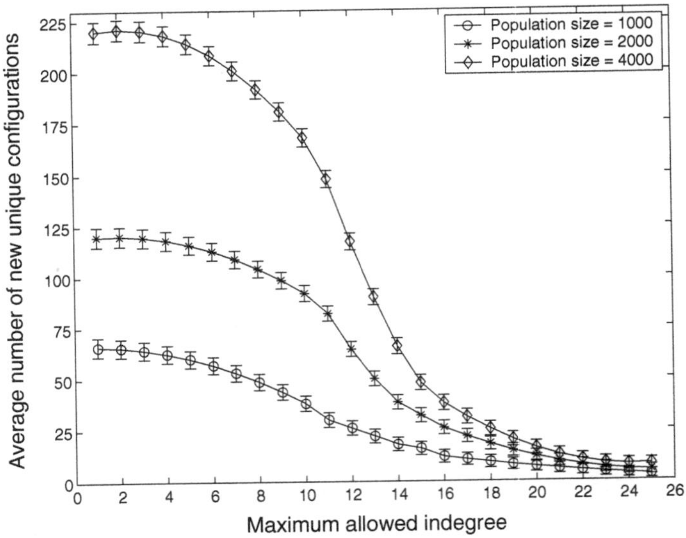

Fig. 4. The BOA applied to a Max-3-SAT problem of size 50. Maximum allowed indegree versus the average of the number of new unique configurations per generation. The results are averaged over 100 independent runs.

model has to be complex enough to identify some of the correlations inside the partial solutions of the problem. But if the model is too complex, an excessive number of spurious correlations may be detected. And when it happens, the diversity in the population of solutions generated by this model falls. Specifying exactly how much complexity the model should have is out of the scope of this work. It seems to depend not only on the structure of the optimization problem being solved, but also on the size of the data set used to construct the BN. A similar behavior is observed for the 1D spin-glass problem as shown next.

4.3 Experiments on the 1D Spin-Glass Problem

We randomly generated an instance of the 1D spin-glass problem with size 50. The maximum fitness value for this problem is equal to 64.34. Three different population sizes were tested, 1000, 2000 and 3000. The maximum allowed indegree varies from 0 to 25.

Fig. 5 shows more evidence that when the probabilistic model used by an EDA overfits the complexity that the structure of the problem requires, the algorithm loses performance. For this problem a maximum allowed indegree value of 1 was sufficient for the BOA to find the optimum to the problem in 100% of the trials for all population sizes tested. This happens because the 1D spin-glass problem has a chain-like structure. Such a structure can easily be encoded by a Bayesian network with maximum allowed indegree 1. When the maximum allowed indegree is greater than 10 the quality of the solutions returned by the BOA decreases for all cases tested.

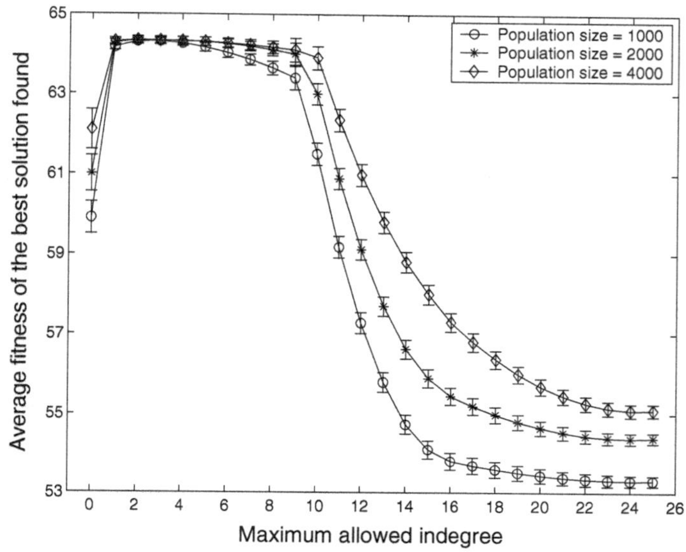

Fig. 5. The BOA applied to a 1D spin-glass problem of size 50. Maximum allowed indegree versus the average value, over 100 independent runs, of the best fitness found. The stopping criterion used was the convergence of all individuals in the population to a unique fitness value.

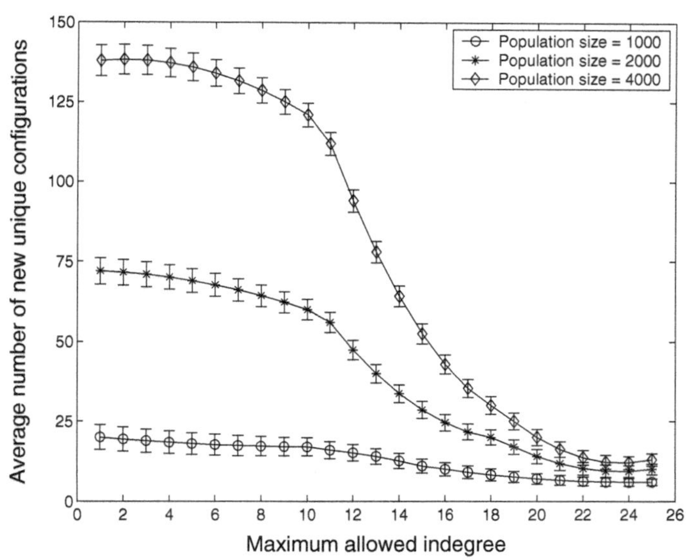

Fig. 6. The BOA applied to a 1D spin-glass problem of size 50. Maximum allowed indegree versus the average, over 100 independent runs, of the number of new unique configurations per generation in a full run of the algorithm.

Again, the average number of new unique configurations of solutions vanishes when the complexity of the model increases. Fig. 6 shows the average number of new unique configurations of the solutions, per run, to this problem. The results indicate that the exploration of the search space diminishes as the complexity of the Bayesian network increases.

Comparing the curves for the population size of 4000 from Figs. 5 and 6 we observe a certain pattern. That is, the average value of the best solution found and the average value of new unique configurations in the population have a downfall on the maximum allowed indegree value of 10. As the only parameter that varies along the plotting of those curves is the maximum allowed indegree value of the BN, what causes the downfall on the quality of the solutions and on the diversity in the population is the increase in the complexity of the BN. The more correlations the Bayesian network encodes the more similar to the solutions used to construct the BN the new sampled solutions will be. As a result, the exploration of the search space is not as good as it could be with a simpler BN.

5 Future Work and Conclusions

The BOA performs better when it identifies enough correlations inside the partial solutions of the problem without identifying an excessive number of spurious correlations. The higher the maximum allowed indegree of its Bayesian network is the more spurious correlations the BOA tends to identify. When the number of spurious correlations detected is too high, it negatively affects the performance of the algorithm. Therefore, a distinction between the complexity of the model and the complexity that the structure of the problem requires should be made. There is a relationship between the complexity that the model in the BOA can reach and BOA's performance.

Every study will have limitations, these have to be addressed. Our empirical experiments did not investigate problems that have partial solutions of different sizes. For instance, some partial solutions of the problem have size 6 while others have size 10, etc. The experiments suggest that the size of the partial solutions of the problem may work as an indication for the complexity necessary for the model. But how to predict this complexity when partial solutions of the problem have different sizes? This is a topic for future research. The analysis of how other scoring metrics, such as the Minimal Description Length, used to measure the goodness-of-fit of the Bayesian network to the data affect the performance of the BOA is also a topic for future investigation. Though other scoring metrics are likely to behave differently, the maximum allowed indegree of the Bayesian network will always be critical for the performance of the BOA.

The Bayesian Optimization Algorithm has improved and has been extended to the so called hierarchical BOA (hBOA). For further research it would be interesting to know how the results presented in this paper affect the performance of this improved version of the algorithm.

References

1. Ludovic Berthier and A. Peter Young. Time and length scales in spin glasses. *Journal of Physics: Condensed Matter*, 16:729–734, 2004.
2. Christian Borgelt and Rudolf Kruse. An empirical investigation of the k2 metric. In *Proceedings of the 6th European Conference on Symbolic and Quantitative Approaches to Reasoning and Uncertainty*, pages 240–251, Toulouse, France, 2001. Springer-Verlag.
3. Remco R. Bouckaert. Properties of Bayesian belief network learning algorithms. In In R. Lopez de Mantaras and editors D. Poole, editors, *Proceedings of the 10th Conference on Uncertainty in Artificial Intelligence*, pages 102–109, Seattle, WA, USA, 1994. Morgan Kaufmann.
4. David M. Chickering, Dan Geiger, and David Heckerman. Learning Bayesian networks is NP-hard. Technical Report MSR-TR-94-17, Microsoft Research, November 1994.
5. Stephen A. Cook. The complexity of theorem proving procedures. In *Proceedings of the third Annual ACM Symposium on Theory of Computing*, pages 151–158, Shaker Heights, Ohio, USA, May 1971.
6. Gregory F. Cooper and Edward Herskovits. A Bayesian method for induction of probabilistic networks from data. Technical Report SMI-91-01, University of Pittsburgh, Pittsburgh, PA, USA, January 1991.
7. Ian P. Gent and Toby Walsh. An empirical analysis of search in GSAT. *Artificial Intelligence Research*, 1:47–59, 1993.
8. Jun Gu, Panos Pardalos, and Ding-Zhu Du. *Satisfiability problem: theory and applications*, volume 35 of *Dimacs Series in Discrete Mathematics and Theoretical Computer Science*. American Mathematical Society, October 1997.
9. Finn V. Jensen. *Bayesian networks and decision graphs.* Springer-Verlag, 1st edition, July 2001.
10. David G. Mitchell, Bart Selman, and Hector J. Levesque. Hard and easy distributions for SAT problems. In Rosenbloom P. and Szolovits P., editors, *Proceedings of the tenth National Conference on Artificial Intelligence*, pages 459–465, Menlo Park, CA, USA, 1992. AAAI Press.
11. Judea Pearl. *Probabilistic reasoning in intelligent systems: networks of plausible inference.* Morgan Kaufmann, 1st edition, September 1988.
12. Martin Pelikan. *Bayesian optimization algorithm: from single level to hierarchy.* PhD thesis, Department of Computer Science at the University of Illinois at Urbana-Champaign, Urbana-Champaign, IL, USA, 2002.
13. Martin Pelikan and David E. Goldberg. Research on the Bayesian optimization algorithm. In Wu A.S., editor, *Workshop of the Genetic and Evolutionary Computation Conference - GECCO-2000*, pages 216–219, Las Vegas, NV, USA, July 2000. Morgan Kaufmann.
14. Martin Pelikan, David E. Goldberg, and Erick Cantú-Paz. BOA: the Bayesian optimization algorithm. In Banzhaf W., Daida J., Eiben A.E., Garzon M.H., Honavar V., Jakiela M., and Smith R.E., editors, *Proceedings of the Genetic and Evolutionary Computation Conference GECCO-1999*, volume 1, pages 525–532, Orlando, Florida, USA, 1999. Morgan Kaufmann.
15. David M. Pennock and Quentin F. Stout. Exploiting a theory of phase transitions in three-satisfiability problems. In *Proceedings of the 13th National Conference on Artificial Intelligence (AAAI-96)*, pages 253–258, Portland, OR, USA, August 1996.

Genetic Programming for Kernel-Based Learning with Co-evolving Subsets Selection

Christian Gagné[1,2], Marc Schoenauer[2], Michèle Sebag[2], and Marco Tomassini[1]

[1] Information Systems Institute, Université de Lausanne, CH-1015 Dorigny, Switzerland
{christian.gagne, marco.tomassini}@unil.ch

[2] Équipe TAO – INRIA Futurs / CNRS UMR 8623, LRI, Bat. 490, Université Paris Sud, 91405 Orsay CEDEX, France
{marc.schoenauer, michele.sebag}@lri.fr

Abstract. Support Vector Machines (SVMs) are well-established Machine Learning (ML) algorithms. They rely on the fact that i) linear learning can be formalized as a well-posed optimization problem; ii) non-linear learning can be brought into linear learning thanks to the *kernel trick* and the mapping of the initial search space onto a high dimensional feature space. The kernel is designed by the ML expert and it governs the efficiency of the SVM approach. In this paper, a new approach for the automatic design of kernels by Genetic Programming, called the Evolutionary Kernel Machine (EKM), is presented. EKM combines a well-founded fitness function inspired from the margin criterion, and a co-evolution framework ensuring the computational scalability of the approach. Empirical validation on standard ML benchmark demonstrates that EKM is competitive using state-of-the-art SVMs with tuned hyper-parameters.

1 Introduction

Kernel methods, including the so-called Support Vector Machines (SVMs), are well-established learning approaches with both strong theoretical foundations and successful practical applications [1]. SVMs rely on two main advances in statistical learning. First, the linear supervised machine learning task is set as a well-posed (quadratic) optimization problem. Second, the above setting is extended to non-linear learning via the *kernel trick*: given a (manually designed) change of representation Φ mapping the initial space onto the so-called feature space, linear hypotheses are characterized in terms of the scalar product in the feature space, or *kernel*. These hypotheses correspond to non-linear hypotheses in the initial space. Although many specific kernels have been proposed in the literature, designing a kernel well suited for an application domain or a dataset so far remains an art more than a science.

This paper proposes a system, the *Evolutionary Kernel Machine* (EKM), for the automatic design of data-specific kernels. EKM applies Genetic Programming

T.P. Runarsson et al. (Eds.): PPSN IX, LNCS 4193, pp. 1008–1017, 2006.

(GP) [2] to construct symmetric functions (kernels), and optimizes a fitness function inspired from the margin criterion [3]. Kernels are assessed within a Nearest Neighbor classification process [4,5]. In order to cope with computational complexity, a cooperative co-evolution governs the prototype subset selection and the GP kernel design, while the fitness case subset selection undergoes a competitive co-evolution.

The paper is organized as follows. Section 2 introduces the formal background and notations on kernel methods. Sections 3 and 4 respectively describe the GP representation and the fitness function proposed for the EKM. Scalability issues are addressed in the co-evolutionary framework introduced in Section 5. Results on benchmark problems are given in Section 6. Finally, related works are discussed in Section 7 before concluding the paper in Section 8.

2 Formal Background and Notations

Supervised machine learning takes as input a dataset $\mathcal{E} = \{(\mathbf{x}_i, y_i),\ i = 1 \ldots n,\ \mathbf{x}_i \in X,\ y_i \in Y\}$, made of n examples; $\mathbf{x}_i$ and y_i respectively stand for the description and the label of the i-th example. The goal is to construct a hypothesis $\mathrm{h}(\mathbf{x})$ mapping X onto Y with minimal generalization error. Only vectorial domains ($X = \mathbb{R}^d$) are considered throughout this paper; further, only binary classification problems ($Y = \{1, -1\}$) are considered in the rest of this section.

Due to space limitations, the reader is referred to [6] for a comprehensive presentation of SVMs. In the simplest (linear separable) case, the hyper-plane $\mathrm{h}(\mathbf{x})$ maximizing the geometrical margin (distance to the closest examples) is constructed. The label associated to example x is the sign of $\mathrm{h}(\mathbf{x})$, with:

$$\mathrm{h}(\mathbf{x}) = \sum_i \alpha_i < \mathbf{x}, \mathbf{x}_i > + b$$

where $< \mathbf{x}, \mathbf{x}_i >$ denotes the scalar product of $\mathbf{x}$ and $\mathbf{x}_i$. Let Φ denotes a mapping from the instance space X onto the feature space and let the kernel $\mathrm{K}(\mathbf{x}, \mathbf{x}')$ be defined as:

$$\mathrm{K} : X \times X \mapsto \mathbb{R}; \qquad \mathrm{K}(\mathbf{x}, \mathbf{x}') =< \Phi(\mathbf{x}), \Phi(\mathbf{x}') >$$

Under some conditions (the kernel trick), non-linear classifiers on X are constructed as in the linear case, and characterized as $\mathrm{h}(\mathbf{x}) = \sum_i \alpha_i \mathrm{K}(\mathbf{x}, \mathbf{x}_i) + b$.

Besides SVMs, the kernel trick can be used to revisit all learning methods involving a distance measure. In the paper, the kernel nearest neighbor (Kernel-NN) algorithm [5], which revisits the k-nearest neighbors (k-NN) [4], is considered. Given a distance (or dissimilarity) function $\mathrm{d}(\mathbf{x}, \mathbf{x}')$ defined on the instance space X, given a set of labelled examples $\mathcal{E} = \{(\mathbf{x}_1, y_1), \ldots, (\mathbf{x}_n, y_n)\}$ and an instance $\mathbf{x}$ to be classified, the k-NN algorithm: i) determines the k examples closest to $\mathbf{x}$ according to $\mathrm{d}(\mathbf{x}, \mathbf{x}')$; ii) outputs the majority class of these k examples. Kernel-NN proceeds as k-NN, where distance $\mathrm{d}_{\mathrm{K}}(\mathbf{x}, \mathbf{x}')$ is defined after the kernel $\mathrm{K}(\mathbf{x}, \mathbf{x}')$ (more on this in Section 4).

Standard kernels on $X = \mathbb{R}^d$ include Gaussian and polynomial kernels[1]. It must be noted that the addition, multiplication and compositions of kernels are kernels, and therefore the standard SVM machinery can find the optimal value of hyper-parameters (e.g. σ, c or k) among a finite set. Quite the opposite, the functional (symbolic) optimization of $\mathrm{K}(\mathbf{x}, \mathbf{x}')$ cannot be tackled to our best knowledge except by Genetic Programming.

3 Genetic Programming of Kernels

The Evolutionary Kernel Machine applies GP to determine symmetric functions $\mathrm{K}(\mathbf{x}, \mathbf{x}')$ on $\mathbb{R}^d \times \mathbb{R}^d$ best suited to the dataset at hand. As shown in Table 1, the main difference compared to standard symbolic regression is that terminals are symmetric expressions of $\mathbf{x}$ and $\mathbf{x}'$ (e.g. $x_i + x'_i$, or $x_i x'_j + x_j x'_i$), enforcing the symmetry of the kernels ($\mathrm{K}(\mathbf{x}, \mathbf{x}') = \mathrm{K}(\mathbf{x}', \mathbf{x})$).

The initialization of GP individuals is done using a ramped half and half procedure [2]. The selection probability of terminals A_i, M_i, I_i and S_i (respectively $C_{i,j}$) is divided by $1/d$ (resp. $2/d(d+1)$), where d is the dimension of the initial instance space ($X = \mathbb{R}^d$).

Indeed the kernel functions built after Table 1 might not satisfy Mercer's condition ($\mathrm{K}(\mathbf{x}, \mathbf{x}) \leq 0 \not\Rightarrow \mathbf{x} = 0$) required for SVM optimization [6]. However these kernels will be assessed along a Kernel-NN classification rule [5]; therefore the fact that they are not necessarily positive is not a limitation. Quite the contrary, EKM kernels can achieve feature selection; typically, terminals associated to non-informative features should disappear along evolution. The use of EKM for feature selection will be examined in a future work.

4 Fitness Measure

Every kernel $\mathrm{K}(\mathbf{x}, \mathbf{x}')$ is assessed after the Kernel-NN classification rule, using the dissimilarity $\mathrm{d_K}$ defined as

$$\mathrm{d_K}(\mathbf{x}, \mathbf{x}')^2 = \mathrm{K}(\mathbf{x}, \mathbf{x}) + \mathrm{K}(\mathbf{x}', \mathbf{x}') - 2\mathrm{K}(\mathbf{x}, \mathbf{x}')$$

Given a prototype set $\mathcal{E}_p = \{(\mathbf{x}_1, y_1), \ldots, (\mathbf{x}_\ell, y_\ell)\}$ and a training example $e = (\mathbf{x}, y)$, let us assuming that $\mathcal{E}_p$ is ordered by increasing dissimilarity to $\mathbf{x}$ ($\mathrm{d_K}(\mathbf{x}, \mathbf{x}_i) \leq \mathrm{d_K}(\mathbf{x}, \mathbf{x}_{i+1})$). Let $\mathrm{p}(e)$ denotes the minimum rank over all prototype examples in the same class as e ($\mathrm{p}(e) = \min\{i,\ y_i = y,\ i = 1 \ldots \ell\}$); let $\mathrm{n}(e)$ denotes the minimum rank over all other prototype examples (not belonging to the same class as e, $\mathrm{n}(e) = \min\{i,\ y_i \neq y,\ i = 1 \ldots \ell\}$).

As noted by [3], the quality of the Kernel-NN classification of e can be assessed from $\delta_\mathrm{K}(e) = \mathrm{n}(e) - \mathrm{p}(e)$. The higher $\delta_\mathrm{K}(e)$, the more confident the classification of e is, e.g. with respect to perturbations of $\mathcal{E}_p$ or $\mathrm{d_K}$; $\delta_\mathrm{K}(e)$ measures the margin of e with respect to Kernel-NN.

---

[1] Respectively $\mathrm{K}(\mathbf{x}, \mathbf{x}') = \exp\left(-\frac{\|\mathbf{x}-\mathbf{x}'\|^2}{\sigma}\right)$ and $\mathrm{K}(\mathbf{x}, \mathbf{x}') = (<\mathbf{x}, \mathbf{x}'> + c)^k$.

Table 1. GP primitives involved in the kernel functions $K(\mathbf{x}, \mathbf{x}')$, $\mathbf{x}, \mathbf{x}' \in \mathbb{R}^d$

Name	# args.	Description
ADD2	2	Addition of two values, $f_{ADD2}(a_1, a_2) = a_1 + a_2$.
ADD3	3	Addition of three values, $f_{ADD3}(a_1, a_2, a_3) = a_1 + a_2 + a_3$.
ADD4	4	Addition of four values, $f_{ADD4}(a_1, a_2, a_3, a_4) = a_1 + a_2 + a_3 + a_4$.
SUB	2	Subtraction, $f_{SUB}(a_1, a_2) = a_1 - a_2$.
MUL2	2	Multiplication of two values, $f_{MUL2}(a_1, a_2) = a_1 a_2$.
MUL3	3	Multiplication of three values, $f_{MUL3}(a_1, a_2, a_3) = a_1 a_2 a_3$.
MUL4	4	Multiplication of four values, $f_{MUL4}(a_1, a_2, a_3, a_4) = a_1 a_2 a_3 a_4$.
DIV	2	Protected division, $f_{DIV}(a_1, a_2) = \begin{cases} 1 & \|a_2\| < 0.001 \\ a_1/a_2 & \text{otherwise} \end{cases}$.
MAX	2	Maximum value, $f_{MAX}(a_1, a_2) = \max(a_1, a_2)$.
MIN	2	Minimum value, $f_{MIN}(a_1, a_2) = \min(a_1, a_2)$.
EXP	1	Exponential value, $f_{EXP}(a) = \exp(a)$.
POW2	1	Square power, $f_{POW2}(a) = a^2$.
$A_i,\ i = 1 \dots d$	0	Add the ith components, $x_i + x'_i$.
$M_i,\ i = 1 \dots d$	0	Multiply the ith components, $x_i x'_i$.
$S_i,\ i = 1 \dots d$	0	Maximum between the ith components, $\max(x_i, x'_i)$.
$I_i,\ i = 1 \dots d$	0	Minimum between the ith components, $\min(x_i, x'_i)$.
$C_{i,j},\ i = 1 \dots d$, $j = 1 \dots i$	0	Crossed multiplication-addition between the ith and j^{th} components, $(x_i x'_j + x_j x'_i)$.
DOT	0	Scalar product of $\mathbf{x}$ and $\mathbf{x}'$, $< \mathbf{x}, \mathbf{x}' >$.
EUC	0	Euclidean distance of $\mathbf{x}$ and $\mathbf{x}'$, $\|\mathbf{x} - \mathbf{x}'\|$.
E	0	Ephemeral random constants, generated uniformly in $[-1, 1]$.

Accordingly, given a prototype set $\mathcal{E}_p = \{(\mathbf{x}_1, y_1), \dots, (\mathbf{x}_\ell, y_\ell)\}$ and a fitness case subset $\mathcal{E}_s = \{(\mathbf{x}'_1, y'_1), \dots, (\mathbf{x}'_m, y'_m)\}$, the fitness function associated to $K(\mathbf{x}, \mathbf{x}')$ is defined as

$$F(K) = \frac{1}{m} \sum_{i=1}^{m} \delta_K(\mathbf{x}'_i, y'_i) - \ell$$

The computation of F has linear complexity in the number ℓ of prototypes and in the number m of fitness cases. In a standard setting, $\mathcal{E}_p$ and $\mathcal{E}_s$ both coincide with the whole training set $\mathcal{E}$ ($\ell = m = n$). However the quadratic complexity of the fitness computation with respect to the number n of training examples is incompatible with the scalability of the approach.

5 Tractability Through Co-evolution

EKM scalability is obtained along two directions, by i) reducing the number ℓ of prototypes used for classification, and ii) reducing the size m of the fitness case subset considered during each generation.

Parameters:
p : GP kernels population size;
ℓ : Size of the prototype subset individuals;
m : Size of the fitness case subset individuals;
λ_p : Number of offsprings in the prototype species;
λ_s : Number of offsprings in the fitness case species;
ρ_p : Fraction of prototype subset individuals replaced by mutation;
ρ_s : Fraction of the fitness case subset individual replaced by mutation.

1. $\mathcal{E}_p^0$: initial prototype subset, stratified uniform sample of size ℓ from $\mathcal{E}$;
2. $\mathcal{E}_s^0$: initial fitness case subset, stratified uniform sample of size m from $\mathcal{E}$;
3. GP^0: initial population of GP kernels, $\{h_i^0,\ i = 1 \dots p\}$;
4. Loop, for $t = 1 \dots T$:
   (a) Apply selection and variation operators to the GP^{t-1} kernel population, constructing $GP^t = \{h_i^t,\ i = 1 \dots p\}$;
   (b) Compute the fitness $\mathrm{F}(h_i^t)$, $i = 1 \dots p$ with prototype subset $\mathcal{E}_s^{t-1}$ and fitness case subset $\mathcal{E}_s^{t-1}$; let $h^{t,*}$ denote the best one;
   (c) Generate λ_p offsprings of $\mathcal{E}_p^{t-1}$, by replacing a fraction ρ_p of the prototypes (uniform stratified sampling); assess these offsprings after $h^{t,*}$ and $\mathcal{E}_s^{t-1}$; set $\mathcal{E}_p^t$ to the best offspring;
   (d) Generate λ_s offsprings of $\mathcal{E}_s^{t-1}$, by replacing a fraction ρ_s of the fitness case (uniform stratified sampling); assess these offsprings after $h^{t,*}$ and $\mathcal{E}_p^t$; set $\mathcal{E}_s^t$ to the best offspring.
5. Output h^{**}, selected among $h^{t,*}$, $t = 0 \dots T$ as the one minimizing the 1-NN error rate on the whole training set $\mathcal{E}$ using the associated $\mathcal{E}_p^t$ prototype subset.

Fig. 1. The Evolutionary Kernel Machine: a co-evolution framework

More precisely, a co-evolutionary framework involving three species is considered, as detailed in Figure 1. The first species includes the GP kernels. The second species includes the prototype subset (fixed-size subsets of the training set), subject to a cooperative co-evolution [7] with the GP kernels. The third species includes the fitness case subset (fixed-size subsets of the training set), subject to a competitive host-parasite co-evolution [8] with the GP kernels.

The prototype species is evolved to find good prototypes such that they maximize the fitness of the GP kernels. The fitness case species is evolved to find hard and challenging examples, such that they minimize the kernel fitness. Of course there is a danger that the fitness case subset ultimately capture the noisy examples, as observed in the boosting framework [9] (see Section 6.2).

Both prototype and selection species are initialized using a stratified uniform sampling with no replacement (the class distribution in the sample is the same as in the whole dataset and all examples are distinct). Both species are evolved using a $(1, \lambda)$ evolution strategy; in each generation, λ offsprings are generated using a uniform stratified replacement of a given fraction of the parent subset,

Table 2. UCI data sets used for the experimentations

Data set	Size	# of features	# of classes	Application domain
bcw	683	9	2	Wisconcin's breast cancer, 65% benign and 35% malignant.
bld	345	6	2	BUPA liver disorders, 58% with disorders and 42% without disorder.
bos	508	13	3	Boston housing, 34 % with median value $v < 18.77$ K$, 33 % with $v \in]18.77, 23.74]$, and 33 % with $v > 23.74$.
cmc	1473	9	3	Contraceptive method choice, 43% not using contraception, 35 % using short-term contraception, and 23 % using long-term contraception.
ion	351	34	2	Ionosphere radar signal, 36 % without structure detected and 64 % with a structure detected.
pid	768	8	2	Pima indians diabetes, 65% tested negative and 35% tested positive for diabetes.

and assessed after the best kernel in the current kernel population. The parent subset is replaced by the best offspring. In each generation, the kernels are assessed after the current prototype and fitness case individuals.

6 Experimental Validation

This section reports on the experimental validation of EKM, on a standard set of benchmark problems [10], detailed in Table 2. The system is implemented using the Open BEAGLE framework[2] for evolutionary computation [11].

6.1 Experimental Setting

The parameters used in EKM are reported in Table 3. The average evolution time for one run is less than one hour (AMD Athlon 2800+).

On each problem, EKM has been evaluated along the standard 10-fold cross validation methodology. The whole data set is partitioned into 10 (stratified) subsets; the training set is made of all subsets but one; the best hypothesis learned from this training set is evaluated on the remaining subset, or test set. The accuracy is averaged over the 10 folds (as the test set ranges over the 10 subsets of the whole dataset); for each fold, EKM is launched 10 times; the 5 best hypotheses (after their accuracy on the training set) are assessed on the test set; the reported accuracy is the average over the 10 folds of these 5 best hypotheses on the test set. In total, EKM is launched 100 times on each problem.

EKM is compared to state of the art algorithms, including k-nearest neighbor and SVMs with Gaussian kernels, similarly assessed using 10-fold cross validation. For k-NN, the underlying distance is the Euclidean one, and scaling normalization option has been considered; the k parameter has been varied in

[2] `http://beagle.gel.ulaval.ca`

Table 3. Tableau of the evolutions parameters

Parameter	Description and parameter values
	GP kernel functions evolution parameters
Primitives	See Table 1.
GP population size	One population of $p = 1000$ individuals
Stop criterion	Evolution ends after $T = 100$ generations.
Replacement strategy	Genetic operations applied following generational scheme.
Selection	Lexicographic parsimony pressure tournaments selection with 7 participants.
Crossover	Classical subtree crossover [2] (prob. 0.7).
Standard mutation	Crossover with a random individual (prob. 0.1).
Swap node mutation	Exchange a primitive with another of the same arity (prob. 0.1).
Shrink mutation	Replace a branch with one of its children and remove the branch mutated and the other children subtrees (if any) (prob. 0.1).
	Prototype subset selection parameters
Prototype subset size	$\ell = 50$ examples in a prototype subset.
Number of offsprings	$\lambda_p = 4$ offsprings per generation.
Mutation rate	$\rho_p = 25$ % of the prototype examples replaced in each mutation.
	Fitness case subset selection parameters
Fitness case subset size	$m = 100$ examples in a fitness case subset.
Number of offsprings	$\lambda_s = 2$ offsprings per generation.
Mutation rate	$\rho_s = 50\%$ of the selection examples replaced in each mutation.

$\{1, 3, 5\}$; the best setting has been kept. For Gaussian SVMs, the Torch3 implementation has been used [12]; the error cost (parameter C) has been varied in $\{10^i,\ i = -3 \ldots 4\}$, the σ parameter is set to 10, and the best setting has been similarly retained.

6.2 Results

Table 4 shows the results obtained by EKM compared with k-NN and Gaussian SVM, together with the optimal parameters for the latter algorithms. The size of the best GP kernel (last column) shows that no bloat occurred, thanks to the lexicographic parsimony pressure. Each algorithm is shown to be the best performing on the half or more of the tested datasets, with frequent ties according to a paired Student's t-test.

Typically, the problems where Gaussian SVMs perform well are those where the optimal C value for cost error is high, suggesting that the noise level in these datasets is high too. Indeed, the fitness case subset selection embedded in EKM might favor the selection of noisy examples, as those are more challenging to GP kernels. A more progressive selection mechanism, taking into account all kernels in the GP population to better filter out noisy examples and outliers, will be considered in further research.

Table 4. Comparative 10-fold results of k-NN, Gaussian SVM and EKM on the UCI data sets, with optimal settings (k and scaling for k-NN, C for SVM). The reported test error is averaged over the 10 folds. For each fold tested with the EKM, the 5 solutions out of 10 runs with best training error are assessed on the test set, and their error is averaged. Test error rates in **bold** denotes the statistically best results according to a 95% two-tails paired Student's t-test. "Average rank" column gives the test error ranking obtained for EKM compared to k-NN and SVM averaged over the 10 folds.

	k-NN				SVM			EKM			
Data set	Best conf. k	Best conf. Scaling	Train error	Test error	Best C	Train error	Test error	Train error	Best-half test error	Mean size	Average rank
`bcw`	5	No	0.027	**0.025**	1	0.030	**0.028**	0.020	**0.030**	167	2.1
`bld`	5	No	0.336	0.353	1	0.329	**0.325**	0.299	**0.309**	158	1.5
`bos`	1	Yes	0.248	**0.235**	0.001	0.224	0.308	0.253	0.281	116	1.8
`cmc`	5	No	0.491	0.486	10	0.273	**0.433**	0.479	0.487	129	2.4
`ion`	1	Yes	0.134	0.134	100	0.070	**0.071**	0.078	**0.095**	156	1.9
`pid`	5	Yes	0.265	**0.255**	0.001	0.315	0.307	0.237	**0.252**	145	1.45

The k-NN outperforms SVM and EKM on the `bos` problem, where the noise level appears to be very low. Indeed, the optimal value for the number k of nearest neighbors is $k = 1$, while the optimal cost error is 10^{-3}, suggesting that the error rate is also low. Still, the fact that the error rate is close to 23% might be explained as the target concept is complex and/or many examples lie close to its frontier. On `bcw`, the differences between the three algorithms are not statistically different and the test error rate is about 2%, suggesting that the problem is rather easy.

EKM is found to outperform the other algorithms on `bld`, demonstrating that Kernel-based dissimilarity can improve on Euclidean distance with and without rescaling. Last, EKM behaves like k-NN on the `pid` problems. Further, it must be noted that EKM classifies the test examples using a 50-examples prototype set, whereas k-NN uses the whole training set (above 300 examples in the `bld` problem and 690 in the `pid` problem).

As the well-known No Free Lunch theorem applies to Machine Learning too, no learning method is expected to be universally competent. Rather, the above experimental validation demonstrates that the GP-evolved kernels can improve on standard kernels in some cases.

7 Related Works

The most relevant work to EKM is the Genetic Kernel Support Vector Machine (GK-SVM) [13]. GK-SVM similarly uses GP within an SVM-based approach, with two main differences compared to EKM. On one hand, GK-SVM focuses on feature construction, using GP to optimize mapping Φ (instead of the kernel). On the other hand, the fitness function used in GK-SVM suffers from a quadratic complexity in the number of training examples. Accordingly, all datasets but one considered in the experimentations are small (less than 200 examples). On a larger dataset, the authors acknowledge that their approach does not improve on a standard SVM with well chosen parameters. Another related work similarly uses GP for feature construction, in order to classify time series [14]. The set of features (GP trees) is further evolved using a GA, where the fitness function is based on the accuracy of an SVM classifier. Most other works related to evolutionary optimization within SVMs (see [15]) actually focus on parametric optimization, e.g. achieving features selection or tuning some parameters.

Another related work is proposed by Weinberger *et al.* [16], optimizing a Mahalanobis distance based on the k-NN margin criterion inspired from [3] and also used in EKM. However, restricted to linear changes of representation, the optimization problem is tackled by semi-definite programming in [16]. Lastly, EKM is also inspired by the Dynamic Subset Selection first proposed by Gathercole and Ross [17] and further developed by [18] to address scalability issues in EC-based Machine Learning.

8 Conclusion

The Evolutionary Kernel Machine proposed in this paper aims to improve kernel-based nearest neighbor classification [5], combining two original aspects. First, EKM implicitly addresses the feature construction problem by designing a new representation of the application domain better suited to the dataset at hand. However, in contrast with [13,14], EKM takes advantage of the kernel trick, using GP to optimize the kernel function. Secondly, EKM proposes a co-evolution framework to ensure the scalability of the approach and control the computational complexity of the fitness computation. The empirical validation demonstrates that this new approach is competitive with well-founded learning algorithms such as SVM and k-NN using tuned hyper-parameters.

A limitation of the approach, also observed in the well-known boosting algorithm [9], is that the competitive co-evolution of kernels and examples tends to favor noisy validation examples. A perspective for further research is to exploit the evolution archive, to estimate the probability for an example to be noisy and achieve a sensitivity analysis. Another perspective is to incorporate ensemble learning, typically bagging and boosting, within EKM. Indeed the diversity of the solutions constructed along population-based optimization enables ensemble learning almost for free.

Acknowledgments. This work was supported by postdoctoral fellowships from the ERCIM (Europe) and the FQRNT (Québec) to C. Gagné. M. Schoenauer and M. Sebag gratefully acknowledge support by the PASCAL Network of Excellence, IST2002506778.

References

1. Shawe-Taylor, J., Cristianini, N.: Kernel Methods for Pattern Analysis. Cambridge University Press, Cambridge, UK (2004)
2. Koza, J.R.: Genetic Programming: On the Programming of Computers by Means of Natural Selection. MIT Press, Cambridge (MA), USA (1992)
3. Gilad-Bachrach, R., Navot, A., Tishby, N.: Margin based feature selection - theory and algorithms. In: Proc. of the 21st Int. Conf. on Machine Learning. (2004) 43–50
4. Duda, R.O., Hart, P.E., Stork, D.G.: Pattern Classification. John Wiley & Sons, Inc., New York (NY), USA (2001)
5. Yu, K., Ji, L., Zhang, X.: Kernel nearest neighbor algorithm. Neural Processing Letters **15**(2) (2002) 147–156
6. Cristianini, N., Shawe-Taylor, J.: An Introduction to Support Vector Machines and Other Kernel-based Learning Methods. Cambridge University Press, Cambridge, UK (2000)
7. Potter, M.A., De Jong, K.A.: Cooperative coevolution: An architecture for evolving coadapted subcomponents. Evolutionary Computation **8**(1) (2000) 1–29
8. Hillis, W.D.: Co-evolving parasites improve simulated evolution as an optimization procedure. Physica D **42** (1990) 228–234
9. Freund, Y., Shapire, R.: Experiments with a new boosting algorithm. In: Proc. of the 13th. Int. Conf. on Machine Learning. (1996) 148–156
10. Newman, D., Hettich, S., Blake, C., Merz, C.: UCI repository of machine learning databases. `http://www.ics.uci.edu/~mlearn/MLRepository.html` (1998)
11. Gagné, C., Parizeau, M.: Genericity in evolutionary computation software tools: Principles and case-study. Int. J. on Artif. Intell. Tools **15**(2) (2006) 173–194
12. Collobert, R., Bengio, S., Mariéthoz, J.: Torch: a modular machine learning software library. Technical Report IDIAP-RR 02-46, IDIAP (2002)
13. Howley, T., Madden, M.G.: The genetic kernel support vector machine: Description and evaluation. Artificial Intelligence Review **24**(3–4) (2005) 379–395
14. Eads, D., Hill, D., Davis, S., Perkins, S., Ma, J., Porter, R., Theiler, J.: Genetic algorithms and support vector machines for time series classification. In: Applications and Science of Neural Networks, Fuzzy Systems, and Evolutionary Computations V. (2002) 74–85
15. Friedrichs, F., Igel, C.: Evolutionary tuning of multiple SVM parameters. Neurocomputing **64** (2005) 107–117
16. Weinberger, K., John, B., Lawrence, S.: Distance metric learning for large margin nearest neighbor classification. In: Neural Information Processing Systems. (2005) 1473–1480
17. Gathercole, C., Ross, P.: Dynamic training subset selection for supervised learning in genetic programming. In: Parallel Problem Solving From Nature. (1994) 312–321
18. Song, D., Heywood, M.I., Zincir-Heywood, A.N.: Training genetic programming on half a million patterns: an example from anomaly detection. IEEE Transactions on Evolutionary Computation **9**(3) (2005) 225–239

Product Geometric Crossover

Alberto Moraglio and Riccardo Poli

Dept. of Computer Science
University of Essex, UK
{amoragn, rpoli}@essex.ac.uk

Abstract. Geometric crossover is a representation-independent definition of crossover based on the distance of the search space interpreted as a metric space. It generalizes the traditional crossover for binary strings and other important recombination operators for the most frequently used representations. Using a distance tailored to the problem at hand, the abstract definition of crossover can be used to design new problem specific crossovers that embed problem knowledge in the search. In this paper, we introduce the important notion of product geometric crossover that allows to build new geometric crossovers combining pre-existing geometric crossovers in a simple way.

1 Introduction

Geometric crossover and geometric mutation are representation-independent search operators that generalize many pre-existing search operators for the major representations used in evolutionary algorithms, such as binary strings [4], real vectors [4], permutations [6], syntactic trees [5] and sequences [7]. They are defined in geometric terms using the notions of line segment and ball. These notions and the corresponding genetic operators are well-defined once a notion of distance in the search space is defined. Defining search operators as functions of the search space is opposite to the standard way [3] in which the search space is seen as a function of the search operators employed. This viewpoint greatly simplifies the relationship between search operators and fitness landscape and has allowed us to give simple *rules-of-thumb* to build crossover operators that are likely to perform well.

Theoretical results of metric spaces can naturally lead to interesting results for geometric crossover. In particular, in this paper we focus on the notion of *metric transformation*. A metric transformation is an operator that constructs new metric spaces from pre-existing metric spaces: it takes one or more metric spaces as input and outputs a new metric space. The notion of metric transformation becomes extremely interesting when considered together with distances firmly rooted in the syntactic structure of the underlaying solution representation (e.g., edit distances). In these cases it gives rise to a simple and *natural interpretation in terms of syntactic transformations*.

In this paper we extend the geometric framework introducing the important notion of cartesian product of geometric crossover, that allows to build new

T.P. Runarsson et al. (Eds.): PPSN IX, LNCS 4193, pp. 1018–1027, 2006.

geometric crossovers combining preexisting geometric crossovers in a very simple way. The metric transformation considered is a simple product of metric spaces and the corresponding induced crossover transformation is the *product geometric crossover*. This may sound very abstract and impractical. However, it actually is not. Indeed, we put the ideas reported in this paper to the test in [8].

The paper is organised as follows. In section 2 we present the geometric framework. In section 3, we extend it with the notion of geometricity-preserving transformation and focus on the notion of product geometric crossover. In section 4, we outline future investigations. In section 5, we draw some conclusions.

2 Geometric Framework

2.1 Geometric Preliminaries

In the following we give necessary preliminary geometric definitions and extend those introduced in [4] and [5]. The following definitions are taken from [2].

The terms *distance* and *metric* denote any real valued function that conforms to the axioms of identity, symmetry and triangular inequality. A simple connected graph is naturally associated to a metric space via its *path metric*: the distance between two nodes in the graph is the length of a shortest path between the nodes.

In a metric space (S, d) a *line segment* (or closed interval) is the set of the form $[x; y] = \{z \in S | d(x, z) + d(z, y) = d(x, y)\}$ where $x, y \in S$ are called extremes of the segment. Metric segment generalises the familiar notions of segment in the Euclidean space to any metric space through distance redefinition. Notice that a metric segment does not coincide to a shortest path connecting its extremes (*geodesic*) as in an Euclidean space. In general, there may be more than one geodesic connecting two extremes; the metric segment is the union of all geodesics.

We assign a structure to the solution set S by endowing it with a notion of distance d. $M = (S, d)$ is therefore a solution *space* and $L = (M, g)$ is the corresponding fitness landscape.

2.2 Geometric Crossover Definition

The following definitions are *representation-independent* therefore applicable to any representation.

Definition 1. *(Image set) The* image set $Im[OP]$ *of a genetic operator* OP *is the set of all possible offspring produced by* OP *with non-zero probability.*

Definition 2. *(Geometric crossover) A binary operator is a geometric crossover under the metric* d *if all offspring are in the segment between its parents.*

Definition 3. *(Uniform geometric crossover) Uniform geometric crossover* UX *is a geometric crossover where all* z *laying between parents* x *and* y *have the same probability of being the offspring:*

$$f_{UX}(z|x,y) = \frac{\delta(z \in [x;y])}{|[x;y]|}$$

$$Im[UX(x,y)] = \{z \in S | f_{UX}(z|x,y) > 0\} = [x;y].$$

A number of general properties for geometric crossover and mutation have been derived in [4] where we also showed that traditional crossover is geometric under Hamming distance.

In previous work we have also studied various crossovers for permutations, revealing that PMX, a well-known crossover for permutations, is geometric under swap distance. Also, we found that Cycle crossover, another traditional crossover for permutations, is geometric under swap distance and under Hamming distance.

2.3 Formal Evolutionary Algorithm and Problem Knowledge

Geometric operators are defined as functions of the distance associated to the search space. However, the search space does not come with the problem itself. The problem consists only of a fitness function to optimize, that defines what a solution is and how to evaluate it, but it does not give any structure on the solution set. The act of putting a structure over the solution set is part of the search algorithm design and it is a designer's choice.

A fitness landscape is the fitness function plus a structure over the solution space. So, for each problem, there is one fitness function but as many fitness landscapes as the number of possible different structures over the solution set. In principle, the designer could choose the structure to assign to the solution set completely independently from the problem at hand. However, because the search operators are defined over such a structure, doing so would make them decoupled from the problem at hand, hence turning the search into something very close to random search.

In order to avoid this one can exploit problem knowledge in the search. This can be achieved by carefully designing the connectivity structure of the fitness landscape. For example, one can study the objective function of the problem and select a neighborhood structure that couples the distance between solutions and their fitness values. Once this is done problem knowledge can be exploited by search operators to perform better than random search, even if the search operators are problem-independent (as is the case of geometric crossover and mutation). Indeed, the fitness landscape is a knowledge interface between the problem at hand and a formal, problem-independent search algorithm.

Under which conditions is a landscape well-searchable by geometric operators? As a rule of thumb, geometric mutation and geometric crossover work well on landscapes where the closer pairs of solutions, the more correlated their fitness values. Of course this is no surprise: the importance of landscape smoothness has been advocated in many different context and has been confirmed in uncountable empirical studies with many neighborhood search meta-heuristics [9]. We operate according to the following rule-of-thumbs:

Rule-of-thumb 1: if we have a good distance for the problem at hand than we have good geometric mutation and good geometric crossover
Rule-of-thumb 2: a good distance for the problem at hand is a distance that makes the landscape "smooth"

3 Product Geometric Crossover

We first introduce the general notion of geometricity-preserving transformations. Then we consider a specific geometricity-preserving transformation associated with the product metric. We introduce product metrics for vector spaces, that are metric preserving transformations, and stress how they can be seen as natural generalization of simple metrics for vector spaces. We then introduce the notion of interval space that naturally bridges the metric and representation aspects of geometric crossover, and recall a few results form interval spaces theory. We use these results to prove our main result of this paper on the product of geometric crossovers. We then give a number of examples of applications. In section 4, we will discuss how to further generalize this theorem to a general structural composition of geometric crossovers.

3.1 Geometricity-Preserving Transformations

In previous work we have proven that a number of important pre-existing recombination operators for the most frequently used representations are geometric crossovers. We have also applied the abstract definition of geometric crossover to distances firmly rooted in a specific solution representation and designed brand-new crossovers. An appealing way to build new geometric crossovers is starting from recombination operators that are known to be geometric and derive new geometric crossovers by *geometricity-preserving transformations/combinations* that when applied to geometric crossovers, return geometric crossovers.

The definition of geometric crossover is based on the notion of metric. Therefore, a natural starting point to seek geometricity-preserving transformations is to consider transformations of the underlying metrics that are known to return metric spaces and study how the geometric crossover associated to the transformed metric space relates with the geometric crossover associated with the original metric space.

There are a number of metric space transformations [2] [10] that are potentially of interest for geometric crossover: sub-metric spaces, product spaces, quotient metric space, gluing metric space, combinatorial transformation, non-negative combinations of metric spaces, Hausdorf transformation, Concave transformation, and Biotope transform.

Geometric crossover is well-defined once a metric space is defined. Let us consider the geometric crossover X associated to the original metric space M, and the geometric crossover X' associated to the transformed metric space $M' = mt(M)$ where mt is the metric transformation. The functional relationship among metric spaces and geometric crossovers can be nicely expressed through a commutative diagram (Fig. 1). gx means application of the formal definition of geometric crossover and gt means *induced geometricity-preserving* crossover transformation associated to the metric transformation mt. This diagram becomes remarkably interesting when the metric transformation mt is associated to an induced geometricity-preserving crossover transformation gt that has a simple interpretation in terms of syntactic manipulation. This indeed allows one to get new geometric crossovers starting from recombination operators that are known to be geometric by simple *geometricity-preserving syntax manipulation.*

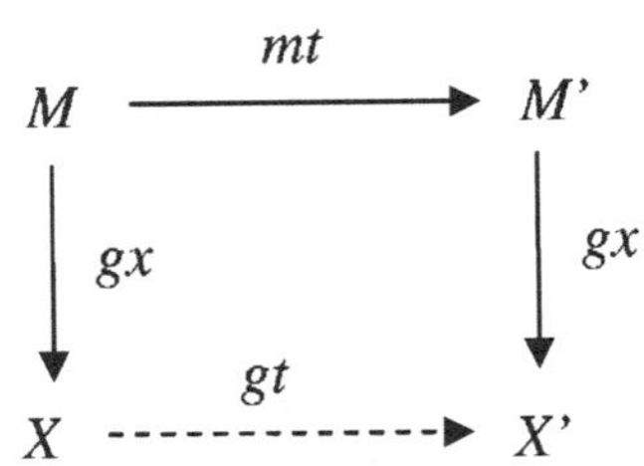

Fig. 1. Commutative diagram linking metric and crossover transformations

We study those metric-preserving transformations which induced geometricity-preserving transformations have a simple and natural interpretation on the solution representation.

3.2 N-Dimensional Real Spaces and Product Metric Spaces

Metric spaces on $\mathbb{R}^2$. Let $S = \mathbb{R}^2$, and $x = (x', x'')$, $y = (y', y'')$. The following are metric spaces on S:

$d_1(x, y) = |x' - y'| + |x'' - y''|$ (Manhattan space)
$d_2(x, y) = \sqrt{|x' - y'|^2 + |x'' - y''|^2}$ (Euclidean space)
$d_\infty(x, y) = Max\{|x' - y'| + |x'' - y''|\}$ (Chessboard space)

These may be proved to be metrics [10]. These definitions may be extended to n-dimensional real spaces.

Product metric spaces. Given two metric spaces $M' = (S', d')$ and $M'' = (S'', d'')$, we may define several metrics on $S' \times S''$. For example, if $x = (x', x'')$ and $y = (y', y'')$ are in $S' \times S''$, let

$d_1(x, y) = d'(x', y') + d''(x'', y'')$ (Manhattan product)
$d_2(x, y) = \sqrt{d'(x', y')^2 + d''(x'', y'')^2}$ (Euclidean product)
$d_\infty(x, y) = Max\{d'(x', y') + d''(x'', y'')\}$ (Chessboard product)

These may be proved to be metrics [10]. These definitions may be extended to the product of any finite number of metric spaces.

It is interesting to notice that product spaces can be considered as generalization of n-dimensional real spaces, where the absolute value metric at each dimension is replaced by a generic metric. This is important because the generalization involves two different types of objects: a *simple metric* for a structured space and a structural *metric transformation* of generic metric spaces. More on this in the section 4.

3.3 Product Interval Spaces

Metric spaces can be associated to geometric interval spaces. The latter are a more natural setting for geometric crossover than the former. We review the notion of interval space and present results that draw a parallel between metric spaces and interval spaces. Then we use them to prove specific results for geometric crossover.

Interval space and Geometric interval space. Let X be a set and let $I : X \times X \to 2^X$ be a function with the following properties:

- *Extensive Law*: $a, b \in I(a, b)$
- *Symmetry Law*: $I(a, b) = I(b, a)$

Then I is called an *interval operator on* X, and $I(a, b)$ is the *interval between* a *and* b. The resulting pair (X, I) is called an *interval space*.
An interval operator I on a set X is *geometric* provided the following hold.

- *Idempotent Law*: $\forall b \in X : I(b, b) = \{b\}$
- *Monotone Law*: if $a, b, c \in X$ and $c \in I(a, b)$, then $I(a, c) \subseteq I(a, b)$
- *Inversion Law*: if $a, b \in X$ and $c, d \in I(a, b)$, then $c \in I(a, d)$ implies $d \in I(c, b)$

A set with a geometric interval operator is called a *geometric interval space*.

Interval space associated to a metric space. The geodesic operator $[\bullet, \bullet]_d$ that associates extremes of a metric segment to all the points that constitute it is a geometric interval operator [1].

Product segment. Let us define the product segment as $[a, b]_{d \times d'} = \{(x_1, x_2) | x_1 \in [a_1, b_1]_d, x_2 \in [a_2, b_2]_{d'}\}$ where $a = (a_1, a_2), b = (b_1, b_2)$
Product segment theorem: The product segment corresponds to the segment of the Manhattan product space: $[(a_1, a_2), (b_1, b_2)]_{d \times d'} = [(a_1, a_2), (b_1, b_2)]_\rho$ where $\rho((a_1, a_2), (b_1, b_2)) = d(a_1, b_1) + d'(a_2, b_2)$ [1]
This result may be extended to the product segment of any finite number of metric spaces.

Interval spaces connect very naturally with the notion of geometric crossover. There is a wealth of results for geometric interval spaces that can easily be transferred to geometric crossover.

3.4 Product Geometric Crossover

A *product geometric crossover* of the geometric crossovers X_i based on the metric spaces (S_i, d_i) is a recombination operator defined over the cartesian product set $\prod_i S_i$ that applies the geometric crossover X_i to the projection S_i.

Example. Let us consider two geometric crossovers $X_1 : S_1 \times S_1 \rightarrow S_1$ and $X_2 : S_2 \times S_2 \rightarrow S_2$. A product geometric crossover of X_1 and X_2 is a recombination operator $X_3 : (S_1, S_2) \times (S_1, S_2) \rightarrow (S_1, S_2)$ that applies the geometric crossover X_1 to elements in the first position and crossover X_2 to elements in the second position.

From the results in the previous section we have the following

Theorem 1. *Any product geometric crossover is a geometric crossover under the distance given by the sum of the distances of the compounding crossovers.*

Proof. This follows immediately from the definition of geometric crossover and the product segment theorem.

The geometric crossovers in each projection of the product geometric crossover do not need to be independent for the product crossover to be geometric. This is because casting any form of dependency between geometric crossovers in different projections results in a reduction of the pool of offspring allowed to be created by the product geometric crossover. From the definition of geometric crossover, such a restriction does not affect its geometricity.

The theorem above is useful because it allows one to build new geometric crossovers combining crossovers that are known to be geometric. In particular, this applies to crossovers for mixed representations. Examples of application of product geometric crossovers include:

- Multi-crossover: same representation same crossover n times
- Hybrid crossover: same representation different crossover for each projection
- Hybrid representation crossover: different representation for each projection (and different crossover)
- Dependent crossover: different projections represent a single entity and they are mutually constrained. This occurs very often in real-world problems. E.g. for neural networks one projection could be a variable-size graph representing the structural part, while a second projection could be a variable-length sequence of reals representing the weights. Clearly recombination of the first projection imposes constraints on the recombination of the second projection to obtain a feasible offspring.

3.5 Simplification and Generalization of Geometricity of Traditional Crossover

Definition 4. *(Discrete metric space) Let A be any non-empty set and*

$$d(x,y) = \begin{cases} 1, \, x \neq y \\ 0, \, x = y \end{cases} \quad \forall x, y \in A$$

This is a metric and is called the discrete metric *of A.*

The discrete metric space is the path metric of a fully-connected graph with A as node set. The interval operator associated with the discrete metric space is: $\forall a, b \in A : [a, b] = \{a, b\}$ (all segments are edges).

We call the geometric crossover associated to the discrete metric, the *discrete metric geometric crossover* (DM-GX). Clearly, the only possible offspring of DM-GX are the parents.

Definition 5. *(Hamming metric space) Let us consider a set A^n whose elements are all vectors of length n over some alphabet A of size $|A|$. The Hamming distance between two vectors is the number of coordinates where they differ. The Hamming space is denoted by $H(n, |A|)$.*

Discrete metrics and Hamming space are linked as follows: the product metric of n discrete metric spaces of the alphabet A is the Hamming space $H(n, |A|)$.

Theorem 2. *Any traditional mask-based crossover for discrete vectors taking values on the alphabet A is geometric under Hamming distance.*

Proof. This follows from the fact that any traditional mask-based crossover is the product crossover of n DM-GX, one for each projection.

When the alphabet A is a set of integers, beside the discrete metric we can consider also the absolute value of their difference (ABD) for each projection as a metric to be used as a basis for a product crossover. It is easy to see that the geometric crossover associated to ABD produces integers between the parents integers as extremes. The product geometric crossover is in this case a blend-type crossover (in contrast with the discrete metric that gives rise to a discrete recombination-type crossover).

3.6 Product Geometric Crossover and the Sudoku Puzzle

In [8] we have designed new geometric crossovers for the Sudoku puzzle that deal in a natural way with its constraints. We have demonstrated the usage of the notion of product geometric crossover to straightforwardly derive (i) new geometric crossovers for the entire grid obtained by employing simple geometric crossovers for each row and (ii) the distance functions associated with them. This has allowed us to analyze the geometric fitness landscape associated to the new geometric crossovers and tell *a priori*, by the way the fitness landscape is constructed, that the new crossovers are very well-suited to the Sudoku puzzle hence likely to perform well. Crossover operators associated with the row-swap distance are the best and produce consistently (near) optimal Sudoku grids, as predicted.

4 Future Investigations

Structural composition of geometric crossovers: The previous results could be generalized in a very interesting way, extending the geometric framework to complex representations. In the following we discuss this.

Basic representations such as vectors, permutations, sequences, trees, graphs and sets, to mention only the most common, can all be seen as structures containing generic objects. These objects do not need to be necessarily numbers or atomic symbols from a given alphabet. Such objects can well be structures themselves, so we can consider derived structures obtained by structural composition, such for example sets of trees. The composition can be repeated recursively with different types of representations thus obtaining a wealth of derived representations, potentially suited to any problem conceivable.

Given geometric crossovers X_A and X_B for the structure A and B associated to the metric spaces M_A and M_B, what is the derived geometric crossover for the derived structure $A \circ B$? What is the derived metric space associated to the derived geometric crossover and the derived structure?

With the product geometric crossover, we have seen that when the structure is a vector, the structural composition with any other representations is connected to a natural derived geometric crossover consisting of a simple geometric crossover for each position in the vector, and associated to a derived metric that is simply the sum of the metric for each position.

In the case of vectors, we have a number of possible structural compositions (a number of metric product operators) but only one notion of metric product that has a natural interpretation on the representation, making it the only one actually useful. In the case of other structures, there could be more than one (or even no) structural composition that has a natural interpretation on the representation. Furthermore, in the case of structures other than vectors, we do not have standard metric transformations such as the metric product that naturally suit them. So, where can we start our generalization from?

There seems to be a way suggested by the case of vectors: we have seen that simple metrics on the vector space (structured objects) can be easily generalized to structural metric transformations of generic metric spaces retaining the overall structure of the original object (vector of metric spaces). We could do the same to generalize metrics for other type of structures to structural metric transformations. The starting point is noticing that distances for structured representations are naturally expressed as some aggregating function of marginal contributions due to the difference in the structural subcomponents. The way of measuring the difference between two components is normally a very simple notion of metric, discrete metric for difference between symbols, or just absolute value for numeric components. In the case of vectors, the aggregating function is a simple sum, and the distance between components is the absolute value. So, the way to pass from metric distance to metric transformation is to replace the simple component-metric with generic metrics, exactly how it was done for the case of vectors.

This seems to be a general and very promising starting point to extend simple metrics on any type of structured object to structural metric transformations naturally associated with its shape. In future work, we will explore these metric transformations and study their induced geometricity-preserving transformations to reveal the effect on the representation of the derived geometric crossovers.

Other metric transformations: Most of the metric transformations listed in the introduction have corresponding syntactic crossover transformations, that can be used for other purposes than actually constructing new geometric crossovers. Indeed, we are currently using some of these transformations to attack the following important open issue regarding geometric crossover. Given a geometric crossover, there is in general more than one distance for which the crossover is geometric (for example, cycle crossover is geometric under Hamming distance and swap distance). The question is: is there a distance that can be said to be the best distance to consider for a specific geometric crossover? If so, what is this distance? The answer relies heavily on the notion of metric transformation.

5 Conclusions

In this paper we have extended the geometric framework introducing the notion of product crossover. This is a very general result that allows one to build new geometric crossovers customized to problems with mixed representations by combining pre-existing geometric crossovers in a straightforward way. We have presented this notion in the more general setting of metric transformations and discussed promising future investigations. Using the product geometric crossover theorem, we have also shown that traditional crossovers for symbolic vectors and blend crossovers for integer and real vectors are geometric crossover.

References

1. M. L. J. Van de Vel, editor. *Theory of Convex Structures.* North-Holland, 1993.
2. M. M. Deza and M. Laurent, editors. *Geometry of Cuts and Metrics.* Springer, 1997.
3. T. Jones. *Evolutionary Algorithms, Fitness Landscapes and Search.* PhD thesis, University of New Mexico, 1995.
4. A. Moraglio and R. Poli. Topological interpretation of crossover. In *Proceedings of Gecco 2004*, pages 1377–1388, 2004.
5. A. Moraglio and R. Poli. Geometric crossover for the permutation representation. *Technical Report CSM-429, Department of Computer Science, University of Essex*, 2005.
6. A. Moraglio and R. Poli. Topological crossover for the permutation representation. In *GECCO 2005 Workshop on Theory of Representations*, 2005.
7. A. Moraglio, R. Poli, and R. Seehuus. Geometric crossover for biological sequences. In *Proceedings of EuroGP 2006*, pages 121–132, 2006.
8. A. Moraglio, J. Togelius, and S. Lucas. Product geometric crossover for the sudoku puzzle. In *Proceedings of IEEE CEC 2006 (to appear)*, 2006.
9. P. M. Pardalos and M. G. C. Resende, editors. *Handbook of Applied Optimization.* Oxford University Press, 2002.
10. W. A. Sutherland, editor. *Introduction to metric and topological spaces.* Oxford University Press, 1975.

Exploration and Exploitation Bias of Crossover and Path Relinking for Permutation Problems

Dirk Thierens

Institute of Information and Computing Sciences
Universiteit Utrecht, The Netherlands
dirk.thierens@cs.uu.nl

Abstract. For most combinatorial optimization problems the computational complexity of evaluating a single solution is much higher than the cost of evaluating an incremental change made by a local search operator. To benefit from this computational gain crossover can be implemented as a path–following algorithm. As a result crossover becomes more similar to path relinking. In this paper we compare the search bias of crossover and path relinking for permutation problems where the absolute position of the elements is decisive. Calculations show that uniform permutation crossover (UPX) can reach many more permutations from a given parent couple than path relinking. UPX is therefore more exploratory than random path relinking, which is itself more exploratory than greedy path relinking. It is important for users to understand the differences in search bias of the operators so they can choose the exploration operator which they deem most fit for their problem. We conclude with a small experiment on an instance of the quadratic assignment problem.

1 Introduction

Genetic local search (GLS) (a.k.a. memetic algorithms) are among the best performing search algorithms for several combinatorial optimization problems such as graph coloring [5], bin packing [3], and quadratic assignment problems [8]. GLS algorithms belong to the class of metaheuristics. Metaheuristics are search techniques that – following a problem independent strategy – try to improve the effectiveness of local search algorithms. Their success depends on whether this strategy - or search bias - coincides with the structure of the fitness landscape of the problem instance. GLS algorithms act on a population of local optima that are generated by a local search algorithm. GLS's search is biased in two ways:

1. The search is focused on the set of best local optima encountered during the optimization process. This bias is implemented by an elitist selection method.
2. The search is also biased by the type of recombination operator applied to generate new starting solutions for the local search.

In this paper we will discuss the latter type of search bias for permutation problems where the absolute position of the elements in the permutation are decisive.

T.P. Runarsson et al. (Eds.): PPSN IX, LNCS 4193, pp. 1028–1037, 2006.

More particularly, we will analyze the differences and similarities between uniform permutation crossover, random path relinking, and greedy path relinking. We apply these three exploration techniques to an instance of the quadratic assignment problem and measure how much they improve upon simple multi-start local search.

The paper is organized as follows. In the next section we define some concepts in permutation problems. Section 3 discusses the crossover and path relinking operators. In Section 4 we compare the exploration operators experimentally on an instance of the quadratic assignment problem. Finally, Section 5 concludes this report.

2 Permutation Problems

To formalize our discussion we need to define the following concepts.

Definition 1. *A permutation P of length n is a random ordering of the set of integers $\{1, \ldots, n\}$. $P(i)$ with $i \in \{1, \ldots, n\}$ denotes the integer located at position i in the permutation P.*

Definition 2. *The distance $d(P_k, P_l)$ between two permutations P_k and P_l of length n is equal to the number of positions where the two permutations have different integer elements:*

$$d(P_k, P_l) = \sum_{i=1}^{n} (1 - \delta_{P_k(i)P_l(i)})$$

where $\delta(i, j)$ is the Kronecker delta function:

$$\delta_{ij} = \begin{cases} 0 \text{ for } i \neq j \\ 1 \text{ for } i = j \end{cases}$$

Definition 3. *A cycle between two permutations P_k and P_l is defined as a subset of the integer elements that can be exchanged between the two permutations such that two (new) valid permutations are obtained.*

Example 1. The two permutations P_k and P_l

$$\begin{array}{llllllllll} P_k: & \mathbf{1} & \mathbf{2} & \mathbf{3} & \mathit{4} & \mathit{5} & \mathit{6} & \mathbf{7} & \mathbf{8} & \mathit{9} \\ P_l: & \mathbf{2} & \mathbf{7} & \mathbf{1} & \mathit{5} & \mathit{9} & \mathit{4} & \mathbf{8} & \mathbf{3} & \mathit{6} \end{array}$$

have two cycles: {1,2,3,7,8} and {4,5,6,9}. Exchanging one or both of the cycles results in two valid permutations. For instance, exchanging the cycle {4,5,6,9} leads to:

$$\begin{array}{llllllllll} P'_k: & \mathbf{1} & \mathbf{2} & \mathbf{3} & \mathit{5} & \mathit{9} & \mathit{4} & \mathbf{7} & \mathbf{8} & \mathit{6} \\ P'_l: & \mathbf{2} & \mathbf{7} & \mathbf{1} & \mathit{4} & \mathit{5} & \mathit{6} & \mathbf{8} & \mathbf{3} & \mathit{9} \end{array}$$

Strictly speaking any individual element that occupies the same position in both permutations represents a separate cycle. However we will focus on the elements that are not shared by the two permutations and only talk about cycles if the subset of integers has at least two elements.

Definition 4. *The cycle distance $c(P_k, P_l)$ between two permutations P_k and P_l is equal to the number of cycles of size 2 or more between P_k and P_l.*

Definition 5. *A path P_kP_l between two permutations P_k and P_l is a sequence of permutations P_i starting at P_k and ending at P_l where each permutation P_i on the path is obtained by swapping two elements from the previous permutation P_{i-1} such that the distance to the goal permutation P_l is reduced:*

$$P_kP_l = \{P_k, P_1, P_2, \ldots, P_{i-1}, P_i, \ldots, P_l\} \quad | \quad d(P_{i-1}, P_l) > d(P_i, P_l)$$

We call the number of permutations in a path P_kP_l the path length $|P_kP_l|$. Obviously, it takes $|P_kP_l| - 1$ swaps to traverse a path of length $|P_kP_l|$.

Proposition 1. *The path length $|P_kP_l|$ of a path between two permutations P_k and P_l that are a distance $d(P_k, P_l)$ and a cycle distance $c(P_k, P_l)$ apart from each other is equal to $d(P_k, P_l) - c(P_k, P_l) + 1$.*

Proof. To reduce the distance between a permutation and the goal permutation at least one of the two swapped elements must be swapped to the location where the element is located in the goal permutation. By the definition of a cycle this means that swaps will only occur between elements of the same cycle. Therefore the cycles remain independent of each other during the path creation. Only when the 2 swapped elements form a cycle of size 2 both elements will be moved simultaneously to their location in the goal permutation. As a result it will take $d_i - 1$ swaps to reorder a cycle of size d_i to the goal cycle. Note that the sum of the sizes d_i of the $c(P_k, P_l)$ cycles equals the distance $d(P_k, P_l)$. The path length $|P_kP_l|$ is one plus the total number of swaps needed to move from P_k to P_l or:

$$|P_kP_l| = 1 + \sum_{i=1}^{c(P_kP_l)} (d_i - 1) = 1 + d(P_k, P_l) - c(P_k, P_l) \qquad \square$$

Local search requires a neighborhood to be defined for a given solution. We generate the neighborhood by swapping two elements of the permutation.

Definition 6. *The swap neighborhood $N(P)$ of a permutation P is the set of all permutations P' that are a distance $d(P, P') = 2$ from P:*

$$N(P) = \{P' \mid \exists i, j \in \{1, \ldots, n\}(i \neq j) \text{ and } \forall k \neq i \neq j \in \{1 \ldots, n\} :$$

$$P'(k) = P(k) \text{ and } P'(i) = P(j) \text{ and } P'(j) = P(i)$$

Obviously, the size of the neighborhood is

$$|N(P)| = \binom{n}{2}$$

3 Exploration Operators

It is often claimed that a disadvantage of crossover is that the generated child has to be evaluated from scratch. For most combinatorial optimization problems the computational cost of evaluating a solution is typically an order $\mathcal{O}(n)$ larger than incrementally updating the cost function after the application of a single local search step. However this disadvantage is only an implementation problem not a structural problem. It is straightforward to implement crossover as a path–following algorithm relinking one (or two) parent(s) with the generated child. The solutions encountered on the path are of course also available to the search process. When applying this path implementation, crossover becomes more similar to path relinking. It is important however to recognize their different exploration behavior. Therefore we need to compute the number of permutations that can be generated from a parent couple by the crossover and path relinking.

3.1 Uniform Permutation Crossover

The standard uniform crossover (UX) operator randomly exchanges the elements of two solutions. UX cannot be used for permutation problems since nearly all offspring would not be valid permutations. The principle of UX is that it preserves the common elements of the parents and generates a random sample in the subspace where the two parents disagree. This principle can easily be applied to permutation problems. We call the uniform permutation crossover (UPX) the operator that preserves the common elements of two permutations and generates a random permutation with the remaining elements. For instance, crossing two permutations P_1 and P_2

$$\begin{array}{llllllllll} P_1: & \mathbf{1} & \mathbf{2} & \mathbf{3} & \mathit{4} & \mathit{5} & \mathit{6} & \mathbf{7} & \mathbf{8} & \mathit{9} \\ P_2: & \mathbf{2} & \mathbf{7} & \mathbf{1} & \mathit{4} & \mathit{5} & \mathit{6} & \mathbf{8} & \mathbf{3} & \mathit{9} \end{array}$$

might result in the offspring:

$$\begin{array}{llllllllll} P': & \mathbf{7} & \mathbf{3} & \mathbf{2} & \mathit{4} & \mathit{5} & \mathit{6} & \mathbf{8} & \mathbf{1} & \mathit{9} \end{array}$$

Call $O^{\text{upx}}(P_k, P_l)$ the set of permutations that can be generated from the permutations P_k and P_l by applying uniform permutation crossover. Obviously, the number of permutations - different from the parents - that can be generated equals:

$$|O^{\text{upx}}(P_k, P_l)| = d(P_k, P_l)! - 2 \tag{1}$$

3.2 Random Path Relinking

Path relinking for combinatorial optimization problems generate new solutions by generating a path between two local optima. One optimum plays the role of initiating solution while the other represents the guiding solution. Starting from the initiating solution a series of local steps are taken each decreasing the distance with the guiding solution.

For our permutation problems the local steps are implemented by selecting an element that has a different position in the guiding solution. The selected element is then swapped with the element on that position thereby reducing the distance between the permutation on the path and the guiding solution. For instance if P_1 is the initiating solution and P_2 the guiding solution a possible path could be:

$$\begin{array}{rccccccccc} P_1: & \mathbf{1} & \mathbf{2} & \mathbf{3} & 4 & 5 & 6 & \mathbf{7} & \mathbf{8} & 9 \\ \downarrow: & \mathbf{3} & \mathbf{2} & 1 & 4 & 5 & 6 & \mathbf{7} & \mathbf{8} & 9 \\ \downarrow: & \mathbf{3} & \mathbf{2} & 1 & 4 & 5 & 6 & 8 & \mathbf{7} & 9 \\ \downarrow: & 2 & \mathbf{3} & 1 & 4 & 5 & 6 & 8 & \mathbf{7} & 9 \\ P_2: & 2 & 7 & 1 & 4 & 5 & 6 & 8 & 3 & 9 \end{array}$$

In random path relinking (RPR) the elements to be swapped are chosen randomly from the set of possible elements. It is important to note that the elements swapped will always belong to the same cycle. If a cycle i has length $d_i(P_k, P_l)$ then we need $d_i(P_k, P_l) - 1$ swaps to reorder all elements in the cycle as specified by the guiding permutation. For each cycle the number of different paths that can be traveled equals $d_i(P_k, P_l)(d_i(P_k, P_l) - 1)(d_i(P_k, P_l) - 2) \ldots 3 = \frac{d_i(P_k, P_l)!}{2}$.

The number of different permutations that can be generated equals

$$\begin{aligned} |O^{\mathrm{rpr}}(P_k, P_l)| &= \binom{d_i(P_k, P_l)}{1} + \binom{d_i(P_k, P_l)}{2} + \ldots + \binom{d_i(P_k, P_l)}{d_i(P_k, P_l) - 2} \\ &= \sum_{j=1}^{d_i(P_k, P_l) - 2} \binom{d_i(P_k, P_l)}{j} \end{aligned}$$

applying the binomial theorem gives us:

$$|O^{\mathrm{rpr}}(P_k, P_l)| = 2^{d_i(P_k, P_l)} - d_i(P_k, P_l) - 2 \tag{2}$$

3.3 Greedy Path Relinking

Random path relinking simply selects the next element to position correctly at random. Greedy path relinking (GPR) also considers the effect on the cost function and generates the path in a steepest descent direction. GPR explores all possible single steps from the current permutation to the guiding permutation and selects the swap that causes the largest decrease of the cost function. If we ignore possible random tie breaking, GPR will generate a unique path from the initiating and the guiding solutions.

For each cycle i the number of permutations on the path between permutations P_k and P_l equals $d_i(P_k, P_l) + (d_i(P_k, P_l) - 1) + \ldots + 3$ or

$$|O^{\mathrm{gpr}}(P_k, P_l)| = \frac{1}{2} d_i(P_k, P_l)(d_i(P_k, P_l) + 1) - 3 \tag{3}$$

In figure 1 we have plotted the number of permutations that can be reached by the UPX, RPR, and GPR operators as a function of the length of the cycles.

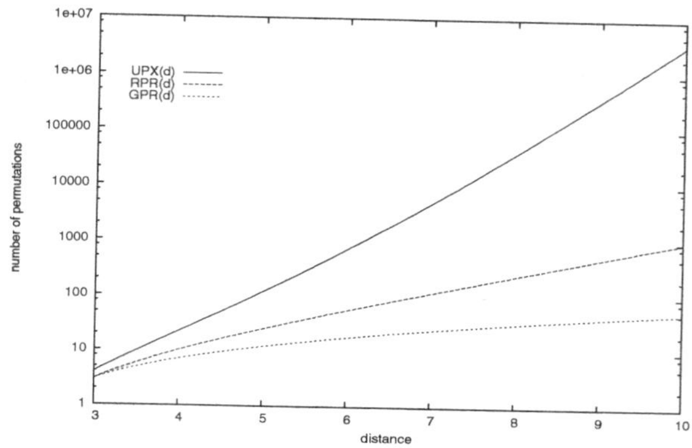

Fig. 1. Number of reachable permutations as a function of the size of 1 cycle for UX, RPR, and GPR

To obtain the total number of reachable permutations the values for each cycle needs to be added together. Clearly, the number of permutations that can be generated by the three operators varies significantly from each other (note the log scale). The number of permutations that can be explored by UPX is vastly larger than the number of permutations available to the path relinking operators.

4 Quadratic Assignment Problem

4.1 QAP

As shown in the previous section, uniform permutation crossover, random path relinking, and greedy path relinking occupy an outspokenly different position on the exploration/exploitation trade-off scale. To illustrate what effect this might have on a given problem we have run the three operators on an instance of the quadratic assignment problem (QAP). The QAP is a notoriously hard combinatorial optimization problem and is relevant for a number of real world problems [2].

Formally, we are given two $n \times n$ matrices A and B. An intuitively clear way to think about the QAP is to consider a set of n facilities that has to be placed at a set of n locations. The elements of the first matrix $A(i,j)$ then represent the distance between location i and location j, while the elements of the second matrix $B(i,j)$ represent the flow of material between facility i and facility j. The permutation P ($P(i) \in \{1,\ldots,n\}$) denotes the assignment of facilities to locations: $P(k) = m$ means that facility k is located at location m. The cost function $C(P)$ that needs to be minimized is specified as:

$$C(P) = \sum_{i=1}^{n}\sum_{j=1}^{n} A(i,j)B(P(i),P(j)) \tag{4}$$

When both matrices A and B are symmetric and have a null diagonal the effect of swapping two elements can be calculated incrementally [11]. This incremental cost evaluation only takes $\mathcal{O}(n)$ time and is given by:

$$\begin{aligned}\Delta C(P_k, P_l) &= C(P_k) - C(P_l) \\ &= 2 \sum_{i=1, i \neq k,l}^{n} (A(k,i) - A(l,i))(B(P(k), P(i)) - B(P(l), P(i)))\end{aligned}$$

4.2 QAP Instance

Many QAP instances found in benchmarks have rather uncorrelated fitness landscapes which makes them uninteresting for investigating the effect of different exploration/exploitation trade-off biases [8]. In fact when there is no structural correlation between local optima no metaheuristic algorithm will improve upon a simple multi-start local search approach. Here we performed experimental tests on a QAP problem instance proposed by Merz and Freisleben [8]. The instance is constructed in such a way that it shows a high correlation and a correlation length close to $n/2$. The distance matrix A of each instance is generated by randomly picking n points in the unit square: $[0 \ldots 1] \times [0 \ldots 1]$. The distance $A(i,j)$ is then defined as 100 times the Euclidean distance between the points i and j. For the matrix B another set of n random points is created in the unit square. The flow $B(i,j)$ is now defined as 100 times the Euclidean distance between the points i and j if this distance is lower than a threshold D_{max}. If the distance is larger than the threshold the matrix entry $B(i,j)$ is set to zero. Note that both the matrices A and B in this class of QAP instances are symmetric and have zero diagonal so we can apply the incremental cost evaluation equation. Note also that the matrix entries obey the triangle inequality, a property usually present in real-world QAP problems but often lacking in randomly generated benchmark problems.

4.3 Experiment

We compare the performance of UPX, RPR, and GPR when embedded in a steady-state genetic local search algorithm using family competition. The population consists of local optima obtained by running the best-improvement local search algorithm with the 2-swap neighborhood. Two parents are randomly selected and a single offspring is generated by applying the exploration operator (either UPX, RPR, or GPR) and the local search algorithm. If the child has a lower cost than any of its two parents it replaces the worst parent. The offspring is created by constructing a path from one parent to the other in case of path relinking, or from one parent to the permutation created by UPX. If there exists a permutation P' on the path whose cost is lower than the cost of the two parents then the local search is started from that permutation. If there is no such permutation the local search will be started from a permutation randomly selected on the path.

ExplorePath(P_k, P_l)

$\overrightarrow{P_kP_l} \leftarrow$ ConstructPath(P_k, P_l)
if $\exists j : C(\overrightarrow{P_kP_l}(j)) < \text{MIN}(C(P_k), C(P_l))$
  then $P_n \leftarrow$ LocalSearch$(\overrightarrow{P_kP_l}(j))$
  else $r \leftarrow$ Random$(2, D(P_k, P_l) - 2)$
    $P_n \leftarrow$ LocalSearch$(\overrightarrow{P_kP_l}(r))$
return P_n

The experiment is run on 5 QAP problem instances of size $n = 50$ and threshold $D_{max} = 0.5$. The population size is $N = 50$. Each algorithm is allowed to call 1000 times the best-improvement 2-swap local search algorithm.

The multi-start local search (MLS) generates 1000 independent local optima. In the table we have also shown how many times the solution with minimal cost has been generated out of 1000 trials. For instance for the QAP instance pmd50(1) the solution with cost 1199982.1 has been generated 8 times.

	pmd50(1)	pmd50(2)	pmd50(3)	pmd50(4)	pmd50(5)
MLS					
min	1199982.1 (8)	1118525.1 (1)	976220.75 (1)	1032839.2 (2)	1105732.5 (1)
mean	1253089.7	1153414.6	1022104.3	1074863.2	1148721.5
std	39682.2	28167.8	21319.3	25837.3	31932.1
UPX					
min	1199982.1 (10)	1118231.6 (4)	925761.3 (7)	1002052.5 (2)	1028371.3 (2)
mean	1199982.1	1128492.8	989726.4	1040764.5	1113962.4
std	0	9285.6	52197.3	23498.2	73401.3
RPR					
min	1199982.1 (10)	1118231.6 (6)	925761.3 (8)	1001836.2 (1)	1028371.3 (3)
mean	1199982.1	11254272.2	975382.4	1034374.5	1078462.4
std	0	7571.3	43672.1	19875.3	52668.3
GPR					
min	1199982.1 (10)	1118231.6 (8)	925761.3 (10)	1001836.2 (3)	1035827.4 (7)
mean	1199982.1	1122322.8	925761.3	1030352.6	1067834.4
std	0	5150.4	0	156821.2	29851.8

The three exploration operators UPX, RPR, and GPR are run for 10 independent runs (each calling the local search method 1000 times). The number between parentheses after the minimal cost values shows the number of runs that reached this value. It is clear from the table that UPX, RPR, and GPR improve upon multi-start local search. This is as expected since the local optima of these QAP instances have a correlated structure. For most instances the GPR reaches the minimal cost permutation more often and has a lower standard deviation. However for the instance pmd50(5) UPX and RPR found a better assignment than GPR. Apparently, for this problem instance the greedy nature of GPR is misled and the more exploratory operators UPX and RPR are able to find lower cost solutions. Even from this small experimental test it is clear that none of the three search methods is consistently better than the others. Of course, this limited set of experiments does not give us enough data to draw any firm conclusions. In future work we intend to set up a full experimental study to highlight the similarities and differences between the path–following implementation of crossover and path relinking.

5 Conclusion

We have discussed the use of uniform permutation crossover, random path relinking, and greedy path relinking for permutation problems where the absolute position of the elements is decisive. By implementing UPX as a path–following algorithm crossover can also benefit from efficient incremental cost evaluations. As a result crossover becomes more similar to path relinking and we have calculated the number of permutations that can be reached by crossover versus random and greedy path relinking. These calculations showed that UPX is a more exploratory operator than random path relinking which is itself more exploratory than greedy path relinking. Performing more exploration and less exploitation (or vice versa) changes the search bias of the metaheuristic. It is important for users to realize the differences in search bias of the operators so they can choose the exploration operator which they deem most fit for their problem.

References

1. D. Corne, F. Glover, and M. Dorigo (eds.). *New Ideas in Optimization*, McGraw-Hill, 1999.
2. E. Cela. *The Quadratic Assignment Problem: Theory and Algorithms.* Kluwer Academic Publishers, 1998.
3. E. Falkenauer. *A Hybrid Grouping Genetic Algorithm for Bin Packing.* Journal of Heuristics, 2:5–30, 1996.
4. C. Fleurent, and J.A. Ferland. *Genetic Hybrids for the Quadratic Assignment Problem.* DIMACS Series on Discrete Mathematics and Theoretical Computer Science, 173–187, 1994.
5. P. Galinier, and J. Hao. *Hybrid evolutionary algorithms for graph coloring.* Journal of Combinatorial Optimization, 3(4), pp. 379–397, 1999.
6. H.H. Hoos, and T. Stützle. *Stochastic Local Search. Foundations and Applications.* Morgan Kaufmann Publishers. 2005.
7. T. James, C. Rego, and F. Glover. *Sequential and Parallel Path-Relinking Algorithms for the Quadratic Assignment Problem.* IEEE Intelligent Systems, pp. 58–65, July/August 2005.
8. P. Merz, and B. Freisleben. *Fitness Landscape Analysis and Memetic Algorithms for the Quadratic Assignment Problem.* IEEE Transaction Evolutionary Computation, 4(4):337–352, 2000.
9. I.H. Osman, and J.P. Kelly (eds.). *Meta-Heuristics: The Theory and Applications*, Kluwer Academic Publishers, Boston, 1996.

10. C.C. Ribeiro, and P. Hansen (eds.). *Essays and Surveys in Metaheuristics*, Kluwer Academic Publishers, Boston, 2001.
11. T. Stützle, and M. Dorigo. *Local Search and Metaheuristics for the Quadratic Assignment Problem.* Technical Report AIDA-01-01, Intellectics Group, Darmstadt University of Technology, Germany. 2001.
12. S. Voss, S. Martello, I.H. Osman, and C. Roucairol (eds.). *Meta-Heuristics: Advances and Trends in Local Search Paradigms for Optimization*, Kluwer Academic Publishers, Boston, 1999.

Geometric Crossover for Sets, Multisets and Partitions

Alberto Moraglio and Riccardo Poli

Department of Computer Science,
University of Essex,
Wivenhoe Park, Colchester, CO4 3SQ, UK
{amoragn, rpoli}@essex.ac.uk

Abstract. This paper extends a geometric framework for interpreting crossover and mutation [5] to the case of sets and related representations. We show that a deep geometric duality exists between the set representation and the vector representation. This duality reveals the equivalence of geometric crossovers for these representations.

1 Introduction

Sets, multisets and partitions are natural representations for many important combinatorial optimization problems such as grouping problems, graph coloring and so on. The set representation for evolutionary algorithms was theoretically studied by Radcliffe [9] within his forma analysis framework.

Geometric crossover and geometric mutation are representation-independent search operators that generalize many pre-existing search operators for the major representations used in evolutionary algorithms, such as binary strings [5], real vectors [5], permutations [7], syntactic trees [6] and sequences [8]. They are defined in geometric terms using the notions of line segment and ball. These notions and the corresponding genetic operators are well-defined once a notion of distance in the search space is defined. Defining search operators as functions of the search space is opposite to the standard way [3] in which the search space is seen as a function of the search operators employed. This viewpoint greatly simplifies the relationship between search operators and fitness landscape and has allowed us to give simple *rules-of-thumb* to build crossover operators that are likely to perform well.

In this paper we use the geometric framework [5] to study and design crossover operators for the set representation and related representations such as multisets and partitions for the fixed-size and variable-size variants. We also show an illuminating isometric duality between the spaces associated to the set representation and the vector representation that enables us to prove the equivalence of geometric crossovers for these representations.

The paper is organised as follows. In section 2 we present the geometric framework. In section 3, we extend it to sets, multisets and partitions of variable-size. In section 4, we consider the fixed-size case. In section 5, we illustrate the duality between sets and vectors. In section 6, we draw some conclusions.

T.P. Runarsson et al. (Eds.): PPSN IX, LNCS 4193, pp. 1038–1047, 2006.

2 Geometric Framework

2.1 Geometric Preliminaries

In the following we give necessary preliminary geometric definitions and extend those introduced in [5] and [6]. The following definitions are taken from [2].

The terms *distance* and *metric* denote any real valued function that conforms to the axioms of identity, symmetry and triangular inequality. A simple connected graph is naturally associated to a metric space via its *path metric*: the distance between two nodes in the graph is the length of a shortest path between the nodes.

In a metric space (S, d) a *line segment* (or closed interval) is the set of the form $[x; y] = \{z \in S | d(x, z) + d(z, y) = d(x, y)\}$ where $x, y \in S$ are called extremes of the segment. Metric segment generalises the familiar notion of segment in the Euclidean space to any metric space through distance redefinition. Notice that a metric segment does not coincide with the shortest path connecting its extremes (*geodesic*) as in an Euclidean space. In general, there may be more than one geodesic connecting two extremes; the metric segment is the union of all geodesics.

We assign a structure to the solution set S by endowing it with a notion of distance d. $M = (S, d)$ is therefore a solution *space* and $L = (M, g)$ is the corresponding fitness landscape.

2.2 Geometric Crossover Definition

The following definitions are *representation-independent* and, therefore, applicable to any representation.

Definition 1. *(Image set) The* image set $Im[OP]$ *of a genetic operator* OP *is the set of all possible offspring produced by* OP *with non-zero probability.*

Definition 2. *(Geometric crossover) A binary operator is a geometric crossover under the metric* d *if all offspring are in the segment between its parents.*

Definition 3. *(Uniform geometric crossover) Uniform geometric crossover* UX *is a geometric crossover where all* z *laying between parents* x *and* y *have the same probability of being the offspring:*

$$f_{UX}(z|x, y) = \frac{\delta(z \in [x; y])}{|[x; y]|}$$

$$Im[UX(x, y)] = \{z \in S | f_{UX}(z|x, y) > 0\} = [x; y].$$

A number of general properties for geometric crossover and mutation have been derived in [5] where we also showed that traditional crossover is geometric under Hamming distance. In previous work we have also studied various crossovers for permutations, revealing that PMX, a well-known crossover for permutations, is geometric under swap distance. Also, we found that Cycle crossover, another traditional crossover for permutations, is geometric under swap distance and under Hamming distance.

3 Geometric Crossover for Variable-Size Sets, Multi-sets and Partitions

We consider problems where solutions are naturally represented as sets of objects taken from a reference set (universal set). We also consider the simple extension to multi-sets, sets that are allowed to contain repetitions of the same object. A set can be seen also as a bipartition of the universal set (objects in the set and remaining objects in the universal set). A natural extension of the notion of set in this sense is to consider generic multi-partitions of the universal set. We will study this case too.

There is a further aspect of the set representation that has a major impact on the associated geometric crossovers: the search being restricted to fixed-size sets versus the variable-size case. In this section, we study sets, multi-sets and partitions for the easier variable-size case. In section 4, we consider the fixed-size case.

3.1 Distances and Crossover for Sets

Let U be the universal set and $A, B \subseteq U$. The *symmetric distance* between sets is $d(A, B) = |A \Delta B|$ where $A \Delta B = A \cup B \setminus A \cap B$ is the symmetric difference between sets. The symmetric distance is a metric [2]. When $A = B$, d(A,B)=0; when $A \cap B = \emptyset$, A and B are at maximum distance and $d(A, B) = |A| + |B|$. The *ins/del edit distance* between A and B is the minimum number of elements that need to be deleted or inserted for A to be transformed into B (and *vice versa*).

Theorem 1. *The symmetric distance is the same as the ins/del edit distance.*

Proof. The edit distance corresponds to the symmetric distance because the minimum number of elements that need to be deleted from A are $|A \setminus B|$ and of those that need to be added are $|B \setminus A|$. It is easy to see that $d(A, B) = |A \Delta B| = |A \setminus B| + |B \setminus A|$.

Corollary: since any edit distance is a metric [1], theorem 1 proves also that the symmetric distance is a metric.

Theorem 2. *Given two parent sets A and B any recombination operator OP that returns offspring O such as $A \cap B \subseteq O \subseteq A \cup B$ is geometric crossover under symmetric distance.*

Proof. Proving geometricity under symmetric distance is equivalent to proving geometricity under ins/del edit distance. Any intermediate set C on the minimal ins/del move path to transform A into B is between A and B (in the segment $[A, B]$) under ins/del edit distance (see Fig. 1). Every O such that $A \cap B \subseteq O \subseteq A \cup B$ belongs to such a path because: A can be transformed into B by inserting in A the elements $O \setminus A$, removing from A the elements $A \setminus O$ and then by inserting in B the elements $B \setminus O$, and removing from B the elements $O \setminus B$. So $d(A, O) = |O \setminus A| + |A \setminus O|$ and $d(B, O) = |O \setminus B| + |B \setminus O|$

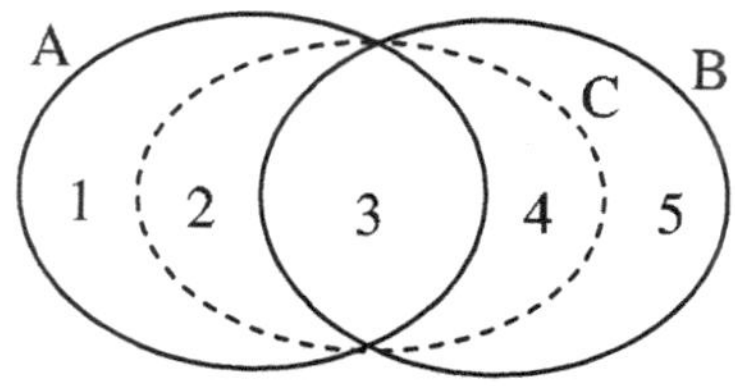

Fig. 1. Venn diagram linking offspring set and parent sets

Example. Let $U = \{a, b, c, d\}$ be the universal set and $A = \{a, b\}$ and $B = \{b, c\}$ two parent sets such that $A, B \subseteq U$. The symmetric distance between A and B is $d_\Delta(A, B) = |A \backslash B| + |B \backslash A| = 1 + 1 = 2$. Let GX_Δ be a geometric crossover under symmetric distance. Any offspring O of A and B, $O = GX_\Delta(A, B)$, respects the condition $A \cap B \subseteq O \subseteq A \cup B$. So, in our example we have: $\{b\} \subseteq O \subseteq \{a, b, c\}$. These are the sets: $\{b\}, \{a, b\}, \{b, c\}, \{a, b, c\}$. It is easy to verify that every O is in the segment between A and B under d_Δ. For example if we consider $O = \{a, b, c\}$ we have $d_\Delta(A, O) + d_\Delta(O, B) = (0 + 1) + (1 + 0) = 2 = d_\Delta(A, B)$.

3.2 Distances and Crossover for Multi-sets

A multi-set (sometimes also called a bag) differs from a set in that each member has a *multiplicity*, which is a natural number indicating how many times it occurs in the multi-set. A multi-set can be formally defined as a pair (A, m) where A is some set and $m : A \to \mathbb{N}$ is a function from A to the set of natural numbers $\mathbb{N}$. The set A is called the underlying set of elements. The *size* of the multi-set (A, m) is the sum of all multiplicities for each element of A: $|(A, m)| = \sum_{a \in A} m(a)$. A *submultiset* (B, n) of a multiset (A, m) is a subset $B \subseteq A$ and a function $n : B \to \mathbb{N}$ such that $\forall b \in B : n(b) \leq m(b)$. The usual operations of union and intersection for sets can easily be generalized to multisets. Suppose (A, m) and (B, n) are multisets. The *union* can be defined as $(A \cup B, f)$ where $f(x) = \max\{m(x), n(x)\}$. The *intersection* can be defined as $(A \cap B, f)$ where $f(x) = \min\{m(x), n(x)\}$.

Hence we can define the *symmetric difference* between multisets as $(A \Delta B, f)$ where $f(x) = \max\{m(x), n(x)\} - \min\{m(x), n(x)\} = |m(x) - n(x)|$. The *symmetric distance* for multisets becomes $d((A, m), (B, n)) = |(A, m) \Delta (B, n)| = \sum_{x \in A \Delta B} |m(x) - n(x)|$. The symmetric distance between multisets can be seen as a simple generalization of the *ins/del edit distance* for sets in which the edit move becomes the insertion or deletion of a *single occurrence* of an element.

The geometricity theorem for sets under symmetric distance can be extended to the case of multisets. Given two parent multisets (A, m) and (B, n) any recombination operator OP that returns offspring (O, f) such as $(A, m) \cap (B, n) \subseteq (O, f) \subseteq (A, m) \cup (B, n)$ is geometric crossover under symmetric distance.

Example. Let $U = \{a, b, c, d\}$ be the universal set, $A = \{a, b\}$ and $B = \{b, c\}$ be two sets such as $A, B \subseteq U$. Let us consider the parent multiset $M_A =$

$\{a, a, b\} = (A, m)$ where $m(a) = 2$ and $m(b) = 1$ and the parent multiset $M_B = \{b, b, c, c\} = (B, n)$ where $n(b) = 2$ and $n(c) = 2$. Their sizes are $|M_A| = 3$ and $|M_B| = 4$. Their union is $M_A \cup M_B = (A, m) \cup (B, n) = (A \cup B, f)$ where $f = max(m, n)$. In our example we have $M_A \cup M_B = \{a, a, b, b, c, c\}$. Their intersection is $M_A \cap M_B = (A, m) \cap (B, n) = (A \cap B, f)$ where $f = min(m, n)$. In our example we have $M_A \cap M_B = \{b\}$. Their symmetric difference is $M_A \Delta M_B = (A \Delta B, f)$ where $f = max(m, n) - min(m, n)$. In our example we have $M_A \Delta M_B = \{a, a, b, c, c\}$. The symmetric distance between M_A and M_B is, therefore, $d_\Delta(M_A, M_B) = |M_A \Delta M_B| = 5$. Let GX_Δ be a geometric crossover under symmetric distance for multisets. Any offspring M_O of M_A and M_B, $M_O = GX_\Delta(M_A, M_B)$, respects the condition $M_A \cap M_B \subseteq M_O \subseteq M_A \cup M_B$. So, in our example we have: $\{b\} \subseteq M_O \subseteq \{a, a, b, b, c, c\}$. Thus, any multiset $M_O = (O, f)$ such as $0 \leq f(a) \leq 2, 1 \leq f(b) \leq 2, 0 \leq f(c) \leq 2$ is a possible offspring of M_A and M_B.

3.3 Distances and Crossover for Partitions

In this paper we restrict our focus on partitioning problems with labeled partitions and a fixed number of partitions. In this section we consider the case where the same partition may have different size in different solutions. In section 4 we will consider the case in which all solutions are required to have the same size for the same partition.

A partition of a set X is a division of X into non-overlapping subsets that cover all of X. When the set X is partitioned into n subsets we say that they form a n-partition of X. A n-partition generalizes the notion of set A seen as partitioning the universal set U in two subsets A and $\overline{A}$ (bipartition).

The symmetric distance between two n-partitions $\mathcal{A} = \{A_1, \ldots, A_n\}$ and $\mathcal{B} = \{B_1, \ldots, B_n\}$ of a set X is a simple generalization of the symmetric distance for sets: $d(\mathcal{A}, \mathcal{B}) = \sum |A_i \Delta B_i|$.

The edit distance between two n-partitions is a natural generalization of the ins/del edit distance for sets. We define the edit distance between two n-partitions as the minimum number of edit moves to transform one partition into the other where the edit move considered is moving one element from one subset to another. This edit move transforms a partition of X into another partition of X for which the conditions of full coverage of X and mutual exclusivity of subsets are respected. This edit distance is a generalization of the ins/del edit distance for sets in that when one considers a set A as a bipartition of the universal set U into A and $\overline{A}$, inserting or deleting one element from A implies respectively deleting or inserting the same element in $\overline{A}$. So, this is equivalent of moving one element from A to $\overline{A}$. The symmetric distance between partitions does not equal their ins/del edit distance (although these distances are related).

Example. Let $X = \{a, b, c, d\}$ be the universal set (the set to be partitioned), and be $\mathcal{A} = (\{a, b\}, \{c, d\})$ and $\mathcal{B} = (\{b, c, d\}, \{a\})$ two ordered (or labeled) bipartitions of X. Since we consider ordered partitions, $(\{a, b\}, \{c, d\}) \neq (\{c, d\}, \{a, b\})$. The edit distance between $\mathcal{A}$ and $\mathcal{B}$ is the minimum number of elements that need to be transferred from one subset to another to transform $\mathcal{A}$ into $\mathcal{B}$ (or viceversa). In our case, in order to transform $\mathcal{A}$ into $\mathcal{B}$, we need to transfer c and d from the second subset to the first subset and transfer a from the first subset to the second for a total of 3 edit moves. So the edit distance $ed(\mathcal{A}, \mathcal{B}) = 3$. The geometric crossover under edit distance requires the offspring partition $\mathcal{O} = (O_1, \ldots, O_n)$ to satisfy $\forall i : A_i \cap B_i \subseteq O_i \subseteq A_i \cup B_i$. Notice that the sets O_i needs to form a partition of X hence need to be chosen so as to be non-overlapping and covering X completely (so their choices cannot be made independently). In our example we have $\{b\} \subseteq O_1 \subseteq \{a, b, c, d\}$ and $\emptyset \subseteq O_2 \subseteq \{a, c, d\}$. Considered independently, O_1 can be any subset of X including b (8 possible subsets) and O_2 can be any subset of $\{a, c, d\}$ (8 possible subsets). However since O_1 and O_2 need to form a partition of X, we have only 8 choices (and not 8^2) which are $\mathcal{O} = (O_1, \overline{O_1})$ where $\{b\} \subseteq O_1 \subseteq \{a, b, c, d\}$.

4 Geometric Crossover for Fixed-Size Sets, Multi-sets and Partitions

Substitution Edit Distance. Let U be the universal set and $\mathcal{X}_n$ the set of all subsets of U of size n, $\mathcal{X}_n = \{A : A \subseteq U, |A| = n\}$, and let $A, B \in \mathcal{X}_n$.

The *edit distance between sets under element substitution move* between A and B is the minimum number of elements of A that need to be substituted with an element in $U \setminus A$ to be transformed into B (or vice versa). Since this distance is an edit distance it is a metric.

For any two sets of the same size, their ins/del edit distance is twice their substitution edit distance because every substitution is equivalent to one deletion and one insertion operation and there are no shorter ways to transform one set into another of the same size using deletions and insertions. The substitution edit distance is well-defined only for sets of the same size because sets of different size cannot be transformed into each other by substitutions only.

Geometric Crossover Under Substitution Edit Distance. Given two parent sets $A, B \in \mathcal{X}_n$ any recombination operator OP that returns offspring $O \in \mathcal{X}_n$ such that $A \cap B \subseteq O \subseteq A \cup B$ is geometric crossover under substitution edit distance. So, this geometric crossover is a geometric crossover under ins/del edit distance restricted to sets of size n.

Proof: If we restrict the image set of a geometric crossover from X to $S \subseteq X$ we obtain a new geometric crossover that for any two parents $a, b \in S$ returns offspring in $[a, b] \cap S$. So, restricting the geometric crossover associated to ins/del edit distance from the set 2^U to the set $\mathcal{X}_n \subseteq 2^U$, we obtain a new geometric crossover based on the ins/del distance that returns offspring of the same size of the parents.

This restricted crossover is also geometric crossover under substitution edit distance because given $A, B \in \mathcal{X}_n$, $O \in [A, B]$ under ins/del edit distance iff $O \in [A, B]$ under substitution edit distance because ins/del edit distance is twice of substitution edit distance and proportional metrics have the same metric intervals.

Example. Let $U = \{a, b, c, d\}$ be the universal set and $A = \{a, b\}$ and $B = \{b, c\}$ two parent sets such as $A, B \subseteq U$. The substitution edit distance between A and B is $d_{sub}(A, B) = 1$: A can be transformed into B by substituting a single element in A, the element b with c. Their ins/del edit distance, which equals their symmetric distance, is $d_{\Delta}(A, B) = 2 \cdot d_{sub}(A, B) = 2$.

Any offspring O of A and B by geometric crossover under ins/del edit distance GX_{Δ}, $O = GX_{\Delta}(A, B)$, respects the condition $A \cap B \subseteq O \subseteq A \cup B$. These are the sets: $\{b\}, \{a, b\}, \{b, c\}, \{a, b, c\}$. The offspring obtained by geometric crossover under substitution edit distance are those that have the same parent size, size 2 in this case: $\{a, b\}, \{b, c\}$. They are in the segment between parents A and B under substitution edit distance (in this case the only offspring are the parents themselves).

5 Geometric Duality of Sets and Vectors

In this section we show that the same metric spaces considered in section 3 and 4, arising from the set and related representations, arise from the vector representation and permutations with repetitions. In other words, set spaces and vector spaces are isometric. This enables us to show that the geometric crossovers considered in section 3 and 4 for sets, multi-sets and partitions all have equivalent dual geometric crossovers based on vectors in the variable-size case and on permutations with repetitions in the fixed-size case (see Table 1).

5.1 Dual Equivalence of Geometric Crossovers for Sets and Vectors

Geometric crossovers based on isometric spaces are equivalent. The space of sets endowed with the symmetric distance is isometric to the space of vectors endowed with Hamming distance. Hence, symmetric crossover for sets is equivalent to the traditional crossover for vectors. In the following, we prove the duality and illustrate it with an example.

Definition 4. *(Indicator function) The indicator function of a subset A of a set U is a function $I_A : U \to \{0, 1\}$ defined as* $I_A(x) = \begin{cases} 1 \text{ if } x \in A, \\ 0 \text{ if } x \notin A. \end{cases}$

Definition 5. *(Isometry) Let X and Y be metric spaces with metrics d_X and d_Y. A map $f : X \to Y$ is called* distance preserving *if for any $x, y \in X$ one has $d_Y(f(x), f(y)) = d_X(x, y)$. A distance preserving map is automatically injective. A* global isometry *is a bijective distance preserving map. Two metric spaces X and Y are called* isometric *if there is a global isometry from X to Y.*

Let U be the universal set, d_{Δ} the symmetric distance between sets and $M = (2^U, d_{\Delta})$ the metric space based on the set of all subsets of U together with the symmetric distance.

Let I_A be the indicator function of $A \subseteq U$ where $U = \{x_1, \cdots, x_n\}$ and V_A be the vector $(I_A(x_1), \cdots, I_A(x_n))$. The map $V : A \to V_A$ mapping a set A and its indicator values vector V_A is bijective.

Table 1. Crossovers dual equivalence

	PRIMAL	DUAL
Representation:	Sets - variable size	Binary vectors
Map:	Indication function	
Distance:	Ins/del edit distance	Hamming distance
Crossover:	Inter/union crossover	Traditional crossover
Representation:	Sets - fixed size	Binary permutations with repetitions
Map:	Indication function	
Distance:	Substitution edit distance	Permutation swap edit distance
Crossover:	Inter/union crossover restricted to fixed size	Sorting crossover by swap
Representation:	Multisets - variable size	Integer vectors
Map:	Multiplicity function	
Distance:	Ins/del edit distance	Absolute value distance
Crossover:	Inter/union crossover	Integer blending crossover
Representation:	Multisets - fixed size	Integer distributions
Map:	Multiplicity function	
Distance:	Substitution edit distance	Absolute value distance
Crossover:	Inter/union crossover restricted to fixed size	Integer blending crossover restricted to constant sum
Representation:	Partitions - variable structure	Multary vectors
Map:	Partition label function	
Distance:	Partition move edit distance	Hamming distance
Crossover:	Partitionwise inter/union crossover restricted to mutual exclusion restricted to complete covering	Traditional crossover
Representation:	Partitions - fixed structure	Permutations with repetitions
Map:	Partition label function	
Distance:	Partition swap edit distance	Permutation swap edit distance
Crossover:	Partitionwise inter/union crossover restricted to mutual exclusion restricted to complete covering restricted to same structure	Sorting crossover by swaps
Representation:	n-partitions of set size n	Permutations
Map:	Partition label function	
Distance:	Partition swap edit distance	Permutation swap edit distance
Crossover:	Partitionwise inter/union crossover restricted to mutual exclusion restricted to complete covering restricted to single element subsets	Sorting crossover by swaps, PMX, Cycle crossover

Let $M' = (\{0,1\}^n, d_H)$ be the metric space of the binary vectors of size n endowed with the Hamming distance d_H.

Theorem 3. *The metric spaces* $M = (2^U, d_\Delta)$ *and* $M' = (\{0,1\}^n, d_H)$ *are isometric.*

Proof. It is sufficient to prove that the the map $V : A \to V_A$ is a distance preserving map. It is immediate to see that for any $A, B \subseteq U$ we have $d_\Delta(A,B) = d_H(V_A, V_B)$. To transform A into B with the minimum number of ins/del operations, the elements that need to be inserted into A are those x_i

for which $V_A(i) = 0$ and $V_B(i) = 1$ and the elements that need to be deleted from A are those x_j for which $V_A(j) = 1$ and $V_B(j) = 0$. These are the only positions in which V_A and V_B differ. Since V is bijective, the opposite implication, $V_A, V_B \in \{0,1\}^n : d_\Delta(V^{-1}(V_A), V^{-1}(V_B)) = d_H(V_A, V_B)$, is also true. This completes the proof.

Example. Let $A = \{a, b\}$ and $B = \{b, c, d\}$. Their offspring O obtained by geometric crossover under symmetric distance are $\{b\} \subseteq O \subseteq \{a, b, c, d\}$. Dually, for the set A the vector of the values of the indicator function is $V_A = (1, 1, 0, 0)$ and for B is $V_B = (0, 1, 1, 1)$. The set of their offspring under traditional crossover is the schema $(*, 1, *, *)$. For the duality, these offspring vectors correspond to the offspring sets above via their indicator functions as it is easy to verify.

5.2 Interesting Uses of the Duality

Thanks to these results we can use the two representations interchangeably. In particular, we can use the most convenient representation, knowing that the search done in one space is equivalent to the search in the other. For example, it is more convenient to work with partitions of both variable structure or fixed structure in their dual spaces based on permutations with repetitions because the constraints of mutual exclusion, full covering and structure preserving are much easier to deal with in operators defined on this space. We have exploited this property in previous work on the graph partitioning problem [4]. On the other hand, it may be more convenient to work with sets of small size (small compared to the size of the universal set) rather than on their dual vectors of fixed size (all the same size of the universal set).

6 Conclusions

We have considered three related representations – sets, multisets and partitions – in their variable size and fixed size variants.

For the variable size case we have considered the ins/del edit distance, that for sets corresponds to the symmetric distance, and its extensions to the case of multi-sets and partitions, for which it becomes the move edit distance.

We have shown that the geometric crossovers associated to the ins/del edit distance for sets is a crossover that requires offspring to be supersets of the intersection of the two parent sets and subsets of their union. The geometric crossovers associated to the ins/del distance for multisets and partitions are simple extensions of the inter/union crossover for sets.

For the fixed size case we have considered the substitution edit distance, that is equivalent to the ins/del edit distance when restricted to set of fixed size. Therefore, geometric crossover under substitution edit distance is a restricted version of the inter/union crossover where all offspring are required to have fixed size. The geometric crossover associated to multisets and partitions for the fixed size case are analogous to the restricted inter/union crossover for sets.

We have proved a duality between geometric crossover for sets, multisets and partitions on the one hand, and binary strings, integer vectors, and permutations with repetitions on the other. Interestingly, this allows the interchangeable use of representations and operators, being equivalent in terms of search, but exploiting their differences in terms of expressing constraints.

References

1. G. Cormode. *Sequence Distance Embeddings.* PhD thesis, University of Warwick, 2003.
2. M. M. Deza and M. Laurent, editors. *Geometry of Cuts and Metrics.* Springer, 1997.
3. T. Jones. *Evolutionary Algorithms, Fitness Landscapes and Search.* PhD thesis, University of New Mexico, 1995.
4. A. Moraglio, Y-H Kim, Y. Yoon, B-R. Moon, and R. Poli. Generalized cycle crossover for graph partitioning. In *Proceedings of Gecco 2006 (to appear)*, 2006.
5. A. Moraglio and R. Poli. Topological interpretation of crossover. In *Proceedings of Gecco 2004*, pages 1377–1388, 2004.
6. A. Moraglio and R. Poli. Geometric crossover for the permutation representation. *Technical Report CSM-429, Department of Computer Science, University of Essex*, 2005.
7. A. Moraglio and R. Poli. Topological crossover for the permutation representation. In *GECCO 2005 Workshop on Theory of Representations*, 2005.
8. A. Moraglio, R. Poli, and R. Seehuus. Geometric crossover for biological sequences. In *Proceedings of EuroGP 2006*, pages 121–132, 2006.
9. N. J. Radcliffe. Genetic set recombination. In *Proceedings of FOGA 1992*, pages 203 – 219, 1992.

Ordinal Regression in Evolutionary Computation

Thomas Philip Runarsson

Science Institute, University of Iceland
tpr@hi.is

Abstract. Surrogate ranking in evolutionary computation using ordinal regression is introduced. The fitness of individual points is indirectly estimated by modeling their rank. The aim is to reduce the number of costly fitness evaluations needed for evolution. The ordinal regression, or preference learning, implements a kernel-defined feature space and an optimization technique by which the margin between rank boundaries is maximized. The technique is illustrated on some classical numerical optimization functions using an evolution strategy. The benefits of surrogate ranking, compared to surrogates that model the fitness function directly, are discussed.

1 Introduction

Evolutionary computation is a biologically inspired iterative process where a population of search points is produced generation after generation. Through parent points a typical evolutionary algorithm will generate a number of new candidate points by reproduction, recombination and mutation. The best of these points will replace some if not all parent points through a selection process. The selection process generally uses an objective function similar to that used in classical methods of search and optimization. In this case the function is referred to as the fitness function. However, unlike classical optimization techniques, the method for selecting the best candidates in evolutionary computation requires only the rank (or partial rank) of the candidates[1]. Alternatively the selection process may be the result of co-evolution where individual points compete for reproduction. In this case there is no explicit fitness function defined, but rather an indirect method of evaluating whether one point is preferable to another.

The current approach in fitness approximation for evolutionary computation involves building surrogate fitness models directly using regression. For a recent review of the state-of-the-art see [1,2,3]. The fitness model is based on a set of evaluated points called the training set. The surrogate model is used to predict the fitness of candidate search points. Commonly a fraction of points are selected and evaluated within each generation (or over some number of generations [4]), added to the training set, and used for updating the surrogate. The goal is to reduce the number of costly true fitness evaluations while retaining a sufficiently accurate surrogate during evolution. Direct models of the fitness function are only possible when a fitness function can be defined. Current methods are therefore unsuitable for co-evolution and interactive evolution. For example, co-evolution has been used to evolve game playing strategies, where

[1] The exception is fitness proportionate selection which is rarely used in practice.

T.P. Runarsson et al. (Eds.): PPSN IX, LNCS 4193, pp. 1048–1057, 2006.

two or more strategies compete by playing a number of games against each other. In interactive evolution a human user may be used to rank candidate points. The approach presented here, based on ordinal regression, is applicable to the cases where no explicit or computable fitness function is available.

In evolutionary computation the surrogate approach should be considered as a preference learning task, where a candidate point $\mathbf{x}_i$ is said to be preferred over $\mathbf{x}_j$ if $\mathbf{x}_i$ has a higher fitness than $\mathbf{x}_j$. The training set for the surrogate model is therefore composed of pairs of points $(\mathbf{x}_i, \mathbf{x}_j)_k$ and a corresponding label $t_k \in [1, -1]$, taking the value $+1$ (or -1) when $\mathbf{x}_i$ has a higher fitness than $\mathbf{x}_j$ (or vice versa). The direct fitness approximation approach does not make full use of the flexibility inherent in the ordering requirement. In classical optimization regression is necessary when the method of search is gradient based, see for example [5]. Evolutionary optimization is a stochastic and direct search method where only the full or partial ordering of the search points is needed. For this reason an ordinal regression offers sufficiently detailed surrogates for evolutionary computation.

The technique presented for ordinal regression is kernel based. This implies that the technique can be readily applied to different data types as long as a kernel can be defined. For example, the search points may be represented by a tree or variable length strings. Section 2 describes the method of ordinal regression using kernel-defined features. The technique is illustrated and tested in section 3 using various kernels to fit Rosenbrock's function. In section 4 a strategy for updating the surrogate during search is discussed and its effectiveness illustrated using the CMA-ES [6] on some numerical optimization functions. This is followed by a discussion and conclusion.

2 Ordinal Regression

The preference learning task of ordinal regression presented here is a variation of the work presented in [7,8]. The modification relates to how the point pairs are selected and the fact that a 2−norm soft margin support vector machine (SVM) is used[2]. The training pairs are selected to reflect the fact that a full ranking surrogate model is required for the work presented here. It is also possible to select the pair by random sampling as is done in [7].

The ranking problem is specified by a set $S = \{(\mathbf{x}_i, y_i)\}_{i=1}^{\ell} \subset X \times Y$ of point/rank pairs, where $Y = \{r_1, \ldots, r_\ell\}$ is the outcome space with ordered ranks $r_1 > r_2, > \ldots > r_\ell$. Now consider the model space $\mathcal{H} = \{h(\cdot) : X \mapsto Y\}$ of mappings from points to ranks. Each such function h induces an ordering $\succ$ on the points by the following rule:

$$\mathbf{x}_i \succ \mathbf{x}_j \quad \Leftrightarrow \quad h(\mathbf{x}_i) > h(\mathbf{x}_j) \tag{1}$$

where the symbol $\succ$ denotes "is preferred to". In ordinal regression the task is to obtain function h^* that can for a given pair $(\mathbf{x}_i, y_i)$ and $(\mathbf{x}_j, y_j)$ distinguish between two different outcomes: $y_i > y_j$ and $y_j > y_i$. The task is therefore transformed into

[2] Initial experiments using the 1−norm soft margin SVM were not entirely satisfactory. This was found to be due to the quadratic programming solver used in the experiments (the PR_LOQO optimizer by A. Smola).

the problem of predicting the relative ordering of all possible pairs of examples [7,8]. However, it is sufficient to consider only all possible pairs of adjacent ranks, see also [9] for yet an alternative formulation. The training set, composed of pairs, is then as follows:

$$S' = \{(\mathbf{x}_k^{(1)}, \mathbf{x}_k^{(2)}), t_k = \text{sign}(y_k^{(1)} - y_k^{(2)})\}_{k=1}^{\ell'}$$

where $(y_k^{(1)} = r_i) \wedge (y_k^{(2)} = r_{i+1})$ (and vice versa $(y_k^{(1)} = r_{i+1}) \wedge (y_k^{(2)} = r_i)$) resulting in $\ell' = 2(\ell - 1)$ possible adjacently ranked training pairs. The rank difference is denoted by $t_k \in [-1, 1]$.

In order to generalize the technique to different point data types and model spaces an implicit kernel-defined feature space with corresponding feature mapping ϕ is applied. Consider the feature vector $\phi(\mathbf{x}) = [\phi_1(\mathbf{x}), \ldots, \phi_m(\mathbf{x})]^T \in \mathbb{R}^m$ where m is the number of features. Then the surrogate considered may be defined by a linear function in the kernel-defined feature space:

$$h(\mathbf{x}) = \sum_{i=1}^{m} w_i \phi_i(\mathbf{x}) = \langle \mathbf{w} \cdot \phi(\mathbf{x}) \rangle. \tag{2}$$

The aim is now to find a function h that encounters as few training errors as possible on S'. Applying the method of large margin rank boundaries of ordinal regression described in [7], the optimal $\mathbf{w}^*$ is determined by solving the following task:

$$\min_{\mathbf{w}} \quad \tfrac{1}{2}\langle \mathbf{w} \cdot \mathbf{w} \rangle + \tfrac{C}{2} \sum_{k=1}^{\ell'} \xi_k^2 \tag{3}$$

subject to $t_k \langle \mathbf{w} \cdot (\phi(\mathbf{x}_k^{(1)}) - \phi(\mathbf{x}_k^{(2)})) \rangle \geq 1 - \xi_k$ and $\xi_k \geq 0$, $k = 1, \ldots, \ell'$. The degree of constraint violation is given by the margin slack variable ξ_k and when greater than 1 the corresponding pair are incorrectly ranked. Note that

$$h(\mathbf{x}_i) - h(\mathbf{x}_j) = \langle \mathbf{w} \cdot (\phi(\mathbf{x}_i) - \phi(\mathbf{x}_j)) \rangle \tag{4}$$

and that minimizing $\langle \mathbf{w} \cdot \mathbf{w} \rangle$ maximizes the margin between rank boundaries, in our case the distance between adjacently ranked pair $h(\mathbf{x}^{(1)})$ and $h(\mathbf{x}^{(2)})$.

In terms of the training data, the optimal $\mathbf{w}^*$ can be expressed as:

$$\mathbf{w}^* = \sum_{k=1}^{\ell'} \alpha^* t_k (\phi(\mathbf{x}_k^{(1)}) - \phi(\mathbf{x}_k^{(2)})) \tag{5}$$

and the function h may be reconstructed as follows:

$$\begin{aligned} h(\mathbf{x}) = \langle \mathbf{w}^* \cdot \phi(\mathbf{x}) \rangle &= \sum_{k=1}^{\ell'} \alpha^* t_k (\langle \phi(\mathbf{x}_k^{(1)}) \cdot \phi(\mathbf{x}) \rangle - \langle \phi(\mathbf{x}_k^{(2)}) \cdot \phi(\mathbf{x}) \rangle) \\ &= \sum_{k=1}^{\ell'} \alpha^* t_k (\kappa(\mathbf{x}_k^{(1)}, \mathbf{x}) - \kappa(\mathbf{x}_k^{(2)}, \mathbf{x})) \end{aligned} \tag{6}$$

where $\kappa(\mathbf{x},\mathbf{z}) = \langle\phi(\mathbf{x})\cdot\phi(\mathbf{z})\rangle$ is the chosen kernel and α_k^* are the Lagrangian multipliers for the constraints that can be determined by solving the dual quadratic programming problem:

$$\max_{\alpha} \sum_{k=1}^{\ell'} \alpha_k - \tfrac{1}{2}\sum_{i=1}^{\ell'}\sum_{j=1}^{\ell'} \alpha_i\alpha_j t_i t_j \big(K(\mathbf{x}_i^{(1)},\mathbf{x}_i^{(2)},\mathbf{x}_j^{(1)},\mathbf{x}_j^{(2)}) + \tfrac{1}{C}\delta_{ij}\big) \quad (7)$$

subject to $\sum_{k=1}^{\ell'} \alpha_k t_k = 0$ and $0 \leq \alpha_k$, $k = 1,\ldots,\ell'$, where $K(\mathbf{x}_i^{(1)},\mathbf{x}_i^{(2)},\mathbf{x}_j^{(1)},\mathbf{x}_j^{(2)}) = \kappa(\mathbf{x}_i^{(1)},\mathbf{x}_j^{(1)}) - \kappa(\mathbf{x}_i^{(1)},\mathbf{x}_j^{(2)}) - \kappa(\mathbf{x}_i^{(2)},\mathbf{x}_j^{(1)}) + \kappa(\mathbf{x}_i^{(2)},\mathbf{x}_j^{(2)})$, where δ_{ij} is the Kronecker δ defined to be 1 if $i = j$ and 0 otherwise [10].

The following section illustrates the technique on a simple problem using common kernels. It is also discussed how the accuracy of the surrogate is evaluated.

3 Model Selection

Model selection in surrogate ranking involves choosing a kernel and it parameters. Furthermore, the regulation parameter C in (3) controlling the balance between model complexity and training errors must be chosen appropriately. A suitable kernel choice is problem specific. For example, consider Rosenbrock's function

$$f(\mathbf{x}) = \sum_{i=2}^{n} 100(x_i - x_{i-1}^2)^2 + (1 - x_{i-1})^2 \quad (8)$$

whose optimal point is located at $\mathbf{x} = (1,\ldots,1)$. Rosenbrock's function is a fourth order polynomial and so the *polynomial kernel*

$$\kappa(\mathbf{x}_i,\mathbf{x}_j) = (1 + \langle\mathbf{x}_i\cdot\mathbf{x}_j\rangle)^d \quad (9)$$

of order $d = 4$ may seem appropriate. Quadratic approximations are also commonly used in local optimization and so a polynomial kernel with $d = 2$ could also be an interesting alternative. However, perhaps the most commonly used kernel in the literature is the *Gaussian kernel*,

$$\kappa(\mathbf{x}_i,\mathbf{x}_j) = \exp\big(-\gamma\|\mathbf{x}_i - \mathbf{x}_j\|^2\big). \quad (10)$$

When applying kernel methods it is also important to scale the points $\mathbf{x}$ first. A standard method of doing so is to scale the training set such that all points are in some range, typically $[-1,1]$. That is, scaled $\tilde{\mathbf{x}}$ is

$$\tilde{x}_i = 2(x_i - \underline{x}_i)/(\overline{x}_i - \underline{x}_i) - 1 \quad i = 1,\ldots,n \quad (11)$$

where $\underline{x}_i$, $\overline{x}_i$ are the maximum and minimum values of variable i in set S. Scaling makes it easier to fix C and kernel parameters during evolution. This is especially important as the evolutionary search zooms in on a particular region of the search space.

Let $n = 2$ and $S = \{\mathbf{x}_i, y_i\}_{i=1}^{\ell}$ be the ℓ training points sampled using a standard normal distribution centered about the origin for Rosenbrock's function. Using

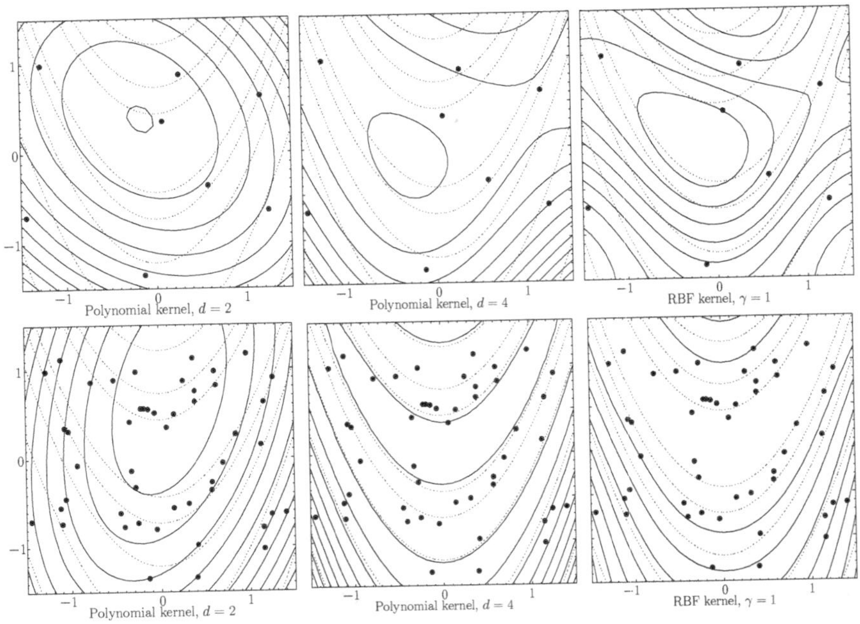

Fig. 1. Contour plots of the true function (dotted lines) versus surrogate (solid lines) for the three different kernels. The $\ell = 10$ (top) and $\ell = 60$ (bottom) training points are depicted as dots.

$\ell = 10, 20, \ldots, 60$ randomly sampled training points the surrogate model h is estimated by ordinal regression. The h contour plots for the extreme cases $\ell = 10$ and $\ell = 60$ and the three different kernels are depicted in Fig. 1. The contours of $f(\mathbf{x})$ are given by the dotted lines in each case. The sampled training points are depicted by dots. In the case of a 4th order polynomial and RBF kernel the training accuracy is 100% for the $2(\ell - 1)$ adjacently ranked point pairs, when $C = 1E6$. However, regardless of how high C is set for the 2nd order polynomial kernel a training accuracy of around 50% is consistently observed. This can be used as an indicator that the current kernel-defined features are not powerful enough to describe the ranking. On the other hand the RBF and 4th order polynomial kernel may overfit the training data. An example of this can be seen in Fig. 1 (top) when $\ell = 10$. However, as the number of training samples increase the chance of overfitting decreases as seen in Fig. 1 (bottom).

When the training accuracy is 100% one way of evaluating the accuracy of the surrogate is through cross validation. The quality of the surrogate is measured as the rank correlation between the surrogate ranking and the true ranking on test data. Here Kendall's τ is used for this purpose. Kendall's τ is computed using the relative ordering of the ranks of all $\ell(\ell - 1)/2$ possible pairs. A pair is said to be concordant if the relative ranks of $h(\mathbf{x}_i)$ and $h(\mathbf{x}_j)$ is the same for $f(\mathbf{x}_i)$ and $f(\mathbf{x}_j)$, otherwise they are discordant. Kendall's τ is the normalized difference in the number of concordant and discordant pairs. Two rankings are the same when $\tau = 1$, completely reversed if $\tau = -1$, and uncorrelated for $\tau \approx 0$.

Table 1. Kendall's τ for surrogate ranking versus true ranking of 1000 testing points generated around point $\mathbf{x} = [0, 0]$ and $\mathbf{x} = [1, 1]$ in Rosenbrock's function for various kernels κ and number of training points ℓ

κ $\ell =$	10	20	30	40	50	60	10	20	30	40	50	60
	$\mathbf{x} = [0, 0]$						$\mathbf{x} = [1, 1]$					
Polynomial, $d = 2$	0.67	0.66	0.67	0.65	0.63	0.60	0.77	0.94	0.93	0.91	0.93	0.93
Training accuracy %	56	58	59	59	47	49	100	100	90	69	69	71
Polynomial, $d = 4$	0.59	0.88	0.90	0.98	0.97	0.98	0.64	0.83	0.90	0.93	0.97	0.98
Training accuracy %	100	100	100	100	100	100	100	100	100	100	100	100
RBF, $\gamma = 1$	0.65	0.85	0.90	0.91	0.93	0.96	0.73	0.84	0.91	0.92	0.94	0.97
Training accuracy %	100	100	100	100	100	100	100	100	100	100	100	100

For our experiment the testing data is created in the same manner as the training data. The testing points are 1000 in total and Kendall's τ computed based on surrogates built using $\ell = 10, 20, \ldots, 60$ training points. Kendall's τ for this study is presented in Table 1 (left) for the all three kernels along with the training accuracy. As anticipated the model accuracy increases with ℓ and the 4th order polynomial kernel appears most suitable.

As the search zooms in on a local minima one may expect that different kernels may be suitable. The experiment is therefore re-run, this time the training and testing samples are sampled centered at the global minima from a Gaussian distribution with variance 0.1^2. In this case the 2nd order polynomial kernel performs much better, even though the training accuracy is not 100% for higher values of ℓ, as shown in Table 1 (right). Using Kendall's τ to evaluate the surrogate ranking of test points forms the basis of our model improvement method presented in the following section.

4 Model Improvement

During evolution different regions of the space are sampled and as a consequence the surrogate ranking model may be insufficiently accurate for new regions of the search space. It is therefore of paramount importance to validate the surrogate during evolution. The accuracy can be validated by generating test points in the new region similarly to the test points used in the previous section. In particular one is interested in validating the accuracy of the ranking of potential parent points during evolution as they are critical for success [11].

The proposed model validation and improvement strategy is as follows:

1. Estimate the ranking of a population of points of unknown fitness using the current surrogate. Let the point with the highest ranking be a test point, $\mathbf{x}_t$. Rank this test point with respect to the points in the training set using the current surrogate.
2. Evaluate the test point using the true fitness function and evaluate its true rank among the training points. In the case where no explicit fitness function can be defined, the test point is evaluated by comparing it with selected points in the training set.

3. Compare the rankings by computing the rank correlation τ_k for the ranking in 1 and 2.
4. Add this new point to the training set.
5. If τ_k is equal to 1 the model is said to be sufficiently accurate. This is a simple cross-validation on a single test point. Creating more test points would be too costly, but plausible.
6. If $\tau_k < 1$ the model is not sufficiently accurate. In this case update the surrogate using the new training set. Repeated the steps above until $\tau = 1$ or all points of unknown fitness have been evaluated.

The frequency by which the model is validated may be at each generation or every $K > 1$ generations. In this work the model is validated at every generation.

Initially at least two known points, $\ell = 2$, must be in the training set for the ordinal regression to work. However, with time the size of the training set grows without limit. In evolutionary computing one is interested in the accurate ranking of points generated in the neighborhood of parent points. If the training set is to have a limited size $\overline{\ell}$ then it would be reasonable to delete the oldest training points from the set first. These deleted points are likely to be representatives of a region of the search space which is no longer of interest.

If the training accuracy is not 100% then clearly $\tau_k < 1$. In this case additional training points will be forced for evaluation. It may be necessary to increase the value of C in order to improve training accuracy or alternatively to select another kernel during

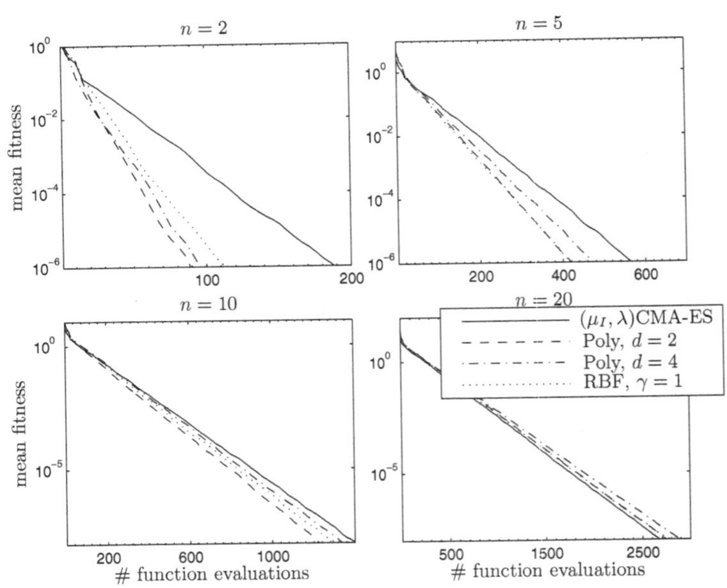

Fig. 2. Mean fitness values versus number of function evaluation for three different kernels and the original CMA-ES for different dimensions n of the sphere model

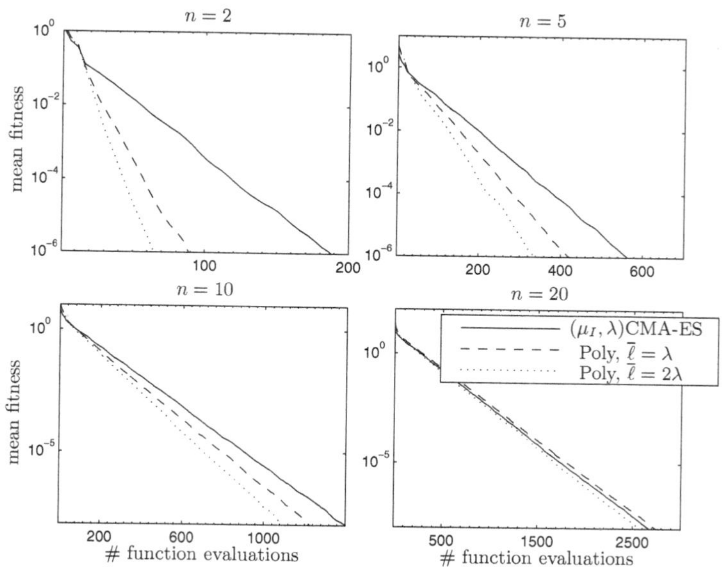

Fig. 3. The 2nd order polynomial kernel versus the original CMA-ES using $\overline{\ell} = \lambda$ and $\overline{\ell} = 2\lambda$ for different dimensions n of the sphere model

search. Decreasing the size of the training data set will also result in 100% training accuracy but at the cost of overfitting.

The surrogate ranking validation and improvement strategy using ordinal regression is now tested using the CMA-ES [6]. The CMA-ES is a very efficient numerical optimization technique but we still expect to reduce the number of function evaluations needed for search. The average fitness for 100 independent runs versus the number of function evaluations are compared to the original CMA-ES for various dimensions $n = 2, 5, 10$ and 20. The parameter setting for the (μ_I, λ) CMA-ES is as recommended in [6] with population size $\lambda = 4 + \lfloor 3\ln(n) \rfloor$ and the number of parents selected $\mu = \lambda/4$. The stopping criteria used are $1000n$ function evaluation or a fitness less than 10^{-10}. The initial mean search point is generated from a uniform distribution between 0 and 1. Unless otherwise specified $\overline{\ell} = \lambda$ and the training set is only pruned to size $\overline{\ell}$ subsequent to the validation and improvement procedure above. During model improvement the data scaling is based on the current training set and new points to be ranked. In all runs presented a 100% training accuracy is achieved by setting $C = 1E6$.

The first experimental results are presented for the infamous sphere model, $f(\mathbf{x}) = \sum_{i=1}^{n} x_i^2$. The average fitness versus the number of function evaluations is presented in Fig. 2. As one may expect for a quadratic function, the 2nd order polynomial performs best. However, as the dimensions increase the performance edge achieved by surrogate ranking, over the original CMA-ES, is lost. The reason for this is that a greater number of training samples are needed at higher dimensions. To illustrate this trend the experiment is repeated with $\overline{\ell} = 2\lambda$ using only the 2nd order polynomial kernel.

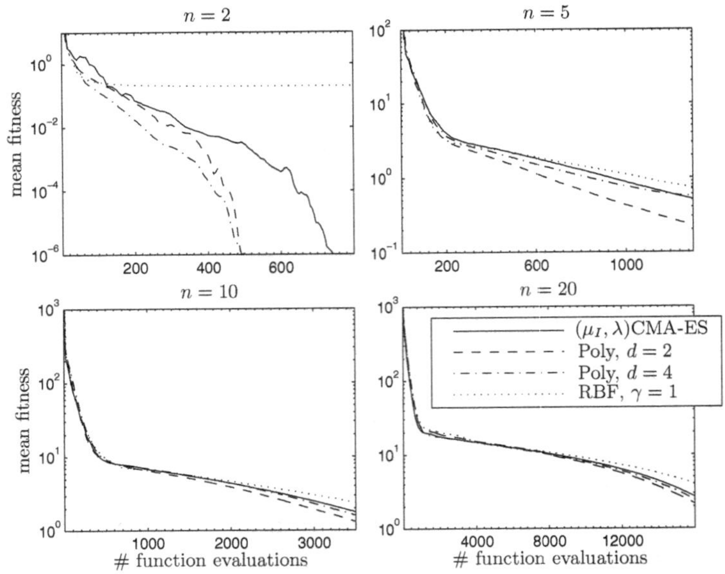

Fig. 4. Mean fitness values versus number of function evaluation for three different kernels and the original CMA-ES for different dimensions n of Rosenbrock's function

A comparison for the different problem dimensions with the original CMA-ES and the case when $\overline{\ell} = \lambda$ is shown in Fig. 3. The performance is improved in all cases when $\overline{\ell} = 2\lambda$ as expected.

The first experiment is now repeated but this time using Rosenbrock's function for different dimensions. The traditional CMA-ES will get stuck in local minima for this problem in around 4 out of 100 experiments. The polynomial kernels again have a performance edge over the original CMA-ES, however, the RBF kernel is more likely to get stuck in the local minima. Overfitting is more of a problem in this case and the simple model (2nd order polynomial kernel) is best at higher dimensions. Clearly the choice of kernel and number of training pairs will influence search performance.

5 Discussion and Conclusion

When building surrogates in evolutionary computation one is interested in the quality of ranking of points only. For this reason the training accuracy and cross validation is a more meaningful measure of quality for the surrogate model. This is in contrast to regression, where the fitness function is modeled directly and the quality estimated in terms of measures such a the least square error.

The technique used to control the number of true fitness evaluations is based on a single test point. The ranking of this test point using the current surrogate is compared with its true ranking in order to determine the quality of the surrogate. This is a simple form of cross-validation. An alternative approach could be to rank all test points along with the training points using the surrogate model. Then update the surrogate ranking model using the single evaluated test point of highest rank. This would then be followed by the re-ranking of training and testing points using the updated surrogate and comparing it with the previous estimate by computing Kendall's τ. This style of heuristic control was applied in [11] with good success. Its aim is to observe a change in ranking between successive updates of the surrogate. In this case it may also be sufficient for τ to be close to 1 or at least the best new candidate points (potential parent points) should be ranked consistently.

A generic framework for surrogate ranking using ordinal regression in evolutionary computation has been presented. To the best of our knowledge this is the first time such a framework has been put forward. The formulation does not need an explicitly defined fitness function, making it suitable for co-evolution and interactive evolution. Choosing a kernel-defined function h also opens up the possibility of using surrogates for other point data types. The only condition is that a kernel can be defined. For example, in genetic programming a tree kernel may potentially be used. In evolutionary art, kernels typically used in pattern recognition may be useful.

The approach reduces the number of fitness evaluation needed, without a loss in performance, as long as an appropriate kernel is selected and a sufficient size of training data is available. The studies presented are exploratory in nature and clearly the approach must be evaluated on a greater range of evolutionary tasks. These investigations are currently underway.

References

1. Ong, Y., Nair, P., Keane, A., Wong, K.W.: 15. Studies in Fuzziness and Soft Computing Series. In: Surrogate-Assisted Evolutionary Optimization Frameworks for High-Fidelity Engineering Design Problems. Springer (2004) 333–358
2. Sobester, A., Leary, S., Keane, A.: On the design of optimization strategies based on global response surface approximation models. Journal of Global Optimization **33**(1) (2005) 31–59
3. Jin, Y.: A comprehensive survey of fitness approximation in evolutionary computation. Soft Computing - A Fusion of Foundations, Methodologies and Applications **9**(1) (2005) 3–12
4. Jin, Y., Olhofer, M., Sendhoff, B.: A framework for evolutionary optimization with approximate fitness functions. IEEE Transactions on Evolutionary Computation **6**(5) (2002)
5. Bandler, J., Cheng, Q., Dakroury, S., Mohamed, A., Bakr, M., Madsen, K., Sondergaard, J.: Space mapping: The state of the art. IEEE Transactions on Microwave Theory and Techniques **52**(1) (2004)
6. Hansen, N., Ostermeier, A.: Completely derandomized self-adaptation in evolution strategies. Evolutionary Computation **9**(2) (2001) 159–195
7. Herbrich, R., Graepel, T., Obermayer, K.: Large margin rank boundaries for ordinal regression. Advances in Large Margin Classifiers (2000) 115–132
8. Joachims, T.: Optimizing search engines using clickthrough data. In: Proceedings of the ACM Conference on Knowledge Discovery and Data Mining (KDD), ACM (2002)
9. Shawe-Taylor, J., Cristianini, N.: Kernel Methods for Pattern Analysis. Cambridge University Press (2004)
10. Christianini, N., Shawe-Taylor, J.: An Introduction to Support Vector Machines. Cambridge University Press (2002)
11. Runarsson, T.P.: Constrained evolutionary optimization by approximate ranking and surrogate models. In: Parallel Problem Solving from Nature VII (PPSN-2004). Volume 3242 of LNCS., Springer Verlag (2004) 401–410

Author Index

Lecture Notes in Computer Science

For information about Vols. 1–4070

please contact your bookseller or Springer

Vol. 4193: T.P. Runarsson, H.-G. Beyer, E. Burke, J.J. Merelo-Guervós, L. D. Whitley, X. Yao (Eds.), Parallel Problem Solving from Nature - PPSN IX. XIX, 1061 pages. 2006.

Vol. 4192: B. Mohr, J.L. Traeff, J. Worringen, J. Dongarra (Eds.), Recent Advances in Parallel Virtual Machine and Message Passing Interface. XVI, 414 pages. 2006.

Vol. 4185: R. Mizoguchi, Z. Shi, F. Giunchiglia (Eds.), The Semantic Web – ASWC 2006. XX, 778 pages. 2006.

Vol. 4184: M. Bravetti, M. Nuñes, G. Zavattaro (Eds.), Web Services and Formal Methods. X, 289 pages. 2006.

Vol. 4180: M. Kohlhase, OMDoc – An Open Markup Format for Mathematical Documents [version 1.2]. XIX, 428 pages. 2006. (Sublibrary LNAI).

Vol. 4178: A. Corradini, H. Ehrig, U. Montanary, L. Ribeiro, G. Rozenberg (Eds.), Graph Transformations. XII, 473 pages. 2006.

Vol. 4176: S.K. Katsikas, J. Lopez, M. Backes, S. Gritzalis, B. Preneel (Eds.), Information Security. XIV, 548 pages. 2006.

Vol. 4168: Y. Azar, T. Erlebach (Eds.), Algorithms – ESA 2006. XVIII, 843 pages. 2006.

Vol. 4165: W. Jonker, M. Petkovic (Eds.), Secure, Data Management. X, 185 pages. 2006.

Vol. 4163: H. Bersini, J. Carneiro (Eds.), Artificial Immune Systems. XII, 460 pages. 2006.

Vol. 4162: R. Královič, P. Urzyczyn (Eds.), Mathematical Foundations of Computer Science 2006. XV, 814 pages. 2006.

Vol. 4159: J. Ma, H. Jin, L.T. Yang, J.J.-P. Tsai (Eds.), Ubiquitous Intelligence and Computing. XXII, 1190 pages. 2006.

Vol. 4158: L.T. Yang, H. Jin, J. Ma, T. Ungerer (Eds.), Autonomic and Trusted Computing. XIV, 613 pages. 2006.

Vol. 4156: S. Amer-Yahia, Z. Bellahsène, E. Hunt, R. Unland, J.X. Yu (Eds.), Database and XML Technologies. IX, 123 pages. 2006.

Vol. 4155: O. Stock, M. Schaerf (Eds.), Reasoning, Action and Interaction in AI Theories and Systems. XVIII, 343 pages. 2006. (Sublibrary LNAI).

Vol. 4153: N. Zheng, X. Jiang, X. Lan (Eds.), Advances in Machine Vision, Image Processing, and Pattern Analysis. XIII, 506 pages. 2006.

Vol. 4152: Y. Manolopoulos, J. Pokorný, T. Sellis (Eds.), Advances in Databases and Information Systems. XV, 448 pages. 2006.

Vol. 4151: A. Iglesias, N. Takayama (Eds.), Mathematical Software - ICMS 2006. XVII, 452 pages. 2006.

Vol. 4150: M. Dorigo, L.M. Gambardella, M. Birattari, A. Martinoli, R. Poli, T. Stützle (Eds.), Ant Colony Optimization and Swarm Intelligence. XVI, 526 pages. 2006.

Vol. 4149: M. Klusch, M. Rovatsos, T.R. Payne (Eds.), Cooperative Information Agents X. XII, 477 pages. 2006. (Sublibrary LNAI).

Vol. 4146: J.C. Rajapakse, L. Wong, R. Acharya (Eds.), Pattern Recognition in Bioinformatics. XIV, 186 pages. 2006. (Sublibrary LNBI).

Vol. 4144: T. Ball, R.B. Jones (Eds.), Computer Aided Verification. XV, 564 pages. 2006.

Vol. 4139: T. Salakoski, F. Ginter, S. Pyysalo, T. Pahikkala, Advances in Natural Language Processing. XVI, 771 pages. 2006. (Sublibrary LNAI).

Vol. 4138: X. Cheng, W. Li, T. Znati (Eds.), Wireless Algorithms, Systems, and Applications. XVI, 709 pages. 2006.

Vol. 4137: C. Baier, H. Hermanns (Eds.), CONCUR 2006 – Concurrency Theory. XIII, 525 pages. 2006.

Vol. 4136: R.A. Schmidt (Ed.), Relations and Kleene Algebra in Computer Science. XI, 433 pages. 2006.

Vol. 4135: C.S. Calude, M.J. Dinneen, G. Păun, G. Rozenberg, S. Stepney (Eds.), Unconventional Computation. X, 267 pages. 2006.

Vol. 4134: K. Yi (Ed.), Static Analysis. XIII, 443 pages. 2006.

Vol. 4133: J. Gratch, M. Young, R. Aylett, D. Ballin, P. Olivier (Eds.), Intelligent Virtual Agents. XIV, 472 pages. 2006. (Sublibrary LNAI).

Vol. 4132: S. Kollias, A. Stafylopatis, W. Duch, E. Oja (Eds.), Artificial Neural Networks – ICANN 2006, Part II. XXXIV, 1028 pages. 2006.

Vol. 4131: S. Kollias, A. Stafylopatis, W. Duch, E. Oja (Eds.), Artificial Neural Networks – ICANN 2006, Part I. XXXIV, 1008 pages. 2006.

Vol. 4130: U. Furbach, N. Shankar (Eds.), Automated Reasoning. XV, 680 pages. 2006. (Sublibrary LNAI).

Vol. 4129: D. McGookin, S. Brewster (Eds.), Haptic and Audio Interaction Design. XII, 167 pages. 2006.

Vol. 4128: W.E. Nagel, W.V. Walter, W. Lehner (Eds.), Euro-Par 2006 Parallel Processing. XXXIII, 1221 pages. 2006.

Vol. 4127: E. Damiani, P. Liu (Eds.), Data and Applications Security XX. X, 319 pages. 2006.

Vol. 4126: P. Barahona, F. Bry, E. Franconi, N. Henze, U. Sattler, Reasoning Web. X, 269 pages. 2006.

Vol. 4124: H. de Meer, J.P. G. Sterbenz (Eds.), Self-Organizing Systems. XIV, 261 pages. 2006.

Vol. 4121: A. Biere, C.P. Gomes (Eds.), Theory and Applications of Satisfiability Testing - SAT 2006. XII, 438 pages. 2006.

Vol. 4119: C. Dony, J.L. Knudsen, A. Romanovsky, A. Tripathi (Eds.), Advanced Topics in Exception Handling Components. X, 302 pages. 2006.

Vol. 4117: C. Dwork (Ed.), Advances in Cryptology - CRYPTO 2006. XIII, 621 pages. 2006.

Vol. 4116: R. De Prisco, M. Yung (Eds.), Security and Cryptography for Networks. XI, 366 pages. 2006.

Vol. 4115: D.-S. Huang, K. Li, G.W. Irwin (Eds.), Computational Intelligence and Bioinformatics, Part III. XXI, 803 pages. 2006. (Sublibrary LNBI).

Vol. 4114: D.-S. Huang, K. Li, G.W. Irwin (Eds.), Computational Intelligence, Part II. XXVII, 1337 pages. 2006. (Sublibrary LNAI).

Vol. 4113: D.-S. Huang, K. Li, G.W. Irwin (Eds.), Intelligent Computing, Part I. XXVII, 1331 pages. 2006.

Vol. 4112: D.Z. Chen, D. T. Lee (Eds.), Computing and Combinatorics. XIV, 528 pages. 2006.

Vol. 4111: F.S. de Boer, M.M. Bonsangue, S. Graf, W.-P. de Roever (Eds.), Formal Methods for Components and Objects. VIII, 447 pages. 2006.

Vol. 4110: J. Díaz, K. Jansen, J.D.P. Rolim, U. Zwick (Eds.), Approximation, Randomization, and Combinatorial Optimization. XII, 522 pages. 2006.

Vol. 4109: D.-Y. Yeung, J.T. Kwok, A. Fred, F. Roli, D. de Ridder (Eds.), Structural, Syntactic, and Statistical Pattern Recognition. XXI, 939 pages. 2006.

Vol. 4108: J.M. Borwein, W.M. Farmer (Eds.), Mathematical Knowledge Management. VIII, 295 pages. 2006. (Sublibrary LNAI).

Vol. 4106: T.R. Roth-Berghofer, M.H. Göker, H. A. Güvenir (Eds.), Advances in Case-Based Reasoning. XIV, 566 pages. 2006. (Sublibrary LNAI).

Vol. 4105: B. Gunsel, A.K. Jain, A. M. Tekalp, B. Sankur (Eds.), Multimedia, Content Representation, Classification and Security. XIX, 804 pages. 2006.

Vol. 4104: T. Kunz, S.S. Ravi (Eds.), Ad-Hoc, Mobile, and Wireless Networks. XII, 474 pages. 2006.

Vol. 4102: S. Dustdar, J.L. Fiadeiro, A. Sheth (Eds.), Business Process Management. XV, 486 pages. 2006.

Vol. 4099: Q. Yang, G. Webb (Eds.), PRICAI 2006: Trends in Artificial Intelligence. XXVIII, 1263 pages. 2006. (Sublibrary LNAI).

Vol. 4098: F. Pfenning (Ed.), Term Rewriting and Applications. XIII, 415 pages. 2006.

Vol. 4097: X. Zhou, O. Sokolsky, L. Yan, E.-S. Jung, Z. Shao, Y. Mu, D.C. Lee, D. Kim, Y.-S. Jeong, C.-Z. Xu (Eds.), Emerging Directions in Embedded and Ubiquitous Computing. XXVII, 1034 pages. 2006.

Vol. 4096: E. Sha, S.-K. Han, C.-Z. Xu, M.H. Kim, L.T. Yang, B. Xiao (Eds.), Embedded and Ubiquitous Computing. XXIV, 1170 pages. 2006.

Vol. 4095: S. Nolfi, G. Baldassare, R. Calabretta, D. Marocco, D. Parisi, J.C. T. Hallam, O. Miglino, J.-A. Meyer (Eds.), From Animals to Animats 9. XV, 869 pages. 2006. (Sublibrary LNAI).

Vol. 4094: O. H. Ibarra, H.-C. Yen (Eds.), Implementation and Application of Automata. XIII, 291 pages. 2006.

Vol. 4093: X. Li, O.R. Zaïane, Z. Li (Eds.), Advanced Data Mining and Applications. XXI, 1110 pages. 2006. (Sublibrary LNAI).

Vol. 4092: J. Lang, F. Lin, J. Wang (Eds.), Knowledge Science, Engineering and Management. XV, 664 pages. 2006. (Sublibrary LNAI).

Vol. 4091: G.-Z. Yang, T. Jiang, D. Shen, L. Gu, J. Yang (Eds.), Medical Imaging and Augmented Reality. XIII, 399 pages. 2006.

Vol. 4090: S. Spaccapietra, K. Aberer, P. Cudré-Mauroux (Eds.), Journal on Data Semantics VI. XI, 211 pages. 2006.

Vol. 4089: W. Löwe, M. Südholt (Eds.), Software Composition. X, 339 pages. 2006.

Vol. 4088: Z.-Z. Shi, R. Sadananda (Eds.), Agent Computing and Multi-Agent Systems. XVII, 827 pages. 2006. (Sublibrary LNAI).

Vol. 4087: F. Schwenker, S. Marinai (Eds.), Artificial Neural Networks in Pattern Recognition. IX, 299 pages. 2006. (Sublibrary LNAI).

Vol. 4085: J. Misra, T. Nipkow, E. Sekerinski (Eds.), FM 2006: Formal Methods. XV, 620 pages. 2006.

Vol. 4084: M.A. Wimmer, H.J. Scholl, Å. Grönlund, K.V. Andersen (Eds.), Electronic Government. XV, 353 pages. 2006.

Vol. 4083: S. Fischer-Hübner, S. Furnell, C. Lambrinoudakis (Eds.), Trust and Privacy in Digital Business. XIII, 243 pages. 2006.

Vol. 4082: K. Bauknecht, B. Pröll, H. Werthner (Eds.), E-Commerce and Web Technologies. XIII, 243 pages. 2006.

Vol. 4081: A. M. Tjoa, J. Trujillo (Eds.), Data Warehousing and Knowledge Discovery. XVII, 578 pages. 2006.

Vol. 4080: S. Bressan, J. Küng, R. Wagner (Eds.), Database and Expert Systems Applications. XXI, 959 pages. 2006.

Vol. 4079: S. Etalle, M. Truszczyński (Eds.), Logic Programming. XIV, 474 pages. 2006.

Vol. 4077: M.-S. Kim, K. Shimada (Eds.), Geometric Modeling and Processing - GMP 2006. XVI, 696 pages. 2006.

Vol. 4076: F. Hess, S. Pauli, M. Pohst (Eds.), Algorithmic Number Theory. X, 599 pages. 2006.

Vol. 4075: U. Leser, F. Naumann, B. Eckman (Eds.), Data Integration in the Life Sciences. XI, 298 pages. 2006. (Sublibrary LNBI).

Vol. 4074: M. Burmester, A. Yasinsac (Eds.), Secure Mobile Ad-hoc Networks and Sensors. X, 193 pages. 2006.

Vol. 4073: A. Butz, B. Fisher, A. Krüger, P. Olivier (Eds.), Smart Graphics. XI, 263 pages. 2006.

Vol. 4072: M. Harders, G. Székely (Eds.), Biomedical Simulation. XI, 216 pages. 2006.

Vol. 4071: H. Sundaram, M. Naphade, J.R. Smith, Y. Rui (Eds.), Image and Video Retrieval. XII, 547 pages. 2006.

FSC
www.fsc.org
MIX
Papier | Fördert gute Waldnutzung
FSC® C083411

Kolibri 360 GmbH
Ferdinand-Jühlke-Straße 7
99095 Erfurt, Deutschland
produktsicherheit@kolibri360.de